c. Overall conclusion/financial reporting objective
Based on your role in the case and the above information, conclude on whether the financial reporting will be more aggressive or conservative or somewhere in between. Note that aggressive accounting tends to overstate net income/assets and present the company in the best light. Conservative accounting ensures that net income/assets are not overstated and that all pertinent information (positive or negative) is disclosed.

2. **Identification and analysis of the financial reporting issues**

   a. Issue identification
   Read the case and look for potential financial reporting issues. To do this, you need to know the accounting principles and rules and have an understanding of the business and the business transactions. Issues are usually about deciding whether or not to **recognize** something (revenues, liabilities etc.), deciding how to **measure** financial statement elements (leave them as they are or write them down or off), or how to **present/disclose** these items in the financial statements (treat them as current or long-term, debt or equity, discontinued or continuing operations, etc.).

   b. Ranking issues
   Focus on the more important issues. In other words, focus first on the issues that are material to the users of the information (those that are more complex and/or those that affect any of the key numbers or ratios identified above). You should identify right away what you consider to be material.

   c. Analysis
   The analysis should consider both qualitative and quantitative aspects. It should also look at the issue from different perspectives. For example, in a revenue recognition issue, should the revenue be recognized now or later? Consider only the relevant alternatives.

   Qualitative:
   - Each perspective must be supported by making reference to GAAP and accounting theory (including the conceptual framework). For example, recognize the revenue now because... or recognize it later because...

   - Make sure the analysis is case specific—i.e., that it refers to the facts of the specific case.

   - Make strong arguments for both sides of the discussion. If the issue is a real issue, there is often more than one way to account for the transaction or event.

   - Make sure that the analysis considers the substance of the transaction from a business and economic perspective.

   Quantitative:
   - Calculate the impact of the different perspectives on key financial statement numbers/ratios. Would this decision be relevant to users?

   - Calculate what the numbers might look like under different accounting methods, if they are relevant.

3. **Recommendations**
   After each issue is analyzed, conclude on how the items should be accounted for. Your conclusion should be based on your role and the financial reporting objective that you identified earlier.

ALL THE HELP, RESOURCES, AND PERSONAL SUPPORT YOU AND YOUR STUDENTS NEED!

2-Minute Tutorials and all of the resources you & your students need to get started
www.wileyplus.com/firstday

Student support from an experienced student user
Ask your local representative for details!

Collaborate with your colleagues, find a mentor, attend virtual and live events, and view resources
www.WhereFacultyConnect.com

Pre-loaded, ready-to-use assignments and presentations
www.wiley.com/college/quickstart

Technical Support 24/7
FAQs, online chat, and phone support
www.wileyplus.com/support

Your *WileyPLUS* Account Manager
Training and implementation support
www.wileyplus.com/accountmanager

www.wileyplus.com

MAKE IT YOURS!

Intermediate Accounting

NINTH CANADIAN EDITION

Intermediate Accounting

Donald E. Kieso, PhD, CPA
KPMG Peat Marwick Emeritus Professor of Accounting
Northern Illinois University
DeKalb, Illinois

Jerry J. Weygandt, PhD, CPA
Arthur Andersen Alumni Professor of Accounting
University of Wisconsin
Madison, Wisconsin

Terry D. Warfield, PhD
Associate Professor
University of Wisconsin
Madison, Wisconsin

Nicola M. Young, MBA, FCA
Saint Mary's University
Halifax, Nova Scotia

Irene M. Wiecek, FCA
University of Toronto
Toronto, Ontario

John Wiley & Sons Canada, Ltd.

Library and Archives Canada Cataloguing in Publication

Intermediate accounting / Donald E. Kieso ... [et al.]. — 9th Canadian ed.

Includes index.
ISBN 978-0-470-16100-5 (v. 1).—ISBN 978-0-470-16101-2 (v. 2)

1. Accounting—Textbooks. I. Kieso, Donald E

HF5636.I57 2010   657'.044   C2009-906922-9

Production Credits
Acquisitions Editor: Zoë Craig
Vice President & Publisher: Veronica Visentin
Vice President, Publishing Services: Karen Bryan
Creative Director, Publishing Services: Ian Koo
Marketing Manager: Aida Krneta
Editorial Manager: Karen Staudinger
Developmental Editor: Daleara Jamasji Hirjikaka
Media Editor: Channade Fenandoe
Editorial Assistant: Laura Hwee
Design & Typesetting: Lakeside Group Inc. (Gail Ferreira Ng-A-Kien)
Cover Design: Ian Koo
Cover Photo: ©iStockphoto.com/Felix Möckel
Printing & Binding: Quad/Graphics

References to the *CICA Handbook* are reprinted (or adapted) with permission from The Canadian Institute of Chartered Accountants, Toronto, Canada. Any changes to the original material are the sole responsibility of the author (and/or publisher) and have not been reviewed or endorsed by the CICA.

Printed and bound in the United States

3 4 5 QG 14 13 12 11

John Wiley & Sons Canada, Ltd.
6045 Freemont Blvd.
Mississauga, Ontario L5R 4J3
Visit our website at: www.wiley.ca

*Dedicated to accounting educators in Canada
and to the students in their Intermediate Accounting classrooms
as we step into a multiple-GAAP world.
Our discipline will be shaped by continuing change
as standards evolve,
making the future an exciting place to be.*

About the Authors

CANADIAN EDITION

Nicola (Nickie) M. Young, MBA, FCA, is a Professor of Accounting in the Sobey School of Business at Saint Mary's University in Halifax, Nova Scotia, where her teaching responsibilities have varied from the introductory offering to final-year advanced financial courses to the survey course in the Executive MBA program. She is the recipient of teaching awards, and has contributed to the academic and administrative life of the university by chairing the Department of Accounting, and membership on the Board of Governors and the Pension and other committees. Nickie was associated with the Atlantic School of Chartered Accountancy for over 25 years in a variety of roles, including program and course development, teaching, and program reform. In addition to contributions to the accounting profession at the provincial level, Nickie has served on national boards of the Canadian Institute of Chartered Accountants (CICA) dealing with licensure and education. She has worked with the CICA's Public Sector Accounting Board (PSAB) for many years as an associate, as a member and chair of the board, and as a chair and member of PSAB task forces. Nickie currently serves on the Board of Directors of the CICA and on its Education and Qualifications Committee. She and Irene Wiecek have also co-authored the *IFRS Primer: International GAAP Basics* (Canadian and U.S. editions).

Irene M. Wiecek, FCA, is a faculty member at the University of Toronto where she is cross-appointed to the Joseph L. Rotman School of Management. She teaches financial reporting in various programs including the Commerce Program (Accounting Specialist) and the Master of Management & Professional Accounting Program (MMPA). The Associate Director of the MMPA Program for many years, she co-founded and is Co-Director of the ICAO (Institute of Chartered Accountants of Ontario)/Rotman Centre for Innovation in Accounting Education, which supports and facilitates innovation in accounting education. Irene has been involved in professional accounting education for over 20 years, currently sitting on the Canadian Institute of Chartered Accountants (CICA) Financial Reporting and Governance Education Committee, as well as developing and directing the CICA IFRS immersion programs for practising accountants. She is an active member of the Ernst & Young Academic Resource Center where she was part of a team that authored a new IFRS curriculum for the Americas. In the area of standard setting, she has chaired the Canadian Academic Accounting Association CICA Financial Reporting Exposure Draft Response Committee. Irene co-authored the *IFRS Primer: International GAAP Basics* (Canadian and U.S. editions) with Nickie Young.

U.S. EDITION

Donald E. Kieso, Ph.D., C.P.A., received his bachelor's degree from Aurora University and his doctorate in accounting from the University of Illinois. He has served as chairman of the Department of Accountancy and is currently the KPMG Emeritus Professor of Accountancy at Northern Illinois University. He has public accounting experience with Price Waterhouse & Co. (San Francisco and Chicago) and Arthur Andersen & Co. (Chicago) and research experience with the Research Division of the American Institute of Certified Public Accountants (New York). He has done postdoctorate work as a Visiting Scholar at the University of California at Berkeley and is a recipient of NIU's Teaching Excellence Award and four Golden Apple Teaching Awards. Professor Kieso is the author of other accounting and business books and is a member of the American Accounting Association, the American Institute of Certified Public Accountants, and the Illinois CPA Society. He is the recipient of the Outstanding Accounting Educator Award from the Illinois CPA Society, the FSA's Joseph A. Silvoso Award of Merit, the NIU Foundation's Humanitarian Award for Service to Higher Education, the Distinguished Service Award from the Illinois CPA Society, and in 2003 received an honorary doctorate from Aurora University.

Jerry J. Weygandt, Ph.D., C.P.A., is Arthur Andersen Alumni Professor of Accounting at the University of Wisconsin-Madison. He holds a Ph.D. in accounting from the University of Illinois. His articles have appeared in *Accounting Review, Journal of Accounting Research, Accounting Horizons, Journal of Accountancy*, and other academic and professional journals. Professor Weygandt is the author of other accounting and financial reporting books and is a member of the American Accounting Association, the American Institute of Certified Public Accountants, and the Wisconsin Society of Certified Public Accountants. He has been actively involved with the American Institute of Certified Public Accountants and has been a member of the Accounting Standards Executive Committee (AcSEC) of that organization. He also served on the FASB task force that examined the reporting issues related to accounting for income taxes. He is the recipient of the Wisconsin Institute of CPAs' Outstanding Educator's Award and the Lifetime Achievement Award. In 2001, he received the American Accounting Association's Outstanding Accounting Educator Award.

Terry D. Warfield, Ph.D., is the Robert and Monica Beyer Professor of Accounting at the University of Wisconsin-Madison. He received a B.S. and M.B.A. from Indiana University and a Ph.D. in accounting from the University of Iowa. Professor Warfield's area of expertise is financial reporting, and prior to his academic career, he worked for five years in the banking industry. He served as the Academic Accounting Fellow in the Office of the Chief Accountant at the U.S. Securities and Exchange Commission in Washington, D.C., from 1995 to 1996. Professor Warfield's primary research interests concern financial accounting standards and disclosure policies. He has published scholarly articles in *The Accounting Review, Journal of Accounting and Economics, Research in Accounting Regulation,* and *Accounting Horizons,* and he has served on the editorial boards of *The Accounting Review, Accounting Horizons,* and *Issues in Accounting Education.* Professor Warfield has served on the Financial Accounting Standards Committee of the American Accounting Association (Chair 1995–1996) and the AAA-FASB Research Conference Committee. He currently serves on the Financial Accounting Standards Advisory Council of the Financial Accounting Standards Board. Professor Warfield has received teaching awards at both the University of Iowa and the University of Wisconsin, and he was named to the Teaching Academy at the University of Wisconsin in 1995. Professor Warfield has developed and published several case studies based on his research for use in accounting classes. These cases have been selected for the AICPA Professor-Practitioner Case Development Program and have been published in *Issues in Accounting Education.*

Preface

This is an edition of *Intermediate Accounting* like no other. Accountants are at the centre of very significant change and accounting educators are leading the charge to equip you with the tools needed to move forward into this exciting arena. The ninth edition has been shaped by the following themes:

- Change
- Choice
- Concepts and core
- Critical thinking
- Complexity

Let's start with the change theme as this one is the most obvious. Canadian accounting standards for publicly accountable enterprises are going global and being replaced by International Financial Reporting Standards (IFRS). This is energizing, especially for students as it gives you a transferrable skill that allows you to go global as well. Accounting standards for private companies are moving to a "made-in-Canada" solution: ASPE or accounting standards for private enterprises, also known as PE GAAP. These standards are more flexible and responsive (from a cost-benefit perspective) to the needs of the numerous and varied private entities that make up much of the economy. Private entities will be able to choose to follow IFRS or ASPE. This edition integrates material from both sets of standards.

As more and more countries move to international accounting standards, the IFRS body of knowledge itself is undergoing unprecedented change. Not only are we moving to a new platform but that platform is shifting at a fairly rapid pace. We have accepted change as a constant in this edition. Although we have tried to ensure that we have the most up-to-date material, we acknowledge that we have to equip you to continue to be able to change with the standards after you leave us.

As always, the core of the textbook rests on foundational principles and concepts. Although these may change, they generally evolve more slowly and many of the basics endure. Much of IFRS and ASPE (and indeed U.S. GAAP) rests upon the same principles. We have attempted to highlight and focus on this core.

Because IFRS and ASPE are principles-based, we continue to encourage you to view things from differing perspectives and to develop professional judgement and critical thinking.

With change and more choice comes more complexity and so we have scaled back in some areas. For instance, in some chapters, we have moved some of the material to the textbook's website (such as that covering instalment sales and cost recovery methods). Many of the perceived complexities in accounting stem from the fact that many accounting students do not really understand the underlying economics and legalities. We have added material that will help you gain a greater understanding of these issues.

New Features

Several new features have been added in this edition.

COMPARISON CHARTS: Our end-of-chapter charts that identify the major differences between IFRS and private enterprise GAAP are a key feature. These charts augment the more detailed charts that have been added to many chapters that also focus on differences. Where there is a new standard being proposed, we have added a column to the end-of-chapter charts so that you understand what may be in store in the future, or provide a Looking Ahead feature to alert you to upcoming changes expected.

FINANCE AND LAW ICONS: In order to help you integrate your knowledge of economics, finance, and law with accounting, we have added new finance and law icons. We have developed the material so that you gain an appreciation for these fundamentals before trying to account for them.

Finance

Law

Books

Cash

Company — Customer

Significant Change

BUSINESS TRANSACTIONS BOXES/ICONS: Many chapters have a new business transactions box and icon. In most business transactions, you give something up and receive something. These boxes and icons are meant to help you understand what has been given up and what has been received in the transaction. As noted earlier, this is tremendously helpful when you are trying to decide how to account for a transaction or economic event.

SIGNIFICANT CHANGE ICON: These icons are meant to catch your attention. Everywhere there has been a significant change in the accounting standard or how it is applied, it has been highlighted with a giant asterisk in the margin.

END-OF-CHAPTER MATERIAL: While not a new feature, this material has been revised to ensure that you have ample opportunity to apply and practise the various methods and models that are acceptable under IFRS and ASPE. Case material allows you to analyze business transactions and situations and apply both sets of standards. We have added new research and writing assignment questions that allow you to explore the nature of GAAP differences and understand why standard setters choose different solutions when different groups of users are considered. New comprehensive coverage problems after chapters 5, 9, 12, 14, 17, and 23 combine material from the current chapter with previous chapters so that you understand how "it all fits together."

Continuing Features

Many things have contributed to the success of Kieso over the years. The following points outline just a few.

Helping Students Practise

The end-of-chapter material includes cases and integrated cases, which draw material from several chapters in order to help you build skills in identifying key accounting issues. In this edition, we have added more than 10 new cases overall and revised all solutions to incorporate IFRS and/or private enterprise standards. Further, a summary guiding you through the case study method appears inside the front cover of this text. This is in addition to the full Case Study Primer available on WileyPLUS and the Student Website.

WILEY PLUS

Analysis doesn't have to be just part of the cases. Our Digging Deeper feature asks you to look more closely at the results you obtain in the problems and exercises. For instance, you might then be asked to comment on results or determine how things might be different if one of the original variables were to change. Digging Deeper questions are identified using the icon shown here.

Digging Deeper

Real-World Emphasis

Since intermediate accounting is a course in which students must understand the application of accounting principles and techniques in practice, we strive to include as many real-world examples as possible.

Real-World Emphasis

Reinforcement of the Concepts

Throughout each chapter you are asked What Do the Numbers Mean? and are presented with discussions applying accounting concepts to business contexts. This feature builds on

What Do
the Numbers
Mean?

the opening feature stories in making the accounting concepts relevant to you. Through current examples of how accounting is applied, you will be better able to relate to and understand the material. The underlying concepts icons in each chapter alert you to remember that the issue under discussion draws on concepts identified in Chapter 2 as part of the conceptual framework. In addition, an Analysis section is present in most chapters. This section discusses the effect on the financial statements of many of the accounting choices made by corporate management, alerting you to look behind the numbers. Finally, the accounting equation appears in the margin next to key journal entries to help you understand the impact of each transaction on the company's financial position and cash flows.

**Underlying
Concept**

Integration of Ethics Coverage

Rather than featuring ethics coverage and problem material in isolation, we use an ethics icon to highlight ethical issues as they are discussed within each chapter. This icon also appears beside each exercise, problem, or case where ethical issues must be dealt with in relation to all kinds of accounting situations.

Ethics

A Complete Package

Kieso continues to provide the most comprehensive and useful technology package available for the intermediate course. Its Student Website continues to expand with new tutorials on bad debts, bonds, and inventory methods. Also featured are a case primer, demonstration problems, expanded ethics coverage, and more. The site can be accessed at www.wiley.com/canada/kieso.

A key feature of every accounting package produced by John Wiley & Sons Canada, Ltd. is *WileyPLUS*. This on-line suite of resources that includes a complete multimedia version of the text will help students come to class better prepared for lectures, and allows instructors to track students' progress throughout the course more easily. Students can take advantage of tools such as quizzes and tutorials to help them study more efficiently. *WileyPLUS* is designed to provide instant feedback as students practise on their own. Students can work through assignments with automatic grading or review custom-made class presentations featuring reading assignments, PowerPoint slides, and interactive simulations.

Currency and Accuracy

Accounting changes at a rapid pace—a pace that has increased in recent years. An up-to-date book is more important than ever. As in past editions, we have endeavoured to make this edition the most current and accurate text available. We have also ensured that new material subject to uncertainty has been vetted by subject matter experts.

The following list outlines the revisions and improvements made in the chapters of this volume.

Chapter 13 Non-Financial and Current Liabilities

- Placed more emphasis on liability definition, in line with the evolving conceptual framework
- Placed more emphasis on the existence of an unconditional obligation at the balance sheet date
- Material on short-term compensated absences now covered in this chapter, including parental leave
- Updated sales tax and HST section
- Updated section using an expense approach and a revenue approach for product guarantees and customer loyalty programs
- New section on upcoming changes for the recognition and measurement of contingencies
- Added real-world illustrations for reporting under IFRS

- New IFRS/ASPE (PE GAAP) comparison chart, including the requirements under the IASB Exposure Draft on the Measurement of Liabilities in IAS 37

Chapter 14 Long-Term Financial Liabilities

- Integrated material on troubled debt and debt settlement/extinguishment (including decision tree) into the body of the chapter instead of in the appendix
- Removed material on impairment as it is covered in earlier chapters
- Incorporated material on measuring liabilities at fair value under the fair value option (own credit risk issue)
- Noted that straight-line amortization of premiums/discounts is acceptable as an accounting policy choice under PE GAAP
- New IFRS/ASPE (PE GAAP) comparison chart
- Noted ongoing projects on derecognition, fair value measurement, and financial instruments with characteristics of equity and conceptual framework

Chapter 15 Shareholders' Equity

- Added new examples for the statement of changes in shareholders' equity and required note disclosures for managing capital
- New IFRS/ASPE (PE GAAP) comparison chart
- Noted ongoing IASB and FASB projects on financial statement presentation and characteristics of equity

Chapter 16 Complex Financial Instruments

- Rearranged the chapter to start with derivatives to lay the foundations for subsequent discussions on hybrid instruments, share-based compensation, and hedging
- Incorporated numerous transactions boxes to help focus on the underlying business transactions and risks transferred
- New material on accounting for purchase commitments as executory contracts versus derivatives
- New material on derivatives involving the entity's own shares (determining if they are equity or derivatives for accounting purposes)
- Used back-to-basics approach regarding compound instruments, looking at basic attributes of debt versus equity
- Added more charts looking at examples of how to account for various complex instruments using basic definitions
- Moved material on discounted cash flow to Chapter 2
- New material on use of more complex fair value measurement models in Appendix 16C (focus on inputs to fair value models)
- Streamlined discussion on hedging in Appendix 16A, incorporating simplified PE GAAP model for hedge accounting (which does not label hedges as cash flow or fair value)
- New IFRS/ASPE (PE GAAP) comparison chart
- Noted IASB projects outstanding including hedging and those mentioned in Chapters 14 and 15

Chapter 17 Earnings per Share

- Noted that IFRS requires presentation of EPS for public entities but there is no guidance in PE GAAP
- Noted that IFRS refers to common shares as "ordinary shares" (the terms are used interchangeably) but IFRS does not refer to senior equity instruments (refers to "preferred shares" instead)
- Deleted references to extraordinary items
- Added paragraph on mandatorily redeemable shares and EPS calculations
- Noted IASB projects outstanding on EPS

Chapter 18 Income Taxes

- Updated to recognize choice allowed by private enterprise standards: taxes payable or future income taxes method

- Updated to explain the very few differences between IFRS (balance sheet liability method) and the future income taxes method
- Used the term "reversing" differences instead of "timing" differences
- Transferred the comprehensive illustration to the appendix
- Updated conceptual questions section for current recognition and measurement issues
- Removed extraordinary item example for intra-period allocation and eliminated reference to available-for-sale, held-to-maturity, and held-for-trading categories of financial instruments
- New IFRS/ASPE (PE GAAP) comparison chart, and update provided on what is on the standard-setting horizon for taxes

Chapter 19 Pensions and Other Employee Future Benefits

- New material on the immediate recognition approach, permitted by ASPE, and the deferral and amortization approach, permitted by ASPE and required by IFRS
- Used new illustrations for the deferral and amortization approach
- Changed illustrations to a spreadsheet format with a clearer distinction between what is recorded on the books and what is in memo accounts
- Reduced emphasis on the transition asset or obligation
- Transferred event accrual accounting situations to Chapter 13
- Added IFRS illustrations
- New IFRS/ASPE (PE GAAP) comparison chart, and update on changing standards

Chapter 20 Leases

- Reorganized chapter to cover existing classification approach for lessees and then lessors
- Introduced the contract-based approach inherent in the new standards expected
- Transferred the four lease illustrations to the website and WileyPLUS
- New spreadsheet-based background for illustrations
- Reduced coverage of cash flow statement differences between operating and capital leases, and lessor's initial direct costs
- New illustration of effect of guaranteed residuals, lease term, and bargain purchase options on depreciation
- Added example of a lease inducement in an operating lease
- New IFRS/ASPE (PE GAAP) comparison chart, with comparison also to expected new standards

Chapter 21 Accounting Changes and Error Analysis

- Transferred error analysis section into an appendix, and clarified when the current taxes payable account is affected
- Revised section on how GAAP is determined under private enterprise standards and IFRS
- Noted that private enterprise standards allow some voluntary changes without the resulting financial statements being "reliable and more relevant"
- Provided illustration of revised equity sections with a statement of changes in equity
- Added a short section on transition to ASPE and IFRS
- Noted that a change in depreciation method is considered a change in estimate throughout
- New IFRS/ASPE (PE GAAP) comparison chart

Chapter 22 Statement of Cash Flows

- Noted that the statement of cash flows is now a required financial statement
- Updated material for changes to other standards, such as financial instruments
- Removed section on cash flow per share
- Changed example from acquisition of treasury shares to the repurchase and cancellation of shares, and eliminated the example of an extraordinary item
- Introduced the situation of a company that starts its worksheet with income before interest and taxes
- New IFRS/ASPE (PE GAAP) comparison chart, and introduction of the proposed new financial statement presentation that may be required in the future

Chapter 23 Other Measurement and Disclosure Issues

- Removed section on differential reporting as there are now two separate sets of GAAP: ASPE/PE GAAP (private entities) and IFRS (publicly accountable entities)
- Noted that PE GAAP does not include guidance for reporting segmented or interim information
- Noted that IFRS does not require related-party transactions to be remeasured
- Retained material on FOFI although Canadian GAAP/IFRS no longer provides guidance
- Retained material on unincorporated business although it is not covered by IFRS
- New IFRS/ASPE (PE GAAP) comparison chart
- Noted IASB projects outstanding

Acknowledgements

We thank the users of our eighth edition, including the many instructors, faculty, and students who contributed to this revision through their comments and instructive criticism. In addition, special thanks are extended to contributors to our ninth edition manuscript and supplements.

Reviewers

Peter Alpaugh, George Brown College

Ann Bigelow, University of Western Ontario

Ralph Cecere, McGill University

Charles Cho, Concordia University

Robert Collier, University of Ottawa

Karen Congo, University of Western Ontario

Helen Farkas, McMaster University

George Fisher, Douglas College

Susan Fisher, Algonquin College

Ian Hutchinson, Acadia University

Stuart Jones, University of Calgary

Jocelyn King, University of Alberta

Cécile Laurin, Algonquin College

Douglas A. Leatherdale, Georgian College

Bruce McConomy, Wilfrid Laurier University

Songlan Peng, York University

Tom Pippy, Conestoga College

Gwen Roberts, Ryerson University

Zvi Singer, McGill University

Rik Smistad, Mount Royal University

Dragan Stojanovic, University of Toronto

Desmond Tsang, McGill University

Helen Vallee, Kwantlen Polytechnic University

Appreciation is also extended to colleagues at the Rotman School of Management, University of Toronto, and the Sobey School of Business, Saint Mary's University, who provided input, suggestions, and support, especially Peter Thomas, for his professionalism and wisdom, and Martha Dunlop, for her expertise and review of the manuscript.

It takes many people and coordinated efforts to get an edition off the ground. Many thanks to the team at John Wiley & Sons Canada, Ltd., who are superb: Zoë Craig, Acquisitions Editor; Veronica Visentin, Publisher; Karen Staudinger, Editorial Manager, who has been an integral part of the last five editions; Karen Bryan, Vice President, Publishing Services; Channade Fenandoe, Media Editor, for managing this increasingly important aspect of the text; Deanna Durnford, Supplements Coordinator; and Aida Krneta, Marketing Manager. Their enthusiasm and support have been invaluable. The contributions of Alison Arnot, Laurel Hyatt, Zofia Laubitz, Gail Ferreira Ng-A-Kien, and Julie van Tol are also very much appreciated. A special thank you goes to Daleara Hirjikaka, our Developmental Editor extraordinaire, who dealt cheerfully with us on an almost daily basis and kept everything on track.

We are particularly grateful to Ann Bigelow, Cécile Laurin, Camillo Lento, Robert Ducharme, Allan Foerster, Ingrid McLeod-Dick, Anu Goel, and Rik Smistad for all their help with the end-of-chapter material and solutions. Thanks also go to Carole Clyne, Laura Cumming, Robert Ducharme, Helen Farkas, Helmut Hauke, Elizabeth Hicks, Cécile Laurin, Camillo Lento, Ingrid McLeod-Dick, Richard Michalski, Peter Secord, Zvi Singer, Marie Sinnott, Rik Smistad, Dragan Stojanovic, and Glenys Sylvestre, who contributed so much to the related supplements.

We appreciate the continuing co-operation of the accounting standards group at the Canadian Institute of Chartered Accountants and of Ron Salole, Vice-President of Standards. The director and principals of the Accounting Standards Board have been as open and helpful as possible in all our dealings with them. For this ninth edition, a special thank you is owed to Tricia O'Malley and Ian Hague. We also thank the CICA itself for allowing us to quote from its materials and Eastern Platinum for permitting us to use its 2009 annual financial statements prepared under IFRS for our specimen financial statements.

We thoroughly enjoy the challenges brought about by change and hope that we are able to transfer some of this enthusiasm to both instructors and students. We hope that this book helps teachers instill in their students an appreciation of the challenges, value, and limitations of accounting, encourages students to evaluate critically and understand financial accounting theory and practice, and prepares students for advanced study, professional examinations, and the successful and ethical pursuit of their careers in accounting or business. If so, then we will have attained our objective.

Suggestions and comments from users of this book are always appreciated. We have striven to produce an error-free text, but if anything has slipped through the variety of checks undertaken, please let us know so that corrections can be made to subsequent printings.

Irene M. Wiecek
TORONTO, ONTARIO
wiecek@rotman.utoronto.ca

Nicola M. Young
HALIFAX, NOVA SCOTIA
nicola.young@smu.ca

May 2010

Brief Contents

Contents

Tracking Points

THESE DAYS almost every retailer seems to be offering points programs to loyal customers.

Hudson's Bay Company's HBC Rewards program offers points for spending at The Bay, Zellers, and Home Outfitters. Once customers have collected enough points, they can redeem them for merchandise or HBC gift cards.

The Shoppers Drug Mart Optimum Program awards points that can be cashed in for discounts on future purchases at the store.

With each purchase, members of the Staples easyRewards program are registered to win prizes, and after spending a certain amount at the store in one year, they can get a small percentage back in rewards.

While each of these programs is slightly different, they all offer the same thing—incentive to spend more money more often in that specific store. And Canadians are taking advantage of these programs. A recent survey of membership in loyalty programs found that 93.6% of Canadian consumers said they belong to at least one program.

But what are the accounting implications for the retailer? The International Financial Reporting Interpretations Committee (IFRIC) issued IFRIC 13 *Customer Loyalty Programmes*, to address how companies "should account for their obligation to provide free or discounted goods or services if and when the customers redeem the points."

IFRIC 13 requires companies to estimate the value of the customers' points and defer this amount of revenue as a liability until they have fulfilled their obligations to supply awards. In the past, some companies would accrue an expense at the time of the initial sale, based on the costs they expected to incur to supply the free or discounted goods. The rationale was that the loyalty awards were incidental costs of securing the first sale that should be recognized when the sale is made. The IFRIC's view is that loyalty awards are separate goods or services that customers have paid for.

IFRIC 13 became mandatory starting in July 2008. So, as Canada adopts IFRS in 2011, many Canadian retailers may be changing the way they account for their loyalty programs. ■

Sources: HBC, Shoppers, and Staples websites; "Canadian Consumer Membership in Loyalty Programs Near Universal: Participation Up 9% Through Recession, Reaching 93.6%," Colloquy news release, August 19, 2009; "Note to Editors," Deloitte Touche Tohmatsu news release, October 5, 2006.

CHAPTER 13

Non-Financial and Current Liabilities

Learning Objectives

After studying this chapter, you should be able to:

1. Define liabilities, distinguish financial liabilities from other liabilities, and identify how they are measured.

2. Define current liabilities and identify and account for common types of current liabilities.

3. Identify and account for the major types of employee-related liabilities.

4. Explain the recognition, measurement, and disclosure requirements for decommissioning and restoration obligations.

5. Explain the issues and account for unearned revenues, product guarantees, and other customer program obligations.

6. Explain and apply two approaches to the recognition of contingencies and uncertain commitments, and identify the accounting and reporting requirements for guarantees and commitments.

7. Indicate how non-financial and current liabilities are presented and analyzed.

8. Identify differences in accounting between private enterprise standards and IFRS and what changes are expected in the near future.

Preview of Chapter 13

This chapter explains the basic principles underlying the accounting and reporting for many common current liabilities and for a variety of non-financial liabilities, such as unearned revenues, product warranty and other customer obligations, and asset retirement obligations. Contingencies, commitments, and guarantees are also addressed. Issues related to long-term financial liabilities are explained in Chapter 14.

The chapter is organized as follows:

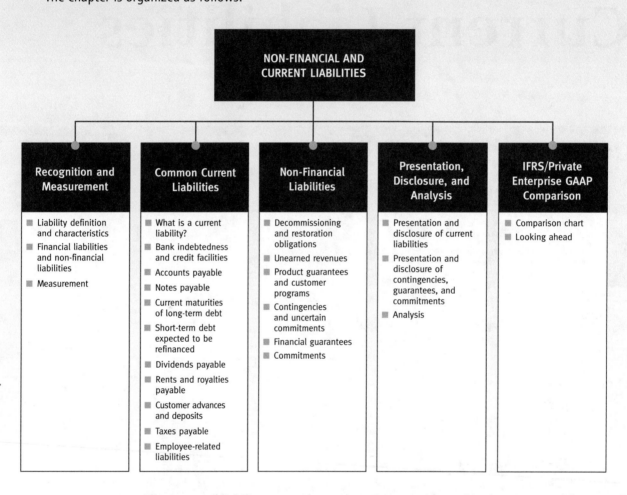

The asset and liability approach to accounting, as evidenced in the conceptual framework, requires that asset and liability definitions govern the recognition of all other accounting elements. Volume 1 of this text concentrated on the recognition and measurement of a variety of assets and Volume 2 continues by beginning with a closer look at liabilities in general, and then several specific types of common liabilities.

The explanations in this chapter about non-financial liabilities under international standards are based on current IAS 37 *Provisions, Contingent Liabilities and Contingent Assets* and materials underlying expected revisions to this standard.[1] While the expected

---

[1] The underlying materials are the 2005 Exposure Draft of Proposed Amendments to IAS 37 *Provisions, Contingent Liabilities and Contingent Assets*, the September 30, 2009 staff summary of decisions reached by the IASB since the exposure draft was published, and the January 2010 Exposure Draft ED/2010/1 *Measurement of Liabilities in IAS 37*.

revisions indicate the current thinking of the IASB as this text went to print, they are not effective until they are incorporated into a final standard. The final standard, expected late in 2010 and effective no earlier than 2012, will be a new IFRS on accounting for liabilities that are not within the scope of other standards, rather than an amendment of existing IAS 37.

RECOGNITION AND MEASUREMENT

Liability Definition and Characteristics

Chapter 2 of this text introduced you to the elements of financial statements and their definitions. It explained that the FASB and IASB were in the process of developing revised definitions of terms such as "assets" and "liabilities" as part of their conceptual framework project and that they had reached tentative conclusions on improved definitions of these terms. In this text, we apply the proposed definitions as they are being used to influence and guide the IASB as it develops new standards, and the AcSB has signalled that it will likely adopt the emerging framework for private entities as well. Illustration 13-1 provides both the definition of liabilities in the existing IFRS and the *CICA Handbook*, Part II as well as what has tentatively been agreed upon for the future.

Underlying Concept

To be able to properly classify specific financial instruments, proper definitions are needed for assets, liabilities, and equities. The conceptual framework definitions are used as the basis for settling difficult classification issues.

1 Objective

Define liabilities, distinguish financial liabilities from other liabilities, and identify how they are measured.

Definition in Existing IFRS and *CICA Handbook*, Part II (a summary)	Current Proposed Definition in Conceptual Framework—Elements and Recognition Project[2]
A liability is an obligation that arises from past transactions or events, which may result in a transfer of assets.	A liability of an entity is a present economic obligation for which the entity is the obligor.
Liabilities have three essential characteristics:	Liabilities have three essential characteristics:
1. They embody a **duty or responsibility**.	1. They exist at the **present** time.
2. The entity has **little or no discretion to avoid the duty**.	2. They represent **economic burdens** or **obligations**.
3. The **transaction** or event that obliges the entity **has occurred**.	3. The obligations are **enforceable on the obligor** entity.

Illustration 13-1

Definitions of Liabilities

The three characteristics of a liability are essential to its definition. First, a liability must exist in the **present**—the economic obligation must exist and the entity must be the obligor **at the balance sheet date**. The existence of a present obligation is not always clear, as we will see later in this chapter. For example, there may be uncertainty about whether an obligating event has occurred, or whether an event that has occurred results in a present obligation, or how a law or regulation applies to that event. Judgement is needed in many circumstances, with management drawing on evidence such as the entity's past experience, other entities' experience with similar items, opinions of experts, and others.[3]

Second, there must be an **economic obligation**—an **unconditional** promise or other requirement to provide or forego economic resources. Obligations in general are either conditional or unconditional. An example of an unconditional obligation is the requirement to pay interest on borrowed money. At each balance sheet date, a company has a present obligation for any accrued but unpaid interest costs to that date. This obligation is not contingent or conditional on a future event. Therefore, any interest accrued (and

---

[2] Taken from *Conceptual Framework—Elements and Recognition Project Update*, FASB and IASB, March 15, 2010.

[3] IASB Staff Paper, *Summary of decisions reached since publishing exposure draft: Liabilities—amendments to IAS 37*, September 30, 2009, p. 5.

unpaid) at the balance sheet date is recognized as a liability—interest payable. Some unconditional obligations are referred to as stand-ready obligations. This means that the obligor "stands ready" to do whatever is required under the terms of a contract, agreement, or law. While there may be uncertainty about the **amount** of future outflows of assets, there is no uncertainty about **whether** a present obligation exists. Examples include insurers or guarantors who stand ready to pay out an amount equal to a loss that may occur under a specific contract if such a loss should occur. A conditional obligation, on the other hand, requires performance to be carried out only if an uncertain future event actually occurs. Unconditional obligations are always recognized as liabilities, whereas conditional obligations on their own are not.

Law

The third characteristic refers to the fact that the entity must have a duty or responsibility to perform in a particular way; it is required to bear the economic obligation, and this requirement can be **enforced by legal or equivalent means**. This means that a law, a contract enforceable by law, or a constructive obligation has to exist. A constructive obligation is one that arises from past or present company practice that signals that the entity acknowledges a potential economic burden. This comes about because the entity has indicated to others that it will accept a specific responsibility and other parties can reasonably expect the entity to perform. For example, a company may be required by provincial legislation to provide 4% vacation pay to its employees, but it may have paid 6% over the past number of years. Therefore, even though the company may not be required by law or contract to pay the extra 2%, the expectation is that it will continue to provide it. This is a constructive obligation, and amounts owing at the balance sheet date are recognized as a liability, based on the 6%.

All entities must comply with the statutes, laws, and regulations in the legal jurisdiction in which they operate; however, these result in liabilities only if the entity violates their provisions. "Present unconditional obligations" cannot result if the provisions are not yet effective or if an obligating event has not yet taken place.

Significant Change

The two definitions in Illustration 13-1 may seem very similar. Going forward, however, there is a marked difference in how the revised definition is applied. Under previous **recognition** requirements, non-financial liabilities were recognized only if it was probable (that is, more likely than not) that the obligation would result in an outflow of cash or other economic resources from the entity. That is, the uncertainty of the amount was an issue in whether the obligation was recognized as a liability. Under the new recognition and measurement requirements, a liability is **recognized** whenever an unconditional obligation exists at the reporting date. Any uncertainty about the amount to be sacrificed in the future is then taken into account in the **measurement** of the liability.

Financial Liabilities and Non-Financial Liabilities

Because a number of accounting standards refer to the recognition, measurement, and reporting of **financial instruments** specifically, it is important to be able to identify those that are financial **liabilities**. Under both accounting standards for private enterprises (ASPE) and IFRS, a financial liability is any liability that is a **contractual obligation**:

1. to deliver cash or other financial assets to another entity; or

2. to exchange financial assets or financial liabilities with another entity under conditions that are potentially unfavourable to the entity.[4]

Note that this definition requires the liability to be based on an obligation that is created by a contract. Liabilities that are created by legislation, such as income taxes payable, do

---

[4] IAS 32 *Financial Instruments: Presentation*, para. 11. Under IFRS, the definition is extended to include certain contracts that may be settled in the entity's own equity instruments; that is, its own shares.

not qualify as financial liabilities and therefore are not covered by the same accounting standards as financial liabilities. In this chapter, most current liabilities are financial in nature, but if the obligation will be met by the delivery of goods or services, such as in the case of unearned revenue and warranty obligations, it is not considered a financial liability.

The distinction between financial and non-financial liabilities is important because the accounting standard that applies depends on how the liability is classified.

Measurement

Financial Liabilities

Financial liabilities are recognized initially at their fair value. After acquisition, though, most of the financial liabilities that are discussed in this and later chapters are accounted for **at their amortized cost**.[5] Consistent with cost-based measurement, transaction costs that are a direct result of the issue of the liability are netted against its original fair value. Alternatively, transaction costs associated with the issue of financial liabilities that are accounted for after acquisition **at fair value** are recognized in net income as they are incurred.

When liabilities are short-term in nature, such as regular trade payables with 30- or 60-day payment terms, they are usually accounted for on practical grounds at their maturity value. This is appropriate because the difference between the liability's fair value and its maturity value is not significant. The slight overstatement of liabilities that results from carrying many current liabilities at their maturity value is accepted if it is immaterial.

Non-Financial Liabilities

Non-financial liabilities, on the other hand, are usually not payable in cash. Therefore, they are measured in a different way. **Private entity** standards or **ASPE** do not separately address the issue of non-financial liabilities, so these are measured in a variety of ways, depending on the specific liability. For example, unearned revenue is usually measured at the fair value of the goods or services to be delivered in the future, and, where matching is an issue, the obligations are measured based on management's best estimate of the cost of the goods or services to be provided in the future.

Under **international standards**, non-financial liabilities are measured initially and at each subsequent reporting date at the best estimate of the amount the entity would rationally pay at the balance sheet date to settle the present obligation. This is usually the present value of the resources needed to fulfill the obligation, measured at the expected value or probability-weighted average of the range of possible outcomes.[6] Proposals to revise the existing standards indicate that any asset outflows used in these calculations are measured at the amount the company would pay to be relieved of the obligation; that is, at their "exit" value or value in sale, not at their cost to the entity.[7]

With this introduction to liabilities, we now take a closer look at specific current liabilities found on most companies' statements of financial position.

---

[5] At the intermediate level of accounting, the only liabilities that are held for trading purposes and later accounted for at fair value are derivatives. These financial liabilities are discussed in Chapter 16.

[6] The standard also addresses the issue of possible reimbursements that apply when an entity settles a provision. In this case, a reimbursement must be virtually certain of being received, so there may be timing differences between when a non-financial liability is recognized and when the corresponding recovery is recognized.

[7] IASB Exposure Draft ED/2010/1 *Measurement of Liabilities in IAS 37* and IASB Staff Paper, *Summary of decisions reached since publishing exposure draft: Liabilities—amendments to IAS 37*, September 30, 2009, pp. 9–10. A limited exception was tentatively agreed on in November 2009. This allows some onerous contracts to be measured at the cost rather than the value of supplying the goods or services.

COMMON CURRENT LIABILITIES

What Is a Current Liability?

Objective 2
Define current liabilities and identify and account for common types of current liabilities.

Because liabilities result in a future disbursement (payment) of assets or services, one of their most important features is the timing of when they are due. Obligations that mature in the short term place a demand on the entity's current assets. They are demands that must be satisfied on time and in the ordinary course of business if operations are to continue. Liabilities with a distant due date generally do not result in a claim on the company's current assets and are therefore classified differently. This difference in timing and the effect on current assets is a major reason for the division of liabilities into (1) current liabilities and (2) noncurrent liabilities.

Another reason for classifying current assets and liabilities separately from long-term assets and liabilities is to provide information about the working capital used by the entity in its normal operating cycle. The normal operating cycle is the period of time between acquiring the goods and services for processing in operations and receiving cash from the eventual sale of the processed goods and services. Industries that manufacture products that go through an aging process and certain capital-intensive industries have an operating cycle of much longer than one year. On the other hand, most retail and service establishments have several operating cycles in a single year. The operating cycle is sometimes referred to as the cash-to-cash cycle. If the length of the cycle is not obvious, accounting standards often assume it is 12 months.

The definition of a current liability and of the length of the operating cycle is directly related to that of a current asset. A liability is classified as current under IFRS when one of the following conditions is met:

1. It is expected to be settled in the entity's normal operating cycle.

2. It is held primarily for trading.

3. It is due within 12 months from the end of the reporting period.

4. The entity does not have an unconditional right to defer its settlement for at least 12 months after the balance sheet date.[8]

Private enterprise standards do not provide a definition of a current asset or current liability, but the examples they provide indicate the intent is similar to that of the IFRS. There may be minor differences in application.

A variety of current liabilities commonly found in the financial statements of companies are illustrated next.

Bank Indebtedness and Credit Facilities

A major element of a company's cash position is its bank indebtedness for current operating purposes and its line of credit or revolving debt arrangements related to this debt. Instead of having to negotiate a new loan every time it needs funds, a company generally enters into an agreement with its bank that allows it to make multiple borrowings up to a negotiated limit. As previous borrowings are partly repaid, the company is permitted to borrow again

---

[8] IAS 1 *Presentation of Financial Statements*, para. 69. The FASB and IASB have made a tentative decision in their joint Financial Statement Presentation project (December 2009) that the current (short-term) and non-current (long-term) classifications should be based only on a fixed period of one year. This part of the project is expected to result in new standards in mid-2011.

under the same contract. Because the financial institution commits itself to making money available to the entity, the bank often charges an additional fee for this service over and above the interest that it charges on the funds that are actually advanced. Under such agreements, the financial institution usually requires collateral and often sets restrictions on the company's activities or financial statement ratios that must be maintained.

The amount of actual bank indebtedness is reported on the balance sheet, while the total funds that the credit arrangement allows the company to borrow and any restrictions that are imposed by the financial institution are disclosed in the notes.

Borrowings and growth must be carefully managed! Maintaining close working relationships with customers, banks, suppliers, and other creditors is central to getting through the crunch. Based in British Columbia, **Pacific Safety Products Inc.** (PSP) enjoyed a 69% increase in sales in one year recently and, along with it, suffered the liquidity problems that often come with such success. The company's annual report indicated that one of PSP's major challenges during the year had been to manage its cash flow so that it could pay suppliers. This was necessary to ensure a continuous flow of raw materials that were needed in the manufacturing process in order to meet customer orders on a timely basis.

What Do the Numbers Mean?

PSP thus reported bank indebtedness of almost $3 million in its current liabilities at the company's year end. Providing details on the indebtedness, a note to the financial statements indicated a maximum operating line of credit of $3 million with the Bank of Nova Scotia, which was secured by accounts receivable, inventory, and an assignment of insurance. The note also reported that the company was not in compliance with the covenants imposed by the bank for its current ratio and tangible net worth, but that the bank was allowing PSP to operate outside its covenants.

Real-World Emphasis

One year later, PSP reported sales that were only 75% of those reported for the preceding fiscal year, but its cash flow from operating activities was almost twice as high as in the earlier period! The uncollected receivables from one year earlier had been collected and this allowed the company to get over the cash crunch. Bank indebtedness was reduced to only $102,417, the operating line was reduced to $2 million, and the company was once again in compliance with the covenants imposed by the bank.

Accounts Payable

Accounts payable, or *trade accounts payable*, are balances owed to others for goods, supplies, or services related to the entity's ordinary business activities that are purchased on open account. This means that evidence of the obligations' existence comes from regular invoices rather than from separate contracts for each transaction. Accounts payable arise because of the time lag between the receipt of goods and services and the payment for them. This period of extended credit is usually stated in the terms of sale and purchase—for example, 2/10, n/30 or 1/10, E.O.M., net 30[9]—and is commonly 30 to 60 days long.

Most accounting systems are designed to record liabilities for purchases of goods when the goods are received. Sometimes there is a delay in recording the goods and the related liability on the books, such as when waiting for an invoice. If title has passed to the purchaser before the goods are received, the transaction should be recorded when the title passes. Attention must be paid to transactions that occur near the end of one accounting period and the beginning of the next so that the goods and services received (the inventory or expense) are recorded in the same accounting period as the liability (accounts payable)

---

[9] As explained in Chapter 7, 2/10, n/30 means there is a 2% discount if the invoice is paid within 10 days with the full amount due in 30 days; and 1/10, E. O. M., net 30 means that there is a 1% discount if the invoice is paid before the 10th of the following month with full payment due by the 30th of the following month.

and both are recorded in the proper period. Chapter 8 discussed this cut-off issue in greater detail and illustrated the entries for accounts payable and purchase discounts.

Notes Payable

Law

Notes payable are written promises to pay a certain sum of money on a specified future date and may arise from purchases, financing, or other transactions. In some industries, instead of the normal procedure of extending credit on an open account, notes (often referred to as trade notes payable) are required as part of the sale/purchase transaction. Notes payable to banks or loan companies are generally created by cash loans. Notes may be classified as current or long-term (noncurrent), depending on the payment due date. Notes may also be interest-bearing or non-interest-bearing (i.e., zero-interest-bearing) and accounting for them is the mirror image of accounting for notes receivable illustrated in Chapter 7.

Interest-Bearing Note Issued

Assume that Provincial Bank agrees to lend $100,000 on March 1, 2011, to Landscape Corp. and the company signs a $100,000, four-month, 12% note. The entry to record the cash received by Landscape Corp. on March 1 is:

A   =   L   + SE
+100,000   +100,000

Cash flows: ↑ 100,000 inflow

| March 1 | Cash | 100,000 | |
| | Notes Payable | | 100,000 |

If Landscape Corp. has a December 31 year end but prepares financial statements semi-annually, an adjusting entry is required to recognize the four months of interest expense and interest payable of $4,000 ($100,000 × 12% × $^4/_{12}$) on June 30. The adjusting entry is:

A =   L   +   SE
    +4,000   −4,000

Cash flows: No effect

| June 30 | Interest Expense | 4,000 | |
| | Interest Payable | | 4,000 |

At maturity on July 1, Landscape Corp. pays the note's face value of $100,000 plus the $4,000 of interest. The entry to record payment of the note and accrued interest is as follows:

A   =   L   + SE
−104,000   −104,000

Cash flows: ↓ 104,000 outflow

July 1	Notes Payable	100,000	
	Interest Payable	4,000	
	Cash		104,000

Zero-Interest-Bearing Note Issued

A zero-interest-bearing note may be issued instead of an interest-bearing note. Despite its name, a **zero-interest-bearing note *does* have an interest component**. The interest is just not added on top of the note's face or maturity value; instead, it is included in the face amount. The interest is the difference between the amount of cash received when the note is signed and the higher face amount that is payable at maturity. The borrower receives the note's present value in cash and pays back the larger maturity value.

To illustrate, assume that Landscape Corp. issues a $100,000, four-month, zero-interest-bearing note payable to the Provincial Bank on March 1. The note's present value is $96,154, based on the bank's discount rate of 12%. Landscape's entry to record this transaction is as follows:

March 1	Cash	96,154	
	Notes Payable		96,154

$$A = L + SE$$
$$+96,154 \quad +96,154$$
Cash flows: ↑ 96,154 inflow

Notes Payable is credited for the note's fair value, which is less than the cash due at maturity. In effect, this is the amount borrowed. If Landscape Corp. prepares financial statements at June 30, the interest expense for the four-month period to June 30 must be recognized along with the increase in the Note Payable: $96,154 \times 12\% \times {}^{4}/_{12} = \$3,846$ as follows:

June 30	Interest Expense	3,846	
	Notes Payable[10]		3,846

$$A = L + SE$$
$$+3,846 \quad -3,846$$
Cash flows: No effect

The Notes Payable account now has a balance of $96,154 + $3,846 = $100,000. This is the amount borrowed plus interest to June 30 at 12%. On July 1 the note is repaid:

July 1	Notes Payable	100,000	
	Cash		100,000

$$A = L + SE$$
$$-100,000 \quad -100,000$$
Cash flows: ↓ 100,000 outflow

The accounting issues related to long-term notes payable are discussed in Chapter 14.

Current Maturities of Long-Term Debt

Bonds, mortgage notes, and other long-term indebtedness that mature within 12 months from the balance sheet date—current maturities of long-term debt—are reported as current liabilities. When only part of a long-term obligation is to be paid within the next 12 months, as in the case of a mortgage or of serial bonds that are to be retired through a series of annual instalments, **only the maturing portion of the principal of the long-term debt is reported as a current liability**. The balance is reported as a long-term liability.

Portions of long-term obligations that will mature in the next 12 months should not be included as current liabilities if, by contract, they are to be retired by assets accumulated for this purpose that properly have not been reported as current assets. In this situation, no current assets are used and no other current liabilities are created in order to repay the maturing liability. Therefore, it is incorrect to classify the liability as current.

---

[10] Alternatively, the note payable could have been recorded at its face value of $100,000, with the $3,846 difference between the cash received and the face value debited to Discount on Notes Payable. Discount on Notes Payable is a contra account to Notes Payable and therefore is subtracted from Notes Payable on the balance sheet.

Law

A liability that is **due on demand** (i.e., callable by the creditor), or that will be due on demand within a year, is also classified as a current liability. Often companies have debt agreements that, while due on demand, have payment schedules set up to pay the obligation over a number of years. The management of these entities argues that only the portion due to be paid within 12 months should be classified as current. Managers further argue that financial statement readers will be misled if the whole of the debt is reported as a current liability, because the company's liquidity position is misrepresented. The standard setters, on the other hand, indicate that all of such callable debt meets the definition of a current liability, and that additional information about the callable debt can be explained in the notes to the financial statements.

Liabilities often become callable by the creditor if there is a violation of a debt agreement. For example, most debt agreements require the borrower to maintain a minimum ratio of equity to debt or, as illustrated in the Pacific Safety Products situation above, specify minimum working capital requirements.

If a long-term debt agreement is violated and the liability becomes payable on demand, the debt is reclassified as current. **Under IFRS**, this position holds, even if the lender agrees between the balance sheet date and the date the financial statements are released that it will not demand repayment because of the violation. This position is consistent with the fact that, at the balance sheet date, the entity did not have an unconditional right to defer the payment beyond 12 months from the reporting date. That right could only be exercised by the lender.

Under ASPE, the liability is reclassified to the current category unless:

1. the creditor waives the covenant (agreement) requirements, **or**

2. the violation has been cured within the grace period that is usually given in these agreements, **and**

3. it is likely that the company will not violate the covenant requirements within a year from the balance sheet date.

Short-Term Debt Expected to Be Refinanced

Significant Change

Short-term debt obligations are amounts scheduled to mature within one year from the balance sheet date. However, a classification issue arises when such a liability is expected to be refinanced on a long-term basis, and therefore current assets are not expected to be needed for them. Where should these short-term obligations expected to be refinanced on a long-term basis be reported?[11]

At one time, the accounting profession generally agreed with not including short-term obligations in current liabilities if they were "expected to be refinanced" on a long-term basis. Because the profession gave no specific guidelines, however, determining whether a short-term obligation was "expected to be refinanced" was usually based solely on management's **intent**. Classification was not clear-cut and the proper accounting was therefore uncertain. For example, take a company that might want a five-year bank loan but handles the actual financing with 90-day notes that it keeps renewing. In this case, is the loan long-term debt or a current liability?

---

[11] Refinancing a short-term obligation on a long-term basis means either replacing it with a long-term obligation or with equity securities, or renewing, extending, or replacing it with short-term obligations for an uninterrupted period that is more than one year from the date of the company's balance sheet.

Consistent with the international standard for callable debt, **IFRS** indicate that if the debt is due within 12 months from the reporting date, it is classified as a current liability. This classification holds even if a long-term refinancing has been completed before the financial statements are released. The only exception accepted for continuing long-term classification is if, at the balance sheet date, the entity expects to refinance it or roll it over **under an existing agreement** for at least 12 months and the decision is **solely at its discretion**.

Also consistent with the **private enterprise standard** for callable debt, the short-term liability expected to be refinanced is classified as a current liability unless either the liability has been refinanced on a long-term basis or there is a non-cancellable agreement to do so before the financial statements are completed and nothing stands in the way of completing the refinancing. That is, if there is irrefutable evidence by the time the financial statements are completed that the debt has been or will be converted into a long-term obligation, PE GAAP allows currently maturing debt to be classified as long-term on the balance sheet.

If an actual refinancing occurs, the amount of the short-term obligation that is excluded from current liabilities cannot be higher than the proceeds from the new obligation or equity securities that are used to retire it. For example, assume that Montavon Winery has $3 million of short-term debt at the reporting date. The company then issues $2 million of long-term debt after the balance sheet date but before the financial statements are issued, and uses the proceeds from the issue to liquidate the short-term liability. If the net proceeds from the issue of the new long-term debt total $2 million, only $2 million of the short-term debt can be excluded from current liabilities.

Under IFRS, the whole $3 million of maturing debt would still be classified as a current obligation. That is, the international standard has a more stringent requirement: the agreement must be firm **at the balance sheet date**.

Another issue is whether a short-term obligation can be excluded from current liabilities if it is paid off after the balance sheet date and then replaced by long-term debt before the financial statements are issued. To illustrate, assume that Marquardt Limited pays off short-term debt of $40,000 on January 17, 2012, and issues long-term debt of $100,000 on February 3, 2012. Marquardt's financial statements dated December 31, 2011, are issued on March 1, 2012. Because the refinancing does not appear to be linked to the short-term debt, private enterprise standards require the debt to be classified as current. In addition, because its repayment occurred **before** funds were obtained through long-term financing, the repayment **used existing** current assets. Illustration 13-2 shows this situation.

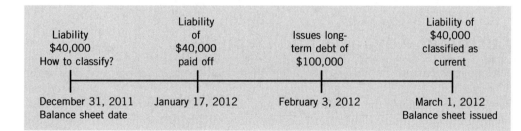

Illustration 13-2

Short-Term Debt Paid Off after Balance Sheet Date and Later Replaced by Long-Term Debt under Both Standards

Dividends Payable

A cash dividend payable is an amount that a corporation owes to its shareholders because the board of directors has authorized a dividend payment. At the dividend declaration date, the corporation incurs a liability that places the shareholders in the position of

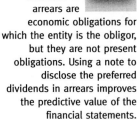

creditors for the amount of dividends declared. Because cash dividends are normally paid within one year of the declaration (generally within three months in actual practice), they are classified as current liabilities.

Accumulated but undeclared dividends on cumulative preferred shares **are not recognized as a liability**, because preferred dividends in arrears are not an obligation until formal action is taken by the board of directors to authorize the distribution. Nevertheless, the company is required to disclose the existence of cumulative dividends that are undeclared in a note to the financial statements.

Dividends that are payable in the form of additional shares **are not recognized as a liability**. Such share or stock dividends (discussed in Chapter 15) do not meet the definition of a liability, because they do not require future outlays of economic resources. In addition, they are not enforceable in that the board of directors can revoke them at any time before they are issued. On declaration, an entry is prepared that reduces (debits) Retained Earnings and credits a contributed capital account such as Stock Dividends Distributable. This latter account is reported in the shareholders' equity section because it represents a transfer of equity from retained earnings to contributed capital.

Law

Rents and Royalties Payable

Law

Rents and royalties payable are another common type of current liability. This obligation may be created by a **contractual agreement in which payments are conditional on the amount of revenue that is earned or the quantity of product that is produced or extracted**. For example, franchisees are usually required to pay franchise fees to the franchisor that are calculated as a percentage of sales, tenants in shopping centres may be obligated to pay additional rents on sales that are above a predetermined amount, and manufacturers may have licensing agreements that require them to pay the holder of a patent a royalty fee for each unit that the manufacturer produces.

Liabilities for expenses that are based on revenues earned or units produced are usually easy to measure. For example, if a lease calls for a fixed rent payment of $500 per month and 1% of all sales over $300,000 per year, the annual rent obligation amounts to $6,000 plus $0.01 of each dollar of revenue over $300,000. Or a royalty agreement may require the accrual of $1.00 per unit that is produced under the patented process, or the accrual of $0.50 on every barrel of oil that is extracted, with the accrued amount then paid to the owner of the mineral rights. As each additional unit of product is produced or extracted, an additional obligation, usually a current liability, is created.

Customer Advances and Deposits

A company's current liabilities may include returnable cash deposits or customer advances that are received from customers and employees. Deposits may be received from customers to guarantee the performance of a contract or service or to guarantee the payment of expected future obligations. For example, telephone companies often require deposits from customers when they install a phone. Some companies require their employees to make deposits for the return of keys or other company property. Deposits may also be received from tenants to cover possible future damage to property.

Are the deposits current or long-term obligations? Their initial classification depends on the conditions attached to the specific deposit. For example, if the entity does not have the right to defer the settlement of the deposit for a period of at least 12 months from the balance sheet date, the deposit is reported as a current liability.

Taxes Payable

Sales Tax

Provincial sales taxes on transfers of tangible property and on certain services must be collected from customers and remitted to the tax authority, usually a provincial or territorial government.[12] The balance in the Sales Taxes Payable account is the liability for sales taxes that have been collected from customers but not yet remitted to the appropriate government. The following entry shows the accounting for a sale on account of $3,000 when a 4% sales tax is in effect:

Accounts Receivable	3,120	
Sales		3,000
Sales Taxes Payable		120

A	=	L	+	SE
+3,120		+120		+3,000

Cash flows: No effect

Goods and Services Tax

Most businesses in Canada are subject to the Goods and Services Tax (GST). The GST, a **value-added tax** of 5% (as of July 1, 2008), is a tax on the value added to the goods and services provided by each taxable entity. The net amount that an entity pays to the Canada Revenue Agency (CRA), which administers this tax, is determined by deducting its input tax credit (the GST the company paid on goods and services it purchased from suppliers) from the amount of GST the company collected, on behalf of the government, on sales to its customers. The Harmonized Sales Tax (HST) is accounted for **in the same way** as the GST in those provinces that have agreed on the combined provincial tax and GST.[13]

Accounting for the GST involves setting up a liability account—GST Payable—that is credited with GST charged on sales, and an asset account—GST Recoverable—that is debited for GST paid to suppliers. Normally, the amount that is collected on sales is higher than the amount paid on purchases, and a net remittance is therefore made to the Canada Revenue Agency. Since GST is also paid on purchases of capital assets, it is possible for the GST Recoverable account to have a larger balance. In these instances, a claim for reimbursement is made to the CRA.

Let's look at the accounting for the GST. Purchases of taxable goods and services are recorded by debiting the GST Recoverable account for the amount of GST to be paid and debiting the appropriate asset or expense account(s) for the purchase price. Since the GST paid is recoverable from the federal government, the GST is not included in the cost of the item(s) acquired. As an example, assume that Bateman Limited purchases merchandise

---

[12] The rate of provincial sales tax varies from province to province. In 2010 (when this text went to print), Alberta and the territories had no sales tax, while Ontario's rate was 8%, Manitoba's and British Columbia's was 7%, and Saskatchewan charged 5%. The tax is usually applied to the sale amount, although in Quebec (7.5%) and Prince Edward Island (10%) it is applied to the selling price plus the GST, increasing the effective provincial rate.

[13] In New Brunswick, Newfoundland and Labrador, and Nova Scotia, the provincial retail sales tax has been combined with the federal Goods and Services Tax (5%) and named the Harmonized Sales Tax (HST). The 13% HST is administered for the most part by the Canada Revenue Agency and is accounted for on the same basis as the GST for the other provinces and territories. Ontario and British Columbia have moved to apply a single HST (13% and 12%, respectively) to replace their existing PST and the federal GST, effective July 1, 2010, and Nova Scotia announced in its 2010 budget that its HST rate is increased to 15%, also effective July 1, 2010. In Quebec, both the Quebec Sales Tax and the GST are administered by the province and both taxes are applied as value-added taxes, similar to the GST.

for $150,000 plus GST of 5% ($7,500). The entry to record this transaction is as follows, assuming a perpetual inventory system is used:

A   =   L   + SE
+157,500   +157,500

Cash flows: No effect

Inventory	150,000	
GST Recoverable	7,500	
Accounts Payable		157,500

If these goods are sold for $210,000 plus GST of 5% ($10,500), the sale entry is:

A   =   L   +   SE
+220,500 +10,500 +210,000

Cash flows: No effect

Accounts Receivable	220,500	
Sales		210,000
GST Payable		10,500

In many cases, GST and sales taxes are levied on the same sale and purchase. Assume, for example, that Smith Ltd. sells supplies to Jones Corp. for $1,000 and both a 7% provincial sales tax and 5% GST are charged on this amount. The entry made by each company follows:

Smith Ltd. (vendor company)			Jones Corp. (purchaser company)		
Accounts Receivable	1,120		Supplies Expense	1,070	
Sales		1,000	GST Recoverable	50	
Sales Taxes Payable		70	Accounts Payable		1,120
GST Payable		50	(To record purchase from Smith Ltd.)		
(To record sale to Jones Corp.)					

Law

Notice that the purchaser includes the provincial sales tax **in the cost** of the goods or services purchased. The provincial sales tax, unlike the GST, is not recoverable by the purchaser.[14] In the provinces with a Harmonized Sales Tax, the full HST amount is treated as shown for the GST.

Because companies are permitted under the legislation to offset the recoverable and payable amounts, only the net balance of the two accounts is reported on the balance sheet. Until a net credit balance is remitted to the Receiver General for Canada, it is reported as a current liability. A net debit balance, on the other hand, is reported as a current asset.

Income Tax

In Canada, federal and provincial income taxes are levied on a company's taxable income. Most businesses consider the amount of income tax payable as an estimate because the calculation of taxable income (and the tax payable on it) has to be reviewed and approved by the CRA. The meaning and application of numerous tax rules, especially new ones, are debatable and often depend on a court's interpretation. Using the best information and advice available, a business prepares its income tax return at the end of its fiscal year and calculates its best estimate of the income tax payable for the period.

---

[14] One exception is in the province of Quebec. The Quebec Sales Tax and the GST are both administered by the province, where all amounts paid are recoverable by the entity through a system of input tax refunds, similar to the input tax credits for the GST.

Assume that Forest Ltd. determines, based on its taxable income for the year, that an income tax liability of $21,000 is payable, and further assume that no accruals have been made during the year. Forest makes the following entry at year end:

Current Income Tax Expense	21,000	
Income Taxes Payable		21,000

A = L + SE
   +21,000 −21,000
Cash flows: No effect

Most corporations are required to make periodic tax instalments (payments) throughout the year based on the previous year's income tax or estimates of the current year's income tax. If Forest Ltd. had made $20,000 of tax instalments during the year, the following entries would also have been made.

Income Taxes Payable	20,000	
Cash		20,000

A = L + SE
−20,000 −20,000
Cash flows: ↓ 20,000 outflow

Assuming the $21,000 tax liability from above, Forest Ltd. would then report an Income Taxes Payable balance of $1,000 in the current liabilities section of its year-end balance sheet ($21,000 − $20,000). Alternatively, if the company had made payments of $23,000, there would be a $2,000 debit balance in the Income Taxes Payable account ($23,000 − $21,000). This is reported as Income Taxes Receivable, a current asset.

An alternative approach that is often used charges (debits) the instalment payments to expense. When the tax return is completed at year end and the actual amount of tax for the year is calculated, the expense is then adjusted. This series of entries is as follows:

Instalment payments of $20,000			**Instalment payments of $23,000**		
Current Income Tax Expense	20,000		Current Income Tax Expense	23,000	
Cash		20,000	Cash		23,000
Income taxes per tax return: $21,000			**Income taxes per tax return: $21,000**		
Current Income Tax Expense	1,000		Income Taxes Receivable	2,000	
Income Taxes Payable		1,000	Current Income Tax Expense		2,000

Regardless of the approach used, the resulting financial statements are identical.

If, in a later year, the CRA assesses an additional tax on an earlier year's income, Income Taxes Payable is credited and the expense is usually charged to current operations. However, if the additional tax was caused by an obvious arithmetic error that occurred when the amount of tax was originally calculated, the error is corrected through retained earnings.

It is common for there to be differences between taxable income **under the tax laws** and accounting income **under generally accepted accounting principles**. Because of these differences, the total income tax payable to the government in any specific year may differ substantially from the total income tax expense reported on the financial statements. Chapter 18 focuses on the problems of accounting for income tax and presents an extensive discussion of related issues that are both complex and interesting.

Unlike corporations, proprietorships and partnerships are not taxable entities. It is the individual proprietor and the members of a partnership, not the business itself, that are subject to personal income taxes on their share of the business's taxable income; therefore, income tax liabilities do not appear on the financial statements of proprietorships and partnerships.

Employee-Related Liabilities

Objective 3
Identify and account for the major types of employee-related liabilities.

Amounts that are owed to employees for salaries or wages at the end of an accounting period are reported as a current liability called Salaries or Wages Payable. The following additional items related to employee compensation are also usually reported as current liabilities:

1. Payroll deductions

2. Short-term compensated absences

3. Profit-sharing and bonuses

Payroll Deductions

The most common types of payroll deductions are employee income taxes, Canada (or Quebec) Pension Plan premiums, employment insurance, and miscellaneous items such as other insurance premiums, employee savings, and union dues. Any amounts that have been deducted but not yet remitted to the proper authority by the end of the accounting period are recognized as current liabilities. This is also true for any matching amounts that the employer itself is required to pay.

Law

Canada (Quebec) Pension Plan (CPP/QPP).   The Canada and Quebec pension plans are financed by the governments through a tax on both the employer and the employee. All employers are required to collect the employee's share of this tax. They deduct it from the employee's gross pay and remit it on a regular basis to the government along with the employer's share. Both the employer and the employee are taxed at the same rate, currently 4.95% each (2010) based on the employee's gross pay up to maximum contributory earnings of $43,700. This maximum amount is determined by subtracting the basic yearly exemption of $3,500 from the maximum amount of pensionable earnings of $47,200. The maximum annual contribution for each of the employee and employer is therefore 4.95% of $43,700, or $2,163.15 in 2010.

Employment Insurance.   Another payroll tax that the federal government levies on both employees and employers is used for a system of employment insurance (EI). Employees must pay a premium of 1.73% (2010) of insurable earnings to an annual maximum contribution of $747.36 while the employer is required to contribute 2.422% or 1.4 times the amount of employee premiums.[15] Insurable earnings are gross wages above a preset minimum and below a maximum amount of $43,200. Both the premium rates and insurable earnings are adjusted periodically.

Income Tax Withholding.   Income tax laws require employers to withhold from each employee's pay the approximate amount of income tax that will be due on those wages. The amount of income tax that is withheld is calculated by the employer according to a government-prescribed formula or a government-provided income tax deduction table, and depends on the length of the pay period and each employee's wages, marital status, claimed dependants, and other permitted deductions.

Illustration of Payroll Deductions.   Assume a weekly payroll of $10,000 that is entirely subject to CPP (4.95%), employment insurance (1.73%), income tax withholdings

---

[15] The Quebec rates are somewhat lower than in the rest of Canada because Quebec separately provides parental benefits under a different plan.

of $1,320, and union dues of $88. The entry to record the wages and salaries paid and the employee payroll deductions is:

Wages and Salaries Expense	10,000	
Employee Income Tax Deductions Payable		1,320
CPP Contributions Payable		495
EI Premiums Payable		173
Union Dues Payable		88
Cash		7,924

A = L + SE
−7,924   +2,076   −10,000

Cash flows: ↓ 7,924 outflow

The required employer payroll taxes are recognized as compensation-related expenses in the same accounting period as the payroll is recorded. The entry for the required employer contributions is as follows:

Payroll Tax Expense	737	
CPP Contributions Payable ($495 × 1.0)		495
EI Premiums Payable ($173 × 1.4)		242

A = L + SE
  +737   −737

Cash flows: No effect

The employer then sends to the Receiver General for Canada the amount of income tax, CPP, and EI deductions withheld from the employees, along with the employer's required contributions for CPP and EI. The entry to record the payment to the CRA for the payroll described above is:

Employee Income Tax Deductions Payable	1,320	
CPP Contributions Payable ($495 + $495)	990	
EI Premiums Payable ($173 + $242)	415	
Cash		2,725

A = L + SE
−2,725   −2,725

Cash flows: ↓ 2,725 outflow

Until they are remitted to the government and the union, these amounts are all reported as current liabilities. In a manufacturing enterprise, all payroll costs (wages, payroll taxes, and fringe benefits) are allocated to appropriate cost accounts such as Direct Labour, Indirect Labour, Sales Salaries, or Administrative Salaries. This abbreviated and somewhat simplified discussion of payroll costs and deductions does not give a clear sense of the large volume of records and clerical work that is involved in maintaining a sound and accurate payroll system.

Short-Term Compensated Absences

Compensated absences are periods of time taken off from active employment for which employees are paid, such as statutory holidays and vacation. The entitlement to such benefits is one of two types:

1. Accumulating; or

2. Non-accumulating.

Underlying Concept

Accounting for obligations for compensated absences is based on liability definition, recognition, and measurement concepts.

Law

Accumulating Rights to Benefits.   Employers are required under provincial law to give each employee vacation equal to a specified number of days, or to pay them in lieu of the vacation. As a result, employers have an unconditional obligation for vacation pay that accrues (or accumulates) as the employees work. This obligation—or liability—is usually satisfied by paying employees their regular salaries when they are absent from work while taking vacation.

Employees may have vested rights to some of their benefits that accumulate with service. This means that the employer is legally required to pay the benefits even if the employee no longer works for the organization; thus, vested rights do not depend on an employee's continued service. For example, assume that you have earned four days of vacation as at December 31, the end of your employer's fiscal year. Because vacation pay is prescribed by law, your employer will have to pay you for these four days even if you resign from your job. In this case, your four days of vacation pay is a vested right and the costs are accrued by the company as expense **in the period in which the benefit is earned by the employee**.

Now assume that a company offers its employees an entitlement to vacation days above the legal requirement. Further assume that this entitlement **is not vested**, but that the right to any unused additional vacation can be carried forward to future periods. If you continue to work for the company, you are entitled to the additional unused vacation days, but if you leave the company, you lose the right to them. Although the rights are not vested, they are accumulated rights and the company will have to honour the majority of those benefits that have been earned. Accumulated rights, therefore, are rights that accrue with employee service. They are not necessarily vested but can still be carried forward to future periods if they are not used in the period in which they are earned. In accounting for accumulated rights, the employer recognizes an expense and a liability for the cost of these compensated absences as they are earned by employees, but the estimated cost and obligation take into account the fact that, because of employee turnover, some of these benefits will never be paid.

Entitlement to **sick pay** varies greatly among employers. In some companies, sick pay vests and employees are allowed to accumulate unused sick time. They can take time off from work with pay even though they are not ill, or they will be paid for the unused sick days when they leave the company. In this case, an obligation exists to pay future amounts; therefore, **the liability and expense are accrued** as the employees earn the benefit. This type of longer term liability is discussed in Chapter 19.

When sick days accumulate with time, but do not vest (i.e., they are paid only when an employee is absent due to illness), it may be very difficult to estimate the expense that is associated with the benefits earned by the employees. In estimating the obligation, management takes into account the likelihood that many of the accumulated benefits will never be paid. Usually if the estimate is an immaterial amount, no accrual is made and the entity accounts for such non-vesting sick pay on a pay-as-you-go basis. This means that the expense is recognized in the accounts as the sick days are taken.

What rate should be used to accrue the compensated absence expense and liability: the current rate or an estimated future rate? The **best measure is the additional amount the entity expects to pay in the future** as a result of the benefits accumulated to the reporting date.[16] Many companies use the current rate of pay as the best estimate of the future amount, but other companies use future amounts that are likely to be paid, or that have already been agreed on under collective agreements, for example.

To illustrate, assume the following information for Amutron Limited that began operations on January 1, 2011:

- The company employs 10 individuals who are paid $480 per week, and this is the best estimate of the following year's wages as well.

---

[16] IAS 19.14 *Employee Benefits* specifies that the "expected cost of accumulating compensated absences" should be measured as "the additional amount that the entity expects to pay as a result of the unused entitlement that has accumulated at the end of the reporting period." Private entity GAAP does not specifically address this issue.

- A total of 20 weeks of vacation is earned by all employees in 2011, but none is taken during the year.

- In 2012, the vacation weeks earned in 2011 are used when the current rate of pay has increased to $500 per week.

The entry at December 31, 2011, to accrue the vacation pay entitlement earned by the employees is as follows:

Wages Expense	9,600	
Vacation Wages Payable ($480 × 20)		9,600

A = L + SE
+9,600 −9,600
Cash flows: No effect

At December 31, 2011, the company reports a current liability of 20 weeks × $480 or $9,600 on its statement of financial position, and an expense of $9,600 for the benefits earned by employees in 2011. In 2012, the vacation time that is paid for (and was earned in 2011) is recorded as follows:

Vacation Wages Payable	9,600	
Wages Expense	400	
Cash ($500 × 20)		10,000

A = L + SE
−10,000 −9,600 −400
Cash flows: ↓ 10,000 outflow

In 2012, the vacation weeks are used and the liability is eliminated. Note that the difference between the cash paid and the reduction in the liability account is recorded as an adjustment to Wages Expense in the period when it is paid. This difference occurs because the liability account was accrued at the lower rate of $480 per week. The cash paid, however, is based on the rate of pay in effect when the benefit is taken. If the future pay rates had been estimated accurately and used to calculate the accrual in 2011, then the cash paid in 2012 would have been the same as the liability.

Non-Accumulating Rights to Benefits. Non-accumulating compensated absences, on the other hand, are benefits that employees are entitled to by virtue of their employment and the occurrence of an obligating event. The rights to these benefits do not vest and are accounted for differently than those that accumulate with service. A good example is the additional compensation and time off for parental (maternity, paternity, and adoption) leave beyond what the government provides, and some short-term disability benefits. Employees' rights to such benefits do not accrue as they work, but only when the requirements of the parental leave or short-term disability plan have been met.[17]

Because the employer has no basis on which to accrue the costs of these benefits and the associated liability, no entry is made until the obligating event occurs. When the parental leave is taken or the employee becomes disabled, the **total** estimated liability and expense associated with the event is recognized at that time. This event accrual method of accounting is applied as follows. Assume that Resource Corp. provides a parental leave benefit plan that promises to pay a qualifying employee for a period of up to one year, an amount equal to the difference between the employee's current salary and the amount paid by employment insurance during the leave. Sue Kim, an employee, applies for and is granted a one-year parental leave to begin on April 18. Resource Corp. calculates that the benefit payable to Sue Kim will be $200 per week. The company makes the following entry when she begins her leave on April 18:

---

[17] In Canada, statutory parental leave comes under the Employment Insurance program. Many companies, however, offer additional paid parental leave benefits to their employees above the regulated absence from the workplace, usually once they are considered permanent employees.

A = L + SE
+10,400   −10,400

Cash flows: No effect

Employee Benefit Expense	10,400	
Parental Leave Benefits Payable		10,400
($200 × 52 weeks = $10,400)		

As the compensated absence (i.e., the parental leave) is taken and Sue Kim is paid, the liability is reduced. Assuming Resource Corp. has a biweekly payroll, the following entry is made each pay period (disregarding payroll deductions):

A = L + SE
−400   −400

Cash flows: ↓ 400 outflow

| Parental Leave Benefits Payable | 400 | |
| Cash | | 400 |

The compensated absences discussed in this section of the chapter are all relatively short-term in nature. When the associated obligations will be met within 12 months from the balance sheet date, there is no need to discount the future cash outflows when measuring the outstanding liability.[18]

Profit-Sharing and Bonus Agreements

Underlying Concept

Accounting follows underlying concepts. For example, in Japan, bonuses to members of boards of directors and to the statutory auditors are considered distributions of profits and therefore are charged against retained earnings.

Many companies have a bonus or a profit-sharing plan for their employees. These plans may be open to all employees or be restricted to those in managerial positions or perhaps only to key officers of the company. Payments under such plans are in addition to the regular salary or wage and may be a percentage of the employees' regular rates of pay, or they may depend on productivity increases or the amount of the company's annual profit. From the entity's viewpoint, **bonus and profit-sharing payments to employees** are considered additional compensation and are therefore a type of wage or salary expense in determining the net income for the year. Obligations for amounts outstanding are usually reported as current liabilities at the reporting date because they relate to and are based on the results of the period just ended, and are usually payable in the near term.

To illustrate, assume that a company has income before bonuses of $100,000 for 2011. The company has an annual bonus plan and determines in January 2012 that it will pay out bonuses of $10,700 related to the prior year. An adjusting entry dated December 31, 2011, is made to record the bonus as follows:

A = L + SE
+10,700   −10,700

Cash flows: No effect

| Employees' Bonus Expense | 10,700 | |
| Bonus Payable | | 10,700 |

In January 2012, when the bonus is paid, the entry is:

A = L + SE
−10,700   −10,700

Cash flows: ↓ 10,700 outflow

| Bonus Payable | 10,700 | |
| Cash | | 10,700 |

It is important to be careful when calculating bonus and profit-sharing amounts, especially if the formula specifies that the bonus is based on **after-tax** income. Because the additional

---

[18] Longer-term employee benefit obligations associated with compensated absences, including post-retirement benefits, are the subject of Chapter 19.

amount to be paid is itself a tax-deductible expense, simultaneous equations may have to be set up and solved to determine both the expense and tax amounts.

NON-FINANCIAL LIABILITIES

Most liabilities that companies incur can be measured fairly accurately by the amount of cash (or the cash equivalent value of other financial assets) that the company must give up to discharge the obligation. In addition, the timing of the payment is usually clear. However, some liabilities are more difficult to measure because the obligations will be met with goods and services (i.e., non-financial resources), and the timing of meeting the obligation and its amount are not fixed. Examples include unearned revenues, product guarantees and warranties, and obligations under customer loyalty programs. Other examples include obligations related to the dismantling and retirement of assets. Prior to the amendments to IAS 37, these were referred to under IFRS as provisions: liabilities of uncertain timing or amount.

Even though the amount and timing of these obligations may not be known, whenever they involve unconditional obligations that are enforceable and that exist at the balance sheet date, they are liabilities. We start by reviewing two such obligations where there is little or no uncertainty about the existence of the liability, although there may be uncertainty about its measurement.

Decommissioning and Restoration Obligations

In many industries, the construction and operation of long-lived assets means taking on obligations that are associated with the eventual retirement of those assets. For example, when a mining company opens up a strip mine, it likely also makes a commitment to restore the land on which the mine is located once the mining activity is completed. Similarly, when an oil company erects an offshore drilling platform, it may be obligated to dismantle and remove the platform at the end of its useful life. Such obligations occur in a variety of ways. For example, they may arise from purchasing an asset before it is used (e.g., the erection of an oil rig), or they may increase over time through normal operations (e.g., a mine site that expands over time). Further examples of restorative activities include the following:

1. Decommissioning nuclear facilities

2. Dismantling, restoring, and reclaiming oil and gas properties

3. Certain closure, reclamation, and removal costs of mining facilities

4. Closure and post-closure costs of landfills

In general, the obligation associated with the retirement of a long-lived asset that results from acquiring, constructing, developing, or operating it must be recognized by the company **in the period when the obligation is incurred.**[19] This liability is known as an asset retirement obligation (ARO) or site restoration obligation.

While this general principle underlies both the IFRS and private enterprise standards, there is a difference in the type of obligation that is recognized and which activities' costs are capitalized as part of the capital asset's cost. A table indicating the differences was presented in Chapter 10, and it is reproduced here as Illustration 13-3.

 4 Objective
Explain the recognition, measurement, and disclosure requirements for decommissioning and restoration obligations.

Law

 **Significant Change**

---

[19] The private entity standard, however, recognizes this type of liability only when a reasonable estimate can be made of the amount.

	IFRS	Private Enterprise Standards
Category of obligations	Recognizes costs of **both legal** and **constructive obligations**, such as when an entity creates an expectation in others through its own actions that it will meet this obligation.	Recognizes costs associated with **legal obligations** only.
Category of activities	Costs included as capital assets are only those related to the acquisition of the asset, not those related to the subsequent production of goods or services (product costs).	Costs included as capital assets are retirement obligations resulting from both the acquisition of the asset and its subsequent use in producing inventory, such as the mining of coal.

The first difference relates to the fact that the IFRS recognizes a broader group of non-financial obligations as liabilities: both legal and constructive obligations. The IFRS position on the second difference is consistent with the concept that costs incurred in the production of goods and services are inventory or product costs. Private enterprise standards recognize all such costs as part of the capital asset. Because the costs capitalized to property, plant, and equipment under private enterprise GAAP are often amortized subsequently as product costs, this GAAP difference may not have a significant effect on financial results.

Measurement

The liability is initially measured at "the best estimate of the expenditure required to settle the present obligation" at the reporting date.[20] Under the proposed revisions to the international standard, a similar measurement objective is identified as the amount the entity "would rationally pay at the end of the reporting period to be relieved of the present obligation." Because the obligation will often be met many years in the future, discounting the future costs is one requirement in determining the present amount required. Significant application guidance is provided on how this measurement should be approached.

Recognition and Allocation

As explained in Chapter 10, the estimated ARO costs associated with the asset's acquisition are added to the carrying amount of the related asset and a liability is recognized for the same amount. An asset retirement cost is recorded as part of the cost of the related asset because it is considered necessary in order to acquire and operate the asset, and to receive its economic benefits. Because no future economic benefit is associated with capitalized asset retirement costs as a stand-alone asset, these costs are not recorded separately from the asset account.

Later, the ARO cost is amortized to expense over the related asset's useful life. While the straight-line method is acceptable, other systematic and rational allocations are also allowed. As the expected retirement obligation and costs increase due to further damage to the site from production activities, private enterprise standards add these to both the recognized liability and to the capital asset account, adjusting the future depreciation rate. Under IFRS, the obligation amount is increased; however, the incremental costs caused by production are added to inventory as production overhead costs.

Note that environmental cleanup costs that are required after such events as a major oil spill or accidental runoff of chemicals into a water table **do not result in an asset retirement obligation and addition to the cost base** of the underlying asset. These

---

[20] *CICA Handbook*, Part II, Section 3110.09 (*Asset Retirement Obligations*) and IAS 37.36 (*Provisions, Contingent Liabilities and Contingent Assets*).

catastrophes do not result in future benefits, and therefore do not justify an increase in any asset's cost.

Illustration of Accounting for Initial Recognition

To illustrate the accounting for the obligation, assume that on January 1, 2011, Wildcat Oil Corp. erects an oil platform off the Newfoundland coast. Wildcat is legally required to dismantle and remove the platform at the end of its five-year useful life. The total cost of dismantling and removal is estimated to be $1 million. Based on a 10% discount rate, the present value of the asset retirement obligation is $620,920 ($1 million × 0.62092). Wildcat makes the following entries to recognize this liability:

Jan. 1, 2011	Drilling Platform	620,920	
	Asset Retirement Obligation		620,920

A = L + SE
+620,920   +620,920
Cash flows: No effect

If only 80% of the $1-million estimate is caused by the asset acquisition itself, with the other 20% caused by the use of the platform over the five years, only 80% of the $620,920 is recognized at January 1, 2011. This is the only part that is a present obligation at that date. Each year as the platform is used and the retirement costs increase due to production, the present value of the estimated increase in the obligation is added to the production overhead costs (IFRS) or to the Drilling Platform asset (ASPE).

Over the asset's life, the retirement cost is depreciated. Using the straight-line method, Wildcat makes the following entry in 2011 and again in 2012, 2013, 2014, and 2015 to record this expense:

Dec. 31, 2011	Depreciation Expense ($620,920 ÷ 5)	124,184	
	Accumulated Depreciation		124,184

A = L + SE
−124,184   −124,184
Cash flows: No effect

In addition, because the liability is measured on a discounted basis, interest on the liability is accrued each period. An entry is made at December 31, 2011, to record the expense and the related increase or **accretion** in the carrying amount of the liability. Under **IFRS**, the interest adjustment to the liability account **due to the passage of time** is recognized as a borrowing cost. Under **PE standards**, it is recognized as an operating expense on the income statement—accretion expense—but not as interest or a borrowing cost.

Dec. 31, 2011	Accretion Expense (ASPE)	62,092	
	or		
	Interest Expense (IFRS)	62,092	
	Asset Retirement Obligation		62,092
	($620,920 × 10%)		

A = L + SE
  +62,092   −62,092
Cash flows: No effect

On January 10, 2016, Wildcat pays Rig Reclaimers, Inc. for dismantling the platform at the contract price of $995,000. Wildcat then makes the following entry to record the settlement of the liability:

Jan. 10, 2016	Asset Retirement Obligation	1,000,000	
	Gain on Settlement of ARO		5,000
	Cash		995,000

A = L + SE
−995,000   −1,000,000   +5,000
Cash flows: ↓ 995,000 outflow

Subsequent Recognition and Measurement of AROs

Private enterprise standards explain how to account for changes in the estimated amount of the obligation or for additional costs and liabilities recognized due to current operations. To summarize, the expense for the interest element is calculated first. This is followed by an adjustment to the carrying amount of the Asset Retirement Obligation account for any increase or decrease in the cost estimates. This adjustment is also made to the carrying amount of the long-lived asset to which it relates and, of course, to the amount of annual depreciation.[21] IFRIC 1 indicates that the **IFRS** is applied in a similar way, except that the change in obligation due to production would be inventoried instead of added to the capital asset's cost.

Unearned Revenues

Objective 5

Explain the issues and account for unearned revenues, product guarantees, and other customer program obligations.

Real-World Emphasis

When a company receives cash or other assets in advance for specific goods or services to be delivered or performed in the future, the entity recognizes the obligation as a liability. For example, a magazine publisher such as **Golf Digest** receives payments from customers when magazine subscriptions are ordered, and an airline such as **Air Canada** usually sells tickets in advance for flights. For their part, retail stores increasingly issue gift certificates that can be redeemed for merchandise. In all these situations, the assets received in advance require the entity to perform in the future. This obligation is a liability that is generally referred to as unearned revenue. The company's liability is measured at the fair value of the outstanding obligation and this revenue is then recognized as the goods are delivered or the services are provided.

To illustrate, assume that the Rambeau Football Club sells 5,000 season tickets at $50 each for its five-game home schedule. The entry for the sale of the season tickets is:

A   =   L   + SE
+250,000   +250,000

Cash flows: ↑ 250,000 inflow

Cash	250,000	
Unearned Football Ticket Revenue		250,000

As each game is completed, the following entry is made to recognize the revenue earned:

A =   L   +   SE
      −50,000   +50,000

Cash flows: No effect

Unearned Football Ticket Revenue	50,000	
Football Ticket Revenue		50,000

The balance in the Unearned Football Ticket Revenue account is reported as a current liability in the balance sheet. As the Rambeau Football Club plays each game, part of the obligation is met, revenue is earned, and a transfer is made from unearned revenue to a revenue account on the income statement. The costs associated with that revenue are deducted as expenses in the same period to determine the period's net income.

Real-World Emphasis

Unearned revenue is material for some companies. In the airline industry, for example, tickets sold for future flights represent a significant portion of total current liabilities. **WestJet's** unearned ticket revenue represented 41.6% of its current liabilities at September 30, 2009, up from 34.0% at December 31, 2008. At the same dates, **Air Canada** reported advance ticket sales equal to 40.8% and 36.2% of current liabilities, respectively. Illustration

---

[21] *CICA Handbook*, Part II, Section 3110 *Asset Retirement Obligations*, paras. 19 – 21.

13-4 shows specific unearned revenue (balance sheet) accounts and earned revenue (income statement) accounts that might be used in different industries.

Industry Type	Account Title	
	Unearned Revenue	**Earned Revenue**
Airline	Advance Ticket Sales	Passenger Revenue
Magazine publisher	Deferred Subscription Revenue	Subscription Revenue
Hotel	Advance Room Deposits	Room Revenue
Equipment maintenance	Unearned Maintenance Contract Fees	Maintenance Contract Revenue

Illustration 13-4
Unearned and Earned Revenue Accounts

Product Guarantees and Customer Programs

Significant Change

Businesses often offer continuing care or other customer programs that require the entity to provide goods and services after the initial product or service has been delivered. This is an area where the accounting for the entity's continuing obligations has been evolving. Historically, an expense approach has been used to account for the outstanding liability, but some recent standards have moved to an approach we call the revenue approach. Let us start with an overview of these two approaches and then see how they are applied in specific situations.

Expense approach. Under some circumstances, the outstanding liability is measured at the cost of the economic resources needed to meet the obligation. The assumption is that along with the liability that is required to be recognized at the reporting date, the associated expense needs to be measured and matched with the revenues of the period. In fact, the need to match expenses has driven this approach over the years. As the actual costs are incurred in subsequent periods, the liability is reduced.

Revenue approach. Under other circumstances, the outstanding liability is measured at the value of the obligation—an output price rather than an input price or cost measure. This is the situation when assets are received in advance for a variety of performance obligations to be delivered in the future. Under this approach, the proceeds received for any goods or services yet to be delivered or performed are unearned at the point of sale. Until the revenue is earned, the obligation—the liability—is reported at its sales or fair value. The liability is then reduced as the revenue is earned. Revenue recognition concerns are at the base of this approach. This is similar in many respects to the contract-based approach to revenue recognition explained in Chapter 6 where the liability represents a performance obligation. Revenue is recognized when the service is provided and the performance obligation is satisfied.

There are two major differences between these approaches:

(a) Under the expense approach, the liability is **measured at the estimated cost** of meeting the obligation. Under the revenue approach, the liability recognized is **measured at the value of the service** to be provided, not at its cost.

(b) Under the expense approach, and assuming the estimate of the cost of the obligation to be met in the future is close to the actual future cost, there is **no effect on future income**.[22] Under the revenue approach, **future income is affected**. Some amount of unearned revenue is recognized as a liability, and this is recognized as revenue in

---

[22] To the extent that the estimates are not exact, future income will be affected by the difference between the estimated expense/liability and the actual costs incurred. These differences are usually minor.

future periods when it is earned or the performance obligation is met. Any expenses associated with that revenue are also recognized in the future. Therefore, **future income amounts are affected** by the profit or loss earned on the delivery of the goods or services provided in subsequent periods.

Product Guarantees and Warranty Obligations

A warranty **(product guarantee)** is a promise made by a seller to a buyer to correct problems experienced with a product's quantity, quality, or performance. Warranties are commonly used by manufacturers to promote sales. Automakers, for example, attract additional business by extending the length of their new-car warranty. For a specified period of time following the date of sale to the consumer, a manufacturer may promise to be responsible for all or part of the cost of replacing defective parts, to perform any necessary repairs or servicing without charge, to refund the purchase price, or even to double your money back. Warranties and product guarantees are stand-ready obligations at the reporting date that result in future costs that are often significant.

Accounting for warranties is in a state of transition. In the past and still applied in some cases, as a holdover from times when the matching principle predominated, the expense approach was widely used. Increasingly today, the asset and liability view and faithful representation drive the accounting model, resulting in the bifurcation or separation of the proceeds received into two or more revenue amounts for the various deliverables promised. Two examples are provided that illustrate how these approaches are applied to warranties.

Expense Approach Illustrated. In this situation, the warranty is **provided with** an associated product or service, with no additional fee being charged for it. All of the revenue from the sale of the product or service is considered earned on delivery of the product or service, but matching requires that all costs associated with that revenue be recognized as an expense in the same accounting period as the sale. Therefore, the future costs to be incurred to make good on the outstanding warranty are estimated and recognized in the same period as the sale, along with the associated obligation (liability) to provide the warranty service in the future. As the actual costs are incurred in subsequent periods, the warranty liability is reduced.

Assume that Denson Corporation begins production of a new machine in July 2011, and sells 100 units for $5,000 each by its year end, December 31, 2011. Denson provides a one-year warranty promising to fix any inherent manufacturing problems. The company has estimated, from experience with a similar machine, that the warranty cost will average $200 per unit. Under IFRS, the estimate is measured using a probability-weighted expected value, while private enterprise GAAP will probably use the value of the most likely estimate.[23] Denson incurs $4,000 in actual warranty costs in 2011 to replace parts on machines that were sold before December 31, 2011, and costs of $16,000 in 2012. Illustration 13-5 shows how the expense approach recognizes these events.

---

[23] For this example, the authors are assuming the result is the same under both methods. These measurements are explained in Chapter 2. In summary, IFRS requires that all possible outcomes be weighted by the probability of their occurrence, and that the sum of these weighted amounts is the expected value to be used as the cost estimate. Private enterprise standards do not dictate any particular method, so the outcome that is most probable could be chosen as the cost estimate.

Illustration 13-5

Expense Approach and Warranty Liability Entries

Sale of 100 machines at $5,000 each, July to December, 2011:

Cash/Accounts Receivable	500,000	
Sales		500,000

Actual warranty costs incurred, July to December, 2011:

Warranty Expense	4,000	
Cash/Inventory/Accrued Payroll		4,000

Year-end adjusting entry to accrue outstanding warranty obligations at December 31, 2011:

Warranty Expense	16,000	
Estimated Liability under Warranty		16,000

December 31, 2011 financial statement amounts reported:

Income Statement	
Warranty Expense	$20,000
Balance Sheet	
Estimated Liability under Warranty	$16,000

Actual warranty costs incurred, 2012:

Warranty Expense	16,000	
Cash/Inventory/Accrued Payroll		16,000

Adjusting entry, December 31, 2012, to adjust liability account to correct balance of $0:

Estimated Liability under Warranty	16,000	
Warranty Expense		16,000

December 31, 2012 financial statement amounts reported:

Income Statement	
Warranty Expense	$0
Balance Sheet	
Estimated Liability under Warranty	$0

The entries illustrate the fact that the actual warranty costs are charged to expense as they are incurred. At the end of the accounting period, the remaining estimated expense associated with the 2011 sales is recognized and the liability account is adjusted for the same amount. At December 31, 2011, the liability was increased to $16,000 as this additional expense was recognized, and at December 31, 2012, it was adjusted to the correct balance at that time of $0, as was the 2012 expense.

In situations where the warranty costs are immaterial or when the warranty period is relatively short, the product guarantee may be accounted for on a cash basis. Under the **cash basis**, warranty costs are charged to expense as they are incurred; that is, they are recognized in expense **in the period when the seller or manufacturer honours the warranty**. No liability is recognized for future costs arising from warranties, and the expense is not necessarily recognized in the period of the related sale. If the cash basis is applied to the facts in the Denson Corporation example, $4,000 is recorded as warranty expense in 2011 and $16,000 as warranty expense in 2012, with the total sales being recorded as revenue in 2011. This method is used for income tax purposes, but not generally for financial reporting purposes.

Underlying Concept

Using the cash method when the costs are immaterial or the warranty period is short is a proper application of the materiality concept.

Revenue Approach Illustrated. Under the revenue approach, the warranty service is considered to be a separate deliverable from the underlying product or service sold. It is either sold as a **separate** service or its price is considered to be **bundled** with the selling price of the associated goods. In the latter case, the amount of revenue attributable to the warranty has to be broken out and recognized separately. Under this method, the proceeds received for (or allocated to) the separate service to maintain the product in good order are unearned at the point of sale. The revenue is earned as the warranty service is provided. This is the same as the contract-based approach to revenue recognition explained in

Chapter 6 where the warranty represents a future performance obligation. Revenue is recognized when the service is provided and the performance obligation is satisfied.

To illustrate, assume that Hamlin Corp. sells equipment for $20,000 on January 2, 2011. Included with the equipment is a warranty agreement for two years, during which time Hamlin agrees to repair and maintain the equipment. Warranty agreements similar to this are available separately and are estimated to have a stand-alone value of $1,200. Therefore, Hamlin allocates $1,200 of the proceeds of the bundled sale to the warranty contract. The entry to record the sale on January 2, 2011, is:

A	=	L	+	SE
+20,000		+1,200		+18,800

Cash flows: ↑ 20,000 inflow

Cash	20,000	
Sales—Equipment		18,800
Unearned Warranty Revenue		1,200

This approach recognizes revenue as Hamlin performs under the warranty contract. Assuming the revenue is earned evenly over the two-year contract term, the entry to remeasure the unearned revenue account to its correct balance at December 31, 2011, is as follows:

A	=	L	+	SE
		−600		+600

Cash flows: No effect

Unearned Warranty Revenue	600	
Warranty Revenue		600

If costs of $423 were incurred in 2011 as a result of servicing this contract, Hamlin's entry is:

A	=	L	+	SE
		+423		−423

Cash flows: No effect

Warranty Contract Expense	423	
Accounts Payable/Accrued Payroll		423

In 2012, the remainder of the unearned warranty revenue is recognized and any costs incurred under the contract are recognized in 2012 expense. If the costs of performing services under the extended warranty contract are not expected to be incurred in a straight-line pattern (as historical evidence might indicate), revenue is recognized over the contract period in the same pattern as the costs are expected to be incurred. In addition, if the costs of providing services under the contract are expected to be more than the remaining unearned revenue (i.e., it is an **onerous contract**), a loss and related liability are recognized for any expected shortfall.

Which approach is considered GAAP? Under both private enterprise standards and IFRS, the principle is clear that revenue that covers a variety of deliverables (bundled sales) should be unbundled and the revenue allocated to the various goods or services that are required to be performed. This method has been used increasingly over the past few years. Even more support for the revenue approach is found in the IFRS draft standards covering these liabilities. These refer to the fact that it is an extremely rare circumstance when a liability cannot be measured reliably, and they require that the liability be measured at the value of the obligation, not its cost. The revenue approach is also consistent with the contract-based view being developed for proposed revenue recognition standards. In the future, this approach will likely be the only one permitted when guarantees are involved.

Customer Loyalty Programs

As indicated in our opening story, customer loyalty programs, such as those offered by Sears, the Bay, and Shoppers Drug Mart, are very popular, with all of them promising future benefits to the customer in exchange for current sales. Canadians' participation in such loyalty programs is high, with over 90% of Canadians belonging to at least one consumer rewards program, up 9 percentage points over two years earlier.[24] Other programs that have been adopted widely include the frequent flyer programs that are used by all major airlines. On the basis of mileage or the number of trips accumulated, frequent flyer members are awarded discounted or free airline tickets. Airline customers can earn miles toward free travel by making long-distance phone calls, staying in hotels, and charging groceries and gasoline on a credit card.

How should such programs be accounted for? As explained in Chapter 6, standard setters now interpret programs where customer loyalty credits are awarded to be revenue arrangements with multiple deliverables. Under **IFRS**, IFRIC Interpretation 13 *Customer Loyalty Programmes* requires the revenue from the original transaction to be allocated between the award credits and the other components of the sale. The fair value of the award credits is recognized as unearned revenue, a liability. This is later recognized in revenue when the credits are exchanged for the promised awards. The issue of accounting for loyalty programs is not explicitly addressed in the **private enterprise standards**; however, the general principle that the revenue recognition criteria should be applied "to the separately identifiable components of a single transaction in order to reflect the substance of the transaction" is carried forward into PE GAAP.[25]

Premiums and Rebates

Many companies offer premiums or other benefits to customers in return for box tops, coupons, labels, wrappers, or other evidence of having purchased a particular product. The premiums may be such items as silverware, dishes, small appliances, toys, or cash values against future purchases.

Printed coupons that can be redeemed for a cash discount on items purchased are extremely popular marketing tools, as is the cash rebate, which the buyer can obtain by returning the store receipt, a rebate coupon, and Universal Product Code (UPC label or bar code) to the manufacturer. **Contests** have also been widely used to get consumers' attention and their sales dollars, with the Tim Hortons "Roll up the Rim to Win" promotion being one of the most successful contests in Canadian history. A wide variety of prizes are offered, including automobiles, vacations, major sporting events tickets, and sweepstake winnings!

Underlying Concept

Similar to warranties, obligations for most premiums and coupons meet the definition of a liability.

With the life of many contests running a few months and the average coupon being valid for an average of approximately six months, many companies have the practical problem of accounting for these marketing costs, as they affect more than one fiscal period. Historically, such programs have been accounted for under the expense approach. The accounting issue relates to the fact that while these promotions **increase current sales revenue**, the associated costs are often incurred **in future periods**. The matching concept requires companies to deduct the total estimated costs against the current period's revenue and the cost is charged to an expense account such as Premium or Promotion Expense. In addition, the obligations existing at the balance sheet date must also be recognized and reported in a liability account such as Estimated Liability for Premiums or Estimated Liability for Coupons Outstanding.

The following hypothetical example illustrates the accounting treatment commonly used for premium offers. In 2011, Fluffy Cakemix Corporation offers its customers a large non-breakable mixing bowl in exchange for $1.00 and 10 box tops. The mixing

---

[24] Based on research by Colloquy, a service provider for the global loyalty-marketing industry, as reported in *CAmagazine*, November 2009, p. 9.

[25] *CICA Handbook*, Part II, Section 3400.08E.

bowl costs Fluffy Cakemix Corporation $2.25, and the company estimates that 60% of the box tops will be redeemed. The premium offer results in the following transactions and entries in 2011:

1. Purchase of 20,000 mixing bowls at $2.25 each:

A = L + SE
0   0   0
Cash flows: ↓ 45,000 outflow

| Inventory of Premium Mixing Bowls | 45,000 | |
| Cash | | 45,000 |

2. Sales of 300,000 boxes of cake mix at $2.10:

A   = L +   SE
+630,000   +630,000
Cash flows: ↑ 630,000 inflow

| Cash | 630,000 | |
| Sales | | 630,000 |

3. Redemption of 60,000 box tops, receiving $1.00 with every 10 box tops, and the delivery of 6,000 mixing bowls (60,000 ÷ 10):

A   = L +   SE
−7,500   −7,500
Cash flows: ↑ 6,000 inflow

Cash [(60,000 ÷ 10) × $1.00]	6,000	
Premium Expense	7,500	
Inventory of Premium Mixing Bowls		13,500
(60,000 ÷ 10) × $2.25 = $13,500		

4. Adjusting entry to recognize the remaining expense and estimated liability for outstanding premiums at the end of the period:

A = L   +   SE
  +15,000   −15,000
Cash flows: No effect

Premium Expense		15,000	
Estimated Liability for Premiums			15,000
Calculation:			
Total boxes sold in 2011		300,000	
Total estimated redemptions (60%)		180,000	
Box tops redeemed in 2011		60,000	
Estimated future redemptions		120,000	
Cost per premium: $2.25 − $1.00 =		$1.25	
Cost of estimated claims outstanding:			
(120,000 ÷ 10) × $1.25 =		$15,000	

The December 31, 2011 balance sheet of Fluffy Cakemix Corporation reports an inventory of premium mixing bowls of $31,500 as a current asset and an estimated liability for premiums of $15,000 as a current liability. The 2011 income statement reports a $22,500 premium expense among the selling expenses.

If the costs associated with premiums and rebates are really **marketing expenses**, the expense approach applied in the illustration is a reasonable way to account for them. On the other hand, the revised international standard covering similar liabilities scheduled to be released in late 2010, is expected to require these obligations to be measured at the amount the entity would rationally pay on the reporting date to be relieved of the obligation. The associated draft *Basis for Conclusions* document indicates that this means measurement at their value, not at the entity's estimated cost of the economic resources to fulfill the obligation itself. If and when this standard becomes effective, and it may not be until 2013, it may change how the accounting for such marketing programs is now widely applied.

Contingencies and Uncertain Commitments

Companies are often involved in situations where it is uncertain whether an obligation to transfer cash or other assets actually exists at the balance sheet date or what amount will be required to settle the obligation. For example, **Research In Motion Limited** provided seven pages of notes to its financial statements for its year ended February 28, 2009, that dealt with lawsuits and claims, mostly involving patent infringements. **Thomson Reuters Corporation** also discussed lawsuits and legal claims in notes to its December 31, 2008 financial statements. In addition, the company referred to the existence of the significant judgement required in determining its tax liabilities and the fact that contingent consideration may become payable as a result of prior business acquisitions.

Broadly speaking, these situations are referred to as contingencies. A contingency is "an existing condition or situation involving uncertainty as to possible gain or loss to an enterprise that will ultimately be resolved when one or more future events occur or fail to occur. Resolution of the uncertainty may confirm the acquisition of an asset or the incurrence of a liability."[26] As indicated in Chapter 5, **gain contingencies** and **contingent assets** are not recorded in the accounts and our discussion is limited to uncertainty and the recognition of liabilities. How the uncertainty is dealt with in accounting is explained below under two approaches. The first approach describes how private enterprises and IFRS currently account for contingencies. The second approach summarizes and reflects the current thinking about liability recognition and measurement that is the basis for proposed revisions to the standard, and a replacement of IAS 37 *Provisions, Contingent Liabilities and Contingent Assets*, to be released in late 2010 and effective two or three years later.

Current Approach to the Recognition and Measurement of Contingencies

Under current private enterprise standards, the term contingent liability includes the **whole population** of existing or possible obligations that depend on the occurrence of one or more future events to confirm either their existence or the amount payable, or both. As we'll see below, some of these contingent liabilities are recognized in the accounts, some require only note disclosure, and others are not referred to at all in the financial statements. Under existing international standards, the term "contingent liability" is used **only** for those existing or possible obligations that are **not** recognized.

The approach taken by current standards to deal with whether a liability should be recognized when there is a contingency is to determine the probability of a future event occurring (or not occurring) that would establish whether the outcome is a loss. How likely it is that a future event will confirm the incurrence of a loss and a liability can range from highly probable to remote or unknown.

Under **private enterprise standards**, the following range is used:

Term	Interpretation
Likely	High
Unlikely	Slight
Not determinable	Cannot be determined

Objective

Explain and apply two approaches to the recognition of contingencies and uncertain commitments, and identify the accounting and reporting requirements for guarantees and commitments.

Real-World Emphasis

---

[26] *CICA Handbook*, Part II, Section 3290.05.

A contingent loss is recognized in income and as a liability **only if both the following conditions** are met:[27]

1. It is **likely** that a future event will confirm that an asset has been impaired or a liability has been incurred at the date of the financial statements.

2. The loss amount can be **reasonably estimated**.

Aside from the "likely" probability, the first condition requires that the liability must relate to events that occurred before the balance sheet date. The second criterion indicates that it has to be possible to make a reasonable and reliable estimate of the liability; otherwise, it cannot be accrued as a liability. The evidence that is used to estimate the liability may be the company's own experience, the experience of other companies in the industry, engineering or research studies, legal advice, or educated guesses by personnel who are in the best position to know. Often, **a range of possible amounts** may be determined. If a specific amount within the range is a better estimate than others, this is the amount that is accrued. If no particular amount is better than another, the bottom of the range is recognized, and the amount of the remaining exposure to possible loss is disclosed in the notes.

When the liability recognition criteria are not met because of the inability to determine a reasonable estimate of the loss amount, or the likelihood of a confirming future event cannot be determined, or when the entity is exposed to loss above the amount accrued, additional information is disclosed in the notes to the statements. Information is disclosed about: (1) the nature of the contingency, (2) the estimated amount of the contingent loss or a statement that an estimate cannot be made, and (3) the extent of exposure to losses in excess of the amount that has been recognized.

Under **current IFRS** requirements, the recognition criterion used to determine the chance of occurrence of a confirming future event is **"probable,"** which is interpreted to mean "more likely than not." This is a somewhat lower hurdle than the "likely" required under private enterprise standards. If the amount cannot be measured reliably, no liability is recognized under IFRS either; however, the standard indicates that it is only in very rare circumstances that this would be the case. If recognized, IAS 37 requires the best estimate and an "expected value" method to be used to measure the liability. This approach assigns weights to the possible outcomes according to their associated probabilities if a range of possible amounts is available. Unless the likelihood of needing future resources to settle a contingent liability is **remote**, disclosures are required about the nature of these uncertain amounts and, if practicable: (1) an estimate of its financial effect, (2) information about the uncertainties related to the amount or timing of any outflows, and (3) whether any reimbursements are possible.

As you might expect, using the terms "likely" or "probable" as a basis for determining the accounting for contingencies involves considerable judgement and subjectivity, as does the requirement that the amounts be "reliably measurable." Practising accountants often express concern over the diversity that exists in the interpretation of these terms. Current accounting practice for these situations relies heavily on the exact language that is used in responses that are received from lawyers—but the language of lawyers may be necessarily biased and protective rather than predictive of the ultimate outcome. As a result, the recognition of losses and liabilities varies considerably in practice. There is agreement,

---

[27] Loss contingencies that result in the incurrence of a liability are the more relevant ones for the discussion in this chapter. Loss contingencies that result in the impairment of an asset (e.g., the collectibility of receivables or a threat of expropriation of assets) are discussed more fully in other chapters of this textbook.

however, that general risks that are inherent in business operations, such as the possibility of war, strike, uninsurable catastrophes, or a business recession, are not accounting "contingencies" and are neither recognized nor reported in the financial statements.

Illustration 13-6 identifies some common examples of potential losses and how they are generally accounted for now.

Illustration 13-6

Accounting Treatment of Loss Contingencies

	Not Accrued	May Be Accrued[a]
Loss Related to		
1. Risk of damage of enterprise property by fire, explosion, or other hazards	X	
2. General or unspecified business risks	X	
3. Risk of damage from catastrophes assumed by property and casualty insurance companies including reinsurance companies	X	
4. Threat of expropriation of assets		X
5. Pending or threatened litigation		X
6. Actual or possible claims and assessments		X
7. Guarantees of indebtedness of others[b]		X
8. Agreements to repurchase receivables (or the related property) that have been sold		X

[a] Will be accrued when all recognition criteria are met regarding likelihood and measurability.
[b] See chapter section on Financial Guarantees

The most common types of loss contingencies have to do with litigation, claims by others, and assessments.[28] To recognize a loss and a liability in the accounts, **the cause for litigation must have occurred on or before the date of the financial statements**. It does not matter that the company did not become aware of the existence or possibility of the lawsuit or claims until after the date of the financial statements.

To evaluate the **likelihood of an unfavourable outcome**, management considers the nature of the litigation, the progress of the case, the opinion of legal counsel, the experience of the company and others in similar cases, and any company response to the lawsuit.[29] **Estimating the amount of loss** from pending litigation, however, can rarely be done with any certainty. And, even if the evidence that is available at the balance sheet date does not favour the defendant, it is not reasonable to expect the company to publish in its financial statements a dollar estimate of the likely negative outcome. Such specific disclosures could weaken the company's position in the dispute and encourage the plaintiff to intensify its efforts. There is a fine line between a shareholder's right to know about potential losses and information that could hurt the company's interests.

Note 17 of the August 31, 2009 year-end financial statements of **CoolBrands International Inc.**, shown in Illustration 13-7, provides a good example of a company's disclosures related to contingent liabilities. All amounts are in thousands of Canadian dollars.

---

[28] The CICA's *Financial Reporting in Canada, 2008 Edition* reports that in 2007 the four most common types of contingent losses disclosed by its sample of 200 Canadian companies were lawsuits, environmental matters, contingent consideration, and possible tax reassessments.

[29] For some companies, litigation presents significant costs in employee time and legal fees, even if the outcomes are positive. For example, in 2003, U.S. giant Wal-Mart Stores Inc. reported that it was the target of 6,649 active lawsuits of all sorts (Associated Press).

Illustration 13-7

Note Disclosure of Contingencies

Real-World Emphasis

Note 17. Contingencies:

Litigation

On October 31, 2006, Capricorn Investors III, L.P. ("Capricorn"), the parent of Americana Foods Corporation, filed a complaint in the Supreme Court of the State of New York against CoolBrands, Integrated Brands, Inc., CBA Foods LLC, CB Americana LLC and certain officers and directors of CoolBrands asserting allegations against the defendants for breaches of contract, breach of fiduciary duty, fraud and conspiracy and seeked injunctive relief and damages of over $60 million. On June 8, 2007, the Company and its co-defendants moved to dismiss the Complaint. On June 13, 2008, the Court granted the Company's motion to dismiss as to seven of the ten claims made by Capricorn in its complaint. The Court provisionally dismissed all of Capricorn's claims against CoolBrands and its subsidiary company Integrated Brands, Inc. but permitted the plaintiff an opportunity to re-plead its case to include these parties. On September 22, 2008, Capricorn filed its submission with the Court to oppose the Court's earlier decision on the defendant's motion to dismiss. On October 6, 2008, the Company filed its reply brief refuting the matters contained in Capricorn's submission and reiterating its position that the case should not continue against CoolBrands and Integrated Brands. On July 16, 2009, the Court rendered its decision and dismissed all claims made by Capricorn against CoolBrands and its affiliated companies. In May 2009 Capricorn filed an appeal of the June 13, 2008 decision. In September 2009 Capricorn filed its Notice to Appeal the Court's July 16, 2009 decision that dismissed the litigation and all remaining claims brought by Capricorn. On October 1, 2009, the Supreme Court, Appellate Division, issued its decision affirming the June 13, 2008 decision previously issued by the Supreme Court. The amount of loss, if any, cannot be determined at this time.

Legal matters

The Company is also a party to other legal proceedings and disputes with former franchisees and others, which arise in the ordinary course of business. In the opinion of the Company, it is unlikely that the liabilities, if any, arising from the legal proceedings and disputes will have a material adverse effect on the consolidated financial position of the Company. The amount of loss, if any, cannot be determined at this time.

Environmental liabilities:

In February 1992, a subsidiary of the Company entered into an agreement with the former owner of the subsidiary whereby the former owner agreed to indemnify the subsidiary for damages or expenses resulting from environmental contamination caused by the former owner and its predecessors on the subsidiary's owned property located in New Jersey. Litigation has commenced by the Company to demand that the former owner abide by the terms of the agreement. In the event the Company is not successful in this litigation, it may be required to pay the costs associated with remediating the environmental contamination on the property. The cost of remediation cannot be reasonably estimated at this time. The subsidiary has provided a self-guarantee to the State of New Jersey in the amount of $370 to cover potential clean up costs.

Future Approach to the Recognition and Measurement of Contingencies

Significant Change

Law

Under the *Exposure Draft of Proposed Amendments to IAS 37 Provisions, Contingent Liabilities and Contingent Assets*, the term "contingent liabilities" is eliminated. This is based on the fact that either a situation results in a liability or it does not; a contingency relates to a future event, not whether the obligation exists at the reporting date. As explained at the beginning of this chapter, liabilities can arise only from **unconditional** (or **non-contingent**) obligations. This highlights a different and more conceptually defensible approach to determining what is recognized as a non-financial liability. Uncertainty about the amounts that might be payable in the future is taken into account in the **measurement** of the liability, not its **existence**.

In general, the approach is applied as follows:

Description of Situation	Liability Recognition Decision at the Reporting Date
There is only an unconditional obligation.	Always recognize because there is a present obligation and it is enforceable.
There is only a conditional obligation.	Do not recognize: it is not a present obligation and therefore not enforceable.
There is an unconditional obligation and a related conditional obligation at the same time.	Always recognize due to the existence of the unconditional obligation.

If a liability is recognized, it is measured, and it is the measurement that takes into account the uncertainties that exist. Let us walk through some examples taken from the IASB exposure draft to see how this works.

> **Situation 1(a) – Product warranty:** A manufacturer sells a product warranty that covers a two-year period. It is uncertain whether the products under warranty will develop faults and have to be replaced or repaired.

Analysis: At the balance sheet date, the entity has an unconditional obligation to stand ready to provide the warranty coverage, and a conditional obligation to repair/replace the products if they develop faults. There is a present and enforceable obligation (to stand ready) as a result of a past event (the sale of the warranty). A liability must be recognized. How will it be measured? While the objective is to measure the obligation at the amount the entity would rationally pay at the balance sheet date to be relieved of the present obligation, this measure may not be evident. Management would consider estimates of the number of claims that might arise from sales prior to the reporting date, the amount and timing of the associated cash flows required, and risks and uncertainties associated with the variability of the possible outcomes.

> **Situation 1(b) – Extended product warranty:** The situation is similar to 1(a) above. In this case, the entity sometimes repairs or replaces the product if defects are found in the third and fourth year after sale, in order to maintain customer goodwill. The entity does not make this practice widely known, and follows a process of carefully comparing the costs of any repairs after the warranty had expired with the potential damage to customer goodwill.

Analysis: In this case, there is no present contractual, legal, or constructive obligation to provide warranty coverage after two years. It is not the entity's policy, it has not told customers this is its general practice, and full discretion about providing the additional service lies solely with the entity. Customers cannot rely on the entity to meet additional claims. This is not an unconditional obligation and no liability is recognized.

> **Situation 2 – Potential lawsuit:** In December 2010, a mistake was made in a hospital operation and the patient dies as a result. The hospital is aware of the mistake, and from past experience and advice from its lawyer, determines that the patient's family is very likely to sue the hospital and would win the case.

Analysis: At December 31, 2010, the hospital has a present obligation as a result of a past event (the operation in which negligence occurred). It is an unconditional obligation and a liability is recognized. While it is uncertain whether the patient's family will initiate court action and, if so, whether they will win the case, this uncertainty is taken into account in the measurement of the liability, not whether there is an unconditional obligation or not.

> **Situation 3(a) – Contaminated land:** After years of contaminating the water system in the foreign country in which it operates, an entity learns in December 2010 that the government, for the first time, has substantively enacted new legislation that requires cleanup of all present and prior contamination by those who pollute.

Analysis: The entity has an unconditional obligation at December 31, 2010. It is a present obligation (the legislation is substantively enacted) as a result of a past event (the past contamination by the entity). A liability is recognized, with any uncertainty about the timing and amount of future expenditures taken into consideration in measuring the liability.

> **Situation 3(b) – Contaminated land:** A company has contaminated a water system in a country without environmental legislation. However, the entity is known through its publications for taking responsibility for cleaning up any contamination it causes.

Analysis: The past event is the contamination of the water system. Although there is no law or formal contract that obligates the entity, honouring its responsibilities in the past and publishing its policies and past actions results in a constructive obligation on the part of the entity. A liability is recognized.

Many situations are not so easily resolved and therefore require a significant degree of judgement. Legal proceedings are particularly difficult situations to assess when determining if a present obligation exists at the balance sheet date, and entities look to their legal advisors, other outside experts, and other evidence for help in determining the existence or non-existence of an obligation at that point in time. No specific probability hurdle is provided to help resolve difficult situations.

Financial Guarantees

Closely related to the topic of contingencies are the requirements for guarantor companies to account for and provide information about a variety of specific types of guarantees that they have provided. One of the most common types is a financial guarantee contract where one party (the guarantor) contracts to reimburse the holder for a loss incurred because another party (the debtor) does not make required payments when due.[30] Such a guarantee qualifies as a financial liability because the guarantor has an unconditional obligation to transfer cash in the future if the debtor fails to meet its obligations. How is such a guarantee reported in the financial statements?

Under **private enterprise GAAP**, such guarantees fall under the loss contingency standards discussed earlier in this section of the chapter, as well as the disclosure provisions for guarantees set out in an accounting guideline.[31] Specific disclosures are required even if the probability of having to make payments under the guarantee is remote. Users are interested in knowing what types of guarantees the company has made, the maximum potential obligation the company is exposed to, how much has been recognized in the accounts as a liability, and the prospects for recovery from third parties.

Under **IFRS**, the guarantee is recognized initially at fair value, usually equal to the premium charged by the guarantor. After this, it is measured at the higher of:

(a) the best estimate of the payment that would be needed to settle the obligation at the reporting date, and

(b) any unamortized premium received as a fee for the guarantee (unearned revenue).

---

[30] IASB, IAS 39.9. The discussion in this chapter does not extend to the revenue recognition issues for insurance contracts.

[31] *CICA Handbook*, Part II, Disclosure of Guarantees, AcG-14.

Similar to warranties, if this is a single obligation, the best estimate would be the "most likely" amount. However, if there is a large number of similar obligations, the expected value of the possible outcomes is determined. The time value of money is taken into consideration if the effects are significant. In addition to reconciling the opening to the closing balance for this type of obligation, the additional disclosures are similar to those under private enterprise standards. The objective under both sets of standards is to give readers better information about the entity's obligations and **particularly about the risks that are assumed as a result of issuing guarantees**.

Illustration 13-8 presents **RONA inc.**'s note disclosure on guarantees from Note 18 of the company's financial statements for its year ended December 28, 2008 (in thousands).

Guarantees

In the normal course of business, the Company reaches agreements that could meet the definition of "guarantees" in AcG-14.

The Company guarantees mortgages for an amount of $1,855. The terms of these loans extend until 2012 and the net carrying amount of the assets held as security, which mainly include land and buildings, is $5,847.

Pursuant to the terms of inventory repurchase agreements, the Company is committed towards financial institutions to buy back the inventory of certain customers at an average of 62% of the cost of the inventories to a maximum of $66,894. In the event of recourse, this inventory would be sold in the normal course of the Company's operations. These agreements have undetermined periods but may be cancelled by the Company with a 30-day advance notice. In the opinion of management, the likelihood that significant payments would be incurred as a result of these commitments is low.

Illustration 13-8

Disclosure of Guarantees—RONA inc.

Additional Disclosures

Real-World Emphasis

Looking ahead, it is likely that accounting for guarantees will be covered by the same recognition and measurement standards as other liabilities, as explained under the "alternative approach" above for contingencies. If there is an unconditional (stand-ready) obligation to make good under the guarantee at the balance sheet date, the liability is recognized and measured for inclusion in the liability section of the statement of financial position.

Commitments

Companies conduct business by entering into agreements with customers, suppliers, employees, and other parties. These executory contracts—contracts where neither party has yet performed—are not recognized as liabilities in the accounts. Although they are not recognized as liabilities at the balance sheet date, unrecognized contractual commitments or contractual obligations commit the company and its assets into the future. While it would not be reasonable or desirable to require companies to disclose all of their outstanding contractual obligations, it is useful to have them highlight commitments that have certain characteristics.

Disclosures are therefore required of commitments to make expenditures that are abnormal relative to the company's financial position and usual operations and for commitments that involve significant risk. Examples include major property, plant, and equipment and intangible asset expenditure commitments, and commitments to make lease payments.

PRESENTATION, DISCLOSURE, AND ANALYSIS

Presentation and Disclosure of Current Liabilities

Objective 7
Indicate how non-financial and current liabilities are presented and analyzed.

Real-World Emphasis

The current liability accounts are commonly presented in Canada as the first classification in the balance sheet's Liabilities and Shareholders' Equity section. Although IFRS illustrates an "upside-down" presentation in IAS 1 *Presentation of Financial Statements* with the long-term assets and liabilities at the top and the current assets and liabilities at the bottom of the statement of financial position, this form of presentation is not required by the standard. In some instances, current liabilities are presented as a group immediately below current assets, with the total of the current liabilities deducted from the current assets total. Although this presentation is not seen often, it is an informative one that focuses on the company's investment in **working capital**.

Within the Current Liabilities section, the accounts may be listed in the order of either their maturity or liquidation preference, whichever provides more useful information to readers of the financial statements. Many companies list notes payable first (sometimes called commercial paper, bank loans, or short-term debt), regardless of their relative amounts, then follow with accounts payable, and then end the section with the current portion of long-term debt. An excerpt from the May 2, 2009 balance sheet of Empire Company Limited is presented in Illustration 13-9. Empire Company has considerable real estate holdings in addition to its activities in the food and grocery industry, and is best known for its Sobeys chain of stores. Compare this with the current liabilities section of IFRS-reporting **Marks & Spencer Group plc** at its March 28, 2009 year end as shown in Illustration 13-10. This company reports in millions of United Kingdom pounds (£). Marks & Spencer is a well-known international retail giant based in the United Kingdom. These excerpts are representative of the types of current liabilities that are found in the reports of many corporations.

Illustration 13-9

Balance Sheet Presentation of Current Liabilities—Empire Company Limited

(in millions)	May 2, 2009	May 3, 2008
LIABILITIES		
Current		
Bank indebtedness (Note 11)	$ 45.9	$ 92.6
Accounts payable and accrued liabilities	1,487.1	1,348.4
Income taxes payable	—	15.5
Future income taxes (Note 18)	42.7	32.9
Long-term debt due within one year (Note 12)	133.0	60.4
Liabilities relating to assets held for sale (Note 9)	—	6.4
	1,708.7	1,556.2

Illustration 13-10

Balance Sheet Presentation of Current Liabilities—Marks & Spencer Group plc

Additional Disclosures

Consolidated balance sheet

	Notes	As at 28 March 2009 £m	As at 29 March 2008 £m
Liabilities			
Current liabilities			
Trade and other payables	20	1,073.5	976.6
Borrowings and other financial liabilities	21	942.8	878.6
Partnership liability to the Marks & Spencer UK Pension Scheme	21	71.9	50.0
Derivative financial instruments	22	76.2	35.1
Provisions	23	63.6	11.1
Current tax liabilities		78.9	37.5
		2,306.9	1,988.9

As indicated earlier in the chapter, IAS 37 uses the term "provisions" to refer to liabilities where there is uncertainty about their timing or the amount of the future expenditure. It requires that companies report provisions separately and provide a reconciliation of the opening and closing balances of each class of provisions. It is likely that anticipated amendments to IAS 37 will replace the term "provision" and use the general term "liability" instead.

Entities should disclose enough supplementary information about their current liabilities so that readers can understand and identify the entity's current needs for cash. Such information usually includes identifying the major classes of current liabilities such as bank loans, trade credit and accrued liabilities, income taxes, dividends, and unearned revenue. Also, amounts owing to officers, directors, shareholders, and associated companies are reported separately from amounts that are owed to enterprises that the reporting entity deals with at arm's length. Secured liabilities and any assets that have been pledged as collateral are identified clearly.

Presentation and Disclosure of Contingencies, Guarantees, and Commitments

Under PE GAAP, companies are required to disclose their contingent liabilities when any of the following are true:

1. It is likely that a future event will confirm the existence of a loss but the loss cannot be reasonably estimated.

2. A loss has been recognized, but there is an exposure to loss that is higher than the amount that was recorded.

3. It is not possible to determine the likelihood of the future confirming event.

Companies reporting under private entity standards are also required to report any contractual obligations that are significant relative to their current financial position of future operations. In addition, guarantors must report information about any guarantees they have made, even if the likelihood of having to make any payments is slight. This includes information about the nature of the guarantees, maximum potential payments, potential recoveries, and the existence of any collateral.

Empire Company Limited, referred to above in Illustration 13-9, provides information in Note 23 to its financial statements for the year ended May 2, 2009, as follows:

Real-World Emphasis

Guarantees and commitments relative to:

- Letters of credit and credit enhancements through standby letters of credit

- Franchisee bank loan guarantees, franchise lease obligation guarantee including equipment leases

- Minimum rent payable under operating lease commitments

Contingencies relative to:

- Canada Revenue Agency reassessments for GST (fiscal years 1999 and 2000)

- Canada Revenue Agency reassessment of the tax treatment of gains realized on the sale of shares of an associated company in 2001

- Existence of possible additional amounts payable under a property redevelopment agreement

- Director, officer, and particular employee indemnification in excess of insurance policy provisions
- Ordinary course of business claims and litigation to which management considers the company's exposure to be immaterial, although unable to predict with certainty

Marks & Spencer Group plc's Note 27 reports on the following contingencies and commitments:

- Capital expenditure commitment related to its interest in a joint venture
- Commitment to purchase property, plant, and equipment if there is a change in trading arrangements with certain warehouse operators
- Commitments for payments under non-cancellable operating leases

Analysis

Because the ability to pay current obligations as they come due is critical to a company's short-term financial health and continued existence, analysts pay particular attention to the current liabilities section of the balance sheet. As with most financial statement items, it is not the absolute dollar amount of the current liabilities that is important, but rather its relationship to other aspects of the company's position and results.

Current liabilities result from **both operating and financing activities**. Trade liabilities, provisions, and other liabilities that **arise from operations**—such as payroll, rent, insurance, and taxes payable—are the most common. In addition, advances from customers are a source of operating credit, and it is important to distinguish them from other operating sources. Why? This liability requires the company to provide a service or product in the future rather than make cash payments, and will therefore result in the recognition of revenue in the future. An increase in this category of liability predicts future revenues, not cash outflows.

Short-term notes and the current portion of long-term debt result **from financing activities**. The company must either generate operating cash flows to repay these liabilities or arrange for their refinancing. Refinancing, however, may not be possible or may come at a higher cost to the borrower than the original note or debt.

Identifying current liabilities separately from long-term obligations is important because it provides information about the company's liquidity. Liquidity refers to a company's ability to convert assets into cash to pay off its current liabilities in the ordinary course of business. The higher the proportion of "assets expected to be converted to cash" to "liabilities currently due," the more liquid the company. A company with higher liquidity is better able to survive financial downturns and has a better chance of taking advantage of investment opportunities that arise.

As indicated in earlier chapters of the text, basic ratios such as net cash flow provided by operating activities to current liabilities and the turnover ratios for receivables and inventory **are useful in assessing liquidity**. Three other key ratios are the current ratio, the acid-test ratio, and the days payables outstanding.

The current ratio is the ratio of total current assets to total current liabilities. The formula is shown in Illustration 13-11.

$$\text{Current ratio} = \frac{\text{Current assets}}{\text{Current liabilities}}$$

Illustration 13-11
Current Ratio Formula

The current ratio shows how many dollars of current assets are available for each dollar of current liabilities. Sometimes it is called the **working capital ratio** because working capital is the excess of current assets over current liabilities. The higher the ratio, the more likely it is that the company can generate cash to pay its currently maturing liabilities.

A company with a large amount of current assets that is made up almost entirely of inventory may have a satisfactory current ratio, but it may not be very liquid. The current ratio does not show whether or not a portion of the current assets is tied up in slow-moving inventories. With inventories—especially raw materials and work in process—there is a question of how long it will take to transform them into finished goods, to convert the finished product into accounts receivable by selling it, and then to collect the amounts that customers owe. Better information may be provided to assess liquidity by eliminating inventories and other non-liquid current assets such as prepaid expenses from the current asset ratio numerator. Many analysts prefer to use the resulting acid-test or quick ratio, shown in Illustration 13-12. This ratio relates quick assets—such as cash, investments held for trading purposes, and receivables—to total current liabilities.

$$\text{Acid-test ratio} = \frac{\text{Cash} + \begin{array}{c}\text{Marketable}\\ \text{securities}\end{array} + \begin{array}{c}\text{Net}\\ \text{receivables}\end{array}}{\text{Current liabilities}}$$

Illustration 13-12
Acid-Test Ratio Formula

The current ratio and quick ratio are useful, especially when analyzing a company over time and when comparing it with other companies in the same industry.

The third ratio, the days payables outstanding, zeroes in on how long it takes a company to pay its trade payables; i.e., it determines the average age of the payables. Trade payables are amounts that the entity owes to suppliers for providing goods and services related to normal business operations; that is, they are amounts that result from operating transactions. When cash is managed well, the payment of payables is delayed as long as possible, but done in time to meet the due date. A trend where the age of the payables outstanding is increasing, particularly if it is above the normal credit period for the industry, may indicate liquidity problems for the company. Illustration 13-13 shows the formula for this ratio.

$$\text{Days payables outstanding} = \frac{\text{Average trade accounts payable}}{\begin{array}{c}\text{Average daily cost of goods sold}\\ \text{or average daily cost of total}\\ \text{operating expenses}\end{array}}$$

Illustration 13-13
Days Payables Outstanding Formula

The formula provides a better result if all the suppliers that are represented in the payables amount (the numerator) provide the goods and services that are captured in the cost of goods sold amount (the denominator). If the trade accounts payable include the suppliers for most of the company's operating goods and services in addition to the inventory purchases, analysts prefer to use the "average daily cost of total operating expenses" as the denominator.

To illustrate the calculation of these ratios, partial balance sheet and income statement information is provided in Illustration 13-14 for the year ended January 31, 2009, for **Reitmans (Canada) Limited**, a women's clothing retailer. The amounts are reported in thousands of Canadian dollars.

Illustration 13-14

*Selected Financial
Statement Information*

**Real-World
Emphasis**

Consolidated Balance Sheets

As at January 31, 2009, and February 2, 2008
(in thousands)

	2009	2008
ASSETS		
CURRENT ASSETS		
Cash and cash equivalents (note 15)	$ 214,054	$ 214,301
Marketable securities (note 5)	32,818	30,053
Accounts receivable	2,689	3,546
Income taxes recoverable	3,826	—
Merchandise inventories (note 2)	64,061	52,441
Prepaid expenses	11,402	22,847
Future income taxes (note 9)	3,598	1,772
Total Current Assets	332,448	324,960
CURRENT LIABILITIES		
Accounts payable and accrued items	$ 70,632	$ 69,189
Income taxes payable	—	16,546
Future income taxes (note 9)	—	761
Current portion of long-term debt (note 8)	1,220	1,146
Total Current Liabilities	71,852	87,642

Consolidated Statements of Earnings

	2009	2008
Sales	$1,050,861	$1,057,720
Cost of goods sold and selling, general and administrative expenses (note 2)	869,930	858,544
	180,931	199,176
Depreciation and amortization	58,184	50,098
Operating earnings before the undernoted	122,747	149,078

The calculation of the current, acid-test, and days payables outstanding ratios for Reitmans is as follows:

$$\text{Current ratio} = \frac{\text{Current assets}}{\text{Current liabilities}} = \frac{\$332,448}{\$71,852} = 4.6$$

$$\text{Acid-test ratio} = \frac{\text{Quick assets}}{\text{Current liabilities}} = \frac{\$214,054 + \$32,818 + \$2,689 + \$3,826}{\$71,852} = 3.5$$

$$\text{Days payables outstanding} = \frac{\text{Average trade accounts payable}}{\text{Average daily cost of goods sold}}$$
or
Average daily total operating expenses

$$= \frac{\dfrac{\$70,632 + \$69,189}{2}}{\dfrac{\$869,930}{365}} = \frac{\$69,911}{\$2,383} = 29.3 \text{ days}$$

While a 4.6-to-1 current ratio and a 3.5-to-1 quick ratio appear in the higher-than-necessary range, it is often difficult to make a definite statement about a company's liquidity from these ratios alone. What amounts to an acceptable ratio depends on the industry and how it operates. In some industries, companies need significant amounts of current and quick assets compared with their current liabilities. In other industries, such as those that generate cash from cash sales or whose receivables and inventory turn over quickly, companies may be very liquid with low current and quick ratios. Too high a ratio may indicate poor deployment of assets in cash, near-cash, receivables, and inventory, as there are carrying costs associated with maintaining these balances. Reitmans probably converts its inventory to cash on a daily basis as customers pay cash or use debit or credit cards such as Visa and MasterCard (credit card slips from these two companies are deposited daily as if they were cash). The length of its cash cycle is reduced because it does not have to carry large receivable balances. For these reasons, Reitmans' working capital ratios could be lower and still indicate ample liquidity. An analyst might question why this company's ratios are so high.

Reitmans' accounts payable are, on average, 29.3 days old. It appears that the company is not experiencing problems keeping up with payments if supplier credit terms are in the 30-day range. It is difficult to draw any definite conclusions about these numbers by themselves. They need to be compared with results from previous years, with credit policies, and with the ratios of other companies in the same industry.

IFRS AND PRIVATE ENTERPRISE GAAP COMPARISON

A Comparison of IFRS and Private Entity GAAP

Illustration 13-15 indicates the differences between private enterprise standards and IFRS as this text went to print, and an indication of what is expected in the revised IFRS on *Liabilities*, a replacement of IAS 37 *Provisions, Contingent Liabilities and Contingent Assets*.

8 Objective

Identify differences in accounting between private enterprise standards and IFRS and what changes are expected in the near future.

Looking Ahead

As indicated throughout the chapter, accounting for a variety of liabilities, including contingencies, is in a state of transition. What underlies the proposed change is the work being carried out by the IASB and the FASB on the conceptual framework—particularly the revised definition of a "liability" and how the recognition criteria are applied. These reflect the shift of the "probability" criterion from being part of the recognition criteria for the element to how an existing obligation is measured. That is, in the existing standards, a liability is recognized if it is **probable** that it will require an outflow of resources in the future. The proposed standards clarify that there must be a present obligation at the reporting date, but no particular degree of certainty of resource outflows is required. The probability of having to give up entity resources in the future becomes part of the measurement aspect. A significant amount of application guidance is expected as part of any revisions, particularly to help in determining if a present obligation exists at the reporting date. As indicated in the chapter, the measurement basis is changing to a "relief" value— the amount the entity would pay a third party to relieve it of its obligation.

As this text went to print, the completion date for the elements and recognition phase of the conceptual framework project was uncertain, with publication of a discussion paper even pushed beyond 2011. A finalized IFRS on Liabilities to replace IAS 37 *Provisions, Contingent Liabilities and Contingent Assets* was planned for late 2010. The Accounting Standards Board is expected to propose changes to the accounting standards in Part II of the *CICA Handbook* every two years, particularly as they affect the conceptual framework.

	Accounting Standards for Private Enterprises (PE GAAP/ASPE)— *CICA Handbook*, Part II, Sections 1510, 1540, 3110, 3280, 3290, 3856, and Accounting Guideline 14	IFRS—IAS 1, 7, 19, 37, and 39; IFRIC 13	IASB Exposure Draft of Proposed Amendments to IAS 37 and IAS 19, June 2005; and Exposure Draft ED/2010/1 *Measurement of Liabilities in IAS 37, Proposed amendments to IAS 37*, January 2010
Scope and definitions – Terminology	A liability is an obligation arising from past transactions and events, the settlement of which may result in the transfer or use of assets, provision of services or other yielding of economic benefits in the future.	A liability is a present obligation arising from past events in which the settlement is expected to result in an outflow of resources that embody economic benefits.	A liability is defined in the same way as in IAS 37. A clarification is made explaining that an obligation only needs to be capable of resulting in an asset outflow; no specific degree of certainty has to exist about that outflow.
	Contingent liability refers to uncertain situations, some of which may be recognized as a liability and others not.	A contingent liability refers only to those that do not meet the recognition criteria.	The contingent liability term is eliminated.
	The term provision is not defined.	A provision is defined as a liability of uncertain timing or amount.	The term "liability" replaces the term "provision."
– Scope	No specific accounting standard addresses non-financial liabilities.	IAS 37 basically addresses non-financial liability issues, including guarantees and onerous contracts	The revised standard will apply to all liabilities unless covered by another IFRS.
	Accounting for financial guarantees is addressed by the loss contingency standards.	Financial guarantees may be covered by insurance standards.	No change.
	Customer loyalty programs are not explicitly addressed in the standards.	Customer loyalty programs are addressed by IFRIC 13, which requires the current proceeds to be split between the original transaction and the award credits (as unearned revenue).	When the IASB completes its revenue recognition project, warranties and refunds will be transferred to a new revenue project
Recognition – Decommissioning and restoration obligations	Recognizes costs associated with legal obligations only.	Recognizes costs of both legal and constructive obligations.	Recognize a liability if it meets the definition of a liability and can be reliably measured; management considers all available evidence to determine the existence of an obligation.
	Costs recognized are capitalized to property, plant, and equipment.	Costs capitalized associated with the asset are recognized as property, plant, and equipment; those that accrue as a result of production are considered product costs and are charged to inventory.	No changes are expected for decommissioning obligations.
– Contingencies and uncertain commitments	Recognize if occurrence of a future confirming event is "likely," meaning a high probability, and measurable.	Recognize if occurrence of a future confirming event is "probable," meaning more likely than not, and measurable—a lower threshold than under PE standards.	Recognize a liability if it meets the definition of a liability and can be reliably measured; management considers all available evidence to determine the existence of an obligation.\n\nThe probability thresholds are removed.

	Accounting Standards for Private Enterprises (PE GAAP/ASPE)— *CICA Handbook*, Part II, Sections 1510, 1540, 3110, 3280, 3290, 3856, and Accounting Guideline 14	IFRS—IAS 1, 7, 19, 37, and 39; IFRIC 13	IASB Exposure Draft of Proposed Amendments to IAS 37 and IAS 19, June 2005; and Exposure Draft ED/2010/1 *Measurement of Liabilities in IAS 37, Proposed amendments to IAS 37*, January 2010
– Contingent gains	Contingent gains are not recognized.	A potential reimbursement is recognized only when virtually certain of recovery.	The right to reimbursement is recognized when it can be reliably measured.
Measurement – Non-financial liabilities	An asset retirement obligation is measured at the best estimate of the expenditure required to settle the present obligation at the balance sheet date or transfer it to a third party.	A provision is measured at the best estimate of the expenditure required to settle the present obligation at the balance date or to transfer it to a third party.	A liability is measured at the amount an entity would rationally pay to be relieved of the present obligation: the lowest of the present value of the resources needed to fulfill the obligation; the amount needed to cancel the obligation; and the amount needed to transfer it to a third party.
	The most likely value is used.	A probability-weighted expected value is required where a large population of items is being measured.	Probability-weighted measures continue to be used.
– Contingencies and uncertain commitments	Measure the amount of the liability at the best estimate in the range of possible outcomes, if none, use lowest point in the range and disclose the remaining exposure to loss.	Measure the amount at the probability-weighted expected value of the loss.	The same measurement as described above applies to all obligations within the scope of IAS 37.
Presentation – Current/noncurrent classification	If long-term debt becomes callable due to a violation of a debt agreement, it can be reported as long-term under certain conditions.	If long-term debt becomes callable due to a violation of a debt agreement, it cannot be reported as long-term even if the creditor agrees not to call the debt before the date the statements are released.	There is no change from existing IFRS.
	Short-term debt expected to be refinanced is reported as long-term if refinanced on a long-term basis before the statements are completed.	Short-term debt expected to be refinanced is reported as a current liability even if refinanced on a long-term basis before the statements are released, unless refinanced under an existing agreement at the reporting date and solely at the entity's discretion.	There is no change from existing IFRS.
Disclosure	There are no general disclosure requirements for liabilities similar to the IFRS provisions. All disclosures are less extensive than required under international standards.	IAS 37 identifies specific disclosures for "provisions" including descriptions and a reconciliation of balances between beginning and ending balances.	Disclosures are similar to those in IAS 37 with increased requirements in situations where liabilities are not recognized due to lack of reliability of measurement and situations of uncertainty of existence.

Illustration 13-15

IFRS and Private Enterprise GAAP Comparison Chart

Summary of Learning Objectives

KEY TERMS

accounting standards for
    private enterprises
    (ASPE), 834
accretion, 853
accumulated rights, 848
acid-test ratio, 871
asset retirement
    obligation (ARO), 851
bifurcation, 856
bonus, 850
callable debt, 840
compensated absences,
    847
conditional obligation,
    834
constructive obligation,
    834
contingency, 861
contingent liability, 861
contractual commitments,
    867
contractual obligations,
    867
current liability, 836
current maturities of
    long-term debt, 839
current ratio, 870
customer advances, 842
days payables
    outstanding, 871
dividend payable, 841
event accrual method,
    849
executory contracts, 867
expense approach, 855
financial liability, 834
guarantees, 866
input tax credit, 843
liability, 833
line of credit, 836
liquidity, 833
loyalty programs, 858
non-accumulating
    compensated
    absences, 849

1 Define liabilities, distinguish financial liabilities from other liabilities, and identify how they are measured.

Liabilities are defined as present obligations of an entity arising from past transactions or events that are settled through a transfer of economic resources in the future. They must be enforceable on the entity. Financial liabilities are a subset of liabilities. They are contractual obligations to deliver cash or other financial assets to another party, or to exchange financial instruments with another party under conditions that are potentially unfavourable. Financial liabilities are initially recognized at fair value, and subsequently either at amortized cost or fair value. Private enterprise standards do not specify how non-financial liabilities are measured. However, unearned revenues are generally measured at the fair value of the goods or services to be delivered in the future, while others are measured at the best estimate of the resources needed to settle the obligation. Under IFRS, non-financial liabilities other than unearned revenues are measured at the best estimate of the amount the entity would rationally pay at the balance sheet date to settle the present obligation.

2 Define current liabilities and identify and account for common types of current liabilities.

Current liabilities are obligations that are payable within one year from the balance sheet date or within the operating cycle if the cycle is longer than a year. IFRS also includes liabilities held for trading and any obligation where the entity does not have an unconditional right to defer settlement beyond 12 months after the balance sheet date. There are several types of current liabilities. The most common are accounts and notes payable, and payroll-related obligations.

3 Identify and account for the major types of employee-related liabilities.

Employee-related liabilities include (1) payroll deductions, (2) compensated absences, and (3) profit-sharing and bonus agreements. Payroll deductions are amounts that are withheld from employees and result in an obligation to the government or other party. The employer's matching contributions are also included in this obligation. Compensated absences earned by employees are company obligations that are recognized as employees earn an entitlement to them, as long as they can be reasonably measured. Bonuses based on income are accrued as an expense and liability as the income is earned.

4 Explain the recognition, measurement, and disclosure requirements for decommissioning and restoration obligations.

A decommissioning, restoration, or asset retirement obligation (ARO) is an estimate of the costs a company is obliged to incur when it retires certain assets. It is recorded as a liability and is usually long-term in nature. Under private enterprise standards, only legal obligations are recognized. They are measured at the best estimate of the cost to settle them at the balance sheet date, and the associated cost is included as part of the cost of property, plant, and equipment. Under IFRS, both legal and constructive obligations are recognized. They are measured at the amount the entity would rationally pay to be relieved of the obligation, and are capitalized as part of PP&E or to inventory, if due to production activities. Over time, the liability is increased for the time value of money and the asset costs are amortized to expense. Entities disclose information about the nature of the obligation and how it is measured, with more disclosures required under IFRS than PE standards.

5 Explain the issues and account for unearned revenues, product guarantees, and other customer program obligations.

When an entity receives proceeds in advance or for multiple deliverables, unearned revenue is recognized to the extent the entity has not yet performed. This is measured at the fair value of the remaining goods or services that will be delivered. When costs remain to be incurred in revenue transactions where the revenue is considered earned and has been recognized, estimated liabilities and expenses are recognized at the best estimate of the expenditures that will be incurred. This is an application of the matching concept.

6 Explain and apply two approaches to the recognition of contingencies and uncertain commitments, and identify the accounting and reporting requirements for guarantees and commitments.

Under existing standards, a loss is accrued and a liability recognized if (1) information that is available before the issuance of the financial statements shows that it is likely (or more likely than not under IFRS) that a liability has been incurred at the date of the financial statements, and (2) the loss amount can be reasonably estimated (under IFRS, it would be a rare situation where this could not be done). Under an alternative approach likely to be required in new standards being developed by the IASB, the probablility of a future confirming event is not considered. Instead, an entity must determine whether it has an unconditional obligation at the reporting date. If so, a liability is recognized and the uncertainty relative to future events is taken into consideration in the measurement of the liability.

Guarantees in general are accounted for similarly to contingencies. Commitments, or contractual obligations, do not usually result in a liability at the balance sheet date. Information about specific types of outstanding commitments is reported at the balance sheet date.

7 Indicate how non-financial and current liabilities are presented and analyzed.

Current liability accounts are commonly presented as the first classification in the liability section of the balance sheet, although under IFRS, a common presentation is to present current assets and liabilities at the bottom of the statement. Within the current liability section, the accounts may be listed in order of their maturity or in order of their liquidation preference. IFRS requires information about and reconciliations of any provisions. Additional information is provided so that there is enough to meet the requirement of full disclosure. Information about unrecognized loss contingencies is reported in notes to the financial statements, including their nature and estimates of possible losses. Commitments at year end that are significant in size, risk, or time are disclosed in the notes to the financial statements, with significantly more information required under IFRS. Three common ratios used to analyze liquidity are the current, acid-test, and days payables outstanding ratios.

8 Identify differences in accounting between private enterprise standards and IFRS and what changes are expected in the near future.

Private enterprise and international standards are substantially the same. However, there are some classification differences, ASPE do not address "provisions," and there are differences related to which decommissioning and restoration liabilities are recognized and how the costs are capitalized, and how the probability and measurement criteria are applied to contingencies. In addition, IFRS require considerably more disclosure. Looking ahead, revisions to the existing standards are being proposed by the IASB and FASB that will likely be applied, at least in part, under *CICA Handbook*, Part II in the future. The major changes relate to the recognition and measurement standards for non-financial liabilities.

Brief Exercises

(LO 2)   **BE13-1**   Roley Corporation uses a periodic inventory system and the gross method of accounting for purchase discounts. On July 1, Roley purchased $60,000 of inventory, terms 2/10, n/30, f.o.b. shipping point. Roley paid freight costs of $1,200. On July 3, Roley returned damaged goods and received a credit of $6,000. On July 10, Roley paid for the goods. Prepare all necessary journal entries for Roley.

(LO 2)   **BE13-2**   Refer to the data for Roley Corporation in BE13-1. Assuming that Roley instead uses the net approach in accounting for its purchases, prepare all necessary journal entries for Roley.

(LO 2)   **BE13-3**   Upland Limited borrowed $40,000 on November 1, 2011, by signing a $40,000, three-month, 9% note. Prepare Upland's November 1, 2011 entry; the December 31, 2011 annual adjusting entry; and the February 1, 2012 entry.

(LO 2)   **BE13-4**   Refer to the data for Upland Limited in BE13-3. Assuming that Upland uses reversing entries, prepare the 2012 journal entry(ies).

(LO 2)   **BE13-5**   Takemoto Corporation borrowed $60,000 on November 1, 2011, by signing a $61,350, three-month, zero-interest-bearing note. Prepare Takemoto's November 1, 2011 entry; the December 31, 2011 annual adjusting entry; and the February 1, 2012 entry.

(LO 2)   **BE13-6**   At December 31, 2011, Burr Corporation owes $500,000 on a note payable due February 15, 2012. Assume that Burr follows IFRS and that the financial statements are completed and released on February 20, 2012. (a) If Burr refinances the obligation by issuing a long-term note on February 14 and by using the proceeds to pay off the note due February 15, how much of the $500,000 should be reported as a current liability at December 31, 2011? (b) If Burr pays off the note on February 15, 2012, and then borrows $1 million on a long-term basis on March 1, how much of the $500,000 should be reported as a current liability at December 31, 2011, the end of the fiscal year? (c) Now assume that Burr follows private enterprise GAAP. Would that affect your answers to (a) and (b)?

(LO 2)   **BE13-7**   DeGroot Limited conducts all its business in a province that has an 8% sales tax as well as the 5% GST, and both taxes are applied on the value of the product or service that is sold. Assume that all of DeGroot's sales attract both types of tax. Prepare the summary journal entry to record the company's sales for the month of July, during which customers purchased $37,000 of goods on account.

(LO 2)   **BE13-8**   Refer to the data for DeGroot Limited in BE13-7. Assume now that DeGroot purchased $29,400 of merchandise inventory in July on which 5% GST was levied. DeGroot uses the periodic inventory system. Prepare the summary entry to record the purchases for July and the subsequent entry to record the payment of any GST owing to the government.

(LO 2)   **BE13-9**   Clausius Ltd. made four quarterly payments of $3,200 each to the CRA during 2011 as instalment payments on its estimated 2011 tax liability. At year end, Clausius's controller completed the company's 2011 tax return, which showed income taxes of $20,000 for its 2011 income. Prepare a summary entry for the quarterly tax instalments and the year-end entry to recognize the 2011 income taxes. Identify any year-end balance sheet amount that is related to income taxes and indicate where it would be reported.

(LO 2)   **BE13-10**   Refer to the information about Clausius Ltd. in BE13-9. Assume instead that the tax return indicated 2011 income taxes of $10,200. Identify any year-end balance sheet amount that is related to income taxes and indicate where it would be reported.

(LO 3)   **BE13-11**   Whirled Corporation's weekly payroll of $23,000 included employee income taxes withheld of $3,426, CPP withheld of $990, EI withheld of $920, and health insurance premiums withheld of $250. Prepare the journal entries to record Whirled's payroll.

(LO 3)   **BE13-12**   Refer to the data for Whirled Corporation in BE13-11. Assume now that the employer is required to match every dollar of the CPP contributions of its employees and to contribute 1.4 times the EI withholdings. Prepare the journal entry to record Whirled Corporation's payroll-related expenses.

(LO 3)   **BE13-13**   Refer to the data for Whirled Corporation in BE13-11 and BE13–12. Prepare Whirled Corporation's entry to record its payroll-related payment to the CRA.

(LO 3)   **BE13-14**   At December 31, 2011, 30 employees of Kasten Inc. have each earned two weeks of vacation time. The employees' average salary is $500 per week. Prepare Kasten's December 31, 2011 adjusting entry.

BE13-15 Laurin Corporation offers parental benefits to its staff as a top-up on employment insurance so that employees end up receiving 100% of their salary for 12 months of parental leave. Ruzbeh Awad, who earns $74,000 per year, announced that he will be taking parental leave for a period of four months starting on December 1, 2011. Assume that the Employment Insurance program pays him a maximum of $720 per week for the four months. Prepare all entries that Laurin Corporation must make during its 2011 fiscal year related to the parental benefits plan as it applies to Ruzbeh Awad. **(LO 3)**

BE13-16 Mayaguez Corporation pays its officers bonuses based on income. For 2011, the bonuses total $350,000 and are paid on February 15, 2012. Prepare Mayaguez's December 31, 2011 adjusting entry and the February 15, 2012 entry. **(LO 3)**

BE13-17 Lu Corp. erects and places into service an offshore oil platform on January 1, 2011, at a cost of $10 million. Lu is legally required to dismantle and remove the platform at the end of its nine-year useful life. Lu estimates that it will cost $1 million to dismantle and remove the platform at the end of its useful life and that the discount rate to be used should be 8%. Prepare the entry to record the asset retirement obligation. **(LO 4)**

BE13-18 Refer to the data for Lu Corp. in BE13-17. Prepare any necessary adjusting entries that are associated with the asset retirement obligation and the asset retirement costs at December 31, 2011, assuming that Lu follows (a) IFRS, and (b) private enterprise GAAP. **(LO 4)**

BE13-19 Sport Pro Magazine Ltd. sold 12,000 annual subscriptions on August 1, 2011, for $18 each. Prepare Sport Pro's August 1, 2011 transaction entry and the December 31, 2011 annual adjusting entry. **(LO 5)**

BE13-20 Jupiter Corp. provides at no extra charge a two-year warranty with one of its products, which was first sold in 2011. In that year, Jupiter sold products for $2.5 million and spent $63,000 servicing warranty claims. At year end, Jupiter estimates that an additional $520,000 will be spent in the future to service warranty claims related to the 2011 sales. Prepare Jupiter's journal entry(ies) to record the sale of the products, the $63,000 expenditure, and the December 31 adjusting entry under the expense approach. **(LO 5)**

BE13-21 Refer to data for Jupiter Corp. in BE13-20. Prepare entries for the warranty that recognize the sale as a multiple deliverable with the warranty as a separate service that Jupiter bundled with the selling price of the product. Warranty agreements similar to this are available separately, are estimated to have a standalone value of $600,000, and are earned evenly over the warranty period. Also prepare the entry(ies) to record the $63,000 expenditure for servicing the warranty during 2011, and the adjusting entry required at year end, if any, under the revenue approach. **(LO 5)**

BE13-22 Henry Corporation sells DVDs. The corporation also offers to sell its customers a two-year warranty contract as a separate service. During 2011, Henry sold 20,000 warranty contracts at $99 each. The corporation spent $180,000 servicing warranties during 2011, and it estimates that an additional $900,000 will be spent in the future to service the warranties. Henry recognizes warranty revenue based on the proportion of costs incurred out of total estimated costs. Prepare Henry's journal entries for (a) the sale of warranty contracts, (b) the cost of servicing the warranties, and (c) the recognition of warranty revenue. **(LO 5)**

BE13-23 Wynn Corp. offers a set of building blocks to customers who send in three UPC codes from Wynn cereal, along with $0.50. The block sets cost Wynn $1.10 each to purchase and $0.60 each to mail to customers. During 2011, Wynn sold 1.2 million boxes of cereal. The company expects 30% of the UPC codes to be sent in. During 2011, 120,000 UPC codes were redeemed. Prepare Wynn's December 31, 2011 adjusting entry. **(LO 5)**

BE13-24 Lawton & Border Inc. is involved in a lawsuit at December 31, 2011. Under existing IFRS standards in IAS 37, (a) prepare the December 31 entry assuming it is probable (and very likely) that Lawton & Border will be liable for $700,000 as a result of this suit. (b) Prepare the December 31 entry, if any, assuming it is probable (although not likely) that Lawton & Border will be liable for a payment as a result of this suit. (c) Would your answer change if it was not probable that Lawton & Border would be liable? (d) How would your answers to parts (a) and (b) change assuming that Lawton & Border follows the proposed amendments to IAS 37? (e) Repeat parts (a) and (b) assuming that Lawton & Border follows private enterprise GAAP. **(LO 6)**

BE13-25 Siddle Corp. was recently sued by a competitor for patent infringement. Lawyers have determined that it is likely that Siddle will lose the case and that a reasonable estimate of damages to be paid by Siddle is $200,000. In light of this case, Siddle is considering establishing a $100,000 self-insurance allowance. Siddle follows private enterprise GAAP. What entry(ies), if any, should Siddle record to recognize this loss contingency? **(LO 6)**

(LO 7)　**BE13-26**　Berry Corporation shows the following financial position and results for the three years ended December 31, 2011, 2012, and 2013 (in thousands):

	2013	2012	2011
Cash	$ 650	$ 700	$ 600
Temporary investments	500	500	500
Accounts receivable	900	1,000	1,300
Inventory	4,900	4,600	4,000
Prepaid expenses	1,300	1,000	900
Total current assets	$ 8,250	$ 7,800	$ 7,300
Accounts payable	$ 1,550	$ 1,700	$ 1,750
Accrued liabilities	2,250	2,000	1,900
Total current liabilities	$ 3,800	$ 3,700	$ 3,650
Cost of goods sold	$15,000	$18,000	$17,000

For each year, calculate the current ratio, quick ratio, and days payables outstanding ratio, and comment on your results.

Exercises

(LO 1)　**E13-1**　**(Balance Sheet Classification of Various Liabilities)** The following items are to be reported on a balance sheet.

1. Accrued vacation pay

2. Income tax instalments paid in excess of the income tax liability on the year's income

3. Service warranties on appliance sales

4. A bank overdraft

5. Employee payroll deductions unremitted

6. Unpaid bonus to officers

7. A deposit received from a customer to guarantee performance of a contract

8. Sales taxes payable

9. Gift certificates sold to customers but not yet redeemed

10. Premium offers outstanding

11. A royalty fee owing on units produced

12. A personal injury claim pending

13. Current maturities of long-term debts to be paid from current assets

14. Cash dividends declared but unpaid

15. Dividends in arrears on preferred shares

16. Loans from officers

17. GST collected on sales in excess of GST paid on purchases

18. An asset retirement obligation

19. The portion of a credit facility that has been used

Instructions

(a) How would each of the above items be reported on the balance sheet according to private enterprise GAAP? If you identify an item as a liability, indicate whether or not it is a financial liability.

(b) Would your classification of any of the above items change if the balance sheet were prepared according to IFRS?

(LO 2)　**E13-2**　**(Accounts and Notes Payable)** The following are selected 2011 transactions of Darby Corporation.

Sept. 1　Purchased inventory from Orion Company on account for $50,000. Darby records purchases gross and uses a periodic inventory system.

Oct. 1　Issued a $50,000, 12-month, 8% note to Orion in payment of Darby's account.

1　Borrowed $75,000 from the bank by signing a 12-month, non-interest-bearing $81,000 note.

Instructions

(a) Prepare journal entries for each transaction.

(b) Prepare adjusting entries at December 31, 2011.

(c) Calculate the net liability, in total, to be reported on the December 31, 2011 balance sheet for the following:

    1. The interest-bearing note

    2. The non-interest-bearing note

(d) Prepare the journal entries for the payment of the notes at maturity.

(e) Repeat part (d) assuming the company uses reversing entries (show the reversing entries at January 1, 2012). Would the use of reversing entries be efficient for both types of notes?

E13-3 (Refinancing of Short-Term Debt) On December 31, 2011, Hornsby Corporation had $1.2 million of short-term debt in the form of notes payable due on February 2, 2012. On January 21, 2012, the company issued 25,000 common shares for $38 per share, receiving $950,000 in proceeds after brokerage fees and other costs of issuance. On February 2, 2012, the proceeds from the sale of the shares, along with an additional $250,000 cash, are used to liquidate the $1.2-million debt. The December 31, 2011 balance sheet is issued on February 23, 2012. **(LO 2)**

Instructions

(a) Assuming that Hornsby follows private enterprise GAAP, show how the $1.2 million of short-term debt should be presented on the December 31, 2011 balance sheet, including the note disclosure.

(b) Assuming that Hornsby follows IFRS, explain how the $1.2 million of short-term debt should be presented on the December 31, 2011 balance sheet.

E13-4 (Refinancing of Short-Term Debt) On December 31, 2011, Zimmer Corporation has $7.9 million of short-term debt in the form of notes payable that will be due periodically in 2012 to Provincial Bank. On January 28, 2012, Zimmer enters into a refinancing agreement with the bank that will permit it to borrow up to 60% of the gross amount of its accounts receivable. Receivables are expected to range between a low of $5.7 million in May and a high of $7 million in October during the year 2012. The interest cost of the maturing short-term debt is 15%, and the new agreement calls for a fluctuating interest rate at 1% above the prime rate on notes due in 2013. Zimmer's December 31, 2011 balance sheet is issued on February 15, 2012. **(LO 2)**

Instructions

(a) Assuming that Zimmer follows private enterprise GAAP, prepare a partial balance sheet for Zimmer Corporation at December 31, 2011, that shows how its $7.9 million of short-term debt should be presented, including any necessary note disclosures.

(b) Assuming that Zimmer follows IFRS, explain how the $7.9 million of short-term debt should be presented on the December 31, 2011 balance sheet.

E13-5 (Liability for Returnable Containers) Diagnostics Corp. sells its products in expensive, reusable containers. The customer is charged a deposit for each container that is delivered and receives a refund for each container that is returned within two years after the year of delivery. When a container is not returned within the time limit, Diagnostics accounts for the container as being sold at the deposit amount. Information for 2011 is as follows: **(LO 2)**

Containers held by customers at December 31, 2010, from deliveries in:	2009	$170,000	
	2010	480,000	$650,000
Containers delivered in 2011			894,000
Containers returned in 2011 from deliveries in:	2009	$115,000	
	2010	280,000	
	2011	310,400	705,400

Instructions

(a) Prepare all journal entries required for Diagnostics Corp. for the reusable containers during 2011.

(b) Calculate the total amount that Diagnostics should report as a liability for reusable containers at December 31, 2011.

(c) Should the liability calculated in (b) be reported as current or long-term? Explain.

(AICPA adapted)

(LO 2)   **E13-6   (Entries for Sales Taxes)** Sararas Corporation is a merchant and operates in the province of Ontario, where the HST rate is 13%. Sararas uses a perpetual inventory system. Transactions for the business for the month of March are as follows:

> Mar. 1   Paid March rent to the landlord for the rental of a warehouse. The lease calls for monthly payments of $5,500 plus 13% HST.
>   3   Sold merchandise on account and shipped merchandise to Marcus Ltd. for $20,000, terms n/30, f.o.b. shipping point. This merchandise cost Sararas $11,000.
>   5   Granted Marcus a sales allowance of $500 (exclusive of taxes) for defective merchandise purchased on March 3. No merchandise was returned.
>   7   Purchased merchandise for resale on account from Tinney Ltd. at a list price of $14,000, plus applicable tax.
>   12   Made a cash purchase at Rona of a desk for the shipping clerk. The price of the desk was $600 before applicable taxes.
>   31   Paid the monthly remittance of HST to the Receiver General.

Instructions

(a) Prepare the journal entries to record these transactions on the books of Sararas Company.

(b) Assume instead that Sararas operates in the province of Alberta, where PST is not applicable. Prepare the journal entries to record these transactions on the books of Sararas.

(c) Assume instead that Sararas operates in the province of Prince Edward Island, where 10% PST is also charged on the 5% GST. Prepare the journal entries to record these transactions on the books of Sararas.

(LO 2)   **E13-7   (Income Taxes)** Shaddick Corp. began its 2011 fiscal year with a debit balance of $11,250 in its Income Taxes Receivable account. During the year, the company made quarterly income tax instalment payments of $8,100 each. In early June, a cheque was received from the CRA for Shaddick's overpayment of 2010 taxes. The refunded amount was exactly as Shaddick had calculated it would be on its 2010 income tax return. On completion of the 2011 income tax return, it was determined that Shaddick's income taxes based on 2011 income were $37,800.

Instructions

(a) Prepare all journal entries that are necessary to record the 2011 transactions and events.

(b) Indicate how the income taxes will be reported on Shaddick's December 31, 2011 balance sheet.

(c) Assume that the cheque from the CRA in early June is for $2,750. The difference arose because of calculation errors on Shaddick's tax return. How would the difference be accounted for and where would it be shown on Shaddick's financial statements?

Digging
Deeper

(LO 3)   **E13-8   (Payroll Tax Entries)** The payroll of Austin Corp. for September 2011 is as follows: Total payroll was $485,000. Pensionable (CPP) and insurable (EI) earnings were $365,000. Income taxes in the amount of $85,000 were withheld, as were $8,000 in union dues. The employment insurance tax rate was 1.73% for employees and 2.42% for employers and the CPP rate was 4.95% for employees and 4.95% for employers.

Instructions

(a) Prepare the necessary journal entries to record the payroll if the wages and salaries paid and the employer payroll taxes are recorded separately.

(b) Prepare the entries to record the payment of all required amounts to the CRA and to the employees' union.

(c) For every dollar of wages and salaries that Austin commits to pay, what is the actual payroll cost to the company?

Digging
Deeper

(d) Discuss any other costs, direct or indirect, that you think would add to the company's costs of having employees.

(LO 3)   **E13-9   (Compensated Absences—Vacation and Sick Pay)** Mustafa Limited began operations on January 2, 2010. The company employs nine individuals who work eight-hour days and are paid hourly. Each employee earns 10 paid vacation days and six paid sick days annually. Vacation days may be taken after January 15 of the year following the year in which they are earned. Sick days may be taken as soon as they are earned; unused sick days accumulate. Additional information is as follows:

Actual Hourly Wage Rate		Vacation Days Used by Each Employee		Sick Days Used by Each Employee	
2010	2011	2010	2011	2010	2011
$10	$11	0	9	4	5

Mustafa Limited has chosen to accrue the cost of compensated absences at rates of pay in effect during the period when they are earned and to accrue sick pay when it is earned.

Instructions

(a) Prepare the journal entry(ies) to record the transactions related to vacation entitlement during 2010 and 2011.

(b) Prepare the journal entry(ies) to record the transactions related to sick days during 2010 and 2011.

(c) Calculate the amounts of any liability for vacation pay and sick days that should be reported on the balance sheet at December 31, 2010 and 2011.

(d) How would your answers to parts (b) and (c) change if the entitlement to sick days did not accumulate?

Digging Deeper

E13-10   (Compensated Absences—Vacation and Sick Pay) Refer to the data in E13-9 and assume instead that **(LO 3)** Mustafa Limited has chosen not to recognize paid sick leave until it is used, and has chosen to accrue vacation time at expected future rates of pay without discounting. The company uses the following projected rates to accrue vacation time:

Year in Which Vacation Time Was Earned	Projected Future Pay Rates Used to Accrue Vacation Pay
2010	$10.75 per hour
2011	$11.60 per hour

Instructions

(a) Prepare the journal entry(ies) to record the transactions related to vacation entitlement during 2010 and 2011.

(b) Prepare the journal entry(ies) to record the transactions related to sick days during 2010 and 2011.

(c) Calculate the amounts of any liability for vacation pay and sick days that should be reported on the balance sheet at December 31, 2010 and 2011.

E13-11   (Compensated Absences—Maternity Benefits) Goldwing Corporation offers enriched parental benefits to its **(LO 3)** staff. While the government provides compensation based on Employment Insurance legislation for a period of 12 months, Goldwing increases the amounts received and extends the period of compensation. The benefit program tops up the amount received to 100% of the employee's salary for the first 12 months, and pays the employee 75% of his or her full salary for another six months after the Employment Insurance payments have ceased.

Zeinab Jolan, who earns $54,000 per year, announced to her manager in early June 2011 that she was expecting a baby in mid-November. On October 29, 2011, nine weeks before the end of the calendar year and Goldwing's fiscal year, Zeinab began her 18-month maternity leave. Assume that the Employment Insurance program pays her a maximum of $720 per week for 52 weeks.

Instructions

Round all answers to the nearest dollar.

(a) Prepare all entries that Goldwing Corporation must make during its 2011 fiscal year related to the maternity benefits plan in regard to Zeinab Jolan. Be sure to include the date of each entry.

(b) Prepare one entry to summarize all entries that the company will make in 2012 relative to Zeinab Jolan's leave.

(c) Calculate the amount of maternity benefits payable at December 31, 2011 and 2012. Explain how these amounts will be shown on the company's balance sheet.

E13-12   (Bonus Calculation and Income Statement Preparation) The incomplete income statement of Perreault **(LO 3)** Corp. follows.

PERREAULT CORP.
Income Statement
For the Year 2011

Revenue		$10,000,000
Cost of goods sold		7,000,000
Gross profit		3,000,000
Administrative and selling expenses	$1,000,000	
Profit-sharing bonus to employees	?	?
Income before income taxes		?
Income taxes		?
Net income		$?

The employee profit-sharing plan requires that 20% of all profits remaining after the deduction of the bonus and income taxes be distributed to the employees by the first day of the fourth month following each year end. The income tax rate is 45%, and the bonus is tax-deductible.

Instructions

(a) Complete the condensed income statement of Perreault Corp. for the year 2011. You will need to develop two simultaneous equations to solve for the bonus amount: one for the bonus and one for the tax.

(b) Prepare the journal entry to record the bonus at December 31, 2011.

(LO 4) E13-13   **(Asset Retirement Obligation)** Crude Oil Limited purchases an oil tanker depot on July 2, 2011, at a cost of $600,000 and expects to operate the depot for 10 years. After the 10 years, the company is legally required to dismantle the depot and remove the underground storage tanks. It is estimated that it will cost $75,000 to do this at the end of the depot's useful life. Crude Oil follows private enterprise GAAP.

Instructions

(a) Prepare the journal entries to record the acquisition of the depot and the asset retirement obligation for the depot on July 2, 2011. Based on an effective interest rate of 6%, the present value of the asset retirement obligation (i.e., its fair value) on the date of acquisition is $41,879.

(b) Prepare any journal entries required for the depot and the asset retirement obligation at December 31, 2011. Crude Oil uses straight-line depreciation. The estimated residual value of the depot is zero.

(c) On June 30, 2021, Crude Oil pays a demolition firm to dismantle the depot and remove the tanks at a cost of $80,000. Prepare the journal entry for the settlement of the asset retirement obligation.

(d) Prepare the schedule to calculate the balance in the asset retirement obligation account for all years from 2011 to 2021, assuming there is no change in the estimated cost of dismantling the depot.

(e) Show how all relevant amounts will be reported on Crude Oil Limited's financial statements at December 31, 2011.

(f) How would the accretion expense be reported on the statement of cash flows?

Digging Deeper

(g) Discuss how Crude Oil would account for the asset retirement costs and obligations if the company reports under IFRS. Be specific.

(LO 5) E13-14   **(Warranties—Expense Approach and Cash Basis)** Winslow Corporation sold 150 colour laser copiers in 2011 for $4,000 each, including a one-year warranty. Maintenance on each machine during the warranty period averages $300.

Instructions

(a) Prepare entries to record the machine sales and the related warranty costs under the expense approach. Actual warranty costs incurred in 2011 were $17,000.

(b) Based on the data above and assuming that the cash basis is used, prepare the appropriate entries.

(c) Is the method in (b) ever acceptable under GAAP? Explain.

(LO 5) E13-15   **(Warranties—Expense Approach)** Cool Sound Corporation manufactures a line of amplifiers that carry a three-year warranty against defects. Based on experience, the estimated warranty costs related to dollar sales are as follows: first year after sale—2% of sales; second year after sale—3% of sales; and third year after sale—4% of sales. Sales and actual warranty expenditures for the first three years of business were:

	Sales	Warranty Expenditures
2010	$ 810,000	$ 6,500
2011	1,070,000	17,200
2012	1,036,000	62,000

Instructions

(a) Calculate the amount that Cool Sound Corporation should report as warranty expense on its 2012 income statement and as a warranty liability on its December 31, 2012 balance sheet. Assume that all sales are made evenly throughout each year and that warranty expenditures are also evenly spaced according to the rates above.

(b) Assume that Cool Sound's warranty expenditures in the first year after sale end up being 4% of sales, which is twice as much as was forecast. How would management account for this change?

Digging
Deeper

E13-16   (Warranties—Expense Approach and Revenue Approach) Selzer Equipment Limited sold 500 Rollomatics **(LO 5)** on account during 2011 at $6,000 each. During 2011, Selzer spent $30,000 servicing the two-year warranties that are included in each sale of the Rollomatic. All servicing transactions were paid in cash.

Instructions

(a) Prepare the 2011 entries for Selzer using the expense approach for warranties. Assume that Selzer estimates that the total cost of servicing the warranties will be $120,000 for two years.

(b) Prepare the 2011 entries for Selzer assuming that the warranties are not an integral part of the sale, but rather a separate service that is considered to be bundled with the selling price. Assume that of the sales total, $160,000 is identified as relating specifically to sales of warranty contracts. Selzer estimates the total cost of servicing the warranties will be $120,000 for two years. Because the repair costs are not incurred evenly, warranty revenues are recognized based on the proportion of costs incurred out of the total estimated costs.

(c) What amounts would be shown on Selzer's income statement under parts (a) and (b)? Explain the resulting difference in the company's net income.

(d) Assume that the equipment sold by Selzer undergoes technological improvements and management now has no past experience on which to estimate the extent of the warranty costs. The chief engineer believes that product warranty costs are likely to be incurred, but they cannot be reasonably estimated. What advice would you give on how to account for and report the warranties?

Digging
Deeper

E13-17   (Warranties—Expense Approach and Revenue Approach) Novack Machinery Corporation manufactures **(LO 5)** equipment to a very high standard of quality; however, it must still provide a warranty for each unit sold, and there are instances where the machines do require repair after they have been put into use. The company started in business in 2011, and as the controller, you are trying to determine whether to use the expense or the revenue approach to measure the warranty obligation. You would like to show the company president how this choice would affect the financial statements for 2011, and advise him of the best choice, keeping in mind that the revenue approach is consistent with the approach being taken under IFRS, and there are plans to take the company public in a few years. You have determined that sales for the year were 1,000 units, with a selling price of $3,000 each. The warranty is for two years, and the estimated warranty cost averages $200 per machine. Actual costs of servicing warranties for the year were $105,000. You have done some research and determined that, if the revenue approach were to be used, the portion of revenue allocated to the warranty portion of the sale would be $350, 40% of which would be earned in the first year of the warranty, with the balance being recognized in the second year.

Instructions

(a) For both the expense and the revenue approach, prepare the necessary journal entries to record all of the transactions described, and determine the warranty liability and expense amounts for 2011.

(b) What are the advantages and disadvantages of the two choices? What do you think is the best choice in this situation? Why?

Digging
Deeper

E13-18   (Premium Entries) Moleski Corporation includes one coupon in each box of soap powder that it packs, and 10 **(LO 5)** coupons are redeemable for a premium (a kitchen utensil). In 2011, Moleski Corporation purchased 8,800 premiums at $0.90 each and sold 120,000 boxes of soap powder at $3.30 per box. In total, 44,000 coupons were presented for redemption in 2011. It is estimated that 60% of the coupons will eventually be presented for redemption.

Instructions

(a) Prepare all the entries that would be made for sales of soap powder and for the premium plan in 2011.

(b) What amounts relative to soap powder sales and premiums would be shown on Moleski's financial statements for 2011?

(LO 5)   E13-19   **(Premiums)** Three independent situations follow.

Situation 1: Marquart Stamp Corporation records stamp service revenue and provides for the cost of redemptions in the year stamps are sold to licensees. The stamps can be collected and then redeemed for discounts on future purchases from Marquart as an incentive for repeat business. Marquart's past experience indicates that only 80% of the stamps sold to licensees will be redeemed. Marquart's liability for stamp redemptions was $13 million at December 31, 2010. Additional information for 2011 is as follows.

Stamp service revenue from stamps sold to licensees	$9,500,000
Cost of redemptions (stamps sold prior to 1/1/11)	6,000,000

If all the stamps sold in 2011 were presented for redemption in 2012, the redemption cost would be $5.2 million.

Instructions

What amount should Marquart report as a liability for stamp redemptions at December 31, 2011?

Situation 2: In packages of its products, ITSS Inc. includes coupons that may be presented at retail stores to obtain discounts on other ITSS products. Retailers are reimbursed for the face amount of coupons redeemed plus 10% of that amount for handling costs. ITSS honours requests for coupon redemption by retailers up to three months after the consumer expiration date. ITSS estimates that 60% of all coupons issued will eventually be redeemed. Information relating to coupons issued by ITSS during 2011 is as follows:

Consumer expiration date	12/31/11
Total face amount of coupons issued	$800,000
Total payments to retailers as at 12/31/11	$330,000

Instructions

(a) What amount should ITSS report as a liability for unredeemed coupons at December 31, 2011?

(b) What amount of premium expense should ITSS report on its 2011 income statement?

Situation 3: Baylor Corp. sold 700,000 boxes of pie mix under a new sales promotion program. Each box contains one coupon that entitles the customer to a baking pan when the coupon is submitted with an additional $4.00 from the customer. Baylor pays $5.00 per pan and $1.00 for handling and shipping. Baylor estimates that 70% of the coupons will be redeemed even though only 250,000 coupons had been processed during 2011.

Instructions

(a) What amount should Baylor report as a liability for unredeemed coupons at December 31, 2011?

(b) What amount of expense will Baylor report on its 2011 income statement as a result of the promotional program?

(c) Prepare any necessary 2011 journal entries to record the coupon liability and redemptions.

(AICPA adapted)

(LO 5)   E13-20   **(Premiums)** Timo operates a very busy roadside fruit and vegetable stand from May to October every year as part of his farming operation, which has a December 31 year end. Each time a customer purchases over $10 of produce, Timo gives them a special fruit-shaped sticker that can't be copied. If a customer collects 10 of these stickers, then they can have $10 worth of produce for no charge. The stickers must be redeemed by June 30 of the following year. During the current year, 25,000 stickers were given out to customers. Timo knows from experience that some stickers will never be cashed in, as the customer may not shop at his stand frequently enough to collect 10 stickers, or they get lost or forgotten. In previous years, 10% of stickers have been redeemed. During the current year, 6% of the stickers given out during the year were redeemed.

Instructions

(a) Determine the amount that should be reported as a sales promotion expense on the December 31 income statement, and the amount of any liability at December 31, assuming the expense approach is used.

(b) Prepare all the necessary journal entries to record the expense associated with the stickers and the related liability at year end.

(LO 5)   E13-21   **(Coupons and Rebates)** St. Thomas Auto Repairs is preparing the financial statements for the year ended November 30, 2010. As the accountant, you are looking over the information regarding short-term liabilities, and determining the amounts that should be reported on the balance sheet. St. Thomas Auto Repairs reports under private enterprise accounting standards. The following information regarding new corporate initiatives has been brought to your attention.

1. The company printed a coupon in the local newspaper in November 2010. The coupon permits customers to take 10% off the cost of any service between November 1, 2010, and January 30, 2011. The newspaper has a circulation of 10,000 customers. In November, 5 coupons were used, resulting in sales reductions of $250. It is expected that 50 more coupons will be used before January 30, and the average sales transaction for the company is $75.

2. In order to reduce the costs associated with sick time, the company developed a new plan in 2010. Employees are permitted up to six sick days per year with pay. If these days are not all used, then 50% of the unused time will be accumulated and can be used as sick pay or the employee can use the time as paid vacation within the next year; otherwise, the rights will expire at the end of the next fiscal year. During 2010, the two employees each used two of their six days. The daily rate of pay for each employee is $100. These two individuals are long-term employees of the company who are unlikely to resign in the near future and who have been relatively healthy in the past.

3. The company is considering starting a customer loyalty program. The program would involve tracking the purchases of each customer on a small card that is retained by the customer. Each time a customer reaches $250 in total purchases, a $10 discount would be offered on the next purchase.

Instructions

(a) For items that affect the 2010 financial statements, determine the amount of any liability that should be reported and the related expense.

(b) Discuss the issues that the proposed customer loyalty program raises from an accounting standpoint. Explain how the program should be accounted for.

E13-22 **(Contingencies and Commitments)** Four independent situations follow. (LO 6)

Situation 1: During 2011, Sugarpost Inc. became involved in a tax dispute with the CRA. Sugarpost's lawyers have informed management that Sugarpost will likely lose this dispute. They also believe that Sugarpost will have to pay the CRA between $900,000 and $1.4 million. After the 2011 financial statements were issued, the case was settled with the CRA for $1.2 million.

Instructions

(a) What amount, if any, should be reported as a liability for this contingency as at December 31, 2011, assuming that Sugarpost follows private enterprise GAAP?

(b) Repeat part (a) assuming that Sugarpost follows proposed IFRS.

Situation 2: Toward the end of Su Li Corp.'s 2011 fiscal year, employer–union talks broke off with the wage rates for the upcoming two years still unresolved. Just before the new year, however, a contract was signed that gave employees a 5% increase in their hourly wage. Su Li had expended $1.2 million in wages on this group of workers in 2011.

Instructions

Prepare the entry, if any, that Su Li Corp. should make at December 31, 2011. Briefly explain your answer.

Situation 3: On October 1, 2011, the provincial environment ministry identified Jackhammer Chemical Inc. as a potentially responsible party in a chemical spill. Jackhammer's management, along with its legal counsel, have concluded that it is likely that Jackhammer will be responsible for damages, and a reasonable estimate of these damages is $5 million. Jackhammer's insurance policy of $9 million has a deductible clause of $500,000.

Instructions

(a) Assuming private enterprise GAAP is followed, how should Jackhammer Chemical report this information in its financial statements at December 31, 2011?

(b) Briefly identify any differences if Jackhammer were to follow existing IFRS.

Situation 4: Etheridge Inc. had a manufacturing plant in Bosnia that was destroyed in the civil war. It is not certain who will compensate Etheridge for this destruction, but Etheridge has been assured by Bosnian government officials that it will receive a definite amount for this plant. The compensation amount will be less than the plant's fair value, but more than its carrying amount.

Instructions

How should the contingency be reported in the financial statements of Etheridge Inc. under private entity GAAP?

E13-23 **(Financial Statement Impact of Liability Transactions)** The following is a list of possible transactions. (LO 2, 3, 5, 6)

1. Purchased inventory for $80,000 on account (assume perpetual system is used).

2. Issued an $80,000 note payable in payment of an account (see item 1 above).

3. Recorded accrued interest on the note from item 2 above.

4. Borrowed $100,000 from the bank by signing a $112,000, six-month, non-interest-bearing note.

5. Recognized four months of interest expense on the note from item 4 above.

6. Recorded cash sales of $75,260, which includes 6% sales tax.

7. Recorded wage expense of $35,000. The cash paid was $25,000; the difference was due to various amounts withheld.

8. Recorded employer's payroll taxes.

9. Accrued accumulated vacation pay.

10. Signed a $2-million contract with Construction Corp. to build a new plant.

11. Recorded bonuses due to employees.

12. Recorded a contingent loss on a lawsuit that the company will probably lose.

13. Accrued warranty expense (assume expense warranty approach).

14. Paid warranty costs that were accrued in item 13 above.

15. Recorded sales of product and separately sold warranties.

16. Paid warranty costs under contracts from item 15 above.

17. Recognized warranty revenue (see item 15 above).

18. Recorded estimated liability for premium claims outstanding.

19. Recorded the receipt of a cash down payment on services to be performed in the next accounting period.

20. Received the remainder of the contracted amount and performed the services related to item 19 above.

Instructions

Set up a table using the format that follows and analyze the effects of the 20 transactions on the financial statement categories in the table using private entity GAAP. Use the following codes: increase (I), decrease (D), or no net effect (NE).

Transaction	Assets	Liabilities	Owners' Equity	Net Income
1				

(LO 7)   E13-24   (Ratio Calculations and Discussion) Kawani Corporation has been operating for several years, and on December 31, 2011, presented the following balance sheet.

KAWANI CORPORATION
Balance Sheet
December 31, 2011

Cash	$ 40,000	Accounts payable	$ 70,000
Receivables	75,000	Mortgage payable	140,000
Inventories	95,000	Common shares (no par)	160,000
Plant assets (net)	220,000	Retained earnings	60,000
	$430,000		$430,000

Cost of goods sold in 2011 was $420,000, operating expenses were $51,000, and net income was $27,000. Accounts payable suppliers provided operating goods and services. Assume that total assets are the same in 2010 and 2011.

Instructions

Calculate each of the following ratios. For each ratio, also indicate how it is calculated and what its significance is as a tool for analyzing the company's financial soundness.

(a) Current ratio

(b) Acid-test ratio

(c) Debt-to-total-assets ratio

(d) Rate of return on assets

(e) Days payables outstanding

E13-25 **(Ratio Calculations and Analysis)** Harold Limited's condensed financial statements provide the following **(LO 7)** information:

HAROLD LIMITED
Balance Sheet

	Dec. 31, 2011	Dec. 31, 2010
Cash	$ 52,000	$ 60,000
Accounts receivable (net)	198,000	80,000
Marketable securities (short-term)	80,000	40,000
Inventories	440,000	360,000
Prepaid expenses	3,000	7,000
Total current assets	773,000	547,000
Property, plant, and equipment (net)	857,000	853,000
Total assets	$1,630,000	$1,400,000
Accounts payable	$ 220,000	$ 145,000
Other current liabilities	20,000	15,000
Bonds payable	400,000	400,000
Common shareholders' equity	990,000	840,000
Total liabilities and shareholders' equity	$1,630,000	$1,400,000

Income Statement
For the Year Ended December 31, 2011

Sales	$1,640,000
Cost of goods sold	(800,000)
Gross profit	840,000
Selling and administrative expense	(440,000)
Interest expense	(40,000)
Net income	$ 360,000

Instructions

(a) Determine the following:
1. Current ratio at December 31, 2011
2. Acid-test ratio at December 31, 2011
3. Accounts receivable turnover for 2011
4. Inventory turnover for 2011
5. Days payables outstanding for 2011
6. Rate of return on assets for 2011
7. Profit margin on sales

(b) Prepare a brief evaluation of the financial condition of Harold Limited and of the adequacy of its profits.

(c) In examining the other current liabilities on Harold Limited's balance sheet, you observe that unearned revenues have declined in the current year compared with the previous year. Is this a positive indicator about the client's liquidity? Explain.

Digging Deeper

E13-26 **(Ratio Calculations and Effect of Transactions)** Financial information for Cao Inc. follows. **(LO 7)**

CAO INC.
Balance Sheet December 31, 2011

Cash		$ 45,000	Notes payable (short-term)	$ 50,000
Receivables	$110,000		Accounts payable	32,000
Less: Allowance	15,000	95,000	Accrued liabilities	5,000
Inventories		170,000	Share capital (52,000 shares)	260,000
Prepaid insurance		8,000	Retained earnings	141,000
Land		20,000		
Equipment (net)		150,000		
		$488,000		$488,000

Income Statement
For the Year Ended December 31, 2011

Sales		$1,400,000
Cost of goods sold		
Inventory, Jan. 1, 2011	$200,000	
Purchases	790,000	
Cost of goods available for sale	990,000	
Inventory, Dec. 31, 2011	170,000	
Cost of goods sold		820,000
Gross profit on sales		580,000
Operating expenses		170,000
Net income		$ 410,000

Instructions

(a) Calculate the following ratios or relationships of Cao Inc. Assume that the ending account balances are representative unless the information provided indicates differently.

1. Current ratio

2. Inventory turnover

3. Receivables turnover

4. Average age of receivables (days sales outstanding)

5. Average age of payables (days payables outstanding)

6. Earnings per share

7. Profit margin on sales

8. Rate of return on assets

(b) For each of the following transactions, indicate whether the transaction would improve, weaken, or have no effect on the current ratio of Cao Inc. at December 31, 2011.

1. Writing off an uncollectible account receivable for $2,200

2. Receiving a $20,000 down payment on services to be performed in 2012

3. Paying $40,000 on notes payable (short-term)

4. Collecting $23,000 on accounts receivable

5. Purchasing equipment on account

6. Giving an existing creditor a short-term note in settlement of an open account owed

Problems

P13-1   The following are selected transactions of Pendlebury Department Store Ltd. for the current year ending December 31.

1. On February 2, the company purchased goods having cash discount terms of 2/10, n/30 from Hashmani Limited for $46,000. Purchases and accounts payable are recorded using the periodic system at net amounts after cash discounts. The invoice was paid on February 26.

2. On April 1, Pendlebury purchased a truck for $50,000 from Schuler Motors Limited, paying $5,000 cash and signing a one-year, 8% note for the balance of the purchase price.

3. On May 1, the company borrowed $83,000 from First Provincial Bank by signing a $92,000 non-interest-bearing note due one year from May 1.

4. On June 30 and December 31, Pendlebury remitted cheques for $19,000 each as instalments on its current year tax liability.

5. On August 14, the board of directors declared a $13,000 cash dividend that was payable on September 10 to shareholders of record on August 31.

6. On December 5, the store received $750 from Jefferson Players as a deposit on furniture that Jefferson Players is using in its stage production. The deposit is to be returned to the theatre company after it returns the furniture on January 15.

7. On December 10, the store purchased new display cases for $8,000 on account. Sales tax of 8% and GST of 5% were charged by the supplier on the purchase price.

8. During December, cash sales of $79,000 were recorded, plus 8% sales tax and 5% GST that must be remitted by the 15th day of the following month. Both taxes are levied on the sale amount to the customer.

9. Pendlebury's lease for its store premises calls for a $2,500 monthly rental payment plus 3% of all sales. The payment is due one week after month end.

10. Pendlebury is legally required to restore the area surrounding one of its store parking lots, at an estimated cost of $100,000, when the store is closed in two years. Pendlebury estimates that the fair value of this obligation at December 31 is $86,000.

11. The corporate tax return indicated taxable income of $205,000. Pendlebury's income tax rate is 20%.

Instructions

(a) Prepare all the journal entries that are necessary to record the above transactions when they occurred and any adjusting journal entries relative to the transactions that would be required to present fair financial statements at December 31. Date each entry.

(b) Identify the current liabilities that will be reported on the December 31 balance sheet, and indicate the amount of each one.

(c) Prepare the journal entries for transactions 7 and 8 above if the 8% sales tax is applied on the purchase or sale amount plus the GST.

(d) Why is the liabilities section of the balance sheet of primary significance to bankers?

(e) How are current liabilities related by definition to current assets?

DD

Digging
Deeper

P13-2 Bian Inc. financed the purchase of equipment costing $85,000 on January 1, 2011, using a note payable. The note requires Bian to make annual $32,389 payments of blended interest and principal on January 1 of the following three years, beginning January 1, 2012. The note bears interest at the rate of 7%.

Instructions

(a) Prepare the debt amortization schedule for the note over its term.

(b) Prepare the journal entry(ies) that are required for the year ended December 31, 2011, and the first instalment payment on January 1, 2012.

(c) Prepare the balance sheet presentation of the note at December 31, 2011 (include both the current and long-term portions).

(d) Prepare the balance sheet presentation of the note at December 31, 2012.

(e) Redo part (c) assuming that the equipment was purchased on July 1, 2011, and the payments are due beginning July 1, 2012.

P13-3 Sultanaly Company Limited pays its office employees each week. A partial list follows of employees and their payroll data for August. Because August is the vacation period, vacation pay is also listed.

Employee	Weekly Pay	Vacation Pay to Be Received in August
Christine Ducharme	$ 450	$ 900
Saul Friedman	110	220
Andrea Gettner	250	
Vijay Gupta	1,250	2,500
Matthew Hartman	480	

Assume that the income tax withheld is 10% of wages and that union dues withheld are 1% of wages. Vacations are taken the second and third weeks of August by Ducharme, Friedman, and Gupta. The employment insurance rate is 1.73% for employees and 1.4 times that for employers. The CPP rate is 4.95% for employee and employer.

Instructions

(a) Make the journal entries that are necessary for each of the four August payrolls. The entries for the payroll and for the company's payroll taxes are made separately.

(b) Make the entry to record the monthly payment of accrued payroll liabilities.

(c) Prepare the entry to accrue the 4% vacation entitlement that was earned by employees in August. (No entitlement is earned on vacation pay.)

P13-4   The following is a payroll sheet for Bayview Golf Corporation for the month of September 2011. The employment insurance rate is 1.73% and the maximum annual amount per employee is $747.36. The employer's obligation for employment insurance is 1.4 times the amount of the employee deduction. Assume a 10% income tax rate for all employees, and a 4.95% CPP premium charged to both the employee and employer, up to an annual maximum of $2,163.15 per employee. Union dues are 1% of earnings.

Name	Earnings to Aug. 31	September Earnings	Income Tax Withholding	CPP	EI	Union Dues
L. Meloche	$ 6,800	$ 800				
P. Groot	6,300	700				
D. Beauchamp	7,600	1,100				
C. Regier	13,600	1,900				

Instructions

(a) Complete the payroll sheet and make the necessary entry to record the payment of the payroll.

(b) Make the entry to record the employer's payroll tax expenses.

(c) Make the entry to record the payment of the payroll liabilities. Assume that the company pays all payroll liabilities at the end of each month.

(d) What is the total expense that the company will report in September 2011 relative to employee compensation?

P13-5   Huang Inc. has a contract with its president, Ms. Shen, to pay her a bonus during each of the years 2011, 2012, and 2013. Assume a corporate income tax rate of 40% during the three years. The profit before deductions for bonus and income taxes was $250,000 in 2011, $308,000 in 2012, and $350,000 in 2013. The president's bonus of 12% is deductible for tax purposes in each year and is to be calculated as follows:

(a) In 2011, the bonus is to be based on profit before deductions for bonus and income tax.

(b) In 2012, the bonus is to be based on profit after deduction of bonus but before deduction of income tax.

(c) In 2013, the bonus is to be based on profit before deduction of bonus but after deduction of income tax.

Instructions

Calculate the amounts of the bonus and the income tax for each of the three years.

P13-6   Brooks Corporation sells portable computer equipment with a two-year warranty contract that requires the corporation to replace defective parts and provide the necessary repair labour. During 2011, the corporation sells for cash 400 computers at a unit price of $2,500. Based on experience, the two-year warranty costs are estimated to be $155 for parts and $185 for labour per unit. (For simplicity, assume that all sales occurred on December 31, 2011.) The warranty is not sold separately from the equipment, and no portion of the sales price is allocated to warranty sales.

Instructions

Answer (a) to (d) based on the information above.

(a) Record the 2011 journal entries, assuming the cash basis is used to account for the warranties.

(b) Record the 2011 journal entries, assuming the accrual basis expense approach is used to account for the warranties.

(c) What liability relative to these transactions would appear on the December 31, 2011 balance sheet and how would it be classified if the cash basis is used?

(d) What liability relative to these transactions would appear on the December 31, 2011 balance sheet and how would it be classified if the accrual basis expense approach is used?

Answer (e) to (h) assuming that in 2012 the actual warranty costs incurred by Brooks Corporation were $21,400 for parts and $39,900 for labour.

(e) Record the necessary entries in 2012, applying the cash basis.

(f) Record the necessary entries in 2012, applying the accrual basis expense approach.

(g) Which method would you recommend to the company? Why?

(h) Assume that the warranty costs incurred by Brooks Corporation in 2013 were substantially higher than estimated. How would the company deal with the discrepancy between the estimated warranty liability and the actual warranty expense?

P13-7 Smythe Corporation sells televisions at an average price of $850 and they come with a standard one-year warranty. The company also offers each customer a separate three-year extended warranty contract for $90 that requires the company to perform periodic services and replace defective parts. The extended warranty begins one year after the purchase date. During 2011, the company sold 300 televisions and 270 extended warranty contracts for cash. Company records indicate that warranty costs in the first year after purchase average $25 per set: $15 for parts and $10 for labour. Smythe estimates the average three-year extended warranty costs as $20 for parts and $40 for labour. Assume that all sales occurred on December 31, 2011, and that all warranty costs are expected to be incurred evenly over the warranty period.

Instructions

Answer (a) and (b) based on the information above.

(a) Record any necessary journal entries in 2011.

(b) What liabilities relative to these transactions would appear on the December 31, 2011 balance sheet and how would they be classified?

Answer (c) and (d) assuming that in 2012 Smythe Corporation incurred actual costs relative to 2011 television warranty sales of $4,410 for parts and $2,940 for labour.

(c) Record any necessary journal entries in 2012 relative to the 2011 television warranties.

(d) What amounts relative to the 2011 television warranties would appear on the December 31, 2012 balance sheet and how would they be classified?

Answer (e) and (f) assuming that in 2013 Smythe Corporation incurred the following costs relative to the extended warranties sold in 2011: $2,000 for parts and $3,000 for labour.

(e) Record any necessary journal entries in 2013 relative to the 2011 television warranties.

(f) What amounts relative to the 2011 television warranties would appear on the December 31, 2013 balance sheet and how would they be classified?

P13-8 Renew Energy Ltd. (REL) manufactures and sells directly to customers a special long-lasting rechargeable battery for use in digital electronic equipment. Each battery sold comes with a guarantee that REL will replace free of charge any battery that is found to be defective within six months from the end of the month in which the battery was sold. On June 30, 2011, the Estimated Liability under Battery Warranties account had a balance of $45,000, but by December 31, 2011, this amount had been reduced to $5,000 by charges for batteries returned.

REL has been in business for many years and has consistently experienced an 8% return rate. However, effective October 1, 2011, because of a change in the manufacturing process, the rate increased to 10%. Each battery is stamped with a date at the time of sale so that REL has developed information on the likely pattern of returns during the six-month period, starting with the month following the sale. (Assume no batteries are returned in the month of sale.)

Month Following Sale	% of Total Returns Expected in the Month
1st	20%
2nd	30%
3rd	20%
4th	10%
5th	10%
6th	10%
	100%

For example, for January sales, 20% of the returns are expected in February, 30% in March, and so on.
Sales of these batteries for the second half of 2011 were:

Month	Sales Amount
July	$1,800,000
August	1,650,000
September	2,050,000
October	1,425,000
November	1,000,000
December	900,000

REL's warranty also covers the payment of the freight cost on defective batteries returned and on new batteries sent as replacements. This freight cost is 10% of the sales price of the batteries returned. The manufacturing cost of a battery is roughly 60% of its sales price, and the salvage value of the returned batteries averages 14% of the sales price. Assume that REL follows IFRS and that it uses the expense approach to account for warranties.

Instructions

(a) Calculate the Battery Warranty Expense that will be reported for the July 1 to December 31, 2011 period.

(b) Calculate the amount of the provision that you would expect in the Estimated Liability under Battery Warranties account as at December 31, 2011, based on the above likely pattern of returns.

P13-9 To stimulate the sales of its Sugar Kids breakfast cereal, Kwiecien Corporation places one coupon in each cereal box. Five coupons are redeemable for a premium consisting of a child's hand puppet. In 2011, the company purchases 40,000 puppets at $1.50 each and sells 480,000 boxes of Sugar Kids at $3.75 a box. From its experience with other similar premium offers, the company estimates that 40% of the coupons issued will be mailed back for redemption. During 2011, 115,000 coupons are presented for redemption.

Instructions

(a) Prepare the journal entries that should be recorded in 2011 relative to the premium plan, assuming that the company follows a policy of charging the cost of coupons to expense as they are redeemed and adjusting the liability account at year end.

(b) Prepare the journal entries that should be recorded in 2011 relative to the premium plan, assuming that the company follows a policy of charging the full estimated cost of the premium plan to expense when the sales are recognized.

(c) How would the accounts resulting from the entries in (a) and (b) above be presented on the 2011 financial statements?

P13-10 The Hwang Candy Corporation offers a CD as a premium for every five chocolate bar wrappers that customers send in along with $2.00. The chocolate bars are sold by the company to distributors for $0.30 each. The purchase price of each CD to the company is $1.80; in addition, it costs $0.50 to mail each CD. The results of the premium plan for the years 2011 and 2012 are as follows (all purchases and sales are for cash):

	2011	2012
CDs purchased	250,000	330,000
Chocolate bars sold	2,895,400	2,743,600
Wrappers redeemed	1,200,000	1,500,000
2011 wrappers expected to be redeemed in 2012	290,000	
2012 wrappers expected to be redeemed in 2013		350,000

Instructions

(a) Prepare the journal entries that should be made in 2011 and 2012 to record the transactions related to the Hwang Candy Corporation's premium plan.

(b) Indicate the account names, amounts, and classifications of the items related to the premium plan that would appear on the balance sheet and the income statement at the end of 2011 and 2012.

(c) For each liability that you identified in (b), indicate whether its account is a financial liability. Explain.

P13-11 Mullen Music Limited (MML) carries a wide variety of musical instruments, sound reproduction equipment, recorded music, and sheet music. MML uses two sales promotion techniques—warranties and premiums—to attract customers.

Musical instruments and sound equipment are sold with a one-year warranty for replacement of parts and labour. The estimated warranty cost, based on experience, is 2% of sales.

A premium is offered on the recorded and sheet music. Customers receive a coupon for each dollar spent on recorded music or sheet music. Customers may exchange 200 coupons plus $20 for a CD player. MML pays $34 for each CD player and estimates that 60% of the coupons given to customers will be redeemed.

MML's total sales for 2011 were $7.2 million: $5.4 million from musical instruments and sound reproduction equipment, and $1.8 million from recorded music and sheet music. Replacement parts and labour for warranty work totalled $164,000 during 2011. A total of 6,500 CD players used in the premium program were purchased during the year and there were 1.2 million coupons redeemed in 2011.

The accrual method is used by MML to account for the warranty and premium costs for financial reporting purposes. The balances in the accounts related to warranties and premiums on January 1, 2011, were:

Inventory of premium CD players	$ 39,950
Estimated premium liability	44,800
Estimated liability for warranties	136,000

Instructions

(a) MML is preparing its financial statements for the year ended December 31, 2011. Determine the amounts that will be shown on the 2011 financial statements for the following:

1. Warranty expense

2. Estimated liability for warranties

3. Premium expense

4. Inventory of premium CD players

5. Estimated premium liability

(b) Assume that MML's auditor determined that both the one-year warranty and the coupons for the CD players were, in fact, revenue arrangements with multiple deliverables that should be accounted for under the revenue approach. Explain how this would change the way in which these two programs were accounted for in part (a).

(CMA adapted)

P13-12   Hamilton Airlines is faced with two situations that need to be resolved before the financial statements for the company's year ended December 31, 2011, can be issued.

1. The airline is being sued for $4 million for an injury caused to a child as a result of alleged negligence while the child was visiting the airline maintenance hangar in March 2011. The suit was filed in July 2011. Hamilton's lawyer states that it is likely that the airline will lose the suit and be found liable for a judgement costing anywhere from $400,000 to $2 million. However, the lawyer states that the most probable judgement is $800,000.

2. On November 24, 2011, 26 passengers on Flight No. 901 were injured upon landing when the plane skidded off the runway. Personal injury suits for damages totalling $5 million were filed against the airline by 18 injured passengers on January 11, 2012. The airline carries no insurance. Legal counsel has studied each suit and advised Hamilton that it can reasonably expect to pay 60% of the damages claimed.

Instructions

(a) Prepare any disclosures and journal entries for the airline required by (1) private enterprise GAAP, and (2) existing IAS 37 under IFRS in the preparation of the December 31, 2011 financial statements.

(b) Ignoring the 2011 accidents, what liability due to the risk of loss from lack of insurance coverage should Hamilton Airlines record or disclose? During the past decade, the company has experienced at least one accident per year and incurred average damages of $3.2 million. Discuss fully.

P13-13   In preparing Sahoto Corporation's December 31, 2011 financial statements under private enterprise GAAP, the vice-president, finance, is trying to determine the proper accounting treatment for each of the following situations.

Ethics

1. As a result of uninsured accidents during the year, personal injury suits for $350,000 and $60,000 have been filed against the company. It is the judgement of Sahoto's legal counsel that an unfavourable outcome is unlikely in the $60,000 case but that an unfavourable verdict for approximately $225,000 is likely in the $350,000 case.

2. In early 2011, Sahoto received notice from the provincial environment ministry that a site the company had been using to dispose of waste was considered toxic, and that Sahoto would be held responsible for its cleanup under provincial legislation. The vice-president, finance, discussed the situation over coffee with the vice-president, engineering. The engineer stated that it would take up to three years to determine the best way to remediate the site and that the cost would be considerable, perhaps as much as $500,000 to $2 million or more. The engineering vice-president advocates recognizing at least the minimum estimate of $500,000 in the current year's financial statements, while the financial vice-president advocates just disclosing the situation and the inability to estimate the cost in a note to the financial statements.

3. Sahoto Corporation owns a foreign subsidiary that has a carrying amount of $5,725,000 and an estimated fair value of $8.7 million. The foreign government has communicated to Sahoto its intention to expropriate the assets and business of all foreign investors. On the basis of settlements other firms have received from this same country, Sahoto expects to receive 40% of the fair value of its properties as a final settlement.

4. Sahoto's chemical product division consists of five plants and is uninsurable because of the special risk of injury to employees and losses due to fire and explosion. The year 2011 is considered one of the safest (luckiest) in the division's history because there were no losses due to injury or casualty. Having suffered an average of three casualties a year during the rest of the past decade (ranging from $60,000 to $700,000), management is certain that next year the company will not be so fortunate.

Instructions

(a) Prepare the journal entries that should be recorded as at December 31, 2011, to recognize each of the situations above.

(b) Indicate what should be reported relative to each situation in the financial statements and accompanying notes. Explain why.

(c) Are there any ethical issues involved in accounting for contingencies?

P13-14   Ramirez Inc., a publishing company, is preparing its December 31, 2011 financial statements and must determine the proper accounting treatment for the following situations. The company has retained your group to assist it in this task.

1. Ramirez sells subscriptions to several magazines for a one-year, two-year, or three-year period. Cash receipts from subscribers are credited to Magazine Subscriptions Collected in Advance, and this account had a balance of $2.3 million at December 31, 2011. Outstanding subscriptions at December 31, 2011, expire as follows:

During 2012	$600,000
During 2013	500,000
During 2014	800,000

2. On January 2, 2011, Ramirez discontinued collision, fire, and theft coverage on its delivery vehicles and became self-insured for these risks. Actual losses of $50,000 during 2011 were charged to delivery expense. The 2010 premium for the discontinued coverage amounted to $80,000 and the controller wants to set up a reserve for self-insurance by a debit to delivery expense of $30,000 and a credit to the reserve for self-insurance of $30,000.

3. A suit for breach of contract seeking damages of $1 million was filed by an author against Ramirez on July 1, 2011. The company's legal counsel believes that an unfavourable outcome is likely. A reasonable estimate of the court's award to the plaintiff is in the range between $300,000 and $700,000. No amount within this range is a better estimate of potential damages than any other amount.

4. Ramirez's main supplier, Bartlett Ltd., has been experiencing liquidity problems over the last three quarters. In order for Bartlett's bank to continue to extend credit, Bartlett has asked Ramirez to guarantee its indebtedness. The bank loan stands at $500,000 at December 31, 2011, but the guarantee extends to the full credit facility of $900,000.

5. Ramirez's landlord has informed the company that its warehouse lease will not be renewed when it expires in six months' time. Ramirez entered into a $2-million contract on December 15, 2011, with Complete Construction Company Ltd., committing the company to building an office and warehouse facility.

6. During December 2011, a competitor company filed suit against Ramirez for industrial espionage, claiming $1.5 million in damages. In the opinion of management and company counsel, it is reasonably possible that damages will be awarded to the plaintiff. However, the amount of potential damages awarded to the plaintiff cannot be reasonably estimated.

Instructions

(a) For each of the above situations, provide the journal entry that should be recorded as at December 31, 2011, under private enterprise GAAP, or explain why an entry should not be recorded. For each situation, identify what disclosures are required, if any.

(b) Would your answer to any of the above situations change if Ramirez followed IFRS (particularly current IFRS standards including IAS 37)?

P13-15   Dungannon Enterprises Ltd. sells a specialty part that is used in widescreen televisions and provides the ultimate in screen clarity. To promote sales of its product, Dungannon initiated a program with some of its smaller customers. In exchange for making Dungannon their exclusive supplier, Dungannon guarantees these customers to their creditors so that Dungannon will assume the customers' long-term debt in the event of non-payment to the creditors. In addition to charging for parts, Dungannon also charges a fee to customers who take the guarantee program, and bases the fee on the time frame that the guarantee covers, which is typically three years. In the current fiscal year, these fees amounted to $30,000 for the three-year coverage period.

Six months before Dungannon's fiscal year end, one of its customers, Hutter Corp., began to experience financial difficulties and missed two months of mortgage payments. Hutter's lender then called on Dungannon to make the mortgage payments. At its fiscal year end on December 31, 2011, Dungannon had recorded a receivable of $15,000 related to the payments made by Dungannon on Hutter's behalf. Hutter owes the lender an additional $30,000 at this point. The lender is contemplating putting a lien on Hutter's assets that were pledged as collateral for the loans but the collateral involves rights on development of new state-of-the-art three-dimensional television technology that is still unproven. Dungannon follows private enterprise GAAP.

Instructions

(a) Prepare all required journal entries and adjusting entries on Dungannon's books to recognize the transactions and events described above.

(b) Identify any disclosures that must be made as a result of this information and prepare the note disclosure for Dungannon for the period ended December 31, 2011.

P13-16   Hrudka Corp. has manufactured a broad range of quality products since 1988. The following information is available for the company's fiscal year ended February 28, 2011.

1. The company has $4 million of bonds payable outstanding at February 28, 2011, that were issued at par in 2000. The bonds carry an interest rate of 7%, payable semi-annually each June 1 and December 1.

2. Hrudka has several notes payable outstanding with its primary banking institution at February 28, 2011. In each case, the annual interest is due on the anniversary date of the note each year (same as the due dates listed). The notes are as follows:

Due Date	Amount Due	Interest Rate
Apr. 1, 2011	$150,000	8%
Jan. 31, 2012	200,000	9%
Mar. 15, 2012	500,000	7%
Oct. 30, 2013	250,000	8%

3. Hrudka has a two-year warranty on selected products, with an estimated cost of 1% of sales being returned in the 12 months following the sale, and a cost of 1.5% of sales being returned in months 13 to 24 following sale. The warranty liability outstanding at February 28, 2010, was $5,700. Sales of warrantied products in the year ended February 28, 2011, were $154,000. Actual warranty costs incurred during the current fiscal year are as follows:

Warranty claims honoured on 2009–2010 sales	$4,900
Warranty claims honoured on 2010–2011 sales	1,100
	$6,000

4. Regular trade payables for supplies and purchases of goods and services on open account are $414,000 at February 28, 2011. Included in this amount is a loan of $23,000 owing to an affiliated company.

5. The following information relates to Hrudka's payroll for the month of February 2011. The company's required contribution for EI is 1.4 times that of the employee contribution; for CPP it is 1.0 times that of the employee contribution.

Salaries and wages outstanding at February 28, 2011	$220,000
EI withheld from employees	9,500
CPP withheld from employees	16,900
Income taxes withheld from employees	48,700
Union dues withheld from employees	21,500

6. Hrudka regularly pays GST owing to the government on the 15th of the month. Hrudka's GST transactions include the GST that it charges to customers and the GST that it is charged by suppliers. During February 2011, purchases attracted $28,000 of GST, while the GST charged on invoices to customers totalled $39,900. At January 31, 2011, the balances in the GST Recoverable and GST Payable accounts were $34,000 and $60,000, respectively.

7. Other miscellaneous liabilities included $50,000 of dividends payable on March 15, 2011; $25,000 of bonuses payable to company executives (75% payable in September 2011, and 25% payable the following March); and $75,000 in accrued audit fees covering the year ended February 28, 2011.

8. Hrudka sells gift cards to its customers. The company does not set a redemption date and customers can use their cards at any time. At March 1, 2010, Hrudka had a balance outstanding of $950,000 in its Unearned Revenues—Gift Cards account. The company received $225,000 in cash for gift cards purchased during the current year and $375,000 in redemptions took place during the year. Based on past experience, 15% of customer gift card balances never get redeemed. At the end of each year, Hrudka recognizes 15% of the opening balance of Unearned Revenues as earned during the year.

Instructions

(a) Prepare the current liability section of the February 28, 2011 balance sheet of Hrudka Corp. Identify any amounts that require separate presentation or disclosure under private enterprise GAAP.

**Digging
Deeper**

(b) For each item included as a current liability, identify whether the item is a financial liability. Explain.

(c) If you have excluded any items from the category of current liabilities, explain why you left them out.

(d) Assume that Hrudka Corp. is not in compliance with the debt covenants in the note payable due October 30, 2013, in item 2 above. How would this affect the classification of the note on the balance sheet?

(e) For a manufacturer such as Hrudka, how should the revenue from unredeemed gift cards be shown on the income statement, as opposed to revenue from redeemed gift cards?

P13-17   Meticulous Corp., a leader in the commercial cleaning industry, acquired and installed, at a total cost of $110,000 plus 15% HST (Harmonized Sales Tax), three underground tanks for the storage of hazardous liquid solutions needed in the cleaning process. The tanks were ready for use on February 28, 2011.

The provincial ministry of the environment regulates the use of such tanks and requires them to be disposed of after 10 years of use. Meticulous estimates that the cost of digging up and removing the tanks in 2021 will be $28,000. An appropriate interest or discount rate is 6%.

Meticulous also manufactures commercial cleaning machines that it sells to dry cleaning establishments throughout Nova Scotia. During 2011, Meticulous sold 20 machines at a price of $12,000 each plus 15% HST. The machines were sold with a three-year warranty for parts and labour. Because Meticulous has been in business since 1983, the company accountant was able to estimate that the warranty costs are likely to be 1% of the selling price in the first year, 1.5% in the second, and 2.5% in the third. Meticulous keeps track of warranty costs by year of manufacture and sale in order to evaluate the performance of company employees.

Instructions

Answer the following, assuming Meticulous follows IFRS and has a December 31 fiscal year end.

(a) Assuming straight-line depreciation and no residual value for the tanks at the end of their 10-year useful life, what is the balance in the asset Storage Tanks account, net of accumulated depreciation, at December 31, 2011?

(b) What is the balance of the asset retirement obligation liability at December 31, 2013, assuming there has been no change to the estimate of the final cost of disposal?

(c) Assume that Meticulous incurred actual warranty expenditures of $1,500 in 2011 and $3,720 in 2012. Determine the balance of the Estimated Liability under Warranties on 2011 sales that would be reported on the December 31, 2012 balance sheet. Ignore HST and assume that Meticulous uses the expense approach to account for warranties.

(d) Determine the Warranty Expense relating to 2011 sales that would be reported on Meticulous's 2011 income statement.

(e) Meticulous follows a policy of filing its HST return on December 31 each year and either sending a cheque or requesting a refund on this date. Assuming there are no other HST transactions during the year, will Meticulous be sending a cheque or requesting a refund on December 31, 2011? What will be the amount of the cheque paid or refund claimed?

Writing Assignments

Ethics

WA13-1   You are the new controller at ProVision Corporation. You are currently preparing the December 31, 2011 financial statements. ProVision manufactures household appliances. It is a private company and has the choice for 2011 to follow private enterprise GAAP or International Financial Reporting Standards. During your review of the accounts and discussion with the lawyer, you discover the following possible liabilities.

1. ProVision began production of a new dishwasher in June 2011, and by December 31, 2011, had sold 100,000 units to various retailers for $500 each. Each dishwasher is sold with a one-year warranty included. The company estimates that its warranty expense per dishwasher will amount to $25. By year end, the company had already paid out $1 million in warranty expenditures on 35,000 units. ProVision's records currently show a warranty expense of $1 million for 2011. Warranties similar to these are available for sale for $75. (Show both the expense approach and the revenue approach as alternatives. Assume that the revenue approach is now used by both PE GAAP and IFRS.)

2. ProVision's retail division rents space from Meadow Malls. ProVision pays a rental fee of $6,000 per month plus 5% on the amount of yearly retail profits that is over $500,000. ProVision's CEO, Burt Wilson, tells you that he had instructed the previous accountant to increase the estimate of bad debt expense and warranty costs in order to keep the retail division's profits at $475,000.

3. ProVision's lawyer, Robert Dowski, informed you that ProVision has a legal obligation to dismantle and remove the equipment used to produce the dishwashers and clean up the rental premises as part of the lease agreement. The equipment, costing $10 million, was put into production on June 1, 2011, and has a useful life of 120 months. The dismantling and removal costs are estimated to be $3 million. In addition, as a result of the production process, there are clean-up costs incurred, estimated to be $5,000 per month during production, which will be totally paid (estimated in total to be $600,000) when the equipment is removed. (The appropriate discount rate to be used for determining the present value of the cash flows is 0.5% per month.)

4. ProVision is the defendant in a patent infringement lawsuit filed by Heidi Golder over ProVision's use of a hydraulic compressor in several of its products. Dowski claims that, if the suit goes against ProVision, the loss may be as much as $5 million. It is more likely than not that ProVision will have to pay some amount on settlement. Although the exact amount is not known, the lawyer has been able to assign probabilities and expected payment amounts as follows: 20% probability that the settlement will be $5 million, 35% probability that the settlement required will be $3 million, and 45% that no settlement will be required.

Instructions

(a) In the form of a memorandum to the CFO, address each of the above issues. Explain what the problem is, and what choices the company has to report these liabilities under PE GAAP or IFRS or under the new proposed exposure draft *Measurement of Liabilities* (IAS 37) released in January 2010. Prepare the journal entries that would be required under adoption of either standard. Explain any differences in the reported income under the various approaches.

(b) Identify any issues that you consider unethical and suggest what should be done.

WA13-2 Antigonish Corporation includes the following items in its liabilities at its year end, December 31, 2011:

1. Accounts payable, $420,000, due to suppliers in January 2012

2. Notes payable, $1.5 million, maturing on various dates in 2014

3. Deposits from customers on equipment ordered from Antigonish, $250,000

4. Salaries payable, $37,500, due on January 14, 2012

5. Bonds payable, $2.5 million, maturing on July 1, 2012. The company has been able to renegotiate an agreement from the bondholders to roll over this maturity date to July 1, 2015. This agreement was settled on January 21, 2012.

Instructions

In answering each of the following, note any differences between IFRS, ASPE, and proposed standards.

(a) What are the essential characteristics that make an item a liability?

(b) What distinguishes a current liability from a long-term liability?

(c) What distinguishes a financial liability from a non-financial liability?

(d) Indicate for each of the above liabilities if it should be reported as current or noncurrent at the December 31, 2011 report date.

WA13-3 City Goods Limited is a sports clothing and equipment retailer, which has a chain of 10 stores across Canada. You have just been hired as the new controller for the company and you are currently meeting with the CFO to discuss some accounting-related topics that have arisen in the preparation of the company's January 31, 2012 financial statements. City Goods is a private company. The following is a summary of your notes from this meeting.

1. Customer loyalty program: In this fiscal year, the company implemented a new customer loyalty program that grants CG points to members based on the amount they spend in the store. The points have no expiry date and can be redeemed against future purchases in the store. The company has already determined that the fair value of each point is $0.50. During the year, 700,000 points were awarded to members, of which 80,000 were subsequently redeemed for purchases in the stores. The company anticipates that 90% of the points will be redeemed at some point in time.

2. The company entered into an agreement on April 1, 2008, to lease a retail location for five years. In December 2011, City Goods decided to close that retail location due to very poor sales. The company has not been able to sublet the premises and is not able to terminate the lease agreement. The monthly lease payment, which includes all operating costs, is $2,300 per month.

3. The company has a policy of refunding purchases by dissatisfied customers, as long as it is within two years from the date of purchase. This refund policy is not documented, but the company has made a practice of doing so in the past. During the year, the company's sales totalled $35 million. From experience, the company has determined the following probabilities for returns: there is a 25% probability that returns will represent 6% of total sales, 55% probability that they will represent 4% of total sales, and 20% probability that they will represent 2% of total sales.

During the year, there were returns on current year's sales of $1.7 million, on which refunds were made.

Instructions

For each of the issues above, explain the situation and the appropriate accounting treatment under ASPE and IFRS. Show any required journal entries. Where necessary, you can use a discount rate of 0.5% per month.

WA13-4   Conduit Corporation has 45 current employees: 5 managers and 40 non-managers. The average wage paid is $250 per day for non-managers. The company has just finished negotiating a new employee contract with the non-managers that would see this increase by 3% effective January 1, 2012. The company's fiscal year end is December 31, 2011. You are the controller for Conduit and are completing the year-end adjusting journal entries. The company has the following employee benefit plans.

1. Non-manager employees are entitled to two sick leave days per month. If any days are not taken, they may accumulate and be taken as vacation or paid in cash. The sick days may be carried forward to the end of the next year. At the end of the year, there were 60 accumulated sick leave days that had not yet been taken.

2. Parental leave: Any employee is entitled to one year's parental leave. The company will pay the amount to top up the unemployment benefits received to make up the employee's annual salary at the time the leave is taken. Currently, there is one employee on parental leave, who started her maternity leave on December 15, 2011. It is expected that the top-up required will be $1,000 per month for 12 months and the employee was paid $500 on December 31, 2011. There is another employee who is trying to adopt a child and has also said that he will want paternity leave at the time the adoption occurs. The top-up is also estimated to be $1,000 per month for this employee.

3. A profit-sharing plan provides for employees to receive a bonus of 3% of net profit before taxes for all employees who worked for the company during the year. The net profit before taxes is estimated to be $2 million. The bonus is allocated 30% to the five managers and 70% to the remaining employees. However, the bonus is not paid until October 31 of the following year, and only to employees who remain with the company. The company expects a 5% turnover by October 31, 2012, for the non-manager group.

4. The company pays on average three weeks' vacation pay, even though Conduit's legal obligation is only for two weeks. This vacation pay accumulates and can be carried over for up to one year. However, if the employee leaves before the vacation is taken, then they are only legally entitled to the two-week rate. At the end of the year, there were 10 non-manager employees who had only taken one week of their annual entitlement during 2011. There is a small probability of 15% that one of these employees will leave before the full vacation accrual is taken.

5. The company is being sued by a former employee. The non-manager employee contends that not enough severance was paid when he was let go in June 2011. The ex-employee's lawyers are asking for a severance payment of two weeks' pay for each year worked, which in this case was 25 years. The company agreed to pay the employee severance of $30,000 when he was asked to leave the company. This $30,000 has already been accrued in the accounting records. The case is still being disputed and will go to arbitration early in March 2012. Conduit's lawyers believe that the probabilities of settlements for additional amounts (over and above the $30,000) are as follows: 25% probability of settling at $20,000, 60% probability of settling at $28,000, and 15% probability of settling at $30,000.

Instructions

You are the controller for Conduit and are completing the year-end adjusting journal entries. Discuss each of the above issues and determine the journal entries that would be required under IFRS and PE GAAP. Also determine whether the benefits are accumulating or non-accumulating and vesting or not vesting.

WA13-5   Write a brief essay highlighting the differences between IFRS and accounting standards for private enterprises noted in this chapter, discussing the conceptual justification for each.

Cases

Refer to the Case Primer on the Student Website to help you answer these cases.

CA13-1   ABC Airlines (ABC) carried more than 11.9 million passengers to over 160 destinations in 17 countries in 2011. ABC is the descendant of several predecessor companies, including AB Air and BC Airlines. The amalgamated company was created in 1999. In the years that followed, the world air travel industry slumped and caused many airlines to go bankrupt or suffer severe financial hardship. ABC weathered the storm by going through a significant restructuring. One of the changes as a result of the restructuring was to have ABC employees take share options as part of their remuneration. This resulted in employees investing $200 million in the company. The company is privately owned.

In 2011, ABC was still suffering losses ($187 million in 2009 and $194 million in 2010) so the CEO announced a new restructuring plan that would hopefully put an end to the continuing losses (which were now partly due to increased competition and falling seat prices). The plan focused on three areas: improved network profitability, decreased overhead costs, and decreased labour costs. For the latter, employees were asked to accept reduced wages over a four-year period.

Just like most companies, ABC is now concerned with increasing market share and maintaining customer loyalty. On the company's website, the following advertisement appears:

"Fly 5, Fly Free—Fly five times with ABC Airlines and its worldwide partners and earn a free trip. The more you fly, the more the world is within reach."

Free flights have been offered by ABC in the past through its well-publicized frequent flyer program. Under the program, customers earn points for flying with ABC and, once they accumulate enough points, they can then use them to take free flights. In the notes to its financial statements, ABC notes that the incremental costs of frequent flyer points are accrued as the entitlements to free flights are earned. The accrual is included as part of accrued liabilities.

Excerpts from the 2011 financial statements follow (in millions):

Total assets (including current assets of $456.5)	$1,866
Current liabilities	765
Long-term debt	841
Preferred shares	289
Common shares	407
Deficit	(436)
Total liabilities and equity	$1,866

Instructions

Adopt the role of company management and discuss the treatment of the "Fly 5, Fly Free" program for financial reporting purposes.

Integrated Cases

IC13-1   Envirocompany Limited (EL) is a pulp and paper company that has been in operation for 50 years. Its shares trade on a major stock exchange. It is located in a small town in Northern Ontario and employs thousands of people. In fact, the town exists mainly because of the jobs created by EL. Its equipment is fairly outdated and pollutes the surrounding water and air with chemicals that have been shown to be carcinogens. The old equipment is part of the reason for the company's "success" since it is all paid for and requires little maintenance. The employees tolerate the pollution because EL gives them good jobs and keeps the local economy going.

Last year, a new chairman of the board of directors was appointed to EL, Charles Champion. He first became aware of the size of the pollution problem before being appointed to the board and he felt that he would like to do something about it. He took this mission as a personal challenge. In the first year of his appointment, he commissioned several in-depth studies on how EL might reduce or eliminate the pollution. He wanted to be careful to protect himself and the other members of the board because directors were increasingly being held personally liable for the actions of companies. The company has begun cultivating an image implying that it would like to become more environmentally conscious while at the same time preserving jobs.

Most studies pointed to the old machinery and recommended that it be replaced by new state-of-the-art equipment. Cost estimates ran into the millions of dollars and the board of directors felt that the company would not be able to survive that type of expenditure. One study proved that the company would not even be in business any more, given the cost of new environmentally friendly equipment, declining demand for unrecycled newsprint, and increasing competition from abroad. That study was quickly put away on a shelf.

Recent environmental studies have shown that the pollutants were seeping into the water table and finding their way into neighbouring communities. The studies showed that there were increasing incidences of birth defects in animals and humans in the affected areas, including increases in sterility for certain aquatic and marine life. This caused several politicians to start grandstanding and calling for tighter pollution controls and steep fines.

In the past year, there have been reports of people living downstream getting sick, apparently from the chemical pollutants from EL. One individual threatened to sue, and EL's lawyers were privately acknowledging the potential for a class action suit. EL has insurance that would cover up to $1 million in damages.

Meanwhile, the accountants were struggling with how to account for the problem in the year-end statements.

Instructions

Adopt the role of the company controller and discuss the financial reporting issues.

IC13-2 Landfill Limited (LL) is a private company that collects and disposes of household garbage. Waste is collected and trucked to local disposal sites where it is dumped and then covered with topsoil. The disposal sites are owned by LL and were financed by debt from Bank Inc. at an average interest rate of 5%.

LL has several disposal sites that will be filled with garbage and later sold as industrial land. LL estimates that the sites will take 20 years on average to fill up. Varying amounts of garbage will be dumped each year. Salvage values are not known at the time although land normally holds its value unless toxic chemicals are found.

Government regulations require that the company perform capping, closure, and post-closure activities. Capping involves covering the land with topsoil and planting vegetation. Closure activities include drainage, engineering, and demolition. Post-closure activities include maintaining the landfill once the government has given final certification. They also include monitoring the ground and surface water, gas emissions, and air quality. If the land is sold, the purchaser reduces the acquisition cost by an estimate of this cost. LL must also guarantee that the land is toxin free and if it is later found to contain toxins, LL will pay for cleanup.

In the past year, one of these landfill sites was sold. However, the company recently received notification from the purchaser's lawyers that high levels of toxins had been found leaking into the water table.

Obtaining new contracts, as well as keeping old ones, depends on many factors. These include competitive bidding, the company's profile in the community, its past work performance, its financial stability, and having a history of adhering strictly to environmental standards. Financial statements are therefore relevant in the process of obtaining new contracts as they are examined by those who award them.

Instructions

Adopt the role of the company auditor and discuss the financial reporting issues. Landfill Limited is one of your new audit clients this year.

IC13-3 Candelabra Limited (CL) is a manufacturing company that is privately owned. The company's production facilities produce a significant amount of carbon dioxide and currently the town is suing CL for polluting the surrounding area. The company is enjoying a period of significant prosperity and earnings have been steadily increasing. CL plans to double in size within the next 10 years. The production facility was financed by a 100-year bond that pays 5% interest annually. The bond includes a covenant that stipulates that the debt to equity ratio must not exceed 2:1. The debt to equity ratio is currently just below this threshold.

The government has recently introduced a system to control pollution whereby each company is allocated a certain number of "carbon credits." The carbon credits allow the company to produce a certain amount of carbon dioxide as a by-product from its production facilities. CL has been allocated a fixed number of these credits by the government at no cost. If CL produces more carbon dioxide than allowed, it will have to pay a fine. CL is pretty sure that it will exceed the amount allowed under the government-allotted carbon credits. Many companies in the surrounding area have extra carbon credits and as a result, the government has established an informal marketplace whereby companies can trade their extra credits. The value of the contracts changes depending on supply and demand.

CL has purchased several carbon credit contracts in the marketplace just in case. At the time it acquired the contracts, there was an oversupply and so CL was able to acquire them at very little cost. Currently, demand for the credits has increased significantly.

As another backup plan, CL is investigating diverting excess carbon dioxide to an underground cave that is situated on company-owned property. Currently, CL has spent a significant amount of funds to investigate the feasibility of diverting and storing the extra carbon dioxide it produces. The engineers working on the project are still not convinced of the feasibility of this type of storage on a larger scale. At present, they have started to store some excess carbon dioxide there on a test basis.

In order to fund the work on the cave, the company has issued shares. The shares are redeemable in cash at the company's option if its carbon dioxide levels (excluding any amounts that will be stored in the cave) reach a certain point. The shares are currently held by a large pension company.

Instructions

Assume the role of CL's auditors and analyze the financial reporting issues.

Research and Financial Analysis

RA13-1 Eastern Platinum Limited

Real-World Emphasis

Eastern Platinum Limited's 2009 annual financial statements can be found at the end of this volume. The company is involved in the mining, exploration, and development of platinum products in South Africa.

Instructions

Review the consolidated statements of financial position and notes to the financial statements of Eastern Platinum Limited and answer the following questions.

(a) What makes up the current liabilities reported at December 31, 2009? Be as specific as possible.

(b) What is the nature of the current liability Provisions? Does the company have any short-term employee benefits included in current liabilities? Why would these amounts related to the employee benefits be included in current liabilities?

(c) Explain the Provision for Environmental Rehabilitation. What is included in this amount and how has it been calculated? Is it a financial or non-financial liability? Explain how the provision changed from January 1, 2008, to December 31, 2009.

(d) Calculate Eastern's current ratio and quick ratio for December 31, 2009, and December 31, 2008. Comment on the company's liquidity.

RA13-2 Canadian Tire Corporation, Limited

Instructions

Refer to the 2008 financial statements and 10-year financial review of Canadian Tire Corporation, Limited found at www.sedar.com. Then answer the following questions.

Real-World Emphasis

(a) What makes up Canadian Tire's current liabilities? Suggest at least five different types of liabilities that are likely included in Accounts Payable and Other. What is included in Deposits?

(b) What were Canadian Tire's working capital, acid-test ratio, and current ratio for the two most recent years of data that are provided? How do these results compare with the measures for five years ago? Comment on the company's current liquidity in general, and compared with its liquidity five years ago. What role does the inventory turnover have in assessing liquidity in general, and for Canadian Tire specifically? What is in the accounts receivable and what role does it play in assessing liquidity for Canadian Tire? Can a turnover ratio be calculated for these accounts receivable?

(c) What is the current portion of long-term debt? Explain clearly what makes up this amount. If the company does not borrow any additional long-term funds during 2009, how much would you expect to see on the 2009 balance sheet as the current portion of long-term debt? Explain clearly what would make up this amount. Are there any concerns arising from this amount?

(d) What types of commitments and contingencies has Canadian Tire reported in its financial statements? Identify which items are commitments and which are contingencies. What is management's reaction to the contingencies?

(e) What covenants does the company have to maintain under its existing debt agreements? Was it in compliance at the year end? (Hint: See the Capital Management Disclosures note.)

RA13-3 lululemon athletica inc. and Costco Wholesale Corporation

lululemon athletica inc. is a vertically integrated designer, manufacturer, and retailer of lifestyle yoga and athletic clothing and accessories for men, women, and children. The company sells its products through its company-owned and operated retail outlets and some franchise and wholesale operators. Costco Wholesale Corporation mainly sells a limited selection of items in a wide variety of product groups at close-to-cost prices in stripped-down big box stores. Its stores have a goal of selling very large volumes of merchandise with little credit risk, and achieving a high inventory turnover. The current asset and current liability sections of the 2009 and 2008 balance sheets of lululemon and Costco follow.

LULULEMON ATHLETICA INC. (IN U.S.$)

	Feb. 1, 2009	Feb. 3, 2008
Current Assets		
Cash	$ 56,796,981	$ 52,544,971
Accounts receivable	4,029,032	4,302,430
Inventories (Note 3)	52,050,891	37,931,990
Prepaid expenses and other current assets	4,111,024	2,518,692
Assets of discontinued operations	–0–	3,038,498
	$116,987,928	$100,336,581
Current Liabilities		
Accounts payable	$ 5,269,423	$ 5,397,102
Accrued liabilities	22,103,034	7,247,055
Accrued compensation and related expenses	5,861,807	7,986,463
Income taxes payable	2,133,036	5,719,804
Unredeemed gift card liability	9,277,536	8,113,953
Other current liabilities	690,081	780,851
Liabilities of discontinued operations	–0–	895,249
	$ 45,334,917	$ 36,140,477
Other Information		
Revenue	$353,488,212	$269,942,362
Cost of sales	174,420,844	125,014,988
Selling, general, and administrative expenses	118,098,347	93,376,167

COSTCO WHOLESALE CORPORATION (MILLIONS OF U.S.$)

	Aug. 30, 2009	Aug. 31, 2008
Current Assets		
Cash and cash equivalents	$ 3,157	$2,619
Short-term investments	570	656
Receivables, net	834	748
Merchandise inventories	5,405	5,039
Deferred income taxes, and other current assets	371	400
Total current assets	$10,337	$9,462
Current Liabilities		
Short-term borrowings	$ 16	$134
Accounts payable	5,450	5,225
Accrued salaries and benefits	1,418	1,321
Accrued sales and other taxes	302	283
Deferred membership income	824	748
Current portion of long-term debt	81	6
Other current liabilities	1,190	1,157
Total current liabilities	$9,281	$8,874
Other Information		
Revenue, net sales	$69,889	$70,977
Merchandise costs	62,335	63,503
Selling, general, and administrative expense	7,252	6,954

Instructions

(a) Calculate the current and quick ratios for lululemon and Costco at their 2009 and 2008 year ends. Which company appears to have better liquidity? Explain the possible reason for this.

(b) Use calculations to estimate the number of days for each stage in the operating cycle of each company and then draw a timeline that shows the cash to cash **operating cycle** of both companies. The cycle includes the following stages: (1) from the receipt of goods from suppliers to the payment to suppliers (average age of payables or days payables outstanding), (2) from the receipt of goods from suppliers to the sale of merchandise (inventory turnover in days), and (3) from the sale of goods to the collection of cash from customers (accounts receivable turnover). What do these measures tell you about each company's cash flow?

(c) Which company do you think is more liquid? Why?

(d) Explain lululemon's treatment of unredeemed gift cards. How much was outstanding as a liability at the end of the 2009 fiscal year end? How much had this amount increased year over year?

RA13-4 Deutsche Lufthansa AG

The financial statements of Deutsche Lufthansa Limited for the year ended December 31, 2008, are available on the www.lufthansa.com website.

Real-World Emphasis

Instructions

(a) What is included in the current liabilities for Lufthansa and how have the percentages of each item to total current liabilities changed from 2007 to 2008?

(b) What specific items are included in Other Provisions, Trade Payables and Other Financial Liabilities, and Advanced Payments Received, Accruals and Deferrals and Other Non-Financial Liabilities? What is included in Liabilities from Unused Flight Documents?

(c) What types of employee benefit liabilities are included in the above numbers? What does "expected losses from uncompleted transactions" represent? How does the company estimate environmental obligations?

(d) What changes have occurred in Other Provisions between December 31, 2007, and December 31, 2008? Prepare a reconciliation of the opening and closing balance for 2008.

(e) How does the company currently account for the bonus miles program, Lufthansa's customer loyalty program? What is the amount in liabilities that represents this obligation? How many miles have been accumulated? For 2009, how will the company be required to account for the customer loyalty program? What is the impact of this change on the 2008 financial reports and the estimated obligation?

(f) What contingencies does the company have? Have any of these been recognized?

(g) What makes up the current portion of borrowings for Lufthansa's most recently reported fiscal year end? Be specific.

(h) Access the British Airways plc annual report for the year ended March 31, 2009, from www.bashares.com. Does the company have any onerous contracts? How much has been recognized and to what do these contracts relate?

RA13-5 Research Topics

There are many interesting company programs and circumstances that relate to the definition, recognition, and measurement of liabilities. Examples include customer loyalty programs, retail gift cards, corporate restructuring obligations, air miles programs, product liability lawsuits, liability accruals on interim financial statements, environmental liabilities, onerous contracts, and many employee benefit programs.

Instructions

Choose one of the programs or circumstances listed above. Research your choice using international and Canadian sources, and prepare a one-page summary of the liability recognition and measurement issues that are involved. If possible, identify any accounting standards that may help resolve the issues.

Intrawest Avoids Major Wipeout

INTRAWEST, the Vancouver-based owner of Whistler-Blackcomb ski resort in British Columbia, among other high-profile vacation destinations, had to navigate some difficult moguls in early 2010 when its owner, Fortress Investment Group, had difficulty keeping up with its long-term financial liabilities. Fortress bought Intrawest in 2006 for U.S. $3.1 billion, financing the deal with U.S. $1.5 billion in new debt. The real estate market then slid down a slippery slope during the economic slump that began in 2008, hitting the North American ski industry hard, as sales of lift tickets and resort condominiums fell.

After Fortress failed to make a U.S. $524-million payment that was due on its debt, its lenders publicly threatened to auction off Intrawest's various properties in B.C., Colorado, California, Florida, and Vermont on February 19—right in the middle of the Winter Olympic Games, during which many skiing events were taking place at Whistler.

Fortress spent the end of 2009 and early 2010 negotiating several deals to sell off various Intrawest assets in order to free up some cash to satisfy its lenders. These included the sale of Copper Mountain in Colorado to Powdr Corp., a Utah-based mountain resort operator; Panorama Mountain Village near Invermere, B.C., including a 50% share in Greywolf Golf Course, to a group of Panorama homeowners and local business people who joined forces to form Panorama Mountain Village Inc. for the purchase; and the Sandestin Golf and Beach Resort in Florida to the Becnel family.

Intrawest said the sales had been planned for some time and were part of the company's long-term strategy to focus on just a few four-season destination resorts, including Whistler-Blackcomb and Mont Tremblant in Quebec. In the end, the foreclosure auction did not take place and Intrawest was ready to ski another day. ∎

Sources: Boyd Erman, "Lenders Plan to Auction Intrawest Assets," *The Globe and Mail*, January 20, 2010; Intrawest news releases, November 17, 2009; January 28, 2010; and February 9, 2010.

CHAPTER 14

Long-Term Financial Liabilities

Learning Objectives

After studying this chapter, you should be able to:

1. Understand the nature of long-term debt.
2. Identify various types of long-term debt.
3. Understand how long-term debt is valued and measured.
4. Apply the effective interest and straight-line bond amortization methods.
5. Value bonds and consideration in special situations.
6. Account for derecognition of debt.
7. Distinguish between and account for debt restructurings that result in extinguishment or in debt continuation.
8. Explain the issues surrounding off–balance sheet financing arrangements.
9. Indicate how long-term debt is presented and analyzed.
10. Identify the major differences in accounting between accounting standards for private enterprises (PE GAAP/ASPE) and IFRS, and what changes are expected in the near future.

Preview of Chapter 14

Long-term debt and financial liabilities continue to play an important role in our capital markets because companies and governments need large amounts of capital to finance their growth. In many cases, the most effective way to obtain capital is by issuing long-term debt. This chapter explains the accounting issues that are related to long-term debt and financial liabilities.

The chapter is organized as follows:

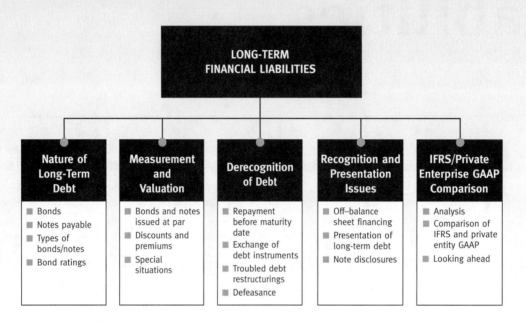

LONG-TERM FINANCIAL LIABILITIES

Nature of Long-Term Debt	Measurement and Valuation	Derecognition of Debt	Recognition and Presentation Issues	IFRS/Private Enterprise GAAP Comparison
▪ Bonds ▪ Notes payable ▪ Types of bonds/notes ▪ Bond ratings	▪ Bonds and notes issued at par ▪ Discounts and premiums ▪ Special situations	▪ Repayment before maturity date ▪ Exchange of debt instruments ▪ Troubled debt restructurings ▪ Defeasance	▪ Off–balance sheet financing ▪ Presentation of long-term debt ▪ Note disclosures	▪ Analysis ▪ Comparison of IFRS and private entity GAAP ▪ Looking ahead

NATURE OF LONG-TERM DEBT

Objective 1
Understand the nature of long-term debt.

Law

Long-term debt **consists of obligations that are not payable within a year or the operating cycle of the business, whichever is longer, and will therefore require probable sacrifices of economic benefits in the future.** Bonds payable, long-term notes payable, mortgages payable, pension liabilities, and lease liabilities are examples of long-term debt or liabilities.[1]

The process that leads to incurring long-term debt is often very formal. For example, the bylaws of corporations usually require that the board of directors and the shareholders give their approval before bonds can be issued or other long-term debt arrangements can be contracted.

What Do the Numbers Mean?

Generally, long-term debt has various **restrictive covenants** (i.e., terms or conditions) that are meant to limit activities and protect both lenders and borrowers. The covenants and other terms of the agreement between the borrower and the lender are stated in a bond indenture or note agreement. The details that are often found in the indenture or agreement include the following: the amount that the corporation is authorized to issue,

---

[1] "Long-term debt" and "long-term liabilities" meet the definition of a financial liability in *CICA Handbook*, Part II, Section 3856 and IAS 32 as they represent contractual obligations to deliver cash. These terms have the same meaning and are used interchangeably throughout the text.

the interest rate, the due date or dates, call provisions, property pledged as security, sinking fund requirements, working capital and dividend restrictions, and limitations on incurring additional debt.

Covenants to restrict the amount of additional debt are common. Additional debt increases the risk of insolvency and there is a limit to the amount of risk that creditors are willing to accept even though some lenders can tolerate more risk than others. Consider what happened to bondholders in the leveraged buyout[2] of **RJR Nabisco**. Solidly rated $9^3/_8\%$ bonds that were due in 2016 plunged 20% in value when management announced the leveraged buyout. The drop occurred because the debt that was added to the capital structure increased the probability of an eventual default.

Real-World Emphasis

Bonds

Bonds are the most common type of long-term debt that companies report on their balance sheets. The main purpose of bonds is to borrow for the long term when the amount of capital that is needed is too large for one lender to supply. **When bonds are issued in $100, $1,000, or $10,000 denominations, a large amount of long-term indebtedness can be divided into many small investing units, which makes it possible for more than one lender to participate in the loan.**

A bond is created by a contract known as a bond indenture and represents a promise to pay both of the following: (1) a sum of money at a designated maturity date, and (2) periodic interest at a specified rate on the maturity amount (face value). Individual bonds are evidenced by a paper certificate and they typically have a $1,000 face value. Bond interest payments are usually made semi-annually, but the interest rate is generally expressed as an annual rate.

An entire bond issue may be sold to an investment banker who acts as a selling agent that markets the bonds. In such arrangements, investment bankers may either underwrite the entire issue by guaranteeing a certain sum to the corporation, thus taking the risk of selling the bonds for whatever price the agent can get (which is known as **firm underwriting**), or the agent may sell the bond issue for a commission that will be deducted from the proceeds of the sale (known as **best efforts underwriting**). Alternatively, the issuing company may choose to place a bond issue privately by selling the bonds directly to a large institution—which may or may not be a financial institution—without the aid of an underwriter. This situation is known as **private placement**.

2 Objective
Identify various types of long-term debt.

Law

Finance

Notes Payable

The difference between **current** notes payable and long-term notes payable is the maturity date. As discussed in Chapter 13, short-term notes payable are expected to be paid within a year or the operating cycle, whichever is longer. **Long-term notes are similar in substance to bonds as both have fixed maturity dates and carry either a stated or implicit interest rate. However, notes do not trade as easily as bonds in the organized public securities markets, and sometimes do not trade at all.** Unincorporated and small corporate enterprises issue notes as their long-term instruments, whereas larger corporations issue both long-term notes and bonds.

Accounting for notes and bonds is quite similar. Like a bond, a note is valued at the present value of its future interest and principal cash flows, and any discount or premium is amortized over the life of the note, just as it is over the life of a bond. Calculating the present value of an interest-bearing note, recording its issuance, and

Underlying Concept

Even though the legal form of a note is different from a bond, the economic substance is the same as they both represent liabilities. They therefore receive substantially the same treatment from an accounting perspective, depending on the features that the specific note or bond carries.

---

[2] A leveraged buyout occurs when a group of individuals, often management, purchases the company. Debt is used to finance the acquisition and it is repaid from company cash flows.

amortizing any discount or premium will be shown for bonds in the next section. As you might expect, the accounting for long-term notes payable mirrors the accounting for long-term notes receivable, which was presented in Chapter 7.

Types of Bonds/Notes

Underlying Concept

Because the various features of debt instruments alter the risk profile, the full disclosure principle would support disclosing specific information about these features.

The following are some of the more common types of long-term debt that are found in practice. Each type of bond has specific contractual features that manage risk for the company and/or the holder. For instance, a secured bond is less risky and therefore often has a lower rate of interest. Any feature that gives the holder more choice or options is generally more desirable to the investor, who may be willing to pay a premium for the flexibility. Where the company has choices and options, such as an option to convert the bond into shares, this may be seen as less desirable by the investors since the choices and options are beyond their control. Each feature noted below changes the riskiness and desirability of the instruments and therefore affects the pricing of the instrument.

The more basic issues regarding bonds and notes will be covered in this chapter, while the more complex instruments will be discussed in Chapter 16.

Finance

Registered and Bearer (Coupon) Bonds.   Bonds that are issued in the owner's name are called **registered bonds**. To sell a registered bond, the current certificate has to be surrendered and a new certificate is then issued. A **bearer** or **coupon bond**, however, is not recorded in the owner's name and may therefore be transferred from one owner to another by simply delivering it to the new owner.

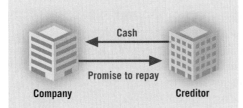

Secured and Unsecured Debt.   **Secured debt** is backed by a pledge of some sort of collateral. **Mortgage bonds or notes** are secured by a claim on real estate. **Collateral trust** bonds or notes are secured by shares and bonds of other corporations. Debt instruments that are not backed by collateral are **unsecured**; e.g., **debenture bonds**. **Junk bonds** are unsecured and also very risky, and therefore pay a high interest rate. These bonds are often used to finance leveraged buyouts.

Term, Serial, and Perpetual Bonds or Notes.   Debt issues that mature on a single date are called **term bonds or notes**, and issues that mature in instalments are called **serial bonds or notes**. Serial bonds are frequently used by schools, municipalities, and provincial or federal governments. **Perpetual bonds or notes** have unusually long terms; i.e., 100 years or more. These are often referred to as century or millennium bonds, depending on the length of the term.

Income, Revenue, and Deep Discount Bonds.   **Income bonds** pay no interest unless the issuing company is profitable. **Revenue bonds** have this name because the interest on them is paid from a specified revenue source. **Deep discount bonds or notes**—which are also referred to as **zero-interest debentures, bonds, or notes**—have very little or no interest and therefore are sold at a large discount that basically provides the buyer with a total interest payoff (at market rates) at maturity.

Commodity-Backed Bonds.   **Commodity-backed debt**, also called **asset-linked debt**, is redeemable in amounts of a commodity, such as barrels of oil, tonnes of coal, or ounces of rare metal.

Callable, Convertible Bonds and Notes and Debt with Various Settlement and Other Options.   **Callable bonds and notes** give the issuer the right to call and retire

the debt before maturity. (These are sometimes referred to as demand loans.) Convertible debt allows the holder or the issuer to convert the debt into other securities such as common shares. Certain bonds or other financial instruments give the issuer the option to repay or settle the principal in either cash or common shares, or give the right to decide to the holder.

One of the more interesting innovations in the bond market is bonds whose interest or principal payments are tied to changes in the weather. The incidence of unusual and extreme weather events has been increasing, along with potential losses from these often unexpected events. Many insurers are feeling the impact of this in terms of profits. The Office of the Superintendent of Financial Institutions, the regulatory body in Canada for financial institutions including insurance companies, has signalled that it is open to allowing insurance companies to issue these weather bonds to help manage risk.

What Do the Numbers Mean?

Holders of the bonds would lose their rights to some or all of the interest and/or principal payments should a triggering event occur. A triggering event could be anything from an excess amount of rainfall to a hail storm or drought. Why would an investor buy this type of security? The instrument would have to be priced to compensate for the riskiness of the instrument by offering a higher interest return or being sold at a discount.

Real-World Emphasis

These instruments are part of a larger group of instruments sometimes referred to as catastrophe bonds ("cat" bonds), which are used globally. The bonds are often sold in private placement offerings, meaning that they are sold to large institutional investors, and since many bonds do not repay the principal if the triggering event occurs, they are referred to as principal-at-risk variable-rate notes.

Bond Ratings

A credit rating is assigned to each new public bond issue by independent credit rating agencies. This rating reflects a current assessment of the company's ability to pay the amounts that will be due on that specific borrowing. The rating may be changed up or down during the issue's outstanding life because the quality is constantly monitored. Note that institutional investors, such as insurance companies and pension funds, invest heavily in what are referred to as investment grade securities. Investment grade securities are high-quality securities (not speculative) and therefore only certain securities qualify. **Because having an investment grade rating on a specific debt offering allows greater access to capital, there is pressure on a company to ensure that its debt instruments are rated investment grade.** Credit rating analysts review many business models and industry factors when they make their determinations. Trends in costs and revenues are especially important.

Two major companies, Moody's Investors Service and Standard & Poor's Corporation, issue quality ratings on every public debt issue. The following table summarizes the categories of ratings issued by Standard & Poor's, along with historical default rates on bonds receiving these ratings.[3] As expected, bonds receiving the highest quality rating of AAA have the lowest historical default rates. Bonds rated below BBB, which are considered below investment grade ("junk bonds"), experience default rates ranging from 20% to 50%.

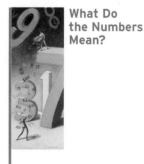

What Do the Numbers Mean?

Original rating	AAA	AA	A	BBB	BB	B	CCC
Default rate	0.52%	1.31	2.32	6.64	19.52	35.76	54.38

---

[3] Data source: Standard & Poor's Corp.

Debt ratings reflect credit quality. The market closely monitors these ratings when determining the required yield and pricing of bonds at issuance and in periods after issuance, especially if a bond's rating is upgraded or downgraded. It is not surprising, then, that bond investors and companies that issue bonds keep a close watch on debt ratings, both when bonds are issued and while the bonds are outstanding.

MEASUREMENT AND VALUATION

Bonds and Notes Issued at Par

Objective 3
Understand how long-term debt is valued and measured.

When a note or bond is issued, it should be recognized at the fair value adjusted by any directly attributable issue costs.[4] When bonds are issued on an interest payment date at **par** (i.e., at **face value**), no interest has accrued and there is no premium or discount. The accounting entry is made simply for the cash proceeds and the bond's face value. To illustrate, assume that a company plans to issue 10-year term bonds with a par value of $800,000, dated January 1, 2011, and bearing interest at an annual rate of 10% payable semi-annually on January 1 and July 1. If it decides to issue them on January 1 at par, the entry on its books would be as follows:

A = L + SE
+800,000 +800,000

Cash flows: ↑ 800,000 inflow

| Cash | 800,000 | |
| Bonds Payable | | 800,000 |

The entry to record the first semi-annual interest payment of $40,000 ($800,000 × 0.10 × ½) on July 1, 2011, would be:

A = L + SE
−40,000 −40,000

Cash flows: ↓ 40,000 outflow

| Bond Interest Expense | 40,000 | |
| Cash | | 40,000 |

The entry to record accrued interest expense at December 31, 2011 (the year end) would be:

A = L + SE
+40,000 −40,000

Cash flows: No effect

| Bond Interest Expense | 40,000 | |
| Bond Interest Payable | | 40,000 |

In Chapter 7, we discussed the recognition of a $10,000, three-year note issued at face value by Scandinavian Imports to Bigelow Corp. In this transaction, the stated rate and the effective rate were both 10%. The time diagram and present value calculation in Chapter 7 for Bigelow Corp. would be the same for the issuer of the note, Scandinavian Imports, in recognizing the note payable. Because the note's present value and its face value are the same ($10,000), no premium or discount is recognized. The issuance of the note is recorded by Scandinavian Imports as follows:

---

[4] *CICA Handbook*, Part II, Section 3856.07 and IAS 39.43. Note that where the liabilities will subsequently be measured at fair value (e.g., under the fair value option), the transaction costs should not be included in the initial measurement. Instead, the costs would be expensed.

Cash	10,000	
Notes Payable		10,000

A   =   L   +   SE
+10,000   +10,000

Cash flows: ↑ 10,000 inflow

Discounts and Premiums

The issuance and marketing of bonds to the public does not happen from one day to the next. It usually takes weeks or even months. Underwriters must be arranged, the approval of the Securities Commission must be obtained, audits and the issuance of a prospectus may be required, and certificates must be printed. Frequently, the terms in a bond indenture are decided well in advance of the bond sale. Between the time the terms are set and the time the bonds are issued, the market conditions and the issuing corporation's financial position may change significantly. Such changes affect the bonds' marketability and, thus, their selling price.

A bond's selling price is set by the supply and demand of buyers and sellers, relative risk, market conditions, and the state of the economy. The investment community values a bond at the **present value of its future cash flows**, which consist of (1) **interest** and (2) **principal**. The rate that is used to calculate the present value of these cash flows is the interest rate that would give an acceptable return on an investment that matches the issuer's risk characteristics.

The interest rate that is written in the terms of the bond indenture (and is ordinarily printed on the bond certificate) is known as the stated, coupon, or nominal rate. This rate, which is set by the bond issuer, is expressed as a percentage of the bond's face value, also called the par value, principal amount, or maturity value. If the rate that is being used by the investment community (i.e., the buyers) is different from the stated rate, when buyers calculate the bond's present value, the result will be different from the bond's face value, and its purchase price will therefore also differ. The difference between the face value and the bond's present value is either a discount or premium.[5] If the bonds sell for less than their face value, they are being sold at a discount. If the bonds sell for more than their face value, they are being sold at a premium.

The interest rate that is actually earned by the bondholders is called the effective yield or market rate. If bonds sell at a **discount**, the **effective yield is higher than the stated rate**. Conversely, if bonds sell at a **premium**, the **effective yield is lower than the stated rate**. While the bond is outstanding, its price is affected by several variables, but especially by the market rate of interest. There is an inverse relationship between the market interest rate and the bond price. That is, when interest rates increase, the bond's price decreases, and vice versa.

To illustrate the calculation of the present value of a bond issue, assume that Discount Limited issues $100,000 in bonds that are due in five years and pay 9% interest

Present Value Concepts

Finance

---

[5] Until the 1950s, it was common for corporations to issue bonds with low, even-percent coupons (such as 4%) to demonstrate their financial soundness. Frequently, the result was larger discounts. More recently, it has become acceptable to set the stated rate of interest on bonds in more precise terms (e.g., $6^7/_8$%). Companies usually try to match the stated rate as closely as possible to the market or effective rate at the time of issue. While discounts and premiums continue to occur, their absolute size tends to be much smaller, and often it is immaterial. A study conducted in the mid-1980s documented that, out of 685 new debt offerings, none were issued at a premium. Approximately 95% were issued either with no discount or at a price above 98. Now, however, zero-interest (deep discount) bonds are more popular, which causes substantial discounts.

annually at year end. At the time of issue, the market rate for such bonds is 11%. Illustration 14-1 shows both the interest and the principal cash flows.

Illustration 14-1
Present Value Calculation of Bond Selling at a Discount

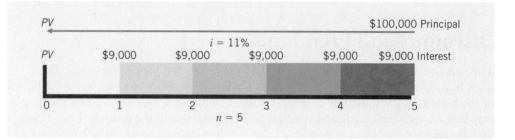

The actual principal and interest cash flows are discounted at an 11% rate for five periods as follows:

Present value of the principal: $100,000 × 0.59345	$59,345
Present value of the interest payments: $9,000 × 3.69590	33,263
Present value (selling price) of the bonds	$92,608

By paying $92,608 at the date of issue, the investors will realize an **effective rate or yield** of 11% over the five-year term of the bonds. These bonds would therefore sell at a discount of $7,392 ($100,000 − $92,608). Note that the price at which the bonds sell is typically stated as a percentage of their face or par value. For example, we would say that the Discount Limited bonds sold for 92.6 (92.6% of par). If Discount Limited had received $102,000, we would say the bonds sold for 102 (102% of par).

When bonds sell below their face value, it means that investors are demanding a rate of interest that is higher than the stated rate. The investors are not satisfied with the stated rate because they can earn a greater rate on alternative investments of equal risk. As they cannot change the stated rate, they therefore refuse to pay face value for the bonds and instead **achieve the effective rate of interest that they want** by lowering the amount invested in the bonds. The result is that the investors receive interest at the stated rate calculated on the face value, but they are essentially earning an effective rate that is higher than the stated rate because they paid less than face value for the bonds. Although notes do not trade as readily as bonds in stock markets, the same issues arise where the stated rate on the notes is different from the market rate at the date of issuance.

Most long-term debt is subsequently measured at amortized cost. Under this method, the interest is adjusted for any premium or discount over the life of the bond.

Objective 4
Apply the effective interest and straight-line bond amortization methods.

Straight-Line Method

If the $800,000 of bonds illustrated earlier were issued on January 1, 2011, at 97 (meaning 97% of par), the issuance would be recorded as follows:

A = L + SE
+776,000 +776,000

Cash flows: ↑ 776,000 inflow

Cash ($800,000 × 0.97)	776,000	
Bonds Payable		776,000

Because of its relationship to interest, discussed above, **the discount is amortized and charged to interest expense over the period of time that the bonds are outstanding.**

Under the straight-line method,[6] the amount that is amortized each year is constant. For example, using the bond discount above of $24,000, the amount amortized to interest expense each year for 10 years is $2,400 ($24,000 ÷ 10 years) and, if amortization is recorded annually, it is recorded as follows:

Bond Interest Expense	2,400	
Bonds Payable		2,400

A   =   L   +   SE
        +2,400   −2,400

Cash flows: No effect

At the end of the first year, 2011, as a result of the amortization entry above, the unamortized balance of the discount is $21,600 ($24,000 − $2,400).

If the bonds were dated and sold on October 1, 2011, and if the corporation's fiscal year ended on December 31, the discount amortized during 2011 would be only $3/12$ of $1/10$ of $24,000, or $600. Three months of accrued interest must also be recorded on December 31.

A premium on bonds payable is accounted for in much the same way as a discount on bonds payable. If the $800,000 of par value, 10-year bonds are dated and sold on January 1, 2011, at 103, the following entry is made to record the issuance:

Cash ($800,000 × 1.03)	824,000	
Bonds Payable		824,000

A   =   L   +   SE
+824,000   +824,000

Cash flows: ↑ 824,000 inflow

At the end of 2011 and for each year that the bonds are outstanding, the entry to amortize the premium on a straight-line basis is:

Bonds Payable	2,400	
Bond Interest Expense		2,400

A   =   L   +   SE
        −2,400   +2,400

Cash flows: No effect

Bond interest expense is increased by amortizing a discount and decreased by amortizing a premium. Amortization of a discount or premium under the effective interest method is discussed later in this chapter.

Some bonds are **callable** by the issuer after a certain date and at a stated price so that the issuing corporation may have the opportunity to reduce its debt or take advantage of lower interest rates. **Whether or not the bond is callable, any premium or discount must be amortized over the bond's life up to the maturity date because it is not certain that the issuer will call the bond and redeem it early.**

Bond interest payments are usually made semi-annually on dates that are specified in the bond indenture. When bonds are not issued on interest payment dates, **bond buyers will pay the seller the interest that has accrued from the last interest payment date to the date of issue**. By paying the accrued interest, the purchasers of the bonds are, in effect, paying the bond issuer in advance for the portion of the full six-month interest payment that the purchasers are not entitled to (but will receive) since they have not held the bonds during the entire six-month period. **The purchasers will receive the full six-month interest payment on the next semi-annual interest payment date.**

---

[6] Although the effective interest method is required under IFRS per IAS 39.47, accounting standards for private enterprises do not specify that this method must be used and therefore the straight-line method is also an option. The straight-line method is valued for its simplicity and might be used by companies whose financial statements are not constrained by GAAP.

To illustrate, assume that $800,000 of par value, 10-year bonds, dated January 1, 2011, and bearing interest at an annual rate of 10% payable semi-annually on January 1 and July 1, are issued on March 1, 2011, at par plus accrued interest. The entry on the books of the issuing corporation is:

A   =   L   +   SE
+813,333   +800,000   +13,333

Cash flows: ↑ 813,333 inflow

Cash	813,333	
Bonds Payable		800,000
Bond Interest Expense ($800,000 × 0.10 × 2/12)		13,333*

*Interest Payable might be credited instead

The purchaser is thus advancing two months of interest because on July 1, 2011, four months after the date of purchase, six months of interest will be received by the purchaser from the issuing company. The issuing company makes the following entry on July 1, 2011:

A   =   L   +   SE
−40,000   −40,000

Cash flows: ↓ 40,000 outflow

Bond Interest Expense	40,000	
Cash		40,000

The expense account now contains a debit balance of $26,667, which represents the proper amount of interest expense: four months at 10% on $800,000.

The above illustration was simplified by having the January 1, 2011 bonds issued on March 1, 2011, at par. If, however, the 10% bonds were issued at 102, the entry on March 1 on the issuing corporation's books would be:

A   =   L   +   SE
+829,333   +816,000   +13,333

Cash flows: ↑ 829,333 inflow

Cash [($800,000 × 1.02) + ($800,000 × 0.10 × 2/12)]	829,333	
Bonds Payable		816,000
Bond Interest Expense		13,333

The premium would be amortized from the date of sale, March 1, 2011, not from the date of the bonds, January 1, 2011.

Effective Interest Method

Significant Change

A common method for amortizing a discount or premium is the **effective interest method**. This method is required under IFRS and allowed as an accounting policy choice under private entity GAAP. Under the effective interest method, the steps are as follows:

1. Interest expense is calculated first by multiplying the **carrying value**[7] of the bonds or notes at the beginning of the period by the effective interest rate.

2. The discount or premium amortization is then determined by comparing the interest expense with the interest to be paid.

Illustration 14-2 shows the formula for the calculation of the amortization under this method.

---

[7] The book value, also called the carrying value, equals the face amount minus any unamortized discount, or plus any unamortized premium. As previously noted, issue costs are deducted as long as the instrument is not subsequently measured using fair value. For simplicity's sake, these costs are assumed to be zero in most of the examples.

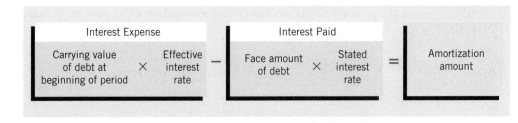

Illustration 14-2

Bond Discount and Premium Amortization Calculation

The effective interest method produces a periodic interest expense that is equal to a **constant percentage of the bonds' or notes' carrying value**.

Both the effective interest and straight-line methods result in the **same total amount of interest expense over the term of the bonds**.

Example: Bonds Issued at a Discount. To illustrate the amortization of a discount using the effective interest method, assume that Master Corporation issued $100,000 of 8% term bonds on January 1, 2011, that are due on January 1, 2016, with interest payable each July 1 and January 1. Because the investors required an effective interest rate of 10%, they paid $92,278 for the $100,000 of bonds, creating a $7,722 discount. The $7,722 discount is calculated as in Illustration 14-3.[8]

Maturity of bonds payable		$100,000
Present value of $100,000 due in 5 years at 10%, interest payable semi-annually [$100,000 × 0.61391]	$61,391	
Present value of $4,000 interest payable semi-annually for 5 years at 10% annually [$4,000 × 7.72173]	30,887	
Proceeds from sale of bonds		92,278
Discount on bonds payable		$ 7,722

Illustration 14-3

Calculation of Discount on Bonds Payable

The five-year amortization schedule appears in Illustration 14-4.

SCHEDULE OF BOND DISCOUNT AMORTIZATION
Effective Interest Method–Semi-Annual Interest Payments
5-Year, 8% Bonds Sold to Yield 10%

Date	Cash Paid	Interest Expense	Discount Amortized	Carrying Amount of Bonds
1/1/11				$ 92,278
7/1/11	$ 4,000[a]	$ 4,614[b]	$ 614[c]	92,892[d]
1/1/12	4,000	4,645	645	93,537
7/1/12	4,000	4,677	677	94,214
1/1/13	4,000	4,711	711	94,925
7/1/13	4,000	4,746	746	95,671
1/1/14	4,000	4,783	783	96,454
7/1/14	4,000	4,823	823	97,277
1/1/15	4,000	4,864	864	98,141
7/1/15	4,000	4,907	907	99,048
1/1/16	4,000	4,952	952	100,000
	$40,000	$47,722	$7,722	

[a] $4,000 = $100,000 × 0.08 × 6/12   [c] $614 = $4,614 − $4,000
[b] $4,614 = $92,278 × 0.10 × 6/12   [d] $92,892 = $92,278 + $614

Illustration 14-4

Bond Discount Amortization Schedule

[8] Because interest is paid semi-annually, the interest rate that is used is 5% (10% × 6/12) and the number of periods is 10 (5 years × 2).

The entry to record the issuance of Master Corporation's bonds at a discount on January 1, 2011, is:

A = L + SE
+92,278 +92,278

Cash flows: ↑ 92,278 inflow

Cash	92,278	
Bonds Payable		92,278

The journal entry to record the first interest payment on July 1, 2011, and amortization of the discount is:

A = L + SE
−4,000 +614 −4,614

Cash flows: ↓ 4,000 outflow

Bond Interest Expense	4,614	
Bonds Payable		614
Cash		4,000

The journal entry to record the interest expense accrued at December 31, 2011 (the year end) and amortization of the discount is:

A = L + SE
   +4,645 −4,645

Cash flows: No effect

Bond Interest Expense	4,645	
Bond Interest Payable		4,000
Bonds Payable		645

Example: Bonds Issued at Premium. If instead it had been a market where the investors were willing to accept an effective interest rate of 6% on the bond issue described above, they would have paid $108,530 or a premium of $8,530, calculated as in Illustration 14-5.

Illustration 14-5

Calculation of Premium on Bonds Payable

Maturity value of bonds payable		$100,000
Present value of $100,000 due in 5 years at 6%, interest payable semi-annually [$100,000 × 0.74409]	$74,409	
Present value of $4,000 interest payable semi-annually for 5 years at 6% annually [$4,000 × 8.53020]	34,121	
Proceeds from sale of bonds		108,530
Premium on bonds payable		$ 8,530

The five-year amortization schedule appears in Illustration 14-6.

Illustration 14-6

Bond Premium Amortization Schedule

SCHEDULE OF BOND PREMIUM AMORTIZATION
Effective Interest Method–Semi-Annual Interest Payments
5-Year, 8% Bonds Sold to Yield 6%

Date	Cash Paid	Interest Expense	Premium Amortized	Carrying Amount of Bonds
1/1/11				$108,530
7/1/11	$ 4,000[a]	$ 3,256[b]	$ 744[c]	107,786[d]
1/1/12	4,000	3,234	766	107,020
7/1/12	4,000	3,211	789	106,231
1/1/13	4,000	3,187	813	105,418
7/1/13	4,000	3,162	838	104,580

Date	Cash Paid	Interest Expense	Premium Amortized	Carrying Amount of Bonds
1/1/14	4,000	3,137	863	103,717
7/1/14	4,000	3,112	888	102,829
1/1/15	4,000	3,085	915	101,914
7/1/15	4,000	3,057	943	100,971
1/1/16	4,000	3,029	971	100,000
	$40,000	$31,470	$8,530	

a $4,000 = $100,000 × 0.08 × $^{6}/_{12}$
b $3,256 = $108,530 × 0.06 × $^{6}/_{12}$
c $744 = $4,000 − $3,256
d $107,786 = $108,530 − $744

The entry to record the issuance of the Master Corporation bonds at a premium on January 1, 2011, is:

Cash	108,530	
Bonds Payable		108,530

A   =   L   + SE
+108,530   +108,530

Cash flows: ↑ 108,530 inflow

The journal entry to record the first interest payment on July 1, 2011, and amortization of the premium is:

Bond Interest Expense	3,256	
Bonds Payable	744	
Cash		4,000

A   =   L   +   SE
−4,000   −744   −3,256

Cash flows: ↓ 4,000 outflow

As the discount or premium should be amortized as an adjustment to interest expense over the life of the bond, it results in a **constant interest rate** when it is applied to the carrying amount of debt that is outstanding at the beginning of any specific period.

Accruing Interest. In our examples up to now, the interest payment dates and the date the financial statements were issued were the same. For example, when Master Corporation sold bonds at a premium, the two interest payment dates coincided with the financial reporting dates. However, what happens if Master wishes to report financial statements at the end of February 2011? In this case, as Illustration 14-7 shows, the premium is prorated by the appropriate number of months to arrive at the proper interest expense.

Interest accrual ($4,000 × $^{2}/_{6}$)	$1,333.33
Premium amortized ($744 × $^{2}/_{6}$)	(248.00)
Interest expense (Jan.–Feb.)	$1,085.33

Illustration 14-7

Calculation of Interest Expense

The journal entry to record this accrual is:

Bonds Payable	248	
Bond Interest Expense	1,085	
Bond Interest Payable		1,333

A   =   L   +   SE
+1,085   −1,085

Cash flows: No effect

If the company prepares financial statements six months later, the same procedure is followed to amortize the premium, as Illustration 14-8 shows.

Premium amortized (Mar.–June) ($744 × ⁴/₆)	$496.00
Premium amortized (July–Aug.) ($766 × ²/₆)	255.33
Premium amortized (Mar.–Aug. 2011)	$751.33

The calculation is much simpler if the straight-line method is used. In the Master situation, for example, the total premium is $8,530 and this amount needs to be allocated evenly over the five-year period. The premium amortization per month is therefore $142 ($8,530 ÷ 60 months).

Special Situations

Non-Market Rates of Interest—Marketable Securities

As previously noted, financial liabilities should initially be recognized at fair value, which is generally the exchange value that exists when two arm's-length parties are involved in a transaction. If a zero-interest-bearing (non-interest-bearing) *marketable* security is issued for cash only, its fair value is the cash received by the security's issuer. The implicit or imputed interest rate is the **rate that makes the cash that is received now equal to the present value of the amounts that will be received in the future**. This rate should also equal the market rate of interest. The difference between the face amount of the security and the present value is **a discount and is amortized to interest expense over the life of the note.**

To illustrate the entries and the amortization schedule, assume that your company is the one that issued the $10,000 three-year, zero-interest-bearing note to Jeremiah Company that was illustrated in Chapter 7. Let's assume further that the note is marketable. The implicit rate that equated the total cash to be paid ($10,000 at maturity) to the present value of the future cash flows ($7,721.80 cash proceeds at the date of issuance) was 9%. Assume that the market rate of interest for a similar note would also be 9%. (The present value of $1 for three periods at 9% is $0.77218.) The time diagram that shows the one cash flow is as follows:

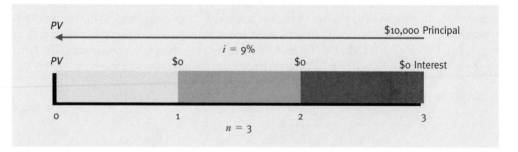

The entry to record issuance of the note would be:

Cash	7,722	
Notes Payable		7,722

The discount is amortized and interest expense is recognized annually. The three-year discount amortization and interest expense schedule is shown in Illustration 14-9 using the effective interest method.

SCHEDULE OF NOTE DISCOUNT AMORTIZATION
Effective Interest Method
0% Note Discounted at 9%

	Cash Paid	Interest Expense	Discount Amortized	Carrying Amount of Note
Date of issue				$ 7,721.80
End of year 1	$-0-	$ 694.96[a]	$ 694.96[b]	8,416.76[c]
End of year 2	-0-	757.51	757.51	9,174.27
End of year 3	-0-	825.73[d]	825.73	10,000.00
	$-0-	$2,278.20	$2,278.20	

[a] $7,721.80 × 0.09 = $694.96
[b] $694.96 − 0 = $694.96
[c] $7,721.80 + $694.96 = $8,416.76
[d] Adjustment to compensate for rounding

Illustration 14-9

Schedule of Note Discount Amortization

Interest expense at the end of the first year using the effective interest method is recorded as follows:

Interest Expense ($7,722 × 9%)	695	
Notes Payable		695

A	=	L	+	SE
		+695		−695

Cash flows: No effect

The total amount of the discount, $2,278 in this case, represents the interest expense to be incurred and recognized on the note over the three years.

Non-Market Rates of Interest—Non-Marketable Loans

If the loans or notes do not trade on a market (i.e., when they are not securities) and the interest rate is a non-market interest rate, the situation must be analyzed carefully. The cash consideration that is given may not be equal to the fair value of the loan or note. Normally, in an arm's-length reciprocal transaction, the loan would be issued with an interest rate approximating the market rate and therefore the consideration would approximate fair value. **If the loan is issued with an interest rate that is less than the market rate, this concession should be accounted for separately.**

In these cases, the entity must measure the value of the loan by discounting the cash flows using the market rate of interest, which is done by considering similar loans with similar terms. Any difference between the cash consideration and the discounted amount (the fair value of the loan) would be booked to net income unless it qualified for some other asset or liability.[9]

For example, assume that a government entity issues at face value a zero-interest-bearing loan that is to be repaid over five years with no stated interest. In doing this, the government is giving an additional benefit to the company beyond the debt financing. It is forgiving the interest that the company would normally be charged. Thus, the company is getting a double benefit—the loan and a grant for the interest that would otherwise be paid. The extra benefit would be accounted for separately as a government grant.

To illustrate, assume that to help a company finance the construction of a building, the government issues a $100,000, five-year, zero-interest-bearing note at face value when the market rate of interest is 10%. To record the loan, the company records a discount of $37,908, which is the difference between the loan's $100,000 face amount and its

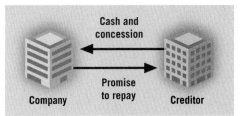

---

[9] *CICA Handbook*, Part II, Section 3856.A8 and IAS 39.AG64.

fair value of $62,092 ($100,000 × the present value factor for five years at 10% = $100,000 × 0.62092). The rest may be booked as a contra account to the related building account under government grant accounting since it relates to the construction of an asset. The issuer's journal entry is:

A	=	L	+ SE			
+100,000		+100,000		Cash	100,000	
				Notes Payable		62,092
Cash flows: ↑ 100,000 inflow				Building—Government Grant		37,908

The discount balance is subsequently amortized to interest expense. The government grant credit balance is amortized to net income as the building is depreciated (in order to offset the costs) or the net value of the building (i.e., net of the government grant) is depreciated.[10] In this situation, the writeoff of the discount and the amortization of the government grant are at different rates.

Notes Issued for Property, Goods, and Services

When a non-marketable debt instrument is exchanged for property, goods, or services in a bargained, arm's-length transaction, there are additional measurement issues. As with other transactions, it should be booked at fair value. But what is the fair value? If the issued debt is a marketable security, the value of the transaction would be easy to determine. If it is not, an attempt must be made to estimate the fair value. Normally, for monetary transactions, we first try to measure the monetary asset or liability and, if this is not possible, we then attempt to value the non-monetary assets in the transaction. In this case, the note is a monetary liability and so we would try to value this first. The note could be valued using a discounting technique. Similar to the previous example, the cash flows from the debt instrument could be discounted using a market rate of interest for similar debt with similar terms. If this is not possible, and if the fair value of the property, goods, or services is readily determinable, this latter value could then be used to value the transaction.

For example, assume that Scenic Development sold land having a cash sale price of $200,000 to Health Spa, Inc. in exchange for Health Spa's five-year, $293,860, zero-interest-bearing note. The $200,000 cash sale price represents the present value of the $293,860 note discounted at 8% for five years. The 8% interest rate is the market rate for a similar loan with similar terms. If both parties were to record the transaction on the sale date at the $293,860 face amount of the note, Health Spa's Land account and Scenic's sales would be overstated by $93,860 because the $93,860 is the interest for five years at an effective rate of 8%. Interest revenue to Scenic and interest expense to Health Spa for the five-year period would also then be correspondingly understated by $93,860.

The transaction could be measured by using a valuation technique to measure the value of the debt or alternatively by using the fair value of the land ($200,000) if it is not possible to measure the debt. In this case, we know the fair value of the land and we also know that the market rate is 8%. Since the present value of the note is equal to the land value, we use $200,000. The difference between the cash sale price of $200,000 and the face amount of the note, $293,860, represents interest at an effective rate of 8% and the transaction is recorded at the exchange date as follows:

---

[10] Note that the deferred credit could also initially be offset against the building assets account, resulting in a lower net book value.

Health Spa, Inc. Books			Scenic Development Company Books		
Land	200,000		Notes Receivable	200,000	
Notes Payable		200,000	Sales		200,000

A = L + SE
+200,000 +200,000

Cash flows: No effect

A = L + SE
+200,000 +200,000

Cash flows: No effect

During the five-year life of the note, Health Spa annually amortizes a portion of the discount of $93,860 as a charge to interest expense. Scenic Development records interest revenue totalling $93,860 over the five-year period by also amortizing the discount.

If a higher interest rate were determined to be the market rate of interest, the land and selling price would be measured at a lower amount since there is an inverse relationship between the discount rate and the present value of the cash flows. This might cause us to question whether the so-called cash sales price of the land has been overstated since the vendor would want to receive consideration equal to the fair value of the land. At some point, a judgement call is required to determine which is more reliable: the imputed interest rate or the stated fair value of the asset.

Fair Value Option

Generally, long-term debt is measured at amortized cost; however, as discussed earlier in the text, there is an option to value financial instruments at fair value (referred to as the fair value option). Although private entity GAAP allows the fair value option for all financial instruments, IFRS explicitly requires that the option be used only where fair value results in more relevant information. This would be the case where the use of fair value eliminates or reduces measurement and/or recognition inconsistencies or where the financial instruments are managed or performance is evaluated on a fair value basis.

One significant issue arises when the fair value option is used for long-term debt. The question is whether the entity should incorporate information about its own liquidity and solvency when measuring the fair value of its own debt. As a general rule, fair value should always incorporate information about the riskiness of the cash flows associated with a particular instrument. However, this gives some peculiar and counterintuitive results; i.e., the riskier the debt, the lower the fair value, thus resulting in recognition of a gain. Therefore, if the company's own credit risk is used when determining the fair value of the company's own debt (where fair value is used to measure the debt), even though the company is worse off, it recognizes a gain. This is an area that is currently the subject of much discussion.

**Significant
Change**

DERECOGNITION OF DEBT

Repayment of debt is often referred to as extinguishment of debt. When debt is repaid or extinguished, it is **derecognized** from the financial statements. If the bonds or any other form of debt security is held to maturity, **no gain or loss is calculated**. This is because any premium or discount and any issue costs will be fully amortized at the date the bonds mature. As a result, the carrying amount will be equal to the bond's maturity (face) value. And as the maturity or face value is also equal to the bond's market value at that time, there is no gain or loss.

From a financial reporting perspective, debt is considered to be extinguished when either of the following occurs:

1. The debtor discharges the liability by paying the creditor.

2. The debtor is legally released from primary responsibility for the liability by law or by the creditor (e.g., cancellation or expiry).[11]

6 Objective
Account for derecognition of debt.

---

[11] *CICA Handbook*, Part II, Section 3856.26 and IAS 39.39.

Repayment before Maturity Date

In some cases, debt is extinguished before its maturity date. The amount paid on extinguishment or redemption before maturity, including any call premium and expense of reacquisition, is called the **reacquisition price**. On any specified date, the bond's **net carrying amount** is the amount that is payable at maturity, adjusted for any unamortized premium or discount and cost of issuance. If the net carrying amount is more than the reacquisition price, the excess amount is a **gain from extinguishment**; conversely, if the reacquisition price exceeds the net carrying amount, the excess is a **loss from extinguishment**. At the time of reacquisition, the **unamortized premium or discount and any costs of issue that apply to the bonds must be amortized up to the reacquisition date**.

To illustrate, assume that on January 1, 2008, General Bell Corp. issued bonds with a par value of $800,000 at 97 (which is net of issue costs), due in 20 years. Eight years after the issue date, the entire issue is called at 101 and cancelled. The loss on redemption (extinguishment) is calculated as in Illustration 14-10, which uses straight-line amortization for simplicity.

Illustration 14-10

*Calculation of Loss on
Redemption of Bonds*

Reacquisition price ($800,000 × 1.01)		$808,000
Net carrying amount of bonds redeemed:		
Face value	$800,000	
Unamortized discount ($24,000[a] × $^{12}/_{20}$)		
(amortized using straight-line basis)	(14,400)	785,600
Loss on redemption		$ 22,400

[a][$800,000 × (1 − 0.97)]

The entry to record the reacquisition and cancellation of the bonds is:

A   =   L   +   SE
−808,000 −785,600 −22,400

Cash flows: ↓ 808,000 outflow

Bonds Payable	785,600	
Loss on Redemption of Bonds	22,400	
Cash		808,000

Exchange of Debt Instruments

Objective 7
Distinguish between and account for debt restructurings that result in extinguishment or in debt continuation.

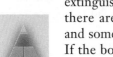

Underlying Concept

If the new debt is substantially the same as the old debt, the economic substance is that it is a continuation of the old debt, even though, legally, the old debt may have been settled.

The replacement of an existing issuance with a new one is sometimes called **refunding**. Generally, an exchange of debt instruments that have **substantially different terms** between a borrower and lender is viewed as an extinguishment of the old debt and the issuance of a new one.[12]

Companies may refund or replace debt to get more favourable terms. These early extinguishments would generally be bound by the initial debt agreement (e.g., whether there are provisions that allow early repayment). The debtor may experience a loss and sometimes a gain depending on the prepayment options in the original agreement. If the bonds are marketable securities, the company can simply buy them back in the marketplace.

Sometimes, however, companies are forced to repay or restructure their debt due to inability to make interest and principal payments. This is sometimes referred to as

---

[12] *CICA Handbook*, Part II, Section 3856.27, IAS 39.40, and IAS 39.AG57.

troubled debt restructuring. An example of the accounting for a settlement through an exchange of debt instruments is noted in the next section.

Troubled Debt Restructurings

A **troubled debt restructuring** occurs when, for economic or legal reasons that are related to the debtor's financial difficulties, a creditor grants a concession to the debtor that it would not offer in ordinary circumstances. This is what separates a troubled debt restructuring from an ordinary early repayment or exchange.

 Law

A troubled debt restructuring can be either one of these two basic types of transactions:

 Finance

1. **Settlement** of the debt at less than its carrying amount

2. **Continuation** of the debt, but with a **modification** of its terms

Settlement of Debt

If the debt is settled, meaning there is early repayment or refunding, the old debt and all related discount, premium, and issuance costs will be removed from the debtor's books (derecognized). Unlike with a normal early repayment or refunding, a gain will usually be recognized in most cases since the creditor generally makes favourable concessions to the debtor in troubled debt situations. The creditor removes the loan receivable from its books and may recognize a further loss.

In order to settle the debt, the debtor may do one of the following:

1. Transfer non-cash assets (real estate, receivables, or other assets).

2. Issue shares.

3. Issue new debt to another creditor and use the cash to repay the existing debt.

If non-cash assets are used to settle the debt, the debtor will recognize a gain or loss on the disposal of the asset for the amount of the difference between the fair value of those assets and their carrying amount (book value). The creditor may force the debtor to transfer the asset if there is a legal charge on the asset (i.e., in the case of collateral or a mortgage). This is referred to as a **loan foreclosure**. The creditor takes the underlying security (the asset) as a replacement for payment of the loan.

To illustrate a transfer of assets, assume that Nova Scotia City Bank has loaned $20 million to Union Trust. Union Trust in turn has invested these monies in residential apartment buildings, but because of low occupancy rates it cannot meet its loan obligations. Nova Scotia City Bank agrees to accept from Union Trust real estate with a fair value of $16 million in full settlement of the $20-million loan obligation. The real estate has a recorded value of $21 million on the books of Union Trust since it is felt that the amount is recoverable. Assume that no prior allowance for doubtful accounts has been set up on the note and no impairment has been recognized on the real estate.[13] The entry to record this transaction on the books of Nova Scotia City Bank (the creditor) is as follows:

Real Estate	16,000,000	
Loss on Loan Impairment	4,000,000	
Note Receivable		20,000,000

A   = L +   SE
−4,000,000   −4,000,000

Cash flows: No effect

---

[13] In reality, a loss should likely have been recognized when the bank first determined that the loan was impaired. This would usually be done before a loan is restructured or settled.

The real estate is recorded at its fair value, and a charge is made to the income statement to reflect the loss.[14]

The entry to record this transaction on the books of Union Trust (the debtor) is as follows:

A   =   L   +   SE
−21,000,000 −20,000,000 −1,000,000

Cash flows: No effect

Note Payable	20,000,000	
Loss on Asset Disposal	5,000,000	
Real Estate		21,000,000
Gain on Restructuring of Debt		4,000,000

Union Trust has a loss on the disposal of real estate in the amount of $5 million, which is the difference between the $21-million book value and the $16-million fair value. In addition, it has a gain on restructuring of debt of $4 million, which is the difference between the $20-million carrying amount of the note payable and the $16-million fair market value of the real estate.

To illustrate the granting of an equity interest (i.e., shares), assume that Nova Scotia City Bank had agreed to accept from Union Trust 320,000 of Union's common shares that have a market value of $16 million, in full settlement of the $20-million loan obligation. Assume also that the bank had previously recognized a loss on impairment of $4 million. The entry to record this transaction on the books of Nova Scotia City Bank (the creditor) is as follows:

A   =   L   +   SE
0

Cash flows: No effect

Investment	16,000,000	
Allowance for Doubtful Accounts	4,000,000	
Note Receivable		20,000,000

The shares that are received by Nova Scotia City Bank are recorded as an investment and at their fair value (equal to market value) on the date of the restructuring.

The entry to record this transaction on the books of Union Trust (the debtor) is as follows:[15]

A   =   L   +   SE
−20,000,000 +20,000,000

Cash flows: No effect

Note Payable	20,000,000	
Common Shares		16,000,000
Gain on Restructuring of Debt		4,000,000

In some cases, a debtor will have serious short-term cash flow problems that lead it to request one or a combination of the following modifications:

1. Reduction of the stated interest rate

2. Extension of the maturity date of the debt's face amount

3. Reduction of the debt's face amount

---

[14] The creditor must decide whether the asset meets the criteria to be classified as held for sale. If it does, the asset will subsequently be valued at its fair value less the costs to sell it.

[15] This type of transaction is sometimes referred to as a debt for equity swap. IFRIC Interpretation 19 deals with the accounting by the debtor (only) and supports the measurement of the common shares issued at fair value. For the debtor, general accounting principles would require the investment in the shares to be initially recognized at fair value. This is supported by *CICA Handbook*, Part II, Section 3856.28.

4. Reduction or deferral of any accrued interest

5. Change in currency

If there are **substantial modifications**, however, **the transaction is treated like a settlement**. The modifications would be considered substantial in either of these two situations:

1. The discounted present value under the new terms (discounted using the original effective interest rate) is at least 10% different from the discounted present value of the remaining cash flows under the old debt.

2. There is a change in creditor and the original debt is legally discharged.[16]

If one of these conditions is met, the transaction is considered a settlement. Otherwise, it is treated as a modification.

When the economic substance is a **settlement**, the old liability is eliminated and a new liability is assumed. The new liability is measured at the present value of the revised future cash flows discounted at the currently prevailing market interest rate, as is done for the initial recording of a bond. The gain is measured as the difference between the current present value of the revised cash flows and the carrying value of the old debt.

Assume that on December 31, 2011, Manitoba National Bank enters into a debt restructuring agreement with Resorts Development Corp., which is experiencing financial difficulties. The bank restructures a $10.5-million loan receivable issued at par (interest paid up to date) by doing all of the following:

1. It reduces the principal obligation from $10.5 million to $9 million.

2. It extends the maturity date from December 31, 2011, to December 31, 2015.

3. It reduces the interest rate from 12% to 8%. (The market rate is currently 9%.)

Is this a settlement or a modification? Has a substantial modification in the debt occurred? The test to establish whether this is a settlement or not involves the cash flows. The present value of both cash flow streams is calculated as follows, using the historic rate as the discount rate for consistency and comparability:

> Old debt: PV = $10,500,000 (since the debt is currently due)
> New debt: PV = $9,000,000 (0.63552) + $720,000 (3.03735) = $7,906,572

The new debt's value differs by more than 10% of the old debt's value, so the renegotiated debt would therefore be considered a settlement, and a gain would be recorded through the following journal entry:

Note Payable—Old	10,500,000		A	=	L	+ SE
Note Payable—New		8,708,468			−1,791,532	+1,791,532
Gain on Restructuring of Debt		1,791,532		Cash flows: No effect		

Because it is new debt, it would be recorded at the present value of the new cash flows at the market interest rate ($9,000,000 × 0.70843) + ($720,000 × 3.23972).

Manitoba National Bank would record any loss on the same basis as an impaired loan, as discussed earlier. That is, the recorded amount of the loan receivable would be reduced

---

[16] *CICA Handbook*, Part II, Section 3856.A52 and IAS 39.40/AG62.

to the amount of the net cash flows receivable (but under the modified terms) discounted at the historical effective interest rate that is inherent in the loan.

Non-Substantial Modification of Terms

Where debt is exchanged but the terms of the new debt are not substantially different (modified) from the old debt, the accounting is different. The old debt is seen to continue to exist but with new terms. A new effective interest rate is imputed by equating the carrying amount of the original debt with the present value of the revised cash flows.

Looking back to our example above for Manitoba National Bank and Resorts Development Corp., if the substantial modification test was not met, the debt would remain on the books at $10.5 million and no gain or loss would be recognized. As a result, no entry would be made by Resorts Development Corp. (debtor) at the date of restructuring. The debtor would **calculate a new effective interest rate**, however, in order to record interest expense in future periods. In this case, the new rate is calculated by relating the pre-restructure carrying amount ($10.5 million) to the total future cash flows ($11,880,000). The rate to discount the total future cash flows ($11,880,000) to the present value that is equal to the remaining balance ($10.5 million) is 3.46613%.

Based on the effective rate of 3.46613%, the schedule in Illustration 14-11 is prepared.

Illustration 14-11

Schedule Showing Reduction of Carrying Amount of Note

	RESORTS DEVELOPMENT CORP. (DEBTOR)			
Date	Interest Paid (8%)	Interest Expense (3.46613%)	Reduction of Carrying Amount	Carrying Amount of Note
12/31/11				$10,500,000
12/31/12	$ 720,000[a]	$ 363,944[b]	$ 356,056[c]	10,143,944
12/31/13	720,000	351,602	368,398	9,775,546
12/31/14	720,000	338,833	381,167	9,394,379
12/31/15	720,000	325,621	394,379	9,000,000
	$2,880,000	$1,380,000	$1,500,000	

[a]$720,000 = $9,000,000 × 0.08
[b]$363,944 = $10,500,000 × 3.46613%
[c]$356,056 = $720,000 − $363,944

Thus, on December 31, 2012 (the date of the first interest payment after the restructuring), the debtor makes the following entry:

A   =   L   +   SE
−720,000   −356,056   −363,944

Cash flows: ↓ 720,000 outflow

December 31, 2012		
Notes Payable	356,056	
Interest Expense	363,944	
Cash		720,000

A similar entry (except for different amounts for debits to Notes Payable and Interest Expense) is made each year until maturity. At maturity, the following entry is made:

A   =   L   + SE
−9,000,000   −9,000,000

Cash flows: ↓ 9,000,000 outflow

December 31, 2015		
Notes Payable	9,000,000	
Cash		9,000,000

In this case also, Manitoba National Bank would account for the restructuring as an impaired loan.

One last point regarding troubled debt situations. Most debt is generally measured at amortized cost. In certain situations, however, the debt may be measured at fair value under the fair value option or in certain hedging situations. If a company is having financial difficulties, its solvency risk increases and the capital markets generally penalize the company with higher cost of capital and interest rates. Where liabilities are carried at fair value, the debt must be continually remeasured. Discounting at a higher interest rate and/or incorporating lower cash flows in the estimation of fair value would mean a lower fair value, thus leading to a gain on revaluation. Should gains be recognized on remeasurement of a company's own debt due to a decline in ability to pay? This question was discussed earlier under the fair value option heading. Currently, the profession supports incorporating the credit risk in the measurement.

The decision tree in Illustration 14-12 summarizes the process for deciding how to account for early retirements and modifications of debt.

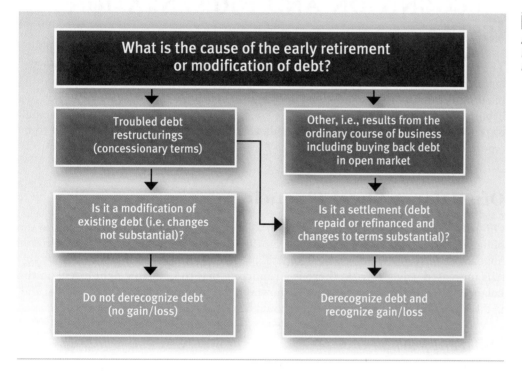

Illustration 14-12

Accounting for Early Retirements and Modifications of Debt

Note that in other than troubled debt situations, companies would generally not exchange debt as there is little economic incentive to do so. They would either buy back the debt in the open market or exercise an early prepayment option, if one existed in the original debt agreement. Thus the accounting would take the form of settlement accounting and the debt would be derecognized.

Defeasance

Occasionally, a company may want to extinguish or pay off debt before its due date but economic factors such as early repayment penalties may stop it from doing so. One option is to set aside the money in a trust or other arrangement and allow the trust to repay the original debt (principal and interest) as it becomes due according to the original agreement. To do this, the company must set aside sufficient funds so that the investment and

Law

any return will be enough to pay the principal and interest directly to the creditor. This is known as defeasance. If the creditor of the original debt agrees to look to the trust for repayment and give up its claim on the company, this is known as **legal defeasance**. Since the company no longer has an obligation to the creditor, the debt may be derecognized.

In some cases, however, the company does not inform the creditor of the arrangement or the creditor does not release the company from the primary obligation to settle the debt. This version of the arrangement is often called **in-substance defeasance**. Does in-substance defeasance result in extinguishment of the debt on the company's books? In essence, if the trust is properly set up—for example, the money is invested in low-risk or risk-free investments in an irrevocable trust—it can be argued that the debt has been pre-paid and there is little risk to the company. On the other hand, the company still has the primary obligation. GAAP does not permit derecognition of debt under in-substance defeasance arrangements since the company still owes the money.

RECOGNITION AND PRESENTATION ISSUES

The reporting of long-term debt is one of the most controversial areas in financial reporting. Because long-term debt has a significant impact on a company's cash flow, reporting requirements must be substantive and informative. One problem is that the definition of a liability and the recognition criteria in the conceptual framework are not precise enough to prevent the argument from being made that certain obligations do not need to be reported as debt.

Off–Balance Sheet Financing

Off–balance sheet financing is an attempt to borrow money in a way that results in the obligations not being recorded as debt on the balance sheet. It is an issue of extreme importance to accountants as well as general management. **Because increased debt signals increased solvency risk, there is a reporting bias to keep low debt levels on the balance sheet.** From a user perspective, however, the amount of debt is very relevant and, in the interest of transparency, all debt should be recognized on the balance sheet.

Different Forms

Off–balance sheet financing can take many different forms. Some examples follow:

1. **Non-consolidated entities.** Under present GAAP, a parent company does not have to consolidate an entity that is less than 50% owned where there is no control. In addition, PE GAAP allows an accounting policy choice even where control does exist (equity method or cost). In such cases, the parent therefore does not report the assets and the liabilities of the entity. Instead, the parent only reports the investment on its balance sheet. As a result, users of the financial statements might not understand that the entity has considerable debt that the parent may ultimately be liable for if the entity runs into financial difficulty. Investments were discussed in Chapter 9.

Finance

2. **Special purpose entities (SPEs) or variable interest entities (VIEs).** A special purpose entity or variable interest entity is an entity that a company creates to perform a special project or function. For example, SPEs or VIEs might be formed to do the following:

(a) Access financing. For example, companies sometimes set up SPEs and VIEs to buy assets such as accounts receivable or investments from the company. The company then sells the assets to the SPE/VIE in return for cash, thus obtaining financing. Investors invest in the SPE/VIE to benefit from the return on the assets and certain tax advantages. This process is known as a securitization of assets. In this way, the company essentially takes a pool of assets and turns it into securities. **Whether the company treats this as a sale or financing was discussed in Chapter 7.**

(b) Take on risk from the company. As in the example above, the sale of the receivables or investments eliminates price and cash flow risks for the company as it now holds cash instead of the riskier receivables or investments. The SPEs/VIEs provide a ready market for buying the assets.

(c) Isolate certain assets from other company assets. For example, the pension assets of company employees are often segregated in a trust fund or SPE. This arrangement allows greater security for the employees and the company gets certain tax advantages when it contributes money to the plan. Recognition of unfunded pension obligations is discussed in Chapter 19.

SPEs and VIEs thus serve valid business functions. **They only become problematic when they are used primarily to make a company's balance sheet look better; i.e., to disguise risk.**[17] As a general rule, these entities should be consolidated when the company is the main beneficiary of the SPE/VIE. Except for what has just been presented, the accounting for SPEs and VIEs is beyond the scope of this book.

3. **Operating leases.** Another way that companies keep debt off the balance sheet is by leasing. Instead of owning the assets, companies lease them. By meeting certain conditions, the company has to report only rent expense each period and provide a note disclosure of the transaction. Accounting for leases is discussed in Chapter 20.

The accounting profession's response to these off–balance sheet financing arrangements has been to tighten up the accounting guidance for guarantees and SPEs and also to mandate **increased disclosure (note) requirements**. This response is consistent with an efficient markets philosophy: the important question is not whether the presentation is off–balance sheet or not, but whether the items are disclosed at all.[18] The standard setters are currently working on this issue of what to include in the economic entity. Definitions for control and the reporting entity are being established as part of the conceptual framework project.

Presentation of Long-Term Debt

Current versus Long-Term

Companies that have large amounts and many issues of long-term debt often report only one amount in the balance sheet and give details about the amount through comments and

9 Objective
Indicate how long-term debt is presented and analyzed.

---

[17] IASB and FASB are currently studying what should be included as part of the reporting entity under the conceptual framework project.

[18] It is unlikely that the accounting profession will be able to stop all types of off–balance sheet transactions. Developing new financial instruments and arrangements to sell to customers is profitable for investment banking firms, especially where there is a demand for them. In the post-Enron era, however, many banks are discontinuing these types of products due to the now highly publicized negative connotations that are associated with them.

Significant Change

schedules in the accompanying notes. Long-term debt that **matures within one year** should generally be reported as a **current liability**, unless it will be retired using something other than current assets. If the debt is to be refinanced, the company must treat it as current unless the refinancing has occurred before the release of the financial statements or a refinancing agreement is in place.[19] IFRS requires that the financing be in place by the balance sheet date.[20]

Where it is more relevant to present information according to liquidity, the entity should present assets and liabilities in order of liquidity. If this is the case, the amounts to be recovered or paid within the next 12 months should be disclosed.[21]

Debt versus Equity

As financial instruments become more complex, the line between what is debt and what is equity is becoming more blurred. As noted above, there is significant pressure on companies to watch their debt levels. The debt-versus-equity issue will be discussed in Chapter 16 when more complex financial instruments are examined.

Note Disclosures

Note disclosures generally indicate the **nature of the liabilities, maturity dates, interest rates, call provisions, conversion privileges, restrictions imposed by the creditors, and assets designated or pledged as security**. Any assets that have been **pledged as security** for the debt should be shown in the assets section of the balance sheet. **The fair value** of the long-term debt should also be disclosed if it is practical to estimate it. Disclosure is required of **future payments** for sinking fund requirements and maturity amounts of long-term debt during each of the next five years. Finally, disclosures are also required regarding risks related to the debt (e.g., solvency, liquidity). The purpose of these disclosures is to **aid financial statement users in evaluating the amounts and timing of future cash flows**.

IFRS AND PRIVATE ENTERPRISE GAAP COMPARISON

Objective 10

Identify the major differences in accounting between accounting standards for private enterprises (PE GAAP/ASPE) and IFRS, and what changes are expected in the near future.

The level of debt that a company holds is a very high-profile number. How much debt is the right amount? It depends. Some debt is good if it allows a company to take advantage of leveraging opportunities; however, too much debt increases the risk to the company. The higher the debt, the greater the risk that the company may not be able to repay it. Capital markets acknowledge this additional solvency risk by increasing the cost of capital and making it more difficult for companies with high debt levels to access additional capital.

In the hope of protecting themselves better, lenders insert covenants into lending agreements that require companies to manage their cash flow risks. Although debt holders assume that the covenants will protect them, covenants are often written in a way that can be interpreted (or misinterpreted) in different ways. Therefore, covenants may provide little or no protection. Note further that covenants normally refer to certain financial tests

---

[19] *CICA Handbook*, Part II, Section 1510.10.

[20] IAS 1.72.

[21] *CICA Handbook*, Part II, Section 1510.02 and IAS 1.61.

and ratios that the borrower must meet or the debt will become payable. **Because of this, the existence of restrictive covenants creates situations that encourage reporting bias.** This may create an environment in which the company feels forced to meet the test even if it means using aggressive accounting to do so.

Ethics

Users of financial statements must be aware of the existence of covenants so that they understand the potential for misstating the financial statements. Whenever these conditions are important for having a complete understanding of the company's financial position and results of operations, they should be described in the body of the financial statements or the accompanying notes.

Analysis

Long-term creditors and shareholders are interested in a company's long-run **solvency**, particularly its ability to pay interest as it comes due and to repay the face value of debt at maturity. Therefore, many debt agreements include covenants that stipulate that certain ratios be met. **Debt to total assets** and **times interest earned** are two ratios that provide information about debt-paying ability and long-run solvency. Companies have a vested interest in making sure that they manage their debt levels in a way that does not weaken their solvency position. The debt to total assets ratio measures the percentage of the total assets that is provided by creditors. It is calculated by dividing total debt (both current and long-term liabilities) by total assets, as shown in the following formula:

$$\text{Debt to total assets} = \frac{\text{Total debt}}{\text{Total assets}}$$

The **higher the percentage** of debt to total assets, the **greater the risk** that the company may be unable to meet its maturing obligations.

The times interest earned ratio indicates the company's ability to meet interest payments as they come due. It is calculated by dividing income before interest expense and income taxes by interest expense:

$$\text{Times interest earned} = \frac{\text{Income before income taxes and interest expense}}{\text{Interest expense}}$$

To illustrate these ratios, we will use data from Eastern Platinum Limited's (EPL) 2009 quarterly report, which disclosed total liabilities of $65.5 million, total assets of $562.9 million, interest income of $0.042 million ($452 thousand in interest expense less interest income of $494 thousand), income tax recovery of $0.680 million, and net income of $2.4 million. EPL's debt to total assets ratio is calculated as follows:

$$\text{Debt to total assets} = \frac{\$65.5}{\$562.9} = 11.6\%$$

EPL has a very moderate debt to total assets percentage of 11.6%. The company is largely capitalized by equity. There is no point in calculating the interest coverage ratio since on a net basis, the company has net interest income. This is due to the fact that debt levels are very low and the company has investments that are generating interest income.

A Comparison of IFRS and Private Entity GAAP

Illustration 14-13 summarizes the differences in accounting for long-term financial liabilities between accounting standards for private enterprises and IFRS.

	Accounting Standards for Private Enterprises (Private Entity GAAP/ASPE)—*CICA Handbook*, Part II, Sections 1510, 1521, and 3856	IFRS—IAS 32 and 39; IFRS 7
Measurement	There is specific guidance on measuring related-party transactions (which will be covered in Chapter 23).	There is no specific guidance on related-party transactions.
	Subsequently, liabilities are generally measured at amortized cost using the effective interest or other method (unless measured at fair value under the fair value option or because it is a derivative, with a few exceptions).	Subsequently, liabilities are generally measured at amortized cost using the effective interest method (unless measured at fair value under the fair value option or because it is a derivative).
Presentation	Normally the balance sheet is segregated into current/noncurrent; however, this may not be appropriate for certain industries.	Normally the balance sheet is segregated into current/noncurrent except where presentation on the basis of liquidity is more relevant (then debt is presented in order of liquidity).
	Refinanced long-term debt may be classified as long-term where refinanced by date of issue of financial statements.	Refinanced long-term debt may be classified as long-term where refinanced by balance sheet date.

Illustration 14-13

IFRS and Private Entity GAAP Comparison Chart

Looking Ahead

The IASB and FASB are currently working on several projects related to long-term debt as follows:

1. **Derecognition project**: This project relates to derecognition of financial assets and liabilities and the intent is to simplify the accounting. This project will primarily affect derecognition of assets.

2. **Fair value measurement project**: The IASB has issued an Exposure Draft on fair value measurement (FV ED). The FV ED presents a common definition of fair value and establishes a hierarchy that helps users measure fair values. The proposed fair value hierarchy has been outlined in Chapter 2. The FV ED also looks at whether to include the entity's own credit risk when measuring impairment of liabilities. Guidance is also provided where the financial liability being issued is not a marketable security. It is expected that the standard will be issued in late 2010.

3. **Financial instruments with the characteristics of equity**: The IASB expected to issue an Exposure Draft on this issue in late 2010. This will affect how debt and equity instruments are classified and presented on the balance sheet.

4. **Conceptual framework project**: As part of this project, the standard setters are trying to circumscribe the economic entity for financial reporting purposes and are looking at the definition of control. This was discussed briefly in Chapter 2.

Summary of Learning Objectives

1 **Understand the nature of long-term debt.**

Incurring long-term debt is often a formal procedure. Corporation bylaws usually require the approval of the board of directors and the shareholders before bonds can be issued or other long-term debt arrangements can be contracted. Generally, long-term debt has various covenants or restrictions. The covenants and other terms of the agreement between the borrower and the lender are stated in the bond indenture or note agreement. Notes are similar in substance to bonds but do not trade as readily in capital markets, if at all.

2 **Identify various types of long-term debt.**

Various types of long-term debt include (1) secured and unsecured bonds; (2) term, serial, perpetual, and callable bonds or notes; (3) convertible and commodity-backed bonds, and bonds that may be settled in common shares; (4) registered and bearer (coupon) bonds; and (5) income, revenue, and deep discount bonds. The variety of types of bonds is a result of attempts to attract capital from different investors and risk takers and to satisfy the issuers' cash flow needs.

3 **Understand how long-term debt is valued and measured.**

The investment community values a bond at the present value of its future cash flows, which consist of interest and principal. The rate that is used to calculate the present value of these cash flows is the interest rate that provides an acceptable return on an investment that matches the issuer's risk characteristics. The interest rate written in the terms of the bond indenture and ordinarily appearing on the bond certificate is the stated, coupon, or nominal rate. This rate, which is set by the issuer of the bonds, is expressed as a percentage of the bond's face value, which is also called the par value, principal amount, or maturity value. If the rate used by the buyers differs from the stated rate, the bond's present value calculated by the buyers will differ from the bond's face value. The difference between the bond's face value and the present value is either a discount or a premium. Long-term debt is measured at fair value on initial recognition, including transaction costs where the instruments will subsequently be valued at amortized cost. Subsequently, the instruments are measured at amortized cost or, in certain limited situations, fair value, under the fair value option.

4 **Apply the effective interest and straight-line bond amortization methods.**

The discount (premium) is amortized and charged (credited) to interest expense over the period of time that the bonds are outstanding. Bond interest expense is increased by amortization of a discount and decreased by amortization of a premium. IFRS requires the effective interest method; however, PE GAAP allows a choice and often smaller private entities use the straight-line method. This method is also used where GAAP is not a constraint. Under the effective interest method, (1) bond interest expense is calculated by multiplying the bond's carrying value at the beginning of the period by the effective interest rate, and (2) the bond discount or premium amortization is then determined by comparing the bond interest expense with the interest to be paid.

5 **Value bonds and consideration in special situations.**

Bonds and notes may be issued with zero interest or for a non-monetary consideration. Measurement of the bonds and the consideration must reflect the underlying substance of the transaction. In particular, reasonable interest rates must be imputed.

Glossary

KEY TERMS

asset-linked debt, 910
bearer bond, 910
bond indenture, 909
callable bonds/notes, 910
carrying value, 916
commodity-backed debt, 910
convertible debt, 911
coupon bond, 910
coupon rate, 913
debenture bonds, 910
debt to total assets ratio, 933
deep discount bonds/notes, 910
defeasance, 930
discount, 913
effective interest method, 916
effective yield, 913
extinguishment of debt, 923
face value, 913
fair value option, 923
imputed interest rate, 920
income bonds, 910
investment grade securities, 911
loan foreclosure, 925
long-term debt, 908
long-term notes payable, 909
market rate, 913
maturity value, 913
mortgage bonds/notes, 910
nominal rate, 913
off-balance sheet financing, 930
par value, 913
perpetual bonds/notes, 910
premium, 913
present value of a bond issue, 913

The fair value of the debt and of the non-monetary consideration should be used to value the transaction.

6 Account for derecognition of debt.

At the time of reacquisition, the unamortized premium or discount and any costs of issue that apply to the debt must be amortized up to the reacquisition date. The amount that is paid on extinguishments or redemption before maturity, including any call premium and expense of reacquisition, is the reacquisition price. On any specified date, the debt's net carrying amount is the amount that is payable at maturity, adjusted for unamortized premium or discount and the cost of issuance. Any excess of the net carrying amount over the reacquisition price is a gain from extinguishment, whereas the excess of the reacquisition price over the net carrying amount is a loss from extinguishment. Legal defeasance results in debt extinguishment. In-substance defeasance does not in itself result in extinguishment.

7 Distinguish between and account for debt restructurings that result in extinguishment or in debt continuation.

Where debt is settled by exchanging the old debt with new debt (generally in troubled debt situations), it is treated as a settlement where the terms of the agreements are substantially different, including a size test, and where the new debt is with a new lender. If not treated as a settlement, it is treated as a modification of the old debt and a new interest rate is imputed.

8 Explain the issues surrounding off–balance sheet financing arrangements.

Off–balance sheet financing is an attempt to borrow funds in such a way that the obligations are not recorded. One type of off–balance sheet financing involves the use of certain variable interest entities. Accounting standard setters are studying this area with the objective of coming up with a new definition of control and the reporting entity.

9 Indicate how long-term debt is presented and analyzed.

Companies that have large amounts and many issues of long-term debt often report only one amount in the balance sheet and support this with comments and schedules in the accompanying notes. Any assets that are pledged as security for the debt should be shown in the assets section of the balance sheet. Long-term debt that matures within one year should be reported as a current liability, unless it will be retired without using current assets. If the debt is to be refinanced, converted into shares, or retired from a bond retirement fund, it should continue to be reported as noncurrent and accompanied by a note explaining the method to be used in its liquidation unless certain conditions are met. Disclosure is required of future payments for sinking fund requirements and maturity amounts of long-term debt during each of the next five years. Debt to total assets and times interest earned are two ratios that provide information about debt-paying ability and long-run solvency.

10 Identify differences in accounting between accounting standards for private enterprises (private entity GAAP) and IFRS, and what changes are expected in the near future.

The international and Canadian standards for long-term debt are largely converged. Small differences relate to whether the debt is presented as current or noncurrent and in measurement; for example, private entity GAAP has measurement standards for related-party transactions. The standard setters are working on several large projects, including fair value measurements, derecognition, and financial instruments with the characteristics of equity.

Brief Exercises

BE14-1   Buchanan Corporation issues $500,000 of 11% bonds that are due in 10 years and pay interest semi-annually. At the time of issue, the market rate for such bonds is 10%. Calculate the bonds' issue price. **(LO 3)**

BE14-2   Chieh, Inc. issued a $300,000, four-year, 8% note at face value to Cedar Bank on January 1, 2011, and received $300,000 cash. The note requires annual interest payments each December 31. Prepare Chieh's journal entries to record (a) the note issuance and (b) the December 31 interest payment. **(LO 3)**

BE14-3   On May 1, 2011, Jadeja Corporation, a publicly listed corporation, issued $200,000 of five-year, 8% bonds, with interest payable semi-annually on November 1 and May 1. The bonds were issued to yield a market interest rate of 6%. Jadeja uses the effective interest method. (a) Calculate the present value (issue price) of the bonds on May 1. (b) Record the issue of the bonds on May 1. (c) Prepare the journal entry to record the first and second interest payments on November 1, 2011, and May 1, 2012. **(LO 3, 4)**

BE14-4   Muszynski Corporation issued a $75,000, four-year, zero-interest-bearing note to Samson Corp. on January 1, 2012, and received $47,664 cash. The implicit interest rate is 12%. (a) Prepare Muszynski's journal entry for the January 1 issuance. (b) Prepare Muszynski's journal entry for the December 31 recognition of interest. (c) Assume that the effective interest of 12% had not been provided in the data. Prove the effective interest rate of 12% using a financial calculator or computer spreadsheet function. (d) Prepare an effective-interest amortization table for the note. **(LO 3, 5)**

BE14-5   Brestovacki Corporation issued a $50,000, four-year, 5% note to Jernigan Corp. on January 1, 2011, and received a computer that normally sells for $38,912. The note requires annual interest payments each December 31. The market interest rate for a note of similar risk is 11%. Prepare Brestovacki's journal entry for (a) the January 1, 2011 issuance and (b) the December 31, 2011 interest payment using the effective interest method. **(LO 3, 5)**

BE14-6   Khajepour Corporation issued a $140,000, four-year, zero-interest-bearing note to Saccomanno Corp. on January 1, 2011, and received $140,000 cash. In addition, the company agreed to sell merchandise to Saccomanno for an amount less than the regular selling price over the four-year period. The market interest rate for similar notes is 8%. Prepare Khajepour's January 1 journal entry. **(LO 3, 5)**

BE14-7   Pflug Ltd. signed an instalment note on January 1, 2011, in settlement of an account payable of $40,000 owed to Mott Ltd. Pflug is able to borrow funds from its bank at 11%, whereas Mott can borrow at the rate of 10%. The note calls for two equal payments of blended principal and interest to be made at December 31, 2011, and 2012. Calculate the amount of the equal instalment payments that will be made to Mott Ltd. **(LO 3)**

BE14-8   Watson Corporation issued $500,000 of 8%, 10-year bonds on January 1, 2011, at face value. The note requires annual interest payments each December 31. Costs associated with the bond issuance were $25,000. Watson follows private enterprise GAAP and uses the straight-line method to amortize bond issue costs. Prepare the journal entry for (a) the January 1, 2011 issuance and (b) the December 31, 2011 interest payment and bond issuance cost amortization. (c) What are the general principles surrounding accounting for transaction costs associated with the issue of note or bonds? **(LO 3)**

BE14-9   Grenier Limited issued $300,000 of 10% bonds on January 1, 2011. The bonds are due on January 1, 2016, with interest payable each July 1 and January 1. The bonds are issued at face value. Prepare the company's journal entries for (a) the January issuance, (b) the July 1, 2011 interest payment, and (c) the December 31, 2011 adjusting entry. **(LO 3)**

BE14-10   Assume that the bonds in BE14–9 were issued at 98. Assume also that Grenier Limited records the amortization using the straight-line method. Prepare the journal entries related to the bonds for (a) January 1, (b) July 1, and (c) December 31. **(LO 4)**

BE14-11   Assume that the bonds in BE14–9 were issued at 103. Assume also that Grenier Limited records the amortization using the straight-line method. Prepare the journal entries related to the bonds for (a) January 1, (b) July 1, and (c) December 31. **(LO 4)**

BE14-12   Stevens Corporation issued $700,000 of 9% bonds on May 1, 2012. The bonds were dated January 1, 2012, and mature on January 1, 2017, with interest payable each July 1 and January 1. The bonds were issued at face value plus accrued interest. Prepare the company's journal entries for (a) the May 1 issuance, (b) the July 1 interest payment, and (c) the December 31 adjusting entry. **(LO 4)**

(LO 4)   **BE14-13**   On January 1, 2012, Quinton Corporation issued $600,000 of 7% bonds that are due in 10 years. The bonds were issued for $559,229 and pay interest each July 1 and January 1. The company uses the effective interest method. Assume an effective rate of 8%. (a) Prepare the company's journal entry for the January 1 issuance. (b) Prepare the company's journal entry for the July 1 interest payment. (c) Prepare the company's December 31 adjusting entry. (d) Assume that the effective interest of 8% was not given in the data. Prove the effective interest rate of 8% using a financial calculator or computer spreadsheet function. (e) Prepare the first three payments of an effective-interest amortization table for the bonds.

(LO 4)   **BE14-14**   Assume that the bonds in BE14–13 were issued for $644,635 and the effective interest rate was 6%. (a) Prepare the company's journal entry for the January 1 issuance. (b) Prepare the company's journal entry for the July 1 interest payment. (c) Prepare the company's December 31 adjusting entry. (d) Assume that the effective interest of 6% was not given in the data. Prove the effective interest rate of 6% using a financial calculator or computer spreadsheet function. (e) Prepare the first three payments of an effective-interest amortization table for the bonds.

(LO 4)   **BE14-15**   Teton Corporation issued $600,000 of 8% bonds on November 1, 2011, for $644,636. The bonds were dated November 1, 2011, and mature in 10 years, with interest payable each May 1 and November 1. The company uses the effective interest method with an effective rate of 6%. Prepare the company's December 31, 2011 adjusting entry.

(LO 6)   **BE14-16**   On January 1, 2011, Henderson Corporation retired $500,000 (face value) of bonds at 99. At the time of retirement, the unamortized premium was $9,750. Prepare the corporation's journal entry to record the reacquisition of the bonds.

(LO 7)   **BE14-17**   What are the types of situations that result in troubled debt? Briefly explain.

(LO 9)   **BE14-18**   At December 31, 2012, Hyasaki Corporation has the following account balances:

Bonds Payable—Due January 1, 2020 (face value, $2,000,000)	$1,912,000
Bond Interest Payable	80,000

Show how the above accounts should be presented on the December 31, 2012 balance sheet, and with the proper classifications.

Exercises

(LO 3)   **E14-1**   **(Entries for Bond Transactions)** Two independent situations follow:

1. On January 1, 2011, Divac Limited issued $300,000 of 10-year, 9% bonds at par. Interest is payable quarterly on April 1, July 1, October 1, and January 1.

2. On June 1, 2011, Verbitsky Inc. issued at par, plus accrued interest, $200,000 of 10-year, 12% bonds dated January 1. Interest is payable semi-annually on July 1 and January 1.

Instructions

For each of these two independent situations, prepare journal entries to record:

(a) The issuance of the bonds

(b) The payment of interest on July 1

(c) The accrual of interest on December 31

(LO 3, 4)   **E14-2**   **(Entries for Bond Transactions—Effective Interest)** Foreman Inc. issued $800,000 of 10%, 20-year bonds on January 1, 2011, at 102. Interest is payable semi-annually on July 1 and January 1. Foreman Inc. uses the effective interest method of amortization for a bond premium or discount. Assume an effective yield of 9.75%. (With a market rate of 9.75%, the issue price would be slightly higher. For simplicity, ignore this.)

Instructions

Prepare the journal entries to record the following. (Round to the nearest dollar.)

(a) The issuance of the bonds

(b) The payment of interest and related amortization on July 1, 2011

(c) The accrual of interest and the related amortization on December 31, 2011

E14-3   (Entries for Bond Transactions—Straight-Line) Foreman Inc. issued $800,000 of 20-year, 10% bonds on January 1, 2011, at 102. Interest is payable semi-annually on July 1 and January 1. The company uses the straight-line method of amortization for any bond premium or discount.   **(LO 3, 4)**

Instructions

(a) Prepare the journal entries to record the following:

  1. The issuance of the bonds

  2. The payment of interest and the related amortization on July 1, 2011

  3. The accrual of interest and the related amortization on December 31, 2011

(b) Briefly explain how the entries would change depending on whether Foreman was to follow IFRS or private enterprise GAAP.

E14-4   (Entries for Non–Interest-Bearing Debt) On January 1, 2012, Guillemette Inc. makes the following acquisitions: **(LO 3, 5)**

  1. Purchases land having a fair market value of $300,000 by issuing a five-year, non–interest-bearing promissory note in the face amount of $505,518.

  2. Purchases equipment by issuing an eight-year, 6% promissory note having a maturity value of $275,000 (interest payable annually).

The company has to pay 11% interest for funds from its bank.

Instructions

(a) Record Guillemette's journal entries on January 1, 2012, for each of the purchases.

(b) Record the interest at the end of the first year on both notes using the effective interest method.

E14-5   (Imputation of Interest) Two independent situations follow.   **(LO 3, 5)**

  1. On January 1, 2012, Spartan Inc. purchased land that had an assessed value of $390,000 at the time of purchase. A $600,000, non–interest-bearing note due on January 1, 2015, was given in exchange. There was no established exchange price for the land, and no ready market value for the note. The interest rate that is normally charged on a note of this type is 12%.

  2. On January 1, 2012, Geimer Furniture Ltd. borrowed $4 million (face value) from Aurora Inc., a major customer, through a non–interest-bearing note due in four years. Because the note was non–interest-bearing, Geimer Furniture agreed to sell furniture to this customer at lower than market price. A 10% rate of interest is normally charged on this type of loan.

Instructions

(a) For situation 1, determine at what amount the land should be recorded at January 1, 2012, and the interest expense to be reported in 2012 related to this transaction. Discuss how the assessed value of the land could be used in this situation.

(b) For situation 2, prepare the journal entry to record this transaction and determine the amount of interest expense to report for 2012.

E14-6   (Purchase of Land with Instalment Note) Desrocher Ltd. issued an instalment note on January 1, 2012, in exchange for land that it purchased from Safayeni Ltd. Safayeni's real estate agent had listed the land on the market for $120,000. The implied interest rate is 9%. The note calls for three equal blended payments of $43,456 that are to be made at December 31, 2012, 2013, and 2014.   **(LO 3, 5)**

Instructions

(a) Discuss how the purchase price of the land will be established.

(b) Using time value of money tables, a financial calculator, or computer spreadsheet functions, prove that the note will cost Desrocher Ltd. 9% interest over the note's full term.

(c) Prepare an effective-interest amortization table for the instalment note for the three-year period.

(d) Prepare Desrocher's journal entry for the purchase of the land.

(e) Prepare Desrocher's journal entry for the first instalment payment on the note on December 31, 2012.

(f) From Safayeni Ltd.'s perspective, what are the advantages of an instalment note compared with a regular interest-bearing note?

Digging
Deeper

(LO 3, 5)   E14-7   (Purchase of Equipment with Non–Interest-Bearing Debt) To meet customer demand for its product, Armada Inc. decided to purchase equipment from Southern Ontario Industries on January 2, 2012, and expand its production capacity. Armada issued an $800,000, five-year, non–interest-bearing note to Southern Ontario Industries for the new equipment when the prevailing market interest rate for obligations of this nature was 12%. The company will pay off the note in five $160,000 instalments that are due at the end of each year over the life of the note.

Instructions

(a) Prepare the journal entry(ies) at the date of purchase. (Round to nearest dollar in all calculations.)

(b) Prepare the journal entry(ies) at the end of the first year to record the payment and interest, assuming that the company uses the effective interest method.

(c) Prepare the journal entry(ies) at the end of the second year to record the payment and interest.

(LO 3, 5)   E14-8   (Purchase of Computer with Non–Interest-Bearing Debt) Soldan Corporation purchased a computer on December 31, 2011, paying $30,000 down and a further $75,000 payment due on December 31, 2014. An interest rate of 10% is implicit in the purchase price. Soldan uses the effective interest method and has a December 31 year end.

Instructions

(a) Prepare the journal entry(ies) at the purchase date. (Round to two decimal places.)

(b) Prepare any journal entry(ies) required at December 31, 2012, 2013, and 2014.

(LO 3, 4)   E14-9   (Entries for Bond Transactions) On January 1, 2011, Osborn Inc. sold 12% bonds having a maturity value of $800,000 for $860,651.79, which provides the bondholders with a 10% yield. The bonds are dated January 1, 2011, and mature on January 1, 2016, with interest payable on January 1 of each year. The company follows IFRS and uses the effective interest method.

Instructions

(a) Prepare the journal entry at the date of issue.

(b) Prepare a schedule of interest expense and bond amortization for 2011 through 2014.

(c) Prepare the journal entry to record the interest payment and the amortization for 2011.

(d) Prepare the journal entry to record the interest payment and the amortization for 2013.

(e) Assume that the company follows private enterprise GAAP. Would there be any other accounting option available to the company with respect to the bond transactions?

(LO 1, 3)   E14-10   (Information Related to Various Bond Issues) Anaconda Inc. has issued three types of debt on January 1, 2011, the start of the company's fiscal year:

1. $10 million, 10-year, 13% unsecured bonds, with interest payable quarterly (the bonds were priced to yield 12%)

2. $2.5 million par of 10-year, zero-coupon bonds at a price to yield 12% per year

3. $15 million, 10-year, 10% mortgage bonds, with interest payable annually to yield 12%

Instructions

Prepare a schedule that identifies the following items for each bond:

(a) The maturity value

(b) The number of interest periods over the life of the bond

(c) The stated rate for each interest period

(d) The effective interest rate for each interest period

(e) The payment amount per period

(f) The present value of the bonds at the date of issue

(g) Each instrument has different features. Comment on how the instruments are different discussing the underlying nature of the debt. Which bonds are most risky and why?

(LO 3, 4, 6)   E14-11   (Entries for Retirement and Issuance of Bonds) Friedman Corporation had bonds outstanding with a maturity value of $500,000. On April 30, 2011, when these bonds had an unamortized discount of $10,000, they were called in at 104. To pay for these bonds, Friedman had issued other bonds a month earlier bearing a lower interest rate. The newly issued bonds had a life of 10 years. The new bonds were issued at 103 (face value $500,000). Issue costs related to the new bonds were $3,000. All issue costs were capitalized.

Instructions

Ignoring interest, calculate the gain or loss and record this refunding transaction.

E14-12 **(Amortization Schedules—Straight-Line)** Minor Inc. sells 10% bonds having a maturity value of $3 million **(LO 4)** for $2,783,724. The bonds are dated January 1, 2011, and mature on January 1, 2016. Interest is payable annually on January 1.

Instructions

Set up a schedule of interest expense and discount amortization under the straight-line method.

E14-13 **(Amortization Schedule—Effective Interest)** Assume the same information as in E14–12. **(LO 4)**

Instructions

Set up a schedule of interest expense and discount amortization under the effective interest method. (Hint: The effective interest rate must be calculated.)

E14-14 **(Determine Proper Amounts in Account Balances)** Three independent situations follow. Answer the ques- **(LO 4)** tions at the end of each situation.

1. Wen Corporation incurred the following costs when it issued bonds: (a) printing and engraving costs, $25,000; (b) legal fees, $69,000; and (c) commissions paid to underwriter, $70,000. What accounting treatment could be given to these costs?

2. Griffith Inc. sold $3 million of 10-year, 10% bonds at 104 on January 1, 2012. The bonds were dated January 1, 2012, and pay interest on July 1 and January 1. If Griffith follows private entity GAAP and uses the straight-line method to amortize bond premium or discount, determine the amount of interest expense to be reported on July 1, 2012, and December 31, 2012.

3. Kennedy Inc. issued $600,000 of 10-year, 9% bonds on June 30, 2011, for $562,500. This price provided a yield of 10% on the bonds. Interest is payable semi-annually on December 31 and June 30. If Kennedy uses the effective interest method, determine the amount of interest expense to record if financial statements are issued on October 31, 2011.

E14-15 **(Entries and Questions for Bond Transactions)** On June 30, 2011, Mosca Limited issued $4 million of 20- **(LO 4, 8)** year, 13% bonds for $4,300,920, which provides a yield of 12%. The company uses the effective interest method to amortize any bond premium or discount. The bonds pay semi-annual interest on June 30 and December 31.

Instructions

(a) Prepare the journal entries to record the following transactions:

1. The issuance of the bonds on June 30, 2011

2. The payment of interest and the amortization of the premium on December 31, 2011

3. The payment of interest and the amortization of the premium on June 30, 2012

4. The payment of interest and the amortization of the premium on December 31, 2012

(b) Show the proper balance sheet presentation for the liability for bonds payable on the December 31, 2011 balance sheet.

(c) Answer the following questions.

1. What amount of interest expense is reported for 2011?

2. Will the bond interest expense that is reported in 2011 be the same as, greater than, or less than the amount that would be reported if the straight-line method of amortization were used?

3. What is the total cost of borrowing over the life of the bond?

4. Will the total bond interest expense for the life of the bond be greater than, the same as, or less than the total interest expense if the straight-line method of amortization were used?

E14-16 **(Entries for Retirement and Issuance of Bonds—Straight-Line)** On June 30, 2004, Auburn Limited issued **(LO 4, 6)** 12% bonds with a par value of $800,000 due in 20 years. They were issued at 98 and were callable at 104 at any date after June 30, 2011.

Because of lower interest rates and a significant change in the company's credit rating, it was decided to call the entire issue on June 30, 2011, and to issue new bonds. New 10% bonds were sold in the amount of $1 million at 102; they mature in 20 years. The company follows private enterprise GAAP and uses straight-line amortization. The interest payment dates are December 31 and June 30 of each year.

Instructions

(a) Prepare journal entries to record the retirement of the old issue and the sale of the new issue on June 30, 2011.

(b) Prepare the entry required on December 31, 2011, to record the payment of the first six months of interest and the amortization of the bond premium.

(LO 4, 6) E14-17 **(Entries for Retirement and Issuance of Bonds—Effective Interest)** Refer to E14–16 and Auburn Limited.

Instructions

Repeat the instructions of E14–16 assuming that Auburn Limited follows IFRS and uses the effective interest method. Provide an effective-interest table for the bonds for the inception of the bond to the date of the redemption. (Hint: it will be necessary to first calculate the effective interest rate on the 2004 and 2011 bonds.)

(LO 5) E14-18 **(Interest-Free Government Loans)** Russell Forest Products Limited needed to upgrade a burner at its sawmill in Cochrane, Ontario, to comply with the new air pollution standards. The new burner, which is used to burn the scrap wood from its sawing operations, will not only reduce the amount of pollution, but will supply heat for the plant facility, including the wood dryer. In order to encourage Russell Forest Products Limited in its compliance with the standards, the Province of Ontario extended an interest-free loan of $400,000 on December 31, 2011. The only conditions in obtaining the interest-free loan are that the loan proceeds be applied directly to the construction costs and that the loan be repaid in full on December 31, 2019. Russell Forest Products Limited borrowed the remaining funds from the bank for the construction of the burner and will be paying interest at the rate of 7% per year.

Instructions

(a) Discuss the issues related to obtaining the interest-free loan from the Province of Ontario.

(b) Prepare an amortization table for the loan using the effective interest method. Present the first three years of the loan.

(c) Prepare the entry on December 31, 2011, to record the interest-free loan.

(d) Prepare any adjusting journal entry that is necessary at December 31, 2012, the company's fiscal year end, concerning any interest on the note.

(LO 4, 6) E14-19 **(Entry for Retirement of Bond; Costs for Bond Issuance)** On January 2, 2006, Brueckner Corporation, a small company that follows private enterprise GAAP, issued $1.5 million of 10% bonds at 97 due on December 31, 2015. Legal and other costs of $110,000 were incurred in connection with the issue. Brueckner Corporation has adopted the policy of capitalizing and amortizing the legal and other costs incurred by including them with the bond recorded at the date of issuance. Interest on the bonds is payable annually each December 31. The $110,000 in issuance costs are being deferred and amortized on a straight-line basis over the 10-year term of the bonds. The discount on the bonds is also being amortized on a straight-line basis over the 10 years. (The straight-line method is not materially different in its effect compared with the effective interest method.)

The bonds are callable at 102 (i.e., at 102% of their face amount), and on January 2, 2011, the company called a face amount of $850,000 of the bonds and retired them.

Instructions

Digging
Deeper

(a) Ignoring income taxes, calculate the amount of loss, if any, that the company needs to recognize as a result of retiring the $850,000 of bonds in 2011. Prepare the journal entry to record the retirement.

(b) How would the amount of the loss calculated in part (a) differ if the policy for Brueckner Corporation had been to carry the bonds at fair value and thus expense the costs of issuing the bonds at January 2, 2006? Assuming that Brueckner Corporation had followed this policy, prepare the journal entry to record the retirement.

(c) How would your answers to (a) and (b) change if Brueckner were to follow IFRS?

(LO 6) E14-20 **(Entries for Retirement and Issuance of Bonds)** Robinson, Inc. had outstanding $5 million of 11% bonds (interest payable July 31 and January 31) due in 10 years. On July 1, it issued $7 million of 15-year, 10% bonds (interest payable July 1 and January 1) at 98. A portion of the proceeds was used to call the 11% bonds at 102 on August 1. The unamortized bond discount for the 11% bonds was $120,000 on August 1.

Instructions

Prepare the necessary journal entries to record the issue of the new bonds and the retirement of the old bonds.

E14-21 (Impairments) On December 31, 2010, Mohr Inc. borrowed $81,241 from Par Bank, signing a $125,000, five-year, non–interest-bearing note. The note was issued to yield 9% interest. Unfortunately, during 2011 Mohr began to experience financial difficulty. As a result, at December 31, 2011, Par Bank determined that it was probable that it would receive only $93,750 at maturity. The market rate of interest on loans of this nature is now 11%. **(LO 7)**

Instructions

(a) Prepare the entry to record the issuance of the loan by Par Bank on December 31, 2010.

(b) Prepare the entry (if any) to record the impairment of the loan on December 31, 2011, by Par Bank.

(c) Prepare the entry (if any) to record the impairment of the loan on December 31, 2011, by Mohr.

E14-22 (Settlement of Debt) Strickland Inc. owes Heartland Bank $200,000 plus $18,000 of accrued interest. The debt is a 10-year, 10% note. During 2011, Strickland's business deteriorated due to a faltering regional economy. On December 31, 2011, the bank agrees to accept an old machine and cancel the entire debt. The machine has a cost of $390,000, accumulated depreciation of $221,000, and a fair value of $180,000. The bank plans to dispose of the machine at a cost of $6,500. **(LO 7)**

Instructions

(a) Prepare the journal entries for Strickland Inc. and Heartland Bank to record this debt settlement.

(b) How should Strickland report the gain or loss on the disposition of the machine and on the restructuring of debt in its 2011 income statement?

(c) Assume that instead of transferring the machine, Strickland decides to grant the bank 15,000 of its common shares, which have a fair value of $190,000. This is in full settlement of the loan obligation. Assuming that Heartland Bank treats Strickland's shares as trading securities, prepare the entries to record the transaction for both parties.

E14-23 (Term Modification—Debtor's Entries) On December 31, 2011, Green Bank enters into a debt restructuring agreement with Troubled Inc., which is now experiencing financial trouble. The bank agrees to restructure a $2-million, 12% note receivable issued at par by the following modifications: **(LO 7)**

1. Reducing the principal obligation from $2 million to $1.9 million

2. Extending the maturity date from December 31, 2011, to December 31, 2014

3. Reducing the interest rate from 12% to 10%

Troubled pays interest at the end of each year. On January 1, 2015, Troubled Inc. pays $1.9 million in cash to Green Bank.

Instructions

(a) Discuss whether or not Troubled should record a gain.

(b) Calculate the rate of interest that Troubled should use to calculate its interest expense in future periods.

(c) Prepare the interest payment entry for Troubled on December 31, 2013.

(d) What entry should Troubled make on January 1, 2015?

E14-24 (Term Modification—Creditor's Entries) Assume the same information as in E14–23 and answer the following questions related to Green Bank (the creditor). **(LO 7)**
Instructions

(a) What interest rate should Green Bank use to calculate the loss on the debt restructuring?

(b) Calculate the loss that Green Bank will suffer from the debt restructuring. Prepare the journal entry to record the loss.

(c) Prepare the amortization schedule for Green Bank after the debt restructuring.

(d) Prepare the interest receipt entry for Green Bank on December 31, 2013.

(e) What entry should Green Bank make on January 1, 2015?

E14-25 (Settlement—Debtor's Entries) Use the same information as in E14–23 but assume now that Green Bank reduced the principal to $1.6 million rather than $1.9 million. On January 1, 2015, Troubled Inc. pays $1.6 million in cash to Green Bank for the principal. **(LO 7)**

Instructions

(a) Can Troubled record a gain under this term modification? If yes, calculate the gain.

(b) Prepare the journal entries to record the gain on Troubled's books.

(c) What interest rate should Troubled use to calculate its interest expense in future periods? Will your answer be the same as in E14–23? Why or why not?

(d) Prepare the amortization schedule of the note for Troubled after the debt restructuring.

(e) Prepare the interest payment entries for Troubled on December 31, 2012, 2013, and 2014.

(f) What entry should Troubled make on January 1, 2015?

(LO 7)   **E14-26   (Settlement—Creditor's Entries)** Use the information in E14–23 and the assumptions in E14–25 and answer the following questions related to Green Bank (the creditor).

Instructions

(a) What interest rate should Green Bank use to calculate the loss on the debt restructuring?

(b) Calculate the loss that Green Bank will suffer under this new term modification. Prepare the journal entry to record the loss on Green Bank's books.

(c) Prepare the amortization schedule for Green Bank after the debt restructuring.

(d) Prepare the interest receipt entry for Green Bank on December 31, 2012, 2013, and 2014.

(e) What entry should Green Bank make on January 1, 2015?

(LO 7)   **E14-27   (Debtor/Creditor Entries for Settlement of Troubled Debt)** Vargo Limited owes $270,000 to First Trust Inc. on a 10-year, 12% note. Because Vargo is in financial trouble, First Trust Inc. agrees to extend the maturity date to December 31, 2013, reduce the principal to $220,000, and reduce the interest rate to 5%, payable annually on December 31.

Instructions

(a) Prepare the journal entry on Vargo's books on December 31, 2011, 2012, and 2013.

(b) Prepare the journal entry on First Trust's books on December 31, 2011, 2012, and 2013.

(LO 7)   **E14-28   (Debtor/Creditor Entries for Settlement of Troubled Debt)** Grumpy Limited owes $137,300 to Bank One Inc. on a 10-year, 11% note. Because Grumpy is in financial trouble, Bank One Inc. agrees to accept some property and cancel the entire debt. The property has a carrying amount of $55,000 and a fair value of $82,500.

Instructions

(a) Prepare the journal entry on Grumpy's books for the debt settlement.

(b) Prepare the journal entry on Bank One's books for the debt settlement.

(LO 9)   **E14-29   (Long-Term Debt Disclosure)** At December 31, 2011, Reddy Inc. has three long-term debt issues outstanding. The first is a $2.2-million note payable that matures on June 30, 2014. The second is a $4-million bond issue that matures on September 30, 2015. The third is a $16.5-million sinking fund debenture with annual sinking fund payments of $3.5 million in each of the years 2013 through 2017.

Instructions

Prepare the note disclosure that is required for the long-term debt at December 31, 2011.

(LO 9)   **E14-30   (Classification of Liabilities)** The following are various accounts:

1. Bank loans payable of a winery, due March 10, 2015 (the product requires aging for five years before it can be sold)

2. $10 million of serial bonds payable, of which $2 million is due each July 31

3. Amounts withheld from employees' wages for income taxes

4. Notes payable that are due January 15, 2014

5. Interest payable on a note payable (the note is due January 15, 2014, and the interest is due June 30, 2012)

6. Credit balance in a customer's account arising from returns and allowances after collection in full of the account

7. Bonds payable of $2 million maturing June 30, 2015

8. An overdraft of $1,000 in a bank account (no other balances are carried at this bank)

9. An overdraft of $1,000 in a bank account (other accounts are carried at this bank and have positive account balances)

10. Deposits made by customers who have ordered goods

Instructions

(a) Indicate whether each of the items above should be classified under IFRS on December 31, 2011, as a current or long-term liability or under some other classification. Consider each one independently from all others; that is, do not assume that all of them relate to one particular business. If the classification of some of the items is doubtful, explain why in each case.

(b) Assume instead that the company follows private enterprise GAAP. Repeat part (a) for the items that would be classified differently.

E14-31   **(Classification)** The following items are found in a company's financial statements: (LO 9)

1. Interest expense (credit balance)

2. Gain on repurchase of debt

3. Mortgage payable (payable in equal amounts over the next three years)

4. Debenture bonds payable (maturing in five years)

5. Notes payable (due in four years)

6. Income bonds payable (due in three years)

Instructions

(a) Indicate how each of these items should be classified in the financial statements under IFRS.

(b) Assume instead that the company follows private enterprise GAAP. Repeat part (a) for the items that would be classified differently.

Problems

P14-1   Four independent situations follow:

1. On March 1, 2012, Wilkie Inc. issued $4 million of 9% bonds at 103 plus accrued interest. The bonds are dated January 1, 2012, and pay interest semi-annually on July 1 and January 1. In addition, Wilkie incurred $27,000 of bond issuance costs.

2. On January 1, 2011, Langley Ltd. issued 9% bonds with a face value of $500,000 for $469,280 to yield 10%. The bonds are dated January 1, 2011, and pay interest annually.

3. Chico Building Inc. has several long-term bonds outstanding at December 31, 2009. These long-term bonds have the following sinking fund requirements and maturities for the next six years:

	Sinking Fund	Maturities
2013	$300,000	$100,000
2014	$100,000	$250,000
2015	$100,000	$100,000
2016	$200,000	–0–
2017	$200,000	$150,000
2018	$200,000	$100,000

4. In the long-term debt structure of Czeslaw Inc., the following three bonds were reported: mortgage bonds payable, $10 million; collateral trust bonds, $5 million; bonds maturing in instalments, secured by plant equipment, $4 million.

Instructions

(a) For situation 1, calculate the net amount of cash received by Wilkie as a result of the issuance of these bonds.

(b) For situation 2, what amount should Langley report for interest expense in 2011 related to these bonds, assuming that it uses the effective interest method for amortizing any bond premium or discount? Could Langley choose to use the straight-line method for amortizing any bond premium or discount?

(c) For situation 3, indicate how this information should be reported in Chico's financial statements at December 31, 2012.

(d) For situation 4, determine the total amount of debenture bonds that is outstanding, if any.

P14-2 The following amortization and interest schedule is for the issuance of 10-year bonds by Capulet Corporation on January 1, 2004, and the subsequent interest payments and charges. The company's year end is December 31 and it prepares its financial statements yearly.

			Amortization Schedule	
Year	Cash	Interest	Amount Unamortized	Carrying Amount
Jan. 1, 2004			$5,651	$ 94,349
2004	$11,000	$11,322	5,329	94,671
2005	11,000	11,361	4,968	95,032
2006	11,000	11,404	4,564	95,436
2007	11,000	11,452	4,112	95,888
2008	11,000	11,507	3,605	96,395
2009	11,000	11,567	3,038	96,962
2010	11,000	11,635	2,403	97,597
2011	11,000	11,712	1,691	98,309
2012	11,000	11,797	894	99,106
2013	11,000	11,894	-0-	$100,000

Instructions

(a) Indicate whether the bonds were issued at a premium or a discount and explain how you can determine this fact from the schedule.

(b) Indicate whether the amortization schedule is based on the straight-line method or the effective interest method and explain how you can determine which method is used. Are both amortization methods accepted for financial reporting purposes?

(c) Determine the stated interest rate and the effective interest rate.

(d) Based on the schedule above, prepare the journal entry to record the issuance of the bonds on January 1, 2004.

(e) Based on the schedule above, prepare the journal entry or entries to reflect the bond transactions and accruals for 2004. (Interest is paid January 1.)

(f) Based on the schedule above, prepare the journal entry or entries to reflect the bond transactions and accruals for 2012. Capulet Corporation does not use reversing entries.

P14-3 Venzuela Inc. is building a new hockey arena at a cost of $2.5 million. It received a down payment of $500,000 from local businesses to support the project, and now needs to borrow $2 million to complete the project. It therefore decides to issue $2 million of 10-year, 10.5% bonds. These bonds were issued on January 1, 2010, and pay interest annually on each January 1. The bonds yield 10% to the investor and have an effective interest rate to the issuer of 10.4053% (increased effective interest rate due to the capitalization of the bond issue costs). Any additional funds that are needed to complete the project will be obtained from local businesses. Venzuela Inc. paid and capitalized $50,000 in bond issuance costs related to the bond issue.

Instructions

(a) Prepare the journal entry to record the issuance of the bonds on January 1, 2010.

(b) Prepare a bond amortization schedule up to and including January 1, 2015, using the effective interest method.

(c) Assume that on July 1, 2013, the company retires half of the bonds at a cost of $1.065 million plus accrued interest. Prepare the journal entry to record this retirement.

Digging Deeper

(d) Assume that the costs incurred by Venzuela Inc. to issue the bonds totalled $50,000 as above. If Venzuela Inc. chose to carry the bonds at fair value and thus expense these costs, how would this affect the amount of interest expense that is recognized by Venzuela Inc. each year and over the 10-year term of the bonds in total, compared with its current accounting practice of capitalizing the bond issue costs?

P14-4 In the following two independent cases, the company closes its books on December 31:

1. Munchousen Inc. sells $2 million of 10% bonds on March 1, 2011. The bonds pay interest on September 1 and March 1. The bonds' due date is September 1, 2014. The bonds yield 12%.

2. Ducharme Ltd. sells $6 million of 11% bonds on June 1, 2011. The bonds pay interest on December 1 and June 1. The bonds' due date is June 1, 2015. The bonds yield 10%. On October 1, 2012, Ducharme buys back $1.2 million worth of bonds for $1.4 million (includes accrued interest).

Instructions

For the two cases above, prepare all of the relevant journal entries from the time of sale until the date indicated (for situation 1, prepare the journal entries through December 31, 2012; for situation 2, prepare the journal entries through December 1, 2013). Use the effective interest method for discount and premium amortization (prepare any necessary amortization tables). Amortize any premium or discount on the interest dates and at year end. (Assume that no reversing entries were made.)

P14-5   Selected transactions on the books of Pfaff Corporation follow:

May 1, 2011   Bonds payable with a par value of $700,000, which are dated January 1, 2011, are sold at 105 plus accrued interest. They are coupon bonds, bear interest at 12% (payable annually at January 1), and mature on January 1, 2021. (Use an interest expense account for accrued interest.)

Dec. 31   Adjusting entries are made to record the accrued interest on the bonds and the amortization of the proper amount of premium. (Use straight-line amortization.)

Jan. 1, 2012   Interest on the bonds is paid.

April 1   Par value bonds of $420,000 are purchased at 103 plus accrued interest and are retired. (Bond premium is to be amortized only at the end of each year.)

Dec. 31   Adjusting entries are made to record the accrued interest on the bonds, and the proper amount of premium amortized.

Instructions

(a) Assume that Pfaff follows private enterprise GAAP. Prepare the journal entries for the transactions above.

(b) How would your answers to the above change if Pfaff were to follow IFRS?

P14-6   On April 1, 2012, Taylor Corp. sold 12,000 of its $1,000 face value, 15-year, 11% bonds at 97. Interest payment dates are April 1 and October 1, and the company uses the straight-line method of bond discount amortization. On March 1, 2013, Taylor took advantage of its favourable share prices to extinguish 3,000 of the bonds by issuing 100,000 shares. At this time, the accrued interest was paid in cash to the bondholders whose bonds were being extinguished. The company's shares were selling for $31 per share on March 1, 2013.

Instructions

Prepare Taylor Corp.'s journal entries to record the following:

(a) April 1, 2012: issuance of the bonds

(b) October 1, 2012: payment of the semi-annual interest

(c) December 31, 2012: accrual of the interest expense

(d) March 1, 2013: extinguishment of 3,000 bonds by the issuance of common shares (no reversing entries are made)

P14-7   Refer to P14–6 and Taylor Corp.

Instructions

Repeat the instructions of P14–6 assuming that Taylor Corp. uses the effective interest method. Provide an effective interest table for the bonds for two interest payment periods. (Hint: it will be necessary to first calculate the effective interest rate on the bonds).

P14-8   On December 31, 2011, Faital Limited acquired a computer software system from Plato Corporation by issuing a $600,000, non–interest-bearing note that is payable in full on December 31, 2015. The company's credit rating permits it to borrow funds from its several lines of credit at 10%. The system is expected to have a five-year life and a $70,000 residual value.

Instructions

(a) Prepare the journal entry for the purchase on December 31, 2011.

(b) Prepare any necessary adjusting entries related to depreciation of the asset (use straight-line) and amortization of the note (use the effective interest method) on December 31, 2012.

(c) Prepare any necessary adjusting entries related to depreciation of the software system and amortization of the bond on December 31, 2013.

P14-9   Sabonis Cosmetics Inc. purchased machinery on December 31, 2011, paying $50,000 down and agreeing to pay the balance in four equal instalments of $40,000 that are payable each December 31. An assumed interest rate of 8% is implicit in the purchase price.

Instructions

(a) Prepare the journal entries that would be recorded for the purchase and for the payments and interest on December 31, 2011, 2012, 2013, 2014, and 2015.

Digging Deeper

(b) From the lender's perspective, what are the advantages of an instalment note compared with an interest-bearing note?

P14-10   On June 1, 2011, MacDougall Corporation approached Silverman Corporation about purchasing a parcel of undeveloped land. Silverman was asking $240,000 for the land and MacDougall saw that there was some flexibility in the asking price. MacDougall did not have the necessary funds to make a cash offer to Silverman and proposed to give, in return for the land, a $300,000, five-year promissory note that bears interest at the rate of 4%. The interest is to be paid annually to Silverman Corporation on June 1 of each of the next five years. Silverman insisted that the note taken in return become a mortgage note. The amended offer was accepted by Silverman, and MacDougall signed a mortgage note for $300,000 due June 1, 2016. MacDougall would have had to pay 10% at its local bank if it were to secure the necessary cash for the land purchase. Silverman, on the other hand, could borrow the funds at 9%. Both MacDougall and Silverman have calendar year ends.

Instructions

(a) Discuss how MacDougall Corporation would determine a value for the land in recording the purchase from Silverman Corporation.

(b) What is the difference between a promissory note payable and a mortgage note payable? Why would Silverman Corporation insist on obtaining a mortgage note payable from MacDougall Corporation?

(c) Calculate the purchase price of the land and prepare an effective-interest amortization table for the term of the mortgage note payable that is given in the exchange.

(d) Prepare the journal entry for the purchase of the land.

(e) Prepare any adjusting journal entry that is required at the end of the fiscal year and the first payment made on June 1, 2012, assuming no reversing entries are used.

Digging Deeper

(f) Assume that Silverman had insisted on obtaining an instalment note from MacDougall instead of a mortgage note. Then do the following:

   1. Calculate the amount of the instalment payments that would be required for a five-year instalment note. Use the same cost of the land to MacDougall Corporation that you determined for the mortgage note in part (a).

   2. Prepare an effective-interest amortization table for the five-year term of the instalment note.

   3. Prepare the journal entry for the purchase of the land and the issuance of the instalment note.

   4. Prepare any adjusting journal entry that is required at the end of the fiscal year and the first payment made on June 1, 2012, assuming no reversing entries are used.

   5. Compare the balances of the two different notes payable and related accounts at December 31, 2011. Be specific about the classifications on the balance sheet.

   6. Why would Silverman insist on an instalment note in this case?

P14-11   Good-Deal Inc. developed a new sales gimmick to help sell its inventory of new automobiles. Because many buyers of new cars need financing, the company offered a low down payment and low car payments for the first year after purchase. It believes that this promotion will bring in some new buyers.

On January 1, 2011, a customer purchased a new $33,000 automobile, making a down payment of $1,000. The customer signed a note indicating that the annual interest rate would be 8% and that quarterly payments would be made over three years. For the first year, the company required a $400 quarterly payment to be made on April 1, July 1, October 1, and January 1, 2012. After this one-year period, the customer was required to make regular quarterly payments that would pay off the loan by January 1, 2014.

Instructions

(a) Prepare a note amortization schedule for the first year.

(b) Indicate the amount that the customer owes on the contract at the end of the first year.

(c) Calculate the amount of the new quarterly payments.

(d) Prepare a note amortization schedule for these new payments for the next two years.

(e) What do you think of Good-Deal Inc.'s new sales promotion?

P14-12 Benoit Inc. issued 25-year, 9% mortgage bonds in the principal amount of $3 million on January 2, 1997, at a discount of $150,000. It then amortized the discount through charges to expense over the life of the issue on a straight-line basis. The indenture securing the issue provided that the bonds could be called for redemption in total but not in part at any time before maturity at 104% of the principal amount, but it did not provide for any sinking fund.

On December 18, 2011, the company issued 20-year, 11% debenture bonds in the principal amount of $4 million at 102 and the proceeds were used to redeem the 25-year, 9% mortgage bonds on January 2, 2012. The indenture securing the new issue did not provide for any sinking fund or for retirement before maturity.

Instructions

(a) Prepare journal entries to record the issuance of the 11% bonds and the retirement of the 9% bonds.

(b) Indicate the income statement treatment of the gain or loss from retirement and the note disclosure that is required. Assume that 2012 income from operations is $3.2 million and that the weighted number of shares outstanding is 1.5 million and the income tax rate is 40%.

P14-13 On January 1, 2011, Batonica Limited issued a $1.2-million, five-year, zero-interest-bearing note to Northern Savings Bank. The note was issued to yield 8% annual interest. Unfortunately, during 2011 Batonica fell into financial trouble due to increased competition. After reviewing all available evidence on December 31, 2011, Northern Savings Bank decided that the loan was impaired. Batonica will probably pay back only $800,000 of the principal at maturity.

Instructions

(a) Prepare journal entries for both Batonica and Northern Savings Bank to record the issuance of the note on January 1, 2011. (Round to the nearest $10.)

(b) Assuming that both Batonica and Northern Savings Bank use the effective interest method to amortize the discount, prepare the amortization schedule for the note.

(c) Under what circumstances can Northern Savings Bank consider Batonica's note to be impaired?

(d) Estimate the loss that Northern Savings Bank will suffer from Batonica's financial distress on December 31, 2011. What journal entries should be made to record this loss?

P14-14 Daniel Perkins is the sole shareholder of Perkins Inc., which is currently under bankruptcy court protection. As a debtor in possession, he has negotiated the following revised loan agreement with United Bank. Perkins Inc.'s $600,000, 10-year, 12% note was refinanced with a $600,000, 10-year, 5% note. Assume the market rate of interest is 12% at the refinancing date.

Instructions

(a) What is the accounting nature of this transaction?

(b) Prepare the journal entry to record this refinancing (1) on the books of Perkins Inc. and (2) on the books of United Bank.

(c) Discuss whether generally accepted accounting principles provide the information that would be useful to managers and potential investors in this situation.

P14-15 Shahani Corporation is having financial difficulty and has therefore asked Bajwa National Bank to restructure its $3-million note outstanding. The present note has three years remaining and pays a current interest rate of 10%. The present market rate for a loan of this nature is 12%. The note was issued at its face value.

Instructions

For each of the following independent situations related to the above scenario, prepare the journal entry that Shahani and Bajwa National Bank would make for the restructuring that is described.

(a) Bajwa National Bank agrees to take an equity interest in Shahani by accepting common shares valued at $2.2 million in exchange for relinquishing its claim on this note.

(b) Bajwa National Bank agrees to accept land in exchange for relinquishing its claim on this note. The land has a carrying amount of $1,050,000 and a fair value of $2.5 million.

(c) Bajwa National Bank agrees to modify the terms of the note so that Shahani does not have to pay any interest on the note over the three-year period.

(d) Bajwa National Bank agrees to reduce the principal balance down to $2.3 million and to require interest only in the second and third year at a rate of 9%.

P14-16   Dilemma Inc. owes Stauskas Bank a $250,000, 10-year, 15% note. The note is due today, December 31, 2011. Because Dilemma Inc. is in financial trouble, Stauskas agrees to accept 60,000 shares of Dilemma's common shares, which are currently selling for $1.40; to reduce the note's face amount to $150,000; to extend the maturity date to December 31, 2015; and to reduce the interest rate to 6%. Interest will continue to be due on December 31 of each year. (Interest is still outstanding as at December 31, 2011.)

Instructions

(a) Prepare all the necessary journal entries on the books of Dilemma Inc. from the time of the restructuring through maturity.

(b) Prepare all the necessary journal entries on the books of Stauskas Bank from the time of the restructuring through maturity.

P14-17   At December 31, 2010, Shutdown Manufacturing Limited had outstanding a $300,000, 12% note payable to Thornton National Bank. Dated January 1, 2008, the note was due on December 31, 2011, with interest payable each December 31. During 2011, Shutdown notified Thornton that it might be unable to meet the scheduled December 31, 2011 payment of principal and interest because of financial difficulties. On September 30, 2011, Thornton sold the note, including interest accrued since December 31, 2010, for $280,000 to Orsini Foundry, one of Shutdown's oldest and largest customers. On December 31, 2011, Orsini agreed to accept inventory that cost $240,000 but was worth $315,000 from Shutdown in full settlement of the note.

Instructions

(a) Prepare the journal entry to record the September 30, 2011 transaction on the books of Thornton, Shutdown, and Orsini. For each company, indicate whether the transaction is a restructuring of troubled debt.

(b) Prepare the journal entries to record the December 31, 2011 transaction on the books of Shutdown and Orsini. For each company, indicate whether this transaction is a restructuring of troubled debt.

P14-18   Mazza Corp. owes Tsang Corp. a $110,000, 10-year, 10% note plus $11,000 of accrued interest. The note is due today, December 31, 2011. Because Mazza Corp. is in financial trouble, Tsang Corp. agrees to forgive the accrued interest and $10,000 of the principal, and to extend the maturity date to December 31, 2014. Interest at 10% of the revised principal will continue to be due on December 31 of each year. Assume the market rate of interest is 10% at refinancing date.

Instructions

(a) Is this a settlement or a modification?

(b) Prepare a schedule of the debt reduction and interest expense for the years 2011 through 2014.

(c) Calculate the gain or loss for Tsang Corp. and prepare a schedule of the receivable reduction and interest revenue for the years 2011 through 2014.

(d) Prepare all the necessary journal entries on the books of Mazza Corp. for the years 2011, 2012, and 2013.

(e) Prepare all the necessary journal entries on the books of Tsang Corp. for the years 2011, 2012, and 2013.

Writing Assignments

WA14-1   On January 1, 2011, Branagh Limited issued for $1,075,230 its 20-year, 13% bonds that have a maturity value of $1 million and pay interest semi-annually on January 1 and July 1. The bond issue costs were not material in amount. Three presentations follow of the balance sheet long-term liability section that might be used for these bonds at the issue date:

1. Bonds payable (maturing January 1, 2031)	$1,075,230
2. Bonds payable principal (face value $1,000,000, maturing January 1, 2031)	97,220[a]
Bonds payable interest (semi-annual payment of $65,000)	978,010[b]
Total bond liability	$1,075,230
3. Bonds payable principal (maturing January 1, 2031)	$1,000,000
Bonds payable interest ($65,000 per period for 40 periods)	2,600,000
Total bond liability	$3,600,000

[a] The present value of $1 million due at the end of 40 (six-month) periods at the yield rate of 6% per period

[b] The present value of $65,000 per period for 40 (six-month) periods at the yield rate of 6% per period

Instructions

(a) Discuss the conceptual merit(s) of each of the three date-of-issue balance sheet presentations shown above.

(b) Explain why investors would pay $1,075,230 for bonds that have a maturity value of only $1 million.

(c) Assuming that, at any date during the life of the bonds, a discount rate is needed to calculate the carrying value of the obligations that arise from a bond issue, discuss the conceptual merit(s) of using the following for this purpose:

    1. The coupon or nominal rate

    2. The effective or yield rate at date of issue

(d) If the obligations arising from these bonds are to be carried at their present value and this is calculated according to the current market rate of interest, how would the bond valuation at dates after the date of issue be affected by an increase or a decrease in the market rate of interest?

WA14-2   Thompson Limited (a private company with no published credit rating) completed several transactions during 2011. In January, the company purchased under contract a machine at a total price of $1.2 million, payable over five years with instalments of $240,000 per year with the first payment due January 1, 2011. The seller considered the transaction to be an instalment sale with the title transferring to Thompson at the time of the final payment. If the company had paid cash for the machine, all at the time of the sale, the machine would have cost $1,050,000. The company could have borrowed funds from the bank to buy the machine at an interest rate between 7% and 7.5%. It is expected that the machine will last 10 years.

On July 1, 2011, Thompson issued $10 million of general revenue bonds priced at 99 with a coupon of 10% payable July 1 and January 1 of each of the next 10 years to a small group of large institutional investors. As a result, the bonds are closely held. The July 1 interest was paid and on December 30 the company transferred $500,000 to the trustee, Holly Trust Limited, for payment of the January 1, 2012 interest.

Thompson purchased $500,000 (face value) of its 6% convertible bonds for $455,000. It expects to resell the bonds at a later date to a small group of private investors.

Finally, due to the economic recession, Thompson was able to obtain some government financing to assist with the purchase of some updated technology to be used in the plant. The government provided a $500,000 loan with an interest rate of 1% on December 31, 2011. The company must repay $500,000 in five years: December 31, 2016. Interest payments of $5,000 are due for the next five years, starting on December 31, 2012. The company could have borrowed a similar amount of funds for an interest rate of 6% on December 31, 2011.

Instructions

(a) As Thompson's accountant, prepare journal entries for the machine purchase and the government loan transactions described above. As Thompson is a private company, indicate any differences in treatment that might arise under PE GAAP and IFRS. For any fair value discussions, outline the level of fair value hierarchy that has been used.

(b) Having prepared the balance sheet as at December 31, 2011, you have presented it to the company president. You are asked the following questions about it. Answer these questions by writing a brief paragraph that justifies your treatment of the items in the balance sheet.

    1. Why is the new machine being valued at $1,050,000 on the books, when we are paying $1.2 million in total? Why has depreciation been charged on equipment being purchased under contract? Title has not yet passed to the company and, therefore, the equipment is not yet our asset. Would it not be more correct for the company to show on the left side of the balance sheet only the amount that has been paid to date instead of showing the full contract price on the left side and the unpaid portion on the right side? After all, the seller considers the transaction an instalment sale.

    2. Bond interest is shown as a current liability. Did we not pay our trustee, Holly Trust Limited, the full amount of interest that is due this period?

    3. The repurchased bonds (sometimes referred to as treasury bonds) are shown as a deduction from bonds payable issued. Why are they not shown as an asset since they can be sold again? Are they the same as bonds of other companies that we hold as investments?

    4. What is this government grant showing on the balance sheet? We received a loan, not a grant, since we have to pay it back. Why is the government loan showing substantially less than the $500,000 that we will have to repay?

WA14-3   **Part I** The appropriate method of amortizing a premium or discount on issuance of bonds is the effective interest method under IFRS. PE GAAP allows either the effective interest rate or the straight-line method.

Part II Gains or losses from the early extinguishment of debt that is refunded can theoretically be accounted for in three ways:

1. They can be amortized over the remaining life of old debt.

2. They can be amortized over the life of the new debt issue.

3. They can be recognized in the period of extinguishment.

Instructions—Part I

(a) What is the effective interest method of amortization and what are the differences and similarities between it and the straight-line method of amortization?

(b) How is interest calculated using the effective interest method? Why and how do amounts that are obtained using the effective interest method differ from amounts that are calculated under the straight-line method?

Instructions—Part II

(a) Provide supporting arguments for each of the three theoretical methods of accounting for gains and losses from the early extinguishment of debt.

(b) Which of the above methods is generally accepted as the appropriate amount of gain or loss that should be shown in a company's financial statements?

WA14-4

Instructions

Write a brief essay highlighting the differences between IFRS and accounting standards for private enterprises noted in this chapter, discussing the conceptual justification for each. As part of this essay, include a discussion of the differences in capital disclosure requirements.

WA14-5   The IASB has been working on determining whether or not an entity's credit risk should be incorporated into the measurement of the liability. The Staff Paper that accompanies the Discussion Paper on Credit Risk in Liability Measurement, dated June 2009, outlines three reasons to support this treatment and three arguments cited against this treatment. (This paper is available at www.iasb.org.) The examples below clarify the issues being addressed.

The example given in the paper discusses a regular bond payable that will be settled in cash and will be valued using an effective rate of interest based on the market's assessment of credit risk and the entity's ability to pay. For example, this might be 7%: in other words, the company would have to pay 7% interest on these bonds and this is used as the effective interest rate to value these bonds at the time the bonds are issued. In addition, suppose that the company also has an asset retirement obligation that will be settled in the provision of services in the future. This will also require some outlay of cash in future and the value of the liability is determined by discounting these future cash flows using a discount rate that incorporates the time value of money and the risks specific to the liability. In many cases, this could be different from the 7% used for the bonds. Should the same discount rate, which incorporates credit risk, be used to determine this liability? Or should the asset retirement obligation be discounted using a default risk-free rate of interest?

Furthermore, as market rates change, should the value of the liabilities also be changing to reflect this? Let's say that the current market rate one year later required for the bond is 8% and this increase is due to a lower credit rating for the entity. Under current accounting standards, the bonds payable does not get revalued since it is reported at amortized cost. Should the bonds payable now be revalued and the effective interest rate changed? The asset retirement obligation would get revalued using the most current discount rates at each reporting period.

Instructions

(a) Explain the meaning of "non-performance risk."

(b) Using the example of a bond payable and an asset retirement obligation, discuss the arguments for and against incorporating credit risk into the measurement of liabilities.

(c) What are the alternatives for measuring liabilities?

Case

Refer to the Case Primer on the Student Website to help you answer these cases.

WILEY
PLUS
Case Primer

CA14-1   Pitt Corporation is interested in building a pop can manufacturing plant next to its existing plant in Montreal. The objective would be to ensure a steady supply of cans at a stable price and to minimize transportation costs. However, the company has been experiencing some financial problems and has been reluctant to borrow any additional cash to fund the project. The company is not concerned about the cash flow problems of making payments; instead, its real concern is the impact of adding long-term debt to its balance sheet.

The president of Pitt, Aidan O'Reilly, approached the president of Aluminum Can Corp. (ACC), its major supplier, to see if some agreement could be reached. ACC was anxious to work out an arrangement, since it seemed inevitable that Pitt would begin its own can production. ACC could not afford to lose the account.

After some discussion, a two-part plan was worked out. First ACC will construct a plant on Pitt's land next to the existing plant, and the plant will initially belong to ACC. Second, Pitt will sign a 20-year purchase agreement. Under the purchase agreement, Pitt will express its intention to buy all of its cans from ACC and pay a unit price that at normal capacity would cover labour and material, an operating management fee, and the debt service requirements on the new plant. The expected unit price, if transportation costs are taken into consideration, is lower than the current market price. If Pitt ends up not taking enough production in any specific year and if the excess cans cannot be sold at a high enough price on the open market, Pitt agrees to make up any cash shortage so that ACC can make the payments on its debt. The bank is willing to make a 20-year loan for the plant, taking the plant and the purchase agreement as collateral. At the end of 20 years, the plant will become Pitt's.

Instructions

Adopt the role of the controller and discuss the financial reporting issues. The company is a private company. (Hint: Use first principles.)

Integrated Cases

Real-World
Emphasis

IC14-1   **Great Canadian Gaming Corporation** (GCGC) has in the past been criticized for its aggressive accounting by the independent research firm Veritas Investment Research. The company's shares trade on the TSX and it operates casinos, racetracks, slot machines, and other entertainment venues.

In British Columbia, the provincial government helps casino operators expand by allowing casinos to keep an additional percentage of gambling revenues until an expansion has been paid for. For instance, if the casino operator spends additional funds on new slot machines, it can keep additional operating profits that would otherwise have been paid to the government. Sometimes, it takes many years for a casino to recoup such an investment. Casino companies also pay into a marketing fund of the provincial lottery corporation and these funds are used to advertise the casinos. GCGC capitalizes the amounts that it pays into the marketing fund.

The following is an excerpt from the notes to the 2008 financial statements of the company:

---

7. RIVER ROCK CANADA LINE PARKING GARAGE

In 2006, the Company entered into a letter of intent with the South Coast British Columbia Transportation Authority ("TransLink") and Canada Line Rapid Transit Inc. ("Canada Line") to build and operate a 1,200 stall multi-level parking garage at Bridgeport Station, across from the River Rock Casino Resort ("River Rock") in Richmond, British Columbia. On August 22, 2008, the Company entered into definitive agreements for this transaction.

Under the terms of the agreements, the Company will reserve 1,200 parking stalls for Canada Line passengers on weekdays between 5:30am and 7:00pm and 600 stalls for all other times. As compensation for the cost of providing these future parking services, TransLink has agreed to provide the Company with approximately 5 acres of land (with an estimated market value of $17.2), 2.6 acres of which is being used for the new parking garage, and $2.5 in cash of which $1.5 has been received as at December 31, 2008. The Company has received legal title to approximately 3.8 acres of the land. The remaining 1.2 acres will be transferred to the Company once the sub-division has been approved by the local municipality. The Company will also receive from TransLink a $2.0 cash payment for an option to purchase the portion of the parking garage used by the 1,200 stalls. TransLink may only exercise this option if certain events defined in the agreement occur. Examples of these include the relocation of the River Rock, or the Company failing to provide Canada Line's passengers access to the parking stalls as set out in the agreement.

Instructions

As an independent analyst, provide a critical analysis of the financial reporting issues related to the above.

IC14-2   Finishing International Enterprises (FIE), a private company based in Vancouver, is Canada's largest dealer of heavy equipment, such as tractors, grapple skidders, and backhoes. The company sells, rents, finances, and provides customer support for all of the heavy equipment it finances.

FIE is owned by Tony Finishing, who provides the strategic vision, while all of the accounting functions are the responsibility of Chen Yi, the controller. Tony has determined that FIE will be expanding into the United States next year. FIE has been able to reduce its debt load over the years but still relies heavily on its creditors for continued support and growth. The bank has never asked for an audit before, but recently, Tony met with the bank to make some routine changes to the banking agreement. He was told the company would have to provide audited statements for the year ended December 31, 2011, given its expansion into the United States. The bank has also stipulated that FIE must maintain a total debt-to-equity ratio of no more than 1 to 1 (i.e., for every $1 in equity, there should be no more than $1 in debt), where debt is defined as all liabilities, including payables and accruals.

Lento & Partners LLP (L&P) has been FIE's accountants for many years. It is now January 2012, and you are the senior accountant at L&P who has been responsible for FIE's year end in the past. Tony has asked you to come in before year end to help Chen establish accounting policies to ensure that FIE is in compliance with GAAP. You meet with Tony and Chen and note the following:

1. During the year, FIE sold 2,000 small tractors for $2,600 each, including a one-year warranty. Maintenance on each machine during the warranty period averages $380. During the year, actual warranty costs incurred were $180,000. FIE is currently using the cash basis to record the warranty expense.

2. On October 1, 2011, the provincial environment ministry identified FIE as a potentially responsible party in a chemical spill in its Hamilton warehouse. Management, along with legal counsel, has concluded that it is likely that they will be responsible for damages, and a reasonable range of these damages is $500,000 to $750,000. FIE's insurance policy of $1 million has a deductible clause of $250,000. Management has yet to record this transaction in the books.

3. The company purchased a new piece of machinery on January 1, 2011. The purchase was financed though an interest-free five-year loan, whereby it is required to pay back $500,000 in each year. Management recorded the asset and liability at $2.5 million in the books. Management was excited about this promotion as the interest rate normally charged on a similar loan would have been 9%. FIE uses the straight-line method to amortize the asset, which has a seven-year useful life.

4. On January 1, 2010, FIE constructed a warehouse on property it leased for a five-year period. FIE will be required to remove the warehouse and restore the property to its original condition at the end of the lease term. Inflation-adjusted costs of removing the warehouse and restoring the property are estimated to be $200,000. In 2010, management recorded a liability for $200,000 in the books. No additional entries have been made.

5. On January 1, 2011, FIE issued 30,000 redeemable and retractable preferred shares at a value of $10 per share. The shares are redeemable by FIE at any time after January 2015. The shares are retractable for $10 per share at any time up to January 2015, after which the retractable feature expires. The preferred shares require the payment of a mandatory dividend of $2 per share during the retraction period, after which the dividends become non-cumulative and non-mandatory (i.e., paid at the discretion of the board).

FIE's balance sheet reveals that the corporation has $1.6 million in debt and $2,850,000 in equity. Tony stated that since equity is greater than debt by $1,250,000, he is planning on paying a large $800,000 dividend on his common shares, which "will still allow the debt-to-equity ratio covenant (1:1) to be maintained." FIE's credit-adjusted risk-free rate is 8%.

Instructions

Provide a report to Tony and Chen outlining your recommendation on accounting policies and other important issues.

Research and Financial Analysis

RA14-1 Radiant Energy Corporation

Access the 2008 annual report for Radiant Energy Corporation for the year ended October 31, 2008, from SEDAR (www.sedar.com).

Real-World Emphasis

Instructions

(a) Review the Consolidated Statement of Loss for October 31, 2008. How much was the gain or loss on debt settlements for each of the years reported? For 2008, review the notes and give explanations of the gain or loss on settlement of debts that are provided in Notes 8, 9, and 11. (Note: you will have unreconciled differences that have no explanation provided.)

(b) Read Note 5 on Discontinued Operations (page 11). How much was the gain on debt settlement for 2008? Using the information in Notes 5 and 11, try to determine how the gains were determined. (Note: you will have unreconciled differences that have no explanation provided.)

RA14-2 Eastern Platinum Limited

Refer to the year-end financial statements and accompanying notes of Eastern Platinum Limited (Eastplats) presented at the end of this volume.

Real-World Emphasis

Instructions

Using ratio and other analyses, prepare an assessment of Eastplats' solvency and financial flexibility for the periods ended December 31, 2009, and December 31, 2008.

RA14-3 Loblaw Companies Limited and Empire Company Limited

Instructions

Access the financial statements for Loblaw Companies Limited for the year ended January 3, 2009, and Empire Company Limited for the year ended May 2, 2009, through SEDAR (www.sedar.com) and then answer the following questions.

Real-World Emphasis

(a) Calculate the debt-to-total-asset ratio and the times interest earned ratio for these two companies. Comment on the quality of these two ratios for both companies.

(b) What financial ratios do both companies use (look in the annual reports) to monitor and present their debt financial condition? Do both companies use the same ratios? Are the ratios calculated in the same way?

(c) Review the type of debt that each company has issued and provide a brief description of the nature of debt issued. What credit rating does each company have? (This can be found in the Management Discussion and Analysis section.) If the credit rating has changed, comment on why this has happened. Compare the debt ratings of the two companies and comment on whether this is what would be expected given the analysis done in part (a).

(d) Review each company's Capital Management Disclosure note. For each company, explain its objectives in managing the capital, what is included in capital and the total of managed capital, the key ratios that are monitored, and any covenants that are imposed on the company.

(e) Do the companies have any variable interest entities? If so, explain the nature of these entities and how they have been reported by the companies.

RA14-4 DBRS

DBRS is a large bond-rating agency in Canada.

Real-World Emphasis

Instructions

Access the agency's website at www.dbrs.com and answer the following.

(a) How does DBRS rate the debt of food retailer companies? In other words, what is its methodology? List the factors considered in assessing the general business risk profile, the general financial risk profile (specific ratios considered), and industry-specific factors.

(b) What ratings has DBRS given to Loblaw Companies Limited and Empire Company Limited?

(d) Comment on why the ratings in (c) might have been given.

(e) Is it possible to have different ratings on different debt instruments in the same company? Explain.

RA14-5 IASB/FASB Joint Projects

Recently the IASB has been working to determine how to report variable interest entities on financial statements.

Instructions

(a) What is a variable interest entity? Why is the accounting problematic? Provide three examples from various company reports.

(b) Review the IASB project on Consolidation. (The exposure draft issued in December 2008 is available at www.iasb.org.) What is the definition of "control" that is considered being proposed? Discuss the issues around the control of a structured entity. Why is it difficult to determine whether or not an entity has control over a variable interest entity? What types of facts and circumstances should be considered in determining control?

Cumulative Coverage: Chapters 13 and 14

The following information is obtained from the 2011 records of Chef's Spoon Incorporated, a company that produces high quality kitchenware. The company has a June 30 year end.

1. The total payroll of Chef's Spoon was $460,000 for the month of June 2011. Income taxes withheld were $110,000. The employment insurance is 1.98% for the employee and 1.4 times the employee premium for the employer. The CPP/QPP contributions are 4.95% for each. No employee earned more than the maximum insurable or pensionable earnings. Payroll is entered at the end of the month, and paid at the first of the next month. The remittance of taxes, CPP, and EI takes place the following month.

2. At the end of May, the vacation pay accrual account had a balance of $50,000. No vacations were taken in June and 70 employees who earned an average salary of $40,000 per year earned 4% vacation pay and another 20 employees earning an average of $125,000 annually qualify for 8% vacation pay.

3. In January 2011 a worker was injured in the factory in an accident partially the result of his own negligence. The worker has sued Chef's Spoon for $800,000. Legal counsel believes it is somewhat possible that the outcome of the suit will be unfavourable and that the settlement would cost the company from $250,000 to $500,000.

4. The company sued one of its suppliers for providing raw materials used in Chef's Spoon products that contained a highly toxic plastic, and it is involved in a pending court case. Chef's Spoon's lawyers believe it is likely that the company will be awarded damages of $1.5 million.

5. On February 1, the company purchased equipment for $90,000 from Culinary Universe Company, paying $30,000 in cash and giving a one-year, 8% note for the balance. This transaction has not been recorded by the company yet because the $30,000 cash payment was made by a personal cheque from a key shareholder. The shareholder is asking to be repaid for this amount by July 15.

6. In order to keep up with the competition, the company needed to modernize its operations by building a new warehouse and production facility. The company had been able to save

$1 million in cash but would need to come up with $4.2 million to finance the balance of the construction costs. After much analysis, the CEO made the decision to issue $4.2-million, 5-year, 6% bonds since it would be cheaper than getting a loan from the bank. The bonds were finally issued February 1, 2011, and would pay interest on February 1 and August 1. The bonds yield 5% and are callable at 103. The company uses the effective interest method to amortize bond discount and premium amounts.

7. During the 2011 fiscal year, the company opened its first retail store. This store sold products manufactured by Chef's Spoon, but also purchased from other suppliers of kitchen products. The retail store is located in a high traffic shopping mall, and the company signed the lease and took control of the space on July 1, 2010. After two months of renovation work, the store opened and has been very successful. Sales in the first 10 months of operations totalled $1,523,000. The lease agreement required monthly rental payments of $15,000 due at the beginning of each month, and, if the total store sales exceeded $1,250,000 during the lease year, the company is required to pay additional rent of 1% of sales over $1,250,000.

8. The retail store sells several premium kitchenware items and gives its customers a coupon with each premium kitchenware item sold. In return for three coupons, customers receive a complementary spice container that the company purchases for $1.20 each (and holds in its Spice Container Inventory account). Chef's Spoon's experience indicates that 60 percent of the coupons will be redeemed. During the 10 months ended June 30, 2011, 100,000 premium kitchenware items were sold, and 45,000 coupons were redeemed. As of June 30, no entries have been recorded with respect to the coupons.

Instructions

(a) For each transaction above, prepare the necessary journal entries to record the liability at year end, and any transactions that have not been properly recorded for the June 30, 2011 year end. If any transaction does not require an entry, explain in detail why no entry is needed. The company follows ASPE.

(b) On August 31, 2012, Chef's Spoon Inc. called 40% of the bonds payable. Prepare the required journal entry for the retirement on this date.

Shaw to Take on Canwest's TV Interests

CANWEST GLOBAL Communications Corp. underwent a financial reorganization in 2010 that saw its television network and related specialty channels go to Shaw Communications Inc.

Canwest and its subsidiary Canwest Limited Partnership started creditor protection proceedings in January 2010 under the *Companies' Creditors Arrangement Act* in order to implement a pre-packaged financial restructuring plan supported by more than 48% of the limited partnership's senior secured debt holders. It initiated a sale and investor solicitation process seeking buyers for or equity investment in its property, assets, and businesses, including various newspapers such as the *National Post*, *The Vancouver Sun*, *Calgary Herald*, *Edmonton Journal*, *Ottawa Citizen*, and *The Gazette*; and a digital media business consisting of approximately 50 websites including canada.com.

In February, Canwest and Shaw entered into a "subscription agreement" in which Shaw agreed to buy the corporation's television interests, which would give the cable TV distributor 80% of the voting interest and 20% of the equity interest in Canwest, upon its emergence from creditor protection. Canwest's newspaper chain was not part of the deal and would remain under bankruptcy protection. Shaw was prepared to fund cash payments to affected creditors and to Canwest's existing shareholders in exchange for additional equity securities of the restructured Canwest.

Under the terms of the recapitalization transaction, affected creditors that would have been entitled to receive at least 5% of the outstanding equity shares in a restructured Canwest would be able to choose to receive shares to satisfy their claims. Otherwise, they and all other affected creditors would receive cash. Existing Canwest shareholders would receive cash in exchange for their shares of Canwest.

After the reorganization is complete, the restructured Canwest will be delisted from the TSX Venture Exchange and will cease to be a reporting issuer under Canadian securities laws.■

Sources: Canwest Global Communications Corp. news releases, January 8, January 12, and February 12, 2010; Dana Flavelle and John Spears, "Shaw Buys Control of Canwest Global," thestar.com, February 12, 2010.

CHAPTER 15

Shareholders' Equity

Learning Objectives

After studying this chapter, you should be able to:

1. Discuss the characteristics of the corporate form of organization.

2. Identify the rights of shareholders.

3. Describe the major features of preferred shares.

4. Explain the accounting procedures for issuing shares.

5. Identify the major reasons for repurchasing shares.

6. Explain the accounting for the reacquisition and retirement of shares.

7. Explain the accounting for various forms of dividend distributions.

8. Explain the effects of different types of dividend preferences.

9. Distinguish between stock dividends and stock splits.

10. Understand the nature of other components of shareholders' equity.

11. Indicate how shareholders' equity is presented.

12. Analyze shareholders' equity.

13. Identify the major differences in accounting between accounting standards for private enterprises (ASPE/PE GAAP) and IFRS, and what changes are expected in the near future.

After studying the appendices to this chapter, you should be able to:

14. Explain the accounting for par value shares.

15. Explain the accounting for treasury shares.

16. Describe the accounting for a financial reorganization.

Preview of Chapter 15

Capital markets are highly important in any economy that functions based on private ownership rather than government ownership. The markets provide a forum where prices are established, and these prices then become signals and incentives that guide the allocation of the economy's financial resources. More and more individuals and entities are investing in the capital marketplace (which includes stock markets and exchanges, as well as other "arenas"). This chapter explains the various accounting issues for different types of shares or equity instruments[1] that corporations issue to raise funds in capital markets. The chapter also examines the accounting issues for retained earnings and other components of shareholders' equity.

The chapter is organized as follows:

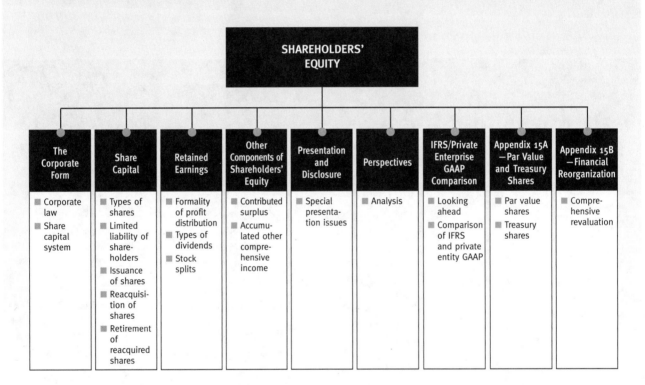

Owners' equity in a corporation is defined as shareholders' equity or corporate capital. The following four categories normally appear as part of shareholders' equity:

1. Common and/or preferred shares

2. Contributed surplus

---

[1] An equity instrument is "any contract that evidences a residual interest in the assets of an entity after deducting its liabilities," according to the *CICA Handbook*, Part II, Section 3856.05(e) and IAS 32.11. Most shares (including common and preferred shares) may be considered equity instruments; however, some preferred shares with debt-like features are classified as financial liabilities. The latter will be discussed in Chapter 16.

3. Retained earnings (deficit)

4. Accumulated other comprehensive income[2]

The first two categories, **shares** and **contributed surplus**, form the **contributed** capital. The third and fourth categories, **retained earnings** and **accumulated other comprehensive income**, represent the enterprise's **earned** capital.

Contributed (paid-in) capital is the total amount that shareholders provide to the corporation for it to use in the business. Earned capital is the capital that is created by the business operating profitably. It consists of all undistributed income that remains invested in the enterprise. The distinction between paid-in capital and earned capital is important from both legal and economic points of view. Legally, there are restrictions on **dividend payouts**. These will be discussed later in the chapter. Economically, management, shareholders, and others want to see earnings for the **corporation's continued existence and growth**. Maintaining the level of contributed capital is also a goal.[3]

Many different meanings are attached to the word "**capital**" because the word is often used differently by various user groups. In corporate **finance**, for example, capital commonly refers to **sources of financing**. In **law**, capital is considered that portion of shareholders' equity that is required by statute to **be retained in the business for the protection of creditors**. Accountants use the word "capital" when referring not only to shareholders' equity but also to long-term assets (capital assets) or when referring to whether an expenditure should be treated as an asset (capitalized) or expensed. It is therefore important to pay careful attention to **the context** in which the term is being used.

Law

Finance

THE CORPORATE FORM

Of the three **primary forms of business organization—the proprietorship, the partnership, and the corporation—**the most common form of business is the corporate form. Although the corporate form has several advantages (as well as disadvantages) over the other two forms, its main advantage is that a corporation is a **separate legal entity** and, therefore, the entity's owners have **greater legal protection** against lawsuits. An additional important advantage is that incorporation involves the issue of shares, which gives **access to capital markets** for companies that choose to raise funds in this way.

Corporations may be classified by the nature of their ownership as follows:

1. **Public-Sector Corporations**

   (a) Government units such as municipalities, cities, and so on. No shares issued.

   (b) Government business enterprises such as Canada Post and provincial liquor control boards (i.e., companies owned by the government and sometimes referred to as Crown corporations). Shares issued.

1 Objective
Discuss the characteristics of the corporate form of organization.

---

[2] Accumulated other comprehensive income is used under IFRS to accumulate other comprehensive income. Accounting standards for private enterprises (ASPE/PE GAAP) does not mention either other comprehensive income or accumulated other comprehensive income.

[3] In Chapter 4, the concept of capital maintenance was discussed. The idea of creating shareholder value is based on at least retaining contributed capital and, ideally, causing it to grow through earnings. Note that the AcSB is moving away from the earned versus contributed distinction, since it is felt that income that is included as other comprehensive income is not really earned by the company nor is it contributed. It might be argued, however, that the income is indeed earned since management made decisions that resulted in these gains/losses.

Significant Change

2. **Private-Sector Corporations**

    (a) Not-for-profit: entities whose main objective is something other than profit (such as churches, charities, and colleges). No shares issued.

    (b) For-profit: companies whose main objective is to increase shareholder value and maximize profit. Shares issued.

        (i) *Private companies:* companies whose shares are held by a few shareholders and are not available for public purchase. These entities are governed by shareholder agreements, which dictate who may hold the shares and how shareholder interests may or may not be transferred or disposed of. These entities may follow PE GAAP but are not required by law to do so. There are many private companies in Canada, from small businesses to large corporate entities such as McCain Foods and Maple Lodge Farms.

        (ii) *Public companies:* companies whose shares are available for purchase by the general public, normally through a stock exchange, such as the Toronto Stock Exchange, or stock market, such as the TSX Venture Exchange.[4] Public companies must follow IFRS,[5] securities laws that have been established by provincial securities commissions, corporations law, and finally rules established by the exchanges and markets that the companies trade on.

This book focuses on the for-profit type of corporation operating in the private sector. Public-sector entities and not-for-profit entities are generally covered in advanced accounting courses.

What Do the Numbers Mean?

Real-World Emphasis

Real estate income or investment trusts (REITs) have created a lot of interest in the last couple of decades. Legally, these funds are often set up as limited purpose **trust funds**. Their activities are restricted and they may be fairly passive. Under the *Income Tax Act*, as long as the trust pays out its income to investors, the trust itself pays no income tax. The investors then pay tax on the cash that they receive from the trust. Investors are referred to as "unitholders" and their liability is normally limited, but not as limited as the liability of a shareholder. It is important for the trustees of the trust (essentially the fund management) to ensure that the trust's insurance and other legal actions protect the unitholders adequately.

    REITs are special purpose entities (SPEs), otherwise known as variable interest entities (VIEs). Their special purpose is to invest in real estate. Canadian Real Estate Investment Trust is the oldest REIT in the Canadian marketplace, having listed on the TSX in 1993. The trust was started in 1984. In Canada, many other industries followed the REIT model in order to take advantage of the tax structure including trusts for Yellow Pages, Swiss Water Decaffeinated, Enbridge, Gateway Casino, Boston Pizza, and A&W. In 2007 the Canadian government passed a law to revoke the tax-free status of these non–real estate trusts. The change in law will be phased in gradually and by 2011 most of these entities will no longer be exempted from taxes. Many observers predict that the number of trusts will fall from just under 300 to about 50 by then, since it will be difficult for them to attract capital.

---

[4] An exchange is a more formal marketplace that is more heavily regulated and uses a specific mechanism for pricing shares. Companies must meet certain requirements to be initially listed on the exchange, and then must continue to meet these ongoing requirements to remain listed. These requirements include numerous financial tests, such as asset and revenue levels. Stock markets use a different share pricing mechanism and are generally less heavily regulated. There is a wide range of types of stock markets. At the more formal end of the range is NASDAQ and at the less formal end are Alternate Trading Systems (ATS), which are unstructured, Internet-based platforms or marketplaces where interested buyers and sellers may meet and trade shares. The TSX is the senior exchange in Canada, whereas the TSX Venture Exchange deals with smaller, start-up companies.

[5] Under Canadian corporations law, public companies must follow GAAP as set out in the *CICA Handbook*. As discussed in Chapter 1, IFRS is now incorporated into the *CICA Handbook* as Part I. This gives IFRS legal status in Canada.

Corporate Law

Anyone who wants to establish a corporation must submit articles of **incorporation** to the provincial or federal government, depending on whether the person wants to do business in a specific province or across Canada. Once the requirements are properly fulfilled, the corporation **charter** is issued, and the corporation is recognized as a **legal entity** under the relevant business corporations act. While the provisions of most provincial business corporations acts are reasonably similar, there are some differences. Consequently, when legal aspects are discussed in this chapter, the discussion will only consider the *Canada Business Corporations Act* (CBCA).

 Law

The articles of incorporation specify such things as the **company name**,[6] place of **registered office, classes and maximum numbers of shares authorized**, restrictions of **rights to transfer shares, number of directors**, and any restrictions on the **corporation's business**. Once it has been incorporated, share certificates are prepared and issued to shareholders.

Share Capital System

A corporation's share capital is generally made up of a large number of units or shares. These shares may be organized into groups or **classes**, such as Class A shares versus Class B shares. Within a class, each share is exactly equal to every other share. The number of shares that are possessed determines each owner's interest. If a company has only one class of shares and it is divided into 1,000 shares, a person owning 500 shares has one half of the corporation's ownership interest, and a person holding 10 shares would have a one-hundredth interest.

2 Objective
Identify the rights of shareholders.

Each share has certain rights and privileges that can only be restricted by provisions in the articles of incorporation. If there are no restrictive provisions, each share gives the following basic or inherent rights:

1. To share proportionately in **profits and losses**

2. To share proportionately in management (i.e., the share gives the **right to vote** for directors)

3. To share proportionately in the corporate **assets upon liquidation** of the corporation

The CBCA allows a corporation to assign a fourth right: this is the right to share proportionately in any new issues of shares of the same class. This right is known as a preemptive right.

The first three rights are expected in the ownership of any business; the last right may be used in a corporation to protect each shareholder's proportional interest in the enterprise. **The preemptive right protects an existing shareholder from the involuntary dilution of the shareholder's ownership interest**. What does this mean? It means that, without this right, the corporation would be able to issue additional shares without notifying the shareholders and at prices that were not favourable to the shareholders, which could result in the shareholders' specific percentage interest (the proportional ownership of the corporation) being reduced. Because the preemptive right that attaches to existing shares makes it inconvenient for corporations to make large issuances of additional shares, as they frequently do in acquiring other companies, many corporations have eliminated it.

The great advantage of the share system is that it makes it very easy to transfer an interest in a business from one individual to another. Individuals who own shares in a

---

[6] Under the CBCA, the name must include the words "Incorporated," "Limited," or "Corporation," or their respective short forms, in either English or French.

corporation may sell them to others **at any time** and **at any price** without obtaining the consent of the company or other shareholders. Each share is the personal property of the owner and may be disposed of at will.[7] For its part, the corporation is only required to maintain a list or **subsidiary ledger of shareholders**, which it needs as a guide to dividend payments, issuance of share rights, voting proxies, and similar elements. Because shares are so easily and frequently transferred, the corporation must update the subsidiary ledger of shareholders periodically, generally before every dividend payment or shareholders' meeting. Major stock exchanges require controls over record keeping that are costly for the typical corporation. As a result, companies generally **outsource** this task to **registrars and transfer agents** that specialize in providing services for recording and transferring shares.

SHARE CAPITAL

Types of Shares

Common Shares

Law

Underlying Concept

Common shares carry the risks and rewards of ownership.

In every corporation, there is one class of shares that represents the basic ownership interest. That class is called common shares. Common shares represent the **residual ownership interest** in the company, suffer the ultimate **risks** of loss, and receive the **benefits** of success. A common shareholder is not guaranteed annual dividends and is not guaranteed assets upon dissolution of the corporation. However, common shareholders generally **control** the corporation management through the **voting rights** attached to these shares.[8] They also tend to profit the most if the company is successful. If a corporation has only one authorized issue of capital shares, that issue is, by definition, common shares, and this is true even if the corporation's charter does not designate the shares as common.

Shares may be in-substance common shares. These are shares that, even though they have the same characteristics as common shares, cannot be or are not called common shares for legal purposes. The following should be considered when deciding whether to treat financial instruments as common shares for financial statement purposes.

- Subordination: The shares do not have a preferred rank over other shares for dividend distributions or for the distribution of company assets upon windup of the company.

- Risks and rewards of ownership: The shares participate in the earnings/losses of the company and the appreciation/depreciation in value of the company.

- Obligation to transfer value: These shares have no obligation to transfer value. Given that they represent a residual interest in the company, they only have value if the company's net assets have value.

- No other common shares: All shares in the class in question have the same features.

- Redemption: The shares are retractable/redeemable only upon windup of the company.[9]

---

[7] The company issuing the shares records a journal entry only when it first issues and sells the shares and when it buys them back. When shareholders buy and sell shares from each other, this is not recorded by the company.

[8] Shareholders who have voting rights elect the board of directors to make major decisions for them.

[9] IAS 32.16A to D and *CICA Handbook*, Part II, Section 3856.A27 and A28.

Preferred Shares

In an effort to attract all types of investors, corporations may offer two or more classes of shares, with each class having **different rights or privileges**. In the preceding section, it was pointed out that each share of a particular issue has the same rights as other shares of the same issue and that there are three inherent rights in every share. By special contracts between the corporation and its shareholders, **some of these rights may be sacrificed by the shareholder in return for other special rights or privileges**. This creates special classes of shares, and because they have certain preferential rights, such shares are usually called preferred shares. In return for any special preference, the preferred shareholder is always required to sacrifice some of the basic rights of common share interests.

A common type of preference is to give the preferred shareholders a **priority claim on earnings and on assets (upon dissolution of the company)**, compared with the claims of the common shareholders. This means that preferred shareholders are assured a dividend, usually at a stated rate, before any amount may be distributed to the common shareholders. They are also assured that if the company goes bankrupt, they rank before the common shareholders in terms of getting their money back. In return for this preference, the preferred shareholders may sacrifice the right to a voice in management or the right to share in profits beyond the stated rate.

Instead of issuing both common and preferred shares, a company may accomplish much the same thing by issuing two classes of shares, Class A shares and Class B shares. In this case, one of the issues is the common share and the other issue has some preference or restriction of basic shareholder rights. Illustration 15-1 is an excerpt about share classes from the notes to the financial statements of Four Seasons Hotels Inc.

11. Shareholders' equity:

(a) Capital stock:

Authorized:

3,725,698 Variable Multiple Voting Shares ("VMVS"), entitling the holder to that number of votes that results in the aggregate votes attaching to the VMVS, representing approximately 65% of the votes attaching to the VMVS and the LVS, in aggregate, which, at December 31, 2006, was 16.45 votes (2005 - 16.09 votes) per VMVS. Changes in the number of votes attaching to the VMVS necessary to maintain this level will occur concurrently with the issue of additional LVS, regardless of whether the number of votes attaching to the VMVS is further increased.

VMVS are convertible into LVS on a one-for-one basis at the option of the holder. The shares automatically convert into LVS upon any transfer outside of the family of Mr. Isadore Sharp, the Chief Executive Officer of FSHI, except a transfer of a majority of the shares to a purchaser who makes an equivalent offer to purchase all outstanding VMVS and LVS.

Unlimited LVS, voting (one vote per share) and ranking equally with the VMVS as to distributions on liquidation, dissolution or winding-up of FSHI.

Unlimited First Preference Shares and Second Preference Shares, issuable in series, non-voting and ranking prior to all other shares with respect to payment of dividends and distributions on liquidation or winding-up of FSHI. The dividend rate, redemption and conversion rights, if any, are to be determined prior to issuance by the directors of FSHI.

In this case, the existence of the VMVS allowed the Sharp family to keep control of the company while it was public, as it would always have the majority of the votes. The company went private in 2007 and the limited voting shareholders were bought out. The following is an excerpt from the material change report filed by the company with the OSC.

3 Objective
Describe the major features of preferred shares.

What Do the Numbers Mean?

Real-World Emphasis

Illustration 15-1

Excerpt from the Notes to the Financial Statements of Four Seasons Hotels Inc.

On April 26, 2007, Four Seasons announced that it had completed the previously announced plan of arrangement pursuant to which Four Seasons was taken private by affiliates of Cascade Investment, L.L.C. (an entity owned by William H. Gates III), Kingdom Hotels International (a company owned by a trust created by His Royal Highness Prince Alwaleed Bin Talal Bin Abdulaziz Alsaud for the benefit of HRH Prince Alwaleed and his family) and Isadore Sharp. Holders of Limited Voting Shares will receive US$82.00 cash per share.

Preferred shares may be issued with a dividend preference that is expressed as a **percentage of the par value or issue price**. Thus, holders of 8% preferred shares issued at $100 are entitled to an annual dividend of $8 per share. This share is commonly referred to as an 8% preferred share. The dividend may also be expressed as a **specific dollar amount** per share; for example, $8 per share. A preference as to dividends does not assure shareholders that dividends will be paid; it only means that the stated dividend rate or amount that applies to the preferred share must be paid before any dividends can be paid on the common shares.

Features of Preferred Shares.   A corporation may attach whatever preferences or restrictions it desires to a preferred share issue, and in whatever combination, as long as the corporation does not specifically violate its incorporation law, and it may issue more than one class of preferred share. Some preferred share features include the following:

1. **Cumulative.** Dividends on cumulative shares that are not paid in any given year are known as dividends in arrears and must be made up in a later year before any profits can be distributed to common shareholders. There is no liability, however, until the board of directors **declares** a dividend. According to common law custom, if the corporate charter is silent about the cumulative feature, the preferred share is considered cumulative.

2. **Convertible.** This feature allows the company or holder to exchange the shares for common shares at a predetermined ratio. Thus, the shareholder has the relative security of the preferred share yet may participate in the appreciation of the company by converting preferred shares to common shares.

Finance

3. **Callable/Redeemable.** The issuing corporation can **call** or redeem at its option (through its own choice) the outstanding preferred shares at specified future dates and at stipulated prices. The callable feature permits the corporation to use the capital that it has obtained through the issuance of such shares until the need has passed or having the issued shares is no longer advantageous. The existence of a call price or prices tends to set a ceiling on the market value of the preferred shares unless they are convertible into common shares. When a preferred share is called for redemption, any dividends in arrears must be paid.

4. **Retractable.** The holders of the shares can **put** or sell their shares to the company, normally after having given adequate notice, and the company must then pay the holders for the shares. The retraction option makes this instrument more attractive to the holders as it gives them more choice.

5. **Participating.** Holders of participating preferred shares share (at the same rate as common shareholders) in any profit distributions that are higher than the prescribed rate of the preferred share. That is, a 5% preferred share, if it is fully participating, will receive not only its 5% return, but also dividends at the same rate that is paid to common shareholders if the latter are paid amounts higher than 5% of par or stated value. Note that participating preferred shares are not always fully participating. That is, they can also be partially participating. For example, provision may be made that a 5% preferred share will be participating up to a maximum total rate of 10%, after

which it ceases to participate in additional profit distributions; or a 5% preferred share may participate only in additional profit distributions that are in excess of a 9% dividend rate on the common share.

Ethics

Preferred shares are often issued instead of debt because a company's debt-to-equity ratio has become too high. The issuing company may structure the instrument such that its legal form represents shares in hopes of avoiding treating the instruments as debt on the financial statements. Accounting for preferred shares can be complex because of their many and varied features and because accountants must account for the instruments in accordance with their economic substance as opposed to their legal form. Chapter 16 discusses the more complex aspects of these financial instruments.

Finally, issuances of common, preferred, or other shares may be made through **private placements**[10] as opposed to through the stock markets and exchanges. The difference between the two is that the company remains private if it has no shares that trade on a stock market or exchange and it is therefore not subject to the same regulations as a public company.

Limited Liability of Shareholders

Those who own a corporation—the shareholders—contribute either property or services to the enterprise in return for ownership shares. **The property or service that has been invested in the enterprise is the limit on a shareholder's possible loss.** That is, if the corporation has losses that are so large that the remaining assets are not enough to pay creditors, the creditors have **no recourse** against the personal assets of the individual shareholders. This is unlike in a partnership or proprietorship, where the owners' personal assets can be accessed to satisfy unpaid claims against the enterprise. Ownership interests in a corporation are legally protected against such a contingency. The shareholders are thus said to have limited liability: they may lose their investment but they cannot lose **more** than their investment.

Law

While the corporate form of organization gives the protective feature of limited liability to the shareholders, it also stipulates that the amount of the shareholders' investment that is represented in share capital accounts cannot be withdrawn unless all prior claims on corporate assets have been paid. This means that the corporation **must maintain this capital until dissolution of the corporation.** Upon dissolution, it must then satisfy all prior claims before distributing any amounts to the shareholders. In a proprietorship or partnership, the owners or partners may withdraw amounts whenever and in whatever amount they choose because all their personal assets can be accessed to protect creditors from loss.

Shares issued by corporations must be **without a nominal or par value** (according to the CBCA). This simply means that all proceeds from the issuance of the shares must be credited to the appropriate share capital account and become part of the shareholders' investment referred to above. In some provinces and in the United States, shares that have a fixed per-share amount printed on each share certificate are called par value shares.[11]

---

[10] The term "private placement" refers to a situation where the shares are only offered privately to a select group of interested investors. In other words, they are not floated for sale on the stock exchange or market. Private placements are often directed at large institutional or individual investors.

[11] *Accounting Trends and Techniques 2007* indicates that its 600 surveyed companies reported 655 issues of outstanding common stock, 579 par value issues, and 55 no-par issues; 8 of the no-par issues were shown at their stated (assigned) values. *Financial Reporting in Canada, 2005* (Toronto, CICA) Chapter 32 noted that, out of 200 companies surveyed, 99.5% either made no reference to par or stated value or they indicated that the shares were without par or stated value.

Par value has only one real significance: it establishes the **maximum responsibility of a shareholder in the event of insolvency** (i.e., in jurisdictions where the concept of par value is legally allowed) or other involuntary dissolution. Par value is thus not value in the ordinary sense of the word. It is merely an amount per share that has been determined by the incorporators of the company and stated in the corporation charter or certificate of incorporation.

Issuance of Shares

Objective 4
Explain the accounting procedures for issuing shares.

In issuing shares, the following procedures are followed: First, the shares must be **authorized**. Next, shares are **offered for sale** and contracts to sell shares are entered into. Finally, amounts to be received for the shares are **collected** and the **shares are issued**.

Share Issue—Basic

Finance

Shares are sold for the price that they will bring in the marketplace. Normally the company will hire specialists (e.g., investment banking firms, underwriters) to value the shares[12] and help **promote and sell them**. As payment for their services, the underwriters take as commission a percentage of the total share consideration that is received from investors. The **net** amount that is received by the company becomes the credit to common or preferred shares. For example, assume that Video Electronics Corporation is organized with 10,000 authorized common shares. The only entry that is made for this authorization is a memorandum entry. There is no journal entry since there is no monetary amount involved in the authorization. If 500 shares are then issued for cash at $10 per share, the entry should be:

A   = L +   SE
+5,000   +5,000

Cash flows: ↑ 5,000 inflow

| Cash | 5,000 | |
| Common Shares | | 5,000 |

Entries for preferred shares are the same as for common shares as long as the preferred shares are classified as equity.[13] As par value shares are relatively uncommon in Canada, the issues that are unique to them are covered in Appendix 15A.

Shares Sold on a Subscription Basis

Underlying Concept
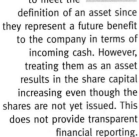

Subscriptions receivable appear to meet the definition of an asset since they represent a future benefit to the company in terms of incoming cash. However, treating them as an asset results in the share capital increasing even though the shares are not yet issued. This does not provide transparent financial reporting.

Shares may also be sold on a subscription basis. Sales of subscribed shares generally occur when new, small companies go public or when corporations offer shares to employees in order to have employees participate in the business ownership. When a share is sold on a subscription basis, its full price is not received immediately. Normally, only a **partial payment** is made, and the share is not issued until the full subscription price is received.

The journal entries for handling shares that are sold on a subscription basis are illustrated by the following example. Assume that Lubradite Corp. offers shares on a subscription basis to selected individuals, giving them the right to purchase 10 common shares at a price of $20 per share. Fifty individuals accept the company's offer and agree to

---

[12] The shares are valued using valuation models that include expected future cash flow or operating income from the company. This often results in pressure on the income numbers since a higher income results in a higher share price.

[13] Some of the more complex features of preferred shares that were noted earlier can result in their being accounted for as debt.

pay 50% down and the remaining 50% at the end of six months. Lubradite's entries would be as follows:

At date of issuance		
Subscriptions Receivable (10 × $20 × 50)	10,000	
Common Shares Subscribed		10,000
(To record receipt of subscriptions for 500 shares.)		
Cash	5,000	
Subscriptions Receivable		5,000
(To record receipt of first instalment representing 50% of total due on subscribed shares.)		

A = L + SE
            0

Cash flows: No effect

A = L + SE
+5,000   +5,000

Cash flows: ↑ 5,000 inflow

In Canada, whether the Subscriptions Receivable account should be presented as an asset or a contra equity account is a matter of professional judgement, although conceptually, it makes sense to record as a reduction of equity. In the United States, the SEC requires the latter treatment. PE GAAP provides guidance for share purchase loan receivables as discussed on page 970.

Ethics

    When the final payment is received and the shares are issued, the entries are:

Six months later		
Cash	5,000	
Subscriptions Receivable		5,000
(To record receipt of final instalment on subscribed shares.)		
Common Shares Subscribed	10,000	
Common Shares		10,000
(To record issuance of 500 shares upon receipt of final instalment from subscribers.)		

A = L + SE
+5,000   +5,000

Cash flows: ↑ 5,000 inflow

A = L + SE
            0

Cash flows: No effect

Defaulted Subscription Accounts

Sometimes a subscriber is unable to pay all instalments and therefore defaults on the agreement. The question is what to do with the balance of the subscription account and the amount that has already been paid in. The answer is determined by the subscription contract, corporate policy, and any applicable law of the jurisdiction of incorporation. The possibilities include returning the amount already paid by the subscriber (possibly after deducting some expenses), treating the amount paid as forfeited and therefore transferring it to the Contributed Surplus account, or issuing fewer shares to the subscriber so that the number of shares issued is equivalent to what the subscription payments already received would have paid for fully.

    For example, assume that a subscriber to 50 Lubradite common shares defaults on the final payment. If the subscription contract stated that amounts paid by the defaulting subscriber would be refunded, Lubradite would make the following entry when the default occurs, assuming that the refund was to be paid at a later date:

Common Shares Subscribed	1,000	
Subscriptions Receivable		500
Accounts Payable		500
(To record default on 50 shares subscribed for $20 each and on which 50% had been paid.)		

A = L + SE
    +500   −500

Cash flows: No effect

If the amount paid by the subscriber were forfeited, there would be a $500 credit to Contributed Surplus as this is a **capital transaction**.

Shares Issued with Other Securities (Lump-Sum Sales)

Generally, corporations sell each **class of shares** separately so that they can determine the proceeds for each class and, ordinarily, even for each lot of shares in the class. Occasionally, however, two or more classes of securities are issued for a single payment or **lump sum**. It is not uncommon, for example, for more than one type or class of security to be issued in the acquisition of another company. The accounting problem in such lump-sum sales is the allocation of the proceeds among the several classes of securities, or determining how to measure the separate classes of shares.

Two possible measurement techniques are used: (1) the **relative fair value method** and (2) the **residual value method**.[14] These measurement techniques are often used in accounting, even for issues that are not lump-sum share issues. The first method values each instrument according to its fair value and then proportionally allocates the lump-sum value to each instrument. The second method values one instrument (often the one that is easier to measure) and then allocates the rest of the amount to the other instrument. These same techniques are used to bifurcate bundled sales for revenue recognition purposes (Chapter 6), allocate the costs of inventory in basket/lump-sum purchases (Chapters 8 and 10), and measure the respective parts of compound financial instruments (Chapter 16). Examples of these methods are presented in Chapters 6, 8, 10, and 16.

Costs of Issuing Shares

Direct incremental costs that are incurred to sell shares, such as underwriting costs, accounting and legal fees, printing costs, and taxes, should be reported as a reduction of the amounts paid in. **Issue costs** are therefore debited to Share Capital because they are **capital transactions** rather than **operating transactions**.

Management salaries and other **indirect costs** related to the share issue should be expensed as they are incurred because it is difficult to establish a relationship between these costs and the proceeds that are received from the sale. In addition, corporations annually incur costs for maintaining the shareholders' records and handling ownership transfers. These recurring costs, which are mainly registrar and transfer agents' fees, are normally charged to expense in the period in which they are incurred.

What Do the Numbers Mean?

Real-World Emphasis

Aside from the case of shares sold on a subscription basis, sometimes companies issue shares but do not require the purchaser to pay right away. This may be the case for instances where the company lends its employees money to buy new shares. There is controversy in such cases about how this receivable should be presented on the balance sheet. Some argue that the receivable should be recorded as an asset like other receivables. Others argue that the receivable should be reported as a reduction of shareholders' equity.

The SEC requires companies to use the latter approach (similar to the accounting for shares sold on a subscription basis) because the risk of collection on these types of transactions is often very high. IFRS is not definitive on this issue but the conceptual framework would support presenting the receivables as a reduction of shareholders' equity unless there is substantial evidence that the company is not at risk for declines in the value of the shares and there is reasonable assurance that the company will collect the amount in cash. PE GAAP specifically supports this approach.[15]

---

[14] These methods are sometimes referred to as the proportional method (relative fair value method) and the incremental method (residual method). Conceptually, the relative fair value method is preferable where fair values are available.

[15] *CICA Handbook*, Part II, Section 3251.10.

Unfortunately, this issue surfaced with Enron. Starting in early 2000, Enron issued shares of its common stock to four "special purpose entities" and in exchange it received notes receivable. Enron then increased its assets and shareholders' equity, a move the company subsequently called an accounting error. As a result, Enron's 2000 audited financial statements overstated assets and shareholders' equity by $172 million. Enron's 2001 unaudited statements overstated them by $828 million. The $1-billion overstatement was 8.5% of Enron's previously reported equity as at June 30—a material amount.

Source: Adapted from Jonathan Weil, "Basic Accounting Tripped Up Enron," "Financial Statements Didn't Add Up," and "Auditors Overlook Simple Rule," *Wall Street Journal*, November 11, 2001, p. C1.

Ethics

Reacquisition of Shares

It is not unusual for companies to buy back their own shares. In fact, share buybacks now exceed dividends as a form of distribution to shareholders.[16] While corporations have varied reasons for purchasing their outstanding shares, some of the major ones are as follows:

5 Objective
Identify the major reasons for repurchasing shares.

1. **To increase earnings per share and return on equity.** By reducing shares outstanding and reducing shareholders' equity, certain performance ratios are often improved, such as earnings per share and return on equity.

2. **To provide shares for employee share compensation contracts or to meet potential merger needs.** Honeywell Inc. reported that part of its purchase of 1 million common shares was to be used for employee share option contracts. Other companies acquire shares to have them available for business acquisitions.

Real-World Emphasis

3. **To stop takeover attempts or to reduce the number of shareholders.** By reducing the number of shares that are held by the public, the current owners and management may find it easier to keep outsiders from gaining control or significant influence. When Ted Turner tried to acquire CBS, CBS started a substantial buyback of its shares.

4. **To make a market in the share.** By purchasing shares in the marketplace, management creates a demand that may stabilize the share price or, in fact, increase it. Over a period of four years, Nexfor Inc., a large North American producer of building materials, repurchased and cancelled 15.5 million shares for $122 million (representing 10% of the company's shares). The company commented that the shares were undervalued and represented a good deal.

5. **To return cash to shareholders.** Pierre Choquette, president and CEO of Methanex, commented in the 2003 annual report: "We continued with our longstanding commitment to return excess cash to our shareholders by distributing close to $150 million in 2003. Over the past four years, nearly half of the more than $1 billion of cash flows from operations has been distributed to shareholders in the form of dividends and share repurchases. This has been accomplished without compromising financial flexibility or our ability to execute strategic projects."

6. **To create value for the shareholders.** If the company feels that the shares are trading at a value that is less than the company's perceived true value, it may buy back the shares as an investment. On October 25, 2006, Brick Brewing Co. Limited

---

[16] At the beginning of the 1990s, the situation was just the opposite; that is, share buybacks were less than half the level of dividends. Companies are extremely reluctant to reduce or eliminate their dividends because they believe that this action is viewed negatively by the market. On the other hand, many companies are no longer raising their dividend per share at the same percentage rate as increases in earnings per share, which effectively reduces the dividend payout over time.

announced that it planned to buy back just over 1 million shares, representing 5% of its outstanding shares. The reason given was that the company felt that the current market price for the shares did not indicate the underlying value of the company and the buyback therefore amounted to an attractive investment at the time.

Some publicly held corporations have chosen to go private; that is, they decided to eliminate public (outside) ownership by purchasing their entire float of outstanding shares. This is often done through a leveraged buyout, which is when management or another employee group purchases the company shares and finances the purchase by using the company assets as collateral.

Once shares are reacquired, they may either be **retired** or held in the treasury for **reissue**. If they are not retired, such shares are referred to as treasury shares. Technically, a treasury share is a corporation's own share that has been reacquired after having been issued and fully paid. In Canada, the CBCA, with minor exceptions, requires that repurchased shares be cancelled and, if the articles limit the number of authorized shares, that the shares be restored to the status of authorized but unissued shares. While some provincial jurisdictions do allow treasury shares to exist, such shares remain relatively uncommon in Canada.[17] This is unlike the United States, where many companies hold treasury shares.[18] Appendix 15A briefly reviews the accounting for these shares.

Retirement of Reacquired Shares

Objective 6
Explain the accounting for the reacquisition and retirement of shares.

When shares are purchased or redeemed by the issuing corporation, it is likely that the price paid will differ from the amount that was received for the shares when they were issued. As this is a **capital transaction**, any gains or losses are booked through equity (rather than through the income statement).

If the acquisition cost is greater than the original cost, then the acquisition cost should be allocated as follows:

1. First, to **share capital**, in an amount equal to the par, stated, or assigned value of the shares

2. Second, for any excess after the first allocation, to **contributed surplus**, to the extent that the contributed surplus was created by a net excess of proceeds over cost on a cancellation or resale of shares of the same class

3. Third, for any excess after the second allocation, to **contributed surplus** in an amount equal to the pro rata share of the portion of contributed surplus that arose from transactions, other than those above, in the same class of shares

4. Last, for any excess after the third allocation, to **retained earnings**

If the acquisition cost is less than the original cost, then the acquisition cost should be allocated as follows:

1. First, to **share capital**, in an amount equal to the par, stated, or assigned value of the shares

2. Second, for the difference after the first allocation, to **contributed surplus**

For shares with **no par value** (i.e., for most shares in Canada), the assigned value is equal to the **average per share amount** in the account for that class of shares at the transaction

---

[17] According to *Financial Reporting in Canada, 2005* (CICA: Toronto), only 13 out of 200 companies reported treasury shares (Chapter 32).

[18] *Accounting Trends and Techniques 2007* indicates that, of its selected list of 600 companies, 389 carried common stock in treasury.

date. The difference between the stated or assigned value and the lower cost of acquisition is credited to contributed surplus and is seen as a contribution by the original shareholders that now accrues to the remaining shareholders.

Applying the formulas noted above, in cases where the acquisition cost is **greater than the assigned cost**, this would normally result in debiting share capital (step 1) and retained earnings (step 4). Contributed Surplus would only be adjusted if there were a **prior balance** in the Contributed Surplus account that related to the shares that are being acquired.

To illustrate, assume that Cooke Corporation has the following in its shareholders' equity accounts:

Share capital:	
Class A, 10,500 shares issued and outstanding	$ 63,000
Class B, 50,000 shares issued and outstanding	100,000
Total share capital	163,000
Retained earnings	300,000
Total shareholders' equity	$463,000

On January 30, 2011, Cooke purchased and cancelled 500 Class A shares at a cost of $4 per share. The required entry is:

Class A Shares [500 ($63,000 ÷ 10,500)]	3,000	
Cash		2,000
Contributed Surplus*		1,000

*Average per share amount (assigned value) = $63,000 ÷ 10,500 = $6. Excess of assigned value over reacquisition cost = $6 − 4 = $2 per share for 500 shares.

A	=	L	+	SE
−2,000				−2,000

Cash flows: ↓ 2,000 outflow

On September 10, 2011, the company purchased and cancelled an additional 1,000 Class A shares. The purchase cost was $8 per share. The transaction is recorded as follows:

Class A shares [1,000 ($60,000 ÷ 10,000)]	6,000	
Contributed Surplus*	1,000	
Retained Earnings	1,000	
Cash		8,000

* Equals the whole amount of the excess from the above

A	=	L	+	SE
−8,000				−8,000

Cash flows: ↓ 8,000 outflow

RETAINED EARNINGS

The basic source of retained earnings—earnings retained for use in the business—is income from operations. Shareholders assume the greatest **risk** in enterprise operations as shareholders' equity declines with any losses. In return, they also reap the **rewards**, sharing in any profits resulting from enterprise activities. Any income that is not distributed among the shareholders becomes additional shareholders' equity. Net income includes a considerable variety of income sources. These include the enterprise's main operation (such as manufacturing and selling a product), plus any secondary activities (such as disposing of scrap or renting out unused space), plus the results of unusual items. All lead to net income that increases retained earnings. The more common items that either increase or decrease retained earnings are expressed in account form in Illustration 15-2.

Illustration 15-2

Transactions That Affect Retained Earnings

RETAINED EARNINGS	
Debits	**Credits**
1. Net loss	1. Net income
2. Prior period adjustments (error corrections) and certain changes in accounting principle	2. Prior period adjustments (error corrections) and certain changes in accounting principle
3. Cash, property, and most stock dividends	3. Adjustments due to financial reorganization
4. Some treasury share transactions	

Formality of Profit Distribution

Legality of Dividend Distribution

Law

An enterprise's owners decide what to do with profits that are realized through operations. Profits may be **left in the business** for a future expansion or simply to have a margin of safety, or they may be **withdrawn and divided among the owners**. In a proprietorship or partnership, this decision is made by the owner or owners informally and requires no specific action. In a partnership, the partnership agreement would usually specify how profits or losses are to be shared. In a corporation, however, profit distribution (referred to as dividends) is controlled by certain **legal restrictions**. Not all shares carry the right to receive dividends.

First, no amounts may be distributed among the owners unless the **corporate capital is kept intact**. This restriction is based on the presumption that there have to be sufficient net assets or security left in the corporation to satisfy the liability holders after any assets have been distributed to shareholders as dividends. Various tests of **corporate solvency** have been used over the years. Under the CBCA, dividends may not be declared or paid if there are reasonable grounds for believing that (1) the corporation is, or would be after the dividend, unable to pay its liabilities as they become due; or (2) the realizable value of the corporation's assets would, as a result of the dividend, be less than the total of its liabilities and stated or legal capital for all classes of shares.

Second, distributions to shareholders must be **formally approved by the board of directors** and recorded in the minutes of the board's meetings. As the top executive body in the corporation, the board of directors must make certain that no distributions are made to shareholders that are not justified by profits, and directors are generally held personally liable to creditors if liabilities cannot be paid because company assets have been illegally paid out to shareholders.

Third, dividends must be in **full agreement with preferences created by the share capital contracts**. Once the corporation has entered into contracts with various classes of shareholders, the stipulations of such contracts must be followed.

Financial Condition and Dividend Distributions

Determining the proper amount of dividends to pay is a difficult financial management decision. Companies that are paying dividends are extremely reluctant to reduce or eliminate their dividends, because they believe that this action could be viewed negatively by the securities market. As a consequence, companies that have been paying cash dividends will make every effort to continue to do so.

Very few companies pay dividends in amounts equal to their legally available retained earnings. The major reasons that companies have for limiting the dividend amount are as follows:

1. Agreements (bond covenants) with specific creditors that require all or a portion of the earnings to be retained in the form of assets in order to build up additional protection against possible loss

Finance

2. The desire to retain assets that would otherwise be paid out as dividends, in order to finance growth or expansion. This is sometimes called internal financing, reinvesting earnings, or ploughing the profits back into the business.

3. The desire to smooth out dividend payments from year to year by accumulating earnings in good years and using such accumulated earnings as a basis for dividends in bad years

4. The desire to build up a cushion or buffer against possible losses or errors in the calculation of profits

Dividend policies vary among corporations. Some older, well-established firms take pride in a long, unbroken string of quarterly dividend payments.[19] They would lower or not declare the dividend only if they were forced to do so by a sustained decline in earnings or a critical shortage of cash. Growth companies, on the other hand, pay few or no cash dividends because their policy is to expand as rapidly as internal and external financing permit. Investors in these companies hope that their share price will appreciate in value and that they will realize a profit when they sell their shares (i.e., they hope to benefit from capital appreciation).

Good business management means paying attention to more than just the legality of dividend distributions. **Economic conditions** also need to be considered and, most importantly, liquidity. Assume the following extreme situation:

Balance Sheet			
Plant assets	$500,000	Share capital	$400,000
		Retained earnings	100,000
	$500,000		$500,000

The company has a retained earnings credit balance, and generally, unless the balance is restricted, the company can therefore declare a dividend of $100,000. But because all its assets are plant assets and used in operations, paying a cash dividend of $100,000 would require selling plant assets or borrowing.

Even if we assume a balance sheet that shows current assets, the question remains whether those cash assets are needed for other purposes.

Balance Sheet				
Cash	$100,000	Current liabilities		$ 60,000
Plant assets	460,000	Share capital	$400,000	
		Retained earnings	100,000	500,000
	$560,000			$560,000

---

[19] **Bank of Montreal** and **Bank of Nova Scotia** have been paying dividends consistently since 1829 and 1833, respectively.

The existence of current liabilities implies very strongly that some of the cash is needed to meet current debts as they mature. In addition, day-to-day cash requirements for payrolls and other expenditures that are not included in current liabilities also require cash.

Thus, before a dividend is declared, management must consider the **availability of funds to pay the dividend**. Other demands for cash should also perhaps be investigated by preparing a cash **forecast**. A dividend should not be paid unless both the present and future financial position appear to justify the distribution. Directors must also consider the effect of inflation and replacement costs before making a dividend commitment. During a period of significant inflation, some costs that are charged to expense under historical cost accounting are understated in terms of **comparative purchasing power** (i.e., the amounts represent older dollars since the asset was purchased earlier when the dollars were likely worth more). Because these costs are not adjusted for inflation, income is therefore **overstated**.

The non-payment of dividends can also significantly impact a company. For instance, Torstar Corporation has Class B shares that are normally non-voting, but if the company does not pay dividends for eight consecutive quarters, the shares then have voting rights.

Types of Dividends

There are basically two classes of dividends:

1. Those that are a return **on** capital (a share of the earnings)

2. Those that are a return **of** capital, referred to as liquidating dividends

The natural expectation of any shareholder who receives a dividend is that the corporation has operated successfully and that he or she is receiving a share of its earnings. A liquidating dividend should therefore be adequately described in the financial statements. This type of dividend will be discussed in greater depth later in the chapter.

Dividends are commonly paid in cash but occasionally they are paid in shares or other assets. **Dividends generally reduce the total shareholders' equity in the corporation**, because the equity is reduced, through an immediate or promised future distribution of assets. Stock dividends are different, however. When a stock dividend is declared, the corporation does not pay out assets or incur a liability. It issues additional shares to each shareholder and nothing more. Both types of dividends are discussed below.

Dividends—Cash

The board of directors votes on the declaration of dividends and if the resolution is properly approved, the dividend is declared. Before the dividend is paid, a current list of shareholders must be prepared. For this reason, there is usually a time lag between the declaration and payment. A resolution approved at the January 10 (**date of declaration**) meeting of the board of directors might be declared payable on February 5 (**date of payment**) to all shareholders of record on January 25 (**date of record**).[20]

The period from January 10 to January 25 gives time for any transfers in process to be completed and registered with the transfer agent. The time from January 25 to February 5

---

[20] Determining the date of record is not always straightforward. It is generally the date prior to what is known as the ex-dividend date. Theoretically, the ex-dividend date is the day after the date of record. However, to allow time for the transfer of shares, stock exchanges generally advance the ex-dividend date by two to four days. Therefore, a party who owns the shares on the day prior to the expressed ex-dividend date receives the dividend, and a party who buys the stock on or after the ex-dividend date does not receive the dividend. Between the declaration date and the ex-dividend date, the market price of the shares includes the dividend.

provides an opportunity for the transfer agent or accounting department, depending on who does this work, to prepare a list of shareholders as at January 25 and to prepare and mail dividend cheques.

To illustrate the declaration and payment of an ordinary dividend that is payable in cash, assume that on June 10 Rajah Corp. declared a cash dividend of 50 cents a share on 1.8 million shares and payable on July 16 to all shareholders of record on June 24. The following entries are required:

At date of declaration (June 10)		
Retained Earnings (Cash Dividends Declared)	900,000	
Dividends Payable		900,000
At date of record (June 24)		
No entry		
At date of payment (July 16)		
Dividends Payable	900,000	
Cash		900,000

A = L + SE
+900,000 −900,000
Cash flows: No effect

A = L + SE
−900,000 −900,000
Cash flows: ↓ 900,000 outflow

To have a ledger account that shows the amount of dividends declared during the year, the company can create and debit Cash Dividends Declared instead of debiting Retained Earnings at the time of declaration. This account is then closed to Retained Earnings at year end. Dividends may be declared either as a certain percentage of par or stated value, such as a 6% dividend, or as an amount per share, such as 60 cents per share. In the first case, the rate is multiplied by the par or stated value of outstanding shares to get the total dividend; in the second, the amount per share is multiplied by the number of shares outstanding. **Cash dividends are not declared and paid on treasury shares since the shares are owned by the company itself.**

Dividends in Kind

Dividends that are payable in corporation assets other than cash are called property dividends or dividends in kind. Property dividends may be merchandise, real estate, or investments, or whatever form the board of directors designates. Because of the obvious difficulties of dividing units and delivering them to shareholders, the usual property dividend is in the form of securities of other companies that the distributing corporation holds as an investment.

A property dividend is a non-reciprocal transfer of non-monetary assets between an enterprise and its owners. These dividends should generally be measured at the fair value of the asset that is given up unless they are considered to represent a spinoff or other form of restructuring or liquidation, in which case they should be recorded at the carrying value of the non-monetary assets or liabilities transferred.[21] No gain or loss would be recorded in the second instance.

When the U.S. Supreme Court decided that **DuPont's** 23% investment in **General Motors** violated antitrust laws, DuPont was ordered to divest itself of the GM shares within 10 years. The shares represented 63 million of GM's 281 million shares then outstanding. DuPont could not sell the shares in one block of 63 million, nor could it sell 6 million shares annually for the next 10 years without severely depressing the value of the

What Do the Numbers Mean?

---

[21] *CICA Handbook*, Part II, Section 3831.14. Note that if the transaction is with a controlling shareholder, then *CICA Handbook*, Part II, Section 3840 dealing with related parties applies. IFRS does not allow related party transactions to be remeasured.

GM shares. At that time, the entire yearly trading volume in GM shares was not even 6 million shares. DuPont solved its problem by declaring a property dividend and distributing the GM shares as a dividend to its own shareholders.

The **fair value** of the non-monetary asset that is distributed is measured by the amount that could be realized if the asset were sold outright at or near the time of the declaration. This amount should be determined by referring to estimated realizable values in cash transactions of the same or similar assets, quoted market prices, independent appraisals, and other available evidence. Often a gain is recognized at this point (on the appreciation of the asset value just prior to the dividend).

Stock Dividends

If management wants to "capitalize" part of the earnings (i.e., reclassify amounts from earned to contributed capital) so that earnings are retained in the business on a permanent basis, it may issue a stock dividend. In this case, **no assets are distributed** and each shareholder has exactly the same proportionate interest in the corporation, and the same total book value, after the issue of the stock dividend as before the declaration. The book value per share is lower, however, because there are now more shares being held.

There is no clear guidance on how to account for stock dividends. The major issue is whether or not they should be treated in the same way as other dividends.[22] If they are treated like other dividends, they should be recorded by debiting Retained Earnings and crediting Share Capital. In terms of measuring the transaction, fair value would be used (measured by looking at the market value of the shares issued, at the declaration date).

Where the stock dividends give the option to the holder to receive them in cash or shares, the stock dividend is considered a non-monetary transaction under GAAP and **must** be treated as a regular dividend, valued at fair value.[23] Where there is no option to receive the dividend in cash, GAAP is silent; however, the CBCA states that for stock dividends, the declared amount of the dividend shall be added to the stated capital account. The CBCA does not allow shares to be issued until they are fully paid for in an amount not less than the fair equivalent of money that the corporation would have received had the shares been issued for cash. Therefore, if the company is incorporated under the CBCA, all stock dividends should be recorded as dividends and measured at fair value.

To illustrate a stock dividend, assume that a corporation has 1,000 common shares outstanding and retained earnings of $50,000. If the corporation declares a 10% stock dividend, it issues 100 additional shares to current shareholders. If it is assumed that the shares' fair value at the time of the stock dividend is $130 per share and that the shareholders had the option to take the dividend in cash but chose not to, the entry is:

A = L + SE
                 0

Cash flows: No effect

At date of declaration		
Retained Earnings (Stock Dividends Declared)	13,000	
Common Shares		13,000

If the dividend is declared before it is distributed, then the journal entry would be a debit to Retained Earnings and a credit to Dividends Payable. Upon share issue, the journal entry would be a debit to Dividends Payable and a credit to Common Shares. Note that no

---

[22] From a tax perspective, the Canada Revenue Agency treats stock dividends received in the same way as other dividends.

[23] *CICA Handbook*, Part II, Section 3831, paras. .05 (f)(ii) and .06.

asset or liability has been affected. The entry merely reflects a reclassification of shareholders' equity. No matter what the fair value is at the time of the stock dividend, each shareholder retains the same proportionate interest in the corporation. Illustration 15-3 proves this point.

Illustration 15-3

Effects of a Stock Dividend

Before dividend:

Common shares, 1,000 shares	$100,000
Retained earnings	50,000
Total shareholders' equity	$150,000

Shareholders' interests:

A—400 shares, 40% interest, book value	$ 60,000
B—500 shares, 50% interest, book value	75,000
C—100 shares, 10% interest, book value	15,000
	$150,000

After declaration and distribution of 10% stock dividend:

If fair value ($130) is used as basis for entry

Shareholders' common shares, 1,100 shares	$113,000
Retained earnings ($50,000 – $13,000)	37,000
Total shareholders' equity	$150,000

Shareholders' interests:

A—440 shares, 40% interest, book value	$ 60,000
B—550 shares, 50% interest, book value	75,000
C—110 shares, 10% interest, book value	15,000
	$150,000

Note, in Illustration 15-3, that the total shareholders' equity has not changed as a result of the stock dividend. Also note that the proportion of the total shares outstanding that is held by each shareholder is unchanged.

Liquidating Dividends

Some corporations use contributed surplus as a basis for dividends. Without proper disclosure of this fact, shareholders may wrongly believe that the corporation has been paying dividends out of profits. We mentioned in Chapter 11 that companies in the extractive industries may pay dividends equal to the total of accumulated income and depletion. The portion of these dividends that is in excess of accumulated income represents a return of part of the shareholders' investment.

For example, assume that McChesney Mines Inc. issued a dividend to its common shareholders of $1.2 million. The cash dividend announcement noted that $900,000 should be considered income and the remainder a return of capital. The entry is:

At date of declaration		
Retained Earnings	900,000	
Contributed Surplus	300,000	
Dividends Payable		1,200,000

A	=	L	+	SE
				+1,200,000 −1,200,000

Cash flows: No effect

In some cases, management may simply decide to cease business and declare a liquidating dividend. In these cases, liquidation may take place over several years to ensure an orderly and fair sale of all assets.

Effects of Dividend Preferences

Objective 8
Explain the effects of different types of dividend preferences.

The examples that now follow illustrate the effects of various dividend preferences on dividend distributions to common and preferred shareholders. Assume that in a given year, $50,000 is to be distributed as cash dividends, outstanding common shares have a value of $400,000, and 1,000 $6-preferred shares are outstanding (issued at $100,000). Dividends would be distributed to each class as follows, under the particular assumptions:

1. If the preferred shares are non-cumulative and non-participating:

Illustration 15-4

Dividend Distribution, Non-Cumulative and Non-Participating Preferred

	Preferred	Common	Total
$6 × 1,000	$6,000	$ –0–	$ 6,000
The remainder to common	–0–	44,000	44,000
Totals	$6,000	$44,000	$50,000

2. If the preferred shares are cumulative and non-participating, and dividends were not paid on the preferred shares in the preceding two years:

Illustration 15-5

Dividend Distribution, Cumulative and Non-Participating Preferred, with Dividends in Arrears

	Preferred	Common	Total
Dividends in arrears,			
$6 × 1,000 for 2 years	$12,000	$ –0–	$12,000
Current year's dividend, $6 × 1,000	6,000	–0–	6,000
The remainder to common	–0–	32,000	32,000
Totals	$18,000	$32,000	$50,000

3. If the preferred shares are non-cumulative and fully participating:[24]

Illustration 15-6

Dividend Distribution, Non-Cumulative and Fully Participating Preferred

	Preferred	Common	Total
Current year's dividend, $6	$ 6,000	$24,000	$30,000
Participating dividend—pro rata	4,000	16,000	20,000
Totals	$10,000	$40,000	$50,000

The participating dividend was determined as follows:

---

[24] When preferred shares are participating, there may be different agreements on how the participation feature is executed. However, if there is no specific agreement, the following procedure is recommended:
(a) After the preferred shares are assigned their current year's dividend, the common shares will receive a "like" percentage. In example (3), this amounts to 6% of $400,000.
(b) If there is a remainder of declared dividends for participation by the preferred and common shares, this remainder will be shared in proportion to the carrying value in each share class. In example (3), the proportion is:

Preferred $100,000/500,000 × $20,000 = $4,000

Common $400,000/500,000 × $20,000 = $16,000

Current year's dividend:
    Preferred, $6 × 1,000 = $6,000
       Common, 6% of $400,000 = $24,000 (= a like amount) $ 30,000
    The 6% represents $6,000 on pref. shares/ $100,000
    Amount available for participation ($50,000 − $30,000) $ 20,000
    Carrying value of shares that are to participate ($100,000 + $400,000) $500,000
    Rate of participation ($20,000/$500,000)   4%
Participating dividend:
    Preferred (4% of $100,000) $ 4,000
    Common (4% of $400,000)   16,000
                                                                  $ 20,000

4. If the preferred shares are cumulative and fully participating, and if dividends were not paid on the preferred shares in the preceding two years (the same procedure that was used in example (3) is used again here to carry out the participation feature):

	Preferred	Common	Total
Dividends in arrears,			
$6 × 1,000 for 2 years	$12,000	$ –0–	$12,000
Current year's dividend, $6	6,000	24,000	30,000
Participating dividend, 1.6%			
($8,000/$500,000)	1,600	6,400	8,000
Totals	$19,600	$30,400	$50,000

Illustration 15-7

Dividend Distribution, Cumulative and Fully Participating Preferred, with Dividends in Arrears

Stock Splits

If a company has undistributed earnings over several successive years and has thus accumulated a sizeable balance in retained earnings, the market value of its outstanding shares is likely to increase. Shares that were issued at prices of less than $50 a share can easily reach a market value of more than $200 a share. The higher the share's market price, the harder it is for some investors to purchase it. The managements of many corporations believe that, for better public relations, the corporation's shares should be widely owned. They wish, therefore, to have a market price that is low enough to be affordable to the majority of potential investors.

9 Objective
Distinguish between stock dividends and stock splits.

To reduce the market value of shares, the common device that is used is the stock split.[25] From an accounting standpoint, no entry is recorded for a stock split; a memorandum note, however, is made to indicate that the number of shares has increased.

Differences between a Stock Split and Stock Dividend

From a **legal** standpoint, a stock split is distinguished from a **stock dividend**, because a stock split results in an increase in the number of shares outstanding with no change in the share capital or the retained earnings amounts. As noted earlier, legally, the **stock**

---

[25] Some companies use reverse stock splits. A reverse stock split reduces the number of shares outstanding and increases the price per share. This technique is used when the share price is unusually low. Note that a company's debt covenants or listing requirements might require that the company's shares trade at a certain level. A reverse stock split might help get the price up to where the company needs it to be.

dividend may result in an increase in both the number of shares outstanding and the share capital while reducing the retained earnings (depending on the legal jurisdiction).

A stock dividend, like a stock split, may also be used to increase the share's marketability. If the stock dividend is large, it has the same effect on market price as a stock split. In the United States, the profession has taken the position that, whenever additional shares are issued to reduce the unit market price, then the distribution more closely resembles a stock split than a stock dividend. **This effect usually results only if the number of shares issued is more than 20%–25% of the number of shares that were previously outstanding.**[26] A stock dividend of more than 20%–25% of the number of shares previously outstanding is called a large stock dividend.

There is no specific guidance under PE GAAP or IFRS. In principle, it must be determined whether the large stock dividend is more like a stock split or a dividend (from an economic perspective). Professional judgement must be used in determining this.

Legal requirements must be considered as a constraint. As noted earlier, for instance, companies that are incorporated under the CBCA must measure any newly issued shares at market (including those issued as stock dividends). This means, therefore, that all stock dividends for such companies are to be treated as dividends and measured at market. On the other hand, in jurisdictions where legal requirements for stated share capital values are not a constraint, the following options would be available for stock dividends:

1. Treat as a dividend (debit retained earnings and credit common shares) and measure at either the market value of the shares or their par or stated value

2. Treat as a stock split (memo entry only)

The SEC supports the second approach for large stock dividends of more than 25%. Illustration 15-8 summarizes and compares the effects of dividends and stock splits.

Illustration 15-8

Effects of Dividends and Stock Splits

Declaration and Distribution of Dividends and Stock Splits

Effect on:	Declaration of Cash Dividend	Payment of Cash Dividend	(Small) Stock Dividend	(Large) Stock Dividend	Stock Split
Retained earnings	Decrease	—	Decrease[a]	Decrease[b]	—
Common shares	—	—	Increase	Increase	—
Contributed surplus	—	—	—	—	—
Total shareholders' equity	Decrease	—	—	—	—
Working capital	Decrease	—	—	—	—
Total assets	—	Decrease	—	—	—
Number of shares outstanding	—	—	Increase	Increase	Increase

[a] Generally equal to market value of shares.

[b] May be equal to par, stated value of shares or market value. Note that some companies may choose to interpret GAAP such that the dividend is treated as a stock split. In Canada, this is a matter of judgement and is governed by legal requirements regarding the value of stated capital and economic substance.

---

[26] *Accounting Research and Terminology Bulletin No. 43*, par. 13.

OTHER COMPONENTS OF SHAREHOLDERS' EQUITY

Contributed Surplus

The term "surplus" is used in an accounting sense to designate the excess of net assets over the total paid-in par or stated value of a corporation's shares. As previously mentioned, this surplus is further divided between earned surplus (retained earnings) and contributed surplus. Contributed surplus may be affected by a variety of transactions or events, as Illustration 15-9 shows.

10 Objective
Understand the nature of other components of shareholders' equity.

- Par value share issue and/or retirement (see Appendix 15A)
- Treasury share transactions (see Appendix 15A)
- Liquidating dividends
- Financial reorganizations (see Appendix 15B)
- Stock options and warrants (Chapter 16)
- Issue of convertible debt (Chapter 16)
- Share subscriptions forfeited
- Donated assets by a shareholder
- Redemption or conversion of shares

Illustration 15-9

Transactions That May Affect Contributed Surplus

Accumulated Other Comprehensive Income

Accumulated other comprehensive income is the cumulative change in equity that is due to the revenues and expenses, and gains and losses that stem from non-shareholder transactions that are excluded from the calculation of net income. It is considered to represent earned income as well. Comprehensive income was previously discussed in Chapters 4, 5, 9, and 10 and will be referred to in Chapter 16. Recall that the concept of comprehensive income is not referred to under PE GAAP.

Significant Change

PRESENTATION AND DISCLOSURE

Numerous disclosures are required under GAAP.[27] For example, basic disclosures include the amounts of authorized share capital, issued share capital, and changes in capital since the last balance sheet date.[28] Under IFRS, the company is required to disclose the changes in all equity accounts including retained earnings, accumulated other comprehensive income, and share capital since the last balance sheet date in the statement of changes in equity (instead of the statements of retained earnings). In many corporations, there are restrictions on retained earnings or dividends and these should be disclosed. The note disclosure should reveal the source of the restriction, pertinent provisions, and the amount of retained earnings that is restricted, or the amount that is unrestricted. Restrictions may be based on maintaining a certain retained earnings balance, the corporation's ability to observe certain working capital requirements, additional borrowing, and other considerations.

11 Objective
Indicate how shareholders' equity is presented.

The following details would normally be disclosed on the face of the balance sheet, in the statement of changes in shareholders' equity (under IFRS), or in the notes:

---

[27] *CICA Handbook*, Part II, Sections 3240, 3251, and 3856 and IFRS 7.

[28] *CICA Handbook*, Part II, Section 3240.20 –.22 and IAS 1.79.

1. The authorized number of shares or a statement noting that this is unlimited

2. The existence of unique rights (e.g., dividend preferences and the amounts of such dividends, redemption and/or retraction privileges, conversion rights, whether or not the dividends are cumulative)

3. The number of shares issued and amount received

4. Whether the shares are par value or no par value

5. The amount of any dividends in arrears for cumulative preferred shares

6. Details of changes during the year (presented in the statement of changes in equity under IFRS)

7. Restrictions on retained earnings

Real-World Emphasis

Under IFRS, companies must also disclose information about their objectives, policies, and processes for managing capital. They must include summary quantitative data about what the company manages as capital and about any changes in capital.[29] The reason for requiring this disclosure is to give users of financial statements better insight into the way the company's capital is managed. Additional detailed disclosures are required under IFRS. Illustration 15-10 shows a sample of these types of disclosures for Methanex.[30]

Illustration 15-10

Example of Required Capital Disclosures

14. Capital disclosures:

The Company's objectives in managing its liquidity and capital are to safeguard the Company's ability to continue as a going concern, to provide financial capacity and flexibility to meet its strategic objectives, to provide an adequate return to shareholders commensurate with the level of risk, and to return excess cash through a combination of dividends and share repurchases.

As at December 31	2008	2007
Liquidity:		
Cash and cash equivalents	$ 328,430	$ 488,224
Undrawn Egypt limited recourse debt facilities	209,426	413,426
Undrawn credit facilities	250,000	250,000
Total liquidity	$ 787,856	$ 1,151,650
Capitalization:		
Unsecured notes	$ 346,700	$ 346,116
Limited recourse debt facilities, including current portion	440,603	251,153
Total debt	787,303	597,269
Non-controlling interest	108,728	41,258
Shareholders' equity	1,281,900	1,335,354
Total capitalization	$ 2,177,931	$ 1,973,881
Total debt to capitalization[1]	36%	30%
Net debt to capitalization[2]	25%	7%

[1] Total debt divided by total capitalization.

[2] Total debt less cash and cash equivalents divided by total capitalization less cash and cash equivalents.

---

[29] IAS 1.134 – .138.

[30] These financial statements were prepared in accordance with pre-2011 Canadian GAAP (which essentially mirrored the requirements under IFRS). Private entity GAAP does not explicitly require these disclosures. This is because many private companies have shares that are closely held and therefore this type of information is not necessarily required in the statements.

The Company manages its liquidity and capital structure and makes adjustments to it in light of changes to economic conditions, the underlying risks inherent in its operations and capital requirements to maintain and grow its operations. The strategies employed by the Company include the issue or repayment of general corporate debt, the issue of project debt, the payment of dividends and the repurchase of shares.

The Company is not subject to any statutory capital requirements and has no commitments to sell or otherwise issue common shares.

The undrawn credit facility in the amount of $250 million is provided by highly rated financial institutions, expires in mid-2010 and is subject to certain financial covenants including an EBITDA to interest coverage ratio and a debt to capitalization ratio.

The credit ratings for the Company's unsecured notes are as follows:

Standard and Poor's Rating Services	BBB– (stable)
Moody's Investor Services	Ba1 (stable)
Fitch Ratings	BBB (negative)

Illustration 15-11 provides an example of a shareholders' equity section on the balance sheet.

FROST CORPORATION
Shareholders' Equity
December 31, 2011

Share Capital	
Preferred shares, $7 cumulative, 100,000 shares authorized, 30,000 shares issued and outstanding	$ 3,000,000
Common shares, no par, stated value $10 per share, 500,000 shares authorized, 400,000 shares issued	4,000,000
Common stock dividend distributable, 20,000 shares	200,000
Total share capital	7,200,000
Contributed Surplus	990,000
Total paid-in capital	8,190,000
Retained Earnings	2,200,000
Accumulated Other Comprehensive Income	2,160,000
Total shareholders' equity	$12,550,000

Illustration 15-11

Example of Shareholders' Equity Section

Changes in shareholders' equity are generally presented in a table in the notes to the financial statements under PE GAAP. Under IFRS, these changes are presented in a statement of changes in shareholders' equity. Illustration 15-12 shows the changes in shareholders' equity for **Methanex**.

Real-World Emphasis

Significant
Change

Consolidated Statements of Shareholders' Equity
(thousands of US dollars, except number of common shares)

	Number of Common Shares	Capital Stock	Contributed Surplus	Retained Earnings	Accumulated Other Comprehensive Income (Loss) (note 1(m))	Total Shareholders' Equity
Balance, December 31, 2006	105,800,942	$ 474,739	$ 10,346	$ 724,166	$ —	$ 1,209,251
Net income	—	—	—	375,667	—	375,667
Compensation expense recorded for stock options	—	—	9,343	—	—	9,343
Issue of shares on exercise of stock options	552,175	9,520	—	—	—	9,520
Reclassification of grant date fair value on exercise of stock options	—	3,668	(3,668)	—	—	—
Payment for shares repurchased	(8,042,863)	(36,287)	—	(168,440)	—	(204,727)
Dividend payments	—	—	—	(55,045)	—	(55,045)
Other comprehensive loss	—	—	—	—	(8,655)	(8,655)
Balance, December 31, 2007	98,310,254	451,640	16,021	876,348	(8,655)	1,335,354
Net income	—	—	—	172,298	—	172,298
Compensation expense recorded for stock options	—	—	8,225	—	—	8,225
Issue of shares on exercise of stock options	224,016	4,075	—	—	—	4,075
Reclassification of grant date fair value on exercise of stock options	—	1,577	(1,577)	—	—	—
Payment for shares repurchased	(6,502,878)	(30,027)	—	(119,829)	—	(149,856)
Dividend payments	—	—	—	(56,833)	—	(56,833)
Other comprehensive loss	—	—	—	—	(31,363)	(31,363)
Balance, December 31, 2008	92,031,392	$ 427,265	$ 22,669	$ 871,984	$ (40,018)	$ 1,281,900

Illustration 15-12

Example of Disclosures of Changes in Shareholders' Equity—Methanex

Special Presentation Issues

Preferred shares generally have no maturity date, and there is therefore no legal obligation to pay the preferred shareholder. As a result, preferred shares have historically been classified as part of shareholders' equity. In the past decade, more and more issuances of preferred shares have features that make the security more like a debt instrument (where there is a legal obligation to pay) than an equity instrument. As mentioned earlier, these will be covered in Chapter 16.

PERSPECTIVES

Analysis

Objective 12
Analyze shareholders' equity.

Several ratios use amounts related to shareholders' equity to evaluate a company's **profitability** and **long-term solvency**. The following four ratios are discussed and illustrated next: (1) rate of return on common shareholders' equity, (2) payout ratio, (3) price earnings ratio, and (4) book value per share.

Financial Statement Analysis Primer

Rate of Return on Common Shareholders' Equity

A widely used ratio that measures profitability from the common shareholders' viewpoint is rate of return on common shareholders' equity. This ratio shows how many dollars of net income were earned for each dollar invested by the owners. It is calculated by dividing net income less preferred dividends by average common shareholders' equity. For example, assume that Garber Inc. had net income of $360,000, declared and paid preferred dividends of $54,000, and had average common shareholders' equity of $2,550,000. Garber's ratio is calculated as follows:

$$\text{Rate of return on common shareholders' equity} = \frac{\text{Net income} - \text{Preferred dividends}}{\text{Average common shareholders' equity}}$$

$$= \frac{\$360,000 - \$54,000}{\$2,550,000}$$

$$= 12\%$$

As the calculation shows, because preferred shares are present, preferred dividends are deducted from net income to calculate the income available to common shareholders. Similarly, the carrying value of preferred shares is deducted from total shareholders' equity to arrive at the amount of common shareholders' equity used in this ratio.

When the rate of return on total assets is lower than the rate of return on the common shareholders' investment, the company is said to be trading on the equity at a gain. Trading on the equity describes the practice of using borrowed money at fixed interest rates or issuing preferred shares with constant dividend rates in hopes of obtaining a higher rate of return on the money used (this is sometimes also referred to as **leverage**). As these debt issues must be given a prior claim on some or all of the corporate assets, the advantage to common shareholders of trading on the equity must come from borrowing at a lower rate of interest than the rate of return that is obtained on the assets that have been borrowed. If this can be done, the capital obtained from bondholders or preferred shareholders earns enough to pay the interest or preferred dividends and to leave a margin for the common shareholders. When this occurs, trading on the equity is profitable.

Payout Ratio

Another measure of profitability is the payout ratio, which is the ratio of cash dividends to net income. If preferred shares are outstanding, this ratio is calculated for common shareholders by dividing cash dividends paid to common shareholders by net income available to common shareholders. Assuming that Troy Corp. has cash dividends of $100,000, net income of $500,000, and no preferred shares outstanding, the payout ratio is calculated as follows:

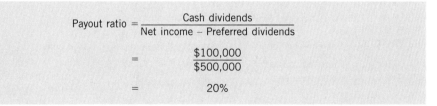

$$\text{Payout ratio} = \frac{\text{Cash dividends}}{\text{Net income} - \text{Preferred dividends}}$$

$$= \frac{\$100,000}{\$500,000}$$

$$= 20\%$$

For some investors, it is important that the payout be high enough to provide a good yield on the shares.[31] However, payout ratios have declined for many companies because many investors now view appreciation in the share value as more important than the dividend amount.

---

[31] Another closely watched ratio is the dividend yield: the cash dividend per share divided by the market price. This ratio gives investors some idea of the rate of return that will be received in the form of cash dividends.

Price Earnings Ratio

The price earnings (P/E) ratio is an oft-quoted statistic that analysts use in discussing the investment potential of an enterprise. It is calculated by dividing the share's market price by the earnings per share. For example, assuming that Soreson Corp. has a market price of $50 and earnings per share of $4, its price earnings ratio would be calculated as follows:

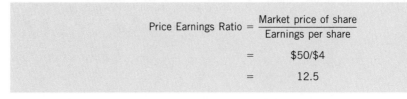

$$\text{Price Earnings Ratio} = \frac{\text{Market price of share}}{\text{Earnings per share}}$$

$$= \$50/\$4$$

$$= 12.5$$

Book Value per Share

A much-used basis for evaluating net worth is the **book** or **equity value per share**. Book value per share is the amount that each share would receive if the company were liquidated, **based on the amounts reported on the balance sheet**. However, the figure loses much of its relevance if the valuations on the balance sheet do not approximate the fair market value of the assets. Book value per share is calculated by dividing common shareholders' equity by the number of common shares outstanding. Assuming that Chen Corporation's common shareholders' equity is $1 million and it has 100,000 shares outstanding, its book value per share is calculated as follows:

$$\text{Book value per share} = \frac{\text{Common shareholders' equity}}{\text{Number of shares outstanding}}$$

$$= \frac{\$1,000,000}{100,000}$$

$$= \$10 \text{ per share}$$

When preferred shares are present, an analysis of the covenants involving the preferred shares should be studied. If preferred dividends are in arrears, the preferred shares are participating, or the preferred shares have a redemption or liquidating value higher than their carrying amount, retained earnings must be allocated between the preferred and common shareholders in calculating book value.

To illustrate, assume that the following situation exists.

Shareholders' equity	Preferred	Common
Preferred shares, 5%	$300,000	
Common shares		$400,000
Contributed surplus		37,500
Retained earnings	–0–	162,582
Totals	$300,000	$600,082
Shares outstanding		4,000
Book value per share		$150.02

In the preceding calculation, it is assumed that no preferred dividends are in arrears and that the preferred shares are not participating. Now assume that the same facts exist except that the 5% preferred shares are cumulative and participating up to 8%, and that dividends for three years before the current year are in arrears. The common shares' book value is then calculated as follows, assuming that no action has yet been taken concerning dividends for the current year.

Shareholders' equity	Preferred	Common
Preferred shares, 5%	$300,000	
Common shares		$400,000
Contributed surplus		37,500
Retained earnings:		
Dividends in arrears (3 years at 5% a year)	45,000	
Current year requirement at 5%	15,000	20,000
Participating additional 3%	9,000	12,000
Remainder to common	–0–	61,582
Totals	$369,000	$531,082
Shares outstanding		4,000
Book value per share		$132.77

In connection with the book value calculation, the analyst must know how to handle the following items: the number of authorized and unissued shares; the number of treasury shares on hand; any commitments with respect to the issuance of unissued shares or the reissuance of treasury shares; and the relative rights and privileges of the various types of shares authorized.

IFRS AND PRIVATE ENTERPRISE GAAP COMPARISON

Looking Ahead

The IASB and FASB are working on several projects including the financial statement project and the project on liabilities and equity. The financial statement project was discussed in Chapter 4.

At the time of writing, several decisions worthy of note had been reached regarding debt and equity instruments. As a general rule, the IASB is trying to reduce the complexity of accounting. Some decisions are noted below and in other chapters including Chapters 14 and 16.

Preliminary Decision Reached by IASB on the Liability and Equity Project	Comments
A cash-settled claim (required to be settled by paying cash or other assets) is a liability unless it has the following characteristics: 1. Its claim on the assets of the company ranks lower than all liability claims. 2. The required payments may occur for one of several stipulated reasons including payout upon liquidation/windup, or where the issuer chooses to distribute all of its assets/pay a dividend or repurchase shares.	This is similar to what IFRS currently states; i.e., where there is an obligation to pay cash, it is a liability except under certain limited situations. Otherwise, the instrument is equity.
Transaction costs on the issuance of financial instruments would be expensed.	This is different from the current practice of recording the instruments net.

Objective 13

Identify the major differences in accounting between accounting standards for private enterprises (ASPE/PE GAAP) and IFRS, and what changes are expected in the near future.

Comparison of IFRS and Private Entity GAAP

Along with the rest of the GAAP relating to financial instruments, GAAP relating to shareholders' equity is also converting with IFRS. Illustration 15-13 summarizes the major differences in accounting for equity between accounting standards for private enterprises and IFRS.

	Accounting Standards for Private Enterprises (Private Entity GAAP/ASPE)—*CICA Handbook*, Part II, Sections 3240, 3251, and 3856	IFRS—IAS 1 and 7
Recognition/ derecognition	Specific guidance is given for reacquisition of shares. The cost should be allocated first to share capital, then to contributed surplus, and then to retained earnings.	No explicit guidance is given.
	Receivables for loans issued to buy shares are recognized as assets if the shareholder is at risk for changes in value of the shares and there is reasonable assurance that the company will be able to collect in cash. Otherwise, they are not recognized or if recognized, are presented as contra equity.	No explicit guidance is given.
Measurement	Specific guidance is given for comprehensive revaluation of assets where a financial reorganization of the company occurs. Assets are revalued, the debt and equity accounts are adjusted to reflect the new capital structure, and any deficit or retained earnings are reclassified to other equity accounts.	No explicit guidance is given for accounting for financial reorganizations. Note that IFRS allows revaluation of property, plant, and equipment and intangibles (using the revaluation method), financial instruments (under the fair value option) and investment properties (under the fair value method). These are covered in other chapters including 10, 14, and 16).
	Dividends in kind that represent a spinoff of assets to shareholders are measured at carrying value unless it is a transaction with controlling shareholders, in which case the transaction is treated as a related party transaction and may be remeasured.	No explicit guidance is given; however, related party transactions are not remeasured.
Presentation	Changes in retained earnings are presented in a retained earnings statement. Changes in capital accounts are presented in the notes. The concept of comprehensive income is not discussed.	Changes in all equity accounts are presented in a separate statement of changes in equity.
Disclosures	Specific disclosures about how a company manages its capital are not explicitly mandated.	Specific disclosures are required regarding how a company manages its capital.

Illustration 15-13

IFRS and Private Entity GAAP Comparison Chart

Summary of Learning Objectives

Glossary

1   Discuss the characteristics of the corporate form of organization.

The three main forms of organization are the proprietorship, partnership, and corporation. Incorporation gives shareholders protection against claims on their personal assets and allows greater access to capital markets.

2   Identify the rights of shareholders.

If there are no restrictive provisions, each share carries the following rights: (1) to share proportionately in profits and losses, (2) to share proportionately in management (the right to vote for directors), and (3) to share proportionately in corporate assets upon liquidation. An additional right to share proportionately in any new issues of shares of the same class (called the preemptive right) may also be attached to the share.

3   Describe the major features of preferred shares.

Preferred shares are a special class of share that possess certain preferences or features that common shares do not have. Most often, these features are a preference over dividends and a preference over assets in the event of liquidation. Many other preferences may be attached to specific shares. Preferred shareholders give up some or all of the rights normally attached to common shares.

4   Explain the accounting procedures for issuing shares.

Shares are recognized and measured at net cost when issued. Shares may be issued on a subscription basis, in which case they are not considered legally issued until they are paid up. Shares may also be issued as a bundle with other securities, in which case the cost must be allocated between the securities. The residual or relative fair value methods (sometimes referred to as the incremental or proportional methods) may be used to allocate the cost.

5   Identify the major reasons for repurchasing shares.

The reasons that corporations have for purchasing their outstanding shares are varied. Some major reasons are (1) to increase earnings per share and return on equity, (2) to provide shares for employee share compensation contracts or to meet potential merger needs, (3) to stop takeover attempts or to reduce the number of shareholders, (4) to make a market in the shares, or (5) to return excess cash to shareholders.

6   Explain the accounting for the reacquisition and retirement of shares.

If the acquisition cost of the shares is greater than the original cost, the difference is allocated to share capital, then contributed surplus, and then retained earnings. If the cost is less, the cost is allocated to share capital (to stated or assigned cost) and to contributed surplus.

7   Explain the accounting for various forms of dividend distributions.

Dividends are generally paid out of earnings or are a return of capital. Dividends paid out of earnings are normally cash, property, or stock dividends. They are recorded at fair value and debited to Retained Earnings. Dividends that are a return of capital are known as liquidating dividends and reduce contributed capital.

KEY TERMS

accumulated other
  comprehensive
  income, 983
basic or inherent
  rights, 963
book value per share, 988
callable/redeemable
  (preferred shares), 966
capital maintenance, 961
common shares, 964
contributed (paid-in)
  capital, 961
convertible (preferred
  shares), 966
cumulative (preferred
  shares), 966
dividends, 974
dividends in kind, 977
earned capital, 961
in-substance common
  shares, 964
large stock dividend, 982
legal capital, 974
leveraged buyout, 972
limited liability, 967
liquidating dividends, 976
lump-sum sales, 970
participating (preferred
  shares), 966
par value shares, 967
payout ratio, 987
preemptive right, 963
preferred shares, 965
price earnings ratio, 988
rate of return on
  shareholders' equity,
  986
retained earnings, 973
retractable (preferred
  shares), 966
shareholders' equity, 960
stock dividend, 978
stock split, 981

8 Explain the effects of different types of dividend preferences.

Dividends paid to shareholders are affected by the dividend preferences of the preferred shares. Preferred shares can be cumulative or non-cumulative, and fully participating, partially participating, or non-participating.

9 Distinguish between stock dividends and stock splits.

A stock dividend is a capitalization of retained earnings that generally results in a reduction in retained earnings and a corresponding increase in certain contributed capital accounts. The total shareholders' equity remains unchanged with a stock dividend. In addition, all shareholders retain their same proportionate share of ownership in the corporation. A stock split results in an increase or decrease in the number of shares outstanding. However, no accounting entry is required. Similar to a stock dividend, the total dollar amount of all shareholders' equity accounts remains unchanged. A stock split is usually intended to improve the shares' marketability by reducing the market price of the shares that are being split. Large stock dividends have the same impact on the markets as stock splits—i.e., the market price of the share declines—and professional judgement is therefore needed in deciding whether they should be treated as a stock split or dividend for accounting purposes. Measurement is also a matter of judgement. Care should be taken to ensure that legal requirements for stated legal capital are met.

10 Understand the nature of other components of shareholders' equity.

Contributed surplus is additional surplus coming from shareholder transactions. Accumulated other comprehensive income is accumulated non-shareholder income that has not been booked through net income. PE GAAP does not discuss this concept.

11 Indicate how shareholders' equity is presented.

The shareholders' equity section of a balance sheet includes Share Capital, Contributed Surplus, Retained Earnings, and Accumulated Other Comprehensive Income. A statement of changes in shareholders' equity is required under IFRS.

12 Analyze shareholders' equity.

Common ratios used in this area are the rate of return on common shareholders' equity, payout ratio, price earnings ratio, and book value per share.

13 Identify the major differences in accounting between accounting standards for private enterprises (ASPE/PE GAAP) and IFRS, and what changes are expected in the near future.

In several cases, PE GAAP provides more guidance, as noted in the comparison chart. IFRS requires a statement of changes in shareholders' equity whereas PE GAAP requires a statement of changes in retained earnings (with additional note disclosure regarding the changes in equity). The IASB and FASB are continuing to work on a financial statements project as well as a liability and equity project.

Appendix 15A

Par Value and Treasury Shares

Neither par value shares nor treasury shares are allowed under the CBCA. As mentioned in the chapter, however, these types of shares are allowed under certain provincial business corporations acts and are common in the United States. For this reason, they will now be discussed in greater detail in this appendix.

Par Value Shares

The par value of a share has no relationship to its fair market value. At present, the par value that is associated with most capital share issuances is very low ($1, $5, or $10). To show the required information for the issuance of par value shares, accounts must be kept for each class of share as follows:

14 Objective
Explain the accounting for par value shares.

1. **Preferred or Common Shares**. These accounts reflect the par value of the corporation's issued shares. They are credited when the shares are originally issued. No additional entries are made in these accounts unless additional shares are issued or shares are retired.

2. **Contributed Surplus (Paid-In Capital in Excess of Par or Additional Paid-In Capital in the United States)**. This account indicates any excess over par value that was paid in by shareholders in return for the shares issued to them. Once it has been paid in, the excess over par becomes a part of the corporation's paid-in capital, and the individual shareholder has no greater claim on the excess paid in than all other holders of the same class of shares.

To illustrate how these accounts are used, assume that Colonial Corporation sold, for $1,100, 100 shares with a par value of $5 per share. The entry to record the issuance is:

Cash	1,100	
Common Shares		500
Contributed Surplus		600

A = L + SE
+1,100   +1,100
Cash flows: ↑ 1,100 inflow

When the shares are repurchased and cancelled, the same procedure is followed as was described in the chapter.

Treasury Shares

Objective **15**
Explain the accounting
for treasury shares.

Treasury shares are created when a company repurchases its own shares but does not cancel them. Generally, the repurchase and resale are treated as a single transaction. The repurchase of treasury shares is the first part of a transaction that is completed when the shares are later resold. Consequently, the holding of treasury shares is viewed as a transitional phase between the beginning and end of a single activity.

When shares are purchased, the total cost is debited to Treasury Shares on the balance sheet. This account is shown as a deduction from the total of the components of shareholders' equity in the balance sheet. An example of such disclosure follows:

Shareholders' equity:	
Common shares, no par value; authorized 24,000,000 shares;	
issued 19,045,870 shares, of which 209,750 are in treasury	$ 27,686,000
Retained earnings	253,265,000
	280,951,000
Less: Cost of treasury shares	(7,527,000)
Total shareholders' equity	$273,424,000

When the shares are sold, the Treasury Shares account is credited for their cost. If they are sold at more than their cost, the excess is credited to Contributed Surplus. If they are sold at less, the difference is debited to Contributed Surplus (if it is related to the same class of shares) and then to Retained Earnings. If the shares are subsequently retired, the journal entries shown in the chapter would be followed.

Note also that dividends on treasury shares should be reversed since a company cannot receive dividend income on its own shares (dr. Dividends Payable, cr. Retained Earnings).

Summary of Learning Objectives for Appendix 15A

14 Explain the accounting for par value shares.

These shares may only be valued at par value in the common or preferred share accounts. The excess goes to contributed surplus. On a repurchase or cancellation, the par value is removed from the common or preferred share accounts and any excess or deficit is booked to contributed surplus or retained earnings, as was discussed for no par shares.

15 Explain the accounting for treasury shares.

Treasury shares are created when a company repurchases its own shares and does not cancel or retire them at the same time; i.e., they remain outstanding. The single-transaction method is used when treasury shares are purchased. This method treats the purchase and subsequent resale or cancellation as part of the same transaction.

Appendix 15B

Financial Reorganization

A corporation that consistently suffers net losses accumulates negative retained earnings, or a deficit. Shareholders generally presume that dividends are paid out of profits and retained earnings and, therefore, a deficit sends a very negative signal about the company's ability to pay dividends. In addition, certain laws in some jurisdictions specify that no dividends may be declared and paid as long as a corporation's paid-in capital has been reduced by a deficit. In these cases, a corporation with a debit balance of retained earnings must accumulate enough profits to offset the deficit before it can pay any dividends.

This situation may be a real hardship on a corporation and its shareholders. A company that has operated unsuccessfully for several years and accumulated a deficit may have finally turned the corner. While the development of new products and new markets, the arrival of a new management group, or improved economic conditions may point to much improved operating results in the future, if the law prohibits dividends until the deficit has been replaced by earnings, the shareholders must wait until such profits have been earned, which can take quite a long time. Furthermore, future success may depend on obtaining additional funds through the sale of shares, but if no dividends can be paid for some time, the market price of any new share issue is likely to be low, assuming the shares can be marketed at all.

Thus, a company with excellent prospects may be prevented from accomplishing its plans because of a deficit, although present management may have had nothing at all to do with the years during which the deficit was accumulated. To permit the corporation to proceed with its plans might well be to the advantage of all interests in the enterprise; to require it to eliminate the deficit through profits might actually force it to liquidate.

A procedure that enables a company that has gone through financial difficulty to proceed with its plans without the encumbrance of having to recover from a deficit is called a financial reorganization. A financial reorganization is defined as a substantial realignment of an enterprise's equity and non-equity interests such that the holders of one or more of the significant classes of non-equity interests and the holders of all of the significant classes of equity interests give up some (or all) of their rights and claims on the enterprise.[32]

A financial reorganization results from negotiation and reaches its conclusion in an eventual agreement between non-equity and equity holders in the corporation. These negotiations may take place under the provisions of a legal act (e.g., *Companies' Creditors Arrangement Act*) or a less formal process.[33] The result gives the company a fresh start and the accounting is often referred to as fresh start accounting.

16 Objective
Describe the accounting for a financial reorganization.

---

[32] *CICA Handbook*, Part II, Section 1625.03.

[33] *CICA Handbook*, Part II, Section 1625.15.

Comprehensive Revaluation

When a financial reorganization occurs, where the same party does not control the company both before and after the reorganization, and where new costs are reasonably determinable, the company's assets and liabilities should undergo a comprehensive revaluation.[34] Under PE GAAP, this requires three steps:[35]

1. The deficit balance (retained earnings) is brought to zero. Any asset writedowns or impairments that existed before the reorganization should be recorded first. The deficit is reclassified to Share Capital, Contributed Surplus, or a separately identified account within Shareholders' Equity.

2. The changes in debt and equity that have been negotiated are recorded. Often debt is exchanged for equity, reflecting a change in control.

3. The assets and liabilities are comprehensively revalued. This step assigns appropriate going concern values to all assets and liabilities based on the negotiations. The difference between the carrying values before the reorganization and the new values after is known as a revaluation adjustment. The revaluation adjustment and any costs incurred to carry out the financial reorganization are accounted for as capital transactions and are closed to Share Capital, Contributed Surplus, or a separately identified account within Shareholders' Equity. Note that the new costs of the identifiable assets and liabilities must not be greater than the entity's fair value if this is known.[36]

Entries Illustrated

The series of entries that follows illustrates the accounting procedures that are applied in a financial reorganization. Assume that New Horizons Inc. shows a deficit of $1 million before the reorganization is effected on June 30, 2011. Under the terms of the negotiation, the creditors are giving up rights to payment of the $150,000 debt in return for 100% of the common shares. The original shareholders agree to give up their shares.

1. **Restate impairments of assets that existed before the reorganization:**

A   = L +   SE
−750,000   −750,000

Cash flows: No effect

Deficit	750,000	
Inventories (loss on writedown)		225,000
Intangible Assets (loss on writedown)		525,000

Elimination of deficit against contributed surplus

A   = L + SE
              0

Cash flows: No effect

Common Shares	1,750,000	
Deficit		1,750,000

---

[34] *CICA Handbook*, Part II, Section 1625.04.

[35] IFRS does not explicitly cover accounting for financial reorganizations although the same accounting principles and procedures may be applied as noted under PE GAAP where legally permissible. IFRS already allows revaluation of investment properties, property, plant, and equipment as well as intangibles. In addition, financial instruments are allowed to be valued at fair value if certain conditions are met.

[36] *CICA Handbook*, Part II, Section 1625.35 – 42.

2. and 3. Restate assets and liabilities to recognize unrecorded gains and losses and to record the negotiated change in control:

Plant Assets (gain on write-up)	400,000	
Long-Term Liabilities (gain on writedown)	150,000	
Common Shares		550,000

A	=	L	+	SE
+400,000		−150,000		+550,000

Cash flows: No effect

Note that, if there is no change in control, PE GAAP does not allow a comprehensive revaluation.

When a financial reorganization occurs and is accounted for as such, the following requirements must be fulfilled:

1. The proposed reorganization should receive the **approval** of the corporation's shareholders before it is put into effect.

2. The new asset and liability valuations should be **fair** and not deliberately understate or overstate assets, liabilities, and earnings.

3. After the reorganization, the corporation must have a zero balance of retained earnings, although it may have contributed surplus arising from the reorganization.

Disclosure

In the period of the reorganization, the following must be disclosed:

1. The date of the reorganization

2. A description of the reorganization

3. The amount of the change in each major class of assets, liabilities, and shareholders' equity resulting from the reorganization

In the following fiscal period, in subsequent reports, the following must be disclosed:

1. The date of the reorganization

2. The revaluation adjustment amount and the shareholders' equity account in which it was recorded

3. The amount of the deficit that was reclassified and the account to which it was reclassified

Summary of Learning Objective for Appendix 15B

16 Describe the accounting for a financial reorganization.

A corporation that has accumulated a large debit balance (deficit) in retained earnings may enter into a process known as a financial reorganization. During a reorganization, creditors and shareholders negotiate a deal to put the company on a new footing. This generally involves a **change in control** and a **comprehensive revaluation** of assets and liabilities. The procedure consists of the following steps: (1) The deficit is reclassified so that the ending balance in Retained Earnings is zero. (2) The change in control is recorded. (3) All assets and liabilities are comprehensively revalued at current values so that the company will not be burdened with having to complete inventory or fixed asset valuations in following years.

WILEY **PLUS**

Glossary

KEY TERMS

comprehensive
   revaluation, 996
financial reorganization,
   995
fresh start accounting,
   995
revaluation adjustment,
   996

Brief Exercises

Note: All assignment material with an asterisk (*) relates to the appendices to the chapter.

(LO 1)   BE15-1   Explain the pros and cons of incorporating.

(LO 2)   BE15-2   Tomlinson Corporation has three classes of shares: Series A, Series B, and Class A. How should Tomlinson classify and present the different classes if the characteristics of each class are as follows?

Series A shares   The shares are mandatorily redeemable and carry a dividend rate of 4%.

Series B shares   The shares are cumulative and carry a dividend rate of $2 per share. They are subordinated to the Series A shares for dividend distribution.

Class A shares   The shares are subordinated to both Series A and Series B shares for dividend distribution and participate in the earnings and losses of the company above a non-cumulative dividend of $0.50 per share. The shares have a voting right of one vote per share.

(LO 4, 14)   *BE15-3   Sportage Limited issued 2,000 shares of no par value common shares for $58,300. Prepare Sportage's journal entry if (a) the stock has no par value, and (b) the stock has a par value of $13 per share.

(LO 4)   BE15-4   Bonata Inc. sells 1,400 common shares on a subscription basis at $65 per share. On June 1, Bonata accepts a 45% down payment. On December 1, Bonata collects the remaining 55% and issues the shares. Prepare the company's journal entries.

(LO 4)   BE15-5   Kramers Inc. sells 1,000 common shares on March 1 to its employees at $25 per share. Kramers lends the money to the employees to buy the new shares. The employees pay 50% of the price on the transaction date and pay the balance in one year. (a) Prepare the company's necessary journal entries. (b) Assuming a December 31 fiscal year end, how should the receivable for the uncollected amount on the share issue be presented on the balance sheet (1) under private enterprise GAAP, and (2) under IFRS?

(LO 4)   BE15-6   Platinum Corporation issued 4,000 of its common shares for $66,000. The company also incurred $1,700 of costs associated with issuing the shares. Prepare the journal entry to record the issuance of the company's shares.

(LO 6)   BE15-7   Marcus Inc. has 52,000 common shares outstanding. The shares have an average cost of $21 per share. On July 1, 2011, Marcus reacquired 800 shares at $56 per share and retired them. Prepare the journal entry to record this transaction.

(LO 6)   BE15-8   Roberts Corporation has 50,000 common shares outstanding, with an average value of $8 per share. On August 1, 2012, the company reacquired and cancelled 600 shares at $40 per share. There was Contributed Surplus of $0.25 per share at the time of the reacquisition (total $12,500). Prepare the journal entry to record this transaction.

(LO 7)   BE15-9   Mortimer Inc. declared a cash dividend of $0.60 per share on its 1.5 million outstanding shares. The dividend was declared on August 1 and is payable on September 9 to all shareholders of record on August 15. Prepare all necessary journal entries for those three dates.

(LO 7)   BE15-10   Mallard Inc. owns shares of Oakwood Corporation that are classified as part of Mallard's trading portfolio and accounted for using fair value through net income. At December 31, 2011, the securities were carried in Mallard's accounting records at their cost of $850,000, which equalled their market value. On September 21, 2012, when the securities' market value was $1.3 million, Mallard declared a property dividend that will result in the Oakwood securities being distributed on October 23, 2012, to shareholders of record on October 8, 2012. Prepare all necessary journal entries for the three dates.

(LO 7)   BE15-11   On April 20, Raule Mining Corp. declared a dividend of $400,000 that is payable on June 1. Of this amount, $150,000 is a return of capital. Prepare the April 20 and June 1 journal entries for Raule.

(LO 7)   BE15-12   Mulligan Golf Corporation has 600,000 common shares outstanding. The corporation declares a 7% stock dividend when the shares' fair value is $30 per share (their carrying value is $18 per share). Prepare the journal entries for the company for both the date of declaration and the date of distribution.

(LO 8)   BE 15-13   List the types of dividends. Why do companies or investors have a preference for one or the other?

(LO 9)   BE15-14   Menzie Corporation has 150,000 common shares outstanding with a carrying value of $12 per share. Menzie declares a 3-for-1 stock split. (a) How many shares are outstanding after the split? (b) What is the carrying value per share after the split? (c) What is the total carrying value after the split? (d) What journal entry is necessary to record the split?

BE15-15 Lu Corporation has the following account balances at December 31, 2012: (LO 11)

Common Shares Subscribed	$ 250,000
Common Shares—No Par Value	310,000
Subscriptions Receivable	80,000
Retained Earnings	1,340,000
Contributed Surplus	320,000
Accumulated Other Comprehensive Income	560,000

Prepare the December 31, 2012 shareholders' equity section of the balance sheet.

BE15-16 The Red Dog Restaurant Limited reported the following balances at January 1, 2012: (LO 11)

Common Shares—No Par Value (32,000 shares issued, unlimited authorized)	$ 800,000
Retained Earnings	1,500,000
Contributed Surplus	540,000
Accumulated Other Comprehensive Income	40,000

During the year ended December 31, 2012, the following summary transactions occurred:

Net income earned during the year	$400,000
Holding gain on investments accounted for using the fair value through other comprehensive income model	25,000
Reduction of contributed surplus during year due to repurchase of common shares	420,000
Reduction of common shares account balance during year due to repurchase of 1,000 common shares	23,000
Dividends paid during the year on common shares	70,000
Issued 2,000 common shares during the year	30,000

(a) Prepare a statement of changes in shareholders' equity for the year as required under IFRS.

(b) Prepare the shareholders' equity section of the balance sheet at December 31.

BE15-17 Arthur Corporation has the following selected financial data: (LO 12)

	2012	2011
Net income	$ 720,000	$ 680,000
Total assets	5,136,000	4,525,000
Preferred shares, 4%, cumulative	600,000	600,000
Common shares	350,000	350,000
Retained earnings	2,786,000	2,190,000
Accumulated other comprehensive income	145,000	130,000
Total shareholders' equity	3,881,000	3,270,000
Cash dividends paid in the year	124,000	170,000
Market price of common shares	$97.46	$64.33
Weighted average number of common shares	80,000	80,000

There were no preferred dividends in arrears. (a) Calculate the following ratios for 2012: (1) rate of return on common shareholders' equity, (2) payout ratio, (3) price earnings ratio, (4) book value, and (5) rate of return on total assets. (b) Is Arthur Corporation trading on the equity?

*BE15-18 Hanover Corporation has 750,000 shares outstanding. The shares have an average cost of $45 per share. On (LO 15) September 5, the company repurchases 1,500 of its own shares at $75 per share and does not cancel them. The shares are classified as treasury shares. On November 20, 2012, the company resells 1,000 of the treasury shares at $80 per share. Prepare the journal entries for the repurchase and subsequent sale of the treasury shares.

*BE15-19 Use the information for Hanover Corporation in BE15-18. Assume now that the company resells the 1,000 (LO 15) treasury shares at $55 per share. Prepare the journal entries for the repurchase and subsequent sale of the treasury shares.

*BE15-20 Tsui Corporation went through a financial reorganization by writing down plant assets by $107,000 and (LO 16) eliminating its deficit, which was $182,000 before the reorganization. As part of the reorganization, the creditors agreed to take back 55% of the common shares in lieu of payment of the debt of $1.8 million. Prepare the entries to record the financial reorganization assuming that Tsui follows private enterprise GAAP.

Exercises

(LO 4) **E15-1** **(Recording Issuance of Common and Preferred Shares)** Vermue Corporation was organized on January 1, 2012. It is authorized to issue 100,000 preferred shares with a $7 dividend, and 400,000 common shares. The following share transactions were completed during the first year:

Jan. 10	Issued 200,000 common shares for cash at $23 per share.
Mar. 1	Issued 17,000 preferred shares for cash at $119 per share.
Apr. 1	Issued 3,000 common shares for land. The asking price for the land was $67,000; its fair value was $60,000.
May 1	Issued 20,000 common shares for cash at $18 per share.
Aug. 1	Issued 1,000 common shares to lawyers in payment of their bill of $19,000 for services rendered in helping the company organize.
Sept. 1	Issued 32,500 common shares for cash at $16 per share.
Nov. 1	Issued 1,500 preferred shares for cash at $125 per share.

Instructions

Prepare the journal entries to record the above transactions.

(LO 4) **E15-2** **(Subscribed Shares)** Callaghan Inc. decided to sell shares to raise additional capital so that it could expand into the rapidly growing service industry. The corporation chose to sell these shares through a subscription basis and publicly notified the investment world. The offering was 40,000 shares at $22 a share. The terms of the subscription were 35% down and the balance at the end of six months. All shares were subscribed for during the offering period.

Instructions

(a) Prepare the journal entries for the original subscription, the collection of the down payments, the collection of the balance of the subscription price, and the issuance of the shares.

(b) Discuss how the Subscriptions Receivable account should be presented on the balance sheet if it is still outstanding at the end of the reporting period.

(c) Discuss how Callaghan should account for the balance in the subscription account and the amounts already collected if the subscriber defaults before making the final payment.

(LO 4, 6) **E15-3** **(Share Issuances and Repurchase)** Kunzig Corporation is authorized to issue 500,000 common shares. During 2012, the company took part in the following selected transactions.

1. Issued 6,000 common shares at $30 per share, less $2,000 in costs related to the issuance of the shares.

2. Issued 3,750 common shares for land appraised at $140,000. The shares were actively traded on a national stock exchange at approximately $32 per share on the date of issuance.

3. Purchased and retired 500 of the company's shares at $29 per share. The repurchased shares have an average per share amount of $38.

Instructions

(a) Prepare the journal entries to record the three transactions listed.

Digging Deeper

(b) When shares are repurchased, is the original issue price of those individual shares relevant? Explain.

(LO 4, 11, 14) ***E15-4** **(Shareholders' Equity Section)** Radford Corporation's charter authorized 1 million shares of $11 par value common shares, and 300,000 shares of 6% cumulative and non-participating preferred shares, with a par value of $100 per share. The corporation engaged in the following share transactions through December 31, 2012: 300,000 common shares were issued for $3.6 million and 10,000 preferred shares were issued for machinery valued at $1,475,000. Subscriptions for 10,500 common shares have been taken, and 30% of the subscription price of $16 per share has been collected. The shares will be issued upon collection of the subscription price in full. In addition, 10,000 common shares have been purchased for $15 and retired. The Retained Earnings balance is $180,000 before considering the transactions above.

Instructions

(a) Prepare the shareholders' equity section of the balance sheet in good form.

(b) Repeat part (a) assuming the common shares and preferred shares are no par.

Digging Deeper

(c) Discuss the alternative presentations of the subscription receivable account. Would the presentation of the receivable affect the book value or the rate of return on shareholders' equity?

E15-5 (Correcting Entries for Equity Transactions) Ramsay Inc. recently hired a new accountant with extensive **(LO 4, 11)** experience in accounting for partnerships. Because of the pressure of the new job, the accountant was unable to review what he had learned earlier about corporation accounting. During the first month, he made the following entries for the corporation's capital shares:

May 12	Cash		221,000	
	Common Shares			221,000
	(Issued 13,000 common shares at $17 per share.)			
10	Cash		400,000	
	Common Shares			400,000
	(Issued 8,000 preferred shares at $50 per share.)			
15	Common Shares		15,000	
	Cash		15,000	
	(Purchased and retired 1,000 common shares at $15 per share.)			
31	Cash		9,000	
	Common Shares			5,000
	Gain on Sale of Shares			4,000
	(Issued 500 shares at $18 per share.)			

Instructions

Based on the explanation for each entry, prepare the entries that should have been made for the capital share transactions. Explain your reasoning.

E15-6 (Participating Preferred and Stock Dividend) The following is the shareholders' equity section of Suozzi **(LO 5, 7)** Corp. at December 31, 2012:

Preferred shares,[a] authorized 100,000 shares; issued 25,000 shares	$ 750,000
Common shares (200,000 authorized, 60,000 issued)	1,800,000
Contributed surplus	1,150,000
Total paid-in capital	3,700,000
Retained earnings	2,470,500
Total shareholders' equity	$6,170,500

[a] The preferred shares have a $5 dividend rate, are cumulative, and participate in distributions in excess of a $3 dividend on the common shares.

Instructions

(a) No dividends were paid in 2010 or 2011. On December 31, 2012, Suozzi wants to pay a cash dividend of $4 a share to common shareholders. How much cash would be needed for the total amount to be paid to preferred and common shareholders?

(b) The company instead decides that it will declare a 15% stock dividend on the outstanding common shares. The shares' market value is $105 per share. Prepare the entry on the date of declaration.

(c) The company decides instead to acquire and cancel 10,500 common shares. The current market value is $105 per share. Prepare the entry to record the retirement, assuming contributed surplus arose from previous cancellations of common shares.

E15-7 (Equity Items on Balance Sheet) The following are selected transactions that may affect shareholders' equity. **(LO 7, 9, 10)**

1. Recorded accrued interest earned on a note receivable.

2. Declared a cash dividend.

3. Effected a stock split.

4. Recorded the expiration of insurance coverage that was previously recorded as prepaid insurance.

5. Paid the cash dividend declared in item 2 above.

6. Recorded accrued interest expense on a note payable.

7. Recorded an increase in the fair value of an investment accounted for using fair value through other comprehensive income (FV-OCI) that will be distributed as a property dividend. The carrying amount of the FV-OCI investment was greater than its cost. The shares are traded in an active market.

8. Declared a property dividend (see item 7 above).

9. Distributed the investment to shareholders (see items 7 and 8 above).

10. Declared a stock dividend.

11. Distributed the stock dividend declared in item 10.

12. Repurchased common shares for less than their initial issue price.

Instructions

(a) In the table below, assuming the company follows IFRS, indicate the effect that each of the 12 transactions has on the financial statement elements that are listed. Use the following codes: increase (I), decrease (D), and no effect (NE).

Item	Assets	Liabilities	Shareholders' Equity	Share Capital	Cont. Surplus	Retained Earnings	Acc. Other Compr. Income	Net Income

(b) Would the effect of any of the above items change if the company were to follow private enterprise GAAP?

(LO 7)   **E15-8   (Preferred Dividends)** The outstanding share capital of Meadowcrest Corporation consists of 3,000 shares of preferred and 7,000 common shares for which $280,000 was received. The preferred shares carry a dividend of $7 per share and have a $100 stated value.

Instructions

Assuming that the company has retained earnings of $95,000 that is to be entirely paid out in dividends and that preferred dividends were not paid during the two years preceding the current year, state how much each class of shares should receive under each of the following conditions.

(a) The preferred shares are non-cumulative and non-participating.

(b) The preferred shares are cumulative and non-participating.

(c) The preferred shares are cumulative and participating.

(LO 7)   **E15-9   (Preferred Dividends)** McNamara Limited's ledger shows the following balances on December 31, 2012:

Preferred shares outstanding: 25,000 shares	$ 625,000
Common shares outstanding: 40,000 shares	3,000,000
Retained earnings	890,000

Instructions

Assuming that the directors decide to declare total dividends in the amount of $445,000, determine how much each class of shares should receive under each of the conditions that follow. Note that one year's dividends are in arrears on the preferred shares, which pay a dividend of $1.50 per share.

(a) The preferred shares are cumulative and fully participating.

(b) The preferred shares are non-cumulative and non-participating.

(c) The preferred shares are non-cumulative and are participating in distributions in excess of a 10% dividend rate on the common shares.

(LO 7, 9)   **E15-10   (Dividend Entries)** The following data were taken from the balance sheet accounts of Bedard Corporation on December 31, 2012:

Current assets	$1,040,000
Investments—trading	824,000
Common shares (no par value, no authorized limit, 600,000 shares issued and outstanding)	6,000,000
Contributed surplus	350,000
Retained earnings	1,840,000

Instructions

Prepare the required journal entries for the following unrelated items.

(a) A 6% stock dividend is declared and distributed at a time when the shares' market value is $48 per share.

(b) A 4-for-1 stock split is effected.

(c) A dividend in kind is declared on January 5, 2012, and paid on January 25, 2012, in bonds that were classified as trading. The bonds have a carrying amount of $100,000 (equal to cost) and a fair value of $165,000.

E15-11 **(Stock Split and Stock Dividend)** The common shares of Hoover Inc. are currently selling at $143 per share. **(LO 9)** The directors want to reduce the share price and increase the share volume before making a new issue. The per share carrying value is $34. There are currently 9 million shares issued and outstanding.

Instructions

(a) Prepare the necessary journal entries assuming that:
1. the board votes a 2-for-1 stock split.
2. the board votes a 100% stock dividend.

(b) Briefly discuss the accounting and securities market differences between these two methods of increasing the number of shares outstanding.

E15-12 **(Entries for Stock Dividends and Stock Splits)** The shareholders' equity accounts of Chatsworth Inc. have **(LO 9)** the following balances on December 31, 2012:

Common shares, 400,000 shares issued and outstanding	$10,000,000
Contributed surplus	2,300,000
Retained earnings	42,400,000

Common shares are currently selling on the Prairie Stock Exchange at $59.

Instructions

Prepare the appropriate journal entries for each of the following cases.

(a) A stock dividend of 10% is declared and issued.

(b) A stock dividend of 100% is declared and issued.

(c) A 2-for-1 stock split is declared and issued.

*E15-13 **(Shareholders' Equity Section)** Brubacher Corporation's post-closing trial balance at December 31, 2012, **(LO 11, 15)** was as follows:

BRUBACHER CORPORATION
Post-Closing Trial Balance
December 31, 2012

	Dr.	Cr.
Accounts payable		$ 310,000
Accounts receivable	$ 480,000	
Accumulated amortization—building and equipment		185,000
Accumulated other comprehensive income		100,000
Contributed surplus—common		1,460,000
Allowance for doubtful accounts		30,000
Bonds payable		300,000
Building and equipment	1,450,000	
Cash	190,000	
Common shares		200,000
Dividends payable on preferred shares (cash)		4,000
Inventories	360,000	
Investments—trading	200,000	
Land	400,000	
Preferred shares		500,000
Prepaid expenses	40,000	
Retained earnings		201,000
Treasury shares (10,000 common shares)	170,000	
Totals	$3,290,000	$3,290,000

At December 31, 2012, Brubacher had the following numbers for its common and preferred shares:

	Common	Preferred
Authorized	600,000	60,000
Issued	200,000	10,000
Outstanding	190,000	10,000

The dividends on preferred shares are $5 cumulative. In addition, the preferred shares have a preference in liquidation of $50 per share.

Instructions

Prepare the shareholders' equity section of Brubacher's balance sheet at December 31, 2012. The company follows IFRS.

(AICPA adapted)

(LO 5, 7, 11)   E15-14   (Dividends and Shareholders' Equity Section) Falkon Corp. reported the following amounts in the shareholders' equity section of its December 31, 2011 balance sheet:

Preferred shares, $8 dividend (10,000 shares authorized, 2,000 shares issued)	$200,000
Common shares (100,000 authorized, 25,000 issued)	100,000
Contributed surplus	155,000
Retained earnings	250,000
Accumulated other comprehensive income	75,000
Total	$780,000

During 2012, the company had the following transactions that affect shareholders' equity.

1. Paid the annual 2011 $8 per share dividend on preferred shares and a $3 per share dividend on common shares. These dividends had been declared on December 31, 2011.

2. Purchased 3,700 shares of its own outstanding common shares for $35 per share and cancelled them.

3. Issued 1,000 shares of preferred shares at $105 per share (at the beginning of the year).

4. Declared a 10% stock dividend on the outstanding common shares when the shares were selling for $45 per share.

5. Issued the stock dividend.

6. Declared the annual 2012 $8 per share dividend on preferred shares and a $2 per share dividend on common shares. These dividends are payable in 2013.

The contributed surplus arose from past common share transactions. The company follows IFRS.

Instructions

(a) Prepare journal entries to record the transactions above.

(b) Prepare the December 31, 2012 shareholders' equity section. Assume 2012 net income was $450,000 and comprehensive income was $455,000.

(c) Prepare the statement of shareholders' equity for the year ended December 31, 2012.

(LO 11)   E15-15   (Statement of Shareholders' Equity) Miss M's Dance Studios Ltd. is a public company, and accordingly uses IFRS for financial reporting. The corporate charter authorizes the issue of up to 1 million common shares and 50,000 preferred shares with a $2 dividend. At the beginning of the December 31, 2012 year, the opening account balances indicated that 25,000 common shares had been issued for $4 per share, and no preferred shares had been issued. Opening retained earnings were $365,000. The transactions during the year were as follows:

Jan. 15	10,000 common shares issued at $6 per share
Feb. 12	2,000 preferred shares issued at $60 per share
June 30	Dividend paid on common shares of $1.50 per share
Sept. 2	Issued 5,000 common shares in exchange for land valued at $25,000
Oct. 31	Dividends declared and paid on preferred shares of $2
Nov. 15	Purchased and retired 500 preferred shares at $62 per share
Dec. 31	Net income reported of $532,000

Instructions

(a) Prepare journal entries to record the transactions above.

(b) Prepare the Statement of Shareholders' Equity.

(LO 11)   E15-16   (Equity Transactions and Statement of Shareholders' Equity) On January 1, 2012, Copeland Ltd. (a public company) had the following shareholders' equity accounts:

Preferred shares, $5-non-cumulative, no par value,	
unlimited number authorized, none issued	–0–
Common shares, no par value, unlimited number	
authorized, 800,000 issued	$5,600,000
Retained earnings	1,323,000
Accumulated other comprehensive income	142,000

The following selected transactions occurred during 2012:

Jan. 2	Issued 100,000 preferred shares at $25 per share.
Mar. 5	Declared the quarterly cash dividend to preferred shareholders of record on March 20, payable April 1.
Apr. 18	Issued 130,000 common shares at $11 per share.
June 5	Declared the quarterly cash dividend to preferred shareholders of record on June 20, payable July 1.
Sept. 5	Declared the quarterly cash dividend to preferred shareholders of record on September 20, payable October 1.
Dec. 5	Declared the quarterly cash dividend to preferred shareholders of record on December 20, payable January 1.
Dec. 31	Net income for the year was $374,000.

Instructions

(a) Prepare journal entries to record the transactions above.

(b) Post the entries to the shareholders' equity T accounts.

(c) Prepare the Statement of Shareholders' Equity for the year.

(d) Prepare the shareholders' equity section of the balance sheet at December 31.

(e) Prepare the financing activities section of the cash flow statement for the year.

(LO 12)

E15-17   (Comparison of Alternative Forms of Financing) What follows are the liabilities and shareholders' equity sections of the balance sheets for Kao Corp. and Bennington Corp. Each has assets totalling $4.2 million.

Kao Corp.		Bennington Corp.	
Current liabilities	$ 300,000	Current liabilities	$ 600,000
Long-term debt, 10%	1,200,000	Common shares	2,900,000
Common shares		(145,000 shares issued)	
(100,000 shares issued)	2,000,000	Retained earnings	
Retained earnings		(Cash dividends, $328,000)	700,000
(Cash dividends, $220,000)	700,000		
	$4,200,000		$4,200,000

For the year, each company has earned the same income before interest and taxes.

	Kao Corp.	Bennington Corp.
Income before interest and taxes	$1,200,000	$1,200,000
Interest expense	120,000	–0–
	1,080,000	1,200,000
Income taxes (45%)	486,000	540,000
Net income	$ 594,000	$ 660,000

At year end, the market price of Kao's shares was $101 per share; it was $63.50 for Bennington's.

Instructions

(a) Which company is more profitable in terms of return on total assets?

(b) Which company is more profitable in terms of return on shareholders' equity?

(c) Which company has the greater net income per share? Neither company issued or reacquired shares during the year.

(d) From the point of view of income, is it advantageous to Kao's shareholders to have the long-term debt outstanding? Why or why not?

(e) What is each company's price earnings ratio?

(f) What is the book value per share for each company?

(LO 16) *E15-18 (Financial Reorganization) The following account balances are available from the ledger of Yutao Shui Corporation on December 31, 2011:

Common Shares (20,000 shares authorized and outstanding)	$1,000,000
Retained Earnings (deficit)	(190,000)

On January 2, 2012, the corporation put into effect a shareholder-approved reorganization by agreeing to pass the common shares over to the creditors in full payment of the $260,000 debt, writing up plant assets by $135,600, and eliminating the deficit. Assume that Yutao Shui follows private enterprise GAAP.

Instructions

Prepare the required journal entries for the financial reorganization of Yutao Shui Corporation.

(LO 16) *E15-19 (Financial Reorganization) The condensed balance sheets of Rockford Limited, a small private company that follows private enterprise GAAP, follow for the periods immediately before, and one year after, it had completed a financial reorganization:

	Before Reorganization	One Year After		Before Reorganization	One Year After
Current assets	$ 300,000	$ 420,000	Common shares	$2,400,000	$1,550,000
Plant assets (net)	1,700,000	1,290,000	Contributed surplus	220,000	
	–0–	–0–	Retained earnings	(620,000)	160,000
	$2,000,000	$1,710,000		$2,000,000	$1,710,000

For the year following the financial reorganization, the company reported net income of $190,000 and depreciation expense of $80,000, and paid a cash dividend of $30,000. As part of the reorganization, the company wrote down inventories by $120,000 in order to reflect circumstances that existed before the reorganization. Also, the deficit, and any revaluation adjustment, was accounted for by charging amounts against contributed surplus until it was eliminated, with any remaining amount being charged against common shares. The common shares are widely held and there is no controlling interest. No purchases or sales of plant assets and no share transactions occurred in the year following the reorganization.

Instructions

Prepare all the journal entries made at the time of the reorganization.

Problems

P15-1   Oregano Corporation's charter authorizes the issuance of 1 million common shares and 500,000 preferred shares. The following transactions involving share issues were completed. Assume that Oregano follows IFRS and that each transaction is independent of the others.

1. Issued 4,200 common shares for machinery. The machinery had been appraised at $74,500, and the seller's carrying amount was $58,600. The common shares' most recent market price is $18 a share.

2. Voted a $6 dividend on both the 17,000 shares of outstanding common and the 40,000 shares of outstanding preferred. The dividend was paid in full.

3. Issued 2,500 shares of common and 1,200 shares of preferred for a lump sum of $125,000. The common had been selling at $13 and the preferred at $80. The company uses the relative fair value method to measure lump-sum share issues.

4. Issued 2,200 shares of common and 135 shares of preferred for furniture and fixtures. The common shares had a fair value of $14 per share and the furniture and fixtures were appraised at $36,000.

5. Issued a $150,000, 7% bond payable at par and gave as a bonus 150 preferred shares, which at that time were selling for $53 a share.

Instructions

Prepare the journal entries to record the transactions.

P15-2   Manitoba Deck System Corporation (MDSC) is a public company whose shares are actively traded on the Toronto Stock Exchange and thus it follows IFRS. The following information relates to MDSC:

Jan. 1, 2012	The company is granted a charter that authorizes the issuance of 500,000 no par value common shares, and 250,000 no par value preferred shares that entitle the holder to a $4 per share annual dividend.
Jan. 10, 2012	15,000 common shares are issued to the founders of the corporation for land that has a fair value of $450,000.
Mar. 10, 2012	4,000 preferred shares are issued for cash for $100 per share.
Apr. 15, 2012	The company issues 110 common shares to a car dealer in exchange for a used vehicle. The asking price for the car is $6,400. At the time of the exchange, the common shares are selling at $55 per share.
Aug. 20, 2012	MDSC decides to issue shares on a subscription basis to select individuals, giving each person the right to purchase 250 common shares at a price of $60 per share. Forty individuals accept the company's offer and agree to pay 10% down and the remainder in three equal instalments.
Oct. 11, 2012	MDSC issues 3,000 common shares and 600 preferred shares for a lump sum of $230,000 cash. At the time of sale, both the common and preferred shares are actively traded. The common shares are trading at $58 each; the preferred shares at $105 each.
Dec. 31, 2012	MDSC declares cash dividends totalling $26,000, payable on January 31, 2013, to holders of record on January 15, 2013.

Instructions

Prepare the general journal entries to record the transactions.

(CGA adapted)

P15-3   Psutka Corporation's general ledger shows the following account balances (the average cost of Psutka's shares is $30 per share), among others. The Contributed Surplus relates to the common shares.

Contributed Surplus	Common Shares	Retained Earnings
Balance $8,000	Balance $270,000	Balance $85,000

Instructions

Assuming that the above balances existed before any of the transactions that follow, record the journal entries for each transaction.

(a) Bought and cancelled 430 shares at $38 per share.

(b) Bought and cancelled 200 shares at $44 per share.

(c) Sold 3,200 shares at $41 per share.

(d) Sold 1,500 shares at $47 per share.

(e) Bought and cancelled 1,000 shares at $50 per share.

P15-4   Stellar Corp. had the following shareholders' equity on January 1, 2012:

Common shares, 300,000 shares authorized, 100,000 shares issued and outstanding	$ 270,000
Contributed surplus	310,000
Retained earnings	2,300,000
Total shareholders' equity	$2,880,000

The following transactions occurred, in the order given, during 2012.

1. Subscriptions were sold for 12,000 common shares at $26 per share. The first payment was for $10 per share.

2. The second payment for the sale in item 1 above was for $16 per share. All payments were received on the second payment except for 2,000 shares.

3. In accordance with the subscription contract, which requires that defaulting subscribers have all their payments refunded, a refund cheque was sent to the defaulting subscribers. At this point, common shares were issued to subscribers who had fully paid on the contract.

4. Repurchased 22,000 common shares at $29 per share. They were then retired.

5. Sold 5,000 preferred shares and 3,000 common shares together for $300,000. The common shares had a market value of $31 per share.

Instructions

(a) Prepare the journal entries to record the transactions for the company for 2012.

(b) Assume that the subscription contract states that defaulting subscribers forfeit their first payment. Prepare the journal entries for items 2 to 4 above.

P15-5   Transactions of Kettle Corporation are as follows.

1. The company is granted a charter that authorizes the issuance of 150,000 preferred shares and 150,000 common shares without par value.

2. The founders of the corporation are issued 10,000 common shares for land valued by the board of directors at $210,000 (based on an independent valuation).

3. Sold 15,200 preferred shares for cash at $110 per share.

4. Repurchased and cancelled 3,000 shares of outstanding preferred shares for cash at $100 per share.

5. Repurchased and cancelled 4,000 preferred shares for cash at $98 per share.

6. Repurchased for cash and cancelled 500 shares of the outstanding common shares issued in item 2 above at $49 per share.

7. Issued 2,000 preferred shares at $99 per share.

Instructions

(a) Prepare entries in journal form to record the transactions listed above. No other transactions affecting the capital share accounts have occurred.

(b) Assuming that the company has retained earnings from operations of $1,032,000, prepare the shareholders' equity section of its balance sheet after considering all the transactions above.

(c) Why is the distinction between paid-in capital and retained earnings important?

(d) How would the repurchase of the preferred shares differ if the preferred shares were retractable or callable/redeemable?

Digging Deeper

P15-6   Armadillo Limited has two classes of shares outstanding: preferred ($6 dividend) and common. At December 31, 2011, the following accounts and balances were included in shareholders' equity:

Preferred shares, 300,000 shares issued (authorized, 1,000,000 shares)	$ 3,000,000
Common shares, 1,000,000 shares (authorized, unlimited)	10,000,000
Contributed surplus—preferred	200,000
Contributed surplus—common	17,000,000
Retained earnings	5,500,000
Accumulated other comprehensive income	250,000

The following transactions affected shareholders' equity during 2012:

Jan. 1	Issued 25,000 preferred shares at $25 per share.
Feb. 1	Issued 50,000 common shares at $20 per share.
June 1	Declared a 2-for-1 stock split (common shares).
July 1	Purchased and retired 30,000 common shares at $15 per share.
Dec. 31	Net income is $2.1 million; comprehensive income is $2,050,000.
Dec. 31	The preferred dividend is declared, and a common dividend of $0.50 per share is declared.

Assume that Armadillo follows IFRS.

Instructions

Prepare the statement of changes in shareholders' equity and the shareholders' equity section of the balance sheet for the company at December 31, 2012. Show all supporting calculations.

P15-7   Original Octave Inc. (OOI) is a widely held, publicly traded company that designs equipment for tuning musical instruments. Information pertaining to its shareholders' equity is as follows.

ORIGINAL OCTAVE INC.
Shareholders' Equity
December 31, 2011

Share capital	
Preferred shares, no par value, $8, cumulative, and participating	
(20,000 authorized; 1,000 issued and outstanding)	$100,000
Common shares, no par value	
(1,000,000 authorized; 40,000 issued and outstanding)	500,000
Contributed capital, preferred share retirement	20,000
	620,000
Retained earnings	280,000
Shareholders' equity	$900,000

The preferred share dividend was not paid in 2011.

Several transactions affecting shareholders' equity took place during the fiscal year ended December 31, 2012, and are summarized in chronological order as follows.

1. Exchanged 10,000 common shares for a prototype piano tuning machine. The machine was appraised at $110,000. On the transaction date, OOI's shares were actively trading at $10 per share.

2. Purchased and retired 10,000 common shares at $15 per share.

3. Paid the annual dividend on the preferred shares. The common shares were then paid a $2 per share dividend.

Instructions

Prepare journal entries for each of the three transactions.

P15-8   Hessenland Corporation had the following shareholders' equity at January 1, 2012.

Preferred shares, 8%, $100 par value, 10,000 shares authorized, 4,000 shares issued	$ 400,000
Common shares, $2 par value, 200,000 shares authorized, 80,000 shares issued	160,000
Common shares subscribed, 10,000 shares	20,000
Contributed surplus—preferred	20,000
Contributed surplus—common	940,000
Retained earnings	780,000
	2,320,000
Less: Common share subscriptions receivable	40,000
Total shareholders' equity	$2,280,000

During 2012, the following transactions occurred.

1. Equipment was purchased in exchange for 100 shares of common. The shares' market value on the exchange date was $12 per share.

2. Sold 1,000 shares of common and 100 shares of preferred for the lump sum price of $24,500. The common shares had a market price of $14 at the time of the sale.

3. Sold 2,000 shares of preferred for cash at $102 per share.

4. All of the subscribers paid their subscription prices into the firm.

5. The common shares were issued.

6. Repurchased and retired 1,000 common shares at $15 per share.

7. Income for 2008 was $246,000.

Instructions

Prepare the shareholders' equity section for the company as at December 31, 2012. (The use of T accounts may help you organize the material.)

P15-9   The books of Binkerton Corporation carried the following account balances as at December 31, 2011:

Cash	$ 1,300,000
Preferred shares, $2 cumulative dividend, non-participating, 25,000 shares issued	750,000
Common shares, no par value, 300,000 shares issued	15,000,000
Contributed surplus (preferred)	150,000
Retained earnings	327,000

The preferred shares have dividends in arrears for the past year (2010). At its annual meeting on December 21, 2011, the board of directors declared the following: The current year dividends shall be $2 per share on the preferred and $0.70 per share on the common; the dividends in arrears shall be paid by issuing one share of common shares for each 20 shares of preferred held.

The preferred is currently selling at $80 per share and the common at $57 per share. Net income for 2011 is estimated at $56,000.

Instructions

(a) Prepare the journal entries that are required for the dividend declaration and payment, assuming that they occur at the same time.

(b) Could the company give the preferred shareholders two years of dividends and common shareholders a $0.70 per share dividend, all in cash? Explain your reasoning.

P15-10   Bablon Corp. has 5,000 preferred shares outstanding (no par value, $2 dividend), which were issued for $150,000, and 30,000 shares of no par value common, which were issued for $550,000.

Instructions

The following schedule shows the amount of dividends paid out over the last four years. Allocate the dividends to each type of share under assumptions (a) and (b). Express your answers in per share amounts and using the format that is shown.

		Assumptions			
		(a) Preferred, non-cumulative, and non-participating		(b) Preferred, cumulative, and fully participating	
Year	Paid-out	Preferred	Common	Preferred	Common
2010	$ 8,000				
2011	$ 24,000				
2012	$ 60,000				
2013	$126,000				

P15-11   Guoping Limited provides you with the following condensed balance sheet information:

Assets		Liabilities and Shareholders' Equity		
Current assets	$ 40,000	Current and long-term liabilities		$100,000
Investments in Geneva Company—		Shareholders' equity		
trading (10,000 shares)	60,000	Common shares[a]	$ 20,000	
Equipment (net)	250,000	Contributed surplus	110,000	
Intangibles	60,000	Retained earnings	180,000	310,000
Total assets	$410,000	Total liabilities and shareholders' equity		$410,000

[a] 10,000 shares issued and outstanding.

Instructions

(a) For each transaction below, indicate the dollar impact (if any) on the following five items: (1) total assets, (2) common shares, (3) contributed surplus, (4) retained earnings, and (5) shareholders' equity. (Each situation is independent.)

1. The company declares and pays a $0.50 per share dividend.

2. The company declares and issues a 10% stock dividend when the shares' market price is $12 per share.

3. The company declares and issues a 40% stock dividend when the shares' market price is $17 per share.

4. The company declares and distributes a property dividend. The company gives one Geneva share for every two company shares held. Geneva is selling for $12 per share on the date when the property dividend is declared.

5. The company declares a 3-for-1 stock split and issues new shares.

(b) What are the differences between a stock dividend and a cash or property dividend?

P15-12 Some of the account balances of Vos Limited at December 31, 2010, are as follows:

$6 Preferred shares (no par, 2,000 shares authorized, 2,000 shares issued and outstanding)	$520,000
Common shares (no par, 100,000 shares authorized, 50,000 shares issued and outstanding)	500,000
Contributed surplus	103,000
Retained earnings	774,000
Accumulated other comprehensive income	22,350

The price of the company's common shares has been increasing steadily on the market; it was $21 on January 1, 2011, and advanced to $24 by July 1 and to $27 at the end of the year 2011. The preferred shares are not openly traded but were appraised at $120 per share during 2011. Vos follows IFRS and had net income of $154,000 during 2011.

Instructions

(a) Prepare the proper journal entries for each of the following.

1. The company declared a property dividend on April 1. Each common shareholder was to receive one share of Waterloo Corp. for every 10 shares outstanding. Vos had 8,000 shares of Waterloo (2% of the outstanding shares), and had purchased them in 2006 for $68,400. The shares were held for sale and are accounted for using fair value through other comprehensive income (FV-OCI) model. The accumulated other comprehensive income relates only to these shares. The fair value of Waterloo shares was $16 per share on April 1. The property dividend was distributed April 21 when the fair value of the Waterloo shares was $18.50. The Waterloo shares stayed at a fair value of $18.50 until year end.

2. On July 1, the company declared a 5% stock dividend to the remaining common shareholders. The stock dividend was distributed July 22.

3. A shareholder, in an effort to persuade Vos to expand into her city, donated to the company a plot of land with an appraised value of $42,000.

(b) Prepare the shareholders' equity section of Vos' balance sheet at December 31, 2011.

(c) How should Vos account for the difference in fair value of the Waterloo shares between the date of declaration and date of distribution? Does the declaration of a property dividend create a financial liability?

P15-13 Perfect Ponds Incorporated is a backyard pond design and installation company. The company was incorporated during 2011, with 1 million common shares, and 50,000 preferred shares with a $3 dividend rate. Perfect Ponds follows private enterprise GAAP. The following transactions took place during the first year of operations with respect to these shares:

Jan. 1	The articles of incorporation are filed and state that 1 million common shares and 50,000 preferred shares are authorized.
Jan. 15	30,000 common shares were sold by subscription to three individuals, who each purchased 10,000 shares for $50 per share. The terms require 10% of the balance to be paid in cash immediately. The balance was to be paid by December 31, 2012, at which time the shares will be issued.
Feb. 20	70,000 common shares were sold by subscription to seven individuals, who each purchased 10,000 shares for $50 per share. The terms require that 10% of the balance be paid in cash immediately, with the balance to be paid by December 31, 2011. Shares are to be issued once the full payment had been received.
Mar. 3	50,000 common shares were sold by an underwriter for $52 per share. The underwriter charged a 5% commission on the sale.
May 10	The company paid $2,000 to a printing company for costs involved in printing common share certificates. As well, an invoice for legal fees related to the issue of common shares was received for $15,000.
Sept. 23	The company issued a combination of 2,000 common and 1,000 preferred shares to a new shareholder for a total price of $200,000. The company was unable to estimate a fair value of the preferred shares, and the most recent sale of common shares was used to estimate the value of the common share portion of the transaction.
Nov. 28	The company wanted to recognize the efforts of a key employee, and offered him the opportunity to purchase 500 common shares for $52, to be paid by December 31, 2012. No interest was to be charged on the outstanding balance; however, the shares were issued immediately.
Dec. 31	Of the seven subscriptions issued on February 20, five subscriptions were paid in full and two subscribers defaulted. According to the subscription contract, the defaulting subscribers would not be issued shares for any amount that had been paid and no money would be refunded.
Dec. 31	The company declared a dividend of $200,000 for 2011. Net income for the year was $800,000.

Instructions

(a) Prepare the journal entries to record the transactions for the year.

(b) Prepare the shareholders' equity section of the balance sheet as of December 31, 2011.

P15-14 Dai Corporation has outstanding $2 million no par value common shares that were issued at $10 per share. The balances at January 1, 2012, were $21 million in its retained earnings account; $4.3 million in its contributed surplus account; and $1.1 million in its accumulated other comprehensive income account. During 2012, the company's net income was $3.2 million and comprehensive income was $3,350,000. A cash dividend of $0.70 a share was paid on June 30, 2012, and a 5% stock dividend was distributed to shareholders of record at the close of business on December 31, 2012. You have been asked to give advice on how to properly account for the stock dividend. The existing company shares are quoted on a national stock exchange. The shares' market price per share has been as follows:

Oct. 31, 2012	$31
Nov. 30, 2012	33
Dec. 31, 2012	38
Average price over the two-month period	35

Instructions

(a) Prepare a journal entry to record the cash dividend.

(b) Prepare a journal entry to record the stock dividend.

(c) Prepare the shareholders' equity section (including a schedule of retained earnings) of the company balance sheet for the year 2012 based on the information given. Write a note to the financial statements that states the accounting basis for the stock dividend and include separate comments on why this basis was chosen.

(d) Prepare a statement of changes in shareholders' equity for the year 2012.

P15-15 Oregano Inc. was formed on July 1, 2009. It was authorized to issue 300,000 shares of no par value common shares and 100,000 shares of cumulative and non-participating preferred stock carrying a $2 dividend. The company has a July 1 to June 30 fiscal year. The following information relates to the company's shareholders' equity account.

Common Shares

Before the 2011–12 fiscal year, the company had 110,000 shares of outstanding common issued as follows:

1. 95,000 shares issued for cash on July 1, 2009, at $31 per share

2. 5,000 shares exchanged on July 24, 2009, for a plot of land that cost the seller $70,000 in 1999 and had an estimated fair value of $220,000 on July 24, 2009

3. 10,000 shares issued on March 1, 2010; the shares had been subscribed for $42 per share on October 31, 2009

Oct. 1, 2011	Subscriptions were received for 10,000 shares at $46 per share. Cash of $92,000 was received in full payment for 2,000 shares and share certificates were issued. The remaining subscription for 8,000 shares was to be paid in full by September 30, 2012, and the certificates would then be issued on that date.
Nov. 30, 2011	The company purchased 2,000 of its own common shares on the open market at $39 per share. These shares were restored to the status of authorized but unissued shares.
Dec. 15, 2011	The company declared a 5% stock dividend for shareholders of record on January 15, 2012, to be issued on January 31, 2012. The company was having a liquidity problem and could not afford a cash dividend at the time. The company's common shares were selling at $52 per share on December 15, 2011.
June 20, 2012	The company sold 500 of its own common shares for $21,000.

Preferred Shares

The company issued 50,000 preferred shares at $44 per share on July 1, 2009.

Cash Dividends

The company has followed a schedule of declaring cash dividends each year in December and June and making the payment to shareholders of record in the following month. The cash dividend declarations have been as follows since the company's first year and up until June 30, 2012:

Declaration Date	Common Shares	Preferred Shares
Dec. 15, 2010	$0.30 per share	$3.00 per share
June 6, 2011	$0.30 per share	$1.00 per share
Dec. 15, 2011	—	$1.00 per share

No cash dividends were declared during June 2012 due to the company's liquidity problems.

Retained Earnings

As at June 30, 2011, the company's retained earnings account had a balance of $690,000. For the fiscal year ending June 30, 2012, the company reported net income of $40,000.

In March 2011, the company received a term loan from Alberta Bank. The bank requires the company to establish a sinking fund and restrict retained earnings for an amount equal to the sinking fund deposit. The annual sinking fund payment of $50,000 is due on April 30 each year; the first payment was made on schedule on April 30, 2012.

Instructions

(a) Prepare the shareholders' equity section of the company's balance sheet, including appropriate notes, as at June 30, 2012, as it should appear in its annual report to the shareholders. (CMA adapted)

(b) Prepare the journal entries for the 2011–12 fiscal year.

(c) Discuss why the common shareholders might be willing to accept a stock dividend during the year rather than a cash dividend.

Digging
Deeper

Writing Assignments

WA15-1 Algonquin Corporation sold 50,000 common shares on a subscription basis for $40 per share. By December 31, 2011, collections on these subscriptions totalled $1.3 million. None of the subscriptions has been paid in full so far. Algonquin is a private company.

Instructions

(a) Discuss the meaning of the account Common Shares Subscribed and indicate how it is reported in the financial statements.

(b) Discuss the arguments in favour of reporting Subscriptions Receivable as a current asset.

(c) Discuss the arguments in favour of reporting Subscriptions Receivable as a contra equity account.

(d) Indicate how these 50,000 shares would be presented on Algonquin's December 31, 2011 balance sheet under the method discussed in (c) above.

(e) Suppose that Algonquin also has a benefit plan that allows employees to purchase shares of the company, and take two years to pay for the shares. When an employee agrees to purchase the shares, the shares are shown as issued and an Employee Share Loan Receivable Account is set up. As payments are made by the employee, this loan receivable account is reduced. Discuss the reporting issues related to this receivable account under IFRS and PE GAAP.

WA15-2 Under IFRS, equity is defined under the Framework for Preparation and Presentation of Financial Statements. Under PE GAAP, a definition of equity is provided in the *CICA Handbook*, Part II, Section 1000.

Instructions

Answer the following questions that relate to these sections and what is reported as equity.

(a) Define and discuss the term "equity."

(b) In reporting equity, various subcategories are required. Outline these equity components under PE GAAP and IFRS and explain why there are differences.

(c) How does PE GAAP report changes in these components? How does IFRS report these changes? Why are these presentations different?

(d) What transactions or events change owners' equity under IFRS? Under PE GAAP?

(e) What are some examples of changes within owners' equity that do not change the total amount of owners' equity under IFRS? Under PE GAAP?

WA15-3   The directors of Amman Corporation are considering issuing a stock dividend. They have asked you to discuss this option by answering the following questions.

Instructions

(a) What is a stock dividend? How is a stock dividend distinguished from a stock split, both from a legal standpoint and from an accounting standpoint?

(b) For what reasons does a corporation usually declare a stock dividend? A stock split?

(c) Discuss the amount of retained earnings, if any, that should be capitalized in connection with a stock dividend.

(AICPA adapted)

WA15-4   Henning Inc. is a medium-sized manufacturer that has been experiencing losses for the five years that it has been in business. Henning is a private company. Although the operations for the year just ended resulted in a loss, several important changes resulted in a profitable fourth quarter, and the company's future operations are expected to be profitable. The treasurer, Peter Henning, suggests that there be a financial reorganization to eliminate the accumulated deficit of $650,000.

Instructions

Ethics

(a) What are the characteristics of a financial reorganization? In other words, what does it consist of?

(b) List the conditions that generally justify a financial reorganization.

(c) Discuss the propriety of the treasurer's proposals to eliminate the deficit of $650,000.

(AICPA adapted)

WA15-5   The definition of equity relies on the definition of a liability. The current definition of equity is that it is the residual amount of the assets after deducting liabilities. Consequently, the definition of a liability is critical to determining what equity is. In addition, financial instruments are classified as equity, only if they do not meet the definition of a liability. FASB, however, has described three approaches for defining an equity instrument from a non-equity instrument: basic ownership, ownership-settlement, and reassessed expected outcomes. FASB decided on the use of "basic ownership" to define an equity instrument.

From the perspective of the conceptual framework, discuss the validity of both this account and the Accumulated Other Comprehensive Income account.

Instructions

Using information available from the IASB website (www.iasb.org), answer the following questions. You may find the following document helpful with this analysis: "Discussion Paper—Financial Instruments with Characteristics of Equity—September 2008."

(a) Explain the three approaches for identifying an equity instrument: basic ownership, ownership settlement, and reassessed expected outcomes.

(b) Explain the IASB's preliminary decision on the characteristics of an equity instrument.

(c) Under each of the above three approaches, assess how a convertible bond that is convertible into a fixed number of shares (regardless of the current share price at the time of conversion) would be classified. How would a convertible bond that was convertible into a variable number of shares, depending on the current share price, be reported under each of the above approaches?

WA 15-6   Write a brief essay highlighting the differences between IFRS and accounting standards for private enterprises noted in this chapter, discussing the conceptual justification for each. As part of this essay, include a discussion of the differences in capital disclosure requirements.

Cases

Refer to the Case Primer on the Student Website to help you answer these cases.

*CA15-1 "You can't write up assets," said Nick Toby, internal audit director of Nadir International Inc., to his boss, Jim Majewski, vice-president and chief financial officer. "Nonsense," said Jim, "I can do this as part of a quasi-reorganization of our company." For the last three years, Nadir International, a farm equipment manufacturing firm, has experienced a downturn in its profits as a result of stiff competition with overseas firms and a general downturn in the North American economy. The company is hoping to turn a profit by modernizing its property, plant, and equipment. This will require Nadir International to raise a lot of money. Management is very optimistic as to the future of the company, as the economy is entering a significant growth period.

Over the past few months, Jim has tried to raise funds from various financial institutions, but they are unwilling to lend capital. The reason they give is that the company's net book value of fixed assets on the balance sheet, based on historic cost, is not large enough to sustain major funding. Jim attempted to explain to bankers and investors that these assets are more valuable than their recorded amounts, especially since the company used accelerated amortization methods and tended to underestimate the useful lives of assets. Jim also believes that the company's land and buildings are substantially undervalued because of rising real estate prices over the past several years.

Jim's proposed solution to raise funds is a simple one: First, declare a large dividend to company shareholders that results in Retained Earnings having a large debit balance. Then, write up the fixed assets of Nadir International to an amount that is equal to the deficit in the Retained Earnings account.

Instructions

Adopt the role of the internal auditor and discuss the financial reporting issues. Nadir is thinking of going public.

CA15-2 Darshan Argrawal, controller for Centre Corporation (a public company), wants to discuss with the company president, Rhonda Santo, the possibility of paying a stock dividend. Argrawal knows that the company does not have a huge amount of cash, but he is certain that Santo would like to give the shareholders something of value this year since it has been a few years since the company has paid any dividends. Argrawal also is concerned that the company's cash position will not improve significantly in the near future. He feels that shareholders look to retained earnings and, if they see a large balance, they believe (erroneously, of course) that the company can pay a cash dividend.

Argrawal wants to propose that the company pay a 100% stock dividend, as opposed to a cash dividend or a 2-for-1 stock split. He reasons (1) that the shareholders will receive something of value, other than cash; and (2) that retained earnings will be reduced by the stock dividend (as opposed to a split, which does not affect retained earnings) so shareholders will be less likely to expect cash dividends in the near future.

For her part, Santo is interested in setting up a program that would have the company make loans to its top executives so that they can purchase new shares that will be issued by the company. This way, there is again no impact on cash yet the executives can participate in increases (hopefully) in the company share price. If all goes well, they can sell the shares, pay back the loans, and keep the difference. The loans are also secured by the company shares. If the share prices decrease, the company would not necessarily enforce collection of the receivable.

Instructions

Adopt the role of the company auditor and discuss the financial reporting issues.

Integrated Case

IC15-1 Sandolin Incorporated (SI) is a global, diversified firm whose shares trade on the major Canadian and U.S. stock markets. It owns numerous toll highways, several companies in the energy business, and an engineering consulting firm. Currently, its shares are trading at a 52-week high and its credit rating on all debt issues is AA. This is partly due to its revenues, which have doubled, and is also due to a recent restructuring. The restructuring is in the energy business and allows the company to position itself as a low-cost competitor in the industry. The restructuring involved laying off 5,000 employees and mothballing several oil and gas wells. The cost to extract oil and gas from the wells is currently too high. The company plans to retain the wells and work on new technology to reduce the extraction costs.

SI is in the process of putting together its annual financial statements and the VP Finance, Santos Suarez, is planning to meet with the company's auditors next week for a preliminary audit planning meeting. Santos is concerned about a phone call that he recently received from the government, as it was threatening legal action relating to the transportation part of the business. Among other things, SI owns a toll highway that stretches approximately 100 kilometres across a major urban centre. The road is very profitable since non-toll roads in the area are very congested and people use the toll road to commute. SI recently raised toll rates on the road and the government is claiming it is prohibited from doing this without government consent, which the government does not plan to give. Santos is concerned that if this news gets out, the credit rating and share price will suffer. SI believes that its contract allows it to change toll rates whenever it wants. SI's lawyers have reviewed the contracts and feel that SI's position is justifiable. The value of the toll road as a business is substantially less if the company loses the right to change the tolls.

While reviewing the company's dramatic increase in revenues, Santos became aware of a new type of transaction that the company has been entering into with increasing frequency in the past two months. As part of the energy business, SI employs a group of traders who make deals that reduce the company's exposure to fluctuating commodity prices. According to several e-mails between the traders, the deals are known as "round trip" trades. Several large trades involved purchases and sales with the same party for the same volume at substantially the same price. They have been treated as sales and account for 40% of the increase in revenues. The trader's position is that the company does make a commission on these deals, which adds up depending on the volume. The company never takes possession of the commodity that is being bought and sold.

Just before year end, the company acquired a mid-sized engineering firm. As part of the deal, the company issued shares to the vendor. The value of the issued shares was higher than the fair value of the engineering firm and the vendor gave SI a one-year note receivable for the difference. If profits from the engineering firm exceed a certain threshold—i.e., if the firm outperforms expectations—the note will not be paid. Currently, SI has recorded the note receivable as an asset.

Instructions

Adopt the role of Santos and analyze the financial reporting issues.

Research and Financial Analysis

RA15-1 Magna International Inc.

The Magna International Inc. financial statements for the year ended December 31, 2009, can be found on SEDAR (www.sedar.com).

Instructions

(a) The company has many different types of shares authorized, issued, and/or outstanding at the end of the 2009 year end. Prepare a chart that shows the following: name of share class, number of authorized shares, number of issued and outstanding shares, number of votes per share, and rights in terms of dividends.

(b) Why would a company structure its capital in this way? Is there a need for the various classes of shares? Who owns the multiple voting shares? (Hint: Look at the Annual Information Form on SEDAR [www.sedar.com].)

(c) Calculate the average book value per share for the 2008 and 2009 year ends. Compare these values with the closing share price at each year end. (Hint: Look at the Annual Information Form.)

(d) Describe the various types of share transactions that occurred during 2007 to 2009.

(e) How much was paid in dividends during 2009, and what kinds of dividends were paid?

(f) For 2008 and 2009, calculate the rate of return on shareholders' equity, the payout ratio, and the price earnings ratio based on the closing share price for the year end. Comment on the amounts calculated.

(g) Examine the Capital Disclosure note. What are the company's objectives in managing its capital? How does it measure its capital and what is included in capital?

RA15-2 Bank of Montreal versus Royal Bank of Canada

The Bank of Montreal and Royal Bank of Canada financial statements for the year ended October 31, 2009, can be found on SEDAR (www.sedar.com).

Instructions

(a) What is the average carrying value of each company's common shares? Compare these values with market prices. What stock exchanges do these banks trade on?

(b) What is the authorized share capital of each company?

(c) Comment on how each company presents its common shares and shareholders' equity.

(d) Describe the changes (number of shares and price) in each company's common share accounts over the past three years. What types of activities are contributing to the changes?

(e) What amounts of cash dividends per share were declared by each company during 2009? What were the dollar amount effects of the cash dividends on each company's shareholders' equity?

(f) What is each company's rate of return on common shareholders' equity for the year ended 2009? Which company gets the higher return on the equity of its shareholders?

RA15-3 Canadian Tire Corporation Limited

Refer to the financial statements and accompanying notes and discussion of Canadian Tire Corporation Limited for the year ended January 3, 2009 (2008 year-end report) and answer the following questions. The financial statements are available on SEDAR at www.sedar.com.

Instructions

(a) What are the issued and authorized shares for both classes of shares that the company has? What percentage of the authorized shares is issued?

(b) Compare the rights that are attached to each share. Are the class A shares more like preferred shares or common shares?

(c) Why does the company repurchase shares every year? How successful was it in achieving its objective in 2008?

(d) How did the company account for the excess of the amount paid on reacquisition over the carrying value of the shares for 2008? Recreate the journal entry.

(e) What was the average carrying value of the shares at the beginning of the year? What average price were the shares repurchased at? Compare this with the market prices of the shares.

(f) Review the capital disclosure note. What are the company's objectives in managing its capital? How does it monitor its capital? What is included in capital for the company?

RA15-4 MDS Inc.

Real-World Emphasis

The following is an excerpt from Note 10 to the financial statements of MDS Inc.

Share Capital

Effective September 26, 2000, the Company declared a one-for-one stock dividend which has essentially the same impact as a two-for-one stock split. Information contained in this note pertaining to dividends, share repurchases, the stock option plan, the stock dividend and share purchase plan and the employee share ownership plan, has been adjusted to reflect the impact of the stock dividend. The tables contained in note 10a) present the number of shares issued, repurchased and converted based on the date of the actual transaction.

(number of shares in thousands)	Common Number	Common Amount
Issued on conversion of Class A to Common	12,945	$ 22.2
Issued on conversion of Class B to Common	47,254	$317.9
Issued subsequent to conversions	9,676	442.6
Stock dividend	69,711	
Repurchases	(116)	(0.4)
Balance October 31, 2000	139,470	$782.3

The Statement of Retained Earnings is noted below:

Years Ended October 31

(millions of Canadian dollars) (restated note 2)	2000	1999	1998
Retained earnings, beginning of year	$324.1	$262.7	$237.6
Net income	110.3	81.9	44.3
Repurchase of shares and options (note 10)	(18.7)	(12.4)	(12.2)
Dividends	(10.3)	(8.1)	(7.0)
Retained earnings, end of year	$405.4	$324.1	$262.7

Instructions

Discuss the financial reporting issues for the stock dividend.

RA15-5 Suncor Energy Inc.

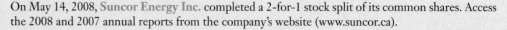

Real-World Emphasis

On May 14, 2008, Suncor Energy Inc. completed a 2-for-1 stock split of its common shares. Access the 2008 and 2007 annual reports from the company's website (www.suncor.ca).

Instructions

(a) Why might Suncor have declared a stock split?

(b) What impact did the stock split have on (1) total shareholders' equity, (2) total book value, (3) number of outstanding shares, and (4) book value per share? Examine the 2007 numbers as originally filed and the restated 2007 comparison numbers in the 2008 year-end annual reports to reflect this change for number of shares outstanding, the total dollar value of common shares outstanding, and earnings per share data.

(c) What impact did the split have on the shares' market value? What has since happened to their market price?

RA15-6 Statements of Changes in Equity

IFRS requires statements of changes in shareholders' equity. PE GAAP only requires a statement of retained earnings.

Instructions

(a) Discuss why these differences occur.

(b) Review the statement of changes of Lufthansa AG (available at www.lufthansa.com) for the year ended December 31, 2009. (1) Explain the various components that are reconciled in the statement of changes. (2) Comment on why users might find the statement of changes in equity more useful than a statement of retained earnings. (3) Which of these components found on Lufthansa's statement for changes in equity would be similar to a private enterprise?

Real-World Emphasis

RA15-7 Impact of Different Legal Systems on IFRS

Companies from many countries have moved to, or are in the process of moving to, IFRS. Evidence has shown that it is preferable to adopt IFRS on a wholesale basis (i.e., with no differences from the standards). This chapter shows how much the legal environment affects the accounting for shares. Different countries will have differing legal systems and environments, which may affect the accounting on a country-by-country basis.

Instructions

How should this situation be dealt with, in your opinion?

RA15-8 Tembec Inc.

Access the 2008 annual report of Tembec Inc. for the period ended September 27, 2008 from SEDAR www.sedar.com.

Real-World Emphasis

Instructions

1. Read Note 1 to Tembec's financial statements for the year ended September 27, 2008 Describe the Plan of Arrangement that was implemented on February 29, 2008. What was the value of the new equity that was issued?

2. Explain what is required to implement "fresh start" accounting. When is it allowed to be done?

3. How was the restructuring completed? Prepare the appropriate journal entries from the information provided in Note 1.

4. How was the "fresh start" accounting applied? Explain the nature of the fair value adjustments and how much was required to adjust each asset and liability account.

Return to Simpler Structures

TD Securities' "structured finance" department focuses on the equity derivative business. Much of its clientele are institutional investors looking for swaps, options, or customized derivatives. Todd Hargarten, vice president and director of TD Securities Inc., describes his work with complex financial instruments as reactive, rather than proactive. "A lot of structured derivatives are bought, not sold," he says.

When working with corporate clients, Hargarten and his colleagues provide information on possible solutions to a business's situation. Often these structures are created for a specific large business; there may occasionally be broadly applicable solutions, but that's rare in Canada, Hargarten says.

Institutional investors make their own decisions. Most large pension plans have in-house expertise to develop their own products. By doing all the pieces themselves and breaking it down to a commodity, the pension funds are isolating the risk, Hargarten adds.

In the past, retail demand for exposure to hot sectors drove structured products. Current interest is not as much in the sector, but in the yield a product provides, Hargarten says.

Principal-protected, equity-linked notes compete with bank-offered, equity-linked guaranteed investment certificates (GICs). The main difference is the term; a note's term can be seven or more years (some have 25-year terms), while a GIC is generally capped at five years. One shortcoming of these structured notes was they were linked to the financial institution, since brokers were reluctant to push a competitor's branded product. As a result, they were limited in size, often ranging from $5 to $25 million. These notes are now sold in other dealers' channels and their size depends on each specific note, Hargarten says.

Adding a bit more structure and flexibility to these instruments can become complicated. For example, covered call-writing funds were first developed in the early 1990s. Then principal protection was added. "Since then a lot of these structures morphed into other areas," Hargarten says. The complexity of these and other financial instruments continued to increase for a number of years. However, following the financial meltdown in 2008, there has been a general trend toward simplicity again. ∎

CHAPTER 16

Complex Financial Instruments

Learning Objectives

After studying this chapter, you should be able to:

1. Understand what derivatives are and why they exist.
2. Explain the various types of financial risks and how they arise.
3. Understand how to account for derivatives.
4. Explain the unique issues associated with derivatives that are settleable using the entity's own equity instruments.
5. Analyze whether a hybrid/compound instrument issued for financing purposes represents a liability, equity, or both (and how to measure).
6. Explain the accounting for the issuance, conversion, and retirement of convertible securities.
7. Describe the various types of stock compensation plans.
8. Explain the differences between employee and compensatory option plans and other options.
9. Describe the accounting for compensatory stock option plans.
10. Identify the major differences in accounting between accounting standards for private enterprises (PE GAAP/ASPE) and IFRS, and what changes are expected in the near future.

After studying the Chapter 16 appendices, you should be able to:

11. Understand how derivatives are used in hedging.
12. Explain what hedge accounting is and identify the qualifying hedge criteria.
13. Explain the difference between a fair value hedge and cash flow hedge.
14. Calculate the impact on net income of using hedge accounting for both types of hedges.
15. Account for stock appreciation rights plans.
16. Explain what performance-type plans are.
17. Understand how options pricing models are used to measure financial instruments.

Preview of Chapter 16

Uncommon in the past, complex financial instruments are now used by companies in many different industries. Companies use these instruments in an effort to manage risk, gain access to pools of financing, and minimize the cost of capital and taxes. In response to this trend, the accounting profession has developed a new framework for dealing with these instruments in the financial statements. Earlier in the text, the accounting was discussed for basic financial instruments, including accounts and notes receivable/payable, investments, loans, and shares. This chapter focuses on complex financial instruments, such as hybrid and compound debt and equity instruments and derivatives.[1] Since employee compensation plans often include such derivatives as stock options, these plans will also be discussed in this chapter.

The chapter is organized as follows:

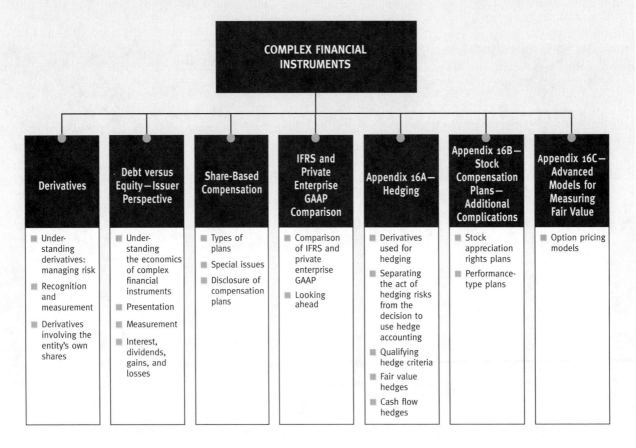

DERIVATIVES

Objective 1
Understand what derivatives are and why they exist.

If you recall from previous chapters, financial instruments are contracts that create both a financial asset for one party and a financial liability or equity instrument for the other party.[2] Financial instruments can be primary or derivative. Primary financial instru-

---

[1] Many derivatives are self-standing but some are embedded in other contracts. Compound and hybrid instruments often contain embedded derivatives.

[2] *CICA Handbook*, Part II, Section 3856.05 and IAS 32.11.

ments include most basic financial assets and financial liabilities, such as receivables and payables, as well as equity instruments, such as shares. The accounting issues for these instruments were covered in earlier chapters. Derivative instruments, on the other hand, are more complex. They are called derivatives because they derive (i.e., get) their value from an **underlying** primary instrument, index, or non-financial item, such as a commodity (called the "underlying"). Derivatives may trade on exchanges such as the Canadian Derivatives Exchange and "over-the-counter" markets. Where there is a market for the derivative, it is easier to value. Certain derivatives do not trade on any exchange or market (for instance, certain executive stock options or tailor-made, as opposed to standardized, foreign exchange forward contracts).

Derivatives are defined by the accounting standards as **financial instruments that create rights and obligations that have the effect of transferring, between parties to the instrument, one or more of the financial risks that are inherent in an underlying primary instrument. They transfer risks that are inherent in the underlying primary instrument without either party having to hold any investment in the underlying.**[3]

 Finance

They have three characteristics:

1. Their value changes in response to the **underlying instrument (the "underlying")**.

2. They require **little or no initial investment**.

3. They are settled at a **future** date.

Options, forwards, and futures are common types of derivatives. Accounting for these common types of derivative instruments will be discussed further in this chapter, along with examples. As a basic rule, derivatives are measured at fair value with gains and losses booked through net income. Special accounting exists for derivatives that are part of a hedging relationship and this is discussed in Appendix 16A. The notion of an **underlying** will be discussed in the context of these examples. Derivatives may be embedded in contracts. This means that the contract has more than one part: a host (non-derivative) part and one or more derivatives. The accounting for embedded derivatives is complex and in flux and is generally beyond the scope of this text. Having said that, the chapter will discuss this area briefly in the context of compound instruments issued by the company.

Understanding Derivatives: Managing Risks

Why do derivatives exist? In short, **they exist to help companies manage risks**. Companies currently operate in an environment of constant change caused by volatile markets, new technology, and deregulation, among other things. This increases overall business risk as well as financial risk. The response from the financial community has been to develop products to manage some of these risks, with one result being the rise of derivatives. Recall from Appendix 5A the differing types of risks that a company faces. Managers of successful companies have always and will continue to manage risks to minimize unfavourable financial consequences and to maximize shareholder value. While managing risk helps keep uncertainty at an acceptable level (which may differ depending on the stakeholders), it also has its costs.

 Finance

There are many layers of costs relating to the use of derivatives. Three categories of costs are as follows:

1. Direct costs

2. Indirect costs

3. Hidden or opportunity costs

---

[3] *CICA Handbook*, Part II, Section 3856.05 and IAS 39.9.

Underlying Concept

As always, the benefits of entering into certain transactions, especially complex ones, should exceed the costs; otherwise, the company will be reducing shareholder value rather than creating it.

In order to enter into contracts that manage risk, such as insurance and derivative contracts, transaction costs are normally incurred, including bank service charges, brokerage fees, and insurance premiums. These are the **direct**, visible costs that are charged by an intermediary or the other party to the transaction. Then there are **indirect**, less visible costs. The activity of researching, analyzing, and executing these transactions uses a significant amount of employee time. As managing risk sometimes results in limiting the potential for gain, there is also a **hidden cost**: the **opportunity cost**. **Use of too many complicated financial instruments increases the complexity of financial statements and therefore reduces their transparency and understandability.** Given the current climate, capital markets may penalize such companies by increasing costs of capital and/or limiting or denying access to capital. This latter aspect also represents a **hidden cost** to the company. Companies must consider all of the costs that are associated with derivatives and weigh them against the benefits.

The growth in use of derivatives has been aided by the development of powerful calculation and communication technology, which provides new ways to analyze information about markets as well as the power to process high volumes of payments. Thanks to these developments, many corporations are now using derivatives extensively and successfully.

What Do the Numbers Mean?

The International Swaps and Derivatives Association (ISDA) was founded in 1985 and has 810 member organizations from 57 countries. The ISDA describes itself as being among the world's largest global financial trade associations as measured by number of member firms. In 2009, the ISDA completed a survey of the world's major companies as identified in the Fortune Global 500. The research show that 471 of the 500 companies use derivatives and that this percentage has been growing since the prior survey was done in 2003. The following chart[4] is taken from the survey and shows the types of derivatives contracts that these companies are entering into. Note the extensive use of foreign currency ("forex") and interest rate derivatives. The numbers reflect percentage of total companies in the survey that use each type of derivative.

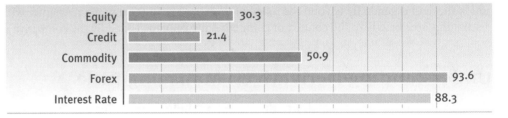

The research shows that there is widespread use of derivatives in many industries. The chart[5] below illustrates this, showing the percentage of surveyed companies in each industry that use derivatives.

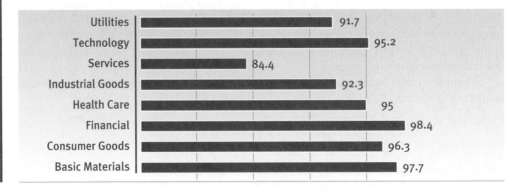

[4] *ISDA Research Notes*, Spring 2009, International Swaps and Derivatives Association, Inc.
[5] Ibid.

Given the widespread use of these instruments, accounting standard setters are striving to ensure that they are properly reflected in the financial statements. Because of the complexity of the derivative contracts and how they are employed by companies to manage risk, the financial reporting issues are significant.

As mentioned above, companies use derivatives to manage risks, and especially financial risks. There are various kinds of financial risks, and they are defined in IFRS as follows.[6]

2 Objective
Explain the various types of financial risks and how they arise.

Finance

1. *Credit risk* The risk that one party to a financial instrument will cause a financial loss for the other party by failing to discharge (respect) an obligation.

2. *Liquidity risk* The risk that an entity will have difficulty meeting obligations that are associated with financial liabilities.

3. *Market risk* The risk that the fair value or future cash flows of a financial instrument will fluctuate because of changes in market prices. There are three types of market risk: currency risk, interest rate risk, and other price risk.

   (a) *Currency risk* The risk that the fair value or future cash flows of a financial instrument will fluctuate because of changes in foreign exchange rates.

   (b) *Interest rate risk* The risk that the fair value or future cash flows of a financial instrument will fluctuate because of changes in market interest rates.

   (c) *Other price risk* The risk that the fair value or future cash flows of a financial instrument will fluctuate because of changes in market prices (other than price changes arising from **interest rate risk** or **currency risk**), whether those changes are caused by factors that are specific to the individual financial instrument or its issuer, or factors that affect all similar financial instruments being traded in the market.

It is important for companies and users of financial statements to identify and understand which risks a company currently has and how it plans to manage these risks. Keep in mind that derivatives often expose the company to additional risks. As long as the company identifies and manages these risks, this is not a problem. **There is a problem, however, when stakeholders do not understand the risk profile of derivative instruments**. The use of derivatives can be dangerous, and it is critical that all the parties that are involved understand the risks and rewards associated with these contracts.[7]

Underlying Concept

Remember from finance courses that increased risk may bring the opportunity for increased rewards. Thus, some companies expose themselves to increased risks in order to maximize shareholder value. This is often referred to as the risk/return trade-off.

An entity might use derivatives to reduce or offset various risks (normally referred to as hedging). It is also possible to enter into derivative contracts to create positions that are expected to be profitable.[8] Both are acceptable strategies and depend on the company's risk tolerance profile; i.e., the nature of the risks that the company can comfortably undertake and the amount of exposure to each risk that it is willing to accept. There are special optional accounting rules that a company can make use of when a derivative is used to hedge certain risk. Although hedging will be discussed in the body of the chapter, **hedge accounting** will be discussed in Appendix 16A due to its added complexity.

---

[6] IFRS 7 Appendix A and *CICA Handbook*, Part II, Section 3856.A66.

[7] There are some well-publicized examples of companies that have suffered sizeable losses as a result of using derivatives, perhaps because they did not fully understand the possible effects of the contracts. For example, companies such as Showa Shell Sekiyu (Japan), Metallgesellschaft (Germany), Proctor & Gamble (United States), and Air Products & Chemicals (United States) have incurred significant losses from investments in derivative instruments. Companies sometimes suffer losses because of taking too much risk or because they do not understand the markets or positions taken. Another reason that a company may suffer losses when using derivatives is because of the timing of closing out the contracts and positions.

[8] When companies create positions that are expected to be profitable, there is often a risk of loss as well. Some refer to this as speculating.

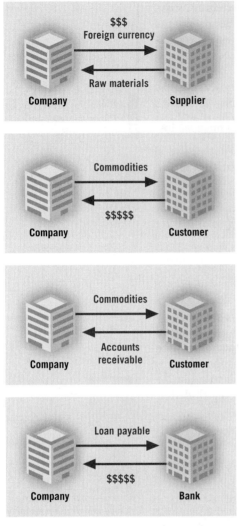

What types of business models and processes generate financial risk? Virtually all business models generate financial (and indeed other) risks. The following are some examples:

- Any business that purchases commodities such as fuel, agricultural products, or renewable resources as inputs has a **market risk** associated with these inputs. These companies know that commodity prices vary significantly depending on supply and demand. This affects the company's profitability and may lead to volatile net income. Often, the commodities are priced in different currencies, which creates a **currency risk**.

- Likewise, any company that sells commodities has a **market risk**. Depending on the commodity pricing when the commodity is sold, the company might make more or less profit, which again can lead to volatile or unpredictable net income.[9]

- Companies that sell on credit have **credit risks**: the risk that the customer or other party (counterparty) may fail to make a payment.

- Companies that borrow money or incur liabilities increase **liquidity risk**: the risk that they will not be able to pay their obligations. Debt also creates **interest rate risk**.

- Companies that buy goods, finance purchases, create inventory, sell goods, and collect receivables have **market risks**: the risk that the value of the assets will change while the company is holding them.

Remember that derivative transactions may be the most efficient way of managing these risks. Alternatively, or in addition, the company may rely on other tools to manage the risks, including internal controls (such as credit checks on customers to reduce or eliminate credit risk).

A company may try to structure its business model such that it is not exposed to certain financial risks and thus does not need to manage them. For instance, by having a policy of selling only for cash, the company is not exposed to credit risk. By using "just-in-time" inventory ordering, a company gets rid of the market risk associated with stockpiling or holding inventory.

Producers and Consumers as Derivative Users

McCain Foods Limited is a large producer of potatoes for the consumer market. Assume that McCain believes that the present price for potatoes is excellent, but that McCain will need two months to harvest its potatoes and deliver them to market. The company has **market risk** related to its inventory. Because the company is concerned that the price of potatoes will drop, it signs a contract in which it agrees to sell its potatoes today at the current market price, but for delivery in two months. This locks in the market price. Known as a forward contract, this type of contract reduces the **market risk** related to the potatoes (both in terms of price and cash flows).

Who would buy this contract? Suppose McDonald's Corporation is on the other side of the contract and it wants to have potatoes (for french fries) in two months and is worried

---

[9] All business inputs have price risks associated with them. There is always a risk that prices to acquire the inputs will vary over time.

that prices will increase.[10] McDonald's also has **market risk**. It therefore agrees to delivery in two months at the current fixed price because it knows that it will need potatoes in two months and that it can make an acceptable profit at the current price level. McDonald's is also managing its **market risk**.

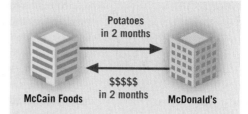

In this situation, if the price of potatoes increases before delivery, you might conclude that McCain loses and McDonald's wins. Conversely, if prices decrease, McCain wins and McDonald's loses. However, the objective is not to gamble on the outcome. In other words, regardless of which way the price moves, both companies should be pleased because both have received a price at which they can make an acceptable profit. In summary:

- Both companies have existing risks because of the way they do business (their business model).

- Both seek to manage these risks.

- Both are using derivatives to reduce these risks.

- Both companies are seen to be hedging their risks because they are reducing uncertainty.

Commodity prices are volatile and depend on factors such as weather, crop disasters, and general economic conditions. For the producer of a product and its consumer to plan effectively, it makes good sense to lock in specific future revenues or input costs in order to run their businesses successfully. This is a key way to manage cash flows to limit the risk of going bankrupt.

Speculators and Arbitrageurs as Derivative Users

In some cases, instead of a company like McDonald's buying the contract, a **speculator** may purchase the contract from McCain. The speculator is not trying to reduce risk, however. Instead the objective is to maximize potential returns by being exposed to greater risks. The speculator is betting that the price of potatoes will increase and that the value of the forward contract will therefore also increase. The speculator, who may be in the market for only a few hours, will then sell the forward contract to another speculator or to a company like McDonald's. The speculator will never take delivery of the potatoes as this was never the intention. The goal was to generate a cash profit from trading in the derivative instrument itself. The difference between this transaction and the earlier hedging transaction is that in the earlier transaction the company was entering into a derivative to reduce a pre-existing risk. In the case of the speculator, there is no pre-existing risk, just a desire to take on additional risk in the hope of increasing profits.

Another user of derivatives is an **arbitrageur**. These market players try to take advantage of inefficiencies in different markets. They try to lock in profits by simultaneously entering into transactions in two or more markets. For example, an arbitrageur might trade in a futures contract and at the same time in the commodity that underlies the futures contract, hoping to achieve small price gains on the difference between the two. Arbitrageurs exist because there is information asymmetry in different markets. This occurs when the same information is not available to all market participants in the different markets. Some markets are more efficient than others. The arbitrageurs force the prices in the different markets to move toward each other since they create demand and supply where previously there might not have been any, thus driving the prices either up or down.

---

[10] Why would one party think that prices will rise and the other that they will fall? The same information is rarely available to all parties. In most contract negotiations, there is information asymmetry, which leads to the parties sometimes expecting different outcomes.

Speculators and arbitrageurs are very important to markets because they keep the market liquid on a daily basis.

Recognition and Measurement of Derivatives

The basic principles regarding accounting for derivatives are as follows:

1. Financial instruments (including financial derivatives) and certain non-financial derivatives represent rights or obligations that meet the definitions of assets or liabilities and should be **recognized in financial statements when the entity becomes party to the contract.**

2. **Fair value is the most relevant measure**.

3. Gains and losses should be booked through net income.

Special optional hedge accounting exists for derivatives and other items that have been designated as being part of a hedging relationship for accounting purposes.

Recall the discussion regarding fair value measurement from Chapter 2 and Appendix 2A. Appendix 16C discusses more advanced measurement techniques and models.

Non-financial Derivatives and Executory Contracts

Note that derivatives may be financial or non-financial. An example of a financial derivative is a forward contract to buy U.S. dollars. An example of a non-financial derivative is a contract to buy pork bellies or potatoes as in the earlier example. GAAP provides accounting guidance for financial instruments (including financial derivatives), as well as certain non-financial derivatives. Thus many commodities futures are accounted for in the same manner as financial derivatives.

 Law

What about purchase commitments? Are they derivatives? For instance, many companies enter into contracts intending to take delivery of raw material as part of locking in a supply of raw materials. These contracts may be structured as commodities futures or forward contracts in legal form (and therefore derivatives from a finance perspective); however, they may also be structured as regular purchase commitments. Under both types of contracts, the company is agreeing to take delivery of the raw materials at an agreed upon price in the future. What separates the two from an accounting perspective? What makes the forwards and futures derivatives from a finance perspective but the purchase commitment not? Should they both be accounted for in a similar manner; i.e., as derivatives?[11]

Purchase commitments are generally labelled as executory contracts: **contracts to do something in the future** (where no cash or product changes hands up front). Note that derivatives are similarly contracts to do something in the future and could arguably also be referred to as executory contracts. In this regard, the two are similar. Purchase commitments are not structured as derivatives contracts from a legal perspective, however, and they do not trade on commodities exchanges (as do futures and options, for instance).[12] Historically, these contracts have not been recognized in the financial statements. An issue exists, however, because technically, purchase commitments meet the

---

[11] Recall that derivatives are contracts themselves just like the purchase commitment and it is the terms of the contract that give rise to contractual rights and obligations that accountants must then account for. Sometimes, accounting is complicated by the fact that accountants like to put labels like "derivatives" on things. This labelling complicates the accounting since standard setters must determine whether it is appropriate to apply the label (and the designated accounting) or not.

[12] Commodities contracts generally trade in liquid markets and by virtue of the fact that they trade on an exchange have a net cash settlement feature. This means that the option exists to close out the position and take cash instead of delivery of the underlying product itself.

accounting definition of derivatives—their value changes with the value of the underlying (in this case the raw material); there is no investment up front and the contract will be settled in future.

Significant Change

Under accounting standards for private enterprises, (ASPE/PE GAAP), purchase commitments are not accounted for as derivatives on the basis that they are not exchange traded and therefore are difficult to measure. They are therefore not recognized until the goods are received. Under IFRS, for contracts that have net settlement features (i.e., can be settled on a net basis by paying cash or other assets as opposed to taking delivery of the underlying product),[13] as long as the company intends to take delivery of the raw materials, the contracts are designated as "expected use," and not accounted for as derivatives. If these contracts do not have net settlement features, they are not accounted for as derivatives either. Where these types of contracts are not accounted for as derivatives, they are accounted for as unexecuted contracts and not recognized until delivery of the underlying non-financial asset takes place (e.g., the inventory is delivered or received).

Illustration 16-1 analyzes the nature of purchase commitments and forwards/futures/options contracts which relate to non-financial assets such as commodities.

	Purchase commitments for non-financial assets (e.g., inventory)	Forward/futures/options to buy/sell non-financial assets (e.g., inventory)
Legal form	Purchase contract/commitment. Generally does not include net settlement clause.	Forward/futures/option contract
Trade on a market (thus establishing liquidity and fair value)?	No	Yes and generally net settleable
Meet the definition of an executory contract (i.e., promise to do something in the future where neither party has yet performed)?	Yes. A contract is signed upfront but no money or goods change hands until later.	Yes. A contract is signed upfront but no money or goods change hands until later.
Meet the definition of a derivative (i.e., value depends on underlying, little or no upfront investments, and settled in future)?	Yes. The value of the contract depends upon the value of the underlying (e.g., inventory), there is no upfront investment, and it will be settled in the future.	Yes. The value of the contract depends upon the value of the underlying (e.g., inventory), there is no upfront investment, and it will be settled in the future.
Perspective for accounting purposes	Generally accounted for as an unexecuted contract and not recognized until the underlying non-financial item is delivered. (Derivative accounting does not apply to these contracts either because they are not exchange traded [PE GAAP] or because they are not settleable on a net basis [IFRS]).	Generally accounted for as a derivative (recognized and measured at FV-NI). Accounted for as an executory contract under IFRS, where there is no net settlement feature or where one exists but company expects to take delivery or deliver the underlying asset.

Illustration 16-1

Accounting for Contracts Involving Non-Financial Assets

---

[13] Per IAS 39.6, there are various ways in which contracts can be settled net in cash or other financial instruments, including:

– where explicitly allowed by contract,
– where there is a history of settling net in cash or taking delivery and immediately selling the item for profit, or
– where the item is readily convertible to cash. (Items are readily convertible to cash where there is a ready market to buy/sell the items.)

The ability to settle net is an important differentiating feature since where it does not exist, the contract will have to settle by delivering or taking delivery of the underlying item. There is no choice. Where net settlement is an option, then an additional hurdle must be cleared to prove that the contract was entered into for expected use.

We will now discuss three basic types of derivatives: options and warrants, forwards, and futures.

Options and Warrants

Objective 3
Understand how to
account for derivatives.

Law

Finance

Options and warrants are derivative instruments. An option or warrant gives the holder the contractual right to acquire or sell an underlying instrument at a fixed price (the exercise or strike price—the agreed-upon price at which the option may be settled) **within a defined term (the** exercise period**).** A good example is an option to purchase shares of a company for a fixed price, on a specified date. The **underlying** is the shares; **i.e., this option derives its value from the share price of the underlying shares.** If the share price goes up, the option is worth more. If it goes down, the option may become worthless.

The option allows the holder to protect himself or herself against declines in the market value of the underlying shares but also allows the holder to participate in increases in the share value without having to hold the actual shares. Derivative instruments do not result in the transfer of the underlying (i.e., the shares in our example) at the contract's inception and perhaps not even when it matures. They also require a relatively low upfront investment (the cost of the option premium). The cost of the option is a fraction of the cost of the actual share itself. Before the end of the option period, the holder may sell the option to capture the value. The holder has the **right to exercise the option but is not obliged** to buy the shares at the exercise price. An example of the use of options in the capital marketplace is noted below. On March 5, 2007, Four Seasons Hotels Inc. (Four Seasons) issued a Notice of Special Meeting and Management Information Circular about the privatization of the company. The privatization was to be effected by three large shareholders buying the shares that were held by the rest of the shareholders. The company would then be owned by these three large shareholders and taken private.

**What Do
the Numbers
Mean?**

**Real-World
Emphasis**

Four Seasons was started as a private company several decades ago by Isadore Sharp, who continued to retain control of the company after it went public. Four Seasons manages 74 luxury hotels and resorts in 31 countries and has several properties under development. The company had two main classifications of common shares: multiple voting shares, which are owned by the Sharp family through a company called Triples Holdings (Triples) and represent a controlling interest in the company, and subordinate/limited voting shares, which are held by the public.

At the time of the announcement, Kingdom Hotels International (Kingdom), owned by Prince Alwaleed, owned 22% of the limited voting shares and Cascade Investment LLC (Cascade), owned by Bill Gates, owned 2% of the limited voting shares. Under the terms of the agreement, the purchasers offered $82 per share, which was priced to represent a premium of 28.4% in excess of the share price just before the announcement. The purchasers were represented by Kingdom, Cascade, and Triples.

The board of directors approved the deal, as did Triples (as controlling shareholder). All that remained for the completion of the transaction was a vote of the limited voting shares. The agreements required that 66.67% of these shareholders vote in favour (the majority of the minority). The vote was to be taken in April. Just before the vote, a major investor, Marisco Capital Management LLC (which owned approximately 19% of the limited voting shares), announced that it would not vote in favour of the privatization and the share price began to fall.

As a result, there was heavy trading in derivative instruments that gave holders of the shares the right to sell the shares for $80 regardless of the outcome of the transaction. The holders of the Four Seasons shares, recognizing that the deal might not go through, were hoping to reduce their market price risk. Non-shareholders were speculating on the outcome of the deal. On the announcement that Marisco would not support the deal, the shares had slumped to $79.

The deal went through and the company is now privately owned.

A Framework for Options.   Options may be purchased (purchased options) or written by a company (written options). If a company **purchases** an option, it will **pay a fee or premium and gain a right** to do something. If a company **writes** an option, it **charges a fee or premium and gives the holder/purchaser the right** to do something. The "right" in question may be either of the following:

Law

1. A right to buy the underlying (a call option)

2. A right to sell the underlying (a put option)

The framework is shown in Illustration 16-2.

Illustration 16-2

A Framework for Options

A written option is riskier for the company because the writer has no control over whether it will be required to deliver something. The company is obligated to perform under the option. This is different from a purchased option, which gives the company the right but not the obligation to do something. Assume that a company writes or sells an option for $5 cash. **Because this creates an obligation for the company that has written the option, the option is generally accounted for as a liability.**

An example of a purchase call option follows.

Illustration of a Purchased Call Option.   Assume that Abalone Inc. purchases a **call option** contract on January 2, 2011, from Baird Investment Corp.[14] The option gives Abalone the right to purchase 1,000 Laredo shares (the underlying) at $100 per share (the exercise/strike price), and it expires April 30, 2011. For the right to buy the shares at this fixed price, Abalone pays a premium of $400. This is a financial derivative because the underlying is a financial asset (i.e., the Laredo shares).

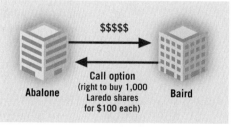

At the time of the transaction, Laredo shares are trading at $100. If the price of Laredo shares increases above $100, Abalone can exercise the option and purchase the shares for $100 per share. Alternatively, Abalone may sell the option to someone else. Here, Baird has the **market risk associated with the shares.** Abalone has **market risk associated with the option** itself, or the $400. At worst, the option becomes

Finance

---

[14] Baird Investment Corp. is referred to as the counterparty. Recall that derivatives are financial instruments. Recall also that financial instruments are a contract between two parties. Counterparties frequently are investment bankers or other entities that hold inventories of financial instruments.

worthless and Abalone loses the $400. If Baird has written the option without holding an investment in Laredo (a "naked" position), it will suffer a loss if the price of Laredo increases. If Baird holds shares in Laredo offsetting the option sold (a "covered call"), its profit on the investment will be limited to the difference between $100 and the price it paid for the shares plus the $400 premium received from Abalone. If Laredo's share price never increases above $100 per share, the call option is worthless and Abalone recognizes a loss equal to the initial price of the call option.

The following journal entry would be made at the acquisition date of January 2, 2011:

A   =   L   +   SE
0

Cash flows: ↓ 400 outflow

| Derivatives—Financial Assets | 400 | |
| Cash | | 400 |

The option premium is composed of two amounts: (1) the intrinsic value and (2) the time value. Illustration 16-3 shows the formula to calculate the option premium.

Illustration 16-3

Option Premium Formula

Option Premium = Intrinsic Value + Time Value

Intrinsic value is the difference between the market price of the underlying and the strike or exercise price at any point in time. It represents the amount that would be realized by the option holder if the option were exercised immediately. On January 2, 2011, the intrinsic value of the option related to the Laredo shares is zero because the market price is equal to the strike price of $100. **Time value** refers to the option's value over and above its intrinsic value. Time value reflects the **possibility that the option will have a fair value greater than zero because there is some expectation that the price of Laredo shares will increase above the strike price during the option term**. As indicated, the option's value is $400.[15]

On March 31, 2011, the price of Laredo shares has increased to $120 per share and the intrinsic value of the call option contract is now $20,000. That is, Abalone could exercise the call option and purchase 1,000 shares from Baird for $100 per share and then sell the shares in the market for $120 per share. This gives Abalone a potential gain of $20,000 ($120,000 – $100,000) on the option contract.

The options may be worth more than this due to the time value component; that is, the shares may increase in value over the remaining month. Assume the options are trading at $20,100. In addition, we must consider the original cost of the option. The entry to record this change in value of the option at March 31, 2011, is as follows:[16]

A   =   L   +   SE
+19,700   +19,700

Cash flows: No effect

Derivatives—Financial Assets	19,700	
Gain		19,700[a]
[a] $20,100 – $400		

[15] The value is estimated using options pricing models, such as the Black-Scholes model. The fair value estimate is affected by the volatility of the underlying stock, the expected life of the option, the risk-free rate of interest, and expected dividends on the underlying shares during the option term. This model is further explained in Appendix 16C.

[16] The decline in value of the time value portion of the options from $400 to $100 reflects both the decreased likelihood that the Laredo shares will continue to increase in value over the option period and the shorter time to maturity of the option contract.

At March 31, 2011, the call option is reported on the balance sheet at its fair value of $20,100 and the net gain increases net income for the period. The options are "in-the-money"; that is, they have value.

On April 1, 2011, assuming the shares are still worth $120 and Abalone settles the option in cash rather than by taking delivery of the shares of Laredo, the entry to record the settlement of the call option contract with Baird is as follows:

Cash	20,000	
Loss	100[17]	
Derivatives—Financial Assets		20,100

A = L + SE
−100   −100

Cash flows: ↑ 20,000 inflow

Illustration 16-4 summarizes the effects of the call option contract on net income.

Date	Transaction	Income (Loss) Effect
March 31, 2011	Net increase in value of call option ($20,100 − $400)	$19,700
April 1, 2011	Settle call option	(100)
	Total net income	$19,600[a]

[a] This amount is net of $400 cost for the right to participate in the increase in the value of the shares.

Illustration 16-4

Effect on Income—Option

On April 1, 2011, Abalone could have taken delivery of the shares under the option contract. The entry to record this is as follows:

Investment	120,000	
Loss	100	
Cash		100,000
Derivatives—Financial Assets		20,100

A = L + SE
−100   −100

Cash flows: ↓ 100,000 outflow

Finance

Abalone could have purchased the Laredo shares directly on January 2 instead of buying an option. To make the initial investment in Laredo shares, Abalone would have had to pay the full cost of the shares upfront and would therefore have had to pay more cash than it did for the option. If the price of the Laredo shares then increased, Abalone would realize a gain; however, Abalone would also be at risk for a loss if the Laredo shares declined in value.

We will return to the discussion of options in Appendix 16A. Chapter 17 will also revisit the option framework when looking at the potentially dilutive impact of options in calculating earnings per share.

Forwards

Law

A forward contract is another type of derivative. Under a forward contract, the parties to the contract each **commit upfront to do something in the future**. For example, one party commits to buy an item (referred to as the underlying) and the other to sell the item at a specified price on a specified date. The price and time period are locked in under the contract. The contracts are specific to the transacting parties based on their needs. These instruments generally do not trade on exchanges as the terms are unique to the parties involved (i.e., the terms are not standardized as most exchange-traded contracts are).

[17] A loss exists due to the decrease in the time value component of the option. As time passes, the time value component declines and is zero at the end of the contract.

Promise to buy
U.S. $1,000 for $1,150
in 30 days

Abalone   Bond

Promise to sell
U.S. $1,000 for $1,150
in 30 days

Finance

Usually banks buy and sell these contracts or act as intermediaries between the parties to the contract. Forwards are measured at the present value of any future cash flows under the contract—discounted at a rate that reflects risk.

Illustration of a Forward Contract.   To illustrate, assume that on January 2, 2011, Abalone Inc. agrees to buy $1,000 in U.S. currency for $1,150 in Canadian currency in 30 days from Bond Bank. The forward contract not only transfers to the holder the right to increases in value of the underlying (in this case, U.S. dollars), it also creates an obligation to pay a fixed amount at a specified date (in this case, $1,150). **This is different than the purchased option, which creates a right but not an obligation: with a purchased option, the holder may choose to exercise the option but does not have to**. The forward contract transfers the **currency risk** inherent in the Canada-U.S. exchange rate. In addition, the contract creates credit risk and liquidity risk. The credit risk is the risk that at the end of the contract, the counterparty (Baird in this case) will not deliver the underlying (U.S. $1,000). The liquidity risk is the risk that Abalone will not be able to honour its commitment to deliver Canadian $1,150 at the end of the contract. This is a financial derivative because the underlying is a financial asset; i.e., foreign currency.

Upon inception, the contract is priced such that the value of the forward contract is zero. Assume in the example above that the date on which the transaction is entered into, U.S. $1 = Canadian $1.10. No journal entry would be recorded at this point because we must consider the fair value of the contract—not just the difference between the spot rate and the forward rate. Like the option, the value of the forward considers both the intrinsic value and the time value component. It is generally valued at the present value of the future net cash flows under the contract.

Under derivatives accounting, subsequently, the forward is remeasured at fair value. The value will vary depending on interest rates as well as on what is happening with the spot prices (the current value) and forward prices (future value as quoted today) for the U.S. dollar. If the U.S. dollar appreciates in value, in general, the contract will have value since Abalone has locked in to pay only $1,150 for the U.S. $1,000. Assuming that the fair value of the contract is $50, on January 5, 2011, Abalone would record the following:

A = L + SE
+50   +50

Cash flows: No effect

Derivatives—Financial Assets/Liabilities	50	
Gain		50

The derivative would be presented as an asset on the balance sheet and measured at fair value with gains and losses, both unrealized and realized, being booked through net income.

Suppose on January 31, there is a negative fair value; i.e., if the contract were settled today, the company would suffer a loss of $30. This might occur for instance if the value of the U.S. currency depreciates. In this case, Abalone is locked in to pay $1,150 for something that is worth less. The following journal entry would be booked:

A = L + SE
−80   −80

Cash flows: No effect

Loss	80	
Derivatives—Financial Assets/Liabilities		80

The original gain is reversed and the additional loss must be booked.

The forward contract meets the definition of a financial liability as it is a **contractual obligation to exchange financial instruments with another party under conditions**

that are potentially unfavourable. The Derivative-Financial Assets/Liabilities account would therefore be presented as a liability on the balance sheet. Since the Derivative contract can sometimes be an asset while at other times it can be a liability, it can be presented as either an asset or a liability on the balance sheet.

Assume that on February 1, the settlement date, the U.S. dollar is worth $1.04 Canadian. The following entry would be booked to settle the contract if it was settled on a net basis:

Loss	80	
Derivatives—Financial Assets/Liabilities	30 (carrying value)	
Cash		110ᵃ
ᵃ U.S. $1,000 × (1.15 − 1.04)		

A = L + SE
−110 −30 −80
Cash flows: ↓ 110 outflow

If Abalone actually took delivery of the U.S. dollars, the following journal entry would be booked:

Cash—U.S. $	1,040 (spot/current exchange rate)	
Derivatives—Financial Assets/Liabilities	30 (carrying value)	
Loss	80	
Cash—Canadian $		1,150

A = L + SE
−110 −30 −80
Cash flows: ↓ 110 outflow

Futures

Futures contracts, another popular type of derivative, are the same as forwards except for the following:

1. They are standardized as to amounts and dates.

2. Futures contracts are exchange traded and therefore have ready market values.

3. They are settled through clearing houses, which generally removes the credit risk.

4. There is a requirement to put up collateral in the form of a "margin" account. The margin account represents a percentage of the contract's value. Daily changes in the value of the contract are settled daily against the margin account by the clearing house (known as marking to market) and resulting deficiencies in the margin account must be made up daily.

The initial margin is treated as a deposit account similar to a bank account, and is increased or decreased as the margin amount changes. The gain or loss on the contract, reflected in the daily change in the account, is recognized in income.

Illustration of a Futures Contract.   For example, assume Forward Inc. entered into a futures contract to sell grain for $1,000. The exchange/broker requires a $100 initial margin (normally a percentage of the market value of the contract or a fixed amount times the number of contracts). This amount is deposited in cash with the exchange/broker. Like the forward, the futures contract would have a zero value up front. This is a non-financial derivative because the underlying is a non-financial commodity; i.e., grain.

At the date when the contract is entered into, the following journal entry would be booked to show the margin that has been deposited with the exchange/broker. The contract is otherwise valued at $0 on inception.

A = L + SE
0

Cash flows: ↓ 100 outflow

| Deposits | 100 | |
| Cash | | 100 |

Finance

Assume that the value of the grain increases after the contract has been entered into. The contract is marked to market by the exchange/broker. Assume that the market value of the contract decreases by $50. This is because Forward has agreed to sell the grain for a fixed amount that is lower than the current market value. The $50 loss is removed from Future's margin account by the exchange/broker. The clearing house then requires Forward to restore the margin account by depositing an additional $50. The entries to record the loss and the additional deposit would be:

A = L + SE
−50   −50

Cash flows: ↓ 50 outflow

Loss	50	
Deposit		50
Deposit	50	
Cash		50

If the contract is closed out (settled net without delivering the grain) with no further changes in value, the following entry would be booked.

A = L + SE
0

Cash flows: ↑ 100 inflow

| Cash | 100 | |
| Deposits | | 100 |

Forward suffered a loss of $50, which was booked to net income already through the journal entries above. This is because it had agreed to sell the grain for $1,000 when it was worth more. Instead of delivering the grain, Forward paid the difference in cash—thus locking in the loss. Note that the net impact is a loss of $50 on the contract.

Derivatives Involving the Entity's Own Shares

Objective 4

Explain the unique issues associated with derivatives that are settleable using the entity's own equity instruments.

Significant Change

Sometimes companies enter into derivative contracts that deal with their own shares. For instance, a company might buy or write options dealing with its own shares or enter into forward contracts to buy or sell its own shares at a future date. Examples of "own equity" derivative instruments include:

1. Options
   (a) Purchased call or put options to buy/sell the entity's own shares
   (b) Written call or put options to buy/sell the entity's own shares
2. Forwards
   (a) To buy the entity's own shares
   (b) To sell the entity's own shares

Illustration of a Contract Involving the Entity's Own Equity Instruments

Assume Abalone paid $400 to Baker for the right to buy 1,000 of its own common shares for $30 each. Assume further that the contract may only be settled by exercising the option and buying the shares. Why would Abalone do this? Perhaps Abalone is looking to buy back its own shares to boost share values.

Should the cost of the option be treated as an investment as in the earlier example where the underlying is a share from another company as opposed to the entity's own shares? This is a **presentation** issue. **IFRS states that this transaction would be presented as a reduction from shareholders' equity and not as an investment.**[18] Contracts where the entity agrees to issue a **fixed *number* of its own shares for a fixed *amount* of consideration** are generally presented as equity (e.g., written call options, forwards to sell shares). This is sometimes referred to as the "fixed for fixed" principle when discussing how to account for derivatives that are settleable with own equity instruments. PE GAAP is silent on this matter but general principles would support presenting the financial instrument as contra equity since it does not meet the definition of an asset.

Not all contracts involving own equity instruments are treated as equity, however. Some end up being treated as financial liabilities or financial assets. This area of accounting is very complex and is beyond the scope of this text. This is also an area of transition. As a general rule, any analysis should go back to basic principles and definitions. The following exceptions exist.

Underlying Concept

Often, complex transactions are best analyzed by looking at basic definitions. This helps by focusing on the substance of the transaction.

1. *Fixed for fixed override.* When a derivative contract is entered into that creates an **obligation to pay cash** or other assets **even if it is for a fixed number of the entity's shares** (e.g., written put option or forward contract to buy shares), it overrides the "fixed for fixed" principle noted earlier and the contract should generally be treated as a financial liability. Therefore, **any time** there is an obligation to pay cash, a financial liability is recognized.

2. *Settlement options.* Where the derivative contract allows **choice** in how the instruments will be settled (e.g., one party can choose to settle net in cash or by exchanging shares), the instrument is a financial asset/liability by default under IFRS unless all possible settlement options result in it being an equity instrument.[19] Under PE GAAP, the instrument would likely be treated as equity if the entity can avoid settling with cash or other assets (i.e., where the entity has the option to choose the way the contract is settled and can avoid paying cash or other assets).

Illustration 16-5 summarizes IFRS requirements for own equity instruments. As mentioned above, PE GAAP is not as explicit in this area and generally the analysis defaults to whether the definition of a liability is met or not.

---

[18] IAS 32 *Financial Instruments: Presentation*, Illustrative Examples. There is quite a comprehensive group of examples presented in IAS 32. This area is currently being studied by the IASB.

[19] IAS 32.26. The IASB made this decision to prevent entities from designing financial instruments so as to achieve a certain accounting outcome per the basis for the Conclusions document for IAS 32. Note that PE GAAP looks to the basic definitions of financial liabilities and equity to resolve the presentation issue. Whether a contract can or may be settled net is an interesting question. If the contract is a non-traded contract between two parties (as opposed to involving instruments that trade in the marketplace) then this would be presumably determined by the terms of the contract. However, when the derivatives are purchased in the capital marketplace (e.g., a stock market/exchange), the entity may trade out of the position (settle net) by selling the contract in the open market. Thus, derivatives that trade in the marketplace involving settlement in own equity instruments are most likely accounted for as financial assets/liabilities and not equity instruments as they effectively allow for net settlement.

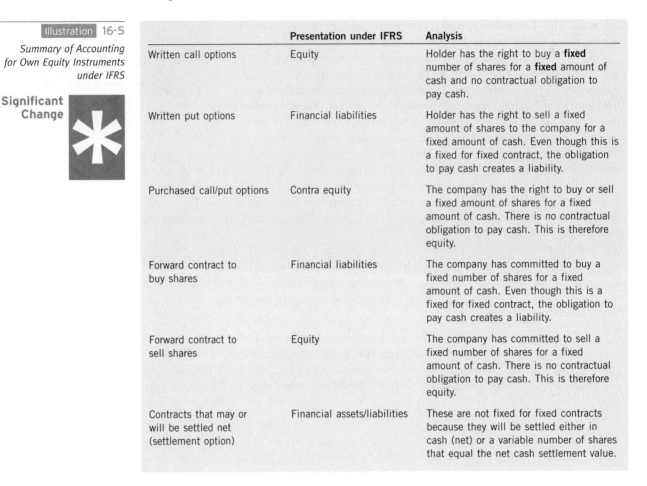

	Presentation under IFRS	Analysis
Written call options	Equity	Holder has the right to buy a **fixed** number of shares for a **fixed** amount of cash and no contractual obligation to pay cash.
Written put options	Financial liabilities	Holder has the right to sell a fixed amount of shares to the company for a fixed amount of cash. Even though this is a fixed for fixed contract, the obligation to pay cash creates a liability.
Purchased call/put options	Contra equity	The company has the right to buy or sell a fixed amount of shares for a fixed amount of cash. There is no contractual obligation to pay cash. This is therefore equity.
Forward contract to buy shares	Financial liabilities	The company has committed to buy a fixed number of shares for a fixed amount of cash. Even though this is a fixed for fixed contract, the obligation to pay cash creates a liability.
Forward contract to sell shares	Equity	The company has committed to sell a fixed number of shares for a fixed amount of cash. There is no contractual obligation to pay cash. This is therefore equity.
Contracts that may or will be settled net (settlement option)	Financial assets/liabilities	These are not fixed for fixed contracts because they will be settled either in cash (net) or a variable number of shares that equal the net cash settlement value.

DEBT VERSUS EQUITY—ISSUER PERSPECTIVE

Understanding the Economics of Complex Financial Instruments

What Is the Economic Reason for the Complexity?

Finance

In companies with very simple capital structures, financing is obtained through debt instruments (loans, bonds, and debentures) and common shares. Both these simple financing vehicles have very different legal and economic characteristics. Debt instruments are generally repaid, pay interest, and rank in preference to common shares upon windup or liquidation. Common shares, on the other hand, are seen as permanent capital, pay dividends, and are residual in nature; i.e., upon windup or liquidation, the shareholders get whatever is left after paying off all debts. These characteristics are summarized in the chart in Illustration 16-6.

	Loan or Bonds Payable	Common Shares
Term	Maturity date/repayment schedule	Permanent capital
Return to investor/lender	Interest, which is a function of the principal amount, time, and risk	Dividends, which are a function of profits, cash flows, and company policy
Seniority in terms of liquidation, windup, or bankruptcy	Often secured by assets of the company. Generally ranks in preference upon liquidation, windup, or bankruptcy.	Unsecured residual interest. Shareholders get whatever is left after other capital providers such as creditors paid out.[20]
Advantages to entity	Interest is tax deductible.	Does not increase solvency or liquidity risk.
	Company does not have to give up ownership.	Do not have to pay out dividends.
	Leverage (maximize profits to shareholders by using the money of creditors).	Unsecured and so assets not at risk except in bankruptcy.
Disadvantages to entity	Too much debt increases liquidity and solvency risk and may result in higher cost of capital and/or lack of access to capital.	Issuance of more shares dilutes existing shareholder base.
		Missed leverage opportunity.

Illustration 16-6

Characteristics of Simple Financing Instruments—Debt and Common Shares

Over the years, the capital markets have sought to profit from the best attributes of both these types of instruments and have created myriad hybrid-type instruments that are neither straight debt (sometimes referred to as plain vanilla debt) nor straight common shares. **Hybrid/compound instruments** have more than one component including debt and equity (such as debt with detachable warrants) or may have the dual attributes of both debt and equity. Preferred shares were probably the first hybrid or compound instrument. They are not quite common shares because they rank in preference to common shares regarding dividend payout and payout upon liquidation, windup, or bankruptcy. They often pay dividends annually similar to debt. Other examples of hybrids or compound instruments are certain convertible debt instruments, term preferred shares, and mandatorily redeemable shares.

From an economic perspective, every time a new instrument is issued, it is priced or benchmarked against the standard instruments of debt and common shares, keeping in mind tax treatments that may be more or less favourable depending on whether the instrument is seen as debt or equity. So companies may, for instance, be able to pay less interest if the instrument also gives the holder some "equity-like" features (for instance, a conversion option). These designer-type financial instruments allow companies to create a specific type of instrument, keeping in mind the amount of capital required, desired risk profile, and acceptable cost of capital. Unfortunately, sometimes one of the design criteria includes a desire to show less debt on the balance sheet.

Ethics

Presentation

Why all the fuss? The capital marketplace focuses on liquidity and solvency and these are calculated using financial statement numbers. Excessive debt on a balance sheet signals increased riskiness and will affect the cost of capital and ultimately access to capital. Given

5 Objective

Analyze whether a hybrid/compound instrument issued for financing purposes represents a liability, equity, or both (and how to measure).

---

[20] This is actually dependent upon the laws in the respective legal jurisdiction.

that demand exists by both companies and investors for these types of instruments, and given the current accounting model that requires separate presentation of debt and equity, accountants must figure out a way to systematically and consistently classify these instruments such that the financial statements provide useful information to users including investors and creditors.

Finance

For this reason, these hybrid/compound instruments must be analyzed carefully for accounting purposes. They may be classified as debt, equity, or as part debt/part equity. The economic substance must be reviewed as well as contractual terms. Does the contract obligate the entity to pay out cash or other assets? If so, some or all of the instrument is a liability.

When analyzing whether the contract is debt, equity, or both, consider the following:

1. Contractual terms

   (a) Does the instrument explicitly **obligate the entity to pay out cash** or other assets?

   (b) Does the instrument give the holder the choice to force the company to pay out cash (in which case it **may create an obligation** for the entity)?

   (c) Are there settlement options (in which case, it **may create an obligation** for the entity)?

2. Economic substance

   Does the instrument contain any **equity-like features** that may need to be separated out? Keep in mind that whenever the instrument gives the holder increased flexibility or choice, the instrument is worth more. For instance, a convertible bond (explained below) is worth more because it allows the holder to have the security of debt but also exposes the investors to the risks and rewards of share ownership. Thus, part of the instrument is equity-like.

3. Definitions of financial statement elements

   A financial liability is defined under both PE GAAP and IFRS as a contractual obligation to do either of the following:

   (a) Deliver cash or another financial asset to another party, or

   (b) Exchange financial instruments with another party under conditions that are potentially unfavourable.

Significant Change

In addition, under IFRS, the definition of a financial liability includes guidance where the instrument is settleable using the entity's shares instead of cash. Essentially, where the company settles the instrument using a variable number of shares (instead of cash), it is still a financial liability. This is supported by PE GAAP as well (although it is not part of the definition).

An equity instrument under both PE GAAP and IFRS is any contract that evidences a residual interest in the assets of an entity after deducting all of its liabilities.

In addition, under IFRS, the guidance includes the following with respect to instruments settleable in the entity's own equity instruments. The instrument is equity only if it will be settled by exchanging a **fixed number** of the issuer's own equity instruments for a **fixed amount** of cash or other assets (and it is not a liability).[21]

These definitions are critical in determining how to present the instruments.

Illustration 16-7 shows some examples of hybrid/compound instruments indicating balance sheet presentation.

---

[21] This was mentioned earlier in this chapter when discussing derivatives. Recall also that Chapter 15 provided a discussion about "in-substance shares," which are treated as equity as long as certain conditions are met even though the holder has the option to require the entity to pay cash.

Contract	Presentation
Convertible debt (convertible at the option of the holder into a fixed number of common shares of the company).	Part liability and part equity. The conversion option is essentially an embedded written call option and this part is equity since a fixed number of shares will be issued. The debt carries with it a contractual obligation to pay interest and principal.*
Puttable shares (holder has the option to require the company to take the instruments back and pay cash).	Liability. This instrument contains a written put option that requires the entity to pay cash or other assets if the option is exercised. The holder has the right to exercise the option and therefore this is beyond the entity's control. The exception to this is noted in the next example below.
Shares that give the holder the option to require the company to surrender a pro rata share of net assets upon windup.	Equity. Although these are technically liabilities because of the put option, they may be presented as equity as long as there are "in-substance common shares." (Recall criteria from Chapter 15.)
Mandatorily redeemable preferred share.	Liability. The mandatory redemption imposes a contractual obligation to deliver cash or other assets. As an exception, High/low preferred shares are presented as equity under PE GAAP (see below).
Debt with detachable warrants. The warrants are for a fixed number of shares.	Liability and equity. Since the warrants are detachable, they are separate financial instruments and are treated as written call options. The instruments allow for a fixed number of shares to be exchanged for a fixed amount of cash. The debt carries with it a contractual obligation to pay interest and principal.*
Preferred shares that must be repaid if certain conditions are met (e.g., if the market price of the common shares exceed a certain threshold).	Liability. Under IFRS, a liability exists since the contingent settlement provision is based on an event outside the company's control. Under PE GAAP, the instrument would be accounted for as a liability only where the contingency is highly likely to occur.[22]
Debt that will be settled by issuing a variable number of common shares equal to the face value of the debt (or where the holder has the option to require settlement in cash or a variable number of shares).	Liability. The common shares are used as currency to settle the obligation, which is equal to the face value of the debt regardless of who has the option to choose.
Perpetual debt.	Liability. The economic value of this instrument is determined by discounting the interest payments (which represent a contractual obligation to pay cash).

*Note that PE GAAP allows the entity to measure the equity portion at $0 as an accounting policy choice. This will be discussed later in the chapter.

Illustration 16-7

Examples of Hybrid/Compound Instruments

Significant Change

Redeemable shares are often used in tax and succession planning. Many small businesses are created and run by individuals who at some point decide that they would like to hand the company over to their children. One orderly way of doing this that minimizes taxes is through the use of redeemable preferred shares, sometimes referred to as **high/low preferred shares**. The business assets can be transferred to a new company, which makes it possible to take advantage of special tax provisions that minimize taxes, and the owner takes redeemable preferred shares as part of the consideration. The children then buy the common shares in the new company for a nominal amount, which allows them to benefit from subsequent increases in the company's value. This also gives them some or all of the voting control since the common shares would normally be voting shares.

What Do the Numbers Mean?

[22] *CICA Handbook*, Part II, Section 3856.A26.

The redemption amount of the preferred shares is set at the company's fair value at the time of the transaction. This means that the fair value is frozen for the individual at a point in time (which is why the label "estate freeze" is sometimes given to this type of transaction). All subsequent increases in value will go to the children through ownership of the common shares. The owner of the former company will eventually get his or her money (which represents the fair value of the assets that he/she put in) out of the new company at a future point by redeeming the preferred shares.

This is a good example of yet another business reason to use complex financial instruments. Note that the redemption feature causes this instrument to be recorded as a (huge) liability since the company has an obligation to deliver cash upon redemption. Many small business owners are not happy with this accounting since it makes the company look highly leveraged when, in fact, the shares will normally not be redeemed in the short- or mid-term. Treating the shares as liabilities on the balance sheet may also cause the company to violate pre-existing debt covenants. As a result of this, PE GAAP requires these particular instruments to be treated as equity.[23]

Offsetting

One last presentation issue is whether the financial instruments should be offset against other financial instruments when presented on the balance sheet. When a company offsets one or more financial instruments, such as financial assets and liabilities, the instruments are generally shown as a net number. For instance, if the company has a receivable of $100 and a payable of $75, and they are presented on a net basis, only net assets of $25 would be presented. The potential problem with this is that it tends to obscure the fact that the $25 asset is really made up of the two components. Therefore there are some restrictions on offsetting.

When can a company show these amounts on a net basis? Only when certain criteria are met, as follows:

1. The company has a legally enforceable right[24] to net the amounts (i.e., if the instruments were to be settled, then they could legally be settled on a net basis).

2. The company intends to settle the instruments on a net basis or simultaneously (i.e., collect the receivable and immediately pay out the payable).[25]

Measurement

Underlying Concept

Well-defined measurement tools help reduce measurement uncertainty. These tools ultimately help in preparing financial information that is more reliable.

Upon initial recognition, financial instruments are measured at fair value, which is generally the exchange value. If they have components of both debt and equity, they may require bifurcation (i.e., splitting into debt and equity). This is therefore a measurement issue. Whatever the classification that is chosen upon inception, this classification continues to be used until the instrument is removed from the balance sheet.

The **measurement** of hybrid/compound instruments is complicated by the fact that the economic value of these instruments can be attributed to **both** the debt and equity components (i.e., the instrument is neither 100% debt nor 100% equity, and instead is **part debt and part equity**). How should these two components be measured?

As noted in previous chapters, there are two approaches to allocating the value of a transaction to its respective parts: the *residual value method* (sometimes referred to as

---

[23] *CICA Handbook*, Part II, Section 3856.23. These types of transactions generally relate more to private entities and not public entities and therefore are not mentioned in IFRS.

[24] The legally enforceable right could exist, for instance, due to the contracts governing the instruments, laws in certain jurisdictions, or rules governing the operation of stock exchanges (if the instruments are traded on a particular exchange).

[25] IAS 32.42 and *CICA Handbook*, Part II, Section 3856.24.

the incremental method) and the relative fair value method (sometimes referred to as the proportional method). These tools have been referred to in earlier chapters and used for instance to help bifurcate bundled sales and purchases. The mechanics are the same. The methods are recapped briefly below:

1. Relative fair value method: Determine the market values of similar individual instruments. For instance, for convertible debt, determine the value of straight debt without the conversion feature and the value of the option to convert. This is easier to do if there are existing markets for both these instruments as separate items. However, measurement of the debt portion can also be done by a PV calculation, discounting at the market rate for similar debt. Measurement of the option portion can be done using an options pricing model.[26] The components are then assigned these values. If the total is greater than or less than the instrument's issue price, the difference is prorated based on the respective market or fair values and is then allocated to each of the components.

2. Residual method: Value only one component (the one that is easier to value, which is often the debt component). The other component is valued at whatever is left.

IFRS requires the use of the residual method with any debt components being valued first and the residual being allocated to the equity components. ASPE allows the equity component to be valued at zero or the residual method to be used, with the more easily measurable component being valued first.[27] Subsequently, debt is measured at amortized costs unless the fair value option is selected (or it is a derivative).

Let's look at a very common financial instrument—convertible debt—and how it is accounted for.

Significant Change

Convertible Debt

A convertible bond is a bond that may be converted into common shares of the company. It combines the benefits of a bond with the privilege of exchanging it for common shares **at the holder's option**. It is purchased by investors who want the security of a bond holding—guaranteed interest—plus the added option of conversion if the value of the common shares increases significantly.

6 Objective
Explain the accounting for the issuance, conversion, and retirement of convertible securities.

Finance

Corporations issue convertible debt for two main reasons. One is the desire to raise equity capital without giving up more ownership control than necessary. To illustrate, assume that a company wants to raise $1 million at a time when its common shares are selling at $45 per share. Such an issue would require selling 22,222 shares (ignoring issue costs). By selling 1,000 bonds at $1,000 par, and with each bond being convertible into 20 common shares, the enterprise may raise $1 million by committing only 20,000 common shares.[28] Investors may be willing to take the bonds since they give the investors greater security (especially if the bonds are secured by company assets) yet allow them to participate in the company growth through the option to convert the bonds to common shares.

A second, more common reason that companies have for issuing convertible securities is to obtain debt financing at cheaper rates. Many enterprises would have to issue debt at higher interest rates unless a convertible feature was attached. The conversion privilege entices the investor to accept a lower interest rate than would normally be the case on a straight debt issue. For example, Amazon.com at one time issued convertible bonds that paid interest at an effective yield of 4.75%, which was much lower than Amazon.com would have had to pay if it had issued straight debt. For this lower interest rate, the investor received the right to buy Amazon.com's common shares at a fixed price until the bonds' maturity.

---

[26] Calculation of this amount using an options pricing model is beyond the scope of this course and would generally be covered in a finance course. Appendix 16C provides a brief recap of options pricing models.

[27] *CICA Handbook*, Part II, Section 3856.22 and IAS.32.31.

[28] In fact, the bonds would sell at a premium due to the embedded stock option.

There are reporting issues in the accounting for convertible debt at all of the following times:

1. Issuance

2. Conversion

3. Retirement

Convertible Debt at Time of Issuance. As previously mentioned, the conversion feature on a convertible bond makes the instrument more valuable to an investor, and, therefore, the option feature itself has value. **The obligation to deliver cash under the bond represents a financial liability and the right to acquire the company's common shares represents an equity instrument**. Under IFRS compound instruments must be split into their components and presented separately in the financial statements. Since the embedded option to convert to common shares is an equity instrument, that part of the instrument is presented as equity. The remaining component is presented as a liability.

For example, assume that Bond Corp. offers three-year, 6% convertible bonds (par $1,000). Each $1,000 bond may be converted into 250 common shares, which are currently trading at $3 per share. Similar straight bonds carry an interest rate of 9%. One thousand bonds are issued at par.

Allocating the proceeds to the liability and equity components under the residual value method involves valuing one component first and then allocating the rest of the value to the other component. Assume that the company decides to use the residual method and measure the debt first. The bond may be measured at the PV of the stream of interest payments ($1 million × 6% for three years) plus the PV of the bond itself ($1 million) all discounted at 9%, which is the market rate of interest. The remainder of the proceeds is then allocated to the option. This allocation is shown in Illustration 16-8.

<table>
<tr><td>Illustration 16-8

Incremental Allocation of Proceeds between Liability and Equity Components</td><td>

Total proceeds at par	$1,000,000
Less:	
Value of bonds (PV annuity 3 years, 9%, $60,000 + PV $1,000,000, in 3 years, 9%)	(924,061)
Incremental value of option	$ 75,939

</td></tr>
</table>

The journal entry to record the issuance would be as follows:

A   =   L   +   SE
+1,000,000   +924,061   +75,939

Cash flows: ↑ 1,000,000 inflow

Cash	1,000,000	
Bonds Payable		924,061
Contributed Surplus—Conversion Rights		75,939

Convertible Debt at Time of Conversion. If bonds are converted into other securities, the main accounting problem is to determine the amount at which to record the securities that have been exchanged for the bond. Assume that holders of the convertible debt of Bond Corp. decide to convert their convertible bonds before the bonds mature. The bond discount will be partially amortized at this point. Assume that the unamortized portion is $14,058. The entry to record the conversion would be as follows:

A   =   L   +   SE
   −985,942   +985,942

Cash flows: No effect

Bonds Payable	985,942	
Contributed Surplus—Conversion Rights	75,939	
Common Shares		1,061,881

This method, referred to as the book value method **of recording the bond conversion, is the method that is required under GAAP.**[29] Support for the book value approach is based on the argument that an agreement was established at the date that the bond was issued either to pay a stated amount of cash at maturity or to issue a stated number of shares of equity securities. Therefore, when the debt is converted to equity in accordance with the pre-existing contract terms, no gain or loss would be recognized upon conversion.[30] Any accrued interest that was forfeited would be treated as part of the new book value of the shares (and credited to Common Shares).

Induced Early Conversions.   Sometimes the issuer wants to induce (cause) a prompt conversion of its convertible debt-to-equity securities in order to reduce interest costs or to improve its debt-to-equity ratio. As a result, the issuer may offer some form of additional consideration—known commonly as a sweetener—such as cash. This situation is referred to as an induced conversion. The additional premium should be allocated between the debt and equity components at the time of the transaction. The approach that is used should be consistent with the method that was used when the debt was originally recorded (e.g., the incremental method).

Assume that Bond Corp. wants to reduce interest costs at some point during the life of the debt. It therefore offers an additional cash premium of $15,000 to the bondholders to convert, and at a time when the carrying amount of the debt was $972,476. Assume further that the **residual method** was used to allocate the issue price originally between debt and equity components, with the debt being measured at its discounted cash flows and the equity being valued as the residual amount. The bond's fair value at the conversion time is $981,462 (ignoring the conversion feature) due to lower market interest rates. The first step in the allocation of the premium is to determine the difference between the fair value and carrying value of the bonds:

$$\$981,462 - \$972,476 = \$8,986$$

Then the residual method would be used to allocate the premium between the debt and equity components (since this method was originally used):

$$\$15,000 - \$8,986 = \$6,014$$

Thus, $8,986 would be treated as a debt retirement cost and $6,014 as a capital transaction similar to a redemption cost. The journal entry would be as follows:

Bonds Payable	972,476	
Expense—Debt Retirement Cost	8,986 (above)	
Contributed Surplus—Stock Options	75,939 (previously calculated)	
Retained Earnings	6,014 (above)	
Common Shares		1,048,415
Cash		15,000

[29] *CICA Handbook*, Part II, Section 3856.A34 and IAS 32.AG32.

[30] An alternative approach that has some conceptual merit uses the market value to record the conversion. Under this method, the common shares would be recorded at market value (their market value or the market value of the bonds); the contributed surplus, bonds payable, and discount amounts would be zeroed out; and a gain/credit or loss/debit would result. Since the CBCA requires shares to be recorded at their cash equivalent value, legal requirements would tend to partially support this approach.

Underlying Concept

Note that the convertible debt in the example above is treated the same as the debt with detachable warrants. This is because the economic substance of the instruments is the same: they both have debt and give the holder the option to hold shares. Recall that PE GAAP allows the entity to allocate $0 to the equity component for simplicity sake.

A	=	L	+	SE
−15,000		−972,476		+957,476

Cash flows: ↓ 15,000 outflow

The shares are now valued at the total carrying value of the bonds, plus the option, as follows:

$$\$972,476 + \$75,939 = \$1,048,415$$

Retirement of Convertible Debt.   The normal retirement of the liability component of convertible debt at maturity (its repayment) is treated the same way as non-convertible bonds, as explained in Chapter 14. The equity component remains in Contributed Surplus. What happens, however, if the instrument is retired early and the company pays off the debt with cash? Assume that Bond Corp. decides to retire the convertible debt early and offers the bondholders $1,070,000 cash, which is the fair value of the instrument at the time of early retirement. The following journal entry would be booked:

Bonds Payable	972,476	
Expense—Debt Retirement Cost	8,986	
Contributed Surplus—Conversion Rights	75,939	
Retained Earnings	12,599	
Cash		1,070,000

A   =   L   +   SE
−1,070,000   −972,476   −97,524

Cash flows: ↓ 1,070,000 outflow

The amounts related to the instrument (including the bonds payable, any remaining discount, and the contributed surplus) are zeroed out and the loss is allocated between the debt portion and the equity portion. The portion allocated to the debt is the same as the amount in the previous example (i.e., the difference between the debt's carrying value and its fair value). If the residual method is used, the rest is allocated to the equity portion. Note that the fair value of $1,070,000 includes the fair value of the bond and the embedded option. The option is also removed from the books as it is seen as settled.

Interest, Dividends, Gains, and Losses

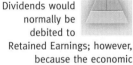

Underlying Concept

Dividends would normally be debited to Retained Earnings; however, because the economic substance of a term preferred share is debt, dividends on term preferred shares are treated as interest or dividend expense.

Once the determination is made to classify something on the balance sheet as debt, equity, or part debt and part equity, the related interest, dividends, gains, and losses must be consistently treated. **For instance, a** term preferred share **would be presented as a liability and, therefore, related dividends would be booked as interest or dividend expense and charged to the income statement (not to Retained Earnings)**.

SHARE-BASED COMPENSATION

Thus far, we have covered off several instances in previous chapters where shares and other equity instruments are used as compensation (instead of cash); for instance, when purchasing inventory and fixed assets. The following material focuses on stock compensation plans that remunerate or compensate employees for services provided.

It is generally agreed that effective compensation programs:

1. Motivate employees to high levels of performance.

2. Help retain executives and recruit new talent.

3. Base compensation on employee and company performance.

4. Maximize the employee's after-tax benefit and minimize the employer's after-tax cost.

5. Use performance criteria that the employee can control.

Although straightforward cash compensation plans (salary and, perhaps, a bonus) are an important part of any compensation program, they are oriented to the short term. Many companies recognize that a more long-run compensation plan is often needed in addition to a cash component.

Long-term compensation plans aim to develop a strong loyalty toward the company. An effective way to accomplish this goal is to give the employees an equity interest based on changes in their company's long-term measures, such as increases in earnings per share, revenues, share price, or market share. These plans come in many different forms. Essentially, they provide the executive or employee with the opportunity to receive shares or cash in the future if the company's performance is satisfactory. Stock-based compensation plans also help companies conserve cash. When they are used, the company does not expend any cash. In fact, if options are used to compensate employees, the employees actually pay cash into the company when they exercise the option. Start-up companies find this aspect very useful since they are often cash-poor in that early phase.

Finance

Types of Plans

Many different types of plans are used to compensate employees and especially management. In all these plans, the reward amount depends on future events. Consequently, continued employment is a necessary element in almost all types of plans. The popularity of a particular plan usually depends on prospects in the stock market and tax considerations. For example, if it appears that appreciation will occur in a company's shares, a plan that offers the option to purchase shares is attractive to an executive.

Conversely, if it appears that price appreciation is unlikely, then compensation might be tied to some performance measure such as an increase in book value or earnings per share.

Four common compensation plans that illustrate different objectives are:

1. Compensatory stock option plans (CSOPs)

2. Direct awards of stock

3. Stock appreciation rights plans (SARs)

4. Performance-type plans

The main accounting issues relate to **recognition** of the plan (when should the cost of the plan be recognized) and **measurement** (how should the cost be measured). SARs and performance-type plans will be discussed in Appendix 16B.

7 Objective
Describe the various types of stock compensation plans.

Underlying Concept

There is no transparency if the costs of compensatory plans are not captured in the income statement.

Stock Options Revisited

Before looking at the accounting for employee stock option plans, it is useful to revisit the earlier discussion about options in this chapter. So far, options have been discussed in the following context:

- as derivatives, used to manage risk (hedge or speculation)

- as debt with detachable warrants (options), used as sweeteners with bonds to access pools of capital and reduce the cost of capital.

The above instruments are sometimes **exchange-traded options**; that is, they trade on an options or stock exchange.

8 Objective
Explain the differences between employee and compensatory option plans and other options.

Companies also use stock options for the following reasons:

1. To **give employees an opportunity to own part of the company**, with the issue being made to a wide group of people (e.g., all employees). Another benefit of these plans if they are widely subscribed to is that the company raises cash. These are generally called employee stock option or purchase plans (ESOPs).

2. To **remunerate management or employees**. These are called compensatory stock option plans (CSOPs).

3. As **compensation in a particular purchase or acquisition transaction**, with the stock options being provided instead of paying cash or another asset, or incurring a liability. For instance, a company might buy another company and pay for the investment with stock options. These are valued at fair value. The accounting is similar to the accounting covered in Chapter 10 under acquisition of assets upon issuance of shares.

Illustration 16-9 reviews the different types of options and option plans. Note that ESOPs and CSOPs are generally not traded on an exchange. As a result, the fair value cannot be measured as readily.

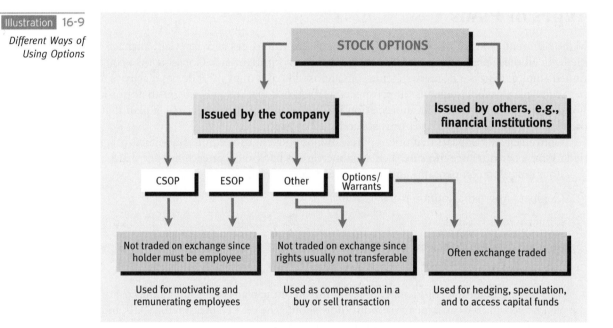

Illustration 16-9

Different Ways of Using Options

What is the difference between ESOPs and CSOPs in terms of accounting? The answer has to do with the underlying nature of the transaction. The main difference between the two plans is that with ESOPs, the employee usually pays for the options (either fully or partially). Thus these transactions are seen as **capital** transactions (charged to equity accounts). The employee is investing in the company. CSOPs, on the other hand, are primarily seen as an **alternative way to compensate** the employees for their services, like a barter transaction. The services are rendered by the employee in the act of producing revenues. This information must be recognized on the income statement as an operating transaction (expensed).

Illustration 16-10 summarizes the difference between CSOPs and non-compensatory plans, or ESOPs.

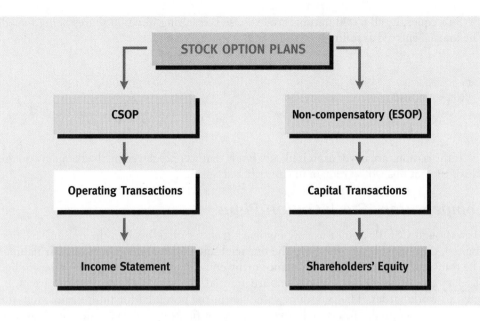

Illustration 16-10

Compensatory versus Non-compensatory Plans

The following factors dictate whether or not a plan is compensatory:

1. **Option terms** (e.g., dealing with enrolment and cancellation). Non-standard terms that give the employees a longer time to enrol and the ability to cancel the option imply that the options are compensatory.

2. **Discount from market price**. A large discount implies that the plan is compensatory.[31]

3. **Eligibility**. Making options available only to certain restricted groups of employees, often management, implies that a plan is compensatory. Plans that are available to all employees are seen as non-compensatory.[32]

Under an ESOP, when an option or share right is sold to an employee, the Cash account is debited and the Contributed Surplus or other equity account is credited for the amount of the premium (i.e., the cost of the option). When the right or option is exercised, the Cash account is again debited for the exercise price, along with the Contributed Surplus account (to reverse the earlier entry) and the Common Shares account is credited to show the issuance of the shares.

To illustrate, assume that Fanco Limited set up an ESOP that gives employees the option to purchase company shares for $10 per share. The option premium is $1 per share and Fanco has set aside 10,000 shares. On January 1, 2011, employees purchase 6,000 options for $6,000. The journal entry is as follows:

Cash	6,000	
Contributed Surplus—Stock Options		6,000

A = L + SE
+6,000   −6,000

Cash flows: ↑ 6,000 inflow

---

[31] Note that a company might offer an option under an ESOP at less than the fair value of the option. As long as this discount is small and effectively represents the issue costs that a company might otherwise have incurred had it done a public offering, this is not seen as compensatory.

[32] IFRS 2.4 and *CICA Handbook*, Part II, Section 3870.28. Note that the wording of the respective standards is different although the substance of the content is the same. IFRS approaches the analysis differently, looking at whether the employee is acting in the role of shareholder or employee.

Subsequently, all 6,000 options are exercised, resulting in 6,000 shares being issued. The journal entry is as follows:

A   = L +   SE
+60,000   +60,000

Cash flows: ↑ 60,000 inflow

Cash	60,000	
Contributed Surplus—Stock Options	6,000	
Common Shares		66,000

If the options are never exercised, any funds that were received by the company on the sale of the options would remain in Contributed Surplus.

Compensatory Stock Option Plans

Objective 9

Describe the accounting for compensatory stock option plans.

Even though CSOPs do not usually involve a transfer of cash when the options are first granted, they are still recognized in the financial statements and measured at **fair value**.[33] The transaction has economic value since many employees accept the stock options in lieu of salary or a bonus. When the options are granted, the employees presumably are motivated to work harder. The economic value lies in the potential for future gain when the options are exercised. How should the fair value of the transaction be measured? **Recall that an option gets its value from two components: the intrinsic value component and a time value component**. While the intrinsic value may be easy to measure (the shares' fair value less the exercise price), the time value component is more difficult to measure. Even though it is difficult to value the stock options themselves, it is even more difficult to value the services rendered by the employees.

The compensation cost that arises from employee stock options should be recognized as the services are being provided.[34]

Determining Expense.   The total compensation expense is calculated on the date when the options are granted to the employee (the grant date) and is based on the fair value of the options that are expected to vest.[35] The grant date is the date when the employee and company agree on the value of what is to be exchanged. **The grant date is therefore the measurement date**. Fair value for public companies is estimated using market prices, and if not available, using a valuation technique (e.g., an options pricing model). No adjustments are made after the grant date for any subsequent changes in the share price, either up or down. The options pricing model incorporates several input measures:

1. The exercise price

2. The expected life of the option

3. The current market price of the underlying stock

4. The volatility of the underlying stock

5. The expected dividend during the option life

6. The risk-free rate of interest for the option life

The **measurement date** may be later for plans that have variable terms (i.e., if the number of shares and/or option price are not known) that depend on events after the date

---

[33] IFRS 2.10 and .11 and *CICA Handbook*, Part II, Section 3870.24.

[34] Stock options that are issued to non-employees in exchange for other goods or services must be measured according to their fair value as non-monetary transactions.

[35] "Vested" means to earn the rights to something. An employee's award becomes vested at the date that the employee's right to receive or retain shares of stock or cash under the award no longer depends on the employee remaining in the employer's service or fulfiling some other prescribed condition.

of grant. For such variable plans, the compensation expense may have to be estimated based on assumptions about the final number of shares and the option price (usually at the exercise date).

Allocating Compensation Expense. In general, compensation expense is recognized in the periods in which the employee performs the service (the service period). Unless something different is specified, the service period is the vesting period: the time between the grant date and the vesting date. Thus, the total compensation cost is determined at the grant date and allocated to the periods that benefit from the employee services. Illustration 16-11 presents the relevant dates and time frames.

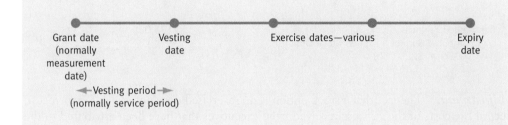

Illustration 16-11

Key Dates in Accounting for Stock Option Plans

To illustrate the accounting for a stock option plan, assume that on November 1, 2011, the shareholders of Chen Corp. approve a plan that grants options to the company's five executives to purchase 2,000 shares each of the company's common shares. The options are granted on January 1, 2012, and may be exercised at any time within the next 10 years. The exercise price per share is $60.

To keep this illustration simple, we will assume that the fair value, as determined using an options pricing model, results in a total compensation expense of $220,000.

At Grant Date. Recall that the option's value is recognized as an expense in the periods in which the employee performs services. In the case of Chen Corp., assume that the documents that are associated with the issuance of the options indicate that the expected period of benefit/service is two years, starting on the grant date. The journal entries to record the transactions related to this option are as follows:

January 1, 2012		
No entry		

December 31, 2012		
Compensation Expense	110,000	
Contributed Surplus—Stock Options ($220,000 ÷ 2)		110,000

A = L + SE
           0

Cash flows: No effect

December 31, 2013		
Compensation Expense	110,000	
Contributed Surplus—Stock Options		110,000

A = L + SE
         −110,000
         +110,000

Cash flows: No effect

The compensation expense is allocated evenly over the two-year service period, assuming that equal service is provided during the entire period.

At Exercise Date. If 20% or 2,000 of the 10,000 options were exercised on June 1, 2015 (three years and five months after date of grant), the following journal entry would be recorded:

A   =   L   +   SE
+120,000   +120,000

Cash flows: ↑ 120,000 inflow

June 1, 2015		
Cash (2,000 × $60)	120,000	
Contributed Surplus—Stock Options (20% × $220,000)	44,000	
Common Shares		164,000

At Expiration.   If the remaining stock options are not exercised before their expiration date, the balance in the Contributed Surplus account would remain. If the company kept several Contributed Surplus accounts, the balance would be shifted to a specific Contributed Surplus account that is used for options that have expired. The entry to record this transaction at the date of expiration is:

A   =   L   +   SE
                0

Cash flows: No effect

Contributed Surplus—Stock Options	176,000	
Contributed Surplus—Expired Stock Options		176,000
(80% × $220,000)		

Significant Change

Adjustment.   The fact that a stock option is not exercised does not make it incorrect to record the costs of the services received from executives that have been attributed to the stock option plan. However, if a stock option is forfeited because an employee fails to satisfy a service requirement (e.g., if the employee leaves the company), the estimate of the compensation expense that has been recorded should be adjusted as a change in estimate (credit Compensation Expense and debit Contributed Surplus). PE GAAP allows a choice, i.e., either estimate forfeitures upfront or account for them as they occur. IFRS requires the former treatment. If estimated upfront, the entity will likely have to adjust subsequently to reflect the actual number of options forfeited.

Direct Awards of Stock

Stock may be awarded directly as compensation for services provided by an employee. This type of transaction is more broadly known as a non-monetary reciprocal transaction. The transaction is non-monetary because it involves little or no cash, and it is reciprocal because it is a two-way transaction. The company gives something up (shares) and gets something in return (the employee's services).

Almost all business transactions are reciprocal. As a **non-monetary** transaction, direct awards of stock are recorded at the fair value of the item that is given up (the stock).[36] For instance, instead of paying cash salary, the company may offer company shares as remuneration. This would be recorded as salary expense at the shares' fair value. The value of the shares is used because it is difficult to value the services provided.

Special Issues

Companies whose shares are traded on stock exchanges are able to measure the value of the options more readily since they can measure volatility. Private companies, however, do not have volatility measures yet must nonetheless attempt to measure it.

Private companies have another issue. If they issue CSOPs to their employees, how do the employees realize the value? If an employee exercises the option and buys the shares, there is no ready market in which to sell the shares and the value is therefore locked in. Often private companies will offer to buy back the shares from the employee.

---

[36] IFRS 2.11 and *CICA Handbook*, Part II, Section 3870.24.

If the company has a policy and past practice of repurchasing the shares, does this create a liability? **This requires professional judgement but a good argument may be made for recognizing a liability instead of equity. In other words, the past practice of repurchasing the shares and the probability that this will be done again (since the employees cannot sell the shares elsewhere) support the recognition of a liability.** The company in substance has an obligation to the employee.[37] The liability would have to be remeasured on an ongoing basis with the difference being charged to income as compensation expense.

Most CSOPs are equity settled; that is, they will be settled by issuing shares to the employee. Sometimes, the CSOPs are cash settled or there is a choice between cash and equity. This will be addressed in Appendix 16B.

Disclosure of Compensation Plans

Full disclosure should be made of the following:

- the accounting policy that is being used

- a description of the plans and modifications

- details of the numbers and values of the options issued, exercised, forfeited, and expired

- a description of the assumptions and methods being used to determine fair values

- the total compensation cost included in net income and contributed surplus

- other[38]

IFRS AND PRIVATE ENTERPRISE GAAP COMPARISON

Many complex financial instruments exist and must be accounted for in the company's financial statements. It is important to understand the nature of the instruments from an economic perspective: why would the company issue this type of instrument and why would an investor invest in it? It is also important to understand what creates the instrument's value. This will help in understanding the economic substance of the instrument. The accounting issues relate to presentation (determining if it is debt or equity, or both) and measurement.

Derivatives have been the focus of some very negative publicity in the past few years with companies suffering significant losses and perhaps even going bankrupt due to derivative instruments. This is partially due to the complexity of these contracts and the fact that they are not well understood by many who use them.

Do complex accounting standards add any value in the capital marketplace? They certainly add to the costs of preparing financial statements. Accountants in industry must stay up to date on these standards, as must the auditors. There is a very real risk that investors and creditors do not understand the standards and perhaps may not even have the educational background that is required to be able to work through the complexities.

10 Objective

Identify the major differences in accounting between accounting standards for private enterprises (PE GAAP/ASPE) and IFRS, and what changes are expected in the near future.

---

[37] *CICA Handbook*, Part II, Section 3870.03.

[38] *CICA Handbook*, Part II, Section 3870.66 -.69 and IFRS 2.44-.52.

Comparison of IFRS and Private Enterprise GAAP

Illustration 16-12 compares Canadian GAAP with the international standards on complex financial instruments, providing additional information relative to the information included in the comparison illustrations in Chapters 14 and 15.

	Accounting Standards for Private Enterprises (Private Entity GAAP/ASPE)—*CICA Handbook*, Part II, Sections 3856 and 3870	IFRS—IAS 32, 39 and IFRS 2
Presentation – Purchase commitments	Accounted for as executory contracts since not exchange traded.	Accounted for as executory contracts unless the contracts allow for net settlement and the entity does not expect to take delivery of the inventory.
– Own equity instruments	Less detailed guidance is provided under PE GAAP. Consider the basic definitions of financial liability and equity. If the definition of a liability is not met, then the instruments is presented as equity.	The definitions of financial liabilities and equity instruments include references to instruments settled in the entity's own instruments. As a general rule, the instrument is equity only if it **will be** settled by issuing a fixed amount of cash for a fixed number of shares **and** there is no contractual obligation.
– Certain puttable shares	Treated as equity if certain criteria are met including under certain tax planning arrangements. The criteria establish whether the instruments are "in-substance" equity instruments. This was also discussed in Chapter 15.	Treated as equity if certain criteria are met. No special treatment for certain tax planning arrangements. The criteria establish whether the instruments are "in-substance" equity instruments. This was also discussed in Chapter 15.
Recognition – Hybrid/compound instruments with contingent settlement provisions	Instruments with contingent settlement provisions are financial liabilities if the contingency is highly likely to occur.	Instruments with contingent settlement provisions represent liabilities where the contingency is outside the control of the issuer.
Measurement – Components of compound instruments	May measure the equity component at $0. Alternatively, measure the component that is most easily measurable and apply the residual to the other component.	Always measure the debt component first (generally at the present value of the cash flows). The rest of the value is assigned to equity since it is a residual item.
	Where a financial liability is indexed to the entity's financial performance or changes in equity, it is measured at the higher of the amortized cost and the amount owing at the balance sheet date given the index feature.	A financial liability that is indexed to the entity's financial performance or changes in equity would be analyzed to determine if an embedded derivative exists. Embedded derivatives are beyond the scope of the text.
	Allowed to value the entire financial instruments at fair value under the fair value option.	Allowed to value the entire financial instruments at fair value under the fair value option as long as certain conditions are met.
– CSOP when using an options pricing model	Volatility is not readily available for private entities but an attempt must be made to measure. May choose whether to recognize forfeitures upfront or later.	Volatility generally measurable. Must estimate forfeitures upfront.

	Accounting Standards for Private Enterprises (Private Entity GAAP/ASPE)—*CICA Handbook,* Part II, Sections 3856 and 3870	IFRS—IAS 32, 39 and IFRS 2
Presentation **– Equity settled CSOP for private entities**	Generally presented as equity although history of repurchasing the shares after the employee has exercised the CSOP may indicate that the CSOP is a liability.	Not applicable.
Recognition and measurement **– Hedge accounting (Appendix 16A)**	Does not specify accounting for fair value hedges or cash flow hedges. Instead, the standard lists certain types of specific hedging transactions that may qualify for hedge accounting including hedges of anticipated transactions and hedges of interest-bearing assets and liabilities. Hedge accounting generally stipulates that the hedging item is not recognized until it is settled (using accrual accounting).	Specifies fair value hedges and cash flow hedges. Under fair value hedge accounting, the hedged item is valued at fair value with gains and losses booked through income. Under cash flow hedge accounting, the gains and losses on the hedging item are booked through OCI and may be recycled to income when the hedged item is booked to net income.
– Accounting for cash-settled and other stock compensation plans (Appendix 16B)	Cash-settled plans such as SARs are measured at intrinsic value. Entities have a choice as to how to measure equity-settled SARs.	Cash-settled plans are measured at fair value (using valuation methods such as options pricing models, which incorporate both intrinsic value and time value). All equity-settled instruments are measured at fair value.

Illustration 16-12

IFRS and Private Enterprise GAAP Comparison Chart

Looking Ahead

A previously mentioned in Chapters 14 and 15, the IASB has been working on numerous projects relating to financial instruments. The project on hedging will attempt to simplify hedge accounting and the project dealing with the definitions of liabilities versus equity will attempt to encourage more consistent application of the standards.

Summary of Learning Objectives

1 **Understand what derivatives are and why they exist.**

Derivatives are financial instruments that derive (get) their value from an underlying instrument. They are attractive since they transfer risks and rewards without having to necessarily invest directly in the underlying instrument. They are used for both speculative purposes (to expose a company to increased risks in the hope of increased returns) and for hedging purposes (to reduce existing risk).

2 **Explain the various types of financial risks and how they arise.**

Financial risks include credit, currency, interest rate, liquidity, market, and other price risks. Credit risk is the risk that the other party to a financial instrument contract will fail to deliver. Currency and interest rate risk are the risk of a change in value and cash flows due to currency or interest rate changes. Liquidity risk is the risk that the company itself will not be able to honour the contract due to cash problems. Finally, market risk is the risk of a change in value and/or cash flows related to market forces.

WILEY PLUS

Glossary

KEY TERMS

book value method, 1045

call option, 1031

compensatory stock option plans (CSOPs), 1048

convertible bonds, 1043

counterparty, 1031

credit risk, 1025

currency risk, 1025

derivative instruments, 1023

3 Understand how to account for derivatives.

Derivatives are recognized on the balance sheet on the date that the contract is initiated. They are remeasured, on each balance sheet date, to their fair value. The related gains and losses are recorded through net income. Written options create liabilities. Futures contracts require the company to deposit a portion of the contracts' value with the broker/exchange. The contracts are marked to market by the broker/exchange daily and the company may have to deposit additional funds to cover deficiencies in the margin account. Purchase commitments that are net settleable and are not "expected use" contracts are accounted for as derivatives under IFRS. Under PE GAAP, purchase commitments are never accounted for as derivatives as they are not exchange-traded futures contracts. Exchange traded derivatives relating to commodities are generally accounted for as derivatives under ASPE. Special hedge accounting may affect how derivatives are accounted for.

4 Explain the unique issues associated with derivatives that are settleable using the entity's own equity instruments.

Under IFRS, derivatives that are settleable in the entity's own equity instruments are accounted for as equity (or contra-equity) if they will be settled by exchanging a fixed number of equity instruments for a fixed amount of cash or other assets and they do not create an obligation to deliver cash or other assets. Otherwise, they are financial assets/liabilities. In general, if the instruments are net settleable or have settlement options, they most often do not meet the criteria for equity presentation and are therefore financial assets/liabilities. IFRS provides significantly more guidance with respect to the accounting for these instruments.

5 Analyze whether a hybrid/compound instrument issued for financing purposes represents a liability, equity, or both (and how to measure).

Complex instruments include compound and hybrid instruments where the legal form may differ from the economic substance. The economic substance dictates the accounting. The main issue is that of presentation: should the instrument be presented as debt or equity? The definitions of debt and equity are useful in analyzing this. It is also important to understand what gives the instruments their value from a finance or economic perspective. If an instrument has both debt and equity components, use of the proportional and incremental methods will help in allocating the carrying value between the two components. There are differences in measuring compound financial instruments under IFRS versus PE GAAP. Related interest, dividends, gains, and losses are treated in a way that is consistent with the balance sheet presentation.

6 Explain the accounting for the issuance, conversion, and retirement of convertible securities.

The method for recording convertible bonds at the date of issuance is different from the method that is used to record straight debt issues. As the instrument is a compound instrument and contains both debt and equity components, these must be measured separately and presented as debt and equity, respectively. Any discount or premium that results from the issuance of convertible bonds is amortized, assuming the bonds will be held to maturity. If bonds are converted into other securities, the principal accounting problem is to determine the amount at which to record the securities that have been exchanged for the bond. The book value method is often used in practice. ASPE allows an entity to value the equity potion of compound instruments at $0.

7 **Describe the various types of stock compensation plans.**

Stock compensation includes direct awards of stock (when a company gives the shares to an employee as compensation), compensatory stock option plans whereby an employee is given stock options in lieu of salary, stock appreciation rights, and performance-type plans. The latter are discussed in Appendix 16B.

8 **Explain the differences between employee and compensatory option plans and other options.**

Employee stock option plans are meant to motivate employees and raise capital for the company. They are therefore capital transactions. Compensatory stock option plans are operating transactions since they are meant to compensate the employee for service provided. Costs relating to the latter are booked as expense.

9 **Describe the accounting for compensatory stock option plans.**

CSOPs are measured at fair value (using an options pricing model) at the grant date. The cost is then allocated to expense over the period that the employee provides service.

10 **Identify the major differences in accounting between accounting standards for private enterprises and IFRS, and what changes are expected in the near future.**

The differences are noted in the comparison chart. The stock-based compensation standards are largely converged and stable; however, the IASB is currently working on several projects relating to financial instruments including defining equity versus liabilities and hedging.

Appendix 16A

Hedging

Derivatives Used for Hedging

Objective **11**
Understand how derivatives are used in hedging.

In the body of the chapter, we discussed basic issues related to derivatives. This appendix will focus on the **accounting for hedging**. How does hedging actually reduce risk from an economic perspective and what are the accounting implications?

Companies that are already exposed to financial risks because of existing business transactions that arise from their business models may choose to protect themselves by managing and reducing those risks. For example, most public companies borrow and lend substantial amounts in credit markets and are therefore exposed to significant financial risks. They face substantial risk that the fair values or cash flows of interest-sensitive assets or liabilities will change if interest rates increase or decrease (**interest rate risk**). These same companies often also have cross-border transactions or international operations that expose them to **exchange rate risk**. The borrowing activity creates **liquidity risk** for the company and the lending activity creates credit risk.

Objective **12**
Explain what hedge accounting is and identify the qualifying hedge criteria.

Because the value and/or cash flows of derivative financial instruments can vary according to changes in interest rates, foreign currency exchange rates, or other external factors, derivatives may be used to offset the associated risks. **Using derivatives or other instruments to offset risks is called hedging**. A properly hedged position should result in no economic loss to the company. It may result in no gain, and there may be costs involved to effect the transactions, but it should limit or eliminate any potential losses. It reduces uncertainty and risk, and therefore volatility, and that is what gives hedging its value.

Separating the Act of Hedging Risks from the Decision to Use Hedge Accounting

It is important to separate the **act of hedging** to reduce economic and financial risks from the **accounting** for these hedges. Hedge accounting is optional and in some cases not even necessary. A company may choose to apply it or not. It is an accounting policy choice.

Why do we need special accounting rules for hedges? They exist in part due to our **mixed measurement model** (fair value, amortized cost, cost) and the **treatment of the related gains and losses where fair value is used**. They also exist because sometimes we **need to hedge future transactions that are not yet recognized on the balance sheet**.

Symmetry in Accounting—No Need for Special Hedge Accounting

Consider the situation where a company has a U.S. $100 receivable that is due in 30 days. The company is exposed to a **foreign currency risk**. Each time the currency rate changes, the economic value of the asset changes. Under existing GAAP, at each balance sheet date, we revalue the asset to reflect the current spot rate for the U.S. dollar. If the U.S. dollar depreciates against the Canadian dollar, the receivable is worth less and the resulting loss gets booked to the income statement. Now let's assume that the company does not want this foreign currency exposure and it enters into a forward contract to sell U.S. dollars for $120 Canadian in 30 days. This provides an **effective (economic) hedge** against changes in the value of the asset. If the U.S. dollar subsequently depreciates in value, then the forward contract increases in value because, under the contract, we can still sell the U.S. $100 for $120 Canadian no matter what happens to the exchange rate. From an **economic perspective**, the gains on the forward offset the losses on the receivable. From an **accounting perspective**, this gain gets booked to the income statement and thus offsets the loss on the receivable. In this case, because the losses on the receivable offset the gains on the forward, **no special hedge accounting is needed**.

No Symmetry in Accounting—Potential Need for Special Hedge Accounting

If instead, the company had an investment in a security classified as Fair Value Through Other Comprehensive Income, losses due to decreases in the value of the security would be booked to Other Comprehensive Income. Suppose the company decided to purchase an option to sell the security at a fixed price. This would protect it against future losses and would therefore be an **effective (economic) hedge against future losses**. If the value of the shares declined, the value of the option to sell at a set price would increase, resulting in a gain. This gain would normally be booked to net income since the option is a derivative. In this case, **even though the gains and losses offset from an economic perspective, there is asymmetry in the accounting because the loss is booked to Other Comprehensive Income and the gain to net income**. The company needs to decide whether it wants to use hedge accounting to ensure that the gains and losses will offset in net income. The journal entries for this example will be looked at later in this appendix.

Underlying Concept

Using hedge accounting increases transparency—reflecting the decrease in income volatility where the company has hedged its positions.

Under IFRS, hedge accounting divides hedges into two basic groups fair value hedges and cash flow hedges:

Under ASPE, hedge accounting is greatly simplified with only certain pre-specified transactions qualifying for optional hedge accounting treatment. These include anticipated purchase/sale of a commodity hedged with a forward contract, anticipated foreign exchange denominated transactions hedged with a forward contract, interest bearing assets/liabilities hedged with interest rate or cross currency swaps and net investments in a foreign subsidiary. Because hedge accounting is designed to ensure that the **timing of the recognition** of gains/losses in net income is the same for both the hedged item and the hedging item, **it will result in recognition and measurement that is different than under normal GAAP. Thus, it is important to ensure that the hedge is effective and properly identified and documented** in order to allow it to qualify for special treatment.

Qualifying Hedge Criteria

Hedges may qualify for optional hedge accounting when the following criteria are met.[39]

1. At the inception of the hedge, the entity must do the following:
   (a) **Identify** the exposure.
   (b) **Designate** that hedge accounting will be applied.

---

[39] *CICA Handbook*, Part II, Section 3856.32 and IAS 39.88.

(c) **Document** the risk management objectives and strategies, the hedging relationship, the items being hedged and used to hedge, the methods of assessing the effectiveness of the hedge, and the method of accounting for the hedge.

2. At the inception and throughout the term, the entity should have reasonable assurance that the relationship is **effective and consistent with the risk management policy**. As a result, all of the following must be respected:

(a) The effectiveness of the hedge should be reliably measurable.[40]

(b) The hedging relationship should be reassessed regularly.

(c) Where the hedge involves forecasted transactions, it should be probable that these transactions will occur.

Fair Value Hedges

Objective 13

Explain the difference between a fair value hedge and cash flow hedge.

Objective 14

Calculate the impact on net income of using hedge accounting for both types of hedges.

Under IFRS, in a fair value hedge, a derivative may be used to hedge or offset the exposure to changes in the fair value of a **recognized asset or liability** (or of a previously unrecognized firm commitment),[41] and thus **reduce market risk**.[42] In a perfectly hedged position, the economic gain/loss on the fair value of the derivative and that of the hedged asset or liability should be equal and offsetting. Hedge accounting modifies the current accounting. Under fair value hedge accounting per IFRS, the hedged item must be recognized on the balance sheet and measured (or remeasured) at fair value and the related gains/losses must be booked through net income. So for instance, if the asset were normally measured at cost, it would have to be remeasured to fair value under hedge accounting. In addition, if the gains/losses were normally booked through OCI, a journal entry would be booked to reclassify them to net income under hedge accounting.

A typical fair value hedge is the use of **put options** (options to sell an investment at a preset price) or a forward contract (to sell the investment at a preset price) to hedge the risk that an investment will decline in value. Let's look at an example.

Using Hedge Accounting—Put Options as Fair Value Hedges

To illustrate, assume that Cathay Inc. purchases an investment for $1,000. This exposes the company to a market risk—the risk that the shares will decline in value. If the investment is designated as Fair Value Through Other Comprehensive Income (FVOCI), it will be carried at its fair value, with gains and losses normally being booked through Other Comprehensive Income. The journal entry to record the initial investment at January 1, 2012, would be as follows:

A = L + SE
0

Cash flows: ↓ 1,000 outflow

Investment—FVOCI	1,000	
Cash		1,000

Significant Change

---

[40] Under IFRS, effectiveness is proven by showing that the changes in the hedged item are highly correlated with the changes in the hedging item. Although no method is specified in the standard, regression analysis is often used. Under PE GAAP, the entity must prove that the critical terms of the contracts for the hedged and hedging items are essentially the same (thus indirectly proving that the hedge will be effective). This is known as the "critical terms match" test.

[41] If a firm commitment such as a purchase commitment is hedged, then the commitment itself must be recognized on the balance sheet so that resulting gains and losses offset the gains and losses generated by the hedging item.

[42] Note that the trade-off to reducing market risk with a derivative is an increase in credit, liquidity, and operational risks. (the risk related to designing and monitoring the hedge position).

Assume that on the same date the company also enters into a derivative contract in which it purchases an option to sell the shares at $1,000 to protect itself against losses in value of the security. The cost of the option is $10. If the value of the shares declines, the company can sell the shares under the option for $1,000—thus limiting any loss. As a derivative, the option will be measured at fair value with subsequent gains and losses booked to net income. The entry would be as follows:

January 1, 2012		
Financial Instrument—Derivative	10	
Cash		10

A = L + SE
0
Cash flows: ↓ 10 outflow

If at December 31, 2012, the fair value of the investment increased by $50, the derivative would decrease in value by $50. (In actual fact, the loss on the option would not exactly offset the gains on the investment as the value of the option incorporates other variables.) The journal entries to record this are as follows:

Investment—FVOCI	50	
Gain/Loss		50
Gain/Loss	50	
Financial Instrument—Derivative		50

A = L + SE
0   0
Cash flows: No effect

As previously mentioned, the derivative is always valued at fair value with the gains/losses being booked to net income. However, normally the gain on the FVOCI investment would be booked to Other Comprehensive Income. There is therefore a mismatch. **Hedge accounting allows the gain on the hedged item to be booked through net income so it may be offset by the loss on the derivative as noted in the journal entry above. Hedge accounting allows us to modify the way we would normally account for the available for sale investment.** This transaction is not eligible for hedge accounitng under PE GAAP.

Using Hedge Accounting—Purchase Commitments as Hedged Items

Assume the company has committed to purchase a certain amount of raw materials at a fixed price denominated in U.S. dollars in order to secure a stable supply of the raw materials. This would create a foreign currency risk as the price is fixed in U.S. dollars, the value of which will vary over time. Normally, a company would not recognize purchase commitments for which it intends to take delivery of the raw materials unless there was a contingent loss that was measurable and probable.[43]

Assume further that the company chooses to hedge the risk by entering into a forward contract to purchase U.S. dollars at a future date at a fixed exchange rate. This would lock in the rate and therefore remove the foreign currency risk. The forward would be recognized on the balance sheet and measured at fair value, with gains and losses being recorded in net income. If the purchase commitment were not recognized on the balance sheet, there

---

[43] If the terms of the contract allowed the contract to be settled net in cash (instead of taking delivery of the raw material), it may meet the definition of a derivative and have to be recognized as being such as noted earlier in the chapter (under IFRS). If the purchase commitment was recognized as a derivative and it was hedged with a derivative, there would be no need for special hedge accounting as both would be recognized and measured at fair value with gains/losses booked through net income such that they offset.

would be a mismatch. **Therefore, per IFRS under hedge accounting, the purchase commitment would also need to be recognized on the balance sheet and measured at fair value** (with gains/losses booked through net income). Since this might be difficult to measure, the entity may choose to account for this under IFRS as a cash flow hedge.

Under PE GAAP hedge accounting, neither the purchase commitment nor the derivative would be recognized until the goods were delivered and the contracts settled. The raw materials would be measured using the locked in forward exchange rate for the U.S. dollars.

Significant Change

Cash Flow Hedges

A cash flow hedge deals with **transactions that offset the effects of future variable cash flows**, such as future interest payments on variable rate debt. Because the debt is variable rate, the interest to be paid out will fluctuate, and this therefore makes future cash flows uncertain. Since the hedged position (i.e., the potential change in future interest payments) is not yet recognized on the balance sheet, the gains/losses related to changes in value (and hence the cash flows) are not captured. **Thus, under hedge accounting per IFRS, any gains/losses on the hedging item should not be included in net income either**. They are therefore recognized in Other Comprehensive Income. Recall that under PE GAAP, there is no such thing as Other Comprehensive Income. Therefore, hedge accounting under PE GAAP for these types of transactions essentially requires that the hedging item not be recognized until the transaction is settled (i.e., it remains off–balance sheet). The purchase commitment example above illustrates this.

In a cash flow hedge, the company is trying to protect itself against variations in future cash flows. Different derivative instruments may be used to effect this. Let's look at an example.

Using Hedge Accounting—Interest Rate Swaps as Cash Flow Hedges

When a company has a series of similar transactions that it wants to hedge, a swap contract may be used. A swap is a transaction between two parties in which the first party promises to make a series of payments to the second party. Similarly, the second party promises to make simultaneous payments to the first party. The parties swap payments. **A swap is a series of forward contracts**. The most common type of swap is the interest rate swap, in which one party makes payments based on a fixed or floating rate and the second party does just the opposite. In most cases, financial institutions and other intermediaries find the two parties, bring them together, and handle the flow of payments between the two parties, as shown in Illustration 16A-1.

Illustration 16A-1

Swap Transaction

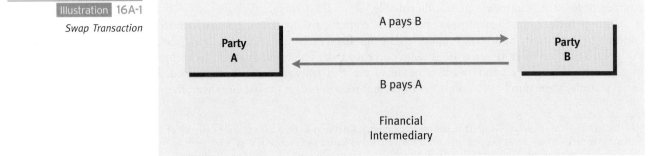

To illustrate the accounting for a cash flow hedge, assume that Jones Corporation issues $1 million of five-year, floating-rate bonds on January 2, 2012. The entry to record this transaction is as follows:

January 2, 2012		
Cash	1,000,000	
Bonds Payable		1,000,000

A = L +   SE
+1,000,000   +1,000,000

Cash flows: ↑ 1,000,000 inflow

A floating interest rate was offered to appeal to investors, but Jones is concerned about the cash flow uncertainty associated with the variable rate interest. To protect against the **cash flow uncertainty**, Jones decides to hedge the risk by entering into a five-year interest rate swap. Under the terms of the swap contract, the following will occur:

1. Jones will pay fixed payments at 8% (based on the $1 million amount) to a counterparty.

2. Jones will receive, from the counterparty, variable or floating rates that are based on the market rate in effect throughout the life of the swap contract.

As Illustration 16A-2 shows, by using this swap Jones can change the interest on the bonds payable from a floating rate to a fixed rate. Jones thus swaps the floating rate, assumed to be 9% in the example, for a fixed rate.

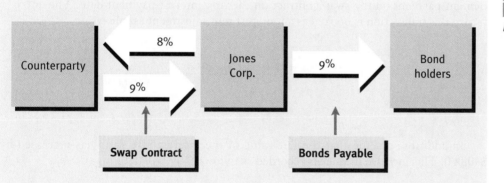

The settlement dates for the swap correspond to the interest payment dates on the debt (December 31). On each interest payment (settlement date), Jones and the counterparty will calculate the difference between current market interest rates (9% in the example) and the fixed rate of 8%, and settle the difference.[44] Both parties will also need to value the swap contract on each balance sheet date using a discounted cash flow model. If interest rates rise, the value of the swap contract to Jones increases (Jones has a gain), while at the same time Jones' floating-rate debt obligation becomes larger (Jones has an economic loss). **The swap is an effective risk management tool in this setting because its value is related to the same underlying (interest rates) that will affect the value of**

Finance

---

[44] The decision to make an interest rate swap is based on a recognized index of market interest rates. The most commonly used index is the London Interbank Offer Rate, or LIBOR. The prime lending rate is another rate that is commonly referenced in loan agreements and other financial instruments. This rate is set periodically by the Bank of Canada. The interest rates that are attached to various instruments are normally above prime (e.g. P + 1% or P + 2%, etc.).

the floating-rate bond payable. Thus, if the swap's value goes up, it offsets the loss related to the debt obligation.

Assuming that the swap was entered into on January 2, 2012 (the same date as the issuance of the debt), the swap at this time has no value and there is therefore no need for a journal entry.

January 2, 2012
No entry required. Memorandum to indicate that the swap contract is signed.

At the end of 2012, the interest payment on the bonds is made. Assume the floating rate is 9%. The journal entry to record this transaction is as follows:

A = L + SE
−90,000   −90,000

Cash flows: ↓ 90,000 outflow

December 31, 2012		
Interest Expense	90,000	
Cash (9% × $1,000,000)		90,000

At the end of 2012, market interest rates have increased substantially to 9%, and the value of the swap contract has therefore increased. Recall (see Illustration 16A-2) that in the swap Jones is to receive a floating rate of 9%, or $90,000 ($1,000,000 × 9%), and pay a fixed rate of 8%, or $80,000. Jones therefore receives $10,000 ($90,000 − $80,000) as a settlement payment on the swap contract on the first interest payment date. The entry to record this transaction is booked as an interest rate adjustment as follows:

A = L + SE
+10,000   +10,000

Cash flows: ↑ 10,000 inflow

December 31, 2012		
Cash	10,000	
Interest Expense		10,000

In addition, assume that the fair value of the interest rate swap has increased by $40,000. This increase in value is recorded as follows:[45]

A = L + SE
+40,000   +40,000

Cash flows: No effect

December 31, 2012		
Financial Instrument—Derivative	40,000	
Other Comprehensive Income—		
Unrealized Holding Gain or Loss		40,000

As a derivative, as previously noted, this swap contract is recognized on the balance sheet, and the gain in fair value is normally reported in net income. **Under IFRS hedge accounting, the gain on the hedging activity is reported in Other Comprehensive Income (as opposed to net income).** This is because there is asymmetry in the accounting under normal GAAP. The losses on the bond payable (due to the fact that it is a variable rate loan and interest rates keep rising) do not get recognized because they are opportunity costs. The gains on the swap do get recognized because the swap is a derivative.

---

[45] Theoretically, this fair value change reflects the present value of expected future differences in variable and fixed interest rates and any changes in the counterparty's credit risk.

The unrealized holding gain will gradually be reflected in net income when the benefit of the locked-in (lower) interest rate is realized as reduced interest expense, as the earlier entries showed. By the end of the swap contract, the value of the contract will be nil and the company will have recorded net interest expense that reflects the fixed rate. Illustration 16A-3 shows the balance sheet presentation of a cash flow hedge.

JONES CORPORATION
Balance Sheet (partial)
December 31, 2012

Financial Asset—Derivatives:	
Swap contract	$ 40,000
Long-term liabilities	
Bonds payable	$1,000,000
Equity	
Other comprehensive income	$ 40,000

The effect on the Jones Corporation balance sheet is the addition of the swap asset. On the income statement, interest expense of $80,000 is reported. Jones has effectively changed the debt's interest rate from variable to fixed (economic substance). That is, by receiving a floating rate and paying a fixed rate on the swap, the floating rate on the bond payable is converted to variable, which results in an effective interest rate of 8% in 2009. The economic gain on the swap offsets the economic loss related to the debt obligation (since interest rates are higher), and therefore the net gain or loss on the hedging activity is zero. **Hedge accounting under IFRS allows us to record the gain outside of net income since the economic substance is that the risk has been neutralized**. Under PE GAAP hedge accounting, the swap contract is not recognized on the balance sheet. Instead only the payments/receipts of interest are accrued as interest expense/income adjustments as shown in the journal entries under IFRS.

One last point on interest rate swaps. **As noted above, they may be used as cash flow hedges. They may also be used as fair value hedges and be eligible for hedge accounting under both IFRS and PE GAAP**. In the latter case, they would protect against changes in fair value of a recorded asset or liability that would occur when market interest rates change and where the asset or liability has a fixed interest rate. They can be used to offset fixed interest rate payments on a debt obligation to take advantage of lower interest rates or to offset a decline in the value of a bond investment when market interest rates are increasing. Interestingly, while this eliminates **risk** created by fixed interest rates, it exposes the company to **cash flow risk**. Financial instruments are bundles of different types of risks. A company must choose which risks, if any, it wants to eliminate, and always keep in mind that the hedging instrument may carry new risks.

Using Hedge Accounting—Derivatives as Cash Flow Hedges of Anticipated Transactions

Another example of a cash flow hedge is a hedge of an anticipated future transaction, such as a raw material purchase.

To illustrate the accounting for cash flow hedges under IFRS, assume that in September 2012, Allied Can Co. anticipates purchasing 1,000 metric tonnes of aluminum in January 2013. Allied is concerned that prices for aluminum will increase in the next few months, and it wants to protect against possible price increases for aluminum inventory. To hedge the risk that it might have to pay for higher prices for inventory in January 2013, Allied enters into a cash-settled aluminum forward contract.

The contract requires Allied to pay any difference between $1,550 per tonne and the spot price for aluminum, if lower, to the counterparty. If the price of aluminum increases, the counterparty will make a payment for the difference to Allied.[46] The contract matures on the expected purchase date in January 2013. The underlying for this derivative is the price of aluminum. If the price of aluminum rises above $1,550, the value of the contract to Allied increases because Allied will be able to purchase the aluminum at the lower price of $1,550 per tonne.

Assume that the contract was entered into on September 1, 2012, and that the price to be paid today for inventory to be delivered in January, the forward price, was equal to the current spot price adjusted for the time between September and January. On a net present value basis, the fair value of this contract will be zero. Therefore no entry is necessary.

September 1, 2012
No entry required. Memorandum to indicate that the contract is signed.

Assume that at December 31, 2012, the price for January delivery of aluminum has increased. The fair value of the contract has therefore also increased, with its value now assumed to be $25,000. Allied would make the following entry to record this increase in the value of the forward contract:

A   =   L   +   SE
+25,000   +25,000

Cash flows: No effect

December 31, 2012		
Financial Instrument—Derivative	25,000	
Other Comprehensive Income—		
Unrealized Holding Gain or Loss		25,000
(Journal entry not booked under PE GAAP hedge accounting)		

The derivative contract is reported on the balance sheet as an asset. The gain on the contract would normally be recorded through net income. **However, under IFRS hedge accounting, it is reported as part of Other Comprehensive Income**. Since Allied has not yet purchased and sold the inventory, this is an **anticipated transaction**. In this type of transaction, gains or losses on the futures contract are accumulated in equity as part of other comprehensive income until the period in which the inventory is sold and earnings is affected.

Under PE GAAP hedge accounting, the derivative contract would not be recognized until it is settled. The gain/loss would be recorded as an adjustment to inventory. Assume now that in January 2013 Allied purchases (separately) 1,000 metric tonnes of aluminum for $1,575. It would make the following entry:

A   =   L   +   SE
0

Cash flows: ↓ 1,575,000 outflow

January 2013		
Aluminum Inventory	1,575,000	
Cash ($1,575 × 1,000 tonnes)		1,575,000
(Booked under both IFRS and PE GAAP hedge accounting)		

At the same time, Allied makes final settlement on the derivative contract and makes the following entry:

---

[46] Under the net settlement feature, the actual aluminum does not have to be exchanged. Rather, the parties to the contract may settle by paying the cash difference between the forward price and the price of aluminum on the settlement date.

January 2013		
Cash	25,000	
Financial Instrument—Derivative		25,000
($1,575,000 − $1,550,000)		
(Credit booked to inventory under PE GAAP hedge accounting)		

A = L + SE
0

Cash flows: ↑ 25,000 inflow

Through use of the derivative contract, Allied has been able to fix the cost of its inventory. The $25,000 contract settlement payment offsets the amount paid to purchase the inventory at the prevailing market price of $1,575,000. The result is that the net cash outflow is at $1,550 per metric tonne, as desired. In this way, Allied has hedged the cash flow for the purchase of inventory, as shown in Illustration 16A-4.

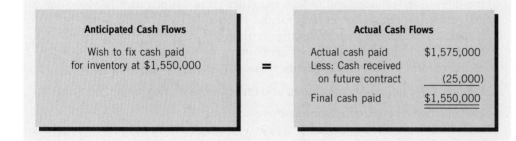

Illustration 16A-4

Effect of Hedge on Cash Flows

There are no income effects at this point. The gain on the futures contract is accumulated in equity as part of Accumulated Other Comprehensive Income under IFRS until the period when the inventory is sold and earnings is affected through cost of goods sold.

For example, assume that the aluminum is processed into cans, the finished goods. The total cost of the cans (including the aluminum purchases in January 2013) is $1.7 million. Allied sells the cans in July 2013 for $2 million. The entry to record the sale is as follows:

July 2013		
Cash	2,000,000	
Sales Revenue		2,000,000
Cost of Goods Sold	1,700,000	
Inventory (Cans)		1,700,000
(Booked under both IFRS and PE GAAP hedge accounting although under		
the latter, the amount would be $1,675,000 versus $1,700,000)		

A = L + SE
+300,000   +300,000

Cash flows: ↑ 300,000 inflow

Since the effect on the anticipated transaction has now affected earnings, Allied makes the following entry related to the hedging transaction:

July 2013		
Other Comprehensive Income—Unrealized Holding		
Gain or Loss	25,000	
Cost of Goods Sold		25,000
(Not booked under PE GAAP hedge accounting)		

A = L + SE
0

Cash flows: No effect

The gain on the futures contract, which was reported as part of Other Comprehensive Income, now reduces the cost of goods sold. As a result, the cost of aluminum included in the overall cost of goods sold is $1,550,000. The derivative contract has worked as planned to manage the cash paid for aluminum inventory and the amount of cost of goods sold. Note that this entry could also be made at the date when the inventory was acquired, except that the credit would be booked to Inventory. Thus, the cost of goods sold in July 2013 would be $1,675,000.

Summary of Learning Objectives for Appendix 16A

11 Understand how derivatives are used in hedging.

Any company or individual that wants to protect itself against different types of business risk often uses derivative contracts to achieve this objective. In general, where the intent is to manage and reduce risk, these transactions involve some type of hedge. Derivatives are useful tools for this since they have the effect of transferring risks and rewards between the parties to the contract. Derivatives can be used to hedge a company's exposure to fluctuations in interest rates, foreign currency exchange rates, equity, or commodity prices.

12 Explain what hedge accounting is and identify the qualifying hedge criteria.

Hedge accounting is optional accounting that ensures that properly hedged positions will reduce volatility in net income created by hedging with derivatives. It seeks to match gains and losses from hedged positions with those of the hedging items so that they may be offset. Since this is special accounting, companies must ensure that there is in fact a real hedge (i.e., that the contract insulates the company from economic loss or undesirable consequences) and that the hedge remains effective. Proper documentation of the risks and risk management strategy is important.

13 Explain the difference between a fair value hedge and cash flow hedge.

A fair value hedge reduces risks relating to fair value changes of recorded assets and liabilities as well as purchase commitments. Cash flow hedges protect against future losses due to future cash flow changes relating to exposures that are not captured on the balance sheet. PE GAAP does not discuss fair value or cash flow hedges but rather stipulates the accounting for certain types of specific hedge transactions.

14 Calculate the impact on net income of using hedge accounting for both types of hedges.

Properly hedged positions reduce income fluctuations because gains and losses are offset. Under IFRS, for cash flow hedges, the gains and losses on the hedging items are booked through Other Comprehensive Income and are brought into net income in the same (future) period that the hedged items are booked to net income. For fair value hedges, hedge accounting adjusts the hedged asset to ensure that it is recognized and measured at fair value and that related gains/losses are booked through net income. Both types of hedges ensure that the gains/losses of the hedged and hedging positions offset. Under PE GAAP hedge accounting, the hedging item (which is generally a derivative) is not recognized on the balance sheet until the hedging item is settled. Thus both the hedged item (usually a future transaction) and the hedging item (the derivative) are off–balance sheet and there is no mismatch. Only certain pre-specified transactions are eligible for hedge accounting under PE GAAP.

Appendix 16B

Stock Compensation Plans–Additional Complications

Two common plans (beyond the stock option plans discussed in the chapter) that illustrate different accounting issues are:

1. Stock appreciation rights plans

2. Performance-type plans

These will be discussed below. In addition, this appendix will discuss briefly accounting where settlement options exist.

Stock Appreciation Rights Plans

One of the main drawbacks of compensatory stock option plans is that in order to realize the stock options benefit, the employees must exercise the options and then sell the shares. This is a somewhat complex process and usually involves incurring transaction costs. One solution to this problem was the creation of stock appreciation rights (SARs). In this type of plan, the executive or employee is given the right to receive compensation equal to the share appreciation, which is defined as the excess of the shares' market price at the date of exercise over a pre-established price. This share appreciation may be paid in cash, shares, or a combination of both.

The major advantage of SARs is that the employee often does not have to make a cash outlay at the date of exercise, and instead receives a payment for the share appreciation. Unlike shares that are acquired under a stock option plan, the shares that constitute the basis for calculating the appreciation in a SARs plan are not issued. The executive is awarded only cash or shares having a market value equivalent to the appreciation.

As indicated earlier, the usual date for measuring compensation related to stock compensation plans is the date of grant. However, with SARs, the final amount of the cash (or shares, or combination of the two) to be distributed is not known until the date of exercise—the measurement date. Therefore, total compensation expense cannot be measured until this date.

How then should compensation expense be recorded during the interim periods from the date of grant to the date of exercise? This determination is not easy because it is impossible to know what the total compensation cost will be until the date of exercise, and the service period will probably not coincide with the exercise date. One way to estimate total compensation cost for the plan at any interim period is the difference between the

15 Objective
Account for stock appreciation rights plans.

Significant Change

current market price of the stock and the option price multiplied by the number of stock appreciation rights outstanding. This approach is supported under PE GAAP. IFRS requires use of an options pricing model to value the SAR and hence the liability.[47]

Regardless of how fair value is estimated for the liability, this total estimated compensation expense is then allocated over the service period, to record an expense (or decrease expense if the market price falls) in each period. At the end of each interim period, the total compensation expense reported to date should equal the percentage of the total service period that has elapsed, multiplied by the estimated compensation cost.

For example, assume that at the end of an interim period the service period is 40% complete and the total estimated compensation is $100,000. At this time, the cumulative compensation expense reported to date should equal $40,000 ($100,000 × 0.40). As a second example, assume the following: In the first year of a four-year plan, the company charges one fourth of the appreciation to date. In the second year, it charges off two fourths or 50% of the appreciation to date, less the amount that was already recognized in the first year. In the third year, it charges off three fourths of the appreciation to date, less the amount recognized previously, and in the fourth year it charges off the remaining compensation expense.

A special problem arises when the exercise date is later than the service period. In the previous example, if the SARs were not exercised at the end of four years, it would be necessary to account for the difference in the market price and the option price in the fifth year. In this case, the compensation expense is adjusted whenever a change in the stock's market price **occurs in subsequent reporting periods until the rights expire or are exercised, whichever comes first**.

Increases or decreases in the market value of those shares between the date of grant and the exercise date, therefore, result in a change in the measure of compensation. Some periods will have credits to compensation expense if the stock's quoted market price falls from one period to the next; the credit to Compensation Expense, however, cannot exceed previously recognized compensation expense. In other words, **cumulative compensation expense cannot be negative**.

To illustrate, assume that Hotels, Inc. establishes a SARs program on January 1, 2012, which entitles executives to receive cash at the date of exercise (anytime in the next five years) for the difference between the shares' market price and the pre-established or stated price of $10 on 10,000 SARs. The shares' market price on December 31, 2012, is $13 and the service period runs for two years (2012 to 2013). Illustration 16B-1 shows the amount

Illustration 16B-1

Compensation Expense, Stock Appreciation Rights

STOCK APPRECIATION RIGHTS
Schedule of Compensation Expense

(1) Date	(2) Market Price	(3) Pre-established Price (10,000 SARs)	(4) Cumulative Compensation Recognizable[a]	(5) Percentage Accrued[b]	(6) Cumulative Compensation Accrued to Date	Expense 2012	Expense 2013	Expense 2014
12/31/12	$13	$10	$30,000	50%	$(15,000) $(55,000)	$15,000	$55,000	
12/31/13	$17	$10	$70,000	100%	$(70,000) $(20,000)			$(20,000)
12/31/14	$15	$10	$50,000	100%	$(50,000)			

[a]Cumulative compensation for unexercised SARs to be allocated to periods of service.
[b]The percentage accrued is based on a two-year service period (2012 to 2013).

---

[47] IFRS 2.30-.33. The ASPE standard refers to the shares' "market price/value". Since the shares of private entities do not trade on exchanges, the standard assumes internal markets for the shares.

of compensation expense to be recorded each period, assuming that the executives exercise their rights after holding the SARs for three years. The company follows PE GAAP.

In 2012, Hotels would record compensation expense of $15,000 because 50% of the $30,000 total compensation cost estimated at December 31, 2012, is allocable to 2012.

In 2013, the market price increased to $17 per share; therefore, the additional compensation expense of $55,000 ($70,000 – $15,000) was recorded. The SARs were held through 2014, during which time the shares decreased to $15. The decrease is recognized by recording a $20,000 credit to Compensation Expense and a debit to Liability under Stock Appreciation Plan. Note that after the service period ends, since the rights are still outstanding, the rights are adjusted to market at December 31, 2014. Any such credit to Compensation Expense cannot exceed previous charges to expense that can be attributed to that plan.

As the compensation expense is recorded each period, the corresponding credit should be to a liability account if the stock appreciation is to be paid in cash. According to GAAP, SARs that call for settlement in cash are indexed liabilities and the measurement date is therefore the settlement date.[48]

If shares are to be issued, then a more appropriate credit would be to Contributed Surplus. The entry to record compensation expense in the first year, assuming that the SARs ultimately will be paid in cash, is as follows:

| Compensation Expense | 15,000 | |
| Liability under Stock Appreciation Plan | | 15,000 |

A = L + SE
+15,000 −15,000
Cash flows: No effect

The liability account would be credited again in 2013 for $55,000 and debited for $20,000 in 2014, when the negative compensation expense is recorded. The entry to record the negative compensation expense is as follows:

| Liability under Stock Appreciation Plan | 20,000 | |
| Compensation Expense | | 20,000 |

A = L + SE
−20,000 +20,000
Cash flows: No effect

At December 31, 2014, the executives receive $50,000; the entry removing the liability is as follows:

| Liability under Stock Appreciation Plan | 50,000 | |
| Cash | | 50,000 |

A = L + SE
−50,000 −50,000
Cash flows: ↓ 50,000 outflow

Complexities

Sometimes there are **choices as to how the instrument will be settled** (in cash or shares). Judgement should be used to determine whether the instrument should be accounted for as an equity-settled instrument (like the CSOP) or a cash-settled instrument (like the SAR above). SARs that **require** equity settlement are presented as equity under PE GAAP and the issuer has a choice in terms of how to measure (measure at fair value or using the intrinsic value method). Equity-settled SARs are presented as equity under IFRS and measured at fair value.

Significant Change

Either way, if the company is unable to measure the cost at the grant date, the measurement date is the exercise date and the amount is continually re-estimated.

---

[48] *CICA Handbook*, Part II, Section 3870.39.

SARs are often issued in combination with compensatory stock options (referred to as tandem or combination plans) and the executive must then select which of the two sets of terms to exercise and which one to cancel. The existence of alternative plans running concurrently poses additional problems. Based on the facts available each period, it must be determined which of the two plans is more likely to be exercised and that plan is then accounted for and the other is ignored.

Performance-Type Plans

Objective 16
Explain what performance-type plans are.

Some executives have become disenchanted with stock compensation plans in which payment depends ultimately on an increase in the common shares' market price. They do not like having their compensation and judgement of performance at the mercy of the stock market's erratic behaviour. As a result, there has been a large increase in the use of **performance-type plans** that award the executives common shares (or cash) if specified performance criteria are attained during the performance period (generally three to five years). Many large companies now have some type of plan that does not rely on share price appreciation. The performance criteria usually include increases in return on assets or equity, growth in sales, growth in earnings per share (EPS), or a combination of these factors.

A performance-type plan's measurement date is the date of exercise because the number of shares that will be issued or the cash that will be paid out when performance is achieved are not known at the date of grant. The company must use its best estimates to measure the compensation cost before the date of exercise. The compensation cost is allocated to the periods involved in the same way as is done with stock appreciation rights; that is, the percentage approach is used.

Tandem or combination awards are popular with these plans. The executive has the choice of selecting between a performance or stock option award. Companies such as General Electric and Xerox have adopted plans of this nature. In these cases, the executive has the best of both worlds: if either the share price increases or the performance goal is achieved, the executive gains. Sometimes, the executive receives both types of plans, so that the monies received from the performance plan can finance the exercise price on the stock option plan.

Summary of Learning Objectives for Appendix 16B

KEY TERMS

combination plans, 1072
stock appreciation rights (SARs), 1069
tandem plans, 1072

15 Account for stock appreciation rights plans.

SARs are popular because the employee can share in increases in value of the company's shares without having to purchase them. The increases in value over a certain amount are paid to the employee as cash or shares. Obligations to pay cash represent a liability that must be remeasured. The cost is therefore continually adjusted, with the measurement date being the exercise date. The related expense is spread over the service period. If the SARs are not exercised at the end of the service period, the liability must continue to be remeasured. Cash-settled SARs are measured using intrinsic values under PE GAAP and fair value under IFRS.

16 Explain what performance-type plans are.

These plans are tied to performance (of the entity, the individual or a group of individuals). There is therefore more measurement uncertainty.

Appendix 16c

Advanced Models for Measuring Fair Value

Options Pricing Models

Chapter 2 introduced the use of a framework for determining fair values. Basic models for calculating fair value include discounted cash flow models, which were reviewed in that chapter. This appendix goes one step further and looks briefly at more advanced models for measuring fair value.

There are numerous **options pricing models** and they are usually covered in more advanced finance texts and courses. The Black-Scholes and binomial tree options pricing models are two of these models.

Options pricing models incorporate the following information (at a minimum) as inputs to the model:

1. The exercise price. This is the price at which the option may be settled. It is agreed upon by both parties to the contract.

2. The expected life of the option. This is the term of the option. It is agreed upon by both parties to the contract. Some options may only be settled at the end of the term (known as European options) while others may be settled at points during the term (known as American options).

3. The current market price of the underlying stock. This is readily available from the stock market.

4. The volatility of the underlying stock. This is the magnitude of future changes in the market price. Volatility looks at how the specific stock price moves relative to the market.

5. The expected dividend during the option life.

6. The risk-free rate of interest for the option life. In general, government bonds carry a return that is felt to be the risk-free return.

Where possible, the fair value is more robust if the inputs make use of external and objective market information. For items such as volatility and dividends, judgement is required in arriving at the input value. Entities look to historical data to help determine these amounts but care should be taken as historical data are not necessarily indicative of the future. In addition, for some entities such as newly listed companies, there will be no history. In this case, the entity may look to similar entities in the same industry. The same problem exists for private entities. For these entities, the company also benchmarks against other similar companies and industries in an attempt to calculate the volatility measure.

17 Objective
Understand how options pricing models are used to measure financial instruments.

Finance

Any other inputs that a knowledgeable market participant would consider in valuing the option would also be taken into account. These include the employees' ability to exercise the option (whether it is restricted or not and whether the option may be exercised early or not).

Recall further that financial instrument values have two components: an **intrinsic value** component and a **time value** component. These two components are used in the Black-Scholes model, which requires the following two amounts to be calculated. Note that this model can be used with published tables.

1. *The standard deviation of proportionate changes in the fair value of the asset underlying the options, multiplied by the square root of the time to expiry of the option.* This amount relates to the time value portion and the potential for the value of the asset underlying the option to change over time. The volatility of the shares as compared with the volatility of the market in general is an important factor here. The more volatile the shares, the greater the fair value of the options. This is because the volatility introduces more risk and the higher the risk, the higher the return.

2. *The ratio of the fair value of the asset underlying the option to the present value of the option exercise price.* This relates to the intrinsic value.

The calculations of the fair value using options pricing models are beyond the scope of this text.

Summary of Learning Objective for Appendix 16C

17 Understand how options pricing models are used to measure financial instruments.

Fair value is most readily determined where there is an active market with published prices. Where this is not the case, a valuation technique is used. More basic techniques include discounted cash flows. More complex techniques include options pricing models such as the Black-Scholes and binomial tree models. Where possible, valuation techniques should use available external inputs to ensure that they are more objective. Having said this, significant judgement goes into determining fair values using options pricing models.

Brief Exercises

Note: All assignment material with an asterisk (*) relates to an appendix to the chapter.

BE16-1   Saver Rio Ltd. purchased options to acquire 1,000 common shares of Spender Limited for $20 per share within the next six months. The premium (cost) related to the options was $500. How should this be accounted for in the financial statements of Saver Rio? Explain which financial risks the transaction exposes the entity to.   **(LO 2, 3)**

BE16-2   Fresh Produce Ltd. entered into a purchase commitment contract to buy apples from Farmers Corp.; however, the contract stipulates that Fresh Produce Ltd. can settle the contact on a net basis. Fresh Produce Ltd. intends to take delivery of the apples so that they can be sold in its grocery stores. How should this be accounted for in Fresh Produce Ltd.'s financial statements if it applies IFRS? Explain which financial risks the transaction exposes the entity to.   **(LO 2, 3)**

BE16-3   On January 1, 2011, Ginseng Inc. entered into a forward contract to purchase U.S. $5,000 for $5,280 Canadian in 30 days. On January 15, the fair value of the contract was $35 (reflecting the present value of the future cash flows under the contract). Assume that the company would like to update its records on January 15. Prepare only necessary journal entries on January 1 and 15, 2011. Explain which financial risks the transaction exposes the entity to.   **(LO 2, 3)**

BE16-4   Refer to BE16–3. Assume the same facts except that the forward contract is a futures contract that trades on the Futures Exchange. Ginseng Inc. was required to deposit $25 with the stockbroker as a margin. On January 15, the broker asked Ginseng to deposit an additional $10. Prepare the journal entries to update the books on January 1 and 15 for the additional margin call as well as the change in value of the futures contract.   **(LO 3)**

BE16-5   On January 1, 2011, Pacer Ltd. paid $1,000 for the option to buy 5,000 of its common shares for $25 each. The contract stipulates that it may only be settled by exercising the option and buying the shares. How should this be accounted for in the financial statements of Pacer Ltd.? Assume that Pacer Ltd. complies with IFRS.   **(LO 4)**

BE16-6   Jamieson Limited, a publicly accountable enterprise, issued century bonds that will not be due until 2104. The bonds carry interest at 5%. Explain how this instrument should be presented on the statement of financial position.   **(LO 5)**

BE16-7   Silky Limited, a private company that complies with accounting standards for private enterprises (ASPE), has redeemable preferred shares outstanding that carry a dividend of 5%. If the shares are not redeemed within five years, the dividend will double every five years from then on. How should Silky account for this instrument? How should Silky treat the dividends associated with the redeemable preferred shares?   **(LO 5)**

BE16-8   Milano Ltd. issued 1,000 preferred shares for $10 per share. The preferred shares pay an annual, cumulative dividend of $0.50 per share, and become mandatorily redeemable if net income drops below $500,000 in any fiscal year. Discuss how Milano Ltd. should account for the preferred shares under IFRS. Would the accounting for the preferred shares differ if Milano Ltd. adopted ASPE?   **(LO 5)**

BE16-9   During 2011, Genoa Limited issued retractable preferred shares. The shares may be presented to the company by the holder for redemption after 2011. Explain how these should be presented in the financial statements under IFRS and ASPE.   **(LO 5)**

BE16-10   Venus Ltd. had 250 $1,000 bonds outstanding, with each one convertible into 20 common shares. The bonds were later converted on December 31, 2011, when the unamortized discount was $14,000, and the shares' market price was $21 per share. The company complies with ASPE, and allocated all of the proceeds to the debt component upon initial recognition. Record the conversion using the book value approach.   **(LO 6)**

BE16-11   Century Ltd. issued 15,000 common shares upon conversion of 10,000 preferred shares. The preferred shares were originally issued at $8 per share and the Contributed Surplus—Conversion Rights account for the preferred shares had a balance of $8,000. The common shares were trading at $13 per share at the time of conversion. Record the conversion of the preferred shares.   **(LO 6)**

BE16-12   Accent Capital Ltd. issued 500 $1,000 bonds at 103. Each bond was issued with one detachable stock warrant. After issuance, the bonds were selling in the market at 97, and the warrants had a market value of $27. Record the issuance of the bonds and warrants assuming that Accent Capital Ltd. applied IFRS.   **(LO 6)**

BE16-13   Refer to BE16–12. Assume that Accent Capital Ltd. applied ASPE. Discuss the two options available to record the issuance of the bonds and warrants. Provide journal entries for each option.   **(LO 6)**

(LO 7)   BE 16-14   List the various types of stock compensation plans.

(LO 8)   BE 16-15   Explain the differences between employee and compensatory option plans and other options.

(LO 9)   BE16-16   On January 1, 2011, Johnson Corporation granted 4,000 options to executives. Each option entitles the holder to purchase one share of Johnson's common shares at $40 per share at any time during the next five years. The shares' market price is $55 per share on the date of grant. The period of benefit is two years. Prepare Johnson's journal entries for January 1, 2011, and December 31, 2011, and 2012. Assume that the options' fair value as calculated using an options pricing model is $106,000. Ignore forfeitures for simplification purposes.

(LO 15)   *BE16-17   Perkins, Inc. established a stock appreciation rights (SARs) program on January 1, 2011, which entitles executives to receive cash at the date of exercise for the difference between the shares' market price and the pre-established price of $20 on 5,400 SARs. The required service period is two years. The shares' fair value is $22 per share on December 31, 2011, and $34 per share on December 31, 2012. The SARs are exercised on January 1, 2013. Calculate Perkins' compensation expense for 2011 and 2012 assuming it complies with ASPE.

(LO 16)   *BE 16-18   Explain what performance-type plans are and how they differ from other types of compensatory plans.

(LO 17)   *BE 16-19   Explain how options pricing models are useful in determining fair value. What are the inputs to such models?

Exercises

(LO 1, 2, 3)   E16-1   **(Derivative Transaction)** On January 2, 2011, Reflow Corporation purchased a call option for $350 on Walter's common shares. The call option gives Reflow the option to buy 1,000 shares of Walter at a strike price of $25 per share. The market price of a Walter share was $25 on January 2, 2011 (the intrinsic value was therefore $0). On March 31, 2011, the market price for Walter stock was $38 per share, and the value of the option was $15,500.

Instructions

(a) Prepare the journal entry to record the purchase of the call option on January 2, 2011.

(b) Prepare the journal entry(ies) to recognize the change in the call option's fair value as of March 31, 2011.

(c) What was the effect on net income of entering into the derivative transaction for the period January 2 to March 31, 2011?

(d) Based on the available facts, explain whether the company is using the option as a hedge or for speculative purposes.

(e) Explain which financial risks the transaction exposes the entity to.

(LO 1, 3)   E16-2   **(Derivative Transaction)** On April 1, 2011, Petey Ltd. paid $150 for a call to buy 500 shares of NorthernTel at a strike price of $25 per share any time during the next six months. The market price of NorthernTel's shares was $20 per share on April 1, 2011. On June 30, 2011, the market price for NorthernTel's stock was $35 per share, and the value of the option was $6,700.

Instructions

(a) Prepare the journal entry to record the purchase of the call option on April 1, 2011.

(b) Prepare the journal entry(ies) to recognize the change in the call option's fair value as of June 30, 2011.

(c) Prepare the journal entry that would be required if Petey Ltd. exercised the call option and took delivery of the shares as soon as the market opened on July 1, 2011.

Digging Deeper

(d) Why is there a loss when the option is exercised?

(LO 1, 3)   E16-3   **(Purchase Commitment)** On January 1, 2011, Fresh Juice Ltd. entered into a purchase commitment contract to buy 10,000 oranges from a local company at a price of $0.50 per orange anytime during the next year. The contract provides Fresh Juice with the option either to take delivery of the oranges at any time over the next year, or to settle the contract on a net basis for the difference between the agreed upon price of $0.50 per orange and the market price per orange for any oranges that have not been delivered. As at January 31, 2011, Fresh Juice Ltd. did not take delivery of any oranges, and the market price for an orange was $0.49.

Instructions

(a) Assuming that IFRS are adopted, how should Fresh Juice Ltd. account for this purchase agreement if it fully intends to take delivery of all 10,000 oranges over the next year? Provide any required journal entries at January 1 and January 31.

(b) How would your answer to part (a) change if Fresh Juice Ltd. did not intend to take delivery of the oranges? Provide any required journal entries at January 1 and January 31.

(c) Assuming that ASPE is adopted, how would Fresh Juice Ltd. account for this purchase agreement if it fully intends to take delivery of all 10,000 oranges over the next year?

E16-4 (Derivatives Involving the Entity's Own Shares) Merry Ltd., a publicly accountable enterprise, paid $250 for **(LO 4)** the option to buy 1,000 of its common shares for $15 each. The contract stipulates that it may only be settled by exercising the option and buying the shares.

Instructions

(a) Provide the journal entry required to account for the purchase of the call option.

(b) Assume that the contract allows both parties a choice to settle the option by either exchanging the shares or settling on a net basis. Would this change your conclusion in part (a)?

E16-5 (Issuance and Conversion of Bonds) The following are unrelated transactions. **(LO 5, 6)**

1. On March 1, 2011, Loma Corporation issued $300,000 of 8% non-convertible bonds at 104, which are due on February 28, 2028. In addition, each $1,000 bond was issued with 25 detachable stock warrants, each of which entitled the bondholder to purchase for $50 one of Loma's no par value common shares. The bonds without the warrants would normally sell at 95. On March 1, 2011, the fair market value of Loma's common shares was $40 per share and the fair market value of each warrant was $2. Loma prepares its financial statements in accordance with IFRS.

2. Grand Corp. issued $10 million of par value, 9%, convertible bonds at 97. If the bonds had not been convertible, the company's investment banker estimates they would have been sold at 93. Grand Corp. has adopted ASPE, and would like to explore all options available to report the convertible bond.

3. Hussein Limited issued $20 million of par value, 7% bonds at 98. One detachable stock purchase warrant was issued with each $100 par value bond. At the time of issuance, the warrants were selling for $6. Hussein Limited had adopted ASPE.

4. On July 1, 2011, Tien Limited called its 9% convertible debentures for conversion. The $10 million of par value bonds were converted into 1 million common shares. On July 1, there was $75,000 of unamortized discount applicable to the bonds, and the company paid an additional $65,000 to the bondholders to induce conversion of all the bonds. The company records the conversion using the book value method. The balance in the account Contributed Surplus—Conversion Rights was $270,000 at the time of conversion.

5. On December 1, 2011, Horton Company issued 500 of its $1,000, 9% bonds at 103. Attached to each bond was one detachable stock warrant entitling the holder to purchase 10 of Horton's common shares. On December 1, 2011, the market value of the bonds, without the stock warrants, was 95, and the market value of each stock warrant was $50. Horton Company prepares its financial statements in accordance with IFRS.

Instructions

Present the required entry(ies) to record each of the above transactions.

E16-6 (Various Complex Financial Statements) The following situations occur independently. **(LO 3, 5, 6)**

1. A company knows that it will require a large quantity of euros to pay for some imports in three months. The current exchange rate is satisfactory, and as a result, the company purchases a forward contract committing it to acquire 10 million euros at the current exchange rate in three months' time.

2. A shipping company uses large quantities of fuel to power its ships. Shipping rates are set well in advance of when the actual transportation of goods will take place. The company purchases forward contracts for fuel to ensure that it knows the price it will have to pay for fuel in the future. The contracts are exchange-traded futures.

3. An exporting company exports a significant amount of wheat to China. In order to protect itself against the risk that prices will drop significantly, it uses a just-in-time inventory management system to keep stock at the lowest possible levels.

4. A manufacturing company uses a large quantity of steel in its products. In order to ensure the cost of this steel is known, the company enters into executory contracts where it agrees to take delivery of predetermined quantities of steel at predetermined prices in the future.

5. A company pays a shareholder $5,000 for the right to buy 500 of its own common shares for $25 per share at a future date. The contract is not net settleable.

6. A company enters into a futures contract with a margin account to sell its grain for $2,500.

7. A company issues preferred shares with the following terms and conditions: the shares are redeemable by the company for $50/share on January 1, 2015, and the redemption price doubles every 12 months after January 1, 2015.

8. A company issues debt with detachable warrants. The warrants can be sold separately, and entitle the holder to purchase one share at a future date for a predetermined price.

9. A company issues debt that, at the option of the holder, can be converted into 100,000 common shares of the company.

10. A company issues shares that can be redeemed for a fixed amount at the request of the shareholder at any time.

Instructions

For each of the above situations, describe the type of financial instrument involved, when it should be recognized in the financial statements, the measurement that should be used for accounting purposes, and how gains or losses should be recorded. Assume the company is not using hedge accounting. Be sure to note if there are differences between ASPE and IFRS for any items.

(LO 6) **E16-7** **(Conversion of Bonds)** Aubrey Inc. issued $6 million of 10-year, 9%, convertible bonds on June 1, 2011, at 98 plus accrued interest. The bonds were dated April 1, 2011, with interest payable April 1 and October 1. Bond discount is amortized semi-annually on a straight-line basis. Bonds without conversion privileges would have sold at 97 plus accrued interest.

On April 1, 2012, $1.5 million of these bonds were converted into 30,000 common shares. Accrued interest was paid in cash at the time of conversion but only to the bondholders whose bonds were being converted. Assume that the company follows IFRS.

Instructions

(a) Prepare the entry to record the issuance of the convertible bonds on June 1, 2011.

(b) Prepare the entry to record the interest expense at October 1, 2011. Assume that accrued interest payable was credited when the bonds were issued. (Round to nearest dollar.)

(c) Prepare the entry(ies) to record the conversion on April 1, 2012. (The book value method is used.) Assume that the entry to record amortization of the bond discount using the straight-line method and interest payment has been made.

Digging Deeper

(d) What do you believe was the likely market value of the common shares as of the date of the conversion of April 1, 2012?

(LO 6) **E16-8** **(Conversion of Bonds)** Vargo Limited had $2.4 million of bonds payable outstanding and the unamortized premium for these bonds amounted to $44,500. Each $1,000 bond was convertible into 20 preferred shares. All bonds were then converted into preferred shares. The Contributed Surplus—Conversion Rights account had a balance of $22,200. Assume that the company follows IFRS.

Instructions

(a) Assuming that the book value method was used, what entry would be made?

(b) From the perspective of the bondholders, what is the likely motive for the conversion of bonds into preferred shares? What are the advantages of each investment that are given up or obtained by the bondholders who chose to convert their investment?

Digging Deeper

(LO 6) **E16-9** **(Conversion of Bonds and Expired Rights)** Dadayeva Inc. has $3 million of 8% convertible bonds outstanding. Each $1,000 bond is convertible into 30 no par value common shares. The bonds pay interest on January 31 and July 31. On July 31, 2011, the holders of $900,000 of these bonds exercised the conversion privilege. On that date, the market price of the bonds was 105, the market price of the common shares was $36, the carrying value of the common shares was $18, and the Contributed Surplus—Conversion Rights account balance was $450,000. The total unamortized bond premium at the date of conversion was $210,000. The remaining bonds were never converted and were retired when they reached the maturity date. Assume that the company follows IFRS.

Instructions

(a) Assuming that the book value method was used, record the conversion of the $900,000 of bonds on July 31, 2011.

(b) Prepare the journal entry that would be required for the remaining amount in Contributed Surplus—Conversion Rights when the maturity of the remaining bonds is recorded.

E16-10 **(Conversion of Bonds)** On January 1, 2011, when its common shares were selling for $80 per share, Plato **(LO 5, 6)** Corp. issued $10 million of 8% convertible debentures due in 20 years. The conversion option allowed the holder of each $1,000 bond to convert the bond into five common shares. The debentures were issued for $10.8 million. The bond payment's present value at the time of issuance was $8.5 million and the corporation believes the difference between the present value and the amount paid is attributable to the conversion feature. On January 1, 2012, the corporation's common shares were split 2 for 1, and the conversion rate for the bonds was adjusted accordingly. On January 1, 2013, when the corporation's common shares were selling for $135 per share, holders of 30% of the convertible debentures exercised their conversion option. The corporation applies ASPE, and uses the straight-line method for amortizing any bond discounts or premiums.

Instructions

(a) Prepare in general journal form the entry to record the original issuance of the convertible debentures.

(b) Using the book value method, prepare in general journal form the entry to record the exercise of the conversion option. Show supporting calculations in good form.

(c) How many shares were issued as a result of the conversion?

(d) From the perspective of Plato Corp., what are the advantages and disadvantages of the conversion of the bonds into common shares?

Digging
Deeper

E16-11 **(Conversion of Bonds)** Shankman Corporation had two issues of securities outstanding: common shares and an **(LO 6)** 8% convertible bond issue in the face amount of $8 million. Interest payment dates of the bond issue are June 30 and December 31. The conversion clause in the bond indenture entitles the bondholders to receive 40 no par value common shares in exchange for each $1,000 bond. The value of the equity portion of the bond issue is $60,000. On June 30, 2011, the holders of $1.2 million of the face value bonds exercised the conversion privilege. The market price of the bonds on that date was $1,100 per bond and the market price of the common shares was $35. The total unamortized bond discount at the date of conversion was $500,000.

Instructions

Prepare in general journal form the entry to record the exercise of the conversion option, using the book value method. Assume the company follows IFRS.

E16-12 **(Conversion of Bonds)** On January 1, 2011, Gottlieb Corporation issued $6 million of 10-year, 7%, convert- **(LO 6)** ible debentures at 104. Investment bankers believe that the debenture would have sold at 102 without the conversion privilege. Interest is to be paid semi-annually on June 30 and December 31. Each $1,000 debenture can be converted into five common shares of Gottlieb Corporation after December 31, 2012. On January 1, 2013, $400,000 of debentures are converted into common shares, which are then selling at $110. An additional $400,000 of debentures are converted on March 31, 2013. The common shares' market price is then $115. Accrued interest at March 31 will be paid on the next interest date. Bond premium is amortized on a straight-line basis.

Instructions

(a) Make the necessary journal entries for:

  1. December 31, 2012

  2. January 1, 2013

  3. March 31, 2013

  4. June 30, 2013

Record the conversions using the book value method.

(b) From the perspective of the debenture holders, why would they be motivated to wait for the conversion of the bonds into common shares? What are the risks involved in waiting and what could the bondholders ultimately give up by waiting too long?

Digging
Deeper

E16-13 **(Issuance of Bonds with Detachable Warrants)** On September 1, 2011, Sands Corp. sold at 102 (plus accrued **(LO 6)** interest) 5,200 of its $1,000 face value, 10-year, 9%, non-convertible bonds with detachable stock warrants. Each bond carried two detachable warrants; each warrant was for one common share at a specified option price of $10 per share. Shortly after issuance, the warrants were quoted on the market for $5 each. Assume that no market value is available for the bonds. Interest is payable on December 1 and June 1. Sands Corp. prepares its financial statements in accordance with ASPE.

Instructions

Prepare in general journal format the entry to record the issuance of the bonds under both options available under ASPE.

(AICPA adapted)

(LO 6)   E16-14   **(Issuance of Bonds with Detachable Warrants)** On January 1, 2011, Tiamund Corp. sold at 103, 100 of its $1,000 face value, 5-year, 9%, non-convertible, retractable bonds. The retraction feature allows the holder to redeem the bonds at an amount equal to three times net income, to a maximum of $1,200 per bond. Tiamund has net income of $250, $350, and $450 for the fiscal years of December 31, 2011, 2012, and 2013, respectively. Tiamund Corp. prepares its financial statements in accordance with IFRS.

Instructions

(a) Prepare in general journal format the entry to record the issuance of the bonds.

(b) Using straight-line amortization, how much would the bond be carried at on the balance sheet for the 2011, 2012, and 2013 year ends?

(LO 7, 8, 9)   E16-15   **(Issuance and Exercise of Stock Options)** On November 1, 2010, Columbo Corp. adopted a stock option plan that granted options to key executives to purchase 45,000 common shares. The options were granted on January 2, 2011, and were exercisable two years after the date of grant if the grantee was still a company employee; the options expire six years from the date of grant. The option price was set at $42 and, using an options pricing model to value the options, the total compensation expense was estimated to be $550,000. Note that the calculation did not take into account forfeitures.

On April 1, 2012, 3,500 options were terminated when some employees resigned from the company. The market value of the shares at that date was $28. All of the remaining options were exercised during the year 2013: 31,500 on January 3 when the market price was $52, and 10,000 on May 1 when the market price was $58 a share. Assume that the entity follows PE GAAP and has chosen not to reflect forfeitures in their upfront estimate of compensation expense.

Instructions

(a) Prepare journal entries relating to the stock option plan for the years 2011, 2012, and 2013. Assume that the employees perform services equally in 2011 and 2012, and that the year end is December 31.

(b) What is the significance of the fact that the pricing model did not take into account forfeitures? Would taking expected forfeitures into account make the estimate of the total compensation expense higher or lower?

(c) List the types of stock compensation plans and when they might be used.

Digging Deeper

(d) How are employee and compensatory option plans different from other options?

(LO 9)   E16-16   **(Issuance, Exercise, and Termination of Stock Options)** On January 1, 2011, Nichols Corporation granted 20,000 options to key executives. Each option allows the executive to purchase one share of Nichols' common shares at a price of $25 per share. The options were exercisable within a two-year period beginning January 1, 2013, if the grantee was still employed by the company at the time of the exercise. On the grant date, Nichols' shares were trading at $20 per share, and a fair value options pricing model determined total compensation to be $750,000. Management has assumed that there will be no forfeitures as they do not expect any of their key executives to leave.

On May 1, 2013, 8,000 options were exercised when the market price of Nichols' shares was $31 per share. The remaining options lapsed in 2014 because executives decided not to exercise their options. Management was indeed correct in their assumption regarding forfeitures in that all executives remained with the company. Assume that the entity follows IFRS.

Instructions

(a) Prepare the necessary journal entries related to the stock option plan for the years ended December 31, 2011, through 2014.

(b) What is the significance of the $20 market price of the Nichols shares at the date of grant? Would the exercise price normally be higher or lower than the market price of the shares on the date of grant?

(c) What is the significance of the $31 market price of the Nichols shares at May 1, 2013, the date of the exercise of the stock options?

(d) What likely happened to the market price of the shares in 2014?

Digging Deeper

(e) What motive might an employee have for delaying the exercise of the stock option? What are the risks involved?

(LO 9)   E16-17   **(Issuance, Exercise, and Termination of Stock Options)** On January 1, 2010, Sorvino Corp. granted stock options to its chief executive officer. This is the only stock option that Sorvino offers and the details are as follows:

Option to purchase:	5,000 common shares
Option price per share:	$62.00
Market price per common share on date of grant:	$57.00
Stock option expiration:	The earlier of eight years after issuance or the employee's cessation of employment with Sorvino for any reason other than retirement
Date when options are first exercisable:	The earlier of four years after issuance or the date on which an employee reaches the retirement age of 65
Fair value at grant date, as determined by an options pricing model:	$10.00

On January 1, 2015, 4,000 of the options were exercised when the market price of the common shares was $78. The remaining stock options were allowed to expire. The CEO remained with the company throughout the period.

Instructions

Record the journal entries at the following dates. Assume that the entity follows PE GAAP and has decided not to include an estimate of forfeitures upon initial recognition of the compensation expense.

(a) January 1, 2010

(b) December 31, 2010, the fiscal year end of Sorvino Inc.

(c) January 1, 2015—the exercise date

(d) December 31, 2017—the expiry date of the options

*E16-18 (Cash Flow Hedge) On January 2, 2011, MacCloud Corp. issued a $100,000, four-year note at prime plus 1% variable interest, with interest payable semi-annually. MacCloud now wants to change the note to a fixed-rate note. As a result, on January 2, 2011, MacCloud Corp. enters into an interest rate swap where it agrees to pay 6% fixed and receive prime plus 1% for the first six months on $100,000. At each six-month period, the variable rate will be reset. The prime interest rate is 5.7% on January 2, 2011, and is reset to 6.7% on June 30, 2011.   **(LO 11, 13, 14)**

Instructions

(a) Calculate the net interest expense to be reported for this note and related swap transaction as of June 30 and December 31, 2011.

(b) Prepare the journal entries relating to the swap for the year ended December 31, 2011.

(c) Explain why this is a cash flow hedge.

*E16-19 (Cash Flow Hedge) On January 2, 2011, Parton Corp. issues a $10-million, five-year note at LIBOR, with interest paid annually. The variable rate is reset at the end of each year. The LIBOR rate for the first year is 5.8%. Parton later decides that it prefers fixed-rate financing and wants to lock in a rate of 6%. As a result, Parton enters into an interest rate swap to pay 6% fixed and receive LIBOR based on $10 million for the remainder of the term of the note. The variable rate is reset to 6.6% on January 2, 2012.   **(LO 11, 13, 14)**

Instructions

(a) Calculate the net interest expense to be reported for this note and related swap transactions as of December 31, 2011, and 2012.

(b) Prepare the journal entries relating to the swap for the years ended December 31, 2011, and 2012.

(c) Explain why this is a cash flow hedge.

*E16-20 (Fair Value Hedge) Sarazan Corp. purchased a $1-million, four-year, 7.5% fixed-rate interest only, non-prepayable bond on December 31, 2011. The bond is actively traded and is held as a fair value through net income (FV-NI) investment. Sarazan later decided to hedge the interest rate and change from a fixed rate to variable rate, so it entered into a swap agreement with M&S Corp. The swap agreement specified that Sarazan will pay a fixed rate of 7.5% and receive variable rate interest with settlement dates that match the interest payments on the instrument. Assume that interest rates increased during 2012 and that Sarazan received $13,000 as a net settlement on the swap for the settlement at December 31, 2012. The loss related to the investment (due to interest rate changes) was $48,000. The value of the swap contract increased by $48,000.   **(LO 11, 13, 14)**

Instructions

(a) Prepare the journal entry to record the receipt of interest on December 31, 2012, from the company that issued the bond.

(b) Prepare the journal entry to record the receipt of the swap settlement on December 31, 2012.

(c) Prepare the journal entry to record the change in the fair value of the swap contract on December 31, 2012.

(d) Prepare the journal entry to record the change in the fair value of the bond on December 31, 2012. Note how this is different from how the fair value change would have been booked if the bond had not been hedged.

(e) Explain why the interest rate swap is a fair value hedge in this situation.

(f) Explain how an interest rate swap can act as both a fair value hedge and a cash flow hedge.

(LO 15) *E16-21 **(Stock Appreciation Rights)** Aoun Limited established a stock appreciation rights program that entitled its new president, Angela Murfitt, to receive cash for the difference between the Aoun Limited common shares' market price and a pre-established price of $32 (also market price) on December 31, 2010, on 40,000 SARs. The date of grant is December 31, 2011, and the required employment (service) period is four years. The common shares' market value fluctuated as follows: December 31, 2011, $36; December 31, 2012, $40; December 31, 2013, $45; December 31, 2014, $36; December 31, 2015, $48. Aoun Limited recognizes the SARs in its financial statements. Angela Murfitt exercised half of the SARs on June 1, 2016. Assume that the entity follows ASPE.

Instructions

(a) Prepare a five-year (2011 to 2016) schedule of compensation expense pertaining to the 40,000 SARs granted to Murfitt.

(b) Prepare the journal entry for compensation expense in 2011, 2014, and 2015 relative to the 40,000 SARs.

(c) Prepare the entry at June 1, 2016, for the exercise of the SARs.

(LO 15) *E16-22 **(Stock Appreciation Rights)** At the end of its fiscal year, December 31, 2011, Beckford Limited issued 200,000 stock appreciation rights to its officers that entitled them to receive cash for the difference between the market price of its stock and a pre-established price of $12. The market price fluctuated as follows: December 31, 2012, $15; December 31, 2013, $11; December 31, 2014, $21; December 31, 2015, $19. The service period is four years and the exercise period is seven years. The company recognizes the SARs in its financial statements. Assume that the entity follows ASPE.

Instructions

(a) Prepare a schedule that shows the amount of compensation expense that is allocable to each year that is affected by the stock appreciation rights plan.

(b) Prepare the entry at December 31, 2015, to record compensation expense, if any, in 2015.

(c) Prepare the entry at December 31, 2015, assuming that all 200,000 SARs are exercised.

(LO 15, 16) *E16-23 **(Stock Appreciation Rights)** Chiu Limited established a stock appreciation rights program that entitled its new president, Brandon Sutton, to receive cash for the difference between the shares' market price and a pre-established price of $32 (also market price) on December 31, 2011, on 50,000 SARs. The date of grant is December 31, 2011, and the required employment (service) period is four years. The president exercised all of the SARs in 2016. The shares' market value fluctuated as follows: December 31, 2012, $36; December 31, 2013, $39; December 31, 2014, $45; December 31, 2015, $36; December 31, 2016, $48. The company recognizes the SARs in its financial statements. Assume that the entity follows ASPE.

Instructions

(a) Prepare a five-year (2012 to 2016) schedule of compensation expense pertaining to the 50,000 SARs granted to Brandon Sutton.

(b) Prepare the journal entry for compensation expense in 2012, 2015, and 2016 relative to the 50,000 SARs.

(c) From the perspective of the employee, contrast the features of a stock appreciation right to the features of compensatory stock options.

(d) Discuss what a performance-type compensation plan is, giving examples.

Digging
Deeper

Problems

P16-1   The treasurer of Hing Wa Corp. has read on the Internet that the stock price of Ewing Inc. is about to take off. In order to profit from this potential development, Hing Wa purchased a call option on Ewing common shares on July 7, 2011, for $240. The call option is for 200 shares (notional value), and the strike price is $70. The option expires on January 31, 2012. The following data are available with respect to the call option:

Date	Fair Value of Option	Market Price of Ewing Shares
Sept. 30, 2011	$1,340	$77 per share
Dec. 31, 2011	$ 825	$75 per share
Jan. 4, 2012	$1,200	$76 per share

Instructions

Prepare the journal entries for Hing Wa for the following dates:

 (a) July 7, 2011: Investment in call option on Ewing shares.

 (b) September 30, 2011: Hing Wa prepares financial statements.

 (c) December 31, 2011: Hing Wa prepares financial statements.

 (d) January 4, 2012: Hing Wa settles the call option net on the Ewing shares (i.e., without buying the shares).

P16-2   Refer to P16–1, but assume that Hing Wa wrote (sold) the call option for a premium of $240 (instead of buying it). Assume that the market price of the shares and the value of the options is otherwise the same.

Instructions

Prepare the journal entries for Hing Wa for the following dates:

 (a) July 7, 2011: Sale of the call option on Ewing shares.

 (b) September 30, 2011: Hing Wa prepares financial statements.

 (c) December 31, 2011: Hing Wa prepares financial statements.

 (d) January 4, 2012: Hing Wa settles the call option net on the Ewing shares (i.e., without selling the shares).

P16-3   Brondon Corp. purchased a put option on Mykia common shares on July 7, 2011, for $480. The put option is for 350 shares, and the strike price is $50. The option expires on January 31, 2012. The following data are available with respect to the put option:

Date	Fair Value of Option	Market Price of Mykia Shares
Sept. 30, 2011	$250	$56 per share
Dec. 31, 2011	$100	$58 per share
Jan. 31, 2012	$ 0	$62 per share

Instructions

Prepare the journal entries for Brondon Corp. for the following dates:

 (a) July 7, 2011: Investment in put option on Mykia shares.

 (b) September 30, 2011: Brondon prepares financial statements.

 (c) December 31, 2011: Brondon prepares financial statements.

 (d) January 31, 2012: Put option expires.

P16-4   Biotech Inc. purchased an option to buy 10,000 of its common shares for $35 each. The option cost $750, and explicitly stipulates that it may only be settled by exercising the option and buying the shares.

Instructions

 (a) Provide the journal entry required to account for the purchase of the call option assuming Biotech Inc. complies with IFRS.

 (b) Assume that the contract allows both parties a choice to settle the option by either exchanging the shares or settling on a net basis. Would this change your conclusion in part (a)?

 (c) Assume that Biotech Inc. complies with ASPE. Would this change your conclusion in part (a)?

P16-5   The shareholders' equity section of McLean Inc. at the beginning of the current year is as follows:

Common shares, 1,000,000 shares authorized, 300,000 shares issued and outstanding	$3,600,000
Retained earnings	570,000

During the current year, the following transactions occurred.

1. The company issued 100,000 rights to the shareholders. Ten rights are needed to buy one share at $32 and the rights are void after 30 days. The shares' market price at this time was $34 per share.

2. The company sold to the public a $200,000, 10% bond issue at par. The company also issued with each $100 bond one detachable stock purchase warrant, which provided for the purchase of common shares at $30 per share. Shortly after issuance, similar bonds without warrants were selling at 96 and the warrants at $8.

3. All but 10,000 of the rights issued in item 1 were exercised in 30 days.

4. At the end of the year, 80% of the warrants in item 2 had been exercised, and the remaining were outstanding and in good standing.

5. During the current year, the company granted stock options for 5,000 common shares to company executives. The company, using an options pricing model, determined that each option is worth $10. The exercise or strike price is $30. The options were to expire at year end and were considered compensation for the current year.

6. All but 1,000 shares related to the stock option plan were exercised by year end. The expiration resulted because one of the executives failed to fulfill an obligation related to the employment contract.

Instructions

(a) Prepare general journal entries for the current year to record each of the transactions. Assume the company follows IFRS.

(b) Prepare the shareholders' equity section of the statement of financial position at the end of the current year. Assume that retained earnings at the end of the current year is $750,000.

P16-6   Lacroix Inc., a publicly accountable enterprise that reports in accordance with IFRS, issued convertible bonds for the first time on January 1, 2011. The $1 million of five-year, 10% (payable annually on December 31, starting December 31, 2011), convertible bonds were issued at 108, yielding 8%. The bonds would have been issued at 98 without a conversion feature, and yielding a higher rate of return. The bonds are convertible at the investor's option.

The company's bookkeeper recorded the bonds at 108 and, based on the $1,080,000 bond carrying value, recorded interest expense using the effective interest method for 2011. He prepared the following amortization table:

Date	Cash Interest (10%)	Effective Interest (8%)	Premium Amortization	Carrying Amount of Bonds
Jan. 1, 2011				$1,080,000
Dec. 31, 2011	$100,000	$86,400	$13,600	1,066,400

You were hired as an accountant to replace the bookkeeper in November 2012. It is now December 31, 2012, the company's year end, and the CEO is concerned that the company's debt covenant may be breached. The debt covenant requires Lacroix to maintain a maximum debt-to-equity ratio of 2.3. Based on the current financial statements, the debt-to-equity ratio would be 2.6. The CEO recalls hearing that convertible bonds should be reported by separating out the liability and equity components, yet he does not see any equity amounts related to the bonds on the current financial statements. He has asked you to look into the bond transactions recorded and make any necessary adjustments. He would also like you to explain how any adjustments that you make affect the debt-to-equity ratio.

Instructions

(a) Determine the amount that should have been reported in the equity section of the statement of financial position at January 1, 2011, for the conversion right, considering that the company must comply with IFRS. Prepare the journal entry that should have been recorded on January 1, 2011.

(b) Explain whether ASPE offers any alternatives that are not available under IFRS.

(c) Using a financial calculator or computer spreadsheet functions, calculate the effective rate (yield rate) for the bonds. Leave at least four decimal places in your calculation.

(d) Prepare a bond amortization schedule from January 1, 2011, to December 31, 2015, using the effective interest method and the corrected value for the bonds.

(e) Prepare the journal entry(ies) dated January 1, 2012, to correct the bookkeeper's recording errors in 2011. Ignore income tax effects.

(f) Prepare the journal entry at December 31, 2012, for the interest payment on the bonds.

(g) Explain the effect that the error correction prepared in part (e) has on the debt-to-equity ratio.

P16-7 On January 1, 2011, Biron Corp. issued $1.2 million of five-year, zero-interest-bearing notes along with warrants to buy 1 million common shares at $20 per share. On January 1, 2011, Biron had 9.6 million common shares outstanding and the market price was $19 per share. Biron Corp. received $1 million for the notes and warrants. If offered alone, on January 1, 2011, the notes would have been issued to yield 12% to the creditor. Assume that the company follows IFRS.

Instructions

(a) Prepare the journal entry(ies) to record the issuance of the zero-interest-bearing notes and warrants for the cash consideration that was received.

(b) Prepare an amortization table for the note using the effective interest method.

(c) Prepare adjusting journal entries for Biron Corp. at the end of its fiscal year of December 31, 2011.

(d) Prepare the journal entry required for Biron Corp. if half of the warrants are exercised on January 1, 2014.

P16-8 On September 30, 2011, Gargiola Inc. issued $4 million of 10-year, 8%, convertible bonds for $4.6 million. The bonds pay interest on March 31 and September 30 and mature on September 30, 2021. Each $1,000 bond can be converted into 80 no par value common shares. In addition, each bond included 20 detachable warrants. Each warrant can be used to purchase one common share at an exercise price of $15. Immediately after the bond issuance, the warrants traded at $3 each. Without the warrants and the conversion rights, the bonds would have been expected to sell for $4.3 million.

The proceeds from the issuance of the bonds with conversion rights and with the detachable warrants included the following:

Gross proceeds	$4,700,000
Underwriting fees	100,000
Net proceeds	$4,600,000

Gargiola Inc. adopted the policy of capitalizing and amortizing the underwriting fees with the bonds' premium, which is accounted for using the effective interest method.

On March 23, 2014, half of the warrants were exercised. The common shares of Gargiola Inc. were trading at $20 each on this day.

Immediately after the payment of interest on the bonds, on September 30, 2016, all bonds outstanding were converted into common shares. Assume the entity follows IFRS.

Instructions

(a) Prepare the journal entry to record the issuance of the bonds on September 30, 2011.

(b) Using a financial calculator or computer spreadsheet functions, calculate the effective rate (yield rate) for the bonds. Leave at least four decimal places in your calculation.

(c) Prepare a bond amortization schedule from September 30, 2011, to September 30, 2016, using the effective interest rate.

(d) Prepare the December 31, 2011 year-end adjusting journal entries and the payment of interest on March 31, 2012. Assume that Gargiola Inc. does not use reversing entries.

(e) Prepare the journal entry to account for the exercise of the warrants on March 30, 2014. How many common shares were issued in this transaction?

(f) Prepare the journal entry to account for the bond redemption on September 30, 2016.

(g) How many shares were issued on September 30, 2016? What do you believe was the likely market value of the common shares as of the date of the conversion, September 30, 2016?

Digging
Deeper

P16-9 Perennial Gardens Incorporated is a nationwide chain of garden centres that operates as a private company. In 2011, it issued three new financial instruments. All three of these instruments are new to you, and you are working on determining how they are to be accounted for under both ASPE and IFRS.

The first financial instrument was a loan. On January 1, 2011, the company borrowed $5 million from a key shareholder at a rate of 3%, at a time when the market rate of interest was 5%. In order to convince the shareholder to loan the money to the company at a rate lower than the market rate of interest, the company agreed that in five years, the shareholder would have the option of either accepting full repayment in debt, or receiving 500,000 shares in the company.

The second financial instrument was one that you benefitted from. The company gave its 10 key management employees a compensatory stock option plan for the first time. The purpose was to provide additional remuneration for key employees at a time when financial constraints were making it difficult for the company to pay additional salaries. The plan allowed the key employees to purchase 5,000 options to purchase shares for $50 each when they were generally considered to be worth $100. The options were granted on January 1, 2011, and could be exercised anytime in the next five years. The options pricing model that was used indicated that the total compensation expense should be $550,000, and the expected period of benefit was two years beginning on the grant date. No other management employee exercised their options during the year, but you exercised all of your options on September 30, 2011.

The final new transaction that you have to determine how to account for is a forward contract. The company had not used these before, but as the Canada/U.S. exchange rate had been very good toward the end of the year, the company decided to purchase its U.S. currency needs for 2012 in advance. The company agreed to buy $7 million in U.S. currency for $7,070,000 (U.S. $1 = Canadian $1.01) on December 15, 2011, from Foreign Currency Inc. Any changes in value of the Canadian dollar would be transferred to Perennial Gardens. On December 31, 2011, the U.S. dollar strengthened in relation to the Canadian dollar, and the new value was U.S. $1 = Canadian $1.02.

Instructions

(a) Prepare the necessary journal entries to account for the three financial instruments under both ASPE (assuming that the company chooses to value the equity component of compound instruments at $0) and IFRS.

(b) Determine the carrying amount for each item at year end, December 31, 2011, under both ASPE and IFRS.

P16-10   ISU Corp. adopted a stock option plan on November 30, 2011, that designated 70,000 common shares as available for the granting of options to officers of the corporation at an exercise price of $8 a share. The market value was $12 a share on November 30, 2011.

On January 2, 2012, options to purchase 28,000 shares were granted to President Don Pedro: 15,000 for services to be rendered in 2012, and 13,000 for services to be rendered in 2013. Also on that date, options to purchase 14,000 shares were granted to Vice-President Beatrice Leonato: 7,000 for services to be rendered in 2012, and 7,000 for services to be rendered in 2013. The shares' market value was $14 a share on January 2, 2012. The options were exercisable for a period of one year following the year in which the services were rendered. The value of the options was estimated at $400,000 at that time.

In 2012, neither the president nor the vice-president exercised their options because the shares' market price was below the exercise price. The shares' market value was $7 a share on December 31, 2013, when the options for 2012 services lapsed.

On December 31, 2014, both the president and vice-president exercised their options for 13,000 and 7,000 shares, respectively, when the market price was $16 a share. The company's year end is December 31.

Instructions

Prepare the necessary journal entries in 2011 when the stock option plan was adopted, in 2012 when the options were granted, in 2013 when the options lapsed, and in 2014 when the options were exercised.

*P16-11   On December 31, 2011, Mercantile Corp. had a $10-million, 8% fixed-rate (based in LIBOR) note outstanding that was payable in two years. It decided to enter into a two-year swap with First Bank to convert the fixed-rate debt to floating-rate debt. The terms of the swap specified that Mercantile will receive interest at a fixed rate of 8% and will pay a variable rate equal to the six-month LIBOR rate, based on the $10-million amount. The LIBOR rate on December 31, 2011, was 7%. The LIBOR rate will be reset every six months and will be used to determine the variable rate to be paid for the following six-month period. Mercantile Corp. designated the swap as a fair value hedge. Assume that the hedging relationship meets all the conditions necessary for hedge accounting and that IFRS is a constraint. The six-month LIBOR rate and the swap and debt fair values were as follows:

Date	6-Month LIBOR Rate	Swap Fair Value	Debt Fair Value
Dec. 31, 2011	7.0%		$10,000,000
June 30, 2012	7.5%	$(200,000)	9,800,000
Dec. 31, 2012	6.0%	60,000	10,060,000

Instructions

(a) Present the journal entries to record the following transactions:

1. The entry, if any, to record the swap on December 31, 2011
2. The entry to record the semi-annual debt interest payment on June 30, 2012
3. The entry to record the settlement of the semi-annual swap amount receivable at 8%, less the amount payable at LIBOR, 7%
4. The entry, if any, to record the change in the debt's fair value at June 30, 2012
5. The entry, if any, to record the change in the swap's fair value at June 30, 2012

(b) Indicate the amount(s) reported on the statement of financial position and income statement related to the debt and swap on December 31, 2011.

(c) Indicate the amount(s) reported on the statement of financial position and income statement related to the debt and swap on June 30, 2012.

(d) Indicate the amount(s) reported on the statement of financial position and income statement related to the debt and swap on December 31, 2012.

*P16-12 LEW Jewellery Corp. uses gold in the manufacture of its products. LEW anticipates that it will need to purchase 500 ounces of gold in October 2011 for jewellery that will be shipped for the holiday shopping season. However, if the price of gold increases, LEW's cost to produce its jewellery will increase, which could reduce its profit margins.

To hedge the risk of increased gold prices, on April 1, 2011, LEW enters into a gold futures contract and designates this contract as a cash flow hedge of the anticipated gold purchase (under IFRS). The notional amount of the contract is 500 ounces, and the terms of the contract require LEW to purchase gold at a price of $300 per ounce on October 31, 2011 (or settle the contract net on the basis of the difference between the $300 and the gold price at October 31). Assume the following data with respect to the price of the futures contract. Ignore margin deposits; i.e., assume none were paid.

Date	Fair Value of Futures Contract
Apr. 1, 2011	$ –0–
June 30, 2011	$5,000
Sept. 30, 2011	$7,500
Oct. 31, 2011	$7,500

Instructions

Prepare the journal entries for the following transactions:

(a) April 1, 2011: Inception of the forward contract.

(b) June 30, 2011: LEW prepares financial statements.

(c) September 30, 2011: LEW prepares financial statements.

(d) October 31, 2011: LEW purchases 500 ounces of gold at $300 per ounce under the forward contract.

(e) December 20, 2011: LEW sells for $350,000 jewellery containing the gold purchased in October 2008. The cost of the finished goods inventory is $200,000.

(f) Indicate the amount(s) reported on the statement of financial position and income statement related to the futures contract on June 30, 2011.

(g) Indicate the amount(s) reported on the income statement related to the futures contract and the inventory transactions on December 31, 2011.

Writing Assignments

WA16-1   For various reasons, a corporation may issue options and warrants that give their holder the right to purchase the corporation's common shares at specified prices that, depending on the circumstances, may be less than, equal to, or greater than the current market price. For example, warrants may be issued to:

1. Existing shareholders on a pro rata basis

2. Certain key employees under an incentive stock option plan

3. Purchasers of the corporation's bonds

Instructions

For each of the three examples of who may receive issues of options and warrants:

(a) Explain why the warrants are used.

(b) Discuss the significance of the price (or prices) at which the warrants are issued (or granted) in relation to (1) the current market price of the company's shares, and (2) the length of time over which they can be exercised.

(c) Describe the information that should be disclosed in the financial statements or notes that are prepared when stock warrants are outstanding in the hands of the three groups of holders listed above.

(AICPA adapted)

WA16-2   Some complex financial instruments require that the Black-Scholes formula be used to measure their fair value. Examples of these complex instruments include derivatives that are options, bonds issued by the entity that are convertible into shares of the entity, and compensatory stock option plans.

Instructions

(a) For each example provided, explain why it requires the use of the Black-Scholes model in measuring fair value. Discuss how these instruments are initially recorded and subsequently measured under IFRS and ASPE.

(b) Discuss the inputs required in using the Black-Scholes formula for compensatory stock option plans and where this information comes from. Discuss the implications in determining the inputs under IFRS and ASPE.

(c) State the impact on the year-over-year compensation expense for newly granted compensatory stock option plans of making the following changes to the inputs used for the Black-Scholes formula, assuming all other inputs remain unchanged:

1. The risk-free rate has increased from 3% to 5%.

2. The volatility has decreased from 45% to 30%.

3. The expected life has increased from four years to six years.

(d) The Black-Scholes formula was originally designed to determine the fair value of options that are exchange traded. As a result, there has been some disagreement as to whether or not the Black-Scholes formula is the appropriate method to be used for measuring compensatory stock options. What are some of the arguments put forth to support this view? (Consider differences between exchange-traded options on shares and compensatory stock options provided to employees.)

WA16-3   Many companies expose themselves to various financial risks, primarily due to their business models (the way they conduct business).

Instructions

(a) Discuss the preceding statement by identifying the various financial risks and giving real life examples. In creating shareholder value, why is it important for a company to manage risk?

(b) Explain what a derivative is. What are the three key characteristics? Give some examples of derivatives.

(c) Explain what is meant by the act of hedging from an economic perspective. What is meant by the use of hedge accounting? When might a company opt for hedge accounting to report an economic hedge? When might a company decide not to use hedge accounting for an economic hedge?

*WA16-4   CopMin Inc. is a private enterprise that is involved in copper mining operations. The company currently owns two operating mines. It is January 1, 2011, and CopMin has recently entered into two types of contracts. For its Papula Mine, it has entered into a sales contract with one of its major customers. As part of this contract, it has agreed to sell 75% of its annual production at a fixed price that increases 1% each year for inflation. The contract is for five years (until December 31, 2015) and cash will be received on delivery of the copper, which will be made on a monthly basis. For its second mine, Minera Mine, the company has purchased a variety of option contracts to sell copper that are exchange traded. The company has options on 60% of the mine's production for 2011 and 40% of the production for 2012. The company has the option to sell copper at a fixed price and all of the contracts can be settled on a net cash basis anytime before expiry. The company paid a fee to buy these option contracts at the time they were purchased.

Instructions

(a) Explain how CopMin would record these two different contracts under IFRS and ASPE.

(b) How would your answer in part (a) change if the contract for the Papula Mine could be settled in net cash?

*WA16-5   Zenon Inc. has recently decided to pay share appreciation rights to its employees as part of their compensation package. The share appreciation rights will be paid in cash. The SARs vest over two years, and expire in five years. The company is a private enterprise that manufactures and sells automotive parts. The CEO has recently come to his controller to ask how these new rights will impact the company's financial statements. In the past the company had used stock options to compensate its employees. It has been determined that the SARs have an intrinsic value of $50,000 and a fair value of $65,000 at the date of grant. If compensatory stock options had been granted in lieu of the SARs, the fair value of the stock options would have been $65,000 with a vesting period of two years, and an expiry date of five years.

Instructions

(a) Explain how SARs are different from compensatory stock options from the employee's point of view.

(b) Explain to the CEO how SARs are measured and reported under IFRS and ASPE. How does this differ from the reporting and measurement of stock options? Explain why there are these differences.

(c) What will be the impact on the statement of financial position and the income statement under these accounting standards for the reporting of the SARs for the initial year of grant and future years? If the compensatory stock options had been granted instead, what would have been the impact on the statements?

*WA16-6   Soron Limited is a private company that uses derivatives to mitigate a variety of risks. Leon Price has just been hired as the new controller and has recently met with the CEO. The CEO has just explained to him the following derivatives that the company is currently party to.

(a) The company recently purchased 10,000 shares in a company. These shares are publicly traded. At the same time, the company purchased exchange-traded options to sell these shares at a future date.

(b) The company recently sold goods to a customer in the United States and the invoice was priced in U.S. dollars, which should be collected in six months. At the same time, to mitigate the loss on the exchange value of this receivable, Soron entered into a forward contract to sell the same amount of U.S. dollars in six months.

(c) Soron has a division that operates in Australia. All of the transactions in this division are translated into Canadian dollars for reporting purposes. In order to mitigate the risk of the exchange rate fluctuation between the Australian dollar and the Canadian dollar, the company has entered into forward contracts to buy Australian dollars in the future at varying amounts over the next year.

Instructions

As Leon Price, explain to the CEO how the three derivatives should be reported under IFRS and ASPE.

WA16-7   Sometimes entities write instruments that require settlement in its own shares. Examples of these include purchased or written options to buy or sell shares, or forward contracts to buy or sell shares.

Instructions

Explain the accounting issues that are created with these instruments. How does IFRS tend to treat these types of instruments? Give examples to support the different treatments that are available under IFRS. Note any differences under ASPE.

WA16-8

Instructions

Write a brief essay highlighting the difference between IFRS and accounting standards for private enterprises noted in this chapter, discussing the conceptual justification for each.

Cases

WILEY
PLUS
Case Primer

Refer to the Case Primer on the Student Website to help you answer these cases.

CA16-1   In 2012, Sanford Corp. adopted a plan to give additional incentive compensation to its dealers to sell its main product: fire extinguishers. Under the plan, Sanford transferred 9,000 of its common shares to a trust with the provision that Sanford would have to forfeit interest in the trust and no part of the trust fund could ever revert to Sanford. Shares were to be distributed to dealers based on each dealer's portion of the total number of fire extinguishers purchased from Sanford (above certain minimum levels per dealer) over the three-year period ending June 30, 2015.

In 2012, the shares of Sanford Corp. were closely held although they did trade on the national stock market. The shares' book value was $7.90 per share as of June 30, 2012, and in 2012 additional shares were sold to existing shareholders for $10 per share.

In 2012, when the shares were transferred to the trust, Sanford charged Deferred Costs for $90,000 ($10 per share market value) and credited Common Shares for the same amount. The deferred cost was charged to operations over a three-year period ended June 30, 2015.

In July 2015, all shares in the trust were distributed to the dealers. The shares' market value at the date of distribution from the trust had risen to $110 per share.

Instructions

Adopt the role of a financial analyst and discuss the financial reporting issues.

Real-World Emphasis

*CA16-2   **Air Canada** is Canada's largest domestic and international airline, providing scheduled and charter air transportation for passengers and cargo. The airline industry has suffered many difficulties and financial setbacks in the past decade. The high costs associated with operating an airline have claimed many "victims," including Canadian Airlines, which was purchased by Air Canada in 2000 in a highly publicized takeover battle. One of the largest cost components on Air Canada's income statement is aircraft fuel.

Since aircraft fuel is a commodity good, its price is subject to significant fluctuations. The cost of a barrel of aircraft fuel is determined by supply and demand relationships and other global economic conditions that affect production. As a result, Air Canada, like all other airlines, faces a high amount of uncertainty about the cost that it will be required to pay for aircraft fuel. In order to reduce the uncertainty and attempt to limit exposure, Air Canada uses a fuel hedging strategy to manage the risk. The notes to the company's financial statements describe the airline's strategy for its fuel hedging and provide additional disclosure as follows:

Fuel Price Risk

In order to manage its exposure to jet fuel prices and to help mitigate volatility in operating cash flows, the Corporation enters into derivative contracts with financial intermediaries. The Corporation uses derivative contracts on jet fuel and other crude oil-based commodities, heating oil and crude oil. Heating oil and crude oil commodities are used due to the relative limited liquidity of jet fuel derivative instruments on a medium to long-term horizon since jet fuel is not traded on an organized futures exchange. The Corporation's policy permits hedging of up to 75% of the projected jet fuel purchases for the next 12 months, 50% for the next 13 to 24 months and 25% for the next 25 to 36 months. These are maximum (but not mandated) limits. There is no minimum monthly hedging requirement. There are regular reviews to adjust the strategy in light of market conditions. The Corporation does not purchase or hold any derivative financial instrument for speculative purposes.

During 2009, the Corporation purchased crude-oil call options. The premium related to these contracts was $6.

As of December 31, 2009, approximately 18% of the Corporation's anticipated purchases of jet fuel for 2010 are hedged at an average West Texas Intermediate ("WTI") capped price of USD$95 per barrel and approximately 10% is subject to an average floor price of USD$96 per barrel. The Corporation's contracts to hedge anticipated jet fuel purchases over the 2010 period are comprised of crude-oil based contracts.

Instructions

Discuss the various accounting issues that arise as a result of Air Canada's aircraft fuel hedging strategy. Specifically, discuss whether or not it makes sense for the company to use hedge accounting (which is optional) and from an accounting perspective, what type of hedge this is.

CA16-3 The executive officers of Coach Corporation have a performance-based compensation plan that links performance criteria to growth in earnings per share. When annual EPS growth is 12%, the Coach executives earn 100% of a predetermined bonus amount; if growth is 16%, they earn 125%. If EPS growth is lower than 8%, the executives receive no additional compensation.

Ethics

In 2011, Joanna Becker, the controller of Coach, reviews year-end estimates of bad debt expense and warranty expense. She calculates the EPS growth at 15%. Peter Reiser, a member of the executive group, remarks over lunch one day that the estimate of bad debt expense might be decreased, increasing EPS growth to 16.1%. Becker is not sure she should do this, because she believes that the current estimate of bad debts is sound. On the other hand, she recognizes that a great deal of subjectivity is involved in the calculation.

Instructions

Discuss the financial reporting issues. Assume this is a public company.

Integrated Cases

IC16-1 Janson Inc. (JI) is in the real estate development business. It buys and sells land and also buys and develops land that it sometimes subsequently sells. The company's shares trade on the Canadian Stock Exchange (CSE) and the company is governed by the Canadian Securities Commission (CSC). The CSC has announced that all Canadian companies that have shares that trade on the CSE will have to follow IFRS for years beginning January 1, 2011. JI's controller is concerned about this and would like to start identifying significant differences that might affect the preparation of the company's financial statements. He is not looking for a list of all differences between PE GAAP and IFRS but rather would like to identify potential alternative accounting treatments under IFRS for major accounting issues that have occurred this year.

During the year, the company purchased several acres of land that it plans to hold for future development or sale purposes. At the purchase date, JI managers were undecided as to intent and thought that they might just wait and see what the market was like. They had architectural plans drawn up during the year that they might use for development of a shopping centre on some of the land. The purchase of the land was financed by a bank loan that included a covenant requiring that the company's annual debt-to-equity ratio not exceed 3 to 1. The company has been paying property taxes on the land, which are quite high. As at year end, JI had a potential buyer who indicated that he might be interested in buying the whole parcel of land. The company would potentially generate a loss if sold to the potential buyer. Negotiations were therefore underway. If the deal went through, it would do so within two months of year end. JI was considering taking the loss since it was worried about a further weakening of the real estate market in that particular area.

JI has several other properties that it has constructed or developed including its head office and several apartment buildings. These were constructed and completed several years ago. Recently, the company received a letter from the tenants' association in one of the buildings noting that radon (a toxic gas) was seeping into the apartments and making the tenants very sick. They were demanding that the problem be fixed or that they be given three months of free rent so that they would have time to look for a new apartment and move out. JI had hired some engineers to assess the problem. The engineers were not sure where the gas was coming from but agreed that they could insulate the building sufficiently such that the gas would not be able to seep in anymore. This would be at a substantial cost. The engineers felt also that the problem might be coming from a building across the road. Their study was inconclusive. JI had its lawyers draft a letter threatening litigation to the owners of the building across the street.

The company has just issued some new financial instruments. The instruments have a maturity date of 2019 and pay interest that is based on company earnings; i.e., the company pays a percentage of after-tax profits. If the company suffers a loss, no interest is payable. The instruments are convertible at the option of the holder to common shares of JI at any time before maturity.

Instructions

Assume the role of an external advisor to the controller and discuss the financial reporting issues.

IC16-2 Saltworks Inc. (SI) produces salt. Its main assets are two pieces of property that have two salt mines in them (mine 1 and mine 2). Both mines are currently in production. The salt exists in a crystalline layer of rock that rests about 50 metres below ground level. In order to mine the salt, tunnels are created by drilling through the rock. When the salt layer is reached, several holes are drilled into the salt layer to the bottom of the layer. Spring water is then fed through the holes. The water dissolves the salt and a cave is gradually created over time that is filled with salty water. The salt water is siphoned out of the hole, concentrated, and dried. It is then ground up and packaged. The life of a salt mine is about 30 years. Mine 1 is almost fully mined, so there is very little salt left. Mine 2 is a new mine and the tunnels are currently being dug. So far, $500,000 of costs have been incurred this year to drill and build tunnels for mine 2.

Mine 1 is completely depreciated and has a zero carrying value (net book value). Recently, SI discovered a new vein of salt in the mountain where mine 1 previously existed. The company's engineers feel that this new mine (mine 3) will produce at least as much salt as mine 1. Costs of $300,000 have been incurred to date to locate and test the salt. The salt from mine 3 is of a different quality and SI is not sure that a market currently exists for this salt nor that the costs of mining will be recoverable from future revenues. Nonetheless, the company plans to continue developing the mine in the meantime to confirm this.

The mountain that houses mine 2 is covered with pine trees. An unrelated company (Logging Co. or LC) has approached SI for the rights to cut the trees down. SI has agreed to sell these rights for $400,000, which has been paid upfront. The contract gives LC the right to cut down a certain number of trees over the next three years. In order to gain access to the trees, logging roads must be built. LC has approached SI about sharing the costs (equally) of building the roads. SI has agreed as it feels it can use the roads later to transport salt. Already, costs of $1 million have been incurred to build the roads. Unfortunately, the work done to date on the roads has to be redone due to excessive rainfall, which led to a huge flood. The flood washed out parts of the new road.

During the year (before the flood), SI had purchased a weather derivative contract. SI paid a premium of $100,000 for the contract. Under the terms of the contract, the counterparty will pay to SI $500,000 if more than 250 mm of rain falls within a certain period (causing flooding). Since this has happened, SI has approached the counterparty for payout.

A local environmental group has discovered that LC will be cutting down trees and is currently in discussions with SI. The group's members are demanding that SI replant the mountain with small seedlings that will grow into trees and eventually replace the trees that will be cut down. Although no contracts have been signed and SI has not specifically agreed to any course of action, SI has assured the group that it is company policy to be environmentally conscientious.

SI's president recently had a meeting with the CEO of a public company that is looking to purchase SI in the next year. The CEO is anxious to have a look at SI's financial statements and has asked that they be prepared in accordance with IFRS.

Instructions

Assume the role of the accountant for SI and discuss the financial reporting issues relating to the above. SI is a private company. (Hint: Use the conceptual framework to analyze any issues that are more complex.)

Research and Financial Analysis

RA16-1 PotashCorp.

Access the financial statements of Saskatoon-based PotashCorp., a global fertilizer producer, from the company's website or SEDAR (www.sedar.com) for the year ended December 31, 2009.

Instructions

(a) The company has several stock-based compensation plans. Compare and contrast these plans, noting such things as who is eligible, whether they have to buy shares to access any benefit, what the benefit or compensation is based on (profits or stock price), vesting periods, expiry periods, how the compensation cost is determined, where the offsetting amounts are reported (equity or liabilities), and when the compensation expense is recorded and whether it is adjusted or not. Prepare a chart to present your findings. (Note: summarize the same type of plans together.)

(b) Review the financial statements and discuss how the stock plans are accounted for. How much was reported to compensation expense, contributed surplus, and liabilities during the year?

(c) Comment on any professional judgement that is used in accounting for the stock option plans. How have these estimates changed from 2005 to 2009? Comment on what the impact on the compensation expense would be as a result of changes in each of these inputs, if all other inputs remained unchanged.

RA16-2 Canadian Tire Corporation

Access the annual report of Canadian Tire Corporation for the year ended January 2, 2010 (2009 annual report), from the company's website or SEDAR (www.sedar.com). According to the annual report, the company operates more than 479 retail stores across Canada, selling automotive parts, accessories, and services; sports and leisure products; and home products.

Instructions

(a) Read the Management Discussion and Analysis portion of the annual report.

(b) Identify and summarize the various business and financial risks that the company is exposed to. Explain how these risks stem from the underlying nature of the business (i.e., the business model).

(c) How is the company dealing with its foreign currency and interest rate risks?

(d) What derivatives are used by the company? What does the company use hedge accounting for? (See Note 1.)

(e) From Note 19, determine the fair values of the derivatives at the year end. In determining the fair value of these derivatives, what fair value hierarchy has been used? Prepare a schedule outlining the fair value of the cash flow hedges, the fair value hedges, and those derivatives not designated as hedges for accounting purposes.

RA16-3 Loblaw Companies Limited

Access the financial statements of Loblaw Companies Limited for the year ended January 2, 2010 (2009 annual report). The statements are available on the company's website or SEDAR (www.sedar.com).

Instructions

(a) During 2008, the company issued second preferred shares—Series A. Describe the terms of these shares and how the company measures and reports these shares. Explain why this presentation is required.

(b) How much were the shares originally issued for? What amount is showing on the statements with respect to these shares at the 2009 year end? Why is the amount different?

(c) How much was paid in dividends on these shares during 2009? How was the cost of these dividends reported?

(d) Review the company's capital management note. How are these preferred shares treated?

RA16-4 Deutsche Lufthansa AG

Access the financial statements of Deutsche Lufthansa AG for the year ended December 31, 2009. These can be found at the company's website (http://investor-relations.lufthansa.com).

Real-World Emphasis

Instructions

(a) Discuss the company's business model (i.e., how it earns income).

(b) Identify and summarize the various financial risks that the company is exposed to. (See the discussion on Financial Opportunities and Risks in the annual report.) How is the company dealing with its financial risks and what are its objectives in managing these risks? What types of derivatives are used for hedging purposes?

(c) Read Note 46 to the financial statements. How much of the various risks noted in part (b) is hedged?

(d) Also from Note 46, what derivative instruments, if any, are being used by the company to hedge its risks related to commodities? Identify which derivatives are designated as cash flow hedges and which are designated as fair value hedges for 2009. Explain why the hedges have been designated as cash flow or fair value.

(e) How have the fair values of the derivatives been determined?

(f) Related to the derivatives, how much was moved from other comprehensive income to earnings during the year?

Open Earnings

WATERLOO, Ontario-based Open Text Corporation has been in the software business for close to 20 years and is the largest software company in Canada. With approximately 4,000 employees, it is the world's largest independent provider of enterprise content management software.

Initially listed on the NASDAQ in 1996, Open Text was one of the first Internet companies to ever go public. "With both our comparable peer companies and the majority of our shareholders being located in the U.S., we choose to report in U.S. GAAP as it is a readily understood standard in the U.S.," explains Greg Secord, Open Text's Vice President of Investor Relations.

For the fiscal year ended 2009, Open Text reported an adjusted net income of U.S. $132.8 million, or $2.49 per share, on a diluted basis. This is up 24% compared with adjusted net income for the previous fiscal year. Net income in accordance with U.S. GAAP was U.S. $56.9 million, or $1.07 per share on a diluted basis, up from fiscal 2008.

"Although we report GAAP-based net income, as required, we also present adjusted net income in our press release and provide reconciliations between GAAP-based net income and adjusted net income," says Secord. "Net income in accordance with GAAP is a defined term with a standardized meaning, whereas adjusted income does not have a standardized meaning."

The reasons for reporting adjusted net income vary from company to company, but most want to provide investors with a snapshot of core operational performance and a perspective on the business without the impact of unusual or infrequent items, Secord explains. "Technology companies generally operate in growth-oriented industries; market repositioning and acquisitions are common strategies. These activities can result in one-time operational expenses, such as restructuring charges. We articulate adjusted net income because we believe that certain expenses like this do not accurately reflect the company's normal day-to-day operations."

Open Text also reports net income per share on both a basic and diluted basis. The diluted figures take into account outstanding options that are in the money; that is, the options that could be exercised, affecting diluted earnings. "For us, reporting on a diluted basis is not just our preferred method, but also the most conservative approach and a mandatory requirement for GAAP," says Secord. ■

CHAPTER 17

Earnings per Share

Learning Objectives

After studying this chapter, you should be able to:

1. Understand why earnings per share (EPS) is an important number.

2. Understand when and how earnings per share must be presented.

3. Identify potential common shares.

4. Calculate earnings per share in a simple capital structure.

5. Calculate diluted earnings per share using the if-converted method.

6. Calculate diluted earnings per share using the treasury stock method.

7. Calculate diluted earnings per share using the reverse treasury stock method.

8. Identify antidilutive potential common shares.

9. Identify the major differences in accounting between accounting standards for private enterprises (PE GAAP/ASPE) and IFRS, and what changes are expected in the near future.

Preview of Chapter 17

Earnings per share data are frequently reported in the financial press and are widely used by shareholders and potential investors in evaluating a company's profitability and value. This chapter examines how basic and diluted earnings per share figures are calculated and what information they contain.

The chapter is organized as follows:

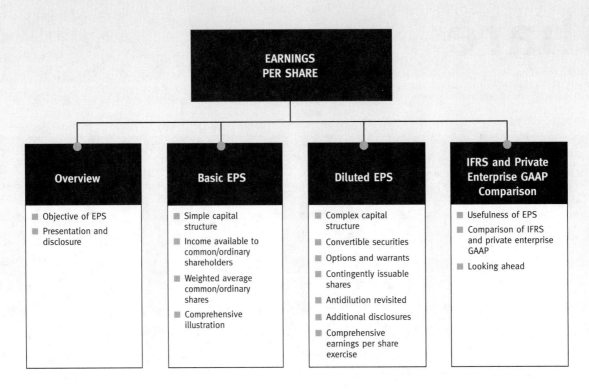

OVERVIEW

Objective of EPS

Objective 1

Understand why earnings per share (EPS) is an important number.

Common[1] shareholders need to know how much of a company's available income can be attributed to the shares that they own. This helps them assess future dividend payouts and the value of each share. As noted in Chapters 15 and 16, common shares are different from other forms of financing, such as debt and preferred shares. Common shareholders have a residual investment in the company. The return on investment does not depend on the passage of time or a face value (as it does for debt). If the company does well, common shareholders are the ones who gain the most. Similarly, if a company does not do well, common shareholders stand to lose the most. (There may not be anything left after a company covers its costs and obligations.) How big is the common shareholders' part of the profit pie? How is it affected by financial instruments such as convertible debt and options? Earnings per share disclosures help investors (both existing shareholders and potential investors) by

---

[1] IFRS refers to common shares as "ordinary shares." The terms will be used interchangeably here.

indicating the amount of income that is earned by each common share: in other words, how big the common shareholders' piece of the earnings pie is. Common shares are sometimes referred to as ordinary shares. The basic calculation is shown in Illustration 17-1.

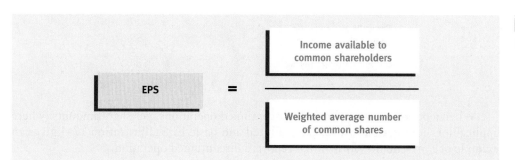

Illustration 17-1

The EPS Formula

Note that EPS is normally calculated only for common shares. The calculation is done for both basic EPS and diluted EPS. Basic EPS looks at actual earnings and the **actual** number of common shares outstanding (with this number prorated for the amount of time that the shares have been outstanding). Diluted EPS is a **"what if"** calculation that takes into account the possibility that financial instruments such as convertible debt and options (and others) might have a negative impact on existing shareholder returns and, therefore, the shares' value. This chapter will deal first with the calculations for basic EPS and then the calculations for diluted EPS.

Presentation and Disclosure

Because of the importance of earnings per share information, companies whose shares trade on a stock exchange or market or companies that are in the process of listing on a stock exchange or market are required to report this information on the face of the income statement.[2] PE GAAP/accounting standards for private enterprises (ASPE) does not require EPS calculations or disclosures in the financial statements. This is because of cost-benefit considerations as well as the fact that these entities may be closely held. Generally, earnings per share information is reported below net income in the income statement.

When the income statement presents discontinued operations, earnings per share should be disclosed for income from continuing operations, discontinued operations, and net income.[3] **The EPS numbers related to discontinued operations may be disclosed on the face of the statement or in the notes.** The EPS data in Illustration 17-2 are representative of this disclosure, and assume that the EPS numbers for discontinued operations and extraordinary items are presented on the face of the income statement.

2 Objective
Understand when and how earnings per share must be presented.

Significant Change

Earnings per share:	
Income from continuing operations	$4.00
Loss from discontinued operations, net of tax	(0.60)
Net income	$3.40

Illustration 17-2

Income Statement Presentation of EPS Components

These disclosures make it possible for users of the financial statements to know the specific impact of income from continuing operations on EPS, as opposed to a single EPS

---

[2] IAS 33 *Earnings per Share* stipulates this in IAS 33.67A.

[3] IAS 33.68.

number, which also includes the impact of a gain or loss from irregular items. If a corporation's capital structure is complex, the earnings per share presentation would include both basic and diluted EPS, as shown in Illustration 17-3.

Illustration 17-3

EPS Presentation—Complex Capital Structure

Earnings per common share:	
Basic earnings per share	$3.80
Diluted earnings per share	$3.35

When a period's earnings include discontinued operations, per share amounts (where applicable) should be shown for both diluted and basic EPS. Illustration 17-4 gives an example of a presentation format that reports a discontinued operation.

Illustration 17-4

EPS Presentation, with Discontinued Operations

Basic earnings per share:	
Income before discontinued operations	$3.80
Discontinued operations	(0.80)
Net income	$3.00
Diluted earnings per share:	
Income before discontinued operations	$3.35
Discontinued operations	(0.65)
Net income	$2.70

IFRS requires the following:

1. Earnings per share amounts must be shown for all periods that are presented.

2. If there has been a stock dividend or stock split, all per share amounts of prior period earnings should be restated using the new number of outstanding shares.

3. If diluted EPS data are reported for at least one period, they should be reported for all periods that are presented, even if they are the same as basic EPS.

4. When the results of operations of a prior period have been restated as a result of a prior period adjustment, the corresponding earnings per share data should also be restated. The restatement's effect should then be disclosed in the year of the restatement.

Basic EPS

Simple Capital Structure

Objective 3
Identify potential common shares.

When a corporation's capital structure consists only of common shares and preferred shares and/or debt without conversion rights, the company is said to have a simple capital structure. In contrast, a company is said to have a complex capital structure if the structure includes securities that could have a dilutive or negative effect (i.e., a lowering effect) on earnings per common share. In the EPS formula given in Illustration 17-1, any increase in the denominator will result in a decrease in EPS. These other, potentially dilutive securities are called potential common shares. A potential common/ordinary share is a security or other contract that may give its holder the right to obtain a common/ordinary share during or after the end of the reporting period. Examples are debt and equity instruments (e.g., preferred shares) that are convertible into common shares, warrants, options, and contingently issuable shares.[4] Contingently issuable shares are shares that are issuable for little or no consideration once a condition involving uncertainty has been resolved.[5] For instance, in an acquisition of another company, the acquirer may promise to issue some additional shares (at a later date) as part of the purchase consideration if the acquired company performs well.

Companies with simple capital structures only need to calculate and present basic EPS. Those with complex capital structures must calculate and present both basic and diluted EPS. The table in Illustration 17-5 summarizes the reporting requirements.

Capital Structure	Major Types of Equity Instruments	Impact on EPS Calculations
Simple	— Common (residual, voting) shares — Preferred shares	— Need only calculate basic EPS

Complex	— Common shares
	— Potential common shares
	  • Convertible preferred shares
	  • Convertible debt
	  • Options/warrants
	  • Contingently issuable shares
	  • Other
		— Must calculate basic and
		  diluted EPS

Illustration 17-5

EPS Reporting Requirements for Different Capital Structures

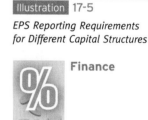

Finance

The calculation of earnings per share for a simple capital structure involves two items: income available to common/ordinary shareholders and the weighted average number of common shares outstanding. These are examined separately in the next sections.

Income Available to Common/Ordinary Shareholders

As noted earlier, basic EPS looks at **actual** earnings that are left or available after paying operating costs (including interest) and after paying or setting aside funds for dividends on shares that rank in preference (most often preferred shares) over the common shares.

Illustration 17-6 shows the concept of income available to common shareholders as a residual component of income.

4 Objective

Calculate earnings per share in a simple capital structure.

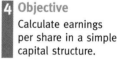

Illustration 17-6

Income Available to Common Shareholders (CSH)

---

[4] IAS 33.5 and .7.

[5] IAS 33.5.

Income available to common shareholders is equal to net income less amounts that have been set aside to cover obligations of other instruments, such as preferred shares that rank in preference over common shares. Since these instruments are senior, they rank in preference in terms of return on investment and these funds must be set aside before looking at how much is available for the common or residual shareholders.

Dividends on Preferred Shares

When a company has both **common and preferred shares outstanding, the dividends for the current year** on these preferred shares **are subtracted from net income** to arrive at **income available to common shareholders**.

In reporting earnings per share information, dividends declared on preferred shares should be subtracted from income from continuing operations **and** from net income to arrive at income available to common shareholders. If dividends on preferred shares are declared and a net loss occurs, the preferred dividend is added to the loss in calculating the loss per share. If the preferred shares are cumulative and the dividend is not declared in the current year, an amount equal to the dividend that should have been declared for the current year only should be subtracted from net income or added to the net loss. Dividends in arrears for previous years should have been included in the previous years' calculations.

Assume, for example, that Michael Limited has net income of $3 million and two classes of preferred shares, in addition to common shares. Class A preferred shares are cumulative and carry a dividend of $4 per share. There are 100,000 shares outstanding throughout the year. No dividend declaration has been made and no dividends have been paid during the year. Class B preferred shares are non-cumulative and carry a dividend of $3 per share. There are 100,000 shares outstanding throughout the year and the dividends have not been declared or paid in the current year. The income available for common shareholders would be calculated as follows:

Net income	$3,000,000
Less:	
Preferred dividends—Class A	
	(400,000)
Income available to common shareholders	$2,600,000

Note that the Class A share dividends are deducted even though they have not been declared or paid. This is because they are cumulative and will eventually have to be paid. No dividends are set aside for the Class B shares since they are non-cumulative and have not been declared. Because they are non-cumulative, the company never has to make up a lost dividend to the Class B shareholders.

Weighted Average Common/Ordinary Shares

In all calculations of earnings per share, the weighted average number of shares outstanding (WACS) during the period is the basis for the per share amounts that are reported. Shares that are issued or purchased during the period affect the amount outstanding and must be weighted by the fraction of the period that they have been outstanding. The rationale for this approach is that the income was generated on the issue proceeds for only part of the year. Accordingly, the number of shares outstanding should be weighted by the same factor. To illustrate, assume that Salomski Inc. has the data in Illustration 17-7 for the changes in its common shares outstanding for the period.

Date	Share Changes	Shares Outstanding
Jan. 1	Beginning balance	90,000
Apr. 1	Issued 30,000 shares for cash	30,000
		120,000
July 1	Purchased 39,000 shares	(39,000)
		81,000
Nov. 1	Issued 60,000 shares for cash	60,000
Dec. 31	Ending balance	141,000

Illustration 17-7

Common Shares Outstanding, Ending Balance—Salomski Inc.

To calculate the weighted average number of shares outstanding, the calculation is done as in Illustration 17-8.

Dates Outstanding	(A) Shares Outstanding	(B) Fraction of Year	(C) Weighted Shares (A × B)
Jan. 1–Mar 31	90,000	3/12	22,500
Apr. 1–June 30	120,000	3/12	30,000
July 1–Oct. 31	81,000	4/12	27,000
Nov. 1–Dec. 31	141,000	2/12	23,500
Weighted average number of shares outstanding			103,000

Illustration 17-8

Weighted Average Number of Shares Outstanding

As illustrated, 90,000 shares were outstanding for three months, which translates to 22,500 whole shares for the entire year. Because additional shares were issued on April 1, the number of shares outstanding changes and these shares must be weighted for the time that they have been outstanding. When 39,000 shares were repurchased on July 1, this reduced the number of shares outstanding and a new calculation again has to be made to determine the proper weighted number of shares outstanding.

Stock Dividends, Splits, and Reverse Splits

When stock dividends or stock splits occur, calculation of the weighted average number of shares requires a restatement of the shares outstanding before the stock dividend or split.[6] For example, assume that a corporation had 100,000 shares outstanding on January 1 and issued a 25% stock dividend on June 30. For purposes of calculating a weighted average for the current year, the additional 25,000 shares outstanding as a result of the stock dividend are assumed to have been outstanding since the beginning of the year. Thus, the weighted average for the year would be 125,000 shares.

The issuance of a stock dividend or stock split requires a restatement (which is applied retroactively), but the issuance or repurchase of shares for cash does not. Why? Stock splits and stock dividends do not increase or decrease the net enterprise's assets; only additional shares are issued. Therefore, the weighted average number of shares must be restated. By restating the number, valid comparisons of earnings per share can be made between periods before and after the stock split or stock dividend. Conversely, the issuance or purchase of shares for cash changes the amount of net assets. The company earns either more or less in the future as a result of this change in net assets. Stated another way, a stock dividend or split does not change the shareholders' total investment; it only increases (unless it is a reverse stock split) the **number** of common shares.

---

[6] IAS 33.28.

To illustrate how a stock dividend affects the calculation of the weighted average number of shares outstanding, assume that Baiye Limited has the data in Illustration 17-9 for the changes in its common shares during the year.

Illustration 17-9

Shares Outstanding, Ending Balance—Baiye Limited

Date	Share Changes	Shares Outstanding
Jan. 1	Beginning balance	100,000
Mar. 1	Issued 20,000 shares for cash	20,000
		120,000
June 1	60,000 additional shares (50% stock dividend)	60,000
		180,000
Nov. 1	Issued 30,000 shares for cash	30,000
Dec. 31	Ending balance	210,000

Illustration 17-10 shows the calculation of the weighted average number of shares outstanding.

Illustration 17-10

Weighted Average Number of Shares Outstanding—Share Issue and Stock Dividend

Dates Outstanding	(A) Shares Outstanding	(B) Restatement	(C) Fraction of Year	(D) Shares Weighted (A × B × C)
Jan. 1–Feb. 28	100,000	1.50	2/12	25,000
Mar. 1–May 31	120,000	1.50	3/12	45,000
June 1–Oct. 31	180,000		5/12	75,000
Nov. 1–Dec. 31	210,000		2/12	35,000
Weighted average number of shares outstanding				180,000

The shares outstanding before the stock dividend must be restated. The shares outstanding from January 1 to June 1 are adjusted for the stock dividend so that these shares are stated on the same basis as shares issued after the stock dividend. Shares issued after the stock dividend do not have to be restated because they are on the new basis. The stock dividend simply restates existing shares. A stock split is treated in the same way.

If a stock dividend or stock split occurs after the end of the year, but before the financial statements are issued, the weighted average number of shares outstanding for the year (and any other years presented in comparative form) must be restated. For example, assume that Hendricks Corp. calculates its weighted average number of shares to be 100,000 for the year ended December 31, 2011. On January 15, 2012, before the financial statements are issued, the company splits its shares 3 for 1. In this case, the weighted average number of shares used in calculating earnings per share for 2011 would be 300,000 shares. If earnings per share information for 2010 is provided as comparative information, it also must be adjusted for the stock split.

Mandatorily Convertible Instruments

Where common shares will be issued in future due to mandatory conversion of a financial instrument that is already outstanding, it is assumed that the conversion has already taken place for EPS calculation purposes. For these instruments, the denominator of the EPS calculation would be adjusted as though the instruments had already been converted to common shares and that the common shares were outstanding. An adjustment may be needed for the numerator depending on how the instruments were presented in the financial statements (i.e., as debt, common, or preferred shares). Note that if the instruments were presented as common share equity already, there would be no need to adjust the numerator and the concern would only be to ensure the number of common shares was adjusted for these shares that were not yet outstanding.

Contingently Issuable Shares

Contingently issuable shares are potential common shares, as mentioned earlier. If these shares are issuable simply with the passage of time (as with the mandatorily convertible instruments noted above), they are not considered contingently issuable since it is certain that time will pass. Where they are issuable based on something else (e.g., profit levels or performance targets), they are included in the calculation of basic EPS when the conditions are satisfied.

Comprehensive Illustration

Leung Corporation has income of $580,000 before discontinued operations (net of tax) of $240,000. In addition, it has declared preferred dividends of $1 per share on 100,000 preferred shares outstanding. Leung Corporation also has the data shown in Illustration 17-11 for changes in its common shares outstanding during 2011.

Dates	Share Changes	Shares Outstanding
Jan. 1	Beginning balance	180,000
May 1	Purchased 30,000 shares	30,000
		150,000
July 1	300,000 additional shares issued (3-for-1 stock split)	300,000
		450,000
Dec. 31	Issued 50,000 shares for cash	50,000
Dec. 31	Ending balance	500,000

Illustration 17-11

Shares Outstanding, Ending Balance—Leung Corp.

To calculate the earnings per share information, the weighted average number of shares outstanding is first determined as in Illustration 17-12.

Dates Outstanding	(A) Shares Outstanding	(B) Restatement	(C) Fraction of Year	(D) Shares Weighted (A × B × C)
Jan. 1–Apr. 30	180,000	3	4/12	180,000
May 1–Dec. 31	150,000	3	8/12	300,000
Weighted average number of shares outstanding				480,000

Illustration 17-12

Weighted Average Number of Shares Outstanding

In calculating the weighted average number of shares, the shares sold on December 31, 2011, are ignored because they have not been outstanding during the year. The weighted average number of shares is then divided into income before discontinued operations and net income to determine the earnings per share. Leung Corporation's preferred dividends of $100,000 are subtracted from income before discontinued operations ($580,000) to arrive at income from continuing operations available to common shareholders of $480,000 ($580,000 − $100,000). Deducting the preferred dividends from the income from continuing operations has the effect of also reducing net income without affecting the amount of the discontinued operations. The final amount is referred to as income available to common shareholders. Illustration 17-13 shows the calculation of income available to common shareholders.

Illustration 17-13

*Calculation of Income
Available to Common
Shareholders*

	(A) Income Information	(B) Weighted Shares	(C) Earnings per Share (A ÷ B)
Income from continuing operations available to common shareholders	$480,000	480,000	$1.00
Income from discontinued operations (net of tax)	240,000	480,000	0.50
Income available to common shareholders	$720,000	480,000	$1.50

Disclosure of the per share amount for the discontinued operations (net of tax) must be reported either on the face of the income statement or in the notes to the financial statements. Income and per share information would be reported as in Illustration 17-14.

Illustration 17-14

*Earnings per Share, with
Discontinued Operations*

Income from continuing operations	$580,000
Income from discontinued operations, net of tax	240,000
Net income	$820,000
Earnings per share:	
Income from continuing operations	$1.00
Income from discontinued operations, net of tax	0.50
Net income	$1.50

DILUTED EPS

Complex Capital Structure

Finance

One problem with a basic EPS calculation is that it fails to recognize the potentially dilutive impact on outstanding shares when a corporation has dilutive securities in its capital structure. **Dilutive securities present a serious problem because their conversion or exercise often decreases earnings per share.** This adverse effect can be significant and, more important, unexpected, unless financial statements call attention to the potential dilutive effect.

A complex capital structure exists when a corporation has potential common shares such as convertible securities, options, warrants, or other rights that could dilute earnings per share if they are converted or exercised. **Therefore, as noted earlier, when a company has a complex capital structure, both basic and diluted earnings per share are generally reported.** The calculation of diluted EPS is similar to the calculation of basic EPS. The difference is that diluted EPS includes the effect of all dilutive potential common shares that were outstanding during the period. The formula in Illustration 17-15 shows the relationship between basic EPS and diluted EPS.

Note that companies with complex capital structures will not report diluted EPS if the securities in their capital structure are antidilutive. Antidilutive securities are securities that, upon conversion or exercise, increase earnings per share (or reduce the loss per

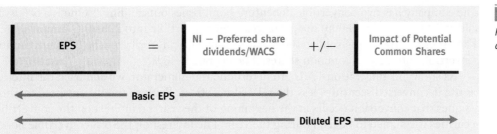

Illustration 17-15

Relationship between Basic and Diluted EPS

share). **The purpose of presenting both EPS numbers is to inform financial statement users of situations that will likely occur and to provide worst-case dilutive situations.** If the securities are antidilutive, the likelihood of conversion or exercise is considered remote. **Thus, companies that have only antidilutive securities report only the basic EPS number.**[7]

The calculation of basic EPS was shown in the previous section. The discussion in the following sections addresses the effects of convertible and other dilutive securities on EPS calculations.

Convertible Securities

At conversion, convertible securities are exchanged for common shares. Convertible securities are therefore potential common shares and may be dilutive. The method that is used to measure the dilutive effects of a potential conversion on EPS is sometimes called the if-converted method.[8]

If-Converted Method

The if-converted method for convertible debt or preferred shares assumes both of the following:

1. It assumes that the convertible securities are converted at the **beginning of the period** (or at the time of the security issuance, if they are issued during the period).[9]

2. It assumes **the elimination of related interest, net of tax** or a preferred share dividend. If the debt/equity had been converted at the beginning of the period, there would be no bond interest expense/preferred dividend. No tax effect is calculated for preferred share dividends, because preferred dividends generally are not tax-deductible.

> **5 Objective**
> Calculate diluted earnings per share using the if-converted method.

Thus the denominator—the weighted average number of shares outstanding—is increased by the additional shares that are assumed to be issued. The numerator—net income—is increased by the amount of interest expense, net of tax or preferred share dividends, that is associated with those potential common shares.

As an example, assume that Field Corporation has net income for the year of $210,000 and a weighted average number of common shares outstanding during the period of 100,000 shares. The basic earnings per share is therefore $2.10 ($210,000 ÷ 100,000).

---

[7] IAS 33.41.

[8] This terminology is used in the United States and was used in pre-2011 Canadian GAAP. IAS 33 does not label the calculations although the calculations themselves are essentially the same.

[9] IAS 33.36.

The company has two convertible debenture bond issues outstanding.[10] One is a 6% issue sold at 100 (total $1,000,000) in a prior year and convertible into 20,000 common shares. The other is a 10% issue sold at 100 (total $1,000,000) on April 1 of the current year and convertible into 32,000 common shares. The tax rate is 40%.

As shown in Illustration 17-16, to determine the numerator, we add back the interest on the if-converted securities less the related tax effect. Because the if-converted method assumes that conversion occurs at the beginning of the year, no interest on the convertible securities is assumed to be paid during the year. The interest on the 6% convertible bonds is $60,000 for the year ($1,000,000 × 6%). The increased tax expense is $24,000 ($60,000 × 0.40), and the interest added back net of taxes is $36,000 [$60,000 − $24,000, or simply $60,000 × (1 − 0.40)].

Because the 10% convertible bonds are issued after the beginning of the year, the shares that are assumed to have been issued on that date, April 1, are weighted as outstanding from April 1 to the end of the year. In addition, the interest adjustment to the numerator for these bonds would only reflect the interest for nine months. Thus, the interest added back on the 10% convertible security would be $45,000 [$1,000,000 × 10% × 9/12 year × (1 − 0.40)]. The calculation of earnings (the numerator) for diluted earnings per share is shown in Illustration 17-16.

<table>
<tr><td>Net income for the year</td><td>$210,000</td></tr>
<tr><td>Add: Adjustment for interest (net of tax)</td><td></td></tr>
<tr><td>6% debentures ($60,000 × [1 − 0.40])</td><td>36,000</td></tr>
<tr><td>10% debentures ($100,000 × 9/12 × [1 − 0.40])</td><td>45,000</td></tr>
<tr><td>Adjusted net income</td><td>$291,000</td></tr>
</table>

Illustration 17-16

Calculation of Adjusted Net Income

The calculation of the weighted average number of shares adjusted for dilutive securities—the denominator in a diluted earnings per share calculation—is shown in Illustration 17-17.

<table>
<tr><td>Weighted average number of shares outstanding</td><td>100,000</td></tr>
<tr><td>Add: Shares assumed to be issued:</td><td></td></tr>
<tr><td>6% debentures (as of beginning of year)</td><td>20,000</td></tr>
<tr><td>10% debentures (as of date of issue,
April 1; 9/12 × 32,000)</td><td>24,000</td></tr>
<tr><td>Weighted average number of shares adjusted for
dilutive securities</td><td>144,000</td></tr>
</table>

Illustration 17-17

Calculation of Weighted Average Number of Shares— Dilutive Securities

Field Corporation would then report earnings per share based on a dual presentation on the face of the income statement; that is, it would present both basic and diluted earnings per share.[11] The presentation is shown in Illustration 17-18.

---

[10] To simplify, the consequences of measuring and presenting the debt and equity components of the convertible debentures separately have been ignored for this example. When initially recognized, convertible debentures would have been recognized as part debt and part equity under IFRS. The interest expense would be calculated using the market interest rate for straight debt; i.e., without the conversion feature.

[11] The conversion of bonds is dilutive because EPS with conversion ($2.02) is less than basic EPS ($2.10).

Net income for the year	$210,000
Earnings per share:	
Basic earnings per share ($210,000 ÷ 100,000)	$2.10
Diluted earnings per share ($291,000 ÷ 144,000)	$2.02

Illustration 17-18

Earnings per Share Disclosure

Other Factors

The example above assumed that Field Corporation's bonds were sold at their face amount. If the bonds were instead sold at a premium or discount, interest expense would have to be adjusted each period to account for this occurrence. Therefore, the amount of interest expense added back, net of tax, to net income is the interest expense reported on the income statement, not the interest paid in cash during the period. Likewise, because the convertible debentures are compound instruments, a portion of the proceeds would actually be allocated to the equity component, and the discount rate on the debt would be the market interest rate on straight debt. (Further discussion of this aspect is beyond the scope of this text.) If financial instruments are settleable in either shares or cash at the issuer option, assume shares.

The conversion rate on a dilutive security may change over the period that the dilutive security is outstanding. In this situation, for the diluted EPS calculation, the most advantageous conversion rate available to the holder is used.[12] For example, assume that a convertible bond was issued January 1, 2009, with a conversion rate of 10 common shares for each bond starting January 1, 2011; beginning January 1, 2014, the conversion rate is 12 common shares for each bond; and beginning January 1, 2019, it is 15 common shares for each bond. In calculating diluted EPS in 2009, the conversion rate of 15 shares to one bond would be used.

Underlying Concept

Showing both basic and diluted EPS reflects the full disclosure principle. The diluted EPS calculation shows the possible negative impact of conversions.

Options and Warrants

Recall from Chapter 16 that stock options allow the holder to buy or sell shares at a preset price (the **exercise price**). The company may either **write** the options or **purchase** them. The options may also allow the holder to buy the shares (**call options**) or sell the shares (**put options**).[13]

Written Options

When the company writes or sells the options, it gives the holder or purchaser the right to either buy (call) or sell (put) the shares. **Thus, if the holder or purchaser decides to exercise the options, the company will have to deliver (either buy or sell the shares).** Generally speaking, the holder of the options will exercise the right if the options are "**in the money.**" They are in the money if the holder of the options will benefit from exercising them. If the option is a call option—giving the holder the right to buy the shares at a

---

[12] IAS 33.39.

[13] Note that IAS 33 was not updated when IAS 32 was revised to provide guidance on accounting for instruments that are settled using the entity's own equity instruments (including options and forwards). IAS 33 therefore is not conceptually consistent with IAS 32 as it relates to these types of instruments and the IASB and FASB have plans to revise the standard. This will be discussed further in the Looking Ahead section at the end of this chapter.

preset price—the holder will exercise it if the preset or exercise price is lower than the current market price. **Written options and their equivalents must be included in the diluted EPS calculations if they are dilutive.** Generally speaking, they are **dilutive when they are written options that are in the money.**

Assume, for example, that Gaddy Limited sold (or wrote) **call options** for $2 that allow the purchaser to buy shares of Gaddy at $10 (the exercise price). At the time, Gaddy shares were trading at $9. Assume further that the market price of Gaddy shares subsequently increases to $15. The options are now in the money since they have value to the holder. If the holder exercises the options, Gaddy will have to issue its own shares for the exercise price ($10). **This will result in dilution for Gaddy and so must be considered in the diluted EPS calculation.** Note that if the shares of Gaddy never go beyond $10, the holder will not exercise them and the options will expire. Expired options as well as options that are not in the money are excluded from the diluted EPS calculation.

Finance

If Gaddy had instead sold **put options** that allow the purchaser to sell shares of Gaddy to Gaddy at an exercise price of $8, these might also be dilutive. Assume that when the put options were issued, Gaddy shares were $9, and that the shares subsequently went down to $6. If the put option is exercised, Gaddy will have to buy the shares from the option holder and will have to pay $8—the exercise price. Again, this must be incorporated in the diluted EPS calculation as it is in the money for the holder. The holder can sell the shares for more than their market value. Once again, if the options expire or are not in the money, they are not included in the diluted EPS calculation (since it is assumed that they will not be exercised).

Written put options, where the company may be forced to buy the shares at an unfavourable price, are the same as **forward purchase contracts.** Forward purchase contracts are included in the calculations if they represent a liability; that is, if the forward purchase price is higher than the average market price. Similarly, written call options are the same as **forward sales contracts.** Forward sales contracts are also included in the calculations if they represent a liability; that is, if the forward selling price is lower than the market price. In both cases, the instruments are in the money to the other party.

Purchased Options

Purchased options, on the other hand, do not result in the company having an obligation (as opposed to written options, which do result in an obligation). When the company buys options, it obtains the right but not the obligation to buy (call) or sell (put) its own shares. When will it exercise these options? Like any option holder, it is assumed that the company will exercise the options when they are **in the money.** Thus, when the underlying shares in a purchased call option have a market value that is greater than the exercise price, they are in the money. Alternatively, when the underlying shares in a purchased put option have a market value that is less than the exercise price, the options are in the money and it is assumed that they will be exercised.

Illustration 17-19 summarizes this.

In-the-Money Options

	Call	Put
Written	In the money when market price is greater than exercise price	In the money when market price is less than exercise price
Purchased	In the money when market price is greater than exercise price	In the money when market price is less than exercise price

Purchased options will always be antidilutive since they will only be exercised when they are in the money and this will always be favourable to the company. They are therefore not considered in the calculation.[14]

Treasury Stock Method

Written options and warrants, and their equivalents, are included in earnings per share calculations through what is sometimes referred to as the treasury stock and/or reverse treasury stock method.

The treasury stock method applies to **written call options and equivalents** and assumes both of the following:

1. that the options and warrants or equivalents are exercised **at the beginning of the year** (or on the date of issue if it is later).

2. that the proceeds are used to purchase common shares for the treasury at the **average market price** during the year.

If the exercise price is lower than the average market price, then the proceeds from exercise are not sufficient to buy back all the shares. This will result in more shares being issued than purchased and the effect will therefore be dilutive. **The excess number of the shares issued over the number of shares purchased is added to the weighted average number of shares outstanding in calculating the diluted earnings per share. Note that no adjustment is made to the numerator.**

Assume, for example, that 1,500 (written) call options are outstanding at an exercise price of $30 for a common share. The average common share market price per share is $50. Because the market price is greater than the exercise price, the options are considered in the money and the holder is assumed to exercise them. The holder can buy the shares for a price that is less than market price—a bargain. By applying the treasury stock method, there would be 600 incremental shares outstanding, calculated as in Illustration 17-20.[15]

Proceeds from exercise of 1,500 options (1,500 × $30)	$45,000
Shares issued upon exercise of options	1,500
Treasury shares purchasable with proceeds ($45,000 ÷ $50)	900
Incremental shares outstanding (additional potential common shares)	600

Objective 6

Calculate diluted earnings per share using the treasury stock method.

Illustration 17-20

Calculation of Incremental Shares

Thus, if the exercise price of the call option or warrant is lower than the shares' market price, dilution occurs because, on a net basis, more common shares are assumed to be outstanding after the exercise. If the exercise price of the call option or warrant is higher than the shares' market price, the options would not be exercised and would therefore be irrelevant to the EPS calculation.[16] As a practical matter, a simple average of the weekly or monthly prices is adequate, as long as the prices do not fluctuate significantly.

---

[14] IAS 33.62.

[15] The incremental number of shares can be calculated in a simpler way: (Market price − Option price) ÷ Market price × Number of options = Number of shares ($50 − $30) ÷ $50 × 1,500 options = 600 shares

[16] It might be noted that options and warrants have basically the same assumptions and problems regarding calculation, although the warrants may allow or require the tendering of some other security, such as debt, in lieu of cash upon exercise. In such situations, the accounting becomes quite complex and is beyond the scope of this book.

To illustrate the application of the treasury stock method, assume that Kubitz Industries, Inc. has net income for the period of $220,000. The average number of shares outstanding for the period was 100,000 shares. Hence, basic EPS, ignoring all dilutive securities, is $2.20. The average number of shares that are outstanding under written call options at an option price of $20 per share is 5,000 shares (although the options are not exercisable at this time). The average market price of the common shares during the year was $28. Illustration 17-21 shows the calculation.

Illustration 17-21

Calculation of Earnings per Share—Treasury Stock Method

	Basic Earnings per Share	Diluted Earnings per Share
Average number of shares outstanding under option:		5,000
Option price per share		× $20
Proceeds upon exercise of options		$100,000
Average market price of common shares		$28
Treasury shares that could be repurchased with proceeds ($100,000 ÷ $28)		3,571
Excess of shares under option over the treasury shares that could be repurchased (5,000 − 3,571)—potential common incremental shares		1,429
Average number of common shares outstanding	100,000	100,000
Total average number of common shares outstanding and potential common shares	100,000 (A)	101,429 (C)
Net income for the year	$220,000 (B)	$220,000 (D)
Earnings per share	$2.20 (B ÷ A)	$2.17 (D ÷ C)

Reverse Treasury Stock Method

Objective 7
Calculate diluted earnings per share using the reverse treasury stock method.

The reverse treasury stock method is used for (written) put options and forward purchase contracts. It assumes both of the following:

1. that the company will issue enough common shares **at the beginning of the year** in the marketplace (at the average market price) to generate sufficient funds to buy the shares under the option/forward.

2. that the proceeds from the above will be used to buy back the shares under the option/forward at the beginning of the year.

If the options are in the money, the company will have to buy the shares back under the options/forward at a higher price than the market price. Thus, it will have to issue more shares at the beginning of the year to generate sufficient funds to meet the obligation under the option/forward.

Assume, for example, that 1,500 (written) put options are outstanding at an exercise price of $30 for a common share. The average market price per common share is $20. Because the market price is less than the exercise price, the options are considered in the money and the holder is assumed to exercise them. The holder can sell the shares for a price that is higher than market price—again, a bargain. By applying the reverse treasury stock method, there would be 750 additional (incremental) shares outstanding, calculated as in Illustration 17-22.

Illustration 17-22

Calculation of Incremental Shares

Amount needed to buy 1,500 shares under put option (1,500 × $30)	$45,000
Shares issued in market to obtain $45,000 ($45,000 ÷ $20)	2,250
Number of shares purchased under the put options	1,500
Incremental shares outstanding (potential common shares)	750

This is dilutive because there will be 750 more shares outstanding. If the market price were higher than the exercise price, the options would never be exercised (the holder could sell the shares in the marketplace for a higher amount). Thus, options that are not in the money are ignored in the diluted EPS calculation. Likewise, when the forward purchase price of a forward purchase contract is lower than the market price, the forward contract is antidilutive because the company would theoretically have to issue fewer shares in the marketplace in order to generate sufficient money to honour the forward contract. In other words, it would issue fewer shares than it would buy back, resulting in fewer common shares outstanding (not more).

Contingently Issuable Shares

Contingently issuable shares are potential common shares, as mentioned earlier. If the shares are issuable upon attaining a certain earnings or market price level for instance, and this level is met at the end of the year, they should be considered as outstanding from the beginning of the year for the calculation of diluted earnings per share. If the conditions have not been met, however, the diluted EPS may still be affected. The number of contingently issuable shares included in the diluted EPS calculation would be based on the number of shares (if any) that would be issuable if the end of the reporting period were the end of the contingency period and if the impact were dilutive.

For example, assume that Walz Corporation purchased Cardella Limited in 2011 and agreed to give the shareholders of Cardella 20,000 additional shares in 2013 if Cardella's net income in 2012 is $90,000. Assume also that in 2011 Cardella's net income is $100,000, which is higher than the $90,000 target for 2012. Because the contingency of stipulated earnings of $90,000 is already being attained in 2011, and because 2011 is treated as though it were the end of the contingency period, Walz's diluted earnings per share for 2011 would include the 20,000 contingent shares in the calculation of the number of shares outstanding.

Antidilution Revisited

In calculating diluted EPS, the combined impact of all dilutive securities must be considered. However, it is necessary to first determine which potentially dilutive securities are in fact individually dilutive and which are antidilutive. As was stated earlier, securities that are antidilutive have to be excluded from EPS calculations; they therefore cannot be used to offset dilutive securities.

8 Objective
Identify antidilutive potential common shares.

Recall that antidilutive securities are securities whose inclusion in earnings per share calculations **would increase earnings per share (or reduce net loss per share)**. Convertible debt is antidilutive if the addition to income of the interest (net of tax) would cause a greater percentage increase in income (the numerator) than a conversion of the bonds would cause a percentage increase in common and potentially dilutive shares (the denominator). In other words, convertible debt is antidilutive if conversion of the security would cause common share earnings to increase by a greater amount per additional common share than the earnings per share amount before the conversion.

To illustrate, assume that Kohl Corporation has a $1-million, 6% debt issue that is convertible into 10,000 common shares. Net income for the year is $210,000, the weighted average number of common shares outstanding is 100,000 shares, and the tax rate is 40%. In this case, assume also that conversion of the debt into common shares at the beginning of the year requires the adjustments to net income and the weighted average number of shares outstanding that are shown in Illustration 17-23.

Illustration 17-23

Test for Antidilution

Net income for year	$210,000	Average number of shares outstanding	100,000
Add: Adjustment for interest (net of tax) on 6% debentures $60,000 × (1 − 0.40)	36,000	Add: Shares issued upon assumed conversion of debt	10,000
Adjusted net income	$246,000	Average number of common and potential common shares	110,000

Basic EPS = $210,000 ÷ 100,000 = $2.10
Diluted EPS = $246,000 ÷ 110,000 = $2.24 (Antidilutive)

As a shortcut, the convertible debt can also be identified as antidilutive by comparing the incremental EPS resulting from conversion, $3.60 ($36,000 additional earnings ÷ 10,000 additional shares), with EPS before inclusion of the convertible debt, $2.10.

With options or warrants, whenever the option or warrant is not in the money, it is irrelevant to the calculations because the holder will not exercise it.

Additional Disclosures

Complex capital structures and a dual presentation of earnings require the following additional disclosures in note form:

1. The amounts used in the numerator and denominator in calculating basic and diluted EPS

2. A reconciliation of the numerators and denominators of basic and diluted per share calculations for income before discontinued operations (including the individual income and share amounts of each class of securities that affects EPS)

3. Securities that could dilute basic EPS in the future but were not included in the calculations because they have antidilutive features

4. A description of common share transactions that occur after the reporting period that would have significantly changed the EPS numbers

Illustration 17-24 presents an example of the reconciliation and related disclosure that is needed to meet the standard's disclosure requirements. Assume that stock options to purchase 1 million common shares at $85 per share were outstanding during the second half of 2011 but that the options are antidilutive.

Illustration 17-24

Reconciliation for Basic and Diluted EPS

	For the Year Ended December 31, 2011		
	Income (Numerator)	Shares (Denominator)	Per Share Amount
Net Income	$7,500,000		
Less: Preferred stock dividends	(45,000)		
Basic EPS			
Income available to common shareholders	7,455,000	3,991,666	$1.87
Warrants		30,768	
Convertible preferred shares	45,000	308,333	
4% convertible bonds (net of tax)	60,000	50,000	
Diluted EPS			
Income available to common shareholders after assumed conversions	$7,560,000	4,380,767	$1.73

Related disclosure: Stock options to purchase 1 million common shares at $85 per share were outstanding during the second half of 2011 but were not included in the calculation of diluted EPS because the options' exercise price was greater than the average market price of the common shares. The options were still outstanding at the end of 2011 and expire on June 30, 2018.

One final note on additional disclosures: an entity may choose to report additional per share calculations based on other reported components of comprehensive income. If this is done, the weighted average number of shares would be the same and the basic and diluted EPS numbers must be presented with equal prominence.

Maple Leaf Foods recognized a charge of $103 million in its 2008 financial statements relating to product recall, restructuring, and other related costs. Of this, $37.5 million related to product recall costs from a voluntary recall of products where bacterial contamination had been discovered. In 2008, the overall net loss was about $37 million, resulting in a loss of 29 cents per share. In the MD&A, management disclosed an "adjusted EPS" figure that was calculated on net income before the recall, restructuring, and other related costs. This resulted in a positive EPS number of 29 cents per share.

What Do the Numbers Mean?

The company wanted to show the results of operations before the one-time costs so users could see how the rest of the business operations were performing. It felt that this additional information would be the most useful. As previously discussed in the text, care should be taken when presenting and using non-GAAP measures as they are non-standardized.

Real-World Emphasis

Comprehensive Earnings per Share Exercise

The purpose of the following exercise is to show the method of calculating dilution when many securities are involved. Illustration 17-25 presents a section of the balance sheet of Andrews Corporation, our assumed company; assumptions about the company's capital structure follow the illustration.

Long-term debt:	
Notes payable, 14%	$ 1,000,000
7% convertible bonds payable	2,000,000
9% convertible bonds payable	3,000,000
Total long-term debt	$ 6,000,000
Shareholders' equity:	
$10 cumulative dividend, convertible preferred shares, no par value; 100,000 shares authorized, 20,000 shares issued and outstanding	$ 2,000,000
Common shares, no par value; 5,000,000 shares authorized, 400,000 shares issued and outstanding	400,000
Contributed surplus	2,100,000
Retained earnings	9,000,000
Total shareholders' equity	$13,500,000

Illustration 17-25

Balance Sheet for Comprehensive Illustration

Notes and Assumptions

December 31, 2011

1. Options were granted or written in July 2009 to purchase 30,000 common shares at $15 per share. The average market price of Andrews' common shares during 2011 was

$25 per common share. The options expire in 2019 and no options were exercised during 2011.

2. The 7% bonds were issued in 2010 at face value. The 9% convertible bonds were issued on July 1, 2011, at face value. Each convertible bond is convertible into 50 common shares (each bond has a face value of $1,000).

3. The $10 cumulative, convertible preferred shares were issued at the beginning of 2008. Each preferred share is convertible into four common shares.

4. The average income tax rate is 35%.

5. The 400,000 common shares were issued at $1 per share and were outstanding during the entire year.

6. Preferred dividends were not declared in 2011.

7. Net income was $1.2 million in 2011.

8. No bonds or preferred shares were converted during 2011.

Instructions

(a) Calculate basic earnings per share for Andrews for 2011.

(b) Calculate diluted earnings per share for Andrews for 2011, following these steps:

1. Determine, for each dilutive security, the incremental per share effect if the security is exercised or converted. Where there are multiple dilutive securities, rank the results from the lowest earnings effect per share to the largest; that is, rank the results from least dilutive to most dilutive. The instruments with the lowest incremental EPS calculation will drag the EPS number down the most and are therefore most dilutive.

2. Beginning with the earnings per share based upon the weighted average number of common shares outstanding, recalculate the earnings per share by adding the smallest per share effects from the first step. If the results from this recalculation are less than EPS in the prior step, go to the next smallest per share effect and recalculate the earnings per share. This process is continued as long as each recalculated earnings per share amount is smaller than the previous amount. The process will end either because there are no more securities to test or because a particular security maintains or increases the earnings per share (i.e., it is antidilutive).

(c) Show the presentation of earnings per share for Andrews for 2011.

Solution to Comprehensive EPS Exercise

(a) **Basic earnings per share**
The calculation of basic earnings per share for 2011 starts with the amount based upon the weighted average number of common shares outstanding, as shown below.

Net income	$1,200,000
Less: $10 cumulative, convertible preferred share dividend requirements	200,000
Income applicable to common shareholders	$1,000,000
Weighted average number of common shares outstanding	400,000
Earnings per common share	$2.50

Note the following points about the above calculation:

1. When preferred shares are cumulative, the preferred dividend is subtracted to arrive at the income that is applicable to common shares, whether or not the dividend is declared.

2. The earnings per share of $2.50 is calculated as a starting point because the per share amount is not reduced by the existence of convertible securities and options.

(b) **Diluted earnings per share**

The steps in calculating diluted EPS are now applied to Andrews Corporation. (Note that net income and income available to common shareholders are not the same if preferred dividends are declared or are cumulative.) Andrews Corporation has four securities (options, 7% and 9% convertible bonds, and the convertible preferred shares) that could reduce EPS.

The first step in the calculation of diluted earnings per share is to determine an incremental per share effect for each potentially dilutive security. Illustrations 17-26 through 17-29 show these calculations. Anything that is less than basic EPS is potentially dilutive.

Number of shares under option	30,000
Option price per share	× $15
Proceeds upon assumed exercise of options	$450,000
Average 2011 market price of common shares	$ 25
Treasury shares that could be acquired with proceeds ($450,000 ÷ $25)	18,000
Excess shares under option over treasury shares that could be repurchased (30,000 − 18,000)	12,000
Per share effect:	
Incremental numerator effect: None	
Incremental denominator effect: 12,000 shares	$ 0
Therefore potentially dilutive	

Illustration 17-26

Incremental Impact of Options

Interest expense for year ($2,000,000 × 7%)	$140,000
Income tax reduction due to interest (35% × $140,000)	49,000
Interest expense avoided (net of tax)	$ 91,000
Number of common shares issued, assuming conversion of bonds (2,000 bonds × 50 shares)	100,000
Per share effect:	
Incremental numerator effect: $91,000	
Incremental denominator effect: 100,000 shares	$ 0.91
Therefore potentially dilutive	

Illustration 17-27

Incremental Impact of 7% Bonds

Interest expense for year ($3,000,000 × 9%)	$270,000
Income tax reduction due to interest (35% × $270,000)	94,500
Interest expense avoided (net of tax)	$175,500
Number of common shares issued, assuming conversion of bonds (3,000 bonds × 50 shares)	150,000
Per share effect (outstanding 1/2 year):	
Incremental numerator effect: $175,500 x 0.5 = $87,750	
Incremental denominator effect: 150,000 shares × 0.5 = 75,000	$ 1.17
Therefore potentially dilutive	

Illustration 17-28

Incremental Impact of 9% Bonds

Illustration 17-29
Incremental Impact of Preferred Shares

Dividend requirement on cumulative preferred (20,000 shares × $10)	$200,000
Income tax effect (dividends not a tax deduction): None	–0–
Dividend requirement avoided	$200,000
Number of common shares issued, assuming conversion of preferred (4 × 20,000 shares)	80,000

Per share effect:
  Incremental numerator effect: $200,000
  Incremental denominator effect: 80,000 shares
	$ 2.50

Therefore neutral	

Illustration 17-30 shows the ranking of all four potentially dilutive securities.

Illustration 17-30

Ranking of Potential Common Shares (Most Dilutive First)

	$ Effect Per Share
Options	–0–
7% convertible bonds	0.91
9% convertible bonds	1.17
$10 convertible preferred	2.50

The next step is to determine earnings per share and, through this determination, to give effect to the ranking in Illustration 17-30. Starting with the earnings per share of $2.50 calculated previously, add the incremental effects of the options to the original calculation, as shown in Illustrations 17-31 to 17-34.

Illustration 17-31

Step-by-Step Calculation of Diluted EPS, Adding Options First (Most Dilutive)

Options	
Income applicable to common shareholders	$1,000,000
Add: Incremental numerator effect of options: None	–0–
Total	$1,000,000
Weighted average number of common shares outstanding	400,000
Add: Incremental denominator effect of options—Illustration 17-26	12,000
Total	412,000
Recalculated earnings per share ($1,000,000 ÷ 412,000 shares)	$ 2.43

Since the recalculated earnings per share is reduced (from $2.50 to $2.43), the effect of the options is dilutive. Again, this effect could have been anticipated because the average market price exceeded the option price ($15).

Illustration 17-32 shows the recalculated earnings per share assuming the 7% bonds are converted.

Illustration 17-32

Step-by-Step Calculation of Diluted EPS, Adding 7% Bonds Next (Next Most Dilutive)

7% Bonds	
Numerator from previous calculation	$1,000,000
Add: Interest expense avoided (net of tax)—Illustration 17-27	91,000
Total	$1,091,000
Denominator from previous calculation (shares)	412,000

Add: Number of common shares assumed issued upon conversion of bonds—Illustration 17-27	100,000
Total	512,000
Recalculated earnings per share ($1,091,000 ÷ 512,000 shares)	$ 2.13

Since the recalculated earnings per share is reduced (from $2.43 to $2.13), the effect of the 7% bonds is dilutive.

Next, in Illustration 17-33, earnings per share is recalculated assuming the conversion of the 9% bonds.

9% Bonds

Numerator from previous calculation	$1,091,000
Add: Interest expense avoided (net of tax)—Illustration 17-28	87,750
Total	$1,178,750
Denominator from previous calculation (shares)	512,000
Add: Number of common shares assumed issued upon conversion of bonds—Illustration 17-28	75,000
Total	587,000
Recalculated earnings per share ($1,178,750 ÷ 587,000 shares)	$ 2.01

Illustration 17-33

Step-by-Step Calculation of Diluted EPS, Adding 9% Bonds Next (Next Most Dilutive)

Since the recalculated earnings per share is reduced (from $2.13 to $2.01), the effect of the 9% convertible bonds is dilutive.

The final step (Illustration 17-34) is the recalculation that includes the 10% preferred shares.

Preferred Shares

Numerator from previous calculation	$1,178,750
Add: Dividend requirements avoided—Illustration 17-29	200,000
Total	$1,378,750
Denominator from previous calculation (shares)	587,000
Add: Number of common shares assumed issued upon conversion of preferred—Illustration 17-29	80,000
Total	667,000
Recalculated earnings per share ($1,378,750 ÷ 667,000 shares)	$ 2.07

Illustration 17-34

Step-by-Step Calculation of Diluted EPS, Adding Preferred Shares Next (Least Dilutive)

The effect of the $10 convertible preferred shares is not dilutive, because the per share effects result in a higher EPS of $2.07. Since the recalculated earnings per share is not reduced, the effects of the convertible preferred shares are not used in the calculation. Diluted earnings per share to be reported is therefore $2.01.

(c) **Presentation of EPS**

The disclosure of earnings per share on the income statement for Andrews Corporation is shown in Illustration 17-35.

Net Income	$1,200,000
Basic earnings per common share	$ 2.50
Diluted earnings per common share	$ 2.01

Illustration 17-35

Presentation of EPS

IFRS AND PRIVATE ENTERPRISE GAAP COMPARISON

Usefulness of EPS

Underlying Concept

The problem with setting standards for calculating EPS is that many of these dilutive financial instruments are very complex and it is not always easy to break them down into their economic components.

EPS is one of the most highly visible standards of measurement for assessing management stewardship and predicting a company's future value. It is therefore a very important number and, because of this importance, GAAP is very specific in regard to its calculation.

Recall Illustration 17-6, which showed the common shareholders' claim on only residual income. Earnings per share provides shareholders with information that helps them predict the value of their shareholdings. The diluted EPS calculation is especially useful since there are many potential common shares outstanding through convertible securities, options and warrants, and other financial instruments, and shareholders need to understand how these instruments can affect their holdings. From an economic perspective, it is therefore important to carefully analyze the potential dilutive impact of the various securities instruments, and the IASB is helping make it possible to do such analyses by continually striving to ensure greater transparency in EPS calculations. Sometimes this is not so easy due to the complexity of the financial statements.

Finance

Earnings per share is also useful in valuing companies. When companies or their shares are valued, "earnings" are often discounted to arrive at an estimated value. While there are many different ways of doing this, discounted cash flow calculations (with earnings often used as a substitute for the calculation) or NPV (net present value) calculations are commonly used to estimate company or share value. Ideally, a **normalized or sustainable cash flow or earnings** number should be used in the valuation calculation since earnings or net income may be of higher or lower quality (as noted in Chapter 4). However, since calculating normalized or sustainable cash flows and earnings requires significant judgement, when valuing common shares the EPS number is sometimes used instead since it is felt to be more reliable and all-inclusinve.

The price earnings ratio provides useful information by relating earnings to the price that the shares are trading at. It is sometimes used to generate a quick estimate of the value of the shares, and therefore the company. It allows an easy comparison with other companies and the information is often readily available. The price earnings ratio divides the price of the share by the earnings per share number. The result is often called the **multiplier**. The multiplier shows the per share value that each dollar of earnings generates. For example, if the share value is $10 and EPS is $1, the multiplier is 10 (10 ÷ 1). **Therefore, each additional dollar of earnings is felt to generate an additional $10 in share price.** This is a very rough calculation only, especially when you think of the judgement that went into calculating that EPS number in the first place. Consider the hundreds of financial reporting choices such as accounting methods, measurement uncertainty, bias, and other judgements. This is one of the major reasons why preparers of financial statements must be aware of the impact of all financial reporting decisions on the bottom line.

Objective 9

Identify the major differences in accounting between accounting standards for private enterprises (PE GAAP/ASPE) and IFRS, and what changes are expected in the near future.

Comparison of IFRS and Private Enterprise GAAP

The main difference between the standards is that PE GAAP does not prescribe standards for calculating EPS at all. The EPS standards therefore only apply to publicly accountable entities in Canada.

Looking Ahead

Where do we go from here? As the accounting for derivatives and financial instruments continues to evolve, standard setters are gradually revisiting other areas to determine the impact of the standards for financial instruments on these other areas. Earnings per share is one such area.

Conversion features included in instruments, such as convertible debt and convertible preferred shares, are in substance embedded options. For instance, in many convertible debt instruments, the conversion feature represents a written call option. Why, then, would we not treat these embedded options as we treat stand-alone options? Why not use the treasury stock or reverse treasury stock method instead of the if-converted method?

Some derivative instruments, such as written put options and forwards to purchase the entity's own shares, are in fact liabilities. How should they be treated for EPS purposes?

With respect to financial instruments that are carried at fair value with gains/losses being booked through net income, many feel that the potentially dilutive impact is already captured when the instruments are revalued to their fair value. This includes some derivatives that are settleable in the entity's own equity instruments, which are treated as financial assets/liabilities.

The IASB and FASB are currently deliberating the responses to an earlier issued Exposure Draft.

Summary of Learning Objectives

1 Understand why earnings per share (EPS) is an important number.

Earnings per share numbers give common shareholders an idea of the amount of earnings that can be attributed to each common share. This information is often used to predict future cash flows from the shares and to value companies.

2 Understand when and how earnings per share must be presented.

Under IFRS, EPS must be presented for all public companies or companies that are intending to go public. The calculations must be presented on the face of the income statement for net income from continuing operations and net income (for both basic EPS and diluted EPS in the case of complex capital structures). When there are discontinued operations the per share impact of these items must also be shown, but it can be shown either on the face of the income statement or in the notes. Comparative calculations must also be shown.

3 Identify potential common shares.

Potential common shares include convertible debt and preferred shares, options and warrants, contingently issuable shares, and other instruments that may result in additional common shares being issued by the company. They are relevant because they may cause the present interests of the common shareholders to become diluted.

4 Calculate earnings per share in a simple capital structure.

Basic earnings per share is an actual calculation that takes income available to common shareholders and divides it by the weighted average number of common shares outstanding during the period.

5 Calculate diluted earnings per share using the if-converted method.

Diluted earnings per share is a "what if" calculation that considers the impact of potential common shares. The if-converted method considers the impact of convertible

Glossary

KEY TERMS

antidilutive securities, 1106
basic EPS, 1099
call options, 1109
complex capital structure, 1100
contingently issuable shares, 1101
diluted EPS, 1099
exercise price, 1109
if-converted method, 1107
income available to common shareholders, 1102
in the money, 1109
potential common/ordinary share, 1100
put options, 1109
reverse treasury stock method, 1112
simple capital structure, 1100

securities such as convertible debt and preferred shares. It assumes that the instruments are converted at the beginning of the year (or issue date, if later) and that any related interest or dividend is thus avoided.

6 **Calculate diluted earnings per share using the treasury stock method.**

The treasury stock method looks at the impact of written call options on EPS numbers. It assumes that the options are exercised at the beginning of the year and that the money from the exercise is used to buy back shares in the open market at the average common share price.

7 **Calculate diluted earnings per share using the reverse treasury stock method.**

The reverse treasury stock method looks at the impact of written put options. It assumes that the options are exercised at the beginning of the year and that the company must first issue shares in the market (at the average share price) to obtain sufficient funds to buy the shares under the option.

8 **Identify antidilutive potential common shares.**

Antidilutive potential common shares are irrelevant since they result in diluted EPS calculations that are higher than the basic EPS; thus, these numbers are antidilutive. Diluted EPS must show the worst possible EPS number. Note that purchased options and written options that are not in the money are ignored for purposes of calculating diluted EPS because they are either antidilutive or will not be exercised.

9 **Identify differences in the accounting standards for private enterprises and IFRS, and what changes are expected in the future.**

PE GAAP does not prescribe accounting standards for EPS. The IASB and FASB are working on a revised plan of action to study the issues.

Brief Exercises

BE17-1 The 2012 income statement of Schmidt Corporation showed net income of $1,230,000 and a loss from discontinued operations of $105,000. Schmidt had 40,000 common shares outstanding all year. Prepare Schmidt's income statement presentation of earnings per share. **(LO 2)**

BE17-2 Hedley Corporation had 2011 net income of $1.4 million. During 2011, Hedley paid a dividend of $5 per share on 100,000 preferred shares. Hedley also had 220,000 common shares outstanding during the year. Calculate Hedley's 2011 earnings per share. **(LO 4)**

BE17-3 Assume the same information as in BE17-2 except that the preferred shares are non-cumulative and the dividend has not been declared or paid. **(LO 4)**

BE17-4 Assume the same information as in BE17-2 except that the preferred shares are cumulative and the dividends have not yet been declared or paid. **(LO 4)**

BE17-5 Bentley Corporation had 120,000 common shares outstanding on January 1, 2011. On May 1, 2011, Bentley issued 65,000 shares. On July 1, Bentley repurchased and cancelled 22,000 shares. Calculate Bentley's weighted average number of shares outstanding for the year ended December 31, 2011. **(LO 4)**

BE17-6 Laurin Limited had 42,000 common shares outstanding on January 1, 2011. On March 1, 2011, Laurin issued 20,000 shares in exchange for equipment. On July 1, Laurin repurchased and cancelled 10,000 shares. On October 1, 2011, Laurin declared and issued a 10% stock dividend. Calculate the weighted average number of shares outstanding for Laurin for the year ended December 31, 2011. **(LO 4)**

BE17-7 Assume the same information as in BE17-6 except that on October 1, 2011, Laurin declared a 3-for-1 stock split instead of a 10% stock dividend. **(LO 4)**

BE17-8 Assume the same information as in BE17-6 except that on October 1, 2011, Laurin declared a 1-for-2 reverse stock split instead of a 10% stock dividend. **(LO 4)**

BE17-9 Tomba Corporation had 300,000 common shares outstanding on January 1, 2011. On May 1, Tomba issued 30,000 shares. (a) Calculate the weighted average number of shares outstanding for the year ended December 31, 2011, if the 30,000 shares were issued for cash. (b) Calculate the weighted average number of shares outstanding for the year ended December 31, 2011, if the 30,000 shares were issued in a stock dividend. **(LO 4)**

BE17-10 Francine Limited was incorporated with a share capital consisting of 100,000 common shares. In January 2011, it issued 20,000 mandatorily convertible preferred shares. The terms of the prospectus for the issuance of the preferred shares require that these convertible preferred shares have to be converted into common shares, at the rate of one preferred share for one common share, during the fourth quarter of 2012. The preferred shares pay an annual dividend of $4 per share. Assume that for the fiscal year ended December 31, 2011, the company made an after-tax profit of $140,000. Calculate the 2011 earnings per share. **(LO 4)**

BE17-11 Sandbox Corporation reported net income of $700,000 in 2011 and had 115,000 common shares outstanding throughout the year. Also outstanding all year were 9,500 of cumulative preferred shares, with each being convertible into two common shares. The preferred shares pay an annual dividend of $5 per share. Sandbox's tax rate is 40%. Calculate Sandbox's 2011 diluted earnings per share. **(LO 4, 5)**

BE17-12 Rockland Corporation earned net income of $300,000 in 2011 and had 100,000 common shares outstanding throughout the year. Also outstanding all year was $800,000 of 10% bonds that are convertible into 16,000 common shares. Rockland's tax rate is 40%. Calculate Rockland's 2011 diluted earnings per share. For simplicity, ignore the IFRS requirement to record the debt and equity components of the bonds separately. **(LO 5)**

BE17-13 Lawrence Limited has 150,000 common shares outstanding throughout the year. On June 30, Lawrence issued 28,000 convertible preferred shares that are convertible into one common share each. Calculate the weighted average common shares for purposes of the diluted EPS calculations. Assume that the preferred shares are dilutive. **(LO 5)**

BE17-14 Bedard Corporation reported net income of $300,000 in 2012 and had 200,000 common shares outstanding throughout the year. Also outstanding all year were 45,000 (written) options to purchase common shares at $10 per share. The average market price for the common shares during the year was $15 per share. Calculate the diluted earnings per share. **(LO 6)**

(LO 6)   **BE17-15**   Glavin Limited purchased 40,000 call options during the year. The options give the company the right to buy its own common shares for $9 each. The average market price during the year was $12 per share. Calculate the incremental shares outstanding for Glavin Limited.

(LO 7)   **BE17-16**   Use the same information as in BE17-15 and assume that Glavin also wrote put options that allow the holder to sell Glavin's shares to Glavin at $13 per share. Calculate the incremental shares outstanding for Glavin Limited.

(LO 8)   **BE17-17**   Assume the same information as in BE17-15 except that Glavin can buy its own common shares for $10 each. How should the options be treated for purposes of the diluted EPS calculation?

(LO 8)   **BE17-18**   Assume the same information as in BE17-16 except that the put options allow the holder to sell Glavin's shares to Glavin at $11 each. How should these options be treated for purposes of the diluted EPS calculation?

Exercises

(LO 2, 4)   **E17-1**   **(EPS—Simple Capital Structure)** On January 1, 2012, Poelman Corp. had 580,000 common shares outstanding. During 2012, it had the following transactions that affected the common share account:

Feb. 1	Issued 180,000 shares.
Mar. 1	Issued a 10% stock dividend.
May 1	Acquired 200,000 common shares and retired them.
June 1	Issued a 3-for-1 stock split.
Oct. 1	Issued 60,000 shares.

The company's year end is December 31.

Instructions

(a) Determine the weighted average number of shares outstanding as at December 31, 2012.

(b) Assume that Poelman earned net income of $3,456,000 during 2012. In addition, it had 100,000 9%, $100 par, non-convertible, non-cumulative preferred shares outstanding for the entire year. Because of liquidity limitations, however, the company did not declare and pay a preferred dividend in 2012. Calculate earnings per share for 2012, using the weighted average number of shares determined in part (a).

(c) Assume the same facts as in part (b), except that the preferred shares were cumulative. Calculate earnings per share for 2012.

(d) Assume the same facts as in part (b), except that net income included a loss from discontinued operations of $432,000, net of applicable income taxes. Calculate earnings per share for 2012.

Digging Deeper

(e) What is the reasoning behind using a weighted average calculation for the number of shares outstanding in the EPS ratio?

(LO 2, 4)   **E17-2**   **(EPS—Simple Capital Structure)** Voisin Inc. had 210,000 common shares outstanding on December 31, 2011. During 2012, the company issued 8,000 shares on May 1 and retired 14,000 shares on October 31. For 2012, the company reported net income of $229,690 after a loss from discontinued operations of $40,600 (net of tax).

Instructions

(a) What earnings per share data should be reported at the bottom of Voisin Inc.'s income statement?

(b) Is it possible for a corporation to have a simple capital structure one fiscal year and a complex capital structure in another fiscal year? If yes, how could this happen?

(LO 2, 4)   **E17-3**   **(EPS—Simple Capital Structure)** Fantino Inc. presented the following data:

Net income	$5,500,000
Preferred shares: 50,000 shares outstanding, $100 par,	
8% cumulative, not convertible	$5,000,000
Common shares: Shares outstanding, Jan. 1, 2012	650,000
Issued for cash, May 1, 2012	100,000
Acquired treasury stock for cash, Sept. 1, 2012 (shares cancelled)	150,000
2-for-1 stock split, Oct. 1, 2012	

Digging
Deeper

Instructions

(a) Calculate earnings per share for the year ended December 31, 2012.

(b) Discuss what the effect would be on your calculation in (a) if the stock split had been declared on January 30, 2013, instead of on October 1, 2012, assuming the financial statements of Fantino Inc. for the year ending December 31, 2012, were issued after January 30, 2013.

E17-4 (EPS—Simple Capital Structure) A portion of the combined statement of income and retained earnings of (LO 2, 4) Simba Inc. for the current year ended December 31 follows:

Income before discontinued operations		$ 30,000,000
Loss from discontinued operations, net of applicable income tax (Note 1)		1,740,000
Net income		28,260,000
Retained earnings at beginning of year		93,250,000
		121,510,000
Dividends declared:		
On preferred shares, $6.00 per share	$ 540,000	
On common shares, $1.75 per share	14,875,000	15,415,000
Retained earnings at end of year		$106,095,000

Note 1. During the year, Simba Inc. suffered a loss from discontinued operations of $1,740,000 after the applicable income tax reduction of $1.2 million.

At the end of the current year, Simba Inc. has outstanding 12.5 million common shares and 90,000 shares of 6% preferred.

On April 1 of the current year, Simba Inc. issued 1 million common shares for $32 per share to help finance the loss.

Instructions

Calculate the earnings per share on common shares for the current year as it should be reported to shareholders.

E17-5 (EPS—Simple Capital Structure) On January 1, 2011, Lui Limited had shares outstanding as follows: (LO 2, 4)

6% cumulative preferred shares, $100 par value,	
10,000 shares issued and outstanding	$1,000,000
Common shares, 200,000 shares issued and outstanding	2,000,000

To acquire the net assets of three smaller companies, the company authorized the issuance of an additional 330,000 common shares. The acquisitions were as follows:

Date of Acquisition	Shares Issued
Company A: April 1, 2011	190,000
Company B: July 1, 2011	100,000
Company C: October 1, 2011	40,000

On May 14, 2011, Lui realized a $97,000 gain (before taxes) on a discontinued operation from a business segment that had originally been purchased in 1994.

On December 31, 2011, the company recorded income of $680,000 before tax and not including the discontinued operation gain. Lui has a 50% tax rate.

Instructions

(a) Calculate the earnings per share data that should appear on the company's financial statements as at December 31, 2011.

(b) What determines that Lui has a simple capital structure?

E17-6 (Weighted Average Number of Shares) On January 1, 2011, Summerhill Distillers Inc. had 475,000 common (LO 4) shares outstanding. On April 1, the corporation issued 47,500 new common shares to raise additional capital. On July 1, the corporation declared and distributed a 20% stock dividend on its common shares. On November 1, the corporation repurchased on the market 45,000 of its own outstanding common shares to make them available for issuances relating to its key executives' outstanding stock options.

Instructions

(a) Calculate the weighted average number of shares outstanding as at December 31, 2011.

(b) Assume that Summerhill Distillers Inc. had a 1-for-5 reverse stock split instead of a 20% stock dividend on July 1, 2011. Calculate the weighted average number of shares outstanding as at December 31, 2011.

(LO 4)   E17-7   (EPS—Simple Capital Structure) At January 1, 2012, Ming Limited's outstanding shares included the following:

> 280,000 $50 par value, 7%, cumulative preferred shares
> 900,000 common shares

Net income for 2012 was $2,130,000. No cash dividends were declared or paid during 2012. On February 15, 2013, however, all preferred dividends in arrears were paid, together with a 5% stock dividend on common shares. There were no dividends in arrears before 2012.

On April 1, 2012, 550,000 common shares were sold for $10 per share and on October 1, 2012, 310,000 common shares were purchased for $20 per share.

The financial statements for 2012 were issued in March 2013.

Instructions

(a) Calculate earnings per share for the year ended December 31, 2012.

(b) What is the significance of the declaration and payment date of February 15, 2013, for the dividend on preferred shares? What effect, if any, will this transaction have on the December 31, 2012 financial statements?

Digging Deeper

(c) Would your answer in part (b) change if the dividend arrears on preferred shares were for two years as at December 31, 2012?

(LO 4)   E17-8   (Weighted Average Number of Shares) Gogeon Inc. uses a calendar year for financial reporting. The company is authorized to issue 10 million common shares. At no time has Gogeon issued any potentially dilutive securities. The following list is a summary of Gogeon's common share activities:

Number of common shares issued and outstanding at December 31, 2010	6,500,000
Shares issued as a result of a 10% stock dividend on September 30, 2011	650,000
Shares issued for cash on March 31, 2012	2,500,000
Number of common shares issued and outstanding at December 31, 2012	9,650,000

A 3-for-1 stock split of Gogeon's common shares occurred on March 31, 2013.

Instructions

(a) Calculate the weighted average number of common shares to use in calculating earnings per common share for 2011 on the 2012 comparative income statement.

(b) Calculate the weighted average number of common shares to use in calculating earnings per common share for 2012 on the 2012 comparative income statement.

(c) Calculate the weighted average number of common shares to use in calculating earnings per common share for 2012 on the 2013 comparative income statement.

(d) Calculate the weighted average number of common shares to use in calculating earnings per common share for 2013 on the 2013 comparative income statement.

(CMA adapted)

(LO 5)   E17-9   (EPS with Convertible Bonds, Various Situations) In 2010, Buraka Inc. issued $75,000 of 8% bonds at par, with each $1,000 bond being convertible into 100 common shares. The company had revenues of $17,500 and expenses of $8,400 for 2011, not including interest and taxes (assume a tax rate of 40%). Throughout 2011, 2,000 common shares were outstanding, and none of the bonds were converted or redeemed. (For simplicity, assume that the convertible bonds' equity element is not recorded.)

Instructions

(a) Calculate diluted earnings per share for the year ended December 31, 2011.

(b) Repeat the calculation in (a), but assume that the 75 bonds were issued on September 1, 2011 (rather than in 2010), and that none have been converted or redeemed.

(c) Repeat the calculation in (a), but assume that 25 of the 75 bonds were converted on July 1, 2011.

E17-10   (EPS with Convertible Bonds) On June 1, 2010, Mohawk Corp. and Shortreed Limited merged to form   **(LO 5)** Livingston Inc. A total of 800,000 shares were issued to complete the merger. The new corporation uses the calendar year as its fiscal year.

On April 1, 2012, the company issued an additional 400,000 shares for cash. All 1.2 million shares were outstanding on December 31, 2012. Livingston Inc. also issued $600,000 of 20-year, 8% convertible bonds at par on July 1, 2012. Each $1,000 bond converts to 40 common shares at any interest date. None of the bonds have been converted to date. If the bonds had been issued without the conversion feature, the annual interest rate would have been 10%.

Livingston Inc. is preparing its annual report for the fiscal year ending December 31, 2012. The annual report will show earnings per share figures based on a reported after-tax net income of $1,540,000 (the tax rate is 40%).

Instructions

(a) Determine for 2012 the number of shares to be used in calculating:
   1. basic earnings per share.
   2. diluted earnings per share.

(b) Determine for 2012 the earnings figures to be used in calculating:
   1. basic earnings per share.
   2. diluted earnings per share.

(CMA adapted)

E17-11   (EPS with Convertible Bonds and Preferred Shares) Ottey Corporation issued $4 million of 10-year, 7%   **(LO 5)** callable convertible subordinated debentures on January 2, 2011. The debentures have a face value of $1,000, with interest payable annually. The current conversion ratio is 14:1, and in two years it will increase to 18:1. At the date of issue, the bonds were sold at 98 to yield a 7.2886% effective interest rate. Bond discount is amortized using the effective interest method. Ottey's effective tax was 35%. Net income in 2011 was $7.5 million, and the company had 2 million shares outstanding during the entire year. For simplicity, ignore the requirement to record the debentures' debt and equity components separately.

Instructions

(a) Prepare a schedule to calculate both basic and diluted earnings per share for the year ended December 31, 2011.

(b) Discuss how the schedule would differ if the security were convertible preferred shares.

(c) Assume that Ottey Corporation experienced a substantial loss instead of income for the fiscal year ending December 31, 2011. How would you respond to the argument made by a friend who states: "The interest expense from the conversion of the debentures is not actually saved, and there are no income taxes to be paid on the additional income that is assumed to have been created from the conversion of the debentures."

Digging
Deeper

E17-12   (EPS with Convertible Bonds and Preferred Shares) On January 1, 2011, Shaylyn Limited issued $2.5 mil-   **(LO 5)** lion of face value, 10-year, 7% bonds at par. Each $1,000 bond is convertible into 15 common shares. Shaylyn's net income in 2011 was $250,000, and its tax rate was 30%. The company had 100,000 common shares outstanding throughout 2011. None of the bonds were exercised in 2011. For simplicity, ignore the requirement to record the bonds' debt and equity components separately.

Instructions

(a) Calculate diluted earnings per share for the year ended December 31, 2011.

(b) Calculate diluted earnings per share for 2011, assuming the same facts as above, except that $1.5 million of 7% convertible preferred shares was issued instead of the bonds. Each $100 preferred share is convertible into four common shares.

E17-13   (EPS with Convertible Bonds and Preferred Shares) Mininova Corporation is preparing earnings per share   **(LO 5)** data for 2012. The net income for the year ended December 31, 2012, was $400,000 and there were 60,000 common shares outstanding during the entire year. Mininova has the following two convertible securities outstanding:

10% convertible bonds (each $1,000 bond is convertible into 25 common shares)	$100,000
5% convertible $100 par value preferred shares (each share is convertible into two common shares)	50,000

Both convertible securities were issued at face value in 2009. There were no conversions during 2012, and Mininova's income tax rate is 34%. The preferred shares are cumulative. For simplicity, ignore the requirement to record the debt and equity components of the bonds separately.

Instructions

(a) Calculate Mininova's basic earnings per share for 2012.

(b) Calculate Mininova's diluted earnings per share for 2012.

(c) Recalculate Mininova's basic and diluted earnings per share for 2012, assuming instead that the preferred shares pay a 14% dividend.

(LO 5)   **E17-14   (EPS with Convertible Bonds with Conversion and Preferred Shares)** Use the same information as in E17-13, except for the changes in part (c). Assume instead that 40% of the convertible bonds were converted to common shares on April 1, 2012.

Instructions

(a) Calculate Mininova's weighted average common shares outstanding.

(b) Calculate Mininova's basic earnings per share for 2012.

(c) Calculate Mininova's diluted earnings per share for 2012.

Digging Deeper

(d) What do you notice about the results of the diluted earnings per share calculation when conversions occur during the year and when they do not occur?

(LO 5)   **E17-15   (EPS with Convertible Bonds and Preferred Shares)** Rao Corporation had a net income of $50,000 for the year ended December 31, 2011, and a weighted average number of common shares outstanding of 10,000. The following information is provided regarding the capital structure:

1. 7% convertible debt, 200 bonds each convertible into 40 common shares. The bonds were outstanding for the entire year. The income tax rate is 40%. The bonds were issued at par ($1,000 per bond). No bonds were converted during the year.

2. 4% convertible, cumulative $100 preferred shares, 1,000 shares issued and outstanding. Each preferred share is convertible into two common shares. The preferred shares were issued at par and were outstanding the entire year. No shares were converted during the year.

Instructions

(a) Calculate the basic earnings per share for 2012.

(b) Briefly explain the if-converted method.

(c) Calculate the diluted earnings per share for 2012, using the if-converted method. For simplicity, ignore the requirement to record the debt and equity components of the bond separately.

(LO 6, 8)   **E17-16   (EPS with Options, Various Situations)** Vimeo Corp.'s net income for 2011 is $90,000. The only potentially dilutive securities outstanding were 1,000 call options issued during 2010, with each option being exercisable for one share at $14. None have been exercised, and 50,000 common shares were outstanding during 2011.
The average market price of the company's shares during 2011 was $20.

Instructions

(a) Calculate diluted earnings per share for the year ended December 31, 2011 (round to nearest cent).

(b) Assuming that the 1,000 call options were instead issued on October 1, 2011 (rather than in 2010), calculate diluted earnings per share for the year ended December 31, 2011 (round to nearest cent). The average market price during the last three months of 2011 was $20.

(c) How would your answers for parts (a) and (b) change if, in addition to the information for parts (a) and (b), the company issued (wrote) 1,000 put options with an exercise price of $10?

(LO 6)   **E17-17   (EPS with Warrants)** Howard Corporation earned $480,000 during a period when it had an average of 100,000 common shares outstanding. The common shares sold at an average market price of $23 per share during the period. Also outstanding were 18,000 warrants that could each be exercised to purchase one common share for $10.

Instructions

(a) Are the warrants dilutive?

(b) Calculate basic earnings per share.

(c) Calculate diluted earnings per share.

E17-18 **(EPS with Contingent Issuance Agreement)** Winnifred Inc. recently purchased Hanover Corp., a large **(LO 7)** home-painting corporation. One of the terms of the merger was that, if Hanover's income for 2011 were $110,000 or more, 10,000 additional shares would be issued to Hanover's shareholders in 2012. Hanover's income for 2010 was $120,000.

Instructions

(a) Would the contingent shares have to be considered in Winnifred's 2010 earnings per share calculations?

(b) Assume the same facts, except that the 10,000 shares are contingent on Hanover achieving a net income of $130,000 in 2011. Would the contingent shares have to be considered in Winnifred's earnings per share calculations for 2010?

Problems

P17-1 Frontline Corporation is a new audit client of yours and has not reported earnings per share data in its annual reports to shareholders in the past. The treasurer, Andrew Benninger, has asked you to provide information about the reporting of earnings per share data in the current year's annual report in accordance with generally accepted accounting principles according to IFRS.

Instructions

(a) Define the term "earnings per share" as it applies to a corporation with a capitalization structure that is composed of only one class of common shares. Explain how earnings per share should be calculated and how the information should be disclosed in the corporation's financial statements.

(b) Discuss the treatment, if any, that should be given to each of the following items in calculating the earnings per share of common shares for financial statement reporting:

1. Outstanding preferred shares issued at a premium with a par value liquidation right

2. The exercise at a price below market value but above carrying amount of a call option on common shares that was issued during the current fiscal year to officers of the corporation

3. The replacement of a machine immediately before the close of the current fiscal year at a cost that is 20% above the original cost of the replaced machine. The new machine will perform the same function as the old machine, which was sold for its carrying amount.

4. The declaration of current dividends on cumulative preferred shares

5. The existence of purchased call options that allow the company to purchase shares of its own common stock at a price that is lower than the average market price

6. The acquisition of some of the corporation's outstanding common shares during the current fiscal year. The shares were classified as treasury stock.

7. A 2-for-1 stock split of common shares during the current fiscal year

8. A provision created out of retained earnings for a contingent liability related to a possible lawsuit

P17-2 Melton Corporation is preparing the comparative financial statements for the annual report to its shareholders for the fiscal years ended May 31, 2011, and May 31, 2012. The income from operations was $1.8 million and $2.5 million, respectively, for each year. In both years, the company incurred a 10% interest expense on $2.4 million of debt for an obligation that requires interest-only payments for five years. The company experienced a loss of $600,000 from the discontinued operation of its Scotland facility in February 2012. The company uses a 40% effective tax rate for income taxes.

The capital structure of Melton Corporation on June 1, 2010, consisted of 1 million common shares outstanding and 20,000 $50, par value, 6% cumulative preferred shares. There were no preferred dividends in arrears, and the company had not issued any convertible securities, options, or warrants.

On October 1, 2010, Melton sold an additional 500,000 common shares at $20 per share. Melton distributed a 20% stock dividend on the common shares outstanding on January 1, 2011. On December 1, 2011, Melton was able to sell an additional 800,000 common shares at $22 per share. These were the only common share transactions that occurred during the two fiscal years.

Instructions

(a) Identify whether the capital structure at Melton Corporation is a simple or complex capital structure, and explain why.

(b) Determine the weighted average number of shares that Melton Corporation would use in calculating earnings per share for the fiscal year ended:

1. May 31, 2011.

2. May 31, 2012.

(c) Prepare, in good form, a comparative income statement that begins with income from operations for Melton Corporation for the fiscal years ended May 31, 2011, and May 31, 2012. This statement will be included in Melton's annual report and should display the appropriate earnings per share presentations.

(CMA adapted)

P17-3   Nazia Gupta of the controller's office of Thompson Corporation was given the assignment of determining the basic and diluted earnings per share values for the year ending December 31, 2012. Gupta has gathered the following information.

1. The company is authorized to issue 8 million common shares. As at December 31, 2011, 2 million shares had been issued and were outstanding.

2. The per share market prices of the common shares on selected dates were as follows:

	Price per Share
July 1, 2011	$20.00
Jan. 1, 2012	21.00
Apr. 1, 2012	25.00
July 1, 2012	11.00
Aug. 1, 2012	10.50
Nov. 1, 2012	9.00
Dec. 31, 2012	10.00

3. A total of 700,000 shares of an authorized 1.2 million convertible preferred shares had been issued on July 1, 2011. The shares were issued at $25, and have a cumulative dividend of $3 per share. The shares are convertible into common shares at the rate of one convertible preferred share for one common share. The rate of conversion is to be automatically adjusted for stock splits and stock dividends. Dividends are paid quarterly on September 30, December 31, March 31, and June 30.

4. Thompson Corporation is subject to a 40% income tax rate.

5. The after-tax net income for the year ended December 31, 2012, was $11,550,000.

The following specific activities took place during 2012:

1. January 1: A 5% common stock dividend was issued. The dividend had been declared on December 1, 2011, to all shareholders of record on December 29, 2011.

2. April 1: A total of 400,000 shares of the $3 convertible preferred shares were converted into common shares. The company issued new common shares and retired the preferred shares. This was the only conversion of the preferred shares during 2012.

3. July 1: A 2-for-1 split of the common shares became effective on this date. The board of directors had authorized the split on June 1.

4. August 1: A total of 300,000 common shares were issued to acquire a factory building.

5. November 1: A total of 24,000 common shares were purchased on the open market at $9 per share and cancelled.

6. Cash dividends to common shareholders were declared and paid as follows:

April 15: $0.30 per share
October 15: $0.20 per share

7. Cash dividends to preferred shareholders were declared and paid as scheduled.

Instructions

(a) Determine the number of shares to use in calculating basic earnings per share for the year ended December 31, 2012.

(b) Determine the number of shares to use in calculating diluted earnings per share for the year ended December 31, 2012.

(c) Calculate the adjusted net income amount to use as the numerator in the basic earnings per share calculation for the year ended December 31, 2012.

P17-4 Cullen Corporation Ltd. has the following capital structure at December 31, 2011, its fiscal year end:

	2011	2010
Number of common shares	375,000	330,000
Number of non-convertible, non-cumulative preferred A shares	10,000	10,000
Amount of 7% convertible bonds	$2,000,000	$2,000,000

The following additional information is available.

1. On July 31, 2011, Cullen Corporation exchanged common shares for a large piece of equipment.

2. Income before discontinued operations for 2011 was $950,000, and a loss from discontinued operations of $150,000 was recorded, net of applicable tax recovery.

3. During 2011, dividends in the amount of $4.00 per share were paid on the preferred A shares.

4. Each $1,000 bond can be converted into 20 common shares.

5. There were unexercised stock options, outstanding since 2008, that allow holders to purchase 20,000 common shares at $40.00 per share.

6. Warrants to purchase 20,000 common shares at $52.00 per share were outstanding at the end of 2012.

7. The average market value of the common shares for 2011 was $50.00.

8. Cullen's tax rate is 40%.

9. Cullen declared and paid a $100,000 dividend to common shareholders on June 1, 2011.

Instructions

(a) Determine the weighted average number of common shares that would be used in calculating earnings per share for the year ended December 31, 2011.

(b) Starting with the heading "Income before discontinued operations," prepare the bottom portion of the income statement for the year ended December 31, 2011, including all necessary earnings per share disclosures.

(AICPA adapted)

P17-5 Denise Laframboise is the controller at Yeung Pharmaceutical Industries, a public company. She is currently preparing the calculation for basic and diluted earnings per share and the related disclosure for Yeung's external financial statements. The following is selected financial information for the fiscal year ended June 30, 2011:

YEUNG PHARMACEUTICAL INDUSTRIES
Selected Statement of Financial Position Information
June 30, 2011

Long-term debt	
Notes payable, 10%	$ 1,000,000
7% convertible bonds payable	5,000,000
10% bonds payable	6,000,000
Total long-term debt	$12,000,000
Shareholders' equity	
Preferred shares, $4.25 cumulative, 100,000 shares authorized,	
25,000 shares issued and outstanding	$ 1,250,000
Common shares, unlimited number of shares authorized,	
1,000,000 shares issued and outstanding	4,500,000
Contributed surplus—conversion rights	500,000
Retained earnings	6,000,000
Total shareholders' equity	$12,250,000

The following transactions have also occurred at Yeung:

1. Options were granted by the company in 2009 to purchase 100,000 shares at $15 per share. Although no options were exercised during 2011, the average price per common share during fiscal year 2011 was $20.

2. Each bond was issued at face value. The 7% convertible debenture will convert into common shares at 50 shares per $1,000 bond. It is exercisable after five years and was issued in 2010. Ignore any requirement to record the bonds' debt and equity components separately.

3. The $4.25 preferred shares were issued in 2009.

4. There are no preferred dividends in arrears; however, preferred dividends were not declared in fiscal year 2011.

5. The 1 million common shares were outstanding for the entire 2011 fiscal year.

6. Net income for fiscal year 2011 was $1.5 million, and the average income tax rate was 40%.

Instructions

(a) For the fiscal year ended June 30, 2011, calculate the following for Yeung Pharmaceutical Industries:

    1. Basic earnings per share

    2. Diluted earnings per share

Digging Deeper

(b) Explain how premiums and discounts on outstanding convertible bonds affect the calculation of diluted earnings per share.

P17-6   An excerpt from the balance sheet of Denomme Limited follows:

DENOMME LIMITED
Selected Balance Sheet Information
At December 31, 2011

Long-term debt	
Notes payable, 10%	$ 2,000,000
4% convertible bonds payable	3,000,000
6% convertible bonds payable	4,000,000
Total long-term debt	$ 9,000,000
Shareholders' equity	
$0.80 cumulative, no par value, convertible preferred shares (unlimited number of shares authorized, 280,000 shares issued and outstanding)	$ 4,000,000
Common shares, no par value (5,000,000 shares authorized, 1,800,000 shares issued and outstanding)	18,000,000
Contributed surplus	100,000
Retained earnings	5,000,000
Total shareholders' equity	$27,100,000

Notes and Assumptions

December 31, 2011

1. Options were granted/written in 2010 that give the holder the right to purchase 50,000 common shares at $12 per share. The average market price of the company's common shares during 2011 was $18 per share. The options expire in 2019 and no options were exercised in 2011.

2. The 4% bonds were issued in 2010 at face value. The 6% convertible bonds were issued on July 1, 2011, at face value. Each convertible bond is convertible into 80 common shares (each bond has a face value of $1,000).

3. The convertible preferred shares were issued at the beginning of 2011. Each share of preferred is convertible into one common share.

4. The average income tax rate is 42%.

5. The common shares were outstanding during the entire year.

6. Preferred dividends were not declared in 2011.

7. Net income was $1,750,000 in 2011.

8. No bonds or preferred shares were converted during 2011.

Instructions

(a) Calculate basic earnings per share for 2011.

(b) Calculate diluted earnings per share for 2011. For simplicity, ignore the requirement to record the debt and equity components of the bonds separately.

P17-7 Lapardy Limited had net income for the fiscal year ending June 30, 2011, of $16.4 million. There were 2 million common shares outstanding throughout 2011. The average market price of the common shares for the entire fiscal year was $75. Lapardy's tax rate was 40% for 2011.

Lapardy had the following potential common shares outstanding during 2011:

1. Options to buy 100,000 common shares at $60 per share

2. 800,000 convertible preferred shares entitled to a cumulative dividend of $8 per share. Each preferred share is convertible into two common shares.

3. 5% convertible debentures with a principal amount of $100 million, issued at par. Each $1,000 debenture is convertible into 20 common shares.

Instructions

For the fiscal year ended June 30, 2011, calculate the following for Lapardy Limited. For simplicity, ignore the requirement to record the debt and equity components separately.

(a) Basic earnings per share

(b) Diluted earnings per share

P17-8 As auditor for Checkem & Associates, you have been assigned to review Tao Corporation's calculation of earnings per share for the current year. The controller, Mac Taylor, has supplied you with the following calculations:

Net income	$3,374,960
Common shares issued and outstanding:	
Beginning of year	1,285,000
End of year	1,200,000
Average	1,242,500
Earnings per share:	

$$\frac{\$3,374,960}{1,242,500} = \$2.72 \text{ per share}$$

You have gathered the following additional information:

1. The only equity securities are the common shares.

2. There are no options or warrants outstanding to purchase common shares.

3. There are no convertible debt securities.

4. Activity in common shares during the year was as follows:

Outstanding, Jan. 1	1,285,000
Shares acquired, Oct. 1	(250,000)
	1,035,000
Shares issued, Dec. 1	165,000
Outstanding, Dec. 31	1,200,000

Instructions

(a) Based on the information, do you agree with the controller's calculation of earnings per share for the year? If you disagree, prepare a revised calculation.

(b) Assume the same facts except that call options had also been issued for 140,000 common shares at $10 per share. These options were outstanding at the beginning of the year and none had been exercised or cancelled during the year. The average market price of the common shares during the year was $20 and the ending market price was $25. Prepare a calculation of earnings per share.

P17-9   The following information is for Blitzen Limited for 2011:

Net income for the year	$1,200,000
8% convertible bonds issued at par ($1,000 per bond), with each bond convertible into 30 common shares	2,300,000
6% convertible, cumulative preferred shares, $100 par value, with each share convertible into 3 common shares	4,000,000
Common shares (600,000 shares outstanding)	6,000,000
Stock options (granted in a prior year) to purchase 75,000 common shares at $20 per share	750,000
Tax rate for 2011	40%
Average market price of common shares	$25 per share

There were no changes during 2011 in the number of common shares, preferred shares, or convertible bonds outstanding. For simplicity, ignore the requirement to book the convertible bonds' equity portion separately.

Instructions

(a) Calculate basic earnings per share for 2011.

(b) Calculate diluted earnings per share for 2011.

P17-10   Cecillia Corporation is preparing the comparative financial statements to be included in the annual report to shareholders. Cecillia's fiscal year ends May 31. The following information is available.

1. Income from operations before income taxes for Cecillia was $1.4 million and $660,000, respectively, for the fiscal years ended May 31, 2012 and 2011.

2. Cecillia experienced a loss from discontinued operations of $500,000 from a business segment disposed of on March 3, 2012.

3. A 41% combined income tax rate applies to all of Cecillia Corporation's profits, gains, and losses.

4. Cecillia's capital structure consists of preferred shares and common shares. The company has not issued any convertible securities or warrants and there are no outstanding stock options.

5. Cecillia issued 150,000 $100 par value, 6% cumulative preferred shares in 2004. All of these shares are outstanding, and no preferred dividends are in arrears.

6. There were 1.5 million common shares outstanding on June 1, 2010. On September 1, 2010, Cecillia sold an additional 300,000 common shares at $17 per share. Cecillia distributed a 15% stock dividend on the common shares outstanding on December 1, 2011.

7. These were the only common share transactions during the past two fiscal years.

Instructions

(a) Determine the weighted average number of common shares that would be used in calculating earnings per share on the current comparative income statement for:

1. the year ended May 31, 2012.

2. the year ended May 31, 2011.

(b) Starting with income from operations before income taxes, prepare a comparative income statement for the years ended May 31, 2012 and 2011. The statement will be part of Cecillia Corporation's annual report to shareholders and should include an appropriate earnings per share presentation.

(c) A corporation's capital structure is the result of its past financing decisions. Furthermore, the earnings per share data that are presented on a corporation's financial statements depend on the corporation's capital structure.

1. Explain why Cecillia Corporation is considered to have a simple capital structure.

2. Describe how earnings per share data would be presented for a corporation that had a complex capital structure.

(CMA adapted)

P17-11   Leviq Enterprises Ltd. has a tax rate of 40% and reported net income of $8.5 million in 2011. The following details are from the balance sheet of Leviq as at December 31, 2011, the end of its fiscal year:

Long-Term Debt:	
Bonds payable due Dec. 31, 2017, 10% (issued at par)	$ 5,000,000
Bonds payable, face value $9,000,000, due Dec. 31, 2021, 7.25%, convertible into common shares at the investor's option at the rate of two shares per $100 of bonds	8,600,000
Shareholders' Equity:	
Preferred shares, $4.50 cumulative, convertible into common shares at the rate of two common shares for each preferred share, 120,000 shares outstanding	$ 5,500,000
Preferred shares, $3.00 cumulative, convertible into common shares at the rate of one common share for each preferred share, 400,000 shares outstanding	10,000,000
Common shares, 1,700,000 shares outstanding	
Contributed surplus—conversion rights for bonds	750,000
Retained earnings	9,500,000

Other information:

1. Quarterly dividends were declared on March 1, June 1, September 1, and December 1 for the preferred shares and paid 10 days after the date of declaration.

2. Dividends paid on common shares amounted to $980,000 during the year and were paid on December 20, 2011.

3. Interest expense on bonds payable totalled $1,465,000, including bond discount amortization, which is recorded using the effective interest amortization method.

4. There were no issuances of common shares during the 2011 fiscal year, and no conversions.

Instructions

(a) Determine the amount of interest expense incurred in 2011 for each of the bonds outstanding at December 31, 2011.

(b) Calculate basic earnings per share for 2011.

(c) Determine the potential for dilution for each security that is convertible into common shares.

(d) Calculate diluted earnings per share for 2011.

(e) What is the significance of the preferred share dividends being paid quarterly? What impact, if any, does this frequency in payment have on the calculation of diluted earnings per share?

Digging
Deeper

P17-12   The following information is available for Noonbeam Inc., a company whose shares are traded on the Toronto Stock Exchange:

Net income	$150,000
Average market price of common shares during 2011 (adjusted for stock dividend)	$20
December 31, 2011 (fiscal year end) market price of common shares	$20
Income tax rate for fiscal year 2011	40%

Transactions in common shares during 2011:	Change	Cumulative shares
Jan. 1, 2011, common shares outstanding		90,000
Mar. 1, 2011, issuance of common shares	30,000	120,000
June 1, 2011, 10% stock dividend	12,000	132,000
Nov. 1, 2011, repurchase of common shares	(30,000)	102,000

Other information:

1. For all of the fiscal year 2011, $100,000 of 6% cumulative convertible bonds have been outstanding. The bonds were issued at par and are convertible into a total of 10,000 common shares (adjusted for the stock dividend) at the option of the holder, and at any time after issuance.

2. Stock options for 20,000 common shares have been outstanding for the entire 2011 fiscal year, and are exercisable at the option price of $25 per share (adjusted for the stock dividend).

3. For all of the fiscal year 2011, $100,000 of 4% cumulative convertible preferred shares have been outstanding. The preferred shares are convertible into a total of 15,000 common shares (adjusted for the stock dividend) at the option of the holder, and at any time after January 2016.

Instructions

(a) Determine the weighted average number of common shares that would be used in calculating earnings per share for the year ending December 31, 2011.

(b) Calculate basic earnings per share for 2011.

(c) Determine the potential for dilution for each security that is convertible into common shares.

(d) Calculate diluted earnings per share for 2011. For simplicity, ignore the requirement to record the debt and equity components of the bonds separately.

P17-13 Audrey Inc. has 1 million common shares outstanding as at January 1, 2011. On June 30, 2011, 4% convertible bonds were converted into 100,000 additional shares. Up to that point, the bonds had paid interest of $250,000 after tax. Net income for the year was $1,298,678. During the year, the company issued the following:

1. June 30: 10,000 call options giving holders the right to purchase shares of the company for $30

2. Sept. 30: 15,000 put options allowing holders to sell shares of the company for $25

On February 1, Audrey also purchased in the open market 10,000 call options on its own shares, allowing it to purchase its own shares for $27. Assume the average market price for the shares during the year was $35.

Instructions

(a) Calculate the required EPS numbers under IFRS. For simplicity, ignore the impact that would result from the convertible debt being a hybrid security.

(b) Show the required presentations on the face of the income statement.

P17-14 Use the same information as in P17-13, but also assume the following.

1. On September 30, 200,000 convertible preferred shares were redeemed. If they had been converted, these shares would have resulted in an additional 100,000 common shares being issued. The shares carried a dividend rate of $3 per share to be paid on September 30. No conversions have ever occurred.

2. There are 10,000 $1,000, 5% convertible bonds outstanding with a conversion rate of three common shares for each bond starting January 1, 2012. Beginning January 1, 2015, the conversion rate is six common shares for each bond; and beginning January 1, 2019, it is nine common shares for each bond. The tax rate is 40%.

Instructions

(a) Calculate the required EPS numbers under IFRS. For simplicity, ignore the impact that would result from the convertible debt being a hybrid security.

(b) Show the required presentations on the face of the income statement.

Writing Assignments

WA17-1 "Earnings per share" (EPS) is the most commonly featured financial statistic for corporations. For many securities, the daily published quotations of share prices include a "times earnings" figure that is based on EPS. Stock analysts often focus their discussions on the EPS of the corporations that they study.

Instructions

(a) Explain how the calculation of EPS is affected by dividends or dividend requirements on classes of preferred shares that may be outstanding.

(b) One of the technical procedures that applies to EPS calculations is the treasury stock method. Briefly describe the circumstances that can make it appropriate to use the treasury stock method.

(c) Convertible debentures are considered potentially dilutive common shares. Explain how convertible debentures are handled in regard to EPS calculations. Does the treatment change if the convertible bond can be settled in cash or shares at the issuer's option?

(d) Recently, an article in *Report on Business* magazine titled "The magic number: The price-to-earnings ratio deserves its favoured status—as long as you use it right," written by Fabrice Taylor (February 2010), noted that the long-term average of all shares for the "times earnings" figure was about 19 times. Taylor went on to state that Maple Leaf Foods Inc. was (currently) trading at a P/E (price-to-earnings) ratio of 100 times EPS for 2008, and Finning International Inc. was trading at a P/E ratio of 442 times the past year's EPS. Maple Leaf Foods in the past year had suffered large losses due to product recalls. Finning is a seller of Caterpillar equipment whose sales and earnings fluctuate with commodity prices.

Are these companies' share prices too high? What might be causing these times earnings multiples to be so high? What other information would be needed before this determination could be made?

(AICPA adapted)

WA17-2 Matt Kacskos is a shareholder of Howat Corporation and has asked you, the firm's accountant, to explain why his employee stock options were not included in diluted EPS. In order to explain this situation, you must briefly explain what dilutive securities are, why they are included in the EPS calculation, and why some securities are antidilutive and therefore are not included in this calculation.

Instructions

(a) Write Kacskos a one-and-a-half page letter explaining why the warrants are not included in the calculation. Use the following data to help you explain this situation.

   1. Howat Corporation earned $228,000 during the period, when it had an average of 100,000 common shares outstanding.

   2. The common shares sold at an average market price of $25 per share during the period.

   3. Also outstanding were 15,000 employee stock options that could be exercised by the holder to purchase one common share at $30 per option.

(b) The IASB proposed in its Exposure Draft issued in 2008 that the year-end price of the shares be used, rather than the average price for the year. Assuming that the year-end market price was $33 per share, would this change your answer in part (a)? Why or why not?

(c) Now assume that the company in the past has made a practice of settling the stock options in cash. Consequently, the stock options have been reported as a liability at fair value, with changes in fair value reflected in net earnings. The 2008 Exposure Draft proposes that, if the options are reported at fair value through profit or loss, then these should not be adjusted for in the diluted EPS. Make arguments to support this new proposed treatment.

(d) Stock options (not just employee stock options) are used for various purposes by companies. Briefly explain the business reasons for companies issuing stock options.

WA17-3   On July 1, 2010, Seaway Tools Limited acquired Marine Machinery from John Tweel. The consideration was paid in 100,000 shares issued to Tweel, in addition to contingent consideration. The agreement also allowed for the following:

1. If Marine's profits for the next three years averaged $5 million or more, 50,000 more shares would be issued to Tweel at December 31, 2011. Marine's profits for 2010, 2011, and 2012 were $7 million, $9 million, and $6 million, respectively.

2. 3,000 new shares for each new customer that Marine attracts with an initial contract value of more than $500,000 during 2010 and 2011. During 2010 and 2011, Marine had two (contracts signed August 1 and November 1) and five new customers (two contracts signed March 1, one contract signed May 1, and two contracts signed September 1), respectively, that met this criterion.

    The consolidated earnings for Seaway were $22 million, $19 million, and $24 million for the years ending December 31, 2010, 2011, and 2012, respectively. The number of shares outstanding for Seaway at January 1, 2010, before the acquisition, was 1 million.

Instructions

Determine the basic and diluted earnings per share for Seaway for 2010 and 2011. (Refer to IAS 33, paragraph 52 to assist you with these calculations.)

WA17-4   IFRS allows per share amounts to be reported on items other than earnings.

Instructions

(a) Write a short essay on the pros and cons of allowing companies to include alternate per share amounts in their annual reports. What other types of per share data might be helpful for investors?

(b) Currently, per share data is only required on the profit or loss for the year. What would be the arguments to support the disclosure of comprehensive income per share also? What would be some arguments to discourage this disclosure?

(c) Find an example of a company's disclosure of per share data for other than earnings per share.

Case

Refer to the Case Primer on the Student Website to help you answer this case.

CA17-1   Canton Products Inc. (CP) has been in business for quite a while. Its shares trade on a public exchange and it is thinking of expanding onto the New York and London stock exchanges. Recently, however, the company has run into cash flow difficulties. The CEO is confident that the company can overcome this problem in the longer term as it has a solid business model; however, in the shorter term CP needs to be very careful in managing its cash flows. Of particular concern is the fact that it has multiple potential common shares outstanding that cause the diluted earnings per share numbers to be significantly lower than the company's basic EPS. This in turn has recently caused CP's stock price to decline and is affecting the company's ability to get the best interest rates on its bank loans.

At a recent meeting with the CFO, the CEO decided to exchange the company's convertible senior subordinated notes (the old notes) for new senior subordinated notes (the new notes). The notes were held by a large institutional investor that agreed to the exchange. The old notes were convertible into 25 shares for each $1,000 note. The new notes have a net share settlement provision that requires that, upon conversion, the company will pay the holders up to $1,000 in cash for each note, plus an excess amount that would be settled in shares at a fixed conversion price (30 shares for each $1,000 note in the total consideration). The notes may only be turned in if the share price exceeds 20% of the fixed conversion price.

It is now year end and the share price is trading above the fixed conversion price but well below the 20% premium level. The note therefore cannot be turned in (i.e., converted). The CEO feels that the share price will not exceed the 20% premium for a couple of years.

Instructions

Adopt the role of the auditors and discuss the issues related to the new notes.

Integrated Case

IC17-1   Toby's Foods Limited (TFL) is in the supermarket business. It is a public company and is thinking of going private (i.e., of buying up all of its shares that are available). The funds will come from a private consortium. The consortium has offered to buy all the shares if the share price hits a certain level. Although the company has come through some tough times, things have been looking up recently. This is partially due to a new strategy to upgrade the stores and increase square footage.

TFL obtains revenues from two sources: in-store sales to customers and fees from sales of new franchises and continuing franchise fees. This year was a banner year for sales of new franchises. The company sold and booked revenues for 10 new franchised stores. Most of these new stores have not yet opened but locations have been found and deposits have been taken from each of the franchisees.

Under the terms of the franchise contracts, TFL has agreed to absorb any losses that the stores suffer for the first five years. Based on market research, however, and the location of the new stores, it is highly unlikely that losses will occur. Just in case, TFL has requested that franchisees deposit a certain amount of money in a trust fund. In addition, TFL has agreed to issue shares of TFL to the franchisees if the stores are profitable in the first two years.

During the year, TFL issued long-term debt that is convertible into common shares of the company. The number of common shares varies depending on the share price. Because of the potential for taking the company private, TFL agreed to certain concessions. If the company goes private, TFL must pay back 120% of the face value of the debt.

Instructions

Assume the role of the controller and discuss the financial reporting issues.

Research and Financial Analysis

RA17-1 British Sky Broadcasting Group plc

Real-World Emphasis

British Sky Broadcasting Group plc (BSkyB) operates the leading pay television broadcast service in the United Kingdom and Ireland. Shares of the company trade on the London Stock Exchange and the NYSE. The company produces financial statements in accordance with IFRS. Access the company's annual report for the year ended June 30, 2009, from its website (http://corporate.sky.com). We know from the annual report (page 63) that the company's shares traded between £3.29 and £5.03 per share.

Instructions

(a) Determine how the company has calculated the basic and diluted earnings per share and verify the calculations, where possible. That is, verify (by examining the relevant notes) the number of shares outstanding, adjustments made to the ordinary shares, and the dilutive shares added. Note any information that is missing in order for you to make this determination. What amounts were determined to be antidilutive? Using the share prices disclosed in the question, determine why the company has concluded that there are some items that are antidilutive.

(b) Assume that all conditions have been met for share option awards. Determine the amount of shares that would be added for the dilution using the treasury stock method for 2009. (Make note of any assumptions you have made.)

(c) BSkyB has also disclosed other information on a per share basis. Explain this other per share data. Why has the company provided this information? If you were an investor, would you find it useful?

RA17-2 Molson Coors Brewing Company

Real-World Emphasis

Molson Coors Brewing Company has a year end of December 26, 2009. Access the company's annual report from the company website (www.molsoncoors.com).

Instructions

(a) What types of per share information does the company provide?

(b) Does the company have a complex or simple capital structure? List the types of shares that the company has outstanding. How has the number of shares been determined for the basic EPS?

(c) Describe the types of share-based compensation the company has. Identify any potential common shares that would be included in the diluted earnings per share calculation.

(d) Discuss how the company calculated its diluted earnings per share and explain any choices that it made. Explain the items that were found to be antidilutive by the company and the reasons provided.

RA17-3 BCE Inc.

Real-World Emphasis

One way of improving a company's EPS is to reduce the number of shares outstanding. Access the financial statements for BCE Inc. for the year ended December 31, 2009, from the company's website or SEDAR. Excerpts from the 2006 financial statements have also been provided below:

Note 10: Earnings Per Share

The following table is a reconciliation of the numerator and the denominator used in the calculation of basic and diluted earnings per common share from continuing operations.

	2006	2005	2004
Earnings from continuing operations (numerator)			
Earnings from continuing operations	1,891	1,834	1,395
Dividends on preferred shares	(70)	(70)	(70)
Earnings from continuing operations – basic	1,821	1,764	1,325
Weighted average number of common shares outstanding (denominator) (in millions)			
Weighted average number of common shares outstanding – basic	861.4	926.8	924.6
Assumed exercise of stock options [(1)]	0.2	0.3	0.6
Weighted average number of common shares outstanding – diluted	861.6	927.1	925.2

(1) The calculation of the assumed exercise of stock options includes the effect of the average unrecognized future compensation cost of dilutive options. It does not include anti-dilutive options. These are options that would not be exercised because their exercise price is higher than the average market value of a BCE Inc. common share for each of the periods shown in the table. The number of excluded options was 18,479,608 in 2006, 24,466,767 in 2005 and 26,693,305 in 2004.

		2006	2005	2004
Net earnings per common share – basic	10			
Continuing operations		2.12	1.90	1.44
Discontinued operations		0.13	0.14	0.14
Extraordinary gain		—	—	0.07
Net earnings		2.25	2.04	1.65
Net earnings per common share – diluted	10			
Continuing operations		2.12	1.90	1.44
Discontinued operations		0.13	0.14	0.14
Extraordinary gain		—	—	0.07
Net earnings		2.25	2.04	1.65
Dividends per common share		1.32	1.32	1.20
Average number of common shares outstanding – basic (millions)		861.4	926.8	924.6

Instructions

(a) What per share information has the company provided each year?

(b) What types of shares does the company have outstanding? What are the dividend payments required on these shares?

(c) How have the earnings from continuing operations been determined for each year from 2004 to 2009? Why has this adjustment been made? Why did the earnings for 2007 and 2006 change significantly from the other years presented?

(d) What has the weighted average number of shares been each year for the period 2004 to 2009 for the basic EPS? Why does this change from year to year? Recalculate the basic earnings per share from continuing operations as if the weighted average number of shares outstanding had remained the same since 2004. Assuming that the company's share price trades at around 12 times earnings, what has been the impact each year of the reduction in the number of shares on the share price?

(e) Review the calculation of the diluted earnings per share. What has caused the dilution impact? What has been excluded from the calculation and why?

RA17-4 EPS Harmonization

The FASB and the IASB have been working together to resolve the remaining differences between FASB Statement 128, *Earnings per Share*, and IAS 33 *Earnings per Share*. In August 2008, the IASB issued an Exposure Draft outlining proposed changes to the earnings per share standard.

Instructions

From the IASB website (www.iasb.org), review the Exposure Draft. Discuss the issues raised and comment on whether the changes will result in better financial reporting.

Cumulative Coverage: Chapters 15 to 17

Cottage Country Corporation is a public company listed on the TSX with a December 31 year end. At the beginning of the current year, there were unlimited common shares authorized with 100,000 issued and outstanding. These shares had a book value of $4 million: $150,000 in retained earnings and $100,000 in contributed surplus of which $75,000 was as a result of common share transactions, and the remainder resulting from the issue of compensatory stock options in 2010.

The following transactions took place during the 2011 fiscal year:

January 1 Cottage Country Corp. issued $5 million of 12%, five-year, convertible bonds, with interest payable annually on December 31. Each $1,000 bond can be converted into 20 common shares. In addition, each $1,000 bond included 10 detachable warrants, where each warrant can be used to purchase one share of common stock at an exercise price of $55. The company intends to use the effective interest amortization method for any bond discount or premium.

Common shares were trading at the time for $45 and a valuator indicated that the warrants had a fair market value of $3. The bond issue with attached warrants sold out at 103. Without the warrants and the conversion rights, the bond issue would have traded at 98.

June 1 By this date, the market price for shares had increased to $55. As a result, 30% of the bonds outstanding were converted into common shares when the market price was $55 per share. The company uses the book value method to record bond conversions.

July 31 50% of the outstanding warrants were exercised when the common shares were trading at $56 per share.

October 1 Cottage Country Corp. granted 2,000 options to executives in 2010. Each option entitled the holder to purchase one common share for $55 during 2011. These options were valued using an option pricing model at $25,000. On October 1, 2011, 1,200 of the options were exercised when the market price was $58.

December 1 Cottage Country Corp. purchased and retired 10,000 shares in the open market for $57 per common share.

December 31 The remaining compensatory stock options expired as the executive to whom they had been issued failed to complete his employment contract. The possibility that someone might not complete their employment contract was not taken into account in the option pricing model that was used to determine the value of these stock options.

The net income from operations after tax was $2.5 million and the tax rate was 40%. The average common share price during 2011 was $52. Income tax expense was $1 million and dividends were paid on December 31 at $2.50 per share.

Instructions

(a) Prepare the appropriate journal entries to record the above transactions.

(b) Prepare any necessary year-end journal entries.

(c) Determine basic and diluted earnings per share, and prepare the presentation of EPS for the income statement.

(d) Complete the statement of shareholders' equity.

A Win-Win Move for the Double-Double

FEW THINGS ARE as quintessentially Canadian as a trip to Tim Hortons for a double-double and maybe a cruller to go. In fact, loyal customers may be surprised to discover that the Canadian icon had actually been a U.S.-registered company for years. However, this is no longer the case now that "Tims" has come home.

Tim Hortons Inc. completed its reorganization as a Canadian public company in September 2009. In addition to operational and administrative benefits, a key reason for the move back across the border was the income tax savings. The federal government plans to reduce the general corporate income tax rate to 15% by 2012. It is also calling on all provinces to reduce their corporate income tax rates to 10%, with the goal of having a statutory corporate tax rate of 25% across Canada, explains Mike Myskiw, Tim Hortons' Vice President, Taxation. In comparison, the U.S. federal rate is 35%. Add state taxes and the U.S. rate could be up to 40%.

The reorganization will not change the way Tim Hortons accounts for income taxes since it is a foreign private issuer listed on the New York Stock Exchange, as well as the Toronto Stock Exchange, and will continue to prepare its financial statements in accordance with U.S. GAAP. It's not certain what effect the conversion to International Financial Reporting Standards will have on accounting for income taxes since the standards of convergence from U.S. GAAP to IFRS have not been finally determined.

While the reorganization includes some discretionary one-time, primarily non-cash charges that will increase Tim Hortons' 2009 tax to approximately 37% to 39%, in the long run, the move is expected to save the company money.

As well, there are a number of other benefits. Head office has always been in Canada, as are most executives, so it makes sense from an operational perspective. It will also make it easier to expand within Canada and internationally. Under Canada's exemption system, companies doing business abroad pay the corporate taxes of that foreign country and, when they repatriate the foreign income, they are exempt from paying Canadian corporate taxes. With the U.S. system, when the company repatriates foreign income, it has to pay the U.S. corporate taxes and then claim a corporate tax credit for the international taxes paid.

All in all, it's a win-win situation for Tim Hortons and its shareholders. ▨

Tim Hortons has not prepared and is not responsible for the substantive content of this article. A full disclaimer and source for information prepared by Tim Hortons is set forth on page 1672.

CHAPTER 18

Income Taxes

Learning Objectives

After studying this chapter, you should be able to:

1. Explain the difference between accounting income and taxable income, and calculate taxable income and current income taxes.

2. Explain what a taxable temporary difference is, determine its amount, and calculate future income tax liabilities.

3. Explain what a deductible temporary difference is, determine its amount, and calculate future income tax assets.

4. Prepare analyses of future income tax balances and record future income tax expense.

5. Explain the effect of multiple tax rates and tax rate changes on income tax accounts, and calculate current and future tax amounts when there is a change in substantively enacted tax rates.

6. Account for a tax loss carryback.

7. Account for a tax loss carryforward, including any note disclosures.

8. Explain why the Future Income Tax Asset account is reassessed at the balance sheet date, and account for the future tax asset with and without a valuation allowance account.

9. Identify and apply the presentation and disclosure requirements for income tax assets and liabilities, and apply intraperiod tax allocation.

10. Identify the major differences between private enterprise standards and IFRS for income taxes.

After studying Appendix 18A, you should be able to:

11. Apply the future income taxes method (balance sheet liability method) of accounting for income taxes in a comprehensive situation.

Preview of Chapter 18

As our opening story about Tim Hortons indicates, companies spend a considerable amount of time and effort to minimize their income tax payments. This is important because income taxes are a major cost of doing business for most corporations. At the same time, companies must present financial information to the investment community that provides a clear picture of present and potential tax obligations and tax benefits. In this chapter, we discuss the basic guidelines that both publicly accountable and private enterprises must follow in reporting income taxes. The content and organization of the chapter are as follows.

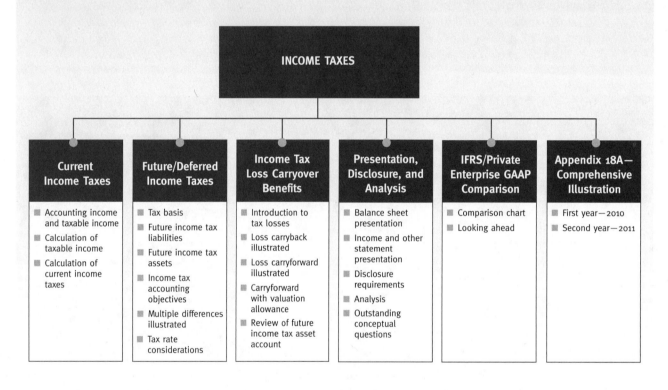

INCOME TAXES

Current Income Taxes	Future/Deferred Income Taxes	Income Tax Loss Carryover Benefits	Presentation, Disclosure, and Analysis	IFRS/Private Enterprise GAAP Comparison	Appendix 18A— Comprehensive Illustration
▪ Accounting income and taxable income ▪ Calculation of taxable income ▪ Calculation of current income taxes	▪ Tax basis ▪ Future income tax liabilities ▪ Future income tax assets ▪ Income tax accounting objectives ▪ Multiple differences illustrated ▪ Tax rate considerations	▪ Introduction to tax losses ▪ Loss carryback illustrated ▪ Loss carryforward illustrated ▪ Carryforward with valuation allowance ▪ Review of future income tax asset account	▪ Balance sheet presentation ▪ Income and other statement presentation ▪ Disclosure requirements ▪ Analysis ▪ Outstanding conceptual questions	▪ Comparison chart ▪ Looking ahead	▪ First year—2010 ▪ Second year—2011

CURRENT INCOME TAXES

Law

Up to this point, you have learned the basic principles that corporations use to report information to investors and creditors. You also recognize that corporations file income tax returns following the *Income Tax Act* (and related provincial legislation), which is administered by the Canada Revenue Agency or CRA.[1] Because GAAP standards and methods differ in several ways from tax regulations, adjustments usually need to be made to the income reported on the financial statements when determining the income that is taxable under tax legislation. That is, the current year's pre-tax income on the **income**

---

[1] Proprietorships and partnerships do not pay income taxes as separate legal entities. Instead, their income is taxed as part of the proprietor's or partners' income as individuals. Organizations that are organized as income trusts also generally do not have their income taxed, because they distribute the income to their unitholders. Taxes that are owed on such distributions are obligations of the unitholders. The favourable tax treatment for most income trusts is scheduled to be phased out by 2011.

statement (i.e., the income amount as determined by applying GAAP) and the company's taxable income usually differ. This is highlighted in Illustration 18-1.

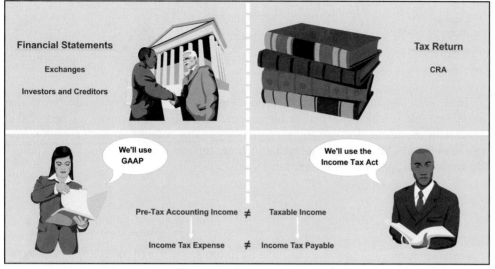

Illustration 18-1

Income Statement Differences between GAAP and Tax Reporting

We start the chapter by taking a closer look at these differences.

Accounting Income and Taxable Income

Accounting income is a financial reporting term that is also known as income before taxes, income for financial reporting purposes, or accounting profit, as it is referred to in IAS 12 *Income Taxes*. In this chapter, it is a pre-tax concept. Accounting income is determined according to GAAP and is measured with the objective of providing useful information to investors and creditors. Taxable income, on the other hand, is a tax accounting term and indicates the amount on which income tax payable is calculated. Taxable income is determined according to the *Income Tax Act and Regulations*, which are designed to raise money to support government operations. It is also referred to as income for tax purposes, or, under IAS 12, as taxable profit.

1 Objective
Explain the difference between accounting income and taxable income, and calculate taxable income and current income taxes.

To illustrate how differences in GAAP and tax rules affect financial reporting and taxable income, assume that Chelsea Inc. reported revenues of $130,000 and expenses of $60,000 on its income statement in each of its first three years of operations. Illustration 18-2 shows the (partial) income statements over these three years.

Illustration 18-2

Accounting Income

CHELSEA INC. GAAP Reporting				
	2010	2011	2012	Total
Revenues	$130,000	$130,000	$130,000	
Expenses	60,000	60,000	60,000	
Accounting income	**$ 70,000**	**$ 70,000**	**$ 70,000**	**$210,000**

Following tax regulations, Chelsea reports the same expenses to the CRA in each of the years. However, the $130,000 of revenue that was reported each year was taxable in different accounting periods: taxable revenues were $100,000 in 2010, $150,000 in 2011, and $140,000 in 2012, as shown in Illustration 18-3.

Illustration 18-3

Taxable Income

CHELSEA INC.
Tax Reporting

	2010	2011	2012	Total
Revenues	$100,000	$150,000	$140,000	
Expenses	60,000	60,000	60,000	
Taxable income	**$ 40,000**	**$ 90,000**	**$ 80,000**	**$210,000**

In reality, companies do not submit revised income statements for the tax return that list only taxable revenues and deductible expenses. Instead, they prepare a schedule that begins with accounting income and they then adjust this amount for each area of difference between GAAP income and taxable income; the result is taxable income. Chelsea's schedules would appear as in Illustration 18-4.

Illustration 18-4

Schedule to Reconcile Accounting Income to Taxable Income

CHELSEA INC.

	2010	2011	2012
Accounting income	**$70,000**	**$70,000**	**$70,000**
Less revenue taxable in a future period	(30,000)		
Add revenue recognized in previous period, taxable in current period		20,000	10,000
Taxable income	**$40,000**	**$90,000**	**$80,000**
Taxes payable (40% assumed rate)	$16,000	$36,000	$32,000

Calculation of Taxable Income

Reversing and Permanent Differences

Let's take a more detailed look at the differences between GAAP income and taxable income. The Chelsea Inc. example above illustrates how to calculate taxable income when there is only one such difference. In reality, many adjustments may be needed. The major reasons for differences between accounting and taxable income follow, and examples of each type are provided.[2]

1. ***Revenues or gains are taxable after they are recognized in accounting income.*** A sale may be recorded in the current accounting period with a debit to a receivable and a credit to revenue, but the revenue may not be included in taxable income until a future year when the receivable is actually collected in cash. There is a timing difference that will reverse in the future. A similar difference may also apply to a gain on sale or to holding gains recognized on assets being held, as these amounts may not be taxable until they have been **realized**; that is, received in cash. Examples include:

   - instalment sales that are recognized when the sale takes place for financial reporting purposes and on the cash basis for tax purposes

---

[2] At the risk of oversimplification, it can be said that the *Income Tax Act* follows a principle of having the tax follow the cash flow. Although taxable income is based mainly on income reported under GAAP, in cases where the timing of cash flows is significantly different from the timing of GAAP recognition, revenues tend to be taxable as they are received in cash and expenses are allowed as deductions when they are paid.

- contracts that are accounted for under the percentage-of-completion method for financial reporting purposes and the completed contract or zero-profit basis for tax purposes, resulting in some or all of the related gross profit being deferred for tax purposes
- unrealized holding gains that are recognized in income or in OCI on investments or other assets carried at fair value, but which are not taxable until the assets are sold and the gains realized

Note for discussions later in the chapter, that in all of these examples, the GAAP balance sheet reports an asset (an account receivable, or construction in process, or an investment account) with a carrying amount that is higher than its tax value would be on a tax balance sheet, if one were prepared.[3] This is the basis for understanding future (or deferred) income taxes later in the chapter.

2. ***Expenses or losses are deductible for tax purposes after they are recognized in accounting income.*** Some expenses or losses that are recognized for accounting purposes are not allowed to be deducted for tax purposes until a future period. For example, for financial statement purposes, an expense may have to be accrued, but for tax purposes it may not be deductible as an expense until it is paid. That is, it is only when the liability is eventually settled that the expense or loss is deductible in calculating taxable income. Examples include the following:

- product warranty liabilities
- estimated losses and liabilities related to restructurings
- litigation accruals
- accrued pension costs
- holding or impairment losses on investments or other assets

In all these examples, notice that a liability (or contra asset or direct asset reduction) is recognized on the balance sheet when the expense or loss is recognized for financial reporting purposes. For tax purposes, however, the expense is not recognized in the current period and, therefore, neither is a tax liability or reduction in the asset's tax value.

3. ***Revenues or gains are taxable before they are recognized in accounting income.*** A company may recognize cash that it received during the year as unearned revenue if it is an advance payment for goods or services to be provided in future years. For tax purposes, the advance payment may have to be included in taxable income when the cash is received. When the entity recognizes this revenue on the income statement in later years when the goods or services are provided to customers, these amounts can be deducted in calculating taxable income. This is because they were included in taxable income in the year the cash was received. They cannot be taxed twice. Examples include the following:

- subscriptions, royalties, and rentals received in advance
- sale and leaseback gains, including a deferral of profit on a sale for financial reporting purposes that would be reported as realized for tax purposes

---

[3] Note that no one prepares a "tax" balance sheet—it is an artificial construct. However, if there were one, the tax values that are referred to here are what would be on that balance sheet, and they would be based on how the transaction is accounted for, for tax purposes. If the revenue is not yet recognized for tax purposes, there would be no receivable either. That is, the tax basis of the receivable is $0. Similarly, the tax value of the investments would be their original cost.

Once again, the balance sheet is also affected. There is a difference between the carrying amount of the liability account Unearned Revenue and its tax basis.

4. ***Expenses or losses are deductible before they are recognized in accounting income***. The cost of assets such as equipment, for example, is deducted for financial statement purposes according to whichever GAAP depreciation method the company uses. For tax purposes, the capital cost allowance (CCA) method must be used. Therefore, depending on which GAAP method was chosen, the asset's cost may be deducted faster for tax purposes than it is expensed for financial reporting purposes. When this happens, taxable income in the early years of the asset's life is lower than the accounting income. Because the asset's capital cost is the total amount that can be depreciated both on the books and for tax purposes, this means that future taxable incomes will be higher than the accounting incomes in those future years. Other examples include the following:

   - property and resources that are depreciated/depleted faster for tax purposes than for financial reporting purposes
   - deductible pension funding that exceeds the pension expense that is recognized
   - prepaid expenses that are deducted in calculating taxable income in the period when they are paid

   These too will result in the carrying amount of a balance sheet account (equipment, at cost less accumulated depreciation, for example) that is different from its tax basis (the equipment's undepreciated capital cost or UCC).

5. ***Permanent differences***. Some differences between taxable income and accounting income are permanent. Permanent differences are caused by items that (1) are included in accounting income but never in taxable income, or (2) are included in taxable income but never in accounting income. Examples include the following:

   - items that are included in accounting income but never in taxable income: **non-tax-deductible expenses** such as fines and penalties, golf and social club dues, and expenses related to the earning of non-taxable revenue; and **non-taxable revenue**, such as dividends from taxable Canadian corporations, and proceeds on life insurance policies carried by the company on key officers or employees
   - items that are included in taxable income but never in accounting income: depletion allowances of natural resources that exceed the resources' cost

   Since **permanent** differences affect only the period in which they occur, there are no deferred or future tax consequences associated with the related balance sheet accounts.

   The situations identified in numbers 1 to 4 above are known as reversible differences or timing differences. Their accounting treatment and tax treatment are **the same**, but the **timing** of when they are included in accounting income and when they are included in taxable income **differs**.

Multiple Differences Illustrated

To illustrate a situation when there are multiple differences between accounting income and taxable income, assume that BT Corporation reports accounting income of $200,000 in each of the years 2010, 2011, and 2012. Assume also that the company is subject to a 30% tax rate in each year, and has the following differences between income reported on the financial statements and taxable income:

Underlying Concept

In some countries, taxable income and accounting income are the same. For entities in such countries, accounting for differences between tax and book income is not an issue.

1. Revenue of $18,000 on a sale to a customer in 2010 is recognized for financial reporting purposes in 2010. The revenue is considered taxable as the customer pays the account—in equal monthly payments over 18 months beginning January 1, 2011.

2. A premium of $5,000 is paid in each of 2011 and 2012 for life insurance that the company carries on key officers. This is not deductible for tax purposes, but is expensed for accounting purposes.

3. A warranty with an estimated cost of $30,000 was provided on sales in 2010. This amount was recognized as expense in the same year. It was expected that $20,000 of the warranty work would be performed in 2011 and $10,000 in 2012, and this is what actually happened. For tax purposes, warranty expenses are not deductible until the expenditures are actually incurred.

The first and third items are **reversible** differences. The second item is a **permanent** difference with no future tax consequences. The reconciliation of BT's accounting income to its taxable income for each year is shown in Illustration 18-5.

	2010	2011	2012
Accounting income	$200,000	$200,000	$200,000
Adjustments:			
Revenue from 2010 sale	(18,000)	12,000	6,000
Warranty expense	30,000	(20,000)	(10,000)
Non-deductible insurance expense		5,000	5,000
Taxable income	$212,000	$197,000	$201,000

Illustration 18-5

Calculation of Taxable Income

The analysis always starts with pre-tax income reported on the income statement. This is adjusted to the taxable amount as follows: revenue items that are not taxable until a future period are deducted, and expenses that are not deductible in the year are added back. This explains the $18,000 deduction of the 2010 sale amount as this was included in 2010's accounting income but is not taxable in 2010. It will be taxable in 2011 and 2012 as the difference reverses, that is, as the receivable is collected. In 2011 and 2012, the amounts collected will be added to the accounting incomes reported to calculate the taxable income for each year.

Starting with pre-tax accounting income and adjusting it to taxable income also explains why the $30,000 of warranty expense is added back to accounting income in 2010. Because BT Corporation did not make any payments under the warranty in 2010, the company cannot deduct any warranty expense for tax purposes. The full amount of $30,000 was deducted in calculating accounting income in 2010, so it is all added back in determining taxable income. The warranty costs are deducted in calculating taxable income in the years they are actually paid by the company (i.e., in 2011 and 2012) even though no warranty expense was deducted in the accounting incomes of those two years.

The original difference and its reversal affect taxable income. The **original** or **originating difference** is the cause of the initial difference between accounting and taxable income amounts. An example is the $30,000 original difference related to warranty expense in 2010. The **reversal**, on the other hand, causes the opposite effect in subsequent years, such as the $20,000 and $10,000 warranty expense differences in 2011 and 2012.

The $5,000 life insurance premium is added back to 2011 and 2012's accounting income because it was deducted as an expense in calculating accounting income in each of those years. It is not a deductible expense for tax purposes in any year and the $5,000 will not affect any future year's taxable income. Its effect is **permanent**.

Calculation of Current Income Taxes

While the calculation of taxable income may sometimes be challenging, the calculation of current income tax expense and income taxes payable in this chapter is straightforward. To determine this amount, the current rate of tax is simply applied to the company's taxable income. Continuing with the BT Corporation example above and the taxable incomes determined in Illustration 18-5, the calculation of the company's current income tax expense and income taxes payable for each of the three years is shown in Illustration 18-6.

<table>
<tr><td></td><td>2010</td><td>2011</td><td>2012</td></tr>
<tr><td>Taxable income</td><td>$212,000</td><td>$197,000</td><td>$201,000</td></tr>
<tr><td>Tax rate</td><td>30%</td><td>30%</td><td>30%</td></tr>
<tr><td>Income tax payable and current
  income tax expense</td><td>$ 63,600</td><td>$ 59,100</td><td>$ 60,300</td></tr>
</table>

Illustration 18-6

BT Corporation's Current Income Tax Expense and Taxes Payable

The year-end adjusting entries to record current income tax each year are as follows:

Dec. 31, 2010	Current Income Tax Expense	63,600	
	Income Tax Payable		63,600
Dec. 31, 2011	Current Income Tax Expense	59,100	
	Income Tax Payable		59,100
Dec. 31, 2012	Current Income Tax Expense	60,300	
	Income Tax Payable		60,300

This method of calculating income tax expense is straightforward and is known as the taxes payable method. It is one of the methods that is permitted under **accounting standards for private enterprises**, or **ASPE.**

Notice that although BT Corporation reported identical accounting income in each year and the tax rate stayed the same, the current **income tax expense differs each year.** This fluctuation is caused mainly by the reversible differences created by the 2010 sale and warranty expense. Conceptually, the income tax expense reported on the income statement **should be directly related to the accounting income that is reported**, not to the amount that is taxable in the period. Therefore, another method, based on an asset and liability approach to income taxes, is required under IFRS and is permitted as the other accounting policy choice under private enterprise standards. This method—the future income taxes method—starts with the calculation of current income taxes as described above. It then adjusts for the effects of any changes in **future income tax assets and liabilities** and recognizes these effects as **future income tax expense.** Note that the terminology used in the international standards for this same approach is the balance sheet liability method; the related tax assets and liabilities are called **deferred income tax assets and liabilities**, and the associated expense is referred to as **deferred income tax expense.** The terms "future" and "deferred" are used interchangeably. This method is explained next.

FUTURE/DEFERRED INCOME TAXES

As indicated above, reversible differences that affect taxable income each year result in an effect on the amount of income taxes payable in the future as the differences reverse. The accumulated tax effects of these differences are recognized on the balance sheet as future tax assets and future tax liabilities. The adjustment of these balance sheet accounts to their correct amount at the balance sheet date dictates the amount of future income tax expense (or deferred income tax expense) to be recognized. The **future income tax expense** and the **current income tax expense** are then both reported on the income statement as components of income tax expense for the period.

The basic principle that underlies future income taxes is as follows: If the recovery of an asset or settlement of a liability that is reported on the balance sheet will result in the company's having to pay income taxes in the future, a future or deferred income tax liability is recognized on the current period's balance sheet. Alternatively, if the recovery or settlement results in future income tax reductions (benefits), a future or deferred income tax asset is recognized on the current balance sheet. This is explained further in the next sections.

Tax Basis

The tax basis or tax base of an asset or liability is similar to a measurement attribute, such as historical cost and fair value. It is the amount attributed to that asset or liability under the rules established by the tax authorities. A good example is the UCC of a depreciable asset. This amount is usually different from the asset's carrying amount in the accounting records. In other words, it is the amount that is attributed for tax purposes to the balance sheet item.

The tax basis of an asset is similar under IFRS and private enterprise standards. It is the amount that can be deducted in determining taxable income when the carrying amount of that asset is recovered. If the proceeds are not taxable, its tax basis is its carrying amount. Examples from *CICA Handbook*, Part II, Section 3465 on *Income Taxes* and IFRS 12 *Income Taxes* will help explain how this is applied.

Example 1. A capital asset was acquired at an original cost (and tax basis) of $1,000. By the end of Year 3, capital cost allowance totalling $424 has been deducted when calculating taxable income for Years 1 to 3. Therefore, the tax basis of this asset at the end of Year 3 is $1,000 − $424 = $576. This is its UCC. Going back to the definition of tax basis provided above, this is the amount that will be deductible for tax purposes in the future as the asset is used to generate cash flows and its carrying amount on the balance sheet is recovered.

Example 2. An investment in another company's shares was purchased at a cost of $1,000. Regardless of whether this investment is accounted for on the balance sheet at fair value or at cost, when it is sold the company has to deduct the cost of the investment from the proceeds received to determine taxable income. The tax basis of the investment is therefore $1,000.

Example 3. A company has trade accounts receivable with a carrying amount of $10,000. The related revenue is taxable as it is earned and is included in taxable income as it is recognized in the accounts. When this asset's carrying amount of $10,000 is recovered (i.e., as the customer pays the account), the full $10,000 can be deducted in determining how much to add to taxable income in the future. Therefore, its tax basis is $10,000.

Example 4. A company holds a life insurance policy on the company president. The policy has a cash surrender value and carrying amount on the balance sheet of $100,000. If the company receives the $100,000 on the president's death, the proceeds are not taxable under the *Income Tax Act*. Based on the definition above, the tax basis of this asset is the same as its carrying amount. There are no tax consequences.

The tax basis of a liability is its carrying amount on the balance sheet reduced by any amount that will be deductible for tax purposes in future periods. The tax basis of revenue received in advance is its carrying amount, less any amount that will not be taxable in the future. When a liability can be settled for its carrying amount without any tax consequences, its tax basis is the same as its carrying amount. Again, let us look at some examples.

Example 1. A company has an accrued liability with a carrying amount of $1,000. The related expense that was included in accounting income when the expense was accrued is deductible for tax purposes only when it is paid. According to the definition above, the tax basis of the accrued liability is its carrying amount ($1,000) less the amount deductible for tax purposes in future periods ($1,000). Therefore, its tax basis is $0.

Example 2. A company receives $1,000 of interest in advance and recognizes this as unearned revenue, a liability. The interest was taxed on a cash basis, when it was received. The tax basis of the unearned revenue is its carrying amount ($1,000) less the amount that will not be taxable in the future ($1,000), thus, $0.

Example 3. A company reports an accrued liability of $200 and the related expenses were deducted for tax purposes in the same period the expense and liability were recognized. The company also reports a loan payable of $500. In both cases, there is no income tax consequence when the liability is paid in the future. The tax basis of the accrued liability and of the loan payable is the same as the carrying amount of each liability on the books.

There may be situations where an item has a tax basis but it is not recognized as an asset or liability on the balance sheet. Consider the example of research and development phase costs that have been expensed in the accounts as incurred, but that are deductible for tax purposes in a future year. Although the carrying amount on the balance sheet is $0, the tax authorities allow the company to reduce future taxable income.

The difference between the tax basis of an asset or liability and its reported amount in the balance sheet is called a temporary difference. There are two types. A taxable temporary difference will result in taxable amounts in future years when the carrying amount of the asset is received or the liability is settled. That is, the effect is an increase in taxable income and income taxes in the future. A deductible temporary difference will decrease taxable income and taxes in the future. We will first look at the effects of **taxable** temporary differences and then discuss **deductible** temporary differences.

Future Income Tax Liabilities

Taxable Temporary Differences

Objective 2
Explain what a taxable temporary difference is, determine its amount, and calculate future income tax liabilities.

In the Chelsea Inc. example in Illustrations 18-2 to 18-4 above, the company reported revenue of $130,000 on its 2010 income statement. For tax purposes, Chelsea reported only $100,000 of taxable revenue, the amount that was collected in cash in the year. At the end of 2010, the carrying amount of accounts receivable on the balance sheet is $30,000 (i.e., $130,000 − $100,000 collected). What is the tax basis of the accounts receivable? Going back to the definition of the tax base of an asset, it is the amount that can be deducted for tax purposes from the $30,000 received. In this case, the full $30,000 will be taxable as it is collected—no amount can be deducted from this. Therefore, the tax value of the accounts receivable is $0.

In the future period when Chelsea collects the $30,000 in accounts receivable, the $30,000 will be taxable and the company will have to pay income tax on it. Therefore, the difference between the carrying amount and tax value of the accounts receivable is a taxable amount—a taxable temporary difference.

What will happen to this $30,000 temporary difference that originated in 2010 for Chelsea Inc.? Assuming that Chelsea expects to collect $20,000 of the receivables in 2011 and $10,000 in 2012, this will result in taxable amounts of $20,000 in 2011 and $10,000 in 2012. These future taxable amounts will cause future taxable income to be increased, along with the amount of income taxes to be paid. Illustration 18-7 presents the original difference, the reversal or turnaround of this temporary difference, and the resulting taxable amounts in future periods.

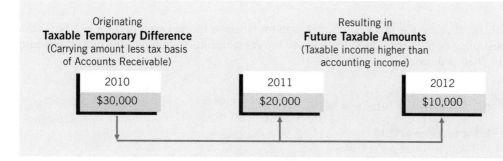

An assumption that underlies a company's GAAP balance sheet is that the assets and liabilities will be recovered and settled, respectively, at least at their reported amounts (carrying amounts). This assumption means that under accrual accounting we need to recognize the future tax consequences of temporary differences in the current year. In other words, it is necessary to recognize in the current period the amount of income taxes that will be payable, reduced, or refunded when the assets' currently reported amounts are recovered or the liabilities are settled.

In our example, we assumed that Chelsea will collect the accounts receivable and report the $30,000 collection as taxable revenue in 2011 and 2012. Based on this, additional income tax will have to be paid in those years. We therefore record the future tax related to the collection of the receivable in Chelsea's books **in 2010.**

Future Income Tax Liability

A future income tax liability or deferred tax liability is the future tax consequence of a taxable temporary difference. It represents the increase in taxes payable in future years as a result of a taxable temporary difference existing at the end of the current year. Recall from the Chelsea example that income tax payable is $16,000 ($40,000 × 40%) in 2010 (Illustration 18-4). In addition, there is a future tax liability at the end of 2010 of $12,000, calculated as shown in Illustration 18-8.

Carrying amount of accounts receivable	$30,000
Tax basis of accounts receivable	–0–
Taxable temporary difference at the end of 2010	30,000
Future tax rate	40%
Future income tax liability at the end of 2010	$12,000

Another way to calculate the future tax liability is to **prepare a schedule that shows the taxable amounts by year** as a result of existing temporary differences, as is shown in Illustration 18-9. A detailed schedule like this is needed when the tax rates in future years are different and the calculations are more complex.

Illustration 18-9

Schedule of Future Taxable Amounts

| | Future Years | | |
	2011	2012	Total
Future taxable amounts	$20,000	$10,000	$30,000
Future tax rate	40%	40%	
Future income tax liability at the end of 2010	$ 8,000	$ 4,000	$12,000

Because it is the first year of operation for Chelsea, there is no future tax liability at the beginning of the year. The calculation of the current, future, and total income tax expense for 2010 is shown in Illustration 18-10.

Illustration 18-10

Calculation of Income Tax Expense, 2010

Current tax expense, 2010 (from Illustration 18-4)		
Taxable income × tax rate ($40,000 × 40%)		$16,000
Future tax expense, 2010		
Future tax liability, end of 2010	$12,000	
Less: Future tax liability, beginning of 2010	–0–	12,000
Income tax expense (total) for 2010		$28,000

This calculation indicates that income tax expense has two components: current tax expense (the amount of income tax payable or refundable for the current period) and deferred or future tax expense. Future or deferred income tax expense is **the change** in the balance sheet future income tax asset or liability account from the beginning to the end of the accounting period.

Journal entries are needed to record both the current and future income taxes. Taxes due and payable are credited to Income Tax Payable, while the increase in future taxes is credited to Future Income Tax Liability. These tax entries could be combined into one entry. However, because disclosure is required of both components, using two entries makes it easier to keep track of the current tax expense and the future tax expense. For Chelsea Inc., the following entries are made at the end of 2010:

A = L + SE		
+16,000 −16,000		

Cash flows: No effect

Current Income Tax Expense	16,000	
Income Tax Payable		16,000

A = L + SE		
+12,000 −12,000		

Cash flows: No effect

Future Income Tax Expense	12,000	
Future Income Tax Liability		12,000

At the end of 2011 (the second year), the taxable temporary difference—the difference between the book value ($10,000) and tax basis ($0) of the accounts receivable—that relates to the 2010 sales is $10,000. (Remember that $20,000 of the 2010 receivable was collected in 2011.) The $10,000 difference is multiplied by the applicable future tax rate to determine the future tax liability of $4,000 ($10,000 × 40%) to be reported at the end of 2011. Both the current and future income tax expense for 2011 are calculated in Illustration 18-11.

Current tax expense, 2011 (from Illustration 18-4)		
Taxable income × tax rate ($90,000 × 40%)		$36,000
Future tax expense, 2011		
Future tax liability, end of 2011 ($10,000 × 40%)	$ 4,000	
Future tax liability, beginning of 2011	12,000	(8,000)
Income tax expense (total) for 2011		$28,000

Illustration 18-11

Calculation of Income Tax Expense, 2011

The journal entries to record income taxes for 2011 are:

Current Income Tax Expense	36,000	
Income Tax Payable		36,000

A = L + SE
   +36,000 −36,000

Cash flows: No effect

Future Income Tax Liability	8,000	
Future Income Tax Benefit		8,000

A = L + SE
   −8,000 +8,000

Cash flows: No effect

Notice in the second entry that an **income tax expense with a credit balance** is often referred to as an income tax benefit, or as indicated in IAS 12, it is a tax income account.

In the entry to record future income taxes at the end of 2012, the Future Income Tax Liability balance is reduced by another $4,000. Illustration 18-12 shows this ledger account as it appears at the end of 2012.

Future Income Tax Liability			
		12,000	2010
2011	8,000		
2012	4,000		
		–0–	Balance

Illustration 18-12

Future Income Tax Liability Account after Reversals

As you can see, the Future Income Tax Liability account has a zero balance at the end of 2012.

Future Income Tax Assets

Deductible Temporary Differences

To help explain deductible temporary differences and future income tax assets, assume that Cunningham Inc. sells microwave ovens on which it offers a two-year warranty accounted for using an expense approach. In 2011, the company estimated its warranty expense related to its 2011 sales of microwave ovens to be $500,000. Cunningham expects that $300,000 of these warranty costs will actually be incurred in 2012, and $200,000 in 2013.

Cunningham reports the $500,000 of warranty expense on its 2011 income statement and a related estimated liability for warranties of $500,000 on its December 31, 2011 balance sheet. For tax purposes, warranty costs are deductible only when the costs are actually

3 Objective
Explain what a deductible temporary difference is, determine its amount, and calculate future income tax assets.

incurred. Therefore, no warranty expense can be deducted in determining 2011's taxable income. Because $500,000 **will be deductible in future periods** when the warranty obligation is settled, the tax basis of the warranty liability at December 31, 2011, is $0. There is a temporary difference of $500,000 related to the warranty liability.

Because of this temporary difference, Cunningham Inc. recognizes **in 2011** the tax benefits (positive tax consequences) associated with the tax deductions in the future. These future deductible amounts will cause taxable income to be less than accounting income in 2012 and 2013. The future tax benefit is reported on the December 31, 2011 balance sheet as a **future income tax asset**.

Cunningham's temporary difference originates in one period (2011) and reverses over two periods (2012 and 2013). This situation is diagrammed in Illustration 18-13.

Illustration 18-13

Reversal of Temporary Difference, Cunningham Inc.

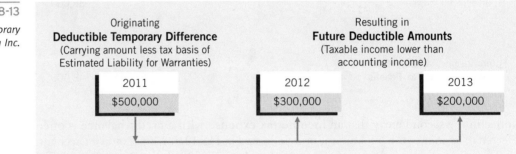

Future Income Tax Assets

A future income tax asset or deferred tax asset is the future tax consequence of a **deductible temporary difference**. In other words, it represents the reduction in taxes payable or the increase in taxes refundable in future years as a result of a deductible temporary difference that exists at the end of the current year.[4]

To illustrate the future income tax asset and income tax benefit, we continue with the Cunningham example. The warranty expense recognized on the income statement in 2011 is not deductible for tax purposes until the period when the actual warranty costs are incurred. Therefore, a deduction will be allowed for tax purposes in 2012 and again in 2013 as the liability for warranties is settled, causing taxable income in those years to be lower than accounting income. The future income tax asset at the end of 2011 (assuming a 40% tax rate for 2012 and 2013) is calculated in Illustration 18-14.

Illustration 18-14

Calculation of Future Income Tax Asset, End of 2011

Carrying amount of warranty liability	$500,000
Tax basis of warranty liability	–0–
Deductible temporary difference at the end of 2011	500,000
Future tax rate	40%
Future income tax asset at the end of 2011	$200,000

Another way to calculate the future tax asset is to prepare a schedule like the one in Illustration 18-15. It shows the deductible amounts that are scheduled for the future as a result of the deductible temporary difference.

---

[4] *CICA Handbook*, Part II, Section 3465.02(d) indicates that future income tax assets also include the income tax benefits that arise through the carryforward of unused tax losses and unused income tax reductions, excluding investment tax credits. IAS 12 *Income Taxes*, para 5, also states that deferred tax assets arise from the carryforward of unused tax losses and tax credits. These are discussed later in the chapter.

	Future Years		
	2012	2013	Total
Future deductible amounts	$300,000	$200,000	$500,000
Future tax rate	40%	40%	
Future income tax asset at the end of 2011	$120,000	$ 80,000	$200,000

Illustration 18-15

Schedule of Future Deductible Amounts

Assuming that 2011 is Cunningham's first year of operations and that income tax payable for this year is $600,000, income tax expense is calculated as shown in Illustration 18-16.

Current tax expense, 2011 (given)		
Taxable income × tax rate		$600,000
Future tax expense/benefit, 2011		
Future tax asset, end of 2011	$200,000	
Less: Future tax asset, beginning of 2011	–0–	(200,000)
Income tax expense (total) for 2011		$400,000

Illustration 18-16

Calculation of Income Tax Expense, 2011

The future tax benefit of $200,000 results from the increase in the future tax asset from the beginning to the end of the accounting period. The future tax benefit captures the fact that the warranty costs are deductible from future taxable income and recognizes this in the accounts in the current period. The total income tax expense of $400,000 on the 2011 income statement is therefore made up of two elements: a current tax expense of $600,000 and the future tax benefit of $200,000. The following journal entries are therefore made at the end of 2011 to recognize income taxes:

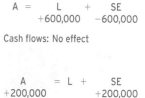

Underlying Concept

The tax benefit is only recognized if it is more likely than not that the company will be able to benefit from the deductions in the future.

Current Income Tax Expense	600,000	
Income Tax Payable		600,000

$$A = \quad L \quad + \quad SE$$
$$+600,000 \quad -600,000$$

Cash flows: No effect

Future Income Tax Asset	200,000	
Future Income Tax Expense/Benefit		200,000

$$A \quad = L + \quad SE$$
$$+200,000 \qquad +200,000$$

Cash flows: No effect

Assuming warranty costs are incurred in the same amounts that were expected, the liability for warranties at the end of 2012 has a carrying amount of $500,000 − $300,000 = $200,000. The tax basis of this liability is still $0 and the future deductible amount is now $200,000. Therefore, the future tax asset at the end of 2012 is 40% of $200,000, or $80,000. Assuming the income tax payable for 2012 is $440,000, income tax expense for the year is calculated as shown in Illustration 18-17.

Current tax expense, 2012 (given)		
Taxable income × tax rate		$440,000
Future tax expense/benefit, 2012		
Future tax asset, end of 2012	$ 80,000	
Less: Future tax asset, beginning of 2012	(200,000)	120,000
Income tax expense (total) for 2012		$560,000

Illustration 18-17

Calculation of Income Tax Expense, 2012

As expected, a reduction in the tax asset account, as with assets in general, results in an increase in the expense to be recognized. The journal entries to record income taxes in 2012 are:

A =   L   +   SE
    +440,000   −440,000

Cash flows: No effect

| Current Income Tax Expense | 440,000 | |
| Income Tax Payable | | 440,000 |

A   = L +   SE
−120,000   −120,000

Cash flows: No effect

| Future Income Tax Expense | 120,000 | |
| Future Income Tax Asset | | 120,000 |

The total income tax expense of $560,000 on the income statement for 2012 is made up of two parts: a current tax expense of $440,000 and a future tax expense of $120,000.

You may have noticed that the future income tax expense of $120,000 that is recognized in 2012 **is not related to future events at all.** In this case, it represents the reversal of a future income tax benefit that originated in a prior year. The future income tax expense or benefit measures the change in the future income tax liability or asset account over the period. It is a combination of originating and reversing temporary differences, changing tax rates, and other events discussed later in this chapter.

At the end of 2013, the Future Income Tax Asset balance is further reduced by $80,000, as shown in the T account in Illustration 18-18. Future income tax expense in 2013 is $80,000.

Illustration 18-18

Future Income Tax Asset Account after Reversals

Future Income Tax Asset			
2011	200,000		
		120,000	2012
		80,000	2013
Balance		–0–	

What Do the Numbers Mean?

Some analysts dismiss future tax assets and future tax liabilities when they assess a company's financial position. However, these accounts meet the conditions set out in the conceptual framework to be recognized as assets and liabilities.

Future Income Tax Asset	Future Income Tax Liability
1. It contributes to future net cash flows.	1. It is an obligation.
2. Access to the benefit is controlled by the entity.	2. It represents a future sacrifice of economic resources.
3. It results from a past transaction or event.	3. It results from a past transaction or event.

A study by B. Ayers[5] found that the market views deferred (i.e., future) tax assets and liabilities in much the same way as it views other assets and liabilities, and that FASB's SFAS No. 109 increased the usefulness of future tax amounts in financial statements.

In addition, the reaction of market analysts to the writeoff of future income taxes in the past supports treating them as assets, as does management's treatment of them. When **Air Canada** ran into financial problems, it reduced its $400-million balance in its future income tax asset account at the end of one year to zero at the end of the next year. The reason? Because the airline was not sure that it would be able to generate enough taxable

---

[5] B. Ayers, "Deferred Tax Accounting Under SFAS No. 109: An Empirical Investigation of Its Incremental Value-Relevance Relative to APB No. 11," *The Accounting Review* (April 1998).

income in the future, its ability to realize any benefits from future deductible amounts was questionable. Like other assets with uncertain benefits, this asset was written down.

Income Tax Accounting Objectives

One objective of accounting for income taxes is to recognize the amount of tax that is payable or refundable for the current year. In Chelsea Inc.'s case, income tax payable is $16,000 for 2010.

A **second objective** is interperiod tax allocation: to recognize the tax effects in the accounting period when the transactions and events are recognized for financial reporting purposes. We saw how this was achieved in the Chelsea example. Accounting for the effect of future taxes on the balance sheet in this way is what underlies the **future income taxes method**, also known as the **balance sheet liability method**. The following table illustrates how the balance sheet amount reported for the warranty liability mirrors the net future cash outflows of Chelsea.

Future Tax Asset	End of 2011	End of 2012
Economic resources needed to settle the obligation:		
Future resources needed to settle the liability	$500,000	$200,000
Future tax savings as liability is settled	200,000	80,000
Net future economic resources needed	$300,000	$120,000
Net liabilities reported on the balance sheet:		
Warranty liability (in liabilities)	$500,000	$200,000
Future income tax asset (in assets)	200,000	80,000
Net liabilities reported	$300,000	$120,000

A similar table could be constructed for Chelsea's receivables and future tax liability to show that the net amount of these two accounts corresponds to the net cash inflow expected as the receivables are collected.

In addition to ensuring that the balance sheet amounts faithfully represent economic reality, future taxes also affect the amount of income tax expense reported in each year. With interperiod tax allocation, the expense amount is related primarily to the revenues and expenses that are reported on each year's income statement. This is shown in Illustration 18-19 for Chelsea Inc. In some years, total income tax expense is greater than taxes payable, and in others it is less. The net result is to report income tax expense that is based on the income statement amounts—in this case 40% of the accounting income, or $28,000. Future taxes affect the tax expense reported in all years where there are originating and reversing differences.

CHELSEA INC. Financial Reporting of Income Tax Expense	2010	2011	2012
Revenues	$130,000	$130,000	$130,000
Expenses	60,000	60,000	60,000
Income before income tax	70,000	70,000	70,000
Less income tax expense:			
Current tax expense	16,000	36,000	32,000
Future tax expense	12,000	(8,000)	(4,000)
	28,000	28,000	28,000
Net income	$ 42,000	$ 42,000	$ 42,000

Illustration 18-19

Accounting Income and Total Income Tax Expense

Multiple Differences Illustrated

A review of recent financial statements of Canadian public companies identifies a variety of causes of temporary differences that result in future tax assets and liabilities. These include differences between the tax basis and carrying amounts of plant and equipment, tax loss carryforwards, pension assets and liabilities, share issue costs, intangible assets, site restoration and asset retirement obligations, and goodwill, among others.

To illustrate the analysis that underlies the accounting for future tax accounts on the balance sheet and future tax expense or benefit on the income statement when there are multiple temporary differences, we return to the BT Corporation example used earlier in the chapter to explain current income taxes. You were asked to assume that BT Corporation reports accounting income of $200,000 in each of the years 2010, 2011, and 2012; that the company is subject to a 30% tax rate in each year; and that it has the following differences between income reported on the financial statements and taxable income:

1. For tax purposes, revenue of $18,000 on a sale made in 2010 is reported over an 18-month period at an equal amount each month as it is collected, beginning January 1, 2011. The entire revenue is recognized for financial reporting purposes in 2010.

2. A premium of $5,000 is paid in each of 2011 and 2012 for life insurance that the company carries on key officers. This is a non-deductible expense for tax purposes, but is considered a business expense for accounting purposes.

3. A warranty with an associated expense of $30,000, provided on sales in 2010, was recognized in the same year. It was expected that $20,000 of the warranty work would be performed in 2011 and $10,000 in 2012, and this is what actually happened.

The calculations of taxable income and current tax expense are shown in Illustrations 18-5 and 18-6. We now continue with the example to see how this information affects the balance sheet and future tax assets and liabilities.

All differences between the accounting income and taxable income are considered in reconciling the income reported on the financial statements to taxable income. However, **only those that result in temporary differences are considered when determining future tax amounts for the balance sheet**. When there are multiple differences, a schedule is prepared of the balance sheet accounts whose carrying and tax bases are different.

For BT Corporation, the revenue from the 2010 sale resulted in an $18,000 difference between the carrying amount and the tax basis of its accounts receivable at the end of 2010. The sale and receivable were recognized in 2010, but no customer payments were received until 2011; no amounts were included in taxable income in 2010. The receivable's tax value is therefore $0. Another way to look at this is that, for tax purposes, neither the account receivable nor the revenue has been recognized.

The life insurance premium expense is a permanent difference. It is not reversible and has no future tax consequences. Therefore, it is not considered in calculating future income taxes.

BT Corporation ended 2010 with a warranty liability on its books of $30,000 because none of the actual warranty work had been carried out as at the end of the year. For tax purposes, however, no warranty expense or associated warranty liability has been recognized at December 31, 2010. The liability's tax value is therefore $0.

The company's analysis and calculation of the temporary differences, the net future tax asset or liability, and the future tax expense or benefit for 2010 are shown in Illustration 18-20. Because the same tax rate is assumed for all periods, calculating the future tax asset and liability is simplified. If the tax rate for future years has been legislated at differing rates, it would be better to use a separate schedule to calculate the future tax amounts as set out in Illustrations 18-9 and 18-15.

Balance Sheet Account	Carrying Amount	− Tax Basis	= (Taxable) Deductible Temporary Difference	× Tax Rate	= Future Income Tax Asset (Liability)
Accounts receivable	$18,000	$–0–	$(18,000)	.30	$(5,400)
Warranty liability	30,000	–0–	30,000	.30	9,000
Net future tax asset, December 31, 2010					3,600
Net future tax asset (liability) before adjustment					–0–
Increase in future tax asset, and future income tax benefit, 2010					$ 3,600

In 2010, BT has two originating differences that result in temporary differences. One results in a future tax asset and the other in a future tax liability. While separate entries could be made to each of these accounts, the analyses and entries in this chapter work with one net account. Balance sheet presentation is covered later in the chapter.

The journal entries to record income taxes for 2010, based on the above analysis and the analysis for current tax expense in Illustration 18-6, are:

Current Income Tax Expense	63,600	
Income Tax Payable (see Illustration 18-6)		63,600

A = L + SE
+63,600 −63,600
Cash flows: No effect

Future Income Tax Asset	3,600	
Future Income Tax Benefit		3,600

A = L + SE
+3,600 +3,600
Cash flows: No effect

Illustration 18-21 sets out the analysis of the temporary differences at the end of 2011. The two differences that originated in 2010 have begun to reverse. The account receivable has been reduced to $6,000 at the end of 2011, and the warranty liability outstanding is now only $10,000. Again, as Illustration 18-21 shows, the future tax expense or benefit is determined **by the change** in the future tax asset or liability account on the balance sheet.

Balance Sheet Account	Carrying Amount	− Tax Basis	= (Taxable) Deductible Temporary Difference	× Tax Rate	= Future Income Tax Asset (Liability)
Accounts receivable	$ 6,000	$–0–	$ (6,000)	.30	$(1,800)
Warranty liability	10,000	–0–	10,000	.30	3,000
Net future tax asset, December 31, 2011					1,200
Net future tax asset before adjustment					3,600
Decrease in future tax asset, and future tax expense, 2011					$(2,400)

The journal entries to record income taxes at December 31, 2011, are:

Current Income Tax Expense	59,100	
Income Tax Payable (see Illustration 18-6)		59,100

A = L + SE
+59,100 −59,100
Cash flows: No effect

A = L + SE
−2,400   −2,400

Cash flows: No effect

| Future Income Tax Expense | 2,400 | |
| Future Income Tax Asset | | 2,400 |

As indicated in Illustration 18-22, by the end of 2012 all differences have reversed, leaving no temporary differences between balance sheet amounts and tax values.

Illustration 18-22

Calculation of Future Tax Asset/Liability and Future Tax Expense—2012

Balance Sheet Account	Carrying Amount	−	Tax Basis	=	(Taxable) Deductible Temporary Difference	×	Tax Rate	=	Future Income Tax Asset (Liability)
Accounts receivable	$ –0–		$ –0–		$ –0–		n/a		$ –0–
Warranty liability	–0–		–0–		–0–		n/a		–0–
Net future tax asset, December 31, 2012									–0–
Net future tax asset before adjustment									1,200
Decrease in future tax asset, and future tax expense, 2012									$(1,200)

The journal entries at December 31, 2012, reduce the Future Income Tax Asset account to zero and recognize $1,200 in future income tax expense for 2012.

A = L + SE
+60,300   −60,300

Cash flows: No effect

| Current Income Tax Expense | 60,300 | |
| Income Tax Payable (see Illustration 18-6) | | 60,300 |

A = L + SE
−1,200   −1,200

Cash flows: No effect

| Future Income Tax Expense | 1,200 | |
| Future Income Tax Asset | | 1,200 |

Illustration 18-23 provides a summary of the bottom portion of the income statements for BT Corporation for each of the three years.

Illustration 18-23

BT Corporation Income Statements—2010, 2011, and 2012

BT CORPORATION
Income Statements (partial) for the Years

	2010	2011	2012
Income before income tax expense	$200,000	$200,000	$200,000
Less income tax expense:			
Current expense	63,600	59,100	60,300
Future expense (benefit)	(3,600)	2,400	1,200
	60,000	61,500	61,500
Net income	$140,000	$138,500	$138,500

Total income tax expense reported in 2010, 2011, and 2012 is $60,000, $61,500, and $61,500, respectively. Although the statutory or enacted rate (i.e., the rate set by government legislation) of 30% applies for all three years, the effective rate is 30% for 2010 ($60,000/$200,000 = 30%) and 30.75% for 2011 and 2012 ($61,500/$200,000 = 30.75%). The **effective tax rate** is calculated by dividing total income tax expense for the period by the pre-tax income reported on the financial statements. The difference between the enacted and effective rates in 2011 and 2012 of 0.75% in this case is caused by the $5,000 non-deductible life insurance expense ([$5,000 × 0.30] ÷ $200,000).

Tax Rate Considerations

In the previous illustrations, the enacted tax rate did not change from one year to the next. To calculate the future tax account reported on the balance sheet, the temporary difference was simply multiplied by the current tax rate because it was expected to apply to future years as well. Tax rates do change, however.

Future Tax Rates

What happens if tax rates (or tax laws) are different for future years? Accounting standards take the position that the income tax rates to use should be the ones that are expected to apply when the tax liabilities are settled or tax assets are realized. These would normally be the rates that have been enacted at the balance sheet date. The accounting standard does recognize, however, that situations may exist where a substantively enacted rate or tax law may be more appropriate.[6] To illustrate the use of different tax rates, we use the example of Warlen Corp. At the end of 2010, this company has a temporary difference of $300,000, as determined in Illustration 18-24.

5 Objective

Explain the effect of multiple tax rates and tax rate changes on income tax accounts, and calculate current and future tax amounts when there is a change in substantively enacted tax rates.

Net carrying amount of depreciable assets	$1,000,000
Tax basis of depreciable assets (UCC)	700,000
Taxable temporary difference	$ 300,000

Illustration 18-24

Calculation of Temporary Difference

This is a **taxable** temporary difference because, to date, Warlen has deducted $300,000 more CCA on its tax returns than it has deducted depreciation expense on its income statements. We know this because the UCC is $300,000 lower than the assets' net carrying amount in the accounts. When Warlen Corp. calculates taxable income in the future, it will have to add back its depreciation expense and deduct a lower amount of CCA. The result will be a taxable income that is higher than the accounting income.

Continuing with this example, assume that the $300,000 will reverse and that the tax rates that are expected to apply in the following years on the resulting taxable amounts are as shown in Illustration 18-25.

	Total	2011	2012	2013	2014	2015
Future taxable amounts	$300,000	$80,000	$70,000	$60,000	$50,000	$40,000
Tax rate		40%	40%	35%	30%	30%
Future tax liability	$108,000	$32,000	$28,000	$21,000	$15,000	$12,000

Illustration 18-25

Future Tax Liability Based on Future Rates

[6] *CICA Handbook*, Part II, Section 3465.51 to .54 and IAS 12 *Income Taxes* paras. 46 to .49. Under private enterprise standards, there must be persuasive evidence that the government is able and committed to enacting the proposed change in the foreseeable future in order to use a substantively enacted rate or tax law. This usually means that the legislation or regulation has to have been drafted in an appropriate form and tabled in Parliament or presented in Council. IFRS indicates that the announced tax rate or law can be used only when the government announcements of tax changes have the substantive effect of actual enactment.

As indicated, the future tax liability is $108,000—the total future tax effect of the temporary difference at the end of 2010.

Because the Canadian tax system provides incentives in the form of reductions in the income tax rates that may be applied to taxable income, the rate used to calculate future tax amounts includes the tax rate reductions, provided it is expected that the company will qualify for the rate reductions in the periods of reversal.[7] The general principle is to use the rates that are expected to apply to the taxable income in the periods when the temporary differences are expected to reverse, provided that the rates are enacted or substantively enacted at the balance sheet date. The Canadian, IASB, and FASB standards all agree that discounting future income tax assets and liabilities **is not permitted**. The issue of discounting remains a contentious one that requires resolution on a broader level.

Revision of Future Tax Rates

When a change in the tax rate is enacted (or substantively enacted) into law, **its effect on the existing future income tax asset and liability accounts is recorded immediately as an adjustment to income tax expense in the period of the change.**

Assume that on September 10, 2010, a new income tax rate is enacted that lowers the corporate rate from 40% to 35%, effective January 1, 2012. To illustrate this change, we use the example of Hostel Corp. If Hostel Corp. has one temporary difference at the beginning of 2010 related to $3 million of excess capital cost allowance, then it has a Future Income Tax Liability account at January 1, 2010, with a balance of $1.2 million ($3,000,000 × 40%). If taxable amounts related to this difference are scheduled to increase the taxable income equally in 2011, 2012, and 2013, the future tax liability at September 10, 2010, is now $1.1 million, calculated as shown in Illustration 18-26.

Illustration 18-26

Schedule of Future Taxable Amounts and Related Tax Rates

	Total	2011	2012	2013
Future taxable amounts	$3,000,000	$1,000,000	$1,000,000	$1,000,000
Tax rate		40%	35%	35%
Revised future tax liability	$1,100,000	$ 400,000	$ 350,000	$ 350,000

An entry is made on September 10, 2010, to recognize the $100,000 decrease ($1,200,000 – $1,100,000) in the future tax liability:

A = L + SE
       −100,000   +100,000

Cash flows: No effect

| Future Income Tax Liability | 100,000 | |
| Future Income Tax Benefit | | 100,000 |

While the private enterprise standard does not require separate disclosure of the future tax expense or benefit due to a change in tax rates, IFRS does.

What Do the Numbers Mean?

When governments change their income tax rates, the effect on corporate Canada can be a substantial hit or a tax windfall! As an example, the last time the federal, Alberta, and Saskatchewan governments significantly reduced future tax rates, it resulted in tax windfalls for many companies in the oil patch. The federal rate fell from 21% in 2007 to a planned 19% in 2010. Companies reporting large future income tax liabilities saw

---

[7] The private enterprise standard indicates that it must be more likely than not that the company will be eligible for the reduced tax rate. Examples of tax incentives include the small business deduction, the manufacturing and processing profits deduction, and the scientific research and development credits.

immediate reductions as they remeasured these liabilities. A concurrent increase in earnings of these companies was reported as the reduction in the future tax liability was taken into income through a future income tax benefit. **Husky Energy Inc.**, an integrated energy and energy-related company, for example, indicated that the reduction in tax rates increased its profits for the second quarter of 2006 by $328 million, helping its profit more than double to $978 million. **Canadian Natural Resources Ltd.**, Canada's second-largest independent petroleum producer at the time, recognized a similar gain from the tax rate change, some $438 million, which brought its reported profit to more than $1 billion!

Basic corporate tax rates do not change often, and the current rate is therefore normally used.[8] However, changes in provincial rates, the small business deduction, foreign tax rates, and surcharges on all levels of income affect the effective rate and may require adjustments to the future tax accounts.

To this point in the chapter, the following topics have been covered:

- Recognition and measurement of current income tax expense (benefit) and the associated income taxes that are currently payable (receivable). This describes the taxes payable approach to accounting for income taxes.

- Explanation of temporary differences and why future tax assets and future tax liabilities are required to be recognized and measured under the future income taxes approach, in addition to the current income taxes.

- Recognition and measurement of future tax assets and future tax liabilities and the associated future tax expense or benefit.

- Explanation of the tax rates to use and how changes in the rates are accounted for.

Appendix 18A provides a comprehensive example to help you cement your understanding of the analyses needed to support the income tax entries for the year. The example illustrates interperiod tax allocation with multiple temporary differences and a tax rate change over a two-year period.

INCOME TAX LOSS CARRYOVER BENEFITS

Introduction to Tax Losses

A loss for income tax purposes or tax loss occurs when the year's tax-deductible expenses and losses exceed the company's taxable revenues and gains. The tax system would be unfair if companies were taxed during profitable periods and received no tax relief during periods of losses. Therefore, a company pays no income tax in a year in which it incurs a tax loss. In addition, the tax laws permit taxpayers to use a tax loss of one year to offset taxable income of other years. This is accomplished through the tax loss carryback and carryforward provisions of income tax legislation, which allow taxpayers to benefit from tax losses—either by recovering taxes that were previously paid or by reducing taxes that will otherwise be payable in the future.

 Law

A corporation can choose to carry a tax loss back against taxable income of the immediately preceding three years. This is a loss carryback. Alternatively, it can choose to carry losses that it earned in tax years ending after 2005 forward to the 20 years that immediately

---

[8] The federal general corporate income tax rate has gradually dropped from 28% to 15% over the period from 2001 to 2011. Federal budgets tabled after the time of writing could change these rates further, one way or the other.

follow the loss. This is a loss carryforward.[9] Or, it may choose to do both. Illustration 18-27 presents a diagram of the carryover periods, assuming a tax loss is incurred in 2010.

Illustration 18-27

Loss Carryback and Carryforward Procedure

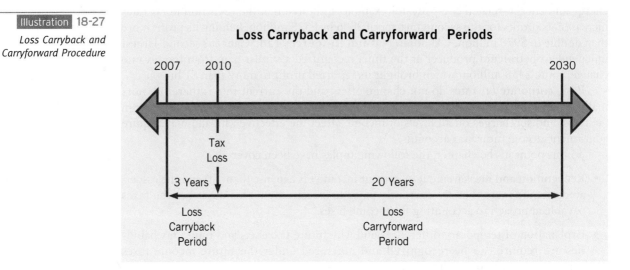

If a loss is carried back, it is usually applied against the earliest available income—2007 in the example above. The **benefit from a loss carryback** is the **recovery of some or all of the taxes** that were paid in those years. The tax returns for the preceding years are refiled; the current-year tax loss is deducted from the previously reported taxable income; and a revised amount of income tax payable is determined for each year. This figure is then compared with the taxes that were actually paid for each of the preceding years, and the government is asked to refund the difference.

If a corporation decides to carry the loss forward, or if the full amount of the loss could not be absorbed in the carryback period, **the tax loss can be used to offset taxable income in the future so that taxes for those future years are reduced or eliminated**. The decision on how to use a tax loss depends on factors such as its size, the results of the previous years' operations, past and anticipated future tax rates, and other factors in which management sees the greatest tax advantage.[10]

Tax losses are relatively common and can be large. Companies that have suffered substantial losses are often attractive merger candidates because, in certain cases, the acquirer may use these losses to reduce its taxable income and, therefore, its income taxes. In a sense, a company that has suffered substantial losses may find itself worth more "dead than alive" because of the economic value related to the tax benefit that another company may be able to use.[11] The following sections discuss the accounting treatment of loss carrybacks and carryforwards.

---

[9] The carryforward period has been increasing. The 2004 federal budget increased it from 7 years to 10, and the 2006 budget increased it again to 20 years. Note also that the references in this chapter to tax losses are limited to non-capital losses. Special rules apply to capital losses.

[10] At one time, it was common practice when refiling prior years' returns to reduce the amount of CCA claimed, thus increasing the amount of taxable income in those prior years. The company could then absorb more of a current year tax loss. With the recent extensions of the carryforward period, now at 20 years, this option is now not commonly allowed.

[11] When Sears Canada Inc. bought 19 Eaton's stores for $80 million, $20 million of the price was for approximately $175 million of tax losses accumulated by Eaton's. The $20 million could not be distributed until five years after Sears had benefited from it. This was because the Canada Revenue Agency could legally appeal the company's use of the losses. The $20 million was finally paid out in 2006.

Loss Carryback Illustrated

To illustrate the accounting procedures for a tax loss carryback, assume that Groh Inc. has the taxable incomes and losses shown in Illustration 18-28 and that there are no temporary or permanent differences in any year.

6 **Objective**
Account for a tax loss carryback.

Illustration 18-28

Income and Loss Data— Groh Inc.

Year	Taxable Income or Loss	Tax Rate	Tax Paid
2007	$ 75,000	30%	$22,500
2008	50,000	35%	17,500
2009	100,000	30%	30,000
2010	200,000	40%	80,000
2011	(500,000)	—	–0–

Underlying Concept

The income tax receivable from the government meets the definition of an asset. Therefore, the asset is recognized on the balance sheet and the benefit associated with this inflow of assets is recognized on the income statement.

In 2011, Groh Inc. incurs a tax loss that it decides to carry back. The carryback is applied first to 2008, the third year preceding the loss year. Any unused loss is then carried back to 2009, and then to 2010. Groh files amended tax returns for each of the years 2008, 2009, and 2010, receiving refunds for the $127,500 ($17,500 + $30,000 + $80,000) of taxes paid in those years.

For accounting purposes, the $127,500 represents the **tax benefit of the loss carryback**. The tax benefit is recognized in 2011, the loss year, because the tax loss gives rise to a tax refund (an asset) that is both measurable and currently realizable. The following journal entry is prepared in 2011:

Income Tax Refund Receivable	127,500	
Current Income Tax Benefit		127,500

A	= L +	SE
+127,500		+127,500

Cash flows: No effect

The Income Tax Refund Receivable is reported on the balance sheet as a current asset at December 31, 2011. The tax benefit is reported on the income statement for 2011 as shown in Illustration 18-29.

Illustration 18-29

Recognition of the Benefit of the Loss Carryback in the Loss Year

GROH INC.	
Income Statement (partial) for 2011	
Income (loss) before income taxes	$(500,000)
Income tax benefit	
Current benefit due to loss carryback	127,500
Net income (loss)	$(372,500)

If the tax loss carried back to the three preceding years is less than the taxable incomes of those three years, the only entry needed is similar to the one above. For Groh Inc., however, the $500,000 tax loss for 2011 is more than the $350,000 in taxable incomes from the three preceding years; **the remaining $150,000 loss can therefore be carried forward**. The accounting for a tax loss carryforward is explained next.

Loss Carryforward Illustrated

7 **Objective**
Account for a tax loss carryforward, including any note disclosures.

If a net operating loss is not fully absorbed through a carryback or if the company decides not to carry the loss back, **the loss can be carried forward for up to 20 years**. Because carryforwards are used to offset expected future taxable income, the tax benefit associated with a loss carryforward is represented by future tax savings: reductions in taxes in the future that would otherwise be payable. In order to actually benefit from this loss, the company must generate future taxable income. In some cases, the ability to do this may be highly uncertain.

The accounting issue, then, is whether the tax benefit of a loss carryforward should be recognized **in the loss year when the potential benefits arise,** or **in future years when the benefits are actually realized.** Private enterprise standards (future income taxes method) take the position that the potential benefit of unused tax losses meets the definition of an asset **to the extent that it is** more likely than not **that the benefit will be realized**; that is, more likely than not that there will be future taxable income against which the losses can be applied. International standards indicate that the potential benefit must be probable. While this term is not defined in the income tax standard, probable is defined as "more likely than not" in another IFRS and the IASB agreed that this was its meaning in its joint project on harmonizing tax standards with U.S. GAAP.

When a tax loss carryforward is more likely than not to result in future economic benefits, it is accounted for in the same way as a deductible temporary difference: a future income tax asset is recognized in an amount equal to the expected benefit.

Future Taxable Income More Likely than Not

To illustrate the accounting for an income tax loss carryforward, we continue with the Groh Inc. example. In 2011, after carrying back as much of the loss as possible to the three preceding years, the company has a $150,000 tax loss available to carry forward. Assuming the company determines **it is more likely than not to generate sufficient taxable income in the future** so that the benefit of the remaining $150,000 loss will be realized, Groh records a future tax asset. If a tax rate of 40% applies to future years, the asset recognized is $60,000 ($150,000 × 40%). The journal entries to record the benefits of the carryback and the carryforward in 2011 are as follows:

A = L + SE
+127,500   +127,500

Cash flows: No effect

To recognize benefit of loss carryback		
Income Tax Refund Receivable	127,500	
Current Income Tax Benefit		127,500

A = L + SE
+60,000   +60,000

Cash flows: No effect

To recognize benefit of loss carryforward		
Future Income Tax Asset	60,000	
Future Income Tax Benefit		60,000

The Future Income Tax Asset account on the balance sheet is a measure of the expected future tax savings from the loss, and because this asset is recognized, a $60,000 future tax benefit is reported on the income statement. The 2011 income statement appears as shown in Illustration 18-30.

Illustration 18-30

Recognition of the Benefit of the Loss Carryback and Carryforward in the Loss Year

GROH INC. Income Statement (partial) for 2011		
Income (loss) before income taxes		$(500,000)
Income tax benefit		
Current benefit due to loss carryback	$127,500	
Future benefit due to loss carryforward	60,000	187,500
Net income (loss)		$(312,500)

For 2012, assume that Groh returns to profitability and has taxable income of $200,000 from the year's operations, subject to a 40% tax rate. In this year, then, Groh can deduct the carryforward loss from the 2012 taxable income, and reduce the tax that would otherwise be payable in the year. In other words, in 2012 Groh **realizes** the benefit of the tax loss carryforward that was **recognized** for accounting purposes in 2011. The income tax payable for 2012 is determined in Illustration 18-31.

Taxable income before loss carryforward, 2012	$ 200,000
Tax loss carryforward deduction	(150,000)
Revised taxable income for 2012	50,000
Tax rate	40%
Income tax payable for 2012 and current tax expense	$ 20,000
Future tax asset, opening balance ($150,000 × 0.4)	$ 60,000
Future tax asset, December 31, 2012 ($0 × 0.4)	–0–
Future tax expense, 2012	$ 60,000

Illustration 18-31

Calculation of Income Tax Payable in the Year the Loss Carryforward Is Realized

The journal entries to record income taxes for 2012 are:

Current Income Tax Expense	20,000	
Income Tax Payable		20,000

A = L + SE
+20,000 −20,000

Cash flows: No effect

Future Income Tax Expense	60,000	
Future Income Tax Asset		60,000

A = L + SE
−60,000 −60,000

Cash flows: No effect

The first entry records income taxes payable for 2012 and, therefore, current income tax expense. The second entry records the using up of the tax benefit that was captured as a future income tax asset the previous year.

The 2012 income statement in Illustration 18-32 shows that the 2012 total income tax expense is based on 2012's reported income. The **benefit of the tax loss** is not reported in 2012. It was already reported in 2011.

GROH INC.
Income Statement (partial) for 2012

Income before income taxes		$200,000
Income tax expense		
Current	$20,000	
Future	60,000	80,000
Net income		$120,000

Illustration 18-32

Presentation When Previously Recognized Tax Benefit Is Realized

Future Taxable Income Not Likely

Let's return to the Groh Inc. example and 2011. A tax asset (Income Tax Refund Receivable) was recognized in 2011 because Groh knew that the company would receive $127,500 of benefits from $350,000 of the tax loss. This left $150,000 of tax losses to carry forward. We assume now that the company's future profitability is uncertain and that at December 31, 2011, there is not enough evidence that there will be future taxable income to deduct these losses against. Therefore, we cannot recognize the potential tax benefit of the loss carryforward as an asset. In this case, the only 2011 income tax entry is:

Income Tax Refund Receivable	127,500
Current Income Tax Benefit		127,500

A   = L +   SE
+127,500   +127,500

Cash flows: No effect

The presentation in the 2011 income statement in Illustration 18-33 reflects the entry made—**only the benefit related to the loss carryback is recognized**. However, the unrecognized potential tax benefit associated with the remaining $150,000 of tax losses is relevant information for financial statement readers. Therefore, the amounts and expiry dates of unrecognized (i.e., unbooked) tax losses are disclosed. This makes readers aware of the possibility of future benefits (reduced future income tax outflows) from the loss, even though the likelihood of realizing these benefits at the reporting date is too uncertain for them to be recognized in the body of the statements.

Illustration 18-33

Recognition of Benefit of Loss Carryback Only

GROH INC.
Income Statement (partial) for 2011

Income (loss) before income taxes	$(500,000)
Income tax benefit	
Current benefit due to loss carryback	127,500
Net income (loss)	$(372,500)

Assume now that in 2012 the company performs better than expected, generating taxable income of $200,000 from its annual operations. After applying the $150,000 loss carryforward, tax is payable on only $50,000 of income. With a tax rate of 40%, the following entry is made:

A =   L   +   SE
     +20,000   −20,000

Cash flows: No effect

Current Income Tax Expense	20,000
Income Tax Payable ($50,000 × 40%)		20,000

This entry recognizes the taxes currently payable in the year. Because the potential tax benefit associated with the loss carryforward **was not recognized in 2011, it is recognized in 2012**, the year it is realized. The $20,000 of current tax expense is actually made up of two components: income taxes of $80,000 accrued on the 2012 income of $200,000, and a $60,000 tax reduction from the realization of the unrecorded loss carryforward. Separate disclosure of the benefit from the loss carried forward is not required under private enterprise standards, but is required under IFRS if it makes up a major component of tax expense.

Illustration 18-34 shows the 2012 income statement.

Illustration 18-34

Recognition of Benefit of Loss Carryforward When Realized

GROH INC.
Income Statement (partial) for 2012

Income before income taxes	$200,000
Current income tax expense (note)	20,000
Net income	$180,000

Note to financial statements (if required): Current tax expense includes a $60,000 benefit from deducting a previously unrecognized tax loss carryforward.

If 2012's taxable income had been less than $150,000, only a portion of the unrecorded tax loss could have been applied. The entry to record 2012 income taxes would have been similar to the entry above. In addition, a note to the financial statements is provided to disclose the amount and expiry date of the remaining unused loss.

Carryforward with Valuation Allowance

In the Groh Inc. example above, we assumed that the company's future was uncertain, and that there was insufficient evidence that the company would be able to benefit from the remaining $150,000 of 2011 tax losses available to be carried forward. As a result, no future income tax asset was recognized in 2011.

There is an alternative recognition approach to this situation. Under it, a future income tax asset is recognized for the full amount of the tax effect on the $150,000 loss carryforward, **along with an offsetting** valuation allowance, a contra account to the future tax asset account. Because the net effect on the financial statements is the same, this valuation allowance approach is also permitted under **private enterprise GAAP** and it is used in pre-2011 reporting in Canada. The valuation allowance approach is not consistent with existing **IAS 12 *Income Taxes***. The international standard allows recognition of a deferred tax asset only to the extent that future benefits are probable.

How does a valuation allowance work? Assuming that the entry for the loss carryback has already been made, the following entries recognize the tax effect of the full $150,000 loss carryforward and the valuation allowance to bring the future tax asset account to its realizable value of zero at December 31, 2011:

Future Income Tax Asset ($150,000 × 40%)	60,000	
Future Income Tax Benefit (re: loss carryforward)		60,000

A   = L +   SE
+60,000   +60,000
Cash flows: No effect

Future Income Tax Expense (re: loss carryforward)	60,000	
Allowance to Reduce Future Income Tax		
Asset to Expected Realizable Value		60,000

A   = L +   SE
−60,000   −60,000
Cash flows: No effect

The latter entry, which sets up the allowance account, indicates that there is insufficient evidence that the company will benefit from the tax loss in the future. The effect on the financial statements is the same whether these two entries are made or the future income tax asset is not recognized in the accounts at all. The income statement under the allowance approach is identical to the statement provided in Illustration 18-33.

Now assume that the company performs better than expected in 2012, generating taxable income of $200,000. After applying the $150,000 loss carryforward, tax is payable on only $50,000 of income. With a tax rate of 40%, the entry for current taxes is:

Current Income Tax Expense	20,000	
Income Tax Payable ($50,000 × 40%)		20,000

A =   L +   SE
   +20,000 −20,000
Cash flows: No effect

Because the amount of tax losses available to carry forward to future years has changed, the Future Income Tax Asset account and its valuation allowance are adjusted. In this case, no tax losses remain.

A	= L +	SE		
−60,000		−60,000		

Cash flows: No effect

Future Income Tax Expense	60,000	
Future Income Tax Asset		60,000

A	= L +	SE		
+60,000		+60,000		

Cash flows: No effect

Allowance to Reduce Future Income Tax		
Asset to Expected Realizable Value	60,000	
Future Income Tax Benefit (loss carryforward)		60,000

The future tax expense of $60,000 (from adjusting the tax asset account) cancels out the $60,000 future tax benefit (from adjusting the allowance account). In this case, the income statement reports only the current income tax expense of $20,000 as set out in Illustration 18-34 when neither the tax asset nor the allowance was recognized.

To summarize, **IFRS currently** requires an "affirmative judgement" approach by recognizing future tax assets only to the extent that it is probable that deductible temporary differences, unused tax losses, and income tax reductions will result in a future tax benefit. This approach differs from the "impairment approach" recommended by the FASB in SFAS 109. The U.S. method recognizes a future income tax asset for all deductible temporary differences, unused tax losses, and income tax reductions and **offsets them with an impairment allowance** for the portion of the asset that does not meet the "more likely than not" threshold. **ASPE—private enterprise GAAP—**permits both approaches. As part of the short-term convergence project between the IASB and the FASB, the IASB had agreed to move to the SFAS 109 valuation allowance approach, and this is expected to be addressed in a 2010 IASB exposure draft.

Review of Future Income Tax Asset Account

Objective 8

Explain why the Future Income Tax Asset account is reassessed at the balance sheet date, and account for the future tax asset with and without a valuation allowance account.

Both private enterprise and international standards recommend recognizing a future income tax asset for most deductible temporary differences and for the carryforward of unused tax losses and other income tax reductions, **to the extent that it is probable that the future income tax asset will be realized**; in other words, as long as taxable income is more likely than not to be available to apply the deductions against. Consistent with the reporting for all assets, the Future Income Tax Asset account must be reviewed at each reporting date to ensure that its carrying amount is appropriate.

Assume that Jensen Corp. has a deductible temporary difference or loss carryforward of $1 million at the end of its first year of operations. Its tax rate is 40% and a future tax asset of $400,000 ($1,000,000 × 40%) is recognized on the basis that it is more likely than not that enough taxable income will be generated in the future. The journal entry to record the future tax benefit and the change in the future tax asset is:

A	= L +	SE		
+400,000		+400,000		

Cash flows: No effect

Future Income Tax Asset	400,000	
Future Income Tax Benefit		400,000

If, at the end of the next period, the deductible temporary difference or loss carryforward remains at $1 million but now only $750,000 meets the criterion for recognition, the future tax asset is recalculated as 40% of $750,000, or $300,000. The entry to be made depends on whether the allowance approach is used or not. Both methods of adjusting the asset account are shown in Illustration 18-35.

Direct Adjustment		Allowance Method	
Future Income Tax Expense	100,000	Future Income Tax Expense	100,000
Future Income Tax Asset	100,000	Allowance to Reduce Future	
		Income Tax Asset to	
		Expected Realizable Value	100,000

Illustration 18-35

Revaluation of Future Tax Asset Account

If a valuation account is used, it is reported on the balance sheet (or is explained in the notes) deducted from the Future Income Tax Asset account. Regardless of approach, the net amount reported is identical. The accounts are reported within the asset section of the statement of financial position as shown in Illustration 18-36.

Direct Adjustment		Allowance Method	
Future income tax asset	$300,000	Future income tax asset	$400,000
		Less: Allowance to reduce	
		future income tax asset to	
		expected realizable value	(100,000)
		Future income tax asset (net)	$300,000

Illustration 18-36

Balance Sheet Presentation of Remaining Future Tax Asset

At the end of the next period when the future tax asset and its realizable value are evaluated, assume it is now more likely than not that $850,000 of the original $1 million will be deductible in the future. This means the tax asset should be reported at $340,000 ($850,000 × 40%). The entry in Illustration 18-37 adjusts the accounts. Notice that a net value of $340,000 means that the allowance needs to be adjusted to $60,000. Once again, the net effect of the two approaches is identical. However, the valuation allowance method has the advantage of retaining the relationship between the Future Income Tax Asset account and the future deductible amounts.

Direct Adjustment		Allowance Method	
Future Income Tax Asset	40,000	Allowance to Reduce Future	
Future Income Tax Benefit	40,000	Income Tax Asset to	
		Expected Realizable Value	40,000
		Future Income Tax Benefit	40,000

Illustration 18-37

Revaluation of Future Tax Asset Account

The accounting standards offer guidance on how to determine whether it is probable that future taxable income of an appropriate nature, and relating to the same taxable entity and the same tax authority, will be available. The following possible sources of taxable income may be available **under the tax law** to realize a tax benefit for deductible temporary differences, tax loss carryovers, and other tax reductions.

 Law

1. Future reversals of existing taxable temporary differences

2. Future taxable income before taking into account reversing temporary differences, tax loss, and other tax reductions

3. Taxable income available in prior carryback years

4. Tax-planning strategies that would, if necessary, be implemented to realize a future tax asset. Tax strategies are actions that are prudent and feasible, and that would be applied.

When an entity has a history of recent tax losses, or circumstances are unsettled, or if the carryforward period allowed by tax law is about to expire, it must look for substantive reasons to justify recognition of a tax asset. Both favourable and unfavourable evidence is considered, with more weight attached to objectively verifiable evidence.[12] If the entity concludes that it is not probable that appropriate future taxable income will be available, a future tax asset is not recognized or a previously recognized tax asset is removed.

The future or deferred tax asset account is also reviewed to determine whether conditions have changed, because it may now be reasonable to recognize a future tax asset that was previously unrecognized. If conditions have changed, the associated tax benefit is recognized in the income statement of the same period. If the entity uses a valuation allowance account, the full future tax asset is already included in the account, and it is the allowance that needs to be adjusted (in this case, reduced).

Agrium Inc., headquartered in Calgary, Alberta, produces and markets agricultural nutrients and industrial products and is a retail supplier of agricultural products and services in both North and South America. As seen in the excerpt from Note 6 to the company's 2008 financial statements in Illustration 18-38, Agrium reports information about its future income tax assets, including those related to its losses available to be carried forward.

Real-World Emphasis

Illustration 18-38

Future Income Tax Assets and Valuation Allowance

As at December 31 (millions of U.S. dollars, except share data)	2008	2007
6. Income Taxes		
Future income tax assets		
Loss carry-forwards expiring through 2028	12	7
Asset retirement obligations and environmental remediation	72	60
Employee future benefits and incentives	42	67
Other	21	13
Future income tax assets before valuation allowance	147	147
Valuation allowance	(32)	(6)
Total future income tax assets, net of valuation allowance	115	141

In this excerpt, Agrium provides information about the sources of the temporary differences that result in future deductible amounts and future income tax assets. Of the U.S. $147 million of future tax assets at December 31, 2008, a valuation allowance of U.S. $32 million was needed.

PRESENTATION, DISCLOSURE, AND ANALYSIS

Balance Sheet Presentation

Objective 9

Identify and apply the presentation and disclosure requirements for income tax assets and liabilities, and apply intraperiod tax allocation.

Because income taxes have a unique nature, income tax assets and liabilities have to be reported separately from other assets and liabilities on the balance sheet.

---

[12] Examples of positive evidence that might support the recognition of a tax asset include a firm sales backlog that will produce more than enough taxable income to realize the future tax asset, or a history of strong earnings and evidence that the loss is due to a specific identifiable and non-recurring cause.

Income Taxes Receivable or Payable Currently

Income tax amounts **currently** receivable or payable are reported separately from **future** or **deferred** tax assets and liabilities. They are reported as current assets or current liabilities, and cannot be netted against one another unless there is a legal right of offset. This means that the receivable and payable usually have to belong to the same taxable entity, they have to relate to the same tax authority, and the authority has to allow a single net payment. This presentation is GAAP whether ASPE or international standards are being applied.

Because corporations are required to make several instalment payments to the Canada Revenue Agency during the year, there could be a debit balance in the Income Tax Payable account. When this occurs, it is reported as a current asset called Prepaid Income Taxes or Income Taxes Receivable. An income tax refund that is the result of carrying a current year's tax loss back against previous years' taxable income is also reported as an income tax receivable and current asset.

Law

Underlying Concept

The principle about netting similar assets and liabilities only when there is a legal right of offset and the intention is to settle them on a net basis is applied consistently through the accounting standards.

Future Tax Assets and Liabilities

The presentation of future or deferred tax asset and liability accounts differs under private enterprise standards and IFRS. The **IFRS requirements** are the easier to apply—all deferred tax assets and liabilities are reported as **noncurrent** items on a classified statement of financial position.

Under private enterprise requirements, however, future tax assets and future tax liabilities are segregated into current and noncurrent categories. The classification of an individual future tax liability or asset **as current or noncurrent** is determined by **the classification of the asset or liability underlying the specific temporary difference**. Let's see what this means.

Step 1.
What is the classification of the asset or liability that resulted in the tax asset or liability? A tax asset or tax liability caused by a temporary difference in an asset or liability classified as noncurrent is identified as noncurrent. A tax asset or tax liability caused by a temporary difference in a current asset or liability account is classified as current. If there is no related asset or liability on the balance sheet, such as with tax losses, the future tax account is classified according to the expected reversal date of the temporary difference: if within 12 months from the reporting date, it is current; otherwise, it is noncurrent.

Step 2.
Determine the *net current* amount by netting the various future tax asset and liability amounts that are classified as current. If the net result is an asset, report it on the balance sheet as a current asset; if it is a liability, report it as a current liability.

Step 3.
Determine the *net noncurrent* amount by netting the various future tax assets and liabilities that are classified as noncurrent. If the net result is an asset, report it on the balance sheet as a noncurrent asset; if it is a liability, report it as a long-term liability.

To illustrate, assume that K. Scoffi Limited has four future tax items at December 31, 2011. K. Scoffi reports under private enterprise GAAP, has chosen to apply the future income taxes payable method of accounting for its income taxes, and operates under a single tax jurisdiction. The analysis in Illustration 18-39 shows how each temporary difference and related future tax asset or liability is classified.

Illustration 18-39

Classification of Temporary Differences as Current or Noncurrent

Temporary Difference Related To:	Resulting Future Tax		Related Balance Sheet Account	Related Balance Sheet Account Classification
	Asset	Liability		
1. **Rent collected in advance:** recognized when earned for accounting purposes and when received for tax purposes	$42,000		Unearned Rent	Current
2. Use of **straight-line depreciation** for accounting purposes and accelerated depreciation for tax purposes		$214,000	Equipment	Noncurrent
3. Recognition of **revenue** in the period of sale for accounting purposes and during the period of collection for tax purposes		45,000	Accounts Receivable	Current
4. **Warranty liabilities:** recognized for accounting purposes at time of sale; for tax purposes at time paid	12,000		Estimated Liability under Warranties	Current
Totals	$54,000	$259,000		

If K. Scoffi has a single future tax liability account with a balance of $259,000 − $54,000 = $205,000 in it, an analysis similar to this is needed to identify each component.

The future taxes to be classified as "current" net to a $9,000 asset ($42,000 + $12,000 − $45,000), and the future taxes to be classified as "noncurrent" net to a $214,000 liability. Consequently, K. Scoffi's future taxes will appear on the December 31, 2011 balance sheet as shown in Illustration 18-40.

Illustration 18-40

Balance Sheet Presentation of Future Income Taxes

Current assets	
Future income tax asset	$9,000
Long-term liabilities	
Future income tax liability	$214,000

As indicated earlier, a future tax asset or liability **may not be related to a specific asset or liability**. One example is research costs that are recognized as expenses in the accounts when they are incurred but deferred and deducted in later years for tax purposes. Another example is a tax loss carryforward. In both cases, a future tax asset is recognized, but there is no related, identifiable asset or liability for financial reporting purposes. In these situations, future income taxes are classified according to the date the temporary difference is expected to reverse or the tax benefit is expected to be realized.

If K. Scoffi reports as a publicly accountable enterprise under IFRS, one net future tax liability of $205,000 is presented as a noncurrent liability.

Similar to taxes currently receivable or payable, **future** or **deferred** tax assets and liabilities also cannot be netted against one another unless they relate to the same taxable entity and the same tax authority and there is a legal right to settle or realize them at the same time. This is required whether private enterprise or international standards are being applied.

Income and Other Statement Presentation

Intraperiod Tax Allocation

Intraperiod tax allocation refers to how and where the income tax expense or benefit for the period—for both current and future taxes—is reported on the income and other statements that reflect transactions that attract income tax. A good place to start is to understand that the objective is to report the tax cost or benefit in the same place as **the underlying transaction or event that gave rise to the tax.** This means that the current and future tax expense (or benefit) of the current period related to **income before discontinued operations, discontinued operations, other comprehensive income, adjustments reported in retained earnings, and capital transactions is reported with the related item.**

To illustrate intraperiod tax allocation, assume that Copy Doctor Inc. has a tax rate of 35% and reports the following pre-tax amounts in 2011:

- a loss from continuing operations of $500,000

- income from discontinued operations of $900,000, of which $210,000 is not taxable

- an unrealized holding gain of $25,000 on investments accounted for at fair value through other comprehensive income (FV-OCI). Assume that this will be taxable as ordinary income when it is realized.

Illustration 18-41 presents an analysis that is useful in determining how and where the current income tax expense or benefit will be reported.

	Continuing Operations	Discontinued Operations	OCI	Total
Accounting income (loss)	($500,000)	$900,000	$25,000	$425,000
Deduct non-taxable permanent difference		(210,000)		(210,000)
Deduct originating difference: gain taxable when realized			(25,000)	(25,000)
Taxable income	($500,000)	$690,000	$-0-	$190,000
Current income tax expense/ tax payable at 35%	($175,000)	$241,500	$-0-	$66,500

Illustration 18-41

Analysis, Intraperiod Tax Allocation—Current Taxes, 2011

Whenever income tax is reported separately so that it appears with a particular component of comprehensive income or in another statement, prepare your analysis by setting up a separate column for each component that attracts tax, as shown in the illustration. Note that the Canada Revenue Agency is not interested in where the company reports various amounts on the GAAP financial statements—it is interested only in the last column of the illustration; that is, in what is taxable in the year and what is not. Based on the analysis, the entry to record current income tax is:

Current Income Tax Expense (discontinued operations)	241,500	
Current Income Tax Benefit (continuing operations)		175,000
Income Tax Payable		66,500

A = L + SE
    +66,500   −66,500

Cash flows: No effect

Future income taxes are also allocated to the financial statement items that attract tax. In this case, we assume that the $25,000 temporary difference between the carrying amount of the FV-OCI investments and their tax basis is the only temporary difference in this and previous years. Illustration 18-42 shows the calculations to determine future income taxes.

Illustration 18-42

Analysis, Intraperiod Tax Allocation—Future Taxes, 2011

	Continuing Operations	Discontinued Operations	OCI	Total
Taxable temporary difference, Dec. 31, 2011	$–0–	$–0–	$25,000	$25,000
Future income tax liability at 35% future rate, Dec. 31, 2011	$–0–	$–0–	$ 8,750	$ 8,750
Less future income tax liability before adjustment	–0–	–0–	–0–	–0–
Future income tax expense, 2011	$–0–	$–0–	$ 8,750	$ 8,750

The calculations are the same as those earlier in the chapter, with added columns for the different parts of the statements that attract tax. In this example, the only temporary difference is related to an item of other comprehensive income. The tax effect therefore is reported there as well. The entry to record future taxes is:

A = L + SE
    +8,750   –8,750

Cash flows: No effect

Future Income Tax Expense (OCI)	8,750	
Future Income Tax Liability		8,750

Illustration 18-43 shows how the income taxes calculated above are reported in the financial statements along with the items that attract the tax. The tax amounts are taken directly from the entries or the analysis.

Illustration 18-43

Statement Presentation— Intraperiod Tax Allocation

COPY DOCTOR INC.
Income Statement
Year Ended December 31, 2011

Income (loss) from continuing operations before tax	$(500,000)	
Less: Current income tax benefit	175,000	$(325,000)
Income from discontinued operations	$ 900,000	
Less: Current income tax expense	(241,500)	658,500
Net income		$ 333,500

Statement of Comprehensive Income
Year Ended December 31, 2011

Net income		$ 333,500
Other comprehensive income:		
Holding gains, FV-OCI investments	$ 25,000	
Less: Future income tax expense	(8,750)	16,250
Comprehensive income		$ 349,750

As far as the Copy Doctor example above goes, accounting under **IFRS** and **private enterprise GAAP** is the same. However, there is a difference in how intraperiod allocation is applied when current and deferred taxes relate to transactions recognized in equity or other comprehensive income of a prior period. **IFRS** requires that, where practical, the tax effect in the current year be traced back to where the transaction was originally reported and be presented in the same statement as in the prior period. Under **PE standards**, income taxes are charged or credited to various equity accounts only for items recognized in the current period. Notice that this difference applies only when there is no current period event or transaction associated with the change in current or future taxes.[13]

In terms of real-world examples, we can look to **CGI Group Inc.**, a Canadian-based company in the business of managing information technology and business process services. For its year ended September 30, 2009, CGI Group Inc. reported income tax expense separately for earnings from continuing operations, income from discontinued operations, and three individual unrealized gain amounts reported in other comprehensive income. A change in accounting policy reported in the statement of retained earnings was also reported net of its tax effect.

Real-World Emphasis

Disclosure Requirements

Taxes Payable Method

If a company reporting under **private enterprise standards** chooses the taxes payable accounting policy to report income taxes, a limited amount of information is required to be disclosed:

- The income tax expense or benefit included in determining income (loss) before discontinued operations; and the amount related to transactions recognized in equity

- A reconciliation of the actual tax rate or expense or benefit to the statutory amount for income (loss) before discontinued operations, with information about major reconciling items

- The amount of capital gain and other reserves to be included in taxable income in each of the next five years; and the amount of unused income tax credits and losses carried forward

This limited information provides a reader with significant information about areas where there are temporary differences and potential increases in taxable income in the medium term.

Future Income Taxes Method

If a company reporting under **private enterprise standards** chooses the future income taxes accounting policy, again, only limited disclosures are required:

- The amounts of current and of future income tax expense or benefit included in income before discontinued operations; and the amount related to capital transactions or transactions recognized in equity

- The amount of unused income tax losses, income tax reductions, and deductible temporary differences for which no future tax asset is recognized

In addition, any enterprise reporting under ASPE whose income is not taxed because it is taxable directly to its owners is required to disclose this fact.

---

[13] Let's look at an example. Assume an entity reports a correction of a prior period error in retained earnings in Year 5. As a result, a future tax liability is recognized on the Year 5 balance sheet and a future tax expense is netted against the retained earnings adjustment in the same year. In Year 6, the tax rate increases, also increasing the balance of the future tax liability recognized in Year 5. Under private enterprise standards, the related future tax expense is reported on the Year 6 income statement. There is no backward tracing to the retained earnings statement. Under IFRS, the increased tax expense in Year 6 is reported in retained earnings. The IASB may change this requirement in the future to harmonize with the FASB approach, which is also similar to ASPE.

The disclosure situation changes for publicly accountable entities reporting under **international GAAP**. The IFRS requirements are extensive, with the following types of information identified:

- Separate disclosure of the major components of income tax expense or benefit, and the source of both current and future taxes

- The amount of current and future tax recognized in equity in the period; and tax expense for each component of OCI

- A reconciliation of the effective tax rate to the statutory rates for the period and an explanation of changes in the statutory rates relative to the prior period

- Information about unrecognized future tax assets and the underlying deductible temporary differences and unused tax losses, as well as supporting evidence for recognized deferred tax assets

- Information about each type of temporary difference and the future tax asset or liability recognized on the statement of financial position

The actual standard, IAS 12 *Income Taxes*, is the best source to refer to for the specific disclosures mandated for publicly accountable enterprises. Excerpts from the 2008 financial statements of Switzerland-based **Nestlé Group** are provided in Illustration 18-44 to indicate what the disclosures entail. The deferred (future) income tax asset and liability accounts on the balance sheet are provided, followed by the company's complete income tax note, Note 7. Nestlé reports amounts in millions of Swiss francs (CHF). Using the bulleted list of required disclosures above, see if you can find the specific information in these excerpts.

Real-World Emphasis

WILEY PLUS
Additional Disclosures

Illustration 18-44
Disclosure of Income Taxes— Nestlé Group

Consolidated balance sheet as at 31 December 2008

In millions of CHF	Notes	2008	2007
Assets			
Non-current assets			
Deferred tax assets	7	2,842	2,224
Liabilities and equity			
Non-current liabilities			
Deferred tax liabilities (a)	7	1,341	1,558

7. Taxes

7.1 Taxes recognised in the income statement

In millions of CHF	2008	2007(a)
Components of taxes		
Current taxes (b)	3,423	3,400
Deferred taxes	(1,090)	156
Taxes reclassified to equity	1,454	(140)
	3,787	3,416

In millions of CHF	2008	2007(a)
Reconciliation of taxes		
Expected tax expense at weighted average applicable tax rate	4,294	3,134
Tax effect of non-deductible or non-taxable items	(873)	(225)
Prior years' taxes	(220)	(58)
Transfers to unrecognised deferred tax assets	61	62
Transfers from unrecognised deferred tax assets	(14)	(46)
Changes in tax rates	(6)	–
Withholding taxes levied on transfers of income	350	403
Other, incl. taxes on capital	195	146
	3,787	3,416

(a) 2007 comparatives have been restated following first application of IFRIC 14.

(b) The adjustment for current taxes of prior years is a benefit of CHF 49 million (2007: expense of CHF 12 million).

The expected tax expense at weighted average applicable tax rate is the result from applying the domestic statutory tax rates to profits before taxes of each entity in the country it operates. For the Group, the weighted average applicable tax rate varies from one year to the other depending on the relative weight of the profit of each individual entity in the Group's profit as well as the changes in the statutory tax rates.

In 2008, the weighted average applicable tax rate is also substantially impacted by the tax free gain resulting from the disposal of the 24.8% stake of Alcon.

7.2 Reconciliation of deferred taxes by types of temporary differences recognised in the balance sheet

In millions of CHF

	Property, plant and equipment	Goodwill and intangible assets	Employee benefits	Inventories, receivables, payables and provisions	Unused tax losses and unused tax credits	Other	Total
At 1 January 2007 (a)	(922)	(655)	1,620	898	288	265	1,494
Currency retranslations	81	15	(85)	(27)	(5)	(10)	(31)
Deferred tax (expense)/ income (a)	(3)	36	(193)	31	(14)	(13)	(156)
Modification of the scope of consolidation	(47)	(453)	80	(11)	9	(219)	(641)
At 31 December 2007 (a)	(891)	(1,057)	1,422	891	278	23	666
Currency retranslations	76	69	(165)	(106)	(26)	(45)	(197)
Deferred tax (expense)/income	(99)	147	654	94	75	219	1,090
Modification of the scope of consolidation	3	(17)	(4)	1	(3)	(38)	(58)
At 31 December 2008	(911)	(858)	1,907	880	324	159	1,501

In millions of CHF	2008	2007(a)
Reflected in the balance sheet as follows:		
Deferred tax assets	2,842	2,224
Deferred tax liabilities	(1,341)	(1,558)
Net assets	1,501	666

(a) 2007 comparatives have been restated following first application of IFRIC 14 (refer to Note 32).

continued on page 1184

7.3 Unrecognised deferred taxes

The deductible temporary differences as well as the unused tax losses and tax credits for which no deferred tax assets are recognised expire as follows:

In millions of CHF	2008	2007
Within one year	80	115
Between one and five years	343	739
More than five years	1,080	890
	1,503	1,744

At 31 December 2008, the unrecognised deferred tax assets amount to CHF 450 million (2007: CHF 520 million).

In addition, the Group has not recognised deferred tax liabilities in respect of unremitted earnings that are considered indefinitely reinvested in foreign subsidiaries. At 31 December 2008, these earnings amount to CHF 17.4 billion (2007: CHF 22.3 billion). They could be subject to withholding and other taxes on remittance.

Analysis

The extensive disclosures related to current and future income taxes are required for several reasons, some of which are now discussed.

Assessment of Quality of Earnings

Ethics

Real-World Emphasis

In trying to assess the quality of a company's earnings, many investors are interested in the reconciliations between accounting and tax numbers. Earnings that are improved by a favourable tax effect should be examined carefully, particularly if the tax effect is non-recurring. Accounting for future income tax assets is an area that requires considerable judgement and may, therefore, be open to abuse. To justify the recognition of future income tax assets on the balance sheet and tax benefits on the income statement, it takes only a small amount of optimism for management to expect flows of future taxable income against which to apply tax losses and other future deductible amounts. Valuation of future income tax assets, either directly or through an adjustment of the valuation allowance account, usually affects bottom-line income on a dollar-for-dollar basis.

A good example of this is the case of **Stelco Inc.**, once a strong Canadian steel producer. In one year, the company's loss of $217 million was reduced by $81 million of future income tax benefits, while $139 million of future income tax assets were reported on its balance sheet. In the next year, the company's $9 million of income was increased by an $11-million future tax benefit, and $161 million of net future tax assets were reported on the balance sheet, $74 million of which was classified as a current asset. The future deductible amounts underlying the tax asset accounts were related to the recognition of employee retirement benefit expenses in excess of amounts paid, and income tax losses carried forward.

To have classified $74 million of the future tax asset as a current asset, management must have expected the upcoming year to be an excellent one for the company! As it turned out, sales volume and prices were down, costs increased, and the cash position deteriorated, resulting in Stelco's obtaining an order to initiate a court-supervised restructuring under the *Companies' Creditors Arrangement Act*.

Regardless of management's motivations in assessing the value of future tax assets, financial statement readers should be aware of how big a part judgement plays in these measurements.

Better Predictions of Future Cash Flows

Examining the future portion of income tax expense provides information about whether taxes payable are likely to be higher or lower in the future. A close examination may provide insight into the company's policies on capitalization of costs and revenue recognition, and on other policies that give rise to differences between the accounting income reported and taxable income. As a result, it may be possible to predict upcoming reductions in future tax liabilities and additional cash required for income tax payments. Such a situation may lead to a loss of liquidity.[14]

Predicting Future Cash Flows from Operating Loss Carryforwards. From disclosures of the amounts and expiration dates of losses being carried forward, analysts can estimate income that a company may recognize in the future and on which it will pay no income tax. For example, Versatile Systems Inc., a British Columbia company, reported in its 2009 financial statements that the company had $26,274,453 of tax losses and deductions that it could use to offset future taxable income. Versatile also provides information about when the operating losses expire, the jurisdiction in which the losses are available for carryforward, and the extent to which a valuation allowance has been provided.

Real-World Emphasis

Outstanding Conceptual Questions

The FASB and IASB believe that the asset-liability method, sometimes referred to as the balance sheet liability approach, is the most conceptually sound method of accounting for income taxes. Its objectives are to recognize the amount of taxes payable or refundable for the current year, and tax liabilities and tax assets for the future tax consequences of events that have been recognized in the financial statements or tax returns.

Although this method is considered to be the most appropriate approach for publicly accountable enterprises, some conceptual questions remain.

No discounting. Without discounting the asset or liability (that is, by not considering its present value), financial statements do not indicate the appropriate benefit of a tax deferral or the burden of a tax prepayment. This impairs the comparability of the financial statements, because a dollar in a short-term deferral is presented as being of the same value as a dollar in a longer-term deferral.

Finance

Recognition of future tax assets. Some professionals believe that future deductible amounts arising from operating loss carryforwards are different from future deductible amounts arising from other causes. One rationale for this view is that a future tax asset arising from normal transactions results in a tax prepayment: a prepaid tax asset. In the case of losses available to carry forward, no tax prepayment has been made. Others argue that realization of a loss carryforward is less likely and thus should require a more severe test than for a net deductible amount arising from normal operations.

These controversies exist within the asset-liability approach. Others argue that a completely different type of approach should be used to report future income taxes. In addition, advances in the conceptual framework project are removing the criterion of "probability" from the definition of both an asset and a liability and incorporating it in the measurement of the elements instead. Questions arise about whether future income tax liabilities are, in fact, "present obligations." And, are future tax assets really "present economic resources"?

---

[14] R.P. Weber and J.E. Wheeler, in "Using Income Disclosures to Explore Significant Economic Transactions," *Accounting Horizons* (September 1992), discuss how deferred (future) tax disclosures can be used to assess the quality of earnings and to predict future cash flows.

When these new concepts are applied to the asset-liability approach to income taxes, it is likely that different recognition and measurement decisions may result.

Objective 10

Identify the major differences between private enterprise standards and IFRS for income taxes.

IFRS AND PRIVATE ENTERPRISE GAAP COMPARISON

A Comparison of IFRS and Private Entity GAAP

Illustration 18-45

IFRS and Private Entity GAAP Comparison Chart

While other differences exist between private enterprise standards and IFRS than those indicated in Illustration 18-45, many relate to complexities in income tax accounting that are beyond the scope of this text.

	Accounting Standards for Private Enterprises (PE GAAP/ASPE)—*CICA Handbook*, Part II, Section 3465	IFRS—IAS 12
Scope, definitions, and terminology	Terminology used: • Accounting income • Taxable income (taxable loss) • Future income tax • Tax expense (tax benefit) • Tax basis • More than likely	Terminology used: • Accounting profit • Taxable profit (tax loss) • Deferred income tax • Tax expense (tax income) • Tax base • Probable
Recognition	A company chooses either the taxes payable method or the future income taxes method as its accounting policy. The future income taxes method is also known as the asset and liability approach and the balance sheet liability method.	No choice is permitted. All companies apply the balance sheet liability method, almost identical to the ASPE future income taxes approach.
	A future tax asset is permitted to be recognized for all deductible temporary differences, unused tax losses, and income tax reductions, with the total offset by a valuation allowance to bring the future tax asset to the amount that is more likely than not to be realized in the future.	A deferred tax asset is permitted to be recognized only to the extent that it is probable that it will be realized in the future. A valuation account is not used.
Presentation	Future income tax assets and liabilities are classified as current or noncurrent based on the classification of the underlying asset or liability that resulted in the future tax amount. When there is no related balance sheet account, the classification is based on when the temporary difference is expected to reverse.	All deferred income tax asset and liability accounts are classified as noncurrent.
	There is no reporting of income taxes in equity accounts unless it is for a current period transaction that affects equity.	IFRS requires "backward tracing" of current period tax changes that relate to items charged or credited to equity or OCI in prior periods. In the current period, the tax effect is reported on the statement the item was originally reported on.
Disclosure	Less information is required to be disclosed under both the taxes payable and future income taxes methods of accounting for income taxes than is required under IFRS.	Considerably more information is required to be reported under IFRS, including details that explain changes in most tax-related accounts, the reasons for temporary differences, and a breakdown of major components of deferred income tax expense for the period.
	An enterprise whose income is not taxed because it is taxed directly to its owners is required to identify this situation.	There is no similar disclosure requirement.

Looking Ahead

In March 2009, the IASB issued an Exposure Draft (ED) of an IFRS to replace IAS 12 *Income Taxes* with the intention of eliminating many of the differences between the IFRS and FASB standards. The ED did not propose to change the fundamental approach to accounting for taxes (the balance sheet liability approach), but it did seek to eliminate differences in the application of and exceptions to this method as used under IFRS, U.S., and Canadian standards.

Examples of harmonization recommended in the ED included moving to the Canadian and U.S. approach to classification of deferred income tax assets and liabilities on the balance sheet, requirement to use a valuation allowance approach for the recognition and measurement of future tax assets, and the removal of the "backward tracing" of current tax changes that relate to a prior-year item in equity or OCI. A major issue dealt with was the approach to accounting for **uncertain tax positions**; that is, how to deal with uncertainty in tax measurements. The proposed position in the ED was not consistent with the approach taken by FASB.

In November 2009, because of other more urgent projects on the IASB agenda and the lack of agreement on the ED positions, the IASB postponed issuing a revised income tax standard. As this text went to print, the Board expected to issue an exposure draft in late 2010 and a revised standard in 2011. The revisions are limited in scope to uncertain tax positions, deferred tax on property remeasurement at fair value, and items that had received support following the March 2009 exposure draft. This latter group includes acceptance of the valuation allowance approach for deferred tax assets.

Summary of Learning Objectives

Present Value Concepts

KEY TERMS

1 Explain the difference between accounting income and taxable income, and calculate taxable income and current income taxes.

Accounting income is calculated in accordance with generally accepted accounting principles. Taxable income is calculated in accordance with prescribed tax legislation and regulations. Because tax legislation and GAAP have different objectives, accounting income and taxable income often differ. To calculate taxable income, companies start with their accounting income and then add and deduct items to adjust the GAAP measure of income to what is actually taxable and tax-deductible in the period. Current income tax expense and income taxes payable are determined by applying the current tax rate to taxable income.

2 Explain what a taxable temporary difference is, determine its amount, and calculate future income tax liabilities.

A taxable temporary difference is the difference between the carrying amount of an asset or liability and its tax basis with the consequence that, when the asset is recovered or the liability is settled in the future for an amount equal to its carrying value, the taxable income of that future period will be increased. Because taxes increase in the future as a result of temporary differences that exist at the balance sheet date, the future tax consequences of these taxable amounts are recognized in the current period as a future tax liability.

3 Explain what a deductible temporary difference is, determine its amount, and calculate future income tax assets.

A deductible temporary difference is the difference between the carrying amount of an asset or liability and its tax basis with the consequence that, when the asset is recovered or the liability is settled in the future for an amount equal to its book value, the taxable income of that future period will be reduced. Because taxes are reduced in the future as a result of temporary differences that exist at the balance sheet date, the future tax consequences of these deductible amounts are recognized in the current period as a future tax asset.

4 Prepare analyses of future income tax balances and record future income tax expense.

The following steps are taken: (1) identify all temporary differences between the carrying amounts and tax bases of assets and liabilities at the balance sheet date; (2) calculate the correct net future tax asset or liability balance at the end of the period; (3) compare the balance in the future tax asset or liability before the adjustment with the correct balance at the balance sheet date—the difference is the future tax expense/benefit; (4) the journal entry is based on the change in the amount of the net future tax asset or liability.

5 Explain the effect of multiple tax rates and tax rate changes on income tax accounts, and calculate current and future tax amounts when there is a change in substantively enacted tax rates.

Tax rates other than the existing rates can be used only when the future tax rates have been enacted into legislation or substantively enacted. Future tax assets and liabilities are measured at the tax rate that applies to the specific future years in which the temporary difference is expected to reverse. When there is a change in the future tax rate, its effect on the future tax accounts is recognized immediately. The effects are reported as an adjustment to future tax expense in the period of the change.

6 Account for a tax loss carryback.

A company may carry a taxable loss back three years and receive refunds to a maximum of the income taxes paid in those years. Because the economic benefits related to the losses carried back are certain, they are recognized in the period of the loss as a tax benefit on the income statement and as an asset (income tax refund receivable) on the balance sheet.

7 Account for a tax loss carryforward, including any note disclosures.

A post-2005 tax loss can be carried forward and applied against the taxable incomes of the next 20 years. If the economic benefits related to the tax loss are more likely than not to be realized during the carryforward period, they are recognized in the period of the loss as a future tax benefit in the income statement and as a future tax asset on the balance sheet. Otherwise, they are not recognized in the financial statements. Alternatively, PE GAAP also allows the use of a contra valuation allowance account, but this approach is not envisaged under current IFRS. Disclosure is required of the amounts of tax loss carryforwards and their expiry dates. If previously unrecorded tax losses are subsequently used to benefit a future period, the benefit is recognized in that future period.

8 Explain why the Future Income Tax Asset account is reassessed at the balance sheet date, and account for the future tax asset with and without a valuation allowance account.

Every asset must be assessed to ensure that it is not reported at an amount higher than the economic benefits that are expected to be received from the use or sale of the asset. The economic benefit to be received from the future income tax asset is a reduction in future income taxes payable. If it is unlikely that sufficient taxable income will be generated in the future to allow the future deductions, the income tax asset may have to be written down. If previously unrecognized amounts are now expected to be realizable, a future tax asset is recognized. These entries may be made directly to the future tax asset account or through a valuation allowance contra account.

9 **Identify and apply the presentation and disclosure requirements for income tax assets and liabilities, and apply intraperiod tax allocation.**

Under all methods, current income taxes payable or receivable are reported separately as a current liability or current asset. Under PE standards and assuming a single tax authority, future tax assets and liabilities are classified as one net current amount and one net noncurrent amount based on the classification of the asset or liability to which the temporary difference relates. Other future tax accounts are classified according to when the temporary differences are expected to reverse. Under IFRS, the deferred tax accounts are all classified as noncurrent. Current and future tax expense is reported separately with income before discontinued operations, discontinued operations, items in OCI, retained earnings, and other capital. Separate disclosure is required of the amounts and expiry dates of unused tax losses, and the amount of deductible temporary differences for which no future tax asset has been recognized. PE GAAP calls for limited disclosures, but under IFRS, additional disclosures are required about temporary differences and unused tax losses, the major components of income tax expense, and the reasons for the difference between the statutory tax rate and the effective rate indicated on the income statement.

10 **Identify the major differences between private enterprise standards and IFRS for income taxes.**

Private enterprise standards allow an accounting policy choice:—the taxes payable method or the future income taxes method—while IFRS requires use of the latter approach, also called the balance sheet liability method. The current differences relate to terminology, the balance sheet classification of future tax assets and liabilities, use of a valuation allowance, and the extent of disclosure.

Appendix 18A

COMPREHENSIVE ILLUSTRATION

The example below walks you through a comprehensive illustration of an income tax problem with several temporary and permanent differences. It assumes the reporting company either reports under IFRS or applies the future income taxes method under accounting standards for private enterprises. The illustration follows one company through two complete years, 2010 and 2011. Study it carefully. It should help cement your understanding of the concepts and procedures presented in the chapter.

First Year—2010

Allman Corporation, which began operations early in 2010, produces various products on a contract basis. The company's year end is December 31. Each contract generates a gross profit of $80,000 and some of Allman's contracts provide for the customer to pay on an instalment basis. In such cases, the customer pays one-fifth of the contract revenue in the year of the sale and one-fifth in each of the following four years. Gross profit is recognized in the year when the contract is completed for financial reporting purposes (accrual basis) and in the year when cash is collected for tax purposes (instalment or cash basis). Information on Allman's operations for 2010 is as follows:

1. In 2010, the company completed seven contracts that allow the customer to pay on an instalment basis. The related gross profit of $560,000 on sales of $1.5 million (to be collected at a rate of $300,000 per year beginning in 2010) is recognized for financial reporting purposes, but only $112,000 of gross profit on these sales is reported on the 2010 tax return. Future collections on the related instalment receivables are expected to result in taxable amounts of $112,000 in each of the next four years.

2. At the beginning of 2010, Allman Corporation purchased depreciable assets with a cost of $540,000. For financial reporting purposes, Allman depreciates these assets using the straight-line method over a six-year service life with no residual value expected. For tax purposes, the assets fall into CCA Class 8, permitting a 20% rate, and for the first year the half-year rule is applied. Any UCC remaining at the end of 2015 is expected to be tax deductible in that year as a terminal loss. The following table shows the depreciation and net asset value schedules for both financial reporting and tax purposes:

	Accounting			Tax	
Year	Depreciation	Carrying Amount, End of Year		CCA	UCC, End of Year
2010	$ 90,000	$450,000		$ 54,000	$486,000
2011	90,000	360,000		97,200	388,800
2012	90,000	270,000		77,760	311,040
2013	90,000	180,000		62,208	248,832
2014	90,000	90,000		49,766	199,066
2015	90,000	—		199,066	—
	$540,000			$540,000	

3. The company guarantees its product for two years from the contract completion date. During 2010, the total product warranty liability accrued for financial reporting purposes was $200,000, and the 2010 expenditures to satisfy the warranty liability were $44,000. The remaining liability of $156,000 is expected to be settled by expenditures of $56,000 in 2011 and $100,000 in 2012.

4. At December 31, 2010, the company accrued non-taxable dividends receivable of $28,000, the only dividend revenue reported for the year.

5. During 2010, non-deductible fines and penalties of $26,000 were paid.

6. The 2010 accounting income before taxes is $412,000.

7. The enacted tax rate for 2010 is 50%, and for 2011 and future years it is 40%.

8. The company is expected to have taxable income in all future years.

Taxable Income, Income Tax Payable, Current Income Tax Expense—2010

The first step in determining the company's income tax payable for 2010 is to calculate its taxable income. Each step in this calculation has to be thought through carefully. Remember that you are starting with what is included in the current year's revenues and expenses (the accounting income) and are adjusting this to what the net taxable amount is. The income taxes levied on the taxable amount are the taxes payable and also the current income tax expense for the year. Illustration 18A-1 shows the results.

Accounting income for 2010	$ 412,000
Permanent differences:	
Non-taxable revenue—dividends	(28,000)
Non-deductible expenses—fines and penalties	26,000
Reversible differences:	
Deferred gross profit for tax purposes ($560,000 – $112,000)	(448,000)
Depreciation per books in excess of CCA ($90,000 – $54,000)	36,000
Warranty expense per books in excess of amount deductible for tax purposes ($200,000 – $44,000)	156,000
Taxable income for 2010	$ 154,000
Income tax payable and current income tax expense for 2010:	
$154,000 × 50%	$ 77,000

Illustration 18A-1

Calculation of Taxable Income and Taxes Payable—2010

Future Tax Assets and Liabilities at December 31, 2010, and 2010 Future Tax Expense

Because future tax expense is the difference between the opening and closing balance of the net future tax asset or liability account, the next step is to determine the net future tax asset or liability at the end of 2010. (The opening balance in this case is $0 because this is the first year of operations.) This represents the net tax effect of all the temporary differences between the carrying amounts and tax bases of related assets and liabilities on December 31, 2010. Illustration 18A-2 summarizes the temporary differences, the future tax asset and liability amounts, the correct balance of the net future tax liability account at December 31, 2010, and the amount required for the future tax expense entry.

Illustration 18A-2

Determination of Future Tax Assets, Liabilities, and Future Income Tax Expense—2010

Balance Sheet Account	Carrying Amount	– Tax Basis	= (Taxable) Deductible Temporary Difference	× Tax Rate	= Future Income Tax Asset (Liability)
Deferred gross profit (contra to A/R)	$ –0–	$448,000	$(448,000)	.40	$(179,200)
Plant and equipment	450,000	486,000	36,000	.40	14,400
Liability for warranties	156,000	–0–	156,000	.40	62,400
Net future tax liability, December 31, 2010					(102,400)
Net future tax asset (liability) before adjustment					–0–
Increase in future tax liability account, and future tax expense for 2010					$(102,400)

Let's review each step in this illustration. Allman Corporation recognized all the profit on the 2010 instalment sales in its 2010 income statement. None of the $560,000 of gross profit is deferred for financial reporting purposes. Therefore, the carrying amount of the deferred gross profit (a contra account to Accounts Receivable) at December 31, 2010, is $0. However, only $112,000 of the gross profit is recognized in taxable income. Therefore, the remaining $448,000 ($560,000 – $112,000) of gross profit is deferred for tax purposes and it will be included in taxable income in the future as the outstanding receivables on the sales are collected. The tax basis of the deferred gross profit account is $448,000. The temporary difference will result in taxable amounts in the future. At the enacted rate of 40%, this will cause an additional $179,200 of income tax to be payable in the future.

The carrying amount of the depreciable assets is $450,000 at the end of 2010, but their undepreciated capital cost, or tax value, is $486,000. Because the company has taken $36,000 **less CCA** than depreciation to the end of 2010, in the future there will be $36,000 **more CCA** deductible for tax purposes than depreciation taken on the books. Therefore, the $36,000 is a deductible temporary difference that will cause future taxes to be reduced by $14,400. Comparing the CCA and depreciation schedules over the next few years reveals that in some years (2011, 2015, and onwards) excess CCA will be claimed, while in others (2012, 2013, and 2014) less CCA than depreciation will be claimed. These net out at December 31, 2010, to $36,000 more CCA than depreciation in the future.

Allman reports a warranty liability of $156,000 on its December 31, 2010 balance sheet. This whole amount will be deductible when calculating taxable income in the future when the actual warranty expenditures are made and the liability settled. Because Allman has not yet recognized the $156,000 of expenses for tax purposes, the tax basis of the liability is $0. This third temporary difference, therefore, is a deductible temporary difference and, at a 40% rate, will result in future tax savings of $62,400.

The key to the analysis is to determine whether taxable income **in a future period will be increased or decreased**. If increased, it is a **taxable** temporary difference; if decreased, it is a **deductible** temporary difference.

The tax effect of each temporary difference is calculated by using the tax rate that applies for each specific future year in which the difference reverses. In this case, because the tax rates for all future years are identical, the future tax amounts can be calculated by simply applying the 40% rate to the temporary differences at the end of 2010 as shown in Illustration 18A-2. If the tax rates for each future year are not the same, a separate schedule setting out when each temporary difference is expected to reverse is needed, such as the one shown in Illustration 18A-3.

(Taxable) deductible temporary differences	Total	Future Years				
		2011	2012	2013	2014	2015
Deferred gross profit	$(448,000)	$(112,000)	$(112,000)	$(112,000)	$(112,000)	
Plant and equipment	36,000	7,200	(12,240)	(27,792)	(40,234)	$109,066
Warranty liability	156,000	56,000	100,000			
Net (taxable) deductible amount	$(256,000)	$ (48,800)	$ (24,240)	$(139,792)	$(152,234)	$109,066
Tax rate enacted for year		40%	40%	40%	40%	40%
Net future tax asset (liability)	$(102,400)	$ (19,520)	$ (9,696)	$ (55,917)	$ (60,894)	$ 43,627

Illustration 18A-3

Schedule of Reversals of Temporary Differences at December 31, 2010

Income Tax Accounting Entries—2010

The entries to record current and future income taxes for 2010 are:

Current Income Tax Expense	77,000	
Income Tax Payable (Illustration 18A-1)		77,000

A = L + SE
+77,000   −77,000
Cash flows: No effect

Future Income Tax Expense	102,400	
Future Income Tax Liability (Illustration 18A-2)		102,400

A = L + SE
+102,400   −102,400
Cash flows: No effect

Financial Statement Presentation—2010

If Allman Corporation reports under **IFRS** (and is a single taxable entity dealing with a single taxation authority), the company is permitted to net its future tax asset of $76,800 ($14,400 + $62,400) and future tax liability of $179,200 to report one net future tax liability of $102,400 as a noncurrent liability. Otherwise, the deferred tax asset and the deferred tax liability are reported separately. IFRS does not permit any deferred tax accounts to be reported in current assets or current liabilities.

Under **private enterprise standards**, however, the future tax assets and liabilities are classified as current and noncurrent on the balance sheet based on the classifications of the related assets and liabilities that underlie the temporary differences. They are then summarized into one net current and one net noncurrent amount (again, assuming a single taxable entity and the same taxation authority). The classification of Allman Corporation's future tax account at the end of 2010 is shown in Illustration 18A-4.

Balance Sheet Account	Classification of Balance Sheet Account	Future Tax Asset (Liability)*	Classification of Future Tax Asset (Liability)	
			Current	Noncurrent
Deferred gross profit (A/R)	Mixed: current and noncurrent	$(179,200)	$(44,800)	$(134,400)
Plant and equipment	Noncurrent	14,400		14,400
Warranty liability	Mixed: current and noncurrent	62,400	22,400	40,000
		$(102,400)	$(22,400)	$ (80,000)

*From Illustration 18A-2

For the first temporary difference, the related account on the balance sheet is the deferred gross profit, a contra account to the accounts receivable. The accounts receivable are classified partially as a current asset and partially as long-term. Because one-fourth of the gross profit relates to the receivable due in 2011, this portion of the receivable is a current asset and the current portion of the future tax liability is $44,800 ($179,200 × 1/4). The $134,400 remainder ($179,200 − $44,800) of the future tax liability is noncurrent.

The plant and equipment are classified as long-term, so the resulting future tax asset is classified as noncurrent. The warranty liability account, like the instalment receivables, is split between the current and long-term categories. Our assumption is that $56,000 of the liability is reported as current and the remaining $100,000 as noncurrent. The current portion of the future tax asset, therefore, is $22,400 ($56,000 ÷ $156,000 × $62,400). The remainder ($62,400 − $22,400 = $40,000) is noncurrent.

Under PE standards for a private entity using the future taxes method of accounting for income taxes, the $102,400 net future tax liability is reported on the balance sheet in two parts: a future tax liability of $22,400 is reported as a **current liability**, and a future tax liability of $80,000 is reported as a **long-term liability**. The balance sheet presentation is shown in Illustration 18A-5 under PE GAAP and under IFRS. The income statement presentation is the same under both standards.

Balance Sheet, December 31, 2010—PE GAAP Presentation

Current liabilities	
Income tax payable	$ 77,000
Future income tax liability	22,400
Long-term liabilities	
Future income tax liability	$ 80,000

Balance Sheet, December 31, 2010—IFRS Presentation

Current liabilities	
Income tax payable	$ 77,000
Long-term liabilities	
Future income tax liability	$102,400

Income Statement, Year Ended December 31, 2010—PE GAAP and IFRS

Income before income tax		$412,000
Income tax expense		
Current	$ 77,000	
Future	102,400	179,400
Net income		$232,600

Second Year—2011

1. During 2011, the company collected one-fifth of the original sales price (or one-quarter of the outstanding receivable at December 31, 2010) from customers for the receivables arising from contracts completed in 2010. Recovery of the remaining receivables is still expected to result in taxable amounts of $112,000 in each of the following three years.

2. In 2011, the company completed four new contracts with a total selling price of $1 million (to be paid in five equal instalments beginning in 2011), earning a gross profit of $320,000. For financial reporting purposes, the full $320,000 is recognized in 2011, whereas for tax purposes the gross profit is deferred and taken into taxable income as the cash is received; that is, one-fifth, or $64,000, in 2011 and one-fifth in each of 2012 to 2015.

3. During 2011, Allman continued to depreciate the assets acquired in 2010 according to the depreciation and CCA schedules that appear on page 1191. Therefore, depreciation expense of $90,000 is reported on the 2011 income statement and CCA of $97,200 is claimed for tax purposes.

4. Information about the product warranty liability and timing of warranty expenditures at the end of 2011 is shown in Illustration 18A-6.

Balance of liability at beginning of 2011	$156,000
Accrual of expense reported on the 2011 income statement	180,000
Expenditures related to contracts completed in 2010	(62,000)
Expenditures related to contracts completed in 2011	(50,000)
Balance of liability at end of 2011	$224,000
Estimated timing of warranty expenditures:	
$ 94,000 in 2012 on 2010 contracts	
50,000 in 2012 on 2011 contracts	
80,000 in 2013 on 2011 contracts	
$224,000	

Illustration 18A-6

Warranty Liability and Expenditure Information

5. During 2011, non-taxable dividend revenue recognized is $24,000.

6. A loss of $172,000 is accrued for financial reporting purposes because of pending litigation. This amount is not tax-deductible until the period when the loss is realized, which is estimated to be 2016.

7. Accounting income for 2011 is $504,800.

8. The tax rate in effect for 2011 is 40%; in late December, revised tax rates of 42% were enacted for 2012 and subsequent years.

Remeasurement of Future Tax Liability Account because of Tax Rate Change

Whenever new tax rates are substantively enacted that affect the measurement of future tax assets and liabilities already on the books, the balances in the future tax accounts are restated. This is recognized at the date the rates are changed. In the case of Allman Corporation, the rates were increased in late December 2011; therefore this is when the adjusting entry is made. The remeasurement is carried out on the temporary differences existing before the rate is changed, in this case those at the beginning of 2011. Illustration 18A-7 indicates how this is done.

Illustration 18A-7

Adjustment for Change in Income Tax Rates

(Taxable) deductible temporary differences	Total	Future Years				
		2011	2012	2013	2014	2015
Net (taxable) deductible amount (from Illustration 18A-3)	$(256,000)	$(48,800)	$(24,240)	$(139,792)	$(152,234)	$109,066
Revised tax rate		40%	42%	42%	42%	42%
Revised net future tax asset (liability)	$(106,544)	$(19,520)	$(10,181)	$ (58,713)	$ (63,938)	$ 45,808
Net future tax liability before change in rates	(102,400)					
Adjustment: increase in future tax liability	$ (4,144)					

The entry to recognize the effect of the change in rates is:

A = L + SE
    +4,144   −4,144

Cash flows: No effect

Future Income Tax Expense	4,144	
Future Income Tax Liability		4,144

Taxable Income, Income Tax Payable, Current Tax Expense—2011

Taxable income, income tax payable, and current income tax expense for 2011 are calculated in Illustration 18A-8.

Illustration 18A-8

Calculation of Taxable Income and Taxes Payable—2011

Accounting income for 2011	$ 504,800
Permanent difference:	
Non-taxable revenue—dividends	(24,000)
Reversible differences:	
Gross profit on 2010 instalment sales, taxable in 2011	112,000
Deferred gross profit for tax—2011 contracts ($320,000 − $64,000)	(256,000)
CCA in excess of depreciation per books ($97,200 − $90,000)	(7,200)
Deductible warranty expenditures from 2010 contracts	(62,000)
Warranty expense per books—2011 contracts in excess of amount deductible for tax purposes ($180,000 − $50,000)	130,000
Loss accrual per books not deductible in 2011	172,000
Taxable income for 2011	$ 569,600
Income tax payable and current income tax expense for 2011: $569,600 × 40%	$ 227,840

Future Tax Assets and Liabilities at December 31, 2011, and 2011 Future Tax Expense

The next step is to determine the correct balance of the net future tax asset or liability account at December 31, 2011. The amount required to adjust this account to its correct balance is future tax expense/benefit for 2011.

Illustration 18A-9 summarizes the temporary differences at December 31, 2011, the future tax effects of these differences, the correct ending balance of the balance sheet future tax account, and the amount required for the future income tax benefit entry.

Balance Sheet Account	Carrying Amount	−	Tax Basis	=	(Taxable) Deductible Temporary Difference	×	Tax Rate	=	Future Income Tax Asset (Liability)
Deferred gross profit (contra to A/R)									
–2010 sales	$ –0–		$336,000		$(336,000)		.42		$(141,120)
–2011 sales	–0–		256,000		(256,000)		.42		(107,520)
Plant and equipment	360,000		388,800		28,800		.42		12,096
Liability for warranties									
–2010 sales	94,000		–0–		94,000		.42		39,480
–2011 sales	130,000		–0–		130,000		.42		54,600
Litigation liability	172,000		–0–		172,000		.42		72,240
Net future tax liability, December 31, 2011									(70,224)
Net future tax asset (liability) before adjustment (102,400) + (4,144)									(106,544)
Decrease in future tax liability, and future tax benefit for 2011									$ 36,320

Illustration 18A-9

Determination of Future Tax Assets, Liabilities, and Future Income Tax Expense/Benefit—2011

The temporary difference caused by deferring the profit on the instalment sales for tax purposes again results in a taxable temporary difference and a future tax liability. The company has no deferred profits in the accounts—it has all been recognized in income. For tax purposes, three-fifths of the 2010 profit of $560,000 (i.e., $336,000) is still deferred at December 31, 2011, while four-fifths of the 2011 profit of $320,000 (i.e., $256,000) is deferred. These amounts will be taxable and increase taxable income in the future.

To the end of 2011, $28,800 less CCA has been claimed than depreciation. This can be seen by comparing the book value of the plant and equipment of $360,000 with its UCC or tax basis of $388,800 at the same date. In the future, there will be $28,800 more CCA deductible for tax purposes than depreciation taken on the books. This will reduce future taxable income. The temporary difference due to warranty costs will result in deductible amounts in each of 2012 and 2013 as this difference reverses, and the $172,000 loss that is not deductible for tax this year will be deductible in the future.

Again, because the future tax rates are identical for each future year, the future tax liability can be calculated by applying the 42% rate to the total of the temporary differences. If instead the rates had been changed to 42% for 2012, 43% for 2013, and 44% thereafter, for example, a schedule similar to the one in Illustration 18A-3 would be prepared.

Income Tax Accounting Entries—2011

The entries to record current and future income taxes for 2011 are:

Current Income Tax Expense	227,840	
Income Tax Payable (Illustration 18A-8)		227,840

A = L + SE
   +227,840 −227,840
Cash flows: No effect

Future Income Tax Liability (Illustration 18A-9)	36,320	
Future Income Tax Benefit		36,320

A = L + SE
   −36,320 +36,320
Cash flows: No effect

Financial Statement Presentation—2011

Continuing the assumptions about Allman set out above Illustration 18A-4, a net future tax liability of $70,224 is reported as a noncurrent liability under IFRS.[15] The private enterprise GAAP classification of Allman Corporation's future tax account at the end of 2011 is shown in Illustration 18A-10.

Illustration 18A-10

Classification of Future Tax Asset/Liability Accounts

Balance Sheet Account	Classification of Balance Sheet Account	Future Tax Asset (Liability)*	Classification of Future Tax Asset (Liability)	
			Current	Noncurrent
Deferred gross profit (A/R)				
–2010 sales	Mixed: current and noncurrent	$(141,120)	$(47,040)	$(94,080)
–2011 sales	Mixed: current and noncurrent	(107,520)	(26,880)	(80,640)
Plant and equipment	Noncurrent	12,096		12,096
Warranty liability				
–2010 sales	Current	39,480	39,480	
–2011 sales	Mixed: current and noncurrent	54,600	21,000	33,600
Litigation liability	Noncurrent	72,240		72,240
		$ (70,224)	$(13,440)	$(56,784)

*From Illustration 18A-9

The future tax accounts related to the deferred gross profit follow the balance sheet classification of the receivables. Of the amounts owed on the 2010 sales, one-third will be collected in 2012 so one-third of the receivable is reported in current assets. One-third of the future tax liability ($1/3 \times $141,120 = $47,040) is also classified as a current item, with the remaining two-thirds reported as noncurrent. The deferred gross profit on the 2011 sales is analyzed the same way—in this case, one-quarter is current and three-quarters noncurrent. The warranty liability related to 2010 sales is all expected to be paid within the next year; therefore it is a current liability on the balance sheet. The related future tax asset is also designated as current. Of the $130,000 warranty liability related to the 2011 sales, $50,000 is expected to be met in 2012 and is included in current liabilities. The current portion of the future tax asset is therefore $21,000 ($50,000 ÷ $130,000 × $54,600), and the remainder is long-term.[16] The litigation liability is reported outside current liabilities and so is its related future tax account.

Under PE standards for a private entity using the future taxes method of accounting for income taxes, the $70,224 net future tax liability is reported on the balance sheet in two parts: a future tax liability of $13,440 is reported as a **current liability**, and a future tax liability of $56,784 is reported as a **long-term liability**. The balance sheet presentation is shown in Illustration 18A-11 under PE GAAP and under IFRS. The income statement presentation is the same under both sets of standards, although there is no PE GAAP requirement to separately disclose the major components of tax expense other than the current tax and future tax expense amounts.

[15] Alternatively, if more than one tax jurisdiction was involved or these were the consolidated financial statements of a number of taxable entities, IFRS requires that the deferred tax assets be reported separately from the deferred tax liabilities. In this case, the future tax liability of $248,640 relating to the deferred gross profit would be reported separately from the total of all the future tax assets of $178,416.

[16] If Allman Corporation classifies all warranty liabilities as current because the company defines the operating cycle as including the two-year warranty period, then the entire future tax asset related to the warranties would be reported as a current amount.

Illustration 18A-11

Financial Statement Presentation—2011

Balance Sheet, December 31, 2011—PE GAAP Presentation

Current liabilities

Income tax payable	$227,840
Future income tax liability	13,440

Long-term liabilities

Future income tax liability	$ 56,784

Balance Sheet, December 31, 2011—IFRS Presentation

Current liabilities

Income tax payable	$227,840

Long-term liabilities

Future income tax liability	$ 70,224

Income Statement, Year Ended December 31, 2011—PE GAAP and IFRS

Income before income tax		$504,800
Income tax expense (benefit)		
Current	$227,840	
Future (see Note 1)	(32,176)	195,664
Net income		$309,136

Note 1. The future tax benefit is the net result of a tax benefit of $36,320 from originating and reversing temporary differences, and a tax expense of $4,144 resulting from a change in tax rates in the year.

Summary of Learning Objective for Appendix 18A

11 **Apply the future income taxes method (balance sheet liability method) of accounting for income taxes in a comprehensive situation.**

In a comprehensive situation, take the following steps: calculate the current income tax expense and payable; determine the taxable and deductible temporary differences as the difference between the carrying amounts and tax bases of the assets and liabilities; calculate the correct balance of the future income tax asset or liability account; and determine the future income tax expense as the adjustment needed to the existing balance. Make an adjusting entry to restate the future tax asset or liability amounts when a change in the future tax rates has been substantively enacted. Classifiy the net future tax asset or liability according to the accounting standards being applied.

Brief Exercises

(LO 2)   **BE18-1**   In 2011, Shafali Corporation had accounting income of $248,000 and taxable income of $198,000. The difference is due to the use of different depreciation methods for tax and accounting purposes. The tax rate is 40%. Calculate the amount to be reported as income taxes payable at December 31, 2011.

(LO 4)   **BE18-2**   At December 31, 2010, Ambuir Corporation had a future tax liability of $35,000. At December 31, 2011, the future tax liability is $52,000. The corporation's 2011 current tax expense is $53,000. What amount should Ambuir report as total 2011 income tax expense?

(LO 4)   **BE18-3**   Nilson Inc. had accounting income of $156,000 in 2011. Included in the calculation of that amount is insurance expense of $5,000, which is not deductible for tax purposes. In addition, the undepreciated capital cost (UCC) for tax purposes is $14,000 lower than the net carrying amount of the property, plant, and equipment, although the amounts were equal at the beginning of the year. Prepare Nilson's journal entry to record 2011 taxes, assuming IFRS and a tax rate of 25%.

(LO 2, 4)   **BE18-4**   At December 31, 2011, Naifa Inc. owned equipment that had a book value of $145,000 and a tax basis of $114,000 due to the use of different depreciation methods for accounting and tax purposes. The enacted tax rate is 30%. Calculate the amount that Naifa should report as a future tax liability at December 31, 2011.

(LO 2, 4)   **BE18-5**   Anugraham Corp. began operations in 2011 and reported accounting income of $275,000 for the year. Anugraham's CCA exceeded its book depreciation by $40,000. Anugraham's tax rate for 2011 and years thereafter is 35%. In its December 31, 2011 balance sheet, what amount of future income tax liability should be reported?

(LO 2)   **BE18-6**   At December 31, 2011, Camille Corporation had an estimated warranty liability of $170,000 for accounting purposes and $0 for tax purposes. (The warranty costs are not deductible until they are paid.) The tax rate is 40%. Calculate the amount that Camille should report as a future tax asset at December 31, 2011.

(LO 3)   **BE18-7**   At December 31, 2010, Chai Inc. had a future tax asset of $40,000. At December 31, 2011, the future tax asset is $62,000. The corporation's 2011 current tax expense is $70,000. What amount should Chai report as total 2011 tax expense?

(LO 4)   **BE18-8**   Using the information from BE18-5, and assuming that the $40,000 difference is the only difference between Anugraham's accounting income and taxable income, prepare the journal entry(ies) to record the current income tax expense, future income tax expense, income taxes payable, and the future income tax liability.

(LO 2, 4)   **BE18-9**   Using the information from BE18-3, calculate the effective rate of income tax for Nilson Inc. for 2011. Also make a reconciliation from the statutory rate to the effective rate, using percentages.

(LO 4)   **BE18-10**   Chua Corporation has a taxable temporary difference related to depreciation of $715,000 at December 31, 2011. This difference will reverse as follows: 2012, $53,000; 2013, $310,000; and 2014, $352,000. Enacted tax rates are 37% for 2012 and 2013, and 43% for 2014. Calculate the amount that Chua should report as a future tax asset or liability at December 31, 2011.

(LO 5)   **BE18-11**   At December 31, 2010, Palden Corporation had a future tax asset of $999,000, resulting from future deductible amounts of $2.7 million and an enacted tax rate of 37%. In May 2011, new income tax legislation is signed into law that raises the tax rate to 39% for 2011 and future years. Prepare the journal entry for Palden to adjust the future tax account.

(LO 6)   **BE18-12**   Ayesha Corporation had the following tax information:

Year	Taxable Income	Tax Rate	Taxes Paid
2008	$390,000	35%	$136,500
2009	325,000	30%	97,500
2010	400,000	30%	120,000

In 2011, Ayesha suffered a net operating loss of $550,000, which it decided to carry back. The 2011 enacted tax rate is 29%. Prepare Ayesha's entry to record the effect of the loss carryback.

(LO 6, 7)   **BE18-13**   Kyle Inc. incurred a net operating loss of $580,000 in 2011. Combined income for 2008, 2009, and 2010 was $460,000. The tax rate for all years is 35%. Prepare the journal entries to record the benefits of the carryback and the carryforward, assuming it is more likely than not that the benefits of the loss carryforward will be realized.

BE18-14 Use the information for Kyle Inc. given in BE18-13, but assume instead that it is more likely than not that the entire tax loss carryforward will not be realized in future years. Prepare all the journal entries that are necessary at the end of 2011 assuming (a) that Kyle does not use a valuation allowance account, and (b) that Kyle does use a valuation allowance account. **(LO 6, 7)**

BE18-15 Use the information for Kyle Inc. given in BE18-14. Assume now that Kyle earns taxable income of $25,000 in 2012 and that at the end of 2012 there is still too much uncertainty to recognize a future tax asset. Prepare all the journal entries that are necessary at the end of 2012 assuming (a) that Kyle does not use a valuation allowance account, and (b) that Kyle does use a valuation allowance account. **(LO 6, 7)**

BE18-16 At December 31, 2011, Aminder Corporation has a future tax asset of $340,000. After a careful review of all available evidence, it is determined that it is more likely than not that $70,000 of this future tax asset will not be realized. Prepare the necessary journal entry assuming (a) that Aminder does not use a valuation allowance account, and (b) that Aminder does use a valuation allowance account. **(LO 6, 7)**

BE18-17 In 2011, Dustin Limited purchased shares of Gurvir Corp. at a cost of $45,000. This was the first time the company had ever acquired an investment to be accounted for at fair value through other comprehensive income (FV-OCI). At December 31, 2011, the Gurvir Corp. shares had a fair value of $41,000. Dustin Limited's income tax rate is 40%. Assume that any gains that are ultimately realized on the sale of the Gurvir Corp. shares will be taxable as ordinary income when the gains are realized. Prepare the necessary journal entries to record the unrealized loss and the related income taxes in 2011. Prepare the statement of comprehensive income for Dustin Limited, beginning with the line for net income of $55,000. Assume Dustin Limited reports under IFRS. **(LO 9)**

BE18-18 Sandeep Corporation had income before income taxes of $230,000 in 2011. Sandeep's current income tax expense is $43,000, and future income tax expense is $41,000. (a) Prepare Sandeep's 2011 income statement, beginning with income before income taxes. (b) Calculate Sandeep's effective tax rate. **(LO 9)**

BE18-19 Kolby Inc. reported income from continuing operations of $71,000 and a loss from discontinued operations of $10,000 in 2011, all before income taxes. All items are fully taxable and deductible for tax purposes. Prepare the bottom of the income statement for Kolby Inc., beginning with income from continuing operations before income taxes. Assume a tax rate of 25%. **(LO 9)**

BE18-20 Sonia Corporation has temporary differences at December 31, 2011, that result in the following balance sheet future tax accounts: **(LO 9)**

Future tax liability, current	$38,000
Future tax asset, current	$52,000
Future tax liability, noncurrent	$96,000
Future tax asset, noncurrent	$27,000

Indicate how these balances will be presented in Sonia's December 31, 2011 balance sheet, assuming (a) Sonia reports under the PE GAAP future income taxes method, and (b) Sonia follows IFRS for reporting purposes.

BE18-21 Using the information from BE18-3, prepare Nilson's journal entry to record 2011 taxes. Assume a tax rate of 25% and that Nilson uses the taxes payable method of accounting for income taxes under PE GAAP. **(LO 10)**

Exercises

E18-1 **(Identifying Reversing or Permanent Differences and Showing Effects)** The accounting for the items in the numbered list that follows is commonly different for financial reporting purposes than it is for tax purposes: **(LO 2)**

1. For financial reporting purposes, the straight-line depreciation method is used for plant assets that have a useful life of 10 years; for tax purposes, the CCA declining-balance method is used with a rate of 20% (ignore the half-year rule).

2. A landlord collects rents in advance. Rents are taxable in the period when they are received.

3. Non-deductible expenses are incurred in obtaining income that is exempt from taxes.

4. Costs of guarantees and warranties are estimated and accrued for financial reporting purposes.

5. Instalment sales are accounted for by the accrual method for financial reporting purposes and the cash basis for tax purposes.

6. For some assets, straight-line depreciation is used for both financial reporting purposes and tax purposes but the assets' lives are shorter for tax purposes.

7. Pension expense is reported on the income statement before it is funded. Pension costs are deductible only when they are funded.

8. Proceeds are received from a life insurance company because of the death of a key officer (the company carries a policy on key officers).

9. The company reports dividends received from taxable Canadian corporations as investment income on its income statement, even though the dividends are non-taxable.

10. Estimated losses on pending lawsuits and claims are accrued for financial reporting purposes. These losses are tax deductible in the period(s) when the related liabilities are settled.

11. Security investments accounted for using the fair value through net income (FV-NI) model are adjusted at the end of the year to their fair value. This is the first year that the company has such investments and the fair value is lower than the cost.

12. An impairment loss is recorded for goodwill in the current accounting period.

Instructions

(a) Match each item in the preceding list to the number below that best describes it:

　i. a reversing difference that will result in future deductible amounts and, therefore, will usually give rise to a future income tax asset

　ii. a reversing difference that will result in future taxable amounts and, therefore, will usually give rise to a future income tax liability

　iii. a permanent difference

(b) For each item in the preceding list, indicate if the amounts that are involved in the current year will be added to or deducted from accounting income to arrive at taxable income.

(LO 2)   E18-2   (Terminology, Relationships, Calculations, Entries)

Instructions

Complete the following statements by filling in the blanks.

(a) In a period in which a taxable temporary difference reverses, the reversal will cause taxable income to be _____ (less than/greater than) accounting income.

(b) In a period in which a deductible temporary difference reverses, the reversal will cause taxable income to be _____ (less than/greater than) accounting income.

(c) If a $76,000 balance in the Future Tax Asset account were calculated using a 40% rate, the underlying temporary difference would amount to $_____ .

(d) Future taxes _____ (are/are not) recorded to account for permanent differences.

(e) If a taxable temporary difference originates in 2011, it causes taxable income of 2011 to be _____ (less than/greater than) accounting income for 2011.

(f) If total tax expense is $50,000 and future tax expense is $65,000, then the current portion of the expense is referred to as a current tax _____ (expense/benefit) of $_____ .

(g) If a corporation's tax return shows taxable income of $100,000 for Year 2 and a tax rate of 40%, how much will appear on the December 31, Year 2 balance sheet for "Income tax payable" if the company has made estimated tax payments of $36,500 for Year 2? $_____

(h) An increase in the Future Tax Liability account on the balance sheet is recorded by a _____ (debit/credit) to the Future Income Tax Expense account.

(i) An income statement that reports current tax expense of $82,000 and a future tax benefit of $23,000 will report total income tax expense of $_____ .

(j) A valuation account may be used whenever it is judged to be more likely than not that a portion of a future tax asset _____ (will be/will not be) realized.

(k) If the tax return shows total taxes due for the period of $75,000 but the income statement shows total income tax expense of $55,000, the difference of $20,000 is referred to as a future tax _____ (expense/benefit).

(l) If a company's income tax rate increases, the effect will be to _____ (increase/decrease) the amount of a future tax liability and _____ (increase/decrease) the amount of a future tax asset.

(m) The difference between the tax basis of an asset or liability and its carrying amount is called a _____ difference. Differences between accounting income and taxable income that will reverse in the future are called _____ differences.

E18-3 **(Permanent and Reversing Differences, Calculating Taxable Income, Entry for Taxes)** Melissa Inc. reports   **(LO 2, 3, 4)** accounting income of $105,000 for 2011. The following items cause taxable income to be different than income reported on the financial statements.

1. Capital cost allowance (on the tax return) is greater than depreciation on the income statement by $16,000.

2. Rent reported on the tax return is $24,000 higher than rent earned on the income statement.

3. Non-deductible fines for pollution appear as an expense of $15,000 on the income statement.

4. Melissa's tax rate is 30% for all years and the company expects to report taxable income in all future years. There are no future taxes at the beginning of 2011. Melissa reports under the PE GAAP future income taxes method.

Instructions

(a) Calculate taxable income and income taxes payable for 2011.

(b) Calculate any future income tax balances at December 31, 2011.

(c) Prepare the journal entries to record income taxes for 2011.

(d) Prepare the income tax expense section of the income statement for 2011, beginning with the line "Income before income taxes."

(e) Reconcile the statutory and effective rates of income tax for 2011.

(f) Provide the balance sheet presentation for any resulting future tax balance sheet accounts at December 31, 2011. Be specific about the classification.

(g) Repeat part (f) assuming Melissa follows IFRS.

E18-4 **(One Reversing Difference, Future Taxable Amounts, One Rate, No Beginning Future Taxes)** Raman   **(LO 2, 4)** Limited had investments in securities on its balance sheet for the first time at the end of its fiscal year ending December 31, 2012. Raman reports under IFRS and its investments in securities are to be accounted for at fair value through net income. During 2012, realized losses and gains on the trading of shares and bonds resulted in investment income, which is fully taxable in the year. Raman also accrued unrealized gains at December 31, 2012, which are not taxable until the investment securities are sold. The portfolio of trading securities had an original cost of $314,450 and a fair value on December 31, 2012, of $318,200. The entry recorded by Raman on December 31, 2012, was as follows:

Investments (FV-NI)	3,750	
Investment Income/Loss (FV-NI)		3,750

Income before income taxes for Raman was $302,000 for the year ended December 31, 2012. There are no other permanent or reversing differences in arriving at the taxable income for Raman Limited for the fiscal year ending December 31, 2012. The enacted tax rate for 2012 and future years is 42%.

Instructions

(a) Explain the tax treatment that should be given to the unrealized gain that Raman Limited reported on its income statement.

(b) Calculate the future income tax balance at December 31, 2012.

(c) Calculate the current income tax for the year ending December 31, 2012.

(d) Prepare the journal entries to record income taxes for 2012.

(e) Prepare the income statement for 2012, beginning with the line "Income before income taxes."

(f) Provide the balance sheet presentation for any resulting income tax balance sheet accounts at December 31, 2012. Be clear on the classification you have chosen and explain your choice.

(g) Repeat part (f) assuming Raman follows the PE GAAP future income taxes method and has chosen the fair value through net income model to account for its securities investments.

(LO 2, 3, 4)   E18-5   (One Temporary Difference, Future Taxable Amount Becomes Future Deductible Amount, One Rate, Change in Rate) Refer to the information for Raman Limited in E18-4. Following the year ended December 31, 2012, Raman continued to actively trade its securities investments until the end of its 2013 fiscal year, when it was forced to sell several of them at a loss, because of the need for cash for operations. By December 31, 2013, the portfolio of investments contained a single investment in shares, which was purchased in November 2013. Raman Limited had paid $42,000 for these remaining shares. At December 31, 2013, the shares' market value was $40,000. Income before income taxes for Raman was $120,000 for the year ended December 31, 2013. There are no other permanent or timing differences in arriving at the taxable income for Raman Limited for the fiscal year ending December 31, 2013. The enacted tax rate for 2013 and future years is 42%.

Instructions

(a) Prepare the necessary journal entry for Raman Limited to accrue the unrealized loss on its securities investments.

(b) Explain the tax treatment that should be given to the unrealized accrued loss that Raman Limited reported on its income statement.

(c) Calculate the future income tax balance at December 31, 2013.

(d) Calculate the current income tax for the year ending December 31, 2013.

(e) Prepare the journal entries to record income taxes for 2013. Assume that there have been no entries to the ending balances of future taxes reported at December 31, 2012.

(f) Prepare the income statement for 2013, beginning with the line "Income before income taxes."

(g) Provide the balance sheet presentation for any resulting future tax balance sheet account at December 31, 2013. Be clear on the classification you have chosen and explain your choice.

(h) Prepare the journal entries in part (e) under the assumption that, late in 2013, the income tax rate changed to 40% for 2014 and subsequent years.

(i) Repeat the balance sheet presentation in part (g) assuming Raman reports under the PE GAAP future income taxes method and has chosen the fair value through net income model to account for its securities investments.

(LO 2, 3, 4)   E18-6   (One Reversing Difference, Future Taxable Amounts, One Rate, No Beginning Future Taxes) Sorpon Corporation purchased equipment very late in 2011. Based on generous capital cost allowance rates provided in the *Income Tax Act*, Sorpon Corporation claimed CCA on its 2011 tax return but did not record any depreciation as the equipment had not yet been put into use. This temporary difference will reverse and cause taxable amounts of $25,000 in 2012, $30,000 in 2013, and $40,000 in 2014. Sorpon's accounting income for 2011 is $200,000 and the tax rate is 40% for all years. There are no future tax accounts at the beginning of 2011.

Instructions

(a) Calculate the future income tax balance at December 31, 2011.

(b) Calculate taxable income and income taxes payable for 2011.

(c) Prepare the journal entries to record income taxes for 2011.

(d) Prepare the income tax expense section of the income statement for 2011, beginning with the line "Income before income taxes."

(LO 2, 3, 4)   E18-7   (One Reversing Difference, Future Taxable Amounts, One Rate, Beginning Future Taxes) Use the information for Sorpon Corporation in E18-6, and assume that the company reports accounting income of $180,000 in each of 2012 and 2013, and no temporary differences other than the one identified in E18-6.

Instructions

(a) Calculate the future income tax balances at December 31, 2012 and 2013.

(b) Calculate taxable income and income taxes payable for 2012 and 2013.

(c) Prepare the journal entries to record income taxes for 2012 and 2013.

(d) Prepare the income tax expense section of the income statements for 2012 and 2013, beginning with the line "Income before income taxes."

Digging
Deeper

(e) What trend do you notice in the amount of net income reported for 2012 and 2013 in part (d)? Is this a coincidence? Explain.

E18-8 **(One Temporary Difference, Future Taxable Amounts, No Beginning Future Taxes, Change in Rate)** **(LO 2, 3, 4)** Use the information for Sorpon Corporation in E18-6, and assume that the company reports accounting income of $180,000 in each of 2012 and 2013, and no reversing differences other than the one identified in E18-6. In addition, assume now that Sorpon Corporation was informed on December 31, 2012, that the enacted rate for 2013 and subsequent years is 35%.

Instructions

(a) Calculate the future income tax balances at December 31, 2012 and 2013.

(b) Calculate taxable income and income taxes payable for 2012 and 2013.

(c) Prepare the journal entries to record income taxes for 2012 and 2013.

(d) Prepare the income tax expense section of the income statements for 2012 and 2013, beginning with the line "Income before income taxes."

E18-9 **(One Reversing Difference, Future Deductible Amounts, One Rate, No Beginning Future Taxes)** Jenny **(LO 2, 3, 4)** Corporation recorded warranty accruals as at December 31, 2011, in the amount of $150,000. This reversing difference will cause deductible amounts of $50,000 in 2012, $35,000 in 2013, and $65,000 in 2014. Jenny's accounting income for 2011 is $135,000 and the tax rate is 25% for all years. There are no future tax accounts at the beginning of 2011.

Instructions

(a) Calculate the future income tax balance at December 31, 2011.

(b) Calculate taxable income and current income taxes payable for 2011.

(c) Prepare the journal entries to record income taxes for 2011.

(d) Prepare the income tax expense section of the income statement for 2011, beginning with the line "Income before income taxes."

E18-10 **(One Reversing Difference, Future Deductible Amounts, One Rate, Beginning Future Taxes)** Use the **(LO 2, 3, 4)** information for Jenny Corporation in E18-9, and assume that the company reports accounting income of $155,000 in each of 2012 and 2013 and the warranty expenditures occurred as expected. No reversing difference exists other than the one identified in E18-9.

Instructions

(a) Calculate the future income tax balances at December 31, 2012 and 2013.

(b) Calculate taxable income and income taxes payable for 2012 and 2013.

(c) Prepare the journal entries to record income taxes for 2012 and 2013.

(d) Prepare the income tax expense section of the income statements for 2012 and 2013, beginning with the line "Income before income taxes."

(e) What trend do you notice in the amount of net income reported for 2012 and 2013 in part (d)? Is this a coincidence? Digging Explain. Deeper

E18-11 **(One Reversing Difference, Future Deductible Amounts, No Beginning Future Taxes, Change in Rate)** **(LO 2, 3, 4)** Use the information for Jenny Corporation in E18-9, and assume that the company reports accounting income of $155,000 in each of 2012 and 2013, and that there is no reversing difference other than the one identified in E18-9. In addition, assume now that Jenny Corporation was informed on December 31, 2012, that the enacted rate for 2013 and subsequent years is 28%.

Instructions

(a) Calculate the future income tax balances at December 31, 2012 and 2013.

(b) Calculate taxable income and income taxes payable for 2012 and 2013.

(c) Prepare the journal entries to record income taxes for 2012 and 2013.

(d) Prepare the income tax expense section of the income statements for 2012 and 2013, beginning with the line "Income before income taxes."

(LO 2, 3, 4, 11) **E18-12** **(Two Reversing Differences, Future Taxable and Deductible Amounts, No Beginning Future Taxes, One Tax Rate)** Sayaka Tar and Gravel Ltd. operates a road construction business. In its first year of operations, the company obtained a contract to construct a road for the municipality of Cochrane West, and it is estimated that the project will be completed over a three-year period starting in June 2011. Sayaka uses the percentage-of-completion method of recognizing revenue on its long-term construction contracts. For tax purposes, and in order to postpone the tax on such revenue for as long as possible, Sayaka uses the completed-contract method allowed by the CRA. By its first fiscal year end, the accounts related to the contract had the following balances:

Accounts Receivable	$320,000
Construction in Process	500,000
Revenue from Long-Term Contract	500,000
Construction Expense	350,000
Billings on Construction in Process	400,000

The accounts related to the equipment that Sayaka purchased to construct the road had the following balances at the end of the first fiscal year ending December 31, 2011, for accounting and tax purposes:

Construction Equipment	$1,100,000
Accumulated Depreciation—Construction Equipment	170,000
Undepreciated Capital Cost	980,000

Sayaka's tax rate is 45% for 2011 and subsequent years. Income before income tax for the year ended December 31, 2011, was $195,000. Sayaka reports under the PE GAAP future income taxes method.

Instructions

(a) Calculate the future income tax asset or liability balances at December 31, 2011.

(b) Calculate taxable income and income taxes payable for 2011.

(c) Prepare the journal entries to record income taxes for 2011.

(d) Prepare the income statement for 2011, beginning with the line "Income before income taxes."

(e) Provide the balance sheet presentation for any resulting future tax balance sheet accounts at December 31, 2011. Be specific about the classification.

(f) Repeat the balance sheet presentation in part (e) assuming Sayaka follows IFRS.

(LO 2, 3, 4, 11) **E18-13** **(Two Reversing Differences, Future Taxable and Deductible Amounts, Beginning Future Taxes, One Tax Rate)** Refer to E18-12 for Sayaka Tar and Gravel Ltd., and assume the same facts for the fiscal year ending December 31, 2011. For the second year of operations, Sayaka made progress on the construction of the road for the municipality. The account balances at December 31, 2012, for the construction project and the accounting and tax balances of accounts related to the equipment used for construction follow (the balances at December 31, 2011, are also listed):

	2012	2011
Accounts Receivable	$ 105,000	$ 320,000
Construction in Process	940,000	500,000
Revenue from Long-Term Contract	440,000	500,000
Construction Expense	410,000	350,000
Billings on Construction in Process	390,000	400,000
Construction Equipment	1,100,000	1,100,000
Accumulated Depreciation—Construction Equipment	460,000	170,000
Undepreciated Capital Cost	620,000	980,000

Sayaka's tax rate continues to be 45% for 2012 and subsequent years. Income before income tax for the year ended December 31, 2012, was $120,000.

Instructions

(a) Calculate the future income tax asset or liability balances at December 31, 2012.

(b) Calculate taxable income and income taxes payable for 2012.

(c) Prepare the journal entries to record income taxes for 2012.

(d) Prepare a comparative income statement for 2011 and 2012, beginning with the line "Income before income taxes."

(e) Provide the comparative balance sheet presentation for any resulting future tax balance sheet accounts at December 31, 2011 and 2012. Be specific about the classification.

(f) Repeat the balance sheet presentation in part (e) assuming Sayaka follows IFRS.

E18-14 (Two Reversing Differences, Future Taxable and Deductible Amounts, Beginning Future Taxes, Change in Tax Rate) Refer to E18-13 for Sayaka Tar and Gravel Ltd., and assume the same facts as in E18-13 for the fiscal year ending December 31, 2012, except that the enacted tax rate for 2013 and subsequent years was reduced to 40% on September 15, 2012. **(LO 2, 3, 4, 11)**

Instructions

(a) Prepare the journal entry to record the effect of the change in the enacted tax rate.

(b) Calculate any future income tax balances at December 31, 2012.

(c) Calculate taxable income and income taxes payable for 2012.

(d) Prepare the journal entries to record income taxes for 2012.

(e) Prepare a comparative income statement for 2011 and 2012, beginning with the line "Income before income taxes" and provide details about the components of income tax expense.

(f) Provide the comparative balance sheet presentation for any resulting future tax balance sheet accounts at December 31, 2011 and 2012. Be specific about the classification.

(g) Repeat the balance sheet presentation in part (e) assuming Sayaka follows IFRS.

E18-15 (Depreciation, Reversing Difference over Five Years, Determining Taxable Income, Taxes Payable Method) Zak Corp. purchased depreciable assets costing $600,000 on January 2, 2010. For tax purposes, the company uses CCA in a class that has a 40% rate. For financial reporting purposes, the company uses straight-line depreciation over five years. The enacted tax rate is 34% for all years. This depreciation difference is the only reversing difference the company has. Assume that Zak has income before income taxes of $340,000 in each of the years 2010 to 2014. **(LO 2, 4, 10)**

Instructions

(a) Calculate the amount of capital cost allowance and depreciation expense from 2010 to 2014, as well as the corresponding balances for carrying amount and undepreciated capital cost of the depreciable assets at the end of each of the years 2010 to 2014.

(b) Determine the amount of taxable income in each year from 2010 to 2014.

(c) Determine the amount of future income taxes that should be reported in the balance sheet for each year from 2010 to 2014.

(d) Prepare the journal entries to record income taxes for each year from 2010 to 2014.

(e) Prepare the income tax entry(ies) to record income taxes for each year, assuming the shareholders have decided on the taxes payable method.

E18-16 (One Reversing Difference through Three Years, One Rate) Aabid Corporation reports the following amounts in its first three years of operations. **(LO 2)**

	2011	2012	2013
Taxable income	$245,000	$121,000	$125,000
Accounting income	160,000	139,000	131,000

The difference between taxable income and accounting income is due to one reversing difference. The tax rate is 35% for all years and the company expects to continue with profitable operations in the future.

Instructions

(a) For each year, (1) identify the amount of the reversing difference originating or reversing during that year, and (2) indicate the amount of the temporary difference at the end of the year.

(b) Indicate the balance in the related future tax account at the end of each year and identify it as a future tax asset or liability.

(LO 2, 3, 4)   E18-17   (Reversing and Permanent Differences, Future Taxable Amount, No Beginning Future Taxes) Christina Inc. follows IFRS and accounts for financial instruments based on IFRS 9. Christina holds a variety of investments, some of which are accounted for at fair value through net income and some of which are accounted for at fair value through other comprehensive income. On January 1, 2011, the beginning of the fiscal year, Christina's accounts and records include the following information:

	Cost	Market Value
Fair value through net income investments	$60,000	$60,000
Fair value through other comprehensive income investments	71,000	71,000

Market values for the FV-NI investments and FV-OCI investments at December 31, 2011, were $58,000 and $75,000, respectively. Computers that are used to track investment performance were purchased during 2011 for $10,000. For tax purposes, assume the computers are in Class 10 with a CCA rate of 30%. Depreciation expense for the year was $2,000. Christina recorded meals and entertainment expenses of $24,000 related to wining and dining clients. The CRA allows 50% of these costs as deductible business expense.

Christina's income before income taxes for 2011 is $110,000. This amount does not include any entries to adjust investments to market values at December 31, 2011. Christina's tax rate for 2011 is 40%, although changes enacted in tax legislation before December 31, 2011, result in an increase in this rate to 45% for 2012 and subsequent taxation years. Assume that these rates apply to all income that is reported. There were no future tax accounts at January 1, 2011.

Instructions

(a) Prepare journal entries to reflect the difference between the carrying amount and market value for the above investments at Christina's year end of December 31, 2011.

(b) Explain the tax treatment that should be given to the unrealized accrued gains or losses reported on Christina's statement of income and statement of comprehensive income.

(c) Calculate the future income tax asset or liability balances at December 31, 2011, and indicate their classification.

(d) Calculate taxable income and income taxes payable for 2011.

(e) Prepare the journal entries to record income taxes for 2011.

(LO 3, 6)   E18-18   (One Difference, Multiple Rates, Beginning Future Taxes, Change in Rates) At the end of 2010, Valerie Corporation reported a future tax liability of $31,000. At the end of 2011, the company had $201,000 of temporary differences related to property, plant, and equipment. Depreciation expense on this property, plant, and equipment has been lower than the CCA claimed on Valerie's income tax returns. The resulting future taxable amounts are as follows:

2012	$ 67,000
2013	50,000
2014	45,000
2015	39,000
	$201,000

The tax rates enacted as of the beginning of 2010 are as follows: 40% for 2010 and 2011; 30% for 2012 and 2013; and 25% for 2014 and later. Taxable income is expected in all future years.

Instructions

(a) Calculate the future tax account balance at December 31, 2011.

(b) Prepare the journal entry for Valerie to record future income taxes for 2011.

(c) Early in 2012, after the 2011 financial statements were released, new tax rates were enacted as follows: 29% for 2012 and 27% for 2013 and later. Prepare the journal entry for Valerie to recognize the change in tax rates.

(LO 2, 5)   E18-19   (Future Tax Liability, Change in Tax Rate) Yen Inc.'s only temporary difference at the beginning and end of 2011 is caused by a $3.3-million deferred gain for tax purposes on an instalment sale of a plant asset. The related receivable (only one half of which is classified as a current asset) is due in equal instalments in 2012 and 2013. The related future tax liability at the beginning of the year is $1,320,000. In the third quarter of 2011, a new tax rate of 39% is enacted into law and is scheduled to become effective for 2013. Taxable income is expected in all future years.

Instructions

(a) Determine the amount to be reported as a future tax liability at the end of 2011. Indicate its proper classification(s).

(b) Prepare the journal entry (if any) that is necessary to adjust the future tax liability when the new tax rate is enacted into law.

E18-20   **(Loss Carryback)** Alliance Inc. reports the following incomes (losses) for both book and tax purposes (assume   **(LO 6)** the carryback provision is used where possible):

Year	Accounting Income (Loss)	Tax Rate
2009	$120,000	40%
2010	90,000	40%
2011	(80,000)	45%
2012	(40,000)	45%

The tax rates listed were all enacted by the beginning of 2009.

Instructions

(a) Prepare the journal entries for each of the years 2009 to 2012 to record income taxes.

(b) Prepare the income tax section of the income statements for each of the years 2009 to 2012, beginning with the line "Income (loss) before income taxes."

E18-21   **(Carryback and Carryforward of Tax Loss)** The accounting income (loss) figures for Farah Corporation are   **(LO 6, 7)** as follows:

2006	$ 160,000 42%
2007	250,000 42%
2008	80,000 38%
2009	(160,000)
2010	(380,000)
2011	130,000
2012	145,000

Accounting income (loss) and taxable income (loss) were the same for all years involved. Assume a 42% tax rate for 2006 and 2007, and a 38% tax rate for the remaining years.

Instructions

Prepare the journal entries for each of the years 2008 to 2012 to record income tax expense and the effects of the tax loss carrybacks and carryforwards, assuming Farah Corporation uses the carryback provision first. All income and losses relate to normal operations and it is more likely than not that the company will generate substantial taxable income in the future.

E18-22   **(Loss Carryback and Carryforward)** Riley Inc. reports the following pre-tax incomes (losses) for both finan-   **(LO 6, 7)** cial reporting purposes and tax purposes:

Year	Accounting Income (Loss)	Tax Rate
2009	$120,000	34%
2010	90,000	34%
2011	(280,000)	38%
2012	220,000	38%

The tax rates listed were all enacted by the beginning of 2009. Riley reports under the PE GAAP future income taxes method.

Instructions

(a) Prepare the journal entries for each of the years 2009 to 2012 to record income taxes, assuming the tax loss is first carried back, and that at the end of 2011, the loss carryforward benefits are judged more likely than not to be realized in the future.

(b) Using the assumption as in (a), prepare the income tax section of the 2011 and 2012 income statements, beginning with the line "Income (loss) before income taxes."

(c) Prepare the journal entries for 2011 and 2012, assuming that it is more likely than not that 25% of the carryforward benefits will not be realized. A valuation allowance is not used by this company.

(d) Using the assumption in (c), prepare the income tax section of the 2011 and 2012 income statements, beginning with the line "Income (loss) before income taxes."

(LO 6, 7, 8) E18-23 (Loss Carryback and Carryforward Using a Valuation Allowance) Refer to the information for Riley Inc. in E18-22.

Instructions

(a) Assume that Riley Inc. uses a valuation allowance to account for future tax assets, and also that it is more likely than not that 25% of the carryforward benefits will not be realized. Prepare the journal entries for 2011 and 2012.

(b) Based on your entries in (a), prepare the income tax section of the 2011 and 2012 income statements, beginning with the line "Income (loss) before income taxes."

(c) Indicate how the future tax asset account will be reported on the December 31, 2011 and 2012 balance sheets.

(d) Assume that on June 30, 2012, the enacted tax rates changed for 2012. Should management record any adjustment to the accounts? If yes, which accounts will be involved and when should the adjustment be recorded?

(e) Repeat part (c) assuming Riley Inc. follows IFRS.

Digging
Deeper

(LO 8, 9) E18-24 (Future Tax Asset—Different Amounts to Be Realized) Brandon Corp. had a future tax asset account with a balance of $101,500 at the end of 2010 due to a single temporary difference of $290,000 related to warranty liability accruals. At the end of 2011, this same temporary difference has increased to $315,000. Taxable income for 2011 is $887,000. The tax rate is 35% for all years.

Instructions

(a) Calculate and record income taxes for 2011, assuming that it is more likely than not that the future tax asset will be realized.

(b) 1. Assuming it is more likely than not that $25,000 of the future tax asset will not be realized, prepare the journal entries to record income taxes for 2011. Brandon does not use a valuation allowance account.

  2. In 2012, prospects for the company improved. While there was no change in the temporary deductible differences underlying the future tax asset account, it was now considered more likely than not that the company would be able to make full use of the temporary differences. Prepare the entry, if applicable, to adjust the future tax asset account.

(LO 8) E18-25 (Future Tax Asset—Different Amounts to Be Realized; Valuation Allowance) Refer to the information provided about Brandon Corp. in E18-24.

Instructions

(a) Assuming that it is more likely than not that $25,000 of the future tax asset will not be realized, prepare the journal entries to record income taxes for 2011. Brandon uses a valuation allowance account.

(b) In 2012, prospects for the company improved. While there was no change in the temporary deductible differences underlying the future tax asset account, it was now considered more likely than not that the company would be able to make full use of the temporary differences. Prepare the entry, if applicable, to adjust the future tax asset and related account(s).

(LO 9) E18-26 (Three Differences, Classification of Future Taxes) Darrell Corporation reports under IFRS and at December 31, 2012, the company had a net future tax liability of $375,000. An explanation of the items that make up this balance follows:

Temporary Differences	Resulting Balances in Future Tax Account
1. Excess of accumulated tax depreciation over book depreciation	$230,000
2. Accrual, for book purposes, of estimated loss contingency from pending lawsuit that is expected to be settled in 2012. The loss will be deducted on the tax return when it is paid.	(80,000)
3. Accrual method (account receivable) used for book purposes and instalment method used for tax purposes for an isolated instalment sale of an investment, due in 2013.	225,000
	$375,000

Instructions

(a) Indicate how future taxes should be presented on Darrell Corporation's December 31, 2012 balance sheet.

(b) How would your response to (a) change if Darrell Corporation followed the PE GAAP future income taxes method?

E18-27 **(Intraperiod Tax Allocation—Other Comprehensive Income)** Hang Technologies Inc. held a portfolio of **(LO 2)** shares and bonds that it accounted for using the fair value through other comprehensive income model at December 31, 2011. This was the first year that Hang had purchased investments. In part due to Hang's inexperience, by December 31, 2011, the market value of the portfolio had dropped below its original cost by $28,000. Hang recorded the necessary adjustments at December 31, 2011, and was determined to hold the securities until the unrealized loss of 2011 could be recovered. By December 31, 2012, Hang's goals of recovery had been realized and the original portfolio of shares and bonds had a fair market value $5,500 higher than the original purchase costs. Hang's income tax rate is 38% for all years. Assume that any gains that will ultimately be realized on the sale of the shares and bonds are taxable as ordinary income when they are realized.

Instructions

(a) Prepare the journal entries at December 31, 2011, to accrue the unrealized loss on Hang's securities and the related income taxes.

(b) Prepare the journal entries at December 31, 2012, to accrue the unrealized gain on the securities and the related income taxes.

(c) Prepare a comparative statement of comprehensive income for the fiscal years ending December 31, 2011 and 2012. Assume net income of $100,000 in each fiscal year.

E18-28 **(Intraperiod Tax Allocation—Discontinued Operations)** Geoff Corp.'s operations in 2011 had mixed **(LO 9)** results. One division, Vincent Group, again failed to earn income at a rate that was high enough to justify its continued operation, and management therefore decided to close the division. Vincent Group earned revenue of $118,000 during 2011 and recognized total expenses of $110,500. The remaining two divisions reported revenues of $273,000 and total expenses of $216,000 in 2011.

In preparing the annual income tax return, Geoff Corp.'s controller took into account the following information:

1. The CCA exceeded depreciation expense by $3,700. There were no depreciable assets in the Vincent Group division.

2. Included in Vincent's expenses is an accrued litigation loss of $5,100 that is not deductible for tax purposes until 2012.

3. Included in the continuing divisions' expenses are the president's golf club dues of $4,500, and included in their revenues are $1,700 of dividends from taxable Canadian corporations.

4. There were no future tax account balances for any of the divisions on January 1, 2011.

5. The tax rate for 2011 and future years is 35%.

6. Geoff Corp. reports under IFRS.

Instructions

(a) Calculate the taxable income and income taxes payable by Geoff Corp. in 2011 and the future income tax asset or liability balances at December 31, 2011.

(b) Prepare the journal entry(ies) to record income taxes for 2011.

(c) Indicate how income taxes will be reported on the income statement for 2011 by preparing the bottom portion of the statement, beginning with "Income before taxes and discontinued operations." Assume that 10,000 common shares were outstanding throughout 2011.

(d) Provide the balance sheet presentation for any resulting future tax balance sheet accounts at December 31, 2011. Be specific about the classification.

(e) How would your response to (d) change if Geoff Corp. followed the PE GAAP future income taxes method?

E18-29 **(Taxes Payable Method)** Refer to the information in E18-4 for Raman Limited. Assume that the company **(LO 9, 10)** reports under private enterprise standards and that the taxes payable method of accounting is used for income taxes.

Instructions

(a) Prepare the journal entry(ies) to record income taxes at December 31, 2012.

(b) Prepare the income statement for 2012, beginning with the line "Income before income taxes."

(c) Provide the balance sheet presentation for any resulting income tax balance sheet accounts at December 31, 2012.

(d) Prepare the disclosures that are necessary because the taxes payable method is being used.

(e) Now that Raman Limited has adopted the taxes payable method, what do you believe would be the reaction of creditors to this accounting policy when they read Raman's financial statements? Explain.

Digging Deeper

(LO 10) E18-30 **(Taxes Payable Method)** Refer to the information in E18-3 for Melissa Inc. Assume that the company follows the taxes payable method of accounting for income taxes under private enterprise GAAP. During the year, Melissa Inc. made tax instalment payments of $42,000.

Instructions

(a) Calculate the taxable income and tax expense for the year ended December 31, 2011.

(b) Prepare the journal entry(ies) to record income taxes at December 31, 2011.

(c) Prepare the income statement for 2011, beginning with the line "Income before income taxes."

(d) Provide the balance sheet presentation for any resulting income tax balance sheet accounts at December 31, 2011.

(LO 10) E18-31 **(Taxes Payable Method)** As the new accountant for Carly's Pet Express Inc., a line of pet boutiques, you are developing the financial statement disclosures for the 2011 financial statement note on Income Taxes. The company uses PE GAAP, and has selected the taxes payable method. The statutory tax rate is currently 38%. During 2011, net income before taxes was $185,000. CCA exceeded depreciation expense by $25,000. The only permanent difference was the non-deductible portion of meals and entertainment costs, 50% of $20,000.

Instructions

(a) Determine the income tax expense to be recorded using the taxes payable method and record the necessary journal entry.

(b) Prepare the reconciliation of actual tax rate to the statutory rate as required for inclusion in the financial statement note on Income Taxes.

Problems

P18-1   Anthony Ltd. began business on January 1, 2011. At December 31, 2011, it had a $3,000 balance in the future tax liability account that pertains to property, plant, and equipment previously acquired at a cost of $1 million. The tax basis of these assets at December 31, 2011, was $940,000; the accounting basis was $950,000. Anthony's income before taxes for 2012 was $80,000. Anthony Ltd. follows the PE GAAP future income taxes method.

The following items caused the only differences between accounting income before income taxes and taxable income in 2012:

1. In 2012, the company paid $75,000 for rent; of this amount, $25,000 was expensed in 2012. The other $50,000 will be expensed equally over the year 2013 and 2014 accounting periods. The full $75,000 was deducted for tax purposes in 2012.

2. Anthony Ltd. pays $12,000 a year for a membership in a local golf club for the company's president.

3. Anthony Ltd. now offers a one-year warranty on all its merchandise sold. Warranty expenses for 2012 were $12,000. Cash payments in 2012 for warranty repairs were $6,000.

4. Meals and entertainment expenses (only 50% of which are ever tax deductible) were $16,000 for 2012.

5. Depreciation expense was $50,000 and CCA was $55,000 for 2012. No new assets were acquired in the year, and there were no asset disposals.

Income tax rates have not changed over the past five years.

Instructions

(a) Calculate the balance in the Future Income Tax Asset/Liability account at December 31, 2012.

(b) Calculate income taxes payable for 2012.

(c) Prepare the journal entries to record income taxes for 2012.

(d) Prepare the income tax expense section of the income statement for 2012, beginning with the line "Income before income taxes."

(e) Indicate how future income taxes should be presented on the December 31, 2012 balance sheet.

(f) How would your response to (e) change if Anthony reported under IFRS?

P18-2   At December 31, 2010, Chloe Corporation had a temporary difference (related to pensions) and reported a related future tax asset of $40,000 on its balance sheet. At December 31, 2011, Chloe has five temporary differences. An analysis reveals the following:

Temporary Difference	Future (Taxable) Deductible Amounts		
	2012	2013	2014
1. Pension liability: expensed as incurred on the books; deductible when funded for tax purposes	$ 30,000	$ 20,000	$ 10,000
2. Royalties collected in advance: recognized when earned for accounting purposes and when received for tax purposes	76,000	—	—
3. Accrued liabilities: various expenses accrued for accounting purposes and recognized for tax purposes when paid	24,000	—	—
4. Deferred gross profit: profits recognized on instalment sales when sold for book purposes, and as collected for tax purposes	(36,000)	(36,000)	(36,000)
5. Equipment: straight-line depreciation for accounting purposes, and CCA for tax purposes	(90,000)	(50,000)	(40,000)
	$ 4,000	$(66,000)	$(66,000)

The enacted tax rate has been 40% for many years. In November 2011, the rate was changed to 38% for all periods after January 1, 2013. Assume that the company has income taxes due of $180,000 on the 2012 tax return and Chloe follows the PE GAAP future income taxes method.

Instructions

(a) Indicate how future income taxes should be presented on Chloe Corporation's December 31, 2011 balance sheet.

(b) How would your response to (a) change if Chloe reported under IFRS?

(c) Calculate taxable income for 2011.

(d) Calculate accounting income for 2011.

(e) Draft the income tax section of the 2011 income statement, beginning with the line "Income before income taxes." Provide as much information as possible about the components of income tax expense.

P18-3   Eloisa Corporation follows the PE GAAP future income taxes method. Information about Eloisa Corporation's income before taxes of $633,000 for its year ended December 31, 2011, includes the following:

1. CCA reported on the 2011 tax return exceeded depreciation reported on the income statement by $100,000. This difference, plus the $150,000 accumulated taxable temporary difference at January 1, 2011, is expected to reverse in equal amounts over the four-year period from 2012 to 2015.

2. Dividends received from taxable Canadian corporations were $15,000.

3. Rent collected in advance and included in taxable income as at December 31, 2010, totalled $60,000 for a three-year period. Of this amount, $40,000 was reported as unearned for book purposes at December 31, 2011. Unearned revenue is reported as a current liability by Eloisa if it will be recognized in income within 12 months from the balance sheet date. Eloisa paid a $2,880 interest penalty for late income tax instalments. The interest penalty is not deductible for income tax purposes at any time.

4. Equipment was disposed of during the year for $90,000. The equipment had a cost of $105,000 and accumulated depreciation to the date of disposal of $37,000. The total proceeds on the sale of these assets reduced the CCA class; in other words, no gain or loss is reported for tax purposes.

5. Eloisa recognized a $75,000 loss on impairment of a long-term investment whose value was considered impaired. The *Income Tax Act* only permits the loss to be deducted when the investment is sold and the loss is actually realized. The investment was accounted for at amortized cost.

6. The tax rates are 40% for 2011, and 35% for 2012 and subsequent years. These rates have been enacted and known for the past two years.

Instructions

(a) Calculate the balance in the Future Income Tax Asset/Liability account at December 31, 2010.

(b) Calculate the balance in the Future Income Tax Asset/Liability account at December 31, 2011.

(c) Prepare the journal entries to record income taxes for 2011.

(d) Indicate how the Future Income Tax Asset/Liability account(s) will be reported on the comparative balance sheets for 2010 and 2011.

(e) Prepare the income tax expense section of the income statement for 2011, beginning with "Income before income taxes."

(f) Calculate the effective rate of tax. Provide a reconciliation and explanation of why this differs from the statutory rate of 40%. Begin the reconciliation with the statutory rate.

(g) How would your response to (d) change if Eloisa reported under IFRS?

P18-4 The accounting income of Stephani Corporation and its taxable income for the years 2011 to 2014 are as follows:

Year	Accounting Income	Taxable Income	Tax Rate
2011	$460,000	$299,000	35%
2012	420,000	294,000	40%
2013	390,000	304,200	40%
2014	460,000	644,000	40%

The change in the tax rate from 35% to 40% was not enacted until early in 2012.

Accounting income for each year includes an expense of $40,000 that will never be deductible for tax purposes. The remainder of the difference between accounting income and taxable income in each period is due to one reversing difference for the depreciation of property, plant, and equipment. No future income taxes existed at the beginning of 2011.

Instructions

(a) Calculate the current and future tax expense or benefit for each of the four years. Also calculate the balance of the future income tax balance sheet account at the end of each fiscal year from 2011 to 2014.

(b) Prepare journal entries to record income taxes in all four years.

(c) Prepare the bottom of the income statement for 2012, beginning with the line "Income before income taxes."

P18-5 Jordan Corporation reports under IFRS. The following information applies to Jordan Corporation.

1. Prior to 2010, taxable income and accounting income were identical.

2. Accounting income was $1.7 million in 2010 and $1.4 million in 2011.

3. On January 1, 2010, equipment costing $1 million was purchased. It is being depreciated on a straight-line basis over eight years for financial reporting purposes, and is a Class 8—20% asset for tax purposes.

4. Tax-exempt interest income of $60,000 was received in 2011.

5. The tax rate is 35% for all periods.

6. Taxable income is expected in all future years.

7. Jordan Corporation had 100,000 common shares outstanding throughout 2011.

Instructions

(a) Calculate the amount of capital cost allowance and depreciation expense for 2008 and 2011, and the corresponding carrying amount and undepreciated capital cost of the depreciable assets at the end of 2010 and 2011.

(b) Determine the amount of current and future income tax expense for 2011.

(c) Prepare the journal entry(ies) to record 2011 income taxes.

(d) Prepare the bottom portion of Jordan's 2011 income statement, beginning with the line "Income before income taxes."

(e) Indicate how future income taxes should be presented on the December 31, 2011 balance sheet.

(f) How would your responses to (d) and (e) change if Jordan Corporation followed the PE GAAP future income taxes method?

P18-6 The accounting records of Steven Corp., a real estate developer, indicated income before taxes of $850,000 for its year ended December 31, 2011, and of $525,000 for the year ended December 31, 2012. The following data are also available.

1. Steven Corp. pays an annual life insurance premium of $11,000 covering the top management team. The company is the named beneficiary.

2. The carrying amount of the company's property, plant, and equipment at January 1, 2011, was $1,256,000, and the UCC at that date was $998,000. Steven recorded depreciation expense of $175,000 and $180,000 in 2011 and 2012, respectively. CCA for tax purposes was $192,000 and $163,500 for 2011 and 2012, respectively. There were no asset additions or disposals over the two-year period.

3. Steven deducted $211,000 as a restructuring charge in determining income for 2010. At December 31, 2010, an accrued liability of $199,500 (reported in current liabilities) remained outstanding relative to the restructuring. This expense is deductible for tax purposes, but only as the actual costs are incurred and paid for. When the actual restructuring of operations took place in 2011 and 2012, the liability was reduced to $68,000 at the end of 2011 and $0 at the end of 2012.

4. In 2011, property held for development was sold and a profit of $52,000 was recognized in income. Because the sale was made with delayed payment terms, the profit is taxable only as Steven receives payments from the purchaser. A 10% down payment was received in 2011, with the remaining 90% expected in equal amounts over the following three years.

5. Non-taxable dividends of $3,250 in 2011 and of $3,500 in 2012 were received from taxable Canadian corporations.

6. In addition to the income before taxes identified above, Steven reported a before-tax gain on discontinued operations of $18,800 in 2011.

7. A 30% rate of tax has been in effect since 2009.

Steven Corp. follows the PE GAAP future income taxes method.

Instructions

(a) Determine the balance of any future income tax asset or liability accounts at December 31, 2010, 2011, and 2012.

(b) Determine 2011 and 2012 taxable income and current income tax expense.

(c) Prepare the journal entries to record current and future income tax expense for 2011 and 2012.

(d) Identify how the future income tax asset or liability account(s) will be reported on the December 31, 2011 and 2012 balance sheets.

(e) Prepare partial income statements for the years ended December 31, 2011 and 2012, beginning with the line "Income from continuing operations before income tax."

(f) How would your response to (d) change if Steven Corp. reported under IFRS?

P18-7 Andrew Weiman and Mei Lee are discussing accounting for income taxes. They are currently studying a schedule of taxable and deductible amounts that will arise in the future as a result of existing temporary differences. The schedule applies to a company that reports under the PE GAAP future income taxes method. The schedule is as follows:

	Current Year	Future Years			
	2011	2012	2013	2014	2015
Taxable income	$50,000				
Taxable amounts		$75,000	$75,000	$ 75,000	$75,000
Deductible amounts				(2,400,000)	
Enacted tax rate	50%	48%	46%	44%	44%

Instructions

(a) Explain the concept of future taxable amounts and future deductible amounts as shown in the schedule.

(b) Determine the balance of the future income tax asset and future income tax liability accounts on the December 31, 2011 balance sheet. Assuming all temporary differences originated in 2011, prepare the journal entry to recognize income tax expense for 2011.

(c) Assume that this company is not expected to perform well in the future due to a sluggish economy and in-house management problems. Identify any concerns you may have about reporting the future tax asset/liability account as calculated.

(d) Company management determines that it is unlikely that the company will be able to benefit from all of the future deductible amounts. Early in 2012, after the entries in (b) have been made, but before the financial statements have been finalized and released, management estimates that $2.0 million of the $2.4 million in future deductible amounts will not be used, and that the remaining amount will be deductible in 2014. Prepare the entry that is required to recognize this, assuming the company uses a valuation allowance to adjust the future income tax asset account.

(e) When finalizing the 2012 financial statements, management estimates that, due to the prospects for an economic recovery, it is now more likely than not that the company will benefit from a total of $2.1 million of the future deductible amounts: $600,000 in 2014 and $1.5 million in 2015. Prepare the journal entry that is required, if any, to adjust the allowance account at December 31, 2012.

(f) Indicate how the future income tax accounts will be reported on the December 31, 2011 and 2012 balance sheets after taking into account the information in (d) and (e) above. Explain how these would differ, if at all, if the company did not use a valuation allowance account.

(g) How would your responses to (f) change if the company followed IFRS?

P18-8   Sarah Corp. reported the following differences between balance sheet carrying amounts and tax values at December 31, 2010:

	Carrying Amount	Tax Value
Depreciable assets	$125,000	$93,000
Warranty liability (current liability)	18,500	–0–
Accrued pension liability (long-term liability)	34,600	–0–

The differences between the carrying amounts and tax values were expected to reverse as follows:

	2011	2012	After 2012
Depreciable assets	$17,500	$12,500	$ 2,000
Warranty liability	18,500	–0–	–0–
Accrued pension liability	11,000	11,000	12,600

Tax rates enacted at December 31, 2010, were 31% for 2010, 30% for 2011, 29% for 2012, and 28% for 2013 and later years.

During 2011, Sarah made four quarterly tax instalment payments of $8,000 each and reported income before taxes on its income statement of $109,400. Included in this amount were dividends from taxable Canadian corporations of $4,300 (non-taxable income) and $20,000 of expenses related to the executive team's golf dues (non-tax-deductible expenses). There were no changes to the enacted tax rates during the year.

As expected, book depreciation in 2011 exceeded the capital cost allowance claimed for tax purposes by $17,500, and there were no additions or disposals of property, plant, and equipment during the year. A review of the 2011 activity in the warranty liability account in the ledger indicated the following:

Balance, Dec. 31, 2010	$18,500
Payments on 2010 product warranties	(18,900)
Payments on 2011 product warranties	(5,600)
2011 warranty accrual	28,300
Balance, Dec. 31, 2011	$22,300

All warranties are valid for one year only. The accrued pension liability account reported the following activity:

Balance, Dec. 31, 2010	$34,600
Payment to pension trustee	(70,000)
2011 pension expense	59,000
Balance, Dec. 31, 2011	$23,600

Pension expenses are deductible for tax purposes, but only as they are paid to the trustee, not as they are accrued for financial reporting purposes.

Sarah Corp. reports under IFRS.

Instructions

(a) Calculate the future tax asset or liability account at December 31, 2010, and explain how it should be reported on the December 31, 2010 balance sheet.

(b) Calculate the future tax asset or liability account at December 31, 2011.

(c) Prepare all income tax entries for Sarah Corp. for 2011.

(d) Identify the balances of all income tax accounts at December 31, 2011, and show how they will be reported on the comparative GAAP balance sheets at December 31, 2011 and 2010, and on the income statement for the year ended December 31, 2011.

(e) How would your responses to (a) and (d) change if Sarah Corp. followed the PE GAAP future income taxes method?

P18-9 The following are two independent situations related to future taxable and deductible amounts that resulted from temporary differences at December 31, 2011. In both situations, the future taxable amounts relate to property, plant, and equipment depreciation, and the future deductible amounts relate to settlements of litigation that were previously accrued in the accounts.

1. Alia Corp. has developed the following schedule of future taxable and deductible amounts:

	2012	2013	2014	2015	2016
Taxable amounts	$300	$300	$300	$ 200	$100
Deductible amount	0	0	0	(1,800)	0

Alia reported a net future income tax liability of $500 at January 1, 2011.

2. Khoi Corp. has the following schedule of future taxable and deductible amounts:

	2012	2013	2014	2015
Taxable amounts	$400	$400	$ 400	$400
Deductible amount	0	0	(3,000)	0

Khoi Corp. reported a net future tax asset of $600 at January 1, 2011.

Both Alia Corp. and Khoi Corp. have taxable income of $4,000 in 2011 and expect to have taxable income in all future years. The tax rates enacted as of the beginning of 2011 are 30% for 2011 to 2014, and 35% for 2015 and subsequent years. All of the underlying temporary differences relate to noncurrent assets and liabilities. Both Khoi and Alia report under the PE GAAP future income taxes method.

Instructions

(a) Determine the future income tax assets or liabilities that will be reported on each company's December 31, 2011 balance sheet.

(b) For each of these two situations, prepare journal entries to record income taxes for 2011. Show all calculations.

(c) Provide the balance sheet presentation of future tax accounts on each company's December 31, 2011 balance sheet, including their correct classification.

(d) How would your response to (c) change if Khoi and Alia followed IFRS?

P18-10 The following information was disclosed during the audit of Shawna Inc.

Year	Amount Due per Tax Return
2011	$140,000
2012	112,000

1. On January 1, 2011, equipment was purchased for $400,000. For financial reporting purposes, the company uses straight-line depreciation over a five-year life, with no residual value. For tax purposes, the CCA rate is 25%.

2. In January 2012, $225,000 was collected in advance for the rental of a building for the next three years. The entire $225,000 is reported as taxable income in 2012, but $150,000 of the $225,000 is reported as unearned revenue on the December 31, 2012 balance sheet. The $150,000 of unearned revenue will be earned equally in 2013 and 2014.

3. The tax rate is 40% in 2011 and all subsequent periods.

4. No temporary differences existed at the end of 2010. Shawna expects to report taxable income in each of the next five years. Its fiscal year ends December 31.

Shawna Inc. follows IFRS.

Instructions

(a) Calculate the amount of capital cost allowance and depreciation expense for 2011 and 2012, and the corresponding carrying amount and undepreciated capital cost of the depreciable assets at December 31, 2011 and 2012.

(b) Determine the balance of the future income tax asset or liability account at December 31, 2011, and indicate the account's classification on the balance sheet.

(c) Prepare the journal entry(ies) to record income taxes for 2011.

(d) Draft the bottom of the income statement for 2011, beginning with "Income before income taxes."

(e) Determine the balance of the future income tax asset or liability account at December 31, 2012, and indicate the account's classification on the December 31, 2012 balance sheet.

(f) Prepare the journal entry(ies) to record income taxes for 2012.

(g) Prepare the bottom of the income statement for 2012, beginning with "Income before income taxes."

(h) Provide the comparative balance sheet presentation for the future tax balance sheet accounts at December 31, 2011 and 2012. Be specific about the classification.

(i) Is it possible to have more than two accounts for future taxes reported on a balance sheet? Explain.

Digging Deeper

(j) How would your response to (h) change if Shawna Inc. reported under the PE GAAP future income taxes method?

P18-11   The following information relates to Pearline Corporation's transactions during 2011, its first year of operations.

1. Income before taxes on the income statement for 2011 was $110,000.

2. In addition, Pearline reported a loss due to the writedown of land of $46,000 for financial reporting purposes.

3. Pearline reported a tax-deductible financing charge of $5,700 on its 2011 statement of retained earnings. The charge is for interest on a financial instrument that is legally debt, but in substance is equity for financial reporting purposes.

4. The tax rate enacted for 2011 and future years is 40%. Since this was Pearline Corporation's first taxation year, no instalments on account of income taxes were required or paid by Pearline.

5. Differences between the 2011 GAAP amounts and their treatment for tax purposes were as follows:

(a) Warranty expense accrued for financial reporting purposes amounted to $15,000. Warranty payments deducted for taxes amounted to $12,000. Warranty liabilities were classified as current on the balance sheet.

(b) Of the loss on writedown of land of $46,000, 25% will never be tax deductible. The remaining 75% will be deductible for tax purposes evenly over the years from 2012 to 2014. The loss relates to the loss in value of company land due to contamination.

(c) Gross profit on construction contracts using the percentage-of-completion method for book purposes amounted to $30,000. For tax purposes, gross profit on construction contracts amounted to $0 as the completed-contract method is used and no contracts were completed during the year. Construction costs amounted to $270,000 during the year.

(d) Depreciation of property, plant, and equipment for financial reporting purposes amounted to $60,000. CCA charged on the tax return amounted to $80,000. The related property, plant, and equipment cost $300,000 when it was acquired early in 2011.

(e) A $3,500 fine paid for a violation of pollution laws was deducted in calculating accounting income.

(f) Dividend revenue earned on an investment was tax exempt and amounted to $1,400.

6. Taxable income is expected for the next few years.

Pearline Corporation follows the PE GAAP future income taxes method.

Instructions

(a) Calculate Pearline Corporation's future income tax asset or liability at December 31, 2011.

(b) Calculate the taxable income for 2011. Show all details of the adjustments to accounting income to arrive at taxable income.

(c) Prepare the journal entry(ies) to record income taxes for 2011.

(d) Prepare a partial 2011 income statement, beginning with "Income before income taxes and extraordinary items."

(e) Prepare a statement of retained earnings for the year ended December 31, 2011, assuming no dividends were declared in the year.

(f) Show how the balance of the future income tax asset or liability account will be reported on the December 31, 2011 balance sheet.

(g) Calculate the effective rate of tax. Provide a reconciliation and explanation of why this differs from the statutory rate of 40%. Begin the reconciliation with the statutory rate.

(h) How would your response to (f) change if Pearline Corporation followed IFRS?

P18-12 Carly Inc. reported the following accounting income (loss) and related tax rates during the years 2006 to 2012:

Year	Accounting Income (Loss)	Tax Rate
2006	$ 70,000	30%
2007	25,000	30%
2008	60,000	30%
2009	80,000	40%
2010	(210,000)	45%
2011	70,000	40%
2012	90,000	35%

Accounting income (loss) and taxable income (loss) were the same for all years since Carly began business. The tax rates from 2009 to 2012 were enacted in 2009.

Instructions

(a) Prepare the journal entries to record income taxes for the years 2010 to 2012. Assume that Carly uses the carryback provision where possible and expects to realize the benefits of any loss carryforward in the year that immediately follows the loss year.

(b) Indicate the effect of the 2010 entry(ies) on the December 31, 2010 balance sheet. Assume Carly follows the PE GAAP future income taxes method. Indicate as well the balance sheet impact if Carly reported under IFRS.

(c) Show how the bottom portion of the income statement would be reported in 2010, beginning with "Loss before income taxes."

(d) Indicate how the bottom portion of the income statement would be reported in 2011, starting with "Income before income taxes."

(e) Prepare the journal entries for the years 2010 to 2012 to record income taxes, assuming that Carly uses the carryback provision where possible but is uncertain if it will realize the benefits of any loss carryforward in the future. Carly does not use a valuation allowance.

(f) Assume now that Carly uses a valuation allowance account along with its future tax asset account. Identify which entries in (e) would differ and prepare them.

(g) Based on your entries in (e), indicate how the bottom portion of the income statements for 2010 and 2011 would be reported, beginning with "Income (loss) before income taxes."

(h) From a cash flow perspective, can you think of any advantage in using the valuation allowance for financial reporting purposes? Can you think of any advantages in not using it?

DD

Digging
Deeper

P18-13 Chen Corporation reported income before taxes for the year ended December 31, 2011, of $1,645,000. In preparing the 2011 financial statements, the accountant discovered an error that was made in 2010. The error was that a piece of land with a cost of $40,000 had been recognized as an operating expense in error. The balance reported as retained earnings at December 31, 2010, was $5,678,000, and the net book value of property, plant, and equipment (excluding land) was $1,352,000 at the same date. During 2011, Chen Corporation acquired additional equipment with a cost of $16,000.

In completing the corporate tax return for the 2011 year, the company controller noted that the 2011 depreciation expense was $365,000, CCA claimed was $300,000, and non-deductible income tax penalties and interest of $2,500 and golf club dues of $4,500 were incurred in the year. In addition, the accounting allowance for doubtful accounts exceeded the tax reserve for uncollectible amounts by $20,000, although they were equal at the beginning of the year. At the end of 2010, the company had temporary differences of $135,000, due to lower depreciation expense than CCA claimed on the corporate tax return. The resulting future taxable amounts and the dates they were expected to reverse at December 31, 2010, were:

2011	$ 65,000
2012	40,000
2013	30,000
	$135,000

The tax rate is 35% for all years. Chen Corporation applies PE GAAP and uses the future income taxes method of accounting.

Instructions

(a) Calculate the balance sheet future tax account balance at December 31, 2010.

(b) Determine the effect of the prior period error on the December 31, 2010 balance sheet and prepare the journal entry to correct the error. Assume that the 2010 income tax return is refiled.

(c) Prepare the journal entries to record income taxes for the 2011 year.

(d) Indicate how the income taxes will be reported on the financial statements for 2011 by preparing the bottom portion of the income statement beginning with "Income before income taxes." Also prepare the Statement of Retained Earnings for the year ended December 31, 2011, assuming no dividends were declared during the year.

P18-14 Aaron Engines Ltd. operates small engine repair outlets and is a tenant in several of Tran Holdings Inc.'s strip shopping malls. Aaron signed several lease renewals with Tran that each called for a three-month rent-free period. The leases start at various dates and are for three to five years each. As with all of Tran's tenants, Aaron pays rent quarterly, three months in advance, and records the payments initially to Prepaid Rent.

The rent-free period obtained in the lease agreement with Tran Holdings Inc. reduces the overall rental costs of the outlets over the term of each lease. Aaron's accounting policy requires the leasing costs of each outlet to be allocated evenly over the term of the lease to fairly match expenses with revenues. Aaron accrues rent expense during the rent-free period to an account called Rent Payable. Following the rent-free period, the Rent Payable account is amortized to Rent Expense over the remaining term of the lease. For tax purposes, Aaron must use the cash basis and is unable to deduct the rent expense accrued during the rent-free periods. On its tax return, Aaron can only deduct the actual rent payments when they are made.

The balances for the accounts related to prepaid rent and rent payable under leases as well as payments for interest to earn tax-exempt income and payments for golf club dues for the years ending December 31, 2013 and 2012, follow:

	2013	2012
Prepaid Rent (assume current classification and no balance at Dec. 31, 2011)	$ 92,000	$ 89,000
Rent Payable (assume noncurrent classification and no balance at Dec. 31, 2011)	133,000	146,000
Golf Dues Expense	11,000	13,000
Interest Expense (incurred to earn tax-exempt income)	6,000	4,000

In 2012, Aaron's tax rate is 43%, and it is 42% for subsequent years. Income before income tax for the year ended December 31, 2012, was $884,000. During 2013, Aaron's tax rate changed to 44% for 2013 and subsequent years. Income before income tax for the year ended December 31, 2013, was $997,000.

Instructions

(a) Calculate the future income tax asset or liability balances at December 31, 2012 and 2013.

(b) Calculate taxable income and income taxes payable for 2012 and 2013.

(c) Prepare the journal entries to record income taxes for 2012 and 2013.

(d) Prepare a comparative income statement for 2012 and 2013, beginning with the line "Income before income taxes."

(e) Provide the comparative balance sheet presentation for any resulting future tax balance sheet accounts at December 31, 2012 and 2013. Be specific about the classification.

(f) Calculate the effective rate of tax for 2013. Provide a reconciliation and explanation of why this differs from the statutory rate of 44%. Begin the reconciliation with the statutory rate.

(g) Repeat the balance sheet presentation in part (e) assuming Aaron follows IFRS.

P18-15 On December 31, 2010, Quirk Inc. has taxable temporary differences of $2,200,000 and a future income tax liability of $924,000. These temporary differences are due to Quirk having claimed CCA in excess of book depreciation in prior years. Quirk's year-end is December 31. At the end of December 2011, Quirk's substantially enacted tax rate for 2011 and future years was changed to 44%.

For the year ended December 31, 2011, Quirk's accounting loss before tax was ($494,000). The following data are also available.

1. Pension expense was $87,000 while pension plan contributions were $111,000 for the year (only actual pension contributions are deductible for tax).

2. Business meals and entertainment were $38,000 (one-half deductible for tax purposes).

3. For the three years ending December 31, 2010, Quirk had cumulative, total taxable income of $123,000 and total tax expense/taxes payable of $51,660.

4. During 2011, the company booked estimated warranty costs of $31,000 and these costs are not likely to be incurred until 2015.

5. In 2011 the company incurred $150,000 of development costs (only 50% of which are deductible for tax purposes).

6. Company management has determined that only one-half of any loss carryforward at the end of 2011 is more likely than not to be realized.

7. In 2011, the amount claimed for depreciation was equal to the amount claimed for CCA.

Instructions

Prepare the journal entries to record taxes for the year ended December 31, 2011, and the tax reconciliation note.

Writing Assignments

WA18-1   The amount of income taxes that is due to the government for a period of time is rarely the same as the amount of income tax expense that is reported on the income statement for that same period under IFRS and one of the alternatives under PE GAAP.

Instructions

(a) Explain the objectives of accounting for income taxes in general purpose financial statements.

(b) Explain the basic principles that are applied in accounting for income taxes at the date of the financial statements to meet the objectives discussed in (a).

(c) Explain how the recognition of future tax accounts on the balance sheet is consistent with the conceptual framework, noting the differences between IFRS and PE GAAP.

(d) Using the definition of an asset and a liability (from Chapter 2), discuss why future income tax assets and future tax liabilities as currently measured and reported might not meet this definition.

WA18-2   The asset-liability approach for recording future income taxes is an integral part of generally accepted accounting principles.

Instructions

(a) Indicate whether each of the following independent situations results in a reversing difference or a permanent difference in the year. Explain your answer. Be sure to note any differences between PE GAAP and IFRS.
 1. Estimated warranty costs (covering a three-year warranty) are expensed for financial reporting purposes at the time of sale but deducted for income tax purposes when they are paid.
 2. Equity investments have a quoted market value that is recorded at fair value through net income and is adjusted to their fair value at the balance sheet date.
 3. The depreciation on equipment is different for book and income tax purposes because of different bases of carrying the asset, which was acquired in a trade-in. The different bases are a result of different rules that are used for book and tax purposes to calculate the cost of assets acquired in a trade-in.
 4. A company properly uses the equity method to account for its 30% investment in another taxable Canadian corporation. The investee pays non-taxable dividends that are about 10% of its annual earnings.
 5. Management determines that the net realizable value of the inventory is below cost, causing a writedown in the current year.
 6. A company reports a contingent loss that it expects will result from an ongoing lawsuit. The loss is not reported on the current year's tax return. Half the loss is a penalty it expects to be charged by the courts. This portion of the loss is not a tax-deductible expenditure, even when it is paid.
 7. The company uses the revaluation model for reporting its land and buildings. Due to current economic conditions, the fair value of the properties declined and the writedown was recorded against the revaluation surplus reported in equity.

8. The company settles its retirement obligation on a drilling platform that is put out of service. The actual settlement was less than the amount accrued, and the company recognizes a gain on settlement in its accounting net income.

(b) Discuss the nature of any future income tax accounts that result from the situations in (a) above, including their possible classifications in the company's balance sheet. Indicate how these accounts should be reported. Note any differences between IFRS and the asset-liability method under PE GAAP.

WA18-3 The following are common items that are treated differently for financial reporting purposes than they are for tax purposes:

1. The excess amount of a charge to the accounting records (allowance method) over a charge to the tax return (direct writeoff method) for uncollectible receivables

2. The excess amount of accrued pension expense over the amount paid

3. The receipt of dividends from a taxable Canadian corporation that are treated as income for accounting purposes but are not subject to tax

4. Expenses incurred in obtaining tax-exempt income

5. A trademark that is acquired directly from the government and is capitalized and amortized over subsequent periods for accounting purposes and expensed for tax purposes

6. A prepaid advertising expense that is deferred for accounting purposes and deducted as an expense for tax purposes

7. Premiums paid on life insurance of officers (where the corporation is the beneficiary)

8. A penalty paid for filing a late tax return

9. Proceeds of life insurance policies on lives of officers

10. Restructuring costs that are recognized as an unusual item on the income statement and are not deductible until actual costs are incurred

11. Unrealized gains and losses that are recognized on investments recorded as FV-NI or FV-OCI and are not taxable or deductible until realized for tax purposes

12. Excess depletion for accounting purposes over the amount taken for tax purposes

13. The estimated gross profit on a long-term construction contract that is reported in the income statement, with some of the gross profit being deferred for tax purposes

Instructions

(a) Indicate for each item above if the situation is a permanent difference, or a reversing difference resulting in a temporary difference.

(b) Indicate for each item above if the situation will usually create future taxable amounts, resulting in a future tax liability; or future deductible amounts, resulting in a future tax asset; or whether it will have no future tax implications.

Ethics

WA18-4 Henrietta Aguirre, CGA, is the newly hired director of corporate taxation for Mesa Incorporated, which is a publicly traded corporation. Aguirre's first job with Mesa was to review the company's accounting practices for future income taxes. In doing her review, she noted differences between tax and book depreciation methods that permitted Mesa to recognize a sizeable future tax liability on its balance sheet. As a result, Mesa did not have to report current income tax expenses.

Aguirre also discovered that Mesa had an explicit policy of selling off plant and equipment assets before they reversed in the future tax liability account. This policy, together with the rapid expansion of Mesa's capital asset base, allowed Mesa to defer all income taxes payable for several years, at the same time as it reported positive earnings and an increasing EPS. Aguirre checked with the legal department and found the policy to be legal, but she is uncomfortable with the ethics of it.

Instructions

(a) Why would Mesa have an explicit policy of selling assets before they reversed in the future tax liability account?

(b) What are the ethical implications of Mesa's deferral of income taxes?

(c) Who could be harmed by Mesa's ability to defer income taxes payable for several years, despite positive earnings?

(d) In a situation such as this, what might be Aguirre's professional responsibilities?

WA18-5   Under the asset-liability method, the tax rates used for future income tax calculations are those enacted at the balance sheet date, based on how the reversal will be treated for tax purposes.

Instructions

For each of the following situations, discuss the impact on future income tax balances.

(a) At December 31, 2010, Golden Corporation has one temporary difference that will reverse and cause taxable amounts in 2011. In 2010, new tax legislation sets tax rates equal to 45% for 2010, 40% for 2011, and 34% for 2012 and the years thereafter.

Explain what circumstances would require Golden to calculate its future tax liability at the end of 2010 by multiplying the temporary difference by:

1. 45%.

2. 40%.

3. 34%.

(b) Record Inc. uses the fair value method for reporting its investment properties. The company has an investment property with an original cost of $5 million and a tax carrying amount of $3.5 million due to cumulative capital cost allowance claimed to date of $1.5 million. This asset is increased to its fair value of $8 million for accounting purposes. No equivalent adjustment is made for tax purposes. The tax rate is 30% for normal business purposes. If the asset is sold for more than cost, the cumulative capital cost allowance of $1.5 million will be included in taxable income as recaptured depreciation, but sale proceeds in excess of cost will be taxable at 15%. Calculate the related future income balance assuming:

1. the value of the asset will be recovered through its use

2. the value of the asset will be recovered by selling the asset

(c) Assume the same above for (a) and (b), but the company is now revaluing a tract of land and a building that are included in property, plant, and equipment. The change in revaluation has been reported in other comprehensive income. All numbers remain the same as discussed in (a) and (b) above. What differences in the tax impact, if any, would be required?

WA18-6   LGS Inc. is a private company. You have recently been hired as the CFO for the company and are currently finalizing the company year-end report for December 31, 2011. The company has an option to follow either IFRS or PE GAAP, and has not yet made the choice. Three situations have arisen affecting the company's reporting of income taxes. These situations are described below (assume that tax rates are 28%).

1. Shortly after you were hired, you found that a prior period adjustment had been made in 2010, and the future income tax liability account was adjusted through retained earnings as part of this error correction. The difference between the accounting value and the tax value of the related asset is $1 million. Originally, the rate used to record the future income tax liability was 25%. In 2011, the enacted tax rate on this difference is now 28% and therefore an adjustment must be made to the financial tax liability account.

2. The company has land with a building that has been recently appraised at a fair value of $10 million. Currently, the building's carrying value is $6.5 million and its original cost was $8 million. Accumulated capital cost allowance booked to date on the building is $2.3 million. (Ignore the one-time adjustments allowed to property, plant, and equipment for first-time adopters for IFRS or PE GAAP.)

3. LGS bought some equity investments during the year that are not publicly traded for a total cost of $340,000. The company purchased these as an investment to be sold in the near future. Currently, the shares have been valued at December 31, 2010, for $510,000. There were no dividends received on this investment during the year.

Instructions

For each of the situations described above, discuss the options for reporting the income tax implications under IFRS and PE GAAP.

WA18-7   Write a brief essay highlighting the difference between IFRS and accounting standards for private enterprises noted in this chapter, discussing the conceptual justification for each.

Case

Refer to the Case Primer on the Student Website to help you answer these cases.

CA18-1   Baker Company Limited (BCL) was founded in 2009 and its first year of operations turned out to be a good one, as start-up years go, since the company not only broke even but actually showed a very small profit. Just as the company was getting established in the market, however, a full-fledged recession hit in 2010 and had devastating effects. Demand for BCL's products in retail markets declined as consumers tightened their purse strings. Through tight cost controls, however, BCL managed to hold its own and still recorded a small profit in 2010.

While the recession finally petered out by the end of 2011, BCL did end up feeling its effects, as the company was unable to remain profitable and suffered large operating losses that year. In fact, the losses were significantly greater than the profits that were reported in the previous two years. Despite this change, BCL management was not overly alarmed by the losses and had the following comments to make:

> The losses were expected given the widespread recession. Since the bulk of our sales are in retail markets, and with unemployment levels being at record highs, it is not surprising that consumer demand has fallen off. If BCL is compared with the industry, you will see that we did much better than our competitors, some of whom went bankrupt.

> Keep in mind that we are a relatively new company and managed to record a profit in two out of our first three years. We attribute this to our strong management team and our ability as a streamlined company to react to the recession with cost control measures and an aggressive, yet flexible sales staff.

> We see ourselves positioned for a new growth spurt given that the economy seems to have recovered and a lot of "dead wood" (i.e., competition) has been cleared out. As a matter of fact, in that regard, the recession will have a positive impact on our short- to mid-term growth potential.

> BCL is on the verge of introducing two new products that will revolutionize the industry and assure us a solid earnings base for the future. These products will be introduced in 2012 and we have already lined up sufficient buyers such that we predict we will at least break even in terms of net income in 2012. This is a very conservative forecast.

Although the effects of the recession were lessening, unemployment was still high in early 2012 and consumer spending had not increased significantly. Some economists were predicting that it would take two or three years for consumer confidence and spending to pick up to pre-recession levels.

Instructions

Adopt the role of the company's auditor and determine whether BCL should recognize the benefits of the losses suffered in the 2011 financial statements. Assume BCL is a private company.

Integrated Case

IC18-1   Cringle Inc. (CI) has just had a planning meeting with its auditors. There were several concerns that had been raised during the meeting regarding the draft financial statements for the December 31, 2011 year end. CI is a public company whose shares list on the TSX. It has recently gone through a major expansion and, as a result, there are several financial reporting decisions that need to be made for the upcoming year-end financial statements. The expansion has been financed in the short term with a line of credit from the bank; however, the company plans to raise capital in the equity markets in the new year. It is hoped that the expansion will increase profitability, although it is too early to tell.

Just before year end, the company purchased a number of investments as follows:

- 20% of the common shares of KL. CI was able to appoint one member to KL's board of directors (which has four members in total). CI is unsure as to whether it will hold on to this investment for the longer term or sell it if the share price increases. The company has currently set a benchmark that if the share price increases by more than 25%, it will liquidate the investment. KL has been profitable over the past few years and the share price is on an upward trend. The original reason for entering into this transaction was to create a strategic alliance with KL that will help ensure a steady supply of high-quality raw materials from KL to CI.

- Corporate bonds. These bonds are five-year bonds that bear interest at 5% (which is in excess of market interest rates). As a result, the company paid a premium for the bonds. The bonds are convertible to common shares of the company. It is CI's intent to hold on to these bonds to maturity, although if there were an unforeseen cash crunch, it might have to cash them in earlier.

The company completed a significant sale to a new U.S. customer on credit on December 31, 2011. Under the terms of the agreement, CI will provide services to the customer over a one-year period. The sales agreement includes a non-refundable upfront fee for a significant amount, which the company has recognized as revenue. As part of the deal, CI will provide access to significant proprietary information (which it has already done) and then provide ongoing analysis and monitoring functions as a service to the customer. It is not specified in the contract whether the rights to the proprietary information are transferable but CI is taking the position that they are. The proprietary information is of no value as a separate item if not transferable. During the year, CI renewed service contracts for some of its other major customers under similar deals.

The receivable for this large sale is in U.S. dollars. Half of this has been hedged using a forward contract to sell U.S. dollars at a fixed rate. The other half is hedged through a natural hedge since the company has some U.S. dollar payables. The auditor has asked that the company prepare some notes analyzing the need for hedge accounting for this transaction and explaining the risks associated with the sales transaction and hedge transactions.

This has been a bad year for the company due to one-time charges on a lawsuit settlement, and currently the draft statements are showing a loss. The company's tax accountants have determined that the company will also have a loss for tax purposes.

Instructions

Assume the role of the controller and analyze the financial reporting issues.

Research and Financial Analysis

RA18-1 Stora Enso Oyj

The complete financial statements of Stora Enso Oyj for the company's year ended December 31, 2009, are available at the company's website (www.storaenso.com). Refer to Stora Enso's financial statements and accompanying notes and answer the following questions.

Instructions

(a) Identify all income tax accounts reported on the December 31, 2009 statement of financial position. Explain clearly what each account represents.

(b) What are the temporary differences that existed at December 31, 2009, and resulted in the deferred taxes? Which of these differences might relate to the deferred tax assets and which ones to the deferred tax liabilities? Explain the reasons for your answers.

(c) Reconcile the opening balance to the closing balance for the income taxes receivable (payable) account and the deferred tax accounts for the year ended December 31, 2009. What are the major transactions causing the balance to change from January 1 to December 31?

(d) Does Stora Enso's management think it is probable that the benefits related to future deductible amounts will be realized? Explain. Discuss the valuation allowance for the deferred taxes and how the company arrived at this valuation allowance. What are the gross amounts of the loss carryforwards that the company has available and what are the expiry dates for these losses?

(e) Has Stora Enso applied intraperiod tax allocation in 2009? Explain.

(f) How much income tax did Stora Enso pay in 2009? Where did you find this information?

(g) What was the effective tax rate for Stora Enso in 2009? In 2008? In 2007? What were the major causes of the differences between the statutory and effective tax rates for 2009 and 2008? For each reason you give, explain whether the effective rate was made higher or lower than the statutory rate.

RA18-2 Gildan Activewear Inc.

Gildan Activewear Inc. is a Canadian company that manufactures and sells activewear, socks, and underwear. Manufacturing is primarily done in Honduras and Dominican Republic and sales are made worldwide.

Instructions

Through SEDAR (www.sedar.com) or Gildan's website (www.gildan.com), obtain a copy of the company's financial statements for its year ended October 4, 2009 (2009 year end), and answer the following questions.

(a) Review the Consolidated Statements of Earnings and Comprehensive Income for 2009 and 2008. What was the income tax expense for each year? Did the company apply intraperiod tax allocation in 2009 or 2008? Why or why not? How much does the company show as income taxes payable on the Balance Sheet for the fiscal year ends 2009 and 2008? What was paid for income taxes in 2009 and 2008, and where did you find this information? Why are the income taxes payable amounts and paid amounts significantly different for 2008 and 2009?

(b) What was the company's effective tax rate for 2009? For 2008? What was the statutory rate in each of these years? What caused the differences? Be specific about whether the effective rate was increased or decreased as a result of each cause that you identify.

(c) For each future income tax account reported on the October 4, 2009 balance sheet, explain what underlies the balance that is reported. For each temporary difference, identify the balance sheet asset or liability where the tax basis and book value differ.

(d) What are the losses that the company has available to carry forward? When do these losses expire? How has the company accounted for these losses?

RA18-3 Comparative Analysis

Alimentation Couche-Tard Inc., Loblaw Companies Limited, and **Empire Company Limited** are three companies in the same industry. Because all three are in the same industry, the expectation is that their operations and financial positions are also similar.

Real-World Emphasis

Instructions

Go to SEDAR (www.sedar.com) or the company websites and, using Alimentation Couche-Tard's financial statements for the year ended April 26, 2009, Loblaw's financial statements for the year ended January 2, 2010, and Empire's financial statements for the year ended May 2, 2009, answer the following questions.

(a) Identify what industry all three companies are in.

(b) Identify all the areas where intraperiod tax allocation was used by the three companies. This requires a careful reading of some of the notes to the financial statements as well as the main statements themselves. Prepare a schedule of the total income tax provision (expense) or recovery (benefit) for each company, and identify where the provision or recovery was reported.

(c) Compare the three companies' future income tax assets and/or future income tax liabilities, and identify, as much as possible, what temporary differences are responsible for these accounts. Would you expect companies in the same industry to have similar types of temporary differences? Do they?

(d) Would you expect the three companies to be subject to similar income tax legislation and tax rates? Are their statutory rates the same? Explain. Compare the companies' statutory and effective rates and explain why there are differences, if there are any.

RA18-4 International Comparison

Different countries have different statutory tax rates. Choose an industry and select five companies that operate in different countries. Access these companies' most recent financial statements and make note of their statutory and effective income tax rates.

    Alternatively, use the railway industry and the following companies:

Real-World Emphasis

Canadian National Railway: Canada

Deutsche Bahn: Germany

East Japan Railway: Japan

NSB Group: Norway

National Railroad Passenger Corporation (Amtrak): United States

Instructions

Access the most recent reports for the five companies you chose. For each company, identify its year end, country of operation, statutory income tax rates, and effective tax rates. Discuss any similarities or differences found.

Automakers Stall on Pension Funding

News REPORTS HAVE been filled with accounts of pension underfunding in recent years. It seems no industry has been safe, including Canada's largest auto manufacturers. Bankruptcy-plagued General Motors of Canada Ltd. faced a pension shortfall of more than $7 billion, and even Canada's healthiest car company, Ford Motor Co. of Canada, reported a $1.8-billion shortfall in its pension plan in 2009.

The most recent public information available, from November 2007, put GM Canada's pension plan deficit at $4.5 billion; this amount would have likely grown to more than $7 billion by the end of 2008, considering the stock market declines that took place that year. It probably regained some ground as the Toronto Stock Exchange recovered about 12% of its value in 2009.

Still, solving GM Canada's pension problems would involve government financial contributions. The Canadian and Ontario governments were prepared to lend the company money once plans for restructuring operations and cutting overall labour costs were made. The company also needed to negotiate a reduction in future retirement benefits for unionized employees still on the job. GM Canada's pension fund was going to face a big hit as more than half its hourly workforce was to be cut by 2014. Based on the figures available, this would translate into a deficit of more than $1 million for every active GM worker by 2014.

While Ford Canada did not seek bailout funding from the government, like GM Canada, it did enter into a cost-cutting agreement with its employees; new employees will now contribute $1 to their own pension for every hour worked.

Ford's pension plan held assets of $2.9 billion as at December 31, 2008, enough to cover just 62% of the plan's liabilities, which means the total liabilities were about $4.7 billion. Ford planned to take advantage of a change in Ontario law that extended the period for addressing pension shortfalls from five years to 10. ■

Sources: Shawn McCarthy, Karen Howlett, and Greg Keenan, "Pension Deficit Threatens GM's viability," *The Globe and Mail*, May 13, 2009; Greg Keenan, "Massive Pension Shortfall Hits Ford," *The Globe and Mail*, September 22, 2009; "Ford Workers Endorse Cost-Cutting Deal," *The Globe and Mail*, Report on Business, November 4, 2009.

CHAPTER 19

Pensions and Other Employee Future Benefits

Learning Objectives

After studying this chapter, you should be able to:

1. Identify and account for a defined contribution benefit plan.

2. Identify and explain what a defined benefit plan is and what the accounting issues are.

3. Explain what the employer's benefit obligation is, identify alternative measures for this obligation, and prepare a continuity schedule of transactions and events that change its balance.

4. Identify transactions and events that change the benefit plan assets, and calculate the balance of the assets.

5. Explain what a benefit plan's funded status is, calculate it, and identify what transactions and events change its amount.

6. Identify the components of pension benefit cost, and account for a defined benefit pension plan under the immediate recognition approach.

7. Identify the components of pension benefit cost, and account for a defined benefit pension plan under the deferral and amortization approach under IFRS and private enterprise standards.

8. Determine the benefit plan accounts reported in the financial statements and explain their relationship to the funded status of the plan.

9. Account for defined benefit plans with benefits that vest or accumulate other than pension plans.

10. Identify the types of information required to be presented and disclosed for defined benefit plans, prepare basic schedules, and be able to read and understand such disclosures.

11. Identify differences between the IFRS and private enterprise accounting standards for employee future benefits and what changes are expected in the near future.

After studying Appendix 19A, you should be able to:

12. Explain and apply basic calculations to determine current service cost, the accrued benefit obligation, and past service cost for a one-person defined benefit pension plan.

Preview of Chapter 19

Since employers are concerned about the current and future well-being of their employees, as are the employees themselves, organizations have established a variety of future benefit programs for their employees. For example, private pension and other post-retirement benefit plans are common in companies of all sizes. In mid-2009, of the 5.9 million Canadian workers who belonged to employer pension plans, about 4.8 million were members of plans whose assets were held in trusteed pension funds. Called trusteed pension funds because they are governed by the provisions of a trust agreement, these funds are impressive in size. The market value of the assets held in trusteed pension funds in Canada peaked at $954.6 billion at the end of 2007 before being hit by the economic downturn in 2008. By the end of the second quarter of 2009, these assets stood at $826.5 billion, up from $791.1 billion three months earlier.[1]

A pension is part of an employee's overall compensation package. Post-retirement health-care and other benefits are also often part of this package. The substantial growth of these plans, in terms of both how many employees are covered and the dollar amount of benefits, has made their costs significantly larger in relation to a company's financial position, results of operations, and cash flows. This is made clear in the opening story about the automakers, but they are not alone in taking steps to reduce such costs. This chapter discusses the accounting issues related to these future benefits.

The chapter is organized as follows:

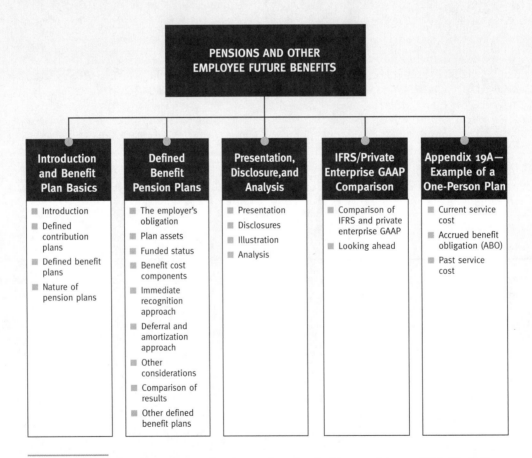

---

[1] Statistics Canada, Employer pension plans (trusteed pension funds), second quarter 2009. *The Daily*, December 15, 2009, available at http://www.statcan.gc.ca/.

INTRODUCTION AND BENEFIT PLAN BASICS

This chapter starts by introducing basic terminology, categories of benefits, and how to account for benefit plans that are relatively straightforward. Because the accounting standards now in place are in the process of being improved and may change by the time many current students are writing professional exams and working as practising professionals, the following section explains the key underlying components of defined benefit plans—such as the company's accrued obligation and assets of pension plans—and what causes them to change. These components and changes in them are the basic building blocks for employee future-benefits accounting. By understanding them, you will understand such topics as pension accounting, even when the accounting standards change later.

After this, we describe two different approaches to the recognition and measurement of the balance sheet benefit liability (or asset) and the period's benefit cost associated with a defined benefit plan. We then set out what constitutes current international and private enterprise accounting standards for such plans. Appendix 19A provides a simplified example of a one-person pension plan to help you better visualize and understand some of the new concepts that are introduced in the chapter.

Introduction

As indicated, this chapter discusses the accounting and reporting for a variety of employee future benefits that are earned by employees and that are expected to be provided to them on a long-term basis. Examples of these benefit plans include:

- Post-retirement plans such as pensions and plans that provide health care or life insurance benefits after an employee's retirement.

- Post-employment plans with benefits that are provided after employment but before retirement. These include long-term disability income benefits, long-term severance benefits, and continuation of benefits such as health care and life insurance.

- Plans covering accumulating and vested compensated absences. This type of benefit includes payments made while an employee is absent from work. It also includes unrestricted sabbatical leaves and accumulated sick days that vest or are taken as paid vacation.

Short-term benefits that are provided while employees are actively employed, such as regular vacations and occasional sick days, were discussed in Chapter 13, as were short-term absences to which employees are entitled by virtue of their employment. Examples of this latter category are parental leave and many short-term disability plans.

Employee future benefit plans can also be described as indicated in Illustration 19-1. The terms used are explained below.

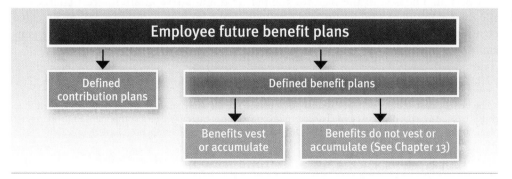

Categories of Employee Future Benefit Plans

Defined contribution plans are fairly straightforward, so we begin with this type of plan. Most of the chapter explains the accounting for defined benefit plans in which the benefits vest or accumulate.

Defined Contribution Plans

Objective 1
Identify and account for a defined contribution benefit plan.

Law

A defined contribution (DC) plan is a post-employment benefit plan that specifies how the entity's contributions or payments into the plan are determined, rather than identifying what benefits will be received by the employee or the method of determining those benefits.[2] The IFRS definition in IAS 19 *Employee Benefits* extends the explanation to include the fact that, once the entity pays those contributions into the fund, it has no further obligation to make additional payments, even if the fund ends up not having enough assets to pay the employee benefits. Under a defined contribution plan, the amounts paid in are usually attributed to specific individuals. The contributions may be a fixed sum—for example, $1,000 per year—or they may be related to salary, such as 6% of regular plus overtime earnings. No promise is made about the ultimate benefit that will be paid out to the employees.

For a DC pension plan, the amounts that are contributed are usually turned over to an independent third party or trustee who acts on behalf of the beneficiaries (the participating employees). The trustee assumes ownership of the pension assets and is responsible for their investment and distribution. The trust is separate and distinct from the employer. The size of the pension benefit that the employee finally collects under the plan depends on the amounts that have been contributed to the pension trust, the income that has accumulated in the trust, the treatment of forfeitures of funds created by the termination of employees before retirement, and the investment alternatives available on retirement.

Because **the contribution is defined**, the accounting for a defined contribution plan is straightforward. The employer's obligation is dictated by the amounts to be contributed. Therefore, a liability is reported on the employer's balance sheet only if the required contributions have not been made in full, and an asset is reported if more than the required amount has been contributed. Discounting is not an issue because amounts due usually fall into the 12-month period following the reporting date. The annual benefit cost (i.e., the pension expense) is simply the amount that the company is obligated to contribute to the plan.[3] The employer generally has no other obligation and assumes no other risk relative to this plan.

The private enterprise standard, or ASPE, speaks to other possible components of the associated cost and liability. When a defined contribution plan is first established, or when it is later amended, the employer may be required to make contributions for employee services that were provided before the start of the plan or its amendment. This obligation is referred to as **prior or past service cost**. Such costs are amortized in a rational and systematic way and are added to the current service cost as part of the annual benefit expense over the period that the organization is expected to realize the economic benefits from the plan change. This period could be as short as just the current period. The cost of the plan for the period might also contain interest charges on any related discounted amounts and a reduction for interest earned on any unallocated plan surplus. Under IFRS, these past service costs, usually fully vested amounts, are generally recognized immediately in expense.

---

[2] *CICA Handbook*, Part II, Section 3461.156.

[3] The benefit **cost** and the benefit **expense** for a period are the same amount unless some portion of the cost is treated as a product cost and charged to inventory, or is capitalized as a component of property, plant, and equipment, for example. In this chapter, these terms are generally used interchangeably.

Defined Benefit Plans

A defined benefit (DB) plan is any benefit plan that is not a defined contribution plan. It is a plan that specifies either the benefits to be received by an employee or the method of determining those benefits. One example is a plan that provides an entitlement to a lump-sum payment of $5,000 on the employee's 10th and 25th anniversaries of employment with the employer company. Another is a plan that provides an annual pension benefit on retirement equal to 2% of the average of the employee's best three years of salary multiplied by the number of years of employment.

2 Objective

Identify and explain what a defined benefit plan is and what the accounting issues are.

Law

The most complex type of benefit plan provides defined benefits that vest in the employee based on the employee's length of service. Employees' rights to post-employment medical benefits, for example, generally vest after the employee has worked a specified number of years, and the amount of pension benefit usually increases with the length of service. Vesting means that an employee keeps the rights to the benefit even if the employee no longer works for the entity. That is, if an employee whose benefits have vested leaves the company, the individual will still receive those benefits. If they are not vested when the employee leaves, the rights to the benefits are lost.

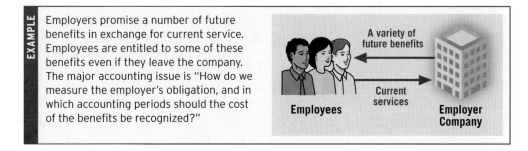

EXAMPLE

Employers promise a number of future benefits in exchange for current service. Employees are entitled to some of these benefits even if they leave the company. The major accounting issue is "How do we measure the employer's obligation, and in which accounting periods should the cost of the benefits be recognized?"

A variety of future benefits

Current services

Employees   **Employer Company**

Other long-term employee benefits, including unrestricted time off for long service or sabbatical leave, deferred compensation, and other compensated absences, may also fit the description of defined benefit plans with benefits that vest or accumulate. All of these benefit plans have something in common: **the entitlement to the benefits increases with the length of the employee's service**. The **objective** in accounting for these plans, therefore, is for the expense and liability related to these plans to be recognized over the accounting periods in which the related services are provided by the employees.

Because DB pension plans will be used extensively in this chapter to explain how to account for this type of plan, basic information about the nature of pension plans is provided next.

Nature of Pension Plans

A pension plan is an arrangement in which an employer provides benefits (payments) to employees after they retire for services that the employees provided while they were working. Pension accounting may refer **either to accounting for the employer** or **accounting for the pension plan.** This chapter focuses on the employer's accounting. The company or employer is the organization that sponsors the pension plan. It incurs the cost and contributes to the pension fund. The fund is the entity that receives the employer contributions (and employee contributions, if any), administers the pension assets, and makes the benefit payments to the pension recipients (the retired employees). Illustration 19-2 sets out the three participants in a pension plan and the flow of cash among them.

Illustration 19-2

Flow of Cash among Pension Plan Participants

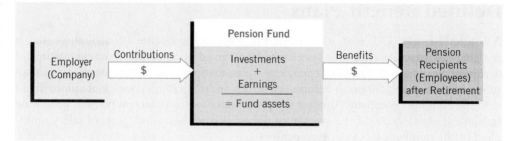

The pension plan in the illustration is **funded**.[4] This means that the employer (company) sets money aside for future pension benefits by making payments to a funding agency that is responsible for accumulating the pension plan assets and for making payments to the recipients as the benefits come due. The assets that are transferred become the assets of the pension plan, which is a separate legal entity. They are not company assets.

In **contributory plans**, the employees pay part of the cost of the stated benefits or voluntarily make payments to increase their benefits. In **non-contributory plans**, the employer bears the entire cost. Companies generally design pension plans in accordance with federal income tax laws that permit deduction of the employer's and employees' contributions to the pension fund and offer tax-free status for earnings on the pension fund assets. The pension benefits are taxable when they are received by the pensioner.

The plan is usually a separate legal and accounting entity for which a set of books is maintained and financial statements are prepared. General purpose financial statements for pension plans are not covered in this chapter but they are set out in Part IV of the *CICA Handbook*. This chapter is devoted to issues that relate to **the employer** as the sponsor of pension and other employee future benefit plans.

What Do the Numbers Mean?

The need for proper administration of pension funds, as well as sound accounting, becomes apparent when one appreciates the size of these funds. The following list shows the pension expense, fund assets, and shareholders' equity of a sample of large Canadian companies.

Company	Year	Pension Expense	Pension Fund Assets	Shareholders' Equity
		in millions	in millions	in millions
ManuLife Financial Corporation	2008	$ 92	$ 2,749	$27,455
Canadian Pacific Railway Limited	2008	41.8	6,118.5	5,993.4
Suncor Energy Inc.	2008	82	613	14,523
Bombardier Inc. (U.S. $)	2009	248	3,833	2,544
BCE Inc.	2008	102	11,510	17,311

As the list shows, pension expense can be a substantial amount, and the fund assets are sometimes larger than the shareholders' equity of the company that sponsors the plan. The two most common types of pension plans are defined contribution plans, discussed earlier, and defined benefit plans, discussed next.[5]

---

[4] When it is used as a verb, **fund** means to pay to a funding agency (for example, to fund future pension benefits or to fund pension cost). Used as a noun or an adjective, it refers to assets that have accumulated in the hands of a funding agency (trustee) for the purpose of meeting pension benefits when they become due.

[5] Increasingly, companies have hybrid plans that have characteristics of both defined contribution and defined benefit plans. As this text went to print, the accounting for this type of plan was expected to be addressed in new pension standards being worked on by the IASB. The PE standard indicates that a plan that has features of both types of plan should account for each component separately according to its substance.

Defined Benefit (DB) Pension Plans

A defined benefit pension plan identifies the pension benefits that an employee will receive after retiring. These benefits typically are a function of an employee's years of service and compensation level in the years approaching retirement. To ensure that appropriate resources are available to pay the benefits at retirement, there is usually a requirement that funds be set aside during the service life of the employees.

Law

The **employees** are the beneficiaries of a defined **contribution** trust, but the **employer** is the beneficiary of a defined **benefit** trust. The trust's main purpose under a defined benefit plan is to safeguard assets and to invest them so that there will be enough to pay the employer's obligation to the employees. **In form**, the trust is a separate entity; **in substance**, the trust assets and liabilities belong to the employer. That is, **as long as the plan continues, the employer is responsible for paying the defined benefits, no matter what happens in the trust**. The employer must make up any shortfall in the accumulated assets held by the trust. If excess assets have accumulated in the trust, it may be possible for the employer to recapture them either through reduced future funding or through a reversion of funds, depending on the trust agreement, plan documents, and governing legislation.[6]

Finance

With a defined benefit plan, the employer assumes the economic risks: the employee is secure because the benefits to be paid on retirement are predefined, but the employer is at risk because the cost is uncertain.[7] The cost depends on factors such as employee turnover, mortality, length of service, and compensation levels, as well as investment returns that are earned on pension assets, inflation, and other economic conditions over long periods of time.

Because the cost to the company is affected by a wide range of uncertain future variables, it is not easy to measure the pension cost and liability that have to be recognized each period as employees provide services to earn their pension entitlement. In addition, an appropriate funding pattern must be established to assure that enough funds will be available at retirement to provide the benefits that have been promised. Whatever funding method is decided on, it should provide enough money at retirement to meet the benefits defined by the plan. Note that **the expense to be recognized each period is not the same as the employer's cash funding contribution,** just as depreciation expense recognized on the use of plant and equipment is not measured in terms of how the asset is financed. The accounting issues related to defined benefit plans are complex, but interesting.

At one time, most employer-sponsored pension plans in Canada were of the defined benefit or DB type. The majority of plans now are DC plans, and the percentage is growing. However, in terms of pension assets, the amount that is in defined benefit plans continues to be disproportionately high.

The Role of Actuaries

The issues that are associated with pension plans involve complicated mathematical considerations. Companies therefore use the services of actuaries to ensure that the plan is appropriate for the employee group covered. Actuaries are individuals who are trained through a long and rigorous certification program to assign probabilities to future events

---

[6] There has been much litigation recently over the ownership of pension fund surpluses. The courts have increasingly determined that pension fund surpluses, or a significant portion of them, should accrue to the benefit of the employee group. Provincial pension legislation increasingly dictates how pension surpluses must be handled.

[7] The employee is not 100% secure, however. If the health of the company sponsor is uncertain, the company's ability to meet any outstanding pension funding requirements may also be uncertain. This was very evident in the economic downturn of 2007 to 2009.

and their financial effects.[8] The insurance industry employs actuaries to assess risks and to advise the industry on the setting of premiums and other aspects of insurance policies. Employers rely heavily on actuaries for help in developing, implementing, and determining the funding of pension plans.

An actuary's chief purpose in pension accounting is to ensure that the company has established an appropriate funding pattern to meet its pension obligations. This calculation requires a set of assumptions to be established and the continued monitoring of these assumptions to ensure that they are realistic. Actuaries make predictions, called **actuarial assumptions**, about mortality rates, employee turnover, interest and earnings rates, early retirement frequency, future salaries, and any other factors that need to be known in order to operate a pension plan. They also calculate the various pension measures that affect the financial statements, such as the pension obligation, the annual cost of servicing the plan, and the cost of amendments to the plan. Defined benefit pension plans rely heavily on information and measurements provided by these specialists.

DEFINED BENEFIT PENSION PLANS

Accounting for employee future benefits such as pensions is in a state of change, with both the FASB and the IASB working on projects to take a fresh look at this area. However, the foundations on which employee future benefit accounting is based are not likely to change significantly. The first is the employer's obligation to pay out benefits in the future for the employees' services up to the balance sheet date. This is estimated by the actuary. The second foundation is the plan assets that have been set aside to fund this obligation. Understanding the nature of the **accrued obligation** (referred to in IAS 19 as the **defined benefit obligation**) and **fund assets (plan assets)**, and the transactions and events that affect their measurement, helps clarify the study of accounting for benefit plans, even as the standards change.

The Employer's Obligation

Alternative Measures of the Obligation

Objective 3

Explain what the employer's benefit obligation is, identify alternative measures for this obligation, and prepare a continuity schedule of transactions and events that change its balance.

Most companies agree that an employer's **pension obligation** is the deferred compensation obligation that it has to its employees for their service under the terms of the pension plan. Measuring that obligation is not so simple, though, because there are different ways of measuring it.

One measure of the pension obligation is based only on the benefits vested to the employees. **Vested benefits** are those that an employee is entitled to receive even if he or she provides no additional services to the company. Most pension plans require a specific minimum number of years of service to the employer before an employee achieves the status of having vested benefits. Actuaries calculate the **vested benefit obligation** using vested benefits only, at current salary levels.

Another way to measure the obligation is using both vested and non-vested benefits. On this basis, the deferred compensation amount is calculated on all years of employees' service —**both vested and non-vested**—using current salary levels. This measurement of the pension obligation is called the **accumulated benefit obligation**.

---

[8] That the general public has little understanding of what an actuary does is illustrated by the following excerpt from *The Wall Street Journal*: "A polling organization once asked the general public what an actuary was and received among its more coherent responses the opinion that it was a place where you put dead actors."

A third method calculates the deferred compensation amount using both vested and non-vested service, and incorporates future salaries projected to be earned over the period to retirement. This measure of the accrued pension obligation is called the projected benefit obligation. Because future salaries are expected to be higher than current salaries, this approach results in the largest measure of the pension obligation.

Deciding which measure to use is a critical choice because it affects the amount of the pension liability and the annual pension expense reported. The diagram in Illustration 19-3 presents the differences in these three measures. Regardless of the approach used, the estimated future benefits to be paid are discounted to their present value.

Finance

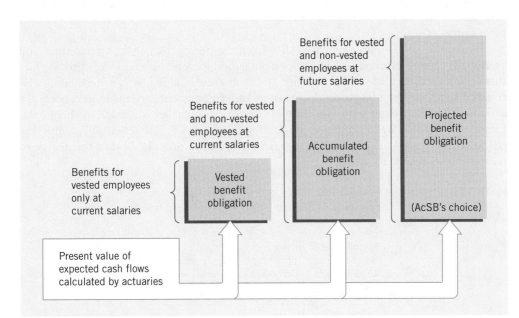

Illustration 19-3

Different Measures of the Pension Obligation

Which of these approaches is generally accepted as the best measure of the obligation? The FASB, IASB, and Canadian Accounting Standards Board have all adopted the projected benefit method as the best measure specifically **for accounting purposes**. The accrued benefit obligation (ABO) for accounting purposes is the present value of vested and non-vested benefits earned to the balance sheet date, with the benefits measured using employees' future salary levels.[9]

Critics of using projected salaries argue that using future salary levels results in future obligations being added to existing ones. Those in favour of the projected benefit obligation counter that a promise by an employer to pay benefits based on a percentage of the employees' future salary is far different from a promise to pay a percentage of their current salary, and that this difference should be reflected in the pension liability and pension expense.

The accrued benefit obligation (ABO) for funding purposes is measured differently. Regardless of the measure of the obligation chosen for accounting purposes, regulators use a variety of different measures for determining the level of contributions that plan sponsors are required by law to remit to the pension fund. This measure of the obligation, designed for a different purpose, tends to focus more on current salary levels and often

Underlying Concept

The FASB and the IASB are studying whether the liability should include estimates of future salaries. This debate will centre on whether a company can have a liability today that is based in part on future salaries that have not yet been earned.

---

[9] When the term "present value of benefits" is used throughout this chapter, it really means the **actuarial present value** of benefits. Actuarial present value is the amount payable adjusted to reflect the time value of money and the probability of payment (by means of decreases for events such as death, disability, withdrawals, or retirement) between the present date and the expected date of payment. For simplicity, we will use the term "present value" instead of "actuarial present value" in our discussion.

uses a different discount rate and other variables. We will see later in the chapter that one of the accounting policy choices permitted under private enterprise standards requires a measure of the accrued benefit obligation based on the funding valuation.

Changes in the Accrued Benefit Obligation

The measurement of the ABO is central to accounting for pension costs. At any point in time, the accrued benefit obligation represents the actuarial present value of the cost of the benefits attributed to employee services that have been provided to date. A simplified example of the measurement of the ABO for accounting purposes in a one-person pension plan is provided in Appendix 19A, and you may find it useful to read this material before proceeding.

Illustration 19-4 summarizes the ABO from the perspective of the transactions and events that change its amount. The accrued obligation increases as employees provide further services and earn additional benefits, and as interest is added to this outstanding discounted liability. The obligation decreases as benefit payments are made to retirees. In addition, the ABO might either increase or decrease as plans are amended to change the future benefits that were promised for prior services, and as the actuarial assumptions change that are used to calculate the obligation. Actuaries provide most of the necessary measurements related to the ABO.

<table>
<tr><td>

Illustration 19-4

*Accrued Benefit Obligation—
Continuity Schedule*

</td><td>

Accrued benefit obligation (ABO), at beginning of period
+ Current service cost
+ Interest cost
− Benefits paid to retirees
± Past service costs of plan amendments during period
± Actuarial gains (−) or losses (+) during period

= Accrued benefit obligation (ABO), at end of period

</td></tr>
</table>

Service Cost.   The current service cost is the cost of the benefits that are to be provided in the future in exchange for the services that the employees provided in the current period. In measuring the service cost to assign to each period, standard setters had to decide on a method of allocating the estimated cost to the individual years during which the entitlement to the benefits builds. Should the total cost be allocated based on the percentage of salary earned by the employee during the year relative to the total estimated career compensation (i.e., **prorated on salaries**) or on an equal amount per year of service (i.e., **prorated on service**)? The standard setters decided on the method that accrues a relatively equal charge for each period—the prorated on service approach.[10]

To calculate current service cost, the actuary predicts the additional benefits that must be paid under the plan's benefit formula as a result of the employees' current year of service and then discounts the cost of these benefits to their present value. For example, consider the following pension benefit formula:

Annual pension benefit on retirement = 2% of salary at retirement × Number of years of service

By working an additional year, the employee earns an entitlement to a larger pension, and the company's pension obligation for accounting purposes increases by the present value of 2% of the employee's estimated final salary for each year of expected retirement.[11] Appendix 19A provides a simplified example of this calculation.

---

[10] IAS 19 *Employee Benefits* refers to this method as the Projected Unit Credit Method.

[11] The service cost for funding purposes is usually calculated on a different basis.

For defined benefit plans where future benefits depend on or are increased by the length of service, the actuary bases the accounting calculations on future salary levels and then attributes the cost of the future benefits to the accounting periods, usually between the date of hire and the date when the employee becomes eligible for full benefits. This is known as the attribution period. The obligation to provide benefits is attributed to the periods in which the employee provides the service that gives rise to the benefits. While the date of hire is the most common date for employees to begin earning benefits, it may be a later date, and eligibility for full benefits may occur before the date of retirement.

Interest Cost.   Because future benefit plans are deferred compensation arrangements—the benefits are essentially elements of wages that are deferred—the time value of money has to be considered. As the obligation is not paid until maturity, it is measured on a discounted basis. As time to maturity passes, **interest accrues on the accrued benefit obligation just as it does on any discounted debt**. The interest is based on the accrued benefit obligation that is outstanding during the period, taking into account any material changes in its balance during that period.

What interest rate should be used? Both **IFRS** and **ASPE** currently require the use of a current market rate, determined by reference to the current yield on high-quality debt instruments such as corporate bonds. The objective is to have the discount rate reflect the estimated timing and amount of the expected benefit payments. **Private enterprise standards** also allow a current settlement rate to be used. This is the rate implied in an insurance contract that could be purchased to effectively settle the pension obligation. The rate to be used is the rate at the end of the reporting period and it is reassessed at each such date. Note that minor changes in the interest rate used to discount pension benefits can dramatically affect the measurement of the employer's obligation. For example, a 1% decrease in the discount rate might increase pension liabilities by 15%!

Benefits Paid to Retirees.   The pension fund trustee is responsible for making payments of the pension benefits to the former employees. Similar to all liabilities, as obligations are met, the balance of the obligation is reduced.

Past Service Costs.   When a defined benefit plan is either initiated (begun) or amended, credit is often given to employees for years of service that they provided before the date of initiation or amendment. As a result of these credits for prior services, the actuary remeasures the accrued benefit obligation, and it usually ends up being larger than it was before the change. The increase in the accrued benefit obligation on the date that the plan is initiated or amended is known as past service cost, the cost of the retroactive benefits. This increase is often substantial. A simplified illustration of how past service cost is calculated is provided in Appendix 19A.

In recent years, because they want to reduce the very significant costs that are associated with post-retirement plans, many companies have been negotiating reductions in some of their plan benefits. When this happens, there is a **decrease** in the accrued benefit obligation that relates to past services, and a **past service benefit** is recognized.

Actuarial Gains and Losses.   Actuarial gains and losses related to the accrued benefit obligation (the liability) can result from either: (1) a change in actuarial assumptions, which means a change in the assumptions about the occurrence of future events that affect the measurement of the future benefit costs and obligations; or (2) an experience gain or loss, which is the difference between what has actually occurred and the previous actuarial assumptions about what would occur. When later events show that assumptions were inaccurate, adjustments are needed.

In estimating the accrued benefit obligation, actuaries make assumptions about such variables as mortality rates, retirement rates, turnover rates, disability rates, and rates of salary escalation (increase). Any difference between these assumed rates and the ones that are actually experienced changes the amount of the accrued benefit obligation. Actual experience is rarely exactly the same as actuarial predictions. An unexpected gain or loss that changes the amount of the ABO is referred to as a liability experience gain or loss. Actuarial gains and losses also occur when the assumptions that are used by the actuary in calculating the ABO are revised, because this too causes a change in the amount of the obligation. An example is the effect of a change in the interest rate used to discount the pension cash flows on the measurement of the obligation. Because experience gains and losses are similar to and affect the ABO in the same way as actuarial gains and losses, both types are referred to as **actuarial gains and losses**.

To illustrate, assume that a company's calculated accrued benefit obligation—based on its opening balance and the year's service cost, interest cost, benefits paid, and plan amendments—was $262,000 at December 31, 2011. If the company's actuaries, using December 31, 2011 estimates in their actuarial calculations, determine that the accrued benefit obligation is $275,000, then the company has suffered an actuarial loss of $13,000 ($275,000 − $262,000). If the actuary calculates a reduced obligation, the result is an actuarial gain. Whatever the result, the ABO is adjusted to its most recent actuarial valuation.

Plan settlements and curtailments also affect the amount of the accrued benefit obligation, but these are outside the scope of this chapter.

Plan Assets

Objective 4
Identify transactions and events that change the benefit plan assets, and calculate the balance of the assets.

The benefit plan assets are the other major foundation on which pension accounting is based. Plan assets are assets that have been set aside in a trust or other legal entity that is separate from the employer company. The assets are restricted and can be used only to settle the related accrued benefit obligation: they cannot be used for meeting the claims of other company creditors. The plan assets are made up mainly of cash and investments in debt and equity securities that are held to earn a reasonable return, generally at a minimum of risk. Other investments, such as real estate investment property, are also common plan holdings.

Changes in Plan Assets

As can be seen in Illustration 19-5, the fund assets change as a result of contributions from the employer (and employee, if the plan is contributory) and from the actual return that is generated on the assets that have been invested. The pool of assets is reduced by payments to retirees.

Illustration 19-5

Plan Assets—Continuity Schedule

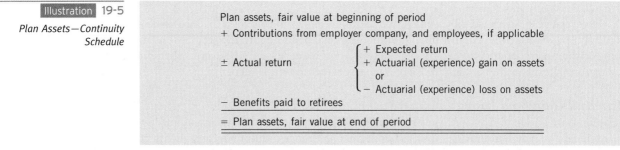

Plan assets, fair value at beginning of period
+ Contributions from employer company, and employees, if applicable
± Actual return
    { + Expected return
      + Actuarial (experience) gain on assets
      or
      − Actuarial (experience) loss on assets
− Benefits paid to retirees
= Plan assets, fair value at end of period

Contributions. The amount of an employer company's contributions to the plan has a direct effect on the plan's ability to pay the accrued obligation. Who and what determines how much a company contributes to the plan? In Canada, pension plans come under either federal or provincial pension legislation as well as regulations of the Canada Revenue Agency (CRA). The CRA stipulates the amount of the contributions that are tax-deductible to the company and the conditions on the payment of benefits out of the plan. Federal and provincial laws dictate the funding requirements.[12]

Actual Return.   The actual return that is earned on the fund assets is the income generated on the assets being held by the trustee, less the cost of administering the fund. The actual return that is earned on these assets usually increases the fund balance. The return is made up of dividends and interest and gains and losses from the sale of investments, as well as profits that are generated on any real estate investments. In addition, because the assets are measured at fair value, holding gains and losses on the assets are included as part of the actual return. Including the holding gains and losses explains why the actual return could increase the plan assets in one year and decrease them in another. In years when stock and/or bond markets decline significantly, such as 2008, the reduction in fair value may be greater than the other forms of income that are reported and the actual return will be a loss.

Because the actual return can be highly variable from one year to the next, actuaries ignore short-term fluctuations when they develop a funding pattern to accumulate assets to pay benefits in the future. Instead, they calculate an expected long-term rate of return and apply it to the fair value of the fund assets to arrive at an expected return on plan assets.[13] As shown in Illustration 19-5, the actual return is made up of two components: (1) the expected return, and (2) the difference between the expected return and the actual return. The plan trustee provides the information on the actual return.

Actuarial Gains and Losses.   The difference between the expected return and the actual return is referred to as an asset experience gain or loss. A gain occurs when the actual return is greater than the expected return. A loss occurs when actual returns are less than expected. The amount of the asset gain or loss is determined at the end of each year by comparing the calculated expected return with the actual return that was earned. For example, if the actuary expected a return of $20,000 based on the long-run average rate, and the actual return earned in the year was only $19,000, the records would indicate an actuarial (or experience) loss of $1,000 in the year. The actual return ($19,000) is made up of the expected return ($20,000) and the actuarial loss ($1,000). Asset experience gains and losses are also referred to as actuarial gains and losses.

Benefits Paid.   The plan trustee pays out benefits to the retirees according to the plan formula and pension agreement.

Funded Status

The measures of the benefit obligation and plan assets are fundamental to pension accounting. Because of this, accounting standards specify that they should be measured as

> **5 Objective**
>
> Explain what a benefit plan's funded status is, calculate it, and identify what transactions and events change its amount.

---

[12] In general, the current service cost has to be funded annually. If a plan is in a surplus position (i.e., fund assets are greater than the accrued obligation), the company may be able to take a contribution holiday; in other words, to temporarily not make any contributions. If there is a funding deficiency, the extent of the shortfall is determined by two different valuations: one based on a going concern assumption and one based on a termination assumption. These dictate the additional funding that is required, and the period over which any deficiency must be funded. With the economic downturn and low interest rates in the latter part of the first decade of this century, many companies had difficulty dealing with unanticipated funding demands as pension obligations increased in value. An ABO based on current salary levels is common in determining the minimum funding requirements.

[13] Under PE GAAP, the expected return may be based, instead, on a market-related value of the assets. The market-related value of plan assets is a calculated value that recognizes changes in fair value in a systematic and rational way over no more than five years (*CICA Handbook*, Part II, Section 3461.089 and .090). Different ways of calculating a market-related value may be used for different asset classes. For example, an employer might use fair value for bonds and a five-year moving average for equities, but the way of determining market-related value should be applied consistently from year to year for each asset class.

at the date of the annual financial statements. Under private enterprise standards, entities may use a date up to three months before the year end if the timing is consistent from year to year.[14] Under IFRS, both the plan assets and ABO are required to represent reporting date values.

As indicated in Illustration 19-6, the difference between the accrued benefit obligation and the pension assets' fair value at a point in time is known as the plan's funded status. A plan with more liabilities than assets is underfunded and has a funded status liability. A plan with accumulated assets that are greater than the related obligation is overfunded and is said to have a funded status asset.[15]

Illustration 19-6

Funded Status

Underlying Concept

Many plans are underfunded but still quite viable. For example, the Royal Bank of Canada had a $1,738-million pension and other benefit plans shortfall. But the Royal Bank at that time had earnings of $3,858 million and a net worth of $36,906 million. Concern over pensions being underfunded is directly related to the financial position and performance of the employer company—the plan sponsor.

| Accrued benefit obligation (ABO), end of period |
| − Fair value of plan assets, end of period |
| = Plan's funded status |

ABO > Plan assets = **underfunded** = a funded status liability
Plan assets > ABO = **overfunded** = a funded status asset

Transition Asset or Obligation

When companies first adopted new GAAP accounting standards for defined benefit plans, they had to determine the funded status of any existing plans at that time. If the change in policy was adopted on a prospective basis, that is, with the effects assigned to future periods, the company had a net transitional asset (if the plan was overfunded) or a transitional obligation or liability (if the benefit plan was underfunded) that had to be accounted for. The transitional asset or liability is merely the funded status of the plan when the accounting standards were applied for the first time. This balance was recognized over time as part of the benefit expense. Transitional balances are now disappearing from the financial statements of many companies.

Accounting for Changes in Funded Status

Now that you have been introduced to most of the components that are needed to account for a DB pension plan, it is time to look at how companies actually account for such plans.

Pension accounting would be relatively straightforward if all the changes in the accrued benefit obligation, as defined for accounting purposes, and in the fund assets (except for the cash contributions made by the employer company to the fund assets) were recognized in accounting entries as part of the benefit expense and as a change in the benefit asset or liability on the balance sheet. The balance sheet account would have the same balance as the funded status, and the income statement account along with the company contributions into the plan would explain the change in the funded status. But this is only one approach to calculating the benefit cost and the net pension asset or liability on the balance sheet. For a variety of reasons, pension accounting has introduced several variations in how and when these amounts are recognized. The methods now in use by IFRS and private enterprise standards are explained next.

---

[14] Under the immediate recognition approach to accounting for defined benefit plans by private enterprises, the measures must represent balance sheet date values.

[15] When Air Canada filed for protection under the *Companies' Creditors Arrangement Act* in 2003, a $1.5-billion unfunded pension liability was listed as one of the key factors behind the company's insolvency. How to deal with this underfunded plan and unbooked liability was central to Air Canada's restructuring negotiations. The company faced similar problems in 2009 with its $3.2-billion pension deficit. In this case, the federal government stepped in with a legislated solution to help extremely troubled companies restructure such problems.

Benefit Cost Components

You have already been introduced to the components that make up the pension benefit cost. They are the events that change the balances of the accrued benefit obligation and the fund assets and, therefore, the funded status:

- Current service cost
- Interest cost
- Return on plan assets
- Past service cost
- Actuarial gains and losses

While there is general agreement that pension costs should be accounted for on the accrual basis and recognized in the accounting periods that benefit from the employees' service, not everyone agrees on when certain cost components should be included in current year expense. Two approaches to accounting for pension expense and the related balance sheet account are:

1. the immediate recognition approach, and
2. the deferral and amortization approach.

Private enterprise GAAP permits companies to make an accounting policy choice between the immediate recognition and deferral and amortization methods, while **IFRS** applies a form of the deferral and amortization approach. Within the IFRS approach, there are areas where choices are permitted.

What differentiates one method from another? There are two major differences:

1. the actuarial valuation method used as the basis for the accrued benefit obligation, and
2. the extent to which some of the costs are deferred and amortized to the expense of later periods instead of being recognized in the benefit cost immediately.

These differences also affect the resulting pension asset or liability reported on the balance sheet. We use the example of Zarle Corporation and its defined benefit pension plan as set out in Illustration 19-8 to explain the immediate recognition approach. The defer-and-amortize method is explained later using details related to the pension plan of Trans Corp. as set out in Illustration 19-15.

Immediate Recognition Approach

Under an immediate recognition approach, the pension benefit expense is made up of all items affecting the funded status during the period except the company contributions into the plan assets:

1. **Current service cost and interest cost.** Both the service cost for benefits earned by employees and the interest cost accrued on the ABO during the current period are recognized and included in pension expense in the same period. If the plan is a contributory one, the service cost is reduced by any contributions made by employees. As you might expect, employee contributions have the effect of reducing the cost of the plan to the employer.

2. **Actual return on plan assets.** The return earned on the fund assets, if a positive amount, reduces the cost to the employer of sponsoring an employee pension plan. If a negative return is generated, the pension cost is increased. Under the immediate recognition approach, the actual return is used in the calculations.

3. **Past service cost.** Plan amendments instantly change the amount of the employer's obligation, and the total cost (or benefit) of the amendment is recognized immediately in pension expense.

4. **Actuarial gains and losses.** When actuarial gains and losses are recognized as a component of pension expense in the same period they are incurred, the reported expense tends to fluctuate significantly from year to year. As you might expect, the immediate recognition approach makes no adjustment for this, but recognizes the full amount of the liability actuarial gain or loss in pension benefit expense each period.

Other components of expense are identified in the accounting standard, including changes to the ABO from plan settlements and curtailments. These are beyond the scope of this text. In addition, some part of the change in the valuation allowance related to the funded status asset is also included. The limit on the carrying amount of a balance sheet accrued benefit asset is explained briefly later in this chapter.

Illustration of Immediate Recognition Approach

A work sheet is used to illustrate how the transactions affecting the ABO and fund assets are accumulated in the accounts. **It is important to note two things:**

1. **Neither the ABO nor the fund assets are recognized in the sponsoring company's accounts; they are both off–balance sheet or memo accounts.** The fund assets belong to the benefit trust, and the ABO is a liability of the sponsoring company only to the extent there are not enough assets in the fund to cover the total obligation.

2. When applying the immediate recognition approach, **the accrued benefit obligation** is based on an actuarial valuation used for **funding purposes**, not the projected benefit obligation used for accounting purposes in the defer-and-amortize approach. It represents the obligation at the balance sheet date.

A unique pension work sheet is used to keep track of pension expense and the accrued benefit asset/liability on the balance sheet, as well as the off–balance sheet amounts. As its name suggests, the work sheet is a working tool; it is not a journal or part of the general ledger. It merely accumulates the information needed to make the pension journal entries. The format of the work sheet that illustrates the relationship among all the components is shown in Illustration 19-7.[16]

Basic Format of Pension Work Sheet

	A	B	C	D	F	G
1		General Journal Entries			Memo Record	
2	Items	Annual Pension Expense	Cash	Accrued Pension Asset/Liability	Accrued Benefit Obligation	Plan Assets
3						
4						
5						
6						

The left-hand columns of the work sheet under "General Journal Entries" determine the entries to be recorded in the formal general ledger accounts. The right-hand "Memo Record" columns maintain balances on the accrued benefit obligation and the fund assets, based on amounts provided by the actuary and pension plan trustee. On the first line of the work sheet, the beginning balances are recorded. Subsequently, transactions and events that relate to the pension plan are entered, using debits and credits and using both sets of

---

[16] This pension entry work sheet is taken from Paul B.W. Miller, "The New Pension Accounting (part 2)," *Journal of Accountancy*, February 1987, pp. 86–94. Copyright 1987. American Institute of Certified Public Accountants, Inc. All rights reserved. Used with permission.

records as if there were just one set for recording the entries. For each transaction or event, the debits must equal the credits and the balance in the Accrued Pension Asset/Liability column must equal the net balance in the Memo Record columns. If the ABO is greater than the plan assets, a pension liability is reported on the balance sheet. If the ABO is less than the plan assets, a pension asset results.

Let's walk through the immediate recognition model by using the facts and circumstances set out in Illustration 19-8 that apply to Zarle's pension plan for the three-year period from 2010 to 2012.

	2010	2011	2012
Fair value of plan assets, first of year	$100,000	$111,000	$134,100
Accrued benefit obligation (ABO) for funding purposes, first of year	100,000	112,000	212,700
Current service cost for year	9,000	9,500	13,000
Interest or discount rate on the liability	10%	10%	10%
Cost of past service benefits granted January 1, 2011	–0–	80,000	–0–
Expected earnings on plan assets for year	10%	10%	10%
Actual earnings on plan assets for year	10,000	11,100	12,000
Employer contributions for year (funding)	8,000	20,000	24,000
Benefits paid to retirees by trustee for year	7,000	8,000	10,500
Actuarial loss due to change in actuarial assumptions	–0–	–0–	28,530
Plan assets, end of year	111,000	134,100	159,600
Accrued benefit obligation (ABO), end of year	112,000	212,700	265,000
Funded status, end of year—over- or (under)-funded	(1,000)	(78,600)	(105,400)

Illustration 19-8

Zarle Corporation Pension Plan, 2010–2012

The Basics—2010 Work Sheet and Entries. Assume that Zarle Corporation begins its 2010 fiscal year with an ABO for funding purposes of $100,000, plan assets of $100,000, and a $0 balance in its Accrued Pension Asset/Liability account on the balance sheet.

Using the information found in Illustration 19-8, Illustration 19-9 presents the work sheet, including the beginning balances and all the pension transactions that Zarle Corporation needs to account for in 2010. The beginning balances of the accrued benefit obligation and the pension plan assets are recorded on the work sheet's first line in the memo record. They are not recorded in the accounts and, therefore, are not reported as a

	A	B	C	D	F	G
1		General Journal Entries			Memo Record	
2	Items	Annual Pension Expense	Cash	Accrued Pension Asset/ Liability	Accrued Benefit Obligation	Plan Assets
3	Balance, Jan. 1, 2010			–0–	100,000 Cr.	100,000 Dr.
4	(a) Service cost	9,000 Dr.			9,000 Cr.	
5	(b) Interest cost	10,000 Dr.			10,000 Cr.	
6	(c) Actual return	10,000 Cr.				10,000 Dr.
7	(d) Contribution		8,000 Cr.			8,000 Dr.
8	(e) Benefits paid				7,000 Dr.	7,000 Cr.
9	Expense entry, 2010	9,000 Dr.		9,000 Cr.		
10	Contribution entry, 2010		8,000 Cr.	8,000 Dr.		
11	Balance, Dec. 31, 2010			1,000 Cr.	112,000 Cr.	111,000 Dr.
12						

Illustration 19-9

Pension Work Sheet—2010

liability and an asset in Zarle Corporation's financial statements. Notice that, although they are "off–balance sheet," the January 1, 2010 funded status of $0 is the same as the balance of $0 in the Accrued Pension Asset/Liability account on the balance sheet on that date. Under the immediate recognition approach, the funded status and the amount of the balance sheet account are the same.[17]

Entry (a) in Illustration 19-9 records the service cost component, which increases the accrued benefit obligation by $9,000 and increases pension expense by $9,000. Entry (b) accrues the interest cost, increasing both the ABO and pension expense by $10,000 (the $100,000 weighted average balance of the accrued benefit obligation multiplied by the discount rate of 10%). Note that in all chapter examples and end-of-chapter problem material, unless specified otherwise, **it is assumed that current service cost is credited at year end and that contributions to the fund and benefits paid to retirees are year-end cash flows**. Such an assumption is needed in order to determine the average balances outstanding for calculating any interest and expected return amounts.

Entry (c) records the actual return on plan assets, which increases the plan assets and decreases pension expense. Entry (d) reflects Zarle Corporation's contribution (funding) of assets to the pension fund; cash is decreased by $8,000 and plan assets are increased by $8,000. Entry (e) records the benefit payments made to retirees, which result in equal $7,000 decreases in the plan assets and the accrued benefit obligation.

Zarle makes a journal entry on December 31, 2010, to formally record the expense for the year:

A = L + SE
     +9,000   −9,000

Cash flows: No effect

| Pension Expense | 9,000 | |
| Accrued Pension Asset/Liability | | 9,000 |

When Zarle Corporation issued its $8,000 cheque to the pension fund trustee late in the year, it made the following entry:

A = L + SE
−8,000   −8,000

Cash flows: ↓ 8,000 outflow

| Accrued Pension Asset/Liability | 8,000 | |
| Cash | | 8,000 |

The credit balance in the Accrued Pension Asset/Liability account of $1,000 represents the funded status—the difference between the ABO of $112,000 and the fund assets of $111,000. This should not be surprising because all the transactions that affected the ABO and plan assets, except for the benefits paid, also affected the balance sheet account. The benefits paid decrease the fund assets and the ABO in equal amounts with no effect on the funded status.

In addition, the balance sheet liability account also represents the excess of the accumulated pension expense recognized to date over the accumulated contributions made to date —a $1,000 liability. Although we are not told what expense was reported and contributions were made in prior years, we can tell that these amounts were equal at January 1, 2010. This is because the Accrued Pension Asset/Liability balance was $0 at that date.

2011 Work Sheet and Entries with Past Service Costs.

One question that standard setters have wrestled with is whether the past service costs or credits that are associated with the adoption or amendment of pension plans should be fully recognized in net

---

[17] There is an exception. As explained later in the chapter, the balance sheet account may have to be adjusted for any valuation allowance that arises from the limit on the carrying amount of an accrued benefit asset.

income when the plan is initiated or amended. Under the immediate recognition approach, the conclusion is that the costs, although significant, all relate to past services and that there is no justification for deferring their recognition to future periods' incomes. We will see this assumption challenged in the deferral and amortization approach explained later.

To illustrate how past service costs affect the pension accounts, we continue with Zarle Corporation's 2011 benefit plan activities as set out in Illustration 19-8 above. Zarle amends its defined benefit pension plan on January 1, 2011, to grant prior service benefits to certain employees. The company's actuaries determine that this causes an increase in the accrued benefit obligation of $80,000.

Illustration 19-10 presents all the pension "entries" and information used by Zarle Corporation in 2011. The work sheet's first line shows the beginning balances of the Accrued Pension Asset/Liability account and the components of the plan's funded status. Entry (f) records Zarle Corporation's granting of prior service benefits by adding $80,000 to the accrued benefit obligation and its immediate recognition in Pension Expense. Entries (g), (h), (i), (j), and (k) are similar to the corresponding entries in 2010. Notice that the interest cost on the ABO is the year's interest at 10% on the average balance outstanding for the year. Because the past service costs were granted effective January 1, the balance outstanding for the year was $112,000 + $80,000 = $192,000.

	A	B	C	D	F	G
1		General Journal Entries			Memo Record	
2	Items	Annual Pension Expense	Cash	Accrued Pension Asset/ Liability	Accrued Benefit Obligation	Plan Assets
3	Balance, Dec. 31, 2010			1,000 Cr.	112,000 Cr.	111,000 Dr.
4	(f) Past service cost	80,000 Dr.			80,000 Cr.	
5	(g) Service cost	9,500 Dr.			9,500 Cr.	
6	(h) Interest cost	19,200 Dr.			19,200 Cr.	
7	(i) Actual return	11,100 Cr.				11,100 Dr.
8	(j) Contribution		20,000 Cr.			20,000 Dr.
9	(k) Benefits paid				8,000 Dr.	8,000 Cr.
10	Expense entry, 2011	97,600 Dr.		97,600 Cr.		
11	Contribution entry, 2011		20,000 Cr.	20,000 Dr.		
12	Balance, Dec. 31, 2011			78,600 Cr.	212,700 Cr.	134,100 Dr.
13						

Illustration 19-10

Pension Work Sheet—2011

An entry is needed on December 31, 2011, to formally record the pension expense for the year.

Pension Expense	97,600	
Accrued Pension Asset/Liability		97,600

$$A = L + SE$$
$$+97{,}600 \quad -97{,}600$$

Cash flows: No effect

When the company made its contributions to the pension fund during the year, the following entry was recorded:

Accrued Pension Asset/Liability	20,000	
Cash		20,000

$$A = L + SE$$
$$-20{,}000 \quad -20{,}000$$

Cash flows: ↓ 20,000 outflow

Because the expense exceeds the funding, the Accrued Pension Liability account increases during the year by the $77,600 difference ($97,600 less $20,000). In 2011, for the same reasons as in 2010, the balance of the Accrued Pension Liability account ($78,600) is equal to the funded status, the difference between the ABO of $212,700 and the plan assets of $134,100.

2012 Work Sheet and Entries with Actuarial Gains/Losses.

Refer back to the pension plan activities for Zarle Corporation in Illustration 19-8 and review what happens during 2012. No additional plan amendments were made in this year; therefore, there are no past service costs to be recognized in 2012. However, there is an actuarial loss in 2012. The loss came about because the actuary updated the underlying actuarial assumptions used in calculating the funding-related ABO at December 31, 2012. The change in assumptions resulted in an increase in the balance of this obligation. If the obligation had been reduced, this would have been an actuarial gain.

Under the immediate recognition approach to pension accounting, the increase in the obligation caused by the actuarial loss is recognized as pension expense in the same accounting period. The immediate recognition in pension cost of both past service costs and actuarial gains and losses can cause significant variability in the pension expense recognized each year. However, both the funded status and balance sheet pension account are reported at up-to-date funding-related values.

Actuarial gains and losses are discussed more fully in the section of this chapter that deals with the deferral and amortization approach to accounting for defined benefit plans.

Illustration 19-11

Pension Work Sheet—2012

	A	B	C	D	F	G
1		General Journal Entries			Memo Record	
2	Items	Annual Pension Expense	Cash	Accrued Pension Asset/ Liability	Accrued Benefit Obligation	Plan Assets
3	Balance, Dec. 31, 2011			78,600 Cr.	212,700 Cr.	134,100 Dr.
4	(l) Service cost	13,000 Dr.			13,000 Cr.	
5	(m) Interest cost	21,270 Dr.			21,270 Cr.	
6	(n) Actual return	12,000 Cr.				12,000 Dr.
7	(o) Contribution		24,000 Cr.			24,000 Dr.
8	(p) Benefits paid				10,500 Dr.	10,500 Cr.
9	(q) Liability loss	28,530 Dr.			28,530 Cr.	
10	Expense entry, 2012	50,800 Dr.		50,800 Cr.		
11	Contribution entry, 2012		24,000 Cr.	24,000 Dr.		
12	Balance, Dec. 31, 2012			105,400 Cr.	265,000 Cr.	159,600 Dr.
13						

The work sheet in Illustration 19-11 presents all the pension transactions and information used by Zarle Corporation in 2012. The beginning balances for this year are identical to the 2011 ending balances from Illustration 19-10.

Entries (l), (m), (n), (o), and (p) are similar to the entries that were explained in 2010 and 2011. Entry (q) records the increase in the accrued benefit obligation that results from a change in actuarial assumptions. Using up-to-date actuarial assumptions at December 31, 2012, the actuary calculates the ending balance to be $265,000. Since the memo record balance at December 31 is $236,470 (equal to $212,700 + $13,000 + $21,270 − $10,500), there is a difference of $28,530 ($265,000 − $236,470). This $28,530 increase in the employer's obligation is the actuarial loss.

The journal entry on December 31, 2012, to formally record pension expense for the year is as follows:

| Pension Expense | 50,800 | |
| Accrued Pension Asset/Liability | | 50,800 |

A = L + SE
  +50,800 −50,800
Cash flows: No effect

The company has already recorded the $24,000 contribution during the year as follows:

| Accrued Pension Asset/Liability | 24,000 | |
| Cash | | 24,000 |

A = L + SE
−24,000 −24,000
Cash flows: ↓ 24,000 outflow

As illustrated previously for the 2010 and 2011 work sheets, the $105,400 credit balance of the Accrued Pension Liability account reported on the statement of financial position at December 31, 2012, is once again equal to the funded status of $265,000 − $159,600 = $105,400. Anyone reading Zarle Corporation's financial statements would expect to see a net liability of $105,400 on the company's balance sheet if the pension fund was actually underfunded by $105,400. This is an advantage of the immediate recognition approach.

On the other hand, pension expense on the income statement is highly variable from year to year due to the immediate recognition of actuarial gains and losses and past service costs directly in expense. Management, however, generally thinks that immediate recognition of these costs gives a false picture of the company's risk. The fluctuations in pension expense are felt to be beyond management's control, and over the longer term many of the actuarial gains and losses are expected to reverse. As a result, there is also support for a deferral and amortization approach to accounting for defined benefit plans.

Deferral and Amortization Approach

One of the major differences between the accounting for defined benefit plans using the deferral and amortization approach and the immediate recognition method is the valuation of the ABO that is used. Under the defer-and-amortize method, the actuarial valuation of the ABO is the one developed specifically for accounting purposes: the projected benefit obligation. The second difference relates to the treatment of the **past service costs** and **actuarial gains and losses**. The deferral and amortization approach provides opportunities to delay the recognition of both as part of the benefit plan expense and as part of the accrued benefit asset/liability on the balance sheet. We begin with a discussion of each of these two components before applying this method to a specific company.

7 Objective

Identify the components of pension benefit cost, and account for a defined benefit pension plan under the deferral and amortization approach under IFRS and private enterprise standards.

Past Service Costs

One question that standard setters have wrestled with is whether the past service costs or credits that are associated with the adoption or amendment of pension plans should be fully recognized in expense, and therefore net income, when the plan is initiated or amended. Those advocating the deferral and amortization approach to pension benefit accounting take the position that these costs should not be recognized immediately in expense. The rationale for deferral is that the employer would not provide credit for past years of service unless it expected to receive benefits in the future; based on this reasoning, the past service costs should not be recognized immediately in expense.

In line with this position, the **private enterprise** defer-and-amortize standard specifies that the past service cost is deferred initially and recognized as an expense on a straight-line basis over the period in which the firm expects to realize the economic benefits from the change in plan. This is normally the expected period from the time of

Underlying Concept

The matching concept is at the core of the deferral and amortization method.

adoption or amendment until the employee is eligible for the plan's full benefits.[18] The period benefiting may actually be shorter than this, justifying a faster recognition of the past service costs. For example, consider a situation in which a company has a history of making plan amendments as a result of renegotiating a union agreement every three years. In this case, writing the costs off to expense on a straight-line basis over three years may be acceptable. If a plan amendment reduces the entity's ABO, the resulting past service **benefit** is amortized in the same way.

IAS 19 *Employee Benefits* also permits some past service costs to be amortized, but on a different basis. For employees whose benefits are already vested, past service costs are recognized immediately in expense and the balance sheet liability. The past service costs that are attributed to employees whose benefits are not yet vested are amortized on a straight-line basis over the average period until the benefits become vested. The international standard provides an example of a company that amended its pension plan on January 1, Year 5, resulting in a past service cost of $270. The vesting period for this company is five years. The $270 cost was attributable to the following employees:

Employees with more than five years' service at Jan. 1, Year 5	$150
Employees with less than five years' service at Jan. 1, Year 5	120
	$270

Assume the average period until vesting is three years for those employees whose benefits are not yet vested. In this situation, $150 of the cost is recognized immediately in expense, while the remaining $120 is deferred and recognized on a straight-line basis over the three-year period beginning January 1, Year 5. Therefore, Year 5's expense is charged with $190 of this cost ($150 + $120/3); Year 6 is assigned $40, as is Year 7.

Under both PE GAAP and IFRS, notice that if only a portion of the past service cost is recognized in expense, that is all that is recognized in the balance sheet liability (or asset) account as well. The remaining unamortized amounts remain off–balance sheet. Past service costs that have not yet been amortized to income are known as unamortized past service costs or unrecognized past service costs. We will come back to this feature when we work through an example later.

Actuarial Gains and Losses

Of great concern to companies that have pension plans are the uncontrollable and unexpected swings in pension expense that can be caused by (1) large and sudden changes in the market value of plan assets, and (2) changes in actuarial assumptions that affect the amount of the accrued benefit obligation. These two events are the sources of actuarial gains and losses. If these gains or losses are fully included in pension expense in the period in which they occur, substantial fluctuations in pension expense result. This was illustrated in the Zarle Corporation example above when the immediate recognition method was used. Therefore, private enterprise standards allow companies to reduce this volatility by choosing the deferral and amortization method of accounting for defined benefit plans, and the IASB's standard incorporates smoothing techniques that dampen and in some cases fully eliminate the fluctuations, as we will see shortly.

Asset Gains and Losses.   The return on plan assets is a component of pension expense that normally reduces the expense amount. Because significant changes in the actual

---

[18] *CICA Handbook*, Part II, Section 3461.093. Note that this accounting treatment is consistent with the upper limit of the attribution period (i.e., the expected period to full eligibility) that is used for attributing current service cost to accounting periods.

return from year to year could result in unacceptable fluctuations in the reported pension expense, the defer-and-amortize approach uses a long-term **expected** rate of return instead of the **actual** rate of return. This is consistent with the actuary's use of a long-run average rate when developing a funding pattern for an employer to ensure that funds are set aside to pay expected benefits in the future.

To determine the expected return component of pension expense, the fair value of plan assets at the beginning of the year is adjusted for additional contributions and payments to retirees during the year and then the weighted average balance of the assets is multiplied by the expected long-term rate of return (the actuary's rate).

As explained earlier in the chapter, the asset actuarial (experience) gain or loss can be determined at the end of each year by comparing the calculated expected return with the actual return that was earned. For example, the **expected return** on Zarle Corporation's pension fund assets for 2011 is 10% of the weighted average balance of the assets during 2011 of $111,000, or $11,100. If the **actual return** on the plan assets for the year 2011 is $12,000, there is an experience **gain** of $900 ($12,000 − $11,100). Plan assets are increased by $12,000, annual expense is credited with $11,100, and an actuarial gain of $900 is noted, **but not recognized**. The gain is deferred, and combined with actuarial gains and losses accumulated in prior years. The accumulated amount is reported in the notes to the financial statements.

Liability Gains and Losses.   Actuarial (experience) gains and losses on plan liabilities, on the other hand, arise from differences between the actuary's assumptions and actual experience, and from changes in the assumptions that are used by the actuary in calculating the ABO.

To illustrate, assume that the expected projected benefit obligation of Zarle Corporation based on adding up the individual components is $212,700 at December 31, 2011. If the company's actuaries, using revised estimates at December 31, 2011, calculate a projected benefit obligation of $213,500, then the company has suffered an actuarial loss of $800 ($213,500 − $212,700). If the actuary calculates a reduced obligation, the result is an actuarial gain. The ABO is adjusted to its most recent estimate and the difference is deferred with actuarial gains and losses (both asset and liability gains and losses) accumulated in prior years. The balance of the accumulated net actuarial gain or loss is reported off–balance sheet, in the notes to the financial statements.

Corridor Amortization for Net Actuarial Gains and Losses.   Because actuarial gains and losses can and are expected to offset each other over time, the accumulated unrecognized or unamortized net actuarial gain or loss may not actually grow very large. In fact, this is the reason that is given for not including these gains and losses directly in pension expense each year. But it is possible that no offsetting will occur and that the balance of the accumulated net gain or loss will continue to grow. To limit its growth, the corridor approach is used to amortize the balance. The corridor approach amortizes the net accumulated gain or loss when its balance is considered too large. It is considered **too large** and must be amortized **only if it exceeds the arbitrarily selected criterion of 10% of the larger of the accrued benefit obligation and the fair value of the plan assets at the first of the year**.[19] That is, the corridor is a range. The accumulated gains or losses only have to be amortized when the total accumulated amount falls outside that range.

Illustration 19-12 presents assumed data on an ABO and plan assets over the six-year period from 2009 to 2014. We use these data to explain how the corridor approach works.

---

[19] Under the deferral and amortization approach in private enterprise standards, the "market-related" value of plan assets could be used instead of their fair value.

Illustration 19-12

Calculation of the Corridor

| | Beginning-of-the-Year Balances | | |
	Accrued Benefit Obligation	Fair Value of Plan Assets	Corridor[a] ± 10%
2009	**$1,000,000**	$ 900,000	$100,000
2010	**1,200,000**	1,100,000	120,000
2011	1,300,000	**1,700,000**	170,000
2012	1,500,000	**2,250,000**	225,000
2013	1,700,000	**1,750,000**	175,000
2014	**1,800,000**	1,700,000	180,000

[a] The corridor is 10% of the larger (in **boldface**) of the accrued benefit obligation and the fair plan asset value.

If the balance of the accumulated net gain or loss stays within the corridor limits for each year, no amortization is required—the balance is carried forward unchanged. This becomes easier to see when the data are shown in a graph as in Illustration 19-13.

Illustration 19-13

Graphic Illustration of the Corridor

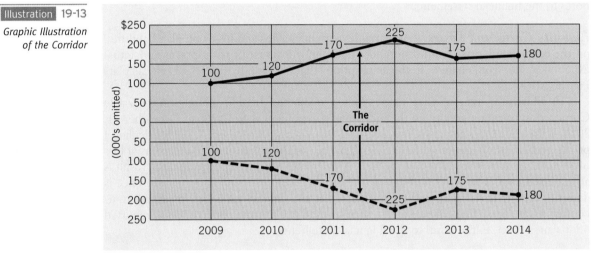

If the accumulated net gain or loss **at the first of the year** is more than the corridor limit, the **amount in excess of the limit** must be amortized. The minimum amortization is the accumulated net gain or loss in excess of the corridor amount divided by the expected average remaining service life of the employee group that is covered by the plan.[20] The expected average remaining service life of an employee group, known as EARSL, is the total number of years of future service that the group is expected to render divided by the number of employees in the group. Any systematic method of amortization may be used instead of the amount determined under this approach, as long as it results in faster recognition of actuarial gains and losses and is used consistently for both gains and losses. It can even be applied to amounts within the range established by the corridor.

Illustration of the Corridor Approach.   In applying the corridor approach, remember that **all calculations are based on beginning-of-the-period balances only**. That is, amortization of the excess is included as a component of pension expense only if the unamortized net gain or loss **at the beginning of the year** exceeds the **beginning-of-the-year corridor**. If there is no accumulated net gain or loss at the beginning of the

---

[20] *CICA Handbook*, Part II, Section 3461.088 and IAS 19 *Employee Benefits*, para. 93.

period, there will be no actuarial gain or loss component of pension expense in the current period.

To illustrate the amortization procedure, assume that a company provides the following information:

	2010	2011	2012
Accrued benefit obligation, January 1	$2,100,000	$2,600,000	$2,900,000
Fair value of fund assets, January 1	2,600,000	2,800,000	2,700,000
Net actuarial loss (gain) in year	400,000	300,000	(170,000)
Corridor: 10% of greater of opening ABO and plan assets	260,000	280,000	290,000

Illustration 19-14 shows how the amortization of the accumulated net loss is determined in each of the three years, assuming the employee group's average remaining service life is five-and-a-half years and remains at that level throughout the three-year period.

Year	(a) Corridor for Year (see above)	(b) Unrecognized net loss (gain), first of year	(c) Excess loss (gain) to be amortized (b) − (a)	(d) Amortization (c) ÷ 5.5	(e) Actuarial loss (gain) in year (see above)	(f) Unrecognized net loss (gain), end of year (b) − (d) + (e)
2010	$260,000	—	—	—	$400,000	$400,000
2011	280,000	$400,000	$120,000	$21,818	300,000	678,182
2012	290,000	678,182	388,182	70,579	(170,000)	437,603

Illustration 19-14

Corridor Test and Gain/Loss Amortization

Notice that the unrecognized net actuarial gain or loss is a cumulative number:

	Opening balance of the accumulated net actuarial gain or loss
±	Asset and liability gains and losses in the current year
−	Current year's amortization and transfer to expense, if any
=	Ending balance of the accumulated net actuarial gain or loss

As Illustration 19-14 shows, the $400,000 accumulated loss at the beginning of 2011 increases pension expense in 2011 by $21,818. This amount is small in comparison with the total loss of $400,000 and indicates that the corridor approach dampens the effects (reduces the volatility) of these gains and losses on pension expense and net income. The rationale for the corridor is that gains and losses result from refinements in estimates as well as real changes in economic value and that, over time, some of these gains and losses will cancel each other out. It therefore seems reasonable that gains and losses should not be recognized fully as a component of pension expense in the period in which they arise.

Note that the gains and losses go through three stages of smoothing. First, the asset gain or loss is smoothed by using the expected return. Then the accumulated net actuarial gain or loss at the beginning of the year is amortized to expense only if it is greater than the corridor. Finally, the excess is spread over the remaining service life of the current employees.

Other Options within the Defer-and-Amortize Approach. Both **private enterprise standards** under the defer-and-amortize approach and **IFRS** allow a company to choose to recognize actuarial gains and losses in income in the same period in which they occur. Unique to the international standard is an option for an entity that recognizes such gains and losses as they occur to report them in other comprehensive income rather than in net income. The entity has to apply this policy, however, to all its defined benefit plans and to all its actuarial gains and losses.

Similar to past service costs that are not recognized immediately, any actuarial gains and losses that are deferred are also not captured in the balance sheet benefit asset or liability account. The unamortized amounts, therefore, are off–balance sheet items.

Illustration of the Deferral and Amortization Approach

We now walk through an example to illustrate the approach permitted as an option by ASPE and required under IFRS. The transactions and events that affect the pension accounts of Trans Corp. over the three-year period 2010 to 2012 are listed in Illustration 19-15.

Illustration 19-15

Trans Corp. Pension Plan, 2010–2012

	2010	2011	2012
Fair value of plan assets, first of year	$150,000	$161,500	$195,500
Accrued benefit obligation (ABO) for accounting purposes, first of year	150,000	289,000	363,300
Current service cost for year	16,000	17,500	19,000
Interest or discount rate on the liability	9%	9%	9%
Cost of past service benefits granted, effective December 31, 2010	120,000	–0–	–0–
Amortization of past service cost	–0–	?	?
Expected earnings on plan assets for year	10%	10%	10%
Actual earnings on plan assets for year	10,000	16,000	28,000
Employer contributions for year (funding)	12,000	30,000	64,000
Benefits paid to retirees by trustee for year	10,500	12,000	15,500
Actuarial loss on liability due to change in actuarial assumptions	–0–	42,790	-0-
Amortization of accumulated actuarial gain/loss	?	?	?
Plan assets, end of year	161,500	195,500	272,000
Accrued benefit obligation (ABO), end of year	289,000	363,300	399,497
Funded status, end of year—over- or (under)-funded	(127,500)	(167,800)	(127,497)

2010 Work Sheet and Entries. The work sheet in Illustration 19-16 sets out the format and information that Trans Corp. needs for 2010. The beginning balances of the accrued benefit obligation and the pension fund assets are recorded on the work sheet's first line in the memo record. They are not recorded in the accounts and, therefore, are not reported as a liability and an asset on Trans Corp.'s balance sheet. Although they are off–balance sheet, the January 1, 2010 funded status of $0 is the same as the balance of $0 in the Accrued Pension Asset/Liability account on the balance sheet on that date. This will happen only when there are no deferred balances relating to past service costs and actuarial gains or losses.

Let's walk through the events of 2010 and see how they are accounted for if Trans Corp. either chooses a deferral and amortization accounting policy under PE GAAP or applies IFRS.

	A	B	C	D	F	G	H	I
1		General Journal Entries			Memo Record			
2	Items	Annual Pension Expense	Cash	Accrued Pension Asset/ Liability	Accrued Benefit Obligation	Plan Assets	Unrecognized Past Service Cost	Unrecognized Actuarial Gain or Loss
3	Balance, Jan. 1, 2010			–0–	150,000 Cr.	150,000 Dr.	–0–	–0–
4	(a) Service cost	16,000 Dr.			16,000 Cr.			
5	(b) Interest cost	13,500 Dr.			13,500 Cr.			
6	(c) Expected return	15,000 Cr.				15,000 Dr.		
7	(d) Asset loss					5,000 Cr.		5,000 Dr.
8	(e) Past service cost				120,000 Cr.		120,000 Dr.	
9	(f) Amortization of past service cost	–0–					–0–	
10	(g) Contribution		12,000 Cr.			12,000 Dr.		
11	(h) Benefits paid				10,500 Dr.	10,500 Cr.		
12	(i) Amortization of actuarial gain/loss	–0–						–0–
13	Expense entry, 2010	14,500 Dr.		14,500 Cr.				
14	Contribution entry, 2010		12,000 Cr.	12,000 Dr.				
15	Balance, Dec. 31, 2010			2,500 Cr.	289,000 Cr.	161,500 Dr.	120,000 Dr.	5,000 Dr.
16								

Illustration 19-16

Trans Corp. Work Sheet—2010

Entries (a), the service cost, and (b), the interest cost, are both recognized directly in expense. Note that the interest is calculated on the weighted average balance of the ABO outstanding for the year. The increase due to the granting of past service benefits was not effective until December 31. No part of it was outstanding during the year, and therefore it is not included in the interest component. Unless stated otherwise, we assume that the service cost, contributions into the fund, and benefits paid are all December 31 transactions.

Items (c) and (d) are related. Item (c), which represents the return on plan assets, is the **expected return**, used to smooth the amount of pension expense. The expected return is 10% of the weighted-average outstanding balance of fund assets for the year, in this case 10% of $150,000 or $15,000. This is higher than the actual return of $10,000. Entry (d) shows the resulting asset actuarial loss of $5,000 ($15,000 – $10,000), which, instead of being recognized in pension expense in 2010, is deferred as an unrecognized actuarial loss in the memo accounts.

The cost of the past service benefits granted effective December 31, 2010, is shown in (e). This is another component that is deferred to an off–balance sheet memo account and later amortized. Because the costs are effective only on the last day of the year, no amount is amortized into pension expense in 2010 in item (f).

The employer contributions and benefits paid by the fund in (g) and (h) are treated the same way as under the immediate recognition method. They do not affect the expense. The last item (i) is the amortization of the net accumulated actuarial gain or loss in the year. Because the amortization is based on the opening balance of this amount, and the opening balance was $0, there is no amortization recognized in expense in 2010.

The expense is made up of five components: the current service cost, interest cost, expected return on assets, and two amortization amounts—for the past service costs and actuarial gains or losses. In this year, both amortization amounts were $0. The entry needed on December 31, 2010, to record the pension expense for the year is:

A =   L   +   SE
       +14,500   −14,500

Cash flows: No effect

Pension Expense	14,500	
Accrued Pension Asset/Liability		14,500

When the company made its contributions to the pension fund late in the year, the following entry was recorded:

A =   L   +   SE
−12,000   −12,000

Cash flows: ↓ 12,000 outflow

Accrued Pension Asset/Liability	12,000	
Cash		12,000

Objective 8

Determine the benefit plan accounts reported in the financial statements and explain their relationship to the funded status of the plan.

Because the expense exceeds the funding, the Accrued Pension Liability account increases during the year by the $2,500 difference ($14,500 less $12,000). At December 31, 2010, the balance of the Accrued Pension Liability account ($2,500) is equal to the balance in the memo accounts. These now include the deferred and unamortized past service costs and actuarial losses:

		At Dec. 31, 2010
Accrued benefit obligation		$289,000 Cr.
Plan assets		161,500 Dr.
Funded status—net liability (underfunded)		127,500 Cr.
Unrecognized past service cost	120,000 Dr.	
Unrecognized actuarial loss	5,000 Dr.	125,000 Dr.
Accrued pension liability on balance sheet		$ 2,500 Cr.

2011 Work Sheet and Entries.   Continuing the Trans Corp. example set out in Illustration 19-15 into 2011, we start by recording the opening balances at January 1, 2011, on the 2011 work sheet in Illustration 19-17. Items (j) and (k) record the current service cost and interest as components of pension expense, and (o) and (p) have been explained previously. The interest cost is 9% of $289,000 or $26,010. The expected return (l) is 10% of $161,500 or $16,150. The actual return of $16,000 was $150 less than what was expected, resulting in an actuarial loss of $150 in (m) that is deferred.

The amortization of the past service costs deferred on December 31, 2010, requires an explanation. On that date, the plan amendment granted employees prior service benefits that had a present value of $120,000. Under the deferral and amortization approach, we need to determine how these costs will be amortized into expense. In this case, we assume either that:

1. the average remaining service life to full benefit eligibility of the employee group covered by the amendment is four years (for PE GAAP), or that

2. no benefits have yet vested in the employees and four years is the average period to vesting (for IFRS).

The annual amortization amount in both cases is $120,000 ÷ 4 = $30,000, effective January 1, 2011. The amortization of these costs in (n) reduces the unamortized balance as they are recognized as part of pension expense in the income statement in each year from 2011 to 2014.

Entry (q) records the increase in the accrued benefit obligation that results from a change in actuarial assumptions. The actuary has calculated the ending balance of the ABO to be $363,300. Since the memo record balance at December 31 is $320,510 (equal

	A	B	C	D		F	G	H	I
1		General Journal Entries				Memo Record			
2	Items	Annual Pension Expense	Cash	Accrued Pension Asset/ Liability		Accrued Benefit Obligation	Plan Assets	Unrecognized Past Service Cost	Unrecognized Actuarial Gain or Loss
3	Balance, Jan. 1, 2011			2,500 Cr.		289,000 Cr.	161,500 Dr.	120,000 Dr.	5,000 Dr.
4	(j) Service cost	17,500 Dr.				17,500 Cr.			
5	(k) Interest cost	26,010 Dr.				26,010 Cr.			
6	(l) Expected return	16,150 Cr.					16,150 Dr.		
7	(m) Asset loss						150 Cr.		150 Dr.
8	(n) Amortization of past service cost	30,000 Dr.						30,000 Cr.	
9	(o) Contribution		30,000 Cr.				30,000 Dr.		
10	(p) Benefits paid					12,000 Dr.	12,000 Cr.		
11	(q) Actuarial loss (liability)					42,790 Cr.			42,790 Dr.
12	(r) Amortization of actuarial gain/loss	–0–							–0–
13	Expense entry, 2011	57,360 Dr.		57,360 Cr.					
14	Contribution entry, 2011		30,000 Cr.	30,000 Dr.					
15	Balance, Dec. 31, 2011			29,860 Cr.		363,300 Cr.	195,500 Dr.	90,000 Dr.	47,940 Dr.
16									

Illustration 19-17

Trans Corp. Work Sheet—2011

to $289,000 + $17,500 + $26,010 − $12,000), there is a difference of $42,790 ($363,300 − $320,510). This $42,790 increase in the employer's obligation is an actuarial loss that is deferred by including it in the unrecognized actuarial gain/loss balance.

Is any amortization of the accumulated actuarial losses needed in 2011? Let's check:

Net accumulated actuarial loss at January 1, 2011	$ 5,000
Corridor: 10% of larger of ABO and fund assets at January 1, 2011 = 10% × 289,000	28,900
Excess of actuarial loss over corridor	$ 0

Assuming Trans Corp. follows a policy of recognizing the minimum amount required under the corridor approach, there is no amortization in 2011.

Again, the pension expense is made up of the same five items: service cost, interest cost, expected return, and any amortization of deferred past service costs and actuarial losses. The entry needed on December 31, 2011, to formally record the expense for the year is:

Pension Expense	57,360	
Accrued Pension Asset/Liability		57,360

A = L + SE
 +57,360 −57,360

Cash flows: No effect

The following entry was recorded in late December 2011:

Accrued Pension Asset/Liability	30,000	
Cash		30,000

A = L + SE
−30,000 −30,000

Cash flows: ↓ 30,000 outflow

Because the expense exceeds the funding, the Accrued Pension Liability account increases during the year by the $27,360 difference ($57,360 less $30,000). In 2011, as in 2010, the balance of the Accrued Pension Liability account ($29,860) is equal to the balances in the memo accounts, as shown in the following reconciliation.

		At Dec. 31, 2011
Accrued benefit obligation		$363,300 Cr.
Plan assets		195,500 Dr.
Funded status—net liability (underfunded)		167,800 Cr.
Unrecognized past service cost	90,000 Dr.	
Unrecognized actuarial loss	47,940 Dr.	137,940 Dr.
Accrued pension liability on balance sheet		$ 29,860 Cr.

2012 Work Sheet and Entries.   We continue with the Trans Corp. data set out in Illustration 19-15. The work sheet in Illustration 19-18 presents the pension information that the company needs for 2012. The beginning balances recorded on the work sheet's first line are the ending balances from the 2011 pension work sheet in Illustration 19-17.

	A	B	C	D	F	G	H	I
1		General Journal Entries			Memo Record			
2	Items	Annual Pension Expense	Cash	Accrued Pension Asset/ Liability	Accrued Benefit Obligation	Plan Assets	Unrecognized Past Service Cost	Unrecognized Actuarial Gain or Loss
3	Balance, Jan. 1, 2012			29,860 Cr.	363,300 Cr.	195,500 Dr.	90,000 Dr.	47,940 Dr.
4	(s) Service cost	19,000 Dr.			19,000 Cr.			
5	(t) Interest cost	32,697 Dr.			32,697 Cr.			
6	(u) Expected return	19,550 Cr.				19,550 Dr.		
7	(v) Asset gain					8,450 Dr.		8,450 Cr.
8	(w) Amortization of past service cost	30,000 Dr.					30,000 Cr.	
9	(x) Contribution		64,000 Cr.			64,000 Dr.		
10	(y) Benefits paid				15,500 Dr.	15,500 Cr.		
11	(z) Actuarial loss (liability)				–0–			–0–
12	(aa) Amortization of actuarial gain/loss	1,451 Dr.						1,451 Cr.
13	Expense entry, 2012	63,598 Dr.		63,598 Cr.				
14	Contribution entry, 2012		64,000 Cr.	64,000 Dr.				
15	Balance, Dec. 31, 2012			29,458 Cr.	399,497 Cr.	272,000 Dr.	60,000 Dr.	38,039 Dr.
16								

Illustration 19-18

Trans Corp. Work Sheet—2012

Entries (s), (t), (w), (x), and (y) are similar to the entries that were explained in 2010 and 2011 for these components. Entries (u) and (v) are related to each other as explained earlier, but this time the company experienced an actuarial gain. The gain is deferred.

Trans Corp. checks to see whether any of the accumulated unrecognized actuarial loss should be amortized to expense in 2012 using the following analysis:

Accumulated actuarial losses at January 1, 2012	$47,940
Corridor: 10% of larger of ABO and fund assets at January 1, 2012 = 10% × 363,300	36,330
Excess of actuarial loss over corridor	$11,610

Now we see that the losses at the first of the year are high enough to be amortized. Assuming an expected average remaining service life of the affected employee group of eight years, the amortization amount in 2012 is $11,610 \div 8 = $1,451.

Note that the pension expense is made up of the same five items: service cost, interest cost, expected return, and any amortization of deferred past service costs and actuarial losses. The entry to record the expense for 2012 is:

Pension Expense	63,598	
Accrued Pension Asset/Liability		63,598

A = L + SE
      +63,598 −63,598

Cash flows: No effect

The company's contribution for the year was:

Accrued Pension Asset/Liability	64,000	
Cash		64,000

A   =   L   + SE
−64,000 −64,000

Cash flows: ↓ 64,000 outflow

The credit balance of the Accrued Pension Liability account reported on the statement of financial position at December 31, 2012, of $29,458 is equal to the net of the balances in the memo accounts at the same date.

		At December 31, 2012
Accrued benefit obligation		$399,497 Cr.
Plan assets		272,000 Dr.
Funded status—net liability (underfunded)		127,497 Cr.
Unrecognized amounts:		
Past service cost	$60,000 Dr.	
Net actuarial losses	38,039 Dr.	98,039 Dr.
Accrued pension liability on balance sheet		$ 29,458 Cr.

Other Considerations

Limit on the Carrying Amount of an Accrued Benefit Asset

Although the illustrations provided in this chapter result in accrued benefit liabilities being reported on the statement of financial position, accrued benefit assets are also found on corporate balance sheets. The accounting standards provide for an asset ceiling test on the balance of any benefit asset reported on the statement of financial position.

Similar to most assets we have studied, there is a limit on the carrying amount of an accrued benefit asset resulting from a defined benefit plan. In general, if the accrued benefit asset recognized is greater than the future benefits the company is expected to receive from the asset, a valuation allowance is needed to reduce the asset's reported amount. Except for minor differences, the limit is determined the same way under IFRS and the deferral and amortization approach of PE GAAP. Under the immediate recognition approach, the objective is the same.

Although the calculations required are not explained in this text, you should be aware that the change in the valuation allowance in the year is recognized as a component of the benefit expense in income in the year. In addition, the accrued benefit asset is reported net of the allowance on the statement of financial position.[21]

Underlying Concept

The measurement of an asset always takes into account the amount of the future benefits expected from the recognized item.

---

[21] The expected future benefits generally represent those that the company can realize from a plan surplus through amounts it can withdraw from the plan or reductions it can make in its future contributions. Under IFRS, the change in the valuation allowance made as a result of actuarial gains and losses recognized in OCI adjusts OCI rather than net income.

Other Benefits

This chapter presents the basics of accounting for employee future benefits. In addition to the valuation of the funded status asset, further complexities arise from temporary deviations from the benefit plan, obligation settlements, benefits provided through insurance contracts or other arrangements, plan curtailments, termination benefits, and multi-employer or multiple-employer plans. The Deutsche Lufthansa AG note disclosures in Illustration 19-21 later in the chapter refer to some of these issues.

Comparison of Results

What is the result of applying the defer-and-amortize approach rather than immediate recognition? You should notice two major differences in the reported results.

First, the expense reported over the three years is smoothed considerably under the deferral approach, making the net income reported less volatile than under the immediate recognition option. The second difference relates to how well the amount reported as the balance sheet liability or asset represents the funded status of the plan. As you saw, the immediate recognition approach tracks the funded status directly, although it incorporates an ABO measured for funding purposes rather than an ABO based on projected salaries. Under the deferral and amortization method, the effects of many of the events that change the funded status are not recognized until future years. This is evident from the reconciliations of the funded status to the accrued pension liability in the Trans Corp. example above.

To resolve the discrepancy between the amount reported on the balance sheet and the funded status while still using the defer-and-amortize approach, the FASB recognizes all the changes in the ABO and plan assets in the balance sheet accrued pension liability/asset account, but reports the unamortized amounts in other comprehensive income (and AOCI) instead of as off–balance sheet items in the notes to the financial statements. Although basically a defer-and-amortize model, the IFRS contains choices that permit entities to recognize items such as actuarial gains and losses immediately in pension expense, and therefore in the balance sheet account as well.

Illustration 19-19 summarizes the private enterprise and IFRS standards as this text went to print, and the Looking Ahead section at the end of the chapter provides a summary of likely changes as the FASB and IASB work on revisions to the employee benefit standards.

Illustration 19-19

Summary of Private Enterprise and International Standards

	Private Enterprise Standards Accounting Policy Choice		IFRS
	Immediate Recognition Approach	Deferral and Amortization Approach	Deferral and Amortization Approach
Actuarial valuation basis for ABO	ABO prepared for funding purposes	ABO used for accounting purposes (projected costs)	ABO used for accounting purposes (projected costs)
Include in expense and balance sheet account:			
Current service cost	Include	Include	Include
Interest cost on ABO	Include	Include	Include
Return on plan assets	Include actual return	Include expected return	Include expected return
Past service cost	Include all	Include only amortization over period to full eligibility, or shorter period that benefits	Include to extent benefits are vested; remainder is amortized over average period to full vesting
Actuarial gains and losses	Include all	Include amortization using corridor approach; minimum is excess amount over the corridor divided by EARSL or shorter period; may recognize immediately.	Include amortization using corridor approach; minimum is excess amount over the corridor divided by EARSL or shorter period. May recognize 100% as incurred; if so, may recognize cost in OCI instead of expense.

Other Defined Benefit Plans

Other Post-Employment and Long-Term Employee Benefit Plans with Benefits That Vest or Accumulate

In addition to pension plans, companies provide their employees with other post-employment benefits as part of their compensation package. These may include such benefits as health care, prescription drugs, life insurance, dental and eye care, legal and tax services, tuition assistance, or free or subsidized travel. In the past, most companies accounted for the cost of these employee future benefits as an expense in the period when the benefits were provided to the retirees, their spouses, dependants, and beneficiaries; that is, on a pay-as-you-go basis. In 2000, the Canadian standard changed to require companies to account for all defined benefit plans where the benefits vest or accumulate on the same basis as they account for defined benefit pension plans.

In 1990 the FASB issued *Statement No. 106*, "Employers' Accounting for Post-Retirement Benefits Other Than Pensions." This standard required a change from the pay-as-you-go method of accounting for these benefits to an accrual basis, similar to pension accounting. When the standard was first applied, the effect on most U.S. companies was significant. For example, General Motors announced a U.S. $20.8-billion charge against its 1992 earnings as a result of adopting the new standard, and this was at a time when the company's net book value before the charge was approximately U.S. $28 billion! The impact of a subsequent change in Canada was not as significant as in the United States because of broader health-care coverage paid for by the government. A Financial Executives Institute Canada (FEI) study estimated a total Canadian unreported liability of $52 billion, almost entirely unfunded. In both countries, the requirement to measure the outstanding obligation and related costs resulted in corporate management paying much closer attention to the benefit packages that are offered to employee groups, supporting the credo that "you only control what gets measured and reported."

Unlike pension benefits, companies tend not to prefund (set aside assets in advance for) their other post-employment benefit plans. The major reason is that payments to prefund health-care costs, for example, are not tax-deductible, unlike contributions to a pension trust. Although these two types of retirement benefits appear similar, there are some significant differences, as indicated in Illustration 19-20.

Objective
Account for defined benefit plans with benefits that vest or accumulate other than pension plans.

What Do the Numbers Mean?

Item	Pensions	Health-Care Benefits
Funding	Generally funded	Generally not funded
Benefit	Well-defined and level dollar amount	Generally uncapped and great variability
Beneficiary	Retiree (maybe some benefit to surviving spouse)	Retiree, spouse, and other dependants
Benefit payable	Monthly	As needed and used
Predictability	Variables are reasonably predictable	Utilization difficult to predict; level of cost varies geographically and fluctuates over time

Illustration 19-20

Differences between Pensions and Post-Retirement Health-Care Benefits

Measuring the net cost of the post-retirement benefits for the period is complex. Due to the uncertainties in forecasting health-care costs, rates of usage, changes in government health programs, and the differences in non-medical assumptions (e.g., the discount rate, employee turnover, rate of early retirement, and spouse-age difference), estimates of post-retirement benefit costs may have a large margin of error. However, not recognizing an obligation and expense before paying the benefits is considered to be an unfaithful representation of financial position and performance.

Under **accounting standards for private enterprises**, the basic concepts, accounting terminology, recognition and measurement criteria, and measurement methods that apply to defined benefit pensions for the most part **also apply to the requirements for other benefits** that vest or accumulate based on the service provided by employees. Examples of such benefits include sabbaticals where unrestricted time off with pay is granted for services provided, service-related long-term disability benefits, or sick days not used that accumulate and are paid out on retirement.[22] Assume, for example, that an employee benefit plan provides a cash bonus of $500 per year of service when an employee retires or has his or her employment terminated for other reasons, on condition that the employee has been employed for at least 10 years. Because the right to the benefit is earned by rendering service and the benefit increases with the length of service provided, the cost and related liability are accrued starting from the date of employment. The measurement of the obligation and expense takes into consideration the probabilities related to employee turnover. The fact that the benefits do not vest for 10 years does not eliminate the need to recognize the cost and liability over the first 10 years of employment.

Under **IFRS**, however, a distinction is made between post-employment plans such as pensions and post-employment health care benefits that are subject to considerable measurement uncertainty and that are amended for past service costs, and other types of long-term employee benefits. Included in this latter group are benefits such as paid leave for long service, unrestricted sabbaticals, long-term disability plans with benefits that increase with service, and deferred compensation, profit-sharing, and bonuses payable more than a year after the end of the period in which the benefits are earned by employees.

For this less complex type of long-term benefit, IFRS uses the **same approach** as for pension plans **except that the actuarial gains and losses and any past service costs are recognized in expense as these costs occur**. This requirement converts the accounting into an immediate recognition approach. The periodic expense is made up of the current service cost (measured taking into account the probability that payment will be required and the length of the payment), interest cost, decreased or increased by the actual return on the assets, and adjusted for any actuarial gains or losses and past service cost in the year. The adjustment to the accrued benefit asset or liability on the balance sheet is made for the same amount. The accrued benefit obligation or ABO, however, is still based on projected cost estimates, not a funding formula valuation. Notice, however, that because actuarial revaluations and past service costs rarely occur for this type of plan, there would be little difference in the accounting treatment under IFRS or PE standards.

Under both standards, benefits such as sick leave that accumulate with service but do not vest in the employee should, in theory, be accrued as the employee provides service. In practical terms, however, because it is difficult to make a reasonable estimate of such benefit amounts, and since the amounts are relatively immaterial, these costs are usually not accrued.

Other Employee Benefit Plans with Benefits That Do Not Vest or Accumulate

Both PE standards and IFRS make no attempt to accrue the benefit costs and liabilities related to employee benefits that do not vest or accumulate with additional service. In this case, there is no basis on which to assign the costs to periods other than the period when the benefits are taken. A good example is costs associated with parental leave or long-term disability benefits that do not change with an employee's length of service. Instead, both the total cost and liability are recognized when the event occurs that obligates the company to

---

[22] Sabbaticals where the employee is expected to use the compensated absence to perform research or engage in other activities to the benefit of the organization do not need to be accrued over the period when the sabbatical is earned.

provide the benefits. This is referred to as an "event accrual" method of accounting for benefits and is explained in Chapter 13.

PRESENTATION, DISCLOSURE, AND ANALYSIS

Presentation

Balance Sheet Presentation of Accrued Benefit Assets/Liabilities

Entities with two or more defined benefit plans are required to separately measure the benefit cost, accrued benefit obligation, and plan assets for each funded benefit plan. If all the plans result in an accrued benefit liability on the balance sheet or all result in an accrued benefit asset, the plans can be reported together in the financial statements. However, because companies generally do not have the legal right to, and do not intend to, use the assets of one plan to pay for the benefits of other plans, an accrued benefit asset of one plan and an accrued benefit liability of another are required to be reported separately on the balance sheet.

Neither IFRS nor accounting standards for private enterprises provide any guidance on how to determine whether accrued benefit assets and liabilities for defined benefit plans are current or long-term, so companies revert to basic underlying principles to determine the classification. Most such assets and liabilities are found in the long-term classifications on both sides of the balance sheet.

Income Statement Presentation of Benefit Cost

Both sets of accounting standards identify the components that make up the benefit costs for the period, and both indicate that a portion of these costs may be required to be treated as a product cost in inventory or capitalized in a property, plant, and equipment asset. However, neither IFRS nor private enterprise GAAP dictates how the components of benefit costs are to be reported on the income statement. Companies therefore have the option of reporting current service cost, interest cost, and the expected return on plan assets as separate components, as part of similar expenses, or in total as a single benefit cost. Many companies report all the components together as a single benefit cost.

Disclosures

For a phenomenon as significant and specialized as pensions and other defined benefit plans, it is not surprising that there are extensive reporting and disclosure requirements. While private enterprise standards require only a limited set of basic information in addition to the accounting policy choices the entity has made, IAS 19 *Employee Benefits* requires a high level of accountability from companies for the effect of such plans on their current and future performance, financial position, and risk.

Under **ASPE**, separate disclosures are required for plans that provide pension benefits and other types of employee future benefits, and most of these are for defined benefit plans. This includes a description of each type of plan and any major changes in the terms of the plan during the year; the effective date of the most recent actuarial valuation for funding purposes; the year-end funded status, including the fair value of the plan assets and accrued benefit obligation; and an explanation of any difference between the amount

10 Objective
Identify the types of information required to be presented and disclosed for defined benefit plans, prepare basic schedules, and be able to read and understand such disclosures.

Underlying Concept
Standard setters make decisions about disclosures in light of the users of the financial statements.

reported on the balance sheet and the plans' funded status. It is expected that any additional information needed by users is available from the company.

The objective under **IFRS** is to provide disclosures for a broad range of users with no access to additional information. The information should help them assess the amounts and likelihood of the cash flows that are associated with future benefits, the relationship between cash flows and pension and other benefits expenses, the impact of employee benefits on the income statement, and the reasonableness of the assumptions that underlie the measurement of the accrued obligation, fund assets, and current expense. In addition, information about unrecognized amounts reported in the notes to the financial statements informs readers about how extensively future earnings may be affected by the obligations to employees to date.

In addition to providing a description of each defined benefit plan or groupings of similar plans and what accounting choices were made where choices are permitted, the following types of information are also required:

- **Reconciliations.** Reconciliations of the opening to closing balances of the present value of the defined benefit obligation and the fair value of the fund assets; and of the funded status to the balance sheet reported benefit asset or liability.

- **Amounts included in periodic net income.** Disclosure is required of the total expense recognized in the period for each of the components that make up the benefit cost, including the line item where each component is reported. In addition, any amounts recognized in OCI must be identified.

- **Underlying assumptions and sensitivity information.** To help in assessing the reasonableness of the amounts reported, the following are required to be disclosed: how the expected return on plan assets is determined and specific information about the principal actuarial assumptions used in determining key plan valuations. The effects of a 1% change in the assumed medical cost trend rates on the related current service and interest cost components and accrued benefit obligation are also required.

- **Other.** The balances of the funded status and its components for the current and preceding four annual periods is required along with experience adjustments that arose from each of the plan assets and liabilities over that time. And, looking forward, the employer's best estimate of the following year's expected funding contributions must be reported.

Illustration

Real-World Emphasis

WILEY PLUS

Additional Disclosures

Companies organize these disclosures in a variety of acceptable ways. Deutsche Lufthansa AG, with group operations including over 400 subsidiaries and associated companies, is a worldwide aviation company based in Germany. Its 2008 accounting policy note and specific balance sheet note on pension provisions set out in Illustration 19-21 provide a comprehensive example of disclosures required under IFRS. As you can tell, the disclosures are extensive! Lufthansa's financial statements for its year ended December 31, 2008, are reported in millions of euros (€m).

It is particularly interesting to note the relationship between the expected rate of return on the plan assets (€281) and the actual return as set out in the reconciliation of the fair value of plan assets. With an actuarial loss of €1,006 in the year, this indicates an actual negative return on the plan assets of €1,006 − €281 = €725 million! This relationship is likely to be found in most companies' pension assets in 2008 because of the significant drop in values on the world's stock exchanges. Look through the other parts of this note and see if you can relate the information to what has been explained in the chapter.

2) Summary of significant accounting policies and valuation methods and estimates used as a basis for measurement

Provisions

Measurement of pension provisions is based on the projected unit credit method prescribed by IAS 19 for defined benefit pension plans. The measurement of pension provisions within the balance sheet is based on a number of estimates and assumptions.

They include, in particular, assumptions about long-term salary and pension trends and average life expectancy. The assumptions about salary and pension trends are based on developments observed in the past and take into account national interest and inflation rates and labour market trends. Estimates of average life expectancy are based on recognised biometric calculation formulas.

The interest rate used for discounting future payment obligations is the country-specific market rate for long-term risk-free cash investments with a comparable time to maturity.

The expected long-term development of existing plan assets is also determined with regard to the country concerned and depending on the fund structure, taking past experience into account.

Changes in estimates and assumptions from year to year and deviations from actual annual effects are reflected in actuarial gains/losses and are, if they exceed 10 per cent of the higher of obligation and plan assets, amortised pro rata via the income statement over the beneficiaries' remaining period of service. The 10 per cent corridor rule prevents fluctuations in the balance sheet and the income statement from year to year.

Actuarial losses not disclosed in the balance sheet as of 31 December 2008 amount to EUR 466m (previous year: EUR 40m). In the 2008 financial year EUR 11m (previous year: EUR 23m) was amortised via staff costs.

37) Pension provisions

A company pension scheme exists for staff working in Germany and staff seconded abroad. For staff who joined the Group before 1995 the supplementary pension scheme for state employees (VBL) was initially retained as the Company's pension scheme. Following collective agreements in 2003 to harmonise retirement benefits for ground and flight staff, the pension scheme for ground and flight staff was also converted to an average salary plan for cockpit staff under the terms of the 4 December 2004 wage settlement. The retirement benefit commitment is now equal to that for staff who joined the Company after 1994. In each case, one salary component is converted into one pension component, retirement benefit being defined as the sum of the accumulated pension components. Under IAS 19 these pension obligations must be regarded as performance-related and therefore taken into account for the amount of obligations and as expenses.

Flight staff are additionally entitled to a transitional pension arrangement covering the period between the end of their active inflight service and the beginning of their statutory/company pension plans. Benefits depend on the final salary before retirement (final salary plans).

Defined contribution retirement benefit schemes also exist within the Group, funded entirely by contributions paid to an external pension provider. Lufthansa runs no financial or actuarial risks from these obligations. In 2008, contributions toward defined contribution pension plans amounted to EUR 339m (previous year: EUR 319m).

Company pension schemes and transitional pension arrangements for Germany are financed mainly by pension provisions. Obligations are measured annually using the projected unit credit method. In the 2004 financial year, work began on building up plan assets to fund future pension payments and transfer them to the Lufthansa Pension Trust. The aim is to outsource the pension obligations in full within 10 to 15 years. In 2008, a further EUR 283m was transferred for staff, taking the total transferred to the pension trust to EUR 3,483m.

Staff abroad are also entitled to retirement benefits and in some cases to medical care, based mainly on length of service and salary earned. As a rule, benefits are financed by means of external funds.

In the course of acquiring Swiss International Air Lines AG on 1 July 2007, pension obligations, mainly statutory obligations, were also taken on. The retirement benefits are funded via pension funds known as collective foundations. The retrospective application of IFRIC 14 had no material effects on the surplus of the previous year at Swiss International Air Lines AG.

In measuring pension provisions and determining pension costs the 10 per cent corridor rule is applied. Actuarial gains and losses are not taken into account unless they exceed 10 per cent of total obligations or 10 per cent of the fair value of existing plan assets. The amount that exceeds the corridor is divided over the expected average remaining years of service of active staff through profit or loss and recognised in the balance sheet.

Pension obligations are calculated on the basis of the following assumptions:

Actuarial assumptions

in %	31.12.2008	31.12.2007	31.12.2006
Interest rate in Germany	6.0	5.5	4.5
Projected salary increase in Germany	2.75	2.75	2.75
Projected pension increase in Germany	1.0 – 2.75	1.0 – 2.75	1.0 – 2.75
Interest rates abroad	3.9 – 6.7	3.4 – 6.0	4.5 – 6.0
Projected salary increases abroad	1.5 – 4.5	1.2 – 4.5	2.9 – 4.25
Projected pension increases abroad	0.0 – 2.8	0.5 – 3.2	1.25 – 3.0
Health care cost trend for pensioners abroad	10.0	11.0	12.0
Expected return on external plan assets in Germany*	5.2	5.75	5.75
Expected return on external plan assets abroad	3.5 – 8.3	3.75 – 8.0	5.2 – 8.25

*Post-tax interest from 2008.

Illustration 19-21

Illustrative Disclosure—Deutsche Lufthansa AG
(continued on page 1266)

Since 31 December 2005 biometric calculations have been based on the 2005 G Heubeck life-expectancy tables, with fluctuation estimated on the basis of age and gender.

The projected return on plan assets is generally based on the plan's investment policy relating to the selection of asset classes. The projected return on equity investments takes into account historic interest rates, future inflation rates, expected dividends and economic growth. The projected return on fixed-interest instruments is based on current interest rates for long-term securities, subject to a risk discount if appropriate. The projected return on property assets corresponds to that of equity investments. For other assets, mainly bank balances, the interest paid on current deposits on the balance sheet date was applied.

An increase or decrease in the assumed health care costs for pensioners by 1 per cent would have the following effects:

in € thousand	Increase	Decrease
Service costs and interest expenses	+ 21	− 23
Health care commitments	+ 404	− 422

On the balance sheet date the present value of pension obligations and the fair values of plan assets were as follows:

in €m	31.12.2008	31.12.2007	31.12.2006
Present value of funded pension obligations in Germany	4,081	4,068	4,455
Plan assets in Germany	3,445	3,580	1,839
Deficit (+)/surplus (−)	636	488	2,616

in €m	31.12.2008	31.12.2007	31.12.2006
Present value of funded pension obligations abroad	1,712	1,603	532
Plan assets abroad	1,476	1,648	469
Deficit (+)/surplus (−)	236	− 45	63
Present value of unfunded pension obligations	1,961	1,948	2,042

On the balance sheet date for 2008 the portfolio of external plan assets is made up as follows:

	Plan assets Germany		Plan assets abroad	
	in €m	in %	in €m	in %
Shares	1,375	39.9	508	34.4
Fixed-income instruments, bonds	1,602	46.5	642	43.5
Real estate	—	—	158	10.7
Other	468	13.6	168	11.4
	3,445	100.0	1,476	100.0

In 2008, the effective loss on plan assets came to EUR 725m (previous year: gain of EUR 107m).

Change in present value of pension obligations

in €m	2008	2007
Carried forward 1.1.	7,619	7,029
Exchange rate differences carried forward	112	− 53
Additions from company acquisitions	—	—
Other changes in the group of consolidated companies	0*	1,084
Current service costs	305	317
Past service costs	− 12	0*
Interest expenses	386	338
Contributions by plan participants	30	10
Actuarial gains/losses	− 450	− 917
Pension payments	− 241	− 209
Plan cuts/settlements	− 4	—
Other**	9	20
Balance on 31.12	7,754	7,619

Change in fair value of plan assets

in €m	2008	2007
Carried forward 1.1.	5,228	2,308
Exchange rate differences carried forward	103	− 45
Additions from company acquisitions	—	—
Other changes in the group of consolidated companies	—	1,160
Projected return on plan assets	281	184
Actuarial gains/losses	− 1,006	− 77
Contributions by plan participants	30	10
Employer contributions	338	1,640
Pension payments	− 53	− 39
Other**	0*	87
Balance on 31.12	4,921	5,228

* Rounded below EUR 1m.
** The amounts in 2008 are almost exclusively for benefit obligations which were measured in accordance with IAS 19 for the first time as of 31.12.2007. The amounts of plan assets in 2007 were almost exclusively assets which qualified as plan assets in 2007.

The carrying amount of pension provisions is lower than the present value of pension obligations due to unrecognised actuarial losses.

Funding status

in €m	2008	2007
Present value of unfunded pension obligations	1,961	1,948
Present value of funded pension obligations abroad	1,712	1,603
Present value of funded pension obligations in Germany	4,081	4,068
External plan assets abroad	− 1,476	− 1,648
External plan assets Germany	− 3,445	− 3,580
Unrecognised actuarial losses	− 466	− 40
Adjustment for asset ceiling	—	110
"Unrealised" asset surpluses	+ 33	—
	2,400	2,461

The year-on-year changes in funding status mainly result from changes in assumptions, especially the rise in interest rates.

In the 2008 and 2007 financial years pension provisions developed as follows:

Pension provisions

in €m	2008	2007
Carried forward	2,461	3,814
Exchange rate differences carried forward	1	− 3
Changes in the group of consolidated companies	0*	26
Pension payments	− 188	− 170
Additions	419	501
Allocation to plan assets / staff changes	− 293	− 1,707
Year-end total	**2,400**	**2,461**

*Rounded below EUR 1m.

The expenses recognised in the income statement due to allocations to the pension provisions are made up as follows:

in €m	2008	2007
Current service costs	305	317
Recognised actuarial losses	11	23
Recognised actuarial gains	0*	—
Past service costs	− 12	0*
Plan cuts/settlements	− 4	—
Interest effect of projected pension obligations	386	338
Projected return on external plan assets	− 281	− 184
Net effect of adjustment for asset ceiling	14	7
	419	**501**

* Rounded below EUR 1m.

Current service costs and actuarial losses/gains are recognised as staff costs, while the interest effect of projected pension obligations less projected external plan asset earnings, is recognised as interest expenses.

Adjustments to pension obligations and plan assets based on past experience were as follows:

Adjustments from past experience

in €m	2008	2007	2006	2005
Pension obligations	+ 122	+ 30	+ 7	− 140
Plan assets	− 1,006	− 77	− 0*	95
Total	**− 1,128**	**− 107**	**− 7**	**+ 235**

* Rounded below EUR 1m.

A minus sign before pension obligations in the table means a reduction in the commitment and, therefore, a gain. A minus sign before plan assets means a loss, however. For the total amount a negative sign signifies an overall loss.

In 2009 an estimated EUR 826m will be transferred to plans. The transfers are made up of planned allocations and benefit payments which are not covered by equivalent reimbursements from plan assets.

Illustration 19-21

*Illustrative Disclosure—
Deutsche Lufthansa AG
(continued)*

Analysis

With all the information that is reported in the notes to the financial statements, what should an analysis focus on? The most important elements are the major assumptions that underlie the calculations, the status of the plan, and the company's future cash requirements.

As was indicated earlier in the chapter, the accrued benefit obligation and benefit expense are based on several estimates that, if altered, can significantly change the amounts. Aside from the actuarial assumptions that were used by the actuary and the rate of compensation and health-care increases—which are both important—the choice of discount rate that was used to measure the ABO, the current service cost, and the interest cost are also key variables. A one-percentage-point difference in rate could have a 10% to 20% effect on the discounted value. This rate is required to be disclosed so that readers can assess it for reasonableness and compare it with those used by other companies in the industry.

The expected rate of return on plan assets also has a direct effect on pension expense. Remember that the difference between the expected and actual returns is recognized through the corridor approach, which considerably reduces the effect, if any, of the actual return on the income statement. This is illustrated well in the Lufthansa example in Illustration 19-21 above.

An analysis of the past service costs and actuarial gains or losses that remain unrecognized provides useful information. These amounts are not included in pension expense when they are incurred, but they are gradually included in pension expense and the balance sheet accrued pension asset/liability account as they are transferred to benefit expense in future periods.

As a company's actual cash flow related to pensions is often very different from the pension costs that are recognized on the income statement, analysts try to determine what the company's future cash commitments are. The disclosure requirements of the standards help somewhat in this regard. They require that the components of the pension costs that were actually incurred in the period be reported separately from those that are a result of accounting allocation (i.e., amortization) adjustments, and also require companies to report the cash impact of the plans in the current period and an estimate of the cash impact for the next fiscal year.

What Do the Numbers Mean?

The new U.S. accounting standards for post-retirement benefits that were issued in 2006 require companies to record their previously unrecognized past service costs, actuarial gains and losses, and any transition costs in Other Comprehensive Income and to recognize the plans' funded status on the balance sheet. Previously, and as is often still the case under the defer-and-amortize approaches used in private enterprise standards and IFRS, the unamortized amounts were simply not recognized in the accounts. As a result, the balance sheet benefit asset or liability cannot portray the entity's real resource or obligation as measured by the funded status of its plan. Would a similar change make much difference to Canadian companies?[23]

For some companies, the adjustment to the new requirements would be minor. For others, it would be very significant. The following table shows the benefit asset or liability that was reported on a sample of Canadian companies' balance sheets; the actual funded status of the benefit plans at the same date; and the unrecognized, unamortized balances related to past service costs, actuarial gains and losses, and, in some cases, transition costs. To put the numbers in perspective, the total shareholders' equity at the balance sheet date is also given.

Company	Year End	Benefit Asset (A) or Liability (L) Reported on Balance Sheet	Funded Status of Plan at Balance Sheet Date	Unrecognized, Unamortized, Off–Balance Sheet Amounts	Total Shareholders' Equity at Balance Sheet Date
		$	$	$	$
Potash Corp. (Cdn. $ million)	Dec. 31, 2008	105 (A)	218.3 (L)	323.3 (L)	4,588.9
Bombardier Inc. (U.S. $ million)	Jan. 31, 2009	271 (A)	1,543 (L)	1,814 (L)	2,544
BCE Inc. (Cdn. $ million)	Dec. 31, 2008	989 (A)	2,092 (L)	3,081 (L)	17,311
Telus Corporation (Cdn. $ million)	Dec. 31, 2008	1,232 (A)	411 (L)	821 (L)	7,182

Law

The major accomplishment of the FASB changes to the accounting standards was to require recognition of the previously "unrecognized" amounts in the balance sheet liability account, instead of just in the notes. They required that the amounts brought onto the balance sheet be recognized in OCI. As you can tell from the numbers presented in the table, such a change to the Canadian standards would have had a significant effect on many public companies' debt-equity ratio and other provisions that underlie existing debt agreements!

---

[23] Canadian companies following pre-2011 Canadian standards applied the deferral and amortization method as described in this chapter for private enterprises.

Hopefully, the effect on private company financial statements is not as significant. Changing from the defer-and-amortize approach to the immediate recognition approach approved by private enterprise standards would have a similar effect on the benefit liability as the change noted above. The effect would be dampened, however, because the funded status under the immediate recognition method is based on a measure of the ABO developed for funding rather than accounting purposes.

IFRS AND PRIVATE ENTERPRISE GAAP COMPARISON

Comparison of IFRS and Private Enterprise GAAP

Both private enterprise standards and IFRS agree on the objective of accounting for the cost of employee future benefits: to recognize a liability and a cost in the reporting period in which an employee has provided the service that gives rise to the benefits. This is based on the fact that the obligation to provide benefits arises as the employees provide the service.[24] Two different approaches are permitted under private enterprise standards, however, and there are minor differences in how the deferral and amortization approach is applied under ASPE and IFRS. These differences are highlighted in Illustration 19-22.

11 Objective

Identify differences between the IFRS and private enterprise accounting standards for employee future benefits and what changes are expected in the near future.

Looking Ahead

In 2006, the IASB added a comprehensive project on post-employment benefits to its agenda, and began by working on an interim standard that would improve IAS 19 *Employee Benefits* by 2011. The board's tentative decisions on recognition and presentation issues released in its April 2010 exposure draft included the following:

- All changes in the plan assets and post-employment benefit obligation should be recognized in the period in which they take place, including recognition of unvested past service cost in the same period as the plan amendment. The net accrued benefit asset or liability therefore is based on the amount of the funded status.

- Changes in the net accrued benefit asset or liability on the balance sheet should be disaggregated into three components: service cost (both current and prior service); net interest income or expense arising from the time value of money related to the net accrued benefit asset or liability; and remeasurements, made up of actuarial gains and losses on the defined benefit obligation, the return on plan assets not recognized in the net interest component, and the effect of the asset ceiling.

- The service cost and interest components should be reported in net income, with the finance component reported as part of other interest costs. The remeasurement component should be presented separately in OCI.

The 2010 exposure draft changes proposed for IAS 19 therefore no longer provide an option for companies to recognize all changes in defined benefit obligations and assets in net income. The final standard, expected to be published in 2011, is likely to create additional differences between the ASPE requirements and those of IFRS, but these may be taken into account in any subsequent review of *CICA Handbook*, Part II, Section 3461. No decision has been made by the IASB and FASB about the timing of a project to comprehensively study the broader issues related to accounting for employee future benefits.

---

[24] *CICA Handbook*, Part II, Section 3461.007.

	Accounting Standard for Private Enterprises (ASPE/ PE GAAP)—*CICA Handbook,* Part II, Section 3461	IFRS—IAS 19 and IFRIC 14 (See Looking Ahead section for exposure draft proposals for change.)
Scope	The standard does not apply to benefits provided during an employee's active employment.	The standard is broader in scope, covering all employee benefits.
Recognition —defined contribution plans	The standard covers treatment of past service costs and the possibility of an interest cost element.	The standard does not make any reference to past service costs and indicates that amounts are undiscounted as they are current in nature.
Recognition —defined benefit plans with benefits that vest or accumulate	Two approaches are permitted: an immediate recognition method and a deferral and amortization method. The immediate recognition model uses a funding valuation measure of the ABO and recognizes past service costs and actuarial gains and losses immediately in the benefit cost and accrued liability, along with current service cost, interest cost, and the actual return on plan assets. The same standards apply generally to all employee future benefit plans with benefits that vest or accumulate.	Only one approach is permitted: a deferral and amortization method. There is no corresponding approach, although IAS 19 provides options to recognize most changes directly in net income. The same standards apply only to post-employment plans that are subject to considerable measurement uncertainty. Other long-term benefit plans use the same approach except that any past service costs or actuarial gains and losses are recognized in expense immediately.
Measurement —ABO and plan assets	While the ABO and plan assets should be measured as at the date of the annual financial statements, a date up to three months earlier may be used as long as it is consistently used. This exception is not indicated when using the immediate recognition approach.	The plan assets and ABO are required to represent reporting date values.
—discount rate	Use of a current rate can be either the current yield on high-quality debt instruments such as corporate bonds or a current settlement rate.	Use of a current rate can only be the current yield on high-quality debt instruments such as corporate bonds.
—past service costs (deferral and amortization approach)	Past service costs are amortized over the period deemed to benefit from the plan initiation or amendment. This is usually the expected period until the employees are eligible for the plan's full benefits, but may be shorter.	Past service costs, if the plan benefits are vested, are recognized immediately. Costs for employees whose benefits are not vested are amortized over the average period until vesting occurs.
—actuarial gains and losses (deferral and amortization approach)	The minimum amount of actuarial gains and losses that are amortized to expense is dictated by the corridor approach. A larger amount can be recognized, even to the extent of immediate recognition. No amount is permitted to be recognized in OCI.	The minimum amount of actuarial gains and losses that are amortized to expense is dictated by the corridor approach. A larger amount can be recognized, even to the extent of immediate recognition. If immediate recognition is applied, the entity can recognize the amount in OCI instead of net income.
Disclosures	Only basic information is required to be disclosed.	Disclosures required, particularly for post-retirement pensions and health-related defined benefit plans, are extensive.

Illustration 19-22

IFRS versus Private Enterprise Comparison Chart

Summary of Learning Objectives

Glossary

1 Identify and account for a defined contribution benefit plan.

Defined contribution plans are plans that specify how contributions are determined rather than what benefits the individual will receive. They are accounted for on close to a cash basis.

2 Identify and explain what a defined benefit plan is and what the accounting issues are.

Defined benefit plans specify the benefits that the employee is entitled to. Defined benefit plans whose benefits vest or accumulate typically provide for the benefits to be a function of the employee's years of service and, for pensions, compensation level. In general, the employer's obligation for such a plan and the associated cost is accrued as an expense as the employee provides the service. An actuary usually determines the required amounts.

3 Explain what the employer's benefit obligation is, identify alternative measures for this obligation, and prepare a continuity schedule of transactions and events that change its balance.

The employer's benefit obligation is the actuarial present value of the benefits that have been earned by employees for services they have rendered up to the balance sheet date. The vested benefit pension obligation is calculated using current salary levels and includes only vested benefits. Another measure of the obligation, the accumulated benefit obligation, bases the calculation of the deferred compensation amount on all years of employee service under the plan, both vested and non-vested, using current salary levels. A third measure, the projected benefit obligation, bases the calculation of the deferred compensation amount on both vested and non-vested service using future salaries. This last measure is used under IFRS and the defer-and-amortize approach under PE GAAP. The funding approach specified by legislation is the measurement of the obligation under PE GAAP's immediate recognition approach. The ABO is increased by the current service cost, the interest cost, plan amendments that usually increase employee entitlements for prior services, and by actuarial losses. It is reduced by the payment of pension benefits and by actuarial gains.

4 Identify transactions and events that change the benefit plan assets, and calculate the balance of the assets.

Plan assets are increased by company and employee contributions and the actual return that is earned on fund assets (that is, the expected return plus the asset experience gain or minus the asset experience loss), and are reduced by pension benefits paid to retirees.

5 Explain what a benefit plan's funded status is, calculate it, and identify what transactions and events change its amount.

A plan's funded status is the difference between the accrued benefit obligation and the plan assets at a point in time. It tells you the extent to which a company has a net obligation (underfunded) or a surplus (overfunded) relative to the benefits that are promised. All items that change the plan assets and ABO with the exception of the payments to retirees change the funded status.

6 Identify the components of pension benefit cost, and account for a defined benefit pension plan under the immediate recognition approach.

Pension cost under the immediate recognition approach is a function of: (1) service cost, (2) interest on the liability, (3) actual return on plan assets, (4) past service costs,

KEY TERMS

accrued benefit obligation (ABO) for accounting purposes, 1237

accrued benefit obligation (ABO) for funding purposes, 1237

accumulated benefit obligation, 1236

actual return, 1241

actuarial assumptions, 1236

actuarial gains and losses, 1239

actuaries, 1235

asset ceiling test, 1259

asset experience gain or loss, 1241

attribution period, 1239

benefit cost, 1232

contributory plans, 1234

corridor approach, 1251

deferral and amortization approach, 1249

defined benefit (DB) plan, 1233

defined benefit obligation, 1236

defined contribution (DC) plan, 1232

EARSL, 1252

expected average remaining service life, 1252

expected return, 1241

experience gain or loss, 1239

funded, 1234

funded status, 1242

funded status asset, 1242

funded status liability, 1242

immediate recognition approach, 1243

liability experience gain or loss, 1240

market-related value of plan assets, 1241

and (5) net actuarial gains or losses. All are immediately included in current expense in their entirety. The pension obligation amount is determined under a funding basis measure.

7   Identify the components of pension benefit cost, and account for a defined benefit pension plan under the deferral and amortization approach under IFRS and private enterprise standards.

Pension cost under the deferral and amortization approach is a function of: (1) service cost, (2) interest on the liability, (3) expected return on plan assets, (4) past service costs, and (5) net actuarial gain or loss. Under PE GAAP and IFRS, items (1) to (3) are included in current expense entirely, while items (4) and (5) are usually recognized through a process of amortization. The unamortized balances of items (4) and (5) are reported in the notes to the financial statements.

8   Determine the benefit plan accounts reported in the financial statements and explain their relationship to the funded status of the plan.

An accrued benefit liability or asset is reported in the balance sheet. Under the immediate recognition approach, this is generally the same as the funded status of the plan. Under the defer-and-amortize approach, the balance is equal to the funded status adjusted for any unamortized past service costs and unamortized actuarial gains and losses. The benefit expense is reported in the income statement, although no guidance is provided on whether it is in total or whether the components can be reported with other similar items.

9   Account for defined benefit plans with benefits that vest or accumulate other than pension plans.

Under PE GAAP, any defined benefit plans with benefits that vest or accumulate are accounted for in the same way as DB pension plans. Under IFRS, because of the reduced uncertainty of the accounting measures, plans other than pensions and health-care-related post-employment plans are accounted for on a different basis. The actuarial gains/losses and past service costs are recognized in expense as they are incurred.

10   Identify the types of information required to be presented and disclosed for defined benefit plans, prepare basic schedules, and be able to read and understand such disclosures.

PE GAAP requires a description of the plans, major changes made in the plans, dates of the actuarial valuations, the fair value of the plan assets, the ABO, and the funded status and how this relates to the balance sheet account. IFRS requires substantial information such as reconciliations, amounts included in net income, underlying assumptions and sensitivity analysis, and other information related to help determine cash flows.

11   Identify differences between the IFRS and private enterprise accounting standards for employee future benefits and what changes are expected in the near future.

IAS 19 is broader based and covers more employee benefits than does *CICA Handbook*, Part II, Section 3461. PE standards permit a choice of the immediate recognition method or the deferral and amortization approach, whereas IFRS permits only the latter method, but with options within it. Within the defer-and-amortize approach, IFRS amortizes past service costs on a different basis and allows actuarial gains and losses to be recognized immediately in expense or OCI. Changes to IAS 19 are expected to recognize all changes in the funded status on the balance sheet with those caused by the time value of money (reported with interest costs) and service costs recognized in net income, and remeasurement changes reported in OCI.

Appendix 19A

EXAMPLE OF A ONE-PERSON PLAN

12 Objective
Explain and apply basic calculations to determine current service cost, the accrued benefit obligation, and past service cost for a one-person defined benefit pension plan.

The following simplified example is provided to help you better visualize and understand some of the new concepts introduced in this chapter. It uses an actuarial valuation for accounting purposes.

Assume that Lee Sung, age 30, begins employment with HTSM Corp. on January 1, 2010, at a starting salary of $37,500. It is expected that Lee will work for HTSM Corp. for 35 years, retiring on December 31, 2044, when Lee is 65 years old. Taking into account estimated compensation increases of approximately 4% per year, Lee's salary at retirement is expected to be $150,000. Further assume that mortality tables indicate the life expectancy of someone age 65 in 2044 is 12 years.

The timeline in Illustration 19A-1 provides a snapshot of much of this information.

Illustration 19A-1
Timeline

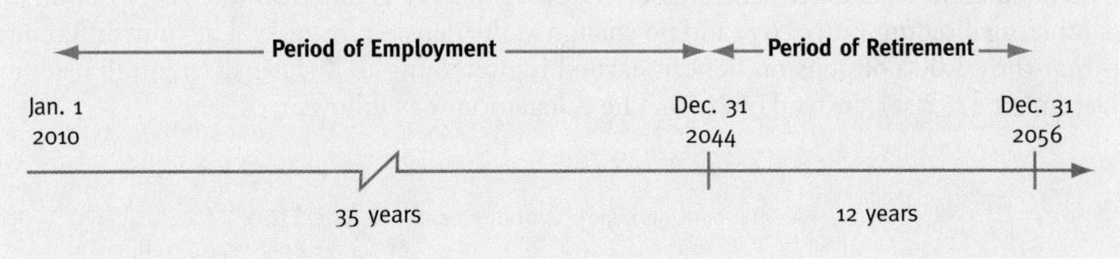

HTSM Corp. sponsors a defined benefit pension plan for its employees with the following **pension benefit formula**:

Annual pension benefit on retirement = 2% of salary at retirement for each year of service, or
= 2% × final salary × years of service

In order to measure 2010 pension costs, dollars paid in the future must be discounted to their present values. Assume a **discount rate of 6%**, which is the current yield on high-quality debt instruments.

Current Service Cost

Year 2010

How much pension does Lee Sung earn for the one year of service in 2010? Applying the pension formula **using projected salaries**:

Annual pension benefit on retirement = 2% × $150,000 × 1 year
= $3,000 per year of retirement

Expanded Discussion:
Present Value Concepts

That is, by virtue of working one year, Lee Sung has earned an entitlement to a pension of $3,000 per year for life.

To determine the company's cost (expense) in 2010 related to this benefit, HTSM discounts these future payments to their present value at December 31, 2010. This is a two-step process. **First**, the pension annuity of $3,000 per year for an estimated 12 years is discounted to its present value on December 31, 2044, the employee's retirement date. Because this is still 34 years in the future at December 31, 2010, the **second** step discounts the annuity's present value at the beginning of retirement to its present value at the end of 2010. The calculations are as follows:

PV of $3,000 annuity ($n = 12$, $i = 6\%$) at Dec. 31, 2044	= $3,000 × 8.38384 (Table A-4)
	= $25,151.52
PV of amount of $25,151.52 ($n = 34$, $i = 6\%$) at Dec. 31, 2010	= $25,151.52 × 0.13791 (Table A-2)
	= $3,469

Therefore the current service cost to HTSM of the pension benefit earned by Lee Sung in 2010 is $3,469. This is a primary component of the period's pension expense.

Year 2011

The calculation of HTSM's current service cost for 2011 is identical to 2010, assuming a continuing discount rate of 6% and no change in the pension formula. The only difference is that the $3,000 of pension benefit earned by Lee Sung in 2011 is discounted back to December 31, 2011, instead of 2010. The calculation is as follows:

Annual pension benefit on retirement	= 2% × $150,000 × 1 year
	= $3,000 per year of retirement
PV of $3,000 annuity ($n = 12$, $i = 6\%$) at Dec. 31, 2044	= $3,000 × 8.38384 (Table A-4)
	= $25,151.52
PV of amount of $25,151.52 ($n = 33$, $i = 6\%$) at Dec. 31, 2011	= $25,151.52 × 0.14619 (Table A-2)
	= $3,677

Therefore the current service cost to HTSM of the pension benefit earned by Lee Sung in 2011 is $3,677.

Accrued Benefit Obligation (ABO)

At December 31, 2011

The accrued benefit obligation calculation is similar to the current service cost calculation except that it represents the present value of the pension benefits that have **accumulated for employee services provided to date as determined under the pension benefit formula**. Because 2010 was the first year of employment, we assume that the ABO at December 31, 2010, is $3,469, the same as the current service cost. At December 31, 2011, the ABO is determined as follows:

$$
\begin{aligned}
\text{Pension benefit earned to Dec. 31, 2011} &= 2\% \times \$150{,}000 \times 2 \text{ years} \\
&= \$6{,}000 \text{ per year of retirement} \\
\text{PV of \$6,000 annuity } (n = 12,\ i = 6\%) \text{ at Dec. 31, 2044} &= \$6{,}000 \times 8.38384 \text{ (Table A-4)} \\
&= \$50{,}303.04 \\
\text{PV of amount of \$50,303.04 } (n = 33,\ i = 6\%) \text{ at Dec. 31, 2011} &= \$50{,}303.04 \times 0.14619 \text{ (Table A-2)} \\
&= \$7{,}354
\end{aligned}
$$

The accrued benefit obligation at the end of 2011 is $7,354. Further, we can reconcile the opening ABO at January 1, 2011, with the ending ABO at December 31, 2011:

ABO, January 1, 2011	$3,469
Add interest on the outstanding obligation: $3,469 × 6% × 1 year	208
Add 2011 current service cost	3,677
ABO, December 31, 2011	$7,354

At December 31, 2040

If Lee Sung works for the full 35 years, assuming no change in the $150,000 final salary estimate, pension benefit formula, discount rate, and life expectancy, the ABO on retirement is as follows:

$$
\begin{aligned}
\text{Pension benefit earned to Dec. 31, 2044} &= 2\% \times \$150{,}000 \times 35 \text{ years} \\
&= \$105{,}000 \text{ per year of retirement} \\
\text{PV of \$105,000 annuity } (n = 12,\ i = 6\%) \text{ at Dec. 31, 2044} &= \$105{,}000 \times 8.38384 \text{ (Table A-4)} \\
&= \$880{,}303
\end{aligned}
$$

At December 31, 2044, HTSM has an obligation with a present value of $880,303. If the company had set aside assets (that is, funded the plan) each year in an amount equal to the current service cost and the funds had earned exactly 6%, the fund assets would have accumulated to $880,303 as well. The company needs to have this amount of cash in order to purchase an annuity that will pay Lee Sung an annual pension of $105,000 for life, which under actuarial calculations is estimated to be 12 years.

Past Service Cost

Now assume that Lee Sung had worked for HTSM's subsidiary company for six years prior to working for HTSM. Further assume that, on December 31, 2014, in determining Lee's pension benefits on retirement, HTSM agrees to give Lee credit for the years that he worked for the subsidiary company before 2010. What is the cost—the past service cost—of this to HTSM? We can determine this by calculating the company's ABO before and after the pension amendment:

	Before credit for prior service	After credit for prior service
Pension benefit earned to Dec. 31, 2014:	2% × $150,000 × 5 yrs = $3,000 × 5 = $15,000 per year	2% × $150,000 × 11 yrs = $3,000 × 11 = $33,000 per year
PV of pension earned to date at Dec. 31, 2044: (PV factor, annuity: $n = 12$, $i = 6$)	$15,000 × 8.38384 = $125,757.60	$33,000 × 8.38384 = $276,666.72
PV of pension earned to date at Dec. 31, 2014: (PV factor, amount: $n = 30$, $i = 6$)	$125,757.60 × 0.17411 = $21,896	$276,666.72 × 0.17411 = $48,170
ABO at Dec. 31, 2014 **after** prior service recognized		$48,170
ABO at Dec. 31, 2014 **before** prior service recognized		21,896
Past service cost incurred		$26,274

Giving credit for prior years of service is not the only event that creates a past service cost. Another common cause of past service cost is a change in the pension benefit formula. For example, if HTSM had agreed to change the formula to 2½% of final salary per year worked, this would have a significant effect on the ABO amount as soon as the formula was changed. A one-half-percentage-point increase on a base rate of 2% is a 25% increase!

Summary of Learning Objective for Appendix 19A

12 Explain and apply basic calculations to determine current service cost, the accrued benefit obligation, and past service cost for a one-person defined benefit pension plan.

The current service cost is a calculation of the present value of the benefits earned by employees that is attributable to the current period. The accrued benefit obligation is the present value of the accumulated benefits earned to a point in time, according to the pension formula and using projected salaries. Past service cost is the present value of the additional benefits granted to employees in the case of a plan amendment.

Brief Exercises

Note: All assignment material with an asterisk (*) relates to the appendix to the chapter.

BE19-1 Ditek Corp. provides a defined contribution pension plan for its employees. Under the plan, the company is **(LO 1)** required to contribute 3% of employees' gross pay to a fund trustee each year. Ditek's total payroll for 2011 was $2,732,864 and the company made all required payments within the year. Prepare a summary journal entry to record Ditek's pension expense for the year.

BE19-2 Unsure Corp. has recently decided to implement a pension plan for its employees; however, it is unsure if it **(LO 1, 2)** would like to structure the pension as a defined contribution plan or a defined benefit plan. As requested by management, prepare a short memo outlining the nature of both plans, along with the accounting treatment of each plan.

BE19-3 Cotter Corp. reports the following information (in hundreds of thousands of dollars) to you about its defined **(LO 3)** benefit pension plan for 2011:

Actual return on plan assets	11	Current service cost	21
Benefits paid to retirees	8	Interest cost	9
Contributions from employer	20	Opening balance, accrued benefit obligation (ABO)	92
Cost of plan amendment in year	13	Opening balance, fund assets	100

Provide a continuity schedule for the ABO for the year.

BE19-4 Refer to the information for Cotter Corp. in BE19–3, and provide a continuity schedule for the plan assets for **(LO 4, 5)** the year. Is the plan overfunded or underfunded?

BE19-5 For Castor Corporation, year-end plan assets were $1,750,000. At the beginning of the year, plan assets were **(LO 4)** $1,350,000. During the year, contributions to the pension fund were $170,000, while benefits paid were $140,000. Calculate Castor's actual return on plan assets.

BE19-6 Potter Corporation is a private enterprise and has elected to use the immediate recognition approach to **(LO 6)** account for its defined benefit pension plan. The following information (in hundreds of thousands of dollars) is available for Potter Corporation for 2011:

Actual return on plan assets	9	Current service cost	19
Benefits paid to retirees	10	Interest cost	11
Contributions from employer	20	Opening balance, ABO, funding basis	100
		Opening balance, fund assets	100

At the end of the year, Potter Corporation revised the terms of its pension plan, which resulted in past service costs of $35.

Determine the pension expense that should be reported on Potter Corporation's December 31, 2011 income statement.

BE19-7 Duster Corporation is a private enterprise and has a defined benefit pension plan that is accounted for under **(LO 6)** the immediate recognition approach. The following information is available for Duster Corporation for 2011:

Service cost	$58,000
Interest on ABO, funding basis	23,000
Expected return on plan assets	25,000
Actual return on plan assets	27,000

Calculate Duster's 2011 pension expense.

BE19-8 At December 31, 2011, Glover Corporation has the following balances: **(LO 5, 7)**

Accrued benefit obligation	$3,400,000
Plan assets at fair value	2,420,000
Unrecognized past service cost	990,000

Determine the account and its balances that should be reported on Glover Corporation's December 31, 2011 balance sheet if it is using the deferral and amortization approach.

(LO 5, 7) BE19-9   Borke Corporation is a public company that uses deferral and amortization to account for the defined benefit pension plan. The following information is available for Borke Corporation for 2011:

Service cost	$29,000
Interest on ABO	22,000
Expected return on plan assets	20,000
Amortization of unrecognized past service cost	15,200
Amortization of unrecognized net actuarial loss	500

Calculate Borke's 2011 pension expense.

(LO 7) BE19-10   At January 1, 2011, Uddin Corporation had plan assets of $250,000 and an accrued benefit obligation of the same amount based on projected costs. During 2011, the service cost was $27,500, discount rate and expected return for plan assets was 10%, actual return on plan assets was $30,000, contributions were $20,000, and benefits paid were $17,500. Prepare a pension work sheet for Uddin Corporation for 2011 assuming that it is a private enterprise that has elected to apply the deferral and amortization approach under private enterprise GAAP.

(LO 6) BE19-11   Refer to BE19-10. Ignoring any differences in the actuarial valuation basis for the ABO, calculate the pension expense for Uddin Corporation assuming that it elected to apply the immediate recognition approach.

(LO 7) BE19-12   On January 1, 2011, Tuesbury Corporation amended its defined benefit pension plan, resulting in $1,125,000 in past service costs. Tuesbury Corporation expects to receive economic benefits, through increased employee productivity and morale, over the next 15 years, at which point the employees will be eligible for their full pension benefits. Currently, all employees who are affected by the plan amendment are already vested.

Calculate the past service costs included in the pension expense for the December 31, 2011 fiscal year under the deferral and amortization method under both PE GAAP and IFRS.

(LO 7) BE19-13   Hunt Corporation had an accrued benefit obligation of $3.1 million and plan assets of $3.3 million at January 1, 2011. Hunt's unrecognized net actuarial loss was $475,000 at that time. The average remaining service period of Hunt's employees is 7.5 years. Calculate Hunt's minimum amortization of the unrecognized actuarial loss for 2011.

(LO 7) BE19-14   Petey Ltd. has a policy of obtaining an actuarial pension valuation every three years. Based on the individual components of its annual pension expense, Petey Ltd.'s accrued benefit obligation as at December 31, 2011, was $356,700. An actuarial valuation revealed that the accrued benefit obligation is actually $388,000. The difference is mostly the result of revised estimates given the recent stock market troubles. Discuss the options available under IFRS to account for the actuarial loss.

(LO 9) BE19-15   Legacy Corporation has the following information available concerning its post-retirement benefit plan for 2011:

Service cost	$80,000
Interest cost	65,500
Expected return on plan assets	48,000

Calculate Legacy's 2011 post-retirement expense.

(LO 9) BE19-16   For 2011, Benjamin Inc. calculated its annual post-retirement expense as $481,800. Benjamin's contribution to the plan during 2011 was $320,000 and amortization of its transition cost was $44,600. Prepare Benjamin's 2011 entry to record post-retirement expense and the entry to record the disbursement for the contribution into the plan.

(LO 12) *BE19-17   Saver Corporation amended its defined benefit pension plan at the beginning of its 2011 fiscal year, resulting in past service costs of $775,000. The vesting period for Saver Corporation is seven years. The plan amendment is attributable to the following employees:

Employees with more than seven years' service as at Jan. 1, 2011	$475,000
Employees with less than seven years' service as at Jan. 1, 2011	$300,000

The average period until vesting for the employees with less than seven years' experience is 3.5 years. Calculate the past service cost that will be included in the fiscal 2011 pension expense.

Exercises

E19-1 **(Defined Contribution Plan)** Jabara Limited provides a defined contribution pension plan for its employees. **(LO 1)** The plan requires the company to deduct 5% of each employee's gross pay for each payroll period as the employee contribution. The company then matches this amount by an equal contribution. Both amounts are remitted to the pension trustee within 10 days of the end of each month for the previous month's payrolls. At November 30, 2011, Jabara reported $26,300 of combined withheld and matched contributions owing to the trustee. During December, Jabara reported gross salaries and wages of $276,100.

Instructions

(a) Prepare the entry to record the December payment to the plan trustee.

(b) What amount of pension expense will the company report for December 2011?

(c) Determine the appropriate pension account and its balance to be reported on the December 31, 2011 balance sheet.

E19-2 **(Defined Contribution Plan)** Ad Venture Ltd. provides a defined contribution pension plan for its employees. **(LO 1)** Currently, the company has 40 full-time and 55 part-time employees. The pension plan requires the company to make an annual contribution of $2,000 per full-time employee, and $1,000 per part-time employee, regardless of their annual salary. In addition, employees can match the employer's contribution in any given year.

At the beginning of the year, 10 full-time and 15 part-time employees elected to contribute to their pension plan by matching the company's contribution. An equal amount of funds was withheld from the employee's cheque in order to fund their pension contribution. Both the employee's and employer's contributions are sent to the plan trustee at year end.

Instructions

(a) What amount of pension expense will the company report?

(b) Prepare a summary journal entry to record Ad Venture Ltd.'s payment to the plan trustee.

E19-3 **(Deferral and Amortization Approach; Immediate Recognition Approach; Changes in Pension Accounts)** **(LO 3, 4)**

Instructions

Complete the following tables by indicating whether the following events increase (I), decrease (D), or have no effect (NE) on the employer's accrued benefit obligation, pension plan assets, the plan's funded status, and the pension expense.

(a) Assume that the company uses the deferral and amortization approach:

	Accrued Benefit Obligation	Pension Plan Assets	Funded Status	Pension Expense
Current service cost				
Actual return on plan assets				
Expected return on plan assets				
Past service costs on date of plan revision (inception)				
Amortization of past service costs				
Actuarial gain/loss				
Amortization of actuarial gain/loss				
Employer contributions				
Benefits paid to retirees				
An increase in the average life expectancy of employees				

(b) Assume that the company uses the immediate recognition approach:

	Accrued Benefit Obligation	Pension Plan Assets	Funded Status	Pension Expense
Current service cost				
Actual return on plan assets				
Expected return on plan assets				
Past service costs on date of plan revision (inception)				
Actuarial gain/loss				
Employer contributions				
Benefits paid to retirees				
An increase in the average life expectancy of employees				

(LO 4)   E19-4   (Calculation of Actual Return) Queensland Importers provides the following pension plan information:

Fair value of pension plan assets, Jan. 1, 2011	$1,418,750
Fair value of pension plan assets, Dec. 31, 2011	1,596,875
Contributions to the plan in 2011	212,500
Benefits paid retirees in 2011	218,750

Instructions

Calculate the actual return on the plan assets for 2011.

(LO 6)   E19-5   (Pension Expense; Immediate Recognition Approach) The following information is in regards to Saverio Corp.'s defined benefit pension, which is accounted for with the immediate recognition approach.

Accrued benefit obligation, funding basis, 1/1/11 (before amendment)	$176,000
Plan assets, 1/1/11	155,000
Discount rate	10%
Annual pension service cost	13,000
Actual return on plan assets	5%
Expected return on plan assets	9%

On January 1, 2011, the company amended its pension plan, which resulted in additional prior service benefits being granted to current employees. The present value of the prior service benefits is $34,000, and the employees are expected to provide future benefits over the next seven years as a result of the pension change.

Instructions

Calculate the pension expense for 2011.

(LO 5, 6, 7)   E19-6   (ABO and Fund Asset Continuity Schedules; Immediate Recognition Approach) The following defined benefit pension data of Datek Corp. apply to the year 2011:

Accrued benefit obligation, funding basis, 1/1/11 (before amendment)	$280,000
Plan assets, 1/1/11	273,100
Accrued pension liability, 1/1/11	6,900
On January 1, 2011, Datek Corp., through plan amendment, grants prior service benefits having a present value of	50,000
Discount rate, and expected return	9%
Annual pension service cost	29,000
Contributions (funding)	27,500
Actual return on plan assets	26,140
Benefits paid to retirees	20,000

The company uses the immediate recognition approach under PE GAAP.

Instructions

(a) Prepare a continuity schedule for the ABO for 2011.

(b) Prepare a continuity schedule for the plan assets for 2011.

(c) Calculate pension expense for 2011 and prepare the entry to record the expense.

(d) Identify the plan's funded status as the asset or liability reported on the December 31, 2011 balance sheet.

(e) Assume that Datek Corp. uses the deferral and amortization method to account for its pension, and that the funding basis valuation and the accounting basis valuation for the ABO are the same at January 1, 2011. Calculate the pension expense for 2011 assuming that the prior service benefits will be amortized over five years.

(f) Reconcile the difference between the pension expense as calculated with the immediate recognition approach versus the deferral and amortization approach.

E19-7 **(Pension Expense)** The following facts apply to the pension plan of Yorke Inc. for the year 2011:   **(LO 7, 10)**

Plan assets, Jan. 1, 2011	$490,000
Accrued benefit obligation, funding basis, Jan. 1, 2011	389,000
Accrued benefit obligation, accounting basis, Jan. 1, 2011	490,000
Interest and expected earnings rate	8.5%
Annual pension service cost	40,000
Contributions (funding)	30,000
Actual return on plan assets	49,700
Benefits paid to retirees	33,400

Instructions

(a) Calculate pension expense for the year 2011, and provide the entries to recognize the pension expense and funding for the year assuming that the deferral and amortization approach is adopted.

(b) Discuss what adjustments would need to be made to your calculation in part (a) if the immediate recognition approach were adopted instead. Provide calculations wherever possible.

E19-8 **(Average Remaining Service Life and Amortization)** Toroton Ltd. has six employees participating in its   **(LO 7)** defined benefit pension plan. The pension plan vests after six years of employment. The current years of service and expected years of future service for these employees at the beginning of 2011 are as follows:

Employee	Current Years of Service	Expected Future Years of Service
Brandon	2	3
Chiara	4	5
Mikayla	5	6
Angela	6	5
Paolo	6	4
Erminia	7	7

On January 1, 2011, the company amended its pension plan, resulting in past service cost of $340,000, of which $200,000 is attributable to employees whose benefits have vested.

Instructions

(a) Calculate the amount of past service cost amortization for the years 2011 through 2016 assuming the company accounts for past service costs with the deferral and amortization method under PE GAAP.

(b) Calculate the amount of past service cost amortization for the years 2011 through 2016 assuming the company accounts for past service costs with the deferral and amortization method under IFRS.

E19-9 **(Application of the Corridor Approach)** Bunker Corp. has the following beginning-of-year present values for   **(LO 7)** its accrued benefit obligation, and fair values for its pension plan assets:

	Accrued Benefit Obligation	Plan Assets
2009	$3,500,000	$ 3,325,000
2010	4,200,000	4,375,000
2011	5,075,000	4,550,000
2012	6,300,000	35,250,000

The average remaining service life per employee in 2009 and 2010 is 10 years, and in 2011 and 2012 is 12 years. The net actuarial gain or loss that occurred during each year is as follows: 2009, $490,000 loss; 2010, $157,500 loss; 2011, $17,500 loss; and 2012, $43,740 gain. There was no opening balance in the accumulated net actuarial gain/loss account on January 1, 2009.

Instructions

Using the corridor approach, calculate the minimum amount of net actuarial gain or loss that should be amortized and charged to pension expense in each of the four years.

(LO 7) E19-10 **(Actuarial Gains and Losses)** The actuary for the pension plan of Brush Inc. calculated the following net actuarial gains and losses:

Net Gain or Loss	
Incurred during the Year	(Gain) or Loss
2010	$ 480,000
2011	300,000
2012	(210,000)
2013	(290,000)

Other information about the company's pension obligation and plan assets is as follows:

As of January 1	Accrued Obligation	Benefit Plan Assets
2010	$4,000,000	$2,400,000
2011	4,520,000	2,200,000
2012	4,980,000	2,600,000
2013	4,250,000	3,040,000

Brush Inc. has a stable labour force of 400 employees who are expected to receive benefits under the plan. Their expected average remaining service life is 12 years. The beginning balance of unrecognized net actuarial gain/loss is zero on January 1, 2010. The plan assets' market-related value and fair value are the same for the four-year period.

Instructions

(a) Prepare a schedule that shows the minimum amount of amortization of the unrecognized net actuarial gain or loss for each of the years 2010, 2011, 2012, and 2013. (Round to the nearest dollar.)

(b) What other options are available under the IFRS deferral and amortization approach to account for the actuarial gains or losses?

(c) What other options are available under the PE GAAP deferral and amortization approach to account for the actuarial gains or losses?

(LO 5, 6, 7, 8) E19-11 **(Pension Expense, Journal Entries)** The following information is available for Huntley Corporation's pension plan for the year 2011:

Expected return on plan assets	$ 15,000
Actual return on plan assets	17,000
Benefits paid to retirees	40,000
Contributions (funding)	95,000
Discount rate	10%
Accrued benefit obligation, Jan. 1, 2011	500,000
Service cost	65,000

Huntley uses the deferral and amortization approach under IFRS to account for its defined benefit plan.

Instructions

(a) Calculate pension expense for the year 2011, and provide the entries to recognize the pension expense and funding for the year, assuming that Huntley accounts for its pension under the deferral and amortization approach.

(b) Calculate pension expense for the year 2011, and provide the entries to recognize the pension expense and funding for the year, assuming that Huntley accounts for its pension with the immediate recognition approach. Assume that the ABO provided at January 1, 2011, for accounting and funding purposes is the same.

(LO 5, 6, 7, 8) E19-12 **(Pension Expense, Journal Entries)** The following information is available for Argust Corporation's pension plan for the 2011 fiscal year:

Accrued benefit obligation, 1/1/11, accounting basis	$315,000
Accrued benefit obligation, 1/1/11, funding basis	255,000
Fair value of plan assets, 1/1/11	297,000
Service cost	63,000
Discount rate	10%
Expected return on plan assets	7%
Actual return on plan assets	8%
Contributions (funding)	79,200
Benefits paid to retirees	43,200

On January 1, 2011, Argust Corp. amended its pension plan, resulting in past service costs with a present value of $140,400. The amendment of the pension plan is expected to provide future benefits for five years.

Instructions

(a) Identify the plan's funded status and the asset or liability reported on the December 31, 2011 balance sheet assuming that Argust Corp. accounts for its pension using the deferral and amortization approach.

(b) Calculate pension expense for 2011 assuming that Argust Corp. accounts for its pension with the deferral and amortization approach.

(c) Identify the plan's funded status and the asset or liability reported on the December 31, 2011 balance sheet assuming that Argust Corp. accounts for its pension with the immediate recognition approach.

(d) Calculate pension expense for 2011, assuming that Argust Corp. accounts for its pension with the immediate recognition approach.

E19-13 (Post-Retirement Benefit Expense Calculation and Entries) Opsco Corp. provides the following informa- **(LO 9)** tion about its non-pension, post-retirement benefit plan for the year 2011:

Service cost	$ 202,500
Past service cost amortization	6,750
Contribution to the plan	47,250
Actual and expected return on plan assets	141,750
Benefits paid	90,000
Plan assets at Jan. 1, 2011	1,597,500
Post-retirement benefit obligation at Jan. 1, 2011	1,822,500
Unrecognized past service cost balance at Jan. 1, 2011	45,000
Amortization of net transition liability	20,250
Unrecognized net transition liability at Jan. 1, 2011	180,000
Discount rate	9%

Instructions

Calculate the post-retirement benefit expense for 2011, and prepare all required journal entries related to the post-retirement benefit plan that were made by Opsco in 2011.

E19-14 (Post-Retirement Benefit Work Sheet) Refer to the information in E19–13. **(LO 9)**

Instructions

(a) Complete a post-retirement work sheet for 2011.

(b) Prepare all required journal entries related to the plan made by Opsco in 2011.

E19-15 (Post-Retirement Benefit Reconciliation Schedule) The following is partial information related to Stanley **(LO 9)** Ltd.'s non-pension, post-retirement benefit plan at December 31, 2011:

Accrued post-retirement benefit obligation, accounting basis	$190,000
Accrued post-retirement benefit obligation, funding basis	160,000
Plan assets (at fair value)	130,000
Past service cost arising in current year	12,000
Transitional liability arising in current year	20,000

Amortization expenses of $1,000 and $3,000 were incurred in the year related to the past service costs and transitional liability, respectively.

Instructions

(a) Prepare a schedule reconciling the funded status with the asset/liability reported on the balance sheet at December 31, 2011, assuming that Stanley Ltd. applies the deferral and amortization approach.

(b) Prepare a schedule reconciling the funded status with the asset/liability reported on the balance sheet at December 31, 2011, assuming that Stanley Ltd. applies the immediate recognition approach.

(LO 9)   E19-16   (Post-Retirement Benefit Expense, Funded Status, and Reconciliation) Rosek Inc. provides the following information related to its post-retirement benefits for the year 2011:

Accrued post-retirement benefit obligation at Jan. 1, 2011	$610,000
Plan assets, Jan. 1, 2011	42,000
Unrecognized net transitional loss, Jan. 1, 2011	568,000
Actual and expected return on plan assets, 2011	3,000
Amortization of transition liability, 2011	35,000
Discount rate	10%
Service cost, 2011	57,000
Plan funding during 2011	22,000
Payments from plan on behalf of retirees	6,000
Actuarial loss on accrued benefit obligation, 2011 (end of year)	88,000

The only unrecognized cost related to this plan at January 1, 2011, was the net transition loss. Rosek Corp. applies the deferral and amortization approach.

Instructions

(a) Calculate the post-retirement benefit expense for 2011.

(b) Determine the December 31, 2011 balance of the fund assets, the accrued obligation, and the funded status.

(c) Determine the balance of the accrued post-retirement benefit asset/liability account on the December 31, 2011 balance sheet.

(d) Reconcile the funded status with the amount reported on the balance sheet at December 31, 2011.

(LO 10)   E19-17   (Pension Calculations and Disclosures) Mila Enterprises Ltd. provides the following information about its defined benefit pension plan:

Balances or Values at December 31, 2011

Accrued benefit obligation, accounting purposes	$2,737,000
Accrued benefit obligation, funding purposes	1,980,000
Vested benefit obligation	1,645,852
Fair value of plan assets	2,278,329
Unrecognized past service cost	205,000
Unrecognized net actuarial loss (1/1/11 balance, –0–)	45,680
Accrued pension liability	207,991
Other pension plan data:	
Service cost for 2011	94,000
Past service cost amortization for 2011	45,000
Actual return on plan assets in 2011	130,000
Expected return on plan assets in 2011	175,680
Interest on Jan. 1, 2011 accrued benefit obligation	253,000
Funding of plan in 2011	92,329
Benefits paid	140,000

Instructions

(a) Prepare the required disclosures for Mila's financial statements for the year ended December 31, 2011, assuming the company is not a public company and does not have broad public accountability.

(b) Prepare the required disclosures that would be required if Mila's common shares were traded on the Toronto Stock Exchange.

Digging Deeper

(c) Calculate the January 1, 2011 balances for the pension-related accounts.

E19-18 **(Continuity Schedules and Calculation of Pension Expense; Deferral and Amortization Approach)** (LO 3, 4, 7, 10)
Rebek Corporation provides the following information about its defined benefit pension plan for the year 2011:

Service cost	$ 225,000
Contribution to the plan	262,500
Past service cost amortization	25,000
Actual and expected return on plan assets	160,000
Benefits paid	100,000
Accrued pension liability at Jan. 1, 2011	25,000
Plan assets at Jan. 1, 2011	1,600,000
Accrued benefit obligation at Jan. 1, 2011	2,000,000
Unrecognized past service cost balance at Jan. 1, 2011	375,000
Settlement rate	10%

Rebek uses the deferral and amortization approach to account for its defined benefit plan.

Instructions

(a) Prepare a continuity schedule for 2011 for the accrued benefit obligation.

(b) Prepare a continuity schedule for 2011 for the plan assets.

(c) Calculate pension expense for the year 2011.

(d) Prepare all pension journal entries recorded by Rebek in 2011.

(e) What pension amount will appear on Rebek's balance sheet at December 31, 2011?

E19-19 **(Preparation of Pension Work Sheet)** Refer to the information in E19–18. (LO 3, 4, 7)

Instructions

(a) Prepare a pension work sheet: insert the January 1, 2011 balances and show the December 31, 2011 balances.

(b) Prepare all journal entries.

E19-20 **(Pension Expense, Journal Entries, Disclosure)** Griseta Limited sponsors a defined benefit pension plan for (LO 5, 7, 10) its employees, which it accounts for using the deferral and amortization approach under PE GAAP. The following data relate to the operation of the plan for the year 2011:

1. The actuarial present value of future benefits earned by employees for services rendered in 2011 amounted to $56,000.

2. The company's funding policy requires a contribution to the pension trustee of $145,000 for 2011.

3. As of January 1, 2011, the company had an accrued benefit obligation of $1 million and an unrecognized past service cost of $400,000. The fair value of pension plan assets amounted to $600,000 at the beginning of the year. The actual and expected return on plan assets was $54,000. The discount rate was 9%.

4. Amortization of past service costs was $40,000 in 2011.

5. No benefits were paid in 2011.

Instructions

(a) Determine the pension expense that should be recognized by the company in 2011.

(b) Prepare the journal entries to record pension expense and the employer's payment to the pension trustee in 2011.

(c) Determine the plan's funded status and reconcile this to the accrued pension asset/liability on the December 31, 2011 balance sheet.

(d) Assuming Griseta is not a public company and does not have broad public accountability, prepare the required disclosures for the 2011 financial statements.

(e) Calculate the January 1, 2011 balance in accrued pension asset/liability.

E19-21 **(Calculation of Actual Return, Gains and Losses, Corridor Test, Past Service Cost, Pension Expense,** (LO 4, 7, 10)
and Reconciliation) Berstler Limited sponsors a defined benefit pension plan, which it accounts for using the deferral and amortization approach under PE GAAP. The corporation's actuary provides the following information about the plan:

	Jan. 1, 2011	Dec. 31, 2011
Vested benefit obligation	$1,200	$1,520
Accumulated and accrued benefit obligation, funding basis	1,520	2,184
Accrued benefit obligation, accounting basis	2,240	2,916
Plan assets (fair value)	1,360	2,096
Discount rate and expected rate of return	10%	10%
Accrued pension asset/liability	0	?
Unrecognized past service cost	880	?
Service cost for the year 2011		320
Contributions (funding in 2011)		640
Benefits paid in 2011		160

The average remaining service life and period to full eligibility is 20 years.

Instructions

(a) Calculate the actual return on the plan assets in 2011.

(b) Calculate the amount of the unrecognized net actuarial gain or loss as of December 31, 2011 (assume the January 1, 2011 balance was zero).

(c) Calculate the amount of actuarial gain or loss amortization for 2011 using the corridor approach. How will 2012's expense be affected, if at all?

(d) Calculate the amount of past service cost amortization for 2011.

(e) Calculate the pension expense for 2011.

(f) Prepare a schedule reconciling the plan's funded status with the amount reported on the December 31, 2011 balance sheet.

(LO 4, 7, 10)   E19-22   **(Preparation of Pension Work Sheet)** Refer to the information in E19–21 about Berstler Limited's defined benefit pension plan.

Instructions

(a) Prepare a 2011 pension work sheet with supplementary schedules of calculations.

(b) Prepare the journal entries at December 31, 2011, to record pension expense and the funding contributions.

(c) Prepare a schedule reconciling the plan's funded status with the pension amounts reported on the balance sheet.

(LO 12)   *E19-23   **(Calculation of Current Service Cost and ABO)** Josit Ltd. initiated a one-person pension plan in January 2005 that promises the employee a pension on retirement according to the following formula: pension benefit = 2.5% of final salary per year of service after the plan initiation. The employee began employment with Josit early in 2002 at age 33, and expects to retire at the end of 2028, the year in which he turns 60. His life expectancy at that time is 21 years.

Assume that this employee earned an annual salary of $40,000 when he joined Josit, that his salary was expected to increase at a rate of 4% per year, and that this remains a reasonable assumption to date. Josit considers a discount rate of 6% to be appropriate.

Instructions

(a) What is the employee's expected final salary?

(b) What amount of current service cost should Josit recognize in 2010 relative to this plan?

(c) What is the amount of the accrued benefit obligation at December 31, 2010?

Problems

P19-1   RWL Limited provides a long-term disability program for its employees through an insurance company. For an annual premium of $18,000, the insurance company is responsible for providing salary continuation to disabled employees on a long-term basis after a three-month waiting period. During the waiting period, RWL continues to pay the employee at full salary. The employees contribute to the cost of this plan through regular payroll deductions that amount to $6,000 for the year. In late October 2011, Tony Hurst, a department manager earning $5,400 per month, was injured and was not expected to be able to return to work for at least one year.

Instructions

Prepare all entries made by RWL in 2011 in connection with the benefit plan, as well as any entries required in 2012.

P19-2 Halifax University recently signed a contract with the bargaining unit that represents full-time professors. The contract agreement starts on April 1, 2011, the start of the university's fiscal year.

The following excerpt outlines the portion of the signed agreement that relates to sabbaticals: "*Professors may apply for a one-year sabbatical leave after seven continuous years of employment, and must outline how their sabbatical plans will benefit the university.*"

After completing the required amount of time, any professor may apply for the leave. The contract notes particular types of activities that the sabbatical is intended to promote, including formal research, continued professional development, and independent study and research. Individual professors are left to make their own choices for whichever of these activities to pursue while on sabbatical leave. As part of their agreement, they must continue to work for Halifax University one year after their sabbatical, or reimburse the university for funds they receive while on leave. The agreement states that professors receive 80% of their salary while on sabbatical leave. Professors may delay, or be asked to delay, their application for sabbatical, in which case they will receive 85% of their salary while on leave.

The issue of sabbatical had long been a point of contention with faculty at Halifax University, which is an independent institution, and they fought vehemently for the right to this paid leave that had not previously been in their collective agreement. The university is phasing in the unfunded sabbatical plan gradually, which means that the first professors will be eligible to apply for their sabbatical in seven years.

The controller has put together the following numbers of professors in each salary group:

Professors with salaries averaging $60,000	55
Professors with salaries averaging $70,000	40
Professors with salaries averaging $100,000	10

The union agreement calls for a wage increase of 2% per year in each of the next seven years. This is consistent with past union agreements for this bargaining unit. Five of the professors with salaries averaging $100,000 are scheduled to retire in four years. Halifax University expects to keep a similar composition of salaried professors in the future. Assume a discount rate of 6%. Halifax University applies the deferral and amortization approach for employee future benefits under ASPE.

Instructions

(a) Prepare any entries that are required at the March 31, 2012 fiscal year end assuming sabbaticals will be granted only if the sabbatical activities proposed by the applicants are expected to benefit the university in some way.

(b) Prepare any entries that are required at the March 31, 2012 fiscal year end assuming sabbaticals will be granted automatically with no restrictions on the professors' activities during the year.

(c) Five employees are granted approval to take sabbatical in the first year that they are eligible under the assumption in (b). Prepare the entry that will be required when the professors are paid, assuming that an amount of $367,000 has correctly been accrued for these employees.

(d) The contract allows employees of the bargaining unit to take up to 10 days of paid sick leave per year. Explain the accounting implications under the following assumptions:

    1. The sick leave is allowed to be carried over for up to a one-year period following year end.

    2. Any unused sick time is not eligible to be carried over to the following fiscal period.

Digging
Deeper

P19-3 Dayte Corporation reports the following January 1, 2011 balances for its defined benefit pension plan, which it accounts for using the deferral and amortization approach under IFRS: plan assets, $460,000; accrued benefit obligation, $460,000. Other data relating to three years of operation of the plan are as follows:

	2011	2012	2013
Annual service cost	$36,800	$ 43,700	$ 59,800
Discount rate and expected rate of return	10%	10%	10%
Actual return on plan assets	39,100	50,370	55,200
Funding of current service cost	36,800	43,700	59,800
Funding of past service cost	—	69,000	80,500
Benefits paid	32,200	37,720	48,300
Past service cost (plan amended, 1/1/11)		368,000	
Past service cost attributable to vested employees		193,000	
Change in actuarial assumptions establishes a Dec. 31, 2013 accrued benefit obligation of			1,196,000

It will take an average of seven years until the pension benefits become vested for employees whose benefits are not yet vested.

Instructions

(a) Prepare a continuity schedule of the projected benefit obligation over the three-year period.

(b) Prepare a continuity schedule of the fund assets over the three-year period.

(c) Determine the pension expense for each of 2011, 2012, and 2013.

(d) Prepare the journal entries to reflect the pension plan transactions and events for each year.

(e) Prepare a schedule reconciling the plan's funded status with the pension amounts reported on the balance sheet over the three-year period.

(f) Determine the pension expense for each of 2011, 2012, and 2013 assuming that the company elects to recognize 100% of the actuarial gains and losses as incurred.

P19-4 The following information is available for Mitten Corporation's pension plan. Mitten reports under private enterprise accounting standards.

	2011	2012	2013
Accrued benefit obligation, funded basis	$155,000	?	?
Accrued benefit obligation, accounting basis	175,000	?	?
Fair value of plan assets	165,000	?	?
Service cost	35,000	47,250	52,500
Discount rate and expected return	7%	7%	7%
Actual return on plan assets	8%	6%	7%
Contributions (funding)	44,000	44,000	44,000
Benefits paid to retirees	24,000	26,000	28,000

On January 1, 2011, Mitten Corp. amended its pension plan, resulting in past service costs with a present value of $78,000. The amendment of the pension plan is expected to provide future benefits for three years.

Instructions

(a) Identify the plan's funded status as the asset or liability reported on the December 31, 2011, 2012, and 2013 balance sheets assuming that Mitten Corp. accounts for its pension with the deferral and amortization approach under PE GAAP.

(b) Calculate pension expense for 2011, 2012, and 2013 assuming that Mitten Corp. accounts for its pension with the deferral and amortization approach under PE GAAP.

(c) Identify the plan's funded status as the asset or liability reported on the December 31, 2011, 2012, and 2013 balance sheets assuming that Mitten Corp. accounts for its pension with the immediate recognition approach.

(d) Calculate pension expense for 2011, 2012, and 2013 assuming that Mitten Corp. accounts for its pension with the immediate recognition approach.

(e) Which method results in a better measure of expense over the three-year period?

(f) Which method results in a better measure of the funded status on the balance sheet?

P19-5 You are the controller of a newly established technology firm that is offering a new pension plan to its employees. The plan was established on January 1, 2011, with an initial contribution by the employer equal to the actuarial estimate of the past service costs for the existing group of employees. These employees are expected to continue to work for the firm for 20 years, on average, prior to retirement. This benefit vested in two employees immediately at a cost of $20,000. The remaining $55,000 was for employees with an average of five years remaining until the benefits are vested. The company is considering going public in the next five years, and the president has asked you to keep her aware of the accounting changes in moving from PE GAAP to IFRS. She wants to be sure that the company always chooses the accounting policies that are closest to IFRS so that changes in the future when the company goes public will be minimized. In addition, she is interested in demonstrating a history of profits so that the company can be taken public successfully. The following information is available for you to work with.

	2011	2012	2013
Fair value of plan assets, beginning of year	$75,000	?	?
ABO for funding purposes, beginning of year	70,000	?	?
ABO for accounting purposes, beginning of year	75,000	?	?
Current service cost for year	12,000	$13,000	$12,500
Interest on the liability	8%	8%	8%
Past service costs granted	75,000	–0–	–0–
Expected earnings on plan assets	8%	8%	8%
Actual earnings on plan assets	6,500	10,000	8,000
Employer contributions for the year	12,000	15,000	12,000
Benefits paid to retirees by trustee	–0–	4,000	5,000

Instructions

(a) Without using the pension work sheet, determine the funded status of the plan and the amount reported on the balance sheet at each year end, and the pension expense for each of the three years using the immediate recognition approach under PE GAAP.

(b) Without using the pension work sheet, determine the funded status of the plan and the amount reported on the balance sheet at each year end, and the pension expense for each of the three years using the deferral and amortization approach under IFRS.

(c) Explain the differences between the two approaches and make a recommendation to your employer about which approach should be used.

P19-6   Branfield Corporation sponsors a defined benefit plan for its 100 employees. On January 1, 2011, the company's actuary provided the following information:

Unrecognized past service cost	$ 390,000
Pension plan assets (fair value)	1,040,000
Accrued benefit obligation	1,430,000

The participating employees' expected average remaining service life (EARSL) and average remaining service period to full eligibility is 8.5 years. All employees are expected to receive benefits under the plan. On December 31, 2011, the actuary calculated that the present value of future benefits earned for employee services rendered in the current year amounted to $213,200; the accrued benefit obligation was $1,825,200; the fair value of pension assets was $1,376,600; and the accumulated benefit obligation amounted to $1,729,000. The expected return on plan assets and the discount rate on the accrued benefit obligation were both 10%. The actual return on plan assets is $80,600. The company funded the current service cost as well as $106,600 of the past service costs in the current year. No benefits were paid during the year. The company accounts for its pension plan with the deferral and amortization approach under PE GAAP.

Instructions

Round all answers to the nearest dollar.

(a) Determine the pension expense that the company will recognize in 2011, identifying each component clearly. (Do not prepare a work sheet.)

(b) Calculate the amount of any 2011 increase/decrease in unrecognized actuarial gains or losses, and the amount to be amortized in 2011 and 2012 under the corridor approach.

(c) Prepare the journal entries to record pension expense and the company's funding of the pension plan in 2011.

(d) Prepare a schedule that reconciles the plan's funded status with the accrued pension asset/liability reported on the December 31, 2011 balance sheet.

(e) Assume that the liability and asset losses on the accrued benefit obligation and plan assets arose because of the disposal of a segment of Branfield's business. How should these losses be reported on the company's 2012 financial statements?

Digging Deeper

P19-7   Manon Corporation sponsors a defined benefit pension plan, which it accounts for with the deferral and amortization approach. The following pension plan information is available for 2011 and 2012:

	2011	2012
Plan assets (fair value), Dec. 31	$380,000	$465,000
Accrued benefit obligation, Jan. 1	600,000	700,000
Accrued pension liability, Jan. 1	40,000	?
Unrecognized past service cost, Jan. 1	250,000	240,000
Unrecognized net actuarial loss, Jan. 1	50,000	?
Service cost	60,000	90,000
Actual and expected return on plan assets	24,000	30,000
Amortization of past service cost	10,000	12,000
Funding of current service costs	60,000	90,000
Funding of past service costs	50,000	30,000
Interest/settlement rate	9%	9%

The pension fund paid out benefits in each year. While there was an unrecognized actuarial gain/loss at January 1, 2011, no additional actuarial gains or losses were incurred in the two-year period.

Instructions

(a) Calculate pension expense for 2011 and 2012.

(b) Prepare all journal entries to record the pension expense and the company's pension plan funding for both years.

(c) Assuming that Manon is not a public company and does not have broad public accountability, prepare the required notes to the financial statements at December 31, 2012.

(d) Prepare the complete pension work sheets for Manon for 2011 and 2012.

P19-8   Bouter Corporation Limited (BCL) began operations in 1990 and in 2000 adopted a defined benefit pension plan for its employees. By January 1, 2010, the accrued benefit obligation was $510,000. The Prepaid/Accrued Pension account on the December 31, 2009 balance sheet was reported as a $190,000 liability balance.

On January 2, 2010, BCL agreed to a new union contract that granted retroactive benefits for services that employees had provided in years before the pension plan came into effect. The actuary informed BCL's chief accountant that, using its normal discount rate of 6%, benefits relating to these past services would cost the company $240,000. The expected average remaining service life of the group expected to receive benefits under this plan at this date was 21 years, the same as the group's period to full eligibility.

On January 1, 2010, the fair value of the pension plan assets was $320,000. The actuary estimates that these assets should earn a long-term rate of return of 7%, although, due to a downturn in the market, the actual return reported for the 2010 year was a loss of $9,500. The workforce is made up of a relatively young group of employees, so payments to those who had retired came to only $48,000 during the year, with these payments being made close to year end. The actuary also reported that the current service cost for BCL's employees for 2010 was $107,500. It is the company's policy, on advice from the actuary, to contribute amounts to the pension plan equal to each year's current service cost and the amount of any expense related to past service costs. This payment was made just before BCL's fiscal year end of December 31, 2010.

At the end of 2010, the actuary revised some key estimates, resulting in an actuarial loss of $15,500 related to the accrued obligation. Assume that the ABO amounts under the funding and accounting basis are the same.

Instructions

(a) Calculate the pension expense that should be reported for BCL's year ended December 31, 2010, under both the immediate recognition approach and the deferral and amortization approach under PE GAAP.

(b) Reconcile the difference in pension expense between the immediate recognition approach and the deferral and amortization approach under PE GAAP.

(c) Calculate the amount in the pension account to be reported on the December 31, 2010 balance sheet under both the immediate recognition approach and the deferral and amortization approach under PE GAAP.

(d) How does the method of accounting for the pension plan (immediate recognition versus deferral and amortization under PE GAAP) impact cash flows in light of the company's policy regarding its contributions to the pension plan?

P19-9   Dubel Toothpaste Corporation initiated a defined benefit pension plan for its 50 employees on January 1, 2011. The insurance company that administers the pension plan provides the following information for the years 2011, 2012, and 2013:

	For Year Ended December 31		
	2011	2012	2013
Plan assets (fair value)	$50,000	$ 85,000	$170,000
Accrued benefit obligation	63,900	?	?
Net actuarial (gain) loss re: ABO	8,900	(24,500)	84,500
Net actuarial (gain) loss re: fund assets	?	?	(18,200)
Employer's funding contribution (made at end of year)	50,000	60,000	95,000

There were no balances as of January 1, 2011, when the plan was initiated. The long-term expected return on plan assets was 8% throughout the three-year period. The settlement rate that was used to discount the company's pension obligation was 13% in 2011, 11% in 2012, and 8% in 2013. The service cost component of net periodic pension expense amounted to the following: 2011, $55,000; 2012, $85,000; and 2013, $119,000. The average remaining service life per employee is 10 years. No benefits were paid in 2011, but $30,000 was paid in 2012, and $35,000 in 2013 (all benefits were paid at the end of the year). The company had elected to use the deferral and amortization approach under IFRS.

Instructions

Depending on what your instructor assigns, do either (a), (b), (c), (e), and (f); or (d), (e), and (f). (Round all answers to the nearest dollar.)

(a) Prepare a continuity schedule for the projected benefit obligation over the three-year period.

(b) Prepare a continuity schedule for the plan assets over the three-year period.

(c) Calculate the amount of net periodic pension expense that the company will recognize in each of 2011, 2012, and 2013.

(d) Prepare and complete a pension work sheet for each of 2011, 2012, and 2013.

(e) Determine the funded status at December 31, 2013, and the balance of the accrued pension asset or liability that will be reported on the December 31, 2013 balance sheet. Fully explain why these amounts differ.

(f) Discuss what options are available for Dubel Toothpaste Corporation in regards to accounting for any actuarial gains or losses.

P19-10   Ekedahl Inc. has sponsored a non-contributory defined benefit pension plan for its employees since 1990. Prior to 2011, the funding of this plan exactly equalled cumulative net pension expense. Other relevant information about the pension plan on January 1, 2011, is as follows:

1. The accrued benefit obligation amounted to $1,250,000 and the fair and market-related value of pension plan assets was $750,000.

2. During 2011, the plan was amended and resulted in unrecognized past service cost of $500,000.

3. The company has 200 employees who are expected to receive benefits under the plan. The employees' expected period to full eligibility is 13 years with an EARSL of 16 years.

4. Of the 200 employees, 95 employees' pension benefits have vested, while the remaining 105 employees' pension benefits will vest over the next 10 years. The amount of past service cost attributed to the 95 employees with vested benefits has been determined to be $245,000.

On December 31, 2011, the accrued benefit obligation was $1,187,500. The fair value of the pension plan assets amounted to $975,000 at the end of the year. A 10% discount rate and an 8% expected asset return rate were used in the actuarial present value calculations in the pension plan. The present value of benefits attributed by the pension benefit formula to employee service in 2011 amounted to $50,000. The employer's contribution to the plan assets was $143,750 in 2011. No pension benefits were paid to retirees during this period.

Instructions

Round all answers to the nearest dollar.

(a) Calculate the amount of past service cost that will be included as a component of pension expense in 2011, 2012, and 2013 under:
1. The immediate recognition approach
2. The deferral and amortization approach under accounting standards for private enterprises
3. The deferral and amortization approach under IFRS

(b) Assuming the deferral and amortization approach is applied, determine the amount of any actuarial gains or losses in 2011 and the amount to be amortized to expense in 2011 and 2012.

(c) Calculate pension expense for the year 2011 under:

   1. The immediate recognition approach

   2. The deferral and amortization approach under accounting standards for private enterprises

   3. The deferral and amortization approach under IFRS

(d) Prepare a schedule reconciling the plan's funded status with the pension amounts reported on the December 31, 2011 balance sheet as accounted for with the deferral and amortization method under both PE GAAP and IFRS.

Digging Deeper

(e) Assume that Ekedahl's pension plan is contributory rather than non-contributory. Would any part of your answers above change? What would be the impact on the company's financial statements of a contributory plan?

P19-11   You are the auditor of Beaton and Gunter Inc., the Canadian subsidiary of a multinational engineering company that offers a defined benefit pension plan to its eligible employees. Employees are permitted to join the plan after two years of employment, and benefits vest two years after joining the plan. You have received the following information from the fund trustee for the year ended December 31, 2011:

Discount rate	5%
Expected long-term rate of return on plan assets	6.5%
Rate of compensation increase	3.5%
Accrued Benefit Obligation	
Accrued benefit obligation at Jan. 1, 2011	$11,375,000
Current service cost	425,000
Interest cost	568,750
Benefits paid	756,250
Actuarial loss for the period	631,250
Plan Assets	
Market value of plan assets at Jan. 1, 2011	9,062,500
Actual return on plan assets, net of expenses	1,125,000
Employer contributions	493,750
Employee contributions	81,250
Benefits paid	756,250

Other relevant information:

   1. The accrued pension liability on January 1, 2011, is $1,601,875.

   2. There is an unrecognized past service cost of $1,991,875 on January 1, 2011.

   3. There is an unrecognized net actuarial gain of $1,281,250 on January 1, 2011.

   4. Employee contributions to the plan are withheld as payroll deductions, and are remitted to the pension trustee along with the employer contributions.

   5. The average vesting period for all employees whose pension has not vested is 20 years.

   6. The EARSL is 20 years.

Instructions

(a) Prepare a pension work sheet for the company.

(b) Prepare the employer's journal entries to reflect the accounting for the pension plan for the year ended December 31, 2011.

(c) Prepare a schedule reconciling the plan's funded status with the pension amounts reported on the December 31, 2011 balance sheet.

(d) Assume that interest rates are falling. Explain what effect this is likely to have on the funded status of the plan.

(e) Discuss any options available to Beaton and Gunter Inc. in accounting for the actuarial gains or losses.

P19-12   Donnie Harpin was recently promoted to assistant controller of Glomski Corporation, having previously served the company as a staff accountant. Glomski is a medium-sized company that reports under private enterprise standards.

   One of Harpin's new responsibilities is to prepare the annual pension accrual. Judy Gralapp, the corporate controller, provided Harpin with last year's working papers and information from the actuary's annual report. The pension work sheet for the prior year is as follows:

	General Journal Entries			**Memo Records**		
	Pension Expense	Cash	Accrued Pension Asset/Liability	Accrued Benefit Obligation	Plan Assets	Unrecognized Past Service Cost
June 1, 2010[1]				$(20,000)	$20,000	
Service cost[1]	$1,800			(1,800)		
Interest[2]	1,200			(1,200)		
Actual return[3]	(1,600)				1,600	
Contribution[1]		$(1,000)			1,000	
Benefits paid[1]				900	(900)	
Past service cost[4]				(2,000)		$2,000
Journal entries	$1,400		($1,400)			
		$(1,000)	1,000			
May 31, 2011 balance			$ (400)	($24,100)	$21,700	$2,000

[1]Per actuary's report.

[2]Beginning accrued benefit obligation × discount rate of 6%.

[3]Expected return was $1,600 (beginning plan assets × expected return of 8%).

[4]A plan amendment that granted employees retroactive benefits for work performed in earlier periods took effect on May 31, 2011. The amendment increased the May 31, 2011 accrued benefit obligation by $2,000. No amortization was recorded in the fiscal year ended May 31, 2011.

The actuary's report for the year ended May 31, 2012, indicated no actuarial gains or losses in the fiscal year ended May 31, 2012. Other pertinent information from the report is as follows:

Contribution	$425	Actual return on plan assets	$1,736
Service cost	$3,000	Benefits paid	$500
Discount rate	6%	Average remaining service life	10 years
Expected return	8%		
Average period to full eligibility	8 years		

Instructions

(a) Prepare the pension work sheet for Glomski Corporation for the year ended May 31, 2012.

(b) Prepare the necessary journal entries to reflect the accounting for Glomski Corporation's pension plan for the year ended May 31, 2012.

P19-13 Hass Foods Inc. sponsors a post-retirement medical and dental benefit plan for its employees. The company adopted the provisions of IAS 19 beginning January 1, 2011. Assume that Hass is permitted to account for any transitional balances on a prospective basis, recognizing the transitional costs on a straight-line basis over five years. The following balances relate to this plan on January 1, 2011:

Plan assets	$ 780,000
Accrued post-retirement benefit obligation	3,439,800
Past service costs	–0–

As a result of the plan's operation during 2011, the following additional data were provided by the actuary:

1. The service cost for 2011 was $273,000.

2. The discount rate was 9%.

3. Funding payments in 2011 were $234,000.

4. The expected return on plan assets was $35,100.

5. The actual return on plan assets was $58,500.

6. The benefits paid on behalf of retirees from the plan were $171,600.

7. The average remaining service life to full eligibility was 20 years.

Instructions

(a) Calculate the post-retirement benefit expense for 2011.

(b) Prepare a continuity schedule for the accrued benefit obligation and for the plan assets from the beginning of the year to the end of 2011.

(c) At December 31, 2011, prepare a schedule reconciling the plan's funded status with the post-retirement amount reported on the balance sheet.

(d) Explain in what ways, if any, the accounting requirements for this plan are different from the requirements for a defined benefit pension plan.

*P19-14 Refer to the example of HTSM Corp. in Appendix 19A and assume it is now 2010, two years after the defined pension plan was initiated. In December 2010, HTSM's actuary provided the company with an actuarial revaluation of the plan. The actuary's assumptions included the following changes:

Estimated final salary on retirement	$145,000
Current settlement/discount rate	7%

Instructions

(a) Calculate the accrued benefit obligation (ABO) at December 31, 2010, and the amount of any actuarial gain or loss.

(b) Based on the revised assumptions at the end of the year, determine what percentage increase or decrease there would be in the ABO for:

1. a 1% increase in the discount rate.

2. a 1% decrease in the discount rate.

(c) Determine the effect of the actuarial revaluation on the plan's funded status at December 31, 2010, and on pension expense for 2010 and for 2011.

(d) Based on the revised assumptions, recalculate the past service cost that was incurred by the company in 2012.

Writing Assignments

WA19-1 Shikkiah Corp. (which is a private enterprise) tries to attract the most knowledgeable and creative employees it can find. To help accomplish this, the company offers a special group of technology employees the right to a fully paid sabbatical leave after every five years of continuous service. It is the company's objective that the employees will come back renewed and with fresh ideas, but there are no restrictions on what they do during the sabbatical year.

Shikkiah hired three employees in early 2011 who were entitled to this benefit. Each new hire agreed to a starting salary of $80,000 per year.

Instruction

(a) Explain generally how this employee benefit should be accounted for by Shikkiah Corp. under PE GAAP and IFRS.

(b) Assume that you are the assistant to the company controller. In response to the controller's request, list all the information you need in order to calculate the amounts and prepare the adjusting entry that is required at December 31, 2011, relative to this plan under ASPE and IFRS.

(c) Assume that the employees' activities during the sixth (the sabbatical) year are specified by the company: the employees must work on research and promotion activities that will benefit the company. Would your answer to (a) change? If yes, explain why and how it would be accounted for. If not, explain why not.

WA19-2 Many business organizations have been concerned with providing for employee retirement since the late 1800s. During recent decades, a marked increase in this concern has resulted in the establishment of private pension and other post-retirement benefit plans in most companies of any size.

The substantial growth of these plans, both in the numbers of employees that they cover and in the types and value of retirement benefits, has increased the significance of the cost of these benefit plans in relation to the financial position, results of operations, and cash flows of many companies. In working with the benefit plans, accountants encounter a variety of terms. Each benefit plan component must be dealt with appropriately if generally accepted accounting principles are to be reflected in the financial statements of entities that offer these plans.

Instructions

(a) How does a contributory plan differ from a non-contributory plan?

(b) Differentiate between accounting for the employer and accounting for the benefit plan.

(c) Explain the terms "funded" and "accrued benefit liability or asset" as they relate to the employer and the benefit plan itself.

(d) Distinguish between each of the following sets of terms as they relate to pension plans and their treatment under ASPE and IFRS:

1. Current service cost and past service cost

2. Asset experience gain/loss and liability experience gain/loss

(e) Explain how the accounting for other post-retirement benefit plans with benefits that vest or accumulate differs from the accounting for defined benefit pension plans, if there is any difference.

WA19-3   Currently, two approaches are available for private enterprises: the immediate recognition approach and the deferral and amortization approach.

Instructions

Describe the advantages and disadvantages of the immediate recognition approach and the deferral and amortization approach. Explain any differences in the impact on the earnings and statement of financial position.

WA19-4

Instructions

Research what Canadian companies have been doing in recent years in response to rising post-employment health care costs and the risks that are associated with defined benefit pension plans. Write a short report on your findings.

WA19-5   The IASB is currently working on proposals that would significantly change the reporting standards for post-employment plans.

Instructions

(a) What is proposed with respect to changes in the discount rates used to calculate the present value of the obligations? See, on the IASB website (www.iasb.org), the Exposure Draft Discount Rate for Employee Benefits, August 2009. Why is the IASB considering changes in this?

(b) As noted in the chapter, the IASB is contemplating changes to the accounting for pension plans. Summarize these changes. Why do you think the IASB is contemplating these changes?

WA19-6   A ceiling test is required for companies that have pension plan assets.

Instructions

Explain how the asset ceiling test would be applied and why is it necessary. (See IFRIC 14 for information).

WA19-7

Instructions

Write a brief essay highlighting the difference between IFRS and accounting standards for private enterprises noted in this chapter, discussing the conceptual justification for each.

Cases

Refer to the Case Primer on the Student Website to help you answer these cases.

CA19-1   Pablo Ltd. (PL) reproduces fine works of art as posters. The company was started 10 years ago with used equipment. Demand for the posters increased recently when PL began to glue the posters onto a wood backing and laminate them. The old equipment has become very expensive to maintain and keeps breaking down, disrupting production. Pietro Pablo, the owner, has decided to go to the bank for a loan to buy new equipment. In preliminary talks with the bank, the manager indicated that financial statements are needed from PL for the year ended December 31, 2011.

While the statements have now been drafted, Pietro is not happy with the net income figure, which is lower than he had expected. Pietro calls you, his accounting manager, and asks if the net income has been correctly calculated. He points to the large payroll expense, which has increased over the last year. You note that the main cause of the increase is that pension expense increased for the following two reasons:

1. The employee pension plan was renegotiated at the beginning of the year and a key change was to increase the amount of pension benefits for each employee for each hour worked. The plan is a defined benefit plan and the amendment provided for retroactive application, so that most of the employees, who were older, would benefit from the plan. The increase in the pension obligation arising from this amendment is being amortized to net income over 14 years, beginning with 2011.

2. The actuary has recently prepared a new actuarial valuation of the pension obligation. In doing so, she suggested that the interest rate used for discounting be changed to reflect recent reductions in interest rates. Short-term interest rates have declined but many economists predict that the mid- to long-term rates will remain more stable at the higher rate. The reduction in the interest rate for discounting has resulted in an increase in the pension obligation. The increase is also being amortized to net income over 14 years, beginning in 2011.

Pietro asks you to determine whether there is any flexibility in applying PE GAAP. The company is a private company.

Instructions

Discuss the financial reporting issues.

CA 19-2   In February 2011, Seaton's Limited filed for protection under the Companies' Creditors Arrangement Act due to liquidity problems. The act gives troubled companies time to restructure their debt and to hopefully avoid bankruptcy. As part of the restructuring process, Seaton's approached its employees and pensioners to split the surplus in the pension plan and allow Seaton's to withdraw a portion of the surplus in cash to help lessen the liquidity problems.

In note 9 to the unaudited financial statements, the following was disclosed with respect to the company's pension plan for the year ended December 31, 2011 (in thousands of dollars):

Plan assets at market	$735,501
Plan assets—four-year moving average market basis	600,662
Projected benefit obligations	327,101
Pension surplus	273,561
Unrecognized actuarial experience adjustment	119,181
Pension surplus per financial statements	154,380

The company further notes that, effective January 1, 2011, the interest rate assumption changed from 9% to 8% to reflect more conservative long-term interest rate expectations.

Instructions

Adopt the role of the pensioners as well as the role of company management and discuss the financial reporting issues related to management's desire to split and withdraw from the pension plan surplus. Assume that Seaton's is a private company.

CA19-3   Farquar Inc. is in the process of going public. The company is in the Canadian oil and gas industry but has decided that it would like to list its shares on the London Stock Exchange. Currently, the company follows pre-2011 Canadian PE GAAP.

Farquar has a significant pension plan that is currently underfunded. For the year ended December 31, 2011, the company (under PE GAAP) did not recognize this large deficit as a liability since it related to past service costs. Farquar's controller, Perry Barta, has on his desk the new U.S. accounting standard and the almost identical proposed Canadian PE Exposure Draft on employee future benefits. Under the new U.S. standard, companies will have to recognize such unfunded amounts through Other Comprehensive Income.

Perry also has on his desk some information about the differences between PE GAAP and IFRS.

Instructions

Adopt the role of the controller and discuss the relative strengths and weaknesses of the three differing views of accounting for the unfunded costs. Perry is very concerned about the impact on the company's debt-to-equity ratio and the earnings per share numbers.

Integrated Cases

Real-World Emphasis

IC19-1   Stelco Inc. is a Canadian steel manufacturing company. In 2004, the company filed for bankruptcy protection, citing the following reasons for declining profits and viability problems:

1. Costs have risen dramatically for inputs such as natural gas and electricity and raw materials, such as coal, coke, and scrap.

2. The cost of employee future benefits—pensions and health care—are also increasing due to improved pension benefits negotiated in contracts with unionized employees, increasing health care costs, lower returns on pension plan assets, and the effect of lower interest rates on the discount factors that are used to determine the Corporation's liabilities under the pension and other benefit plans.

3. Global steelmaking overcapacity has created downward pressure on selling prices due to significant and continued import penetration of the Canadian market by steel products offered, in management's opinion, at unfairly low prices over the last several years.

4. The appreciation in the value of the Canadian dollar during 2003 further negatively affected selling prices. Selling prices strengthened in the early part of 2004, due in part to increased demand, particularly in China. However, the Corporation believes that these price increases are not sustainable and therefore are not expected to be sufficient to offset growing cost issues.

5. Several North American steel producers have emerged from court-supervised bankruptcy protection with a cost structure that is more competitive than that of the Corporation. The Corporation cannot compete effectively in this new environment unless it takes steps to reduce its liabilities and lower its overall costs.

6. In addition, the Corporation requires additional funding to complete strategically critical capital projects at its Hamilton and Lake Erie business units. The Corporation is unable to raise additional funds to complete these projects.

The protection afforded by the Companies' Creditors Arrangement Act (CCAA) was challenged by the United Steelworkers of America (USWA). The president of USWA Local 1005 was quoted in the newspapers as saying, "We are not going to allow them to blackmail us by using CCAA as a way to convince us to give up our wages and benefits. It amounts to legalized corruption. In my opinion, the CCAA process is an abuse of power." The USWA challenged the courts as to whether Stelco should be protected by CCAA.

Stelco's assets had a book value of $2.74 billion and liabilities of $2.09 billion in the bankruptcy documents. The following is an excerpt from the 2003 financial statements:

Note 18. Employee Future Benefits (continued)

Accrued benefit obligation and plan assets

Information about the Corporation's defined benefit plans, other than the multiemployer defined benefit plan, in aggregate, is as follows:

(in millions)	2003 Pension benefit plans	2003 Other benefit plans	2002 Pension benefit plans	2002 Other benefit plans
Accrued benefit obligation				
Balance at beginning of year	$ 3,263	$ 1,082	$ 2,748	$ 924
Increase (decrease) in ownership of joint venture	(18)	(8)	11	2
Current service cost	53	15	49	14
Interest cost	200	72	192	62
Benefits paid	(195)	(55)	(181)	(52)
Actuarial losses	244	156	189	135
Plan curtailments	6	(2)	–	–
Plan amendments	1	2	255	(1)
Other	2	2	–	(2)
Balance at end of year	3,556	1,264	3,263	1,082
Plan assets				
Fair value at beginning of year	2,613	9	2,822	9
Increase (decrease) in ownership of joint venture	(13)	–	11	–
Actual return on plan assets	342	1	(76)	(1)
Administrative expenses paid	(8)	–	(6)	–
Employer contributions	62	1	41	1
Benefits paid	(195)	(1)	(181)	–
Other	3	–	2	–
Fair value at end of year	2,804	10	2,613	9

continued on page xx

Funded status – plan surplus (deficit)	(752)	(1,254)	(650)	(1,073)
Unamortized net actuarial loss	773	328	679	186
Unamortized past service costs	253	2	272	–
Accrued benefit asset (liability)	274	(924)	301	(887)
Valuation allowance	–	–	(2)	–
Accrued benefit asset (liability) net of valuation allowance	$ 274	$ (924)	$ 299	$ (887)

The accrued benefit asset (liability) is reflected in the Consolidated Statement of Financial Position as follows:

	2003			2002
(in millions)	Pension benefit plans	Other benefit plans	Pension benefit plans	Other benefit plans
Deferred pension cost	$ 274	$ –	$ 299	$ –
Employee future benefits liability – current	–	(49)	–	(47)
Employee future benefits liability – non-current	–	(875)	–	(840)
Total	$ 274	$ (924)	$ 299	$ (887)

In 2002, when the company was first experiencing the cash flow difficulties that led to the current situation, it issued $90 million of 9.5% convertible unsecured subordinated debentures that were due in 2007. The effective interest rate on the debentures was 16.65% and they were convertible into common shares at the option of the holder. They were also redeemable by the corporation after February 2005 and the company had the option of paying the interest in cash or by issuing shares to a trustee, with the proceeds being used to settle the interest. The principal could also be paid in shares.

Although the CCAA proceedings have triggered defaults under virtually all debt obligations, the CCAA generally protects companies from attempts by creditors to collect the loans.

Instructions

Adopt the role of the company and analyze the financial reporting issues. (Although the company would have been following pre-2011 PE GAAP, use IFRS to analyze the financial reporting issues for purposes of this case).

Real-World Emphasis

IC19-2 **Canadian Utilities Limited** is based in Alberta and is involved in power generation, utilities, logistics, and energy services and technologies. The company was incorporated in 1927 and its shares trade on the TSX. PricewaterhouseCoopers is the current auditor.

According to the notes to the 2009 financial statements, the company accounts for employee future benefits and stock-based compensation as follows:

Employee Future Benefits

The Corporation accrues for its obligations under defined benefit pension and other post employment benefit ("OPEB") plans. Costs of these benefits are determined using the projected benefits method prorated on service and reflects management's best estimates of investment returns, wage and salary increases, age at retirement and expected health care costs.

Pension plan assets at the end of the year are reported at market value. The expected long term rate of return on plan assets is determined at the beginning of the year on the basis of the long bond yield rate at the beginning of the year plus an equity and management premium that reflects the plan asset mix.

Expected return on plan assets for the year is calculated by applying the expected long term rate of return to the market related value of plan assets, which is the average of the market value of plan assets at the end of the preceding three years.

Accrued benefit obligations at the end of the year are determined using a discount rate that reflects market interest rates on high quality corporate bonds that match the timing and amount of expected benefit payments.

Experience gains and losses and the effect of changes in assumptions in excess of 10% of the greater of the accrued benefit obligations or the market value of plan assets, adjustments resulting from plan amendments and the net transitional liability or asset, which arose upon the adoption in 2000 of the current accounting standard, are amortized over the estimated average remaining service life of employees.

Pursuant to an AUC decision effective January 1, 2000, the regulated operations, excluding Alberta Power (2000), are required to expense contributions for other post employment benefit and certain other defined benefit pension plans as paid. The difference between the amounts accrued and paid is deferred in non-current regulatory assets.

Employer contributions to the defined contribution pension plans are expensed as paid.

Stock Based Compensation Plans

The Corporation expenses stock options granted on and after January 1, 2002; no compensation expense is recorded for stock options granted prior to January 1, 2002 as permitted by GAAP. The Corporation determines the fair value of the options on the date of grant using an option pricing model and recognizes the fair value over the vesting period of the options granted as compensation expense and contributed surplus. Contributed surplus is reduced as the options are exercised and the amount initially recorded in contributed surplus is credited to Class A and Class B share capital.

No compensation expense is recognized when share appreciation rights are granted. Prior to vesting, compensation expense arising from an increase or decrease in the market price of the shares over the base value of the rights is accrued equally over the remaining months to the date of vesting. After that date, compensation expense arising from an increase or decrease in the market price of the shares is recognized monthly in earnings.

Instructions

Adopt the role of the auditor and discuss any financial reporting issues. Assume the company is interested in how the move to IFRS will affect it. Even though it will not follow ASPE, it is also interested in how the accounting differs. Therefore, specifically, discuss the differences between ASPE and IFRS for the issues raised.

Research and Financial Analysis

RA19-1 BCE Inc.

Obtain the annual statements for BCE Inc. for the year ended December 31, 2009, from the company's website or SEDAR (www.sedar.com).

Real-World Emphasis

Instructions

Refer to the 2009 financial statements of BCE Inc and answer the following questions.

(a) Determine what the funded status is of the defined benefit plans and what the dollar amount of the over- or underfunding is at December 31, 2009, and December 31, 2008. Has the status improved or deteriorated since the end of the preceding year? What is the major reason for the change in BCE's funded status? What is the status of the plans in the net deficit position and what is the status of the plans in a net surplus position at December 31, 2009?

(b) What is the amount of the pension asset or liability reported on BCE's December 31, 2009 balance sheet? Provide reconciliation to the funded status reported in (a). Comment on this representation.

(c) What was the expected return on the plan assets in 2009? What was the actual return on the plan assets for the year? What amount of actuarial gains and losses, if any, were amortized to pension expense in 2009? What was the total amount of actuarial gains and losses arising during the year? How much has not yet been recognized in the accounts at December 31, 2009? How much was recognized for past service costs during the year? What was the total amount of past service costs arising during the year? How much has not yet been recognized in the accounts at December 27, 2009?

(d) What was the expense that the company reported for its defined benefit plans? Estimate the amount of expense that would have been reported under the immediate recognition approach for December 31, 2009. Comment on any differences.

(e) What type of post-retirement plans does the company have? Are these in a surplus or deficit position? What were the balances reported for these plan obligations? How do these balances compare with the actual deficits or surpluses in the plans and why?

(f) What is the total expense for the defined contribution plans during 2009? 2008?

RA19-2 Canadian National Railway Company

Real-World
Emphasis

Ethics

Below is an excerpt from the note disclosure (excerpts from Note 12) of the Canadian National Railway Company's December 31, 2008 annual report.

(v) Components of net periodic benefit cost (income)

		Pensions		
In millions	*Year ended December 31,*	**2008**	2007	2006
Service cost		$ **136**	$150	$146
Interest cost		**801**	742	713
Curtailment gain		—	—	—
Expected return on plan assets		**(1,004)**	(935)	(903)
Amortization of prior service cost		**19**	19	19
Recognized net actuarial loss (gain)		**—**	53	91
Net periodic benefit cost (income)		$ **(48)**	$ 29	$ 66

(i) Obligations and funded status

		Pensions	
In millions	*Year ended December 31,*	**2008**	2007
Change in benefit obligation			
Benefit obligation at beginning of year		**$14,419**	$14,545
Amendments		**—**	—
Adoption of SFAS No. 158 measurement date provision (Note 2)		**—**	3
Interest cost		**801**	742
Actuarial gain		**(2,274)**	(195)
Service cost		**136**	150
Curtailment gain		**—**	—
Plan participants' contributions		**52**	54
Foreign currency changes		**45**	(33)
Benefit payments and transfers		**(853)**	(847)
Benefit obligation at end of year		**$12,326**	$14,419
Component representing future salary increases		**(397)**	(618)
Accumulated benefit obligation at end of year		**$11,929**	$13,801
Change in plan assets			
Fair value of plan assets at beginning of year		**$16,000**	$15,625
Employer contributions		**127**	75
Plan participants' contributions		**52**	54
Foreign currency changes		**27**	(26)
Actual return on plan assets		**(1,742)**	1,119
Benefit payments and transfers		**(853)**	(847)
Fair value of plan assets at end of year		**$13,611**	$16,000
Funded (unfunded) status (Excess of fair value of plan assets over benefit obligation at end of year)		**$1,285**	$1,581

Measurement date for all plans is December 31.

Instructions

Using the above disclosure notes, answer the following questions.

(a) Is the company's pension plan in a surplus or deficit status position at December 31, 2008? 2007?

(b) What is the amount reported for the pension expense for December 31, 2008, and 2007? What could cause these trends?

(c) What was the amount of cash flow used to fund the plan for 2008 and 2007? Why would there be differences in the annual funding amounts? How does this compare with the expense that is showing for the company for the related years?

(d) Discuss whether or not you believe that the pension expense is faithfully presented in the profit or loss statement for the years 2008 and 2007.

RA19-3 Research Topic

RONA Inc., Bank of Montreal, and Air Canada are all Canadian companies with defined benefit plans. Access these companies' financial statements for the 2009 fiscal year ends from SEDAR at www.sedar.com.

Real-World Emphasis

Instructions

Analyze the notes to the financial statements of each of the three companies, and provide answers to the following questions.

(a) For each company, identify the following three assumptions:

1. The discount rate

2. The rate of compensation increase that was used to measure the projected benefit obligation

3. The expected long-term rate of return on plan assets

(b) Comment on any significant differences between the assumptions that are used by each firm.

(c) Did any of the companies change their assumptions during the period covered by the notes? If yes, what was the effect on each of the following: the current year's accrued benefit obligation, the plan assets, and the pension expense? Explain.

(d) Identify the types of plans and the assumptions that underlie any future benefit plans other than pensions. Are these similar across the three companies? Comment on how any differences would affect an intercompany analysis.

(e) Are the pension plans and post-retirement plans in a deficit or surplus position? What are the amounts that have been reported on the statement of financial position?

(f) Calculate the debt to total assets ratio for each company using the reported numbers, and then using the actual funded status for the accrued benefit rather than the amounts originally reported. Comment.

RA19-4 Other Employee Future Benefits

Companies provide other employee future benefits in addition to defined benefit pension plans. In many cases, these obligations and expenses can be significant, but often are ignored. Access the 2009 fiscal year-end statements for the following companies from SEDAR (www.sedar.com): BCE Inc., Potash Corp., Canadian Pacific Railway, and Air Canada.

Real-World Emphasis

Instructions

(a) For each company, outline the other employee future benefits that are provided. Detail the assumptions that have been used to account for these other employee future benefits.

(b) For each company, provide the following:

1. Funded status of the pension plans

2. Pension expense

3. Funded status of the other employee future benefits

4. Other employee future benefit expense and any plan assets to support the other employee future benefits

(c) Comment on the relative amounts of the deficit and expenses of the pension plans and the other benefits. What impact does this have on any analysis completed for companies?

RA19-5 Research Topic

Real-World Emphasis

The IASB is proposing changes in the accounting of defined pension plans as outlined in the chapter material. Using the reports of three Canadian companies in the telecommunications industry, determine the impact of these changes on the companies' financial statements.

Access the 2009 fiscal year-end reports for **BCE Inc.**, **Rogers Communications Inc.**, and **TELUS**.

Instructions

Using the financial statements for the three companies:

(a) Prepare a schedule that reports for each company:

1. The balance of the benefit asset/liability reported on the statement of financial position (be sure to identify the asset impact separately from the liability impact)

2. The funded status

3. The total of the unrecognized (unamortized) past service costs, net actuarial gains/losses, and transition balances at the balance sheet date

4. Total assets

5. Total liabilities

6. Total shareholders' equity

(b) Calculate the current total debt-to equity ratio and the debt to total assets ratio for each of the three companies at the report date.

(c) Determine revised balances for the total liabilities and total shareholders' equity, assuming the companies implement the proposals.

(d) Recalculate the total debt-to-equity ratios using the revised balances from part (c), and comment on your findings.

(e) What is the amount that is recorded as the pension cost? What would be the amounts under the new proposals for the service cost, interest cost, and the remeasurement costs to OCI (ignoring income taxes)?

RA19-6 Immediate Recognition Approach

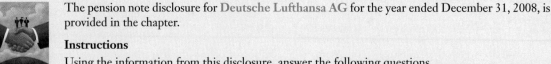

Real-World Emphasis

The pension note disclosure for **Deutsche Lufthansa AG** for the year ended December 31, 2008, is provided in the chapter.

Instructions

Using the information from this disclosure, answer the following questions.

Ethics

(a) If Lufthansa could adopt the immediate recognition approach, determine what the amounts recognized as the accrued benefit liability would be for the years ended December 31, 2007, and 2008. Reconcile this balance with the balance recognized under the deferral and amortization approach. (Assume that the asset benefit obligation would be the same under the projected benefit approach and the actuarial funding approach.) Calculate the expense under the immediate recognition approach for 2008. Show a reconciliation of the opening and closing balances of the deficit balance under the immediate recognition approach for 2008.

(b) Given the information in part (a), discuss the impact of the different reporting approaches on the statement of financial position and the profit or loss statement for the 2008 fiscal year end. Explain what has caused the major differences in both approaches. Which method do you believe most faithfully represents the pension plans in the financial reports for the company? What is the cash flow required for the company in 2008 and how does this relate to the statement presentation?

(c) Review the assumptions that Lufthansa has used for the discount rate and expected return on the plan assets. How does the company determine the expected rate of return on the plan assets? Comment on the trends over the past few years, and whether you believe these are fair and reasonable assumptions.

Change in Flight Path for Lease Reporting

WITH A FLEET of more than 80 aircraft, about 40% of which is leased, WestJet has significant lease obligations. The reason the Calgary-based airline leases a good portion of its fleet is simple: airplanes are expensive. "It's a big capital commitment when you purchase an aircraft," says Robert Palmer, WestJet's Vice-President, Controller. "Leasing allows us to be more flexible with our fleet planning." After the term of the lease, the company can return the plane or extend the lease.

Another advantage is off-balance sheet reporting. When WestJet signs a lease, it tests the lease to determine if it's an operating lease or a capital lease. All of WestJet's current aircraft leases do not qualify as capital leases and therefore are considered operating leases: the airline will not own the aircraft at the end of the lease's term; the leases range from 8 to 14 years, just a portion of the aircraft's economic lives; and the lease payments are only a portion of the aircraft's fair value. WestJet does not include the future operating lease payments on the balance sheet, but instead includes them in the notes to the financial statements as a commitment. The aircraft rental expense–i.e., the lease payment–is included in the statement of earnings.

This may change, however, with WestJet's move to IFRS as of January 2011. "The IASB and FASB have put out a discussion paper on removing the concept of operating leases," explains Palmer. "Every lease would become a capital lease, so therefore, the asset and corresponding liability would be on your balance sheet." This will affect WestJet's reporting of its liabilities since, as of September 2009, it had approximately $1.6 billion in lease commitments that were not included in liabilities.

"The big concern," says Palmer, "is what it will do to your covenants and ratios," such as the debt-to-equity ratio. But WestJet isn't too worried since it considers off–balance sheet obligations relating to aircraft operating leases when doing these calculations.

WestJet will have to make changes to its balance sheet and educate users about those changes. "But nothing has really changed in the business," Palmer stresses. "It's just the way it's being presented." ∎

CHAPTER 20

Leases

Learning Objectives

After studying this chapter, you should be able to:

1. Explain the conceptual nature, economic substance, and advantages of lease transactions.
2. Identify and apply the criteria that are used to determine the type of lease for accounting purposes for a lessee under the classification approach.
3. Calculate the lease payment that is required for a lessor to earn a specific return.
4. Account for a lessee's basic capital (finance) lease.
5. Determine the effect of, and account for, residual values and bargain purchase options in a lessee's capital (finance) lease.
6. Account for an operating lease by a lessee and compare the operating and capitalization methods of accounting for leases.
7. Determine the balance sheet presentation of a capital (finance) lease and identify other disclosures required.
8. Identify and apply the criteria that are used to determine the type of lease for a lessor under the classification approach.
9. Account for and report basic financing and sales-type leases by a lessor.
10. Account for and report financing and sales-type leases with guaranteed values or a bargain purchase option by a lessor.
11. Account for and report an operating lease by a lessor.
12. Explain and apply the contract-based approach to a basic lease for a lessee and lessor.
13. Identify differences in accounting between accounting standards for private enterprises and IFRS, and what changes are expected in the near future.

After studying Appendix 20A, you should be able to:

14. Describe and apply the lessee's accounting for sale-leaseback transactions.
15. Explain the classification and accounting treatment for leases that involve real estate.

Preview of Chapter 20

Leasing continues to grow in popularity as a form of asset-based financing.[1] Instead of borrowing money to buy an airplane, a computer, a nuclear core, or a satellite, a company leases the item. Railroads lease huge amounts of equipment, many hotel and motel chains lease their facilities, most retail chains lease the bulk of their retail premises and warehouses, and, as indicated in the opening vignette, most airlines lease their airplanes! The popularity of leasing is shown by the fact that 189 of 200 companies surveyed in *Financial Reporting in Canada—2008* disclosed lease data.[2] Small and medium-sized enterprises also use leases as an important form of debt financing.

Because of the significance and popularity of lease arrangements, consistent accounting and complete reporting of these transactions are crucial. In this chapter, we look at these important issues related to leasing.

The chapter is organized as follows:

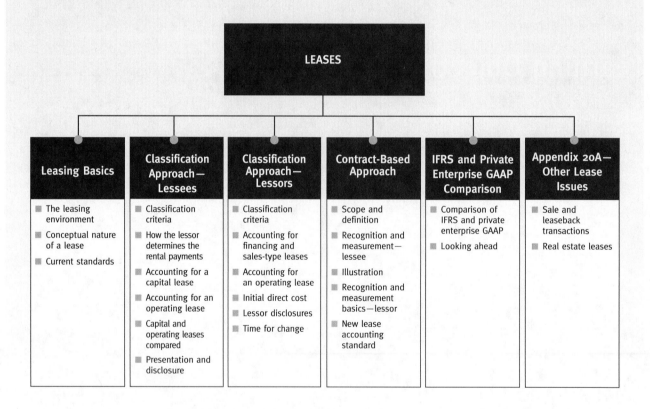

---

[1] Asset-based financing is the financing of equipment through a secured loan, conditional sales contract, or lease.

[2] CICA, *Financial Reporting in Canada—2008*, p. 301.

LEASING BASICS

The Leasing Environment

Aristotle once said, "Wealth does not lie in ownership but in the use of things"! Many Canadian companies have clearly come to agree with Aristotle as, rather than owning assets, they now are heavily involved in leasing them.

A **lease** is a contractual agreement between a **lessor** and a **lessee** that gives the lessee, for a specified period of time, the right to use specific property owned by the lessor in return for specified, and generally periodic, cash payments (rents). An essential element of the lease agreement is that the lessor transfers less than the total interest in the property. Because of the financial, operating, and risk advantages that the lease arrangement provides, many businesses and other types of organizations lease substantial amounts of property as an alternative to ownership. Any type of equipment or property can be leased, such as rail cars, helicopters, bulldozers, schools, golf club facilities, barges, medical scanners, computers, and so on. The largest class of leased equipment is information technology equipment. Next are assets in the transportation area, such as trucks, aircraft, and rail cars.

1 Objective
Explain the conceptual nature, economic substance, and advantages of lease transactions.

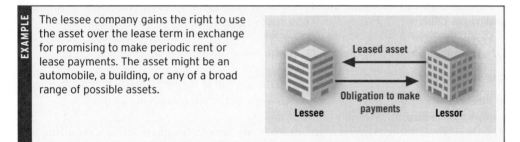

EXAMPLE — The lessee company gains the right to use the asset over the lease term in exchange for promising to make periodic rent or lease payments. The asset might be an automobile, a building, or any of a broad range of possible assets.

Leased asset

Obligation to make payments

Lessee   Lessor

Because a lease is a contract, the provisions that the lessor and lessee agree to can vary widely from lease to lease. Indeed, they are limited only by the ingenuity of the two parties to the contract and their advisors. The lease's duration—lease term—may be anything from a short period of time to the entire expected economic life of the asset. The **rental payments** may be the same amount from year to year, or they may increase or decrease; further, they may be predetermined or may vary with sales, the prime interest rate, the consumer price index, or some other factor. In many cases, the rent is set at an amount that enables the lessor to recover the asset's cost plus a fair return over the life of the lease.

Law

The obligations for taxes, insurance, and maintenance (executory costs) may be the responsibility of either the lessor or the lessee, or they may be divided. In order to protect the lessor from default on the rents, the lease may include restrictions—comparable to those in bond indentures—that limit the lessee's activities in making dividend payments or incurring further debt. In addition, the lease contract may be non-cancellable or may grant the right to early termination on payment of a set scale of prices plus a penalty. In case of default, the lessee may be liable for all future payments at once, and receive title to the property in exchange; or the lessor may have the right to sell the asset to a third party and collect from the lessee all or a portion of the difference between the sale price and the lessor's unrecovered cost.

When the lease term ends, several alternatives may be available to the lessee. These may range from simple termination, to the right to renew or buy the asset at a nominal price.

Who Are the Players?

Who are the lessors referred to above? In Canada, lessors are usually one of three types of company:

1. Manufacturer finance companies

2. Independent finance companies

3. Traditional financial institutions

Manufacturer finance companies, or captive leasing companies as they are also called, are subsidiaries whose main business is to perform leasing operations for the parent company. **General Motors Acceptance Corporation of Canada, Limited** is an example of a captive leasing company. As soon as the parent company receives a possible order, its leasing subsidiary can quickly develop a lease-financing arrangement that facilitates the parent company's sale of its product.

An **independent finance company** acts as a financial intermediary by providing financing for transactions for manufacturers, vendors, or distributors. Your dentist, for example, when acquiring specialized equipment for his or her practice, may order the equipment through the manufacturer or distributor, who in turn may outsource the financing to a lessor such as an independent finance company.

Subsidiaries of domestic and foreign banks are examples of **traditional financial institutions** that provide leasing as another form of financing to their customers.

Advantages of Leasing

Although leasing does have disadvantages, the growth in its use suggests that it often has a genuine advantage over owning property. Some of the advantages are as follows:

1. 100% Financing at Fixed Rates. Leases are often signed without requiring any money down from the lessee, helping to conserve scarce cash—an especially desirable feature for new and developing companies. In addition, lease payments often remain fixed (i.e., unchanging), which protects the lessee against inflation and increases in the cost of money. The following comment about a conventional loan is typical: "Our local bank finally agreed to finance 80% of the purchase price but wouldn't go any higher, and they wanted a floating interest rate. We just couldn't afford the down payment and we needed to lock in a payment we knew we could live with."

Turning to the lessor's point of view, financial institutions and leasing companies find leasing profitable because it provides attractive interest margins.

2. Protection Against Obsolescence. Leasing equipment reduces the risk of obsolescence to the lessee, and in many cases passes the risk of residual value to the lessor. For example, a company that leases computers may have a lease agreement that permits it to turn in an old computer for a new model at any time, cancelling the old lease and writing a new one. The cost of the new lease is added to the balance due on the old lease, less the old computer's trade-in value. As one treasurer remarked, "Our instinct is to purchase." But when new computers come along in a short time, "then leasing is just a heck of a lot more convenient than purchasing."

On the other hand, the lessor can benefit from the property reversion (i.e., the return of the asset) at the end of the lease term. Residual values can produce very large profits. For example, **Citicorp** at one time assumed that the commercial aircraft it was leasing to the airline industry would have a residual value of 5% of their purchase price. As it turned out, however, the planes were worth 150% of their cost—a handsome price appreciation. Three years later these same planes slumped to 80% of their cost, but this was still a far greater residual value than the projected 5%.

3. *Flexibility.* Lease agreements may contain less restrictive provisions than other debt agreements. Innovative lessors can tailor a lease agreement to the lessee's specific needs. For instance, a ski lift operator using equipment for only six months of the year can arrange rental payments that fit well with the operation's revenue streams. In addition, because the lessor retains ownership and the leased property is the collateral, it is usually easier to arrange financing through a lease.

4. *Less Costly Financing for Lessee, Tax Incentives for Lessor.* Some companies find leasing cheaper than other forms of financing. For example, start-up companies in depressed industries or companies in low tax brackets may lease as a way of claiming tax benefits that might otherwise be lost. Investment tax credits and capital cost allowance deductions offer no benefit to companies that have little or no taxable income. Through leasing, these tax benefits are used by the leasing companies or financial institutions. They can then pass some of these tax benefits back to the asset's user through lower rental payments.

Underlying Concept

Some companies "double-dip" at the international level. The leasing rules of the lessor's and lessee's countries may differ, permitting both parties to own the asset. In such cases, both the lessor and lessee can receive the tax benefits related to amortization.

5. *Off–Balance Sheet Financing.* Certain leases do not add debt on a balance sheet or affect financial ratios, and may add to borrowing capacity.[3] Off–balance sheet financing has been critical to some companies. For example, airlines use lease arrangements extensively and this results in a great deal of off–balance sheet financing. Illustration 20-1 indicates that debt levels are understated by WestJet Airlines Ltd., Air Canada, and Helijet International Inc., a sample of Canadian companies in the transportation industry.

	WestJet December 31, 2009 ($ thousands)	Air Canada December 31, 2009 ($ millions)	Helijet August 31, 2009 ($ thousands)
Long-term liabilities, excluding future income taxes and deferred credits	$1,056,838	$5,465	$ 944
Shareholders' equity	1,388,928	1,446	(2,794)
Unrecognized future minimum lease payments under existing operating leases	1,613,350	2,630	7,948

Illustration 20-1

Reported Debt and Unrecognized Operating Lease Obligations

Conceptual Nature of a Lease

If an airline borrows $80 million on a 10-year note from the bank to purchase a Boeing 787 jet plane, it is clear that an asset and related liability should be reported on the company's balance sheet at that amount. If the airline purchases the 787 for $80 million directly from Boeing through an instalment purchase over 10 years, it is equally clear that an asset and related liability should be reported (i.e., the instalment purchase transaction should be "capitalized"). However, if the Boeing 787 is leased for 10 years through a non-cancellable lease transaction with payments of the same amount as the instalment purchase, there are differences of opinion about how this transaction should be reported. Three views on accounting for leases can be summarized as follows.

Underlying Concept

The issue of how to report leases is the classic case of substance versus form. Although legal title does not technically pass in lease transactions, the benefits from the use of the property do transfer.

Do Not Capitalize Any Leased Assets—An Executory Contract Approach. Because the lessee does not own the property, it is not appropriate to capitalize the lease.

---

[3] As shown in this chapter, some lease arrangements are not capitalized on the balance sheet. This keeps the liabilities section free from large commitments that, if recorded, would have a negative effect on the debt-to-equity ratio. The reluctance to record lease obligations as liabilities is one of the main reasons that some companies resist capitalized lease accounting.

Furthermore, a lease is an executory contract that requires continuing performance by both parties. Because other executory contracts (such as purchase commitments and employment contracts) are not currently capitalized, leases should not be capitalized either. The lessor should continue to recognize the leased item as an asset.

Capitalize Leases That Are Similar to Instalment Purchases—A Classification Approach.   The classification approach says that transactions should be classified and accounted for according to their economic substance. Because instalment purchases are capitalized as property, plant, and equipment assets, leases that have similar characteristics to instalment purchases should be accounted for in the same way. In our earlier example, the airline is committed to the same payments over a 10-year period for either a lease or an instalment purchase; lessees simply make rental payments, whereas owners make mortgage payments. The financial statements should classify and report these transactions in the same way: recognizing the physical asset on the lessee's balance sheet where appropriate. Transactions not recognized as in-substance acquisitions of assets are classified as operating leases and accounted for differently.

Law

Capitalize All Leases—A Contract-Based Approach.   Under the contract-based approach, the leased asset that is acquired is not the physical property; rather, it is the **contractual right to use** the property that is conveyed under the lease agreement. The liability is the contractual obligation to make lease payments. Under this view, also called a property rights or right-of-use approach, it is justifiable to capitalize the fair value of the rights and obligations associated with a broad range of leases.[4]

In short, the various viewpoints range from no capitalization to capitalization of all leases.

Current Standards

What do the current standards require? The FASB, private enterprise, and international standards in effect when this text went to print are consistent with the **classification approach** that capitalizes leases that are similar to an instalment purchase. These are classified as capital or finance leases and usually are recognized as items of property, plant, and equipment. The accounting treatment is based on the concept that **a lease that transfers substantially all of the benefits and risks of property ownership should be capitalized**.

By capitalizing the present value of the future rental payments, the **lessee** records an asset and a liability at an amount that is generally representative of the asset's fair value. The **lessor**, having transferred substantially all the benefits and risks of ownership, removes the asset from its balance sheet, and replaces it with a receivable. The typical journal entries for the lessee and the lessor, assuming the leased equipment is capitalized, are shown at the top of Illustration 20-2. If the benefits and risks of ownership **are not transferred** from one party to the other, the lease is classified as an operating lease. The accounting for an operating lease by the lessee and lessor is shown in the bottom of Illustration 20-2.

---

[4] The property rights approach was originally recommended in *Accounting Research Study No. 4* (New York: AICPA, 1964), pp. 10–11. More recently, this view has received additional support. See Warren McGregor, "Accounting for Leases: A New Approach," Special Report (Norwalk, Conn.: FASB, 1996).

Illustration 20-2

Journal Entries for Capital and Operating Leases

	Lessee			Lessor		
Capital or Financial Lease	Leased Equipment	xx		Lease Receivable (net)	xx	
	Lease Obligation		xx	Equipment		xx
	Depreciation Expense	x				
	Accumulated Depreciation		x			
	Lease Obligation	x		Cash	x	
	Interest Expense	x		Interest Income		x
	Cash		x	Lease Receivable		x
Operating Lease	Rent Expense	x		Cash	x	
	Cash		x	Rental Income		x

When the asset is capitalized as an item of property, plant, and equipment, the lessee recognizes the depreciation. The lessor and lessee treat the lease rentals as the receipt and the payment of interest and principal. If the lease is not capitalized, no asset is recorded by the lessee and no asset is removed from the lessor's books. When a lease payment is made, the lessee records rent or lease expense and the lessor recognizes rental or lease income.

While the CICA, FASB, and IASB standards were all consistent with the classification approach as this text went to print, these standards are expected to have a limited life going forward. Current thinking supports the **contract-based approach** and it is this concept that underlies the 2010 Exposure Draft issued by the IASB and FASB for a new converged lease accounting standard.

The contract-based approach simply states that "lease contracts create assets and liabilities that should be recognized in the financial statements of lessees."[6] The most significant change that would result from the adoption of this approach is the recognition on the statement of financial position of rights and obligations as assets and liabilities for what are now termed "operating" leases. These leases, as you can tell from Illustration 20-2, are now off–balance sheet items and are reported as an expense only as the lease payments are made. Under the contractual right-of-use approach, all leases covered by the expected standard are recognized as a type of intangible asset along with the contractual obligation (liability) to make lease payments in the future.

The next section of this chapter explains the basics of the classification approach that is currently in use. This is followed by an explanation of the basics of the contract-based approach as set out in the 2010 Exposure Draft, expected to be published as an IFRS standard in 2011.

Underlying Concept

"According to the World Leasing Yearbook 2009, in 2007 the annual volume of leases amounted to U.S. $760 billion. However, the assets and liabilities arising from many of these contracts cannot be found" on entities' balance sheets.[5]

CLASSIFICATION APPROACH— LESSEES

Classification Criteria

Before discussing the accounting for the two classifications of leases required by current accounting standards, we begin by looking at how the classification decision is made by the lessee. From the lessee's standpoint, all leases are classified for accounting purposes as either operating leases or capital leases. As indicated previously, when the risks and benefits of ownership are transferred from the lessor to the lessee, the lease is accounted for as

2 Objective

Identify and apply the criteria that are used to determine the type of lease for accounting purposes for a lessee under the classification approach.

---

[5] IASB, Snapshot: *Leases—Preliminary Views* (of Discussion paper DP/2009/1), March 2009, page 2.

[6] Ibid., page 4.

a capital lease (described as a finance lease under IFRS); otherwise, it is accounted for as an operating lease. The terms "capital lease" and "finance lease" are used interchangeably in this chapter.

What are the risks and benefits (or rewards) of ownership? Benefits of ownership are the ability to use the asset to generate profits over its useful life, to benefit from any appreciation in the asset's value, and to realize its residual value at the end of its economic life. The risks, on the other hand, are the exposure to uncertain returns, and to risk of loss from use or idle capacity and from technological obsolescence.

Guidance is provided to help preparers determine the substance of the lease transaction under both accounting standards for private enterprises (ASPE) and IAS 17 *Leases*, and the objective under both standards is the same. The IFRS identifies numerous qualitative indicators to help in identifying whether a lease is a finance (capital) lease or not. Section 3065 of Part II of the *CICA Handbook*, on the other hand, provides fewer qualitative indicators, but includes a few quantitative indicators that end up being used extensively in making the classification decision. These quantitative factors are known as "bright lines" and they are key to the financial engineering of leases so they will meet the accounting method preferred by the entity. The net effect is that entities applying IFRS make the classification decision based on principles; and those applying private enterprise standards, as all Canadian reporters did prior to 2011, look to whether certain numerical thresholds have been met or missed.

IFRS Criteria

Significant Change

Under IFRS, any one or a combination of the following situations **normally indicates** that the risks and rewards of ownership are transferred to the lessee, and supports classification as a finance lease:

1. There is reasonable assurance that the lessee will obtain ownership of the leased property by the end of the lease term. If there is a bargain purchase option in the lease, it is assumed that the lessee will exercise it and obtain ownership of the asset.[7]

2. The lease term is long enough that the lessee will receive substantially all of the economic benefits that are expected to be derived from using the leased property over its life.

3. The lease allows the lessor to recover substantially all of its investment in the leased property and to earn a return on the investment. Evidence of this is provided if the present value of the minimum lease payments is close to the fair value of the leased asset.

4. The leased assets are so specialized that, without major modification, they are of use only to the lessee.

Other indicators that might suggest a transfer of the risks and benefits of ownership include situations where the lessee absorbs the lessor's losses if the lessee cancels the lease, or the lessee assumes the risk associated with the amount of the residual value of the asset at the end of the lease, or where there is a bargain renewal option—when the lessee can renew the lease for an additional term at significantly less than the market rent.

The standard also states that these indicators are not always conclusive. The decision has to be made on the substance of each specific transaction. If the lessee determines that the risks and benefits of ownership have not been transferred to it, the lease is classified as an operating lease.

---

[7] Bargain purchase options will be defined in the next section.

ASPE Criteria

The private enterprise standards assume that the risks and benefits of ownership **are normally transferred to the lessee**, and the lessee should classify and account for the arrangement as a capital lease if **any one or more of** the following criteria is met:

1. There is reasonable assurance that the lessee will obtain ownership of the leased property, including through a bargain purchase option. This is identical to the first IFRS situation described above.

2. The lessee will benefit from most of the asset benefits due to the length of the lease term—identical to the second IFRS situation. **In addition, a numerical threshold is included**: this is usually assumed to occur if the lease term is 75% or more of the leased property's economic life.

3. The lessor recovers substantially all of its investment and earns a return on that investment as explained in the third IFRS criteria above. **In addition, a numerical threshold is included**: this is usually assumed if the present value of the minimum lease payments is equal to 90% or more of the fair value of the leased asset.

Under U.S. and pre-2011 Canadian GAAP, and under the new private enterprise standards, the numerical thresholds tend to take over from professional judgement in applying the capitalization criteria.

IFRS and ASPE Requirements—A Closer Look

Aside from how the classification decision is made and the use of different terms (to mean the same thing), the remainder of lease accounting under both sets of standards is very similar.

Transfer of Ownership Test.   The transfer of ownership criterion is not controversial and is easily applied in practice. The transfer may occur at the end of the lease term with no additional payment or through a bargain purchase option. A bargain purchase option is a provision that allows the lessee to purchase the leased asset for a price that is significantly lower than the asset's expected fair value when the lessee can exercise the option. At the beginning of the lease, the difference between the option price and the expected fair value in the future must be large enough to make it reasonably sure that the option will be exercised.

For example, assume that you were to lease a car for $599 per month for 40 months with an option to purchase it for $100 at the end of the 40-month period. If the car's estimated fair value is $3,000 at the end of the 40 months, the $100 option to purchase is clearly a bargain and, therefore, capitalization is required. It is assumed that an option that is a bargain will be acted on. In other situations, it is not so clearly evident whether the option price in the lease agreement is a bargain.

Economic Life Test.   Under IFRS, the decision of whether the lease term is long enough to allow the lessee to derive most of the benefits offered by the asset requires judgement. Under PE GAAP, if the lease period is equal to or greater than 75% of the asset's economic life, it is assumed that most of the risks and rewards of ownership are going to accrue to the lessee.

The lease term is **generally considered the fixed, non-cancellable term of the lease**. However, this period can be extended if a bargain renewal option is provided in the lease agreement. A bargain renewal option is a provision that allows the lessee to renew the lease for a rental amount that is lower than the expected fair rental at the date when the option becomes exercisable. At the beginning of the lease, the difference between the renewal rental and the expected fair rental must be large enough to provide reasonable

Underlying Concept

In lease accounting, the importance of good definitions is clear. If the lease fits the definition of an asset in that it gives the lessee the economic benefits that flow from the possession or use of the leased property, then an asset should be recognized.

assurance that the option to renew will be exercised. With bargain renewal options, as with bargain purchase options, it is sometimes difficult to determine what is a bargain.

Estimating the economic life can also be a problem, especially if the leased item is a specialized asset or has been used for a long period of time. For example, determining the economic life of a nuclear core is extremely difficult because it is affected by much more than normal wear and tear.

Recovery of Investment by Lessor Test.   The rationale for the recovery of investment by the lessor criterion is that if the present value of the payments is reasonably close to the asset's market price, the lessor is recovering its investment in the asset plus earning a return on the investment through the lease. The economic substance, therefore, is that the lessee is purchasing the asset. Applying this test requires an understanding of additional specific terms. For example, to calculate the present value of the minimum lease payments, three important factors are involved: (1) the minimum lease payments, (2) any executory costs, and (3) the discount rate.

Minimum Lease Payments. Minimum lease payments from a lessee's perspective include the following:[8]

1. *Minimum rental payments:* The payments that the lessee is making or can be required to make to the lessor under the lease agreement, excluding contingent rent and executory costs (defined below).

2. *Amounts guaranteed:* Any amounts guaranteed by the lessee related to the residual value of the leased asset. The residual value is the asset's estimated fair value at the end of the lease term. The lessor often transfers the risk of loss in value to the lessee or to a third party by requiring a guarantee of the estimated residual value, either in whole or in part. The guaranteed residual value from the lessee's perspective is the maximum amount the lessor can require the lessee to pay at the end of the lease. The unguaranteed residual value is the portion of the residual value that is not guaranteed by the lessee or is guaranteed solely by a party that is related to the lessor. Often, no part of the residual is guaranteed.

3. *Bargain purchase option:* As explained above, this is an option that allows the lessee to acquire the leased asset at the end of the lease term for an amount considerably below the asset's value at that time. This may or may not be included in the lease conditions.

Executory Costs. Like most assets, leased property needs to be insured and maintained, and it may require the payment of property tax. These ownership-type expenses are called executory costs. If the lessor pays these costs, any portion of each lease payment that represents a recovery of executory costs from the lessee **is excluded** from the rental payments used in calculating the minimum lease payments. If the amount of the payment that represents executory costs cannot be determined from the lease contract, the lessee makes an estimate of the executory costs and excludes that amount. Many lease agreements, however, require the lessee to pay the executory costs directly. In these cases, the rental payments can be used without any adjustment in the minimum lease payments calculations.

Finance

Discount Rate. What discount rate should be used by the lessee in determining the present value of the minimum lease payments: the rate implicit in the lease, or the lessee's incremental borrowing rate? The interest rate implicit in the lease is the lessor's internal rate of return at the beginning of the lease that makes the present value of the minimum lease payments plus any unguaranteed residual values equal to the fair value of the

---

[8] "Minimum lease payments" is defined differently for a lessor.

leased asset.[9] The lessee's incremental borrowing rate is the interest rate that, at the beginning of the lease, the lessee would incur to borrow the funds needed to purchase the leased asset, assuming a similar term and using similar security for the borrowing.[10]

IFRS requires the interest rate implicit in the lease to be used whenever it is reasonably determinable; otherwise the incremental borrowing rate is used. **PE GAAP** specifies that the lower of the two rates is used.

There are two reasons for using these rates. First, the lessor's implicit rate is generally a more realistic rate to use in determining the amount, if any, to report as the asset and related liability for the lessee. Second, the private enterprise standard ensures that the lessee does not use an artificially high incremental borrowing rate **that would cause the present value of the minimum lease payments to be less than 90% of the property's fair value. This might make it possible to avoid capitalization of the asset and related liability!** Remember that the higher the discount rate that is used, the lower the discounted value. The lessee may argue that it cannot determine the implicit rate of the lessor and therefore the higher rate should be used. However, in many cases, the implicit rate that is used by the lessor is disclosed or can be estimated. Determining whether or not a reasonable estimate can be made requires judgement, particularly when using the incremental borrowing rate comes close to meeting the 90% test. **Because the leased property cannot be capitalized at more than its fair value**, the lessee is prevented from using an excessively low discount rate.

Specialized Nature of Leased Asset.   When the leased assets are so specialized that they are useful only to the lessee except at great incremental cost, the substance of the transaction is one of financing the asset acquisition, with the risks and benefits associated with ownership of the asset transfered to the lessee.

How the Lessor Determines the Rental Payments

The lessor determines the rental amount to charge based on the rate of return—the implicit rate—that the lessor needs to receive in order to justify leasing the asset.[11] The key variables considered in deciding on the rate of return are the lessee's credit standing, the length of the lease, and the status of the residual value (guaranteed or unguaranteed).

Assume Lessor Corporation wants to earn a 10% return on its investment of $100,000 in an asset that is to be leased to Lessee Corporation for five years with the annual rental due in advance each year. Illustration 20-3 shows how Lessor determines the amount of the rental payment, assuming there is no bargain purchase option or residual value at the end of the lease.[12]

3 Objective
Calculate the lease payment that is required for a lessor to earn a specific return.

Finance

---

[9] IAS 17 *Leases* requires the **interest rate implicit in the lease** to be the rate that equates the inflows with the fair value of the leased asset **plus any initial direct costs of the lessor**. If the lessor is a manufacturer or dealer, the initial direct costs are not included.

[10] IAS 17 *Leases* uses this as a secondary definition. It prefers the interest rate that the lessee would have to pay on a similar lease.

[11] In lease-versus-buy decisions and in determining the lessor's implicit rate, income tax consequences must be factored in. A major variable is whether the CRA requires the lease to be accounted for as a conditional sale: this is usually established based on whether the title is transferred by the end of the lease term or the lessee has a bargain purchase option. Tax shields that relate to the rental payment and capital cost allowance significantly affect the return and an investment's net present value.

[12] Alternatively, use Excel or other spreadsheet program to calculate the required payments. With Excel, use the following series of keystrokes: INSERT/FUNCTION/PMT. Fill in the variables that you are prompted to enter.

Investment to be recovered[13]	$100,000.00
Less: Present value of the amount to be recovered through a bargain purchase option or residual value at end of the lease term	–0–
Equals the present value of amount to be recovered through lease payments	$100,000.00
Five beginning-of-the-year lease payments to yield a 10% return: ($100,000 ÷ 4.16986[a])	$ 23,981.62

[a] PV of an annuity due (Table A-5); $i = 10\%$, $n = 5$

If there is a bargain purchase option or a residual value, guaranteed or not, the lessor does not have to recover as much through the rental payments. In such cases, the present value of these other recoveries is deducted before determining the present value of the amount to be recovered through lease payments. This is illustrated later in the chapter in more detail.

What Do the Numbers Mean?

Lease this year's model for just $199 per month! Or 0% financing! Sometimes leasing just looks too good to be true...and sometimes it is. It pays to be familiar with what is involved in a typical leasing agreement such as you might encounter in a vehicle lease, and to do your homework before signing on the dotted line.

First, there is often an upfront payment required to cover freight costs and pre-delivery expenses, plus taxes on these. Add to this a requirement for an initial down payment plus the first month's rent in advance. Increasing this payment, of course, will lower your monthly rental. Do you have to pay a security deposit similar to one you would pay on an apartment you rent? Some leasing companies also charge an administration fee for acquiring the vehicle and processing the paperwork for you.

Check out all the conditions. How reasonable is the annual mileage allowance? How much do you have to pay per kilometre if you exceed the "free" amount? What happens at the end of the lease term? Do you have to ensure that the vehicle has a reasonable residual value at the end? What price will you have to pay to purchase the leased asset if that is an option?

Finally, what alternatives are there of acquiring the same asset? What are the cash flows associated with the financing of a direct purchase? Or borrowing the money elsewhere and paying cash for the car? The 0% financing might be at the expense of a sales price that is higher than you could otherwise negotiate. A $2,000 or more rebate today for a cash deal may make a difference to your decision. The bottom line: get familiar with the agreements, look at your options, schedule the cash flows, and make your decision with full knowledge and understanding of what is involved.

We now turn to how **the lessee** accounts for agreements classified as capital or finance leases.

Accounting for a Capital Lease

Capital Lease Basics

Asset and Liability Are Recognized. In a capital or finance lease transaction, the lessee uses the lease **as a source of financing**. The lessor provides the leased asset to the lessee and finances the transaction by accepting instalment payments. The lessee accounts for the transaction as if an asset is purchased and a long-term obligation is entered into.

---

[13] If the lessor is not a manufacturer or dealer, then any initial direct costs of negotiating and arranging the lease are added to this amount.

Over the life of the lease, the rental payments made by the lessee are a repayment of principal and interest on the outstanding balance.

The lessee recognizes the asset and liability at the lower of (1) **the present value of the minimum lease payments** as defined above and (2) the fair value of the leased asset at the lease's inception. The reason for this is that, like other assets, a leased asset cannot be recorded at more than its fair value.

Depreciable Amount, Period, and Method.   Having capitalized the asset, its "cost" is allocated over its useful life.[14] You need to understand the terms of the lease and what is included in the capitalized value—the present value of the minimum lease payments—to determine the depreciable amount and its useful life.

For example, if it is a simple lease that transfers title to the asset at the end of the lease term for no additional payments, then the full capitalized value less any estimated residual value at the end of its useful life to the lessee is depreciated over the full useful life to the entity. If the lease contains a bargain purchase option, the assumption is that the lessee will acquire legal title to the asset and it will continue to use the asset. Once again, the entity allocates the full capitalized cost over the full useful life of the asset. It is a matter of thinking about it in terms of what physically happens to the asset.

Now consider a situation in which the lessee is obligated to make rental payments over the lease term and then return the asset to the lessor in whatever condition it is in at that time. All that is capitalized are the lease payments because this is all the lessee is responsible for. In this case, the full capitalized value is amortized over the time to the end of the lease. This changes if the lessee also takes on an obligation to guarantee the residual value of the asset at the end of the lease. Now the capitalized value includes the present value of the guaranteed residual. (You may want to review the definition of **minimum lease payments** to see that only the residual value guaranteed by the lessee is included!) Now, what will the entity depreciate? Because the guaranteed residual value is expected to be returned to the lessor, the lessee depreciates only the capitalized amount less the guaranteed residual amount over the period to the end of the lease.

Illustration 20-4 summarizes the depreciable amounts and depreciation period, and you are encouraged to understand the reason for each.

	Included in Capitalized Asset Cost	Depreciable Amount	Depreciation Period
Asset reverts to lessor at end of lease term:			
– Lessee does not guarantee any residual value	Minimum rental payments	Full capitalized amount	Lease term
– Lessee guarantees a residual value	Minimum rental payments plus residual value guarantee	Full capitalized amount minus undiscounted guaranteed residual value	Lease term
Lessee retains asset at end of lease term:			
– Title is transferred, no purchase option	Minimum rental payments	Full capitalized amount minus estimated residual value, if any, at end of useful life	Useful life of asset
– Title is transferred when bargain purchase option is exercised	Minimum rental payments plus bargain purchase option	Full capitalized amount minus estimated residual value, if any, at end of useful life	Useful life of asset

Illustration 20-4

Depreciable Amount and Period

---

[14] An exception to measuring the leased asset at amortized cost is made when a lessee leases investment property under a finance lease. In such a case, the investment property may be accounted for at fair value under IAS 40 *Investment Property*.

The lessee amortizes the leased asset by applying conventional depreciation methods that it uses for assets it owns.

Effective Interest Method.   Over the term of the lease, the effective interest method is used to allocate each lease payment between principal and interest. In this way, the periodic interest expense is equal to a constant percentage of the obligation's outstanding balance. The discount rate used to determine how much of each payment represents interest is the same one the lessee used to calculate the present value of the minimum lease payments.

Capital Lease Method Illustration 1

We use the example of a lease agreement between Lessor Corporation and Lessee Corporation to illustrate the accounting for a capital lease. The contract calls for Lessor Corporation to lease equipment to Lessee Corporation beginning January 1, 2010. The lease agreement's provisions and other pertinent data are given in Illustration 20-5.

Illustration 20-5

Lease Agreement Terms and Conditions

1. The lease term is five years, the lease agreement is non-cancellable, and it requires equal rental payments of $25,981.62 at the beginning of each year (annuity due basis), beginning January 1, 2010. The lease contains no renewal options, and the equipment reverts to Lessor Corporation at the end of the lease.
2. The equipment has a fair value of $100,000 on January 1, 2010, an estimated economic life of five years, and no residual value. Lessee Corporation uses straight-line depreciation for similar equipment that it owns.
3. Lessee Corporation pays all executory costs directly to third parties except for maintenance fees of $2,000 per year, which are included in the annual payments to the lessor.
4. Lessee Corporation's incremental borrowing rate is 11% per year. Lessor Corporation set the annual rental to earn a rate of return on its investment of 10% per year; this fact is known to Lessee Corporation.

The lease meets the criteria for classification as a capital lease under both IFRS and private enterprise standards for two reasons: (1) Lessor Corporation uses up all the benefits the leased asset has to offer over the five-year lease term. The 75% threshold in the PE standard is well met; and (2) the present value of the minimum lease payments is $100,000 (calculated below) and this is the same as the asset's fair value. It also exceeds the 90% of fair value threshold set out in the PE standard. Only one of the capitalization criteria has to be met to justify classification as a capital or finance lease.

Finance

The **minimum lease payments** are $119,908.10 ($23,981.62 × 5), and the present value of the minimum lease payments is $100,000, as calculated in Illustration 20-6.[15] This is the amount that is capitalized as the leased asset and recognized as the lease obligation.

Illustration 20-6

Present Value of Minimum Lease Payments

PV of minimum   = ($25,981.62 − $2,000) × present value of an annuity due of $1 for
lease payments   5 periods at 10% (Table A-5)
                = $23,981.62 × 4.16986
                = $100,000

The lessor's implicit interest rate of 10% is used in this case instead of the lessee's incremental borrowing rate of 11% either because (1) Lessee Corp. is a public company

---

[15] Alternatively, using Excel or another spreadsheet program, enter the following series of key strokes: INSERT/FUNCTION/PV. Fill in the required variables that the program asks for. Note that the interest rate must be provided with the % sign or be in decimal form.

and this is the IFRS preferred rate, or (2) Lessee Corp. applies private enterprise standards and this rate is lower than its incremental borrowing rate.[16]

The entry to record the lease on Lessee Corporation's books on January 1, 2010, is:

Equipment under Capital Leases	100,000	
Obligations under Capital Leases		100,000

A   =   L   +   SE
+100,000   +100,000

Cash flows: No effect

The journal entry to record the first lease payment on January 1, 2010, is:

Maintenance Expense (or Prepaid Expense)	2,000.00	
Obligations under Capital Leases	23,981.62	
Cash		25,981.62

A   =   L   +   SE
−25,981.62   −23,981.62   −2,000.00

Cash flows: ↓ 25,981.62 outflow

Each lease payment of $25,981.62 consists of three elements: (1) a reduction in the principal of the lease obligation, (2) a financing cost (interest expense), and (3) executory costs (maintenance). The total financing cost of $19,908.10 over the lease's term is the difference between the present value of the minimum lease payments ($100,000) and the actual cash payments excluding the executory costs ($119,908.10). These amounts, along with the annual interest expense, are shown in the lease amortization schedule in Illustration 20-7.[17]

	A	B	C	D	E
1		**Lessee Corporation** **Lease Amortization Schedule** **(Annuity due basis)**			
2	**Date**	**Annual Lease Payment**	**Interest (10%) on Unpaid Obligation**	**Reduction of Lease Obligation**	**Balance of Obligation**
3		**(a)**	**(b)**	**(c)**	**(d)**
4	1/1/10				$100,000.00
5	1/1/10	$ 23,981.62	$ –0–	$ 23,981.62	76,018.38
6	1/1/11	23,981.62	7,601.84	16,379.78	59,638.60
7	1/1/12	23,981.62	5,963.86	18,017.76	41,620.84
8	1/1/13	23,981.62	4,162.08	19,819.54	21,801.30
9	1/1/14	23,981.62	2,180.32*	21,801.30	–0–
10		$119,908.10	$19,908.10	$100,000.00	
12	(a) Lease payment as required by lease, excluding executory costs. (b) 10% of the preceding balance of (d) except for 1/1/10; since this is an annuity due, no time has elapsed at the date of the first payment and no interest has accrued. (c) (a) minus (b). (d) Preceding balance minus (c). *Rounded by 19 cents.				

Illustration 20-7

Lease Amortization Schedule for Lessee—Annuity Due Basis

---

[16] If Lessee Corporation had an incremental borrowing rate of 9% (lower than the 10% rate used by Lessor Corporation) or it did not know the rate used by Lessor, the present value calculation yields a capitalized amount of $101,675.35 ($23,981.62 × 4.23972). Because this amount exceeds the asset's fair value, Lessee Corporation capitalizes the $100,000 and uses 10% as its effective rate for amortization of the lease obligation.

[17] This is a perfect task for Excel or other spreadsheet program. Set up the schedule headings, and use formulas to perform the calculations for you.

Accrued interest is recorded at Lessee Corporation's fiscal year end, December 31, 2010, as follows:

A = L + SE
     +7,601.84   −7,601.84

Cash flows: No effect

Interest Expense	7,601.84	
Interest Payable		7,601.84

Using Lessee Corporation's normal depreciation policy, the following entry is made on December 31, 2010, to record the current year's depreciation of the leased equipment:

A   = L + SE
−20,000   −20,000

Cash flows: No effect

Depreciation Expense—Leased Equipment	20,000	
Accumulated Depreciation—Leased Equipment		20,000
($100,000 ÷ 5 years)		

At December 31, 2010, the assets recorded under capital leases are identified separately on the lessee's balance sheet, or in a note cross-referenced to the balance sheet. Similarly, the related obligations are identified separately. The principal portion that is due within one year is classified with current liabilities and the remainder is reported with noncurrent liabilities. For example, the current portion of the December 31, 2010 total obligation of $76,018.38 **is the principal of the obligation that will be paid off within the next 12 months**. Therefore, the current portion is $16,379.78, as indicated on the amortization schedule. Illustration 20-8 shows the liability section of the December 31, 2010 balance sheet for the lease obligation and related accrued interest.

Illustration 20-8

Reporting Current and Noncurrent Lease Liabilities

Current liabilities	
Interest payable	$ 7,601.84
Obligations under capital leases, current portion	16,379.78
Noncurrent liabilities	
Obligations under capital leases	$59,638.60

The journal entry to record the lease payment on January 1, 2011, is as follows:

A   = L   + SE
−25,981.62   −23,981.62   −2,000.00

Cash flows: ↓ 25,981.62 outflow

Maintenance Expense (or Prepaid Expense)	2,000.00	
Interest Payable[18]	7,601.84	
Obligations under Capital Leases	16,379.78	
Cash		25,981.62

Entries through to 2014 follow the same pattern as above. Other executory costs (insurance and maintenance) that are assumed by Lessee Corporation are recorded in the same way as the company records operating costs incurred on assets that it owns.

At the end of the lease, the amount capitalized as leased equipment is fully depreciated and the lease obligation is fully discharged. If the equipment is not purchased, the lessee returns it to the lessor and removes the equipment and related accumulated depreciation accounts from the books. If instead the lessee purchases the equipment at the end of the lease for $5,000, and expects to use it for another two years, the following entry is made:

---

[18] This entry assumes that the company does not prepare reversing entries. If reversing entries are used, Interest Expense is debited for this amount.

Equipment ($100,000 + $5,000)	105,000	
Accumulated Depreciation—Leased Equipment	100,000	
Equipment under Capital Leases		100,000
Accumulated Depreciation—Equipment		100,000
Cash		5,000

A = L + SE
0   0   0

Cash flows: ↓ 5,000 outflow

Capital Lease Method Illustration 2

The Lessor/Lessee Corporation example above illustrates the lessee's accounting for a basic lease. Let's now see what the effects are of including residual value requirements in the lease agreement. If title does not pass to the lessee and there is no bargain purchase option, the lessee returns the asset to the lessor at the end of the lease. There is often a significant residual value at the end of the lease term, especially when the leased asset's economic life is longer than the lease.[19]

5 Objective
Determine the effect of, and account for, residual values and bargain purchase options in a lessee's capital (finance) lease.

Guaranteed versus Unguaranteed.   The residual value may be unguaranteed or guaranteed by the lessee. If the lessee agrees to pay for any loss in value below a stated amount at the end of the lease, the stated amount is the guaranteed residual value.

The guaranteed residual value is used in lease arrangements for good reason: It protects the lessor against any loss in estimated residual value, and so ensures that the lessor will get its desired rate of return on its investment. For **capital leases**, residual values guaranteed by the lessee affect the amounts that are recognized as the leased asset and lease obligation.

Effect on Lease Payments.   A guaranteed residual value—by definition—is more likely to be realized than an unguaranteed residual value. As the risk of non-recovery is reduced, the lessor may reduce the required rate of return, and therefore the rental payments required.

Assume the same data as in the Lessee Corporation/Lessor Corporation example above in Illustration 20-5: Lessor wants to recover its net investment in the leased asset of $100,000 and earn a 10% return.[20] The asset reverts to Lessor at the end of the five-year lease term. Now assume that the asset is expected to have a residual value of $5,000 at the end of the lease. **Whether the residual value is guaranteed or not**, Lessor Corporation calculates the lease payments using the same approach set out in Illustration 20-3. Illustration 20-9 shows the calculations when the residual value is included.

 Finance

LESSOR'S CALCULATION OF LEASE PAYMENTS (10% ROI)	
Guaranteed or Unguaranteed Residual Value	
(Annuity due basis)	
Investment in leased equipment to be recovered	$100,000.00
Less amount to be recovered through residual value, end of year 5:	
Present value of residual value ($5,000 × 0.62092, Table A-2)	3,104.60
Amount to be recovered by lessor through rental payments	$ 96,895.40
Five periodic lease payments ($96,895.40 ÷ 4.16986, Table A-5)	$ 23,237.09

Illustration 20-9

Lessor's Calculation of Lease Payment

---

[19] When the lease term and the economic life are not the same, the asset's residual value at the end of the lease and at the end of its useful life will differ. The residual value at the end of an asset's economic life is sometimes referred to as salvage value, and it is generally a small amount.

[20] Technically, the rate of return that is demanded by the lessor would differ depending on whether the residual value was guaranteed or unguaranteed. To simplify the illustrations, we ignore this difference in this chapter.

Contrast this lease payment with the lease payment of $23,981.62 that was calculated in Illustration 20-3 when there was no residual value. The payments are lower because a portion of the lessor's net investment of $100,000 is recovered through the residual value. The residual value amount is discounted in the calculation because it will not be received for five years.

Lessee Accounting with a Residual Value.   If the residual value is guaranteed by the lessee, there are both economic and accounting consequences. The accounting difference is that the minimum lease payments that are capitalized as the leased asset are defined to **include the guaranteed** residual value. Unguaranteed residual values are excluded from "minimum lease payments." If the residual value is not guaranteed by the lessee, the lessee has no responsibility or obligation for the asset's condition at the end of the lease. The unguaranteed residual value, therefore, is not included in the calculation of the lease obligation either.

Finance

A guaranteed residual is similar to an additional lease payment that will be paid in property or cash, or both, at the end of the lease. Using the rental payments as calculated by the lessor in Illustration 20-9, the lessee's **minimum lease payments** are $121,185.45 ([$23,237.09 × 5] + $5,000). Illustration 20-10 shows the calculation of the present value of the minimum lease payments. This amount is capitalized as the leased asset and recognized as the lease liability.

Illustration 20-10

Calculation of Lessee's Capitalized Amount— Guaranteed Residual Value

LESSEE'S CAPITALIZED AMOUNT (10% RATE)
(Annuity due basis; guaranteed residual value)

Present value of five annual rental payments of $23,237.09, $i = 10\%$: ($23,237.09 × 4.16986, Table A-5)	$ 96,895.40
Add: present value of guaranteed residual value of $5,000 due at end of five-year lease term: ($5,000 × 0.62092, Table A-2)	3,104.60
Lessee's capitalized amount	$100,000.00

Illustration 20-11

Lease Amortization Schedule for Lessee—Guaranteed Residual Value

	A	B	C	D	E
1			Lessee Corporation Lease Amortization Schedule (Annuity due basis, guaranteed residual value)		
2	Date	Lease Payment	Interest (10%) on Unpaid Obligation	Reduction of Lease Obligation	Lease Obligation
3		(a)	(b)	(c)	(d)
4	1/1/10				$100,000.00
5	1/1/10	$ 23,237.09	$ –0–	$ 23,237.09	76,762.91
6	1/1/11	23,237.09	7,676.29	15,560.80	61,202.11
7	1/1/12	23,237.09	6,120.21	17,116.88	44,085.23
8	1/1/13	23,237.09	4,408.52	18,828.57	25,256.66
9	1/1/14	23,237.09	2,525.67	20,711.42	4,545.24
10	12/31/14	5,000.00*	454.76**	4,545.24	–0–
11		$121,185.45	$21,185.45	$100,000.00	

13   (a) Annual lease payment as required by lease, excluding executory costs.
   (b) Preceding balance of (d) × 10%, except 1/1/10.
   (c) (a) minus (b).
   (d) Preceding balance minus (c).
   *Represents the guaranteed residual value.
   **Rounded by 24 cents.

As Illustration 20-11 shows, Lessee Corporation's schedule of interest expense and amortization of the $100,000 lease obligation results in a $5,000 guaranteed residual value payment at the end of five years, on December 31, 2014.

The journal entries in the first column of Illustration 20-16 are based on a **guaranteed residual value**. The format of these entries is the same as illustrated earlier, but the amounts are different because of the capitalized residual value. As you might expect, the guaranteed residual value is subtracted from the cost of the leased asset in determining the depreciable amount. Assuming the straight-line method is used, the depreciation expense each year is $19,000 ([$100,000 − $5,000] ÷ 5). Note that the **undiscounted residual value is used** in this calculation, consistent with Chapter 11 and your introductory accounting course.

Illustration 20-12 shows how the leased asset and obligation are reported on the December 31, 2014 balance sheet, just before the lessee transfers the asset back to the lessor.

Property, plant, and equipment		Current liabilities	
Equipment under capital leases	$100,000.00	Interest payable	$ 454.76
Less: Accumulated depreciation—		Obligations under	
capital leases	95,000.00	capital leases	4,545.24
	$ 5,000.00		$5,000.00

Illustration 20-12

Account Balances on Lessee's Books at End of Lease— Guaranteed Residual Value

If the equipment's fair value is less than $5,000 at the end of the lease, Lessee Corporation records a loss. For example, assume that Lessee Corporation depreciated the leased asset down to its residual value of $5,000 but the asset's fair value at December 31, 2014, is only $3,000. In this case, Lessee Corporation records the following entry, assuming cash is paid to make up the residual value deficiency:

Loss on Capital Lease	2,000.00	
Interest Payable	454.76	
Obligations under Capital Leases	4,545.24	
Accumulated Depreciation—Capital Leases	95,000.00	
Equipment under Capital Leases		100,000.00
Cash		2,000.00

A   =   L   +   SE
−7,000   −5,000   −2,000

Cash flows: ↓ 2,000 outflow

If the fair value is more than $5,000, a gain may or may not be recognized. Gains on guaranteed residual values are shared between the lessor and lessee in whatever ratio the parties initially agreed to.

Lessee Accounting with an Unguaranteed Residual Value.

From the lessee's viewpoint, an unguaranteed residual value has the same effect as no residual value on its calculation of the minimum lease payments, the leased asset, and lease obligation. Assume the same facts as those above except that the $5,000 residual value is **unguaranteed**. The annual lease payment is the same ($23,237.09) because, whether the residual is guaranteed or unguaranteed, Lessor Corporation's amount to be recovered through lease rentals is the same: $96,895.40. Lessee Corporation's minimum lease payments are $116,185.45 ($23,237.09 × 5). Illustration 20-13 calculates the capitalized amount for the lessee.

Finance

Illustration 20-13

Calculation of Lessee's Capitalized Amount— Unguaranteed Residual Value

LESSEE'S CAPITALIZED AMOUNT (10% RATE) (Annuity due basis, unguaranteed residual value)	
Present value of five annual rental payments of $23,237.09 *i* = 10%, $23,237.09 × 4.16986 (Table A-5)	$96,895.40
Unguaranteed residual value is not included in minimum lease payments	–0–
Lessee's capitalized amount	$96,895.40

With an unguaranteed residual, Lessee Corporation's amortization table for the $96,895.40 obligation is provided in Illustration 20-14.

Illustration 20-14

Lease Amortization Schedule for Lessee—Unguaranteed Residual Value

	A	B	C	D	E
1			Lessee Corporation Lease Amortization Schedule (10%) (Annuity due basis, unguaranteed residual value)		
2	Date	Lease Payment	Interest (10%) on Unpaid Obligation	Reduction of Lease Obligation	Lease Obligation
3		(a)	(b)	(c)	(d)
4	1/1/10				$96,895.40
5	1/1/10	$ 23,237.09	$ –0–	$23,237.09	73,658.31
6	1/1/11	23,237.09	7,365.83	15,871.26	57,787.05
7	1/1/12	23,237.09	5,778.71	17,458.38	40,328.67
8	1/1/13	23,237.09	4,032.87	19,204.22	21,124.45
9	1/1/14	23,237.09	2,112.64*	21,124.45	–0–
10		$116,185.45	$19,290.05	$96,895.40	

12	(a) Annual lease payment as required by lease, excluding executory costs.
	(b) Preceding balance of (d) × 10%, except Jan. 1, 2010.
	(c) (a) minus (b).
	(d) Preceding balance minus (c).
	*Rounded by 19 cents.

With no guarantee of the residual value, the journal entries needed to record the lease agreement and subsequent depreciation, interest, property tax, and payments are provided in the right-hand column of Illustration 20-16. The format of these entries is the same as illustrated earlier. Note that the leased asset is recorded at $96,895.40 and is depreciated over five years. Using straight-line depreciation, the depreciation expense each year is $19,379.08 ($96,895.40 ÷ 5). Illustration 20-15 shows how the asset and obligation are reported on the December 31, 2014 balance sheet, just before the lessee transfers the asset back to the lessor.

Illustration 20-15

Account Balances on Lessee's Books at End of Lease— Unguaranteed Residual Value

Property, plant, and equipment		Current liabilities	
Equipment under capital leases	$96,895	Obligations under capital leases	$–0–
Less: Accumulated depreciation capital leases	96,895		
	$ –0–		

Whether the asset's fair value at the end of the lease is $3,000 or $6,000, the only entry required is one to remove the asset and its accumulated depreciation from the books. There is no gain or loss to report.

Lessee Entries Involving Residual Values.   Lessee Corporation's entries for both a guaranteed and an unguaranteed residual value are shown side by side in Illustration 20-16.

Guaranteed Residual Value			Unguaranteed Residual Value		
Capitalization of Lease (January 1, 2010):					
Equipment under Capital Leases	100,000.00		Equipment under Capital Leases	96,895.40	
Obligations under Capital Leases		100,000.00	Obligations under Capital Leases		96,895.40
First Payment (January 1, 2010):					
Maintenance Expense	2,000.00		Maintenance Expense	2,000.00	
Obligations under Capital Leases	23,237.09		Obligations under Capital Leases	23,237.09	
Cash		25,237.09	Cash		25,237.09
Adjusting Entry for Accrued Interest (December 31, 2010):					
Interest Expense	7,676.29		Interest Expense	7,365.83	
Interest Payable		7,676.29	Interest Payable		7,365.83
Entry to Record Depreciation (December 31, 2010):					
Depreciation Expense—Capital Leases	19,000.00		Depreciation Expense—Capital Leases	19,379.08	
Accumulated Depreciation—			Accumulated Depreciation—		
Capital Leases		19,000.00	Capital Leases		19,379.08
([$100,000 − $5,000] ÷ 5 years)			($96,895.40 ÷ 5 years)		
Second Payment (January 1, 2011):					
Maintenance Expense	2,000.00		Maintenance Expense	2,000.00	
Obligations under Capital Leases	15,560.80		Obligations under Capital Leases	15,871.26	
Interest Payable	7,676.29		Interest Payable	7,365.83	
Cash		25,237.09	Cash		25,237.09

Illustration 20-16

Comparative Entries for Guaranteed and Unguaranteed Residual Values, Lessee Corporation

Lessee Accounting with a Bargain Purchase Option.   Based on the examples above, you may be able to deduce how the lessee would account for a lease when the terms include a bargain purchase option. The lessor gets a return on its investment in the leased asset from the option amount it will receive at the end of the lease (similar to the residual value calculations) and from the lease payments. Therefore the option amount is taken into consideration in determining the amount of the lease payments.

The lessee's accounting **assumes that the option will be exercised** and that the title to the leased property will be transferred to the lessee. Therefore, the bargain option price is included in the minimum lease payments and its present value is included as part of the leased asset and lease obligation.

There is **no difference** between the lessee's calculations and the amortization schedule for the lease obligation for a $5,000 **bargain purchase option** and those shown previously for the $5,000 **guaranteed residual value**. The only accounting difference is the calculation of the **annual depreciation of the asset**. In the case of a guaranteed residual value, the lessee depreciates the asset over the lease term because the asset will be returned to the lessor. In the case of a bargain purchase option, the lessee uses the asset's economic life and its estimated remaining value at the end of that time because it is assumed that the lessee will acquire title to the asset by exercising the option, and will then continue to use it.

Accounting for an Operating Lease

6 Objective

Account for an operating lease by a lessee and compare the operating and capitalization methods of accounting for leases.

In a lease agreement where the risks and benefits of ownership of the leased asset are not considered to be transferred to the lessee, a non-capitalization method is appropriate. Under this type of lease, **neither the leased asset nor the obligation to make lease**

Expanded Discussion: Illustrations
of Lease Arrangements

payments is recognized in the accounts. It is treated as an executory contract, and the lease payments are treated as rent expense. You were introduced to rent expense in your introductory accounting course.[21]

Refer back to the Lessor Corporation and Lessee Corporation example in Illustration 20-5 and assume now that the lease described there does not qualify as a finance or capital lease and, by default, is an operating lease. The charge to the income statement for rent expense each year is $25,981.62, the amount of the rental payment. The journal entry to record the payment each January 1 is as follows:

A = L + SE
0   0   0

Cash flows: ↓ 25,981.62 outflow

| Prepaid Rent | 25,981.62 | |
| Cash | | 25,981.62 |

Assuming that adjusting entries are prepared only annually, the following entry is made at each December 31 fiscal year end:

A   = L +   SE
−25,981.62   −25,981.62

Cash flows: No effect

| Rent Expense | 25,981.62 | |
| Prepaid Rent | | 25,981.62 |

Both **private enterprise standards** and **IFRS** agree that lease rentals are recognized on a straight-line basis over the term of the lease unless another systematic basis better represents the pattern of the benefits received. Complexities can arise, however, such as when lease inducements are offered. Assume that to motivate a lessee to sign a new five-year lease for office space at $3,000 each month, a lessor agrees to a three-month rent-free period at the beginning of the lease and a two-month rent-free period at the end. How much rent expense should be recognized in each accounting period?

The straight-line method is applied to the lease inducement example in the following way:

Lease term: 5 years × 12 months = 60 months
Total rent: 60 − 3 − 2 = 55 months × $3,000 = $165,000
Rent expense to be recognized each month: $165,000 ÷ 60 months = $2,750

That is, the total rent is recognized evenly over the lease term.

Capital and Operating Leases Compared

As indicated above, if the lease in Illustration 20-5 had been accounted for as an operating lease, the first-year charge to operations would have been $25,981.62, the amount of the rental payment. As a capital lease, however, the first-year charge is $29,601.84: straight-line depreciation of $20,000, interest expense of $7,601.84, and executory expenses of $2,000. Illustration 20-17 shows that, while the total charges to operations are the same over the lease term whether the lease is accounted for as a capital lease or as an operating lease, the charges are higher in the earlier years and lower in the later years under the

---

[21] Under IAS 40 *Investment Property*, a lessee is able to classify a property interest under an operating lease as an investment property. If this option is taken, the investment property must be accounted for under the fair value model. There is no corresponding private enterprise concept.

capital lease treatment. The higher expense in the early years, along with the recognition of the lease obligation as a liability, are two reasons that lessees are reluctant to classify leases as capital leases. Lessees, especially when real estate leases are involved, claim that it is no more costly to operate the leased asset in the early years than in the later years; thus, they prefer an even charge like the operating method offers.

	A	B	C	D	E		G	H
1			**Lessee Corporation** **Schedule of Charges to Operations** **Capital Lease versus Operating Lease**					
2		**Capital Lease**					**Operating Lease**	
3	**Year**	**Depreciation**	**Executory Costs**	**Interest**	**Total Expense**		**Expense**	**Difference**
4	2010	$ 20,000	$ 2,000	$ 7,601.84	$ 29,601.84		$ 25,981.62	$3,620.22
5	2011	20,000	2,000	5,963.86	27,963.86		25,981.62	1,982.24
6	2012	20,000	2,000	4,162.08	26,162.08		25,981.62	180.46
7	2013	20,000	2,000	2,180.32	24,180.32		25,981.62	(1,801.30)
8	2014	20,000	2,000	–0–	22,000.00		25,981.62	(3,981.62)
9		$100,000	$10,000	$19,908.10	$129,908.10		$129,908.10	$ –0–
10								

Illustration 20-17

Comparison of Charges to Operations—Capital vs. Operating Leases

If an accelerated depreciation method is used, the difference between the amounts that are charged to operations under the two methods is even larger in the earlier and later years.

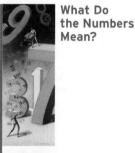

What Do the Numbers Mean?

The most important and significant difference between the two approaches, however, is the effect on the balance sheet. The capital lease approach initially reports an asset and related liability of $100,000 on the balance sheet, **whereas no such asset or liability is reported under the operating lease method.** Refer back to Illustration 20-1 to understand the significance of the amounts that are left off the statement of financial position for WestJet, Air Canada, and Helijet. It is not surprising that the business community resists capitalizing leases, as the resulting **higher debt-to-equity ratio, reduced total asset turnover**, and **reduced rate of return on total assets** are seen as having a detrimental effect on the company.

Ethics

And resist this they have! The intention of the Canadian standard was to have the accounting for leases based on whether or not the risks and benefits of ownership were transferred, similar to how the international standard works. However, because the standard specifies 75% of the asset's useful life and 90% of its fair value, management often interprets these numbers as "rates to beat." That is, leases are specifically engineered to ensure that ownership is not transferred and to have them come in just under the 75% and 90% hurdles so that the capitalization criteria are not met.

The experience with how this standard has been applied remains one of the key reasons why Canadian and international standard setters shy away from identifying specific numerical criteria in standards. They prefer to rely on principles-based, rather than rules-based, guidance.

Whether this resistance is reasonable is a matter of opinion. From a cash flow point of view—and excluding any cash flow effects that are associated with income tax differences—a company is in the same position whether the lease is accounted for as an operating or a capital lease. The reasons that managers often give when they argue against capitalization are that capitalization can more easily lead to violation of loan covenants; can affect the amount of compensation that is received (for example, a stock compensation plan tied to earnings); and can lower rates of return and increase debt-to-equity relationships, thus making the company less attractive to present and potential investors.[22]

Presentation and Disclosure

Current versus Noncurrent Classification

The classification of the lessee's lease obligation was presented earlier for an **annuity due** situation. As indicated in Illustration 20-8, the lessee's current portion of the lease obligation is the reduction in its principal balance within 12 months from the balance sheet date **plus** interest accrued to the balance sheet date. Coincidentally, the total of these two amounts in the example is the same as the rental payment of $23,981.62 that will be made one day later on January 1 of the next year. In this example, the balance sheet date is December 31 and the due date of the lease payment is January 1, so the total of the principal reduction on January 1 and the interest accrued to December 31 is the same as the rental payment ($23,981.62). **This will happen only when the payment is due the day following the balance sheet date.** Understandably, this is not a common situation.

The following questions might now be asked. What happens if the lease payments fall as an **ordinary annuity** rather than an annuity due, and what if the lease payment dates do not coincide with the company's fiscal year? To illustrate, assume that the lease in our original example from Illustration 20-5 was signed and effective on September 1, 2010, with the first lease payment to be made on September 1, 2011—an ordinary annuity situation. Assume also that we continue to use the other facts of the Lessee Corporation/Lessor Corporation example, excluding the executory costs. Because the rents are paid at the end of the lease periods instead of at the beginning, the five rents are set at $26,379.73 to earn the lessor an interest rate of 10%.[23] With both companies having December 31 year ends, Illustration 20-18 provides the appropriate lease amortization schedule for this lease, based on the September 1 lease anniversary date each year.

Finance

	A	B	C	D	E
1			**Lessee Corporation** Lease Amortization Schedule (10%) (Ordinary annuity basis)		
2	Date	Annual Lease Payment	Interest (10%)	Reduction of Principal	Balance of Lease Obligation
3	1/9/10				$100,000.00
4	1/9/11	$ 26,379.73	$10,000.00	$ 16,379.73	83,620.27
5	1/9/12	26,379.73	8,362.03	18,017.70	65,602.57
6	1/9/13	26,379.73	6,560.26	19,819.47	45,783.10
7	1/9/14	26,379.73	4,578.31	21,801.42	23,981.68
8	1/9/15	26,379.73	2,398.05*	23,981.68	–0–
9		$131,898.65	$31,898.65	$100,000.00	
11	*Rounded by 12 cents.				

---

[22] One study indicates that management's behaviour did change as a result of the profession's requirements to capitalize certain leases. Many companies restructured their leases to avoid capitalization; others increased their purchases of assets instead of leasing; and others, faced with capitalization, postponed their debt offerings or issued shares instead. It is interesting to note that the study found no significant effect on share or bond prices as a result of capitalization of leases. A. Rashad Abdel-khalik, "The Economic Effects on Lessees of *FASB Statement No. 13*, Accounting for Leases," Research Report (Stamford, Conn.: FASB, 1981).

[23] The rent is now calculated as $100,000 ÷ 3.79079 = $26,379.73. The denominator is the factor for $n = 5$ and $i = 10$ for an ordinary annuity (Table A-4).

At December 31, 2010, the lease obligation is still $100,000. How much should be reported in current liabilities on the December 31, 2010 balance sheet and how much in long-term liabilities? The answer here is the same as earlier: **the current portion is the principal that will be repaid within 12 months from the balance sheet date** (i.e., $16,379.73). **In addition, any interest that has accrued up to the balance sheet date** (i.e., 10% of $100,000 × 4/12 = $3,333) is reported in current liabilities. The long-term portion of the obligation is the principal that will **not** be repaid within 12 months from the balance sheet date, or $83,620.27. It helps if you can first correctly describe in words what makes up the current portion, then determine the numbers that correspond.

On December 31, 2011, the long-term portion of the lease is $65,602.57. The principal due within 12 months from December 31, 2011, or $18,017.70, is included as a current liability along with interest accrued to December 31, 2011, of $2,787 (10% of $83,620.27 ×4/12).

Lessee Disclosures

Capital/Finance Leases.   Because a capital or finance lease recognizes the leased capital asset and a long-term liability, most of the required disclosures are identified in or are similar to those in the standards that cover property, plant, and equipment; intangible assets; impairment; financial instruments; and/or long-term liabilities. IFRS requires additional disclosures related to:

1. The net carrying amount of each class of leased asset

2. A reconciliation of the future minimum lease payments to their present value in total, and for the next year, years two to five, and beyond five years from the balance sheet date

3. The entity's material lease arrangements, especially concerning contingent rents, sublease payments, and restrictions imposed by lease agreements

Operating Leases.   Both ASPE and IFRS require disclosure of the minimum lease payments for their operating leases extending into the future. Private enterprises report the total at the balance sheet date and those payable in each of the next five years. The IFRS requirement is similar, but extends the disclosures to include a description of significant lease arrangements and information about subleases and contingent rents.

Real-World Emphasis

WILEY PLUS

Additional Disclosures

Illustration of Lease Disclosures by a Lessee.   The excerpts from the financial statements of **Canadian Pacific Railway Limited** (CPR) for the year ended December 31, 2009, in Illustration 20-19 show how this lessee company met the disclosure requirements for its leases under pre-2011 Canadian GAAP, similar to the new private enterprise requirements. The company reports in millions of Canadian dollars.

14 Net properties

(in millions of Canadian dollars)	Annual rate	2009			2008 Restated (note 2)		
		Cost	Accumulated depreciation	Net book value	Cost	Accumulated depreciation	Net book value
Track and roadway	2.9%	$11,590.1	$3,197.5	$ 8,392.6	$11,862.4	$3,195.0	$ 8,667.4
Buildings	2.8%	357.3	115.4	241.9	366.5	126.8	239.7
Rolling stock	2.9%	3,369.7	1,327.1	2,042.6	3,497.4	1,340.2	2,157.2
Information systems(1)	8.2%	639.7	276.2	363.5	609.9	240.0	369.9
Other	4.7%	1,339.7	412.5	927.2	1,418.0	467.6	950.4
Total net properties		$17,296.5	$5,328.7	$11,967.8	$17,754.2	$5,369.6	$12,384.6

(1) Additions during 2009 were $42.9 million (2008 – $55.6 million; 2007 – $48.8 million) and depreciation expense was $47.5 million (2008 – $44.5 million; 2007 – $50.5 million).

CAPITAL LEASES INCLUDED IN PROPERTIES

(in millions of Canadian dollars)	2009			2008		
	Cost	Accumulated depreciation	Net book value	Cost	Accumulated depreciation	Net book value
Buildings	$ 0.5	$ 0.1	$ 0.4	$ —	$ —	$ —
Rolling stock	536.2	139.3	396.9	604.3	152.6	451.7
Other	4.5	1.8	2.7	5.6	1.3	4.3
Total assets held under capital lease	$541.2	$141.2	$ 400.0	$609.9	$153.9	$456.0

During 2009, properties were acquired under the Company's capital program at an aggregate cost of $722.2 million (2008 – $922.3 million; 2007 – $850.9 million), $0.8 million of which were acquired by means of capital leases (2008 – $79.5 million; 2007 – $12.1 million). Cash payments related to capital purchases were $722.4 million in 2009 (2008 – $832.9 million; 2007 – $836.0 million). At December 31, 2009, $11.0 million (2008 – $9.4 million; 2007 – $2.1 million) remained in accounts payable related to the above purchases.

18 Long-term debt

(in millions of Canadian dollars)

	Maturity	Currency in which payable	2009	2008
Obligations under capital leases (5.20% – 9.38%) (H)	2010-2026	US$	319.7	406.4
Obligations under capital leases (5.64% – 5.65%) (H)	2013-2031	CDN$	12.0	12.8

Annual maturities and principal repayments requirements, excluding those pertaining to capital leases, for each of the five years following 2009 are (in millions): 2010 – $381.6; 2011 – $289.2; 2012 – $38.1; 2013 – $148.3; 2014 – $44.2.

H. At December 31, 2009, capital lease obligations included in long-term debt were as follows:

(in millions of Canadian dollars)	Year	Capital leases
Minimum lease payments in:	2010	$ 33.4
	2011	33.4
	2012	33.8
	2013	31.9
	2014	177.1
	Thereafter	213.1
Total minimum lease payments		522.7
Less: Imputed interest		(191.0)
Present value of minimum lease payments		331.7
Less: Current portion		(10.5)
Long-term portion of capital lease obligations		$321.2

The carrying value of the assets collateralizing the capital lease obligations was $400.0 million at December 31, 2009.

28 Commitments and contingencies

Minimum payments under operating leases were estimated at $930.1 million in aggregate, with annual payments in each of the five years following 2009 of (in millions): 2010 – $148.1; 2011 – $128.1; 2012 – $114.6; 2013 – $100.0; 2014 – $78.7.

29 Guarantees

In the normal course of operating the railway, the Company enters into contractual arrangements that involve providing certain guarantees, which extend over the term of the contracts. These guarantees include, but are not limited to:
❑ residual value guarantees on operating lease commitments of $167.3 million at December 31, 2009

Illustration 20-19

Capital Lease Disclosures by a Lessee—CPR

Illustration 20-20 provides an additional example of disclosure related to lessees, this time under IFRS. The excerpts are taken from the December 31, 2008 financial statements of **Barclays Bank PLC**. Barclays is an internationally renowned financial services provider engaged in all aspects of the industry, particularly in Europe, United States, Africa, and Asia. The company reports amounts in millions of British pounds (£m).

38 Leasing (continued)

(b) As Lessee

Finance lease commitments
The Group and the Bank lease items of property, plant and equipment on terms that meet the definition of finance leases. Finance lease commitments are included within other liabilities (see Note 25).

Obligations under finance leases were as follows:

	The Group		The Bank	
	2008	2007	2008	2007
	Total future minimum payments £m	Total future minimum payments £m	Total future minimum payments £m	Total future minimum payments £m
Not more than one year	35	12	2	7
Over one year but not more than two years	13	14	3	2
Over two years but not more than three years	14	13	1	3
Over three years but not more than four years	17	12	—	2
Over four years but not more than five years	14	15	—	—
Over five years	3	17	—	—
Net obligations under finance leases	**96**	83	6	14

The carrying amount of assets held under finance leases at the balance sheet date was:

	The Group		The Bank	
	2008	2007	2008	2007
	£m	£m	£m	£m
Cost	87	94	—	—
Accumulated depreciation	(67)	(24)	—	—
Net book value	**20**	70	—	—

Operating lease commitments
The Group and the Bank lease various offices, branches and other premises under non-cancellable operating lease arrangements. The leases have various terms, escalation and renewal rights. There are no contingent rents payable. The Group and the Bank also lease equipment under non-cancellable lease arrangements.

Where the Group and the Bank are the lessees the future minimum lease payment under non-cancellable operating leases are as follows:

	The Group				The Bank			
	2008		2007		2008		2007	
	Property £m	Equipment £m	Property £m	Equipment £m	Property £m	Equipment £m	Property £m	Equipment £m
Not more than one year	275	5	191	6	45	2	44	5
Over one year but not more than two years	354	1	396	1	223	—	252	—
Over two years but not more three years	334	1	357	1	213	—	233	—
Over three years but not more four years	315	—	323	—	197	—	219	1
Over four years but not more than five years	465	5	287	—	185	—	195	—
Over five years	2,744	1	2,225	—	1,782	—	1,869	—
Total	**4,487**	**13**	3,779	8	**2,645**	**2**	2,812	6

The total of future minimum sublease payments to be received under non-cancellable subleases at the balance sheet date is £158m (2007: £167m) for the Group and £148m (2007: £167m) for the Bank.

Illustration 20-20

Lessee Disclosures under IFRS—Barclays Bank PLC

CLASSIFICATION APPROACH— LESSORS

Classification Criteria

Objective 8

Identify and apply the criteria that are used to determine the type of lease for a lessor under the classification approach.

From the **lessor's** standpoint, all leases are classified for accounting purposes as follows:

Type	Private enterprise standards terminology	IFRS terminology
Operating	Operating lease	Operating lease
Sales-type	Sales-type lease	Finance lease: = Manufacturer or dealer lease
	or	or
Financing-type	Direct financing lease	= Other finance lease

The lessor considers the same factors as the lessee in determining whether the risks and benefits of ownership of the leased property are transferred. If they **are not transferred** to the lessee, the lessor accounts for the lease contract as an operating lease. If instead the risks and benefits of ownership **are transferred** to the lessee, the lessor accounts for the lease under private enterprise terminology as either a sales-type or direct financing lease. Under IFRS, non-operating leases are called finance leases, mirroring the terminology used by the lessee. The substance of the types of non-operating leases is exactly the same under both—IFRS's manufacturer or dealer lease is equivalent a sales-type lease, and an other finance lease is equivalent to a direct-financing lease.

Under **IFRS**, the criteria to assess whether a lease is an operating lease or a finance lease are identical to the criteria used by the lessee, as explained earlier in this chapter. Under **private enterprise standards**, the same criteria are also used, with the addition of two revenue recognition-based tests that must be passed:

1. Is the credit risk associated with the lease normal when compared with the risk of collection of similar receivables?

2. Can the amounts of any unreimbursable costs that are likely to be incurred by the lessor under the lease be reasonably estimated?

If collectibility of the amounts that are due under the contract is not reasonably assured or if the lessor still has to absorb an uncertain amount of additional costs associated with the agreement, then it is not appropriate to remove the leased asset from the lessor's books and recognize revenue. In short, if any one of the three private enterprise criteria for classification as a capital lease is met and the answer to both of these additional two questions is also yes, then the arrangement is not an operating lease—it is either a sales-type or a direct financing lease.

How do you distinguish between a sales-type and a financing-type lease? This depends on the specific situation. Some manufacturers enter into lease agreements either directly or through a subsidiary captive leasing company as a way of facilitating the sale of their product. These transactions are usually sales-type lease arrangements. Other companies are in business to provide financing to the lessee for the acquisition of a variety of assets in order to generate financing income. They usually enter into direct financing, or other finance leases.

The difference between these classifications **is the presence or absence of a manufacturer's or dealer's profit (or loss)**. A sales-type lease (a manufacturer or dealer lease) includes in the rental amount the recovery of a manufacturer's or dealer's profit as well as the asset's cost. The profit (or loss) to this lessor is the difference between the fair value of the leased property at the beginning of the lease, and the lessor's cost or carrying amount (book value). As indicated earlier, sales-type leases normally arise when manufacturers or dealers use leasing as a way of marketing their products.

Direct financing leases (or other financing leases), on the other hand, generally result from arrangements with lessors that are engaged mostly in financing operations, such as lease-finance companies and a variety of financial intermediaries, such as banks or their finance subsidiaries. These lessors acquire the specific assets that lessees have asked them to acquire. Their business model is to earn interest income on the financing arrangement with the lessee.

All leases that are not financing or sales-type leases are classified and accounted for by the lessor as **operating leases**. Under PE standards, when both revenue recognition criteria are not met, it is possible that a lessor will classify a lease as an **operating** lease while the lessee will classify the same lease as a **capital** lease. When this happens, both the lessor and lessee carry the asset on their books and both depreciate the capitalized asset.

Accounting for Financing and Sales-Type Leases

For all leases that are not operating leases, the lessor recognizes the leased assets on the balance sheet as a receivable equal to its net investment in the lease. This applies under both sets of standards.

9 Objective
Account for and report basic financing and sales-type leases by a lessor.

Lessor Accounting for a Financing-Type Lease

Direct or other financing leases are, in substance, the financing of an asset by the lessee. The lessor removes the asset from its books and replaces it with a receivable. The accounts and information that are needed to record this type of lease are as follows.

LESSOR TERMINOLOGY		
Term	Account	Explanation
Gross investment in lease	Lease Payments Receivable	The undiscounted rental/lease payments (excluding executory costs) plus any guaranteed or unguaranteed residual value that accrues to the lessor at the end of the lease or any bargain purchase option.[a]
Unearned finance or interest income	Unearned Interest Income (contra account to Lease Payments Receivable)	The difference between the undiscounted Lease Payments Receivable and the fair value of the leased property.
Net investment in lease	Net of the two accounts above	The gross investment (the Lease Payments Receivable account) less the Unearned Interest Income; i.e., the gross investment's present value.

[a] This is equal to the lessor's minimum lease payments, as defined, plus any unguaranteed residual value. To a lessor, the minimum lease payments are the **minimum lease payments** as defined for the lessee plus any residual amounts guaranteed by parties unrelated to the lessee or lessor.

The net investment is the present value of the items that make up the gross investment. The difference between these two accounts is the unearned interest. The unearned interest income is amortized and taken into income over the lease term by applying the effective interest method, using the interest rate implicit in the lease. This results in a constant rate of return being produced on the net investment in the lease.

Illustration of a Financing-Type Lease (Annuity Due).   The following lease example uses the same data as the Lessor Corporation/Lessee Corporation example in Illustration 20-5. The relevant information for Lessor Corporation from the illustration follows.

1. The lease has a **five-year term** that begins January 1, 2010, is non-cancellable, and requires equal **rental payments of $25,981.62** at the beginning of each year. Payments include **$2,000 of executory costs** (maintenance fee).

2. The equipment has a **cost and fair value of $100,000** to Lessor Corporation, an estimated **economic life of five years**, and **no residual value**. No initial direct costs are incurred in negotiating and closing the lease contract.

3. The lease contains no renewal options and the **equipment reverts to Lessor Corporation** at the end of the lease.

4. **Collectibility is reasonably assured** and **no additional costs** (with the exception of the maintenance fees being reimbursed by the lessee) are to be incurred by Lessor Corporation.

5. The interest rate implicit in the lease is 10%. Lessor Corporation set the annual lease payments to ensure a **10% return** on its investment, shown previously in Illustration 20-3.

The lease meets the criteria for classification as a financing-type lease as set out above. It is not a sales-type or manufacturer/dealer lease, because **there is no dealer profit** between the equipment's fair value and the lessor's cost.

Illustration 20-21 calculates the initial gross investment in the lease, which is the amount to be recognized in Lease Payments Receivable.

Illustration 20-21 *Calculation of Lease Payments Receivable*	Gross investment in the lease and lease payments receivable = Total lease payments (excluding executory costs) plus residual value or bargain purchase option[24] = [($25,981.62 − $2,000) × 5] + $0 = $119,908.10

The net investment in the lease is the present value of the gross investment, as determined in Illustration 20-22.

Illustration 20-22 *Calculation of Net Investment in the Lease*	Net investment in the lease = Gross investment in the lease discounted at the rate implicit in the lease = $23,981.62 × 4.16986 (*n* = 5, *i* = 10) (Table A-5) + $0 × 0.62092 (*n* = 5, *i* = 10) (Table A-2) = $100,000

The unearned interest or finance income is the interest that will be earned over the term of the lease. It is the difference between the gross investment and the net investment—$119,908.10 minus $100,000, or $19,908.10.

The acquisition of the asset by the lessor, its transfer to the lessee, the resulting receivable, and the unearned interest income are recorded on January 1, 2010, as follows:

---

[24] Under IFRS, a lessor who is not a manufacturer or dealer also includes any intial direct costs associated with negotiating and arranging the lease. In this example, these costs are $0.

Equipment Purchased for Lease	100,000	
Cash[25]		100,000

A = L + SE
0   0   0

Cash flows: ↓ 100,000 outflow

Lease Payments Receivable	119,908.10	
Equipment Purchased for Lease		100,000.00
Unearned Interest Income—Leases		19,908.10

A = L + SE
0   0   0

Cash flows: No effect

The Unearned Interest Income account is classified on the balance sheet as a contra account to the receivable account. Generally, the lease payments receivable amount, although it is **recorded** at the gross investment amount, is **reported** on the balance sheet at the "net investment" amount and entitled "Net investment in capital leases."[26]

As a result of this entry, Lessor Corporation replaces its investment in the asset that it acquired for Lessee Corporation at a cost of $100,000, with a net lease receivable of $100,000. Similar to Lessee's treatment of interest, Lessor Corporation applies the effective interest method and recognizes interest income according to the unrecovered net investment balance, as shown in Illustration 20-23.

	A	B	C	D	E
1			**Lessor Corporation** **Lease Amortization Schedule** **(Annuity due basis)**		
2	Date	Annual Lease Payment	Interest (10%) on Net Investment	Net Investment Recovery	Net Investment
3		(a)	(b)	(c)	(d)
4	1/1/10				$100,000.00
5	1/1/10	$ 23,981.62	$ –0–	$ 23,981.62	76,018.38
6	1/1/11	23,981.62	7,601.84	16,379.78	59,638.60
7	1/1/12	23,981.62	5,963.86	18,017.76	41,620.84
8	1/1/13	23,981.62	4,162.08	19,819.54	21,801.30
9	1/1/14	23,981.62	2,180.32*	21,801.30	–0–
10		$119,908.10	$19,908.10	$100,000.00	
12	(a) Annual rental that provides a 10% return on net investment (exclusive of executory costs). (b) 10% of the preceding balance of (d) except for 1/1/10. (c) (a) minus (b). (d) Preceding balance minus (c). *Rounded by 19 cents.				

Illustration 20-23

Lease Amortization Schedule for Lessor—Annuity Due Basis

On January 1, 2010, the entry to record the receipt of the first year's lease payment is as follows:

---

[25] The lessor usually finances the purchase of this asset over a term that generally coincides with the term of the lease. Because the lessor's cost of capital is lower than the rate that is implicit in the lease, the lessor earns a profit represented by the interest spread.

[26] While lessees may record and report the lease obligation on a net basis, lessors tend to recognize the gross amount in receivables. Unlike the lessee, lessors may have hundreds or thousands of lease contracts to administer and the amounts to be collected are the gross receivables. Therefore, for administrative simplicity, the amounts that are received are a direct reduction of the receivable, and the interest is determined and adjusted for separately.

A	=	L	+	SE
+2,000				+2,000

Cash flows: ↑ 25,981.62 inflow

Cash	25,981.62	
Lease Payments Receivable		23,981.62
Maintenance Expense		2,000.00

On December 31, 2010, the interest income earned during the first year is recognized:

A	=	L	+	SE
+7,601.84				+7,601.84

Cash flows: No effect

Unearned Interest Income—Leases	7,601.84	
Interest Income—Leases		7,601.84

T accounts for the receivable and its unearned interest contra account, and the effect on the net investment after these entries are made and posted, are shown in Illustration 20-24.

Illustration 20-24

General Ledger Lease
Asset Accounts

	Lease Payments Receivable		Unearned Interest Income		Net Investment in Lease
Jan. 1/10	$119,908.10			$19,908.10	$100,000.00
Jan. 1/10		23,981.62			(23,981.62)
	95,926.48			19,908.10	76,018.38
Dec. 31/10			7,601.84		7,601.84
	95,926.48			12,306.26	83,620.22

At December 31, 2010, the net investment in capital leases is reported in Lessor Corporation's balance sheet among current and noncurrent assets, as appropriate. The principal portion that is due within 12 months is classified as a current asset and the remainder is reported with noncurrent assets.

The net investment at December 31, 2010, is $83,620.22, which is the balance at January 1, 2010, of $76,018.38 plus interest earned up to the balance sheet date of $7,601.84. The **current portion** is determined as follows:

Recovery of net investment within 12 months from Dec. 31, 2010	$16,379.78
Interest accrued to Dec. 31, 2010	7,601.84
Current portion of net investment	$23,981.62

The **long-term portion** is the $59,638.60 remainder. The lease amortization schedule in Illustration 20-23 indicates that this is the net investment that will still have to be recovered after 12 months from the balance sheet date.

Illustration 20-25 shows how the lease assets appear on the December 31, 2010 balance sheet.

Illustration 20-25

Balance Sheet Reporting
by Lessor

Current assets	
Net investment in capital leases	$23,981.62
Noncurrent assets	
Net investment in capital leases	$59,638.60

The following entries record the receipt of the second year's lease payment and recognition of the interest earned in 2011:

Jan. 1, 2011	Cash	25,981.62	
	Lease Payments Receivable		23,981.62
	Maintenance Expense		2,000.00

A = L + SE
+2,000   +2,000
Cash flows: ↑ 25,981.62 inflow

| Dec. 31, 2011 | Unearned Interest Income—Leases | 5,963.86 | |
| | Interest Income—Leases | | 5,963.86 |

A = L + SE
+5,963.86   +5,963.86
Cash flows: No effect

Journal entries through to 2014 follow the same pattern except that no entry is recorded in 2014, the last year, for earned interest. Because the receivable is fully collected by January 1, 2014, there is no outstanding investment balance during 2014 for Lessor Corporation to earn interest on. When the lease expires, the gross receivable and the unearned interest have been fully written off. Note that Lessor Corporation records no depreciation. If the equipment is sold to Lessee Corporation for $5,000 when the lease expires, Lessor Corporation recognizes the disposition of the equipment as follows:

| Cash | 5,000 | |
| Gain on Sale of Leased Equipment | | 5,000 |

A = L + SE
+5,000   +5,000
Cash flows: ↑ 5,000 inflow

Lessor Accounting for a Sales-Type Lease

Accounting for a lease entered into by a manufacturer or dealer lessor is very similar to the accounting for a financing-type lease. The major difference is that the lessor in the sales-type lease has usually manufactured or acquired the leased asset in order to sell it and is looking, through the lease agreement, to make a profit on the "sale" of the asset as well as earn interest on the extended payment terms. The lessor expects to recover the asset's selling price through the lease payments. The cost or carrying amount on the lessor's books is usually less than the asset's fair value to the customer. The lessor, therefore, records a sale and the related cost of goods sold in addition to the entries made in the direct financing lease.

In addition to the gross investment in the lease, the net investment in the lease and the unearned interest income, the following information must be determined:

LESSOR TERMINOLOGY (continued)		
Term	Account	Explanation
Selling price of the asset	Sales	The present value of the Lease Payments Receivable account reduced by the present value of any unguaranteed residual.[a]
Cost of the leased asset being sold	Cost of Goods Sold	The cost of the asset to the lessor, reduced by the present value of any unguaranteed residual.

[a] This is the present value of the minimum lease payments.

The same data from the earlier Lessor Corporation/Lessee Corporation example are used to illustrate the accounting for a sales-type lease. There is one exception: instead of the leased asset having a cost of $100,000 to Lessor Corporation, the assumption is that **Lessor Corporation manufactured the asset and that it is in Lessor's inventory at a cost of $85,000**. Lessor's regular selling price for this asset—its fair value—is $100,000, and Lessor wants to recover this amount through the lease payments.

The lessor's accounting entries to record the lease transactions are the same as the entries illustrated earlier for a financing-type lease, except for the entry at the lease's inception. **Sales and cost of goods sold are recorded in a sales-type lease.** The entries are as follows:

	January 1, 2010		
Lease Payments Receivable ($23,981.62 × 5)		119,908.10	
Unearned Interest Income—Leases			19,908.10
Sales			100,000.00

A = L + SE
+100,000   +100,000
Cash flows: No effect

Cost of Goods Sold	85,000.00	
Inventory		85,000.00

A = L + SE
−85,000   −85,000
Cash flows: No effect

Cash	25,981.62	
Lease Payments Receivable		23,981.62
Maintenance Expense		2,000.00

A = L + SE
+2,000   +2,000
Cash flows: ↑ 25,981.62 inflow

	December 31, 2010	
Unearned Interest Income—Leases	7,601.84	
Interest Income—Leases		7,601.84

A = L + SE
+7,601.84   +7,601.84
Cash flows: No effect

Compare the January 1, 2010 entries above with the entries for the financing-type lease. The sales-type lease recognizes that what is being recovered is the asset's selling price, so a sale is recorded. The cost of the inventory is transferred to cost of goods sold. With a sales-type lease, the lessor recognizes **a gross profit from the sale**, which is reported at the lease's inception, and also recognizes **interest** or **finance income** over the period of the lease until the receivable is no longer outstanding. A lessor with a financing-type lease reports **only finance income.**

Lessor Accounting for Residual Value and Bargain Purchase Option

Objective 10

Account for and report financing and sales-type leases with guaranteed values or a bargain purchase option by a lessor.

Assume the same data as in the Lessee Corporation/Lessor Corporation example above and in Illustration 20-5: Lessor wants to recover its net investment in the leased asset of $100,000 and earn a 10% return.[27] The asset reverts to Lessor at the end of the five-year lease term. Now assume that the asset is expected to have a residual value of $5,000 at the end of the lease. **Whether the residual value is guaranteed or not**, Lessor Corporation calculates the lease payments using the same approach set out in Illustration 20-3. Illustration 20-9 shows the calculations when the residual value is included. As you can see from the Lessee Corporation/Lessor Corporation example, the lease payment was $23,237.09, both with the guarantee and without it.

Please note that the accounting result is exactly **the same whether the situation involves a residual value or a bargain purchase option.** At the end of the lease term, the

---

[27] Technically, the rate of return that is demanded by the lessor would differ depending on whether the residual value was guaranteed or unguaranteed. To simplify the illustrations, we ignore this difference in the chapter.

lessor either recovers an asset expected to have a value of $5,000, or the lessor expects to get a payment of $5,000 from the lessee for the residual value. In either case, the lessor expects to recover an additional $5,000 at the end of the lease term.

Financing-Type Lease.   Illustration 20-26 provides the calculations that are the basis for the lessor's accounting for a financing-type lease, whether the residual value of $5,000 is guaranteed or unguaranteed or whether there is a $5,000 bargain purchase option. The example continues with the Lessee Corporation/Lessor Corporation data.

Gross investment	= ($23,237.09 × 5) + $5,000	= $121,185.45
Net investment:		
PV of lease payments +	= $23,237.09 × 4.16986 (Table A-5) +	
PV of residual value	$5,000 × 0.62092 (Table A-2)	= 100,000.00
Unearned interest income		$ 21,185.45

Illustration 20-26

Calculation of Financing-Type Lease Amounts by Lessor

Illustration 20-27 shows the lessor's amortization schedule, which is the same whether the residual value is guaranteed or unguaranteed.

	A	B	C	D	E
1			**Lessor Corporation** **Lease Amortization Schedule** **(Annuity due basis, residual value or bargain purchase option)**		
2	**Date**	**Lease Payment Received**	**Interest (10%) on Net Investment**	**Net Investment Recovery**	**Net Investment**
3		**(a)**	**(b)**	**(c)**	**(d)**
4	1/1/10				$100,000.00
5	1/1/10	$ 23,237.09	$ –0–	$ 23,237.09	76,762.91
6	1/1/11	23,237.09	7,676.29	15,560.80	61,202.11
7	1/1/12	23,237.09	6,120.21	17,116.88	44,085.23
8	1/1/13	23,237.09	4,408.52	18,828.57	25,256.66
9	1/1/14	23,237.09	2,525.67	20,711.42	4,545.24
10	12/31/14	5,000.00*	454.76**	4,545.24	–0–
11		$121,185.45	$21,185.45	$100,000.00	

13   (a) Lease payment as required by lease, excluding executory costs.
     (b) Preceding balance of (d) × 10%, except January 1, 2010.
     (c) (a) minus (b).
     (d) Preceding balance minus (c).
     *Represents the residual value or bargain purchase option.
     **Rounded by 24 cents.

Illustration 20-27

Lease Amortization Schedule for Lessor—Residual Value or Bargain Purchase Option

Lessor Corporation's entries during the first year for this lease are shown in Illustration 20-28. Note the similarity between these entries and those of Lessee Corporation in Illustration 20-16.

Inception of Lease (January 1, 2010):		
Lease Payments Receivable	121,185.45	
Equipment Purchased for Lease		100,000.00
Unearned Interest Income—Leases		21,185.45

Illustration 20-28

Entries for Residual Value or Bargain Purchase Option, Lessor Corporation

First Payment Received (January 1, 2010):		
Cash	25,237.09	
Lease Payments Receivable		23,237.09
Maintenance Expense		2,000.00
Adjusting Entry for Accrued Interest (December 31, 2010):		
Unearned Interest Income—Leases	7,676.29	
Interest Income—Leases		7,676.29

Sales-Type Lease. The gross investment and the original amount of unearned interest income are the same for a sales-type lease and a financing-type lease, whether or not the residual value is guaranteed or whether there is a bargain purchase option of the same amount.

When recording **sales revenue** and **cost of goods sold**, however, there is a difference in accounting, **but only in the situation of an unguaranteed residual value**. A guaranteed residual value or bargain purchase option can be considered part of sales revenue because the lessor either knows or is fairly certain that the entire amount will be realized. There is less certainty, however, that any unguaranteed residual will be realized; therefore, **sales and cost of goods sold are only recognized for the portion of the asset that is sure to be realized**. The gross profit amount reported on the asset's sale **is the same** whether the residual value is guaranteed or not, but the present value of any unguaranteed residual is not included in the calculation **of either the sales amount or the cost of goods sold**.

To illustrate a sales-type lease (a) with a guaranteed residual value or bargain purchase option and (b) without a guaranteed residual value, assume the same facts as in the preceding examples: the estimated residual value or option amount is $5,000 (the present value of which is $3,104.60); the annual lease payments are $23,237.09 (the present value of which is $96,895.40); and the leased equipment has an $85,000 cost to the manufacturer, Lessor Corporation. In the case of residual values, assume that the leased asset's actual fair value at the end of the lease is $3,000.

Illustration 20-29 provides the calculations that are needed to account for this sales-type lease.

Illustration 20-29

Calculation of Lease Amounts by Lessor Corporation—Sales-Type Lease

	Sales-Type Lease	
	Guaranteed Residual Value or Bargain Purchase Option	Unguaranteed Residual Value
Gross investment	$121,185.45 ([$23,237.09 × 5] + $5,000)	$121,185.45
Unearned interest income	$21,185.45 ($121,185.45 − [$96,895.40 + $3,104.60])	$21,185.45
Sales	$100,000 ($96,895.40 + $3,104.60)	$96,895.40
Cost of goods sold	$85,000	$81,895.40 ($85,000 − $3,104.60)
Gross profit	$15,000 ($100,000 − $85,000)	$15,000 ($96,895.40 − $81,895.40)

The $15,000 gross profit that is recorded by Lessor Corporation at the point of sale is the same whether there is a $5,000 bargain purchase option or a residual value that is guaranteed or unguaranteed. However, the **sales revenue** and **cost of goods sold** amounts reported are **different**.

The 2010 and 2011 entries and the entry to record the asset's return at the end of the lease are provided in Illustration 20-30. The only differences are in the original entry that recognizes the lease and the final entry to record the asset's return to the lessor.

Guaranteed Residual Value/Bargain Purchase Option			Unguaranteed Residual Value		
To record sales-type lease at inception on January 1, 2010:					
Cost of Goods Sold	85,000.00		Cost of Goods Sold	81,895.40	
Lease Payments Receivable	121,185.45		Lease Payments Receivable	121,185.45	
Sales Revenue		100,000.00	Sales Revenue		96,895.40
Unearned Interest Income		21,185.45	Unearned Interest Income		21,185.45
Inventory		85,000.00	Inventory		85,000.00
To record receipt of the first lease payment on January 1, 2010:					
Cash	25,237.09		Cash	25,237.09	
Lease Payments Receivable		23,237.09	Lease Payments Receivable		23,237.09
Maintenance Expense		2,000.00	Maintenance Expense		2,000.00
To recognize interest income earned during the first year, December 31, 2010:					
Unearned Interest Income	7,676.29		Unearned Interest Income	7,676.29	
Interest Income		7,676.29	Interest Income		7,676.29
(See lease amortization schedule, Illustration 20-27)					
To record receipt of the second lease payment on January 1, 2011:					
Cash	25,237.09		Cash	25,237.09	
Lease Payments Receivable		23,237.09	Lease Payments Receivable		23,237.09
Maintenance Expense		2,000.00	Maintenance Expense		2,000.00
To recognize interest income earned during the second year, December 31, 2011:					
Unearned Interest Income	6,120.21		Unearned Interest Income	6,120.21	
Interest Income		6,120.21	Interest Income		6,120.21
To record receipt of residual value at end of lease, December 31, 2014:					
Inventory	3,000		Inventory	3,000	
Cash	2,000		Loss on Capital Lease	2,000	
Lease Payments Receivable		5,000	Lease Payments Receivable		5,000

Illustration 20-30

Entries for Residual Values, Lessor Corporation— Sales-Type Lease

If the situation included a $5,000 bargain purchase option that was exercised at the end of the lease, all the entries would be the same as those in the "Guaranteed Residual Value" column with one exception. The entry for the exercise of the option on December 31, 2014, is:

Cash	5,000	
Lease Payments Receivable		5,000

The estimated unguaranteed residual value in all leases needs to be reviewed periodically by the lessor and the usual impairment standards apply to the lease-related accounts. If the estimate of the unguaranteed residual value declines, the accounting for the transaction must be revised using the changed estimate. The decline represents a reduction in the lessor's net investment and is recognized as a loss in the period when the residual estimate is reduced. Upward adjustments in estimated residual value are not recognized.

Accounting for an Operating Lease

11 Objective
Account for and report an operating lease by a lessor.

With an operating lease, the lessor records each rental receipt as rental income. The leased asset remains on the lessor's books and is depreciated in the normal manner, with the depreciation expense of the period matched against the rental income. An equal (straight-line) amount of rental income is recognized in each accounting period regardless of the lease provisions, unless another systematic and rational basis better represents the pattern in which the leased asset provides benefits. In addition to the depreciation charge, maintenance and other operating costs that are incurred during the period are also charged to expense.

To illustrate operating lease accounting, assume that the Lessor Corporation/Lessee Corporation lease agreement used throughout the chapter does not meet the capitalization criteria and is therefore classified as an operating lease. The entry to record the cash rental receipt, assuming the $2,000 is to cover the lessor's maintenance expense, is as follows:

A = L + SE
+25,981.62 +25,981.62

Cash flows: ↑ 25,981.62 inflow

Cash	25,981.62	
Rental Income		25,981.62

Lessor Corporation records depreciation as follows, assuming the straight-line method, a cost basis of $100,000, and a five-year life with no residual value:

A = L + SE
−20,000 −20,000

Cash flows: No effect

Depreciation Expense—Leased Equipment	20,000	
Accumulated Depreciation—Leased Equipment		20,000

If property taxes, insurance, maintenance, and other operating costs during the year are the lessor's obligation, they are recorded as expenses that are chargeable against the gross rental revenues reported.

Initial Direct Costs

Underlying Concept

The accounting treatment for the lessor's initial direct costs applies the matching concept.

Initial direct costs are generally defined as costs incurred by a lessor that are directly associated with negotiating and arranging a specific lease. Examples of such costs include commissions, legal fees, and costs of preparing and processing lease documents.

Because initial direct costs are treated somewhat differently between IFRS and private enterprise standards in ways that do not result in material differences in the amount of income or assets reported, we do not provide details of the accounting for each classification of lease in this chapter. The important issue is that they are accounted for similar to other costs in that their effect is matched with the revenue of the accounting period benefitting from the lease.

In a **financing-type lease**, the initial direct costs are recognized in such a way that they are spread over the term of the lease. For a **sales-type lease**, the costs are recognized as an expense in the year they are incurred; that is, they are expensed in the same period that the gross profit on the sale is recognized. For **operating leases**, the lessor defers the initial direct costs and allocates them over the lease term in proportion to the amount of rental income that is recognized.

Lessor Disclosures

Financing and Sales-Type Leases

The **ASPE** requirements are limited to disclosure of the entity's net investment in direct financing and sales-type leases and the interest rate implicit in them, as well as the carrying amount of any impaired leases including the amount of the related impairment allowance.

The requirements of **IAS 17 *Leases*** are more extensive. In addition to providing a reconciliation between the gross investment in the lease and the present value of the minimum lease payments, the amounts of both of these due within the next year, between years two and five, and beyond five years is required. Additional requirements include the amount of unearned finance income, unguaranteed residual values, contingent rental income in the year, the allowance for doubtful receivables, and general information about the lessor's leasing arrangements.

Operating Leases

Under **private enterprise standards**, disclosures are limited to the cost and related accumulated depreciation of property that is held for leasing purposes, along with the carrying amount of any impaired lease receivables and related allowance provided for impairment.

The **IFRS** disclosures for operating leases are similar to those for finance leases. Lessors report the future minimum lease payments in total as well as the amounts due within one year, between years two and five, and beyond five years. The contingent rental income for the period and general information about the entity's leasing arrangements are also reported. For operating leases as well as for those that are not classified as operating in nature, additional requirements are imposed by other standards. These include the standards on property, plant, and equipment; financial instruments; investment property; and impairment; among others.

Time for Change

As indicated at the beginning of this chapter, lease accounting is an area of accounting that is much abused through efforts by preparers to circumvent the provisions of the standards. In practice, the accounting rules for capitalizing leases have been rendered partly ineffective by the strong motivation of lessees to resist capitalization. Leasing generally involves large dollar amounts that, if capitalized, materially increase reported liabilities and weaken debt-to-equity and other ratios. Lease capitalization is also resisted because charges to expense in the early years of the lease are higher when leases are capitalized than when they are treated as operating leases, often with no corresponding tax benefit.

As a consequence, much effort has been devoted, particularly in North America, to "beating" the profession's lease capitalization rules. To avoid asset capitalization, lease agreements are designed, written, and interpreted so that none of the three criteria is satisfied from the lessee's viewpoint. Under IFRS, similar leases are accounted for in different ways, and new positions being taken on asset and liability definition are driving standard setters to change the existing requirements. We now take a look at what is being proposed.

CONTRACT-BASED APPROACH

The IASB and the FASB have been working since 2006 on a joint project to replace their accounting standards on leases. They released a discussion paper in 2009 that set out preliminary views on significant aspects of a new accounting model for lessee accounting and identified issues that need to be addressed for the lessor. After studying the responses and further discussion, the IASB expected to issue an Exposure Draft of a revised, and common, lease accounting standard in mid-2010.[28] The final standard is expected to be released in 2011.

12 Objective
Explain and apply the contract-based approach to a basic lease for a lessee and lessor.

Significant Change

---

[28] The description of the proposed standards included in this text are based on the tentative decisions reached by the FASB and IASB that were reported in the February 19, 2010 and May 14, 2010 *Leases Project Update*, the latter accessed at <www.fasb.org> on May 19, 2010.

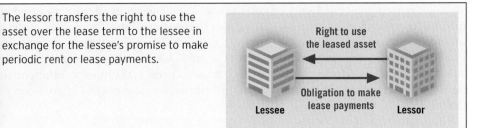

EXAMPLE

The lessor transfers the right to use the asset over the lease term to the lessee in exchange for the lessee's promise to make periodic rent or lease payments.

Law

The accounting model proposed is a contract-based approach first introduced to you in Chapter 6 and then discussed again earlier in this chapter. In essence, the lessee recognizes an asset representing its contractual right to use the leased item over the lease term along with a contractual liability that captures its obligation to pay rentals. While this looks similar to the capital/finance lease situation in the preceding section, it is a very different concept. Under the **classification approach**, the lessee recognizes a lease as the leased property itself when there is a transfer of the risks and benefits of ownership and when this is an in-substance instalment purchase of the asset. The **contract-based approach** sees the asset taken on by the lessee as the contractual right to use the asset, not the transfer of the asset itself. In addition, this approach is much broader, capturing most arrangements that are now considered operating leases.

Let's see what the basics of this new approach are.

Scope and Definition

A lease is defined in the joint FASB-IASB project as "a contract in which the right to use a specified asset is conveyed, for a period of time, in exchange for consideration."[29] While this definition is broad enough to encompass a variety of types of assets, the standard is effective for property, plant, and equipment assets only.

The intent of the revision is to set out the accounting treatment for all non-cancellable lease contracts where the contractual **right to use** the asset is transferred from a lessor to a lessee. For this reason, contracts that actually transfer **control of the underlying asset** itself or almost all of the risks and benefits associated with ownership **are excluded from the new standard**. Such in-substance purchases by the lessee include contracts in which the title to the property is transferred automatically at the end of the lease, those with a bargain purchase option that is reasonably certain to be exercised, those in which the contract is expected to cover almost all of the useful life of the asset, and contracts where the lessor's return is fixed. These situations are excluded because they are in-substance acquisitions of the asset itself. In such cases, the accounting would be similar to present day capital or finance leases.

Recognition and Measurement—Lessee

Initial Measurement

Under the contract-based approach, the assets and liabilities arise and are recognized when the lease contract is first signed. At this point, the contractual rights and contractual obligations are usually equal and, until the right-of-use asset is delivered, the contractual rights and obligations are both recognized, but are reported net on the balance sheet.

---

[29] FASB-IASB *Leases Project Update*, May 14, 2010; accessed at <www.fasb.org> on May 19, 2010.

The Contractual Lease Obligation.   The contractual obligation recognized by the lessee is measured at the present value of the lease payments.[30] While this sounds straightforward at first, a number of decisions need to be made before the resulting amounts are determined and then discounted:

1. Do contingent rentals—additional rents that become payable based on the level of sales or other variable—have to be considered?

2. How are any guarantees of residual values at the end of the lease factored into the calculations?

3. Lease contracts often contain renewal or purchase options, sometimes at bargain prices and other times at market rates; or options to end the lease early. Are these considered?

4. What discount rate is used?

The new proposals take the position that the contractual obligation to pay rent **includes amounts payable under contingent rental arrangements** over the term of the lease and **amounts expected to be payable under residual value guarantees or purchase options**. Therefore, such amounts are estimated in advance, are measured using probability-weighted expected values, and are included in the lease payments as part of the initial liability recognized. Note, however, that it is only the cash flows that are expected to be made in the future related to these items that is included, not the full amount of the residual value, for example, unless that is expected to be the amount of the deficiency.

An associated issue is one of determining the **term of the lease**. This decision, in turn, affects the number of periods over which the minimum and contingent rentals are payable, as well as the amount of any residual value deficiency or purchase option amount to be received. Taking all relevant factors into account, including the possibility of early termination and the renewal of the lease at market rates, an entity identifies the **longest possible lease term that is "more likely than not" to occur**, and uses this in its calculations.

The third variable in measuring the lease payments is the discount rate itself. Here the standard setters propose the use of the lessee's incremental borrowing rate. However, if the rate implicit in the lease can be readily determined, this alternative rate can be used.

The Contractual Right-of-Use Asset.   The asset recognized under the contract-based approach is measured initially at cost, based on the present value of the lease payments as described above for the lease obligation. Consistent with a cost model, any of the lessee's direct costs of negotiating and arranging the lease are also capitalized.

Measurement after Recognition

The Contractual Lease Obligation.   After the leased asset is delivered and the lease begins, the contractual rights and obligations are no longer reported net on the balance sheet.

The lease obligation is accounted for at amortized cost. As lease payments are made, the contractual obligation is reduced, with each payment separated into interest and principal reduction amounts. Interest is calculated using the original discount rate established when the obligation was first recognized, applied to the outstanding principal balance.

The estimates used to determine the lease term and rental amounts are reassessed at every reporting date if new events or circumstances indicate that there might be a material change in the amount of the obligation. If there is, the liability is remeasured.

---

[30] The proposals allow an exemption for short-term leases. A short-term lease is an agreement with an expected total term of less than 12 months. From the lessee's point of view, the right-of-use asset and lease obligation are both reported gross; that is, on an undiscounted basis. The lessor also has an option to use this simplified accounting.

Illustration 20-31 sets out the accounting proposals for any resulting changes in the amount of the obligation.

Illustration 20-31

Changes in Contractual Lease Obligation—Accounting Requirements

	Remeasurement of Contractual Lease Obligation	
Cause	A change in the obligation from changes in amounts payable for rentals, residual value guarantees, and purchase options	A change in the obligation to pay rentals as a result of a reassessment of the lease term
Accounting	Change related to current or prior periods: – Recognize in net income Change relating to future periods: – Adjust the carrying amount of the contractual right-of-use asset	All changes: – Adjust the carrying amount of the contractual right-of-use asset

The Contractual Right-of-Use Asset.   Accounting for the right-of-use asset after initial recognition and measurement is consistent with its nature; it is similar to the accounting requirements for an intangible asset. Most contractual rights (assets) will continue to be accounted for at amortized cost, taking into account any changes in amount resulting from remeasurements of the lease obligation.

Although not addressed in the May 2010 *Leases Project Update* provided by the IASB and FASB, the asset's cost will likely be amortized to expense on a systematic basis over the term of the lease (consistent with the term used in determining the obligation) using a method that best represents the pattern of benefits received from the asset used. The proposals do specify, however, that "amortization" expense, not "rent" expense, is recognized on the income statement.

Also consistent with other standards, right-of-use assets can be revalued using the revaluation model in IAS 38 *Intangible Assets*, and are considered for impairment under the requirements of IAS 36 *Impairment of Assets*.

Illustration

We now walk through an example of how a lease is accounted for under the contract-based approach. Assume that EE Corporation, a lessee, enters into a non-cancellable lease contract with OR Limited, a lessor, on September 1, 2011. Assume that the signing and delivery of the lease happened on the same day. The terms and conditions of the lease are set out in Illustration 20-32.

Illustration 20-32

Terms, Conditions, and Other Information Related to the Lease Contract

Leased asset	Manufacturing equipment
Economic life of equipment	7 years
Lease term	September 1, 2011, to August 31, 2015
Lease payment per year, payable in advance	$5,000
Contingent rental payments	Not required
Renewal option	Renewable for additional 2 years at option of lessee at $4,500 per year
Expected value of asset (not guaranteed)	
– August 31, 2015	$6,000
– August 31, 2017	$1,000
Title to leased equipment	Retained by lessor
Rate implicit in the lease	9%
Lessee's incremental borrowing rate	9%
Fair value of leased asset, September 1, 2011	$24,000
Lessor's initial direct costs	$365

Lessee's expectations:
- Most likely lease term (option will be taken to renew lease for additional 2 years)   Lease will expire on August 31, 2017; lease term is 6 years.

Lessor's expectations:
- Most likely lease term   Lessee will renew the lease for 2 years on August 31, 2015; a 6-year lease term
- Probability-weighted expected value of residual at end of lease term $1,000

Lessee Accounting

Because EE Corporation now has the right to use the manufacturing equipment owned by OR Limited (an asset) and an obligation to make lease payments (a liability), the contractual rights and obligations at acquisition are measured and recognized. The obligation is the minimum lease payments, including contingent rentals and possible payments under guarantees, all discounted using the lessee's incremental borrowing rate over the longest possible term that is more likely than not to occur. Illustration 20-33 shows that the initial measure of the obligation and asset, taking into account the lessee's expectations identified in Illustration 20-32, is $23,769.

Contractual Rights and Obligations under Lease, September 1, 2011		
Present value of amounts payable under the lease contract, $i = 9$:		
$5,000 annuity due × 3.53130 ($n = 4$) [Table A-5]	=	$17,656
$4,500 sum × 0.70843 ($n = 4$) [Table A-2]	=	3,188
$4,500 sum × 0.64993 ($n = 5$) [Table A-2]	=	2,925
		$23,769

Illustration 20-33

Initial Measurement of Contractual Rights and Obligations

The initial entries to recognize the contract and the first payment on September 1, 2011, are:

Contractual Lease Rights	23,769	
Contractual Lease Obligations		23,769

A   =   L   +   SE
+23,769   +23,769
Cash flows: No effect

Contractual Lease Obligation	5,000	
Cash		5,000

A   =   L   +   SE
−5,000   −5,000
Cash flows: ↓ 5,000 outflow

At December 31, 2011, EE Corporation's year end, the company recognizes the amortization of lease rights that have been used up and interest expense on the obligation since September 1, 2011:

Amortization Expense	3,961	
Contractual Lease Rights[a]		3,961
($23,769 ÷ 6 years)		

A   =   L   +   SE
−3,961   −3,961
Cash flows: No effect

[a]The May 2010 *Leases Project Update* made no reference to separate disclosures of accumulated amortization amounts, although it indicated that the asset was to be reported with property, plant, and equipment assets. Use of an accumulated amortization account would also be correct.

A = L + SE
      +563   −563

Cash flows: No effect

Interest Expense	563
Interest Payable	563
[($23,769 − $5,000) × .09 × 4/12]	

Recognition and Measurement Basics—Lessor

The standard setters have initially decided that the lessor should take a performance obligation approach to accounting for the lease contract. That is, the transaction is represented by the following illustration.

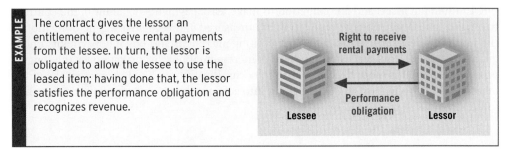

EXAMPLE

The contract gives the lessor an entitlement to receive rental payments from the lessee. In turn, the lessor is obligated to allow the lessee to use the leased item; having done that, the lessor satisfies the performance obligation and recognizes revenue.

Lessee — Right to receive rental payments → Lessor

Performance obligation

    Similar to the lessee's accounting, the contractual rights and obligations are recognized when the contract is signed and reported net until the asset is delivered and performance begins.

Lease Assets

The lessor measures the contract-based lease receivable at the present value of the rental payments to be received, discounted at the interest rate the lessor is charging the lessee, increased by any initial direct costs incurred by the lessor. Although the lease term chosen by the lessor is also the "longest possible term that is more likely than not to occur," its expectations may differ from those of the lessee. The measurement of the expected value of contingent rents, expected residual values or purchase options, mirror those of the lessee, but here again, different amounts may result. Also note that amounts are recognized by the lessor only to the extent that they can be measured reliably.

    After its initial recognition, the lease receivable is accounted for at amortized cost, using the effective interest method. Subsequent adjustments made to the receivable as a result of changes in either the expected values of the amounts to be received or the lease term are accounted for as set out in Illustration 20-34. The leased asset itself remains in the accounts, depreciated over its useful life.

Illustration 20-34

Changes in Contractual Lease Receivable—Accounting Requirements

	Remeasurement of Contractual Lease Obligation	
Cause	A change in the receivable from changes in expected rent payments and residual value	A change in the receivable as a result of a reassessment of the lease term
Accounting	Treat as an adjustment to the original transaction price. For a change related to a satisfied performance obligation: – Recognize in net income For a change related to an unsatisfied performance obligation: – Adjust the carrying amount of the performance obligation	All changes: – Adjust the carrying amount of the performance obligation

The Performance Obligation

Initially, the lessor's obligation to allow the lessee to use an asset it owns is measured at the present value of the lease payments that are also recognized in the lease receivable. After this, as the lessor meets the performance obligation, the obligation is decreased and revenue is recognized in a systematic and rational manner based on the pattern of the asset's use by the lessee.

Under a performance obligation approach to lessor accounting, the leased asset itself remains on the balance sheet of the lessor at the same time that the lessor recognizes the new Lease Receivable asset and the performance obligation liability. All three accounts are reported separately on the balance sheet, but totalled to one net lease asset or net lease liability amount. Interest income, lease income, and depreciation expense are presented separately in the income statement.

Lessor Accounting—A Derecognition Approach

Another approach, a **derecognition approach**, is also being studied. This approach removes the portion of the underlying leased asset that is given up in the lease agreement from the balance sheet and recognizes a lease receivable. The derecognition approach is expected to be expanded upon and explained in the Exposure Draft as well.

New Lease Accounting Standard

As members of the IASB (and FASB) decide what positions to include in the Exposure Draft a number of other positions have been taken and other issues discussed. These include such topics as an alternative derecognition approach to lessor accounting, lessee and lessor disclosures, sale-leaseback transactions, the unit of accounting, impairment, long-term leases of land, and transitional requirements. After the preferred positions are exposed and due process completed, a revised IFRS is expected to be released in 2011. The application of lease accounting in an IFRS world will change considerably from what has been practised for many years.

IFRS and Private Enterprise GAAP Comparison

A Comparison of IFRS and Private Enterprise GAAP

Illustration 20-35 sets out material differences between existing IFRS and private enterprise accounting standards for lessees and lessors. In general, except for some terminology differences, the classification approach is applied in much the same way under both sets of standards after the initial classification of the lease has been made. Illustration 20-35 also sets out the major differences between this approach and the IFRS proposals that support a contract-based method.

> **13 Objective**
> Identify differences in accounting between accounting standards for private enterprises and IFRS, and what changes are expected in the near future.

Looking Ahead

As indicated earlier in the chapter, the FASB and IASB have been working together to develop a new leasing standard. The proposals were being put in exposure draft form just as this text went to print, with a final standard due in 2011.

The new standards will differ from the existing classification approach, as the highlights of the contract-based method summarized in Illustration 20-35 indicate. Contracts

	Accounting Standards for Private Enterprises (Private Enterprise GAAP/ASPE)—*CICA Handbook*, Part II, Section 3065	IFRS—IAS 17	IASB Proposed Model—A Contract-Based Approach
Scope and Definitions	Applies primarily to property, plant, and equipment assets.	Applies to a broader group of assets, including intangible assets.	Applies only to property, plant, and equipment assets.
	Leases are either a capital or an operating lease to a lessee.	Leases are either a finance or an operating lease to a lessee.	No classification is needed, except that those leases that are an in-substance purchase and sale of the underlying asset do not qualify for treatment under the proposed standard.
	Leases are either operating or a sales-type or direct financing lease to a lessor.	Leases are either an operating or a finance lease to a lessor.	
Recognition – By lessee	Leases where the risks and benefits of ownership are transferred to the lessee are capital leases to the lessee. The classification criteria include numerical thresholds that are often used.	Leases where the risks and benefits of ownership are transferred to the lessee are finance leases to the lessee. The degree to which the asset is specialized and of use only to the lessee without major expense to the lessor is an additional criterion considered, but no numerical thresholds are given for any criterion.	Lessee recognizes its contractual right to use the leased asset as an asset, and its obligation to make rental payments as a liability.
	Private enterprise standards do not recognize investment property outside the regular classification requirements.	A property interest under an operating lease may be recognized as an investment property and accounted for under the fair value model.	
– By lessor	Classification criteria include numerical thresholds; plus two revenue recognition criteria must be met to qualify as a sales-type or a direct financing lease rather than an operating lease.	A lessor considers the same criteria as the lessee to determine whether the lease is a finance lease or an operating lease. A finance lease could be one entered into by a manufacturer or dealer, or not. The result is similar to PE GAAP.	Under the performance obligation approach, the lessor recognizes the contract-based rental payments as a lease receivable and the obligation to provide the lessee with a right to use the asset as a liability. Revenue is recognized as a transfer from the liability as performance takes place.
Measurement	For capital leases, the lessee uses the lower of the lessee's incremental borrowing rate and the rate implicit in the lease to determine the capitalized amount of the leased asset.	For finance leases, the lessee uses the interest rate implicit in the lease whenever it can be reasonably determined; otherwise the incremental borrowing rate is used.	Measurement by both lessee and lessor take into account probability-weighted expected outcomes of rental payments, residual values and options; and a lease term equal to the longest possible term that is more likely than not to occur. Lessee and lessor measurements will differ on the expected payments/receipts, for example, where the lessor recognizes only the amounts that can be reliably measured.

	Accounting Standards for Private Enterprises (Private Enterprise GAAP/ASPE)—*CICA Handbook*, Part II, Section 3065	IFRS—IAS 17	IASB Proposed Model—A Contract-Based Approach
Disclosure – Lessee	Most capital lease disclosures are similar to the disclosures required for plant and equipment assets and long-term liabilities in general.	Most finance lease disclosures are similar to the disclosures covering the asset and liability in other IFRS. Additional disclosures are required about material lease arrangements including contingent rents, sub-lease payments, and lease-imposed restrictions for both operating and finance leases.	Lease rights are reported with property, plant, and equipment on the statement of financial position.
– Lessor	For operating leases, the lessor discloses only the cost and net carrying amount of assets held for leasing purposes and impairment information.	For operating leases, the lessor reports information about the future minimum lease payments due within one year, years two to five, and after five years, as well as about the entity's leasing arrangements in general.	The leased asset, lease receivable, and performance obligation are reported separately, but presented as one net asset or net obligation on the statement of financial position under the performance obligation approach.
	There are minimum requirements related to the net investment in direct financing and sales-type leases, the interest rate implicit in the lease, and impairment information.	For finance leases, a reconciliation is required between gross investment and net investment; the amounts of both due within one year, years two to five, and after five years; and supplementary information about unguaranteed residual values, unearned finance income, contingent rentals, impairments, and general lease arrangement information.	
Appendix 20A—Sale-Leaseback transactions: – Recognition	The deferred gain on sale recognized by a lessee on a capital leaseback is amortized on the same basis as the depreciation of the leased asset.	The deferred gain on sale recognized by a lessee on a finance leaseback is recognized over the lease term.	The transaction is accounted for as a sale and leaseback only if the underlying asset has been "sold."
	The gain on an operating leaseback is deferred and amortized unless the lease is for only a minor portion of the original asset.	The gain on an operating leaseback is deferred and amortized only for that portion of the sales price that exceeds fair value of the asset sold. A loss is recognized immediately, unless subsequent rents are less than market rates. In this case, the loss is deferred and amortized.	Gains and losses are recognized if all assets are at fair value, otherwise the asset, liabilities, gains, and losses are adjusted to reflect current market rental amounts.
Appendix 20A—Real estate leases: – Recognition	When ownership of the leased asset is not expected to be transferred to the lessee by the end of the lease either directly or through a bargain purchase option and the fair value of the land is significant relative to the building, a lease involving both land and building is treated as two separate leases based on the relative fair value of each.	A bargain purchase option is not considered in determining whether title will be transferred by the end of the lease. Ordinarily, a lease of land and building are treated as two separate leases, with the lease payments separated based on the relative fair value of the leasehold interests, rather than the fair value of the leased property.	

Illustration 20-35

IFRS and Private Enterprise GAAP Comparison Chart

in which the substance of the lease is a purchase and sale will be accounted for as such; but most all other non-cancellable leases will be recognized on both the lessee's and lessor's statement of financial position as contract-based rights and obligations.

Summary of Learning Objectives

WILEY
PLUS
Glossary

KEY TERMS

asset-based financing, 1306

bargain purchase option, 1313

bargain renewal option, 1313

capital leases, 1310

classification approach, 1310

contract-based approach, 1310

direct financing leases, 1333

effective interest method, 1318

executory contract, 1310

executory costs, 1314

finance leases, 1310

gross investment in lease, 1333

guaranteed residual value, 1314

incremental borrowing rate, 1315

initial direct costs, 1342

interest rate implicit in the lease, 1314

lease, 1307, 1344

lease term, 1313

lessee, 1307

lessor, 1307

manufacturer or dealer lease, 1332

manufacturer's or dealer's profit, 1332

minimum lease payments, 1314

1 Explain the conceptual nature, economic substance, and advantages of lease transactions.

A lease is a contract between two parties that gives the lessee the right to use property that is owned by the lessor. In situations where the lessee obtains the use of the majority of the economic benefits inherent in a leased asset, the transaction is similar in substance to acquiring an asset. Therefore, the lessee recognizes the asset and associated liability and the lessor transfers the asset under one of the approaches to lease accounting. The major advantages of leasing for the lessee relate to the cost and flexibility of the financing, and protection against obsolescence. For the lessor, the finance income is attractive.

2 Identify and apply the criteria that are used to determine the type of lease for accounting purposes for a lessee under the classification approach.

Where the risks and benefits of owning the leased asset are transferred to the lessee—which is evidenced by the transfer of title, or the use of the majority of the asset services inherent in the leased asset, or the recovery by the lessor of substantially all of its investment in the leased asset plus a return on that investment, or, under IFRS, in some cases the degree of specialization of the specific asset—the lease is classified as a capital or finance lease. If none of these criteria is met, the lease is classified as an operating lease.

3 Calculate the lease payment that is required for a lessor to earn a specific return.

The lessor determines the investment that it wants to recover from a leased asset. If the lessor has acquired an asset for the purpose of leasing it, the lessor usually wants to recover the asset's cost. If the lessor participates in leases as a way of selling its product, it usually wants to recover the sales price. The lessor's investment in the cost or selling price can be recovered in part through a residual value if the asset will be returned to the lessor, or through a bargain purchase price that it expects the lessee to pay, if a bargain purchase is part of the lease agreement. In addition to these sources, the lessor recovers its investment through the lease payments. The periodic lease payment, therefore, is the annuity amount whose present value exactly equals the amount to be recovered through lease payments.

4 Account for a lessee's basic capital (finance) lease.

As a capital lease, called a finance lease under IFRS, the asset is capitalized on the lessee's balance sheet and a liability is recognized for the obligation owing to the lessor. The amount capitalized is the present value of the minimum lease payments (in effect the payments, excluding executory costs) that the lessee has agreed to take responsibility for. The asset is then depreciated in the same way as other capital assets owned by the lessee. Payments to the lessor are divided into an interest portion and a principal payment, using the effective interest method.

5 Determine the effect of, and account for, residual values and bargain purchase options in a lessee's capital (finance) lease.

When a lessee guarantees a residual value, it is obligated to return either the leased asset or cash, or a combination of both, in an amount that is equal to the guaranteed value. The lessee includes the guaranteed residual in the lease obligation and leased asset value. The asset is depreciated to this value by the end of the lease term. If the residual is unguaranteed, the lessee takes no responsibility for the residual and it is excluded from the lessee's calculations.

6 Account for an operating lease by a lessee and compare the operating and capitalization methods of accounting for leases.

A lessee recognizes the lease payments that are made as rent expense in the period that is covered by the lease, usually based on the proportion of time. Over the term of a lease, the total amount that is charged to expense is the same whether the lease has been treated as a capital/finance lease or as an operating lease. The difference relates to the timing of recognition for the expense (more is charged in the early years for a capital lease), the type of expense that is charged (depreciation and interest expense for a capital lease versus rent expense for an operating lease), and the recognition of an asset and liability on the balance sheet for a capital lease versus non-recognition for an operating lease. Aside from any income tax differences, the cash flows for a lease are the same whether it is classified as an operating or capital lease.

7 Determine the balance sheet presentation of a capital (finance) lease and identify other disclosures required.

The current portion of the obligation is the principal that will be repaid within 12 months from the balance sheet date. The current portion also includes the amount of interest that has accrued up to the balance sheet date. The long-term portion of the obligation or net investment is the principal balance that will not be paid within 12 months of the balance sheet date. Lessees disclose the same information as is required for capital assets and long-term debt in general. In addition, details are required of the future minimum lease payments for each of the next five years, and under IFRS, information about its leasing arrangements is required.

8 Identify and apply the criteria that are used to determine the type of lease for a lessor under the classification approach.

If a lease, in substance, transfers the risks and benefits of ownership of the leased asset to the lessee (decided in the same way as for the lessee) and revenue recognition criteria related to collectibility and ability to estimate any remaining unreimbursable costs are met, the lessor accounts for the lease as either a direct financing or a sales-type lease. Under IFRS, it is classified either as a financing, or a manufacturer or dealer lease. The existence of a manufacturer's or dealer's profit on the amount to be recovered from the lessee is the difference between a sales-type lease and a direct financing lease, as the objective is only to generate finance income in the latter. If any one of the capitalization or revenue recognition criteria is not met, the lessor accounts for the lease as an operating lease. While these are not set out in the international standard, they would be applied in general before any revenue is recognized by the lessor.

9 Account for and report basic financing and sales-type leases by a lessor.

In a finance lease, the lessor removes the cost of the leased asset from its books and replaces it with its net investment in the lease. This is made up of two accounts: (1)

the gross investment or lease payments receivable, offset by (2) the portion of these amounts that represents unearned interest. The net investment represents the present value of the lease payments and the residual value or bargain purchase option amounts. As the lease payments are received, the receivable is reduced. As time passes, the unearned interest is taken into income based on the implicit rate of return that applies to the net investment. Under a sales-type lease, the accounting is similar except that the net investment represents the sale amount the lessor wants to recover. The lessor also transfers the inventory "sold" to cost of goods sold.

10 **Account for and report financing and sales-type leases with guaranteed values or a bargain purchase option by a lessor.**

For both types of lease, the net investment in the lease includes the estimated residual value whether it is guaranteed or not, or the bargain purchase option amount. Under a sales-type lease, both the sale and cost of goods sold amounts are reduced by any unguaranteed residual values.

11 **Account for and report an operating lease by a lessor.**

The lessor records the lease payments received from the lessee as rental income in the period covered by the lease payment. Because the leased asset remains on the lessor's books, the lessor records depreciation expense. Separate disclosure is required of the cost and accumulated amortization of property held for leasing purposes, and the amount of rental income earned.

12 **Explain and apply the contract-based approach to a basic lease for a lessee and lessor.**

The contract-based approach to lease accounting assumes that the asset transferred by the lease contract from the lessor to the lessee is the right to use the leased property. The lessee recognizes this right-of-use as an asset and recognizes the obligation to make rental payments as an obligation. The lessor recognizes the contractual right to receive lease payments as an asset—a receivable—and recognizes its performance obligation to permit the lessee to use the asset as a liability. As performance takes place, the lessor recognizes revenue.

13 **Identify differences in accounting between accounting standards for private enterprises and IFRS, and what changes are expected in the near future.**

Under the classification approach, private enterprise GAAP is substantially the same as the IFRS requirements. Different terminology is used and the classification requirements that differentiate between a capital/finance lease and an operating lease under IFRS are more principles-based than under the PE standards. A new lease standard is expected to be issued by the IASB and FASB in 2011 that will significantly change the approach to lease accounting. Under the revisions planned, a contract-based or right-of-use approach is used by both lessee and lessor.

Appendix 20A

Other Lease Issues

Sale and Leaseback Transactions

Sale-leaseback describes a transaction in which a property owner (the seller-lessee) sells a property to another party (the purchaser-lessor) and, at the same time, leases the same asset back from the new owner. The property generally continues to be used without any interruption. This type of transaction is fairly common.[31]

For example, a company buys land, constructs a building to its specifications, sells the property to an investor, and then immediately leases it back. From the seller's viewpoint, the advantage of a sale and leaseback usually has to do with financing. If an equipment purchase has already been financed, and rates have subsequently decreased, a sale-leaseback can allow the seller to refinance the purchase at lower rates. Alternatively, a sale-leaseback can also provide additional working capital when liquidity is tight.

To the extent that, after the sale, the seller-lessee continues to use the same asset it has sold, **the sale-leaseback is really a form of financing**, and therefore it is reasonable that no gain or loss is recognized on the transaction. In substance, the seller-lessee is simply borrowing funds. On the other hand, if the seller-lessee gives up the ownership risks and benefits associated with the asset, the transaction is clearly a sale, and gain or loss recognition is appropriate. Accounting standards indicate that the lease should be accounted for as a capital or operating lease by the seller-lessee and as a direct finance or operating lease by the purchaser-lessor, as appropriate under the lease accounting standards.

When a seller-lessee leases back only a portion of the asset sold, such as one floor of a 10-floor building sold, or a lease term of two years when the remaining useful life is six years, then the transaction does not meet the definition of a sale-leaseback transaction. In such a case, the sale and the lease are accounted for as separate transactions based on the underlying substance of each.

Seller-Lessee Accounting

If the lease meets the criteria to be classified as a **capital or finance lease**, the seller-lessee accounts for the transaction as a sale, and the lease as a capital or finance lease. Any profit on the sale of the assets that are leased back **is deferred and amortized** over the lease term (under **IFRS**) or on the same basis as the depreciation of the leased assets (if **PE GAAP**). If the leased asset is land only, the amortization is on a straight-line basis over the lease term.

[31] *Financial Reporting in Canada—2008* (CICA, 2008) reports that out of 200 companies surveyed, 27 companies provided disclosure related to current (2007) or prior years' sale-leaseback transactions.

14 Objective

Describe and apply the lessee's accounting for sale-leaseback transactions.

Underlying Concept

A sale-leaseback may be similar in substance to the parking of inventories discussed in Chapter 8. As the ultimate economic benefits remain under the control of the "seller," the definition of an asset is satisfied.

For example, if Lessee Inc. sells equipment having a book value of $580,000 and a fair value of $623,110 to Lessor Inc. for $623,110 and leases the equipment back for $50,000 a year for 20 years, the profit of $43,110 (i.e., $623,110 − $580,000) is deferred and amortized over the 20-year period. The $43,110 is credited originally to a Deferred Profit on Sale-Leaseback account.

If none of the capital lease criteria is met, the seller-lessee accounts for the transaction as a sale, and the lease as an **operating lease**. Under **IFRS** if the terms of the transaction are clearly fair value amounts, the profit or loss on disposal is recognized in net income immediately. If the selling price is less than fair value, the same rule applies unless the future rentals are also below a market rent to compensate. If so, the loss is deferred and amortized over the period the asset is expected to be used. If the selling price is more than fair value, the amount above fair value is deferred and amortized over the same period.

Under **private enterprise standards**, the profit or loss on sale of a property sold and leased back under an operating lease arrangement is deferred and amortized in proportion to the rental payments over the period of time that it is expected the lessee will use the assets.

The standards require, however, that when there is a legitimate loss on the sale of an asset—that is, when the asset's **fair value is less than its carrying amount**—the loss is recognized immediately. For example, if Lessee Inc. sells equipment that has a book value of $650,000 and a fair value of $600,000, the difference of $50,000 is charged directly to a loss account.

Purchaser-Lessor Accounting

Under a sale and leaseback transaction, the purchaser-lessor applies the regular lease standards. This type of transaction results in either an operating or direct-financing type lease on the part of the lessor.

Sale-Leaseback Illustration

To illustrate the accounting treatment for a sale-leaseback transaction, assume that on January 1, 2011, Lessee Inc. sells a used Boeing 767, having a cost of $85.5 million and a carrying amount on Lessee's books of $75.5 million, to Lessor Inc. for $80 million, and then immediately leases the aircraft back under the following conditions:

1. The term of the non-cancellable lease is 15 years, and the agreement requires equal annual rental payments of $10,487,443, beginning January 1, 2011.

2. The aircraft has a fair value of $80 million on January 1, 2011, and an estimated economic life of 15 years.

3. Lessee Inc. pays all executory costs.

4. Lessee Inc. depreciates similar aircraft that it owns on a straight-line basis over 15 years.

5. The annual payments assure the lessor a 12% return, which is the same as Lessee's incremental borrowing rate.

6. The present value of the minimum lease payments is $80 million, or $10,487,443 × 7.62817 (Table A-5: $i = 12$, $n = 15$).

This is a capital or finance lease to Lessee Inc. because the lease term covers the entire useful life of the asset and because the lessor recovers its investment in the aircraft and earns the required rate of return from the minimum lease payments. Assuming that the appropriate revenue recognition criteria are met, Lessor Inc. classifies this arrangement as a direct financing lease.

Illustration 20A-1 shows the journal entries related to this lease for both Lessee Inc. and Lessor Inc. for the first year.

Lessee Inc.			Lessor Inc.		
Sale of aircraft by Lessee Inc. to Lessor Inc., January 1, 2011, and leaseback transaction:					
Cash	80,000,000		Aircraft	80,000,000	
Accumulated Depreciation	10,000,000		Cash		80,000,000
Aircraft		85,500,000			
Deferred Profit on					
Sale-Leaseback		4,500,000			
Aircraft under Capital Leases	80,000,000		Lease Payments Receivable	157,311,645[a]	
Obligations under Capital Leases		80,000,000	Aircraft		80,000,000
			Unearned Interest Income		77,311,645
			[a]($10,487,443 × 15 = $157,311,645)		
First lease payment, January 1, 2011:					
Obligations under			Cash	10,487,443	
Capital Leases	10,487,443		Lease Payments		
Cash		10,487,443	Receivable		10,487,443
Executory costs incurred and paid by Lessee Inc. throughout 2011:					
Insurance, Maintenance,			(No entry)		
Taxes, etc., Expense	XXX				
Cash or Accounts Payable		XXX			
Depreciation expense for 2011 on the aircraft, December 31, 2011:					
Depreciation Expense	5,333,333		(No entry)		
Accumulated Depreciation—					
Leased Aircraft		5,333,333			
($80,000,000 ÷ 15)					
Amortization of deferred profit on sale-leaseback by Lessee Inc., December 31, 2011:					
Deferred Profit on			(No entry)		
Sale-Leaseback	300,000				
Depreciation Expense[b]		300,000			
($4,500,000 ÷ 15)					
[b]alternatively a gain account could be credited					
Interest for 2011, December 31, 2011:					
Interest Expense	8,341,507		Unearned Interest Income	8,341,507	
Interest Payable		8,341,507[c]	Interest Income		8,341,507[c]
[c] Lease obligation or net investment in the lease of ($80,000,000 − $10,487,443) × 12% × 12/12					

Illustration 20A-1

Comparative Entries for Sale-Leaseback for Lessee and Lessor

Looking ahead to expected changes in the lease accounting standards, it is likely that the standards on sale-leasebacks will also change. One area of controversy is the reporting of a deferred gain as a liability when there is no obligation to a creditor or other party. As recent standards support an asset-liability approach to income measurement, deferred charges and deferred credits that do not meet the definitions of assets and liabilities, respectively, are not likely to remain. Also, the international lease standard considers an issue that the private enterprise standard does not. IAS 17 *Leases* recognizes that if the leaseback is an operating lease, the sale has actually transferred the risks and benefits of ownership to the purchaser. The international standard therefore allows a gain to be recognized, but only if the transaction takes place at fair value.

Real-World Emphasis

Disclosure and Example

There are no specific disclosure requirements for a sale-leaseback transaction other than the ones that are required for financial reporting and leases in general. Illustration 20A-2 provides an example of how Netherlands-based Koninklijke Ahold N.V. reports its sale-leaseback transaction. Ahold is an international food retailing group of companies with supermarket operations in Europe and the United States.

Illustration 20A-2

Example of Sale-Leaseback Disclosure

3 Significant accounting policies —

Sale and leaseback

The gain or loss on sale and operating leaseback transactions is recognized in the income statement immediately if (i) Ahold does not maintain or maintains only minor continuing involvement in these properties, other than the required lease payments and (ii) these transactions occur at fair value. Any gain or loss on sale and finance leaseback transactions is deferred and amortized over the term of the lease. In classifying the leaseback in a sale and leaseback transaction, similar judgments have to be made as described under "Leases."

In some sale and leaseback arrangements, Ahold sells a property and only leases back a portion of that property. These properties generally involve shopping centers, which contain an Ahold store as well as other stores leased to third-party retailers. Ahold recognizes a sale and the resulting profit on the portion of the shopping center that is not leased back to the extent that (i) the property is sold for fair value and (ii) the risks and rewards of owning stores, which are not leased back to Ahold, have been fully transferred to the buyer. The leaseback of the Ahold store and any gain on the sale of the Ahold store is accounted for under the sale and leaseback criteria described above.

In some sale and leaseback arrangements, Ahold subleases the property to third parties (including franchisees) or maintains a form of continuing involvement in the property sold, such as earn-out provisions or obligations or options to repurchase the property. In such situations, the transaction generally does not qualify for sale and leaseback accounting, but rather is accounting for as a financing transaction ("financing"). The carrying amount of the asset remains on the balance sheet and the sale proceeds are recorded as a financing obligation. The financing obligation is amortized over the lease term, using either the effective interest rate or Ahold's cost of debt rate, whichever is higher. Once Ahold's continuing involvement ends, the sale is accounted for under the sale and leaseback criteria described above.

25 Other non-current liabilities

€ million	January 3, 2010	December 28, 2008
Step rent accruals	141	117
Deferred income	47	55
Other	14	12
Total other non-current liabilities	202	184

Step rent accruals relate to the equalization of rent payments from lease contracts with scheduled fixed rent increases throughout the life of the contract.

Deferred income predominantly represents the non-current portions of deferred gains on sale and leaseback transactions.

Real Estate Leases

Objective 15
Explain the classification and accounting treatment for leases that involve real estate.

When a capital or finance lease involves land, and ownership of the land will not be transferred to the lessee, capitalizing the land on the lessee's balance sheet would result in no expense (such as depreciation) being recognized for its use over the term of the lease. Then, at the end of the lease, a loss equal to the capitalized value of the land would be recognized when the land is transferred back to the lessor. This explains why **special guidance is needed for leases that involve land**.

Land

If land is the only leased asset, and title to the property is transferred to the lessee by the end of the lease, the **lessee** accounts for the arrangement as a capital or finance lease, and the **lessor** accounts for it either as a dealer or manufacturer sales-type or as a direct financing lease, whichever is appropriate. If the title is not transferred, it is accounted for as an operating lease. It is interesting to note that under IFRS, the existence of a bargain purchase option does not provide evidence of the future transfer of title, but under PE GAAP, it does.

Land and Building

If land and a building are leased together, **IFRS** requires that each be considered separately when classifying the lease. The minimum lease payments are allocated on the basis of the relative fair values of the leasehold interest in each component.[32] If this can't be determined reliably, the entire lease is classified as a finance lease, unless it is clear that both are operating leases. If the portion determined to be for the land is immaterial, the whole arrangement may be accounted for as a single unit.

Under **private enterprise standards**, the lessee can capitalize land separately from the building when title is expected to be transferred, either directly or through a bargain purchase option. The minimum lease payments in this case are allocated based on the relative fair values of the land and the building. If title is not expected to be transferred, the accounting depends on the fair value of the land relative to the building. If it is minor, the land and building are treated as a single unit when classifying the lease; if significant, the land and building are considered separately, with the land portion classified as an operating lease.

Summary of Learning Objectives for Appendix 20A

Glossary

KEY TERM

sale-leaseback, 1355

14 Describe and apply the lessee's accounting for sale-leaseback transactions.

A sale and leaseback is accounted for by the lessee as if the two transactions were related. In general, any gain or loss, with the exception of a real (economic) loss, is deferred by the lessee and recognized in income over the lease term. For an operating lease under PE GAAP, the seller-lessee takes the deferred gain or loss into income in proportion to the rental payments made; under IFRS, the gain or loss may be taken to income immediately. For a capital lease, the deferred gain or loss is taken into income over the same period and basis as the depreciation of the leased asset (PE GAAP) or over the term of the lease (IFRS).

15 Explain the classification and accounting treatment for leases that involve real estate.

Because the capitalization of land by the lessee in a capital or finance lease that does not transfer title results in an unwanted and unintended effect on the lessee's financial statements, the portion of such leases that relates to land is accounted for as an operating lease. If the relative value of the land is minor, however, the minimum lease payments are fully capitalized as building.

---

[32] Allocating on the basis of the value of leasehold interests is not the same thing as on the basis of relative fair values of the underlying assets. Because the land will revert to the lessor and maintain its value, unlike the building, the rental payments charged for the land will not be based on recovering its full fair value.

Brief Exercises

Note: All assignment material with an asterisk (*) relates to the appendix to the chapter.

(LO 2)   **BE20-1**   Piper Corporation recently signed a lease for equipment from Photon Inc. The lease term is five years and requires equal rental payments of $32,000 at the beginning of each year. The equipment has a fair value at the lease's inception of $140,000, an estimated useful life of eight years, and no residual value. Piper pays all executory costs directly to third parties. Photon set the annual rental to earn a rate of return of 8%, and this fact is known to Piper. The lease does not transfer title or contain a bargain purchase option. How should Piper classify this lease using private enterprise GAAP?

(LO 4)   **BE20-2**   Lalonde Ltd., a public company following IFRS, recently signed a lease for equipment from Costner Ltd. The lease term is five years and requires equal rental payments of $25,173 at the beginning of each year. The equipment has a fair value at the lease's inception of $112,400, an estimated useful life of five years, and no residual value. Lalonde pays all executory costs directly to third parties. The appropriate interest rate is 6%. Prepare Lalonde's journal entries at the inception of the lease.

(LO 3)   **BE20-3**   Use the information for Lalonde and Costner from BE20–2. Explain, using numbers, how Costner determined the amount of the lease payment of $25,173.

(LO 4)   **BE20-4**   McCormick Corporation Ltd., a public company following IFRS, recorded a finance lease at $150,000 on May 1, 2011. The interest rate is 10%. McCormick Corporation made the first lease payment of $25,561 on May 1, 2011. The lease requires a total of eight annual payments. The equipment has a useful life of eight years with no residual value. Prepare McCormick Corporation's December 31, 2011 adjusting entries.

(LO 4)   **BE20-5**   Use the information for McCormick Corporation from BE20–4. Assume that at December 31, 2011, McCormick made an adjusting entry to accrue interest expense of $8,296 on the lease. Prepare McCormick's May 1, 2012 journal entry to record the second lease payment of $25,561. Assume that no reversing entries are made.

(LO 5)   **BE20-6**   Merrill Corporation, which uses private enterprise GAAP, enters into a six-year lease of machinery on September 13, 2011, that requires six annual payments of $28,000 each, beginning September 13, 2011. In addition, Merrill guarantees the lessor a residual value of $17,000 at lease end. The machinery has a useful life of six years. Prepare Merrill's September 13, 2011 journal entries, assuming an interest rate of 9%.

(LO 5)   **BE20-7**   Use the information for Merrill Corporation from BE20–6. Assume that a residual value of $17,000 is expected at the end of the lease, but that Merrill does not guarantee the residual value. Prepare Merrill's September 13, 2011 journal entries, assuming an interest rate of 9% and that Merrill also uses private enterprise GAAP.

(LO 10)   **BE20-8**   Use the information for Merrill Corporation from BE20–6. Assume that for Moxey Corporation, the lessor, collectibility is reasonably predictable, there are no important uncertainties concerning costs, and the machinery's carrying amount is $121,000. Prepare Moxey's September 13, 2011 journal entries.

(LO 6)   **BE20-9**   Wing Corporation enters into a lease with Sharda Inc, a lessor, on August 15, 2011, that does not transfer ownership or contain a bargain purchase option. Both Wing and Sharda use IFRS. The lease covers three years of the equipment's eight-year useful life, and the present value of the minimum lease payments is less than 90% of the equipment's fair market value. Prepare Wing's journal entry to record its August 15, 2011 annual lease payment of $31,500. Wing has a November 30 year end.

(LO 11)   **BE20-10**   Use the information for Wing Corporation and Sharda Inc. from BE20–9. Assume that Sharda, the lessor, has a June 30 year end. Prepare Sharda's entry on August 15, 2011, and any adjusting entry needed on June 30, 2012.

(LO 8, 9)   **BE20-11**   Lai Corporation, which uses private enterprise GAAP, leased equipment that was carried at a cost of $175,000 to Swander Inc., the lessee. The term of the lease is five years, beginning January 1, 2011, with equal rental payments of $40,584 at the beginning of each year. Swander pays all executory costs directly to third parties. The equipment's fair value at the lease's inception is $175,000. The equipment has a useful life of six years with no residual value. The lease has an implicit interest rate of 8%, no bargain purchase option, and no transfer of title. Collectibility is reasonably assured, with no additional costs to be incurred by Lai. Prepare Lai Corporation's January 1, 2011 journal entries at the inception of the lease.

(LO 9)   **BE20-12**   Use the information for Lai Corporation from BE20–11. Assume that the direct financing lease was recorded at a present value of $175,000. Prepare Lai's December 31, 2011 entry to record interest.

BE20-13 Use the information for Lai Corporation from BE20–11. Assume that instead of costing Lai $175,000, the equipment was manufactured by Lai at a cost of $137,500 and the equipment's regular selling price is $175,000. Prepare Lai Corporation's January 1, 2011 journal entries at the inception of the lease and the entry at December 31, 2011, to record interest. **(LO 8, 9)**

BE20-14 Regina Corporation, which uses private enterprise GAAP, manufactures replicators. On May 29, 2011, it leased to Barnes Limited a replicator that cost $265,000 to manufacture and usually sells for $410,000. The lease agreement covers the replicator's five-year useful life and requires five equal annual rentals of $95,930 each, beginning May 29, 2011. The equipment reverts to Regina at the end of the lease, at which time it is expected that the replicator will have a residual value of $40,000, which has been guaranteed by Barnes, the lessee. An interest rate of 12% is implicit in the lease agreement. Collectibility of the rentals is reasonably assured, and there are no important uncertainties concerning costs. Prepare Regina's May 29, 2011 journal entries. **(LO 10)**

BE20-15 Use the information for Regina Corporation from BE20–14. Assume instead that the residual value is not guaranteed. Prepare Regina's May 29, 2011 journal entries. **(LO 10)**

BE20-16 Langlois Services Inc. is using the contract-based approach to account for a lease of a truck. The lease includes a residual value guarantee at the end of the term of the lease of $16,000. Langlois estimates that the likelihood for the residual value of $16,000 has a 50% certainty. Langlois feels that there is a 30% chance that the residual value will be $12,000 and a 20% chance that it will be $10,000. Calculate the probability weighted value of the residual guarantee that needs to be included in the lease obligation recorded by Langlois when the lease is signed. **(LO 12)**

*BE20-17 On January 1, 2011, Ryan Animation Ltd., which uses IFRS, sold a truck to Letourneau Finance Corp. for $65,000 and immediately leased it back. The truck was carried on Ryan Animation's books at $53,000, net of $26,000 of accumulated depreciation. The term of the lease is five years, and title transfers to Ryan Animation at lease end. The lease requires five equal rental payments of $17,147, with each payment made at year end. The appropriate rate of interest is 10%, and the truck has a useful life of five years with no salvage value. Prepare Ryan Animation's 2011 journal entries. **(LO 14)**

*BE20-18 Lessee Corp. agreed to lease property from Lessor Corp. effective January 1, 2011, for an annual payment of $23,576.90, beginning January 1, 2011. The property is made up of land with a fair value of $100,000 and a two-storey office building with a fair value of $150,000 and a useful life of 20 years. The implicit interest rate is 8%, the lease term is 20 years, and title to the property is transferred to Lessee at the end of the lease term. Prepare the required entries made by Lessee Corp. on January 1, 2011, and at its year end of December 31, 2011. Both Lessee and Lessor use private enterprise GAAP. **(LO 15)**

*BE20-19 Use the information provided in BE20–18 about Lessee Corp. Assume that title to the property will not be transferred to Lessee by the end of the lease term and that there is also no bargain purchase option, but that the lease does meet other criteria to qualify as a capital lease. Prepare the required entries made by Lessee Corp. on January 1, 2011, and at its year end of December 31, 2011. **(LO 15)**

Exercises

E20-1 (Type of Lease and Amortization Schedule) Victoria Leasing Corporation, which uses private enterprise GAAP, leases a new machine that has a cost and fair value of $95,000 to Black Corporation on a three-year, non-cancellable contract. Black Corporation agrees to assume all risks of normal ownership, including such costs as insurance, taxes, and maintenance. The machine has a three-year useful life and no residual value. The lease was signed on January 1, 2011, and Victoria Leasing Corporation expects to earn a 9% return on its investment. The annual rentals are payable on each December 31, beginning December 31, 2011. Black Corporation has an excellent credit rating and so Victoria Leasing is reasonably assured of the collections under the lease. **(LO 2, 3, 8, 13)**

Instructions

(a) Discuss the nature of the lease arrangement and the accounting method that each party to the lease should apply.

(b) Use a computer spreadsheet to prepare an amortization schedule that would be suitable for both the lessor and the lessee and that covers all the years involved.

(c) Discuss the differences, if any, in the classification of the lease to Victoria Leasing Corporation (the lessor) or to Black Corporation (the lessee) if both were using IFRS in their financial reporting.

(LO 2, 4, 5)   **E20-2**   **(Lessee Entries and Capital Lease with Unguaranteed Residual Value—Lease and Fiscal Year Differ)** On September 1, 2011, Wong Corporation, which uses private enterprise GAAP, signed a five-year, non-cancellable lease for a machine. The terms of the lease called for Wong to make annual payments of $13,668 at the beginning of each lease year, starting September 1, 2011. The machine has an estimated useful life of six years and a $9,000 unguaranteed residual value. The machine reverts back to the lessor at the end of the lease term. Wong uses the straight-line method of depreciation for all of its plant assets, has a calendar year end, prepares adjusting journal entries at the end of the fiscal year, and does not use reversing entries. Wong's incremental borrowing rate is 10%, and the lessor's implicit rate is unknown.

Digging
Deeper

Instructions

(a) Explain why this is a capital lease to Wong.

(b) Using time value of money tables, a financial calculator, or computer spreadsheet functions, calculate the present value of the minimum lease payments for the lessee.

(c) Prepare all necessary journal entries for Wong for this lease, including any year-end adjusting entries through September 1, 2012.

(d) Would this also be a capital lease if the lessee reported under IFRS?

(LO 6)   **E20-3**   **(Lessee Entries, Operating Lease, Comparison)** Refer to the data and other information provided in E20–2. Assume that the machine has an estimated economic life of seven years and that its fair value on September 1, 2011, is $79,000.

Instructions

(a) Explain why this lease is now considered an operating lease.

(b) Prepare all necessary journal entries for Wong Corporation for this lease, including any year-end adjusting entries through December 31, 2012.

(c) Identify what accounts will appear on Wong's December 31, 2011 statement of financial position and income statement relative to this lease.

(d) How would Wong's December 31, 2011 statement of financial position and income statement differ from your answer to (c) if the lease were a capital lease as described in E20–2?

(e) What major financial statement ratios would be different if Wong accounted for this lease as an operating lease rather than as a capital lease? Explain.

(LO 2, 4, 7)   **E20-4**   **(Lessee Calculations and Entries; Capital Lease; Disclosure)** On December 31, 2011, Xu Ltd., which uses private enterprise GAAP, entered into an eight-year lease agreement for a conveyor machine. Annual lease payments are $28,500 at the beginning of each lease year, which ends December 31, and Xu made the first payment on January 1, 2012. At the end of the lease, the machine will revert to the lessor. However, conveyor machines are only expected to last for eight years and have no residual value. At the time of the lease agreement, conveyor machines could be purchased for approximately $166,000 cash. Equivalent financing for the machine could have been obtained from Xu's bank at 10.5%. Xu's fiscal year coincides with the calendar year and Xu uses straight-line depreciation for its conveyor machines.

Instructions

(a) Calculate the present value of the minimum lease payments using a financial calculator or work sheet functions.

(b) Explain why this is a capital lease to Xu Ltd. Document your calculations in arriving at your explanation.

(c) Prepare an amortization schedule for the term of the lease to be used by Xu Ltd. Use a computer spreadsheet.

(d) Prepare the journal entries on Xu Ltd.'s books to reflect the signing of the lease agreement and to record the payments and expenses related to this lease for the years 2012 and 2010 as well as any adjusting journal entries at its fiscal year ends of December 31, 2012, and 2010.

(e) Prepare a partial comparative balance sheet at December 31, 2010, and 2012, for all of the accounts related to this lease for Xu Ltd. Be specific about the classifications that should be used.

(f) Provide Xu Ltd.'s required note disclosure concerning the lease for the fiscal year ending December 31, 2010.

(g) What is the significance of the difference between the amount of the present value of the minimum lease payments calculated in part (a) and the approximate selling price of the machine of $166,000?

Digging
Deeper

(LO 2, 4, 5)   **E20-5**   **(Lessee Calculations and Entries; Capital Lease with Guaranteed Residual Value)** New Bay Corporation leases an automobile with a fair value of $21,500 from Simon Motors, Inc. on the following lease terms:

1. It is a non-cancellable term of 55 months.

2. The rental is $425 per month at the end of each month (the present value at 1% per month is $17,910).

3. The estimated residual value after 55 months is $2,500 (the present value at 1% per month is $1,446). New Bay Corporation guarantees the residual value of $2,500.

4. The automobile's estimated economic life is 72 months.

5. New Bay Corporation's incremental borrowing rate is 12% a year (1% a month). Simon's implicit rate is unknown.

Instructions

(a) Assuming that New Bay Corporation reports under private enterprise standards, explain why this is a capital lease.

(b) What is the present value of the minimum lease payments for New Bay?

(c) Record the lease on New Bay Corporation's books at the date of inception.

(d) Record the first month's depreciation on New Bay Corporation's books (assume the straight-line depreciation method).

(e) Record the first month's lease payment.

(f) Would this lease be considered a capital lease if the company reported under IFRS?

Digging
Deeper

E20-6   (Lessee Entries; Finance Lease with Executory Costs and Unguaranteed Residual Value) On January 1, 2011, Fine Corp., which uses IFRS, signs a 10-year, non-cancellable lease agreement to lease a specialty loom from Sheffield Corporation. The following information concerns the lease agreement. **(LO 2, 4, 5)**

1. The agreement requires equal rental payments of $73,580 beginning on January 1, 2011.

2. The loom's fair value on January 1, 2011, is $450,000.

3. The loom has an estimated economic life of 12 years, with an unguaranteed residual value of $12,000. Fine Corp. depreciates similar equipment using the straight-line method.

4. The lease is non-renewable. At the termination of the lease, the loom reverts to the lessor.

5. Fine's incremental borrowing rate is 12% per year. The lessor's implicit rate is not known by Fine Corp.

6. The yearly rental payment includes $2,470.29 of executory costs related to insurance on the loom.

Instructions

(a) Prepare an amortization schedule for the term of the lease to be used by Fine. Use a computer spreadsheet.

(b) Prepare the journal entries on Fine Corp.'s books to reflect the signing of the lease agreement and to record the payments and expenses related to this lease for the years 2011 and 2012 as well as any adjusting journal entries at its fiscal year ends of December 31, 2011, and 2012.

(c) Prepare Fine Corp.'s required note disclosure on the lease for the fiscal year ending December 31, 2012.

Digging
Deeper

E20-7   (Lessee Entries; Finance Lease with Executory Costs and Unguaranteed Residual Value—Lease and Fiscal Years Differ) **(LO 2, 4, 5)**

Instructions

Refer to the data and other information provided in E20–6, but now assume that Fine's fiscal year end is May 31. Prepare the journal entries on Fine Corp.'s books to reflect the lease signing and to record payments and expenses related to this lease for the calendar years 2011 and 2012. Fine does not prepare reversing entries.

E20-8   (Amortization Schedule and Journal Entries for Lessee) Oakridge Leasing Corporation, which uses private enterprise GAAP, signs an agreement on January 1, 2011, to lease equipment to LeBlanc Limited. The following information relates to the agreement: **(LO 2, 3, 7)**

1. The term of the non-cancellable lease is five years, with no renewal option. The equipment has an estimated economic life of six years.

2. The asset's fair value at January 1, 2011, is $80,000.

3. The asset will revert to the lessor at the end of the lease term, at which time the asset is expected to have a residual value of $7,000, which is not guaranteed.

4. LeBlanc Limited assumes direct responsibility for all executory costs, which include the following annual amounts: $900 to Rocky Mountain Insurance Corporation for insurance and $1,600 to James County for property taxes.

5. The agreement requires equal annual rental payments of $18,142.95 to the lessor, beginning on January 1, 2011.

6. The lessee's incremental borrowing rate is 11%. The lessor's implicit rate is 10% and is known to the lessee.

7. LeBlanc Limited uses the straight-line depreciation method for all equipment.

8. LeBlanc uses reversing entries when appropriate.

Instructions

Answer the following, rounding all numbers to the nearest cent.

(a) Use a computer spreadsheet to prepare an amortization schedule for LeBlanc Limited for the lease term.

(b) Prepare all of LeBlanc's journal entries for 2011 and 2012 to record the lease agreement, the lease payments, and all expenses related to this lease. Assume that the lessee's annual accounting period ends on December 31.

(c) Provide the required note disclosure for LeBlanc Limited concerning the lease for the fiscal year ending December 31, 2012.

Digging
Deeper

(d) Would this lease be considered a capital lease if the company reported under IFRS? Would the note disclosure required in (c) above need to be modified under IFRS?

(LO 6, 11)   E20-9   (Accounting for an Operating Lease—Lease and Fiscal Year Differ) On January 1, 2011, Morrison Corp. leased a building to Wisen Inc. Both companies use IFRS. The relevant information on the lease is as follows:

1. The lease arrangement is for 10 years.

2. The leased building cost $5.5 million and was purchased by Morrison for cash on July 1, 2011.

3. The building is amortized on a straight-line basis. Its estimated economic life is 40 years.

4. Lease payments are $325,000 per year and are made at the end of the lease year, and so the first lease payment was made June 30, 2012.

5. Property tax expense of $57,000 and insurance expense of $11,000 on the building were incurred by Morrison for the 2011 fiscal year. Payment for these two items was made on July 1, 2011.

6. Both the lessor and the lessee have their fiscal years on a calendar-year basis.

Instructions

(a) Prepare the journal entries and any year-end adjusting journal entries made by Morrison Corp. in 2011.

(b) Prepare the journal entries and any year-end adjusting journal entries made by Wisen Inc. in 2011.

Digging
Deeper

(c) If Morrison paid $30,000 to a real estate broker on July 1, 2011, as a fee for finding the lessee, how much should Morrison Corp. report as an expense for this fee item in 2011?

(d) Would any of the accounting treatment you have provided in (a) through (c) above change if Morrison had been using private enterprise GAAP?

(LO 6, 11)   E20-10   (Accounting and Disclosure for an Operating Lease—Lessee and Lessor) On May 1, 2011, a machine was purchased for $1,750,000 by Pomeroy Corp. The machine is expected to have an eight-year life with no salvage value and is to be depreciated on a straight-line basis. The machine was leased to St. Isidor Inc. on May 1, 2011, at an annual rental of $480,000. Other relevant information is as follows:

1. The lease term is three years.

2. Pomeroy Corp. incurred maintenance and other executory costs of $61,000 for the fiscal year ending December 31, 2011, related to this lease.

3. The machine could have been sold by Pomeroy Corp. for $1,850,000 instead of leasing it.

4. St. Isidor is required to pay a rent security deposit of $65,000 and to prepay the last month's rent of $40,000 on signing the lease.

5. Both Pomeroy and St. Isidor use IFRS.

Instructions

(a) How much should Pomeroy Corp. report as income before income tax on this lease for 2011?

(b) What amount should St. Isidor Inc. report for rent expense for 2011 on this lease?

(c) What financial statement disclosures relative to this lease are required for each company's December 31, 2011 year end assuming private enterprise GAAP had been used for each company?

(d) What additional disclosures, if any, apply if both companies use IFRS?

E20-11 **(Operating Lease for Lessee and Lessor with Initial Costs)** On February 20, 2011, Sigouin Inc. purchased **(LO 6, 11)** a machine for $1.6 million for the purpose of leasing it. The machine is expected to have a 10-year life with no residual value, and will be amortized on the straight-line basis. The machine was leased to Densmore Corporation on March 1, 2011, for a four-year period at a monthly rental of $26,500. There is no provision for the renewal of the lease or purchase of the machine by the lessee at the expiration of the lease term. Sigouin paid $36,000 to a third party for commissions associated with negotiating the lease in February 2011. Both Sigouin Inc. and Densmore Corporation use private enterprise GAAP.

Instructions

(a) What expense should Densmore Corporation record based on the above facts for the year ended December 31, 2011? Show supporting calculations in good form.

(b) What income or loss before income taxes should Sigouin record based on the above facts for the year ended December 31, 2011?

(c) Would your answer to (a) and (b) above be different if both companies used IFRS?

(AICPA adapted)

E20-12 **(Operating Lease vs. Capital Lease)** You are auditing the December 31, 2011 financial statements of Deng, **(LO 6)** Inc., a manufacturer of novelties and party favours and a user of private enterprise GAAP. During your inspection of the company garage, you discovered that a 2010 Shirk automobile is parked in the company garage but is not listed in the equipment subsidiary ledger. You ask the plant manager about the vehicle, and she tells you that the company did not list the automobile because the company was only leasing it. The lease agreement was entered into on January 1, 2011, with Quick Deal New and Used Cars. You decide to review the lease agreement to ensure that the lease should be given operating lease treatment, and you discover the following lease terms:

1. It is a non-cancellable term of 50 months.

2. The rental is $220 per month at the end of each month (the present value at 1% per month is $8,623).

3. The estimated residual value after 50 months is $2,100 (the present value at 1% per month is $1,277). Deng guarantees the residual value of $1,100.

4. The automobile's estimated economic life is 60 months.

5. Deng's incremental borrowing rate is 12% per year (1% per month).

Instructions

You are a senior auditor writing a memo to your supervisor, the audit partner in charge of this audit, to discuss the situation. Be sure to include (a) why you inspected the lease agreement, (b) what you determined about the lease, and (c) how you advised your client to account for this lease. Explain every journal entry that you believe is necessary to record this lease properly on the client's books.

E20-13 **(Lease Payment Calculation and Lessee-Lessor Entries—Capital/Sales-Type Lease)** On January 1, 2011, **(LO 2, 3, 8,** Lavery Corporation leased equipment to Flynn Corporation. Both Lavery and Flynn use private enterprise GAAP and **9, 13)** have calendar year ends. The following information pertains to this lease.

1. The term of the non-cancellable lease is six years, with no renewal option. The equipment reverts to the lessor at the termination of the lease, at which time it is expected to have a residual value (not guaranteed) of $6,000. Flynn Corporation depreciates all its equipment on a straight-line basis.

2. Equal rental payments are due on January 1 of each year, beginning in 2011.

3. The equipment's fair value on January 1, 2011, is $144,000 and its cost to Lavery is $111,000.

4. The equipment has an economic life of seven years.

5. Lavery set the annual rental to ensure a 9% rate of return. Flynn's incremental borrowing rate is 10% and the lessor's implicit rate is unknown to the lessee.

6. Collectibility of lease payments is reasonably predictable and there are no important uncertainties about any unreimbursable costs that have not yet been incurred by the lessor.

Instructions

(a) Explain clearly why this lease is a capital lease to Flynn and a sales-type lease to Lavery.

(b) Using time value of money tables, a financial calculator, or computer spreadsheet functions, calculate the amount of the annual rental payment.

(c) Prepare all necessary journal entries for Flynn for 2011.

(d) Prepare all necessary journal entries for Lavery for 2011.

(e) Discuss the differences, if any, in the classification of the lease to Lavery Corporation (the lessor) or to Flynn Corporation (the lessee) if both were using IFRS in their financial reporting.

(LO 3, 4, 9, 10) **E20-14   (Lessor Entries, Financing Lease with Option to Purchase, Lessee Capitalizable Amount)** Castle Leasing Corporation, which uses IFRS, signs a lease agreement on January 1, 2011, to lease electronic equipment to Wai Corporation, which also uses IFRS. The term of the non-cancellable lease is two years and payments are required at the end of each year. The following information relates to this agreement.

1. Wai Corporation has the option to purchase the equipment for $13,000 upon the termination of the lease.

2. The equipment has a cost and fair value of $135,000 to Castle Leasing Corporation. The useful economic life is two years, with a residual value of $13,000.

3. Wai Corporation is required to pay $5,000 each year to the lessor for executory costs.

4. Castle Leasing Corporation wants to earn a return of 10% on its investment.

5. Collectibility of the payments is reasonably predictable, and there are no important uncertainties surrounding the costs that have not yet been incurred by the lessor.

Instructions

(a) Using time value of money tables, a financial calculator, or computer spreadsheet functions, calculate the lease payment that Castle Leasing would require from Wai Corporation.

(b) What classification will Wai Corporation give to the lease? What classification will be given to the lease by Castle Leasing Corporation?

(c) What classification would be adopted by Wai Corporation and Castle Leasing Corporation had they both been using private enterprise GAAP?

(d) Prepare a lease amortization table for Castle Leasing for the term of the lease.

(e) Prepare the journal entries on Castle Leasing's books to reflect the payments received under the lease and to recognize income for the years 2011 and 2012.

(f) Assuming that Wai Corporation exercises its option to purchase the equipment on December 31, 2012, prepare the journal entry to reflect the sale on Castle Leasing's books.

(g) What amount would Wai Corporation capitalize and recognize as a liability on signing the lease? Explain.

(LO 3, 9, 10) **E20-15   (Rental Amount Calculation, Lessor Entries, Disclosure—Financing Lease with Unguaranteed Residual Value)** On January 1, 2011, Vick Leasing Inc., a lessor that uses IFRS, signed an agreement with Rock Corporation, a lessee, for the use of a compression system. The system cost $415,000 and was purchased from Manufacturing Solutions Ltd. specifically for Rock Corporation. Annual payments are made each January 1 by Rock. In addition to making the lease payment, Rock also reimburses Vick $4,000 each January 1 for a portion of the maintenance expenditures, which cost Vick Leasing a total of $6,000 per year. At the end of the five-year agreement, the compression equipment will revert to Vick and is expected to have a residual value of $25,000, which is not guaranteed. Collectibility of the rentals is reasonably predictable, and there are no important uncertainties surrounding the costs that have not yet been incurred by Vick Leasing Inc.

Instructions

(a) Assume that Vick Leasing Inc. has a required rate of return of 8%. Calculate the amount of the lease payments that would be needed to generate this return on the agreement if payments were made each:

1. January 1
2. December 31

(b) Use a computer spreadsheet to prepare an amortization table that shows how the lessor's net investment in the lease receivable will be reduced over the lease term if payments are made each:

1. January 1

2. December 31

(c) Assume that the payments are due each January 1. Prepare all journal entries and adjusting journal entries for 2011 and 2012 for the lessor, assuming that Vick has a calendar year end. Include the payment for the purchase of the equipment for leasing in your entries and the annual payment for maintenance.

(d) Provide the note disclosure concerning the lease that would be required for Vick Leasing Inc. at December 31, 2012. Assume that payments are due each January 1.

E20-16 **(Lessor Entries—Sales-Type Lease)** Pucci Corporation, a machinery dealer whose stock trades on the (LO 8, 9) Toronto Stock Exchange, and so uses IFRS, leased a machine to Ernst Corporation on January 1, 2011. The lease is for a six-year period and requires equal annual payments of $24,736 at the beginning of each year. The first payment is received on January 1, 2011. Pucci had purchased the machine during 2010 for $99,000. Collectibility of lease payments is reasonably predictable, and no important uncertainties exist about costs that have not yet been incurred by Pucci. Pucci set the annual rental amount to ensure an 8% rate of return. The machine has an economic life of six years, with no residual value, and reverts to Pucci at the termination of the lease.

Instructions

(a) Using time value of money tables, a financial calculator, or computer spreadsheet functions, calculate the amount of each of the following:

1. Gross investment

2. Unearned interest income

3. Net investment in the lease

(b) Prepare all necessary journal entries for Pucci for 2011.

E20-17 **(Type of Lease, Lessee Entries with Bargain Purchase Option)** The following facts are for a non- (LO 2, 4, 5, cancellable lease agreement between Hebert Corporation and Russell Corporation, a lessee:　10, 13)

Inception date	July 1, 2011
Annual lease payment due at the beginning of each year, starting July 1, 2011	$20,066.26
Bargain purchase option price at end of lease term	$ 4,500.00
Lease term	5 years
Economic life of leased equipment	10 years
Lessor's cost	$60,000.00
Fair value of asset at July 1, 2011	$88,000.00
Lessor's implicit rate	9%
Lessee's incremental borrowing rate	9%

The collectibility of the lease payments is reasonably predictable, and there are no important uncertainties about costs that have not yet been incurred by the lessor. The lessee assumes responsibility for all executory costs. Both Russell and Hebert use private enterprise GAAP.

Instructions

Answer the following, rounding all numbers to the nearest cent.

(a) Discuss the nature of this lease to Russell Corporation, the lessee.

(b) Discuss the nature of this lease to Hebert Corporation, the lessor.

(c) Prepare a lease amortization schedule for the lease obligation using a computer spreadsheet for Russell Corporation for the five-year lease term.

(d) Prepare the journal entries on the lessee's books to reflect the signing of the lease and to record the payments and expenses related to this lease for the years 2011 and 2012. Russell's annual accounting period ends on December 31, and Russell does not use reversing entries.

(e) Discuss the differences, if any, in the classification of the lease to Russell Corporation (the lessor) or to Hebert Corporation (the lessee) if both were using IFRS in their financial reporting.

E20-18 **(Lessor Entries with Bargain Purchase Option)** A lease agreement between Hebert Corporation and (LO 5, 8, Russell Corporation is described in E20-17.　9, 10)

Instructions

Provide the following for Hebert Corporation, the lessor, rounding all numbers to the nearest cent.

(a) Calculate the amount of gross investment at the inception of the lease.

(b) Calculate the amount of net investment at the inception of the lease.

(c) Prepare a lease amortization schedule using a computer spreadsheet for Hebert Corporation for the five-year lease term.

(d) Prepare the journal entries to reflect the signing of the lease and to record the receipts and income related to this lease for the years 2011, 2012, and 2013. The lessor's accounting period ends on December 31, and Hebert Corporation does not use reversing entries.

(LO 3, 8, 9) E20-19 (Calculation of Rental, Amortization Table, Journal Entries for Lessor—Lease and Fiscal Year Differ) Zoppas Leasing Corporation, which has a fiscal year end of October 31 and uses IFRS, signs an agreement on January 1, 2011, to lease equipment to Irvine Limited. The following information relates to the agreement.

1. The term of the non-cancellable lease is six years, with no renewal option. The equipment has an estimated economic life of eight years.

2. The asset's cost to Zoppas, the lessor, is $305,000. The asset's fair value at January 1, 2011, is $305,000.

3. The asset will revert to the lessor at the end of the lease term, at which time the asset is expected to have a residual value of $45,626, which is not guaranteed.

4. Irvine Limited, the lessee, assumes direct responsibility for all executory costs.

5. The agreement requires equal annual rental payments, beginning on January 1, 2011.

6. Collectibility of the lease payments is reasonably predictable. There are no important uncertainties about costs that have not yet been incurred by the lessor.

Instructions

Answer the following, rounding all numbers in parts (b) and (c) to the nearest cent.

(a) Assuming that Zoppas Leasing desires a 10% rate of return on its investment, use time value of money tables, a financial calculator, or computer spreadsheet functions to calculate the amount of the annual rental payment that is required. Round to the nearest dollar.

(b) Prepare an amortization schedule using a computer spreadsheet that would be suitable for the lessor for the lease term.

(c) Prepare all of the journal entries for the lessor for 2011 and 2012 to record the lease agreement, the receipt of lease payments, and the recognition of income. Assume that Zoppas prepares adjusting journal entries only at the end of the fiscal year.

(LO 3, 8, 9, 10) E20-20 (Lessor Entries, Determination of Type of Lease, Lease Payment Calculation, Spreadsheet Application, Financial Statement Amounts) Turpin Corp., which uses private enterprise GAAP, leases a car to Jaimme DeLory on June 1, 2011. The term of the non-cancellable lease is 48 months. The following information is provided about the lease:

1. The lessee is given an option to purchase the automobile at the end of the lease term for $5,000.

2. The automobile's fair value on June 1, 2011, is $29,500. It is carried in Turpin's inventory at $21,200.

3. The car has an economic life of seven years, with a $1,000 residual value at the end of that time. The car's estimated fair value is $10,000 after four years, $7,000 after five years, and $2,500 after six years.

4. Turpin wants to earn a 12% rate of return (1% per month) on any financing transactions.

5. Jaimme DeLory represents a reasonable credit risk and no future costs are anticipated in relation to this lease.

6. The lease agreement calls for a $1,000 down payment on June 1, 2011, and 48 equal monthly payments on the first of each month, beginning June 1, 2011.

Instructions

(a) Determine the amount of the monthly lease payment using present value tables, a financial calculator, or computer spreadsheet functions.

(b) What type of lease is this to Turpin Corp.? Explain.

(c) Prepare a lease amortization schedule for the 48-month lease term using a computer spreadsheet.

(d) Prepare the entries that are required, if any, on December 31, 2011, Turpin's fiscal year end.

(e) How much income will Turpin report on its 2011 income statement relative to this lease?

(f) What is the net investment in the lease to be reported on the December 31, 2011 statement of financial position? How much is reported in current assets? In non-current assets?

E20-21 **(IRFS vs. Contract-Based Lease and Journal Entries for Lessee)** Cuomo Mining Corporation, a public **(LO 2, 6, 12)** company whose stock trades on the Toronto Stock Exchange, uses IFRS. The Vice-President of Finance has asked you, the assistant controller, to prepare a comparison of the company's current accounting of a lease with the contract-based approach, which is expected to be implemented in the near future. The lease you are going to use for this comparison was signed by Cuomo on April 1, 2011, with Bertrand Ltd. for a piece of excavation equipment. The following information relates to the agreement.

1. The term of the non-cancellable lease is three years, with a renewal option of one additional year at the annual rate of 125% of the initial payment. The equipment has an estimated economic life of 10 years.

2. The asset's fair value at April 1, 2011, is approximately $1 million.

3. The asset will revert to Bertrand at the end of the initial term of the lease, or at the end of the renewal period should Cuomo exercise that option. The excavation equipment is expected to have a fair value of $600,000 on March 31, 2013, and $500,000 on March 31, 2014, which is not guaranteed.

4. Cuomo assumes direct responsibility for all executory costs for the excavation equipment.

5. The initial term of the lease agreement requires equal annual rental payments of $135,000 to Bertrand, beginning on April 1, 2011.

6. The lessee's incremental borrowing rate is 9%. Bertrand's implicit rate is 8% and is known to Cuomo.

7. Cuomo has a calendar year end.

You have established that it has always been Cuomo's intention to exercise the renewal period on account of the nature of the asset. Cuomo's operations manager says that there is a 70% chance that the renewal period will be exercised.

Instructions

Answer the following, rounding all numbers to the nearest dollar.

Part 1

Using the current accounting under IFRS:

(a) Determine the accounting treatment of the lease agreement and obligation to Cuomo. What were the conditions that would need to be in place for the lease to be classified as a financing lease?

(b) Record all transactions concerning the lease for Cuomo for the fiscal year 2011.

Part 2

Using the proposed contract-based approach:

(c) Determine the amount of lease obligation at the signing of the lease.

(d) Use a computer spreadsheet to prepare an amortization schedule for Cuomo for the lease term including the expected lease renewal.

(e) Prepare all of Cuomo's journal entries for fiscal years 2011 and 2012 to record the lease agreement and the lease payments.

Part 3

Prepare a table of Cuomo's balance sheet disclosure of all of the amounts that would appear concerning the right and the obligation at December 31, 2012. Follow with the statement of income disclosure for the fiscal year ending December 31, 2012. Be specific concerning classifications. Include a second column to show the amounts Cuomo reports for the same period following IFRS.

*E20-22 **(Sale-Leaseback—Lessee and Lessor Entries)** On January 1, 2011, Hein Corporation sells equipment to **(LO 14)** Liquidity Finance Corp. for $720,000 and immediately leases the equipment back. Both Hein and Liquidity use private enterprise GAAP. Other relevant information is as follows:

1. The equipment's carrying value on Hein's books on January 1, 2011, is $640,000.

2. The term of the non-cancellable lease is 10 years. Title will transfer to Hein at the end of the lease.

3. The lease agreement requires equal rental payments of $117,176.68 at the end of each year.

4. The incremental borrowing rate of Hein Corporation is 12%. Hein is aware that Liquidity Finance Corp. set the annual rental to ensure a rate of return of 10%.

5. The equipment has a fair value of $720,000 on January 1, 2011, and an estimated economic life of 10 years, with no residual value.

6. Hein pays executory costs of $11,000 per year directly to appropriate third parties.

Digging
Deeper

Instructions

(a) Prepare the journal entries for both the lessee and the lessor for 2011 to reflect the sale and leaseback agreement. No uncertainties exist and collectibility is reasonably certain.

(b) What is Hein's primary objective in entering a sale-leaseback arrangement with Liquidity Finance Corp.? Would you consider this transaction to be a red flag to creditors, demonstrating that Hein is in financial difficulty?

(LO 14)   *E20-23   (Lessee-Lessor, Sale-Leaseback) Presented below are four independent situations. All the companies involved use private enterprise GAAP.

1. On December 31, 2011, Zarle Inc. sold equipment to Daniell Corp. and immediately leased it back for 10 years. The equipment's selling price was $520,000, its carrying amount $400,000, and its estimated remaining economic life 12 years.

2. On December 31, 2011, Tessier Corp. sold a machine to Cross Ltd. and simultaneously leased it back for one year. The machine's selling price was $480,000, its carrying amount was $420,000, and it had an estimated remaining useful life of 14 years. The rental payments' present value for one year is $35,000.

3. On January 1, 2011, McKane Corp. sold an airplane with an estimated useful life of 10 years. At the same time, McKane leased back the plane for 10 years. The airplane's selling price was $500,000, the carrying amount $379,000, and the annual rental $73,975.22. McKane Corp. intends to amortize the leased asset using the straight-line depreciation method.

4. On January 1, 2011, Barnes Corp. sold equipment with an estimated useful life of five years. At the same time, Barnes leased back the equipment for two years under a lease classified as an operating lease. The equipment's selling price (fair value) was $212,700, the carrying amount was $300,000, the monthly rental under the lease was $6,000, and the rental payments' present value was $115,753.

Instructions

(a) For situation 1: Determine the amount of deferred profit to be reported by Zarle Inc. from the equipment sale on December 31, 2011.

(b) For situation 2: At December 31, 2011, how much should Tessier report as deferred profit from the sale of the machine?

(c) For situation 3: Discuss how the gain on the sale should be reported by McKane at the end of 2011 in the financial statements.

(d) For situation 4: For the year ended December 31, 2011, identify the items that would be reported on Barnes's income statement related to the sale-leaseback transaction.

(LO 14)   *E20-24   (Land Lease, Lessee and Lessor) On September 15, 2011, Local Camping Products Limited, the lessee, entered into a 20-year lease with Sullivan Corp. to rent a parcel of land at a rate of $30,000 per year. Both Local and Sullivan use private enterprise GAAP. The annual rental is due in advance each September 15, beginning in 2011. The land has a current fair value of $195,000. The land reverts to Sullivan at the end of the lease. Local Camping's incremental borrowing rate and Sullivan's implicit interest rate are both 8%.

Instructions

(a) Prepare Local Camping Products' required journal entries on September 15, 2011, and at December 31, 2011, its year end.

(b) Explain how and why these entries might differ if Local were leasing equipment instead of land.

(c) Prepare the entries required on Sullivan's books at September 15, 2011, and at December 31, 2011, its year end.

E20-25   (Real Estate Lease) Rancour Ltd., which uses private enterprise GAAP, recently expanded its operations   (LO 14, 15)
into an adjoining municipality and, on March 30, 2011, signed a 15-year lease with its Municipal Industrial Commission
(MIC). The property has a total fair value of $150,000 on March 30, 2011, with one third of the amount attributable to
the land and two thirds to the building. The land is expected to double in value over the next 15 years, while the building
will depreciate by 60%. The lease includes a purchase option at the end of the lease that allows Rancour to receive title to
the property for a payment of $90,000.

Rancour is required to make rental payments of $10,000 annually, with the first payment due March 30, 2011. The
MIC's implicit interest rate, known to all, is 7%. The building's economic life is estimated at 20 years, at which time it will
have a small residual value of $10,000.

Instructions

(a) Prepare the entries required by Rancour on the signing of the lease and the payment of the first lease payment.

(b) Assuming that Rancour's year end is December 31, prepare the entries that are required on December 31, 2011;
March 30, 2012; and December 31, 2012. Rancour does not use reversing entries.

Problems

P20-1   Interior Design Inc. (ID) is a privately owned business that produces interior decorating options for consumers.
ID has chosen to follow private enterprise GAAP. The software that it purchased 10 years ago to present clients with
designs that are unique to their offices is no longer state-of-the-art, and ID is faced with making a decision on the replacement of its software. The company has two options:

1. Enter into a lease agreement with Precision Inc. whereby ID makes an upfront lease payment of $12,000 on January
   1, 2012, and annual payments of $4,500 over the next five years on each December 31. At the end of the lease, ID has
   the option to buy the software for $5,000. The first annual lease payment is on December 31, 2012.

2. Enter into a lease agreement with Graphic Design Inc. on January 1, 2012, whereby ID makes five annual lease payments of $6,500, beginning on January 1, 2012. ID may purchase the software at the end of the lease period for $200.
   This is considered a bargain price compared with the offer of $5,000 in the proposal from Precision Inc.

Under both options, the software will require annual upgrades that are expected to cost $1,500 per year. These upgrade
costs are in addition to the lease payments that are required under the two independent options. As this additional cost is
the same under both options, ID has decided to ignore it in making its choice.

The Precision agreement requires a licensing fee of $1,000 to be renewed annually. If ID decides on the Precision
option, the licensing fee will be included in the annual lease payment of $4,500. Both Precision Inc. and Graphic Design
Inc. offer software programs of similar quality and ease in use, and both provide adequate support. The software under
each offer is expected to be used for up to eight years, although this depends to some extent on technological advances in
future years. Both offers are equivalent in terms of the product and service.

It is now early October 2011, and ID hopes to have the software in place by its fiscal year end of December 31, 2011.
ID is currently working on preparing its third-quarter financial statements, which its bank is particularly interested in see-
ing in order to ensure that ID is respecting its debt-to-equity ratio covenant in its loan agreement with the bank. The
interest rate on the bank loan, which is ID's only source of external financing, is 10% per year. ID would have preferred to
be in a position where it could buy rather than lease the software, but the anticipated purchase price of $30,000 exceeds
the limits that the bank set for ID's borrowing.

Instructions

(a) Discuss the nature of the lease arrangement under each of the two lease options offered to Interior Design and the
corresponding accounting treatment that should be applied.

(b) Prepare all necessary journal entries and adjusting journal entries for Interior Design under the Precision Inc. option,
from lease inception on January 1, 2012, through to December 31, 2012.

(c) Prepare an amortization schedule using a computer spreadsheet that would be suitable for the lease term in the
Graphic Design Inc. option.

(d) Prepare all necessary journal entries and adjusting journal entries for Interior Design under Graphic Design's option,
from lease inception on January 1, 2012, through to January 1, 2013.

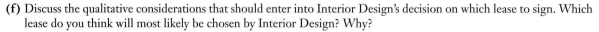

Digging Deeper

(e) Summarize and contrast the effects on Interior Design's financial statements for the year ending December 31, 2012, using the entries prepared in parts (b) and (d) above. Include in your summary the total cash outflows that would be made by Interior Design during 2012 under each option.

(f) Discuss the qualitative considerations that should enter into Interior Design's decision on which lease to sign. Which lease do you think will most likely be chosen by Interior Design? Why?

(g) What are the long-term and short-term implications of the choice between these two options? How do these implications support the direction in which GAAP is headed in the future concerning the accounting for leases?

P20-2   You have just been hired as the new controller of SWT Services Inc., and on the top of the stack of papers on your new desk is a bundle of draft contracts with a note attached. The note says "please help me to understand which of these leases would be best for our situation." The note is signed by the president of SWT Services Inc. You have reviewed the proposed contracts, and asked a few questions, and in the process have become aware that the company is facing a large cutback in capital spending to deal with the effect of competitive pressure in the industry. A new customer service system that is heavily IT based is critical in meeting the challenge head on. In order to meet this commitment, you need to identify the lease that will have the lowest total cost in the coming year and overall. As well you will need to address the cash demands of each choice. The leases are for telecommunications and computer equipment and software, and the following information is available.

Lease One: The equipment and software has a fair value of $487,694 and an expected life of six years. The lease has a five-year term. Annual rent is paid each January 1, beginning in 2011, in the amount of $104,300. The implicit rate of the lease is not known by SWT. Insurance and operating costs of $23,500 are to be paid directly by SWT to the lessor in addition to the lease payments. At the end of the lease term, the equipment will revert to the lessor, who will be able to sell it for $85,000. If the lessor is unable to sell the equipment for this amount, SWT will be required to make up the difference. SWT will likely purchase the equipment for $85,000 if any payments are required under this clause of the lease.

Lease Two: The equipment and software have a fair value of $444,412 and an expected life of seven years. The lease has a five-year term beginning January 1, 2011, with a two-year renewal period. Annual lease payments are made beginning December 31, 2011, in the amount of $137,500. This lease has an implicit rate of 8%. Insurance and operating costs of $26,500 are included in the lease payment. At the end of the initial lease term, the equipment can be leased for another two years for $27,500 per year, including insurance and operating costs, and then at the end of that two-year period, the equipment will belong to SWT.

SWT uses private enterprise GAAP and has a December year end. SWT's incremental borrowing rate is 10%.

Instructions

(a) Prepare a memo to the president explaining which lease will have the lowest cost in the initial year of the lease and overall cost for the full term of the lease, including any renewal period for Lease Two. Include in your analysis a comparison of the cash flow requirement under each option for the term of the lease including any renewal option.

(b) Which lease do you recommend the company sign, assuming both will meet the company's requirements and the equipment proposed in both leases is similar? Bring as many arguments to your recommendation as possible to allow the president to be fully advised of the factors leading to your recommendation.

P20-3   On January 1, 2011, Hunter Ltd. entered into an agreement to lease a truck from Situ Ltd. Both Hunter and Situ use IFRS. The details of the agreement are as follows:

Carrying value of truck for Situ Ltd.	$20,691
Fair value of truck	$20,691
Economic life of truck	5 years
Lease term	3 years
Rental payments (at beginning of each month)	$620
Executory costs included in rental payments each month for insurance	$20
Incremental borrowing rate for Hunter Ltd.	12%
Hunter Ltd. guarantees Situ Ltd. that at the end of the lease term Situ Ltd. will realize $3,500 from selling the truck.	

Additional information:

1. There are no abnormal risks associated with the collection of lease payments from Hunter.

2. There are no additional unreimbursable costs to be incurred by Situ in connection with the leased truck.

3. At the end of the lease term, Situ sold the truck to a third party for $3,200, which was the truck's fair value at December 31, 2010. Hunter paid Situ the difference between the guaranteed residual value of $3,500 and the proceeds obtained on the resale.

4. Hunter knows the interest rate that is implicit in the lease.

5. Hunter knows the amount of executory costs included in the minimum lease payments.

6. Hunter uses straight-line depreciation for its trucks.

Instructions

(a) Discuss the nature of this lease for both Hunter Ltd. (the lessee) and Situ Ltd. (the lessor).

(b) Assume that the effective interest of 12% had not been provided in the data. Prove the effective interest rate of 12% using a financial calculator or computer spreadsheet function.

(c) Prepare a lease amortization schedule for the full term of the lease using a computer spreadsheet.

(d) Prepare the journal entries that Hunter would make on January 1, 2011, and 2012, and any year-end adjusting journal entries at December 31, 2011, related to the lease arrangement, assuming that Hunter does not use reversing entries.

(e) Identify all accounts that will be reported by Hunter Ltd. on its comparative balance sheet at December 31, 2012, and 2011, and comparative income statement for the fiscal years ending December 31, 2012, and 2011. Include all the necessary note disclosures on the transactions related to this lease for Hunter and be specific about the classifications in each statement.

(f) Prepare the journal entry for Hunter's payment on December 31, 2013, to Situ to settle the guaranteed residual value deficiency. Assume that no accruals for interest have been recorded as yet during 2013, but that the 2013 depreciation expense for the truck has been recorded.

(g) Prepare Hunter's partial comparative statement of cash flows for the years ended December 31, 2012, and 2011, for all transactions related to the above information. Be specific about the classifications in the financial statement.

Digging Deeper

P20-4   Refer to the information in P20–3.

Instructions

(a) Prepare the journal entries that Situ would make on January 1, 2011, and the adjusting journal entries at December 31, 2011, to record the annual interest income from the lease arrangement, assuming that Situ has a December 31 fiscal year end.

(b) Identify all accounts that will be reported by Situ Ltd. on its comparative income statement for the fiscal years ending December 31, 2012, and 2011, and its comparative statement of financial position at December 31, 2012, and 2011. Be specific about the classifications in each statement.

Digging Deeper

(c) Prepare a partial comparative statement of cash flows for Situ for the years ended December 31, 2012, and 2011, for all transactions related to the information in P20-3. Be specific about the classifications in the financial statement.

Digging Deeper

P20-5   LePage Manufacturing Ltd. agrees to lease machinery to Labonté Corporation on July 15, 2011. Both LePage and Labonté use private enterprise GAAP. The following information relates to the lease agreement.

1. The lease term is seven years, with no renewal option, and the machinery has an estimated economic life of nine years.

2. The machinery's cost is $420,000 and the asset's fair value on July 15, 2011, is $560,000.

3. At the end of the lease term, the asset reverts to LePage, the lessor. The asset is expected to have a residual value of $80,000 at this time, and this value is guaranteed by Labonté. Labonté depreciates all of its equipment on a straight-line basis.

4. The lease agreement requires equal annual rental payments, beginning on July 15, 2011.

5. LePage usually sells its equipment to customers who buy the product outright, but Labonté was unable to get acceptable financing for an outright purchase. LePage's credit investigation on Labonté revealed that the company's financial situation was deteriorating. Because Labonté had been a good customer many years ago, LePage agreed to enter into this lease agreement, but used a higher than usual 15% interest rate in setting the lease payments. Labonté is aware of this rate.

6. LePage is uncertain about what additional costs it might have to incur in connection with this lease during the lease term, although Labonté has agreed to pay all executory costs directly to third parties.

7. LePage incurred legal costs of $4,000 in early July 2011 in finalizing the lease agreement.

Instructions

(a) Discuss the nature of this lease for both the lessee and the lessor.

(b) Using time value of money tables, a financial calculator, or computer spreadsheet functions, calculate the amount of the annual rental payment that is required.

(c) Prepare the journal entries that Labonté would make in 2011 and 2012 related to the lease arrangement, assuming that the company has a December 31 fiscal year end and that it does not use reversing entries.

(d) From the information you have calculated and recorded, identify all balances related to this lease that would be reported on Labonté's December 31, 2011 balance sheet and income statement, and where each amount would be reported.

(e) Prepare the journal entries that LePage would make in 2011 and 2012 related to the lease arrangement, assuming that the company has a December 31 fiscal year end and does not use reversing entries.

(f) From the information you have calculated and recorded, identify all balances related to this lease that would be reported on LePage's December 31, 2011 balance sheet and income statement, and where each amount would be reported.

(g) Comment briefly on the December 31, 2011 reported results in (d) and (f) above.

P20-6   Synergetics Inc. leased a new crane to Gumowski Construction under a six-year, non-cancellable contract starting February 1, 2011. The lease terms require payments of $21,500 each February 1, starting February 1, 2011. Synergetics will pay insurance, taxes, and maintenance charges on the crane, which has an estimated life of 12 years, a fair value of $160,000, and a cost to Synergetics of $160,000. The crane's estimated fair value is $50,000 at the end of the lease term. No bargain purchase or renewal options are included in the contract. Both Synergetics and Gumowski adjust and close books annually at December 31 and use IFRS. Collectibility of the lease payments is reasonably certain and there are no uncertainties about unreimbursable lessor costs. Gumowski's incremental borrowing rate is 8% and Synergetics' implicit interest rate of 7% is known to Gumowski.

Instructions

(a) Identify the type of lease that is involved and give reasons for your classification. Also discuss the accounting treatment that should be applied by both the lessee and the lessor.

(b) Would the classification of the lease have been different if Synergetics and Gumowski had been using private enterprise GAAP?

(c) Prepare all the entries related to the lease contract and leased asset for the year 2011 for the lessee and lessor, assuming the following executory costs: insurance of $450 covering the period February 1, 2011, to January 31, 2012; taxes of $200 for the remainder of calendar year 2011; and a one-year maintenance contract beginning February 1, 2011, costing $1,200. Straight-line depreciation is used for similar leased assets. The crane is expected to have a residual value of $20,000 at the end of its useful life.

(d) Identify what will be presented on the balance sheet and income statement, and in the related notes, of both the lessee and the lessor at December 31, 2011.

P20-7   Ramey Corporation is a diversified public company with nationwide interests in commercial real estate development, banking, copper mining, and metal fabrication. The company has offices and operating locations in major cities throughout Canada. With corporate headquarters located in a metropolitan area of a western province, company executives must travel extensively to stay connected with the various phases of operations. In order to make business travel more efficient to areas that are not adequately served by commercial airlines, corporate management is currently evaluating the feasibility of acquiring a business aircraft that can be used by Ramey executives. Proposals for either leasing or purchasing a suitable aircraft have been analyzed, and the leasing proposal was considered more desirable.

The proposed lease agreement involves a twin-engine turboprop Viking that has a fair value of $1 million. This plane would be leased for a period of 10 years, beginning January 14, 2011. The lease agreement is cancellable only upon accidental destruction of the plane. An annual lease payment of $141,780 is due on January 14 of each year, with the first payment to be made on January 14, 2011. Maintenance operations are strictly scheduled by the lessor, and Ramey will pay for these services as they are performed. Estimated annual maintenance costs are $6,900. The lessor will pay all insurance premiums and local business taxes, which amount to a combined total of $4,000 annually and are included in the annual lease payment of $141,780. Upon expiration of the 10-year lease, Ramey can purchase the Viking for $44,440. The plane's estimated useful life is 15 years, and its value in the used plane market is estimated to be $100,000 after 10 years. The residual value probably will never be less than $75,000 if the engines are overhauled and maintained as prescribed by the manufacturer. If the purchase option is not exercised, possession of the plane will revert to the lessor; there is no provision for renewing the lease agreement beyond its termination on December 31, 2020.

Ramey can borrow $1 million under a 10-year term loan agreement at an annual interest rate of 12%. The lessor's implicit interest rate is not expressly stated in the lease agreement, but this rate appears to be approximately 8% based on 10 net rental payments of $137,780 per year and the initial market value of $1 million for the plane. On January 14, 2011, the present value of all net rental payments and the purchase option of $44,440 is $886,215 using the 12% interest rate. The present value of all net rental payments and the $44,440 purchase option on January 14, 2011, is $1,019,061 using the 8% interest rate implicit in the lease agreement. The financial vice-president of Ramey Corporation has established that this lease agreement is a financing lease as defined by the IFRS standards followed by Ramey.

Instructions

(a) IFRS indicates that the crucial accounting issue is whether the risks and benefits of ownership are transferred from one party to the other, regardless of whether ownership is transferred. What is meant by "the risks and benefits of ownership," and what factors are general indicators of such a transfer?

(b) Have the risks and benefits of ownership been transferred in the lease described above? What evidence is there?

(c) What is the appropriate amount for Ramey Corporation to recognize for the leased aircraft on its balance sheet after the lease is signed?

(d) Independent of your answer in part (c), assume that the annual lease payment is $141,780 as stated above, that the appropriate capitalized amount for the leased aircraft is $1 million on January 14, 2011, and that the interest rate is 9%. How will the lease be reported on the December 31, 2011 balance sheet and related income statement? (Ignore any income tax implications.)

(CMA adapted, in part)

P20-8 The following facts pertain to a non-cancellable lease agreement between Woodhouse Leasing Corporation and McKee Electronics Ltd., a lessee, for a computer system:

Inception date	October 1, 2011
Lease term	6 years
Economic life of leased equipment	6 years
Fair value of asset at October 1, 2011	$150,690
Residual value at end of lease term	–0–
Lessor's implicit rate	8.5%
Lessee's incremental borrowing rate	8.5%
Annual lease payment due at the beginning of each year, beginning October 1, 2011	$30,500

The collectibility of the lease payments is reasonably predictable, and there are no important uncertainties about costs that have not yet been incurred by the lessor. McKee Electronics Ltd., the lessee, assumes responsibility for all executory costs, which amount to $2,500 per year and are to be paid each October 1, beginning October 1, 2011. (This $2,500 is not included in the rental payment of $30,500.) The asset will revert to the lessor at the end of the lease term. The straight-line depreciation method is used for all equipment.

The following amortization schedule for the lease obligation has been prepared correctly for use by both the lessor and the lessee in accounting for this lease using private enterprise GAAP. The lease is accounted for properly as a capital lease by the lessee and as a direct financing lease by the lessor.

Date	Annual Lease Payment/ Receipt	Interest (8.5%) on Unpaid Obligation/ Net Investment	Reduction of Lease Obligation/ Net Investment	Balance of Lease Obligation/ Net Investment
10/01/11				$150,690
10/01/11	$ 30,500	–0–	$ 30,500	120,190
10/01/12	30,500	$10,216	20,284	99,906
10/01/13	30,500	8,492	22,008	77,898
10/01/14	30,500	6,621	23,879	54,019
10/01/15	30,500	4,592	25,908	28,111
10/01/16	30,500	2,389	28,111	–0–
	$183,000	$32,310	$150,690	

Instructions

Answer the following questions, rounding all numbers to the nearest dollar.

(a) Assuming that McKee Electronics' accounting period ends on September 30, answer the following questions with respect to this lease agreement.

1. What items and amounts will appear on the lessee's income statement for the year ending September 30, 2012?
2. What items and amounts will appear on the lessee's statement of financial position at September 30, 2012?
3. What items and amounts will appear on the lessee's income statement for the year ending September 30, 2013?
4. What items and amounts will appear on the lessee's statement of financial position at September 30, 2013?

(b) Assuming that McKee Electronics' accounting period ends on December 31, answer the same questions as in (a) above for the years ending December 31, 2011, and 2012.

(c) Discuss the differences, if any, in the classification of the lease to McKee Electronics Ltd. if the company were using IFRS in its financial reporting.

P20-9 Assume the same information as in P20–8.

Instructions

Answer the following questions, rounding all numbers to the nearest dollar.

(a) Assuming that Woodhouse Leasing Corporation's accounting period ends on September 30, answer the following questions with respect to this lease agreement.

1. What items and amounts will appear on the lessor's income statement for the year ending September 30, 2012?
2. What items and amounts will appear on the lessor's statement of financial position at September 30, 2012?
3. What items and amounts will appear on the lessor's income statement for the year ending September 30, 2013?
4. What items and amounts will appear on the lessor's statement of financial position at September 30, 2013?

(b) Assuming that Woodhouse Leasing Corporation's accounting period ends on December 31, answer the same questions as in (a) above for the years ending December 31, 2011, and 2012.

(c) Discuss the differences, if any, in the classification of the lease to Woodhouse Leasing Corporation if the company were using IFRS in its financial reporting.

P20-10 In 2008, Yin Trucking Corporation, which follows private enterprise GAAP, negotiated and closed a long-term lease contract for newly constructed truck terminals and freight storage facilities. The buildings were erected to the company's specifications on land owned by the company. On January 1, 2009, Yin Trucking Corporation took possession of the leased properties. On January 1, 2009, and 2010, the company made cash payments of $1,048,000 that were recorded as rental expenses.

Although the useful life of each terminal is 40 years, the non-cancellable lease runs for 20 years from January 1, 2009, with a purchase option available upon expiration of the lease.

The 20-year lease is effective for the period January 1, 2009, through December 31, 2028. Advance rental payments of $900,000 are payable to the lessor on January 1 of each of the first 10 years of the lease term. Advance rental payments of $320,000 are due on January 1 for each of the last 10 years of the lease. The company has an option to purchase all of these leased facilities for $1 million on December 31, 2028, although their fair value at that time is estimated at $3 million. At the end of 40 years, the terminals and facilities will have no remaining value. Yin Trucking must also make annual payments to the lessor of $125,000 for property taxes and $23,000 for insurance. The lease was negotiated to assure the lessor a 6% rate of return.

Instructions

Answer the following questions, rounding all numbers to the nearest dollar.

(a) Using time value of money tables, a financial calculator, or computer spreadsheet functions, calculate for Yin Trucking Corporation the amount, if any, that should be capitalized on its January 1, 2009 balance sheet.

(b) Assuming a capital lease and a capitalized value of terminal facilities at January 1, 2009, of $8.7 million, prepare journal entries for Yin Trucking Corporation to record the following:

1. The cash payment to the lessor on January 1, 2011
2. Depreciation of the cost of the leased properties for 2011 using the straight-line method
3. The accrual of interest expense at December 31, 2011

(c) What amounts would appear on Yin's December 31, 2011 balance sheet for the leased asset and the related liabilities under the lease arrangement described in part (b)?

P20-11 Lee Industries and Lor Inc. enter into an agreement that requires Lor Inc. to build three diesel-electric engines to Lee's specifications. Both Lee and Lor follow private enterprise GAAP. Upon completion of the engines, Lee has agreed to lease them for a period of 10 years and to assume all costs and risks of ownership. The lease is non-cancellable, becomes effective on January 1, 2011, and requires annual rental payments of $620,956 each January 1, starting January 1, 2011.

Lee's incremental borrowing rate is 10%, and the implicit interest rate used by Lor Inc. is 8% and is known to Lee. The total cost of building the three engines is $3.9 million. The engines' economic life is estimated to be 10 years, with residual value expected to be zero. Lee depreciates similar equipment on a straight-line basis. At the end of the lease, Lee assumes title to the engines. Collectibility of the lease payments is reasonably certain and there are no uncertainties about unreimbursable lessor costs.

Instructions

Answer the following questions, rounding all numbers to the nearest dollar.

(a) Discuss the nature of this lease transaction from the viewpoints of both the lessee (Lee Industries) and lessor (Lor Inc.).

(b) Prepare the journal entry or entries to record the transactions on January 1, 2011, on the books of Lee Industries.

(c) Prepare the journal entry or entries to record the transactions on January 1, 2011, on the books of Lor Inc.

(d) Prepare the journal entries for both the lessee and lessor to record interest expense (income) at December 31, 2011. (Prepare a lease amortization schedule for the lease obligation for two years using a computer spreadsheet.)

(e) Show the items and amounts that would be reported on the balance sheet (ignore the notes) at December 31, 2011, for both the lessee and the lessor.

(f) Identify how the lease transactions would be reported on each company's statement of cash flows in 2011.

(g) Provide the note disclosure concerning the lease that would be required for the lessee, Lee Industries, on its financial statements for the fiscal year ending December 31, 2011.

(h) Provide the note disclosure concerning the lease that would be required for the lessor, Lor Inc., on its financial statements for the fiscal year ending December 31, 2011.

P20-12 Dubois Steel Corporation, as lessee, signed a lease agreement for equipment for five years, beginning January 31, 2011. Annual rental payments of $41,000 are to be made at the beginning of each lease year (January 31). The taxes, insurance, and maintenance costs are the lessee's obligation. The interest rate used by the lessor in setting the payment schedule is 9%; Dubois' incremental borrowing rate is 10%. Dubois is unaware of the rate being used by the lessor. At the end of the lease, Dubois has the option to buy the equipment for $4,000, which is considerably below its estimated fair value at that time. The equipment has an estimated useful life of seven years with no residual value. Dubois uses straight-line depreciation on similar equipment that it owns, and follows IFRS.

Instructions

Answer the following questions, rounding all numbers to the nearest dollar.

(a) Prepare the journal entry or entries, with explanations, that should be recorded on January 31, 2011, by Dubois.

(b) Prepare any necessary adjusting journal entries at December 31, 2011, and the journal entry or entries, with explanations, that should be recorded on January 31, 2012, by Dubois. (Prepare the lease amortization schedule for the lease obligation using a computer spreadsheet for the minimum lease payments.) Dubois does not use reversing entries.

(c) Prepare any necessary adjusting journal entries at December 31, 2012, and the journal entry or entries, with explanations, that should be recorded on January 31, 2013, by Dubois.

(d) What amounts would appear on Dubois' December 31, 2012 balance sheet relative to the lease arrangement?

(e) What amounts would appear on Dubois' statement of cash flows for 2011 relative to the lease arrangement? Where would the amounts be reported?

(f) Assume that the leased equipment had a fair value of $200,000 at the inception of the lease, and that no bargain purchase option is available at the end of the lease. Determine what amounts would appear on Dubois' December 31, 2012 balance sheet and what amounts would appear on the 2012 statement of cash flows relative to the leasing arrangements.

P20-13 CHL Corporation manufactures specialty equipment with an estimated economic life of 12 years and leases it to Provincial Airlines Corp. for a period of 10 years. Both CHL and Provincial Airlines follow private enterprise GAAP. The equipment's normal selling price is $210,482 and its unguaranteed residual value at the end of the lease term is estimated to be $15,000. Provincial Airlines will pay annual payments of $25,000 at the beginning of each year and all maintenance, insurance, and taxes. CHL incurred costs of $105,000 in manufacturing the equipment and $7,000 in negotiating and closing the lease. CHL has determined that the collectibility of the lease payments is reasonably predictable, that no additional costs will be incurred, and that the implicit interest rate is 8%.

Instructions

Answer the following questions, rounding all numbers to the nearest dollar.

(a) Discuss the nature of this lease in relation to the lessor and calculate the amount of each of the following items:
1. Gross investment
2. Unearned interest income
3. Sales price
4. Cost of sales

(b) Prepare a 10-year lease amortization schedule for the lease obligation using a computer spreadsheet.

(c) Prepare all of the lessor's journal entries for the first year of the lease, assuming the lessor's fiscal year end is five months into the lease. Reversing entries are not used.

(d) Determine the current and non-current portion of the net investment at the lessor's fiscal year end, which is five months into the lease.

(e) Assuming that the $15,000 residual value is guaranteed by the lessee, what changes are necessary to parts (a) to (d)?

P20-14 Assume the same data as in P20–13 and that Provincial Airlines Corp. has an incremental borrowing rate of 8%.

Instructions

Answer the following questions, rounding all numbers to the nearest dollar.

(a) Discuss the nature of this lease in relation to the lessee.

(b) What classification will Provincial Airlines Corp. give to the lease?

(c) What difference, if any, would occur in the classification of the lease if Provincial were using IFRS?

(d) Using time value of money tables, a financial calculator, or computer spreadsheet functions, calculate the amount of the initial obligation under capital leases.

(e) Prepare a 10-year lease amortization schedule for the lease obligation using a computer spreadsheet.

(f) Prepare all of the lessee's journal entries for the first year, assuming that the lease year and Provincial Airlines' fiscal year are the same.

(g) Prepare the entries in (f) again, assuming that the residual value of $15,000 was guaranteed by the lessee.

(h) Prepare the entries in (f) again, assuming a residual value at the end of the lease term of $45,000 and a purchase option of $15,000.

P20-15 Jennings Inc., which uses IFRS, manufactures an X-ray machine with an estimated life of 12 years and leases it to SNC Medical Centre for a period of 10 years. The machine's normal selling price is $343,734, and the lessee guarantees a residual value at the end of the lease term of $15,000. The medical centre will pay rent of $50,000 at the beginning of each year and all maintenance, insurance, and taxes. Jennings incurred costs of $210,000 in manufacturing the machine and $14,000 in negotiating and closing the lease. Jennings has determined that the collectibility of the lease payments is reasonably predictable, that there will be no additional costs incurred, and that its implicit interest rate is 10%.

Instructions

Answer the following questions, rounding all numbers to the nearest dollar.

(a) Discuss the nature of this lease in relation to the lessor and calculate the amount of each of the following items:
1. Gross investment
2. Sales price
3. Unearned interest income
4. Cost of sales

(b) Prepare a 10-year lease amortization schedule for the lease obligation.

(c) Prepare all of the lessor's journal entries for the first year.

(d) Identify the amounts to be reported on Jennings's balance sheet, income statement, and statement of cash flows one year after signing the lease, and prepare any required note disclosures.

(e) Assume that SNC Medical Centre's incremental borrowing rate is 12% and that the centre knows that 10% is the rate implicit in the lease. Determine the depreciation expense that SNC will recognize in the first full year that it leases the machine.

(f) Assuming instead that the residual value is not guaranteed, what changes, if any, are necessary in parts (a) to (d) for the lessor and in part (e) for the lessee?

(g) Discuss how Jennings would have determined the classification of the lease if the company were using private enterprise GAAP for its financial reporting.

P20-16 Lanier Dairy Ltd. leases its milk cooling equipment from Green Finance Corporation. Both companies use IFRS. The lease has the following terms.

1. The lease is dated May 30, 2011, with a lease term of eight years. It is non-cancellable and requires equal rental payments of $30,000 due each May 30, beginning in 2011.

2. The equipment has a fair value and cost at the inception of the lease of $211,902, an estimated economic life of 10 years, and a residual value (which is guaranteed by Lanier Dairy) of $23,000.

3. The lease contains no renewal options and the equipment reverts to Green Finance Corporation on termination of the lease.

4. Lanier Dairy's incremental borrowing rate is 6% per year; the implicit rate is also 6%.

5. Lanier Dairy uses straight-line depreciation for similar equipment that it owns.

6. Collectibility of the payments is reasonably predictable, and there are no important uncertainties about costs that have not yet been incurred by the lessor.

Instructions

(a) Describe the nature of the lease and, in general, discuss how the lessee and lessor should account for the lease transaction.

(b) Prepare the journal entries for the lessee and lessor at May 30, 2011, and at December 31, 2011, which are the lessee's and lessor's year ends, respectively.

(c) Prepare the journal entries at May 30, 2012, for the lessee and lessor. Assume reversing entries are not used.

(d) What amount would have been capitalized by the lessee upon inception of the lease if:
   1. the residual value of $23,000 had been guaranteed by a third party, not the lessee?
   2. the residual value of $23,000 had not been guaranteed at all?

(e) On the lessor's books, what amount would be recorded as the net investment at the inception of the lease, assuming:
   1. Green Finance had incurred $1,200 of direct costs in processing the lease?
   2. the residual value of $23,000 had been guaranteed by a third party?
   3. the residual value of $23,000 had not been guaranteed at all?

(f) Assume that the milk cooling equipment's useful life is 20 years. How large would the residual value have to be at the end of 10 years in order for the lessee to qualify for the operating method? Assume that the residual value would be guaranteed by a third party. (Hint: The lessee's annual payments will be appropriately reduced as the residual value increases.)

(g) Discuss how Jennings would have determined the classification of the lease if the company were using private enterprise GAAP for its financial reporting.

P20-17 Fram Fibreglass Corp. (FFC) is a private New Brunswick company, using private enterprise GAAP, that manufactures a variety of fibreglass products for the fishing and food services industry. With the traditional fishery in decline over the past few years, FFC found itself in a tight financial position in early 2011. Revenues had levelled off, inventories were overstocked, and most operating costs were increasing each year.

The Royal Montreal Bank, which FFC has dealt with for 20 years, was getting anxious as FFC's loans and line of credit were at an all-time high, the most recent loan carrying an interest rate of 15%. In fact, the bank had just recently imposed stipulations on FFC that prevented the company from paying out any dividends or increasing its debt-to-equity ratio above current levels without the bank's prior approval.

The Vice-President of Finance, Joe Blowski, CMA, knew that with aggressive investment in new equipment the company could go after new markets in the construction industry. He had investigated the cost of the necessary equipment and found that $50,000 of new capital investment would allow the company to get started. All it needed was the financing. Joe set up appointments with Kirk Cullen, the loans officer at the provincial Industrial Development Bank, and with Heidi Hazen, the manager of the local office of Municipal Finance Corp.

Kirk Cullen was very receptive to Joe's request. He indicated that the Industrial Development Bank would be interested in working with FFC, and could provide him with a lease on the equipment he identified. Heidi Hazen also welcomed the business, suggesting a lease arrangement between Municipal Finance Corp. and FFC as well. Two days later, Joe had proposals from both lenders on his desk.

You are an accounting major and co-op student placed with FFC for your final work term. On his way out of the office for a meeting, Joe provides you with the two proposals and asks, just before the elevator door closes, "Would you please review these and give me your analysis and recommendation on which proposal to accept, if either?" The details of the two proposals are as follows:

	Industrial Development Bank Proposal	Municipal Finance Corp. Proposal
Selling price of equipment	$50,000	$50,000
Lease term	April 23, 2011 to April 22, 2013	May 1, 2011 to April 30, 2013
Economic life of equipment	7 years	7 years
Residual value, end of lease term	$10,000	$10,000
Residual value guaranteed	no	by lessee
Annual rental payment	$12,000 in advance	$11,681 in advance
Executory costs	$1,020 per year included in rent	$300 per year in addition to rent
Interest rate implicit in lease	12%	unknown
Equipment returned at end of lease	yes	yes

Instructions

Prepare the required report.

P20-18 Mulholland Corp., a lessee, entered into a non-cancellable lease agreement with Galt Manufacturing Ltd., a lessor, to lease special purpose equipment for a period of seven years. Both Mulholland and Galt follow private enterprise GAAP. The following information relates to the agreement:

Lease inception	May 2, 2011
Annual lease payment due at the beginning of each lease year	$?
Residual value of equipment at end of lease term, guaranteed by an independent third party	$100,000
Economic life of equipment	10 years
Usual selling price of equipment	$415,000
Manufacturing cost of equipment on lessor's books	$327,500
Lessor's implicit interest rate, known to lessee	12%
Lessee's incremental borrowing rate	12%
Executory costs per year to be paid by lessee, estimated	$ 14,500

The leased equipment reverts to Galt Manufacturing at the end of the lease, although Mulholland has an option to purchase it at its expected fair value at that time.

Instructions

(a) Using time value of money tables, a financial calculator, or computer spreadsheet functions, calculate the lease payment determined by the lessor to provide a 12% return.

(b) Prepare a lease amortization table for Galt Manufacturing, the lessor, covering the entire term of the lease.

(c) Assuming that Galt Manufacturing has a December 31 year end, and that reversing entries are not made, prepare all entries made by the company up to and including May 2, 2013.

(d) Identify the balances and classification of amounts that Galt Manufacturing will report on its December 31, 2011 balance sheet, and the amounts on its 2011 income statement and statement of cash flows related to this lease.

(e) Assuming that Mulholland has a December 31 year end, and that reversing entries are not made, prepare all entries made by the company up to and including May 2, 2013. Assume payments of executory costs of $14,000, $14,400, and $14,950 covering fiscal years 2011, 2012, and 2013, respectively.

(f) Identify the balances and classification of amounts that Mulholland will report on its December 31, 2011 balance sheet, and the amounts on its 2011 income statement and statement of cash flows related to this lease.

(g) On whose balance sheet should the equipment appear? On whose balance sheet does the equipment currently get reported?

P20-19   Your employer, Wagner Inc., is a large Canadian public company that uses IFRS. You are working on a project to determine the effect of the proposed contract-based approach on the corporate accounting for leases. To get started on the project, you have collected the following information with respect to a lease for a fleet of trucks used by Wagner to transport completed products to warehouses across the country. The trucks have an economic life of eight years. The lease term is from July 1, 2011, to June 30, 2018, and the company intends to lease the equipment for this period of time, so the lease term is seven years. The lease payment per year is $545,000, payable in advance, with no other payments required, and no renewal option or bargain purchase option available. The expected value of the fleet of trucks at June 30, 2018, is $450,000; this value is guaranteed by Wagner. The leased trucks must be returned to the lessor at the end of the lease. Wagner's management is confident that with an aggressive maintenance program, Wagner has every reason to believe that the asset's residual value will be more than the guaranteed amount at the end of the lease term. Wagner's incremental borrowing rate is 8%, and the rate implicit in the lease is not known. At the time the lease was signed, the fair value of the leased trucks was $3,064,470.

Instructions

(a) Based on the original information:

1. Using time value of money tables, a financial calculator, or computer spreadsheet functions, determine the contractual obligations and rights under the lease at July 1, 2011.

2. Prepare an amortization schedule for the obligation over the term of the lease.

3. Prepare the journal entries and any year-end (December 31) adjusting journal entries made by Wagner Inc. in 2011 and up to and including July 1, 2012.

(b) Immediately after the July 1, 2012 leased payments, based on the feedback of the staff in operations, management reassesses its expectations for the guaranteed residual value. Management now estimates the fleet of trucks to have a value of $400,000 with a 60% probability and $300,000 with a 40% probability.

1. Calculate the probability-weighted expected value of the residual at the end of the lease term. Also calculate the present value at July 1, 2012, of any additional cash flows related to the residual value guarantee.

2. Prepare any necessary entry to implement the revision to the contractual lease rights and obligation at July 1, 2012.

3. Revise the amortization schedule effective January 1, 2013, for the lease, including any liability related to the residual value guarantee.

4. Prepare the year-end adjusting journal entries made by Wagner Inc. for fiscal year 2012.

P20-20   Sanderson Inc., a pharmaceutical distribution firm, is providing a BMW car for its Chief Executive Officer as part of a remuneration package. Sanderson has a calendar year end, issues financial statements annually, and follows private enterprise GAAP. You have been assigned the task of calculating and reporting the financial statement effect of several options Sanderson is considering in obtaining the vehicle for its CEO.

Option 1: Obtain financing from Western Bank to finance an outright purchase of the BMW from BMW Canada, which regularly sells and leases luxury vehicles.

Option 2: Sign a lease with BMW Canada and exercise the option to renew the lease at the end of the initial term.

Option 3: Sign a lease with BMW Canada and exercise the option to purchase at the end of the lease. The amount of the option price is financed with a bank loan.

For the purpose of your comparison, you can assume a January 1, 2011 purchase and you can also exclude all amounts for any provincial sales taxes, GST, and HST on all the proposed transactions. You can also assume that Sanderson uses the straight-line method of depreciating automobiles. Assume that for options 1 and 2, the BMW is sold on January 1, 2016, for $10,000.

Sanderson does not expect to incur any extra kilometre charges because it is likely that the BMW won't be driven that much by the CEO. However, there is a 10% chance that an extra 10,000 km will be driven and a 15% chance that an extra 20,000 km will be used.

Terms and values concerning the asset that are common to all options:

Date of purchase or signing of lease	January 1, 2011
Purchase price equal to fair value at January 1, 2011	$79,000
Cost to BMW Canada	$70,000
Physical life	8 years
Useful life to Sanderson	5 years
Residual value at January 1, 2016, equal to fair value	$10,000
Fair value at January 1, 2014	$39,500

Borrowing terms with Western Bank for purchase: Option 1

Loan amount	$79,000
Fixed bank rate for loan to purchase	7%
Term of loan to purchase	5 years
Repayment terms	Quarterly instalment note
First payment due	April 1, 2011

For Option 2:

Terms, conditions, and other information related to the initial lease with BMW Canada:

Lease term	36 months
First lease payment date	January 1, 2011
Monthly lease payment	$1,392.21
Maximum number of kilometres allowed under lease	72,000
Excess kilometre charge beyond 72,000 km	25 cents
Option to purchase price at end of lease	50% of original fair value
Date of payment for option to purchase	January 1, 2014
Maintenance and insurance	paid by Sanderson
Interest rate stated in lease—annual	6%
Sanderson's incremental borrowing rate	7%

Terms, conditions, and other information related to the renewal option for lease with BMW Canada:

Renewal lease term	24 months
Renewal option first lease payment date	January 1, 2014
Monthly lease payment	$1,371.00
Maximum number of kilometres allowed under renewal lease	48,000
Excess kilometre charge beyond 48,000 km	25 cents
Option to purchase at end of renewal option	none
Maintenance and insurance	paid by Sanderson
Renewal option	none
Interest rate stated in renewal lease	7%
Sanderson's incremental borrowing rate (projected)	8%

Borrowing terms with Western Bank to exercise option to purchase: Option 3

Loan amount	$39,500
Bank rate January 1, 2014	8%
Term of loan January 1, 2014	2 years
Repayment terms	Quarterly instalment note
First payment due	April 1, 2014

Instructions

(a) For Option 1:

1. Using a financial calculator or computer spreadsheet, calculate the quarterly blended payments that will be due to Western Bank on the instalment note.

2. Prepare an amortization schedule for the loan with Western Bank for the term of the lease.

3. Record all of the necessary transactions on January 1, 2011, the first loan payment, and for any adjusting journal entries at the end of the fiscal year 2011.

(b) For Option 2:

1. Using a financial calculator or computer spreadsheet, determine how BMW Canada arrived at the amounts of the monthly payment for the original lease and the lease renewal option, allowing it to recover its investment.

2. Assume that the original lease is signed and Sanderson Inc. has no intention of exercising the lease renewal. Determine the classification of the three-year lease for Sanderson Inc.

3. Assume that Sanderson fully intends to exercise the renewal option offered by BMW Canada. Determine the classification of the lease for Sanderson Inc.

4. Prepare a lease amortization schedule for the term of the lease for Sanderson Inc.

5. Record all of the necessary transactions on January 1, 2011, for the first two lease payments and for any adjusting journal entries at the end of the fiscal year 2011 for Sanderson Inc.

(c) For Option 3:

   1. Determine the classification of the lease for Sanderson Inc.

   2. Record all of the necessary transactions concerning the lease on January 1, 2011, and for any adjusting journal entries at the end of the fiscal year ending December 31, 2011.

   3. Using a financial calculator, or computer spreadsheet functions, calculate the quarterly blended payments that will be due to Western Bank on the instalment note used to finance the purchase.

   4. Prepare an amortization schedule for the loan with Western Bank.

   5. Record all of the necessary transactions concerning exercising the option to purchase on January 1, 2014, the signing of the instalment note payable to the bank, the first loan payment, and any adjusting journal entries at the end of the fiscal year ending December 31, 2014.

(d) Using the contract-based approach in the proposed standards, assuming the information in Option 2, update, if necessary, and reproduce the amortization table needed under this approach, for the first 13 payments of the lease. Prepare the journal entries on January 1 and February 1, 2011, and for any adjusting journal entries at the end of the fiscal year ending December 31, 2011.

(e) Assume that the amount paid by Sanderson on July 1, 2014, equals the amount calculated based on probability weighting for the excess charge for kilometres driven. How would you account for the penalty Sanderson expects to pay?

(f) Prepare a table of the financial statement results from the above three options and the contract-based approach of part (d). Your table should clearly show all of the classifications and amounts for the statement of financial position at December 31, 2011, and the income statement for the 2011 fiscal year.

(g) Calculate the amount of the expense for the BMW for the total five-year period based on each of the three assumptions, as well as under the contract-based approach assuming that Sanderson follows Option 2. Include any penalty payment for excess kilometres driven for Option 2.

(h) Based on the results obtained in part (g), provide Sanderson with additional considerations that should be taken into account before making a choice between the different options.

P20-21 Use the information for P20–20.

Instructions

Under Option 2:

(a) Assume that at the signing of the original lease, Sanderson Inc. has no intention of exercising the lease renewal. Determine the classification of the three-year lease for BMW Canada, which follows private enterprise GAAP.

(b) Prepare the journal entry to show how BMW Canada records the collection of the first lease payment on January 1, 2011.

(c) Assume now that Sanderson Inc. signs the renewal option at the same time that it enters into the original lease agreement.

   1. Prepare a lease amortization schedule including the renewal period for BMW Canada.

   2. Determine the classification of the lease for BMW Canada.

   3. Record all of the necessary transactions on January 1, 2011, for the first two lease payments collected and for any adjusting journal entries at the end of the fiscal year ending December 31, 2011, for BMW Canada.

*P20-22 The head office of North Central Ltd. has operated in the western provinces for almost 50 years. North Central uses IFRS. In 1995, new offices were constructed on the same site at a cost of $9.5 million. The new building was opened on January 4, 1996, and was expected to be used for 35 years, at which time it would have a value of approximately $2 million.

In 2011, as competitors began to consider merger strategies among themselves, North Central felt that the time was right to expand the number of its offices throughout the province. This plan required significant financing and, as a source of cash, North Central looked into selling the building that housed its head office. On June 29, 2011, Rural Life Insurance Company Ltd. purchased the building (but not the land) for $8 million and immediately entered into a 20-year lease with North Central to lease back the occupied space. The terms of the lease were as follows:

1. It is non-cancellable, with an option to purchase the building at the end of the lease for $1 million.

2. The annual rental is $838,380, payable on June 29 each year, beginning on June 29, 2011.

3. Rural Life expects to earn a return of 10% on its net investment in the lease, the same as North Central's incremental borrowing rate.

4. North Central is responsible for maintenance, insurance, and property taxes.

5. Estimates of useful life and residual value have not changed significantly since 1993.

Instructions

(a) Prepare all entries for North Central Ltd. from June 29, 2011, to December 31, 2012. North Central has a calendar year fiscal period.

(b) Assume instead that there was no option to purchase, that $8 million represents the building's fair value on June 29, 2011, and that the lease term was 12 years. Prepare all entries for North Central from June 29, 2011, to December 31, 2012.

Digging Deeper

(c) Besides the increase in cash that it needs from the sale of the building, what effect should North Central expect to see on the net assets appearing on its balance sheet immediately after the sale and leaseback?

*P20-23   Zhou Ltd. is a private corporation, which uses private enterprise GAAP, and whose operations rely considerably on a group of technology companies that experienced operating difficulties from 2008 to 2010. As a result, Zhou suffered temporary cash flow problems that required it to look for innovative means of financing. In 2011, Zhou's management therefore decided to enter into a sale and leaseback agreement with a major Canadian leasing company, Intranational Leasing.

Immediately after its September 30, 2011 year end, Zhou sold one of its major manufacturing sites to Intranational Leasing for $1,750,000, and entered into a 15-year agreement to lease back the property for $175,000 per year. The lease payment is due October 1 of each year, beginning October 1, 2011.

Zhou's carrying amount of the property when sold was $250,000. The lease agreement gives Zhou the right to purchase the property at the end of the lease for its expected fair value at that time of $2.5 million. In 2011, the land is estimated to be worth 40% of the total property value, and the building, 60%. Zhou uses a 10% declining-balance method of amortizing its buildings, and has a 7% incremental borrowing rate.

Instructions

(a) Prepare all entries that are needed by Zhou to recognize the sale and leaseback transaction on October 1, 2011; any adjusting entries that are required on September 30, 2012; and the October 1, 2012 transaction. Reversing entries are not used.

(b) Prepare all necessary note disclosures and amounts that are to be reported on Zhou's September 30, 2012 balance sheet, income statement, and statement of cash flows for its year ended September 30, 2012.

(CICA adapted)

Writing Assignments

WA20-1   Cuby Corporation entered into a lease agreement for 10 photocopy machines for its corporate headquarters. The lease agreement qualifies as an operating lease in all ways except that there is a bargain purchase option. After the five-year lease term, the corporation can purchase each copier for $1,000, when the anticipated market value of each machine will be $2,500.

Ethics

Glenn Beckert, the financial vice-president, thinks the financial statements must recognize the lease agreement as a finance lease because of the bargain purchase clause. The controller, Tareek Koba, disagrees: "Although I don't know much about the copiers themselves, there is a way to avoid recording the lease liability." She argues that the corporation might claim that copier technology advances rapidly and that by the end of the lease term—five years in the future—the machines will most likely not be worth the $1,000 bargain price.

Instructions

Answer the following questions.

(a) Is there an ethical issue at stake? Explain.

(b) Should the controller's argument be accepted if she does not really know much about copier technology? Would your answer be different if the controller were knowledgeable about how quickly copier technology changes?

(c) What should Beckert do?

(d) What would be the impact of these arguments on the company's statement of financial position under the contract-based approach for reporting leases? What impact would Koba's argument have in this case?

WA20-2   Sporon Corp. is a fast-growing Canadian private company in the manufacturing, distribution, and retail of specially designed yoga and leisure wear. Sporon has recently signed 10 new leases for new retail locations and is looking to sign about 30 more over the next year as the company grows and expands its retail outlets. All of these leases are for five years with a renewal option for five more years. All of the leases also have a contingent rent that is based on a percentage of the excess of annual sales in each location over a certain amount. The threshold and the percentage vary between locations. The contingent rent is payable annually on the anniversary date of the lease. The company has currently assessed these to be operating, as they have no conditions that meet the capitalization criteria under accounting standards for private enterprises. All of these payments on these leases are expensed as incurred.

The company has also moved into a new state-of-the-art manufacturing and office facility designed specifically for its needs, and signed a 20-year lease with PPS Pension Inc., the owner. As this building lease also does not meet any of the criteria for a capital lease under accounting standards for private enterprises, Sporon accounts for this lease as an operating lease. As a result, it expenses both the monthly rental and the annual payment that it agreed on with PPS to cover property tax increases above the 2010 base property tax cost. The tax increase amount is determined by PPS and is payable by September 30 each year.

The small group of individuals who own the company are very interested in the company's annual financial statements as they expect, if all goes well, to take the company public by 2012. For this and other reasons, Sporon's chief financial officer, Louise Bren, has been debating whether or not to adopt IFRS or ASPE for the 2011 year end.

Louise has also been following the new changes that are being proposed by the IASB to adopt the contract-based approach.

Instructions

(a) Explain to Louise Bren to what extent, if any, adjustments will be needed to Sporon's financial statements for the leases described above, based on **existing** private enterprise accounting standards and international accounting standards.

(b) Assume that the joint IASB-FASB study group supports the contract-based approach for leases. Prepare a short report for the CFO that explains the conceptual basis for this approach and that identifies how Sporon Corp.'s statement of financial position, statement of comprehensive income, and cash flow statement will likely differ under revised leasing standards based on this approach.

(c) Prepare a short, but informative, appendix to your report in (b) that addresses how applying such a revised standard might affect a financial analyst's basic ratio analysis of Sporon Corp.'s profitability (profit margin, return on assets, return on equity); risk (debt-to-equity, times interest earned); and solvency (operating cash flows to total debt).

WA20-3   As the IASB-FASB joint international working group began its study of lease accounting in late 2006 and early 2007, it had a number of staff documents prepared to help observers at their meetings follow the working group's discussions. These documents are available on the IASB website (www.iasb.org) by following the "Projects" link for "Leases." They cover a wealth of information, including the results of prior academic research on lease accounting and its potential implications for the lease accounting project.

Obtain the Information for Observers document for the February 15, 2007 and March 22, 2007 meetings of the IASB-FASB joint committee that deals with academic research on lease accounting. Alternatively, research and read up on the academic accounting literature on lease accounting.

Instructions

(a) Summarize the issues that have been addressed by academic research on lease accounting.

(b) In general, what were the findings of this research on each issue?

(c) Identify what the implications are of the research findings for the development of new accounting standards for leases.

WA20-4   In March 2010, the IASB decided to look at two models for lessor accounting. One model is the performance obligation model and one is called the derecognition model. Both of these models are discussed in the document *Discussion Paper Preliminary Views: Leases*, July 17, 2009. The discussion paper is available on the IASB website at www.iasb.org.

Instructions

(a) Describe the "performance obligation approach" for lessor accounting with respect to its concept, impact on the statement of financial position, and its impact on the statement of comprehensive income.

(b) Describe the "derecognition approach" for lessor accounting with respect to its concept, impact on the statement of financial position, and its impact on the statement of comprehensive income.

(c) Using the information below, determine what the statement of financial position would look like at the inception of the lease under the two alternatives:

The Lessor has entered into a six-year lease for a piece of machinery. The Lessor carries the machinery on its books at $100,000. The present value of the lease payments to be received for the lease is determined to be $92,900. Show the assets and liabilities that would be shown on the statement of financial position under the two different alternatives.

WA20-5 On October 30, 2011, Truttman Corp. sold a five-year-old building with a carrying value of $10 million at its fair value of $13 million and leased it back. There was a gain on the sale. Truttman pays all insurance, maintenance, and taxes on the building. The lease provides for 20 equal annual payments, beginning October 30, 2011, with a present value equal to 85% of the building's fair value and sales price. The lease's term is equal to 73% of the building's useful life. There is no provision for Truttman to reacquire ownership of the building at the end of the lease term. Truttman has a December 31 year end.

Instructions

(a) Why would Truttman have entered into such an agreement?

(b) In reaching a decision on how to classify a lease, why is it important to compare the equipment's fair value with the present value of the lease payments, and its useful life to the lease term? What does this information tell you under ASPE and IFRS?

(c) Assuming that Truttman would classify this as an operating lease, determine how the initial sale and the sale-leaseback transaction would be reported under ASPE and IFRS for the 2011 year. What would be the implications if the selling price had been $14 million, $1 million greater than the fair value of the building?

(d) Assuming that Truttman would classify this as a finance lease, determine how the initial sale and the sale-leaseback transaction would be reported under ASPE and IFRS for the 2011 year.

WA20-6 Write a brief essay highlighting the difference between IFRS and accounting standards for private enterprises and the contract-based approach noted in this chapter, discussing the conceptual justification for each.

Cases

Refer to the Case Primer on the Student Website to help you answer these cases.

CA20-1 Crown Inc. (CI) is a private company that manufactures a special type of cap that fits on a bottle. At present, it is the only manufacturer of this cap and therefore enjoys market security. The machinery that makes the cap has been in use for 20 years and is due for replacement. CI has the option of buying the machine or leasing it. Currently, CI is leaning toward leasing the machine since it is expensive to buy and funds would have to be borrowed from the bank. The company's debt-to-equity ratio is currently marginal, and if the funds were borrowed, the debt-to-equity ratio would surely worsen. CI's top management is anxious to maintain the ratio at its present level.

The dilemma for CI is that if it leases the machine, it may have to set up a long-term obligation under the lease and this would also affect the debt-to-equity ratio. Since this is clearly unacceptable, CI decided to see if the leasing company, Anchor Limited, could do anything to help with the situation. After much negotiation, the following terms were agreed upon and written into the lease agreement:

1. Anchor Limited would manufacture and lease to CI a unique machine for making caps.

2. The lease would be for a period of 12 years.

3. The lease payments of $150,000 would be paid at the end of each year.

4. CI would have the option to purchase the machine for $850,000 at the end of the lease term, which is equal to the expected fair market value at that time; otherwise, the machine would be returned to the lessor.

5. CI also has the option to lease the machine for another eight years at $150,000 per year.

6. The rate that is implicit in the lease is 9%.

The new machine is expected to last 20 years. Since it is a unique machine, Anchor Limited has no other use for it if CI does not either purchase it at the end of the lease or renew the lease. If CI had purchased the asset, it would have cost $1.9 million. Although it was purposefully omitted from the written lease agreement, there was a tacit understanding that CI would either renew the lease or exercise the purchase option.

Instructions

Assume the role of CI's auditors and discuss the nature of the lease, noting how it should be accounted for. The company controller has confided in you that the machine will likely be purchased at the end of the lease. Assume that you are aware of top management's position on adding debt to the balance sheet. Management has also asked you to compare the accounting under ASPE and IFRS.

CA20-2 Kelly's Shoes Limited used to be a major store in Canada before it went bankrupt and was bought by Bears Shoes Limited. Many of the stores were anchor tenants in medium- to large-sized retail shopping malls. This space was primarily leased under non-cancellable real estate leases as disclosed in note 16 to the consolidated financial statements. Aggregate commitments under both capital and operating leases amounted to over $1.3 million.

As part of Kelly's restructuring and downsizing plans prior to its bankruptcy, the company announced at the beginning of the year that it planned to close down 31 of its 85 stores by June 30. Subsequently, it announced that it might keep certain stores open until February in the following year if the landlords were prepared to provide an appropriate level of financial support. Kelly's also announced that landlords who allowed the stores to close June 30 (the earlier date) would be given a bonus of three months of rent.

Instructions

Assume the role of Kelly's management and discuss the financial reporting issues that the company had to deal with before its bankruptcy. Discuss any differences between IFRS and ASPE.

Integrated Cases

IC20-1 Air Canada is Canada's largest airline, operating domestic and international flights on a full-service basis. During 2003, the company ran into financial difficulty and took steps to reorganize its operations and rethink its business model. The company needed to obtain significant additional financing and was looking to undergo a financial reorganization under which control of the company would likely change hands.

In March 2004, the company set up voluntary separation programs, which allowed for up to 300 non-unionized employees to "retire" with severance payments. Unionized employees were covered by a separate similar plan. In addition, it was planned that certain employees would be terminated and receive severance payments under pre-existing contracts.

Real-World Emphasis

Many lease contracts were renegotiated and/or terminated. While operating under bankruptcy protection court orders, the company had ceased to pay its lessors. GE Capital Corporation and its subsidiaries leased, managed the leases of, or had an interest in 108 aircraft—the bulk of Air Canada's aircraft. GE's lawyers notified the airline that it must either pay the back rent or return the planes, noting that the company should not be allowed to hide behind the bankruptcy protection and use the planes for free. The company had many of its leased planes recorded as operating leases. Aircraft operating lease rentals over the lease term were amortized to operating expense on a straight-line basis. The difference between the straight-line aircraft rent expense and the payments as stipulated under the lease agreement was included in deferred charges and deferred credits ($1.8 billion).

The following is an excerpt from the financial statements:

11. Convertible Subordinated Debentures

In December 1999, the Corporation issued $150 convertible subordinated debentures which have an annual interest rate of 7.25%, payable quarterly, and are convertible at $16.00, at the holder's option, into Air Canada common shares and Class A non-voting common shares ("Class A shares") at any time up to and including maturity in December 2009. This equals a rate of 6.25 shares per $100.00 principal amount of convertible subordinated debentures. There are no principal payments until maturity in 2009. The Corporation can force conversion into common shares and Class A shares at any time following the seventh anniversary of the issue if the weighted average closing price of the shares of the Corporation for the 20 trading days prior to the date of the redemption provides the holder an internal rate of return of at least 12% for the period commencing from the date of issuance of the convertible subordinated debentures and ending on the redemption date. The internal rate of return calculation includes interest payments made by the Corporation under the convertible subordinated debentures and the excess of the weighted average closing price above $16.00.

The company entered into a new cobranding agreement with CIBC regarding Aeroplan points and the Aerogold Visa card. The agreement revised a prior agreement with CIBC increasing the amount that CIBC would pay for the Aeroplan points (by 24%). As a result of revising the old agreement, CIBC is seeking damages of $209 million. In addition, the new CIBC contract also provides the Company with a borrowing facility under which the Company received financing of $315. During the year, at CIBC's option, the principal portion of the loan was reduced through the offset of amounts owing from CIBC for Aeroplan miles purchased.

Instructions

Adopt the role of Air Canada's auditors and discuss the financial reporting issues. For simplicity sake, use IFRS in the analysis.

IC20-2   Imax Corporation is a Canadian company whose shares trade on the TSX and NASDAQ. The company files its statements in U.S. GAAP (as allowed by the Ontario Securities Commission). The company is one of the world's leading entertainment technology companies, specializing in large-format and three-dimensional film presentations. It designs, manufactures, sells, and leases projection systems. Most IMAX theatres are operated by third parties under lease and licensing agreements. The company also produces films.

The following excerpts from the December 31, 2008 financial statements explain various transactions that have been entered into:

Terminations, Consensual Buyouts and Concessions

The Company enters into theater system arrangements with customers that contain customer payment obligations prior to the scheduled installation of the theater system. During the period of time between signing and the installation of the theater system, which may extend several years, certain customers may be unable to, or elect not to, proceed with the theater system installation for a number of reasons including business considerations, or the inability to obtain certain consents, approvals or financing. Once the determination is made that the customer will not proceed with installation, the arrangement may be terminated under the default provisions of the arrangement or by mutual agreement between the Company and the customer (a "consensual buyout"). Terminations by default are situations when a customer does not meet the payment obligations under an arrangement and the Company retains the amounts paid by the customer. Under a consensual buyout, the Company and the customer agree, in writing, to a settlement and to release each other of any further obligations under the arrangement or an arbitrated settlement is reached. Any initial payments retained or additional payment received by the Company are recognized as revenue when the settlement arrangements are executed and the cash is received, respectively. These termination and consensual buyout amounts are recognized in Other revenues.

In addition, with the introduction of the IMAX digital theater system in July 2008, the Company could agree with customers to convert their obligations for other theater system configurations that have not yet been installed to arrangements to acquire or lease the IMAX digital theater system. The Company considers these situations to be a termination of the previous arrangement and origination of a new arrangement for the IMAX digital theater system. The Company continues to defer an amount of any initial fees received from the customer such that the aggregate of the fees deferred and the net present value of the future fixed initial and ongoing payments to be received from the customer equals the fair value of the IMAX digital theater system to be leased or acquired by the customer. Any residual portion of the initial fees received from the customer for the terminated theater system is recorded in Other revenues at the time when the obligation for the original theater system and the IMAX digital theater system arrangement is signed.

The Company may offer certain incentives to customers to complete theater system transactions including payment concessions or free services and products such as film licenses or 3D glasses. Reductions in, and deferral of, payments are taken into account in determining the sales price either by a direct reduction in the sales price or a reduction of payments to be discounted in accordance with SFAS 13 or Accounting Principle Board Opinion No. 21, "Interest on Receivables and Payables" ("APB 21"). Free products and services

are accounted for as separate units of accounting. Other consideration given by the Company to customers are accounted for in accordance with Emerging Issues Task Force Abstract No. 01-09, "Accounting for Consideration Given by a Vendor to a Customer (Including a Reseller of the Vendor's Products)" (EITF 01-09").

Maintenance and Extended Warranty Services

Maintenance and extended warranty services may be provided under a multiple element arrangement or as a separately priced contract. Revenues related to these services are deferred and recognized on a straight-line basis over the contract period and are recognized in Services revenues. Maintenance and extended warranty services includes maintenance of the customer's equipment and replacement parts. Under certain maintenance arrangements, maintenance services may include additional training services to the customer's technicians. All costs associated with this maintenance and extended warranty program are expensed as incurred. A loss on maintenance and extended warranty services is recognized if the expected cost of providing the services under the contracts exceeds the related deferred revenue.

Film Production and IMAX DMR Services

In certain film arrangements, the Company produces a film financed by third parties whereby the third party retains the copyright and the Company obtains exclusive distribution rights. Under these arrangements, the Company is entitled to receive a fixed fee or to retain as a fee the excess of funding over cost of production (the "production fee"). The third parties receive a portion of the revenues received by the Company on distributing the film which is charged to costs and expenses applicable to revenues-services. The production fees are deferred, and recognized as a reduction in the cost of the film based on the ratio of the Company's distribution revenues recognized in the current period to the ultimate distribution revenues expected from the film. Film exploitation costs, including advertising and marketing totaled $0.9 million in 2008 (2007—$1.2 million, 2006—$0.7 million) and are recorded in costs and expenses applicable to revenues-services as incurred.

Revenue from film production services where the Company does not hold the associated distribution rights are recognized in Services revenues when performance of the contractual service is complete, provided there is persuasive evidence of an agreement, the fee is fixed or determinable and collection is reasonably assured.

Revenues from digitally re-mastering (IMAX DMR) films where third parties own or hold the copyrights and the rights to distribute the film are derived in the form of processing fees and recoupments calculated as a percentage of box-office receipts generated from the re-mastered films. Processing fees are recognized as Services revenues when the performance of the related re-mastering service is completed provided there is persuasive evidence of an arrangement, the fee is fixed or determinable and collection is reasonably assured. Recoupments, calculated as a percentage of box-office receipts, are recognized as Services revenue when box-office receipts are reported by the third party that owns or holds the related film rights, provided collection is reasonably assured.

Losses on film production and IMAX DMR services are recognized as costs and expenses applicable to revenues-services in the period when it is determined that the Company's estimate of total revenues to be realized by the Company will not exceed estimated total production costs to be expended on the film production and the cost of IMAX DMR services.

The company has various financing agreements that contain restrictive covenants, including restrictions on debt levels.

Instructions

Adopt the role of a potential investor and analyze the financial reporting issues. Use IFRS for the analysis (as opposed to U.S. GAAP).

Research and Financial Analysis

RA20-1 Eastern Platinum Limited

Refer to the 2009 year-end financial statements and accompanying notes of Eastern Platinum Limited (Eastplats) at the end of this volume, and then answer the following questions about the company. (Note that Eastplats follows IFRS.)

Real-World Emphasis

Instructions

(a) Review the notes and determine how Eastplats accounts for its leasing transactions. Is Eastplats the lessor or lessee and what types of leases does it have?

(b) Identify all accounts on the consolidated statements of financial position and the consolidated income statement, along with their dollar amounts, that relate to any lease agreements that the company is a party to. Explain briefly what each lease agreement covers.

(c) Identify the line account(s) on the Consolidated Statements of Cash Flows where the cash lease payments are reported. Explain your answer.

(d) Calculate Eastplats's return on total assets and total debt-to-equity ratios for 2009.

(e) Assume the IASB develops a revised lease accounting standard using the contract-based approach. Would there be any impact to the financial statement of Eastplats? If so, what would the impact be?

RA20-2 Canadian National Railway Company and Canadian Pacific Railway Limited

The accounting for operating leases is a controversial issue. Many observers argue that firms that use operating leases are using significantly more assets and are more highly leveraged than their balance sheets indicate. As a result, analysts often use footnote disclosures to reconstruct and then capitalize operating lease obligations. One way to do so is to increase a firm's assets and liabilities by the present value of all its future minimum rental payments.

Real-World Emphasis

Instructions

Go to the SEDAR website (www.sedar.com) or the websites of the companies and access the financial statements of Canadian National Railway Company (CNR) and Canadian Pacific Railway Limited (CPR) for their years ended December 31, 2009. Refer to the financial statements and notes to the financial statements and answer the following questions.

(a) Identify all lease arrangements that are indicated in each company's financial statements and notes. For each lease arrangement, give the title and balances of the related lease accounts that are included in the financial statements.

(b) Have CNR and CPR provided all the lease disclosures as required by the accounting standards?

(c) What are the terms of these leases?

(d) What amount did each company report as its future minimum annual rental commitments under capital leases? Under operating leases? Are there significant differences between the two companies and the way they provide for their physical operating capacity, or are they basically similar?

(e) Calculate the debt-to-equity ratio for each company at December 31, 2009.

(f) Assuming that the contract-based approach is adopted by both companies, estimate the impact on the statement of financial position using 7% as the lessee's implied borrowing rate. What information is missing from the companies' notes to make a more accurate calculation of the impact of adopting the contract-based approach?

(g) Recalculate the ratios in part (e), incorporating the adjustments made in (f) above. Comment on your results.

(h) What do you believe are the advantages of adopting the contract-based approach when trying to compare companies? Relate your discussion to your analysis above for CNR and CPR.

RA20-3 Indigo Books & Music Inc.

Real-World Emphasis

Indigo Books & Music Inc., operating under Indigo Books, Music More, Chapters, Coles, The World's Biggest Bookstore, SmithBooks, The Book Company, and chapters.indigo.ca, has 245 stores across Canada. Through the SEDAR website (www.sedar.com) or the company's website, access the financial statements of Indigo Books & Music Inc. for its 52 weeks ending March 28, 2009. Refer to the financial statements and notes to the financial statements and answer the following questions.

Instructions

(a) Identify all lease arrangements that are indicated in the company's financial statements, including the notes. Indicate any balances related to these leases that are reported on the income statement and balance sheet.

(b) Calculate the following ratios for Indigo based on the 2009 published financial statements:

1. Debt-to-equity ratio

2. Capital asset turnover ratio

3. Total asset turnover ratio

4. Return on investment (net income to total assets)

(c) Assume that the company adopts the contract-based approach. Assuming an interest rate of 7%, estimate the impact of the adoption on the 2008 and 2009 balance sheet. Also, estimate the impact on the 2009 income statement and cash flow statement. List any assumptions that you have made. To assist with the analysis, below is the information on operating lease payments that were committed to as of March 29, 2008 (excerpts from note 12) and the capital lease interest rates (excerpt from note 6).

The Company's contractual obligations due over the next five fiscal years and thereafter are summarized below:

(millions of dollars)	Operating leases	Capital leases	Total
2009	58.3	2.6	60.9
2010	52.0	2.3	54.3
2011	43.4	0.9	44.3
2012	37.7	0.1	37.8
2013	28.1	0.1	28.2
Thereafter	47.5	—	47.5
Total obligations	267.0	6.0	273.0

The Company has entered into capital lease agreements for certain equipment. The obligation under these capital leases is $6.0 million, of which $2.6 million is included in the current portion of long-term debt. These capital leases have an average interest rate of 5.2% and an average term of 51 months.

(d) Using your estimate of the amount to capitalize for Indigo, recalculate the ratios in (b) above. Compare the recalculated ratios with the original results and comment on the differences.

RA20-4 Research an Automobile Lease

Instructions

Contact an automobile dealership and find out the full out-of-pocket cost of purchasing a specific model of car if you were to pay cash for it. Also find out the details of the costs that are associated with leasing the same model car. Answer the following questions.

(a) What terms and conditions are associated with the lease? In other words, specify the lease term, residual values and whether they are guaranteed by the lessee or not, the lessor's implicit interest rate, any purchase options, etc.

(b) What cash flows are associated with the lease?

(c) Which do you think is the better deal? Briefly explain.

Continuous Change

OVER THE PAST DECADE, the financial press has reported on multitudes of companies having to restate their financial statements due to changes in accounting standards or to adjust for accounting errors. But, for Canada, no change has been as significant as the decision by the Canadian Accounting Standards Board (AcSB) to adopt International Financial Reporting Standards (IFRS) for publicly accountable enterprises in Canada. This has affected, and will continue to affect, all public entities that follow Canadian GAAP.

"We're going through the biggest upheaval in accounting standards that I have ever seen in my career," says Tricia O'Malley, Chair of the AcSB. "The shift to IFRS is huge."

The continuous review and updating of accounting standards is not new, though it has increased in recent years. "One of the things that has changed significantly over the course of my career is the speed with which accounting standards change," says O'Malley. "Something that a lot of accountants still haven't gotten used to is the fact that change is inevitable and the world is just moving faster than it did."

Every time a new business structure or transaction is invented, the related accounting needs to be worked out. "The first securitization deals I worked on were in the early 1990s, and by the year 2008, they practically brought down the global economy," O'Malley quips. "Things change pretty quickly."

One might think that once the January 1, 2011 IFRS adoption deadline has passed, most of the change will be done. But this is not necessarily the case. "The IASB's work program is very, very full, with very aggressive timing," O'Malley stresses. "So there will be inevitably a whole lot of new standards to learn over the next five years. They are addressing so many enormous issues—really basic, fundamental important topics, such as revenue recognition and when investments should be consolidated." Once these are taken care of, O'Malley expects the pace of change will slow down after 2013 or 2014.

Expect the IASB to issue more changes to accounting standards as the business world, thus the accounting world, continues to evolve. ■

CHAPTER 21

Accounting Changes and Error Analysis

Learning Objectives

After studying this chapter, you should be able to:

1. Identify and differentiate among the types of accounting changes.

2. Identify and explain alternative methods of accounting for accounting changes.

3. Identify the accounting standards for each type of accounting change under private enterprise and international standards.

4. Apply the retrospective application method of accounting for a change in accounting policy and identify the disclosure requirements.

5. Apply retrospective restatement for the correction of an accounting error and identify the disclosure requirements.

6. Apply the prospective application method for an accounting change and identify the disclosure requirements for a change in an accounting estimate.

7. Identify economic motives for changing accounting methods and interpret financial statements where there have been retrospective changes to previously reported results.

8. Identify differences in the accounting standards for private enterprises and IFRS related to accounting changes.

After studying Appendix 21A, you should be able to:

9. Correct the effects of errors and prepare restated financial statements.

Preview of Chapter 21

As our opening story indicates, the number of changes in accounting standards has increased substantially in recent years. When new standards are adopted and when accounting errors are uncovered and changes in accounting estimates are made, companies must follow specific accounting and reporting requirements. To ensure comparability, standard setters have standardized how accounting changes, error corrections, and related earnings per share information are accounted for and reported. In this chapter, we discuss these reporting standards which help investors better understand a company's financial condition and performance. In the appendix, we look at how to analyze and correct the accounts when there have been numerous errors. The chapter is organized as follows:

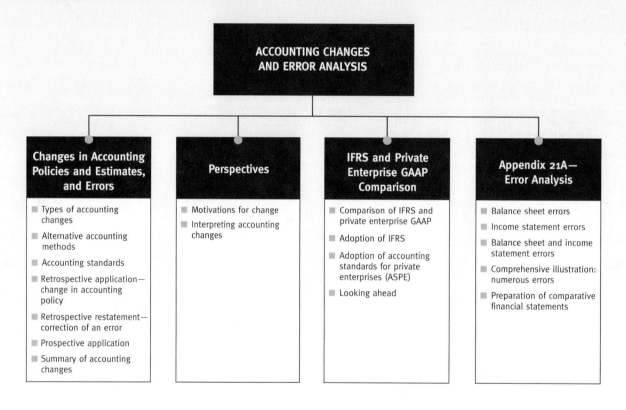

CHANGES IN ACCOUNTING POLICIES AND ESTIMATES, AND ERRORS

Financial press readers regularly see headlines about companies that report accounting changes and related events. Why do these accounting changes occur?

First, the accounting profession may mandate new accounting methods or standards. Quite apart from the major changes as Canadian companies adopt either IFRS or private enterprise standards in 2011, specific standards change from time to time. For example, revisions were made to inventory standards and to the requirements for goodwill and intangible assets in 2008, and even to the accounting standard for accounting changes itself, effective a year earlier. Second, changing economic conditions may cause a company to revise its methods of accounting. Third, changes in technology and in operations may require a company to revise estimates of the service lives, depreciation method, or expected residual value of depreciable assets. Lastly, corrections are needed when accounting errors are discovered. How should all these changes be accounted for and disclosed so that the financial information's usefulness is maintained?

Before the existence of a standard for accounting changes, companies had considerable flexibility and were able to use alternative accounting treatments for what were basically equivalent situations. The overall objectives of accounting and disclosure standards for accounting changes, therefore, are to limit the types of changes permitted, standardize the reporting for each type of change, and ensure that readers of accounting reports have the necessary information to understand the effects of such changes on the financial statements.

> **Underlying Concept**
>
> While the qualitative characteristic of usefulness may be improved by changes in accounting methods, the characteristics of comparability and consistency may be weakened.

Types of Accounting Changes

Accounting standards for private enterprises (ASPE) and IFRS have established reporting frameworks that cover three types of accounting changes:

> **1 Objective**
>
> Identify and differentiate among the types of accounting changes.

1. A change in accounting policy. Changes in the choice of "specific principles, bases, conventions, rules, and practices applied by an entity in preparing and presenting financial statements" are all changes in accounting policies.[1] The initial adoption of a new accounting standard and a change from a weighted average cost flow formula to one based on FIFO are both examples of a change in policy.

2. A change in accounting estimate. A change in an accounting estimate is an adjustment to the carrying amount of an asset or a liability or the amount of an asset's periodic consumption, and results from either an assessment of the present status of or the expected future benefits and obligations associated with an asset or liability.[2] Examples include a change in the estimate of the service life of an asset that is subject to depreciation, and a change in the estimate of the net realizable value of accounts receivable.

3. Correction of a prior period error. Prior period errors are omissions from or mistakes in the financial statements of one or more prior periods that are caused by the misuse of, or failure to use, reliable information that existed when those financial statements were completed and could reasonably have been found and used in their preparation and presentation.[3] An example is the failure to recognize depreciation on a group of capital assets that were used in operations for a specific prior period.

Each of these classifications is discussed separately below.[4]

Another major type of change occurs when the specific entities making up the reporting entity change due to a business combination or the disposal of a major part of a company's operations. These are not included in this chapter. Discontinued operations were explained in Chapter 4 and business combinations and other reporting entity changes are covered in most advanced accounting courses.

---

[1] *CICA Handbook*, Part II, Section 1506.05 and IAS 8 *Accounting Policies, Changes in Accounting Estimates and Errors*, para. 5.

[2] Ibid.

[3] Ibid.

[4] *Financial Reporting in Canada—2008* (CICA) reports that 188 of the 200 companies surveyed in 2007 reported a change in accounting policy. This reflects the large number of new or amended standards that became effective in that year. Only two of the 200 companies reported a change in accounting estimate in 2007. No changes were identified as the correction of an error.

Accounting Policies

What Is GAAP?   Before discussing what is involved in a **change in accounting policy**, it is a good idea to review the issues related to the **initial choice of accounting policy**.

Under **private enterprise standards**, *CICA Handbook*, Part II, Section 1100 on Generally Accepted Accounting Principles describes what makes up GAAP and the GAAP hierarchy. The GAAP hierarchy is the guidance to follow when there is no primary source of generally accepted accounting principles that covers a specific situation. Section 1100 identifies two levels of GAAP:

1. Primary sources of GAAP

2. Policies that are consistent with the primary sources of GAAP, and are developed by exercising professional judgement and applying concepts set out in Section 1000, Financial Statement Concepts

The first level, the primary sources of GAAP, lists these sources in order of authority, as follows:

(i) Sections 1400 to 3870, including Appendices; and

(ii) Accounting Guidelines, including Appendices.

The second level—policies consistent with the primary sources, applying professional judgement, and the concepts in Section 1000—is used only when primary sources of GAAP do not deal with the specific issue. Section 1100 provides additional guidance on applying secondary sources and addresses the topic of consistency in accounting policies. It indicates that similar transactions, events, and circumstances are accounted for and presented in a consistent manner in an entity's financial statements.

International standards require a similar **hierarchy**. The **primary sources** to look to are the IFRS and guidance that is an integral part of the specific standard. When no such source exists, judgement is used to determine the accounting treatment. Judgement takes into account the definitions of elements, recognition criteria, and measurement concepts and the underlying qualities of financial statement information found in the Framework for the Preparation and Presentation of Financial Statements. It ensures that the method chosen results in consistency with the treatment that primary sources would require for similar situations.

Under both ASPE and IFRS, if GAAP specifically requires or permits categorization of items and different policies to be used, such as with depreciation methods, different methods may be used. Once an appropriate method is chosen from among those allowed, this method is then applied consistently to each category. Both sets of standards also identify other sources such as the pronouncements of standard-setting bodies with similar conceptual frameworks that could be considered and applied, as long as the result is consistent with the hierarchy set out above.

Changes in Accounting Policies.   Having been introduced to the original choice of policy, we can now ask what conditions must exist for an entity to be allowed to change its policy. Under **IFRS**, one of the following two situations is required for a change in an accounting policy to be acceptable:

1. The change is required by a primary source of GAAP.

2. A voluntary change results in the financial statements presenting reliable and more relevant information about the effects of the transactions, events, or conditions on the entity's financial position, financial performance, or cash flows.[5]

---

[5] IAS 8.4. If an entity changes its accounting policy by following a source other than a primary source of GAAP, this is treated as a voluntary change in policy (IAS 8.21). Under both sets of GAAP, early adoption of a new accounting standard is not considered a voluntary change in policy.

Accounting standards for private enterprises permit a third type of accounting policy change to be made without having to meet the "reliable, but more relevant" test in the second situation above. It allows the following voluntary changes in policy to be made:

3. Between or among alternative private enterprise GAAP methods of accounting and reporting for investments in subsidiary companies, and in companies where the investor has significant influence or joint control; for expenditures during the development phase on internally generated intangible assets; for defined benefit plans; for accounting for income taxes; and for measuring the equity component of a financial instrument that has both a liability and equity component at zero

Significant Change

Specific transitional provisions that indicate how any changes are to be accounted for are often identified in new or revised standards and other documents that qualify as a primary source of GAAP. The second situation permitting a change in policy—a voluntary change—underscores one of the principles underlying both private enterprise and international standards: for a change in accounting policy to be acceptable, the new policy chosen must result in financial information that remains reliable and is more relevant than under the previous policy. In other words, the change would be unacceptable if it produces more reliable but less relevant information. The assumption, therefore, is also that the use of another method that remains reliable and is equally relevant would not meet the criterion for being an acceptable change. The onus is on management to explain why a different method is more relevant than the method that is currently being applied.

Underlying Concept

Relevance and reliability are used in accounting standards as criteria in the choice of accounting methods.

A change in the measurement basis of an asset or liability is clearly a change in accounting policy. An IFRS example of an acceptable voluntary change might be the move from a cost basis to the fair value model for measuring investment property. Another possible example, this time related to private enterprise accounting, is the change made by a company that constructs its own long-lived assets if it moves from expensing all interest charges as they are incurred to capitalizing interest during construction. In both cases, management can likely explain in what way the resulting financial information has become more relevant and remains reliable.

But determining what is "more relevant" is not always obvious in financial reporting. How is relevance measured? One enterprise might argue that a change in accounting policy from FIFO to an average cost formula better matches current costs and current revenues, providing more predictive, and therefore more relevant, information. Conversely, another enterprise might change from an average cost formula to FIFO because it wants to report a more current and relevant ending inventory amount that also has better predictive value. The decision has to be made based on the situation in each specific case.

The requirement based on relevance and reliability (or faithful representation under the changing conceptual framework) links back to the two primary qualitative characteristics of accounting information that make it useful. The main purpose of the qualitative characteristics is their use as evaluative criteria in choosing among accounting alternatives. Any new or revised standard that is issued as a primary source of GAAP has been evaluated against these characteristics as part of the process of its development.

The third situation allowed under **private enterprise** accounting standards as an acceptable change in accounting policy refers to standards where accounting policy choices have to be made. These changes are treated as voluntary changes, but they do not have to meet the "reliable and more relevant" hurdle required of other voluntary changes. Although not specifically stated in the actual standard, once that choice has been made, the same policy is followed consistently.

It is not always obvious whether an accounting change is, in fact, a change in accounting policy. It is clearly **not** a change in policy if either one of the following two situations is evident:

1. A different policy is applied to transactions, events, or conditions that are different in substance from those that previously occurred.

2. A different policy is applied to transactions, events, or conditions that either did not occur previously or that were immaterial.

Consider, for example, a company that begins to capitalize interest during the construction of its own long-lived assets. If the company was not involved in any self-construction activities previously, the new policy of capitalizing interest would not be considered a change in accounting policy. Another example is applying a new "defer and amortize" policy for development expenditures. If these costs were immaterial previously but are now significant, the change in materiality justifies the new policy. This is not a change in methods of accounting for similar events and circumstances. In each of these examples, the method that was used previously was appropriate for the circumstances that existed then; the new policy is appropriate for the changed circumstances.

What happens if the accounting policy that was previously followed was not acceptable, or if the policy was applied incorrectly? Rather than being a change in accounting policy, these changes to a generally accepted accounting method are considered corrections of an error. A switch from the cash basis of accounting to the accrual basis is considered an error correction. If a company incorrectly deducted residual values when calculating double-declining depreciation on tangible capital assets and later recalculates the depreciation without deducting the estimated residual value, the change is considered the correction of an error.

Finally, companies often change how they allocate or group items within categories on the financial statements. When an item is reclassified on the financial statements of the prior period(s) in order to make the statements comparable, this is considered a change in presentation only and not, in itself, a change in accounting policy. IAS 1 *Presentation of Financial Statements* requires that an "extra" balance sheet—an opening balance sheet for the earlist comparative period presented—be provided in such a case.

Changes in Accounting Estimates

In preparing financial statements, estimates of the effects of future conditions and events are often made. As future conditions and events and their effects cannot be known with certainty, estimation requires the use of judgement. The following are a few of the many examples of accounting items that require estimates:

1. Uncollectible receivables

2. Inventory obsolescence

3. Fair value of financial assets or financial liabilities

4. Useful lives of, the pattern of consumption of the future economic benefits that are embodied in, and the residual values of depreciable assets

5. Liabilities for warranty costs

The use of reasonable estimates is considered an essential part of the accounting process. And it is normal to expect that accounting estimates will change over time as new events occur, circumstances change, more experience is acquired, or additional information is obtained. By its very nature, a change in estimate does not relate to past periods. Instead, and as its definition reinforces, the change is brought about by assessing the present status and future expectations associated with specific assets and liabilities.

Sometimes it is difficult to differentiate between a change in an estimate and a change in an accounting policy. Assume, for example, that a company changes its method of depreciation for its property, plant, and equipment. At first glance, this clearly appears to be a change in an accounting policy. Or does the new method result from a change in the estimate of the pattern in which the assets' benefits are used by the entity? Assume that a company changes from deferring and amortizing certain development costs to recording them as expenses as they are incurred because the future benefits associated with these costs have become doubtful. Is this a change in policy or a change in estimate?

The definition of a change in accounting estimate clearly includes both of these scenarios. Further, **in cases where it is unclear whether a change is one of policy or of estimate,** the change is treated as a change in estimate. A revision of an estimate, such as a prior year's tax assessment not caused by errors, is given change-in-estimate treatment. It is clearly not the same thing as a correction of an error, which is discussed next.

Correction of an Error in Prior Period Financial Statements

No business, large or small, is immune from errors. The risk of material errors, however, may be reduced by installing good internal controls and applying sound accounting procedures. The accounting standards define prior period errors and make a distinction between errors and changes in accounting estimates. Estimates, by their nature, are approximations whose values change as circumstances and conditions change and more information becomes available. Errors, on the other hand, are omissions or mistakes, either intentional or through oversight, that are not discovered until after the financial statements for a period have been issued.

The following are examples of accounting errors:

1. A change from an accounting policy that is not generally accepted to an accounting policy that is acceptable. The rationale adopted is that the prior periods were incorrectly presented. Example: a change from the cash basis of accounting to the accrual basis.

2. Arithmetic mistakes. Example: the incorrect totalling of the inventory count sheets in calculating total inventory cost.

3. Previous estimates were not prepared in good faith. Example: based on information that was available when an amortization rate was determined, an entity used a clearly unrealistic rate.

4. An omission due to an oversight. Example: the failure to accrue certain revenues at the end of the period.

5. A recognition error. Example: the recognition of a cost as an asset instead of as an expense.

6. A misappropriation of assets. Example: the correction of a previous year's financial statements because inventory theft was discovered.

A problem may arise in distinguishing between the correction of an accounting error and a change in estimate. What is the correct treatment of the settlement of litigation (not previously accrued) related to a reassessment of a prior year's income taxes? How do we determine whether the information was overlooked in earlier periods (an error) or whether it results from new information, more experience, or subsequent developments (a change in estimate)? This decision is important because, depending on the answer, a different accounting treatment is applied. The general rule is that when a careful estimate later proves to be incorrect, the change is considered a change in estimate. This is the case with most unaccrued tax litigation settlements. Only when the estimate was obviously calculated incorrectly because of lack of expertise or it was done in bad faith should the adjustment be considered an error correction. There is no clear separating line here. Good judgement must take all the circumstances into account.

Alternative Accounting Methods

Objective 2
Identify and explain alternative methods of accounting for accounting changes.

Three approaches have been suggested for reporting changes in the accounts:

1. **Retrospective.** Retrospective application (also known as retroactive application) requires applying a new accounting policy in the accounts as if the new method had always been used. The cumulative effect of the change on the financial statements at the beginning of the period is calculated and an adjustment is made to the financial statements. In addition, all prior years' financial statements that are affected are restated on a basis that is consistent with the newly adopted policy. Advocates of this position argue that only by restating prior periods can accounting changes lead to comparable information. If this approach is not used, the years before the change will be reported using one method and the current and following years will present financial statements on a different basis. Consistency is considered essential in providing meaningful earnings-trend data and other financial relationships that are necessary to evaluate a business.

2. **Current.** The cumulative effect of the change on the financial statements at the beginning of the period is calculated. This **"catch-up" adjustment** is then reported in the current year's income statement. Advocates of this position argue that restating financial statements for prior years results in a loss of confidence by investors in financial reports. How will a present or prospective investor react when told that the earnings reported five years ago have changed? Restatement, if permitted, might also upset many contractual and other arrangements that were based on the old figures. For example, profit-sharing arrangements based on the old policy might have to be recalculated and completely new distributions made. This might create numerous legal problems. Many practical difficulties also exist: the cost of restatement may be excessive, or restatement may be impossible based on the data available.

3. **Prospective** (in the future). With prospective application, previously reported results remain; no change is made. Opening balances are not adjusted, and no attempt is made to correct or change past periods. Instead, the new policy or estimate is applied to balances existing at the date of the change, with effects of the change reported in current and future periods. Supporters of this position argue that once management presents financial statements based on acceptable accounting principles, methods, and estimates, they are final; management cannot change prior periods by adopting new methods and calculations. According to this line of reasoning, a cumulative adjustment in the current year is not appropriate, because such an approach includes amounts that have little or no relationship to the current year's income or economic events.

Objective 3
Identify the accounting standards for each type of accounting change under private enterprise and international standards.

Accounting Standards

Illustration 21-1 identifies the accounting standards for each type of accounting change. These are more fully explained and illustrated below.

Illustration   21-1
Accounting Changes—GAAP Accounting Methods

Type of Accounting Change	Accounting Method Applied
Change in accounting policy—on adoption of a primary source of GAAP	Apply the method that is approved in the transitional provisions of the primary source.
	If there is none, use retrospective application to the extent that it is practicable.
	If retrospective application is impracticable, apply prospectively.
Change in accounting policy—voluntary	Use retrospective application to the extent practicable.

Type of Accounting Change	Accounting Method Applied
	If impracticable, apply prospectively.
Change in accounting estimate	Apply prospectively.
Correction of an error	Use retrospective restatement.

As indicated, **only two of the general approaches are permitted: retrospective and prospective treatment**. When new or revised primary sources of GAAP are adopted, recommendations are usually included that specify how an entity should handle the transition. The transitional provisions are sometimes complex. Those involving new disclosures (e.g., Financial Instruments—Disclosures) tend to be applied prospectively. Those that require existing balance sheet items to be remeasured (e.g., Financial Instruments—Recognition and Measurement) tend to require retrospective application by adjusting the opening asset and liability measurements and retained earnings and other equity balances. Some particularly major changes, such as when other post-retirement benefits were first recognized for accounting purposes in Canada, permit a choice of either prospective or retrospective application. The transitional provisions also set out specific disclosures that are required when the new or revised primary sources are adopted.

For all accounting changes, the requirements apply to each incident—it is not appropriate to net the effects of two or more changes when considering materiality. Let's turn now to how these methods are applied. Retrospective application and restatement are discussed first, followed by prospective application.

Underlying Concept

Until the United States harmonized its policies with the IASB in 2004, the FASB required the current or "catch-up" method to be used for changes in accounting principles. The cumulative effect was recognized on the income statement just above the net income number.

Retrospective Application—Change in Accounting Policy

When an entity voluntarily changes one of its accounting policies, retrospective application is considered the most informative method of accounting for these changes and reporting their effects on the financial statements. This method is often recommended in the specific transitional provisions of a new or revised primary source of GAAP as well.

The underlying principle of the retrospective application method is that all comparative periods are presented as if the new accounting policy had always been used. This outcome provides the best information to users who assess trends in financial information for prediction purposes. Specifically, retrospective application means that the opening balance of each affected component of equity is adjusted for the earliest prior period that is presented. In addition, all other affected comparative amounts that are disclosed for each prior period that is provided are presented as if the new accounting policy had always been in use.

Faced with having to retrospectively restate its financial statements of prior periods, an entity may find that data from specific prior periods may not be available, or may only be available at too high a cost. If it is impracticable to do the restatements—i.e., if the entity cannot determine the effects on a specific prior period or the cumulative effect of the change in policy for all comparative prior periods after making all reasonable efforts to do so—a limited version of retrospective application may need to be applied.

The accounting standards clearly explain what is meant by impracticable. It is considered impracticable to apply a change to a particular prior period if any of the following situations are true:

1. The effects of the retrospective application cannot be determined.

2. Assumptions are needed about what management's intents were in that prior period.

3. Significant estimates must be made that need to take into account circumstances that existed in that prior period, and it is no longer possible to do this.

Objective

4 Apply the retrospective application method of accounting for a change in accounting policy and identify the disclosure requirements.

Underlying Concept

The cost-benefit constraint is always considered by standard setters in determining appropriate accounting policies.

Partial retrospective application is allowed only when one or more of these three limitations exist. If the cumulative effect cannot be determined even on the opening balances of the current period, then a change in accounting policy is accounted for prospectively.

Retrospective Application with Full Restatement of Comparative Information

Retrospective application with full restatement of all comparative information is applied as follows:

1. An accounting entry is made to recognize the effects of the new accounting policy that is being applied retrospectively, along with any related income tax effects.

2. Financial statement amounts for prior periods that are included for comparative purposes are restated to give effect to the new accounting policy. The entity adjusts the opening balance of the specific components of equity that are affected for the earliest prior period included in the report, along with other relevant accounts affected for each period.

3. Disclosures are made that enable users of the financial statements to understand the effects of any changes on the financial statements so that the statements remain comparable to those of other years and of other entities.

To illustrate full retrospective application, assume that Denson Ltd. has expensed all interest costs incurred on self-constructed assets since beginning its major capital upgrading project in 2009. In 2011, the company changes its accounting policy to one of capitalizing all avoidable interest costs related to the self-constructed assets. Management believes that this approach provides a more relevant measure of income earned as well as a better reflection of the asset's cost. Shareholders and financial analysts are better able to assess a period's operating performance and prospects for the future with information that is reported under this changed accounting policy. The company is subject to a 40% tax rate. Denson has also expensed interest for tax purposes and plans to continue using this method in the future.

Illustration 21-2 provides the information for analysis.

Illustration 21-2

Data for Full Retrospective Application Example

	Interest Expensed Policy Reported in Prior Years		
	2011	2010	2009
Income Statement			
Income before income tax	$190,000	$160,000	$400,000
Income tax—40%	76,000	64,000	160,000
Net income	$114,000	$96,000	$240,000
Statement of Retained Earnings			
Opening balance	$1,696,000	$1,600,000	$1,360,000
Net income	114,000	96,000	240,000
Closing balance	$1,810,000	$1,696,000	$1,600,000

	Incomes if **Interest Capitalization Policy** Had Been Used		
	2011	2010	2009
Income Statement			
Income before income tax	$200,000	$180,000	$600,000
Income tax—40%	80,000	72,000	240,000
Net income	$120,000	$108,000	$360,000

| | Differences in Income, Income Tax, and Net Income | | |
| | Using Interest Capitalization Policy | | |
	2011	2010	2009
Increase in income before tax	$10,000	$20,000	$200,000
Increase in income tax expense	4,000	8,000	80,000
Increase in net income	$ 6,000	$12,000	$120,000

Accounting Entry to Recognize the Change.   The first step is to make the accounting entry to recognize this change in accounting policy. Because the 2011 accounts have not yet been closed, any adjustments that are needed to 2011's income are made to the income statement and balance sheet accounts themselves, while any changes to prior years are made through retained earnings.

The entry to record the change effective January 1, 2011, is:

Property, Plant, and Equipment (net)	220,000	
Future Income Tax Liability		88,000
Retained Earnings—Change in Accounting Policy		132,000

A   =   L   +   SE
+220,000   +88,000   +132,000

Cash flows: No effect

The Property, Plant, and Equipment account, net of its accumulated depreciation, is increased by $220,000. This represents the additional costs charged to the capital asset account for interest, less the related increase in the accumulated depreciation account from the increased depreciation expense since the assets were completed and used in operations ($200,000 + $20,000). The $220,000 adjustment brings these accounts to what the January 1, 2011 balances would have been if the revised policy had been in effect since the beginning of construction. In reality, both the asset account and its contra account—the accumulated depreciation—are affected. The adjustment is shown as a net amount so you can focus on the other balance sheet effects.

The Future Income Tax Liability credit recognizes the tax effects of the taxable temporary difference; that is, the difference between the carrying amount and tax basis of the capital asset account. In future periods, because taxable income will be higher than accounting income as a result of this temporary difference at January 1, 2011, a future tax liability is recognized.[6] The adjustment to Retained Earnings is the accumulated after-tax effect of the new policy up to the beginning of the current year and represents all changes to prior years' incomes ($120,000 + $12,000 = $132,000). The entry corrects the accounts to January 1, 2011, and the revised policy is applied to the current year's operations.

The next step is to prepare the comparative financial statements by restating them as if the new policy had been in use from the beginning of 2009, the first year that Denson Ltd. incurred interest costs on self-constructed assets.

Financial Statement Presentation.   Illustration 21-3 shows what the bottom portion of the income statement for Denson Ltd. looks like after giving effect to the retrospective change in accounting policy. It also presents the restated statements of retained earnings.[7]

---

[6] Think this through. The book value of the PP&E asset has just been increased, but no change has been made to the UCC. Future depreciation expense is based on the larger carrying amount, but this won't be permitted for tax purposes; the costs were actually deducted for tax purposes previously. Therefore, future taxable income will be higher than accounting income.

[7] Although accounting standards for private enterprises refer to the preparation of a statement of retained earnings, there is no requirement to prepare it in this form. Because changes in all shareholders' equity accounts are required to be reported, it is equally acceptable to prepare a statement of changes in equity. An example of this is shown in Illustration 21-6.

Illustration 21-3
*Comparative Income
Statements and Statements of
Retained Earnings*

DENSON LTD.
Statement of Income
Year Ended December 31

	2011	2010 (restated)	2009 (restated)
Income before income tax	$200,000	$180,000	$600,000
Income tax—40%	80,000	72,000	240,000
Net income	$120,000	$108,000	$360,000

DENSON LTD.
Statement of Retained Earnings
Year Ended December 31

	2011 (restated)	2010 (restated)	2009 (restated)
Opening balance	$1,828,000	$1,720,000	$1,360,000
Net income	120,000	108,000	360,000
Closing balance	$1,948,000	$1,828,000	$1,720,000

Underlying Concept

Applying full retrospective treatment and providing the related disclosures that are required is an attempt to restore the comparability of the income statements.

The Property, Plant, and Equipment; Accumulated Depreciation; and Future Income Tax Liability accounts on the comparative balance sheet now appear as if the new accounting policy had always been used. This is the objective of retrospective application. However, it is important for the financial statement reader to be alerted to the fact that Denson did change a key policy in the year. The disclosure requirements are identified after our next illustration.

Retrospective Application with Partial Restatement of Comparative Information

Impracticability. As indicated earlier, retrospectively restating the financial statements of a prior year requires information that may, in many cases, be impracticable to obtain, even though the cumulative effect can be determined. For example, when the AcSB adopted the current accounting standards for post-retirement benefits other than pensions, many companies accounted for the change retroactively. Before the new standard took effect, companies had recognized payments made for medical premiums for retirees as an expense as the payments were made—a pay-as-you-go method. Under the revised standard, the expense was required to be estimated and charged to the period in which the employees earn the entitlement to the future benefit—an accrual approach. For many reasons, however, it was not practicable for some companies to retroactively determine the effect of the new standard on specific prior years—a necessary condition for restatement. The standard's transitional provisions therefore permitted a partial retrospective application.

Thus, if the effect of a change in policy can be determined for some of the prior periods, the change in policy is applied retrospectively with restatement to the carrying amounts of assets, liabilities, and affected components of equity at the beginning of the earliest period for which restatement is possible. This could even be the current year. An adjustment is made to the opening balances of the equity components for that earliest period, similar to the adjustments in the full restatement that was illustrated above.

While estimates can be used to allow some restatements to be made retrospectively, estimates should not be made for this purpose after the fact if it is impossible to objectively assess circumstances and conditions in prior years that need to be known in order to develop those estimates. It is not appropriate to apply hindsight in developing measurements that need to be used. Measurements must be based on conditions that existed and were known in the prior period.

If the entity cannot practicably determine the cumulative effect of the change even at the beginning of the current period, retrospective treatment cannot be applied. Instead, the entity applies the new accounting policy **prospectively** from the earliest date that is practicable. This situation may arise if the necessary data were not collected and cannot be recreated appropriately.

Example—Statement of Retained Earnings.   In the Denson Ltd. example in Illustrations 21-2 and 21-3, the company was able to determine the effect of the change in accounting policy on each prior year affected. What would happen if the company had been using a policy of expensing interest on self-constructed assets for many years and management concluded that it was impracticable to determine the effects on specific years any further back than 2010? It knows what the effect is on the January 1, 2010 capital assets, future income tax liability, and retained earnings, but it does not know the income effects on specific years prior to that date. In this case, management is only able to determine the information provided in Illustration 21-4.

	Interest Expensed Policy Reported in Prior Years			Illustration 21-4
	2011	2010	2009	*Data for Partial Retrospective Application Example*
Income Statement				
Income before income tax	$190,000	$160,000	$400,000	
Income tax—40%	76,000	64,000	160,000	
Net income	$114,000	$96,000	$240,000	
Statement of Retained Earnings				
Opening balance	$1,696,000	$1,600,000	$1,360,000	
Net income	114,000	96,000	240,000	
Closing balance	$1,810,000	$1,696,000	$1,600,000	

	Incomes if **Interest Capitalization Policy** Had Been Used		
	2011	2010	2009
Income Statement			
Income before income tax	$200,000	$180,000	Unknown
Income tax—40%	80,000	72,000	
Net income	$120,000	$108,000	

	Differences in Income, Income Tax, and Net Income Using Interest Capitalization Policy		
	2011	2010	2009
Increase in income before tax	$10,000	$20,000	Unknown
Increase in income tax expense	4,000	8,000	Unknown
Increase in net income	$ 6,000	$12,000	

When it is impracticable to determine the effects on a specific period that is presented for comparative purposes, the accounting standard indicates that the relevant assets and liabilities of the earliest prior period for which the effect is known should be adjusted, along with the opening balances of that period's equity accounts.

The journal entry to record the change in accounting policy is the same as the one that was made for the full restatement above:

A	=	L	+	SE
+220,000		+88,000		+132,000

Cash flows: No effect

Property, Plant, and Equipment (net)	220,000	
Future Income Tax Liability		88,000
Retained Earnings—Change in Accounting Policy		132,000

Illustration 21-5 shows how the comparative financial statements are presented when only partial retrospective restatement is possible.

Illustration 21-5

Partial Retrospective Application: Comparative Income Statements and Statements of Retained Earnings

DENSON LTD.
Statement of Income
Year Ended December 31

	2011	2010 (restated)	2009
Income before income tax	$200,000	$180,000	$400,000
Income tax—40%	80,000	72,000	160,000
Net income	$120,000	$108,000	$240,000

DENSON LTD.
Statement of Retained Earnings
Year Ended December 31

	2011 (restated)	2010 (restated)	2009
Opening balance, as previously reported		$1,600,000	
Change in capitalization of interest accounting policy		120,000	
Opening balance, as restated	$1,828,000	1,720,000	$1,360,000
Net income	120,000	108,000	240,000
Closing balance	$1,948,000	$1,828,000	$1,600,000

As the illustration shows, the 2009 financial statements are not restated. Instead, the effect of the policy change is carried back only to January 1, 2010, and the retained earnings amount at that date is adjusted for the cumulative effect of the change to that date. The new policy is applied in the 2010 and 2011 comparative income statements and balance sheets, and is supported by the required disclosures.

An expanded retained earnings statement is included in this presentation to show the type of adjustment that is needed to restate the beginning balance of retained earnings for the earliest prior period that is presented. In 2010, the beginning balance is adjusted for the excess of the "capitalization of interest" incomes over the "interest expensed" incomes prior to 2010 ($120,000). The restated balance is the amount that the opening balance would have been if the new policy had always been in effect. In 2011, the restated opening balance is what would have been in the accounts if the new policy had always been applied.

Partial Retrospective Application Example—Statement of Changes in Equity.
Let us assume now that Denson Ltd. prepares a statement of changes in equity rather than a statement of retained earnings. The same requirements apply, but the statement is formatted in a different way. We assume that Denson Ltd. has had share capital outstanding of $2 million since the beginning of it 2009 fiscal year, and the same change in interest

capitalization policy applies.[8] Illustration 21-6 shows how the change would be presented in a comparative statement of changes in equity.

Illustration 21-6

Partial Retrospective Application: Statement of Changes in Equity

	Share Capital	Retained Earnings	Total
DENSON LTD.			
Statement of Changes in Equity			
Year Ended December 31, 2011			
Balance, January 1, 2009	$2,000,000	$1,360,000	$3,360,000
Net income 2009		240,000	240,000
Balance December 31, 2009, as previously reported	$2,000,000	$1,600,000	$3,600,000
Cumulative effect of change in interest capitalization accounting policy		120,000	120,000
Balance January 1, 2010, as restated	$2,000,000	$1,720,000	$3,720,000
Net income 2010 (restated)		108,000	108,000
Balance December 31, 2010, as restated	$2,000,000	$1,828,000	$3,828,000
Net income 2011		120,000	120,000
Balance December 31, 2011	$2,000,000	$1,948,000	$3,948,000

This adjustment process might appear complicated at first. It may be helpful at this point for you to try to develop the revised income and retained earnings statements on your own assuming the interest capitalization policy had always been used. You should end up with the results in Illustrations 21-3, 21-5, and 21-6.

Is there any **effect on the statement of cash flows**? As you might expect, past cash flows for prior periods do not change just because we change an accounting policy in 2011. However, the category of cash flow will change in our example. Instead of all the interest paid being reported as an operating outflow, the restated financial statements report the capitalized interest as an investing outflow, thereby increasing the cash flow from operations above the amount previously reported. In other situations the cash flow from operations does not change. In the Canadian Pacific Railway Limited example in Illustration 21-7, the pension prior service cost accounting change did not affect cash flows, and the locomotive overhauls change resulted in an equal adjustment between operating and investing cash flows. The cash flow amount did not change in total.

Continuing with our Denson Ltd. example, if the company had been unable to determine the effect on 2010's income, the adjustment would have been made instead to the opening balance of 2011's retained earnings. In the most limited circumstances, if it were not practicable to determine the cumulative effect even at the beginning of 2011, retrospective application is not possible and Denson would apply the new accounting policy on a prospective basis from the earliest possible date in the current year. The prospective method is explained later in the chapter where it is applied to changes in estimates.

---

[8] IFRS 23 *Borrowing Costs* actually changed, effective January 1, 2009, from allowing a choice of policy to requiring capitalization on qualifying assets. Although the transitional provisions stated that prospective treatment was to be used, they allowed companies to choose an earlier date and make the change effective from that earlier date. Therefore, the situation described in the chapter might have been applied by several companies complying with IFRS, although the dates would have been different.

What Do the Numbers Mean?

Changes in accounting policy, whether they are mandated or voluntary, can have a significant effect on reported incomes and therefore on trend data for analysis.

Consider the following data about Canadian companies from an article in *Canadian Business* magazine after the AcSB approved an accounting standard that required companies to charge the cost of stock options to expense based on their fair values rather than their lower intrinsic values.

Company	Earnings before Change in Policy*	Earnings after Change in Policy*	Percentage Drop
QLT	$ 12,405	$ −13,120	205.8
Certicom	−4,900	−11,922	143.3
Cott	3,900	−1,500	138.5
Imax	11,972	−1,207	110.1
Pivotal	−27,646	−42,135	52.4
Shaw Communications	−47,828	−68,664	43.6
Cognos	73,144	46,005	37.1
Open Text	27,757	19,397	30.1
Nortel Networks	−3,585,000	−4,537,000	26.6
Zarlink Semiconductor	−57,900	−73,100	26.3

Source: John Gray, "Out of Options," *Canadian Business*, Jan. 19–Feb. 1, 2004. Vol. 77, issue 2, p.57.
*All figures in U.S. dollars, except Shaw

Application of the new standard, however, did not have such a dramatic effect on other companies, such as the Canadian banks, which began expensing options before being required to do so.

The expense is measured using an options pricing model that requires several assumptions, including the expected option life, stock volatility, dividends, and a risk-free rate of return. Because each of these variables is an estimate, companies have some latitude in the expense calculation.

Disclosures Required for a Change in Accounting Policy

Whether the change in accounting policy is due to an initial application of a primary source of GAAP or to a voluntary change, considerable information is required to be reported under both private enterprise standards and IFRS. This helps readers understand why the change was made and what its effects are on previous and the current period financial statements. The information below is required to be disclosed in the period of the change, if practicable, regardless of whether the change was accounted for retrospectively or currently:

1. For an initial application of an IFRS or primary source, its title, the nature of the change and that it is made according to its transitional provisions, and what the provisions are

2. The nature of any voluntary change, and why the new policy provides reliable and more relevant information

3. The effects of the change, to the extent practicable, on each financial statement line item affected in the current period, and on periods before those presented

4. Where full retrospective application is impracticable, additional information about why that is so, the periods affected, and how the change was handled

As indicated earlier in the chapter, under **private enterprise GAAP** some voluntary accounting policy choice changes are exempt from having to provide "reliable and more relevant" information.

Under **IFRS**, the information set out above is also required when a transitional provision or voluntary change might have an **effect on future periods**. Related to this disclosure is a requirement to report information about new standards that have been issued but are not yet effective and have not been applied. The entity discloses any reasonably reliable information that would be useful in assessing the effect of the new primary source on its financial statements when it will be first applied.

A limited amount of additional information is required to be disclosed under **IFRS**. This includes line-item adjustments for all prior periods presented and, for entities required to report earnings per share amounts, the adjustments needed to basic and fully diluted EPS because of the accounting change. An opening balance sheet at the beginning of the earliest comparative period is also required.

Example of Disclosures

Canadian Pacific Railway Limited (CPR) is a well-known Canadian transportation icon. Illustration 21-7 provides excerpts from CPR's financial statements for its year ended December 31, 2009, that indicate its disclosures related to a variety of accounting policy changes. These provide good examples of the retrospective application of voluntary

Real-World Emphasis

Illustration 21-7

Example of Disclosure of Changes in Accounting Policy

Additional Disclosures

CONSOLIDATED STATEMENT OF CHANGES IN SHAREHOLDERS' EQUITY

(in millions of Canadian dollars)	Share capital	Contributed surplus	Accumulated other comprehensive income	Retained income	Total Shareholders' equity
Balance at December 31, 2006, as previously reported	$1,175.7	$32.3	$80.4	$3,586.1	$4,874.5
Adjustment for change in accounting policies (Note 2)			0.4	(197.5)	(197.1)
Balance at December 31, 2006, as restated	1,175.7	32.3	80.8	3,388.6	4,677.4
Net income				932.1	932.1
Other comprehensive income (loss)			(39.4)		(39.4)
Dividends declared				(138.4)	(138.4)
Shares purchased (Note 23)	(24.5)			(206.6)	(231.1)
Stock compensation expense		11.3			11.3
Shares issued under stock option plans	37.4	(1.2)			36.2
Balance at December 31, 2007	1,188.6	42.4	41.4	3,975.7	5,248.1
Net income				607.2	607.2
Other comprehensive income (loss)			36.3		36.3
Dividends declared				(152.2)	(152.2)
Stock compensation expense		7.8			7.8
Shares issued under stock option plans	32.2	(10.0)			22.2
Balance at December 31, 2008	1,220.8	40.2	77.7	4,430.7	5,769.4
Net income				612.4	612.4
Other comprehensive income (loss)			(28.2)		(28.2)
Dividends declared				(166.5)	(166.5)
Shares issued (Note 23)	495.2				495.2
Stock compensation (recovery) expense		(1.6)			(1.6)
Shares issued under stock option plans	30.4	(5.1)			25.3
Balance at December 31, 2009	$1,746.4	$33.5	$49.5	$4,876.6	$6,706.0

See Notes to Consolidated Financial Statements.

continued on pages 1410 and 1411

NOTES TO CONSOLIDATED FINANCIAL STATEMENTS
December 31, 2009

2 Accounting changes

PENSION PRIOR SERVICE COSTS

During 2009, CP changed its accounting policy for the treatment of prior service pension costs for unionized employees. In previous periods, CP had amortized these costs over the expected average remaining service period for employees. CP now amortizes these costs over the remaining contract term. The change in policy was made to provide more relevant information by amortizing the costs based on the contract term as CP generally renegotiates union contracts on a routine and consistent basis that is substantially shorter than the expected average remaining service period. The change has been accounted for on a retrospective basis. As a result of the change the following increases (decreases) to financial statement line items occurred:

(in millions of Canadian dollars, except per share data)	Year ended December 31			As at December 31		As at January 1
	2009	2008	2007	2009	2008	2007
Compensation and benefits	$0.9	$0.1	$(10.1)			
Income tax expense	1.2	0.3	7.3			
Net income	$(2.1)	$(0.4)	$2.8			
Basic earnings per share	$(0.01)	$—	$ 0.02			
Diluted earnings per share	$(0.01)	$—	$ 0.02			
Prepaid pension costs and other assets				$(105.1)	$(104.2)	$(114.2)
Future income tax liability				(27.0)	(28.2)	(35.8)
Retained income				(78.1)	(76.0)	(78.4)

LOCOMOTIVE OVERHAULS

During 2009, CP changed its accounting policy for the treatment of locomotive overhaul costs. In prior periods, CP had capitalized such costs and depreciated them over the expected economic life of the overhaul. These costs are now expensed to better represent the nature of overhaul expenditures on locomotives. This policy aligns the treatment of locomotive costs with CP's current operational practices, which have changed over recent years and gradually shifted to be more in the nature of a repair. The change has been accounted for on a retrospective basis. As a result of the change, the following increases (decreases) to financial statement line items occurred:

(in millions of Canadian dollars, except per share data)	Year ended December 31			As at December 31		As at January 1
	2009	2008	2007	2009	2008	2007
Depreciation and amortization	$(43.5)	$(48.8)	$(44.5)			
Compensation and benefits	0.1	0.5	0.9			
Materials	13.8	35.0	36.7			
Purchased services and other	29.3	23.8	19.6			
Total increases	43.2	59.3	57.2			
Total operating expenses	(0.3)	10.5	12.7			
Equity income in DM&E	—	(0.4)	(1.1)			
Income tax expense	1.3	(2.6)	2.5			
Net income	$(1.0)	$(8.3)	$(16.3)			
Basic earnings per share	$(0.01)	$(0.05)	$(0.11)			
Diluted earnings per share	$(0.01)	$(0.05)	$(0.11)			
Other comprehensive income	2.1	(2.4)	1.4			
Comprehensive income	$1.1	$(10.7)	$(14.9)			
Cash provided by operating activities	$(43.2)	$(59.3)	$(57.2)			
Cash used in investing activities	$43.2	$59.3	$57.2			
Net properties				$(187.9)	$(191.8)	$(164.4)
Future income taxes liability				(51.5)	(54.3)	(52.6)
Accumulated other comprehensive income				1.5	(0.6)	0.4
Retained income				(137.9)	(136.9)	(112.2)

GOODWILL AND INTANGIBLE ASSETS

In February 2008, the Canadian Institute of Chartered Accountants ("CICA") issued accounting standard Section 3064 "Goodwill and intangible assets", replacing accounting standard Section 3062 "Goodwill and other intangible assets" and accounting standard Section 3450 "Research and development costs". Section 3064, which replaces Section 3062, establishes standards for the recognition, measurement, presentation and disclosure of goodwill subsequent to its initial recognition and of intangible assets by profit-oriented enterprises. Various changes have been made to other sections of the CICA Handbook for consistency purposes. The new Section was applicable to financial statements relating to fiscal years beginning on or after October 1, 2008. Accordingly, the Company adopted the new standards for its fiscal year beginning January 1, 2009. The provisions of Section 3064 were adopted retrospectively, with restatement of prior periods.

As a result of this adoption, the Company has retroactively expensed certain expenditures related to pre-operating periods of a facility, rather than recording them as assets in "Prepaid pension costs and other assets" and "Net properties". The adoption of Section 3064 resulted in a reduction to opening retained income of $6.9 million at January 1, 2007, $7.4 million at January 1, 2008 and $10.4 million at January 1, 2009. For the year ended December 31, 2008, the adoption of this section resulted in an increase to "Purchased services and other" expense of $5.0 million (2007 – $0.8 million), a decrease to "Income tax expense" of $2.0 million (2007 – $0.3 million), and a $0.02 (2007 – $nil) decrease to previously reported basic and diluted earnings per share.

CREDIT RISK AND THE FAIR VALUE OF FINANCIAL ASSETS AND FINANCIAL LIABILITIES

On January 20, 2009 the Emerging Issues Committee ("EIC") issued a new abstract EIC 173 "Credit risk and the fair value of financial assets and financial liabilities". This abstract concludes that an entity's own credit risk and the credit risk of the counterparty should be taken into account when determining the fair value of financial assets and financial liabilities, including derivative instruments.

This abstract applies to all financial assets and liabilities measured at fair value in interim and annual financial statements for periods ending on or after January 20, 2009. The adoption of this abstract did not impact the Company's financial statements.

FINANCIAL INSTRUMENTS – DISCLOSURES

The CICA amended Section 3862 "Financial Instruments – Disclosures", to include additional disclosures about fair value measurements and to enhance liquidity risk disclosures associated with financial instruments. This standard is effective for the annual period ending December 31, 2009. The adoption of this standard did not impact the amounts reported in the Company's financial statements as it relates to disclosure.

Illustration 21-7

Example of Disclosure of Changes in Accounting Policy (continued)

changes in accounting policy as well as changes under the transitional requirements of primary sources of GAAP. The company's statement of income, balance sheet, and statement of cash flows all report numbers presented for 2007 and 2008 as "restated."

In addition to the excerpts reproduced here, CPR also reported on future accounting changes. The company described the upcoming changes to primary GAAP as well as the change to IFRS for Canadian public companies. CPR has decided to adopt U.S. GAAP for its financial reporting in 2011.[9] Therefore, it will not be affected by the transition to IFRS.

You will learn in the discussion of accounting errors that is covered next that retrospective restatements to correct errors are handled in the same way as retrospective application of a change in accounting policy. The Canadian Pacific Railway Limited example can be reviewed for that type of change as well. In addition, notice that retained earnings is not the only equity account that may be subject to restatement. CPR's Statement of Changes in Shareholders' Equity indicates that the company's **accumulated other comprehensive income** was also adjusted for changes preceding December 31, 2006, in the same way as retained earnings was adjusted, and Note 2 identifies changes to other comprehensive income in each of 2007, 2008, and 2009.

---

[9] The Canadian Accounting Standards Board required Canadian publicly accountable enterprises to adopt IFRS on January 1, 2011, unless, as permitted by Canadian securities regulators, registrants adopted U.S. GAAP on or before that same date.

Retrospective Restatement—Correction of an Error

Although the general approach to accounting for an error correction is similar to accounting for a change in accounting policy, the accounting standards make a distinction between the two: prior financial statements with material errors were never prepared in accordance with GAAP, unlike those that used a different, but acceptable, accounting policy. The term retrospective restatement is used in the case of an error correction. The result is the correction of amounts that were reported in the financial statements of prior periods as if the error had never occurred. Specifically, retrospective restatement takes place in the first set of financial statements that is completed after the error's discovery by:

- restating the comparative amounts for the prior period(s) presented in which the error occurred; or

- if the error took place before the earliest prior period provided, restating the opening amounts of assets, liabilities, and equity for the earliest period presented

Accounting standards for **private enterprises** allow only full retrospective restatement. An accounting error, by its definition and nature, can be traced to a specific prior year; therefore, full retrospective changes to all prior years that are affected is required.

IFRS, on the other hand, accept that there may be situations where it may be impracticable to determine the accounting adjustment needed for a specific prior period or for the cumulative effect of an error. In such a case, partial retrospective restatement is allowed, similar to the requirements for an accounting policy change:

- If the effect on each prior period presented cannot be determined, the opening amounts of the balance sheet elements for the earliest period the effects can be determined are restated. This may be the current period.

- If the cumulative effect on prior periods cannot be determined at the beginning of the current period, the error is corrected from the earliest possible date practicable.

Retrospective Restatement—Affecting One Prior Period

As soon as they are discovered, errors are corrected retrospectively by proper entries in the accounts and are reflected in the financial statements. In the year in which the error is discovered, the correction is recorded as an adjustment to the beginning balance of retained earnings. **If comparative statements are presented, the prior statements that are affected are restated to correct the error so that they appear as if the error had never occurred.** The accounting and reporting is similar to the examples of retrospective application for a voluntary change in accounting policy.

To illustrate, assume that the bookkeeper for Selectric Corporation discovered in 2011 that in 2010 the accountant had failed to record in the accounts $20,000 of depreciation expense on a newly constructed building. Selectric's tax rate is 40%.

As a result of the $20,000 depreciation error in 2010, the following balances are incorrect:

Depreciation expense (2010) was understated by:	$20,000
Accumulated depreciation at December 31, 2010/January 1, 2011, was understated by:	20,000
Future income tax expense (2010) was overstated by ($20,000 × 40%):	8,000
Net income (2010) was overstated by ($20,000 − $8,000):	12,000
Future income tax liability at December 31, 2010/January 1, 2011, was overstated by ($20,000 × 40%):	8,000

The entry needed in 2011 to correct the omission of $20,000 of depreciation in 2010, assuming the books for 2010 have been closed, is:

Retained Earnings	12,000	
Future Income Tax Asset/Liability	8,000	
Accumulated Depreciation—Buildings		20,000

A	=	L	+	SE
−20,000		−8,000		−12,000

Cash flows: No effect

The Retained Earnings account is adjusted because all 2010 income statement accounts were closed to retained earnings at the end of that year. The journal entry to record the error correction is the same whether single-period or comparative financial statements are prepared; however, presentation on the financial statements will differ. If single-period financial statements are presented, the error is reported as an adjustment to the opening balance of retained earnings of the period in which the error is discovered, as Illustration 21-8 shows.

Retained earnings, January 1, 2011		
As previously reported (assumed)		$350,000
Correction of an error (depreciation)	$(20,000)	
Less: Applicable income tax reduction	8,000	(12,000)
Restated balance of retained earnings, January 1, 2011		338,000
Add: Net income 2011 (assumed)		400,000
Retained earnings, December 31, 2011		$738,000

Illustration 21-8

Reporting an Error—Single-Period Financial Statements

If comparative financial statements are prepared, adjustments are made to correct the amounts of all affected accounts in the statements of all periods that are reported. The data for each year that is presented are restated to the correct amounts. In addition, the opening balance of retained earnings for the earliest period being reported is adjusted for any cumulative change in amounts that relates to periods that are prior to the reported periods. In the case of Selectric Corporation, the error of omitting the depreciation of $20,000 in 2010, which was discovered in 2011, results in restating the 2010 financial statements when they are presented for comparison with those of 2011. Illustration 21-9 shows the changes that need to be made to the previously reported amounts on the comparative statements.

Comparative Balance Sheet (restated)
December 31, 2010

Accumulated depreciation, buildings	+$20,000	Future income tax liability	−$ 8,000
		Retained earnings	− 12,000

Comparative Income Statement (restated)
Year ended December 31, 2010

Depreciation expense	+$20,000
Future income tax expense	− 8,000
Net income	− 12,000

Comparative Statement of Retained Earnings
Years ended December 31, 2010 (restated)

Opening balance, January 1	no change
Net income	−$12,000
Ending balance, December 31	−$12,000

Illustration 21-9

Reporting an Error Correction—Changes to the Comparative Financial Statements

Selectric's 2011 financial statements (presented in comparative form with those of 2010) are prepared as if the error had not occurred; the only exception to this is the restated opening balance of retained earnings at January 1, 2011. In addition, a note to the 2011 financial statements is required that provides all appropriate disclosures.

Retrospective Restatement—Affecting Multiple Prior Periods

Assume that when preparing the financial statements for the year ended December 31, 2011, the controller of Shilling Corp. discovered that a property purchased in mid-2008 for $200,000 had been charged entirely to the Land account in error. The $200,000 cost should have been allocated between Land ($50,000) and Building ($150,000). The building was expected to be used for 20 years and then sold for $70,000 (not including the land). Prior to discovery of this error, Shilling Corp.'s accounting records reported the information in Illustration 21-10.

Illustration 21-10

Accounting Records before Restatement

	2011 (books not closed)	2010
Revenues	$402,000	$398,000
Expenses	329,000	320,000
Income before tax	73,000	78,000
Income tax expense (30%)	21,900	23,400
Net income	$ 51,100	$ 54,600
Retained earnings, January 1	$294,000	$242,000
Net income for year	51,100	54,600
Dividends declared	(2,100)	(2,600)
Retained earnings, December 31	$343,000	$294,000

Retrospective restatement is required, so the first step is to determine the effect of this error on all prior periods. Preparing an appropriate analysis provides backup for the required correcting entry and helps in the restatement of the financial statements. The specific analysis differs for each situation encountered. However, each analysis requires identifying two things: first, what is in the books and records now; and second, what would have been in the accounts if the error had not occurred. The correcting entry then adjusts what is there now to what should be there. Illustration 21-11 shows the analysis that underlies the correcting entry to Shilling's accounts. Assume that the tax records were not updated for the building acquisition and therefore no CCA was claimed on the building over the years. Go through each line, making sure that you understand the source of each number.

Illustration 21-11

Analysis of Error on Shilling's Records

	2011	2010	2009	2008
Income statement effects:				
Correct amount of depreciation expense ($150,000 − $70,000) ÷ 20 = $4,000 per year	$ 4,000	$ 4,000	$ 4,000	$ 2,000
Correct amount of tax benefit related to depreciation = 30% of depreciation expense	1,200	1,200	1,200	600
Income was overstated each year by:	$ 2,800	$ 2,800	$ 2,800	$ 1,400

Balance sheet effects, end of each year:				
Land reported	$200,000	$200,000	$200,000	$200,000
Correct land balance	50,000	50,000	50,000	50,000
Building reported	–0–	–0–	–0–	–0–
Correct building balance	150,000	150,000	150,000	150,000
Accumulated depreciation reported	–0–	–0–	–0–	–0–
Correct accumulated depreciation	14,000	10,000	6,000	2,000
Future tax asset reported re: building	–0–	–0–	–0–	–0–
Correct future tax asset balance				
(= 30% of accumulated depreciation				
at year end)[10]	4,200	3,000	1,800	600

The correcting entry needed at the 2011 year end when the error is discovered is taken directly from the analysis in Illustration 21-11.

Building (150,000 − 0)	150,000	
Depreciation Expense (4,000 − 0)	4,000	
Future Tax Asset (4,200 − 0)	4,200	
Retained Earnings (Jan. 1, 2011: 2,800 + 2,800 + 1,400)	7,000	
Land (200,000 − 50,000)		150,000
Accumulated Depreciation (14,000 − 0)		14,000
Income Tax Expense (1,200 − 0)		1,200

$$A \ = \ L \ + \ SE$$
$$-9,800 \qquad\qquad -9,800$$

Cash flows: No effect

Let's review this entry. The objective is to correct the accounts so the amounts in the records are the same as they would have been if there had been no error. The Building account would have had a $150,000 balance, but now stands at $0, so we need to debit $150,000 to Building. Depreciation expense should have been taken on the building in 2011 but was not, so the current year's expense needs to be recognized. With income statement items, because all accounts get closed out each year to Retained Earnings, the correction to depreciation expense for 2008 to 2010 must be to Retained Earnings. The depreciation expense for 2011 has not yet been closed out, so the adjustment is made directly to the expense. The same explanation applies to the adjustment to Income Tax Expense. In 2011, the adjustment is made to the expense account but for 2008 to 2010, it is made to Retained Earnings. In effect, the $7,000 adjustment to decrease the January 1, 2011 Retained Earnings balance represents the 2008 to 2010 Depreciation Expense correction of $10,000, net of the related Income Tax Expense correction for the same three-year period of $3,000.

Three other balance sheet accounts need correcting. The Land account, now at $200,000, must be reduced to $50,000. The Accumulated Depreciation now stands at $0 but should be $14,000. Lastly, the Future Tax Asset account related to the temporary deductible difference between the tax basis (UCC) of the building and its revised carrying amount is recognized.

Now that the records have been adjusted, the accounting error has to be reported on the comparative statements for 2010, assuming that only one year's comparative statements are provided. These financial statements are presented "as if the error had never

---

[10] The correct future tax asset amount is actually 30% of the difference between the asset's tax basis and its carrying amount. Because no CCA has been claimed, the correct tax basis at December 31, 2011, is $150,000, its capital cost. The correct carrying amount at December 31, 2011, is $150,000 − $14,000 = $136,000. The temporary difference is $150,000 − $136,000 = $14,000 and the future tax asset is $14,000 × 30% = $4,200.

occurred." If the error occurred before the earliest period that is presented, as in this situation, then the opening balances of the related assets, liabilities, and equity for the earliest prior period presented are restated. The required income statements and statements of retained earnings are presented in Illustration 21-12.

Illustration 21-12

Retrospective Restatement of Comparative Statements— Shilling Corp.

Income Statement	2011	2010 (restated)
Revenues	$402,000	$398,000
Expenses	333,000[a]	324,000[b]
Income before tax	69,000	74,000
Income tax expense	20,700[c]	22,200[d]
Net income	$ 48,300	$ 51,800

[a]$329,000 + $4,000   [c]$21,900 − $1,200

[b]$320,000 + $4,000   [d]$23,400 − $1,200

Statement of Retained Earnings		
Retained earnings, January 1, as previously reported		$242,000
Cumulative effect of accounting error, net of tax benefit of $1,800		(4,200)
Retained earnings, January 1, as restated	$287,000	237,800
Net income	48,300	51,800
Less: Dividends declared	(2,100)	(2,600)
Retained earnings, December 31	$333,200	$287,000

The adjustments to the income statement are relatively straightforward as the expenses and income tax lines are simply changed to the corrected amounts. The earliest retained earnings balance that is reported now has to be restated to what it would have been if the error had never occurred.

For the 2010 statement of retained earnings, the previously reported opening retained earnings balance (i.e., the 2009 ending balance) is adjusted for the effects on income (and therefore retained earnings) prior to January 1, 2010. The cumulative adjustment at this date is $4,200. This reflects the $6,000 of additional depreciation expense ($2,000 + $4,000) reduced by the $1,800 of related income tax benefit ($600 + $1,200) to January 1, 2010. If the error had not been made, the balance of retained earnings at January 1, 2010, would have been $237,800. The revised 2010 net income of $51,800 is added to this and the 2010 dividends are deducted in determining the corrected December 31, 2010 balance of retained earnings.

For 2011, the restated opening retained earnings for 2011 of $287,000 is the balance that would have been reported if the error had never occurred. The correct income for 2011 is added to this and the 2011 dividends are deducted to give the retained earnings at the end of 2011. It is not an accounting error in the current year.

The comparative balance sheet for 2010 is designated as "restated" and information is disclosed about the effect on each financial statement line item that has been affected. Under **IFRS**, an opening January 1, 2010 comparative balance sheet must also be presented with the correct amounts reported.

It may be useful to revisit the Canadian Pacific Railway Limited example in Illustration 21-7 to review how this company applied retrospective adjustments. Although the examples provided were not error corrections, the general approach is the same. Also notice that equity accounts other than retained earnings are changed using the same approach when changes affect them.

Disclosures Required for the Correction of an Accounting Error

The disclosures required when a company corrects an error in a prior period are few, but informative. The following are disclosed in the year of the correction, but are not necessary in subsequent periods:

1. The nature of the error

2. The amount of the correction made to each affected financial statement item for each prior period presented

3. The amount of the correction made at the beginning of the earliest prior period presented

IAS 8 *Accounting Policies, Changes in Accounting Estimates and Errors* requires two additional disclosures. Because IAS 8 recognizes that it may not be practicable to determine the correction's effect on each specific prior period, an entity is required to provide information about the circumstances leading to any impracticality and how such an error has been corrected. Also, the effect of the correction on both basic and fully diluted earnings per share is reported for each prior period presented. IAS 1 *Presentation of Financial Statements* also requires an opening balance sheet for the earliest comparative period presented.

Prospective Application

As explained above, the effects of changes in estimates are handled prospectively. That is, no changes are made to previously reported results—they are made forward from the time of the change in estimate. Changes in estimates are viewed as normal recurring corrections and adjustments—the natural result of the accounting process—and retrospective treatment is therefore not appropriate. Opening balances are not adjusted, and no attempt is made to "catch up" for prior periods. The financial statements of prior periods are not restated.

> **6 Objective**
>
> Apply the prospective application method for an accounting change and identify the disclosure requirements for a change in an accounting estimate.

Instead, the effect of a change in estimate is accounted for by including it in net income or comprehensive income, as appropriate, in (1) the period of change if the change affects that period only, or (2) the period of change and future periods if the change affects both. If the estimate relates to the balance of an asset, liability, or equity item, the item's carrying amount is changed.

The circumstances related to a change in estimate are different from those related to a change in accounting policy. If changes in estimates were handled on a retroactive basis, continual adjustments of prior years' income would occur. It seems proper to accept the view that, because new conditions or circumstances exist, the revision fits the new situation and should be handled in the current and future periods only.

As indicated earlier in the chapter, **it is also appropriate to apply prospective treatment to a change in accounting policy** if it is impracticable to determine the effect of the change even as far back as the beginning of the current period. In such a situation, the new accounting policy is only applied to transactions and events that occur after the accounting policy is changed.

Illustration—Change in Estimate

To illustrate the accounting for a change in estimate, assume that Underwriter Labs Inc. purchased a building for $300,000 that was originally estimated to have a useful life of 15 years and no residual value. Depreciation of $20,000 per year has been recorded for five years on a straight-line basis. In 2011, the total useful life estimate is revised to 25 years. The accounts at the beginning of the sixth year are as follows:

Building	$300,000
Less accumulated depreciation at end of 2010: 5 × $20,000 =	100,000
Carrying amount of building, January 1, 2011	$200,000

Assuming no entry has yet been made in 2011, the entry to record depreciation for 2011 is:

A   =   L   +   SE
−10,000   −10,000

Cash flows: No effect

Depreciation Expense	10,000	
Accumulated Depreciation—Building		10,000

The $10,000 depreciation charge is calculated in Illustration 21-13.

Illustration 21-13

Depreciation after Change in Estimate

$$\text{Depreciation charge} = \frac{\text{Carrying amount of asset} - \text{Residual value}}{\text{Remaining service life}} = \frac{\$200,000 - \$0}{25 \text{ years} - 5 \text{ years}} = \$10,000$$

Prospective treatment applied to a change in accounting policy simply means that the new policy is applied to the current balance of the related asset, liability, and/or equity item after the date of change.

Disclosure Requirements for a Change in an Accounting Estimate

Disclosures for changes in estimates have the same objective as other types of changes: to provide information that is useful in assessing the effects of the change on the financial statements. In addition to reporting the nature and amount of any change in estimate that affects the current period as required under accounting standards for **private enterprises**, **IFRS** also requires reporting of the nature and amount of any change that is expected to affect future periods, unless it is impracticable to estimate its effect. If impracticable to estimate, this fact is disclosed.

Do companies have to disclose changes in accounting estimates made as part of normal operations, such as bad debt allowances or inventory obsolescence? Materiality plays an important role here, as it does with other accounting standards. Although the change may have little effect in the current year, the effect on future periods has to be considered.

Example of Disclosure of a Change in Estimate

Real-World Emphasis

Qantas Airways Limited, an international airline headquartered in Sydney, Australia, reports under international reporting standards. Illustration 21-14 captures Qantas' disclosure about a change in accounting estimate it reported in its financial statements for its year ended June 30, 2009.

Illustration 21-14

Example of Disclosure of a Change in Accounting Estimate

Additional Disclosures

QANTAS AIRWAYS LIMITED
NOTES TO THE FINANCIAL STATEMENTS
(in Australian dollars)

1. Statement of Significant Accounting Policies

(C) CRITICAL ACCOUNTING ESTIMATES AND JUDGEMENTS

Change in accounting estimate — Software
Effective 1 July 2008, the estimated useful lives of core system software were revised from five years to 10 years. The net effect of the changes in the current financial year was a decrease in amortisation expense of the Qantas Group of $17 million (Qantas: $17 million).

Assuming the assets are held until the end of their revised useful lives, amortisation of the Qantas Group in future years in relation to these assets will decrease by between $10 million and $26 million each year from 2010 to 2013 and increase by between $15 million to $20 million each year from 2014 to 2018.

Summary of Accounting Changes

Developing recommendations for reporting accounting changes has helped resolve several significant and long-standing accounting problems. Yet, because of the diversity of situations and of characteristics of the items that are encountered in practice, applying professional judgement is still very important. The primary objective is to serve the user of the financial statements. Achieving this requires accuracy, full disclosure, and the avoidance of any misleading inferences.

The major accounting approaches that were presented in earlier discussions are summarized in Illustration 21-15.

Illustration 21-15

Accounting Approaches to Accounting Changes

Accounting Change	Accounting Method to Apply			
	Method Indicated in the Standard	Retrospective		
		Full Retrospective	Partial Retrospective	Prospective
CHANGE IN ACCOUNTING POLICY On adoption of, or change in, a primary source of GAAP—transitional provision included: IFRS and PE GAAP	✓			
On adoption of, or change in, a primary source of GAAP—no transitional provision or if it is a voluntary change: IFRS and PE GAAP		✓ if practicable	✓ if full retrospective treatment is not practicable	✓ if partial retrospective treatment is not practicable
Change within the allowed accounting policy choices identified in *CICA Handbook*, Part II, Section 1506: PE GAAP only		✓ if practicable	✓ if full retrospective treatment is not practicable	✓ if partial retrospective treatment is not practicable
CORRECTION OF AN ERROR IFRS only		✓ if practicable	✓ if full retrospective treatment is not practicable	✓ if partial retrospective treatment is not practicable
PE GAAP only		✓		
CHANGE IN ACCOUNTING ESTIMATE IFRS and PE GAAP				✓

PERSPECTIVES

Motivations for Change

Objective **7**

Identify economic motives for changing accounting methods and interpret financial statements where there have been retrospective changes to previously reported results.

Understanding how an entity chooses its accounting methods and procedures is complex. The complexity is due to the fact that managers, and others, have an interest in how the financial statements make the company appear. Managers naturally want to show their financial performance in the best light. A favourable profit picture can influence investors, and a strong liquidity position can influence creditors. Too favourable a profit picture, however, can provide union negotiators with ammunition during bargaining talks. Also, if the federal government has established price controls, managers might believe that a trend of lower profits might persuade the regulatory authorities to grant their company a price increase. Hence, managers might have varying profit motives, depending on the economy and who they want to impress.

Research has provided insights into why companies may prefer certain accounting methods.[11] Some of these reasons are as follows.

1. **Political costs**. As companies become larger and more politically visible, politicians and regulators devote more attention to them. The larger the firm, the more likely it is to become subject to legislation such as anti-competition regulations and the more likely it is to be required to pay higher taxes. Therefore, companies that are politically visible may try to report income numbers that are low in order to avoid the scrutiny of regulators. By reporting low income numbers, companies hope to reduce their exposure to being viewed as a monopoly power.[12] This practice can have an effect on other concerned parties as well. For example, labour unions may be less eager to demand wage increases if reported income is low. Researchers have found that the larger a company is, the more likely it is to adopt approaches that decrease income when it selects its accounting methods.

2. **Capital structure**. Several studies have found that a company's capital structure can affect the selection of accounting methods. For example, a company with a high debt-to-equity ratio is more likely to be constrained by debt covenants. That is, a company may have a debt covenant that indicates that it cannot pay any dividends if retained earnings fall below a certain level. As a result, this type of company is more likely to select accounting methods that will increase net income—such as capitalizing interest instead of expensing it, or using the full cost method instead of the successful efforts approach for exploration and development costs in the oil and gas industry.

3. **Bonus payments**. Studies have found that if compensation plans tie managers' bonus payments to income, management will select accounting methods that maximize bonus payments.

4. **Smooth earnings.** Substantial increases in earnings attract the attention of politicians, regulators, and competitors. In addition, large increases in income create problems for management because the same results are difficult to achieve in subsequent

---

[11] See Ross L. Watts and Jerold L. Zimmerman, "Positive Accounting Theory: A Ten-Year Perspective," *The Accounting Review* (January 1990) for an excellent review of research findings related to management incentives in selecting accounting methods.

[12] "There's an old saw on Bay Street that the Royal Bank earned a billion dollars three years before it told the world," indicates Kim Shannon of Sionna Investment Managers Inc. Although the comment was made in the context of a discussion on income smoothing, the authors believe that this was directly related to the appearance of the situation at a time when banks were heavily under fire for allegedly "gouging" consumers with fees and closing branches. "A Beautiful Find," *Globe and Mail* on-line, Jan. 30, 2004, <www.globeandmail.com>.

years. Compensation plans may adjust to these higher numbers as a baseline and make it difficult for management to achieve its profit goals and receive bonuses in the following years. On the other hand, decreases in earnings might signal that the company is in financial trouble. Furthermore, significant decreases in income raise concerns on the part of shareholders, lenders, and other interested parties about the competency of management. For all these reasons, companies have an incentive to "manage" or "smooth" their earnings. Management typically believes that steady growth of 10% each year is much better than 30% growth one year followed by a 10% decline the next. In other words, management usually prefers to report gradually increasing income and it sometimes changes accounting methods to ensure such a result.

Management pays careful attention to the accounting it follows and often changes accounting methods, not for conceptual reasons, but rather for economic reasons. As indicated throughout this textbook, such arguments have come to be known as economic consequences arguments, since they focus on the supposed impact of accounting on the behaviour of investors, creditors, competitors, governments, and the managers of the reporting companies themselves, rather than address the conceptual justification for accounting standards.[13]

To counter these pressures, standard setters have declared, as part of their conceptual framework, that they will assess the merits of proposed standards from a position of neutrality. That is, the soundness of standards should not be evaluated on the grounds of their possible impact on behaviour. It is not the standard setter's place to choose standards according to the kinds of behaviour that they want to promote or discourage. At the same time, the reality is that accounting numbers influence behaviour. Nonetheless, the justification for accounting choices should be conceptual, and not viewed in terms of their economic impact.

Underlying Concept

Neutrality is an aspect of reliability and faithful representation.

Interpreting Accounting Changes

What effect do accounting changes have on financial statement analysis? Not surprisingly, they often make it difficult to develop meaningful trend data, which undermines one of the major reasons that accounting information has been found useful in the past.

The former **Alliance Atlantis Communications Inc.** reported numerous accounting changes. In one year, the company adopted three revised accounting policies, and during the next fiscal period, it adopted three more. All but one of the six changes were initial applications of a primary source of GAAP. The voluntary change transferred what had been classified as investing expenditures to the operating classification, reducing previously reported cash from operations by hundreds of millions of dollars!

Another note to the financial statements indicated that the company changed its method of accounting for its "investment in the two CSI television series," but failed to adequately explain the reason. Was this an error? What may not be clear to readers is that while certain income (revenues of $77.1 million and income of $32.8 million) was reported in the financial statements of the two prior years, these amounts were pulled out of retained earnings in the current year, and, one assumes, must have been available to include in revenue and income at a later date.

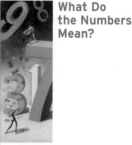

What Do the Numbers Mean?

Real-World Emphasis

---

[13] Economic consequences arguments—and there are many of them—constitute manipulation through the use of lobbying and other forms of pressure brought on standard setters. We have seen examples of these arguments in the oil and gas industry about successful efforts versus full cost, in the technology area with the issue of mandatory expensing of research and most development costs, and with stock options, and so on.

International Hi-Tech Industries Inc., based in Vancouver, provided another example. The company announced it was restating its aggregate revenue for the previous seven years by more than $6 million and reducing its income over the past two and a half years by about $3 million. At issue was the fact that the company had determined that revenue related to non-refundable fees and deposits had been recognized earlier than it should have been. Here, too, the restatement cancelled out previously reported earnings, leaving them available to be reported on the income statement again in the future! To be fair, the new revenue recognition policy appeared to be a more appropriate policy.

These situations highlight the difficulty that investors may experience when they are trying to identify trend data for analysis and the challenge that standard setters have in determining best practices for reporting accounting changes. The accounting standards covering these issues attempt to limit the changes to situations where they are well warranted, and they require disclosures of the effects of each change on the previously reported financial statements.

Financial statement readers should look closely at all accounting changes and adjust any trend data appropriately. Although most adjustments result in no change in the company's cash position, some adjustments can end up converting previously reported operating cash flows to investment or financing flows. Most changes tend to shift earnings from one accounting period to another. The disclosures required by the accounting standards are the best source of input for the analysis.

IFRS AND PRIVATE ENTERPRISE GAAP COMPARISON

Comparison of IFRS and Private Enterprise GAAP

Objective 8

Identify differences in the accounting standards for private enterprises and IFRS related to accounting changes.

Private enterprise and international accounting standards covering how to choose accounting policies initially and how to account for changes in policy, corrections of errors, and changes in estimates are very similar. The significant differences between the two sets of GAAP are identified in Illustration 21-16.

Adoption of IFRS

The most significant accounting change in Canadian accounting history is the move from the application by publicly accountable enterprises of accounting standards set by the Canadian Accounting Standards Board to the adoption of those issued by the IASB. How is this 2011 change applied?

IFRS 1 *First-time Adoption of International Financial Reporting Standards* is the standard for an entity's preparation of its first IFRS financial statements. IAS 8 does not deal with changes in accounting policies for a first-time adoption. IFRS 1 states that its objective is to ensure that these first statements contain high quality, cost-effective information that is comparable for all periods presented, is transparent for users, and provides the appropriate base for application of IFRS in the future.

With a January 1, 2011 changeover date and an entity's first reporting date of December 31, 2011, transition to IFRS actually took place at the beginning of business on January 1, 2010. One full year of comparative information is required in the first reporting period, incuding an opening comparative IFRS balance sheet. Canadian companies have invested many years in this transition.

	Accounting Standards for Private Enterprises (Private Entity GAAP/ASPE)—*CICA Handbook*, Part II, Sections 1100 and 1506	IFRS—IAS 1 and 8
Accounting policies	Accounting policies applied are determined by applying the primary sources of GAAP—the principles and policies set out in Part II of the *CICA Handbook*, first in Sections 1400 to 3870, and then in the Accounting Guidelines. If not dealt with in a primary source or if additional guidance is needed, management uses policies consistent with the primary sources, and that are developed using professional judgement and the concepts in Section 1000.	Accounting policies applied are determined by applying the IFRS. If there is no specific IFRS that applies, management applies judgement in determining a policy that is relevant to the needs of users and is reliable. Judgement considers first the requirements of IFRS in similar situations, and then the definitions, recognition criteria, and elements in the *Framework for the Preparation and Presentation of Financial Statements*.
Changes in accounting policy	Other than a change in accounting policy that is required by a primary source of GAAP, an accounting policy can be changed under two circumstances: (1) when it results in reliable and more relevant information; and (2) when the choice is related to a change in GAAP methods within a number of specifically identified accounting standards.	Other than a change in accounting policy that is required by an IFRS, an accounting policy can be changed only under one circumstance: when it results in reliable and more relevant information.
Correction of an error	PE GAAP assumes that the correction can be made to each specific prior period. No allowance is made for impracticability.	IFRS permits other than full retrospective restatement in the situation that it is impracticable to determine the period-specific effects or cumulative effect of the error.
Presentation and disclosure	There is no requirement for an additional balance sheet for retrospective treatment of an accounting policy or retrospective restatement, or reclassification of items in the financial statements.	When applying retrospective treatment for a change in accounting policy or restatement due to correction of an error, or when an entity reclassifies items in the financial statements, an opening balance sheet must be presented for the earliest comparative period reported.
	There is no requirement to report on issued standards that are not yet effective.	Information about the effect of issued standards that are not yet effective is required to be disclosed.

Illustration 21-16

IFRS and Private Enterprise GAAP Comparison Chart

In general, the accounting policies used in reporting the assets, liabilities, and equity items on an entity's opening IFRS balance sheet and in all periods covered by its first set of statements are required to comply with the IFRS in effect on the first reporting date. The adjustments needed to bring the entity's previous GAAP measures in line with IFRS balance sheet recognition and measurement standards are recognized directly in retained earnings (or some other category of equity, if applicable). Retrospective application to specific prior periods is not applied.

IFRS 1 identifies various exemptions from some IFRS requirements, prohibits retrospective application of certain aspects of other IFRS, and sets out presentation and disclosure requirements. It also allows some one-time opportunities to reconsider accounting decisions, such as the classification and revaluation of certain assets.

Adoption of Accounting Standards for Private Enterprises (ASPE)

Similar to the transition provisions for the first-time adoption of IFRS, *CICA Handbook*, Part II, Section 1500 entitled First Time Adoption sets out the requirements for the first-time adoption of accounting standards for private enterprises, or ASPE. Its objectives are identical to those of IFRS 1.

Canadian private enterprises have to choose a new basis of accounting by January 1, 2011, at the latest. If an entity changes effective January 1, 2011, its first reporting date is December 31, 2011, and its date of transition to ASPE is January 1, 2010. Again, similar to the IFRS changeover, a full year of comparative information is required in the first reporting period and this includes an opening comparative balance sheet prepared on the basis of accounting standards for private enterprises. Exemptions from some requirements of specific standards are permitted, and there are one-time opportunities here as well to reclassify and remeasure certain assets.

Section 1500 requires retrospective application of the new standards, but also provides relief from applying certain individual standards where retrospective application does not meet the cost-benefit test. In general, adjustments are made to retained earnings.

Looking Ahead

The accounting standards covering accounting changes as identified in this chapter have been updated relatively recently and no significant changes are expected to these standards—IFRS or ASPE—in the immediate future.

KEY TERMS

change in accounting estimate, 1395

change in accounting policy, 1395

correction of a prior period error, 1395

economic consequences, 1421

full retrospective application, 1402

GAAP hierarchy, 1396

impracticable, 1401

neutrality, 1421

partial retrospective application, 1404

primary sources of GAAP, 1396

prior period errors, 1395

prospective application, 1400

retroactive application, 1400

retrospective application, 1400

Summary of Learning Objectives

1 Identify and differentiate among the types of accounting changes.

There are three types of accounting changes. (1) Change in accounting policy: a change in the specific principles, bases, rules, or practices that an entity applies in the preparation of its financial statements. (2) Change in an accounting estimate: a change in the carrying amount of an asset or liability or the amount of an asset's periodic consumption from reassessing the current status of the asset or liability or the expected future benefits or obligations associated with it. (3) Correction of a prior period error: a change caused by an omission from or misstatement in prior years' financial statements from the misuse of or failure to use reliable information that existed at the time the statements were completed and that could have been used in their preparation and presentation.

2 Identify and explain alternative methods of accounting for accounting changes.

Accounting changes could be accounted for retrospectively, currently, or prospectively. The retrospective method requires restatement of prior periods as if the accounting change had been used from the beginning or the error had never been made. The current method calculates a catch-up adjustment related to the effect on all prior years, and reports it in the current period. Prospective treatment requires making no adjustment for past effects, but instead, beginning to use the new method in the current and future periods.

3 Identify the accounting standards for each type of accounting change under private enterprise and international standards.

A change in accounting policy due to the initial application of a new primary source of GAAP is accounted for according to the transitional provisions of that standard. If none is provided, or if it is a voluntary change, retrospective application is used. A change in an accounting estimate is accounted for prospectively. Errors are corrected through full retrospective restatement.

4 Apply the retrospective application method of accounting for a change in accounting policy and identify the disclosure requirements.

Comparative periods are presented as if the new accounting policy had always been applied. The opening balance of each affected component of equity is adjusted for the earliest prior period presented, and all other affected comparative amounts for each prior period provided are restated. When the effects on particular prior periods are impracticable to determine, the cumulative effect of the change is shown as an adjustment to the beginning retained earnings of the earliest prior period possible. Required disclosures therefore include identifying the nature of the change, the effect on each financial statement item affected, the amounts relating to periods prior to those that are presented, and why full retrospective application was not applied, if applicable. If the change resulted from applying transitional provisions, information about the standards and the provisions is provided, including, if under IFRS, the effects on future periods. If it is a voluntary change, excluding specific PE accounting changes, the reasons why the new policy results in more relevant information are disclosed. Information about the future effect of changes in primary sources of GAAP that are issued but not yet effective is also required under IFRS.

5 Apply retrospective restatement for the correction of an accounting error and identify the disclosure requirements.

Comparative amounts for prior periods affected are restated, unless under IFRS it is not practicable to identify the effect on specific past periods. If the error is in a period before the earliest comparative statements included, the opening balances of the earliest comparative period are restated. An opening balance sheet is required under IFRS for the earliest comparative period presented as is information about the nature of any impracticality. The nature of the error and the amount of the adjustment to each comparative financial statement line item and to EPS are all required disclosures.

6 Apply the prospective application method for an accounting change and identify the disclosure requirements for a change in an accounting estimate.

Under prospective treatment, only the current and future fiscal periods are affected. There is no adjustment of current-year opening balances and no attempt is made to "catch up" for prior periods. The nature and amount of a change in an accounting estimate that affects the current period or, under IFRS, if it expected to affect future periods, is required to be disclosed.

7 Identify economic motives for changing accounting methods and interpret financial statements where there have been retrospective changes to previously reported results.

Some of the aspects that affect decisions about the choice of accounting methods are (1) political costs, (2) the capital structure, (3) bonus payments, and (4) the desire to smooth earnings. Financial statement users should analyze the information presented about accounting changes and adjust any trend information affected.

8 Identify differences in the accounting standards for private enterprises and IFRS related to accounting changes.

The accounting standards for private enterprises are very similar to international standards. Minor differences exist, such as IAS 8's permitting partial retrospective treatment for the correction of an accounting error, ASPE allowing specific voluntary changes without justification on a "reliable and more relevant" basis, and IFRS requiring additional disclosures.

retrospective restatement, 1412
transitional provisions, 1401
voluntary change, 1397

Appendix 21A

Error Analysis

Objective 9
Correct the effects of errors and prepare restated financial statements.

In the past, it was unusual to see the correction of material errors in the financial statements of large corporations. Internal control procedures and the diligence of the accounting staff were normally sufficient to find and correct any major errors in the system before the statements were released. However, in the decade just past, there were a number of well-publicized cases of major companies restating past results. For example, numerous companies in the United States and Canada, including Apple Inc., Pixar Inc., and Research In Motion, restated past financial statements for a number of years due to improper dating of stock option grants. Many top executives have signed settlements for large sums of money with their shareholders over these events. Smaller businesses may face different problems. These enterprises may not be able to afford an internal audit staff or be able to implement the necessary control procedures to ensure that accounting data are recorded accurately.

What Do the Numbers Mean?

Investor research firm Glass, Lewis & Co. recently reported that the number of error restatements made by U.S. public companies with market values of U.S. $250 million or more in 2008 was the lowest in the past five years: 172 companies filed a total of 185 financial restatements, with services and technology companies filing the most. This was in sharp contrast to two years earlier when it reported that 2006 numbers were 12 times higher than those in 1997. The top categories they identified at that time were as follows:

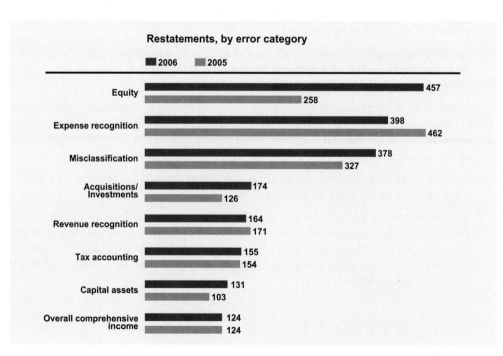

Restatements, by error category

■ 2006 ■ 2005

Category	2006	2005
Equity	457	258
Expense recognition	398	462
Misclassification	378	327
Acquisitions/Investments	174	126
Revenue recognition	164	171
Tax accounting	155	154
Capital assets	131	103
Overall comprehensive income	124	124

What caused the turnaround? Glass, Lewis & Co. attributes it to the work done within companies to improve their internal control systems, a process undertaken to comply with the requirements of the *Sarbanes-Oxley Act* of 2002. It also points to the fact that the SEC relaxed its materiality standards so that companies could avoid making restatements.

What causes these restatements in the first place? The complexity of corporate transactions—especially increasingly sophisticated financing techniques—provides fertile ground for making errors. In addition, the increased number and complexity of accounting standards and other regulations, low budgets for the internal audit function, and reduced levels of spending on external audit fees all contributed to the need for restatements. Trent Gazzaway, the U.S. national managing partner of corporate governance for audit firm Grant Thornton, LLP, suggested that "[c]ompanies are in business to produce their product and sell it at a profit, and the reporting of the processes around that is a secondary goal. In some cases, it's become too secondary." And, of course, some errors are due to "just plain dumb mistakes."[14]

In practice, firms do not correct errors that are discovered unless they have a significant effect on the financial statements. For example, the failure to record accrued wages of $5,000 when the total payroll for the year is $1,750,000 and net income is $940,000 is not considered significant, and no correction is made. Obviously, defining materiality is difficult, and experience and judgement are used to determine whether adjustment is necessary for a given error. All errors discussed in this section are assumed to be material and to require adjustment. For simplicity, we have chosen to ignore the tax effects initially so that you can focus instead on the direct effects of the errors themselves.

The accountant must answer three questions in error analysis:

1. What type of error is involved?

2. What entries are needed to correct the error?

3. How are financial statements to be restated once the error is discovered?

As indicated earlier, the standards usually require that errors be corrected retrospectively with restatement, meaning that the elements of the financial statements are adjusted as if the error had never occurred. Three types of errors can occur. Because each type has its own peculiarities, it is important to understand their differences.

Balance Sheet Errors

Balance sheet errors affect only the presentation of an asset, liability, or shareholders' equity account. Examples are classifying a short-term receivable as part of the investment section, a note payable as an account payable, or plant assets as inventory. Reclassification of the item to its proper position is needed when the error is discovered. If comparative statements that include the error year are prepared, the balance sheet for the error year is restated correctly.

Income Statement Errors

These errors affect only income statement accounts. Errors involve the improper classification of revenues or expenses, such as recording interest revenue as part of sales, pur-

---

[14] *Source:* Glass, Lewis & Co. press release, March 19, 2009. "Glass Lewis Releases 2008 Financial Restatement Data," <www.glasslewis.com>; Roy Harris, "Say Again? An Explosion in Accounting Errors—in Part Reflecting the Difficulties of Today's Complex Rules—Has Forced Nearly a Quarter of U.S. Companies to Learn the Art of the Restatement," *CFO Magazine*, April 2007.

chases as bad debt expense, or amortization expense as interest expense. An income statement classification error has no effect on the balance sheet or on net income. If a reclassification error is discovered in the year the error is made, an entry is needed to correct it. If the error occurred in prior periods, no entry is needed at the date of discovery because the accounts for the year of the misclassification have all been closed to retained earnings and the current year is correctly stated. If comparative statements that include the error year are prepared, the income statement for the error year is restated correctly.

Balance Sheet and Income Statement Errors

The third type of error involves both the statement of financial position and the income statement. For example, assume that accrued wages were overlooked by the accounting staff at the end of the accounting period. The error's effect is to understate expenses and liabilities, and overstate net income for that accounting period. This type of error affects both the balance sheet and the income statement and is either a counterbalancing or a non-counterbalancing error.

Counterbalancing errors are errors that will be offset or that will self-correct over two periods. In the previous illustration, the failure to record accrued wages is considered a counterbalancing error because, after a two-year period, the error will no longer be present. In other words, the failure to record accrued wages in year one means that (1) wages expense for the first period is understated, (2) net income for the first period is overstated, (3) accrued wages payable (a liability) at the end of the first period is understated, and (4) retained earnings at the end of the first period is overstated. In period two, wages expense is overstated and net income is understated, but both accrued wages payable (a liability) and retained earnings at the end of the second period **are now correct. For the two years combined**, both wages expense and net income are correct, as are the ending balance sheet amounts of wages payable and retained earnings. Most errors in accounting that affect both the balance sheet and income statement are counterbalancing errors.

Non-counterbalancing errors are errors that are not offset in the next accounting period. An example is the failure to capitalize equipment that has a useful life of five years. If we expense this asset immediately, expenses will be overstated in the first period but understated in the next four periods. At the end of the second period, the error's effect is not fully offset. Net income is only correct overall at the end of five years, because the asset will have been fully depreciated at this point, assuming it has no residual value. Thus, **non-counterbalancing errors are those that take longer than two periods to correct themselves.**

Only in rare instances is an error never reversed. This would occur, for example, if land were initially expensed. Because land is not subject to depreciation, the error is not offset until the land is sold.

Counterbalancing Errors

The usual types of counterbalancing errors are illustrated on the following pages. In studying these illustrations, several points should be remembered. **First—and this is key— the entries will differ depending on whether or not the books have been closed for the period in which the error is found.**

1. When **the books have been closed**:
    (a) If the error is already counterbalanced, no entry is necessary.
    (b) If the error is not yet counterbalanced, an entry is necessary to adjust the present balance of retained earnings and the other affected balance sheet account(s).

2. When **the books have not been closed**:

    (a) If the error is already counterbalanced and the company is in the second year, an entry is necessary to correct the current period income statement account(s) and to adjust the beginning balance of retained earnings.

    (b) If the error is not yet counterbalanced, an entry is necessary to adjust the beginning balance of retained earnings and correct the affected current period income statement account(s) **and balance sheet account(s)**.

Second, if comparative statements are presented, it is necessary to restate the amounts for comparative purposes. **Restatement is necessary even if a correcting journal entry is not required**. To illustrate, assume that Sanford Cement Ltd. failed to accrue revenue in 2009 when it was earned, but recorded the revenue in 2010 when it was received. The error is discovered in 2012. No entry is necessary to correct this error, because the effects have been counterbalanced by the time the error is discovered in 2012. However, if comparative financial statements for 2009 through to 2012 are presented, the accounts and related amounts for the years 2009 and 2010 are restated correctly for financial reporting purposes.

The following are examples of counterbalancing errors. Income tax effects have been ignored for now. Work with the entries until you understand each one. In addition, the 2011 comparative financial statements would need to be restated.

1. **Failure to record accrued wages**. On December 31, 2011, accrued wages of $1,500 were not recognized. The entry in 2012 to correct this error, assuming that the books have not been closed for 2012, is:

Retained Earnings	1,500	
Wages Expense		1,500

A = L + SE
0   0   0
Cash flows: No effect

The rationale for this entry is as follows: When the accrued wages relating to 2011 were paid in 2012, an additional debit of $1,500 was made to 2012 Wages Expense, overstating this account by $1,500. Because 2011 accrued wages were not recorded as Wages Expense for 2011, net income for 2011 was overstated by $1,500. Because 2011 net income was overstated by $1,500, the 2012 opening Retained Earnings were also overstated by $1,500, because net income is closed to Retained Earnings.

If the books have been closed for 2012, no entry is made, because the error is counterbalanced.

2. **Failure to record prepaid expenses**. In January 2011, a two-year insurance policy costing $1,000 was purchased; Insurance Expense was debited, and Cash was credited. No adjusting entries were made at the end of 2011. The entry on December 31, 2012, to correct this error, assuming that the books have not been closed for 2012, is:

Insurance Expense	500	
Retained Earnings		500

A = L + SE
0   0   0
Cash flows: No effect

If the books are closed for 2012, no entry is made, because the error is counterbalanced.

3. **Understatement of unearned revenue**. On December 31, 2011, cash of $50,000 was received as a prepayment for renting office space for the following year. The entry

that was made when the rent payment was received was a debit to Cash and a credit to Rent Revenue. No adjusting entry was made as at December 31, 2011. The entry on December 31, 2012, to correct this error, assuming that the books have not been closed for 2012, is:

A = L + SE
0   0   0

Cash flows: No effect

Retained Earnings	50,000	
Rent Revenue		50,000

If the books are closed for 2012, no entry is made, because the error is counterbalanced.

4. **Overstatement of accrued revenue.** On December 31, 2011, interest income of $8,000 was accrued that applied to 2012. The entry made on December 31, 2011, was to debit Interest Receivable and credit Interest Income. The entry on December 31, 2012, to correct this error, assuming that the books have not been closed for 2012, is:

A = L + SE
0   0   0

Cash flows: No effect

Retained Earnings	8,000	
Interest Income		8,000

If the books have been closed for 2012, no entry is made, because the error is counterbalanced.

5. **Overstatement of purchases.** The accountant recorded a purchase of merchandise for $9,000 in 2011 that applied to 2012. The physical inventory for 2011 was correctly stated. The company uses the periodic inventory method. The entry on December 31, 2012, to correct this error, assuming that the books have not been closed, is:

A = L + SE
0   0   0

Cash flows: No effect

Purchases	9,000	
Retained Earnings		9,000

If the 2012 books were closed, no entry is made, because the error is counterbalanced.

6. **Understatement of ending inventory.** On December 31, 2011, the physical inventory count was understated by $25,000 because the inventory crew failed to count one section of a merchandise warehouse. The entry on December 31, 2012, to correct this error, assuming the 2012 books have not yet been closed and the ending inventory has not yet been adjusted to the inventory account, is:

A = L + SE
+25,000   +25,000

Cash flows: No effect

Inventory (beginning)	25,000	
Retained Earnings		25,000

If the books are closed for 2012, no entry needs to be made, because the error has been counterbalanced.

7. **Overstatement of purchases and inventories.** Sometimes, both the physical inventory and the purchases are incorrectly stated. Assume that 2012 purchases of $9,000 were incorrectly recorded as 2011 purchases and that 2011 ending inventory was overstated by the same amount. The entry on December 31, 2012, to correct this

error before the 2012 books are closed and the correct ending inventory is adjusted to the inventory account is:

Purchases	9,000	
Inventory (beginning)		9,000

A = L + SE
−9,000   −9,000
Cash flows: No effect

The net income for 2011 is correct because the overstatement of purchases was offset by the overstatement of ending inventory in cost of goods sold. Similar to the other examples of counterbalancing errors, no entry is required if the 2012 books have already been closed. Regardless, the 2011 comparative statements need to be restated.

Non-counterbalancing Errors

Because non-counterbalancing errors do not self-correct over a two-year period, the entries for them are more complex, and correcting entries are needed even if the books have been closed. The best approach is to identify what the relevant account balances are in the accounts, what they should be, and then bring them to the correct balances through correcting entries. Examples follow. Here, as well, the prior year's financial statements need to be restated.

1. **Failure to record depreciation**. Assume that a machine with an estimated five-year useful life was purchased on January 1, 2011, for $10,000. The accountant incorrectly expensed this machine in 2011 and the error was discovered in 2012. If we assume that the company uses straight-line depreciation on similar assets, the entry on December 31, 2012, to correct this error, given that the 2012 books are not yet closed, is:

Machinery	10,000	
Amortization Expense (2012)	2,000	
Retained Earnings		8,000
Accumulated Depreciation		4,000
Retained Earnings:		
Expense reported in 2011	$10,000	
Correct depreciation for 2011 (20% × $10,000)	(2,000)	
Retained earnings understated as at Dec. 31, 2011, by	$ 8,000	
Accumulated Depreciation, Dec. 31, 2012:		
Accumulated depreciation (20% × $10,000 × 2)	$ 4,000	

A = L + SE
+6,000   +6,000
Cash flows: No effect

If the books are closed for 2012, the entry is:

Machinery	10,000	
Retained Earnings		6,000
Accumulated Depreciation		4,000
Retained Earnings:		
Retained earnings understated as at Dec. 31, 2011, by	$ 8,000	
Correct depreciation for 2012 (20% × $10,000)	(2,000)	
Retained earnings understated as at Dec. 31, 2012, by	$ 6,000	

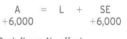

A = L + SE
+6,000   +6,000
Cash flows: No effect

2. **Failure to adjust for bad debts**. Assume that a company has been using the direct writeoff method when the allowance method should have been applied. Thus, the

following bad debt expense has been recognized as the debts have actually become uncollectible.

	2011	2012
From 2011 sales	$550	$690
From 2012 sales		700

The company estimates that an additional $1,400 will be written off in 2013, of which $300 applies to 2011 sales and $1,100 to 2012 sales.[15] The entry on December 31, 2012, to correct the accounts for bad debt expense, assuming that the books have not been closed for 2012, is:

$$
\begin{array}{l}
A = L + SE \\
-1,400 \quad\quad -1,400
\end{array}
$$

Cash flows: No effect

Bad Debt Expense	410	
Retained Earnings	990	
Allowance for Doubtful Accounts		1,400

Allowance for doubtful accounts:
Additional $300 for 2011 sales and $1,100 for 2012 sales = $1,400.

Bad debt expense corrections needed:	2011	2012
Accounts written off by year of sale ($550 + $690 = $1,240)	$1,240	$ 700
Additional bad debts anticipated (total of $1,400)	300	1,100
Correct amount of bad debt expense each year	1,540	1,800
Bad debt expense previously recorded	(550)	(1,390)
Bad debt expense adjustment needed	$ 990	$ 410

If the books have been closed for 2012, the entry is:

$$
\begin{array}{l}
A = L + SE \\
-1,400 \quad\quad -1,400
\end{array}
$$

Cash flows: No effect

Retained Earnings	1,400	
Allowance for Doubtful Accounts		1,400

Income Tax Effects

As mentioned earlier, the income tax effects are not reported with the above correcting entries in order to make it easier for you to focus on the effects of the errors themselves. Once you understand the correcting entries, it is easier to add the income tax effects, as we will do now.

If a correction **increases a previous year's income** (either by an increase in revenue or a decrease in expense), the income tax expense for that period will usually be increased: more income, more tax. If the correction **reduces a previous year's income** (either by a decrease in revenue or an increase in expense), the income tax expense for that period will usually be reduced: less income, less tax. The net correction to retained earnings, therefore, is made net of tax. Note that for counterbalancing errors, the income tax effects also offset each other over the two-year period, assuming tax rates have not changed.

---

[15] Note that this example may be using hindsight in order to derive the amounts needing correction in each specific year, and therefore, the entity may contend that it is impracticable to retrospectively restate past amounts. Retrospective restatement does not endorse the use of hindsight, so the adjustment may actually need to be made on a partial retrospective basis or even only in the current year.

Because the tax return for the previous period has already been filed, most adjustments of the previous year's income affects Income Tax Payable. The Future Tax Asset/Liability account is affected only when the treatment for income taxes in the previous year is a permitted tax treatment. Examples include the depreciation and bad debt non-counterbalancing error situations below. In both these cases, taxable income was correct as it was calculated in the prior year, but now the amount of the related temporary difference has changed.

Illustration 21A-1 identifies the **correcting entries** that are needed, including the tax effects for the counterbalancing and non-counterbalancing examples we just walked through. A 40% income tax rate is assumed for all years.

Illustration 21A-1

Correcting Entries with Income Tax Effects

BOOKS FOR 2012					
Error	**Not Closed**		**Closed**		
COUNTERBALANCING ERRORS					
1. Accrued Wages					
Retained Earnings	900		–No Entry–		
Income Tax Payable	600				
Wages Expense		1,500			
2. Prepaid expenses					
Insurance Expense	500		–No Entry–		
Retained Earnings		300			
Income Tax Payable		200			
3. Unearned Revenue					
Retained Earnings	30,000		–No Entry–		
Income Tax Payable	20,000				
Rent Revenue		50,000			
4. Accrued Revenue					
Retained Earnings	4,800		–No Entry–		
Income Tax Payable	3,200				
Interest Income		8,000			
5. Overstatement of Purchases					
Purchases	9,000		–No Entry–		
Retained Earnings		5,400			
Income Tax Payable		3,600			
6. Understatement of Ending Inventory					
Inventory (beginning)	25,000		–No Entry–		
Retained Earnings		15,000			
Income Tax Payable		10,000			
7. Overstatement of Purchases and Inventories					
Purchases	9,000		–No Entry–		
Inventory (beginning)		9,000			
NON-COUNTERBALANCING ERRORS					
1. Depreciation					
Machinery	10,000		Machinery	10,000	
Depreciation Expense	2,000		Accumulated Depreciation		4,000
Accumulated Depreciation		4,000	Retained Earnings		3,600
Retained Earnings		4,800	Future Tax Asset/Liability		2,400
Future Tax Asset/Liability		3,200			
2. Bad Debts					
Bad Debt Expense	410		Retained Earnings	840	
Retained Earnings	594		Future Tax Asset/Liability	560	
Future Tax Asset/Liability	396		Allowance for Doubtful		1,400
Allowance for Doubtful		1,400	Accounts		
Accounts					

Comprehensive Illustration: Numerous Errors

In some circumstances, a combination of errors occurs, and a work sheet is prepared to help with the analysis. To demonstrate the use of a work sheet, the following problem is presented for solution. The mechanics of how the work sheet is prepared should be clear from the format of the solution. The tax effects are omitted.

The income statements of Hudson Corporation for the three years ended December 31, 2010, 2011, and 2012, show the following net incomes:

2010	$17,400
2011	20,200
2012	11,300

An examination of the company's accounting records for these years reveals that several errors were made in arriving at the net incomes reported. The following errors were discovered:

1. Wages earned by workers but not paid at December 31 were consistently omitted from the records. The amounts omitted were:

December 31, 2010	$1,000
December 31, 2011	1,400
December 31, 2012	1,600

These amounts were recorded as expenses when they were paid; that is, in the year following the year when they were earned by the employees.

2. The merchandise inventory on December 31, 2010, was overstated by $1,900 as a result of errors made in the footings (totals) and extensions on the inventory sheets.

3. Insurance of $1,200 that is applicable to 2012 was expensed on December 31, 2011.

4. Interest receivable in the amount of $240 was not recorded on December 31, 2011.

5. On January 2, 2011, a piece of equipment costing $3,900 was sold for $1,800. At the date of sale, the equipment had accumulated depreciation of $2,400. The proceeds on the sale were credited to Miscellaneous Income in 2011. In addition, depreciation was recorded for this equipment in both 2011 and 2012 at the rate of 10% of cost.

The **first** step in preparing the work sheet is to prepare a schedule showing the corrected net incomes for each of the years ended December 31, 2010, 2011, and 2012. Each correction of the amount that was originally reported is clearly labelled. The **next step** is to indicate the balance sheet accounts affected as at December 31, 2012, if any. The completed work sheet for Hudson Corporation is provided in Illustration 21A-2.

	A	B	C	D	E	G	H	I
1		**Hudson Corporation**						
		Work Sheet to Correct Income and Balance Sheet Errors						
2		**Work Sheet Analysis of Changes in Net Income**				**Balance Sheet Correction at December 31, 2012**		
3	Year	2010	2011	2012	Totals	Debit	Credit	Account
4	Net income as reported	$17,400	$20,200	$11,300	$48,900			
5	Wages unpaid, 12/31/10	(1,000)	1,000		–0–			
6	Wages unpaid, 12/31/11		(1,400)	1,400	–0–			
7	Wages unpaid, 12/31/12			(1,600)	(1,600)		$1,600	Wages Payable
8	Inventory overstatement, 12/31/10	(1,900)	1,900		–0–			
9	Unexpired insurance, 12/31/11		1,200	(1,200)	–0–			
10	Interest receivable, 12/31/11		240	(240)	–0–			
11	Correction for entry made on sale of equipment, 1/2/11[a]		(1,500)		(1,500)	$2,400		Accumulated Depreciation
12							3,900	Machinery
13	Overcharge of depreciation, 2011		390		390	390		Accumulated Depreciation
14	Overcharge of depreciation, 2012			390	390	390		Accumulated Depreciation
15	Corrected net income	$14,500	$22,030	$10,050	$46,580			
16								
17	[a]Calculations							
	Cost	$ 3,900						
	Accumulated depreciation	2,400						
	Carrying amount	1,500						
	Proceeds from sale	1,800						
	Gain on sale	300						
	Income reported	1,800						
	Adjustment	$(1,500)						
18								

Illustration 21A-2

Work Sheet to Correct Income and Balance Sheet Errors

Correcting entries **if the books have not been closed for 2012** are:

Retained Earnings	1,400	
Wages Expense		1,400

(To correct wages expense charged to 2012 that should have been charged to prior year.)

Wages Expense	1,600	
Wages Payable		1,600

(To record wages expense and accrual for wages at 2012 year end.)

| Insurance Expense | 1,200 | |
| Retained Earnings | | 1,200 |

(To correct insurance expense charged to 2011 that should have been charged to 2012.)

| Interest Income | 240 | |
| Retained Earnings | | 240 |

(To correct interest income recognized in 2012 that should have been reported in 2011.)

Retained Earnings	1,500	
Accumulated Depreciation	2,400	
Machinery		3,900

(To record writeoff of machinery and correction of the gain reported in 2011.)

Accumulated Depreciation	780	
Depreciation Expense		390
Retained Earnings		390

(To correct charges made in error to depreciation expense in 2011 and 2012.)

If the books have been closed for 2012, the correcting entries are:

| Retained Earnings | 1,600 | |
| Wages Payable | | 1,600 |

(To correct the cumulative effect of accrued wages errors to December 31, 2012.)

Retained Earnings	1,500	
Accumulated Depreciation	2,400	
Machinery		3,900

(To record writeoff of machinery and correction of the gain reported in 2011.)

| Accumulated Depreciation | 780 | |
| Retained Earnings | | 780 |

(To correct charges made in error to depreciation expense in 2011 and 2012.)

Preparation of Comparative Financial Statements

Up to now, our discussion of error analysis has been concerned with identifying the type of error involved and then accounting for its correction in the accounting records. Equally important is how the corrections are presented on comparative financial statements. In annual reports or other documents, five- or 10-year financial summaries are often provided. Illustration 21A-3, explained below, shows how a typical year's financial statements are restated, assuming that many different errors have been corrected. Dick & Wally's Outlet Ltd. is a small retail outlet in the town of Priestly Sound. Lacking expertise in accounting, its management does not keep adequate records. As a result, numerous errors occurred in recording accounting information:

1. The bookkeeper, by mistake, failed to record a cash receipt of $1,000 on the sale of merchandise in 2012.

2. Accrued wages at the end of 2011 were $2,500; at the end of 2012, $3,200. The company does not accrue wages; all wages are charged to Administrative Expense.

3. The 2012 beginning inventory was understated by $5,400 because goods in transit at the end of last year were not counted. The purchase entry was made early in 2012.

4. No allowance had been set up for estimated uncollectible receivables. Dick and Wally decided to set up such an allowance for the estimated probable losses at December 31, 2012, for 2011 accounts of $700, and 2012 accounts of $1,500. They also decided to correct the charge against each year so that it shows the losses (actual and estimated) relating to that year's sales. Accounts have been written off to bad debt expense (selling expense) as follows:

	In 2011	In 2012
2011 accounts	$400	$2,000
2012 accounts		1,600

5. Unexpired insurance not recorded at the end of 2011 was $600, and at the end of 2012, $400. All insurance is charged to Administrative Expense.

6. An account payable at the end of 2012 of $6,000 should have been a note payable.

7. During 2011, an asset that cost $10,000 and had a carrying amount of $4,000 was sold for $7,000. At the time of sale, Cash was debited and Miscellaneous Revenue was credited for $7,000.

8. As a result of transaction 7, the company overstated depreciation expense (an administrative expense) in 2011 by $800 and in 2012 by $1,200.

9. In a physical count, the company determined the 2012 ending inventory to be $40,000.

Illustration 21A-3 presents a work sheet that begins with the unadjusted trial balance of Dick & Wally's Outlet. The correcting entries and their effect on the financial statements can be determined by examining the work sheet. The numbers in parentheses show which transaction number the correction relates to.

Dick & Wally's Outlet
Work Sheet Analysis to Adjust Financial Statements for the Year 2012

	Trial balance Unadjusted		Adjustments		Income Statement Adjusted		Balance Sheet Adjusted	
	Debit	Credit	Debit	Credit	Debit	Credit	Debit	Credit
Cash	3,100		(1) 1,000				4,100	
Accounts Receivable	17,600						17,600	
Notes Receivable	8,500						8,500	
Inventory, Jan. 1, 2012	34,000		(3) 5,400		39,400			
Property, Plant, and Equipment	112,000			(7) 10,000[a]			102,000	
Accumulated Depreciation		83,500	(7) 6,000[a]					75,500
			(8) 2,000					
Investments	24,300						24,300	
Accounts Payable		14,500	(6) 6,000					8,500
Notes Payable		10,000		(6) 6,000				16,000
Share Capital		43,500						43,500
Retained Earnings		20,000	(4) 2,700[b]	(3) 5,400				
			(7) 4,000[a]	(5) 600				
			(2) 2,500	(8) 800				17,600
Sales		94,000		(1) 1,000		95,000		
Purchases	21,000				21,000			
Selling Expenses	22,000			(4) 500[b]	21,500			
Administrative Expenses	23,000		(2) 700	(5) 400	22,700			
			(5) 600	(8) 1,200				
Totals	265,500	265,500						
Wages Payable				(2) 3,200				3,200
Allowance for Doubtful Accounts				(4) 2,200[b]				2,200
Unexpired Insurance			(5) 400				400	
Inventory, Dec. 31, 2012						(9) 40,000	(9) 40,000	
Net Income					30,400			30,400
Totals			31,300	31,300	135,000	135,000	196,900	196,900

[a] Machinery			[b] Bad Debts	For Sales in	
				2011	2012
Proceeds from sale	$ 7,000		Bad debts charged	$2,400	$1,600
Carrying amount of machinery	4,000		Other bad debts anticipated	700	1,500
Gain on sale	3,000			3,100	3,100
Income credited	7,000		Charges made in year	400	3,600
Retained earnings adjustment	$(4,000)		Bad debt adjustment	$2,700	$ (500)

Illustration 21A-3

Work Sheet to Adjust Financial Statements

Summary of Learning Objective for Appendix 21A

Glossary

9 Correct the effects of errors and prepare restated financial statements.

Three types of errors can occur: (1) Errors that affect only the balance sheet. (2) Errors that affect only the income statement. (3) Errors that affect both the balance sheet and the income statement. This last type of error is classified either as (a) a counterbalancing error, where the effects are offset or corrected over two periods; or (b) a non-counterbalancing error, where the effects take longer than two periods to correct themselves.

KEY TERMS

counterbalancing errors, 1428

non-counterbalancing errors, 1428

Brief Exercises

Note: All assignment material with an asterisk (*) relates to the appendix to the chapter.

BE21-1 Mann Corporation decided at the beginning of 2011 to change from the capital cost allowance (CCA) method of depreciating its capital assets (a declining-balance method that is a non-GAAP method because CCA does not remove the asset's carrying amount on disposition) to straight-line depreciation because the straight-line method will result in more relevant financial information and is a GAAP compliant method. The company will continue to use the capital cost allowance method for tax purposes. For years prior to 2011, total depreciation expense under the two methods is as follows: capital cost allowance, $117,000; and straight-line, $76,000. The tax rate is 30%. Mann follows accounting standards for private enterprises (ASPE). Prepare Mann's 2011 journal entry to record the accounting change. **(LO 4)**

BE21-2 Use the information in BE21-1, but assume instead that the change to the straight-line method was made because straight-line better represents the pattern of benefits provided by the capital assets. Prepare Mann's 2011 journal entry, if any, to record the change in estimate. **(LO 3)**

BE21-3 Bailey Corp. changed depreciation methods in 2011 from straight-line to double-declining-balance because management argued that the change would improve the relevance of the information to financial statement readers. The assets involved were acquired early in 2008 for $185,000 and had an estimated useful life of eight years, with no residual value. The 2011 income using the double-declining-balance method was $490,000. Bailey had 10,000 common shares outstanding all year. What is the effect of the accounting change on the reported income and EPS for 2011? Bailey follows IFRS. Ignore income taxes. **(LO 4)**

BE21-4 Bronson, Inc. changed from the average cost formula to the FIFO cost formula in 2011. The increase in the prior year's income before taxes as a result of this change is $435,000. The tax rate is 35%. Prepare Bronson's 2011 journal entry to record the change in accounting principle, assuming that the company's financial statements were determined to have better predictive value as a result of the change. **(LO 4)**

BE21-5 Corning Corporation purchased a computer system for $60,000 on January 1, 2010. It was depreciated based on a seven-year life and an $18,000 residual value. On January 1, 2012, Corning revised these estimates to a total useful life of four years and a residual value of $10,000. Prepare Corning's entry to record 2012 depreciation expense. Assume that Corning follows IFRS and uses straight-line depreciation. **(LO 3)**

BE21-6 In 2012, Dody Corporation discovered that equipment purchased on January 1, 2010, for $75,000 was expensed in error at that time. The equipment should have been depreciated over five years, with no residual value. The tax rate is 32%. Prepare Dody's 2012 journal entry to correct the error and record 2012 depreciation. **(LO 5)**

BE21-7 Roundtree Manufacturing Corp. is preparing its year-end financial statements following IFRS and is considering the accounting for the following items: **(LO 3, 4, 5, 6)**

1. The vice president of sales had indicated that one product line has lost its customer appeal and will be phased out over the next three years. Therefore, a decision has been made to lower the estimated lives on related production equipment from the remaining five years to three years.

2. The Hightone Building was converted from a sales office to offices for the Accounting Department at the beginning of this year. Therefore, the expense related to this building will now appear as an administrative expense rather than a selling expense on the current year's income statement.

3. Estimating the lives of new products in the Leisure Products Division has become very difficult because of the highly competitive conditions in this market. Therefore, the practice of deferring and amortizing preproduction costs has been abandoned in favour of expensing such costs as they are incurred.

Explain whether each of the above items is a change in principle, a change in estimate, or an error.

(LO 3, 4, 5, 6) **BE21-8** Palmer Corp. is evaluating the appropriate accounting for the following items under ASPE:

1. Management has decided to switch from the FIFO inventory valuation method to the average cost inventory valuation method for all inventories.

2. When the year-end physical inventory adjustment was made for the current year, the controller discovered that the prior year's physical inventory sheets for an entire warehouse were mislaid and excluded from last year's count.

3. Palmer's Custom Division manufactures large-scale, custom-designed machinery on a contract basis. Management decided to switch from the completed-contract method to the percentage-of-completion method of accounting for long-term contracts.

Explain whether each of the above items is a change in accounting principle, a change in estimate, or an error.

(LO 5, 9) ***BE21-9** At January 1, 2011, Motteray Corp. reported retained earnings of $2 million. In 2011, Motteray discovered that 2010 depreciation expense was understated in error by $500,000. In 2011, net income was $900,000 and dividends declared were $250,000. The tax rate is 40%. Motteray follows accounting standards for private enterprises. (a) Prepare a 2011 statement of retained earnings for Motteray Corp. (b) Briefly explain how your answer would change if Motteray were to follow IFRS.

(LO 9) ***BE21-10** Indicate the effect—Understated (U), Overstated (O), or No Effect (NE)—that each of the following errors has on 2011 net income and 2012 net income:

	2011	2012
Wages payable were not recorded at Dec. 31, 2011.	____	____
Equipment purchased in 2010 was expensed.	____	____
Equipment purchased in 2011 was expensed.	____	____
Ending inventory at Dec. 31, 2011, was overstated.	____	____
Patent amortization was not recorded in 2012.	____	____

Exercises

(LO 3, 4, 5, 6) **E21-1** **(Accounting for Accounting Changes)** The following are various types of accounting changes:

____ **1.** Change in a plant asset's residual value

____ **2.** Change due to an overstatement of inventory

____ **3.** Change from sum-of-the-years'-digits to straight-line method of depreciation because of a change in the pattern of benefits received

____ **4.** Change in a primary source of GAAP

____ **5.** Change in decision by management from not capitalizing interest during construction to capitalizing it because the change increases the relevance of the resulting information. The company is reporting a self-constructed asset for the first time.

____ **6.** Change in the rate used to calculate warranty costs

____ **7.** Change from an unacceptable accounting principle to an acceptable accounting principle

____ **8.** Change in a patent's amortization period

____ **9.** Change from the zero-profit method to the percentage-of-completion method on construction contracts because the company now accepts longer commercial contracts rather than shorter residential contracts

____ **10.** Recognition of additional income taxes owing from three years ago as a result of improper calculations by the accountant, who was not familiar with income tax legislation and income tax returns

Instructions

(a) For each change or error, use the following code letters to indicate how it would be accounted for assuming the company follows IFRS:

Accounted for in the current year only (CY)
Accounted for prospectively (P)
Accounted for retrospectively (R)
None of the above, or unable to tell. Explain. (NA)

(b) Identify the type of change for each of the situations in items 1 to 10.

(c) Now assume that the company follows ASPE. Identify the situations in part (a) that would be accounted for differently under ASPE than IFRS.

(d) What are the conditions that must exist for an entity to be allowed to change an accounting policy?

Digging
Deeper

E21-2 **(Error and Change in Estimate—Depreciation)** Makins Ltd. purchased a machine on January 1, 2009, for **(LO 4, 5, 6)**
$1,350,000. At that time, it was estimated that the machine would have a 10-year life and no residual value. On December
31, 2012, the firm's accountant found that the entry for depreciation expense had been omitted in 2010. In addition, management informed the accountant that it planned to switch to double-declining-balance depreciation because of a change
in the pattern of benefits received, starting with the year 2012. At present, the company uses the straight-line method for
depreciating equipment.

Instructions

(a) Prepare the general journal entries, if any, the accountant should make at December 31, 2012. (Ignore tax effects.)

(b) Assume the same information as above, but factor in tax effects. The company has a 34% tax rate for 2009 to 2012.

E21-3 **(Change in Policy and Change in Estimate—Depreciation)** Khim Inc. acquired the following assets in **(LO 4, 6)**
January 2008:

Equipment: estimated service life, 5 years; residual value, $15,000	$465,000
Building: estimated service life, 30 years; no residual value	$780,000

The equipment was depreciated using the double-declining-balance method for the first three years for financial reporting purposes. In 2011, the company decided to change the method of calculating depreciation to the straight-line method
for the equipment because of a change in the pattern of benefits received, but no change was made in the estimated service life or residual value. It was also decided to change the building's total estimated service life from 30 years to 40 years,
with no change in the estimated residual value. The building is depreciated on the straight-line method.

Instructions

(a) Prepare the journal entry to record depreciation expense for the equipment in 2011. (Ignore tax effects and round to
the nearest dollar.)

(b) Prepare the journal entry to record the depreciation expense for the building in 2011. (Ignore tax effects and round
to the nearest dollar.)

E21-4 **(Depreciation Changes)** On January 1, 2007, Zui Corporation purchased a building and equipment that had **(LO 4, 6)**
the following useful lives, residual values, and costs:

Building: 40-year estimated useful life, $50,000 residual value, $1,200,000 cost
Equipment: 12-year estimated useful life, $10,000 residual value, $130,000 cost

The building was depreciated under the double-declining-balance method through 2010. In 2011, the company decided
to switch to the straight-line method of depreciation because of a change in the pattern of benefits received. In 2012, Zui
decided to change the equipment's total useful life to nine years, with a residual value of $5,000 at the end of that time.
The equipment is depreciated using the straight-line method.

Instructions

(a) Prepare the journal entry(ies) necessary to record the depreciation expense on the building in 2011. (Ignore tax
effects.)

(b) Calculate the depreciation expense on the equipment for 2011. (Ignore tax effects.)

(LO 4, 5) **E21-5** **(Accounting Change—Inventory)** Linden Corporation started operations on January 1, 2006, and has used the FIFO method of inventory valuation since its inception. In 2012, it decides to switch to the average cost method. You are provided with the following information.

	Net Income		Retained Earnings (Ending Balance)
	Under FIFO	Under Average Cost	Under FIFO
2006	$100,000	$ 92,000	$100,000
2007	70,000	65,000	160,000
2008	90,000	85,000	235,000
2009	120,000	130,000	340,000
2010	300,000	293,000	590,000
2011	305,000	310,900	780,000

Instructions

(a) What is the beginning retained earnings balance at January 1, 2008, if Linden prepares comparative financial statements starting in 2008?

(b) What is the beginning retained earnings balance at January 1, 2011, if Linden prepares comparative financial statements starting in 2011?

(c) What is the beginning retained earnings balance at January 1, 2012, if Linden prepares single-period financial statements for 2012?

(d) What is the net income reported by Linden in the 2011 income statement if it prepares comparative financial statements starting in 2009?

(LO 4, 6) **E21-6** **(Change in Estimate—Depreciation)** Ingles Corp. changed from the straight-line method of depreciation on its plant assets acquired early in 2009 to the double-declining-balance method in 2011 because of a change in the pattern of benefits received (before finalizing its 2011 financial statements). The assets had an eight-year life and no expected residual value. Information related to both methods follows:

Year	Double-Declining-Balance Depreciation	Straight-Line Depreciation	Difference
2009	$250,000	$125,000	$125,000
2010	187,500	125,000	62,500
2011	140,625	125,000	15,625

Net income for 2010 was reported at $270,000; net income for 2011 before depreciation and income tax is $300,000. Assume an income tax rate of 30%.

Instructions

The change from the straight-line method to the double-declining-balance method is considered a change in estimate.

(a) What net income is reported for 2011?

(b) What is the amount of the adjustment to opening retained earnings as at January 1, 2011?

(c) What is the amount of the adjustment to opening retained earnings as at January 1, 2010?

(d) Prepare the journal entry(ies), if any, to record the adjustment in the accounting records, assuming that the accounting records for 2011 are not yet closed.

(LO 2, 4, 6) **E21-7** **(Determine Type of Change and Method of Accounting; Prepare Journal Entries)** Goodwin Corp., which began operations in January 2008, follows IFRS and is subject to a 40% income tax rate. In 2011, the following events took place:

1. The company switched from the zero-profit method to the percentage-of-completion method of accounting for its long-term construction projects. This change was a result of hiring an experienced estimator, which made it possible to estimate completion costs.

2. Due to a change in maintenance policy, the estimated useful life of Goodwin's fleet of trucks was lengthened.

3. It was discovered that a machine with an original cost of $100,000, residual value of $10,000, and useful life of four years was expensed in error on January 23, 2010, when it was acquired. This situation was discovered after preparing the 2011 adjusting entries but prior to calculating income tax expense and closing the accounts. Goodwin uses straight-line depreciation and takes a full year in the year of acquisition. The asset's cost had been appropriately added to the CCA class in 2010 before the CCA was calculated and claimed.

4. As a result of an inventory study early in 2011 after the accounts for 2010 had been closed, management decided that the average costing method would provide a more relevant presentation in the financial statements than does FIFO costing. In making the change to average cost, Goodwin determined the following:

Date	Inventory—FIFO Cost	Inventory—Average Cost
Dec. 31, 2010	$ 90,000	$ 80,000
Dec. 31, 2009	130,000	100,000
Dec. 31, 2008	200,000	150,000

Instructions

(a) Analyze each of the four 2011 events described above. For each event, identify the type of accounting change that has occurred, and indicate whether it should be accounted for with full retrospective application, partial retrospective application, or prospectively.

(b) Prepare any necessary journal entries that would be recorded in 2011 to account for events 3 and 4.

(ASCA adapted)

E21-8 **(Change in Policy—Long-Term Contracts)** Talia Construction Company Ltd. changed from the completed- **(LO 1, 4)** contract to the percentage-of-completion method of accounting for long-term construction contracts during 2011. For tax purposes, the company uses the completed-contract method and will continue this approach in the future. Talia follows ASPE. The appropriate information related to this change is as follows:

	Pre-Tax Income Using:		
	Percentage-of-Completion	Completed-Contract	Difference
2010	$820,000	$620,000	$200,000
2011	700,000	480,000	220,000

Instructions

(a) Assuming that the change qualifies as a change in accounting policy and that the tax rate is 35%, calculate the net income to be reported in 2011.

(b) Provide the necessary entry(ies) to adjust the accounting records for the change in accounting policy.

(c) If this change was made to reflect changed circumstances, how should the change be accounted for?

E21-9 **(Various Changes in Policy—Inventory Methods)** Avery Instrument Corp., a small company that follows **(LO 4, 5)** ASPE, began operations on January 1, 2008, and uses a periodic inventory system. The following net income amounts were calculated for Avery under three different inventory methods:

	FIFO	Average Cost	LIFO
2008	$26,000	$24,000	$20,000
2009	30,000	25,000	21,000
2010	28,000	27,000	24,000
2011	34,000	30,000	26,000

Instructions

Answer the following, ignoring tax considerations.

(a) Assume that in 2011 Avery changed from the average cost method to the FIFO method of costing inventories and it was agreed that the FIFO method provided more relevant financial statement information. Prepare the necessary journal entry for the change that took place during 2011, and provide all the information that is needed for reporting on a comparative basis.

(b) Assume that in 2011 Avery, which had been using the LIFO method since incorporation in 2008, changed to the FIFO method of costing inventories in order to comply with *CICA Handbook*, Part II, Section 3031, since LIFO is no longer a permitted inventory cost flow assumption under GAAP. The company applies the new policy retrospectively in accordance with the transitional provisions of the *Handbook* section. Prepare the necessary journal entry for the change, and provide all the information that is needed for reporting on a comparative basis.

E21-10 **(Change in Estimate, Error Correction)** Hollington Corp.'s controller was preparing the year-end adjusting **(LO 6, 7,** entries for the company's year ended December 31, 2011, when the V.P. Finance called him into her office. **8, 9)**

"Jean-Pierre," she said, "I've been considering a couple of matters that may require different treatment this year. First, the patent we acquired in early January 2009 for $410,000 will now likely be used until the end of 2013 and then be sold for $110,000. We previously thought that we'd use it for 10 years in total and then be able to sell it for $50,000. We've been using straight-line amortization on the patent.

"Secondly, I just discovered that the property we bought midway through 2008 for $135,000 was charged entirely to the Land account instead of being allocated between Land ($33,750) and Building ($101,250). The building should be of use to us for a total of 20 years. At that point, it'll be sold and we should be able to realize at least $37,000 from the sale of the building.

"Please let me know how these changes should be accounted for and what effect they will have on the financial statements."

Instructions

(a) Briefly identify the accounting treatment that should be applied to each accounting change that is required.

(b) Assuming that no amortization has been recorded as yet for the patent for 2011, prepare the December 31, 2011 entries that are necessary to make the accounting changes and to record patent amortization expense for 2011.

(c) Identify, and calculate where possible, the required disclosures for each change.

Digging Deeper

(d) Discuss the timing of applying the change in the patent's useful life and residual value. Since the determination of the change was done as part of the year-end process, should the change be applied to 2011 going forward, or to 2012 going forward? What are the implications of each approach?

(e) Could Hollington's controller consider the patent to be impaired instead of revising its useful life and residual value? What criteria should the controller look at to determine the appropriate treatment?

(ASCA adapted)

(LO 1, 5) E21-11 (Error Correction Entries) The first audit of the books of Gomez Limited was recently carried out for the year ended December 31, 2011. Gomez follows IFRS. In examining the books, the auditor found that certain items had been overlooked or might have been incorrectly handled in the past:

1. At the beginning of 2009, the company purchased a machine for $450,000 (residual value of $45,000) that had a useful life of six years. The bookkeeper used straight-line depreciation, but failed to deduct the residual value in calculating the depreciation base for the three years.

2. At the end of 2010, the company accrued sales salaries of $36,000 in excess of the correct amount.

3. A tax lawsuit that involved the year 2009 was settled late in 2011. It was determined that the company owed an additional $73,000 in taxes related to 2009. The company did not record a liability in 2009 or 2010, because the possibility of losing was considered remote. The company charged the $73,000 to retained earnings in 2011 as a correction of a prior year's error.

4. Gomez purchased another company early in 2007 and recorded goodwill of $450,000. Gomez amortized $22,500 of goodwill in 2007, and $45,000 in each subsequent year.

5. In 2011, the company changed its basis of inventory costing from FIFO to weighted average cost. The change's cumulative effect was to decrease net income of prior years by $39,000. The company debited this cumulative effect to Retained Earnings. The average cost method was used in calculating income for 2011.

6. In 2011, the company wrote off $87,000 of inventory that it discovered, in 2011, had been stolen from one of its warehouses in 2010. This loss was charged to a loss account in 2011.

Instructions

(a) Prepare the journal entries in 2011 to correct the books where necessary, assuming that the 2011 books have not been closed. Assume that the change from FIFO to weighted average cost can be justified as resulting in more relevant financial information. Disregard the effects of corrections on income tax.

(b) Identify the type of change for each of the six items.

(c) Redo part (a) but include the effects of income tax, assuming the company has a tax rate of 25%.

(LO 4, 5) E21-12 (Change in Estimate and Error, Financial Statements) The comparative statements for Hessey Inc. follow:

	2011	2010
Sales	$340,000	$270,000
Cost of sales	200,000	142,000
Gross profit	140,000	128,000
Expenses	88,000	50,000
Net income	$ 52,000	$ 78,000

	2011	2010
Retained earnings (Jan. 1)	$125,000	$ 72,000
Net income	52,000	78,000
Dividends	(30,000)	(25,000)
Retained earnings (Dec. 31)	$147,000	$125,000

The following additional information is provided:

1. In 2011, Hessey decided to change its depreciation method from sum-of-the-years'-digits to the straight-line method. The assets were purchased at the beginning of 2010 for $90,000 with an estimated useful life of four years and no residual value. (The 2011 income statement contains depreciation expense of $27,000 on the assets purchased at the beginning of 2010.)

2. In 2011, the company discovered that the ending inventory for 2010 was overstated by $20,000; ending inventory for 2011 is correctly stated.

Hessey follows ASPE.

Instructions

(a) Prepare the revised statements of retained earnings for 2010 and 2011, assuming comparative statements (ignore income tax effects). Do not prepare notes to the financial statements.

(b) Identify other possible accounting treatments for the change in depreciation method under alternative circumstances.

E21-13   (Accounting Change—Measurement Model for Investment Property) Holdem Properties Corporation **(LO 4)** purchased a parcel of land in 2010 for $1 million with the intent to construct a building on the property in the near future. At the time of purchase, and in the subsequent financial statements for the years ended December 31, 2010, and 2011, Holdem applied the cost model and measured and reported the land at its acquisition cost as allowed in IAS 16. Holdem follows IFRS and management decided in early 2012 that the land qualifies as an investment property under IAS 40 and that Holdem is to apply the fair value model of accounting for investment properties effective immediately because the company believes that changing the measurement model will provide more relevant information. Independent appraisals indicate that the land's fair value at December 31, 2010, and 2011, was $980,000 and $1,050,000, respectively. Holdem's reported retained earnings at December 31, 2010, and 2011, were $230,000 and $290,000, respectively.

Instructions

(a) Prepare the original balance sheets and income statements for the affected accounts.

(b) Prepare Holdem's journal entry, if any, to record the change in accounting policy.

(c) Prepare the restated balance sheets and income statements for the affected accounts.

E21-14   (Political Motivations for Policies) Ever since the unethical actions of some employees of Enron Corp. first **(LO 7)** came to light, ethics in accounting has been in the news with increasing frequency. The unethical actions of the employees essentially involved their selection of certain accounting policies for the company.

In many instances, GAAP does allow firms some flexibility in their choice of legitimate accounting policies. This is true, for example, in choosing an inventory cost formula. However, the company's choice of policies may ultimately be influenced by several specific factors.

Instructions

State three of these factors and explain why each of them may influence an accounting policy choice.

(CGA adapted)

(LO 9) *E21-15   **(Error Analysis and Correcting Entry)** You have been engaged to review the financial statements of Lindsay Corporation. In the course of your examination of the work of the bookkeeper hired during the year that just ended, you noticed a number of irregularities for the past fiscal year:

1. Year-end wages payable of $4,100 were not recorded, because the bookkeeper thought that "they were immaterial."

2. Accrued vacation pay for the year of $29,400 was not recorded, because the bookkeeper "never heard that you had to do it."

3. Insurance that covers a 12-month period and was purchased on November 1 was charged to insurance expense in the amount of $2,760 "because the amount of the cheque is about the same every year."

4. Reported sales revenue for the year was $2,310,000 and included all sales taxes charged for the year. The sales tax rate is 5%. Because the sales tax is forwarded to the provincial ministry of revenue, the bookkeeper thought that "the sales tax is a selling expense" and therefore debited the Sales Tax Expense account. At the end of the fiscal year, the balance in the Sales Tax Expense account was $101,300.

Instructions

Prepare the necessary correcting entries, assuming that Lindsay Corporation uses a calendar-year basis and that the books for the fiscal year that just ended are not yet closed.

(LO 9) *E21-16   **(Error Analysis)** Hennesey Tool Corporation's December 31 year-end financial statements contained the following errors:

	December 31, 2010	December 31, 2011
Ending inventory	$9,600 overstated	$8,100 understated
Depreciation expense	$2,300 overstated	—

An insurance premium of $66,000 covering the years 2010, 2011, and 2012 was prepaid in 2010, with the entire amount charged to expense that year. In addition, on December 31, 2011, fully depreciated machinery was sold for $15,000 cash, but the entry was not recorded until 2012. There were no other errors during 2010 or 2011, and no corrections have been made for any of the errors. Hennesey follows accounting standards for private enterprises.

Instructions

Answer the following, ignoring income tax considerations.

(a) Calculate the total effect of the errors on 2011 net income.

(b) Calculate the total effect of the errors on the amount of Hennesey's working capital at December 31, 2011.

(c) Calculate the total effect of the errors on the balance of Hennesey's retained earnings at December 31, 2011.

(d) Assume that the company has retained earnings on January 1, 2010 and 2011, of $1,250,000 and $1,607,000, respectively; net income for 2010 and 2011 of $422,000 and $375,000, respectively; and cash dividends declared for 2010 and 2011 of $65,000 and $45,000, respectively, before adjustment for the above items. Prepare a revised statement of retained earnings for 2010 and 2011.

Digging Deeper

(e) Outline the accounting treatment required by ASPE in this situation and explain how these requirements help investors.

(CGA adapted)

(LO 9) *E21-17   **(Error Analysis and Correcting Entries)** A partial trial balance of Kapoor Corporation at December 31, 2011, follows:

	Dr.	Cr.
Supplies on hand	$ 4,100	
Accrued salaries and wages		$ 3,900
Interest receivable on investments	5,500	
Prepaid insurance	93,000	
Unearned rent		–0–
Accrued interest payable		15,000

Additional adjusting data:

1. A physical count of supplies on hand on December 31, 2011, totalled $2,100. Through an oversight, the Accrued Salaries and Wages account was not changed during 2011. Accrued salaries and wages on December 31, 2011, amounted to $5,100.

2. The Interest Receivable on Investments account was also left unchanged during 2011. Accrued interest on investments amounted to $4,750 on December 31, 2011.

3. The unexpired portions of the insurance policies totalled $65,000 as at December 31, 2011.

4. A cheque for $44,000 was received on January 1, 2011, for the rent of a building for both 2011 and 2012. The entire amount was credited to rental income.

5. Depreciation for the year was recorded in error as $5,350 rather than the correct figure of $53,500.

6. A further review of prior years' depreciation calculations revealed that depreciation of $13,500 had not been recorded. It was decided that this oversight should be corrected by adjusting prior years' income.

Assume that Kapoor applies IFRS.

Instructions

(a) Assuming that the books have not been closed, what adjusting entries are necessary at December 31, 2011? Ignore income tax considerations.

(b) Assuming that the books have been closed, what adjusting entries are necessary at December 31, 2011? Ignore income tax considerations.

(c) Discuss the nature of the adjustments that are needed and how the situations could have occurred. Are they all accounting errors, or are they part of the normal accounting cycle? (Hint: Revisit the topic of adjusting entries in Chapter 3.) How should management present the adjustments for these items on its financial statements and in the notes?

Digging Deeper

*E21-18 **(Error Analysis)** The before-tax income for Luanne Hensall Corp. for 2010 was $101,000; for 2011, it was **(LO 9)** $77,400. However, the accountant noted that the following errors had been made:

1. Sales for 2010 included $38,200 that had been received in cash during 2010, but for which the related products were delivered in 2011. Title did not pass to the purchaser until 2011.

2. The inventory on December 31, 2010, was understated by $8,640.

3. The bookkeeper, in recording interest expense for both 2010 and 2011 on bonds payable, made the following entry each year:

| Interest Expense | 15,000 | |
| Cash | | 15,000 |

The bonds have a face value of $250,000 and pay a stated interest rate of 6%. They were issued at a discount of $15,000 on January 1, 2010, to yield an effective interest rate of 7%. (Use the effective interest method.)

4. Ordinary repairs to equipment had been charged in error to the Equipment account during 2010 and 2011. In total, repairs in the amount of $8,500 in 2010 and $9,400 in 2011 were charged in this way. The company applies a rate of 10% to the balance in the Equipment account at year end in determining its depreciation charges.

Assume that Luanne Hensall Corp. applies IFRS.

Instructions

(a) Prepare a schedule showing the calculation of corrected income before taxes for 2010 and 2011.

(b) Prepare the journal entries that the company's accountant would prepare in 2011, assuming the errors are discovered while the 2011 books are still open. Ignore income taxes.

*E21-19 **(Error Analysis)** When the records of Hilda Corporation were reviewed at the close of 2011, the following **(LO 9)** errors were discovered.

	2010			2011		
	Over-statement	Under-statement	No Effect	Over-statement	Under-statement	No Effect
1. Failure to record amortization of patent in 2011						
2. Failure to record the correct amount of ending 2010 inventory (the amount was understated because of a calculation error)						
3. Failure to record merchandise purchased in 2010 (it was also omitted from ending inventory in 2010 and remained unsold at the end of 2011)						
4. Failure to record accrued interest on notes payable in 2010 (the amount was recorded when paid in 2011)						
5. Failure to reflect supplies on hand on balance sheet at end of 2010						

Instructions

For each item, indicate by a check mark in the appropriate column whether the error resulted in an overstatement or understatement, or had no effect on net income for the years 2010 and 2011.

Problems

P21-1   Shawn Kimble Enterprises Ltd. follows IFRS and reported income before income taxes of $176,000, $180,000, and $198,000 in each of the years 2009, 2010, and 2011, respectively. The following information is also available.

1. In 2011, Shawn Kimble lost a court case in which it was the defendant. The case was a patent infringement suit, and Shawn Kimble must now pay a competitor $25,000 to settle the suit. No previous entries had been recorded in the books relative to this case as Shawn Kimble's management felt the company would win.

2. A review of the company's provision for uncollectible accounts during 2011 resulted in a determination that 1% of sales is the appropriate amount of bad debt expense to be charged to operations, rather than the 1.5% used for the preceding two years. Bad debt expense recognized in 2010 and 2009 was $25,000 and $17,500, respectively. The company would have recorded $22,500 of bad debt expense under the old rate for 2011. No entry has yet been made in 2011 for bad debt expense.

3. Shawn Kimble acquired land on January 1, 2008, at a cost of $40,000. The land was charged to the equipment account in error and has been depreciated since then on the basis of a five-year life with no residual value.

4. During 2011, the company changed from the double-declining-balance method of depreciation for its building to the straight-line method. Shawn Kimble changed to the straight-line method because its parent company uses straight-line, and it was required to match its policies to those of its parent company. Total depreciation under both methods for the past three years is as follows. Double-declining-balance depreciation has been used in 2011.

	Straight-Line	Double-Declining-Balance
2009	$32,000	$60,000
2010	32,000	57,000
2011	32,000	54,150

5. Late in 2011, Shawn Kimble determined that a piece of specialized equipment purchased in January 2008 at a cost of $54,000 with an estimated life of five years and residual value of $4,000 is now expected to continue in use until the end of 2015 and have a residual value of $2,000 at that time. The company has been using straight-line depreciation for this equipment, and depreciation for 2011 has already been recognized based on the original estimates.

6. The company has determined that a $225,000 note payable that it issued in 2009 has been incorrectly classified on its balance sheet. The note is payable in annual instalments of $25,000, but the full amount of the note has been shown as a long-term liability with no portion shown in current liabilities. Interest expense relating to the note has been properly recorded.

Instructions

(a) For each of the accounting changes, errors, or transactions, present the journal entry(ies) that Shawn Kimble needs to make to correct or adjust the accounts, assuming the accounts for 2011 have not yet been closed. If no entry is required, write "none" and briefly explain why. Ignore income tax considerations.

(b) Prepare the entries required in (a) but assume an income tax rate of 25% throughout the fiscal periods that are identified.

(c) For each of the accounting changes, identify the type of change involved and whether retrospective or prospective treatment is required.

Digging Deeper

P21-2 As at December 31, 2011, Oatfield Corporation is having its financial statements audited for the first time ever. The auditor has found the following items that might have an effect on previous years.

1. Oatfield purchased equipment on January 2, 2008, for $130,000. At that time, the equipment had an estimated useful life of 10 years, with a $10,000 residual value. The equipment is depreciated on a straight-line basis. On January 2, 2011, as a result of additional information, the company determined that the equipment had a total useful life of seven years with a $6,000 residual value.

2. During 2011, Oatfield changed from the double-declining-balance method for its building to the straight-line method because the company thinks the straight-line method now more closely follows the benefits received from using the assets. The current year depreciation was correctly calculated using the new method following straight-line depreciation. In case the following information was needed, the auditor provided calculations that present depreciation on both bases. The building had originally cost $1.2 million when purchased at the beginning of 2009 and has a residual value of $120,000. It is depreciated over 20 years. The original estimates of useful life and residual value are still accurate.

	2011	2010	2009
Straight-line	$54,000	$ 54,000	$ 54,000
Double-declining-balance	97,200	108,000	120,000

3. Oatfield purchased a machine on July 1, 2008, at a cost of $160,000. The machine has a residual value of $16,000 and a useful life of eight years. Oatfield's bookkeeper recorded straight-line depreciation during each year but failed to consider the residual value.

4. Prior to 2011, staff training costs were expensed immediately because they were immaterial, even though the company would benefit for at least three years because of improved worker efficiency. With the spurt in growth, these costs have now become material and management has decided to depreciate them over three years. Amounts expensed in 2008, 2009, and 2010 were $300, $500, and $1,000, respectively. During 2011, $4,500 was spent and the amount was debited to Deferred Training Costs (an asset account).

Instructions

Answer the following, ignoring income tax considerations.

(a) Prepare the necessary journal entries to record each of the changes or errors. The books for 2011 have not been closed.

(b) Calculate the 2011 depreciation expense on the equipment.

(c) Calculate the comparative net incomes for 2010 and 2011, starting with income before the effects of any of the changes identified above. Income before depreciation expense was $600,000 in 2011 and $420,000 in 2010.

P21-3 On December 31, 2011, before the books were closed, management and the accountant at Madrasa Inc. made the following determinations about three depreciable assets.

1. Depreciable asset A was purchased on January 2, 2008. It originally cost $540,000 and the straight-line method was chosen for depreciation. The asset was originally expected to be useful for 10 years and have no residual value. In 2011, the decision was made to change the depreciation method from straight-line to double-declining-balance, and the estimates relating to useful life and residual value remained unchanged.

2. Depreciable asset B was purchased on January 3, 2007. It originally cost $180,000 and the straight-line method was chosen for depreciation. The asset was expected to be useful for 15 years and have no residual value. In 2011, the decision was made to shorten this asset's total life to nine years and to estimate the residual value at $3,000.

3. Depreciable asset C was purchased on January 5, 2007. The asset's original cost was $160,000 and this amount was entirely expensed in 2007 in error. This particular asset has a 10-year useful life and no residual value. The straight-line method is appropriate.

Additional data:

1. Income in 2011 before depreciation expense amounted to $400,000.

2. Depreciation expense on assets other than A, B, and C totalled $55,000 in 2011.

3. Income in 2010 was reported at $370,000.

4. In both 2010 and 2011, 100,000 common shares were outstanding. No dividends were declared in either year.

Madrasa follows IFRS.

Instructions

Answer the following questions, ignoring all income tax effects.

(a) Prepare all necessary entries in 2011 to record these determinations.

(b) Calculate the adjusted net income and earnings per share for 2010 and 2011.

(c) Prepare comparative retained earnings statements for Madrasa Inc. for 2010 and 2011. The company reported retained earnings of $200,000 at December 31, 2009.

(d) Prepare the required note disclosures for each of these changes.

Digging
Deeper

(e) How would the changes to Madrasa's depreciable assets be reflected on the statement of cash flows?

P21-4   Both the management of Kimmel Instrument Corporation, a small company that follows IFRS, and its independent auditors recently concluded that the company's results of operations will have greater predictive value in future years if Kimmel changes its method of costing inventory from FIFO to average cost. The following data are a five-year income summary and a schedule of what the inventories might have been if they had been stated using the average cost method.

KIMMEL INSTRUMENT CORPORATION
Statement of Income and Retained Earnings for the Years Ended May 31

	2007	2008	2009	2010	2011
Sales—net	$13,964	$15,506	$16,673	$18,221	$18,898
Cost of goods sold					
Beginning inventory	1,000	1,100	1,000	1,115	1,237
Purchases	13,000	13,900	15,000	15,900	17,100
Ending inventory	(1,100)	(1,000)	(1,115)	(1,237)	(1,369)
Total	12,900	14,000	14,885	15,778	16,968
Gross profit	1,064	1,506	1,788	2,443	1,930
Administrative expenses	700	763	832	907	989
Income before taxes	364	743	956	1,536	941
Income taxes (50%)	182	372	478	768	471
Net income	182	371	478	768	470
Retained earnings—beginning	1,206	1,388	1,759	2,237	3,005
Retained earnings—ending	$ 1,388	$ 1,759	$ 2,237	$ 3,005	$ 3,475
Earnings per share	$ 1.82	$ 3.71	$ 4.78	$ 7.68	$ 4.70

KIMMEL INSTRUMENT CORPORATION
SCHEDULE OF INVENTORY BALANCES USING AVERAGE COST METHOD
Year Ended May 31

2006	2007	2008	2009	2010	2011
$950	$1,124	$1,091	$1,270	$1,480	$1,699

Instructions

(a) Prepare comparative statements for the five years that would be suitable for inclusion in the historical summary portion of Kimmel's annual report, assuming that Kimmel had changed its inventory costing method to average cost in 2011. Indicate the effects on net income and earnings per share for the years involved. (All amounts except EPS are rounded up to the nearest dollar.)

(b) Prepare the statement of retained earnings for 2011, with comparative statements for 2010 and 2009 to be issued to shareholders, assuming retrospective treatment.

(c) Identify all balance sheet accounts that require restatement on the comparative May 31, 2010 and 2009 balance sheets issued to shareholders in 2011.

(d) Assume that the data for the years 2006 to 2010 were not available. Briefly explain how to account for this inability to apply full retrospective application under both ASPE and IFRS, and prepare the statement of retained earnings for 2011, with a comparative statement for 2010 to be issued to shareholders as an illustration to aid in the explanation.

P21-5 McIntosh Corporation has decided that, in preparing its 2011 financial statements under IFRS, two changes should be made from the methods used in prior years:

1. **Depreciation.** McIntosh has always used the CCA method for tax and financial reporting purposes (as a variant of the declining-balance method). Prior to 2011, the company's only investors were members of the McIntosh family. Accordingly, the company did not have audited financial statements in the past, and it used CCA for financial reporting purposes as many private companies do that do not need their statements audited. The CCA method was more efficient in preparing financial information. During 2011, however, the company obtained financing through a share issuance. With the larger number of investors now using its financial statements, the company reviewed its depreciation method in preparation for an audit. Management has decided that the declining balance method would have been a more appropriate method for financial reporting, and the following schedule identifies the excess of CCA claimed in the past and expected for the current year over the declining balance amounts that should have been reported.

	Excess of CCA for Tax Purposes over Declining-Balance Depreciation Calculated for Financial Statement Purposes
Prior to 2010	$1,365,000
2010	106,050
2011	103,950
	$1,575,000

Depreciation is charged to cost of sales and to selling, general, and administrative expenses on the basis of 75% and 25%, respectively.

2. **Bad debt expense.** In the past, McIntosh recognized bad debt expense equal to 1.5% of net sales. After careful review, it has been decided that a rate of 1.75% is more appropriate for 2011. Bad debt expense is charged to selling, general, and administrative expenses. The following information is taken from preliminary financial statements, which were prepared before including the effects of the two changes.

McINTOSH CORPORATION
Condensed Balance Sheet
December 31, 2011

Assets	2011	2010
Current assets*	$43,561,000	$43,900,000
Plant assets, at cost	45,792,000	43,974,000
Less: Accumulated depreciation	23,761,000	22,946,000
	$65,592,000	$64,928,000
Liabilities and Shareholders' Equity		
Current liabilities	$21,124,000	$23,650,000
Long-term debt	15,154,000	14,097,000
Share capital	11,620,000	11,620,000
Retained earnings	17,694,000	15,561,000
	$65,592,000	$64,928,000

*Includes future income tax asset of $225,000 (2011) and $234,000 (2010), with the latter amount being the result of deductible temporary differences that occurred before 2010.

McINTOSH CORPORATION
Income Statement
Year Ended December 31, 2011

	2011	2010
Net sales	$80,520,000	$78,920,000
Cost of goods sold	54,847,000	53,074,000
	25,673,000	25,846,000
Selling, general, and administrative expenses	19,540,000	18,411,000
	6,133,000	7,435,000
Other expense, net	(1,198,000)	(1,079,000)
Income before income taxes	4,935,000	6,356,000
Income taxes	2,220,750	2,860,200
Net income	$ 2,714,250	$ 3,495,800

There have been no temporary differences between any book and tax items prior to the above changes except for those that involve the allowance for doubtful accounts. For tax purposes, bad debts are deductible only when they are written off. The tax rate is 45%.

Instructions

(a) For each of the items that follow, calculate the amounts that would appear on the comparative (2011 and 2010) financial statements of McIntosh Corporation after adjustment for the two accounting changes. Show amounts for both 2011 and 2010, and prepare supporting schedules as necessary.

   1. Accumulated depreciation

   2. Future tax asset/liability

   3. Selling, general, and administrative expenses

   4. Current portion of income tax expense

   5. Future portion of income tax expense

(b) Prepare the comparative financial statements that will be issued to shareholders for McIntosh's year ended December 31, 2011.

P21-6   The founder, president, and major shareholder of Hawthorne Corp. recently sold his controlling interest in the company to a national distributor in the same line of business. The change in ownership was effective June 30, 2011, halfway through Hawthorne's current fiscal year.

During the due diligence process of acquiring the company and over the last six months of 2011, the new senior management team had a chance to review the company's accounting records and policies. Hawthorne follows accounting standards for private enterprises. Although EPS are not part of ASPE, management calculates EPS for its own purposes and applies the IFRS guidelines. By the end of 2011, the following decisions had been made:

   1. Hawthorne's policy of expensing all interest as incurred will be changed to correspond to the policy of the controlling shareholder whereby interest on self-constructed assets is capitalized. This policy will be applied retrospectively, and going forward it will simplify the consolidation process for the parent company. The major effect of this policy is to reduce interest expense in 2009 by $9,200 and to increase the cost of equipment by the same amount. The equipment was put into service early in 2010. Hawthorne uses straight-line depreciation for equipment and a five-year life. Because the interest has already been deducted for tax purposes, the change in policy results in a taxable temporary difference.

   2. Deferred charges of $12,000 remained in long-term assets at December 31, 2010. These were being written off on a straight-line basis with another three years remaining at that time. On reviewing the December 31, 2011 balances (after an additional year of depreciation), management decided that there were no further benefits to be received from these deferrals and there likely had not been any benefits for the past two years. The original costs were tax deductible when incurred.

   3. A long-term contract with a preferred customer was completed in December 2011. When discussing payment with the customer, it came to light that a down payment of $30,000 made by the customer on the contract at the end of 2009 had been taken into revenue (and into taxable income) when received. The revenue should have been recognized in 2011 on completion of the contract.

Hawthorne's financial statements (summarized) were as follows at December 31, 2010 and 2011, before any corrections related to the information above. The December 31, 2011 statements are in draft form only and the 2011 accounts have not yet been closed.

Statement of Financial Position
December 31

Assets	2011	2010	Liabilities and Equity	2011	2010
Current assets	$192,300	$168,400	Current liabilities	$117,000	$103,000
Long-term assets	322,000	311,000	Long-term liabilities	166,000	153,000
	$514,300	$479,400	Share capital (10,000 shares)	50,000	50,000
			Retained earnings	181,300	173,400
				$514,300	$479,400

Income Statement
Year Ended December 31

	2011	2010
Revenues	$475,000	$460,000
Expenses	378,000	376,000
	97,000	84,000
Income tax (30% effective rate)	29,100	25,200
Net income	$ 67,900	$ 58,800
Earnings per share	$ 6.79	$ 5.88
Dividends declared, per share	$ 6.00	$ 2.50

Instructions

(a) Prepare any December 31, 2011 journal entries that are necessary to put into effect the decisions made by senior management.

(b) Prepare the comparative statement of financial position, income statement, and statement of retained earnings that will be issued to shareholders for the year ended December 31, 2011.

(c) Prepare the required note disclosures for the accounting changes.

(d) Assume now that Hawthorne follows IFRS instead of ASPE. Briefly comment on the changes, if any, to the accounting treatment for the three decisions in items 1 to 3 above.

P21-7 Aston Corporation performs year-end planning in November each year before its fiscal year ends in December. The preliminary estimated net income following IFRS is $3 million. The CFO, Rita Warren, meets with the company president, Jim Aston, to review the projected numbers. She presents the following projected information.

Ethics

ASTON CORPORATION
Projected Income Statement
Year Ended December 31, 2011
($000s)

Sales		$29,000
Cost of goods sold	$14,000	
Depreciation	2,600	
Operating expenses	6,400	23,000
Income before income taxes		6,000
Provision for income taxes		3,000
Net income		$ 3,000

SELECTED BALANCE SHEET INFORMATION
December 31, 2011
($000s)

Estimated cash balance $ 5,000
Investment securities (FV-OCI) (at cost)   10,000

Security	Cost	Estimated Fair Value
A	$ 2,000	$ 2,200
B	4,000	3,900
C	3,000	3,000
D	1,000	1,800
Total	$10,000	$10,900

Other information ($000s) at December 31, 2011:
Equipment $ 3,000
Accumulated depreciation (5 years, straight-line)   1,200
New robotic equipment (purchased 1/1/11)   5,000
Accumulated depreciation (5 years, double-declining-balance)   2,000

The corporation has never used robotic equipment before, and Warren assumed an accelerated method because of the rapidly changing technology in robotic equipment. The company normally uses straight-line depreciation for production equipment. The investment securities held at year end were purchased during 2011, and are accounted for using the fair value through other comprehensive income (FV-OCI) model.

Aston explains to Warren that it is important for the corporation to show a $7-million net income before taxes because Aston receives a $1-million bonus if the income before taxes and bonus reaches $7 million. He also cautions that he will not pay more than $3 million in income taxes to the government.

Instructions

Digging
Deeper

(a) What can Warren do within IFRS to accommodate the president's wishes to achieve $7 million of income before taxes and bonus? Present the revised income statement based on your decision.

(b) Are the actions ethical? Who are the stakeholders in this decision, and what effect does Aston's actions have on their interests?

(c) Are there any cash flow implications of the choices made to achieve the president's wishes?

(d) Assume instead that Aston Corporation follows ASPE instead of IFRS. Briefly comment on the changes, if any, to the accounting treatment of the items discussed above.

P21-8 Kesterman Corporation is in the process of negotiating a loan for expansion purposes. Kesterman's books and records have never been audited and the bank has requested that an audit be performed and that IFRS be followed. Kesterman has prepared the following comparative financial statements for the years ended December 31, 2011 and 2010.

KESTERMAN CORPORATION
Statement of Financial Position
as at December 31, 2011 and 2010

	2011	2010
Assets		
Current assets		
Cash	$163,000	$ 82,000
Accounts receivable	392,000	296,000
Allowance for doubtful accounts	(37,000)	(18,000)
Trading investments, at cost	78,000	78,000
Merchandise inventory	207,000	202,000
Total current assets	803,000	640,000

Plant assets		
Property, plant, and equipment	167,000	169,500
Accumulated depreciation	(121,600)	(106,400)
Plant assets (net)	45,400	63,100
Total assets	$848,400	$703,100

Liabilities and Shareholders' Equity

Liabilities		
Accounts payable	$121,400	$196,100
Shareholders' equity		
Common shares, no par value,		
50,000 authorized, 20,000 issued and		
outstanding	260,000	260,000
Retained earnings	467,000	247,000
Total shareholders' equity	727,000	507,000
Total liabilities and shareholders' equity	$848,400	$703,100

KESTERMAN CORPORATION
Statement of Income
for the Years Ended December 31, 2011 and 2010

	2011	2010
Sales	$1,000,000	$900,000
Cost of sales	430,000	395,000
Gross profit	570,000	505,000
Operating expenses	210,000	205,000
Administrative expenses	140,000	105,000
	350,000	310,000
Net income	$ 220,000	$195,000

During the audit, the following additional facts were determined:

1. An analysis of collections and losses on accounts receivable during the past two years indicates a drop in anticipated bad debt losses. After consulting with management, it was agreed that the loss experience rate on sales should be reduced from the recorded 2% to 1.5%, beginning with the year ended December 31, 2011.

2. An analysis of the trading investments revealed that the total fair value for these investments as at the end of each year was as follows:

Dec. 31, 2010	$78,000
Dec. 31, 2011	$65,000

3. The merchandise inventory at December 31, 2010, was overstated by $8,900 and the merchandise inventory at December 31, 2011, was overstated by $13,600.

4. On January 2, 2010, equipment costing $30,000 (estimated useful life of 10 years and residual value of $5,000) was incorrectly charged to operating expenses. Kesterman records depreciation on the straight-line basis. In 2011, fully depreciated equipment (with no residual value) that originally cost $17,500 was sold as scrap for $2,800. Kesterman credited the $2,800 in proceeds to the equipment account.

5. An analysis of 2010 operating expenses revealed that Kesterman charged to expense a four-year insurance premium of $4,700 on January 15, 2010.

6. The analysis of operating expenses also revealed that operating expenses were incorrectly classified as part of administrative expenses in the amount of $15,000 in 2010 and $35,000 in 2011.

Instructions

(a) Prepare the journal entries to correct the books at December 31, 2011. The books for 2011 have not been closed. Ignore income taxes.

(b) Beginning with reported net income, prepare a schedule showing the calculation of corrected net income for the years ended December 31, 2011 and 2010, assuming that any adjustments are to be reported on comparative statements for the two years. Ignore income taxes. (Do not prepare financial statements.)

(c) Prepare a schedule showing the calculation of corrected retained earnings at January 1, 2011.

(AICPA adapted)

P21-9 You have been assigned to examine the financial statements of Picard Corporation for the year ended December 31, 2011, as prepared following IFRS. You discover the following situations:

1. The physical inventory count on December 31, 2010, improperly excluded merchandise costing $26,000 that had been temporarily stored in a public warehouse. Picard uses a periodic inventory system.

2. The physical inventory count on December 31, 2011, improperly included merchandise with a cost of $15,400 that had been recorded as a sale on December 27, 2011, and was being held for the customer to pick up on January 4, 2012.

3. A collection of $6,700 on account from a customer received on December 31, 2011, was not recorded until January 2, 2012.

4. Depreciation of $4,600 for 2011 on delivery vehicles was not recorded.

5. In 2011, the company received $3,700 on a sale of fully depreciated equipment that originally cost $25,000. The company credited the proceeds from the sale to the Equipment account.

6. During November 2011, a competitor company filed a patent infringement suit against Picard, claiming damages of $620,000. The company's legal counsel has indicated that an unfavourable verdict is probable and a reasonable estimate of the court's award to the competitor is $450,000. The company has not reflected or disclosed this situation in the financial statements.

7. A large piece of equipment was purchased on January 3, 2011, for $41,000 and was charged in error to Repairs Expense. The equipment is estimated to have a service life of eight years and no residual value. Picard normally uses the straight-line depreciation method for this type of equipment.

8. Picard has a portfolio of temporary investments reported as trading investments at fair value. No adjusting entry has been made yet in 2011. Information on carrying amounts and fair value is as follows:

	Carrying Amount	Fair Value
Dec. 31, 2010	$95,000	$95,000
Dec. 31, 2011	$94,000	$82,000

9. At December 31, 2011, an analysis of payroll information showed accrued salaries of $10,600. The Accrued Salaries Payable account had a balance of $16,000 at December 31, 2011, which was unchanged from its balance at December 31, 2010.

10. An $18,000 insurance premium paid on July 1, 2010, for a policy that expires on June 30, 2013, was charged to insurance expense.

11. A trademark was acquired at the beginning of 2010 for $36,000. Through an oversight, no amortization has been recorded since its acquisition. Picard expected the trademark to benefit the company for a total of approximately 12 years.

Instructions

Assume that the trial balance has been prepared, the ending inventory has not yet been recorded, and the books have not been closed for 2011. Assuming also that all amounts are material, prepare journal entries showing the adjustments that are required. Ignore income tax considerations.

P21-10 Penn Company, a small company following accounting standards for private enterprises, is adjusting and correcting its books at the end of 2011. In reviewing its records, it compiles the following information.

1. Penn has failed to accrue sales commissions payable at the end of each of the last two years, as follows:

Dec. 31, 2010	$3,500
Dec. 31, 2011	$2,500

2. In reviewing the December 31, 2011 inventory, Penn discovered errors in its inventory-taking procedures that have caused inventories for the last three years to be incorrect, as follows:

Dec. 31, 2009	Understated $16,000
Dec. 31, 2010	Understated $19,000
Dec. 31, 2011	Overstated $ 6,700

Penn has already made an entry that established the incorrect December 31, 2011, inventory amount.

3. In 2011, Penn changed the depreciation method on its office equipment from double-declining-balance to straight-line. The equipment had an original cost of $100,000 when purchased on January 1, 2009. It has a 10-year useful life and no residual value. Depreciation expense recorded prior to 2011 under the double-declining-balance method was $36,000. Penn has already recorded 2011 depreciation expense of $12,800 using the double-declining-balance method.

4. Before 2011, Penn accounted for its income from long-term construction contracts on the completed-contract basis because it was unable to reliably measure the degree of completion or the estimated costs to complete. Early in 2011, Penn's growth permitted the company to hire an experienced cost accountant and the company changed to the percentage-of-completion basis for financial accounting purposes. The completed-contract method will continue to be used for tax purposes. Income for 2011 has been recorded using the percentage-of-completion method. The following information is available:

	Pre-Tax Income	
	Percentage-of-Completion	Completed-Contract
Prior to 2011	$150,000	$105,000
2011	60,000	20,000

Instructions

(a) Prepare the necessary journal entries at December 31, 2011, to record the above corrections and changes as appropriate. The books are still open for 2011. As Penn has not yet recorded its 2011 income tax expense and payable amounts, tax effects for the current year may be ignored. Penn's income tax rate is 40%.

(b) If there are alternative methods of accounting for any items listed above, explain what the options are and why you chose the particular alternative.

P21-11 On May 5, 2012, you were hired by Gavin Inc., a closely held company that follows ASPE, as a staff member of its newly created internal auditing department. While reviewing the company's records for 2010 and 2011, you discover that no adjustments have yet been made for the items listed below.

1. Interest income of $18,800 was not accrued at the end of 2010. It was recorded when received in February 2011.

2. Equipment costing $18,000 was expensed when purchased on July 1, 2010. It is expected to have a four-year life with no residual value. The company typically uses straight-line depreciation for all fixed assets.

3. Research costs of $36,000 were incurred early in 2010. They were capitalized and were to be amortized over a three-year period. Amortization of $12,000 was recorded for 2010 and $12,000 for 2011. For tax purposes, the research costs were expensed as incurred.

4. On January 2, 2010, Gower leased a building for five years at a monthly rental of $9,000. On that date, the company paid the following amounts, which were expensed when paid for both financial reporting and tax purposes:

Security deposit	$35,000
First month's rent	9,000
Last month's rent	9,000
	$53,000

5. The company received $42,000 from a customer at the beginning of 2010 for services that it is to perform evenly over a three-year period beginning in 2010. None of the amount received was reported as unearned revenue at the end of 2010. The $42,000 was included in taxable income in 2010.

6. Merchandise inventory costing $16,800 was in the warehouse at December 31, 2010, but was incorrectly omitted from the physical count at that date. The company uses the periodic inventory method.

Instructions

Using the table that follows, enter the appropriate dollar amounts in the appropriate columns to indicate the effect of any errors on the net income figure reported on the income statement for the year ending December 31, 2010, and the retained earnings figure reported on the balance sheet at December 31, 2011. Assume that all amounts are material and that an income tax rate of 25% is appropriate for all years. Assume also that each item is independent of the other items. It is not necessary to total the columns on the grid.

	Net Income for 2010		Retained Earnings at Dec. 31, 2011	
Item	Understated	Overstated	Understated	Overstated
	————	————	————	————
	————	————	————	————
	————	————	————	————

(CIA adapted)

P21-12 Kitchener Corporation has followed IFRS and used the accrual basis of accounting for several years. A review of the records, however, indicates that some expenses and revenues have been handled on a cash basis because of errors made by an inexperienced bookkeeper. Income statements prepared by the bookkeeper reported $29,000 net income for 2010 and $37,000 net income for 2011. Further examination of the records reveals that the following items were handled improperly:

1. Rent of $1,300 was received from a tenant in December 2010, but the full amount was recorded as income at that time even though the rental related to 2011.

2. Wages payable on December 31 have been consistently omitted from the records of that date and have been entered instead as expenses when paid in the following year. The amounts of the accruals that were recorded in this way were as follows:

Dec. 31, 2009	$1,100
Dec. 31, 2010	1,500
Dec. 31, 2011	940

3. Invoices for office supplies purchased have been charged to expense accounts when received. Inventories of supplies on hand at the end of each year have been ignored, and no entry has been made for them. The inventories were as follows:

Dec. 31, 2009	$1,300
Dec. 31, 2010	740
Dec. 31, 2011	1,420

Instructions

(a) Prepare a schedule that shows the corrected net income for the years 2010 and 2011. All listed items should be labelled clearly. Ignore income tax considerations.

(b) Prepare the required journal entries to correct the 2011 net income. Assume that the books are open and ignore income tax considerations.

(c) Assume that Kitchener had unadjusted retained earnings of $95,000 at January 1, 2010, and of $124,000 at January 1, 2011. Prepare a schedule that shows the corrected opening retained earnings balances.

P21-13 You have been asked by a client to review the records of Inteq Corporation, a small manufacturer of precision tools and machines that follows ASPE. Your client is interested in buying the business, and arrangements were made for you to review the accounting records. Your examination reveals the following:

1. Inteq Corporation commenced business on April 1, 2008, and has been reporting on a fiscal year ending March 31. The company has never been audited, but the annual statements prepared by the bookkeeper reflect the following income before closing and before deducting income taxes:

Year Ended March 31	Income Before Taxes
2009	$ 71,600
2010	111,400
2011	103,580

2. A relatively small number of machines have been shipped on consignment. These transactions have been recorded as ordinary sales and billed in this way, with the gross profit on each sale being recognized when the machine was shipped. On March 31 of each year, the amounts for machines billed and in the hands of consignees were as follows:

2009	$6,500
2010	none
2011	5,590

The sales price was determined by adding 30% to cost. Assume that the consigned machines are sold the following year.

3. On March 30, 2010, two machines were shipped to a customer on a C.O.D. basis. The sale was not entered until April 5, 2010, when $6,100 cash was received. The machines were not included in the inventory at March 31, 2010. (Title passed on March 30, 2010.)

4. All machines are sold subject to a five-year warranty. It is estimated that the expense ultimately to be incurred in connection with the warranty will amount to 0.5% of sales. The company has charged an expense account for actual warranty costs incurred. Sales per books and warranty costs were as follows:

Year Ended March 31	Sales	Actual Warranty Costs Incurred for Sales Made in			
		2009	2010	2011	Total
2009	$ 940,000	$760			$ 760
2010	1,010,000	360	$1,310		1,670
2011	1,795,000	320	1,620	$1,910	3,850

5. A review of the corporate minutes reveals that the manager is entitled to a bonus of 0.5% of the income before deducting income taxes and the bonus. The bonuses have never been recorded or paid.

6. Bad debts have been recorded on a direct writeoff basis. Experience of similar enterprises indicates that losses will approximate 0.25% of sales. Bad debts written off and expensed were as follows:

	Bad Debts Incurred on Sales Made in			
	2009	2010	2011	Total
2006	$750			$ 750
2007	800	$ 520		1,320
2008	350	1,800	$1,700	3,850

7. The bank deducts 6% on all contracts that it finances. Of this amount, 0.5% is placed in a reserve to the credit of Inteq Corporation and is refunded to Inteq as financed contracts are paid in full. The reserve established by the bank has not been reflected in Inteq's books. On the books of the bank for each fiscal year, the excess of credits over debits (the net increase) to the reserve account for Inteq were as follows:

2009	$ 3,000
2010	3,900
2011	5,100
	$12,000

8. Commissions on sales have been entered when paid. Commissions payable on March 31 of each year were as follows:

2009	$1,400
2010	800
2011	1,120

Instructions

(a) Present a schedule showing the revised income before income taxes for each of the years ended March 31, 2009, 2010, and 2011. Make calculations to the nearest dollar.

(b) Prepare the journal entry or entries that you would give the bookkeeper to correct the books. Assume that the books have not yet been closed for the fiscal year ended March 31, 2011. Disregard corrections of income taxes.

(AICPA adapted)

P21-14 You are the auditor of Vegatron Services Inc., a privately owned full-service cleaning company following ASPE that is undergoing its first audit for the period ending September 30, 2011. The bank has requested that Vegatron have its statements audited this year to satisfy a condition of its debt covenant. It is currently October 1, 2011, and the company's books have been closed. As part of the audit, you have found the following situations:

1. Despite having high receivables, Vegatron has no allowance for doubtful accounts, and cash collections have slowed dramatically. Unfortunately, Vegatron is owed $5,000 by Brad's Fast Foods at the end of fiscal 2011. Brad's has received substantial media attention during the past year due to Department of Health investigations that ultimately resulted in the closure of the company's operations; the owner has apparently moved to the Bahamas. No adjustment has been made for this balance. Company management estimates that an allowance for doubtful accounts of

$47,000 is required. During the 2011 fiscal year, the company wrote off $38,000 in receivables, and it estimates that its September 30, 2010 allowance for doubtful accounts should have been $30,000.

2. Vegatron's only capital asset on its books is an advanced cleaning system that has a cost of $35,000 and a carrying amount of $20,825. Vegatron has been depreciating this asset using the capital cost allowance used for tax purposes for the two years prior to the 2011 fiscal year, at the rate of 30%. Useful life at the time of purchase was estimated to be 10 years. Vegatron would like to change to a straight-line approach to provide more relevant information to its statement users. Management anticipates that the asset will continue to be of use for four years after the September 30, 2011 year end and will have no residual value. Since the company's accountant was uncertain about how to deal with the change in policy, depreciation expense has not been recorded for the fiscal year.

3. Vegatron purchased a computer at the beginning of the fiscal year and immediately expensed its $3,000 cost. Upon questioning, one of the owners said he thought the computer would likely not need to be replaced for at least two more years.

4. You notice that there are no supplies on the statement of financial position. Company management explains that it expenses all supplies when purchased. The company had $1,500 of cleaning supplies on hand at the end of September 2011, which is about $500 higher than the balance that was on hand at the end of the previous year.

5. Vegatron started this year to keep a small amount of excess cash in trading investments. At the end of September 2011, the fair value of this portfolio was $15,000 and the cost of the investments was $12,000.

Instructions

(a) Assuming that the company's books are closed, prepare any journal entries that are required for each of the transactions. Ignore income tax considerations.

(b) For each of the items, discuss the type of change that is involved and how it is accounted for on the current and comparative financial statements.

(c) If Vegatron elected to follow IFRS, discuss how this might change your answers to (a).

(d) Repeat part (a) assuming that the books are open.

Writing Assignments

WA21-1   It is December 2011 and Cranmore Inc. recently hired a new accountant, Jodie Larson. Although Cranmore is a private company, it adopted IFRS for its reporting standards in 2010. As part of her preparation of the 2011 financial statements for Cranmore Inc., Jodie has proposed the following accounting changes.

1. At December 31, 2010, Cranmore had a receivable of $250,000 from Michael Inc. on its statement of financial position that had been owed since mid-2009. In December 2011, Michael Inc. was declared bankrupt and no recovery is expected. Jodie proposes to write off the receivable in 2011 against retained earnings as a correction of a 2009 error.

2. Jodie proposes to change from double-declining-balance to straight-line depreciation for the company's manufacturing assets because of a change in the pattern in which the assets provide benefits to the company. If straight-line depreciation had been used for all prior periods, retained earnings would have been $380,800 higher at December 31, 2010. The change's effect just on 2011 income is a reduction of $48,800.

3. For equipment in the leasing division, Jodie proposes to adopt the sum-of-the-years'-digits depreciation method, which the company has never used before. Cranmore began operating its leasing division in 2011. If straight-line depreciation were used, 2011 income would be $110,000 higher.

4. Cranmore has decided to adopt the revaluation method for reporting and measuring its land, with this policy being effective from January 1, 2011. At December 31, 2010, the land's fair value was $900,000. The land's book value at December 31, 2010, was $750,000. (Hint: Refer to IAS 8 for the treatment of this specific change in policy.)

5. Cranmore has investments that are recorded at fair value through OCI. At December 31, 2010, an error was made in the calculation of the fair values of these investments. The amount of the error was an overstatement of the fair value by $200,000.

Cranmore's income tax rate is 30%.

Instructions

(a) For each of the changes described above, identify whether the situation is a change in policy, a change in estimate, or the correction of an error. Justify your answer.

(b) For each of the changes described above, determine whether a restatement of January 1, 2011 retained earnings is required. What is the amount of the adjustment, if any? Prepare the required journal entries to record any adjustments.

(c) Prepare the statement of changes in equity. An excerpt from the statement of changes in equity for December 31, 2010, is provided below:

	Share Capital	Retained Earnings	AOCI Investments at FV through OCI	Total
Opening—January 1, 2010	$1,000,000	$2,500,000	$ 650,000	$4,150,000
Comprehensive Income	–0–	910,000	475,000	1,385,000
Closing balance—December 31, 2010	$1,000,000	$3,410,000	$1,125,000	$5,535,000

The profit or loss is $1,350,000 and the other comprehensive income is $150,000 for the 2011 year. There were no shares issued or repurchased during the year. There are no other changes to the equity accounts for 2011.

(d) Identify what disclosures are required in the notes to the financial statements as a result of each of these changes.

WA21-2   Various types of accounting changes can affect the financial statements of a private business enterprise differently. Assume that each item on the following list would have a material effect on the financial statements of a private enterprise in the current year:

1. A change to the income taxes payable method from the tax liability method

2. A change in the estimated useful life of previously recorded capital assets where the straight-line depreciation method is used

3. A change from deferring and amortizing development costs to immediate recognition. The change to immediate recognition arises because the company does not have the resources to market the new product adequately

4. A change from including the employer share of CPP premiums with Payroll Tax Expenses to including it with Salaries and Wages Expense on the income statement

5. The correction of a mathematical error in inventory costing that was made in a prior period

6. A change from straight-line amortization to a double-declining method in recognition of the effect that technology has on the pattern of benefits received from the asset's use

7. A change from presenting unconsolidated statements (using the cost method for the subsidiaries) to presenting consolidated statements for the company and its two long-held subsidiaries

8. A change in the method of accounting for leases for tax purposes to conform with the financial accounting method; as a result, both future and current taxes payable changed substantially

9. A change from the periodic inventory method to the perpetual method with the introduction of scanning equipment and updated computer software

10. A change in an accounting method due to a change in a primary source of GAAP

Instructions

Identify the type of accounting change that is described in each item, and indicate whether the prior years' financial statements must be restated when they are presented in comparative form with the current year's statements. Also indicate if the company is required to justify the change.

WA21-3   Ali Reiners, a new controller of Luftsa Corp., is preparing the financial statements for the year ended December 31, 2011. Luftsa is a publicly traded entity and therefore follows IFRS. As a result of this review, Ali has found the following information.

Ethics

1. Luftsa has been offering a loyalty rewards program to its customers for about five years. In the past, the company has not recorded any accrual related to the accumulated points as the amounts were not significant. However, with recent changes to the plan in 2011, the loyalty points are now accumulating much more rapidly and have become material. Ali has decided that effective January 1, 2011, the company will defer the revenue related to these points at the time of each sale, which will result in a liability.

2. In 2011, Luftsa decided to change its accounting policy for depreciating property, plant, and equipment to depreciate based on components and also to adopt the revaluation model. The company hired specialized appraisers at January 1, 2011, to determine the fair values, useful lives, and depreciable amounts for all of the components of the assets. In

prior years, the company did not have sufficient documentation to be able to apply component accounting, and the appraisers were not able to determine this information.

3. One division of Luftsa Corp., Rosentiel Co., has consistently shown an increasing net income from period to period. On closer examination of its operating statement, Ali Reiners noted that inventory obsolescence charges are much lower than in other divisions. In discussing this with the division's controller, Ali learned that the controller knowingly makes low estimates related to the writeoff of inventory in order to manage his bottom line.

4. In 2011, the company purchased new machinery that is expected to increase production dramatically, particularly in the early years. The company has decided to depreciate this machinery on an accelerated basis, even though other machinery is depreciated on a straight-line basis.

5. All products sold by Luftsa are subject to a three-year warranty. It has been estimated that the expense ultimately to be incurred on these machines is 1% of sales. In 2011, because of a production breakthrough, it is now estimated that 0.5% of sales is sufficient. In 2009 and 2010, warranty expense was calculated as $64,000 and $70,000, respectively. The company now believes that warranty costs should be reduced by 50%.

6. In reviewing the capital asset ledger in another division, Usher Division, Ali found a series of unusual accounting changes in which the useful lives of assets were substantially reduced when halfway through the original life estimate. For example, the useful life of one truck was changed from 10 to 6 years during its fifth year of service. The divisional manager, who is compensated in large part by bonuses, indicated on investigation, "It's perfectly legal to change an accounting estimate. We always have better information after time has passed."

Instructions

Ali Reiners has come to you for advice about each of the situations. Prepare a memorandum to the controller, indicating the appropriate accounting treatment that should be given to each situation. For any situations where there might be ethical considerations, identify and assess the issues and suggest what should be done.

WA21-4 Rydell Manufacturing Ltd. is preparing its year-end financial statements. Rydell is a private enterprise. The controller, Theo Kimbria, is confronted with several decisions about statement presentation for the following items.

1. The company has decided to change its depreciation method for the machinery to units of production rather than the straight-line method.

2. Trying to meet the criteria for capitalization of the development costs has become very difficult because of the highly competitive conditions in this market. Therefore, the practice of deferring and amortizing development costs has been abandoned in favour of expensing these costs as they are incurred.

3. The company has decided to change from using the corridor approach for accounting for actuarial gains and losses to recording these directly to OCI in each reporting period (or directly to net income if the company follows accounting standards for private enterprises, or ASPE).

4. When the year-end physical inventory adjustment was made for the current year, the controller discovered that the prior year's physical inventory sheets for an entire section of warehouse had been mislaid and left out of last year's count.

5. The method of accounting that is used for financial reporting purposes for certain receivables has been approved for tax purposes during the current tax year by the CRA. This change for tax purposes will cause both current taxes payable and future tax liabilities to change substantially.

6. Management has decided to switch from the FIFO inventory valuation method to the average cost inventory valuation method for all inventories.

Instructions

For each of the six changes that Rydell Manufacturing Ltd. made in the current year, advise Theo on whether the change is a change in accounting policy, a change in estimate, the correction of an error, or none of these. Explain if the accounting treatment would be different under ASPE or IFRS. Provide a short explanation for your choice. Determine if retrospective or prospective application would be required in each case and what information would be required in any note disclosure. If the information that is provided is insufficient for you to determine the nature of the change, identify what additional information you need and how this might affect your response.

(CMA adapted)

WA21-5 ASPE does not permit the correction of an error to be accounted for using partial retrospective restatement or prospective restatement. However, IAS 8 does allow partial retrospective restatement or even prospective treatment for error corrections.

Instructions

(a) Write a short memorandum that is suitable for being presented to your class in support of the Canadian position for private enterprises.

(b) Write a short memorandum suitable for presentation to your class in support of the international position.

WA21-6 At a recent conference on financial accounting and reporting, three participants provided examples of similar accounting changes that they had encountered in the last few months. They all involved the current portion of long-term debt.

The first participant explained that it had just recently come to her attention that the current portion of long-term debt was incorrectly calculated in the last three years of her company's financial statements due to an error in an accounting software product. The second participant explained that his company had just decided to change its definition of what is "current" to make it closer to the "operating cycle," which is approximately 18 months. The company had been using "12 months from the balance sheet date." The third participant also acknowledged that her company has decided to change from a "12 months from the balance sheet date" definition to one based on the company's operating cycle, which is now close to two years. She explained that the company's strategic plan over the last three years had moved the company into bidding on and winning significant longer-term contracts and that the average life of these contracts has now lengthened to about two years.

Instructions

(a) As a panellist at this conference who is expected to respond to the participants, prepare a brief report on the advice you would give on how each situation should be handled under GAAP. Identify what steps each participant should take and what disclosures, if any, each would be required to report.

(b) Under proposals for new financial statement presentation, the IASB is considering making the change that "current" would now mean 12 months, regardless of the company's operating cycle. This is believed to make the statements more comparable across different companies. If this new change is accepted, what would likely be the accounting treatment required on implementing this change?

WA21-7

Instructions

Write a brief essay highlighting the differences between IFRS and accounting standards for private enterprises noted in this chapter, discussing the conceptual justification for each.

Case

Refer to the Case Primer on the Student Website to help you answer the case.

CA21-1 Andy Frain is an audit senior of a large public accounting firm who has just been assigned to the Usher Corporation's annual audit engagement. Usher is a public company and has been a client of Frain's firm for many years. Usher is a fast-growing business in the commercial construction industry. In reviewing the fixed asset ledger, Frain discovered a series of unusual accounting changes, in which the useful lives of assets, depreciated using the straight-line method, were substantially lowered near the mid-point of the original estimate. For example, the useful life of one dump truck was changed from 10 to 6 years during its fifth year of service. Upon further investigation, Andy was told by Vince Nasab, Usher's accounting manager, "I don't really see your problem. After all, it's perfectly legal to change an accounting estimate. Besides, our CEO likes to see big earnings!"

Instructions

Discuss the issues.

Integrated Cases

IC21-1 Temple Limited is in the real estate business. After several years of economic growth, most of the company's assets are now worth significantly more than the amount that is recognized on the financial statements. Wanting to capitalize on this positive trend, the company is ready to expand and is looking at developing a new property in the Bahamas that will cost $300 million. Currently, the company's debt-to-equity ratio is 5:1 and the company needs to raise funds for the expansion. Lendall Bank, the company's primary lender, understands that there is hidden value in the balance sheet and is willing to finance the project.

Temple is now concerned about how the capital markets will react to this increase in debt. The company's shares list on the TSX and, therefore, GAAP is a constraint. Terry Temple, the company's CEO, attended a conference on international GAAP where the speakers noted that Canadian companies that are publicly accountable will move to IFRS for fiscal years beginning on or after January 1, 2011.

Under IFRS, fair value accounting is permitted for real estate as an accounting policy choice. The following handout was given to conference attendees. It represents a tentative timeline for the rollout of international standards in Canada for Canadian companies (the handout was modified and taken from a publication issued by the CICA on transitioning to IFRS).

December 31, 2008	Possible disclosure of an enterprise's plan for convergence and what effects the enterprise anticipates will arise with the change to IFRS.
December 31, 2009	Same disclosure required as in 2008, but with a greater degree of quantification of the effects of the change to IFRS.
January 1, 2010	First year for collection of comparative information for inclusion with 2011 financial statements under new IFRS-based requirements. Opening balance sheet for 2010 on IFRS basis required. Valuations on certain items may be advisable for the opening balance sheet preparation, depending on accounting policy choices under IFRS 1.
December 31, 2010	Last year of reporting under current Canadian GAAP.
January 1, 2011	Changeover. First year reporting under new IFRS-based standards. Opening balance sheet for 2011 on IFRS basis required.
March 31, 2011	Enterprises issuing interim financial statements prepare their first IFRS-based statements for the three months ended March 31, 2011.
December 31, 2011	End of first annual reporting period in accordance with new IFRS-based requirements including IFRS-based comparatives for 2010.

Instructions

Adopt the role of Temple Limited's controller and write a memo to address the CEO's concerns. Hint: review Chapters 10 and 11 regarding asset valuation. You might also wish to review IFRS 1 to see what choices the company has regarding valuing its assets at January 1, 2010 (opening balance sheet date for comparative balance sheet for 2011 financial statements).

IC21-2   Sunlight Equipment Manufacturers (SEM) makes barbecue equipment. The company has historically been very profitable; however, in the last year and a half, things have taken a turn for the worse due to higher consumer interest rates and a slowdown in the economy. On its 2011 draft year-end statements, the company is currently showing a break-even position before any final year-end adjustments. The company had fired its CEO, Sam Lazano, at the beginning of the year and a turnaround specialist was hired—Theo Lundstrom. Theo has a reputation of being able to come into companies that are suffering and make them profitable within two years. Theo has agreed with SEM's board of directors that he will be paid a $1-million bonus if the company has a combined two-year profit of $5 million by the end of 2013.

Among other things, Theo instituted a more aggressive sales policy for its customers, who are mainly retailers, as well as a new remuneration policy for sales staff. Theo attributed the company's poor performance to untrained sales staff whose remuneration and bonus scheme was not properly aligned to maximize sales. Under the new remuneration policy, sales staff is paid salary as well as a bonus, which is a percent of gross sales as at year end. The sales staff has responded well and sales have increased by 20%.

The new sales policy is as follows:

- Cash down payment of 20% with remaining payment for shipment once the barbecues are sold by the customer to a third party.

- If the customers order double their normal order, no down payment is required.

- The barbecues may be stored on the premises of SEM. Many customers have taken the company up on this offer in order to double the size of their purchase.

- Any unsold barbecues are allowed to be returned after year end.

Under the new policy, sales have increased dramatically, with many customers taking advantage of the new terms. As at year end, legal title to all barbecues has passed to the customers. Only customers with excellent credit history have been allowed to purchase under the new policy. The company has accrued bonuses for almost all its sales staff.

The increased profits from these sales have been offset by the accrual of $500,000 of Theo's bonus. He is very confident that he will be able to turn the company around and so has accrued part of his bonus. He has also decided to change several accounting policies, including the following:

- Depreciation on machinery switched to straight-line from double-declining-balance. Note that the equipment is about 2 years old with an estimated life of 10 years. Theo felt that the double-declining-balance method was arbitrary and noted that several of their competitors used the straight-line method. Machinery is most useful when new since it requires less downtime for fixing.

Another problem that Theo had identified was in inventory management. Theo was convinced that inventory was being stolen and/or "lost" due to poor tracking. The company had therefore hired a company, Software Limited, to install a new inventory tracking system during the year. Midway through the year, Software Limited had gone bankrupt and was not able to finish the installation. The installation was a customized job and as at year end, the system was not functioning yet. SEM has not been able to find a company to replace Software Limited. To date, $2 million has been spent on the new system. Theo had capitalized the costs and noted he was confident that he would be able to find a company that could successfully complete the installation.

Instructions

Adopt the role of the company's auditors and discuss the financial reporting issues for the 2011 year end. The company is a private company but would like the statements to be prepared in accordance with IFRS.

Research and Financial Analysis

RA21-1 Eastern Platinum

Refer to the 2009 year-end financial statements and accompanying notes of Eastern Platinum Limited (Eastplats) that have been reproduced at the end of this volume and on the book companion site. In Eastplats's notes, the company refers to accounting standards that have been retrospectively applied, standards that have been prospectively applied, and standards that have been issued but are not yet effective.

Real-World Emphasis

Instructions

(a) Review note 25 from the financial statements that appear on the book companion site, and explain how the IFRS standards have been adopted and retrospectively applied. Indicate and explain the following:

   1. On what date did the company adopt IFRS?

   2. What exemptions to retrospective restatement were applied?

   3. What items required restatement and what was their impact on the income statement for 2008, and the statement of financial position at January 1, 2008, and December 31, 2008? Consider putting the solution in table format.

(b) What disclosure did the company provide on standards that were issued, but were not effective?

RA21-2 Research In Motion Limited

In recent years, many well-known companies, including Apple and Home Depot, have been accused of backdating options. A February 2009 *National Post* article titled "OSC, RIM in tentative settlement" explained that the Ontario Securities Commission was charging Research In Motion Limited (RIM) with the backdating of options. The following are some excerpts from the article:

Real-World Emphasis

"According to a statement of allegations filed by the OSC late yesterday, the total 'in the money' benefit resulting from the incorrect dating practices for all employees was about $66-million, including $33-million that has not been reimbursed or repaid to RIM or otherwise forfeited. The regulator said 1,400 of 3,200 option grants made between 1998 and 2006 were made using incorrect dating practices...

"An internal investigation at RIM revealed that options had been 'backdated'—or set at earlier lower prices that would give the recipient an immediate gain on paper—leading to improper accounting treatment in the company's books. As a result of the internal probe and earnings restatement, Mr. Balsillie left his chairman's post and Mr. Kavelman was assigned to a different job within the company. Some directors were also replaced...

"According to the OSC's statement of allegations, the directors and officers involved 'did not take reasonable steps to provide proper oversight in relation to RIM's options granting practices or to ensure that RIM's public disclosure reflected those practices.'

"The regulator alleged that the grant dates selected resulted in more favourable pricing for the options or 'in the money' grants.

"'In many instances, the lowest share price in a period was chosen using hindsight in order to set the grant date and, therefore, the exercise price,' the OSC said.

"Between July, 1998, and August, 2006, 'RIM repeatedly made statements in many of its filings, including prospectuses, financial statements, annual reports, and management information circulars, that contained the misleading or untrue statement that options were priced at the fair market value of RIM's common shares at the date of the grant and were granted in accordance with the terms of the plan,' the OSC said in its final statement of allegations released yesterday."*

In settlement of this case, four senior executives (Kavelman, Loberto, Balsillie and Lazaridis) were required to pay $77 million in fines to the OSC and restitution to RIM. In addition, the executives were required to pay $1.76 million to the SEC for penalties plus give back more than $800,000 in profits made on the sale of the backdated options.

Instructions

Access the financial statements of Research In Motion Limited for the fiscal year ended March 3, 2007, from SEDAR (www.sedar.com) or from the company's website.

(a) Explain the nature of the errors that the company has made. Describe the process that the company undertook to determine the extent and nature of these errors. What is meant by backdating of the options?

(b) What was the impact of these errors on the net income and cumulatively on retained earnings for each of the years 1999 to 2006? In what years does this restatement appear to have the largest impact?

(c) For the years ended March 4, 2006, and February 26, 2005, explain the impact on cost of sales; research and development; and selling, marketing, and administration expenses. What percentage of net income did total restatements represent for each of these years? What is the impact on the EPS for each year?

(d) What is the impact on the balance sheet for March 4, 2006? What is the impact on the current ratio and debt-to-equity ratio before and after these restatements?

(e) What is the impact on the operating cash flows for the years ended March 4, 2006, and February 26, 2005?

RA21-3 Canadian Tire Corporation, Limited

Real-World
Emphasis

Access the annual report for Canadian Tire Corporation, Limited for the year ended January 2, 2010, from SEDAR (www.sedar.com).

Instructions

(a) Reviewing the Consolidated Statement of Changes in Shareholders' Equity, discuss whether Canadian Tire reported any accounting changes in the years presented. Which accounts were impacted and by how much?

(b) Identify and explain each accounting change that the company implemented in 2009. How was each accounting change applied? If the change was due to an amendment of the standards, provide the details of the effective date of the changes. Classify each change as being one of the following:

1. A change in accounting policy mandated by a change in a primary source of GAAP

2. A voluntary change in accounting policy

3. A change in estimate

(c) For each change reported in (a) above, explain whether the change was retrospectively or prospectively applied. What was the impact of each change on the financial reports of Canadian Tire in each year presented?

(d) The company also provides details for future accounting changes. Describe the note disclosure provided for these.

(e) In the Management Discussion and Analysis, the company has also provided details on its adoption of IFRS. Explain the different phases that the company has developed to adopt IFRS. Summarize the relevant accounting standards and preliminary findings as to their impact on Canadian Tire's financial statements.

*Material reprinted with the express permission of: "The National Post Company", a Canwest Partnership.

(f) Upon adoption of IFRS, companies will be required to adopt all the standards on a retrospective basis. However, to ease this transition, IFRS 1 provides exemptions that first-time adopters may apply to be exempt from retrospective application of certain identified standards. In the Management Discussion and Analysis, Canadian Tire has provided information on the exemptions that it will likely apply for. List each exemption and provide a short explanation of the exemption and the company's intention with respect to this exemption.

RA21-4 Research Case–Adoption of IFRS

Canadian public companies are to adopt IFRS for years starting on or after January 1, 2011. The AcSB and Ontario Securities Commission have been actively communicating with Canadian public companies since then, stressing the importance of looking ahead to prepare for the change to IFRS and to determine what effect the changeover is likely to have on each company. Documentation of this process and estimates of the impact are to be disclosed in the financial reports as early as possible to assist users' understanding.

Choose a sample of three public Canadian companies that you are interested in. Locate a copy of each company's annual reports for its prior two years.

Instructions

(a) Summarize what each company disclosed about the change to IFRS in both years' financial statements and Management Discussion and Analysis.

(b) Compare the disclosures in each company's two financial reports. What additional information has been provided to assist the user in determining the impact? Is this change expected to have much of an effect on each company? Summarize, to the extent possible, what each company identifies as the standards having the most relevance during the changeover.

(c) If the 2011 financial statements have been released, review the note disclosures related to the change to IFRS. How have the companies disclosed the transition to IFRS? What standards have had the greatest impact on the opening assets, liabilities, and net earnings for these companies?

RA21-5 Research Case–L'Oréal

Real-World Emphasis

Companies must disclose changes in accounting policies and the impact of these changes in the notes to their financial statements. Access the annual report (or financial statements) for cosmetics company L'Oréal for the year ended December 31, 2009, from its website (www.loreal.com).

Instructions

Using the consolidated financial statements for L'Oreal, answer the following questions.

(a) List all changes in IFRS that L'Oreal identified in its notes to the financial statements. How were these changes in policies implemented? What was the impact on the company's financial statements for the current and prior years, if any?

(b) Why has the company provided comparisons for four different dates for the Statement for the Financial Position?

(c) Describe any changes in presentation the company has reported.

RA21-6 Research Case–Transitional Provisions

The IASB is working to update a major portion of the standards and has a put a project plan in place that outlines the timelines for these various updates. The items below are examples of topics where new standards are proposed to be released (or already have been released).

Consolidations—IAS 27, *Financial Instruments*—IFRS 9, *Joint Arrangements*—IAS 31, Non-financial liabilities, Fair value measurements

Instructions

Using the IASB website (www.iasb.org), identify new standards that have been recently released. Review the transitional provisions, if any, for each of these standards identified. Write a report on the accounting requirements for each change in the year when it becomes effective. Discuss whether the requirements seem reasonable, and whether they are consistent from one standard to another.

Cash Flow Is Key

CLEARWATER SEAFOODS has continued to thrive and provide quality seafood products for more than 30 years, and has done so in part because it knows about cash flows. "The ability to sustain and grow cash flows is key," says Tyrone Cotie, director of corporate finance and investor relations at the Bedford, N.S.–based company. Clearwater operates a large fleet of vessels in Canada and Argentina and owns several processing plants throughout Eastern Canada.

"The statement of cash flows ties together the information contained on the balance sheet and income statement," Cotie explains. "It provides an accurate picture of the cash flows of the business by removing the non-cash items from the earnings statement and by adding the investments noted on the balance sheet to cash outflows. It shows you the cash that was generated during the year and where it was used."

In 2009, Clearwater management focused on controlling costs and increasing vessel operations and productivity. The company generated cash by disposing of non-core quotas that were not earning an adequate return on capital. These sales of non-core quotas generated proceeds of $15.3 million in the first three quarters of 2009, while the sale of other surplus assets generated another $1.3 million. The sale of non-core quotas is part of Clearwater's strategy to maintain liquidity, including tightly managing its working capital, limiting capital spending, and limiting distributions.

As an income fund, Clearwater has distributed a significant amount of cash to unit holders since it went public in July 2002. However, the company has limited cash distributions to unit holders in recent years, paying none in 2008 and 2009, and not planning any in 2010.

The IASB has been discussing moving to the direct method of reporting cash flows; however, currently the majority of public issuers in Canada use the indirect method, Cotie points out. "Although these potential changes will not impact the net change in cash, they have the potential to dramatically increase the amount of effort required to produce the statement," he adds. "Further, I do not believe the direct method is useful as it would not be reflective of how companies actually manage their cash resources." ■

CHAPTER 22

Statement of Cash Flows

Learning Objectives

After studying this chapter, you should be able to:

1. Describe the purpose and uses of the statement of cash flows.

2. Define cash and cash equivalents.

3. Identify the major classifications of cash flows and explain the significance of each classification.

4. Prepare the operating activities section of a statement of cash flows using the direct method.

5. Prepare the operating activities section of a statement of cash flows using the indirect method.

6. Prepare a statement of cash flows using the direct method.

7. Prepare a statement of cash flows using the indirect method.

8. Identify the financial presentation and disclosure requirements for the statement of cash flows.

9. Read and interpret a statement of cash flows.

10. Identify differences in the accounting standards for private enterprises and IFRS, and explain what changes are expected to standards for the statement of cash flows.

After studying Appendix 22A, you should be able to:

11. Use a work sheet to prepare a statement of cash flows.

Preview of Chapter 22

Examining a company's income statement may provide insights into its profitability, but it does not provide much information about its liquidity and financial flexibility. The purpose of this chapter is to highlight the requirements for the reporting of cash flow statements found in accounting standards for private enterprises (ASPE) and in IFRS. We explain the main components of this statement and the type of information it provides; and demonstrate how to prepare, report on, and interpret such a statement. The chapter ends with a comparison of ASPE and international GAAP.

The chapter is organized as follows:

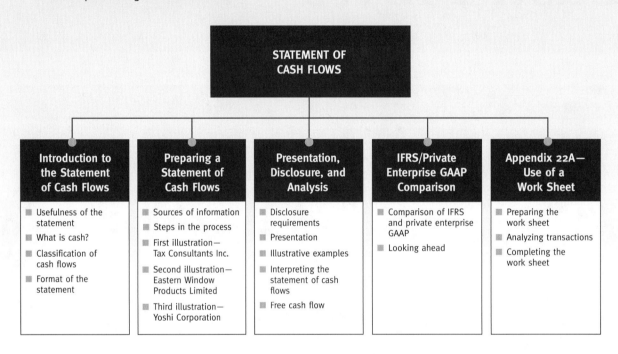

STATEMENT OF CASH FLOWS

Introduction to the Statement of Cash Flows	Preparing a Statement of Cash Flows	Presentation, Disclosure, and Analysis	IFRS/Private Enterprise GAAP Comparison	Appendix 22A— Use of a Work Sheet
▪ Usefulness of the statement ▪ What is cash? ▪ Classification of cash flows ▪ Format of the statement	▪ Sources of information ▪ Steps in the process ▪ First illustration— Tax Consultants Inc. ▪ Second illustration— Eastern Window Products Limited ▪ Third illustration— Yoshi Corporation	▪ Disclosure requirements ▪ Presentation ▪ Illustrative examples ▪ Interpreting the statement of cash flows ▪ Free cash flow	▪ Comparison of IFRS and private enterprise GAAP ▪ Looking ahead	▪ Preparing the work sheet ▪ Analyzing transactions ▪ Completing the work sheet

INTRODUCTION TO THE STATEMENT OF CASH FLOWS

Objective 1
Describe the purpose and uses of the statement of cash flows.

Will the company be able to continue to pay dividends? How did it finance the acquisition of its new subsidiary? Will the company have sufficient cash to meet the significant amount of debt that is maturing next year? How did cash increase when there was a net loss for the period? How were the proceeds of the bond issue used? How was the expansion in plant and equipment financed? Or, as the opening story discusses, how are cash management activities related to corporate strategy? These questions cannot be answered by reviewing the statement of financial position and statement of income or comprehensive income alone. A statement of cash flows is needed.

The primary purpose of the statement of cash flows is to provide information about an entity's cash receipts and cash payments during a period. A secondary objective is to provide information on a cash basis about its operating, investing, and financing activities. The statement of cash flows therefore reports cash receipts, cash payments, and the net change in cash resulting from an enterprise's operating, investing, and financing activities during a period, and does so in a format that reconciles the beginning and ending cash balances.

Usefulness of the Statement

The information in a statement of cash flows enables investors, creditors, and others to assess the following:

1. **Liquidity and solvency of an entity—its capacity to generate cash and its needs for cash resources.** To assess an entity's ability to generate cash to pay maturing debt, to maintain and increase productive capacity, and to distribute a return to owners, it is important to determine both the timing and degree of certainty of expected cash inflows.

2. **Amounts, timing, and uncertainty of future cash flows.** Historical cash flows are often useful in helping to predict future cash flows. By examining the relationships between items such as sales and net income and the cash flow from operating activities, or cash flow from operating activities and increases or decreases in cash, it is possible to make better predictions of the amounts, timing, and uncertainty of future cash flows than is possible using accrual-based data alone.

3. **Reasons for the difference between net income and cash flow from operating activities.** The net income number is important because it provides information on an enterprise's success or failure from one period to another. But some people are critical of accrual basis income because so many estimates are needed to calculate it. As a result, the number's reliability is often challenged. This usually does not occur with cash. Readers of the financial statements benefit from knowing the reasons for the difference between net income and cash flow from operating activities. It allows them to make their own assessment of the income number's reliability.

Because of the importance of this information, the statement of cash flows is required to be included in all private enterprise GAAP or IFRS financial statements.

Underlying Concept

The statement of cash flows is another example of relevant information—information that is useful in assessing and predicting future cash flows.

Significant Change

What Is Cash?

As part of a company's cash management system, short-term, near-cash investments are often held instead of cash alone because this allows the company to earn a return on cash balances that exceeds its immediate needs. It is also common for an organization to have an agreement with the bank that permits the entity's account to fluctuate between a positive balance and an overdraft. Because a company's cash activity and position are more appropriately described by including these other cash management activities, cash flows are defined in terms of inflows and outflows of cash and cash equivalents.

Cash is defined as cash on hand and demand deposits. Cash equivalents are short-term, highly liquid investments that are readily convertible to known amounts of cash and have an insignificant risk of change in value.[1] Cash equivalents are made up of **non-equity investments** that are acquired with short maturities—generally less than three months when they are acquired—and include such short-term investments as treasury bills, commercial paper, and money market funds that are acquired with cash in excess of current needs. IAS 7 *Statement of Cash Flows* does permit preferred shares acquired close to their maturity date to be included on the basis that they are cash equivalents in substance. In

2 Objective
Define cash and cash equivalents.

Underlying Concept

In their joint financial statement presentation project, the FASB and the IASB have tentatively decided to discontinue the use of the term "cash equivalents." Instead, they are suggesting that all non-cash securities be presented and classified in the same way as other short-term investments.

---

[1] *CICA Handbook*, Part II, Section 1540.06(a) and (b), and IAS 7.6.

addition, **bank overdrafts** that are repayable on demand and fluctuate often between positive and negative balances are included in cash and cash equivalents under both sets of standards if they result from and are an integral part of an organization's cash management policies.

Throughout this chapter, the use of the term "cash" should be interpreted generally to mean "cash and cash equivalents."

Classification of Cash Flows

Objective 3

Identify the major classifications of cash flows and explain the significance of each classification.

The statement of cash flows classifies cash receipts and cash payments according to whether they result from an operating, investing, or financing activity. The transactions and other events that are characteristic of each kind of activity and the significance of each type of cash flow are as follows.

1. Operating activities are the enterprise's principal revenue-producing activities and other activities that are not investing or financing activities. Operating flows generally involve the cash effects of transactions that determine net income, such as collections from customers on the sale of goods and services, and payments to suppliers for goods and services acquired, to the CRA for income taxes, and to employees for salaries and wages.

   The amount of cash that is provided by or used in operations is key information for financial statement users. Like blood flowing through the veins and arteries of our bodies, operating cash flows—derived mainly from receipts from customers—are needed to maintain the organization's systems: to meet payrolls, to pay suppliers, to cover rentals and insurance, and to pay taxes. In addition, surplus cash flows from operations are needed to repay loans, to take advantage of new investment opportunities, and to pay dividends without having to seek new external financing.

2. Investing activities involve the acquisition and disposal of long-term assets and other investments that are not included in cash equivalents or those acquired for trading purposes. Investing cash flows are a result of such activities as making and collecting loans and acquiring and disposing of investments and productive long-lived assets. They also include cash payments for and receipts from a variety of derivative products, unless such contracts are entered into for trading or financing purposes.

   The use of cash in investing activities tells the financial statement reader whether the entity is ploughing cash back into additional long-term assets that will generate profits and increase cash flows in the future, or whether the stock of long-term productive assets is being decreased by conversion into cash.

3. Financing activities result in changes in the size and composition of the enterprise's equity capital and borrowings. Financing cash flows include obtaining cash from issuing debt and repaying amounts borrowed, and obtaining capital from owners and providing them with a return on, and a return of, their investment.

   Details of cash flows related to financing activities allow readers to assess the potential for future claims to the organization's cash and to identify major changes in the form of financing, especially between debt and equity.

   Illustration 22-1 identifies an enterprise's typical cash receipts and payments and classifies them, according to ASPE, as to whether they result from operating, investing, or financing activities. Note that the *operating* cash flows are related almost entirely to **working capital accounts** (i.e., **current asset** and **current liability accounts**), the *investing* cash flows generally involve **long-term asset items**, and the *financing* flows are derived mainly from changes in **long-term liability and equity accounts**. IFRS' requirements are similar, but not identical.

Illustration 22-1

Classification of Typical Cash Inflows and Outflows

Types of Cash Flows	Relationship to the Balance Sheet
OPERATING	
Cash inflows	
From cash sales and collections from customers on account	
From returns on loans (interest) and equity securities (dividends)	Generally related
From receipts for royalties, rents, and fees	to changes in
Cash outflows	non-cash current
To suppliers on account	assets and
To, and on behalf of, employees for services	current liabilities
To governments for taxes	
To lenders for interest	
To others for expenses	
INVESTING	
Cash inflows	
From proceeds on the sale of property, plant, and equipment	
From proceeds on the sale of debt or equity securities of other entities	Generally related
From the collection of principal on loans to other entities	to changes in
Cash outflows	long-term assets
For purchases of property, plant, and equipment	
For purchases of debt or equity securities of other entities	
For loans to other entities	
FINANCING	
Cash inflows	
From proceeds on the issuance of equity securities	
From proceeds on the issuance of debt (bonds and notes)	Generally related
Cash outflows	to changes in
For payments of dividends to shareholders	long-term liabilities
For redemptions of long-term debt or reacquisitions of share capital	and equity
For reductions of capital lease obligations	

Some transactions that you might think are investing or financing activities may actually be operating cash flows. Under accounting standards for private enterprises (ASPE), for example, cash dividends and interest received and cash dividends and interest paid **that are included in determining net income** are classified as **operating** flows. Any dividends or interest paid **that are charged directly against retained earnings, however,** are reported as **financing** flows.[2]

Under **IFRS**, however, a choice is allowed. Interest paid and received and dividends received (excluding those received from an associate—a significant influence investment[3]) can be recognized as operating flows on the basis they are included in determining net income. Alternatively, interest paid could be a financing outflow while interest and dividends received could be considered investment flows. A choice is also permitted for dividends paid: a financing flow as a return to equity holders, or an operating flow as a measure of the ability of operations to cover returns to shareholders. However management views these specific flows, once the choice is made, it is applied consistently from period to period. Illustration 22-2 summarizes this type of cash flow.

[2] Dividend payments that are recognized in the income statement relate to equity securities that are determined to be liabilities in substance; and interest payments that are charged to retained earnings relate to debt securities that are judged to be equity instruments in substance. The statement of cash flows, therefore, treats returns to in-substance equity holders as financing outflows and to those designated as creditors as operating outflows.

[3] IAS 7 *Statement of Cash Flows*, para .20, indicates that the undistributed income of an associate is an adjustment in determining cash from operations under the indirect method.

Illustration 22-2

*Interest and Dividends:
Classification*

	Interest and dividends paid	Interest and dividends received
ASPE/PE GAAP	Operating: if recognized in net income Financing: if charged to retained earnings	Operating
IFRS	Choice: Operating or Financing	Choice: Operating or Investing

Although they are reported on the income statement, some items are the result of an investing or financing activity. For example, the sale of property, plant, and equipment is an investing activity even though the gain or loss on sale is reported in income. In this case, the cash proceeds received on the sale are properly classified as an investing cash inflow. The gain or loss, therefore, must be **excluded** in determining cash flows from operating activities. Similarly, the repayment (extinguishment) of debt is not an operating activity, and the gain or loss on repayment is not an operating cash flow. The cash paid to redeem the debt, not the amount of the gain or loss, is the actual cash flow and the repayment is clearly a financing activity.

Outflows to purchase investments and loans that are acquired specifically **for trading purposes**, and the proceeds on their sale, are treated the same as flows related to inventories acquired for resale; that is, as operating cash flows. If investments are acquired for other purposes, the cash flows are investing flows.

Income taxes present another complexity. While income tax expense can be identified with specific operating, investing, and financing transactions, the related cash payments for taxes usually cannot. For this reason, income tax payments are classified as operating cash flows unless they can be specifically identified with financing and investing activities.

How should significant non-cash transactions that affect an organization's assets and capital structure, such as those listed below, be handled?

1. The acquisition of assets by assuming directly related liabilities (including capital lease obligations) or by issuing equity securities

2. Exchanges of non-monetary assets

3. The conversion of debt or preferred shares to common shares

4. The issue of equity securities to retire debt

Because the statement of cash flows reports only the cash effect of activities, significant investing and financing transactions that do not affect cash are excluded from the statement. They are required to be disclosed elsewhere in the financial statements.[4]

Underlying Concept

Not requiring taxes to be allocated to the various activities is an application of the cost-benefit constraint. While the information may be beneficial, the cost of providing it exceeds the benefits.

What Do the Numbers Mean?

Generally, companies move through several life-cycle stages of development, and each stage has implications for its cash flows. As the following graph shows, the pattern of flows from operating, financing, and investing activities varies depending on the stage of the cycle.

---

[4] Note that an asset that is acquired and financed through a third party when the lender pays the seller directly is considered a cash inflow (financing) followed by a cash outflow (investing). If an existing mortgage is assumed when an asset is acquired, however, this does not result in a cash flow.

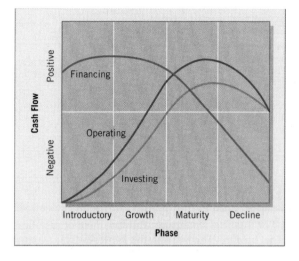

In the introductory phase, the product is likely not generating much revenue, although significant cash is being spent to build up the company's inventories. Therefore, operating cash flow is negative. Because the company is making heavy investments to get a product off the ground, the cash flow associated with investing activities is also negative. Financing cash flows are positive as funds are raised to pay for the investments and cover the operating shortfall.

As the product moves to the growth and maturity phases, these relationships reverse. The product generates more cash from operations, which is used to cover investments that are needed to support the product, and less cash is needed from financing. So is a negative operating cash flow bad? Not always. It depends to a great extent on the product life cycle.

Source: Adapted from Paul D. Kimmel, Jerry J. Weygandt, and Donald E. Kieso, *Financial Accounting: Tools for Business Decision Making*, 5th ed. (New York: John Wiley & Sons, 2009), p. 606.

Format of the Statement

The three activities discussed in the preceding section guide the general format of the statement of cash flows. The operating activities section usually appears first, and is followed by the investing and financing activities sections. The individual inflows and outflows from investing and financing activities are reported separately; that is, they are reported gross, not netted against one another. Thus, a cash outflow from the purchase of property is reported separately from the cash inflow from the sale of property. Similarly, the cash inflow from issuing debt is reported separately from the cash outflow for the retirement of debt. If they are not reported separately, it is harder to see how extensive the enterprise's investing and financing activities are and therefore it is more difficult to assess future cash flows.[5]

Illustration 22-3 sets out a basic or "skeleton" format of a statement of cash flows. Note that the statement also provides a reconciliation between the beginning-of-the-period cash and the end-of-the-period cash reported in the comparative balance sheets.

4 Objective
Prepare the operating activities section of a statement of cash flows using the direct method.

5 Objective
Prepare the operating activities section of a statement of cash flows using the indirect method.

---

[5] Netting is permitted in limited and specific circumstances. See *CICA Handbook*, Part II, Section 1540.25–.26 and IAS 7.22 – .24.

Illustration 22-3

Format of the Statement of Cash Flows

COMPANY NAME
Statement of Cash Flows
Period Covered

Cash flows from operating activities		
Net income		XXX
Adjustments to reconcile net income to cash provided by (used in)		
operating activities: (List of individual items)	XX	XX
Net cash provided by (used in) operating activities		**XXX**
Cash flows from investing activities		
(List of individual inflows and outflows)	XX	
Net cash provided by (used in) investing activities		**XXX**
Cash flows from financing activities		
(List of individual inflows and outflows)	XX	
Net cash provided by (used in) financing activities		**XXX**
Net increase (decrease) in cash		**XXX**
Cash at beginning of period		**XXX**
Cash at end of period		**XXX**

Illustration 22-3 presents the net cash flow from operating activities indirectly by making the necessary adjustments to the net income reported on the income statement. This is referred to as the **indirect method** (or reconciliation method). The cash flow from operating activities could be calculated directly by identifying the sources of the operating cash receipts and payments. This approach, explained in Illustration 22-4, is referred to as the **direct method**.

Illustration 22-4

Cash Flows from Operating Activities—Direct Method

Cash flows from operating activities	
Cash receipts from customers	XX
Cash receipts from other revenue sources	XX
Cash payments to suppliers for goods and services	(XX)
Cash payments to and on behalf of employees	(XX)
Cash payments of income taxes	(XX)
Net cash provided by (used in) operating activities	**XXX**

Standard setters have wrestled with the issue of which method should be used. Both IFRS and PE GAAP encourage, but do not require, use of the direct method because it provides additional information.[6]

Direct versus Indirect

In general, public companies tend to prefer the indirect method, although commercial lending officers and other investors tend to prefer the direct method because of the additional information that it provides.

In Favour of the Direct Method.   The main advantage of the direct method is that it shows operating cash receipts and payments. That is, it is more consistent with the

Underlying Concept

FASB also encourages use of the direct rather than the indirect method. If the direct method is used, a reconciliation between net income and cash flow from operating activities must be provided as this information is otherwise not available.

---

[6] Unfortunately, use of the direct method is the exception. Companies suggest that it is costly for them to generate the information required by the direct method, but it may also be due in part to the fact that instructors tend to teach the indirect method because that is what is used, and the indirect method is used because that is what accountants have been taught!

objective of a statement of cash flows—to provide information about the entity's cash receipts and cash payments—than the indirect method.

Supporters of the direct method argue that knowing the specific sources of operating cash receipts and the purposes that operating cash payments were made for in past periods is useful in estimating future operating cash flows. Furthermore, information about the amounts of major classes of operating cash receipts and payments is more useful than information only about their arithmetic sum (the net cash flow from operating activities).

Many preparers of financial statements say that they do not currently collect information in a manner that allows them to determine amounts such as cash received from customers or cash paid to suppliers. But supporters of the direct method believe that the incremental cost of assimilating such operating cash receipts and payments data is not significant, especially with sophisticated database accounting systems underlying companies' financial reporting modules.[7]

In Favour of the Indirect Method.　　The main advantage of the indirect method is that it focuses on the differences between net income and cash flow from operating activities. That is, it provides a useful link between the statement of cash flows, the income statement, and the statement of financial position.

Preparers of financial statements argue that it is less costly to develop information that adjusts net income to net cash flow from operating activities. Supporters of the indirect method also state that the direct method, which effectively reports income statement information on a cash rather than an accrual basis, may suggest incorrectly that net cash flow from operating activities is as good as, or better than, net income as a measure of performance.

As the indirect method has been used almost exclusively in the past, both preparers and users are more familiar with it and this helps perpetuate its use. Each method provides useful information. The best solution may lie in mandating the direct method, which comes closer to meeting the statement's objectives, and requiring supplementary disclosure of a reconciliation of net income to cash flow from operations. The FASB and IASB have been working on a joint project dealing with financial statement presentation that includes significant changes to the statement of cash flows. An update on this project is provided in the Looking Ahead section at the end of this chapter.

PREPARING A STATEMENT OF CASH FLOWS

Sources of Information

The statement of cash flows was previously called the Statement of Changes in Financial Position.[8] By analyzing the changes in all non-cash accounts on the statement of financial position from one period to the next, it is possible to identify and summarize the sources of all cash receipts and all cash disbursements. Illustration 22-5 explains why this is true.

---

[7] *CICA Handbook*, Part II, Section 1540 also provides and explains, in an appendix, a simplified work sheet approach for companies to use in developing the information needed to present operating cash flows under the direct method.

[8] Prior to the current standard on cash flows, significant non-cash transactions **were included** in the statement because of their effect on the entity's asset and capital structure. This difference shows the change in focus from a statement of changes in financial position (old terminology) to a statement of cash flows (new terminology), where only cash effects are reported.

Illustration 22-5

Relationship of Changes in Cash to Other Balance Sheet Accounts

$$A = L + SE$$
$$\Delta A = \Delta(L + SE)$$
$$\Delta A = \Delta L + \Delta SE$$
$$\Delta(\text{Cash} + \text{non-cash } A) = \Delta L + \Delta SE$$
$$\Delta \text{Cash} + \Delta \text{non-cash } A = \Delta L + \Delta SE$$
$$\Delta \text{Cash} = \Delta L + \Delta SE - \Delta \text{non-cash } A$$

Note: Δ is a symbol meaning "change in."

Unlike the other financial statements, which are prepared directly from the adjusted trial balance, the statement of cash flows is usually based on an analysis of the changes in the accounts on the balance sheet over the accounting period. Information to prepare this statement comes from the following three sources.

1. **Comparative balance sheets** provide the amount of the changes in each asset, liability, and equity account from the period's beginning to end.

2. **The current income statement** provides details about the most significant changes in the balance sheet retained earnings account and information about expenses that did not use cash and revenues that did not generate cash.

3. **Selected transaction data** from the general ledger provide additional information needed to determine how cash was generated or used during the period.

The preparation of the cash flow statement by manually accumulating these three sources of information is still very common today in small and medium-sized enterprises, in spite of advances made in technology. Alternatively, some companies have unique spreadsheet programs that generate the cash flow statement from a combination of their income statement data, changes in balance sheet accounts, and other cash flow details provided as input. Larger organizations with sophisticated enterprise resource planning systems and multi-dimensional databases have created template-based cash flow reports using their financial statement reporting modules, or have the ability to generate server-based cash flow calculations in real time.

Steps in the Process

Whether you are preparing a cash flow statement manually, developing a spreadsheet template for use in its preparation, or interpreting a completed statement that has been presented to you, familiarity with the manual steps involved in the statement's preparation explained below will increase your understanding of this important financial statement.

Step 1:   Determine the change in cash. This procedure is straightforward because the difference between the beginning and ending balances of cash and cash equivalents can easily be calculated by examining the comparative balance sheets. **Explaining this change is the objective of the analysis that follows.**

Step 2:   Record information from the income statement on the statement of cash flows.[9] This is the starting point for calculating cash flows from operating activities. **Whenever subsequent analyses indicate that the actual operating cash flow and the amount reported on the income statement are different, the income statement number is adjusted.**

---

[9] Income statement information is used rather than information from the statement of comprehensive income because other comprehensive income amounts are non-cash and non-operating in nature.

Most adjustments fall into one of three categories:

Category 1. Amounts that are reported as revenues and expenses on the income statement are not the same as cash received from customers and cash paid to suppliers of goods and services. Companies receive cash from customers for revenue reported in a previous year, and do not receive cash for all the revenue reported as earned in the current period. Similarly, cash payments are made in the current period to suppliers for goods and services acquired, used, and recognized as expense in a preceding period. In addition, not all amounts that are recognized as expense in the current year are paid for by year end. Most of the adjustments for these differences are related to receivables, payables, and other working capital accounts.

Category 2. Some expenses, such as depreciation and amortization, represent costs that were incurred and paid for in a previous period. While there was a cash flow associated with the original acquisition of the asset (an investing flow), there is no cash flow associated with the amortization of these assets over the periods they are used.

Category 3. Amounts that are reported as gains or losses on the income statement are not usually the same as the cash amount from the transaction and, in many cases, the underlying activity is not an operating transaction. For example, gains and losses on the disposal of long-term assets and on the early retirement of long-term debt are reported on the income statement. The first results from an investing transaction and the second from a financing transaction—neither is an operating activity. Also, the cash flow amounts are the **proceeds on disposal** of the asset and the **payment to retire the debt, not the amount of the reported gain or loss**.

Step 3: ***Analyze the change in each balance sheet account, identify all cash flows associated with changes in the account balance, and record the effect on the statement of cash flows.*** This analysis identifies all investing and financing cash flows, and all adjustments that are needed to convert income reported on the income statement to cash flow from operations. Analyze the balance sheet accounts one at a time until all the changes have been explained and the related cash flows identified.

Step 4: ***Complete the statement of cash flows.*** Calculate subtotals for the operating, investing, and financing categories and ensure that the net change in cash you determined is equal to the actual change in cash for the period.[10]

We now work through these four steps to prepare the statements of cash flows for three different companies of increasing complexity.

First Illustration—Tax Consultants Inc.

Tax Consultants Inc. began operations on January 1, 2011, when it issued 60,000 common shares for $60,000 cash. The company rented its office space and furniture and equipment, and performed tax consulting services throughout its first year. The 2011 comparative balance sheets and the income statement and additional information for 2011 are presented in Illustration 22-6.

---

[10] On occasion, even experienced accountants get to this step and find that the statement does not balance! Don't despair. Determine the amount of your error and review your analysis until you find it.

Illustration 22-6

Comparative Balance Sheets and Income Statement—Tax Consultants Inc., 2011

COMPARATIVE BALANCE SHEETS

Assets	Dec. 31, 2011	Jan. 1, 2011	Change Increase/Decrease
Cash	$49,000	$-0-	$49,000 increase
Accounts receivable	36,000	-0-	36,000 increase
	$85,000	$-0-	
Liabilities and Shareholders' Equity			
Accounts payable	$ 5,000	$-0-	5,000 increase
Common shares	60,000	-0-	60,000 increase
Retained earnings	20,000	-0-	20,000 increase
	$85,000	$-0-	

INCOME STATEMENT
For the Year Ended December 31, 2011

Revenues	$125,000
Operating expenses	85,000
Income before income taxes	40,000
Income tax expense	6,000
Net income	$ 34,000

Additional information:
An examination of selected data indicates that a dividend of $14,000 was declared during the year.

Step 1: **Determine the change in cash.** This first step is a straightforward calculation. Tax Consultants Inc. had no cash on hand at the beginning of 2011 and $49,000 on hand at the end of 2011; thus, the change in cash was an increase of $49,000.

Step 2: **Record information from the income statement on the statement of cash flows.** Most cash activity in any organization is related to operations, so the second step takes information from the operating statement (the income statement) and reports it on the statement of cash flows under the heading "Cash flows from operating activities." The specific information that is taken from the income statement and reported on the statement of cash flows in this step **depends on whether the indirect or the direct approach is used**. Regardless of the approach, this information will be converted from the accrual basis to the cash basis through adjustments in Step 3.

Objective 6

Prepare a statement of cash flows using the direct method.

Direct Method. Under this approach, skeleton headings similar to the ones in Illustration 22-4 are set up under "Cash flows from operating activities." The number and descriptions of these headings vary from company to company. Amounts reported on the income statement are then transferred on a line-by-line basis to the heading that comes closest to representing the type of cash flow, until all components of net income have been transferred.

Illustration 22-7

Direct Approach

DIRECT APPROACH

Cash flows from operating activities

Cash received from customers	+125,000
Cash paid to suppliers	− 85,000
Income taxes paid	− 6,000
	+ 34,000

Cash flows from investing activities
Cash flows from financing activities

The three headings in Illustration 22-7 are appropriate for Tax Consultants Inc. Because all income statement amounts are transferred to the Operating Activities section, the net amount transferred is equal to the amount of net income—the same as under the indirect approach.

In Step 3, adjustments are made to the appropriate line within the Operating Cash Flow section whenever the analysis indicates an operating cash flow that is not equal to the revenue or expense amount reported on the income statement. Revenues of $125,000 will be converted into the amount of cash received from customers; operating expenses of $85,000 will be adjusted to the amount of cash payments made to suppliers; and income tax expense of $6,000 will become income tax payments remitted to the government. Under this approach, the specific revenue and expense lines are adjusted. Under the indirect method discussed below, it is only the bottom-line net income number that is adjusted, **but they are identical adjustments**.

Indirect Method. The indirect approach transfers the net income amount reported on the income statement to the operating section of the statement of cash flows, as indicated in Illustration 22-8. Whenever the analysis in Step 3 indicates an operating cash inflow or outflow that differs from the amount of revenue or expense included in the net income figure, the net income number is adjusted to correct it to the operating cash effect.

7   **Objective**
Prepare a statement of cash flows using the indirect method.

INDIRECT APPROACH

Cash flows from operating activities	
Net income	+34,000
Adjustments:	
Cash flows from investing activities	
Cash flows from financing activities	

Illustration   22-8

Indirect Approach

Step 3: Analyze the change in each balance sheet account, identify all cash flows associated with changes in the account balance, and record the effect on the statement of cash flows. By analyzing the change in each account, transactions that involve cash can be identified and their effects can be recorded on the statement of cash flows.

Because the change in each account on the statement of financial position has to be explained, begin with the first non-cash asset and work down systematically through each asset, liability, and equity account. The results of Step 3 are provided in Illustration 22-9, where each item is referenced to the analysis that follows.

Illustration   22-9

Preparation of Statement of Cash Flows—Tax Consultants Inc.

CASH FLOWS FROM OPERATING ACTIVITIES

Indirect Method

Net income	+34,000
Adjustments: Increase in accounts receivable	−36,000(a)
Increase in accounts payable	+ 5,000(b)
	+ 3,000

Direct Method

Cash received from customers	+125,000	−36,000(a)	+89,000
Cash paid to suppliers	− 85,000	+ 5,000(b)	−80,000
Income taxes paid	− 6,000		− 6,000
	+ 34,000		+ 3,000

CASH FLOWS FROM INVESTING ACTIVITIES	–0–
CASH FLOWS FROM FINANCING ACTIVITIES	
Proceeds from issue of common shares	**+60,000(c)**
Dividends paid	**−14,000(d)**
	+46,000
Increase in cash	+49,000

(a) **Accounts Receivable.** During the year, Tax Consultants' receivables increased by $36,000. Because this account increases by the amount of revenue that is recognized and decreases by cash received from customers, the cash received from customers must have been $36,000 less than the revenue reported on the 2011 income statement. Therefore, an adjustment is needed in the Operating Activities section of the statement of cash flows. Under the indirect method, $36,000 is deducted from the net income number because $36,000 less cash came in than is included in the revenue component of the net income reported. Using the direct method, the revenue line is reduced directly.

(b) **Accounts Payable.** Accounts Payable increases by purchases on account and decreases by payments on account. Tax Consultants' purchases must have been $5,000 higher than payments during 2011. A $5,000 adjustment is needed to convert the purchases included in net income to the amount paid to suppliers.

Under the indirect method, $5,000 is added back to net income because the amount deducted as expense did not use an equivalent amount of cash. Under the direct approach, the $5,000 adjustment is made to the operating expense line where the cost of the goods and services purchased was presented.

(c) **Common Shares.** The increase in this account resulted from the issue of shares that was recorded in this entry:

Cash	60,000	
Common Shares		60,000

The $60,000 inflow of cash is reported on the statement of cash flows as a financing inflow.

(d) **Retained Earnings.** In this account, $34,000 of the increase is explained by net income. We already recognized this on the statement as the starting point in calculating cash flows from operations. The remaining change in the account is explained by the entry:

Retained Earnings	14,000	
Cash		14,000

Assuming Tax Consultants Inc. reports under ASPE, the $14,000 dividend payment is reported as a financing outflow. The entire dividend must have been paid in cash because the company does not report a Dividends Payable account.

The changes in all balance sheet accounts have been explained and their cash effects have been reported appropriately on the statement of cash flows. The statement can now be completed.

Step 4: ***Complete the statement of cash flows.*** Calculate subtotals for each of the operating, investing, and financing sections, and then the change in cash for the year. This should agree with the change identified in Step 1.

The completed statement illustrating both the indirect and the direct method is shown in Illustration 22-10.

Illustration 22-10

Completed Statement of Cash Flows—Tax Consultants Inc.

STATEMENT OF CASH FLOWS
Year Ended December 31, 2011

Indirect Method			Direct Method			
Cash flows from operating activities			**Cash flows from operating activities**			
Net income		$34,000	Cash received from customers			$89,000
Less: Increase in accounts			Less cash payments:			
receivable		(36,000)	To suppliers		$80,000	
Add: Increase in accounts payable		5,000	For income taxes		6,000	86,000
		3,000				3,000
Cash flows from investing activities		–0–	**Cash flows from investing activities**			–0–
Cash flows from financing activities			**Cash flows from financing activities**			
Proceeds on issue of common shares		60,000	Proceeds on issue of common shares			60,000
Payment of dividends		(14,000)	Payment of dividends			(14,000)
		46,000				46,000
Increase in cash during year		49,000	**Increase in cash during year**			49,000
Opening cash balance		–0–	Opening cash balance			–0–
Cash, December 31, 2011		$49,000	Cash, December 31, 2011			$49,000

The $49,000 cash increase came from a combination of net operating inflows of $3,000 and net financing inflows (primarily from the sale of common shares) of $46,000. Note that net cash provided by operating activities is the same whether the direct or indirect method is used. The indirect method explains how the company could report a healthy income of $34,000 yet have an operating cash inflow of only $3,000. The main reason is that $36,000 of the revenue reported has not yet been collected. The direct method provides different insights. The $3,000 contribution to cash from operations is a result of cash collections from customers ($89,000) being only a little more than the operating cash outflows to suppliers ($80,000) and to the government for taxes ($6,000).

Second Illustration—Eastern Window Products Limited

To illustrate the preparation of a more complex statement of cash flows, we use the operations of Eastern Window Products Limited (EWPL) for its 2012 year. EWPL has been operating for several years, and the company's comparative balance sheets at December 31, 2012 and 2011, its statement of income and retained earnings for the year ended December 31, 2012, and other information are provided in Illustration 22-11.

For purposes of this example, EWPL could be reporting under either ASPE or IFRS. Assume, if a publicly accountable enterprise, that company management has chosen to present interest paid as an operating flow and dividends paid as a financing flow.

BALANCE SHEETS – DECEMBER 31

	2012 $	2011 $	Change Increase/Decrease $
Cash	37,000	59,000	22,000 decrease
Accounts receivable	46,000	56,000	10,000 decrease
Inventory	82,000	73,000	9,000 increase
Prepaid expenses	6,000	7,500	1,500 decrease
Land	70,000	-0-	70,000 increase
Building	200,000	-0-	200,000 increase
Accumulated depreciation—building	(6,000)	-0-	6,000 increase
Equipment	68,000	63,000	5,000 increase
Accumulated depreciation—equipment	(19,000)	(10,000)	9,000 increase
	484,000	248,500	
Accounts payable	70,000	59,100	10,900 increase
Income taxes payable	4,000	1,000	3,000 increase
Wages payable	2,000	2,700	700 decrease
Mortgage payable	152,400	-0-	152,400 increase
Bonds payable	50,000	40,000	10,000 increase
Common shares	80,000	72,000	8,000 increase
Retained earnings	125,600	73,700	51,900 increase
	484,000	248,500	

STATEMENT OF INCOME AND RETAINED EARNINGS
Year Ended December 31, 2012

Sales revenue		$592,000
Less: Cost of goods sold		355,000
Gross profit		237,000
Salaries and wages expense	$55,000	
Interest expense	16,200	
Depreciation expense	15,000	
Other operating expenses	51,000	137,200
Income before income tax		99,800
Income tax expense		39,900
Net income		59,900
Retained earnings, January 1		73,700
Dividends declared		(8,000)
Retained earnings, December 31		$125,600

Additional information:
The company assumed an existing mortgage of $155,000 on acquiring a building and land during 2012.

Step 1: **Determine the change in cash**. Cash decreased by $22,000 during the year. There are no cash equivalents.

Step 2: **Record information from the income statement on the statement of cash flows**. Under the **indirect approach**, record the $59,900 net income in the Operating Activities section of the statement of cash flows.

Under the **direct approach**, set up skeleton headings for the types of operating cash flows involved. Illustration 22-12 suggests that six headings are likely appropriate for EWPL, including an "Other expenses/losses" section that includes items such as depreciation expense that do not fall under the other headings. Because all income statement amounts are transferred to the Operating Activities section, the net amount transferred is the same as under the indirect approach.

As you proceed through Step 3 using the direct approach, the following will occur:

- sales revenue of $592,000 will be converted into cash received from customers,

- cost of goods sold of $355,000 and other operating expenses of $51,000 will be adjusted to an amount that represents cash payments to suppliers for goods and services acquired,

- salaries and wages expense of $55,000 will become cash payments made to and on behalf of employees,

- interest expense of $16,200 becomes interest payments made, and

- income tax expense of $39,900 becomes income tax payments remitted to the government.

Illustration 22-12

Statement of Cash Flows Working Paper—EWPL

CASH FLOWS FROM OPERATING ACTIVITIES

Indirect Method

Net income	+ 59,900
Adjustments: Decrease in accounts receivable	+ 10,000(a)
Increase in inventory	− 9,000(b)
Decrease in prepaid expenses	+ 1,500(c)
Depreciation expense—building	+ 6,000(e)
Depreciation expense—equipment	+ 9,000(g)
Increase in accounts payable	+ 10,900(h)
Increase in income taxes payable	+ 3,000(i)
Decrease in wages payable	− 700(j)
	+ 90,600

Direct Method

Cash received from customers	+592,000	+10,000(a)	+602,000
Cash paid to suppliers			
for goods and services	−355,000	− 9,000(b)	
	− 51,000	+ 1,500(c)	−402,600
		+10,900(h)	
Cash paid to employees	− 55,000	− 700(j)	− 55,700
Cash interest paid	− 16,200		− 16,200
Income taxes paid	− 39,900	+ 3,000(i)	− 36,900
Other expenses/losses—depreciation	− 15,000	+ 6,000(e)	—
		+ 9,000(g)	
	+ 59,900		+ 90,600

CASH FLOWS FROM INVESTING ACTIVITIES

Purchase of land and building	−115,000(d)
Purchase of equipment	− 5,000(f)
	−120,000

CASH FLOWS FROM FINANCING ACTIVITIES

Mortgage payable	− 2,600(k)
Bonds issued	+ 10,000(l)
Shares issued	+ 8,000(m)
Dividends paid	− 8,000(n)
	+ 7,400
CHANGE IN CASH	− 22,000

Step 3:   Analyze the change in each balance sheet account, identify any cash flows associated with a change in the account balance, and record the effect on the statement of cash flows. The results of this step are provided in Illustration 22-12 above, where each item is referenced to the analysis that follows.

(a) **Accounts Receivable.** During the year, EWPL's receivables decreased by $10,000. Because Accounts Receivable is increased by revenue that is recognized and decreased by cash received from customers, the cash inflow from customers must have been $10,000 more than the revenue reported on the 2012 income statement. Under the indirect method, $10,000 is added to the net income number. Under the direct method, the revenue number is increased directly.

(b) **Inventory.** Inventory increased by $9,000. Because Inventory is increased by the purchase of goods and is reduced by transferring costs to cost of goods sold, EWPL must have purchased $9,000 more inventory than it sold and, therefore, $9,000 more than the costs included in cost of goods sold on the income statement. The first part of this analysis does not tell us how much cash was paid for the purchases; it only converts cost of goods sold to the cost of purchases in the year. The analysis of Accounts Payable (see item [h] below) converts the amount purchased to the cash payments to suppliers.

Cost of goods sold of $355,000 was deducted in calculating net income. Under the indirect method, net income must be further reduced by $9,000 to adjust for the additional $9,000 of goods purchased that are still in inventory. Under the direct method, the $9,000 adjustment is made directly to the cost of goods sold line to adjust it to the cost of goods purchased.

(c) **Prepaid Expenses.** Prepaid Expenses decreased by $1,500. Because this account is increased by the acquisition of goods and services before they are used and decreased by transferring the cost of the goods and services used up to expense—the same as for inventory—EWPL must have recognized $1,500 more expense than the amount purchased. The expenses reported on the income statement, therefore, have to be reduced by $1,500 to convert them to the cost of goods and services purchased. Under the indirect method, $1,500 is added back to the income reported. Under the direct method, the appropriate expense is reduced directly for the $1,500. When the Accounts Payable account is analyzed below, the purchases will be adjusted to cash paid to suppliers.

(d) **Land, Building.** The balance sheets indicate an increase in Land of $70,000 and an increase in the Building account of $200,000, suggesting an investing cash outflow of $270,000. The investment in real property, however, is often financed by directly assuming a mortgage note payable that results in a lower net cash outlay. A review of the records indicates that EWPL assumed a $155,000 mortgage in acquiring the land and building, so the actual cash outflow is only $115,000 (the $270,000 cost of the land and building less the financing provided by the mortgage of $155,000). It is often useful to prepare the underlying journal entry:

Land	70,000	
Building	200,000	
Mortgage Payable		155,000
Cash		115,000

This entry explains the change in the Land and the Building accounts on the balance sheet. It also explains part of the change in the Mortgage Payable account (see item [k] below), and identifies the actual outflow of cash of $115,000. This is reported as an **investing** cash flow on the statement.

(e) **Accumulated Depreciation—Building**. The $6,000 increase in this account is due entirely to the recognition of depreciation expense for the year:

Depreciation Expense	6,000	
Accumulated Depreciation—Building		6,000

The entry records a non-cash event. Under the indirect approach, $6,000 is added back to net income because depreciation expense did not use up any cash. Under the direct approach, depreciation expense is adjusted directly.

(f) **Equipment**. EWPL purchased $5,000 of equipment during 2012. This resulted in an investing outflow of cash of $5,000.

(g) **Accumulated Depreciation—Equipment**. The $9,000 increase in this account is due to depreciation expense for the year. As explained in item (e), the operating activities section is adjusted for this non-cash expense.

(h) **Accounts Payable**. The Accounts Payable account is increased by the cost of purchases and decreased by payments on account. EWPL's cash payments to suppliers, therefore, must have been $10,900 less than the goods and services purchased during the year. In steps (b) and (c) above, cost of goods sold and other expenses were adjusted to convert them to the cost of goods and services purchased. A further adjustment of $10,900 is required to adjust the purchases to the amount of cash that was actually paid.

Under the indirect method, $10,900 is added back to net income to reflect the fact that the amounts deducted for purchases did not use an equivalent amount of cash. Under the direct approach, the $10,900 adjustment reduces the cost of goods and services purchased to the cash outflow for these purchases.

(i) **Income Taxes Payable.** This liability account is increased by the current income tax expense reported and is decreased by payments to the government. Income tax expense, therefore, was $3,000 higher than the payments. Under the indirect method, the $3,000 difference is added back to net income. Under the direct method, an adjustment is made to the income tax expense line.

(j) **Wages Payable.** Similar to other current payables, this account is increased by amounts recognized as expense and decreased by payments; in this case, to employees. The $700 decrease indicates that cash outflows were $700 more than wages expense. Under the indirect method, an additional $700 is deducted from the reported income. Salaries and wages expense is adjusted under the direct approach.[11]

(k) **Mortgage Payable.** The cash flow associated with part of the change in this account was identified above in item (d). If the account increased by $155,000 when the property was acquired, principal payments of $2,600 must have been made to reduce the balance to $152,400. The entry underlying this transaction is:

Mortgage Payable	2,600	
Cash		2,600

[11] For all current asset and current liability account changes that adjust accrual basis net income to cash flows from operations, a simple check can be made. The adjustment for all increases in current asset accounts should have the same effect within the Operating Activities section of the statement of cash flows. All decreases in current asset accounts should have the same effect. All increases and decreases in current liability accounts should have the opposite effect of increases and decreases, respectively, in current asset accounts. This is a useful mechanical procedure to double-check your adjustments.

This is a financing outflow.

(l) **Bonds Payable.** The increase in this account is explained by the following entry:

Cash	10,000	
Bonds Payable		10,000

The $10,000 cash received from the bond issue is a financing cash inflow.

(m) **Common Shares.** The $8,000 increase in this account resulted from the issue of shares.

Cash	8,000	
Common Shares		8,000

The $8,000 cash received is a financing inflow.

(n) **Retained Earnings.** Net income accounts for $59,900 of the increase in retained earnings. We recognized this on the statement of cash flows already as the starting point in calculating cash flows from operations. The remainder of the change is explained by the entry for dividends:

Retained Earnings	8,000	
Cash		8,000

The payment of dividends that is charged to retained earnings is classified as a financing outflow. This treatment is required under **private enterprise** standards, and permitted under **IFRS**—the alternative being to recognize it as an operating outflow.

As the changes in all balance sheet accounts have now been explained and all cash flows have been identified, the statement can be completed.

Step 4: **Complete the statement of cash flows.** Subtotals are calculated for each section of the statement and the calculated change in cash is compared with the change identified in Step 1. Both indicate a $22,000 decrease in EWPL's cash balance during 2012.

A statement in good form is then prepared from the working paper developed in Illustration 22-12, using more appropriate descriptions and explanations. Illustration 22-13 shows what the final statement might look like if the indirect method is chosen. The additional disclosures that are provided are discussed in a later section of the chapter.

Illustration 22-13

EWPL Statement of Cash Flows, 2012—Indirect Method

EASTERN WINDOW PRODUCTS LIMITED
Statement of Cash Flows
Year Ended December 31, 2012

Cash provided by (used in) operations		
Net income		$ 59,900
Add back non-cash expense—depreciation		15,000
Add (deduct) changes in non-cash working capital[a]		
– accounts receivable	$10,000	
– inventory	(9,000)	

– prepaid expenses	1,500	
– accounts payable	10,900	
– income taxes payable	3,000	
– wages payable	(700)	15,700
		90,600
Cash provided by (used in) investing activities		
Purchase of property, plant, and equipment		(120,000)
Cash provided by (used in) financing activities		
Payment on mortgage payable	(2,600)	
Proceeds on issue of bonds	10,000	
Dividends paid	(8,000)	
Proceeds on issue of common shares	8,000	7,400
Decrease in cash		(22,000)
Cash balance, beginning of year		59,000
Cash balance, end of year		$ 37,000

Notes:
1. Cash consists of cash on hand and balances with banks.
2. Cash payments during the year for interest and income taxes were $16,200 and $36,900, respectively.
3. During the year, property was acquired at a total cost of $275,000 (land $70,000; building $200,000;[b] equipment $5,000), of which $155,000 was financed directly by the assumption of a mortgage.

[a] Many companies provide only the subtotal on the statement of cash flows and report the details in a note to the financial statements.
[b] IFRS requirement only.

Illustration 22-14 presents the Operating Activities section of the statement of cash flows if the direct method had been used.

Cash provided by (used in) operations	
Received from customers	$ 602,000
Payments to suppliers	(402,600)
Payments to and on behalf of employees	(55,700)
Interest payments	(16,200)
Income taxes paid	(36,900)
	$ 90,600

Illustration 22-14

Operating Activities Section, Direct Method—EWPL

Third Illustration—Yoshi Corporation

The next step is to see how the same principles are applied to more complex situations. Some of these complexities are illustrated through our next example of a **publicly accountable entity**, Yoshi Corporation, as we use the same approach as in the two previous examples. Although Yoshi Corporation applies IFRS, almost all of the situations are treated the same as if the company applied private enterprise standards. If you prefer a more structured method of accumulating the information for the statement of cash flows than what is shown here, we recommend that you refer to the work sheet approach in Appendix 22A or the T account method illustrated on the Student Website.

Illustrations 22-15, 22-16, 22-17, and 22-18 provide the comparative balance sheets of Yoshi Corporation at December 31, 2012 and 2011; the statement of comprehensive income; the statement of changes in equity for the year ended December 31, 2012; and selected additional information.

Illustration 22-15

Comparative Balance Sheets—Yoshi Corporation

YOSHI CORPORATION
Comparative Balance Sheets
December 31, 2012 and 2011

	2012 $	2011 $	Change Increase/Decrease $
Assets			
Cash	5,000	32,000	27,000 decrease
Cash equivalents	14,000	4,000	10,000 increase
Temporary investments	25,000	30,000	5,000 decrease
Accounts receivable	106,500	52,700	53,800 increase
Allowance for doubtful accounts	(2,500)	(1,700)	800 increase
Inventories	303,000	311,000	8,000 decrease
Prepaid expenses	16,500	17,000	500 decrease
Investment in shares of Portel Corp.	18,500	15,000	3,500 increase
Investment in shares of Hyco Ltd.	17,500	13,000	4,500 increase
Deferred development costs	190,000	30,000	160,000 increase
Land	131,500	82,000	49,500 increase
Equipment	187,000	142,000	45,000 increase
Accumulated depreciation—equipment	(29,000)	(31,000)	2,000 decrease
Buildings	262,000	262,000	–0–
Accumulated depreciation—buildings	(74,100)	(71,000)	3,100 increase
Goodwill	7,600	10,000	2,400 decrease
Total assets	1,178,500	897,000	
Liabilities			
Accounts payable	130,000	131,000	1,000 decrease
Dividends payable, term preferred shares	2,000	–0–	2,000 increase
Accrued liabilities	43,000	39,000	4,000 increase
Income taxes payable	3,000	16,000	13,000 decrease
Bonds payable	97,800	97,500	300 increase
Term preferred shares	60,000	–0–	60,000 increase
Future income tax liability	10,000	6,000	4,000 increase
Total liabilities	345,800	289,500	
Shareholders' Equity			
Common shares	225,400	88,000	137,400 increase
Retained earnings	602,800	518,500	84,300 increase
AOCI	4,500	1,000	3,500 increase
Total shareholders' equity	832,700	607,500	
Liabilities and shareholders' equity	1,178,500	897,000	

Illustration 22-16

Statement of Comprehensive Income—Yoshi Corporation

YOSHI CORPORATION
Statement of Comprehensive Income
Year Ended December 31, 2012

Net sales		$923,200
Equity in earnings of Portel Corp.		5,500
Investment income, temporary investments		1,300
Gain on sale of land		10,500
		940,500
Expenses		
Cost of goods sold	$395,400	
Salaries and wages	200,000	
Selling and administrative	134,600	
Depreciation	14,600	
Interest and dividend expense	11,300	

Impairment loss—goodwill	2,400	
Other expenses and losses	12,000	770,300
Income before income tax		170,200
Income tax: Current	49,500	
Future	3,000	52,500
Net income		117,700
Other comprehensive income		
Unrealized gain on FV-OCI investment,		
net of future income tax of $1,000		3,500
Comprehensive income		$121,200

Illustration 22-17

Statement of Changes in Equity—Yoshi Corporation

YOSHI CORPORATION
Statement of Changes in Equity
Year Ended December 31, 2012

	Common Shares $	Retained Earnings $	Accumulated Other Comprehensive Income $	Total $
Balance, January 1, 2012	88,000	518,500	1,000	607,500
2% stock dividend issued	15,000	(15,000)		–0–
Proceeds on sale of shares	144,000			144,000
Shares purchased and cancelled	(21,600)	(12,400)		(34,000)
Net income		117,700		117,700
Cash dividend declared		(6,000)		(6,000)
Unrealized gain, FV-OCI investment			3,500	3,500
Balance, December 31, 2012	225,400	602,800	4,500	832,700

Illustration 22-18

Additional Information—Yoshi Corporation

YOSHI CORPORATION
Additional Information

1. Cash equivalents represent money-market instruments with original maturity dates of less than 90 days.
2. Temporary investments held at the beginning of the year were sold during the year for $32,300. Additional investments, also accounted for at FV-NI, were acquired at a cost of $26,000.
3. During 2012, bad debts of $1,450 were written off.
4. Yoshi accounts for its 22% interest in Portel Corp. using the equity method. Portel Corp. paid a dividend in 2012.
5. The investment in shares of Hyco Ltd. was purchased in 2011 for $12,000 and classified for accounting purposes at FV-OCI.
6. During 2012, Yoshi incurred $200,000 of development costs that met the criteria for deferral as an intangible asset. During the year, $40,000 of this asset was amortized.
7. Land in the amount of $54,000 was purchased by issuing term preferred shares. The term preferred shares are classified as financial liabilities.
8. An analysis of the Equipment account and related accumulated depreciation indicates the following:

Equipment:	
Balance, January 1, 2012	$142,000
Cost of equipment purchased	73,000
Cost of equipment sold (sold at a loss of $1,500)	(28,000)
Balance, December 31, 2012	$187,000

continued on page 1492

Accumulated depreciation:

Balance, January 1, 2012	$ 31,000
Accumulated depreciation on equipment sold	(13,500)
Depreciation expense, 2012	11,500
Balance, December 31, 2012	$ 29,000

9. The bonds payable, issued in 2010, were issued at a discount and have a maturity value of $100,000.
10. Changes in other balance sheet accounts resulted from usual transactions and events.

Step 1:   **Determine the change in cash**. Yoshi's cash and cash equivalents include holdings of money-market instruments as well as cash balances, with a decrease in cash of $17,000 that needs to be explained. This is the difference between the opening cash and cash equivalents of $36,000 ($32,000 + $4,000) and the ending cash and cash equivalents of $19,000 ($5,000 + $14,000).

Step 2:   **Record information from the income statement on the statement of cash flows**. Under the **indirect method**, the net income of $117,700 is inserted as the starting point, as shown in Illustration 22-19.

Illustration 22-19

Statement of Cash Flows Working Paper—Yoshi Corporation

CASH FLOWS FROM OPERATING ACTIVITIES

Indirect Method

Net income	+117,700
Adjustments: Decrease in trading investments	+ 5,000(a)
Increase in accounts receivable, net of write-offs	− 55,250(b)
Bad debt expense	+ 2,250(c)
Decrease in inventories	+ 8,000(d)
Decrease in prepaid expenses	+ 500(e)
Equity method investment income	− 5,500(f)
Dividend from equity method investment	+ 2,000(f)
Amortization of development costs	+ 40,000(h)
Gain on sale of land	− 10,500(i)
Loss on disposal of equipment	+ 1,500(j)
Depreciation expense—equipment	+ 11,500(j)
Depreciation expense—buildings	+ 3,100(k)
Impairment loss—goodwill	+ 2,400(l)
Decrease in accounts payable	− 1,000(m)
Increase in dividends payable on term preferred shares	+ 2,000(n)
Increase in accrued liabilities	+ 4,000(o)
Decrease in income taxes payable	− 13,000(p)
Amortization of bond discount	+ 300(q)
Increase in future income tax liability (net income)	+ 3,000(s)
	+118,000

Direct Method

Receipts from customers	+923,200	−55,250(b)	+867,950
Received from investment in Portel Corp.	+ 5,500	− 5,500(f) + 2,000(f)	+ 2,000
Received on temporary investment transactions	+ 1,300	+ 5,000(a)	+ 6,300
Payments for goods and services	−395,400	+ 2,250(c)	
	−134,600	+ 8,000(d)	
	− 12,000	+ 500(e)	
		+40,000(h)	−490,750
		+ 1,500(j)	
		− 1,000(m)	

Payments to employees	−200,000	+ 4,000(o)	− 196,000
Interest and dividend payments	− 11,300	+ 2,000(n) ⎫	− 9,000
		+ 300(q) ⎭	
Income taxes paid	− 52,500	−13,000(p) ⎫	− 62,500
		+ 3,000(s) ⎭	
Other items:			
Depreciation expense	− 14,600	+11,500(j) ⎫	—
		+ 3,100(k) ⎭	
Impairment loss	− 2,400	+ 2,400(l)	—
Gain on sale of land	+ 10,500	−10,500(i)	—
	+117,700		+118,000

CASH FLOWS FROM INVESTING ACTIVITIES

Development costs incurred	−200,000(h)
Proceeds on sale of land	+ 15,000(i)
Purchase of equipment	− 73,000(j)
Proceeds on sale of equipment	+ 13,000(j)
	−245,000

CASH FLOWS FROM FINANCING ACTIVITIES

Proceeds on issue of term preferred shares	+ 6,000(r)
Proceeds on issue of common shares	+144,000(t)
Dividends paid on common shares	− 6,000(u)
Payment to repurchase common shares	− 34,000(t)
	+110,000
CHANGE IN CASH	− 17,000

Using the **direct method**, skeleton headings that cover each potential type of cash flow—from customer receipts to income taxes—are set up within the Operating Activities section of the statement of cash flows working paper, as shown in Illustration 22-19. The statement of comprehensive income provides clues about the types of operating cash flows and how they should be described. For example, the equity basis income from the investment in Portel Corp. is not a cash flow, but it will be replaced after adjustment with any dividends received from the investment.

Each amount that makes up the net income of $117,700 is transferred to the most appropriate skeleton heading on the work sheet. Amounts reported as cost of goods sold, selling and administrative expense, and other expenses and losses form the base for what will eventually be "Cash paid to suppliers for goods and services." Income tax expense is included on the line that will be adjusted to "Income taxes paid." The holding gain on the FV-OCI investment and the tax on it are not included, but will be taken into account later.

Note that this illustration begins with **net income**, consistent with the international standard. Other companies, however, may decide to begin with comprehensive income, or even income before taxes. As long as the relationship of the beginning number to net income is obvious, the objective of the standard is met. If a number other than net income is used, the adjustments that follow will also be different, but the final statement will report the same amounts and types of cash flows and change in cash balances as under the approach used here.

*Step 3: **Analyze the change in each balance sheet account, identify any cash flows associated with a change in the account balance, and record the effect on the statement of cash flows.*** The analysis begins with the temporary investments that are held for trading purposes.

(a) **Temporary Investments.** Based on information provided in Illustration 22-18, we can reproduce the entries made during the year to this account:

Cash	32,300	
Temporary Investments		30,000
Investment Income, Temporary Investments		2,300
Temporary Investments	26,000	
Cash		26,000
Investment Income, Temporary Investments	1,000	
Temporary Investments		1,000

These entries tell us three things:

1. They explain the change in the Temporary Investments account during the year.

2. They indicate what makes up the investment income on the temporary investments of $1,300.

3. They indicate that the cash effect of these transactions is +$32,300 − $26,000 = +$6,300.

The net cash flow is an **operating** flow because the securities were acquired for trading purposes. We have already included an inflow of $1,300 in the operating section, so an adjustment is needed there for an additional $5,000.

Under the indirect method, $5,000 is added to the net income number to increase the cash inflow from the $1,300 already included to the actual $6,300 net cash inflow that was generated. Under the direct approach, the $5,000 adjustment is made to the line item identifying the trading investment activity.

(b) **Accounts Receivable.** Unlike the previous two company illustrations, Yoshi reports both the receivable and its contra allowance account. The receivable control account is increased by sales on account and reduced by accounts written off and cash received on account. The 2012 receivable T account is shown below, with the Sales amount taken from the income statement. The cash received on account, the only missing information, must have been $867,950. This was determined by solving for the one unknown credit entry: $52,700 + $923,200 − $1,450 − x = $106,500. The cash received, therefore, was $923,200 − $867,950 = $55,250 less than the revenue reported on the income statement.

Accounts Receivable			
Jan.1	52,700		
Sales on account	923,200	1,450	Accounts written off (given)
		?	Cash received on account
Dec. 31	106,500		

Using the indirect approach, $55,250 is deducted from the net income reported. Under the direct method, the revenue of $923,200 is adjusted directly by $55,250 to convert it to cash received from customers.

(c) **Allowance for Doubtful Accounts.** This account had an opening balance of $1,700, was increased by bad debt expense, reduced by accounts written off, and ended the year at $2,500. With accounts written off of $1,450, bad debt expense must have been $2,250 ($1,700 + bad debt expense − $1,450 = $2,500; or prepare a T account to determine this). Because bad debt expense does not use cash, the net income number in the Operating Activities section must be adjusted.

Under the indirect method, $2,250 is added back to net income. Under the direct method, the $2,250 adjustment reduces the expense line that includes bad debt expense. In this example, it is assumed to be in selling expenses.

The only time it is necessary to analyze the Accounts Receivable and the Allowance account separately is when the direct method is used. This is because two adjustments are needed: one to adjust the revenue reported ($55,250) and the other to adjust the non-cash bad debt expense ($2,250). When the indirect method is used, both adjustments correct the one net income number. The analysis is easier, therefore, if you focus on the change in the net accounts receivable and make one adjustment to the net income number.[12]

(d) **Inventories.** Because the Inventory account is increased by the cost of goods purchased and decreased by the transfer of costs to cost of goods sold, the $8,000 decrease in the Inventory account indicates that purchases were $8,000 less than cost of goods sold. Using the indirect approach, $8,000 is added back to the net income number. The direct approach adjusts cost of goods sold directly to convert it to the cost of goods purchased. The analysis of Accounts Payable in step (m) will convert the purchases to cash paid to suppliers.

(e) **Prepaid Expenses.** This account decreased by $500 because the costs that were charged to the income statement were $500 more than the costs of acquiring prepaid goods and services in the year. For reasons similar to the inventory analysis in step (d), $500 is either added back to net income under the indirect approach, or used to adjust the expense line associated with the prepaid expense under the direct approach. We assume that the prepaid expenses were charged to selling and administrative expenses when they were used.

(f) **Investment in Shares of Portel Corp.** The journal entries that explain the increase of $3,500 in this account are:

Investment in Portel Corp.	5,500	
Equity in Earnings of Portel Corp.		5,500
(To record investment income using the equity method.)		
Cash	2,000	
Investment in Portel Corp.		2,000
(To record the dividend received from Portel Corp.)		

The $5,500 investment income amount is reported on the income statement and the dividend amount is derived from the change in the account balance. Cash did not change as a result of the investment income; therefore, an adjustment is needed to reduce the net income number. Under the indirect method, the $5,500 is deducted to offset the $5,500 reported; under the direct approach, the $5,500 adjustment is made to the specific revenue line. This adjustment eliminates the equity-method income reported.

The second entry indicates a dividend cash inflow of $2,000. In this case, an adjustment is needed to the net income reported because it does not include the cash dividend. Unlike dividends received from other types of investments, those received

---

[12] For Yoshi Corporation, net receivables increased $53,000, from $51,000 ($52,700 − $1,700) at the beginning of the year to $104,000 ($106,500 − $2,500) at year end. The increase means that $53,000 of income was recognized that did not result in a corresponding cash flow. On the statement of cash flows under the indirect method, one adjustment to reduce net income by $53,000 is all that is needed.

from associates (significantly influenced investees) are reported in operating flows. Using the indirect method, $2,000 is added to net income. Under the direct approach, $2,000 is added to the same line as the $5,500 deduction above, as this completes the adjustment of the non-cash equity-basis income to cash received from the investment in Portel.

(g) **Investment in Shares of Hyco Ltd.** The entry that explains the change in this investment classified as an FV-OCI investment is:

Investment in Shares of Hyco Ltd.	4,500	
Holding Gain on Investment (OCI)		4,500
(To adjust investment to fair value at year end.)		

The entry explains the change in the investment account and the source of $4,500 of other comprehensive income. No cash flow is involved and no income statement amount is affected. Therefore, no amounts are reported on the statement of cash flows and no adjustment is needed in the operating section.

If an FV-OCI investment had been acquired or sold in the year, there would be investing cash flows to capture on the statement. In the case of a disposal, any realized holding gain or loss transferred (recycled) from OCI to net income would need to be eliminated in the operating activities section.

(h) **Deferred Development Costs.** The two transactions that affected this intangible asset account in the current year are summarized in the following journal entries:

Deferred Development Costs	200,000	
Cash		200,000
(To record capitalized development costs.)		
Development Expenses	40,000	
Deferred Development Costs		40,000
(To record the amortization of deferred development costs.)		

The first entry indicates a cash outflow of $200,000. This is an investing outflow and is recognized in the statement's Investing Activities section.

The second entry did not affect cash. As explained earlier, it is important to be alert to non-cash amounts that are included in net income. This $40,000 expense did not use any cash; an adjustment to net income is therefore needed under the indirect approach. Under the direct method, the adjustment is made to the specific expense: in this case, assumed to be the general operating expenses line.

(i) **Land.** This account increased by $49,500. Because you know that land was purchased at a cost of $54,000 during the year, there must have been a disposal of land with a cost of $4,500. Knowing there was a gain on sale of land of $10,500, the entries that affect this account in 2012 must have been:

Land	54,000	
Term Preferred Shares		54,000
(To record purchase of land through issue of term preferred shares.)		
Cash	15,000	
Land		4,500
Gain on Disposal of Land		10,500
(To record disposal of land costing $4,500.)		

The first entry indicates that there were no cash flows associated with this transaction. Although this investment and financing transaction is not reported on the statement of cash flows, information about such non-cash transactions is a required disclosure elsewhere in the financial statements.

The second entry identifies a cash inflow of $15,000 on land disposal. This is an investing inflow because it affects the company's stock of non-current assets, so it is included on the statement of cash flows in the investing cash flow section.

The second transaction also results in a gain of $10,500 on the income statement. By starting with "net income" in the statement's Operating Cash Flow section in Step 2, the $10,500 gain is included in income as if the gain had generated $10,500 of operating cash flows. This is incorrect for two reasons. First, the cash inflow was $15,000, not $10,500. Second, the cash flow was an investing, not an operating, flow. An adjustment is needed, therefore, to deduct $10,500 from the income reported using the indirect method or from the gain on sale of land line if the direct method is used.

(j) **Equipment and Accumulated Depreciation—Equipment.** All the information that is needed to reproduce the entries made to these accounts in 2012 was provided in Illustrations 22-15, 22-16, and 22-18.

Equipment	73,000	
Cash		73,000
Cash	13,000	
Loss on Disposal of Equipment	1,500	
Accumulated Depreciation—Equipment	13,500	
Equipment		28,000
Depreciation Expense	11,500	
Accumulated Depreciation—Equipment		11,500

The first entry explains a cash outflow of $73,000 due to the purchase of equipment, an investing activity.

The second entry records the disposal of an asset that cost $28,000 and has accumulated depreciation of $13,500; that is, a carrying amount of $14,500. To be sold at a loss of $1,500, the proceeds on disposal must have been $13,000.

The analysis of this entry is similar to the land disposal in step (i):

1. The cash effect is an inflow of $13,000. This is an investing receipt.

2. The transaction results in a loss of $1,500 that is reported in 2012 income. Because the cash effect was not a $1,500 payment and because it was not an operating flow, an adjustment is needed in the Operating Cash Flow section. The $1,500 loss is added back to net income under the indirect method, or to the appropriate line (other expenses and losses) under the direct approach.

The third entry reflects the annual depreciation expense. Depreciation does not use cash, so an adjustment is needed to add this amount back to net income. Under the direct method, the depreciation line itself is corrected.

(k) **Buildings and Accumulated Depreciation—Buildings.** There was no change in the asset account during the year and, since there is no additional information, the increase in the accumulated depreciation account must have been due entirely to the depreciation recorded for the year. The $3,100 non-cash expense is an adjustment in the Operating Activities section.

(l) **Goodwill.** The $2,400 decrease in Goodwill is the result of the following entry:

Impairment Loss—Goodwill	2,400	
Goodwill		2,400

There was no effect on cash. Under the indirect method, $2,400 is added back to net income; under the direct approach, the impairment loss line itself is reduced.

(m) **Accounts Payable.** Because Accounts Payable is increased by purchases on account for operations and decreased by payments to suppliers, cash outflows to suppliers must have been $1,000 higher than purchases in 2012. Previous adjustments to the work sheet in (d) and (e) converted expenses reported on the income statement to the cost of goods and services purchased. The analysis of accounts payable completes this by converting the purchases' amount to the cash paid for purchases. The indirect method deducts an additional $1,000 from the net income reported, while the direct method adjusts the expense line.

(n) **Dividends Payable on Term Preferred Shares.** The $2,000 increase indicates that dividends paid were $2,000 less than the dividends declared on these shares. Because the term preferred shares are liabilities in substance, the dividends on these shares are treated the same as interest on debt: they are deducted as dividend expense on the income statement. Under the indirect approach, $2,000 is added back to net income because the cash outflow was less than the dividend expense reported. Under the direct approach, the line item that includes the dividend expense is reduced. This assumes Yoshi reports interest paid as an operating outflow, and this treatment is required by PE GAAP.

    If Yoshi follows a policy of reporting interest paid (and dividends on in-substance financial liabilities) as financing outflows, as also permitted under IFRS, the amount recognized in net income and reported in operating flows on the work sheet is eliminated and the correct cash outflow is reported in the financing activities section.

(o) **Accrued Liabilities.** This account is increased by expenses recognized and decreased by payments of the accrued amounts. During 2012, the payments must have been $4,000 less than the expenses reported: $4,000 is therefore added back to net income under the indirect method. Using the direct approach, you must determine which expenses should be adjusted. If it was interest expense that was accrued and paid, the interest expense line is adjusted; if it was wages and salaries payable, the salaries and wages expense is adjusted. In Illustration 22-19, we assume the accruals relate to accrued payroll costs.

(p) **Income Taxes Payable.** This account is increased by current tax expense and decreased by payments to the tax authorities. The $13,000 reduction indicates that the cash outflows were $13,000 more than the expense recognized. Net income is adjusted downward by $13,000 under the indirect approach and the income tax line is adjusted under the direct method.

(q) **Bonds Payable.** In the absence of other information, we assume the change in the Bonds Payable account was increased through amortization of the remaining discount:

Interest Expense	300	
Bonds Payable		300

The entry results in an expense with no corresponding use of cash. An adjustment of $300 is added back to net income under the indirect method, or to the interest expense line under the direct method.[13] The adjustment is identical if Yoshi accounts for the discount as a separate contra account.

(r) **Term Preferred Shares.** Term preferred shares of $60,000 were issued during the year, with $54,000 of this amount issued in exchange for land. This transaction was analyzed in (i) above. Without information to the contrary, the remaining issue of shares must have been for cash and recorded with this entry:

Cash	6,000	
Term Preferred Shares		6,000

This is reported as a financing inflow.

(s) **Future Income Tax Liability.** The increase in this account's credit balance was a result of the following two entries:

Future Income Tax Expense	3,000	
Future Income Tax Liability		3,000
Future Income Tax Expense (OCI)	1,000	
Future Income Tax Liability		1,000

No part of the expense reported used cash. Therefore the $3,000 tax expense included in net income is added back under the indirect approach and a similar adjustment is made to the income tax expense line under the direct method. The $1,000 amount reported in OCI did not use cash and it is not on the work sheet; therefore no adjustment needs to be made for it.

(t) **Common Shares.** The following entries summarize the changes to this account:

Retained Earnings	15,000	
Common Shares		15,000
Cash	144,000	
Common Shares		144,000
Common Shares	21,600	
Retained Earnings	12,400	
Cash		34,000

The first entry records the stock dividend, which neither used nor provided cash. The issue of a stock dividend is not a financing and/or investing transaction, and therefore, is **not** required to be reported. The second entry records a $144,000 inflow of cash as a result of issuing shares, so it is reported as a financing inflow on the work sheet.

The third entry records the purchase and cancellation of shares in the year. Although IFRS does not provide specific guidance on the repurchase of a company's

---

[13] *CICA Handbook*, Part II, Sections 1540.32 and .33 explain how the amortization of a financial asset or financial liability acquired or issued at a premium or discount is reflected on the statement of cash flows. In general, any discount amortization is not a cash flow; while the amount received or paid in the case of a premium is split between interest (an operating flow) and repayment of principal (an investing or financing flow, as appropriate). IAS 7 *Statement of Cash Flows* does not make specific reference to this matter.

own shares, these entries are reasonable based on the information provided in Illustration 22-17. As the entry shows, the transaction used $34,000 cash. This financing flow is reported on the work sheet.

(u) **Retained Earnings.** The statement of changes in equity also explains the $84,300 increase in this account. The $15,000 decrease due to the stock dividend was analyzed above as having no effect on cash flow. The cash flow associated with the $12,400 "loss" on the repurchase and cancellation of the common shares has already been dealt with in (t). The $117,700 increase due to net income and the cash flows associated with it have already been included in the Operating Activities section of the statement of cash flows. The $6,000 decrease due to dividends paid on the common shares could be either a financing or an operating outflow. This depends on the company's policy and how it has reported the dividend in the past. We assume it is a financing flow.

Private enterprise standards require this dividend to be reported as a financing flow. Under IFRS, if the dividend on common shares is treated as an operating flow, the net income number (or the specific line item affected) is adjusted for the outflow.

The changes in all balance sheet accounts have now been analyzed and those that affect cash have been recorded on the statement of cash flows working paper. **The following general statements summarize the approach to the analysis.**

1. For most current asset and current liability accounts, focus on the transactions that increase and decrease each account. Compare the effect on the income statement with the amount of the related cash flow, and then adjust the income number(s) in the Operating Activities section of the statement accordingly.

2. For non-current asset and non-current liability accounts in general, reconstruct summary journal entries that explain how and why each account changed. Then analyze each entry as follows:

   (a) What is the cash flow? The cash effect is the amount of the debit or credit to cash (or cash equivalents) in the entry.

   (b) Is the cash flow an investing or financing flow? If so, update the work sheet.

   (c) Identify all debits or credits to income statement accounts where the operating cash flow is not equal to the amount of revenue, gain, expense, or loss that is reported. Each of these requires an adjustment to the income number(s) that were originally reported in the Operating Activities section. Update the work sheet.

While the transactions entered into by Yoshi Corporation represent a good cross-section of common business activities, they do not cover all possible situations. The general principles and approaches used in the above analyses, however, can be applied to most other transactions and events.

Step 4: ***Complete the statement of cash flows.*** Determine subtotals for each major classification of cash flow and ensure that the statement reconciles to the actual change in cash identified in Step 1.

The working paper prepared in Illustration 22-19 is presented with more appropriate descriptions and complete disclosure to comply with GAAP and to enable readers to better interpret the information. Illustration 22-20 presents a completed statement of cash flows for Yoshi Corporation, using the direct method to explain the operating flows.

Illustration 22-20

Statement of Cash Flows—Yoshi Corporation (Direct Method)

YOSHI CORPORATION
Statement of Cash Flows
Year Ended December 31, 2012

Cash provided by (used in) operations

Received from customers		$ 867,950
Dividends received on equity method investment		2,000
Net cash received on temporary investment transactions		6,300
Payments to suppliers		(490,750)
Payments to and on behalf of employees		(196,000)
Payments for interest, and dividends on term preferred shares		(9,000)
Income taxes paid		(62,500)
		118,000

Cash provided by (used in) investing activities

Investment in development costs	$(200,000)	
Purchase of equipment	(73,000)	
Proceeds on sale of land	15,000	
Proceeds on sale of equipment	13,000	(245,000)

Cash provided by (used in) financing activities

Proceeds on issue of common shares	144,000	
Proceeds on issue of term preferred shares	6,000	
Repurchase and cancellation of common shares	(34,000)	
Dividends paid on common shares	(6,000)	110,000
Decrease in cash and cash equivalents (Note 1)		(17,000)
Cash and cash equivalents, January 1		36,000
Cash and cash equivalents, December 31		$ 19,000

Note 1. Cash and cash equivalents are defined as cash on deposit and money-market instruments with original maturity dates of less than 90 days.

Note 2. Term preferred shares valued at $54,000 were issued during the year as consideration for the purchase of land.

For those who prefer the indirect method of reporting operating cash flows, Illustration 22-21 indicates how the statement's Operating Activities section might look.

Illustration 22-21

Cash Provided by Operations—Yoshi Corporation (Indirect Method)

Cash provided by (used in) operations

Net income		$117,700
Add back non-cash expenses:		
Depreciation expense	$ 14,600	
Impairment loss—goodwill	2,400	
Amortization of discount on bond	300	
Amortization of development costs	40,000	
Future income taxes	3,000	60,300
Equity in income of Portel Corp. in excess of dividends received		(3,500)
Deduct non-operating gains (net):		
Gain on sale of land	(10,500)	
Loss on disposal of equipment	1,500	(9,000)
Changes in non-cash working capital accounts (see Note A)		(47,500)
		$118,000

Note A—changes in non-cash working capital:		
Temporary investments	$ 5,000	
Accounts receivable	(53,000)	
Inventory	8,000	

continued on page 1502

Prepaid expenses	500
Accounts payable	(1,000)
Dividends payable, term preferred shares	2,000
Accrued liabilities	4,000
Income taxes payable	(13,000)
	($47,500)

How would this statement differ if **private enterprise standards** had been followed instead of **IFRS**? Because we assumed that Yoshi follows the same reporting options for interest and dividends paid **permitted** under IFRS that are **required** under PE standards, the statements could be identical. The amount of cash generated or used by each type of activity and the change in cash are the same. Alternative presentations are permitted under IFRS, however, so the way the information is presented may differ. If the company had chosen different policies for reporting interest and dividends paid, the cash amounts in the operating and financing categories would change, but the net change in cash would not.

PRESENTATION, DISCLOSURE, AND ANALYSIS

Objective 8

Identify the financial presentation and disclosure requirements for the statement of cash flows.

Disclosure Requirements

The specific items that require disclosure are similar in IFRS and private enterprise standards, with the latter requiring less disclosure. In addition to reporting cash flows according to operating, investing, and financing classifications, the standards call for disclosure of the items set out in Illustration 22-22.

Illustration 22-22

Disclosures Required for the Statement of Cash Flows

IFRS	Private Enterprise Standards
Separately disclose interest received and paid and dividends received and paid.	Separately present interest and dividends paid and charged to retained earnings as a financing activity; otherwise disclosure is not required.
Separately disclose taxes on income.	Not required.
Disclose and provide relevant information about significant non-cash investing and financing transactions.	Same as IFRS requirement.
Report policy on what makes up cash and cash equivalents, and reconcile the change in amounts to the same amounts reported on the balance sheet.	Same as IFRS requirement.
Report and explain amount of cash and cash equivalents that have restrictions on their use.	Disclosure of restricted amount is all that is required.

The international standard also identifies other information that may be helpful to users in assessing an entity's financial position and liquidity, and encourages the disclosure of this information along with a related commentary. Examples include the amount of additional cash available under existing borrowing agreements; investing cash flows related to maintaining operating capacity and those for increasing operating capacity; and the operating, investing, and financing cash flows of each reportable segment.

Presentation

As indicated earlier in the chapter, entities can choose between the direct and indirect methods of presenting operating cash flows on the statement, although the direct approach is preferred and encouraged by standard setters. Both the PE standard and IFRS describe the indirect method as reconciling the net income (or, under IFRS, the profit and loss) to cash flow from operating activities, but it is common in IFRS-prepared statements to see companies begin with **income before tax** or **income before interest and taxes**. The reason for this approach is that all other adjustments can be made and then the cash actually paid out for taxes and interest can be reported as separate figures. This allows entities to meet some of the disclosure requirements on the face of the statement.[14]

Illustration 22-23 provides an example of this presentation by British Airways plc in its financial statements for the year ended March 31, 2009 (reported in millions of pounds, £). Notice that the opening "operating (loss)/profit" is actually before interest and income tax expense. The actual cash flows for these two costs are reported at the bottom of the operating activities section.

Real-World Emphasis

Cash flow statements

For the year ended March 31, 2009

Illustration 22-23

Operating Cash Flows Alternative Presentation— British Airways plc

		Group	
		2009	2008
£ million	Note		Restated
Cash flow from operating activities			
Operating (loss)/profit		**(220)**	878
Operating loss from discontinued operations			(2)
Depreciation, amortisation and impairment		**694**	692
Operating cash flow before working capital changes		**474**	1,568
Movement in inventories, trade and other receivables		**32**	96
Movement in trade and other payables and provisions		**(136)**	(325)
Payments in respect of restructuring		**(64)**	(32)
Cash payment to NAPS pension scheme	36		(610)
Payment to DOJ in settlement of competition investigation			(149)
Other non-cash movement		**1**	3
Cash generated from operations		**307**	551
Interest paid		**(177)**	(182)
Taxation		**3**	(66)
Net cash flow from operating activities		**133**	303

Both sets of standards require, for the most part, the reporting of gross cash inflows and outflows from investing and financing activities rather than netted amounts. Other significant requirements relate to financial institutions, foreign currency cash flows, and business combinations and disposals. These are left to a course in advanced financial accounting.

---

[14] Another presentation alternative identified in IAS 7.20, although not widely used, is a variation of the indirect method: revenues and expenses are presented along with the changes in inventories and operating receivables and payables in the period.

Illustrative Examples

Real-World Emphasis

WILEY PLUS

Additional Disclosures

Stantec Inc.'s Consolidated Statements of Cash Flow for its years ended December 31, 2009 and 2008, are provided in Illustration 22-24. Stantec, a Canadian-based company, provides professional engineering consulting services primarily related to infrastructure and facilities projects in North America and the Caribbean. Note that this company uses the direct method to present its operating cash flows, and its financial statements are presented in accordance with pre-2011 Canadian GAAP—very similar to IFRS and PE standards. Some of the required disclosures are presented on the face of the statement itself, although many companies provide them in notes to the financial statements. Although not required, Stantec also provides a reconciliation of its net income with the cash flows from operations in Note 20. This is shown in Illustration 22-24 as well. Take a minute to review the statement of cash flows for the differences in cash activity from one year to the next.

Illustration 22-24

Statement of Cash Flows—
Stantec Inc.

Consolidated Statements of Cash Flows

Years ended December 31 *(In thousands of Canadian dollars)*	**2009** **$**	2008 $
CASH FLOWS FROM (USED IN) OPERATING ACTIVITIES		
Cash receipts from clients	**1,564,415**	1,222,566
Cash paid to suppliers	**(545,671)**	(276,862)
Cash paid to employees	**(852,459)**	(737,931)
Dividends from equity investments	**1,283**	150
Interest received	**2,192**	1,857
Interest paid	**(12,383)**	(6,597)
Income taxes paid	**(65,731)**	(50,037)
Income taxes recovered	**8,331**	6,884
Cash flows from operating activities (note 20)	**99,977**	160,030
CASH FLOWS FROM (USED IN) INVESTING ACTIVITIES		
Business acquisitions, net of cash acquired (note 2)	**(73,078)**	(92,087)
Restricted cash used for acquisitions	**—**	—
Cash held in escrow (note 2)	**—**	(6,178)
Decrease (increase) in investments held for self-insured liabilities	**(11,040)**	5,820
Proceeds on disposition of investments	**—**	9
Purchase of intangible assets	**(3,062)**	(2,846)
Purchase of property and equipment	**(17,366)**	(32,791)
Proceeds on disposition of property and equipment	**1,331**	410
Cash flows used in investing activities	**(103,215)**	(127,663)
CASH FLOWS FROM (USED IN) FINANCING ACTIVITIES		
Repayment of long-term debt	**(147,902)**	(164,602)
Proceeds from long-term borrowings	**68,771**	228,337
Repayment of acquired bank indebtedness (note 2)	**(4,596)**	(1,788)
Repayment of capital lease obligations	**(2,759)**	(438)
Repurchase of shares for cancellation (note 14)	**—**	(8,914)
Proceeds from issue of share capital (note14)	**2,346**	1,199
Cash flows from (used in) financing activities	**(84,140)**	53,794
Foreign exchange gain (loss) on cash held in foreign currency	**(1,911)**	3,643
Net increase (decrease) in cash and cash equivalents	**(89,289)**	89,804
Cash and cash equivalents, beginning of the year	**103,979**	14,175
Cash and cash equivalents, end of the year	**14,690**	103,979

20. Cash Flows From Operating Activities

Cash flows from operating activities determined by the indirect method are as follows:

(In thousands of Canadian dollars)	2009 $	2008 $
CASH FLOWS FROM OPERATING ACTIVITIES		
Net income for the year	**55,940**	29,017
Add (deduct) items not affecting cash:		
Depreciation of property and equipment (note 1b)	**24,547**	21,820
Amortization of intangible assets (note 1b)	**19,820**	14,264
Impairment of goodwill and intangible assets	**35,000**	58,369
Future income tax	**(5,873)**	(5,731)
Loss (gain) on dispositions of investments and property and equipment	**2,520**	(520)
Stock-based compensation expense (note 14)	**3,985**	5,118
Provision for self-insured liability (note 9)	**9,443**	12,470
Other non-cash items	**(9,446)**	(3,445)
Share of income from equity investments	**(3,690)**	(160)
Dividends from equity investments	**1,283**	150
	133,529	131,352
Change in non-cash working capital accounts:		
Accounts receivable	**37,298**	23,987
Costs and estimated earnings in excess of billings	**(8,486)**	21,305
Prepaid expenses	**(1,953)**	2,499
Accounts payable and accrued liabilities	**(49,800)**	(20,088)
Billings in excess of costs and estimated earnings	**6,522**	2,728
Income taxes payable/recoverable	**(17,133)**	(1,753)
	(33,552)	28,678
Cash flows from operating activities	**99,977**	160,030

Contrast the direct method approach in the operating activities section of Stantec's Cash Flow Statements in Illustration 22-24 with the same section prepared under the indirect method. It is surprising that the cash flow from operations determined under two such different approaches actually has the same meaning!

Interpreting the Statement of Cash Flows

As you can tell, companies have some flexibility in how information is reported in the statement of cash flows. The way in which the information is summarized and described can improve the information content and help users interpret and understand the significance of the cash flow data.

One way to approach an analysis of the statement is to begin by focusing on the three subtotals and determining what they tell you about which activities (operating, investing, and financing) generated cash for the company and which used cash. After this general assessment, delve deeper into the details within each section.

As an example, the statement of cash flows of Stantec Inc. in Illustration 22-24 indicates that, in 2009, excess operating cash flows of almost $100,000 thousand allowed the company to internally finance almost all of its investment activities of $103,215 thousand during the year. Due to healthy cash balances at the start of the year, Stantec also used over $84,000 thousand to reduce its debt. The net result was an $89,289 thousand reduction in cash over the year, with the ending balance considerably less than the opening amount.

9 Objective
Read and interpret a statement of cash flows.

Underlying Concept

Consolidated statements of cash flows may be of limited use to analysts evaluating multinational entities. With so much data brought together, users of the statements are not able to determine "where in the world" the funds are sourced and used.

The 2008 story was different. In **2008**, Stantec's cash from operations was much stronger than in 2009. The operating cash flows of a little over $160,000 thousand, along with financing activities that generated another $53,794 thousand, was more than enough to cover the company's needs for investment capital of $127,663 thousand. This resulted in an increase in cash of almost $90,000 thousand over the year. Each company and each statement of cash flows tells a different story, but the questions they answer remain the same: where did the cash come from, and how was it used? Each story has to be read and interpreted in conjunction with the other financial statements and the MD&A.

Operating Activities

Whether a company uses the direct or indirect method, the **net operating cash flows tell you the same thing: the extent to which cash receipts from customers and other operating sources were able to cover cash payments to suppliers of goods and services, to employees, and for other operating expenditures**. This is how the approximately $100 million cash provided by operating activities at Stantec in 2009 and the $160 million in 2008 are interpreted.

Stantec has a growth strategy that it identifies as combining internal growth and acquisition of firms that will help move it toward becoming a global design firm. This means that it wants to generate cash from operations and use those flows to finance its business acquisitions. As a service provider, the company is not capital intensive; that is, it does not have large investments in property, plant, and equipment assets. The company, therefore, does not have a significant physical asset base to use as collateral for long-term borrowing. Instead, goodwill from its many acquisitions is the largest asset on its balance sheet.

While the direct method provides more detail about the specific sources and uses of cash and is particularly useful in comparisons with previous years, the indirect method explains the relationship between the accrual-based net income and the cash from operations. Stantec's largest adjustment between these two numbers, as is the case with many companies, is the add-back of depreciation and amortization expense, and, in this company's case, impairment charges related to goodwill and its intangible assets. This explains the major reason why its operating cash flows are so much higher than the net income the company reports.

Future income taxes and a variety of other expenses are adjusted because their cash effects are felt in different periods than their income statement effects. A positive adjustment in the current year often means that the related cash outflow will be felt in a subsequent year.[15]

An adjustment for the "changes in non-cash working capital balances" is found in the operating activities section of almost every statement of cash flows prepared under the indirect method and this can have a significant effect on the operating cash flow reported. The details, such as those provided in Note 20 in Illustration 22-24, should be reviewed. The change in these accounts reduced the operating cash flows otherwise generated, in sharp contrast to the working capital changes in the preceding year. Although accounts receivable collections added to the cash flow, the paydown of accounts payable and income taxes and the acquisition of prepaid expenses had the opposite effect. These changes need to be analyzed carefully. For example, consider the case of Axcan Pharma Inc., which reported cash flow from operating activities of more than U.S. $56.5 million in a recent year, up substantially from U.S. $35.3 million in the previous year. Almost

---

[15] A good example of this type of adjustment that one should be aware of is the adjustment for unfunded pension and other post-employment benefits expense. The current year adjustment has a positive effect—it increases operating cash flows above the net income reported as no cash was paid out. However, very large amounts of operating cash outflows will be required in the future when these claims are eventually paid.

U.S. $12.8 million of the increase, however, came from changes in working capital made up of higher than usual collections of accounts receivable and lower than usual payments on its payables. In that case, the operating cash flows in the period under review do not represent operating cash flows that are likely to be replicated; that is, repeated in subsequent years.

Users of financial statements need to look beyond the amount of cash generated or used in operations, and analyze the reasons for the operating cash flows. The objective of the analysis is to assess whether the cash flow levels are sustainable and likely to be repeated in the future, or whether they are the result of payment deferrals and one-time events.

Investing Activities

Consistent with its strategic goals, Stantec reports significant cash outlays for business acquisitions, explained in more detail in another note. Because investments in new business assets are the source of future operating cash flows, it is important to understand whether the new investment just maintains the existing capacity of a company, or whether the investment increases the potential for higher levels of operating cash flows in the future. For companies with substantial property, plant, and equipment, how do the new amounts invested compare with the stock of existing property, plant, and equipment, and with the depreciation charges for the year? Also, what types of assets have been purchased? Are they investments in new technologies and development expenditures? Or are existing assets being disposed of, reducing the potential for operating flows in the future?

Stantec appears to be investing in the future by making acquisitions consistent with its growth strategy. These, in turn, are generating operating cash flows to allow for the internal financing of further acquisitions.

Financing Activities

The operating and investing flows just tell part of a company's cash story for the period. The financing activities section completes the picture. It clearly captures what changes took place to the firm's capital structure and whether the entity increased or reduced the claims of creditors to cash in the future.

In contrast to its 2008 financing activities, Stantec used the excess cash balances it had built up plus an additional $68,771 thousand to repay about $147,902 thousand of its long-term debt. This almost $80,000 thousand net reduction in debt, combined with repayments of bank loans and capital lease obligations, accounted for almost all of the cash used in financing activities. With only minor amounts of cash proceeds from the sale of shares, the result was a reduction in the company's debt ratios in the year.

As indicated above, the methods of financing are usually related to the types of assets acquired. For example, purchases of intangibles and development expenditures are often difficult to use as collateral and, therefore, they are generally financed internally from operating cash flows or externally through new equity.

Details of cash flows related to financing activities allow readers to assess the potential for future claims on the organization's cash and, as indicated above, to identify major shifts in the form of financing, especially between debt and equity. Will there be increased demand for future cash for interest claims and debt repayment? Companies in a growth stage may report significant amounts of cash generated from financing activities—financing that is needed to handle the significant investment activity. As growth levels off and operations begin to generate positive cash flows, financing flows tend to reverse as debt is repaid and, if appropriate, shares are redeemed. The required disclosure of long-term debt repayments over the next five years is an excellent source of information about upcoming demands on an organization's cash for financing purposes.

Due to recent concerns about a decline in the quality of earnings, some investors have been focusing more on cash flow. Management has an incentive to make cash flow look good, because the capital markets pay a premium for companies that generate a lot of cash from operations rather than through borrowings. However, just as they can with earnings, companies have ways to pump up cash flow from operations.

One way that companies can boost their operating cash flow is by securitizing receivables. Chapter 7 discussed how companies can speed up cash collections by selling their receivables. For example, Oxford Industries, an apparel company, recently reported a $74 million increase in cash flow from operations. This seemed impressive until you read the fine print, which indicated that a major portion of the increase was due to the sale of receivables. While it originally appeared that the company's core operations had improved, Oxford did little more than accelerate collection of its receivables. In fact, operating cash flow would have been negative without the securitization.

Operating cash flows can also be manipulated by having too liberal a policy of capitalizing expenditures as property, plant, and equipment instead of expensing them as incurred. Such a policy leads to these costs being treated as investment flows. They are not deducted in determining net income or cash from operations. Even when depreciated, the costs end up having no effect on operating cash flow. WorldCom was able to conceal almost U.S. $4 billion of decline in its operations this way; Adelphia Communications overstated its operating cash flow by U.S. $102 million this way; and closer to home, Atlas Cold Storage later reported a similar situation, although on a smaller scale.

The moral: Operating cash flow, like earnings, can be of high or low quality.

Caution should also be exercised in comparing companies' operating cash flows, even if they are in the same industry. Consider the different effect on operating cash flow of one company that rents its premises under operating leases with another that owns its property or has capital lease arrangements. Or compare one company that capitalizes interest and overhead as part of self-constructed assets to another that expenses these costs, or one company that capitalizes internal-use computer software versus another that absorbs the costs as they are incurred. In all cases, one set of policies results in investing or financing outflows of cash, while the other set reports reduced operating cash flows. And, unlike revenue and expense accruals and deferrals that are reported on an income statement, where the effect reverses over time, the effects on the classifications in the statement of cash flows are permanent.[16]

Free Cash Flow

Introduced in Chapter 5 and publicized by many companies in recent years, a non-GAAP performance measure used by many companies is free cash flow (FCF). As the name suggests, this is an indicator of financial flexibility that uses information provided on the statement of cash flows. Free cash flow is net operating cash flows reduced by the capital expenditures that are needed to sustain the current level of operations. The resulting cash flow is the discretionary cash that a company has available for increasing its capacity and acquiring new investments, paying dividends, retiring debt, repurchasing its shares, or simply adding to its liquidity.

The calculation of this measure varies by company as some entities deduct all capital expenditures on the basis that it is impossible to separate sustaining expenditures from the total. Others also deduct current dividends. FCF measures are more useful to investors if information is also provided about how they are calculated.

---

[16] Gerald I. White, Ashwinpaul C. Sondhi, and Dov Fried, *The Analysis and Use of Financial Statements*, 3rd ed. (New York: John Wiley & Sons, Inc., 2003), p. 96.

In general, companies with significant free cash flow have a strong degree of financial flexibility. They are able to take advantage of new opportunities or cope well during poor economic times without jeopardizing current operations.

IFRS AND PRIVATE ENTERPRISE GAAP COMPARISON

Comparison of IFRS and Private Enterprise GAAP

10 Objective

Identify differences in the accounting standards for private enterprises and IFRS, and explain what changes are expected to standards for the statement of cash flows.

Because the most recent pre-2011 Canadian standard on the statement of cash flows was based on the international standard of the same name, private enterprise GAAP and IAS 7 are very similar. Illustration 22-25 sets out the few areas where there are differences between them.

	Accounting Standards for Private Enterprises (PE GAAP/ASPE)—*CICA Handbook*, Part II, Section 1540	IFRS—IAS 7
Definitions and Scope	Cash equivalents exclude all equity investments.	Preferred shares acquired close to their maturity date may be included in cash equivalents.
Presentation	Interest and dividends received are presented as operating cash flows. Interest and dividends paid are operating flows if recognized in net income. If charged directly to retained earnings, they are presented as financing cash flows.	Interest and dividends received may be classified and presented as either operating or investing cash flows. Interest and dividends paid are either operating or financing outflows.
Disclosure	Interest and dividends paid and charged to retained earnings must be disclosed separately as a financing activity.	Separate disclosure is required for each of interest and dividends received and paid.
	Income taxes paid are not required to be disclosed.	Income taxes paid are required to be disclosed.
	The amount of restriction on cash and cash equivalents' use is required to be disclosed.	Restrictions on the use of cash and cash equivalents and an explanation of the restrictions are required to be disclosed.

Illustration 22-25

IFRS and Private Enterprise GAAP Comparison

Looking Ahead

The most influential event on the horizon that affects the reporting of cash flows is Phase B of the joint FASB-IASB *Financial Statement Presentation* project.[17] From the IASB's perspective, Phase B is intended to replace existing IAS 1 *Presentation of Financial Statements* and IAS 7 *Statement of Cash Flows*. With an exposure draft in 2010 and a final standard expected in 2011, the revisions to our present financial reporting model are extensive and imminent! A reasonable period will be provided, however, before the new requirements must be applied.

---

[17] Phase A dealt with the question of what makes up a complete set of financial statements and is now complete and embedded in IAS 1. Phase B looks at how information is presented on the face of the financial statements, and Phase C will cover interim financial reporting.

Chapter 4 in Volume 1 of this text introduced the major changes expected to our reporting model by presenting the chart in Illustration 22-26, taken from an October 2008 presentation of the preliminary views document by the IASB.

Proposed format for the presentation of financial statements

Statement of financial position	Statement of comprehensive income	Statement of cash flows
Business • Operating assets and liabilities • Investing assets and liabilities	Business • Operating income and expenses • Investing income and expenses	Business • Operating cash flows • Investing cash flows
Financing • Financing assets • Financing liabilities	Financing • Financing asset income • Financing liability expenses	Financing • Financing asset cash flows • Financing liability cash flows
Income taxes	Income taxes on continuing operations (business and financing)	Income taxes
Discontinued operations	Discontinued operations net of tax	Discontinued operations
	Other comprehensive income, net of tax	
Equity		Equity

Illustration 22-26

Financial Statement Presentation Proposals

Since this proposed format was developed, the FASB and IASB have tentatively agreed on minor revisions, but the cohesiveness of the financial picture of an entity's activities among and across the statements continues to be a primary goal.[18] What would the statement of cash flows look like under these proposals? Illustration 22-27 sets out the proposed format from the 2008 Discussion Paper. As you can see, the cash flow information provided about business-related operating activities is expected to increase significantly.[19]

Illustration 22-27

Proposed Statement of Cash Flows Presentation

TOOLCO STATEMENT OF CASH FLOWS
(proposed format)

	For the year ended 31 December	
	2010	2009
BUSINESS		
Operating		
Cash received from wholesale customers	2,108,754	1,928,798
Cash received from retail customers	703,988	643,275
Total cash collected from customers	*2,812,742*	*2,572,073*
Cash paid for goods		
Materials purchases	(935,544)	(785,000)
Labour	(418,966)	(475,313)

[18] For example, there is a tentative agreement to add a "financing arising from operating activities" category to the business section in the statement of financial position and statement of cash flows. The related cash flows would be included in the operating section of the cash flow statement. IASB *Project Update*, March 2010.

[19] Illustration 22-27 is taken from the IASB Discussion Paper: *Preliminary Views on Financial Statement Presentation*, October 2008, p. 110. Other comments related to tentative decisions to date are based on IASB *Updates* to April 30, 2010.

Overhead—transport	(128,640)	(108,000)
Pension	(170,100)	(157,500)
Overhead—other	(32,160)	(27,000)
Total cash paid for goods	*(1,685,409)*	*(1,552,813)*
Cash paid for selling activities		
Advertising	(65,000)	(75,000)
Wages, salaries and benefits	(58,655)	(55,453)
Other	(13,500)	(12,500)
Total cash paid for selling activities	*(137,155)*	*(142,953)*
Cash paid for general and administrative activities		
Wages, salaries and benefits	(332,379)	(314,234)
Contributions to pension plan	(170,100)	(157,500)
Capital expenditures	(54,000)	(50,000)
Lease payments	(50,000)	—
Research and development	(8,478)	(7,850)
Settlement of share-based remuneration	(3,602)	(3,335)
Other	(12,960)	(12,000)
Total cash paid for general and administrative activities	*(631,519)*	*(544,919)*
Cash flow before other operating activities	*358,657*	*331,388*
Cash from other operating activities		
Disposal of property, plant and equipment	37,650	—
Investment in associate A	—	(120,000)
Sale of receivable	8,000	10,000
Settlement of cash flow hedge	3,402	3,150
Total cash received (paid) for other operating activities	*49,052*	*(106,850)*
Net cash from operating activities	**407,709**	**224,538**
Investing		
Purchase of available-for-sale financial assets	—	(130,000)
Sale of available-for-sale financial assets	56,100	51,000
Dividends received	54,000	50,000
Net cash from investing activities	**110,100**	**(29,000)**
NET CASH FROM BUSINESS ACTIVITIES	**517,809**	**195,538**

Other tentative decisions reached include eliminating the term "cash equivalents" and treating them instead in the same way as other short-term investments, presenting bank overdrafts in the debt category of the financing section of the statement, and requiring the direct method for reporting operating cash flows. A reconciliation between operating income and operating cash flows and information about significant non-cash transactions are elevated in importance and reported on the face of the statement rather than being disclosed only in the notes.

Summary of Learning Objectives

1　Describe the purpose and uses of the statement of cash flows.

The primary purpose of this statement is to provide information about an entity's cash receipts and cash payments during a period. A secondary objective is to report the entity's operating, investing, and financing activities during the period. The statement's objective is to provide information about historical changes in an enterprise's cash so that investors and creditors can assess the amount, timing, and degree of certainty associated with an entity's future cash flows, as well as the organization's needs for cash and how cash will be used.

Glossary

KEY TERMS

cash, 1471
cash equivalents, 1471
cash flows, 1471
direct method, 1476
financing activities, 1472

2   Define cash and cash equivalents.

The definition of cash is related to an organization's cash management activities. Cash and cash equivalents include cash on hand, demand deposits, and short-term, highly liquid non-equity investments that are convertible to known amounts of cash with insignificant risk of changes in value. These amounts are reduced by bank overdrafts that fluctuate from positive to negative balances and that are repayable on demand. IFRS allows preferred shares acquired within a short period of their maturity to be included as a cash equivalent.

3   Identify the major classifications of cash flows and explain the significance of each classification.

Cash flows are classified into those resulting from operating, investing, and financing activities. A company's ability to generate operating cash flows affects its capacity to pay dividends to shareholders, to take advantage of investment opportunities, to provide internal financing for growth, and to meet obligations when they fall due. The amount of cash spent on investing activities affects an organization's potential for future cash flows. Cash invested in increased levels of productive assets forms the basis for increased future operating cash inflows. Financing cash activities affect the firm's capital structure and, therefore, the requirements for future cash outflows.

4   Prepare the operating activities section of a statement of cash flows using the direct method.

The direct method presents operating cash flows in a manner similar to a condensed cash basis income statement. The accrual amounts are listed and adjusted whenever the cash received or paid out differs from the revenues, gains, expenses, and losses reported in net income, and for non-operating gains and losses.

5   Prepare the operating activities section of a statement of cash flows using the indirect method.

The indirect method begins with the net income reported. This number is adjusted whenever the cash received or paid out for operating items differs from the amount reported as a revenue or expense in net income. Non-operating gains and losses are also adjusted out.

6   Prepare a statement of cash flows using the direct method.

This involves determining the change in cash and cash equivalents during the period, inserting line items from the income statement as the starting point within the statement's Operating Activities section, and analyzing the changes in all accounts on the statement of financial position to identify all transactions that have an impact on cash. Those with a cash impact are recorded on the statement of cash flows. To ensure that all cash flows have been identified, the results recorded on the statement are compared with the change in cash during the period. The statement is then prepared with required disclosures.

7   Prepare a statement of cash flows using the indirect method.

The steps using the indirect method are the same as in Objective 6 above, with one exception. Rather than starting with line items from the income statement in the Operating Activities section, the net income amount is the beginning point. All the same adjustments are then made to adjust net income to a cash basis.

8   Identify the financial presentation and disclosure requirements for the statement of cash flows.

Under IFRS, disclosure is required of cash flows associated with interest and dividends received and paid, the definition and components of cash and cash equivalents reconciled to the amounts reported on the balance sheet, and the amount of and explanation for cash and cash equivalents not available for use. All income tax cash flows are reported as operating flows unless they can be linked directly to investing or financing flows. Choices are available under IFRS for the reporting of interest and dividends received (operating or investing) and interest and dividends paid (operating or financing). Gross amounts should be reported except in specifically permitted circumstances, and non-cash investing and financing transactions are excluded from the statement of cash flows, but details about these are reported elsewhere on the financial statements. PE GAAP presentation requirements are very similar, but disclosures are limited to interest and dividends paid and charged to retained earnings and the amount of any restricted cash. In addition, interest and dividends received are both operating flows, and interest and dividends paid are operating flows unless they were charged directly to retained earnings.

9   Read and interpret a statement of cash flows.

The first step is to look at the subtotals for the three classifications of activities and the overall change in cash. This provides a high-level summary of the period's cash flows. Next, analyze the items within each section for additional insights, keeping alert for accounting policies that affect the type of cash flow reported. Familiarity with the company's business and strategic direction is very useful in interpreting the statement.

10 Identify differences in the accounting standards for private enterprises and IFRS, and explain what changes are expected to standards for the statement of cash flows.

There are no significant differences between ASPE and IFRS related to the statement of cash flows except for the definition of cash equivalents and the presentation and disclosure requirements identified above.

Appendix 22A

Use of a Work Sheet

Objective **11**
Use a work sheet to prepare a statement of cash flows.

When many adjustments are needed or there are other complicating factors, a work sheet is often used to assemble and classify the data that will appear on the statement of cash flows. The work sheet (a spreadsheet when using computer software) is merely a device that aids in the preparation of the statement; using one is optional. The skeleton format of the work sheet for preparing the statement of cash flows using the indirect method is shown in Illustration 22A-1.

Illustration 22A-1

*Format of Work Sheet for
Preparing Statement
of Cash Flows*

	A	B	C	E	F
1		Statement of Cash Flows for the Year Ended...			
2	**Balance Sheet Accounts**	**End of Last Year Balances**	**Debits**	**Credits**	**End of Current Year Balances**
3	Debit balance accounts	XX	XX	XX	XX
4		XX	XX	XX	XX
5	Totals	XX			XX
7	Credit balance accounts	XX	XX	XX	XX
8		XX	XX	XX	XX
9	Totals	XX			XX
11	Cash Flows				
12	**Operating activities**				
13	Net income		XX		
14	Adjustments		XX	XX	
15	**Investing activities**				
16	Receipts (dr.) and payments (cr.)		XX	XX	
17	**Financing activities**				
18	Receipts (dr.) and payments (cr.)		XX	XX	
19	Totals		XX	XX	
20	**Increase (cr.) or decrease (dr.) in cash**		XX or	XX	
21	Totals		XX	XX	
22					

The following guidelines are important in using a work sheet:

1. In the Balance Sheet Accounts section, accounts with debit balances are listed separately from those with credit balances. This means, for example, that Accumulated Depreciation is listed under credit balances and not as a contra account under the debit balances. The beginning and ending balances of each account are entered. As the analysis proceeds, each line that relates to a balance sheet account should balance. That is, the beginning balance plus or minus the reconciling item(s) must equal the ending balance. When all balance sheet accounts agree in this way, all changes in account balances have been identified and reconciled and the analysis is complete.

2. The bottom portion of the work sheet is an area to record the operating, investing, and financing cash flows. This section provides the detail for the change in the cash balance during the period—information that is used to prepare the formal statement of cash flows. Inflows of cash are entered as debits in the reconciling columns and outflows of cash are entered as credits in the reconciling columns. Thus, in this section, the sale of equipment for cash at book value is entered as a debit under inflows of cash from investing activities. Similarly, the purchase of land for cash is entered as a credit under outflows of cash for investing activities.

3. The reconciling items shown in the work sheet are not entered in any journal or posted to any account. They do not represent either adjustments or corrections of the balance sheet accounts. They are only used to make it easier to prepare the statement of cash flows.

Preparing the Work Sheet

The preparation of a work sheet involves a series of steps.

Step 1. Enter the balance sheet accounts and their beginning and ending balances in the appropriate Balance Sheet Accounts section.

Step 2. Enter the debits and credits from the summary entries that explain the changes in each balance sheet account (other than cash); identify all entries that affect cash, and enter these amounts in the reconciling columns at the bottom of the work sheet.

Step 3. After the analysis is complete and the changes in all balance sheet accounts have been reconciled, enter the increase or decrease in cash on the balance sheet cash line (or lines, if cash equivalents) and at the bottom of the work sheet. The totals of the reconciling columns should balance.

To illustrate the procedure for preparing the work sheet, we use the same comprehensive illustration for Yoshi Corporation, a publicly accountable enterprise reporting under IFRS, that was used in the chapter. The indirect method serves initially as the basis for calculating net cash provided by operating activities. An illustration of the direct method is also provided. The financial statements and other data related to Yoshi Corporation for its year ended December 31, 2012, are presented in Illustrations 22-15, 22-16, 22-17, and 22-18. Most of the analysis was discussed earlier in the chapter and additional explanations related to the work sheet are provided in the discussion here.

Analyzing Transactions

Before the analysis begins, Yoshi's balance sheet accounts are transferred to the work sheet's opening and ending balance columns. The following discussion explains the individual adjustments that appear on the work sheet in Illustration 22A-2. The discussion assumes that you are familiar with the analysis of the Yoshi illustration earlier in the chapter.

	A	B	C	D	E	F	G
1			**Work Sheet for Preparation of Statement of Cash Flows** **Year Ended December 31, 2012**				
2		**Balance** **12/31/11**		**Reconciling Items—2012** **Debits Credits**			**Balance** **12/31/12**
3	**Debits**						
4	Cash	32,000			(24)	27,000	5,000
5	Cash equivalents	4,000	(24)	10,000			14,000
6	Temporary investments	30,000			(2)	5,000	25,000
7	Accounts receivable	52,700	(3)	55,250	(3)	1,450	106,500
8	Inventories	311,000			(4)	8,000	303,000
9	Prepaid expenses	17,000			(5)	500	16,500
10	Investment in shares of Portel Corp.	15,000	(6)	5,500	(6)	2,000	18,500
11	Investment in shares of Hyco Ltd.	13,000	(7)	4,500			17,500
12	Deferred development costs	30,000	(8)	200,000	(8)	40,000	190,000
13	Land	82,000	(9)	54,000	(9)	4,500	131,500
14	Equipment	142,000	(10)	73,000	(10)	28,000	187,000
15	Buildings	262,000					262,000
16	Goodwill	10,000			(11)	2,400	7,600
17	**Total debits**	1,000,700					1,284,100
18							
19	**Credits**						
20	Allowance for doubtful accounts	1,700	(3)	1,450	(12)	2,250	2,500
21	Accumulated depreciation— equipment	31,000	(10)	13,500	(13)	11,500	29,000
22	Accumulated depreciation— buildings	71,000			(14)	3,100	74,100
23	Accounts payable	131,000	(15)	1,000			130,000
24	Dividends payable, term preferred shares	—			(16)	2,000	2,000
25	Accrued liabilities	39,000			(17)	4,000	43,000
26	Income taxes payable	16,000	(18)	13,000			3,000
27	Bonds payable	97,500			(19)	300	97,800
28	Term preferred shares	—			(9)	54,000	60,000
29					(20)	6,000	
30	Future income tax liability	6,000			(21)	3,000	10,000
31					(21)	1,000	
32	Common shares	88,000	(22)	21,600	(22)	15,000	225,400
33					(22)	144,000	
34	Retained earnings	518,500	(22)	12,400	(1)	117,700	602,800
35			(22)	15,000			
36			(23)	6,000			
37	Accumulated other						
38	comprehensive income	1,000	(21)	1,000	(7)	4,500	4,500
39	**Total credits**	1,000,700					1,284,100
40							
41	**Cash Flows**						
42	**Operating activities:**						
43	Net income		(1)	117,700			
44	Decrease in temporary investments		(2)	5,000			
45	Increase in accounts receivable				(3)	55,250	
46	Decrease in inventories		(4)	8,000			
47	Decrease in prepaid expenses		(5)	500			
48	Equity in earnings of Portel Corp.				(6)	5,500	
49	Dividend from Portel Corp.		(6)	2,000			
50	Amortization, deferred						
51	development costs		(8)	40,000			

52	Gain on sale of land			(9)	10,500
53	Loss on disposal of equipment	(10)	1,500		
54	Impairment loss—goodwill	(11)	2,400		
55	Bad debt expense	(12)	2,250		
56	Depreciation expense—equipment	(13)	11,500		
57	Depreciation expense—buildings	(14)	3,100		
58	Decrease in accounts payable			(15)	1,000
59	Dividend, term preferred shares	(16)	2,000		
60	Increase in accrued liabilities	(17)	4,000		
61	Decrease in income taxes payable			(18)	13,000
62	Amortization of bond discount	(19)	300		
63	Future income tax liability	(21)	3,000		
64					
65	**Investing activities:**				
66	Development costs incurred			(8)	200,000
67	Proceeds on disposal of land	(9)	15,000		
68	Purchase of equipment			(10)	73,000
69	Proceeds on sale of equipment	(10)	13,000		
70					
71	**Financing activities:**				
72	Proceeds on issue of term preferred shares	(20)	6,000		
73	Proceeds on sale of common shares	(22)	144,000		
74	Repurchase of common shares			(22)	34,000
75	Dividend on common shares			(23)	6,000
76	Decrease in cash	(24)	17,000		
77			885,450		885,450
78					
79					

Illustration 22A-2

Work Sheet for Preparation of Statement of Cash Flows— Yoshi Corporation

1. **Net Income.** Because so much of the analysis requires adjustments to convert accrual basis income to the cash basis, the net income number is usually the first reconciling item put in the work sheet. The entry to reflect this and the balance sheet account affected is:

Operating—Net Income	117,700	
Retained Earnings		117,700

The credit to Retained Earnings explains part of the change in that account. We know that net income did not generate $117,700 of cash, so this number is considered a temporary one that will be adjusted whenever the subsequent analysis identifies revenues and expenses whose cash impact is different from the revenue and expense amounts that are included in net income. It is a starting point only.

2. **Temporary Investments.** Based on the activity and adjustments in this account during 2012, the entry to explain the net change in its balance is as follows:

Cash ($32,300 – $26,000)	6,300	
Temporary Investments		5,000
Investment Income, Temporary Investments ($2,300 – $1,000)		1,300

Because the cash flows related to investments held for trading purposes are all operating cash flows, the Operating Activities section should report $6,300 of net cash inflows. However, all that is reported so far is the $1,300 of investment income. Therefore, an adjustment of $5,000 is needed to adjust the investment income number to the cash flows from these temporary investments. This explains the $5,000 decrease in this account's balance during the year.

3. **Accounts Receivable.** The following two entries summarize the net change in this account and identify the other accounts that are affected:

Accounts Receivable	55,250	
Revenue		55,250
Allowance for Doubtful Accounts	1,450	
Accounts Receivable		1,450

Accounts Receivable increased by $53,800 during the year after writing off accounts totalling $1,450. The increase due to reporting revenue in excess of cash receipts therefore must have been $55,250. This requires an adjustment to the net income reported in the work sheet's Operating Activities section. The other entry explains changes in two balance sheet accounts with no cash impact. Enter these on the work sheet.

4. **Inventories.** The entry to explain the net change in the Inventory account is as follows:

Cost of Goods Sold	8,000	
Inventories		8,000

The credit to inventories explains the change in that account. The debit is an expense of $8,000 that was deducted in calculating net income, but which did not use cash. This requires a debit column adjustment to the net income in the Operating Activities section.[20]

5. **Prepaid Expenses.** Assuming the prepaid expenses were selling and administrative in nature, the following entry summarizes the change in this account:

Selling and Administrative Expense	500	
Prepaid Expenses		500

The credit entry explains the change in the Prepaid Expenses account. The debit represents a non-cash expense deducted on the income statement, requiring an adjustment to the net income reported in the Operating Activities section.

6. **Investment in Shares of Portel Corp.** Entries explaining the change in this account are:

Investment in Shares of Portel Corp.	5,500	
Equity in Earnings of Portel Corp.		5,500
Cash	2,000	
Investment in Shares of Portel Corp.		2,000

---

[20] This is consistent with the analysis earlier in the chapter. If $8,000 of cost of goods sold came from a reduction in inventory levels, purchases for the year must have been $8,000 less than cost of goods sold. Therefore both analyses equally well convert the cost of goods sold to the level of purchases in the year.

The first entry explains part of the change in the investment account and identifies a non-cash revenue included in net income. The entry to adjust net income for this is a $5,500 credit. The second entry credit explains the remainder of the change in the balance sheet account. The debit portion of the entry represents an operating inflow of cash that has not been included in net income. The Operating Activities section is adjusted to reflect this $2,000 operating cash inflow.

7. **Investment in Shares of Hyco Ltd.** A single entry explains the change in this investment accounted for at FV-OCI.

Investment in Shares of Hyco Ltd.	4,500	
Holding Gain on Investment (OCI/AOCI)		4,500

The entry explains the change in two balance sheet accounts. The $4,500 was not an income statement item and it is not a cash transaction.

8. **Deferred Development Costs.** The entries to summarize the changes in this account are as follows:

Deferred Development Costs	200,000	
Cash		200,000
Development Expense	40,000	
Deferred Development Costs		40,000

The first entry identifies an outflow of cash related to the investment in this non-current asset—an investing flow. The second entry recognizes the amortization of these deferred costs—a non-cash expense—reported in net income. The adjustment adds back (debits) $40,000 to the net income number. Remember to enter the transactions that explain changes in the balance sheet accounts as you proceed.

9. **Land.** The entries affecting the Land account are:

Land	54,000	
Term Preferred Shares		54,000
Cash	15,000	
Land		4,500
Gain on Disposal of Land		10,500

The first entry explains changes in both the Land and Term Preferred Shares accounts—a significant non-cash transaction. The second entry identifies a $15,000 investing inflow of cash, a reduction of $4,500 in the Land account, and a gain reported in net income that does not correspond to the actual cash flow. Net income is adjusted.

10. **Equipment.** The entries that affect the Equipment account are as follows:

Equipment	73,000	
Cash		73,000
Cash	13,000	
Loss on Disposal of Equipment	1,500	
Accumulated Depreciation—Equipment	13,500	
Equipment		28,000

The first entry identifies a $73,000 investing outflow of cash. The second entry explains the remainder of the change in the asset account and part of the change in the Accumulated Depreciation account, and identifies a $13,000 investing inflow of cash and a $1,500 non-cash loss that is reported in net income and needs to be adjusted.

11. **Goodwill.** The decrease in Goodwill is an impairment loss, recreated with this entry:

Impairment Loss—Goodwill	2,400	
Goodwill		2,400

The impairment loss is a non-cash charge to the income statement. It therefore requires an adjustment to the net income included in the Operating Activities section.

12. **Allowance for Doubtful Accounts.** Part of the change in this account was explained previously in item 3 above. The remaining entry to this account recognized bad debt expense:

Bad Debt Expense	2,250	
Allowance for Doubtful Accounts		2,250

This completes the explanation of changes to the allowance account. In addition, it identifies a non-cash expense of $2,250, which requires an adjustment to net income in the Operating Activities section.

13. **Accumulated Depreciation—Equipment.** One of the changes in the Accumulated Depreciation account was explained previously in item 10. The other entry affecting this account is:

Depreciation Expense	11,500	
Accumulated Depreciation—Equipment		11,500

The entry identifies an $11,500 non-cash expense requiring an adjustment to net income and the cash flows from operations.

14. **Accumulated Depreciation—Buildings.** With no change in the Buildings account during the year, the only entry needed to explain the change in the Accumulated Depreciation account is:

Depreciation Expense	3,100	
Accumulated Depreciation—Buildings		3,100

This $3,100 non-cash expense requires an adjustment to the net income number in the Operating Activities section.

15. **Accounts Payable.** The summary entry to explain the net change in this account is:

Accounts Payable	1,000	
Cash		1,000

The reduction in the payables balance resulted from paying out $1,000 more cash than was recorded in purchases. Cost of goods sold and other expenses have already been adjusted to represent the goods and services purchased, so a $1,000 credit adjustment is needed to convert the purchases to the amount paid; that is, to the operating cash outflow.

16. **Dividends Payable on Term Preferred Shares.** The summary entry explaining the net change in this account is as follows:

Dividend Expense (income statement expense)	2,000	
Dividends Payable on Term Preferred Shares		2,000

The increase in the liability account results from recognizing more dividends as an expense (these shares are a financial liability in substance) than dividends paid in the year. Therefore, $2,000 is added back to net income to adjust the operating cash flows to equal cash dividends paid in 2012.

17. **Accrued Liabilities.** The $4,000 increase in this account was caused by recognizing $4,000 more expense than payments in the year. The entry is as follows:

Salaries and Wages Expense (assumed)	4,000	
Accrued Liabilities		4,000

To adjust, $4,000 is added back (debited) to the cash provided by net income as reported.

18. **Income Taxes Payable.** The decrease in this account occurred because Yoshi Corporation paid out more cash than the expense reported, reflected by this entry:

Income Taxes Payable	13,000	
Cash		13,000

Because the expense reported has been deducted in determining the income number, an additional $13,000 outflow is deducted or credited on the work sheet.

19. **Bonds Payable.** The change in the Bonds Payable account is assumed to be explained by the following entry as a result of amortizing the bond discount netted with the liability:

Interest Expense	300	
Bonds Payable		300

That is, $300 of the interest expense did not require any cash, so an adjustment is needed to the net income in the operating activities section.

20. **Term Preferred Shares.** $54,000 of the increase has already been explained above. The remaining increase is assumed to have resulted from the following entry, a $6,000 financing inflow:

Cash	6,000	
Term Preferred Shares		6,000

21. **Future Income Tax Liability.** The increase in this account is due to the deferral of the tax liability to future periods, reflected in this entry:

Future Income Tax Expense	3,000	
Future Income Tax Liability		3,000
Future Income Tax Expense (AOCI)	1,000	
Future Income Tax Liability		1,000

The change in the balance sheet account is explained, and the non-cash portion of income tax expense is adjusted by adding back $4,000 to net income.

22. **Common Shares.** The following entries explain the change in this account over the year:

Retained Earnings	15,000	
Common Shares		15,000
Cash	144,000	
Common Shares		144,000
Common Shares	21,600	
Retained Earnings	12,400	
Cash		34,000

The first entry records the stock dividend. As discussed earlier, this is a non-cash activity that, although explaining the change in two balance sheet accounts, is not part of the statement of cash flows. The second entry records the inflow of cash for shares sold—a financing activity. The third entry records the repurchase and cancellation of the company's own shares.

23. **Retained Earnings.** Most of the changes in this account have already been dealt with above. One additional entry is needed to explain the remainder of the change:

Retained Earnings (dividends)	6,000	
Cash		6,000

This entry records a financing outflow of cash for dividends on common shares.

Completing the Work Sheet

All that remains to complete the balance sheet portion of the work sheet is to credit the Cash account by $27,000 and debit the Cash Equivalents by $10,000, netting to a $17,000 credit or decrease in cash. The $17,000 debit to balance this work sheet entry is inserted at the bottom of the work sheet. The debit and credit columns of the reconciling items are then totalled and balanced.

If the direct method of determining cash flows from operating activities is preferred, one change is needed to the above procedures. Instead of debiting the net income of \$117,700 and using this as the starting point to represent cash inflows from operations, the individual revenues, expenses, gains, and losses (netting to \$117,700) are transferred to the Operating Activities section on a line-by-line basis. When income statement items differ from the actual cash generated or used, adjustments are made to the specific line items affected.

The analysis is simplified if items that will be reported together on the final statement are grouped together, and if all income tax amounts are grouped as well. This step and the adjustments that are needed in the Operating Activities section are shown in Illustration 22A-3. The adjustments in the Operating Activities section are exactly the same as the ones that were made using the indirect approach, except that they are made to a specific line item instead of net income.

Illustration 22A-3

Operating Activities Work Sheet—Direct Method

DIRECT METHOD

		Debits (inflows)		Credits (outflows)
Cash Flows				
Operating activities:				
Receipts from customers	(1)	923,200	(3)	55,250
Received from investment in Portel Corp.	(1)	5,500	(6)	5,500
	(6)	2,000		
Received on temporary investment transactions	(1)	1,300		
	(2)	5,000		
Payments for goods and services	(4)	8,000	(1)	395,400
	(5)	500	(1)	134,600
	(8)	40,000	(1)	12,000
	(10)	1,500	(15)	1,000
	(12)	2,250		
Payments to employees	(17)	4,000	(1)	200,000
Interest and dividend payments	(19)	300	(1)	11,300
	(16)	2,000		
Impairment loss—goodwill	(11)	2,400	(1)	2,400
Income taxes paid	(21)	3,000	(1)	52,500
			(18)	13,000
Depreciation expense	(13)	11,500	(1)	14,600
	(14)	3,100		
Cash received on sale of land	(1)	10,500	(9)	10,500

The bottom part of the work sheet provides the necessary information to prepare the formal statement shown in Illustrations 22-20 (direct method) and 22-21 (indirect method).

Summary of Learning Objective for Appendix 22A

11 Use a work sheet to prepare a statement of cash flows.

A work sheet can be used to organize the analysis and cash flow information needed to prepare a statement of cash flows. This method accounts for all changes in the balances of non-cash balance sheet accounts from the period's beginning to the end, identifying all operating, investing, and financing cash flows in the process. The statement of cash flows is prepared from the cash flow information accumulated at the bottom of the work sheet.

Brief Exercises

All assignment material with an asterisk (*) relates to the appendix to the chapter.

(LO 2) **BE22-1**   Mullins Corp. reported the following items on its June 30, 2011 trial balance and on its comparative trial balance one year earlier:

	June 30, 2011	June 30, 2010
Cash in bank	$12,100	$ 9,460
Petty cash	100	125
Investment in shares of GTT Ltd. (to be sold within 60 days)	6,500	–0–
Investment in Canada 60-day treasury bills	22,000	28,300
Accounts payable	66,300	69,225
Temporary bank overdraft, chequing account	13,800	1,000

Determine the June 30, 2011 cash and cash equivalents amount for the 2011 statement of cash flows, and calculate the change in cash and cash equivalents since June 30, 2010.

(LO 3, 8) **BE22-2**   In 2011, Abbotsford Inc. issued 1,000 common shares for land worth $149,000.

(a) Prepare Abbotsford's journal entry to record the transaction.

(b) Indicate the effect that the transaction has on cash.

(c) Indicate how the transaction is reported on the statement of cash flows.

(LO 3, 8) **BE22-3**   Wong Textiles Ltd. entered into a capital lease obligation during 2012 to acquire a cutting machine. The amount recorded to the Leased Equipment account and the corresponding Lease Obligation account was $85,000 at the date of signing the lease. Wong paid the first annual lease payment of $2,330 at the date of signing, and by the end of 2012 had recorded depreciation of $1,100 for the machine. Using the direct format, provide the necessary disclosure for these transactions on the statement of cash flows.

(LO 3) **BE22-4**   Flin Flon Corporation, which follows IFRS, had the following activities in 2011.

1. Sold land for $140,000.

2. Purchased temporary investment in common shares for $15,000 with the intention of trading.

3. Purchased inventory for $845,000.

4. Received $73,000 cash from bank borrowings.

5. Retired $76,000 of bonds payable.

6. Purchased equipment for $495,000.

7. Issued common shares for $350,000.

8. Recorded a holding gain of $3,000 on investments accounted for using the fair value through net income (FV-NI) model.

9. Purchased investments in bonds, reported at amortized cost for $61,000.

10. Declared and paid a dividend of $18,000 (charged to retained earnings).

11. Investments in bonds reported at amortized cost, with a carrying amount of $410,000, were sold for $415,000.

12. Dividends were received for $4,000.

Calculate the amount that Flin Flon should report as net cash provided (used) by investing activities in its statement of cash flows. Flin Flon has adopted the policy of classifying dividends paid as financing activities and dividends received as investing activities on the cash flow statement.

(LO 3) **BE22-5**   Tang Corporation, which follows accounting standards for private enterprises (ASPE), had the following activities in 2011.

1. Paid $870,000 of accounts payable.

2. Paid $12,000 of bank loan interest.

3. Issued common shares for $200,000.

4. Paid $170,000 in dividends (charged to retained earnings).

5. Collected $150,000 in notes receivable.

6. Issued $410,000 of bonds payable.

7. Paid $20,000 on bank loan principal.

8. Issued a stock dividend in the amount of $11,000.

9. Received $5,000 in interest from an investment in bonds.

10. Purchased at a cost of $47,000 the corporation's own shares.

Calculate the amount that Tang should report as net cash provided (used) by financing activities in its 2011 statement of cash flows.

BE22-6 Watson Corporation, which uses accounting standards for private enterprises (ASPE), is using the indirect **(LO 3)** method to prepare its 2011 statement of cash flows. A list of items that may affect the statement follows:

_____ **(a)** Increase in accounts receivable

_____ **(b)** Decrease in accounts receivable

_____ **(c)** Issue of shares

_____ **(d)** Depreciation expense

_____ **(e)** Sale of land at carrying amount

_____ **(f)** Sale of land at a gain

_____ **(g)** Payment of dividends charged to retained earnings

_____ **(h)** Purchase of land and building

_____ **(i)** Purchase of long-term investment in bonds, reported at amortized cost

_____ **(j)** Increase in accounts payable

_____ **(k)** Decrease in accounts payable

_____ **(l)** Loan from bank by signing note payable

_____ **(m)** Purchase of equipment by issuing a note payable

_____ **(n)** Increase in inventory

_____ **(o)** Issue of bonds

_____ **(p)** Retirement of bonds

_____ **(q)** Sale of equipment at a loss

_____ **(r)** Purchase of corporation's own shares

_____ **(s)** Acquisition of equipment using a capital/finance lease

_____ **(t)** Conversion of bonds into common shares

_____ **(u)** Impairment loss on goodwill

Match each code in the list that follows to the items above to show how each item will affect Watson's 2011 statement of cash flows. Unless stated otherwise, assume that the transaction was for cash.

Code Letter	Effect
A	Added to net income in the operating section
D	Deducted from net income in the operating section
R-I	Cash receipt in investing section
P-I	Cash payment in investing section
R-F	Cash receipt in financing section
P-F	Cash payment in financing section
N	Non-cash investing and/or financing activity disclosed in notes to the financial statement

BE22-7 At January 1, 2011, Apex Inc. had accounts receivable of $72,000. At December 31, 2011, the accounts receiv- **(LO 4)** able balance was $59,000. Sales for 2011 were $420,000. Sales returns and allowances for the year were $10,000. Purchase discounts were in the amount of $4,200 and sales discounts $1,000. Calculate Apex's 2011 cash receipts from customers.

(LO 4)   BE22-8   Ciao Corporation had January 1 and December 31 balances as follows:

	1/1/11	12/31/11
Inventory	$90,000	$113,000
Accounts payable	61,000	69,000

For 2011, the cost of goods sold was $550,000. Calculate Ciao's 2011 cash paid to suppliers of merchandise.

(LO 4)   BE22-9   Tercek Inc., which uses accounting standards for private enterprises (ASPE), had the following balances and amounts appear on its comparative financial statements at year end:

	Dec. 31, 2012	Dec. 31, 2011
Income taxes payable	$1,200	$1,400
Future income tax asset—current	300	–0–
Future income tax liability—non-current	1,950	1,600
Income tax expense	2,500	2,100
Future income tax benefit	(600)	(200)

Calculate the amount that should appear as cash paid for income taxes.

(LO 4)   BE22-10   Azure Corporation had the following 2011 income statement data:

Sales	$205,000
Cost of goods sold	120,000
Gross profit	85,000
Operating expenses (includes depreciation of $21,000)	50,000
Net income	$ 35,000

The following accounts increased during 2011 by the amounts shown: Accounts Receivable, $17,000; Inventory, $11,000; Accounts Payable, $13,000; Mortgage Payable, $40,000. Prepare the cash flows from operating activities section of Azure's 2011 statement of cash flows using the direct method.

(LO 5)   BE22-11   Using the information from BE22–10 for Azure Corporation, prepare the cash flows from operating activities section of Azure's 2011 statement of cash flows using the indirect method.

(LO 4, 5)   BE22-12   Majestic Corporation had the following 2011 income statement data:

Revenues	$100,000
Expenses	60,000
	$ 40,000

In 2011, Majestic had the following activity in selected accounts:

Accounts Receivable					Allowance for Doubtful Accounts			
1/1/11	20,000						1,200	1/1/11
Revenues	100,000	1,000		Writeoffs	Writeoffs	1,000	1,540	Bad debt expense
		90,000		Collections				
12/31/11	29,000						1,740	12/31/11

Prepare Majestic's cash flows from operating activities section of the statement of cash flows using (a) the direct method, and (b) the indirect method.

(LO 5)   BE22-13   October Corporation reported net income of $46,000 in 2012. Depreciation expense was $17,000 and unrealized holding losses on temporary investments (FV-NI) were $3,000. The following accounts changed as indicated in 2012:

Accounts Receivable	$11,000 increase
Investments in Bonds, at Amortized Cost	16,000 increase
Future Income Tax Assets	2,000 decrease
Inventory	7,400 increase
Non-Trade Note Payable	15,000 decrease
Accounts Payable	9,300 increase

Calculate the net cash provided by operating activities.

BE22-14 In 2011, Oswald Corporation reported a net loss of $56,000. Oswald's only net income adjustments were **(LO 5)** depreciation expense of $87,000 and an increase in accounts receivable of $8,100. Calculate Oswald's net cash provided (used) by operating activities.

*BE22-15 Indicate in general journal form how the following items would be entered in a work sheet to prepare the **(LO 11)** statement of cash flows.

(a) Net income is $207,000.

(b) Cash dividends declared (charged to retained earnings) and paid totalled $60,000.

(c) Equipment was purchased for $114,000.

(d) Equipment that originally cost $40,000 and had accumulated depreciation of $32,000 was sold for $13,000.

Exercises

E22-1 **(Classification of Major Transactions and Events)** Dunrobin Industries Ltd., which uses IFRS, had the fol- **(LO 3, 8, 10)** lowing transactions during its most recent fiscal year.

1. Acquired raw materials inventory.

2. Declared a cash dividend on common shares.

3. Collected cash from tenants for rents.

4. Acquired a 4% interest in a supplier company's shares accounted as FV-NI. (Management's intention is not to trade the shares.)

5. Made the annual contribution to the employees' pension plan.

6. Leased new equipment under a finance lease.

7. Leased additional office space under an operating lease.

8. Paid the semi-annual interest on outstanding debentures and amortized the associated premium.

9. Paid the supplier for the acquisition in (1.) above.

10. Acquired land by issuing preferred shares.

11. Paid the car dealership for a new fleet of vehicles for the sales staff.

12. Collected a dividend on the investment made in (4.) above.

13. Sold the old fleet of sales vehicles at an amount in excess of their carrying amount.

14. Distributed additional shares following a declaration of a 5% stock dividend.

Dunrobin Industries Ltd. has adopted the policy of classifying dividends received as investing activities, dividends paid as operating activities, and interest paid as a financing activity on the cash flow statement.

Instructions

Identify each transaction listed above as

(a) an operating activity,

(b) an investing activity,

(c) a financing activity,

(d) a significant non-cash investing or financing activity, or

(e) none of these options.

Where there are choices or options in the classification, provide details of the options available.

E22-2 **(Classification of Transactions)** Bonilla Corp., which uses IFRS, had the following activity in its most recent **(LO 3, 8, 10)** year of operations:

1. Purchase of equipment

2. Redemption of bonds

3. Conversion of bonds into common shares

4. Sale of building

5. Depreciation of equipment

6. Exchange of equipment for furniture of equal fair value

7. Issue of common shares

8. Amortization of intangible assets

9. Purchase of company's own shares

10. Issue of bonds for land

11. Impairment loss on goodwill

12. Holding loss on investment accounted at fair value with gains and losses in net income

13. Payment of dividends on common shares

14. Increase in interest receivable on notes receivable

15. Pension expense in excess of amount funded

16. Signing of a finance lease agreement for equipment

17. Payment of a monthly finance lease obligation

18. Purchase of a treasury bill as a cash equivalent

19. Payment on an operating lease agreement

20. Holding gain accrued on FV-NI equity security investments

21. Redemption of preferred shares classified as debt

22. Payments of principal on an operating line of credit

23. Payment of interest on an operating line of credit

Bonilla Corp. has adopted the policy of classifying dividends received as operating activities, dividends paid as operating activities, interest received as investing activities, and interest paid as a financing activity on the cash flow statement.

Instructions

Using the indirect method, classify the items as

  (a) an operating activity, added to net income;

  (b) an operating activity, deducted from net income;

  (c) an investing activity;

  (d) a financing activity;

  (e) a significant non-cash investing or financing activity; or

  (f) none of these options.

Where there are choices or options in the classification, provide details of the options available.

(LO 3, 8)   E22-3   (Statement Presentation of Transactions—Indirect Method) Each of the following items must be considered in preparing a statement of cash flows (indirect method) for Bastille Inc., which uses ASPE, for the year ended December 31, 2011.

1. Plant assets that cost $40,000 six years before and were being depreciated on a straight-line basis over 10 years with no estimated residual value were sold for $5,300.

2. During the year, 10,000 common shares were issued for $41 cash per share.

3. Uncollectible accounts receivable in the amount of $27,000 were written off against the allowance for doubtful accounts.

4. The company sustained a net loss for the year of $10,000. Depreciation amounted to $22,000. A gain of $9,000 was reported on the sale of land for $39,000 cash.

5. A three-month Canadian treasury bill was purchased for $50,000 on November 13, 2011. The company uses a cash and cash-equivalent basis for its statement of cash flows.

6. Patent amortization for the year was $18,000.

7. The company exchanged common shares for a 40% interest in TransCo Corp. for $900,000.

8. The company accrued a holding loss on investments accounted for at FV-NI.

Instructions

Identify where each item is reported in the statement of cash flows, if at all.

E22-4 (Statement Presentation of Transactions—Equity Accounts) The following selected account balances are **(LO 3, 8)** taken from the financial statements of Mandrich Inc. at year end prepared using IFRS:

	2012	2011
Preferred shares classified as equity	$145,000	$145,000
Common shares: 9,000 shares in 2012, 10,000 shares in 2011	122,000	140,000
Contributed surplus—reacquisition of common shares	3,500	–0–
Cash dividends—preferred	6,250	6,250
Stock dividends—common	14,000	4,000
Retained earnings (balance after closing entries)	300,000	240,000

At December 31, 2012, the following information is available:

1. Mandrich Inc. repurchased 2,000 common shares during 2012. The repurchased shares had a weighted average cost of $32,000.

2. During 2012, 1,000 common shares were issued as a stock dividend.

3. Mandrich Inc. chooses to classify dividends paid as financing activities.

Instructions

(a) Calculate net income for the fiscal year ending December 31, 2012.

(b) Provide the necessary disclosure for all of Mandrich Inc.'s transactions on the statement of cash flows. Also state the section of the cash flow statement in which each item is reported. Where there are choices or options in the classification, provide details of the options available.

(c) Does Mandrich Inc. have other choices in classifying dividends paid on the cash flow statement?

E22-5 (Statement Presentation of Transactions—Investment Using Equity Method) The following selected **(LO 3, 4,** account balances were taken from the financial statements of Blumberg Inc. concerning its long-term investment in shares **8, 9, 10)** of Black Inc. over which it has had significant influence since 2009:

	Dec. 31, 2012	Dec. 31, 2011
Investment in Black Inc.	$494,600	$422,000
Investment income recorded for Black	13,200	11,800

At December 31, 2012, the following information is available:

1. Blumberg purchased additional common shares in Black Inc. on January 2, 2012, for $65,000. As a result of this purchase, Blumberg's ownership interest in Black increased to 40%.

2. Black reported income of $33,000 for the year ended December 31, 2012.

3. Black declared and paid total dividends of $14,000 on its common shares for the year ended December 31, 2012.

Instructions

(a) Prepare a reconciliation of the Investment in Black Inc. account from December 31, 2011, to December 31, 2012, assuming Blumberg Inc. uses the equity method for this investment.

(b) Prepare a table that contrasts the direct and indirect methods for presenting all transactions related to the Black Inc. investment on Blumberg's statement of cash flows based on the assumption that Black uses IFRS and adopts the policy of classifying dividends received as investing activities. Be specific about the classification in the statement for each item that is reported.

(c) Prepare a table that contrasts the direct and indirect methods for presenting all transactions related to the Black Inc. investment on Blumberg's statement of cash flows based on the assumption that Black uses ASPE and must therefore classify dividends received as operating cash flows.

E22-6 (Classification of Transactions and Calculation of Cash Flows) The following are selected balance sheet **(LO 3, 10)** accounts of Strong Ltd. at December 31, 2010, and 2011, and the increases or decreases in each account from 2010 to 2011. Also presented is the selected income statement and other information for the year ended December 31, 2011.

Balance Sheet (selected accounts)

	2011	2010	Increase (Decrease)
Assets			
Accounts receivable	$ 84,000	$ 74,000	$10,000
Temporary investments reported at FV-NI	41,000	49,000	(8,000)
Property, plant, and equipment	177,000	147,000	30,000
Accumulated depreciation	(78,000)	(67,000)	11,000
Liabilities and shareholders' equity			
Bonds payable	149,000	146,000	3,000
Dividends payable	8,000	5,000	3,000
Common shares	31,000	22,000	9,000
Retained earnings	104,000	91,000	13,000

Income Statement (selected information)
For the Year Ended December 31, 2011

Sales revenue	$295,000
Depreciation expense	33,000
Gain on sale of FV-NI investments	5,000
Holding loss on FV-NI investments	3,000
Gain on sale of equipment	14,500
Net income	31,000

Additional information:

1. During 2011, equipment costing $45,000 was sold for cash.

2. Accounts receivable relate to sales of merchandise.

3. During 2011, $20,000 of bonds payable were issued in exchange for property, plant, and equipment. All bonds were issued at par.

4. During the year, temporary investments accounted at FV-NI were sold for $22,000. Additional investments were purchased.

Instructions

Determine the category (operating, investing, or financing) and the amount that should be reported in the statement of cash flows for the following items, assuming Strong Ltd. follows ASPE:

(a) Cash received from customers

(b) Payments for purchases of property, plant, and equipment

(c) Proceeds from the sale of equipment

(d) Cash dividends paid

(e) Redemption of bonds payable

(f) Proceeds from the sale of investments

(g) Purchase of investments

(LO 3)　E22-7　(Partial Statement of Cash Flows—Indirect Method) The following accounts appear in the ledger of Tanaka Limited, which uses IFRS and has adopted the policy of classifying dividends paid as operating activities:

Retained Earnings		Dr.	Cr.	Bal.
Jan. 1, 2011	Credit balance			$ 42,000
Aug. 15	Dividends (cash)	$15,000		27,000
Dec. 31	Net income for 2011		$40,000	67,000

Machinery		Dr.	Cr.	Bal.
Jan. 1, 2011	Debit balance			$140,000
Aug. 3	Purchase of machinery	$62,000		202,000
Sept. 10	Cost of machinery constructed	48,000		250,000
Nov. 15	Machinery sold		$56,000	194,000

Accumulated Depreciation—Machinery		Dr.	Cr.	Bal.
Jan. 1, 2011	Credit balance			$84,000
Nov. 15	Accumulated depreciation on machinery sold	25,200		58,800
Dec. 31	Depreciation for 2011		$16,800	75,600

Instructions

Show how the information posted in the accounts is reported on a statement of cash flows by preparing a partial statement of cash flows using the indirect method. The loss on sale of machinery (November 15) was $5,800.

E22-8 **(Analysis of Changes in Capital Asset Accounts and Related Cash Flows)** MacAskill Mills Limited, which uses ASPE, engaged in the following transactions in 2011. **(LO 3, 7)**

1. The Land account increased by $58,000 over the year: Land that originally cost $60,000 was exchanged along with a cash payment of $3,000 for another parcel of land valued at $91,000. Additional land was acquired later in the year in a cash purchase.

2. The Furniture and Fixtures account had a balance of $67,500 at the beginning of the year and $62,000 at the end. The related accumulated depreciation account decreased over the same period from a balance of $24,000 to $15,200. Fully depreciated office furniture that cost $10,000 was sold to employees during the year for $1,000. In addition, fixtures that cost $3,000 and had a carrying amount of $700 were written off, and new fixtures were acquired and paid for.

3. A five-year capital lease for specialized machinery was entered into halfway through the year; under the terms of the lease the company agreed to make five annual payments (in advance) of $25,000, after which the machinery will revert to the lessor. The present value of these lease payments at the 10% rate that is implicit in the lease was $104,247. The first payment was made as agreed.

Instructions

For each listed item:

(a) Prepare the underlying journal entries that were made by MacAskill Mills during 2011 to record all information related to the changes in each capital asset account and associated accounts over the year.

(b) Identify the amount(s) of the cash flows that result from the transactions and events recorded, and determine the classification of each one.

(c) Prepare the corresponding amounts to those prepared in part (b) for the operating activities section of the statement of cash flows prepared using the indirect method.

(d) Comment on the results obtained in (b) and (c) above.

E22-9 **(Statement of Cash Flows—Direct and Indirect Methods)** Angus Farms Ltd., which uses ASPE, had the following transactions during the fiscal year ending December 31, 2011. **(LO 3, 8)**

1. On May 1, a used tractor was sold at auction. The information concerning this transaction included:

Original cost of the tractor	$52,000
Carrying amount of tractor at date of sale	14,000
Cash proceeds obtained at sale	22,500

2. After the seeding season, on June 15, 2011, a plough with an original cost of $6,000 and a carrying amount of $500 was discarded.

3. On September 1, 2011, a new plough was purchased for $7,700.

4. On December 30, a section of land was sold to a neighbouring farm called Clear Pastures Ltd. The original cost of the land was $45,000. To finance the purchase Clear Pastures gave Angus a three-year mortgage note in the amount of $75,000 that carries interest at 5%, with interest payable annually each December 30.

5. On December 31, 2011, depreciation was recorded on the farm equipment in the amount of $12,600.

Instructions

(a) Prepare the journal entries that recorded the transactions during the year.

(b) Prepare the sections of the cash flow statement of Angus Farms Ltd. to report the transactions provided, using the indirect format.

(c) Prepare the sections of the cash flow statement of Angus Farms Ltd. to report the transactions provided, using the direct format.

(d) What results do you notice when comparing the information arrived at in parts (b) and (c) above?

(LO 3, 4, 8, 9) E22-10 (Partial Statement of Cash Flows—Operating and Finance Leases) Wagner Inc. is a large Canadian public company that uses IFRS. A lease for a fleet of trucks has been capitalized and the lease amortization schedule for the first three lease payments appears below. The trucks have an economic life of eight years. The lease term is from July 1, 2011, to June 30, 2018, and the trucks must be returned to the lessor at the end of this period of time.

WAGNER INC.
Lease Amortization Schedule

Date	Annual Lease Payments	Interest (8%) on Unpaid Obligation	Reduction of Lease Obligation	Balance of Lease Obligation
				$3,064,470
July 1, 2011	$545,000		$545,000	2,519,470
July 1, 2012	545,000	$201,558	343,442	2,176,028
July 1, 2013	545,000	174,082	370,918	1,805,110

Instructions

(a) Prepare the journal entries and any year-end (December 31) adjusting journal entries made by Wagner Inc. in 2011 and 2012.

(b) Prepare a partial comparative statement of cash flows for the 2011 and 2012 fiscal years along with any additional disclosure notes. Wagner Inc. has adopted the policy of classifying any interest paid as operating activities on the statement of cash flows.

(c) Repeat parts (a) and (b) assuming that the lease must be recorded as an operating lease.

(d) From the perspective of an external user, which cash flow statement seems to present a more favourable picture of Wagner Inc.'s financial performance? Comment briefly.

(LO 4) E22-11 (Convert Net Income to Operating Cash Flow—Indirect Method) Shen Limited reported net income of $32,000 for its latest year ended March 31, 2012.

Instructions

For each of the five different situations involving the balance sheet accounts that follow, calculate the cash flow from operations:

	Accounts Receivable March 31		Inventory March 31		Accounts Payable March 31	
	2012	2011	2012	2011	2012	2011
(a)	$20,000	$21,500	$16,500	$17,900	$ 9,000	$ 9,300
(b)	$23,000	$20,000	$17,300	$20,500	$14,600	$10,200
(c)	$20,000	–0–	$12,000	–0–	$ 7,000	–0–
(d)	$19,500	$21,000	$19,500	$15,600	$10,200	$14,100
(e)	$21,500	$24,000	$12,900	$14,000	$13,300	$11,300

(LO 4) E22-12 (Statement of Cash Flows—Direct Method) El Lobos Corp. uses the direct method to prepare its statement of cash flows and follows IFRS. El Lobos' trial balances at December 31, 2011, and 2010, were as follows:

	Dec. 31, 2011	Dec. 31, 2010
Debits		
Cash	$ 55,000	$ 57,000
Accounts Receivable	33,000	30,000
Inventory	31,000	47,000
Property, Plant, and Equipment	95,000	90,000
Cost of Goods Sold	253,000	380,000
Selling Expenses	138,000	172,000
General and Administrative Expenses	140,000	151,300
Interest Expense	15,600	2,600
Income Tax Expense	20,200	56,200
	$780,800	$986,100

Digging Deeper

	Dec. 31, 2011	Dec. 31, 2010
Credits		
Allowance for Doubtful Accounts	$ 1,300	$ 1,100
Accumulated Depreciation	26,500	25,000
Accounts Payable	25,000	15,500
Income Taxes Payable	21,000	29,100
Deferred Income Tax Liability	5,300	4,600
8% Callable Bonds Payable	46,000	45,500
Common Shares	53,600	22,000
Retained Earnings	44,700	64,600
Sales	557,400	778,700
	$780,800	$986,100

Additional information:

1. El Lobos purchased $5,000 of equipment during 2011.

2. El Lobos allocated one third of its depreciation expense to selling expenses and the remainder to general and administrative expenses.

3. Bad debt expense for 2011 was $5,000 and writeoffs of uncollectible accounts totalled $4,800.

4. El Lobos has adopted the policy of classifying the payments of interest as financing activities on the statement of cash flows.

Instructions

Determine what amounts El Lobos should report in its statement of cash flows for the year ended December 31, 2011, for the following:

(a) Cash collected from customers

(b) Cash paid to suppliers of goods and services (excluding interest and income taxes)

(c) Cash paid for interest

(d) Cash paid for income taxes

E22-13 (Preparation of Operating Activities Section—Direct Method) Ellis Corp.'s income statement for the year **(LO 4)** ended December 31, 2011, had the following condensed information:

Revenue from fees		$778,000
Operating expenses (excluding depreciation)	$499,000	
Depreciation expense	66,000	
Holding loss on temporary investments (FV-NI)	4,000	
Loss on sale of equipment	14,000	583,000
Income before income taxes		195,000
Income tax expense		61,000
Net income		$134,000

There were no purchases or sales of temporary investments during 2011.

Ellis's balance sheet included the following comparative data at December 31:

	2011	2010
Temporary investments (FV-NI)	$22,000	$26,000
Accounts receivable	35,000	54,000
Accounts payable	44,000	31,000
Income taxes payable	6,000	8,500

Instructions

Prepare the operating activities section of the statement of cash flows using the direct method.

E22-14 (Preparation of Operating Activities Section—Indirect Method) Data for Ellis Corp. are presented in **(LO 5)** E22-13.

Instructions

Prepare the operating activities section of the statement of cash flows using the indirect method.

(LO 4, 5)   E22-15   (Cash Provided by Operating, Writeoff, and Recovery of Accounts Receivable) The following are the transactions from Izzy Inc. concerning the allowance for doubtful accounts.

1. Writeoff of accounts receivable	$5,000
2. Recovery of accounts previously written off	3,500
3. Accrual for bad debt expense	4,400

Assume these are the only transactions for the year.

Instructions

(a) Record the above transactions.

(b) Prepare the reporting necessary on a partial statement of cash flows using

    1. the direct method, and

    2. the indirect method.

(LO 6, 7)   E22-16   (Accounting Cycle, Financial Statements, Cash Account, and Statement of Cash Flows) The following are transactions of Albert Sing, an interior design consultant, for the month of September 2011.

Sept.	1	Albert Sing begins business as an interior design consultant, investing $31,000 for 8,000 common shares of the company, A.S. Design Limited.
	2	Purchased furniture and display equipment from Green Jacket Co. for $17,280.
	4	Paid rent for office space for the next three months at $680 per month.
	7	Employed a part-time secretary, Michael Bradley, at $300 per week.
	8	Purchased office supplies on account from Mann Corp. for $1,142.
	9	Received cash of $1,690 from clients for services performed.
	10	Paid miscellaneous office expenses, $430.
	14	Invoiced clients for consulting services, $5,120.
	18	Paid Mann Corp. on account, $600.
	19	Paid a dividend of $1.00 per share on the 5,000 outstanding shares.
	20	Received $980 from clients on account.
	21	Paid Michael Bradley two weeks of salary, $600.
	28	Invoiced clients for consulting services, $2,110.
	29	Paid the September telephone bill of $135 and miscellaneous office expenses of $85.

At September 30, the following information is available.

1. The furniture and display equipment has a useful life of five years and an estimated residual value of $1,500. Straight-line depreciation is appropriate.

2. One week's salary is owing to Michael Bradley.

3. Office supplies of $825 remain on hand.

4. Two months of rent has been paid in advance.

5. The invoice for electricity for September of $195 has been received, but not paid.

Instructions

(a) Prepare journal entries to record the transaction entries for September. Set up a T account for the Cash account and post all cash transactions to the account. Determine the balance of cash at September 30, 2011.

(b) Prepare any required adjusting entries at September 30, 2011.

(c) Prepare an adjusted trial balance at September 30, 2011.

(d) Prepare a balance sheet and income statement for the month ended September 30, 2011.

(e) Prepare a statement of cash flows for the month of September 2011. Use the indirect method for the cash flows from operating activities.

(f) Recast the cash flow from operating activities section using the direct method.

(g) Compare the statement of cash flows in parts (e) and (f) with the Cash account prepared in part (a) above.

(h) As a creditor, what would you consider to be an alarming trend that is revealed by the statement of cash flows prepared using the indirect method as required in part (e) above? Is this trend as easy to notice when the statement is prepared using the direct method as required in part (f) above?

E22-17 **(Statement of Cash Flows—Indirect and Direct Methods)** Condensed financial data of Tobita Limited,   **(LO 6, 7, 9)** which follows ASPE, for 2011 and 2010 follow:

TOBITA LIMITED
Comparative Balance Sheet
December 31

	2011	2010
Cash	$1,800	$1,150
Receivables	1,750	1,300
Inventory	1,600	1,900
Plant assets	1,900	1,700
Accumulated depreciation	(1,200)	(1,170)
Long-term investments (FV-NI)	1,300	1,420
	$7,150	$6,300
Accounts payable	$1,200	$ 900
Accrued liabilities	200	250
Bonds payable	1,400	1,550
Share capital	1,900	1,700
Retained earnings	2,450	1,900
	$7,150	$6,300

TOBITA LIMITED
Income Statement
Year Ended December 31, 2011

Sales		$6,900
Cost of goods sold		4,700
Gross margin		2,200
Selling and administrative expense		910
Income from operations		1,290
Other expenses and gains		
Interest expense	$(20)	
Gain on sale of investments (FV-NI)	80	60
Income before tax		1,350
Income tax expense		540
Net income		$ 810

Additional information: During the year, $70 of common shares were issued in exchange for plant assets. No plant assets were sold in 2011.

Instructions

(a) Prepare a statement of cash flows using the indirect method.

(b) Prepare a statement of cash flows using the direct method.

(c) Does Tobita Limited have any options on how to classify interest and dividends paid on the statement of cash flows?

(d) What would you consider to be an alarming trend that is revealed by the statements that you have prepared? Is it as easy to notice this trend using the direct method, as in part (b)?

Digging
Deeper

E22-18 **(Statement of Cash Flows—Direct and Indirect Methods)** Tuit Inc., a greeting card company that follows   **(LO 6, 7)** ASPE, had the following statements prepared as of December 31, 2012:

TUIT INC.
Comparative Balance Sheet
December 31

	2012	2011
Cash and cash equivalents	$ 51,000	$ 25,000
Accounts receivable	58,000	51,000
Inventories	40,000	60,000
Prepaid rent	5,000	4,000
Printing equipment	154,000	130,000
Accumulated depreciation—equipment	(35,000)	(25,000)
Goodwill	20,000	50,000
Total assets	$293,000	$295,000
Accounts payable	$ 46,000	$ 40,000
Income taxes payable	4,000	6,000
Wages payable	8,000	4,000
Short-term loans payable	8,000	10,000
Long-term loans payable	60,000	69,000
Common shares	130,000	130,000
Retained earnings	37,000	36,000
Total liabilities and shareholders' equity	$293,000	$295,000

TUIT INC.
Income Statement
Year Ending December 31, 2012

Sales		$338,150
Cost of goods sold		165,000
Gross margin		173,150
Operating expenses		120,000
Operating income		53,150
Interest expense	$11,400	
Impairment loss—goodwill	30,000	
Gain on sale of equipment	(2,000)	39,400
Income before tax		13,750
Income tax expense		6,750
Net income		$ 7,000

Additional information:

1. Dividends on common shares in the amount of $6,000 were declared and paid during 2012.

2. Depreciation expense is included in operating expenses, as are salaries and wages expense of $69,000.

3. Equipment with a cost of $20,000 that was 70% depreciated was sold during 2012.

Instructions

(a) Prepare a statement of cash flows using the direct method.

(b) Prepare a statement of cash flows using the indirect method.

(c) Does Tuit Inc. have any options on how to classify interest and dividends paid on the statement of cash flows?

(LO 6, 7, 8,   E22-19   (Statement of Cash Flows—Direct and Indirect Methods) Guas Inc., a major retailer of bicycles and acces-
9, 10)   sories, operates several stores and is a publicly traded company. The company is currently preparing its statement of cash
flows. The comparative balance sheet and income statement for Guas as of May 31, 2012, are as follows:

GUAS INC.
Balance Sheet
May 31, 2012, and May 31, 2011

	2012	2011
Current assets		
Cash	$ 33,250	$ 20,000
Accounts receivable	74,800	55,600
Merchandise inventory	188,700	199,000
Prepaid expenses	8,800	7,000
Total current assets	305,550	281,600
Plant assets		
Plant assets	596,500	501,500
Less: Accumulated depreciation	148,000	122,000
Net plant assets	448,500	379,500
Total assets	$754,050	$661,100
Current liabilities		
Accounts payable	$123,000	$115,000
Salaries payable	61,000	72,000
Interest payable	24,700	22,600
Total current liabilities	208,700	209,600
Long-term debt		
Bonds payable	75,000	100,000
Total liabilities	283,700	309,600
Shareholders' equity		
Common shares	335,750	280,000
Retained earnings	134,600	71,500
Total shareholders' equity	470,350	351,500
Total liabilities and shareholders' equity	$754,050	$661,100

GUAS INC.
Income Statement
For the Year Ended May 31, 2012

Sales		$1,345,800
Cost of merchandise sold		814,000
Gross margin		531,800
Expenses		
Salary expense		207,800
Interest expense		66,700
Other expenses		24,800
Depreciation expense		26,000
Total expenses		325,300
Operating income		206,500
Income tax expense		65,400
Net earnings		$ 141,100

The following is additional information about transactions during the year ended May 31, 2012, for Guas Inc., which follows IFRS:

1. Plant assets costing $95,000 were purchased by paying $44,000 in cash and issuing 5,000 common shares.

2. The "other expenses" relate to prepaid items.

3. In order to supplement its cash, Guas issued 4,000 additional common shares.

4. There were no penalties assessed for the retirement of bonds.

5. Cash dividends of $78,000 were declared and paid at the end of the fiscal year.

Instructions

(a) Compare and contrast the direct method and the indirect method for reporting cash flows from operating activities.

(b) Prepare a statement of cash flows for Guas Inc. for the year ended May 31, 2012, using the direct method. Support the statement with appropriate calculations, and provide all required disclosures.

(c) Using the indirect method, calculate only the net cash flow from operating activities for Guas Inc. for the year ended May 31, 2012.

(d) Does Guas Inc. have a choice in how it classifies dividends paid on the statement of cash flows?

(LO 6, 7, 8, 10) **E22-20** **(Statement of Cash Flows—Direct and Indirect Methods)** Information from the balance sheet and statement of income are given below for North Road Inc., a company following ASPE, for the year ended December 31.

Comparative Balance Sheet, at December 31

	2011	2010
Cash	$ 92,700	$ 47,250
Accounts receivable	90,800	37,000
Inventories	121,900	102,650
Investments in land	84,500	107,000
Property, plant, and equipment	290,000	205,000
Accumulated depreciation	(49,500)	(40,000)
	$630,400	$458,900
Accounts payable	$ 52,700	$ 48,280
Accrued expenses payable	12,100	18,830
Notes payable	140,000	70,000
Common shares	250,000	200,000
Retained earnings	175,600	121,790
	$630,400	$458,900

Statement of Income, Year Ended December 31, 2011

Revenues		
Sales		$297,500
Gain on sale of equipment		8,750
		306,250
Expenses		
Cost of goods sold	$ 99,460	
Depreciation expense	58,700	
Operating expenses	14,670	
Income tax expense	39,000	
Interest expense	2,940	214,770
Net income		$ 91,480

Additional information:

1. Investments in land were sold at cost during 2011.

2. Equipment costing $56,000 was sold for $15,550, resulting in a gain.

3. Common shares were issued in exchange for some equipment during the year. No other shares were issued.

4. The remaining purchases of equipment were paid for in cash.

Instructions

(a) Prepare a cash flow statement for the year ended December 31, 2011, using the indirect method.

(b) Prepare the operating activities section of the cash flow statement using the direct method.

(c) Does North Road Inc. have a choice in how it classifies dividends paid on the statement of cash flows?

(LO 1, 7, 9) **E22-21** **(Prepare Statement from Transactions, and Explain Changes in Cash Flow)** Strong House Inc. had the following condensed balance sheet at the end of operations for 2010:

STRONG HOUSE INC.
Balance Sheet
For the Year Ended December 31, 2010

Cash	$ 10,000	Current liabilities	$ 14,500
Current assets (non-cash)	34,000	Long-term notes payable	30,000
Investment in bonds, at amortized cost	40,000	Bonds payable	32,000
Plant assets	57,500	Share capital	80,000
Land	38,500	Retained earnings	23,500
	$180,000		$180,000

Strong House Inc. follows IFRS and chooses to classify dividends paid as financing activities and interest paid as operating activities on the statement of cash flows.

During 2011, the following occurred:

1. Strong House Inc. sold part of its investment portfolio in bonds for $15,500, resulting in a gain of $500.

2. Dividends totalling $19,000 were paid to shareholders.

3. A parcel of land was purchased for $5,500.

4. Common shares with a fair value of $20,000 were issued.

5. Bonds payable of $10,000 were retired at par.

6. Heavy equipment was purchased through the issuance of $32,000 of bonds.

7. Net income for 2011 was $42,000 after allowing for depreciation on Strong House's plant assets of $13,550. The amount of interest paid during 2011 was $4,150 and the amount of income taxes paid was $19,500.

8. Both current assets (other than cash) and current liabilities remained at the same amount.

Instructions

(a) Prepare a statement of cash flows for 2011 using the indirect method.

(b) Draft a one-page letter to Mr. Gerald Brauer, president of Strong House Inc., in which you briefly explain the changes within each major cash flow category. Refer to the statement of cash flows whenever necessary.

(c) Prepare a balance sheet at December 31, 2011, for Strong House Inc.

(d) Comment briefly about why the statement of cash flows used to be called a statement of changes in financial position.

*E22-22 **(Work Sheet Analysis of Selected Transactions)** The following transactions took place during the year (LO 11) 2011 for Mia Inc.

1. Convertible bonds payable with a carrying amount of $300,000 along with conversion rights of $9,000 were exchanged for unissued common shares.

2. The net income for the year was $410,000.

3. Depreciation charged on the building was $90,000.

4. Recorded the investment income earned from investment in Transot Ltd. using the equity method. Transot earnings for the year were $123,000 and Mia Inc. owns 28% of the outstanding common shares.

5. Old office equipment was traded in on the purchase of new equipment, resulting in the following entry:

Office Equipment	50,000	
Accumulated Depreciation—Office Equipment	30,000	
Office Equipment		40,000
Cash		34,000
Gain on Disposal of Plant Assets*		6,000

*The gain on disposal of plant assets was credited to current operations as ordinary income.

6. Dividends in the amount of $123,000 were declared. They are payable in January 2012.

Instructions

For each item, use journal entries to show the adjustments and reconciling items that would be made on Mia Inc.'s work sheet for a statement of cash flows.

(LO 11) *E22-23   (Work Sheet Preparation) The comparative balance sheet for Cosky Corporation follows:

	Dec. 31, 2012	Dec. 31, 2011
Cash	$ 16,500	$ 21,000
Temporary investments, at fair value through net income	25,000	19,000
Accounts receivable	43,000	45,000
Allowance for doubtful accounts	(1,800)	(2,000)
Prepaid expenses	4,200	2,500
Inventories	81,500	65,000
Land	50,000	50,000
Buildings	125,000	73,500
Accumulated depreciation—buildings	(30,000)	(23,000)
Equipment	53,000	46,000
Accumulated depreciation—equipment	(19,000)	(15,500)
Delivery equipment	39,000	39,000
Accumulated depreciation—delivery equipment	(22,000)	(20,500)
Patents	15,000	–0–
	$379,400	$300,000
Accounts payable	$ 26,000	$ 16,000
Short-term notes payable (trade)	4,000	6,000
Accrued payables	3,000	4,600
Mortgage payable	73,000	53,400
Bonds payable	50,000	62,500
Share capital	150,000	106,000
Retained earnings	73,400	51,500
	$379,400	$300,000

Additional information:

1. Dividends of $15,000 were declared and paid in 2012.

2. There were no unrealized gains or losses on the temporary investments, at fair value through net income.

Instructions

Based on the information, prepare a work sheet for a statement of cash flows. Make reasonable assumptions as appropriate.

Problems

P22-1   Gao Limited, a publicly traded company, uses IFRS and had the following events and transactions occur in its fiscal year ending October 31, 2011. Although no dates are given, the events described are in chronological order.

1. Gao Limited repurchased common shares on the open market to allow stock options to its key employees to be exercised without a dilution effect resulting to the remaining shareholders. The weighted average issue price of the outstanding shares on the date of reacquisition was $34.20, and 4,000 shares were repurchased at a price of $44.40. On the date of declaration, Gao had contributed surplus for preferred share repurchases of $84,600 and contributed surplus for common share repurchases of $22,700.

2. Common shares were issued in partial settlement of a purchase of land. Gao paid $33,000 and 5,000 common shares for the land. On the date of the transaction, the common shares were trading at $41.50.

3. Gao has 8,000 preferred shares outstanding. These shares are limited in number and are not traded on the public stock exchange. Gao declared a property dividend to be paid to the preferred shareholders. Shareholders will receive for each preferred share held one share of Trivex Corp. Gao holds 8,000 shares of Trivex (2% of the outstanding shares), and had purchased them in 2009 for $68,400 (or $8.55 per share). The shares were held as an investment since 2009 and accounted for using the fair value through other comprehensive income (FV-OCI) model with recycling (transference). At the beginning of the fiscal year, the accumulated other comprehensive income had a debit balance in the amount of $2,350 relating only to the Trivex shares. The fair value of Trivex shares was $7.80 per share on the date of declaration of the property dividend. On the date of the dividend distribution, the fair value of the Trivex shares was $7.95. There being no longer any investments accounted for at FV-OCI, the reclassification entry needed to be recorded, in accordance with Gao's practice.

4. Gao declared a 5% stock dividend to the common shareholders. There were 43,200 common shares outstanding on the date of declaration and the market price of the common shares on that date was $39.70. The stock dividend was later distributed.

5. A shareholder, in an effort to persuade Gao to expand into her city, donated to the company a plot of land with an appraised value of $42,000.

6. Gao sold by subscription to an investment institution 10,000 common shares for $38.50 per share. The terms require 10% of the balance to be paid in cash immediately. The remainder is expected to be paid in fiscal year 2012.

7. Gao has term preferred shares on its statement of financial position. These shares are classified as debt. Gao declared a cash dividend of $3,800 on these shares. The dividend will be paid in the first week of the fiscal year 2012.

Instructions

(a) Prepare the underlying journal entries that were made by Gao Limited during 2011 to record all information related to the changes in each equity account and associated accounts over the year.

(b) Prepare the captions that would appear on Gao's statement of cash flows for the year ended October 31, 2011, using the indirect format. Include all necessary additional disclosures required under IFRS.

(c) How would your answer to parts (a) and (b) above change if the investments in Trivex were accounted for using the fair value through net income model?

(d) How would your answer to parts (a) and (b) above change if Gao were using ASPE?

P22-2 The following accounts appear in the ledger of Samson Inc. Samson's shares trade on the Toronto and New York stock exchanges and so the company uses IFRS. Samson made a special election to account for shares held in Anderson Corp. as FV-OCI and to reclassify out of OCI and into net income investment holding gains that are realized. It also chooses to classify dividends received as operating cash flows. Samson's investment in Anderson Corp. is not strategic and is classified as a long-term investment.

Investment in Anderson Corp.		Dr.	Cr.	Bal.
Dec. 1, 2010	Purchase of 40,000 shares	$893,500		$893,500
Dec. 31, 2010	Fair value adjustment 40,000 shares		$10,100	883,400
Aug. 15, 2011	Fair value adjustment of 3,000 shares	4,350		887,750
Aug. 15, 2011	Sale of 3,000 shares		63,850	823,900
Nov. 3, 2011	Purchase of 2,000 shares	35,480		859,380
Dec. 31, 2011	Fair value adjustment 39,000 shares	19,620		879,000

Accumulated Other Comprehensive Income		Dr.	Cr.	Bal.
Dec. 31, 2010	Closing entry	$ 10,100		$ 10,100
Dec. 31, 2011	Closing entry		18,620	(8,520)

Dividend Income		Dr.	Cr.	Bal.
June 30, 2011	Dividends from Anderson Corp.		$35,700	$ (35,700)

Gain on Sale of Anderson Corp. Shares		Dr.	Cr.	Bal.
Aug. 15, 2011	Reclassification adjustment—3,000 shares		$ 5,350	$ (5,350)

Holding Gain/Losses on FV-OCI Investments		Dr.	Cr.	Bal.
Dec. 31, 2010	Fair value adjustment 40,000 shares	$ 10,100		$ 10,100
Dec. 31, 2010	Closing entry		$10,100	–0–
Aug. 15, 2011	Fair value adjustment of 3,000 shares		4,350	(4,350)
Aug. 15, 2011	Reclassification adjustment—3,000 shares	5,350		1,000
Dec. 31, 2011	Fair value adjustment 39,000 shares		19,620	(18,620)
Dec. 31, 2011	Closing entry	18,620		–0–

Instructions

(a) Prepare a partial comparative statement of financial position for Samson Inc. at the fiscal year end of December 31, 2011.

(b) Prepare an income statement, a statement of comprehensive income, and a statement of changes in accumulated other comprehensive income for the year ended December 31, 2011.

(c) Prepare the journal entries dated June 30, August 15, and November 3, 2011. Provide explanations to the entries.

(d) Using the direct and the indirect methods, prepare a table that contrasts the presentation of all transactions recorded in the ledger accounts provided on Samson's statement of cash flows. Be specific about the classification within the statement for each item that is reported. What other choices could Samson have used in the classification of cash flows?

(e) How would your answer to parts (b) and (d) above change if the investments were accounted for using the fair value through net income model?

(f) What would be the reason why Samson would not use the fair value through other comprehensive income model?

P22-3   MFI Holdings Inc. follows IFRS and applies the FV-OCI model without recycling. MFI's balance sheet contained the following comparative data at December 31:

Balance sheet accounts:

	2011	2010
Investments (at fair value with gains and losses in OCI)	$24,000	$37,900
Accumulated other comprehensive income (loss)	400	(2,400)

Partial statement of income and comprehensive income, 2011:

Dividend income	$ 200
Loss on sale of investments at fair value with gains and losses in OCI	300
Net income	XXX
Other comprehensive income	
Holding gain on FV-OCI investments during the year	2,500
Comprehensive income	$ XXX

At December 31, 2011, the following information is available:

1. MFI Holdings had a single investment in shares at December 31, 2010. The investment cost $40,300 and was sold during 2011 for $40,000.

2. During 2011, dividends of $200 were received on shares classified as investments at fair value with gains and losses in OCI.

3. Another investment, with the same classification, was purchased at a cost of $23,600. The fair value of this new investment at December 31, 2011, was $24,000.

Instructions

(a) Calculate and reconcile the transactions that were recorded to the accounts Fair Value through Other Comprehensive Income Investment and Accumulated Other Comprehensive Income.

(b) Using the direct and the indirect methods, prepare a table that contrasts the presentation of all transactions related to the above financial statements and related investment transactions on MFI's statement of cash flows. Be specific about the classification within the statement for each item that is reported.

(c) How would your answer to parts (a) and (b) above change if the investments were accounted for using the fair value through net income model?

(d) What would be the reason why MFI would not use the fair value through other comprehensive income model?

P22-4   Neilson Corp. reported $145,000 of net income for 2011. In preparing the statement of cash flows, the accountant noted several items that might affect cash flows from operating activities.

1. During 2011, Neilson reported a sale of equipment for $7,000. The equipment had a carrying amount of $23,500.

2. During 2011, Neilson sold 100 Lontel Corporation common shares at $200 per share. The acquisition cost of these shares was $145 per share. This investment was shown on Neilson's December 31, 2010 balance sheet as an investment at fair value with gains and losses in net income.

3. During 2011, Neilson made a correction of an error for ending inventory of December 31, 2010. The debit to opening retained earnings was $14,600.

4. During 2011, Neilson revised its estimate for bad debts. Before 2011, Neilson's bad debt expense was 1% of its net sales. In 2011, this percentage was increased to 2%. Net sales for 2011 were $500,000, and net accounts receivable decreased by $15,000 during 2011.

5. During 2011, Neilson issued 500 common shares for a patent. The shares' market value on the transaction date was $23 per share.

6. Depreciation expense for 2011 was $38,000.

7. Neilson Corp. holds 40% of Nirbana Corporation's common shares as a long-term investment and exercises significant influence. Nirbana reported $27,000 of net income for 2011.

8. Nirbana Corporation paid a total of $2,800 of cash dividends to all shareholders in 2011.

9. During 2011, Neilson declared a 10% stock dividend, distributing 1,000 common shares. The market price at the date of issuance was $20 per share.

10. Neilson Corp. paid $10,000 in dividends: $2,500 of this amount was paid on term preferred shares classified as a long-term liability.

Instructions

(a) Prepare a schedule that shows the net cash flow from operating activities using the indirect method. Assume that no items other than the ones listed affected the calculation of 2011 cash flow from operating activities. Also assume that Neilson Corp. follows ASPE.

(b) Assume now that Neilson Corp. follows IFRS. What possible amounts might be reported?

P22-5 Comparative balance sheet accounts of Laflamme Inc., which follows ASPE, and its statement of income for the year ending December 31, 2012, follow:

Comparative Balance Sheet Data

	December 31		
	2012	2011	Change
Cash	$ 46,000	$ 56,000	$ (10,000)
Cash equivalents (note 1)	36,000	45,000	(9,000)
Accounts receivable	348,000	271,000	77,000
Prepaid insurance	16,000	35,000	(19,000)
Inventory	398,000	350,000	48,000
Supplies	13,000	17,000	(4,000)
Long-term investment, at equity (note 7)	418,000	400,000	18,000
Land	640,000	500,000	140,000
Building (note 3)	1,310,000	1,280,000	30,000
Accumulated depreciation—building	(400,000)	(360,000)	(40,000)
Equipment (note 4)	632,000	640,000	(8,000)
Accumulated depreciation—equipment	(160,000)	(135,000)	(25,000)
Patent	100,000	100,000	
Accumulated amortization	(40,000)	(35,000)	(5,000)
	$3,357,000	$3,164,000	$193,000
Bank overdrafts (temporary)	$ –0–	$ 93,000	$ (93,000)
Accounts payable	165,000	150,000	15,000
Taxes payable	26,000	35,000	(9,000)
Accrued liabilities	57,000	41,000	16,000
Dividends payable	20,000	50,000	(30,000)
Long-term notes payable	420,000	460,000	(40,000)
Bonds payable	999,000	995,000	4,000
Preferred shares	504,000	380,000	124,000
Common shares	746,000	666,000	80,000
Retained earnings	420,000	294,000	126,000
	$3,357,000	$3,164,000	$193,000

Income Statement

Revenues		
Sales revenue	$999,000	
Investment income	90,000	$1,089,000
Expenses and Losses		
Cost of goods sold	314,000	
Commissions expense	108,000	
Operating expenses (note 5)	166,000	
Wages expense	104,000	
Interest expense	95,000	
Loss on sale of equipment (note 4)	11,000	
Income tax expense	96,000	894,000
Net Income		$ 195,000

The following is additional information about Laflamme's transactions during the year ended December 31, 2012.

1. The cash equivalents are typically term deposits that are very liquid and mature on average in 60 days. The bank overdrafts are temporary and reverse within a few days. Laflamme has opted to show these as cash and cash equivalents on its statement of cash flows.

2. A stock dividend on common shares for $18,000 was declared and distributed during the year.

3. There were no disposals of buildings during the year 2012.

4. Equipment with an original cost of $46,000 and carrying amount of $14,000 was sold at a loss during the year.

5. All depreciation and amortization expense is included in operating expenses.

6. During the year, Laflamme obtained land with a fair value of $100,000 in exchange for its preferred shares.

7. Investment income includes the equity earnings of $62,000 from a long-term investment accounted for using the equity method and from interest revenue on the short-term investments referred to in item 1 above.

Instructions

(a) Prepare the statement of cash flows for the year ended December 31, 2012, for Laflamme Inc. using the indirect method. Prepare any additional disclosure notes that are required, including a table that shows the details of the cash and cash equivalents accounts at the end of each period.

(b) Prepare the operating activities section of the statement using the direct format.

(c) Does Laflamme Inc. have any options available to it concerning the classification of interest and dividends paid or received?

Digging Deeper

(d) If Laflamme Inc. chose to not treat the cash equivalents and the temporary bank overdrafts as cash and cash equivalents, how would transactions related to these accounts be reported on the statement of cash flows?

P22-6 Comparative balance sheet accounts of Jensen Limited, which follows IFRS, appear below:

JENSEN LIMITED
Balance Sheet Accounts
December 31, 2011, and 2010

Debit balances	2011	2010
Cash	$ 80,000	$ 51,000
Accounts receivable	138,500	119,000
Merchandise inventory	75,000	61,000
Long-term investments (FV-NI)	59,000	80,000
Deferred income tax asset	6,500	11,000
Equipment	70,000	48,000
Building	145,000	145,000
Land	40,000	25,000
	$614,000	$540,000

Credit balances	2011	2010
Allowance for doubtful accounts	$ 10,000	$ 8,000
Accumulated depreciation—equipment	21,000	14,000
Accumulated depreciation—building	37,000	28,000
Accounts payable	72,500	60,000
Income taxes payable	12,000	10,000
Long-term notes payable	62,000	70,000
Accrued pension liability	7,500	10,000
Common shares	300,000	250,000
Retained earnings	92,000	90,000
	$614,000	$540,000

Data from Jensen's 2011 income statement follow:

Sales		$960,000
Less: Cost of goods sold		600,000
Gross profit		360,000
Less: Operating expenses		
(includes depreciation and bad debt expense)		250,000
Income from operations		110,000
Other revenues and expenses		
Interest expense	$ (10,000)	
Gain on investments (FV-NI)	24,000	
Loss on sale of equipment	(3,000)	11,000
Income before taxes		121,000
Income taxes		45,000
Net income		$ 76,000

Additional data:

1. Equipment that cost $10,000 and was 40% depreciated was sold in 2011.

2. Cash dividends were declared and paid during the year.

3. Common shares were issued in exchange for land.

4. FV-NI investments that had cost $35,000 and had a fair value of $37,000 at December 31, 2010, were sold during the year for proceeds of $50,000. Additional purchases of FV-NI investments were made during 2011.

5. Cost of goods sold includes $115,000 of direct labour and benefits and $11,700 of pension costs. Operating expenses include $76,000 of wages and $8,000 of pension expense.

6. Jenson has adopted the policy of classifying interest paid as operating activities and dividends paid as financing activities on the statement of cash flows.

Instructions

(a) Prepare a statement of cash flows using the indirect method, including all required disclosures.

(b) Prepare the "Cash provided by (or used in) operating activities" section under the direct method.

(c) Does Jensen Limited have any options available for the classification of interest and dividends paid or received?

(d) Comment on the company's cash activities during the year.

(e) Assume that you are a shareholder of Jensen Limited. What do you think of the dividend payout ratio that is highlighted in the statement of cash flows?

Digging Deeper

P22-7 The unclassified balance sheet accounts for Sorkin Corporation, which is a public company using IFRS, for the year ended December 31, 2011, and its statement of comprehensive income and statement of cash flows for the year ended December 31, 2012, are as follows:

SORKIN CORPORATION
Balance Sheet Accounts
December 31, 2011
($ in millions)

Cash	$ 21
Accounts receivable	194
Inventory	200
Prepaid expenses	12
Long-term investment in shares of Stoker Inc.	125
Land	150
Buildings and equipment	400
Accumulated depreciation	(120)
Patents	60
Accumulated amortization patent	(28)
Goodwill	60
Total assets	$1,074
Accounts payable	$ 65
Salaries and wages payable	11
Bond interest payable	4
Income taxes payable	14
Future income tax liability	8
Bonds payable	250
Common shares	495
Retained earnings	227
Total liabilities and shareholders' equity	$1,074

SORKIN CORPORATION
Statement of Income
Year Ended December 31, 2012
($ in millions)

Revenues:		
Sales revenue	$410	
Holding gain on investments (FV-NI)	5	
Investment income	11	$426
Expenses and losses:		
Cost of goods sold	158	
Administrative expenses	22	
Salaries and wages expense	65	
Depreciation and amortization expense	21	
Bond interest expense	28	
Loss from damaged equipment	18	
Loss on impairment of goodwill	20	332
Income before income taxes		94
Income taxes		39
Net income		$ 55

SORKIN CORPORATION
Statement of Cash Flows (Indirect Method)
For the Year Ended December 31, 2012

Cash flows from operating activities		
Net earnings		$55
Add back (deduct) non-cash revenues and expenses:		
Investment revenue from equity investment in Stoker Inc.	(11)	
Dividends received from equity investment in Stoker Inc.	6	
Loss from damaged equipment	18	
Depreciation expense	19	
Holding gain on investments at FV-NI	(5)	
Amortization of patent	2	
Amortization of bond discount	3	
Loss on impairment of goodwill	20	52
Add (deduct) changes in non-cash working capital:		
Decrease in accounts receivable	4	
Increase in inventories	(5)	
Decrease in prepaid expenses	2	
Decrease in accounts payable	(15)	
Decrease in salaries and wages payable	(5)	
Increase in future income tax liability	3	
Increase in bond interest payable	4	
Decrease in income taxes payable	(2)	(14)
Net cash provided by operating activities		93
Cash flows from investing activities:		
Proceeds from disposal of damaged equipment	10	
Purchase of land (note 1)	(23)	
Purchase of long-term investments (FV-NI)	(25)	
Net cash used by investing activities		(38)
Cash flows from financing activities:		
Dividends paid	(7)	
Redemption of serial bonds	(60)	
Issuance of preferred shares	75	
Repurchase of common shares	(9)	
Net cash used by financing activities		(1)
Net increase in cash		54
Cash, January 1, 2012		21
Cash, December 31, 2012		$75

Note 1. Non-cash investing and financing activities

(a) During the year, land was acquired for $46 million in exchange for cash of $23 million and a $23-million, four-year, 15% note payable to the seller.

(b) Equipment was acquired through a finance lease that was capitalized initially at $82 million.

Additional information from the accounting records:

1. The investment income represents Sorkin's reported income in its 35%-owned, significantly influenced investment in Stoker Inc. Sorkin received a dividend from Stoker during the year.

2. Early in 2012, Sorkin purchased shares for $25 million as a long-term investment at fair value with gains and losses in net income. There were no purchases or sales of these shares during 2012, nor were there any dividends received from this investment.

3. A machine that originally cost $70 million became unusable due to a flood. Most major components of the machine were unharmed and were sold together for $10 million. Sorkin had no insurance coverage for the loss because of the nature of this casualty.

4. Reversing differences in the year between pre-tax accounting income and taxable income resulted in an increase in future taxable amounts, causing the future income tax liability to increase by $3 million.

5. On December 30, 2012, land costing $46 million was acquired by paying $23 million cash and issuing a $23-million, four-year, 15% note payable to the seller.

6. Equipment was acquired through a 15-year financing lease. The present value of minimum lease payments was $82 million when signing the lease on December 31, 2012. Sorkin made the initial lease payment of $2 million on January 1, 2013.

7. Serial bonds with a face value of $60 million were retired at maturity on June 20, 2012. In order to finance this redemption and have additional cash available for operations, Sorkin issued preferred shares for $75 million cash.

8. In February, Sorkin issued a 4% stock dividend (four million shares). The market price of the common shares was $7.50 per share at that time.

9. In April 2012, 1 million common shares were repurchased for $9 million. The weighted average original issue price of the repurchased shares was $12 million.

Instructions

(a) Prepare the unclassified balance sheet accounts for Sorkin Corporation for the year ended December 31, 2012, as a check on the statement of cash flows. Add whichever accounts you consider necessary.

Digging Deeper

(b) Prepare the operating activities section of the statement of cash flows for Sorkin Corporation using the direct method.

(c) How would the statement of cash flows differ if the terms on the purchase of land had been essentially the same except that the financing for the note payable had been negotiated with a mortgage company instead of the seller of the land?

P22-8   Ashley Limited, which follows ASPE, had the following information available at the end of 2011:

ASHLEY LIMITED
Comparative Balance Sheet
December 31, 2011, and 2010

	2011	2010
Cash	$ 15,000	$ –0–
Accounts receivable	17,500	16,950
Temporary investments (FV-NI)	20,000	30,000
Inventory	42,000	35,000
Prepaid rent	3,000	12,000
Prepaid insurance	2,100	900
Office supplies	1,000	750
Land	125,000	175,000
Building	350,000	350,000
Accumulated depreciation	(105,000)	(87,500)
Equipment	525,000	400,000
Accumulated depreciation	(130,000)	(112,000)
Patent	90,000	90,000
Accumulated amortization	(45,000)	(40,000)
Total assets	$910,600	$871,100
Temporary bank overdraft	$ –0–	$ 12,000
Accounts payable	22,000	20,000
Income taxes payable	5,000	4,000
Wages payable	5,000	3,000
Short-term notes payable (trade)	10,000	10,000
Long-term notes payable (non-trade)	60,000	70,000
Future income tax liability	30,000	25,000
Bonds payable	375,000	375,000
Common shares	260,000	237,500
Retained earnings	143,600	114,600
Total liabilities and shareholders' equity	$910,600	$871,100

ASHLEY LIMITED
Income Statement
Year Ended December 31, 2011

Sales revenue		$1,160,000
Cost of goods sold		(748,000)
Gross margin		412,000
Operating expenses		
Selling expenses	$ 19,200	
Administrative expenses	124,700	
Salaries and wages expense	92,000	
Depreciation and amortization expense	40,500	
Total operating expenses		(276,400)
Income from operations		135,600
Other revenues/expenses		
Gain on sale of land	8,000	
Investment income (note 1)	6,400	
Interest expense	(51,750)	(37,350)
Income before taxes		98,250
Income tax expense		(39,400)
Net income		$ 58,850

Note 1: Investment income for the temporary investments includes dividend income of $2,400 and unrealized holding gains of $4,000 from investments at FV-NI.

Instructions

(a) Prepare a statement of cash flows for Ashley Limited using the direct method, accompanied by all required disclosures and a schedule that reconciles net income to cash flow from operations.

(b) Does Ashley Limited have any options available for the classification of interest and dividends paid or received?

(c) Prepare a memo for top management that summarizes and comments on the cash activities of Ashley in 2011.

(d) Management wants to provide more captions (headings) in the section for cash flow from operating activities. Recommend one additional caption that would help achieve this goal.

Digging
Deeper

P22-9 Davis Inc. is a privately held company that uses ASPE. Davis had the following information available at March 31, 2012:

DAVIS INC.
Income Statement
For the Year Ended March 31, 2012

Sales		$450,000
Cost of goods sold		260,000
Gross profit		190,000
Operating expenses		
Salaries and wages	$64,500	
Depreciation expense	7,500	
Rent expense	18,000	
Other general and administrative expenses	21,000	
Amortization of patents	1,500	112,500
Operating income		77,500
Other revenues and expenses		
Bond interest expense	(6,750)	
Unrealized gains on FV-NI investments	3,000	
Investment income	12,500	
Gain on retirement of bonds	16,600	25,350
		102,850
Income tax expense—current	19,900	
Income tax expense—future	10,300	30,200
Net income		$ 72,650

Davis Inc.'s partial list of comparative account balances as of March 31, 2012, and 2011, is as follows:

	March 31		
	2012	2011	Change
Cash	$ 5,200	$ 4,400	$ 800
Temporary investment in 30-day treasury bills	20,000	6,200	13,800
Accounts receivable	46,400	43,600	2,800
Inventory	35,800	29,600	6,200
Prepaid expenses	2,650	2,800	(150)
Investments recorded at FV-NI	5,230	2,230	3,000
Prepaid rent—long-term	4,000	-0-	4,000
Accounts payable, trade	22,800	24,200	(1,400)
Salaries and wages payable	500	1,300	(800)
Income taxes payable	13,000	29,500	(16,500)
Interest payable	3,000	1,500	1,500
Accrued pension cost liability	8,500	6,900	1,600
Future income tax liability	12,900	2,600	10,300

Additional data:

1. Bond interest expense includes $750 of bond discount amortized.

2. The investment income represents Davis Inc.'s reported income in its 40%-owned, significantly influenced investment in Jessa Ltd. Davis received a $2,000 dividend from Jessa on February 15, 2012.

3. During the year, the company retired $500,000 of its outstanding bonds payable, paying out $16,600 less than the price at which the bonds were carried on the books.

4. In early January 2012, Davis renewed and signed a four-year operating lease, agreeing to pay $4,000 each month in rent. The lessor required the payment of the rent for the first and last months of the lease at that time.

5. The change in investment at FV-NI is from the change in the market value of the securities for the fiscal year 2012. There were no purchases or sales of these securities during the 2012 fiscal year.

Note: There is insufficient information to allow you to prepare a complete statement of cash flows.

Instructions

(a) What is the amount of Davis Inc.'s change in cash to be explained on the statement of cash flows for the year ended March 31, 2012?

(b) Prepare the "Cash provided by (used in) operations" section of the statement of cash flows, assuming that the indirect method is used and all necessary information has been provided.

(c) Identify the amounts that would be reported within this section if the direct method were used for the following items:

1. Cash paid to and on behalf of employees
2. Cash received from customers
3. Income taxes paid
4. Cash paid to suppliers for goods and services
5. Interest paid

Digging
Deeper

(d) Calculate the sum of the cash flows in part (c). Should the sum of the cash flows in the direct format equal the amount arrived at in part (a) for "Cash provided by (used in) operations"? If not, why not? If it should, do the amounts equal each other? Why or why not?

P22-10 Comparative balance sheet accounts of Secada Inc., which follows IFRS, follow:

SECADA INC.
Comparative Balance Sheet Accounts
December 31, 2011, and 2010

	December 31	
Debit accounts	2011	2010
Cash	$ 45,000	$ 33,750
Accounts receivable	67,500	60,000
Merchandise inventory	30,000	24,000
Long-term investments (FV-NI)	23,250	40,500
Machinery	30,000	18,750
Buildings	67,500	56,250
Land	7,500	7,500
	$270,750	$240,750
Credit accounts		
Allowance for doubtful accounts	$ 2,250	$ 1,500
Accumulated depreciation—machinery	5,625	2,250
Accumulated depreciation—buildings	13,500	9,000
Accounts payable	30,000	24,750
Accrued payables	2,375	1,125
Income taxes payable	1,000	1,500
Long-term note payable—non-trade	26,000	31,000
Common shares	150,000	125,000
Retained earnings	40,000	44,625
	$270,750	$240,750

Additional data:

1. Cash dividends declared during the year were $21,125.

2. A 20% stock dividend was declared during the year and $25,000 of retained earnings was capitalized.

3. Investments at FV-NI that cost $20,000 and had a fair value at December 31, 2010, of $22,500 were sold during the year for $23,750.

4. Machinery that cost $3,750 and had $750 of depreciation accumulated was sold for $2,200.

Secada's 2011 statement of income is as follows:

Sales		$640,000
Less cost of goods sold		380,000
Gross margin		260,000
Less: Operating expenses (includes $8,625 depreciation, and $5,400 bad debts)		180,450
Income from operations		79,550
Other: Holding loss on investments (FV-NI)	$ (1,000)	
Loss on sale of machinery	(800)	(1,800)
Income before taxes		77,750
Income tax expense		40,000
Net income		$37,750

Instructions

(a) Calculate net cash flow from operating activities using the direct method.

(b) Prepare a statement of cash flows using the indirect method.

(c) Assume that your investment club is considering investing in Secada Inc. Write a memo to the other members of the club about the company's cash activities during 2011.

(d) Management wants to provide more captions (headings) in the section on cash flow from operating activities. Recommend one additional caption that would help achieve that goal.

Digging
Deeper

P22-11   Jeopardy Inc.'s CFO has just left the office of the company president after a meeting about the draft balance sheet at April 30, 2011, and income statement for the year ended. (Both are reproduced below.) "Our liquidity position looks healthy," the president had remarked. "Look at the current and acid-test ratios, and the amount of working capital we have. And between the goodwill writeoff and depreciation, we have almost $23 million of non-cash expenses. I don't understand why you've been complaining about our cash situation."

The CFO turns the draft financial statements over to you, the newest member of the accounting staff, along with extracts from the notes to the financial statements.

JEOPARDY INC.
Consolidated Balance Sheet
April 30, 2011, and 2010
(in $000s)

	2011	2010
Assets		
Cash and 60-day treasury bills	$ 3,265	$ 3,739
Accounts receivable	23,744	18,399
Inventories	26,083	21,561
Income taxes recoverable	145	–0–
Prepaid expenses	1,402	1,613
	54,639	45,312
Investments (Note 1)	5,960	6,962
Property, plant, and equipment (Note 2)	37,332	45,700
Future income tax asset	4,875	2,245
Franchise fees (Note 3)	4,391	1,911
Goodwill	–0–	12,737
	$107,197	$114,867
Liabilities		
Current		
Bank overdraft (temporary)	$ 6,844	$ 6,280
Accounts payable and accrued (Note 4)	3,243	4,712
Current portion of long-term debt	1,800	1,200
	11,887	12,192
Long-term debt (Note 5)	14,900	14,500
Shareholders' Equity		
Share capital (Note 6)	79,257	62,965
Retained earnings	1,153	25,210
	80,410	88,175
	$107,197	$114,867

Consolidated Statement of Income and Retained Earnings
Year Ended April 30, 2011, and 2010
(in $000s)

	2011	2010
Revenue		
Operating	$89,821	$68,820
Interest and other	1,310	446
	91,131	69,266
Expenses		
Operating*	76,766	62,455
General and administrative*	13,039	12,482
Depreciation and amortization	10,220	11,709
Goodwill writeoff	12,737	–0–
Interest	1,289	1,521
Loss on sale of capital assets	394	–0–
	114,445	88,167

Loss before equity loss and income taxes	(23,314)	(18,901)
Equity income (loss) (Note 1)	(2,518)	100
Loss before income taxes	(25,832)	(18,801)
Income taxes	2,775	5,161
Net loss	(23,057)	(13,640)
Retained earnings, beginning of year	25,210	38,850
	2,153	25,210
Stock dividend	(1,000)	–0–
Retained earnings, end of year	$ 1,153	$25,210

*The operating and general and administrative expenses for 2011 include salaries and wages of $37,509 and $9,115, respectively.

Draft Notes to the Financial Statements
For the Year Ended April 30, 2011

Note 1. Investments

The company's investments at April 30 are as follows (in $000s):

	2011	2010
Compuco Ltd. (fair value 2011, $4.3 million)		
Shares, opening balance at equity	$6,962	$5,862
Equity income (loss)	(2,518)	100
Shares, ending balance at equity	4,444	5,962
Other investments, at amortized cost	1,516	1,000
	$5,960	$6,962

Note 2. Property, Plant, and Equipment

Additions to property, plant, and equipment for the current year amounted to $2,290,000. Proceeds from the disposal of property, plant, and equipment amounted to $250,000.

Note 3. Franchise Fees

Franchise fees are amortized over the term of 10 years using the straight-line method.

Note 4. Accounts Payable and Accrued (in $000s)

	2011	2010
Accounts payable—suppliers	$3,102	$4,562
Accrued salaries and wages payable	141	150
	$3,243	$4,712

Note 5. Long-Term Debt (in $000s)

	2011	2010
Debentures	$12,500	$12,500
Bank term loans, due April 30, 2012,		
principal repayable at $150,000 a month		
(2010, at $100,000 a month)	4,200	3,200
	16,700	15,700
Current maturities	(1,800)	(1,200)
	$14,900	$14,500

Debentures bear interest at 12% per annum and are due in 2011. Bank term loans bear interest at 8% and the bank advanced $2.2 million during the year.

Note 6. Share Capital

On September 14, 2010, Jeopardy Inc. issued 3.8 million shares with special warrants. Net proceeds from issuing 3.8 million shares amounted to $14,393,000. Net proceeds from issuing 3.8 million warrants amounted to $899,000. On April 30, 2011, a stock dividend of $1 million was issued.

Instructions

Based on the assumption that Jeopardy Inc. follows ASPE:

(a) Prepare a statement of cash flows for the year ended April 30, 2011, on a non-comparative basis from the information provided. The CFO wants to use the direct method to report the company's operating cash flows this year. Include all required disclosures.

(b) Prepare a reconciliation of the 2011 net loss to cash provided from (used in) operations. This reconciliation is to be included in a note to the financial statements.

(c) Write a memo to the president of Jeopardy Inc. that explains why the company is experiencing a cash crunch when its liquidity ratios look acceptable and it has significant non-cash expenses.

(CICA adapted)

P22-12   The following is Mann Corp.'s comparative balance sheet at December 31, 2011, and 2010, with a column showing the increase (decrease) from 2010 to 2011:

MANN CORP.
Comparative Balance Sheet

	2011	2010	Increase (Decrease)
Cash	$ 28,300	$ 44,400	$ (16,100)
Accounts receivable	846,400	766,700	79,700
Inventories	717,600	675,000	42,600
Property, plant, and equipment	3,066,400	2,866,400	200,000
Accumulated depreciation	(1,165,000)	(1,010,000)	155,000
Investment in Bligh Corp., at equity	288,000	266,000	22,000
Loan receivable	251,500	–0–	251,500
Total assets	$4,033,200	$3,608,500	
Bank loan	$ 142,600	$ 72,900	69,700
Accounts payable	753,600	814,600	(61,000)
Income taxes payable	37,000	46,000	(9,000)
Dividends payable	65,000	85,000	(20,000)
Lease obligation	270,000	–0–	270,000
Share capital, common	900,000	900,000	–0–
Retained earnings	1,865,000	1,690,000	175,000
Total liabilities and shareholders' equity	$4,033,200	$3,608,500	

Additional information:

1. On December 31, 2010, Mann acquired 25% of Bligh Corp.'s common shares for $266,000. On that date, the carrying value of Bligh's assets and liabilities was $1,064 thousand, which approximated their fair values. Bligh reported income of $88,000 for the year ended December 31, 2011. No dividend was paid on Bligh's common shares during the year.

2. During 2011, Mann loaned $285,000 to TMC Corp., an unrelated company. TMC made the first semi-annual principal repayment of $33,500, plus interest at 10%, on December 31, 2011.

3. On January 2, 2011, Mann sold equipment costing $70,000, with a carrying amount of $44,000, for $42,000 cash.

4. On December 31, 2011, Mann entered into a finance lease for equipment. The present value of the annual lease payments is $270,000, which equals the equipment's fair value. Mann made the first rental payment of $47,000 when due on January 2, 2012.

5. Net earnings for 2011 were $240,000. The amount of income taxes paid was $151,000.

6. The amount of interest paid during the year was $14,900 and the amount of interest earned was $9,400. Mann has adopted the policy of classifying interest received and interest paid as operating cash flows.

7. Mann declared and paid cash dividends for 2011 and 2010 as follows:

	2011	2010
Declared	Dec. 15, 2011	Dec. 15, 2010
Paid	Feb. 28, 2012	Feb. 28, 2011
Amount	$65,000	$85,000

8. The bank loan listed in the comparative balance sheet represents a line of credit used to finance operating cash demands of the business. The limit set on the operating line by the lender is $600,000. Although the operating line functions similar to a bank overdraft, at no time during 2011 did the operating line become reduced to nil.

Instructions

(a) Prepare a statement of cash flows for Mann Corp. for the year ended December 31, 2011, using the indirect method, including any necessary additional note disclosures.

(b) Prepare a reconciliation of the change in property, plant, and equipment's carrying amount to the amounts appearing on the statement of cash flows and corresponding notes.

(c) Financial statement preparers often use reconciliations of changes in major categories of balance sheet accounts to balance the statement of cash flows, as required in part (b) above. What additional insight does this reconciliation reveal to a reader of the statement that is not as evident from the statement of cash flows?

(d) What other choices did Mann Corp. have available for the classification of interest received and paid? Would your opinion of Mann's liquidity position and ability to generate cash change from these alternative classifications?

(e) Is Mann Corp. in financial difficulty from a poor liquidity position and extremely small cash reserves?

(AICPA adapted)

P22-13 Seneca Corporation, which uses IFRS, has contracted with you to prepare a statement of cash flows. The controller has provided the following information:

	December 31	
	2011	2010
Cash	$ 38,700	$13,000
Accounts receivable	11,600	9,750
Inventory	10,600	9,100
Investments (FV-NI)	–0–	2,500
Building	–0–	27,700
Equipment	40,500	18,500
Patent	14,000	14,000
	$115,400	$94,550
Allowance for doubtful accounts	$ 1,400	$ 1,500
Accumulated depreciation—equipment	2,000	3,300
Accumulated depreciation—building	–0–	5,700
Accumulated amortization—patent	9,000	7,750
Accounts payable	4,400	3,300
Dividends payable	–0–	6,000
Notes payable, short-term (non-trade)	3,400	4,000
Long-term notes payable	30,500	25,000
Share capital	43,000	33,000
Retained earnings	21,700	5,000
	$115,400	$94,550

Additional data related to 2011 are as follows:

1. Equipment that cost $10,500 and was 50% depreciated at the time of disposal was sold for $2,600.
2. Common shares were issued to pay $10,000 of the long-term note payable.
3. Cash dividends paid were $6,000. Seneca has adopted the policy of classifying dividends paid as operating activities.
4. On January 1, 2011, a flood destroyed the building. Insurance proceeds on the building were $23,000.
5. Long-term investments in shares, reported at fair value with gains and losses in net income, were sold at $3,300 above their cost. The fair value of these investments at December 31, 2010, equalled their original cost.
6. Cash of $17,000 was paid to acquire equipment.
7. A long-term note for $15,500 was issued in exchange for equipment.
8. Interest of $2,200 and income taxes of $5,600 were paid in cash. Seneca has adopted the policy of classifying interest paid as financing activities.

Instructions

(a) Use the indirect method to analyze the above information and prepare a statement of cash flows for Seneca.

(b) Prepare a reconciliation of the change in property, plant, and equipment's carrying amount to the amounts appearing on the statement of cash flows and corresponding notes.

(c) Financial statement preparers often use reconciliations of changes in major categories of balance sheet accounts to balance the statement of cash flows, as required in part (b) above. What additional insight does this reconciliation reveal to a reader of the statement that is not as evident from the statement of cash flows?

(d) Prepare a short analysis of Seneca's cash flow activity for 2011. The analysis is to be given to the controller.

(e) What choices, if any, are available for classifications for interest and dividends paid or received by Seneca?

(f) What kind of company would you expect to be revealed by the operating, investing, and financing sections of Seneca's statement of cash flows: a company that is severely troubled financially or a recently formed company that is experiencing rapid growth?

Writing Assignments

WA22-1   HTM Limited is a young and growing producer of electronic measurement instruments and technical equipment. You have been retained by HTM to advise it in preparing a statement of cash flows using the indirect method. For the fiscal year ended October 31, 2011, you have obtained the following information about certain HTM events and transactions. The company reports under IFRS.

1. Earnings reported for the fiscal year were $800,000.

2. Depreciation expense of $315,000 was included in the earnings reported.

3. Uncollectible accounts receivable of $40,000 were written off against the allowance for doubtful accounts. Also, $51,000 of bad debt expense was included in determining income for the year and was added to the allowance for doubtful accounts.

4. A gain of $9,000 was realized on the sale of a machine; it originally cost $75,000, of which $30,000 was depreciated to the date of sale.

5. The company has investments that are recorded at FV through OCI. The increase in the value of these investments that was included in other comprehensive income for the year was $30,000.

6. The company has an investment property, which is measured at fair value. At October 31, 2011, it was determined that the fair value of the building had declined by $45,000 and the appropriate adjustment was made.

7. On July 3, 2011, equipment was purchased for $700,000; HTM gave in exchange a payment of $75,000 cash, previously unissued common shares with a $200,000 market value, and a $425,000 mortgage note payable for the remainder.

8. On August 3, 2011, $800,000 in face value of HTM's 10% convertible debentures were converted into common shares. The bonds were originally issued at face value.

9. Bonds payable with a par value of $100,000, on which there was an unamortized bond discount of $2,000, were redeemed at 99.5.

10. On September 21, 2011, a new issue of $500,000 par value, 8% convertible bonds was issued at 101. Without the conversion feature, the bonds would have been issued at 99.

11. HTM's employees accrue benefits related to the company's unfunded post-retirement medical plan each year. At October 31, 2011, HTM recognized $49,000 of accrued expense for the current year.

Instructions

(a) Explain whether each of the 11 numbered items is a source of cash, a use of cash, or neither.

(b) Explain how each item that is a source or use of cash should be reported in HTM's statement of cash flows for the fiscal year ended October 31, 2011, assuming HTM uses the indirect approach for the Operating Activities section. For items that are neither a source nor use of cash, explain why this is true, and indicate the disclosure, if any, that should be made of the item in the company's statement of cash flows for the year ended October 31, 2011.

WA22-2   The past few years have seen numerous changes in Canadian accounting standards, such as for investments, asset retirement obligations, and stock options. Assume that IFRS has been adopted.

Instructions

For each accounting situation listed below, identify any related cash flows, and explain how the statement of cash flows is affected for companies with this type of transaction.

(a) Investments of securities purchased for trading held by a company are classified as fair value through net income. The investments do not meet the definition of cash equivalents, but are used to earn a return on excess cash until the cash is needed for operations. Small amounts of gains and losses on disposal, interest and dividends received, and changes in their fair values are reported in income.

(b) A company holds equity investments that are classified as fair value through OCI (without recycling). One security was disposed of at a gain during the year and the others have fair values that are higher than they were at the previous year end. Dividends have been received and reported in income.

(c) An investment in another company's bonds is recorded at amortized cost. The investment was acquired at a premium because the bond pays a higher rate of interest than the market rate.

(d) A company began development activities for a new mine site. As a result, it incurred an obligation related to the mine's eventual retirement, reporting it as an asset retirement liability and as a portion of the mine's cost on its balance sheet. The following year, the obligation was increased due to expanded mine activity as well as the accretion of the amount that was recognized in the preceding year representing interest.

(e) Stock options with a two-year vesting period were issued to the top executive team at the beginning of the current fiscal period. The fair value of the stock options was determined using the Black-Scholes formula.

(f) Stock options that were granted three years ago were exercised in the current year when the fair value of the company's shares was at an all-time high. The option or strike price was approximately half of the market share price when the options were exercised.

WA22-3   Durocher Guitar Corp. is in the business of manufacturing top-quality, steel-string folk guitars. Durocher is a private enterprise and follows ASPE. In recent years, the company has experienced working capital problems resulting from investments in new factory equipment, the unanticipated buildup of receivables and inventories, and the payoff of a mortgage on one of its manufacturing plants. The founder and president of the company, Laraine Durocher, has tried to raise cash from various financial institutions, but she has been unsuccessful because of the company's poor performance in recent years. In particular, the company's lead bank, First Provincial, is especially concerned about Durocher's inability to maintain a positive cash position. The commercial loan officer from First Provincial told Laraine Durocher, "I can't even consider your request for capital financing unless I see that your company is able to generate positive cash flows from operations."

Ethics

Thinking about the banker's comment, Laraine Durocher came up with what she believes is a good plan: with a more attractive statement of cash flows, the bank might be willing to provide long-term financing. To "window dress" cash flows, the company can sell its accounts receivables to factors, liquidate its raw material inventories, and arrange a sale and leaseback for major components of its equipment. These rather costly transactions would generate lots of cash. As the chief accountant for Durocher Guitar, it is your job to advise Laraine Durocher on this plan.

Instructions

(a) Explain how each of these "solutions" would affect Durocher Guitar Corp.'s statement of cash flows. Be specific.

(b) Are there any ethical issues related to Laraine Durocher's idea?

(c) What would you advise Laraine Durocher to do?

WA22-4   The statement of cash flows is one of the four main statements required in the preparation of a company's financial statements.

Instructions

(a) Explain what the purpose is of the statement of cash flows, and identify at least three reasons users might find it helpful.

(b) What is the definition of cash? What can be included in cash equivalents? How are bank overdrafts treated? State any differences between IFRS and ASPE.

(c) Identify and describe the three categories of activities that must be reported in the statement of cash flows. What is the relationship between these activities and a company's statement of financial position?

(d) Identify two methods of reporting cash flows from operations. Are both permitted under GAAP? Explain. Which method do you prefer? Why?

(e) Provide two examples of a non-cash investing and financing transaction, and describe the financial reporting requirements for such transactions.

(f) Assume that you overhear the following comment by an investor in the stock market: "You can't always trust the net income number reported, because of all the estimates and judgement that go into its determination. That's why I only look at the cash flow from operations in analyzing a company." Comment.

WA22-5   In October 2008, the IASB published a Discussion Paper entitled "Preliminary Views on Financial Statement Presentation" (see www.iasb.org). Since then, there have been various meetings to discuss the comments received and proposed changes. This discussion paper made various proposals about changes to the statement of cash flows.

Instructions

Locate and read the Discussion Paper entitled "Preliminary Views on Financial Statement Presentation" and any Financial Statement Presentation project summaries and updates on the IASB website that relate to the statement of cash flows. Write a short report that you can present to your class on the decisions that have been made to date on this project that will affect the statement of cash flows and why. Describe how the statement will be different from what is now reported and any reconciliations that are proposed.

WA22-6

Instructions

Write a brief essay highlighting the difference between IFRS and accounting standards for private enterprises noted in this chapter, discussing the conceptual justification for each.

Case

Refer to the Case Primer on the Student Website to help you answer these cases.

WILEY PLUS
Case Primer

CA22-1   Papadopoulos Limited (PL) sells retail merchandise in Canada. The company was incorporated last year and is now in its second year of operations. PL is owned and operated by the Papadopoulos family, and Iris Papadopoulos, the company president, has decided to expand into the American marketplace. In order to do this, bank financing will be necessary.

The books have been kept by Iris's daughter Tonya, who is studying accounting in university. Financial statements had only been prepared for tax purposes in the past. For the year ended December 31, 2011, Tonya prepared the following statement showing cash inflows and cash outflows:

Sources of cash:	
From shareholder loan	$150,000
From sales of merchandise	350,000
From truck financing	50,000
From term deposit cashed in	100,000
From interest income	10,000
Total sources of cash	$660,000
Uses of cash:	
For fixed asset purchases	$100,000
For inventory purchases	250,000
Operating expenses, including depreciation of $70,000	160,000
For purchase of investment	55,000
For purchase of truck	50,000
For interest on debt	30,000
Total uses of cash	$645,000
Net increase in cash	$ 15,000

Tonya showed the statement to her mother, noting that the bank was sure to give them a loan, especially since they were profitable in their second year and since cash had increased over the year, which shows that it had been a good year. Iris was not convinced, however, and decided to have the statement looked at by a "real" accountant.

Instructions

Adopt the role of the accountant and redraft the statement, if necessary, in good form for the bank. Discuss the company's financial position. Consider PE GAAP to be a constraint.

Integrated Case

IC22-1   Earthcom Inc. (EI) is in the telecommunications industry. The company builds and maintains telecommunication lines that are buried in the ground. The company is a public company and has been having some bad luck. One of its main underground telecommunications lines was cut by accident and the company cannot determine the exact location of the problem. As a result, many of the company's customers have lost service. Because EI did not have a backup plan, it is uncertain about how long it will take to restore service. The affected customers are not happy and are threatening to sue. In order to try to calm them down, EI has managed to purchase some capacity from a competitor. Unfortunately, the cost of the service is much higher than the revenues from EI's customers. EI is also currently spending quite a bit on consulting fees (on lawyers and damage control consultants).

In addition, EI is spending a significant amount of money trying to track down the problem with its line, and although it has had no luck so far the company recently announced that it was confident that services would be restored imminently. As a result of the work being done, EI feels that it will be in a better position to restore service if this ever happens again.

The company has been upgrading many of its very old telecommunications lines that were beginning to degrade due to age. It has capitalized these amounts and they are therefore showing up as investing activities on the cash flow statement. The company's auditors have questioned this as they feel that the amounts should be expensed.

As a result of all this, EI's share price has plummeted, making its stock options worthless. Management has historically been remunerated solely based on these stock options, however. The company's CFO meanwhile has just announced that he is leaving and is demanding severance pay for what he is calling constructive dismissal. He feels that because the stock options are worthless, he is working for free—which he cannot afford to do—and that the company has effectively fired him.

Instructions

Adopt the role of the company controller and discuss the financial reporting issues.

Research and Financial Analysis

RA22-1 Eastern Platinum Limited

Eastern Platinum Limited's 2009 financial statements can be found at the end of this volume. The company is involved in the mining, exploration, and development of platinum products in South Africa.

Real-World Emphasis

Instructions

Review the financial statements and notes of Eastern Platinum Limited (Eastplats) and answer the following questions.

(a) How does Eastplats define cash and cash equivalents? Do the cash and cash equivalents reported on the statement of cash flows reconcile to the statement of financial position amounts that are reported? Provide details of the reconciliation.

(b) Prepare a summary analysis of Eastplats's sources and uses of cash at the level of operating, investing, and financing subtotals only, for 2009 and 2008. Based on this, comment on the similarities and differences in the company's needs for cash and how they were met over the past three years.

(c) What method of reporting operating cash flows does Eastplats use in the statement of cash flows? Do you think this approach provides useful information to a potential investor?

(d) Using the information provided in the statement of cash flows, determine the balances of the Trade Receivables, Inventories, and Accounts Payable and Accrued Liabilities that would have been reported on the January 1, 2008 statement of financial position. Compare this with the actual balance at January 1, 2008, provided in the notes and explain any differences.

(e) From the statement of cash flows, it appears that share-based payments provided U.S. $582 thousand of cash from operations and that environmental expense provided an additional U.S. $301 thousand. Explain.

(f) Explain why interest income has been deducted and finance costs have been added on the statement of cash flows. Companies have a choice in classifying interest income and finance costs. What choice did Eastplats make with respect to this?

(g) Based only on the information in the Financing Activities section of the statement of cash flows, can you tell whether the debt-to-equity ratio increased or decreased during the years ended December 31, 2009, and 2008? Explain.

(h) Is Eastplats's operating capability expanding or contracting? What type of assets is the company investing in? What is the likely effect of these investments on Eastplats's future operating and financing cash flows?

(i) Comment briefly on the company's solvency and financial flexibility.

RA22-2 Bombardier Inc.

Real-World Emphasis

Access the financial statements of Bombardier Inc. for the year ended January 31, 2010, and January 31, 2008, from the company's website or SEDAR (www.sedar.com).

Instructions

Changes in non-cash working capital items can have a significant impact on operating cash flows. Using the financial statements, answer the following questions.

(a) What does Bombardier do? When is revenue and related costs recognized? Comment on the timing of revenue and expenses, and cash receipts and payments related to operating activities.

(b) What were Bombardier's net earnings from 2007 to 2010? What were the operating cash flow amounts for the same periods? Calculate the difference between net income and operating cash flows for each year. In which years was the operating cash flow higher or lower than net earnings? Calculate the year over year percentage changes in net earnings. Calculate the year over year percentage changes in operating cash flows. Comment on these differences in dollar amounts and year over year percentage changes.

(c) What is causing these differences in net income and operating cash flows to occur? Highlight significant differences and explain why these arise.

(d) Comment on the ability to predict cash flows for this company. Which approach in preparing operating cash flows (direct or indirect) would be most useful to potential investors?

RA22-3 AltaGas Income Trust

Real-World Emphasis

AltaGas Income Trust is an income trust that has interests in natural gas extraction and transmission along with coal-fired, gas-fired, and hydro power generation; natural gas field gathering and processing; and energy services. The entity also provides services including natural gas and natural gas liquids marketing, gas transportation, and the wholesale marketing of power. Its objective is to ensure stable cash flows that can be used to pay out a steady distribution to its unitholders. Income trusts are investment vehicles that hold income-producing assets. Income trusts generally pay a monthly cash distribution to their unitholders, which is one of the primary reasons that investors would purchase units.

Instructions

Access the financial statements for AltaGas Income Trust for the year ended December 31, 2009, from the entity's website or from SEDAR (www.sedar.com) and answer the following questions.

(a) For the period 2005 to 2009, what have been AltaGas's distributions per unit, the net income per unit, and the funds from operations per unit? Compare the amounts each year and comment. Why would the trust provide all this information on a per-unit basis? Are the distributions sustainable?

(b) Review the statement of cash flows for the two years 2008 and 2009. What are the total cash flows from (or used by) operations, investing activities, and financing activities? What sources of cash are available to fund the annual distributions and capital investments? Do you think that the distributions are sustainable?

(c) Using information from Note 21 and the statement of cash flows only, determine the 2009 balances for accounts receivable, inventory, accounts payable and accrued liabilities, customer deposits, and deferred revenues, starting with the December 31, 2008 balances. Compare with the actual amounts for December 31, 2009, and explain any differences.

(d) Using the net book value of capital assets at December 31, 2008, as the opening balance and items from the statement of cash flows, statement of earnings, and related note disclosures, try to reconcile the opening and closing balance for capital assets for 2009.

RA22-4 Allon Therapeutics Inc. versus Oncothyreon Inc.— Comparative Analysis

Allon Therapeutics Inc. and Oncothyreon Inc. are both involved in the discovery, research, and development of therapeutic products. Allon Therapeutics focuses mainly on discovering and developing first drugs that impact the progression of neurodegenerative diseases, while Oncothyreon researches and develops therapeutic products for the treatment of cancer.

 Real-World Emphasis

Instructions

From the company websites, obtain the comparative financial statements of Allon for its year ended December 31, 2009, and of Oncothyreon for its year ended December 31, 2009. Review the financial statements and answer the following questions.

(a) Compare the companies' statements of operations and comment on their results over the past two fiscal periods. What is the major reason for the results that are reported?

(b) How would you expect companies in this industry and stage of development to be financed? Why? Is this consistent with what is reported on their statement of financial position? Comment.

(c) For the two most recent years reported by each company, write a brief explanation of their cash activities at the subtotal level of operating, investing, and financing flows. Note any similarities and differences.

(d) How do the investments that Allon and Oncothyreon make differ from the investments made by companies in other industries? Describe the difference in general, and then specifically explain how it affects each of the financial statements.

(e) Are the companies liquid? Explain. On what does the solvency and financial flexibility of companies in this industry depend?

RA22-5 Nestlé Group

Nestlé Group is one of the world's largest food and beverage companies, selling 10,000 different products ranging from milk and diary, to chocolate and pet food. Access a copy of the company's comparative financial statements for the year ended December 31, 2009, from the company's website (www.nestle.com).

 Real-World Emphasis

Instructions

(a) Prepare a summary report of Nestlé's cash activities during its year ended December 31, 2009, and 2008, at the subtotal level of operating, investing, and financing activities, and a comparative report for the preceding fiscal year. Are there major differences at this level between the two periods? Explain. How is the company using any excess operating cash flows after investing activities?

(b) Identify what major differences there are between the company's accrual-based income and its cash flow from operating activities over the past two years.

(c) Prepare a short report summarizing Nestlé's investing cash transactions and its financing cash transactions for 2009.

(d) How has the company classified interest paid, interest received, income taxes paid, dividends received, and dividends paid? What were the amounts for these items during 2009?

The Importance of the Auditor's Opinion

FOLLOWING FINANCIAL SCANDALS in the United States and the subsequent increase in legislative and regulatory initiatives, full disclosure in financial reporting has become highly important for public companies. There is more focus at the audit committee level; there's been an increased effort in management's discussion and analysis; and, with increased directors' responsibilities, full disclosures have been received more readily.

Three members of the Audit and Assurance Group of professionals at PricewaterhouseCoopers LLP in Toronto have commented on these changes. "GAAP has evolved to the point where the disclosures are extensive," says Gino Scapillati, National Managing Partner. "Statements disclose a lot more than they used to."

Serge Gattesco, partner and national leader of the Audit and Assurance Group, adds that the role of the auditor is "to provide an opinion on the financial statements of a company on whether the financial statements are prepared fairly in accordance with GAAP. The auditor also provides a detailed reporting to audit committees to support them in their governance role." For certain U.S. registrants, an auditor must also attest to the effectiveness of internal controls.

As of 2011, Canadian GAAP for publicly accountable enterprises is transitioning to International Financial Reporting Standards. Gattesco does not foresee much impact of this change on the volume of the disclosures in the financial statements, or on the role of the auditor, other than in the year of transition, where things are more complicated. "Broadly speaking," he says, "it doesn't much matter whose standards you're looking at, they all impose a significant disclosure burden."

While questionable financial reporting has come under increased media scrutiny, instances of actual fraud are rare. "There is a big distinction between fraudulent financial reporting and errors in financial statements that get caught at a later date," clarifies Lisa Simeoni, another Audit and Assurance Group Partner. While there are the deliberate acts where the intent is to get a certain financial result, more common are the other instances such as where there has been an interpretation of GAAP, and a different view is later taken that results in changes to past financials.

For public companies, a qualified opinion is not an option, says Scapillati. When auditors identify a problem, they work with management to address it. They then meet with the audit committee to explain how problems have been resolved and adjusted for. ◼

CHAPTER 23

Other Measurement and Disclosure Issues

Learning Objectives

After studying this chapter, you should be able to:

1. Review the full disclosure principle and describe problems of implementation.

2. Explain the use of accounting policy notes in financial statement preparation.

3. Describe the disclosure requirements for major segments of a business.

4. Describe the accounting problems associated with interim reporting.

5. Discuss the accounting issues for related-party transactions.

6. Identify the difference between the two types of subsequent events.

7. Identify issues related to financial forecasts and projections.

8. Identify the major disclosures found in the auditor's report.

9. Identify the major differences in accounting between accounting standards for private enterprise GAAP (PE GAAP/ASPE) and IFRS, and what changes are expected in the near future.

Preview of Chapter 23

It is very important to read not only a company's financial statements and related information, but also the president's letter and management discussion and analysis (MD&A). In this chapter, we cover several disclosures that must accompany the financial statements to ensure that the statements are not misleading.

The chapter is organized as follows:

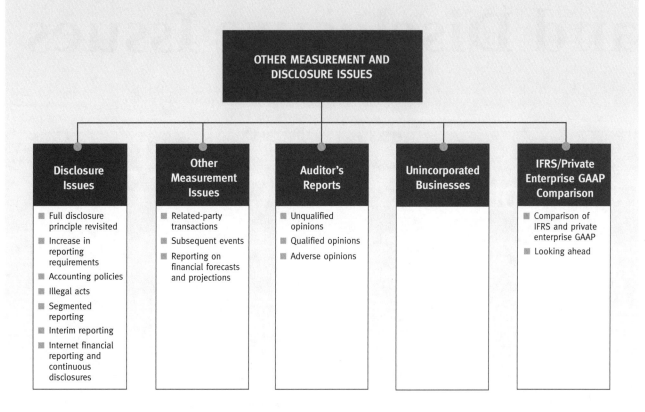

DISCLOSURE ISSUES

Full Disclosure Principle Revisited

Some information is best provided in the financial statements and some is better provided by other means of financial reporting. For example, earnings and cash flows are readily available in financial statements, but investors might do better to look at comparisons with other companies in the same industry, which can be found in news articles or brokerage house reports.

Financial statements, notes to the financial statements, and supplementary information are all areas that are directly affected by GAAP. Other types of information that are found in the annual report, such as the management discussion and analysis, are not subject to GAAP. Illustration 23-1 shows the various types of financial information.

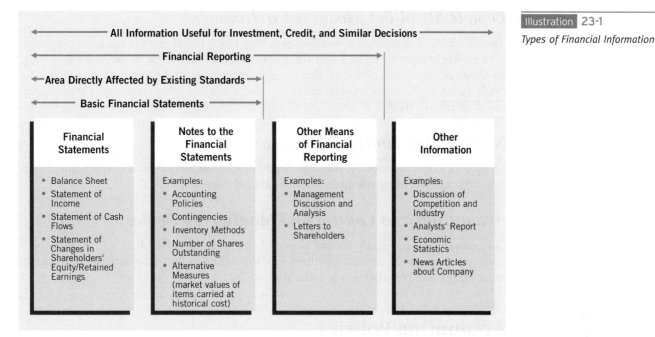

Illustration 23-1

Types of Financial Information

As indicated in Chapter 2, the accounting profession has adopted a full disclosure principle that calls for reporting of any financial facts that are significant enough to influence the judgement of an informed reader. In some situations, the benefits of disclosure may be apparent while the costs are uncertain. In other instances, the costs may be certain but the benefits of disclosure are less apparent. How much information is enough information? This is a difficult question to answer. While not enough information is clearly problematic, sometimes too much—often referred to as information overload—is equally problematic.

Different users want different information, and it becomes exceedingly difficult to develop disclosure policies that meet their varied objectives.

Underlying Concept

This is a good example of the trade-off between the cost-benefit constraint and the full disclosure principle.

Increase in Reporting Requirements

Disclosure requirements for public companies have increased substantially over the past several decades.[1] As illustrated throughout this textbook, the accounting profession has issued many standards in the last two decades that have substantial disclosure provisions.

Accounting standards for private enterprises (referred to here as ASPE or PE GAAP) have fewer disclosure requirements.[2] This is due to the fact that many private enterprises have less complex business models and transactions as well as the fact that many private companies are closely held, thus giving stakeholders greater access to information that may not be presented in the financial statements.

The reasons for the increase in disclosure requirements for public companies are varied. Some of them are as follows.

1 Objective

Review the full disclosure principle and describe problems of implementation.

---

[1] When European Union countries switched to IFRS from their national GAAP in 2005, it was felt that the required disclosures were 30% more than in their prior national GAAP (see "IFRS Conversions—What CFOs Need to Know and Do" by the CICA, August 2009).

[2] It is generally felt that disclosure requirements under PE GAAP/ASPE should be approximately 40%–50% less than under prior Canadian GAAP (see "Private Matters" by Jeff Buckstein, *CA Magazine*, May 2009).

Complexity of the Business Environment

The difficulty of distilling economic events into summarized reports has been magnified by the increasing complexity of business operations in such areas as derivatives, leasing, business combinations, pensions, financing arrangements, and revenue recognition. As a result, notes to the financial statements are used extensively to explain these transactions and their future effects.

Necessity for Timely Information

Today, more than ever before, users are demanding information that is current and predictive. For example, more complete interim data are required.

Accounting as a Control and Monitoring Device

Governments have recently sought more information and public disclosure of such phenomena as management compensation, environmental pollution, related-party transactions, errors and irregularities, and illegal activities.

Accounting Policies

Objective 2
Explain the use of accounting policy notes in financial statement preparation.

As mentioned previously, notes are an integral part of a business enterprise's financial statements. However, they are frequently overlooked because they are highly technical and often appear in small print. Notes are the accountant's means of amplifying or explaining items that are presented in the main body of the statements. Information that is relevant to specific financial statement items can be explained in qualitative terms in notes, and additional quantitative data can be provided to expand the information in the financial statements. Notes can also be used to give information about restrictions that are imposed by financial arrangements or basic contractual agreements. Although notes may be technical and difficult to understand, they provide meaningful information for the financial statement user.

The accounting policies of any particular entity are the specific accounting principles and methods that are currently employed and considered most appropriate to present fairly the enterprise's financial statements. Information about the accounting policies that have been adopted and followed by a reporting entity is essential for financial statement users in making economic decisions. The accounting policies disclosure should be given either as the first note or in a separate Summary of Significant Accounting Policies section that immediately precedes the notes to the financial statements. The Summary of Significant Accounting Policies answers such questions as: What method of depreciation is used on plant assets? What valuation method is employed on inventories? What amortization policy is followed in regard to intangible assets? How are marketing costs handled for financial reporting purposes?

Refer to the audited financial statements of Eastern Platinum Limited found at the end of this volume for an illustration of a note disclosure of accounting policies and other notes. Analysts carefully examine the summary of accounting policies section to determine whether the company is using conservative or liberal accounting practices. For example, recognizing revenues prior to delivery of products might be considered liberal or aggressive. On the other hand, using the successful efforts method for an oil and gas company would generally be viewed as following a conservative practice.

As discussed in previous chapters, ASPE allows greater choice in accounting policies to allow for flexibility for private entities of differing sizes and complexity. In addition, ASPE allows entities to change accounting policies in certain instances without having to meet the criteria of providing more relevant and reliable information. The IASB has been attempting to reduce accounting policy choice to promote comparability. If there are any changes in accounting policy, the entity must prove that the new policy provides more relevant and reliable information.

Illegal Acts

Accounting errors are unintentional mistakes, whereas irregularities are intentional distortions of financial statements. As indicated in this textbook, when errors are discovered, the financial statements should be corrected. The same treatment should be given to irregularities. When an accountant or auditor discovers irregularities, however, a whole different set of suspicions, procedures, and responsibilities comes into play.

Illegal acts have been defined in the past as "a violation of a domestic or foreign statutory law or government regulation attributable to the entity ... or to management or employees acting on the entity's behalf."[3] The term "illegal act" is not meant to include personal misconduct by the entity's management or employees that may be unrelated to the enterprise's business activities. The accountant or auditor must evaluate the adequacy of disclosure in the financial statements and may have to assess whether the item should be recognized in the balance sheet or income statement. For example, if revenue is derived from an illegal act that is considered material in relation to the financial statements, this information should be disclosed. Furthermore, if the illegal act creates a liability to pay a fine, this would need to be reflected in the balance sheet and income statement.

Segmented Reporting

In the last several decades, business enterprises have at times had a tendency to diversify their operations by investing in various other businesses. As a result of such diversification efforts, investors and investment analysts have sought more information about the details behind conglomerate financial statements. Particularly, they want income statement, balance sheet, and cash flow information on the individual segments that together result in the total business income figure. Illustration 23-2 presents segmented (disaggregated) financial information for British Airways plc.

3 Objective
Describe the disclosure requirements for major segments of a business.

Real-World Emphasis

Illustration 23-2

Segmented Information Note—British Airways plc

---

3 Segment information

a Business segments

The Group's network passenger and cargo operations are managed as a single business unit. The Management Board makes resource allocation decisions based on route profitability, which considers aircraft type and route economics, with only limited reference to the strength of the cargo business. The objective in making resource allocation decisions is to optimise consolidated financial results. While the operations of OpenSkies and CityFlyer are considered to be separate operating segments, their activities are considered to be sufficiently similar in nature to aggregate the two segments and report them together with the network passenger and cargo operations. Therefore, based on the way the Group treats the network passenger and cargo operations, and the manner in which resource allocation decisions are made, the Group has only one reportable operating segment for financial reporting purposes, reported as the 'airline business'.

Financial results from other operating segments are below the quantitative threshold for determining reportable operating segments and consist primarily of Air Miles Travel Promotions Limited, British Airways Holidays Limited and Speedbird Insurance Company Limited.

continued on pages 1568 and 1569

---

[3] *CICA Handbook*, Section 5136.03.

For the year ended March 31, 2009

£ million	Airline business	All other segments	Unallocated	Total
Revenue				
Sales to external customers	8,840	152		**8,992**
Inter-segment sales	18			**18**
Segment revenue	8,858	152		**9,010**
Segment result	(240)	20		**(220)**
Other non-operating expense	(30)			**(30)**
(Loss)/profit before tax and finance costs	(270)	20		**(250)**
Net finance costs	78	(59)	(182)	**(163)**
Profit on sale of assets	8			**8**
Share of associates' profit	4			**4**
Tax			43	**43**
Loss after tax	(180)	(39)	(139)	**(358)**
Assets and liabilities				
Segment assets	10,164	115		**10,279**
Investment in associates	209			**209**
Total assets	10,373	115		**10,488**
Segment liabilities	3,842	381		**4,223**
Unallocated liabilities*			4,419	**4,419**
Total liabilities	3,842	381	4,419	**8,642**
Other segment information				
Property, plant and equipment – additions (note 15d)	643	2		**645**
Intangible assets – additions (excluding L'Avion – note 18c)	21			**21**
Purchase of subsidiary (net of cash acquired – note 6c)	34			**34**
Depreciation, amortisation and impairment (note 4a)	693	1		**694**
Impairment of available-for-sale financial asset – Flybe (note 21)	13			**13**
Exceptional items (note 4b):				
Restructuring	78			**78**
Unused tickets (note 2)	(109)			**(109)**
Impairment of OpenSkies goodwill	5			**5**

*Unallocated liabilities primarily include deferred taxes of £652 million and borrowings of £3,763 million which are managed on a Group basis.

For the year ended March 31, 2008, Restated

£ million	Continuing operations				Discontinued operations*	Total
	Airline business	All other segments	Unallocated	Total		
Revenue						
Sales to external customers	8,570	188		8,758		8,758
Inter-segment sales	31			31		31
Segment revenue	8,601	188		8,789		8,789
Segment result	857	21		878	(2)	876
Other non-operating income	9			9		9
Profit/(loss) before tax and finance costs	866	21		887	(2)	885
Net finance income/(costs)	181	(11)	(175)	(5)		(5)
Profit/(loss) on sale of assets	16	(2)		14		14
Share of associates' profit	26			26		26
Tax			(194)	(194)		(194)
Profit/(loss) after tax	1,089	8	(369)	728	(2)	726
Assets and liabilities						
Segment assets	10,966	99		11,065		11,065
Investment in associates	227			227		227
Total assets	11,193	99		11,292		11,292
Segment liabilities	3,479	298		3,777		3,777
Unallocated liabilities**			4,253	4,253		4,253
Total liabilities	3,479	298	4,253	8,030		8,030

Other segment information

Property, plant and equipment – additions (note 15d)	*636*	*1*	*637*	*637*
Intangible assets – additions (note 18c)	*40*		*40*	*40*
Depreciation, amortisation and impairment (note 4a)	*690*	*2*	*692*	*692*
Impairment of available-for-sale financial asset – Flybe (note 21)	*6*		*6*	*6*
Exceptional items (note 4b):				
Restructuring	*1*		*1*	*1*
Unused tickets (note 2)	*(36)*		*(36)*	*(36)*

*As disclosed in note 5, BA Connect, which previously comprised the majority of the 'Regional airline business' segment, was disposed of in March 2007.

**Unallocated liabilities primarily include deferred taxes of £1,075 million and borrowings of £3,174 million which are managed on a Group basis.

b Geographical segments – by area of original sale

£ million	Group 2009	2008 Restated
Europe:	**5,617**	*5,581*
UK	**4,197**	*4,362*
Continental Europe	**1,420**	*1,219*
The Americas	**1,719**	*1,697*
Africa, Middle East and Indian sub-continent	**875**	*821*
Far East and Australasia	**781**	*659*
Revenue	**8,992**	*8,758*

Total of non-current assets excluding available-for-sale financial assets, employee benefit assets, derivative financial instruments and prepayments and accrued income located in the UK is £7,337 million (2008: £7,336 million) and the total of these non-current assets located in other countries is £372 million (2008: £375 million).

Illustration 23-2

Segmented Information Note—British Airways plc (continued)

If the analyst only has access to the consolidated figures, information about the composition of these figures is hidden in aggregated totals. There is no way to tell from the consolidated data how much each product line contributes to the company's profitability, risk, and growth potential. For example, in the case of British Airways, the segmented data reveal that the airline business segment yields 50% of the operating loss while contributing 98% of the revenues, whereas all other segments generate 2% of revenues yet 50% of losses.

Companies have always been somewhat hesitant to disclose segmented data for several reasons, including the following:

1. Without a thorough knowledge of the business and an understanding of such important factors as the competitive environment and capital investment requirements, the investor may find the segmented information meaningless or may even draw improper conclusions about the segments' reported earnings.

2. Additional disclosure may harm reporting firms because it may be helpful to competitors, labour unions, suppliers, and certain government regulatory agencies.

3. Additional disclosure may discourage management from taking intelligent business risks because segments that report losses or unsatisfactory earnings may cause shareholder dissatisfaction with management.

4. The wide variation among firms in the choice of segments, cost allocation, and other accounting problems limits the usefulness of segmented information.

5. The investor is investing in the company as a whole and not in the particular segments, and it should not matter how any single segment is performing if the overall performance is satisfactory.

6. Certain technical problems, such as classification of segments and allocation of segment revenues and costs (especially "common costs"), are challenging.

On the other hand, the advocates of segmented disclosures offer these reasons in support of the practice:

1. Segmented information is needed by the investor to make an intelligent investment decision regarding a diversified company:

   (a) Sales and earnings of individual segments are needed to forecast consolidated profits because of the differences among segments in growth rate, risk, and profitability.

   (b) Segmented reports disclose the nature of a company's businesses and the relative size of the components, which aids in evaluating the company's investment worth.

2. The absence of segmented reporting by a diversified company may put its unsegmented, single-product-line competitors at a competitive disadvantage because the conglomerate may obscure information that its competitors must disclose.

The advocates of segmented disclosures appear to have a much stronger case. Many users indicate that segmented data are the most useful financial information provided, aside from the basic financial statements.

Significant Change

The development of accounting standards for segmented financial information has been a continuing process during the past quarter century. The basic reporting requirements are discussed next. Note that PE GAAP/ASPE does not contain guidance for reporting segmented information.

Objective of Reporting Segmented Information

The objective of reporting segmented financial data is to provide information about the different types of business activities in which an enterprise engages and the different economic environments in which it operates[4] so that users of financial statements can

1. better understand the enterprise's performance,

2. better assess its prospects for future net cash flows, and

3. make more informed judgements about the enterprise as a whole.

Basic Principles

A company might meet the segmented reporting objective by providing complete sets of financial statements that are disaggregated in several ways: for example, by products or services, by geography, by legal entity, or by type of customer. However, it is not feasible to provide all that information in every set of financial statements. The IASB instead requires that financial statements include selected information on a single basis of segmentation. The method chosen is sometimes referred to as the management approach. The management approach is based on the way that management segments the company for making operating decisions, which is made evident by the company's organization structure. As this approach focuses on information about the components of the business that management looks at in making its decisions about operating matters, the components are referred to as operating segments.

---

[4] IFRS 8.1.

Identifying Operating Segments

An operating segment is a component of an enterprise that has all of the following characteristics:

1. It engages in business activities from which it earns revenues and incurs expenses.

2. Its operating results are regularly reviewed by the company's chief operating decision-maker to assess segment performance and allocate resources to the segment.

3. There is discrete financial information available on it.[5]

Information about two or more operating segments may only be aggregated if the segments have the same basic characteristics in all of the following areas:

1. The nature of the products and services provided

2. The nature of the production process

3. The type or class of customer

4. The methods of product or service distribution

5. If applicable, the nature of the regulatory environment

After the company decides on the segments for possible disclosure, a quantitative materiality test is made to determine whether the segment is significant enough to warrant actual disclosure. An operating segment is regarded as significant, and is therefore identified as a reportable segment, if it satisfies one or more of the following quantitative thresholds:[6]

1. Its reporting revenue (including both sales to external customers and intersegment sales or transfers) is 10% or more of the combined revenue of all the enterprise's operating segments.

2. The absolute amount of its reported profit or loss is 10% or more of the greater, in absolute amount, of:

   (a) the combined reported operating profit of all operating segments that did not incur a loss, and

   (b) the combined reported loss of all operating segments that did report a loss.

3. Its assets are 10% or more of the combined assets of all operating segments.

In applying these tests, three additional factors must be considered. First, segment data must explain a significant portion of the company's business. Specifically, the segmented results must equal or exceed 75% of the combined sales to unaffiliated customers for the entire enterprise. This test prevents a company from providing limited information on only a few segments and lumping all the rest into one category.[7]

Second, as the profession recognizes that reporting too many segments may overwhelm users with detailed information, it has therefore proposed 10 segments as an upper limit benchmark for the number of segments that a company should be required to disclose.[8]

Third, if an operating segment does not meet any of the tests but management believes separate information would be useful to users, then the segment may be presented separately.

---

[5] IFRS 8.5.

[6] IFRS 8.12 and .13.

[7] IFRS 8.13–.15.

[8] IFRS 8.19.

To illustrate these requirements, assume that a company has identified the six possible reporting segments shown in Illustration 23-3 (amounts in 000s).

Illustration 23-3

Data for Different Possible Reporting Segments

Segments	Total Revenue (Unaffiliated)	Operating Profit (Loss)	Assets
A	$ 100	$10	$ 60
B	50	2	30
C	700	40	390
D	300	20	160
E	900	18	280
F	100	(5)	50
	$2,150	$85	$970

The respective tests may be applied as follows:

Revenue test:
10% × $2,150 = $215; C, D, and E meet this test.

Operating profit (loss) test:
10% × $90 = $9 (note that the $5 loss is excluded as it is a loss); A, C, D, and E meet this test.

Assets tests:
10% × $970 = $97; C, D, and E meet this test.

The reportable segments are therefore A, C, D, and E, assuming that these four segments have enough sales to meet the test of 75% of combined sales. The 75% test is calculated as follows:

75% of combined sales test: 75% × $2,150 = $1,612; the sales of A, C, D, and E total $2,000 ($100 + $700 + $300 + $900); therefore, the 75% test is met.

Measurement Principles

The accounting principles that an entity uses for segment disclosure do not need to be the same principles that are used to prepare the consolidated statements. This flexibility may at first appear inconsistent. But preparing segment information in accordance with generally accepted accounting principles would be difficult because some principles are not expected to apply at a segment level. Examples include accounting for the cost of company-wide employee benefit plans and accounting for income taxes in a company that files one overall tax return.

Allocations of joint, common, or company-wide costs solely for external reporting purposes are not required. Common costs are defined as any costs that are incurred for the benefit of more than one segment and whose interrelated nature prevents a completely objective division of the costs among the segments. For example, the company president's salary is difficult to allocate to various segments. Allocations of common costs are inherently arbitrary and may not be meaningful if they are not used for internal management purposes. There is a presumption instead that allocations to segments are either directly attributable to the segment or reasonably allocable to it. There should be disclosure of the choices that were made in measuring segmented information.

Segmented and Enterprise-Wide Disclosures

The IASB requires that an enterprise report the following:[9]

---

[9] IFRS 8.23, .27, .28 and .31–.34.

1. **General information** about its reportable segments. This includes factors that management considers most significant in determining the company's reportable segments, and the types of products and services from which each operating segment derives its revenues.

2. **Segment revenues, profit and loss, assets, liabilities, and related information.** This states total profit or loss and total assets and liabilities for each reportable segment. In addition, the following specific information about each reportable segment must be reported if the amounts are regularly reviewed by management:

   (a) Revenues from external customers (revenues from customers attributed to individual material foreign countries should be separately disclosed)

   (b) Revenues from transactions with other operating segments of the same enterprise

   (c) Interest revenue

   (d) Interest expense

   (e) Depreciation and amortization

   (f) Unusual items

   (g) Equity in the net income of investees and joint ventures that are accounted for using the equity method

   (h) Income tax expense or benefit

   (i) Significant non-cash items other than depreciation and amortization expense

   Note that the amount that is reported should be the amount reviewed by management (otherwise referred to as the chief operating decision-maker). Information about the basis of accounting and other details should be disclosed.

3. **Reconciliations.** An enterprise must provide a reconciliation of the total of the segments' revenues to total revenues; a reconciliation of the total of the operating segments' profits and losses to its income before income taxes and discontinued operations; and a reconciliation of the total of the operating segments' assets and liabilities to total assets and liabilities. Reconciliations for other significant items that are disclosed should also be presented and all reconciling items should be separately identified and described for all of the above.

4. **Products and services.** The amount of revenues from external customers.

5. **Geographic areas.** Revenues from external customers (Canada versus foreign) and capital assets and goodwill (Canada versus foreign) should be stated. Foreign information must be disclosed by country if the amounts are material.

6. **Major customers.** If 10% or more of the revenues are derived from a single customer, the enterprise must disclose the total amount of revenues from each of these customers by segment.

Interim Reporting

One further source of information for the investor is interim reports. Interim reports cover periods of less than one year. While at one time annual reporting was considered sufficient in terms of providing timely information, demand quickly grew for quarterly information and now capital markets are moving rapidly to even more frequent disclosures. IFRS does not mandate which entities should provide interim information; however, it provides guidance (which entities are encouraged to follow) if the entity does provide the information. If the interim report is in compliance with IFRS, this should be disclosed. PE GAAP/ASPE does not include standards for interim reporting.

Illustration 23-4 presents the disclosure of selected quarterly data for Torstar Corporation. The media company also disclosed a balance sheet, statement of comprehensive income, statement of changes in shareholders' equity, and statement of changes in cash flows (along with the related notes). The statements were accompanied by a management discussion of the operations, liquidity and capital resources, outlook, and recent developments. With such comprehensive coverage, the report gives a significant amount of information.

Illustration 23-4

Disclosure of Selected Quarterly Data—Torstar Corporation

Real-World Emphasis

Torstar Corporation Consolidated Statements of Income (Dollars in Thousands) (Unaudited)		
	Three months ended March 31	
	2010	2009
Operating revenue		
Newspapers and digital	**$221,444**	$214,529
Book publishing	**112,775**	124,478
	$334,219	$339,007
Operating profit		
Newspapers and digital	**$13,229**	($4,836)
Book publishing	**22,677**	20,617
Corporate	**(3,327)**	(4,153)
Restructuring and other charges	**(8,332)**	(25,900)
	24,247	(14,272)
Interest	**(4,289)**	(5,558)
Foreign exchange	**(844)**	(250)
Loss of associated businesses	**(4,300)**	(7,005)
Income (loss) before taxes	**14,814**	(27,085)
Income and other taxes	**(7,400)**	5,700
Net income (loss)	**$7,414**	($21,385)
Earnings (loss) per Class A and Class B share:		
Net income (loss) – Basic and Diluted	**$0.09**	($0.27)

Objective 4

Describe the accounting problems associated with interim reporting.

Because of the short-term nature of the information in these reports, however, there is considerable controversy about the general approach that should be taken. Supporters of the discrete view believe that each interim period should be treated as a separate accounting period. Deferrals and accruals would therefore follow the same principles that are used for annual reports. Accounting transactions should be reported as they occur, and expense recognition should not change with the period of time covered. Proponents of the integral view, on the other hand, believe that the interim report is an integral part of the annual report and that deferrals and accruals should take into consideration what will happen for the entire year. In this approach, estimated expenses are assigned to parts of a year based on the sales volume or some other activity base. IFRS generally favours the discrete view.

Significant Change

One notable exception to the discrete view is in calculating tax expense. Normally a company would prepare its tax return at year end and assess taxes payable and related tax balances. It is neither cost-effective nor feasible to do this for each interim period (since tax rates are often graduated and therefore increase with increasing taxable income), so annual estimates are made instead. Specifically, an estimate is made of interim taxable income and temporary differences and then the annual estimated tax rate is applied. **Another exception relates to the employer's portion of payroll taxes.** Although these taxes may be remitted by the employer early in the year (as required by law), they are assessed by the government on an annual basis. Therefore, for interim reporting periods, the total estimated annual amount is allocated to the interim periods, which means that the expense is recognized on an accrual basis as opposed to a cash basis.

Interim Reporting Requirements

As a general rule, the profession indicates that the same accounting principles that are used for annual reports should be used for interim reports. Revenues should be recognized in interim periods on the same basis as they are for annual periods. For example, if the percentage-of-completion method is used for recognizing revenue on an annual basis, then the same method should be applied to interim reports as well. Also, costs that are directly associated with revenues (product costs), such as materials, labour and related fringe benefits, and manufacturing overhead, should be treated in the same manner for interim reports as for annual reports.

Underlying Concept

For information to be relevant, it must be available to decision-makers before it loses its capacity to influence their decisions (timeliness). Interim reporting is an excellent example of this concept.

Companies should also generally use the same inventory cost formulas (FIFO, weighted average, etc.) for interim reports that they use for annual reports.

At a minimum, a condensed balance sheet, comprehensive income statement, statement of changes in equity, statement of cash flows, and notes are required.[10] Note that the standard provides for condensed statements at a minimum but does not preclude more detailed presentations. Condensed financial statements should include at a minimum the same headings and subtotals as the most recent annual statements. The balance sheet should be presented as at the end of the current interim period with a comparative balance sheet as at the end of the immediately preceding fiscal year. A balance sheet should also be presented for the beginning of the earliest comparative period when an entity applies an accounting policy retrospectively or makes a retrospective restatement.

Significant Change

The income statement should be presented for the current interim period and interim year to date with like comparatives (i.e., comparable information for the previous period or year). For the statement of changes in equity, the information should be presented cumulatively for the current fiscal year to date with comparatives. Finally, for the cash flow statement, information should be presented cumulatively for the current fiscal year to date with like comparatives.[11] Earnings per share (EPS) information is also required if an enterprise must present this information in its annual information.[12]

Regarding disclosure, the following interim data should be reported as a minimum:[13]

1. Whether the statements comply with IFRS

2. A statement that the company follows the same accounting policies and methods as the most recent annual financial statements including a description of new or changed policies

3. A description of any seasonality or cyclicality of interim period operations

4. The nature and amount of any unusual items

5. The nature and amount of changes in estimates

6. Issuances, repurchases, and repayments of debt and equity securities

7. Dividends paid

---

[10] IAS 34.8.

[11] IAS 34.20.

[12] IAS 34.11 and 11A.

[13] IAS 34.16.

8. Information about reportable segments including revenues from external customers, intersegment revenues, segment profit or loss, total assets for which there is a material change, a description of differences from the last annual statements in the basis of segmentation, and reconciliation of segment profit or loss to the entity's total profit or loss before taxes and discontinued operations

9. Events subsequent to the interim period

10. Specific information about changes in the composition of the entity

11. Information about contingencies

12. Any other information that is required for fair presentation and/or is material to an understanding of the interim period

Unique Problems of Interim Reporting

Changes in Accounting.   What happens if a company decides to change an accounting principle in the third quarter of a fiscal year? Should the adjustment for the cumulative effect of the change be charged or credited to that quarter? Presentation of a cumulative effect in the third quarter may be misleading because of the inherent subjectivity that is associated with the reported income of the first two quarters. In addition, a question arises as to whether such a change might not be used to manipulate a particular quarter's income. These changes should therefore be reflected by retroactive application to prior interim periods unless the data are not available. The comparable interim periods of prior fiscal years should also be restated.[14]

Earnings per Share. Interim reporting of earnings per share numbers has all the problems that are inherent in calculating and presenting annual earnings per share figures, and more. If shares are issued in the third period, EPS for the first two periods will not be indicative of year-end EPS. For purposes of calculating earnings per share and making the required disclosure determinations, each interim period should stand alone. That is, all applicable tests should be made for that single period.

Seasonality. Seasonality occurs when sales are compressed into one short period of the year while certain costs are fairly evenly spread throughout the year. For example, the natural gas industry has its heavy sales in the winter, while the beverage industry has its heavy sales in the summer.

In a seasonal business, wide fluctuations in profits occur because off-season sales do not absorb the company's fixed costs (for example, manufacturing, selling, and administrative costs that tend to remain fairly constant regardless of sales or production). Revenues and expenses should be recognized and accrued when they are earned or incurred according to GAAP. This also holds for interim periods. Thus, a company would only defer recognition of costs or revenues if it would be appropriate to do so at year end (i.e., the same tests are applied). As mentioned earlier in the text, deferral of costs is not appropriate unless the costs meet the definition of an asset.

Continuing Controversy. The profession has developed the stringent standards noted above for interim reporting and this has alleviated much of the controversy that existed regarding the discrete and integral perspectives.

There is still controversy, however, in regard to the independent auditor's involvement in interim reports. Many auditors are reluctant to express an opinion on interim financial information, arguing that the data are too tentative and subjective. Conversely,

---

[14] IAS 34.43.

an increasing number of individuals are arguing for some type of examination of interim reports. A compromise may be a limited review of interim reports that provides some assurance that an examination has been conducted by an outside party and that the published information appears to be in accordance with generally accepted accounting principles.

Analysts want financial information as soon as possible, before it becomes old news. We may not be far from a continuous database system in which corporate financial records can be accessed by computer. Investors might be able to access a company's financial records via computer whenever they wish and put the information in the format they need. Thus, they could learn about sales slippage, cost increases, or earnings changes as they happen, rather than waiting until after the quarter has ended.[15]

A steady stream of information from the company to the investor could be very positive because it might alleviate management's continual concern with short-run interim numbers. It would also alleviate many of the allocation problems that plague current GAAP.

Internet Financial Reporting and Continuous Disclosures

How can companies improve the usefulness of their financial reporting practices? Many companies are using the Internet's power and reach to provide more useful information to financial statement readers. Most large companies have Internet sites, and a considerable proportion of these companies' websites contain links to their financial statements and other disclosures. The increased popularity of such reporting is not surprising, since the costs of printing and disseminating paper reports are reduced.

How does Internet financial reporting improve the overall usefulness of a company's financial reports? First, dissemination of reports via the Internet can allow firms to communicate with more users than is possible with traditional paper reports. In addition, Internet reporting allows users to take advantage of tools such as search engines and hyperlinks to quickly find information about the firm and, sometimes, to download the information for analysis, perhaps in computer spreadsheets. Finally, Internet reporting can help make financial reports more relevant by allowing companies to report expanded disaggregated data and more timely data than is possible through paper-based reporting. For example, some companies voluntarily report weekly sales data and segment operating data on their websites.

Given these benefits and ever-improving Internet tools, will it be long before electronic reporting entirely replaces paper-based financial disclosure? The main obstacles to achieving complete electronic reporting are **equality of access to electronic financial reporting and the reliability of the information that is distributed** via the Internet. Although companies may practise Internet financial reporting, they must still prepare traditional paper reports because some investors may not have Internet access. These investors would receive differential (less) information relative to wired investors if companies were to eliminate paper reports. In addition, at present, Internet financial reporting is a voluntary means of reporting. As a result, there are no standards for the completeness of reports on the Internet, nor is there a requirement that these reports be audited. One concern in this regard is that computer hackers could invade a company's website and corrupt the financial information that is there.

---

[15] A step in this direction is the OSC's mandate for companies to file their financial statements electronically through SEDAR (similar to the SEC requirement to use EDGAR in the United States). SEDAR provides interested parties with computer access to financial information such as periodic filings, corporate prospectuses, and proxy materials.

A great example of the use of technology and continuous reporting is the current practice of releasing quarterly results via the company website through video and live streaming. Investors and analysts can visit the company website and hear the earnings announcements first-hand.

While Internet financial reporting is gaining in popularity, until issues related to differential access to the Internet and the reliability of web-based information are addressed, we will continue to see traditional paper-based reporting.

OTHER MEASUREMENT ISSUES

Related-Party Transactions

Objective 5
Discuss the accounting issues for related-party transactions.

Significant Change

Related-party transactions present especially sensitive and difficult problems. The accountant or auditor who has responsibility for reporting on these types of transactions has to be extremely careful to ensure that the rights of the reporting company and the needs of financial statement users are properly balanced.

IFRS deals only with disclosure requirements whereas PE GAAP/ASPE requires that some related-party transactions be remeasured.

Related-party transactions arise when a business engages in transactions in which one of the transacting parties has the ability to significantly influence the policies of the other, or in which a non-transacting party has the ability to influence the policies of the two transacting parties. Related parties include but are not limited to the following:

(a) Companies or individuals who control, or are controlled by, or are under common control with the reporting enterprise

(b) Investors and investees where there is significant influence or joint control

(c) Company management

(d) Members of immediate family of the above

(e) The other party when a management contract exists[16]

Transactions among related parties cannot be presumed to be carried out at arm's length since there may not be the required conditions of competitive, free-market dealings. Transactions such as borrowing or lending money at abnormally low or high interest rates, real estate sales at amounts that differ significantly from appraised values, exchanges of non-monetary assets, and transactions involving enterprises that have no economic substance ("shell corporations") suggest that related parties may be involved. **In each case, there is a measurement issue.** A basic assumption about financial information is that it is based on transactions that are between arm's-length parties. **Consequently, if this condition is not met, the transactions should at least be disclosed as being between related parties. Furthermore, special measurement principles exist for related-party transactions and these may require a transaction to be remeasured under PE GAAP/ASPE.**

The accountant is expected to report the **economic substance rather than the legal form** of these transactions and to make adequate disclosures. The following disclosures are recommended:[17]

---

[16] *CICA Handbook*, Part II, Section 3840.04, and IAS 24.9.

[17] *CICA Handbook*, Part II, Section 3840.51.

1. The nature of the relationship(s) involved

2. A description of the transactions

3. The recorded amounts of transactions

4. The measurement basis that was used

5. Amounts due from or to related parties and the related terms and conditions

6. Contractual obligations with related parties

7. Contingencies involving related parties

8. Under IFRS, management compensation and the name of the entity's parent company as well as its ultimate controlling entity/individual

Significant Change

Under PE GAAP/ASPE, certain related-party transactions must be remeasured to the carrying amount of the underlying assets or services that were exchanged. Carrying amount is defined as the amount of the item transferred as recorded in the books of the transferor. **This is the case if the transaction is not in the normal course of business, there is no substantive change in ownership, and/or the exchange amount is not supported by independent evidence.** The argument to support remeasurement rests on the premise that, if the transaction is not an ordinary transaction for the enterprise, there might not be a reasonable measure of fair value. Furthermore, if there is no change in ownership, then no bargaining has taken place and, therefore, the price that is arrived at for the exchange may not represent a value that would have been arrived at had the transaction been at arm's length.

Transactions that are in the normal course of business that have no commercial substance must also be remeasured. This argument rests on the premise that, if the transaction is not bona fide or authentic, there is no real exchange of risks and rewards of ownership and, therefore, no gain or loss should be recognized. **This is only an issue where the transaction is also a non-monetary transaction.** A transaction has commercial substance when the entity's cash flows are expected to be significantly different after and as a result of the transaction. In making this determination, consider the risk, timing, and amount of cash flows. Finally, where products or properties are exchanged in the normal course of business to facilitate sales, the transaction is also recorded at carrying value.

Where transactions are remeasured to their carrying value, the difference between the carrying amounts of the items that have been exchanged is booked as a charge or credit to equity.[18] To illustrate, assume that Knudson Limited, a manufacturing company, sells land worth $20,000 to Bay Limited. The companies are related because the same shareholder has a 90% equity interest in each company (the rest of the shares are publicly traded). The land has a carrying value of $15,000 on Knudson's books. In exchange, Bay Limited, also a manufacturing company, transfers to Knudson a building that has a net book value of $12,000. This transaction is not in the **ordinary (normal) course of business** since both companies are manufacturers and would not normally be selling capital assets such as land and buildings. Based on this assessment, therefore, the transaction merits further analysis.

Illustration 23-5 is a decision tree[19] of the judgement that is necessary when determining how to treat related-party transactions.

---

[18] *CICA Handbook*, Part II, Section 3840.09.

[19] *CICA Handbook*, Part II, Section 3840 DT.

Illustration 23-5

*Related-Party Transactions—
Decision Tree*

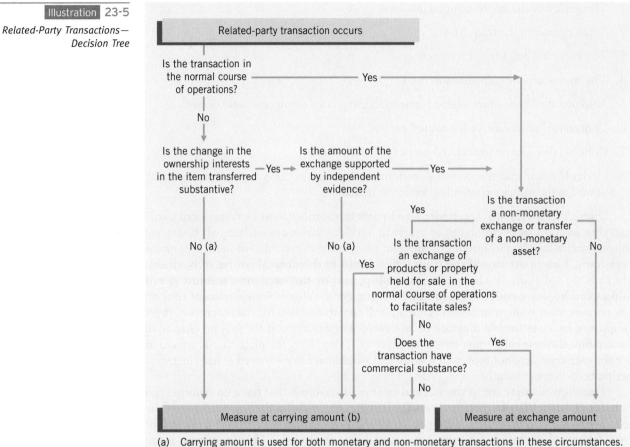

(a)   Carrying amount is used for both monetary and non-monetary transactions in these circumstances.
(b)   In rare circumstances, when the carrying amount of the item received is not available,
       a reasonable estimate of the carrying amount, based on the transferor's original cost, may be
       used to measure the exchange.

Looking at the decision tree, the next question is **whether there has been a substantive change in ownership**. Do different parties own the exchanged items after the transaction? Since the same controlling shareholder owns both assets before and after the transaction (even if indirectly through the companies), there is no substantive change in ownership.[20] The transaction would therefore be remeasured to carrying values with the following journal entry on the Knudson books:

A	=	L	+	SE
−3,000				−3,000

Cash flows: No effect

Property, plant, and equipment	12,000	
Retained earnings	3,000	
Land		15,000

[20] As a benchmark, a substantive change in ownership may be deemed to have occurred if an unrelated party has gained or given up more than a 20% interest in the exchanged items (*CICA Handbook*, Part II, Section 3840.35). In the example above, if the controlling shareholder only owned, say, 70% of both companies and the shares were publicly traded, then one might argue that a substantive change in ownership may be evident—i.e., the other 30% of the shareholders now own (indirectly, through their shareholdings) part of the asset where they did not before the transaction. This is not so clear-cut, however, since the majority shareholders still have a controlling interest, and no real bargaining would have happened between the non-controlling interest shareholders and the majority shareholders. The resolution of this issue would be a matter of judgement.

Bay would record the land at $15,000 and take the building off its books. The resulting credit would be booked to Contributed Surplus. Note that the difference between the carrying values is generally viewed as an equity contribution or distribution and is therefore booked through equity.

If, on the other hand, the transaction had been in the normal course of business, and the transaction had commercial substance, it would have been recorded at the exchange value. The exchange value is defined as the amount of consideration paid or received and agreed to by the related parties.[21] In this case, assume that the agreed upon exchange value is $20,000. Note that the exchange value is not necessarily equal to the fair value but it could be. It is whatever value the two parties agree on. PE GAAP/ASPE notes that it is possible that the transaction value may approximate fair value but it is not necessary to establish what fair value would be if the transaction value is not an approximation. If cash were exchanged, this would determine the exchange value.

In this case, the transaction would be treated like a sale by both parties and Knudson would recognize a gain of $5,000 ($20,000 − $15,000). Likewise, Bay would also recognize a gain of $8,000 ($20,000 − $12,000).

Subsequent Events

Events that take place after the formal balance sheet date but before the financial statements are complete must be considered. Under IFRS, this date is the date that the statements are considered authorized for issue, whereas under ASPE, the date is a matter of judgement, taking into account management structure and procedures followed in completing the statements. These events are referred to as subsequent events since they occur subsequent to the balance sheet date. The subsequent events period is time-diagrammed in Illustration 23-6.

6 Objective
Identify the difference between the two types of subsequent events.

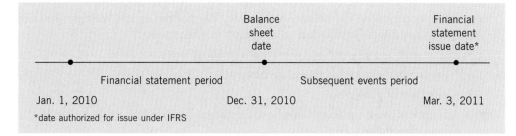

Illustration 23-6

Time Periods for Subsequent Events

Significant Change

A period of several weeks, and sometimes months, may lapse after the end of the year before the financial statement completion date. Taking and pricing the inventory, reconciling subsidiary ledgers with controlling accounts, preparing necessary adjusting entries, assuring that all transactions for the period have been entered, obtaining an audit of the financial statements by independent public accountants, and printing the annual report all take time. **During the period between the balance sheet date and distribution of the financials to shareholders and creditors, important transactions or other events may occur that materially affect the company's financial position or operating situation.**

Many readers of a recent balance sheet believe that the balance sheet condition is constant and they therefore project it into the future. Readers therefore need to be made aware if the company has sold one of its plants, acquired a subsidiary, suffered extraordinary losses, settled significant litigation, or experienced any other important event in the

---

[21] *CICA Handbook*, Part II, Section 3840.03.

post–balance sheet period. Without an explanation in a note, the reader might be misled and draw inappropriate conclusions.

Two types of events or transactions that occur after the balance sheet date may have a material effect on the financial statements or may need to be considered to interpret these statements accurately:

1. **Events that provide additional evidence about conditions that existed at the balance sheet date, affect the estimates used in preparing financial statements, and, therefore, result in needed adjustments.** All information that is available prior to the issuance of the financial statements is used to evaluate previously made estimates. To ignore these subsequent events is to skip an opportunity to improve the financial statements' accuracy. This first type of event encompasses information that would have been recorded in the accounts if it had been known at the balance sheet date. For example, if a loss on an account receivable results from a customer's bankruptcy subsequent to the balance sheet date, the financial statements are adjusted before their issuance. The bankruptcy stems from the customer's poor financial health, which existed at the balance sheet date.

   The same criterion applies to settlements of litigation. The financial statements must be adjusted if the events that gave rise to the litigation, such as personal injury or patent infringement, took place prior to the balance sheet date. If the event giving rise to the claim took place subsequent to the balance sheet date, no adjustment is necessary, but the event must still be disclosed. Thus, a loss resulting from a customer's fire or flood after the balance sheet date is not indicative of conditions that existed at that date. Accordingly, adjustment of the financial statements is not appropriate.

Underlying Concept

The periodicity or time period assumption implies that an enterprise's economic activities can be divided into artificial time periods for purposes of analysis.

2. **Events that provide evidence about conditions that did not exist at the balance sheet date but arise subsequent to that date and do not require adjustment of the financial statements.** Some of these events may have to be disclosed to keep the financial statements from being misleading. These disclosures take the form of notes, supplemental schedules, or even pro forma "as if" financial data prepared as if the event had occurred on the balance sheet date. The following are examples of such events that require disclosure (but do not result in adjustment):

   (a) Events such as a fire or flood that results in a loss

   (b) A decline in the market value of investments

   (c) A purchase of a business

   (d) A commencement of litigation where the cause of action arose subsequent to the balance sheet date

   (e) Changes in foreign currency rates

   (f) An issuance of shares or debt

   Illustration 23-7 presents an example of subsequent events disclosure from the 2009 annual report of Nestlé S.A., which reports in Swiss francs (CHF).

Real-World Emphasis

Illustration 23-7

Subsequent Events Note Disclosure—Nestlé S.A.

31. Events after the balance sheet date

On 4 January 2010, the Group announced its intention to launch an additional Share Buy-Back programme of CHF 10 billion commencing in 2010 for two years, once the existing programme launched in 2007 has been completed.

On 5 January 2010, the Group announced the acquisition of Kraft Food's frozen pizza business in the US and Canada for USD 3.7 billion in cash. The frozen pizza business will enhance Nestlé's frozen food activities in North America, where the Group has already established a leadership in prepared dishes and hand-held product categories.

The estimated sales 2009 of this business amount to USD 2.1 billion with an estimated EBIT of USD 279 million. The transaction is expected to be completed in 2010 as well as the major part of valuation of assets and liabilities of this business acquisition.

At 18 February 2010, date of approval of the Financial Statements by the Board of Directors, the Group had no subsequent events that warrant a modification of the value of the assets and liabilities or an additional disclosure.

Many subsequent events or developments are not likely to require either adjustment of the financial statements or disclosure. Typically, these are non-accounting events or conditions that management normally communicates by other means. These events include legislation, product changes, management changes, strikes, unionization, marketing agreements, and loss of important customers. What to include in the financial statements is a matter of professional judgement since all changes to the business will eventually affect performance one way or another.

Sometimes subsequent events are so pervasive—such as a rapid deterioration of the entity's financial health—that they call into question the going concern assumption. Recall from earlier chapters that the going concern assumption presumes that an entity will continue to operate and will be able to realize its assets and discharge its liabilities in an orderly manner. This supports the use of the mixed fair value/historical cost measurement model. If the subsequent event calls the going concern assumption into question, the measurement model would perhaps change. The company would have to make a decision as to whether it should include additional note disclosures or whether the assets and liabilities should be remeasured to reflect net realizable values in a liquidation market.

Illustration 23-8 presents an excerpt from Quintain Estates and Development plc's annual report and accounts for the year 2009. Quintain lists on the London Stock Exchange. This note illustrates the concept of going concern. In this case, the value of the company's property has declined significantly and, if it declines further, it may result in debt covenants being breached and loans being called.

Real-World Emphasis

---

ii) GOING CONCERN

The Group's financial statements have been prepared on a going concern basis which assumes that the Group will continue to meet its liabilities as they fall due. The Group's cashflow forecasts show that it is expected to have adequate resources available to continue in operational existence for the foreseeable future. In preparing these forecasts, the Directors have had regard to the impact of a continued reduction in property values upon the financial covenants which are contained in the Group's loan documents. If values were to fall by more than 11% by 30 September 2009 or more than 9% by 31 March 2010, compliance with bank covenants would depend on the successful outcome to one or more of several options being explored to provide additional financial flexibility for the Group. These include disposals of properties and non-current investments, debt renegotiation and equity raising. Further details are given in the section on Risk Management in the Operating and Financial Review.

Although the Directors have no reason to believe that they will not be able to complete these initiatives successfully if necessary, and therefore believe that it is appropriate to prepare these financial statements on a going concern basis, they consider that this gives rise to a material uncertainty which may cast significant doubt on the ability of the Group to continue as a going concern. As a result, the Group may therefore be unable to continue realising its assets and discharging its liabilities in the normal course of business.

Illustration 23-8

Potential Going Concern Issues—Quintain Estate and Development plc

Reporting on Financial Forecasts and Projections

In recent years, the investing public's demand for more and better information has focused on disclosure of corporate expectations for the future.[22] These disclosures take one of two forms, as explained next.

---

[22] Some areas in which companies are using financial information about the future are equipment lease-versus-buy analysis, analysis of a company's ability to successfully enter new markets, and an examination of merger and acquisition opportunities. In addition, forecasts and projections are also prepared for use by third parties in public-offering documents (which require financial forecasts), tax-oriented investments, and financial feasibility studies. Use of forward-looking data has been enhanced by the increased capability of computers to analyze, compare, and manipulate large quantities of data.

Financial Forecast

Objective 7
Identify issues related
to financial forecasts
and projections.

A financial forecast consists of prospective financial statements that present, to the best of the responsible party's knowledge and belief, an entity's expected financial position, results of operations, and cash flows. A financial forecast is based on the responsible party's assumptions about conditions that it expects to exist and the course of action it expects to take.

Financial Projection

A financial projection consists of prospective financial statements that present—to the best of the responsible party's knowledge and belief, given one or more hypothetical assumptions—an entity's expected financial position, results of operations, and cash flows. A financial projection is based on the responsible party's assumptions about conditions that it expects would exist and the course of action it expects would be taken, if one or more hypothetical assumptions occurred.

The difference between a financial forecast and a financial projection is that a forecast attempts to provide information on what is expected to happen, whereas a projection provides information on what is not necessarily expected to happen, but might.

Financial forecasts are the subject of intensive discussion among journalists, corporate executives, securities commissions, financial analysts, accountants, and others. Predictably, there are strong arguments on each side. Listed below are some of the arguments.

Arguments for requiring published forecasts:

1. Investment decisions are based on future expectations; therefore, information about the future facilitates better decisions.

2. Forecasts are already circulated informally, but are uncontrolled, frequently misleading, and not available equally to all investors. This confused situation should be brought under control.

3. Circumstances now change so rapidly that historical information is no longer adequate for prediction.

Arguments against requiring published forecasts:

1. No one can foretell the future. Therefore, forecasts, while conveying an impression of precision about the future, will inevitably be wrong.

2. Organizations will strive only to meet their published forecasts, not to produce results that are in the shareholders' best interest.

3. When forecasts are not proved to be accurate, there will be recriminations and probably legal actions.[23]

4. Disclosure of forecasts will be detrimental to organizations because it will fully inform not only investors, but also competitors (foreign and domestic).

The AcSB had previously issued a statement on standards for accountants' services on prospective financial information. This statement established procedures and reporting standards for presenting financial forecasts and projections. It requires all of the following:

---

[23] This issue is serious. Over a recent three-year period, 8% of the companies on the NYSE were sued because of an alleged lack of financial disclosure. Companies complain that they are subject to lawsuits whenever the stock price drops. As one executive noted, you can even be sued if the stock price goes up because you did not disclose the good news fast enough. Nortel Networks was the subject of numerous lawsuits alleging that it misled investors and shareholders.

1. That appropriate assumptions be used

2. That the time period not extend beyond the point in time for which such information can be reasonably estimated

3. That the information be presented in accordance with the accounting policies that are expected to be used in the historical financial statements

4. That the statements include at least an income statement

5. That there be a cautionary note attached

6. That the information be clearly labelled as a forecast or projection

7. Various other disclosures, including assumptions, accounting policies, and the extent to which actual results versus estimated results are incorporated

Note that when Canada moved to IFRS, this standard was removed since publicly accountable entities are bound to follow IFRS beginning in 2011. It is useful to note the requirements of this former standard, however, to understand the types of information that might be included in forward-looking information.

Significant Change

To encourage management to disclose this type of information, securities law has a safe harbour rule. This rule gives protection to an enterprise that presents an inaccurate forecast as long as the forecast is prepared on a reasonable basis and is disclosed in good faith. However, many companies note that the safe harbour rule does not actually work in practice, since it does not cover oral statements and it has not kept them out of court.

The United States has permitted financial forecasts for years, and the results have been fairly successful. There are some significant differences between the British and North American business and legal environments, but these could probably be overcome if influential interests cooperated to produce an atmosphere that supports quality forecasting. Illustration 23-9 shows a typical British forecast that has been adapted from a construction company's report to support a public offering of shares.

Profits have grown substantially over the past 10 years and directors are confident of being able to continue this expansion ... While the rate of expansion will be dependent on the level of economic activity in Ireland and England, the group is well structured to avail itself of opportunities as they arise, particularly in the field of property development, which is expected to play an increasingly important role in the group's future expansion.

Profits before taxation for the half year ended 30th June 2011 were £402,000. On the basis of trading experiences since that date and the present level of sales and completions, the directors expect that, in the absence of unforeseen circumstances, the group's profits before taxation for the year to 31st December 2011 will be not less than £960,000.

No dividends will be paid in respect of the year ended 31st December, 2011. In a full financial year, on the basis of above forecasts (not including full year profits), it would be the intention of the board, assuming current rates of tax, to recommend dividends totalling 40% (of after-tax profits), of which 15% payable would be as an interest dividend in November 2012 and 25% as a final dividend in June 2013.

Illustration 23-9

Financial Forecast of a British Company

Questions of Liability

What happens if a company does not meet its forecasts? Are the company and the auditor going to be sued? If a company, for example, projects an earnings increase of 15% and achieves only 5%, should the shareholders be allowed to sue the company? One court case involving **Monsanto Chemical Corporation** has provided some guidelines. In this case, Monsanto predicted that sales would increase by 8% to 9% and that earnings would rise by 4% to 5%. In the last part of the year, however, the demand for Monsanto's products dropped as a result of a business turndown, and instead of increasing, the company's earnings declined. The company was sued because the projected earnings figure was

Real-World Emphasis

erroneous, but the judge dismissed the suit, ruling that the forecasts were the best estimates of qualified people whose intents were honest.

Safe harbour rules are intended to protect enterprises that provide good-faith projections. However, much concern exists as to how securities commissions and the courts will interpret such terms as "good faith" and "reasonable assumptions" when inaccurate forecasts mislead users of this information.

AUDITOR'S REPORTS

Objective 8
Identify the major disclosures found in the auditor's report.

Another important source of information that is often overlooked is the auditor's report. An auditor is an accounting professional who conducts an independent examination of the accounting data presented by a business enterprise. If the auditor is satisfied that the financial statements present the financial position, results of operations, and cash flows fairly in accordance with generally accepted accounting principles, an unqualified opinion is expressed, as shown in Illustration 23-10.

Illustration 23-10

Example of Auditors' Report under Canadian Auditing Standards

Real-World Emphasis

INDEPENDENT AUDITOR'S REPORT

[Appropriate Addressee]

We have audited the accompanying financial statements of ABC Company, which comprise the balance sheet as at December 31, 20X1, and the income statement, statement of changes in equity and cash flow statement for the year then ended, and a summary of significant accounting policies and other explanatory information.

Management's Responsibility for the Financial Statements

Management is responsible for the preparation and fair presentation of these financial statements in accordance with Canadian generally accepted accounting principles, and for such internal control as management determines is necessary to enable the preparation of financial statements that are free from material misstatement, whether due to fraud or error.

Auditor's Responsibility

Our responsibility is to express an opinion on these financial statements based on our audit. We conducted our audit in accordance with Canadian generally accepted auditing standards. Those standards require that we comply with ethical requirements and plan and perform the audit to obtain reasonable assurance about whether the financial statements are free from material misstatement.

An audit involves performing procedures to obtain audit evidence about the amounts and disclosures in the financial statements. The procedures selected depend on the auditor's judgment, including the assessment of the risks of material misstatement of the financial statements, whether due to fraud or error. In making those risk assessments, the auditor considers internal control relevant to the entity's preparation and fair presentation of the financial statements in order to design audit procedures that are appropriate in the circumstances, but not for the purpose of expressing an opinion on the effectiveness of the entity's internal control. An audit also includes evaluating the appropriateness of accounting policies used and the reasonableness of accounting estimates made by management, as well as evaluating the overall presentation of the financial statements.

We believe that the audit evidence we have obtained is sufficient and appropriate to provide a basis for our audit opinion.

Opinion

In our opinion, the financial statements present fairly, in all material respects, the financial position of ABC Company as at December 31, 20X1, and its financial performance and its cash flows for the year then ended in accordance with Canadian generally accepted accounting principles.

[Auditor's signature]
[Date of the auditor's report]
[Auditor's address]

Source: Reproduced with permission from *Reporting on Financial Statements under Canadian Auditing Standards,* Canadian Institute of Chartered Accountants, (Toronto: CICA, 2009).

In preparing a report, an auditor follows these reporting standards in accordance with the reporting standards articulated in the *Canadian Auditing Standards*:

1. **The auditor's report shall be in writing.**

2. **The report should have a title.**

3. **The report should be addressed as required by the engagement.**

4. **The introductory paragraph should identify the entity, state that the statements have been audited, refer to the significant accounting policies and specify the period covered.**

5. **The report should articulate management's responsibility for the financial statements.**

6. **The report should articulate the auditor's responsibility for the financial statements including that the audit was conducted in accordance with Canadian generally accepted auditing standards, that the standards require the auditor to comply with ethical requirements, and that the auditor must plan the audit to ensure that there is reasonable assurance that the statements are free from material misstatements.**

7. **The report should describe what an audit entails and whether the auditor believes that they have obtained sufficient appropriate audit evidence.**

8. **The report should obtain an audit opinion which states (if unqualified) that the financial statements present fairly in all material respects the results of operations and financial position in accordance with GAAP or gives a true and fair view** (if there is a reservation, the report should explain it).

9. **The report should be signed and dated.**

Unqualified Opinions

In most cases, the auditor issues a standard unqualified or clean opinion; that is, the auditor expresses the opinion that the financial statements present fairly, in all material respects, the entity's financial position, results of operations, and cash flows in conformity with generally accepted accounting principles. Certain circumstances, although they do not affect the auditor's unqualified opinion, may require the auditor to add an explanatory paragraph to the audit report.

Qualified Opinions

In some situations, however, the auditor is required to express a qualified opinion. A qualified opinion contains an exception to the standard opinion. Ordinarily the exception is not significant enough to invalidate the statements as a whole; if it were, an adverse opinion would be rendered. The usual circumstances in which the auditor may deviate from the standard unqualified short-form report on financial statements are when there is a departure from GAAP.

A qualified opinion states that, except for the effects of the matter related to the qualification, the financial statements present fairly, in all material respects, the financial position, results of operations, and cash flows in conformity with generally accepted accounting principles.

A qualified opinion might also be given where there is a scope limitation; that is, where the auditor has not been able to obtain sufficient and appropriate audit evidence, which might happen for instance if there has been an inadvertent destruction by fire of company records. In this case, there would be a disclaimer of opinion that would note that the auditor is unable to give an opinion.

Adverse Opinions

An adverse opinion is required in any report in which the exceptions to fair presentation are so pervasive that in the independent auditor's judgement a qualified opinion is not justified. In such a case, the financial statements taken as a whole are not presented in accordance with generally accepted accounting principles. Adverse opinions are rare, because most enterprises change their accounting to conform to the auditor's desires.

UNINCORPORATED BUSINESSES

Throughout this text, the primary emphasis has been on incorporated businesses. Partnerships and sole proprietorships are another significant business form. These businesses are unincorporated and thus do not have share capital. This form of business has in the past decade become very popular as a tax shelter in the form of income trusts or investment trusts. Interestingly enough, while ownership of partnerships is generally private, ownership of income and investment trusts is often public. The partnership or trust units trade on various stock exchanges.

The accounting issues related to these types of entities are generally similar to those of incorporated companies, with a few exceptions:

1. It is critical to define the economic entity since unincorporated businesses are not separate legal entities. The financial statements should indicate clearly the name under which the business is conducted and it should be clear that the business is unincorporated and that the statements do not include the assets and liabilities of the owners.

2. Salaries, interest, or similar items accruing to owners should be clearly indicated.

3. No provision for income taxes should be made. Since the businesses are not separate legal entities, the income is taxed in the hands of the unitholders.

Note that the owners' equity section would also include different terminology; e.g., owners' equity versus share capital, and withdrawals versus dividends. PE GAAP provides guidance in Section 1800 of Part II of the *CICA Handbook*, whereas there is no specific guidance under IFRS.

IFRS AND PRIVATE ENTERPRISE GAAP COMPARISON

Objective 9
Identify the major differences in accounting between accounting standards for private enterprises (PE GAAP/ASPE) and IFRS, and what changes are expected in the near future.

Comparison of IFRS and Private Enterprise GAAP

Illustration 23-11 compares PE GAAP/ASPE with the international standards.

	Accounting Standards for Private Enterprises (PE GAAP/ASPE)—*CICA Handbook,* Part II, Sections 1100, 1701, 1751, 3820, and 3840	IFRS—IAS 8, 10, 24, and 34; IFRS 8
Disclosures	Generally less disclosure requirements due to the fact that many private entities have less complex business transactions and stakeholders who have greater access to information about the entity.	Increased level of disclosures.
Accounting policies	Greater range of choice of policies to account for differing sizes and complexities of business entities. Entities need not meet the test of providing more relevant and reliable information in certain situations where accounting policies are changed.	The IASB is attempting to reduce choice in terms of accounting policies to promote comparability. Where there is an accounting change, the entity must prove that the new policy provides more relevant and reliable information.
Segmented reporting	No guidance provided	Separate information should be presented for reportable segments including information about revenues, profits and loss, and assets and liabilities. These numbers must be reconciled to reported financial statements. In addition, information about the segment products and services as well as material customers and information by geographical areas should be disclosed.
Interim reporting	No guidance provided.	IFRS does not mandate which entities should provide interim information; however, it provides guidance (which entities are encouraged to follow) if the entity does provide the information. If the interim report is in compliance with IFRS, this should be disclosed. Basically, each interim period is considered a discrete period. The same accounting policies should be used as for the annual financial statements.
Related party transactions	Related-party transactions are remeasured under certain situations (basically where the transaction has no economic substance or is not measurable).	IFRS only requires additional disclosures regarding related parties. It does not require remeasurement. In addition to the disclosure requirement under ASPE, management compensation, and the name of the entity's parent company, as well as its ultimate controlling entity or individual are required to be disclosed.
Subsequent events	The subsequent event period ends when the statements are complete. The date is a matter of judgement, taking into account management structure and procedures followed in completing the statements.	The subsequent event period ends when the statements are authorized for issue.
Unincorporated business	Specific guidance includes requiring the statements to define the entity and disclose salaries and other items accruing to owners. Income taxes are not provided for.	IFRS does not provide guidance.

Illustration 23-11

IFRS and Private Enterprise GAAP Comparison Chart

Looking Ahead

IFRS has developed its own standards for private enterprises: small and mid-sized entity GAAP.

Throughout this textbook, we have stressed the need to provide information that is useful to predict the amounts, timing, and uncertainty of future cash flows. To achieve this objective, judicious choices of alternative accounting concepts, methods, and means of disclosure must be made. You are probably surprised by the large number of choices among acceptable alternatives that accountants are required to make.

You should be aware, however, as Chapter 1 indicated, that accounting is greatly influenced by its environment. Because it does not exist in a vacuum, it seems unrealistic to assume that alternative presentations of certain transactions and events will be eliminated entirely. Nevertheless, we are hopeful that by developing a conceptual framework the profession will be able to focus on the needs of financial statement users and eliminate diversity where appropriate. The profession must continue its efforts to develop a sound foundation upon which financial standards and practice can be built.

WILEY
PLUS
Glossary

KEY TERMS

accounting errors, 1567

accounting policies, 1566

adverse opinion, 1588

auditor's report, 1586

carrying amount, 1579

chief operating
    decision-maker, 1573

clean opinion, 1587

commercial substance,
    1579

common costs, 1572

disaggregated financial
    information, 1567

discrete view, 1574

financial forecast, 1584

financial projection, 1584

full disclosure principle,
    1565

illegal acts, 1567

integral view, 1574

interim reports, 1573

management approach,
    1570

operating segments, 1570

qualified opinion, 1587

related-party
    transactions, 1578

Summary of Learning Objectives

1 Review the full disclosure principle and describe problems of implementation.

The full disclosure principle calls for financial reporting of any financial facts that are significant enough to influence the judgement of an informed reader. Implementing the full disclosure principle is difficult because the cost of disclosure can be substantial and the benefits difficult to assess. Disclosure requirements for public entities have increased because of (1) the growing complexity of the business environment, (2) the necessity for timely information, and (3) the use of accounting as a control and monitoring device. For private entities, disclosure requirements have decreased due to the lesser complexity of many private entities and the fact that many stakeholders of private entities have greater access to information.

2 Explain the use of accounting policy notes in financial statement preparation.

Notes are the accountant's means of amplifying or explaining the items presented in the main body of the statements. Information that is pertinent to specific financial statement items can be explained in qualitative terms, and supplementary quantitative data can be provided to expand the information in the financial statements. Accounting policy notes explain the accounting methods and policies chosen by the company, thus allowing greater comparability between companies.

3 Describe the disclosure requirements for major segments of a business.

If only the consolidated figures are available to the analyst, much information regarding the composition of these figures is hidden in aggregated figures. There is no way to tell from the consolidated data how much each product line contributes to the company's profitability, risk, and growth potential. As a result, segment information is required by the profession for public entities.

4 Describe the accounting problems associated with interim reporting.

Interim reports cover periods of less than one year. There are two viewpoints regarding interim reports. The discrete view holds that each interim period should be treated as a separate accounting period. In contrast, the integral view holds that the interim report is an integral part of the annual report and that deferrals and accruals should take into consideration what will happen for the entire year. IFRS encourages the discrete view approach. The same accounting principles that are used for annual reports should generally be employed for interim reports; however, there are several unique reporting problems. Interim reporting is not mandated by accounting standard setters even for public entities.

5 Discuss the accounting issues for related-party transactions.

Related-party transactions pose special accounting issues. Since the transactions are not at arm's length, they may have to be remeasured under ASPE, as the exchange value is not necessarily representative of the market or fair value. In the absence of reliable information, the transaction may have to be remeasured to reflect historical values or costs. IFRS does not require remeasurement of related-party transactions whereas ASPE does.

6 Identify the difference between the two types of subsequent events.

Type 1 events provide additional evidence about an event that existed at the balance sheet date. These events should be reflected in the balance sheet and income statement. Type 2 events provide evidence about events or transactions that did not exist at the balance sheet date. These should be disclosed in notes if they will have a material impact on the future of the company.

7 Identify issues related to financial forecasts and projections.

There is a concern that companies will be sued if their financial forecasts are not met. To encourage management to disclose this type of information, securities commissions have issued "safe harbour" rules. The safe harbour rule generally provides protection to an enterprise that presents an inaccurate forecast as long as the projection was prepared on a reasonable basis and was disclosed in good faith. However, the safe harbour rule has not always worked well in practice.

8 Identify the major disclosures found in the auditor's report.

If the auditor is satisfied that the financial statements present the financial position, results of operations, and cash flows fairly in accordance with generally accepted accounting principles, an unqualified opinion is expressed. A qualified opinion contains an exception to the standard opinion; ordinarily, the exception is not significant enough to invalidate the statements as a whole. An adverse opinion is required in any report in which the exceptions to fair presentation are so pervasive that a qualified opinion is not justified. A disclaimer of an opinion is appropriate when the auditor has gathered so little information on the financial statements that no opinion can be expressed.

9 Identify differences in accounting between private enterprise GAAP and IFRS, and what changes are expected in the near future.

Differences are noted in the chapter and the comparison chart.

Brief Exercises

(LO 1)   **BE23-1**   An annual report of Crawford Industries states: "The company and its subsidiaries have long-term leases expiring on various dates after December 31, 2011. Amounts payable under such commitments, without reduction for related rental income, are expected to average approximately $5,711,000 annually for the next three years. Related rental income from certain subleases to others is estimated to average $3,094,000 annually for the next three years." What information is provided by this note?

(LO 1)   **BE23-2**   An annual report of Ford Motor Company states: "Net income a share is computed based upon the average number of shares of capital stock of all classes outstanding. Additional shares of common stock may be issued or delivered in the future on conversion of outstanding convertible debentures, exercise of outstanding employee stock options, and for payment of defined supplemental compensation. Had such additional shares been outstanding, net income a share would have been reduced by 10¢ in the current year and 3¢ in the previous year. …As a result of capital stock transactions by the company during the current year (primarily the purchase of Class A Stock from Ford Foundation), net income a share was increased by 6¢." What information is provided by this note?

(LO 1)   **BE23-3**   What type of disclosure or accounting is necessary for each of the following items?

  (a) Because of a general increase in the number of labour disputes and strikes, both within and outside the industry, there is more chance that a company will suffer a costly strike in the near future.

  (b) A company reports a discontinued operation (net of tax) correctly on the income statement. No other mention is made of this item in the annual report.

  (c) A company expects to recover a substantial amount in connection with a pending refund claim for a prior year's taxes. Although the claim is being contested, the company's lawyers have confirmed that they expect their client to recover the taxes.

(LO 3)   **BE23-4**   Bronwyn Mantini, a student of intermediate accounting, was heard to remark after a class discussion on segmented reporting: "All this is very confusing to me. First we are told that there is merit in presenting the consolidated results and now we are told that it is better to show segmented results. I wish they would make up their minds." Evaluate this comment.

(LO 3)   **BE23-5**   Penner Corporation has seven industry segments with total revenues as follows:

	(thousands)		(thousands)
Gamma	$600	Suh	$225
Kennedy	650	Tsui	200
RGD	250	Nuhn	700
Red Moon	375		

Based only on the revenues test, which industry segments are reportable under IFRS?

(LO 3)   **BE23-6**   Operating profits and losses for the seven industry segments of Penner Corporation are as follows:

	(thousands)		(thousands)
Gamma	$90	Suh	$ (20)
Kennedy	(40)	Tsui	34
RGD	25	Nuhn	100
Red Moon	50		

Based only on the operating profit (loss) test, which industry segments are reportable under IFRS?

(LO 3)   **BE23-7**   Assets for the seven industry segments of Penner Corporation are as follows:

	(thousands)		(thousands)
Gamma	$500	Suh	$200
Kennedy	550	Tsui	150
RGD	400	Nuhn	475
Red Moon	400		

Based only on the assets test, which industry segments are reportable under IFRS?

BE23-8 What are the accounting problems related to the presentation of interim data?   (LO 4)

BE23-9 How does seasonality affect interim reporting and how should companies overcome the seasonality problem?   (LO 4)

BE23-10 McNamara Limited purchases land from its president for $390,000 in cash. The land was purchased by the   (LO 5)
president 15 years ago for $45,000. (a) Assume that McNamara follows accounting standards for private enterprises
(ASPE). Prepare the journal entry to record the purchase of the land. Use the decision tree in Illustration 23-5 to explain
the basis for your answer. What information should be disclosed for this transaction? (b) How would your answer to part
(a) change if McNamara were to follow IFRS?

BE23-11 Textile manufacturer Peterson Corp. exchanges computer software having a carrying amount of $11,000 with   (LO 5)
the real estate company Frederick Corp. The software that is received in exchange from Frederick Corp. has a carrying
amount of $15,100, performs different functions, and has a fair value of $20,800. Both companies are 100% owned by the
same individual and since they are closely held companies they both follow ASPE. Discuss how this transaction should be
measured and prepare the journal entries for both companies to record the exchange. Use the decision tree in Illustration
23-5 to explain the reasoning for your answer.

BE23-12 How would the transaction in BE23–11 be recorded if it were arm's-length?   (LO 5)

BE23-13 How would the transaction in BE23–11 be recorded if the individual shareholder only owned 40% of the   (LO 5)
shares of each company? Assume that there is independent evidence to support the value of the computer software.
Discuss and prepare journal entries. Use the decision tree in Illustration 23-5 to explain the reasoning for your answer.

BE23-14 The following information was described in a note of Cruton Packing Co., a public company that follows   (LO 5)
IFRS: "During August, Bigelow Products Corporation purchased 212,450 shares of the Company's common shares,
which constitutes approximately 35% of the shares outstanding. Bigelow has since obtained representation on the Board
of Directors. An affiliate of Bigelow Products Corporation acts as a food broker for Cruton Packing in the Toronto marketing area. The commissions for such services after August amounted to approximately $33,000."
   Why is this information disclosed?

BE23-15 Tonoma Corporation, a public company that follows IFRS, is preparing its December 31, 2011 financial   (LO 6)
statements. The following two events occurred between December 31, 2011, and March 10, 2012, when the statements
were completed and authorized for issue. (a) A liability, estimated at $140,000 at December 31, 2011, was settled on
February 26, 2012, at $190,000. (b) A flood loss of $80,000 occurred on March 1, 2012.
   What effect do these subsequent events have on 2011 net income?

BE23-16 What are the major types of subsequent events? Indicate how each of the following subsequent events would   (LO 6)
be reported:

 (a) Collection of a note written off in a prior period

 (b) Issuance of a large preferred share offering

 (c) Acquisition of a company in a different industry

 (d) Destruction of a major plant in a flood

 (e) Death of the company's chief executive officer

 (f) Additional wage costs associated with the settlement of a four-week strike

 (g) Settlement of a federal income tax case at considerably more tax than was anticipated at year end

 (h) Change in the product mix from consumer goods to industrial goods

BE23-17 Olga Conrad, a financial writer, noted recently, "There are substantial arguments for including earnings pro-   (LO 7)
jections in annual reports and the like. The most compelling is that it would give anyone interested something now available to only a relatively select few—like large stockholders, creditors, and attentive bartenders." Identify some arguments
against providing earnings projections.

BE23-18 The following comment appeared in the financial press: "Inadequate financial disclosure, particularly with   (LO 7)
respect to how management views the future and its role in the marketplace, has always been a stone in the shoe. After all,
if you don't know how a company views the future, how can you judge the worth of its corporate strategy?" What are some
arguments for reporting earnings forecasts?

BE23-19 What is the difference between an auditor's unqualified opinion or "clean" opinion and a qualified one?   (LO 8)

Exercises

(LO 2) **E23-1** **(Illegal Acts)** The detection and reporting of illegal acts by management or other employees is a difficult task. To fulfill their responsibilities, auditors must have a good knowledge of the client's business, including an understanding of the laws and regulations that govern the business and activities of their clients. In addition, accountants and auditors must be sensitive to factors in the company that may indicate an abnormally high risk of illegal acts by the company or its employees.

Instructions

(a) Identify some examples of illegal acts that may be committed by a company or its employees that, if violated, could reasonably be expected to result in a material misstatement in the financial statements.

(b) Explain how, if at all, an undetected illegal act by a client (for example, paying bribes to secure business, or violating pollution control laws and regulations) could affect the company's financial statements.

(c) Identify some factors that could indicate that the risk of violation of laws and regulations is greater than normal and that evaluation of note disclosure, or possibly recognition, of an illegal act may be required.

(LO 3) **E23-2** **(Segmented Reporting)** LaGraca Inc. is involved in five separate industries. The following information is available for each of the five industries:

Operating Segment	Total Revenue	Operating Profit (Loss)	Assets
A	$140,000	$25,000	$240,000
B	40,000	8,000	11,000
C	26,000	(5,000)	36,000
D	190,000	(2,000)	49,000
E	2,000	500	15,000
	$398,000	$26,500	$351,000

Instructions

Determine which of the operating segments are reportable under IFRS based on each of the following:

(a) Revenue test

(b) Operating profit (loss) test

(c) Assets test

(LO 5) **E23-3** **(Related-Party Transaction)** Maffin Corp. owns 75% of Grey Inc. Both companies are in the mining industry. During 2011, Maffin Corp. purchased a building from Grey Inc. for $1,000. The building's carrying amount in Grey Inc.'s financial statements is $700. Maffin's contributed surplus account contains a credit balance of $200 from previous related-party transactions. Grey's contributed surplus account is nil. There is no available independent evidence of the value of the building as it is a unique building in a remote part of the country. Maffin subsequently sold the building, during 2012, to an unrelated party for $1,100. Both Maffin and Grey follow ASPE.

Instructions

Using the related-party decision tree in Illustration 23-5, answer the following.

(a) How would both Maffin and Grey record the purchase and sale of the building during 2011?

(b) Record the subsequent sale of the building by Maffin during 2011.

(c) Assume that Maffin purchased the building from Grey for $500. How would your answer to part (a) change?

(d) Assume that the transaction is in the normal course of operations for both Maffin and Grey and that it has commercial substance. How would your answers to parts (a) and (b) change?

DD

Digging Deeper

(e) Calculate the total impact on income of the purchase and sale of the building for 2011 and 2012 for the consolidated reporting unit of the two companies. What can you conclude from your calculation?

(LO 5) **E23-4** **(Related-Party Transaction)** Verez Limited owns 90% of Consior Inc. During 2011, Verez acquired a machine from Consior in exchange for its own used machine. Both companies are in the consulting business. The agreed exchange amount is $1,000, although the transaction is non-monetary. Consior Inc. carries its machine on its books at a carrying amount of $700, whereas Verez carries its machine on its books at a carrying amount of $900. Neither company has a balance in the contributed surplus account relating to previous related-party transactions. Both Verez and Consior follow ASPE.

Instructions

Using the related-party decision tree in Illustration 23-5, prepare the journal entries to record the exchange for both Verez and Consior under the following assumptions.

(a) The transaction is not in the normal course of operations for either company, and the transaction has commercial substance.

(b) The transaction is not in the normal course of operations for either company, and the transaction does not have commercial substance.

(c) The transaction is in the normal course of operations for each company, and the transaction has commercial substance.

(d) The transaction is in the normal course of operations for each company, and the transaction does not have commercial substance.

(e) Briefly explain how your answers to parts (a) through (d) would change if both companies were to follow IFRS.

E23-5 **(Post-Balance Sheet Events)** Mackay Corporation completed, authorized, and issued its financial statements following IFRS for the year ended December 31, 2011, on March 10, 2012. The following events took place early in 2012. **(LO 6)**

1. On January 10, 19,000 common shares were issued at $45 per share.

2. On March 1, Mackay determined after negotiations with the Canada Revenue Agency that income taxes payable for 2011 should be $1.2 million. At December 31, 2011, income taxes payable were recorded at $1 million.

Instructions

Discuss how these post-balance sheet events should be reflected in the 2011 financial statements.

E23-6 **(Post-Balance Sheet Events)** The following are subsequent (post-balance sheet) events. **(LO 6)**

____ 1. Settlement of a federal tax case at a cost considerably higher than the amount expected at year end

____ 2. Introduction of a new product line

____ 3. Loss of an assembly plant due to fire

____ 4. Sale of a significant portion of the company's assets

____ 5. Retirement of the company president

____ 6. Prolonged employee strike

____ 7. Loss of a significant customer

____ 8. Issuance of a significant number of common shares

____ 9. Material loss on a year-end receivable because of a customer's bankruptcy

____ 10. Hiring of a new president

____ 11. Settlement of a prior year's litigation against the company

____ 12. Merger with another company of similar size

Instructions

For each of the above events, indicate whether the company should

(a) adjust the financial statements,

(b) disclose the event in notes to the financial statements, or

(c) neither adjust nor disclose.

Problems

P23-1 Your firm has been engaged to examine the financial statements of Samson Corporation for the year 2011. The bookkeeper who maintains the financial records has prepared all the unaudited financial statements for the corporation since its organization on January 2, 2005. The client provides you with the information that follows:

SAMSON CORPORATION
Balance Sheet
As of December 31, 2011

Assets		Liabilities	
Current assets	$1,881,100	Current liabilities	$ 962,400
Other assets	5,121,900	Long-term liabilities	1,390,000
		Capital	4,650,600
	$7,003,000		$7,003,000

An analysis of current assets discloses the following:

Cash (restricted in the amount of $400,000 for plant expansion)	$ 571,000
Investments in land	185,000
Accounts receivable less allowance of $30,000	480,000
Inventories (FIFO flow assumption)	645,100
	$1,881,100

Other assets include:

Prepaid expenses	$ 47,400
Plant and equipment less accumulated depreciation of $1,430,000	4,130,000
Cash surrender value of life insurance policy	84,000
Notes receivable (short-term)	162,300
Goodwill	252,000
Land	446,200
	$5,121,900

Current liabilities include:

Accounts payable	$ 510,000
Notes payable (due 2013)	157,400
Estimated income taxes payable	145,000
Premium on common shares	150,000
	$ 962,400

Long-term liabilities include:

Unearned revenue	$ 489,500
Dividends payable (cash)	200,000
8% bonds payable (due May 1, 2016)	700,500
	$1,390,000

Capital includes:

Retained earnings	$2,810,600
Common shares; 200,000 authorized, 184,000 issued	1,840,000
	$4,650,600

The following supplementary information is also provided:

1. On May 1, 2011, the corporation issued at 93.4, $750,000 of bonds to finance plant expansion. The long-term bond agreement provided for the annual payment of interest every May 1. The existing plant was pledged as security for the loan. Use the effective interest method for discount amortization.

2. The bookkeeper made the following mistakes:

   (a) In 2009, the ending inventory was overstated by $183,000. The ending inventories for 2010 and 2011 were correctly calculated.

   (b) In 2011, accrued wages in the amount of $275,000 were omitted from the balance sheet and these expenses were not charged on the income statement.

   (c) In 2011, a gain of $175,000 (net of tax) on the sale of certain plant assets was credited directly to retained earnings.

3. A major competitor has introduced a line of products that will compete directly with Samson's primary line, which is now being produced in a specially designed new plant. Because of manufacturing innovations, the competitor's line will be of similar quality but priced 50% below Samson's line. The competitor announced its new line on January 14, 2012. Samson indicates that the company will meet the lower prices; the lower prices are still high enough to cover Samson's variable manufacturing and selling expenses, but will permit only partial recovery of fixed costs.

4. You learned on January 28, 2012, prior to completion of the audit, of heavy damage from a recent fire at one of Samson's two plants and that the loss will not be reimbursed by insurance. The newspapers described the event in detail.

Instructions

(a) Analyze the above information to prepare a corrected balance sheet for Samson in accordance with IFRS. Prepare a description of any notes that might need to be prepared. The books are closed and adjustments to income are to be made through retained earnings.

(b) "The financial statements of a company are management's responsibility, not the accountant's." Discuss the implications of this statement.

Digging Deeper

P23-2 In an examination of Kelsey Corporation Ltd. as of December 31, 2011, you have learned that the following situations exist. No entries have been made in the accounting records for these items. Kelsey follows IFRS.

1. The corporation erected its present factory building in 1996. Depreciation was calculated by the straight-line method, using an estimated life of 35 years. Early in 2011, the board of directors conducted a careful survey and estimated that the factory building had a remaining useful life of 25 years as of January 1, 2011.

2. An additional assessment of 2011 income taxes was levied and paid in 2012.

3. When calculating the accrual for officers' salaries at December 31, 2011, it was discovered that the accrual for officers' salaries for December 31, 2010, had been overstated.

4. On December 15, 2011, Kelsey Corporation Ltd. declared a stock dividend of 1,000 common shares per 100,000 of its common shares outstanding, distributable February 1, 2012, to the common shareholders of record on December 31, 2011.

5. Kelsey Corporation Ltd., which is on a calendar-year basis, changed its inventory method as of January 1, 2011. The inventory for December 31, 2010, was costed by the average method, and the inventory for December 31, 2011, was costed by the FIFO method. Kelsey is changing its inventory method as it presented more reliable and more relevant information.

6. Kelsey has guaranteed the payment of interest on the 20-year first mortgage bonds of Bonbee Inc., an affiliate. Outstanding bonds of Bonbee Inc. amount to $150,000 with interest payable at 10% per annum, due June 1 and December 1 of each year. The bonds were issued by Bonbee Inc., on December 1, 2007, and all interest payments have been met by the company with the exception of the payment due December 1, 2011. Kelsey states that it will pay the defaulted interest to the bondholders on January 15, 2012.

7. During the year 2011, Kelsey Corporation Ltd. was named as a defendant in a suit for damages by Anand Shahid Corporation for breach of contract. The case was decided in favour of Anand Shahid Corporation, which was awarded $80,000 damages. At the time of the audit, the case was under appeal to a higher court.

Instructions

Describe fully how each of the items should be reported in the financial statements of Kelsey Corporation Ltd. for the year 2011.

P23-3 Three independent situations follow.

Situation 1

A company offers a one-year warranty for the product that it manufactures. A history of warranty claims has been compiled and the probable amount of claims on sales for any particular period can be determined.

Situation 2

Subsequent to the date of a set of financial statements, but before the date of authorization for issuing the financial statements, a company enters into a contract that will probably result in a significant loss to the company. The loss amount can be reasonably estimated.

Situation 3

A company has adopted a policy of recording self-insurance for any possible losses resulting from injury to others by the company's vehicles. The premium for an insurance policy for the same risk from an independent insurance company would have an annual cost of $4,000. During the period covered by the financial statements, there were no accidents involving the company's vehicles that resulted in injury to others.

Instructions

Discuss the accrual or type of disclosure that is necessary under ASPE (if any) and the reason(s) why the disclosure is appropriate for each of the three independent situations.

(AICPA adapted)

P23-4 Leopard Corporation is currently preparing its annual financial statements for the fiscal year ended April 30, 2011, following IFRS. The company manufactures plastic, glass, and paper containers for sale to food and drink manufacturers and distributors. Leopard maintains separate control accounts for its raw materials, work-in-process, and finished goods inventories for each of the three types of containers. The inventories are valued at the lower of cost and net realizable value.

The company's property, plant, and equipment are classified in the following major categories: land, office buildings, furniture and fixtures, manufacturing facilities, manufacturing equipment, and leasehold improvements. All fixed assets are carried at cost. The depreciation methods that are used depend on the type of asset (its classification) and when it was acquired.

Leopard plans to present the inventory and fixed asset amounts in its April 30, 2011 balance sheet as follows:

Inventories	$4,814,200
Property, plant, and equipment (net of depreciation)	$6,310,000

Instructions

What information regarding inventories and property, plant, and equipment must be disclosed by Leopard Corporation in the audited financial statements issued to shareholders, either in the body or the notes, for the 2010–11 fiscal year?

(CMA adapted)

P23-5 Radiohead Inc. produces electronic components for sale to manufacturers of radios, television sets, and digital sound systems. In connection with her examination of Radiohead's financial statements for the year ended December 31, 2011, Marg Zajic, CA, completed field work two weeks ago. Ms. Zajic now is evaluating the significance of the following items prior to preparing her auditor's report. Except as noted, none of these items has been disclosed in the financial statements or notes.

Item 1

A 10-year loan agreement that the company entered into three years ago provides that, subsequent to the date of the agreement, dividend payments may not exceed net income earned after taxes. The balance of retained earnings at the date of the loan agreement was $420,000. From that date through December 31, 2011, net income after taxes has totalled $570,000 and cash dividends have totalled $320,000. Based on these data, the staff auditor who was assigned to this review concluded that there was no retained earnings restriction at December 31, 2011.

Item 2

Recently, Radiohead interrupted its policy of paying cash dividends quarterly to its shareholders. Dividends were paid regularly through 2010, discontinued for all of 2011 to finance the purchase of equipment for the company's new plant, and resumed in the first quarter of 2012. In the annual report, dividend policy is to be discussed in the president's letter to shareholders.

Item 3

A major electronics firm has introduced a line of products that will compete directly with Radiohead's primary line, which is now being produced in Radiohead's specially designed new plant. Because of manufacturing innovations, the competitor's line will be of similar quality but priced 50% below Radiohead's line. The competitor announced its new line during the week following the completion of Ms. Zajic's field work. Ms. Zajic read the announcement in the newspaper and discussed the situation by telephone with Radiohead executives. Radiohead will meet the lower prices as they are still high enough to cover variable manufacturing and selling expenses, although they will permit only partial recovery of fixed costs.

Item 4

The company's new manufacturing plant, which cost $2.4 million and has an estimated life of 25 years, is leased from Armadillo National Bank at an annual rental of $600,000. The company is obligated to pay property taxes, insurance, and maintenance. At the conclusion of its 10-year non-cancellable lease, the company has the option of purchasing the property for $1. In Radiohead's income statement, the rental payment is reported on a separate line.

Instructions

For each of the items, discuss any additional disclosures in the financial statements and notes that the auditor should recommend to her client. The client follows IFRS. (The cumulative effect of the four items should not be considered.)

P23-6 You have completed your audit of Khim Inc. and its consolidated subsidiaries for the year ended December 31, 2011, and are satisfied with the results of your examination. You have examined the financial statements of Khim for the past three years. The corporation follows IFRS and is now preparing its annual report to shareholders. The report will include the consolidated financial statements of Khim and its subsidiaries, and your short-form auditor's report. During your audit, the following matters came to your attention.

1. A vice-president who is also a shareholder resigned on December 31, 2011, after an argument with the president. The vice-president is soliciting proxies from shareholders and expects to obtain sufficient proxies to gain control of the board of directors so that a new president will be appointed. The president plans to have a note prepared that would include information of the pending proxy fight, management's accomplishments over the years, and an appeal by management for the support of shareholders.

2. The corporation decides in 2011 to adopt the straight-line method of depreciation for plant equipment. The straight-line method will be used for new acquisitions and for previously acquired plant equipment that was being depreciated on an accelerated basis.

3. The Canada Revenue Agency is currently examining the corporation's 2009 federal income tax return and is questioning the amount of a deduction claimed by the corporation's domestic subsidiary for a loss sustained in 2009. The examination is still in process, and any additional tax liability is indeterminable at this time. The corporation's tax counsel believes that there will be no substantial additional tax liability.

Instructions

(a) Prepare the notes, if any, that you would suggest for each of the items.

(b) For each item that you decided did not require note disclosure, explain your reasons for not making the disclosure.

(AICPA adapted)

P23-7 Franklin Corporation is a diversified company that operates in five different industries: A, B, C, D, and E. The following information relating to each segment is available for 2011. Sales of segments B and C included intersegment sales of $20,000 and $100,000, respectively.

	A	B	C	D	E
Sales	$40,000	$ 80,000	$580,000	$35,000	$55,000
Cost of goods sold	19,000	50,000	270,000	19,000	30,000
Operating expenses	10,000	40,000	235,000	12,000	18,000
Total expenses	29,000	90,000	505,000	31,000	48,000
Operating profit (loss)	$11,000	$ (10,000)	$ 75,000	$ 4,000	$ 7,000
Assets	$35,000	$ 60,000	$500,000	$65,000	$50,000
Liabilities	$22,000	$ 31,000	$443,000	$12,000	$29,000

Instructions

(a) Determine which of the segments are reportable under IFRS based on each of the following:

1. Revenue test

2. Operating profit (loss) test

3. Assets test

(b) Prepare the necessary disclosures.

(c) The corporation's accountant recently commented, "If I have to disclose our segments individually, the only people who will gain are our competitors and the only people who will lose are our present shareholders." Evaluate this comment.

Digging Deeper

P23-8 You are compiling the consolidated financial statements for Vu Corporation International (VCI), a public company. The corporation's accountant, Timothy Chow, has provided you with the following segment information.

Note 7: Major Segments of Business

VCI conducts funeral service and cemetery operations in Canada and the United States. Substantially all revenues of VCI's major segments of business are from unaffiliated customers. Segment information for fiscal 2011, 2010, and 2009, follows:

(thousands)							
	Funeral	Floral	Cemetery	Corporate	Dried Whey	Limousine	Consolidated
Revenues:							
2011	$302,000	$10,000	$ 83,000	$ –0–	$7,000	$14,000	$416,000
2010	245,000	6,000	61,000	–0–	4,000	8,000	324,000
2009	208,000	3,000	42,000	–0–	1,000	6,000	260,000
Operating Income:							
2011	$79,000	$ 1,500	$18,000	$(36,000)	$ 500	$ 2,000	$ 65,000
2010	64,000	200	12,000	(28,000)	200	400	48,800
2009	54,000	150	6,000	(21,000)	100	350	39,600
Capital Expenditures:*							
2011	$ 26,000	$ 1,000	$ 9,000	$ 400	$ 300	$ 1,000	$ 37,700
2010	28,000	2,000	60,000	1,500	100	700	92,300
2009	14,000	25	8,000	600	25	50	22,700
Depreciation and Amortization:							
2011	$ 13,000	$ 100	$ 2,400	$ 1,400	$ 100	$ 200	$ 17,200
2010	10,000	50	1,400	700	50	100	12,300
2009	8,000	25	1,000	600	25	50	9,700
Identifiable Assets:							
2011	$334,000	$ 1,500	$162,000	$114,000	$ 500	$ 8,000	$620,000
2010	322,000	1,000	144,000	52,000	1,000	6,000	526,000
2009	223,000	500	78,000	34,000	500	3,500	339,500
Liabilities:							
2011	$222,000	$ 1,230	$132,000	$ 99,000	$ 340	$ 6,000	$460,570
2010	209,000	900	119,000	74,000	750	4,100	407,750
2009	121,000	350	56,000	27,000	320	2,400	207,070

*Includes $4,520,000, $111,480,000, and $1,294,000 for the years ended April 30, 2011, 2010, and 2009, respectively, for purchases of businesses.

Instructions

Determine which of the segments must be reported separately and which can be combined under the category "Other." Then write a one-page memo to the company's accountant, Timothy Chow, that explains all of the following:

(a) Which segments must be reported separately and which ones can be combined

(b) Which criteria you used to determine the reportable segments

(c) What major items must be disclosed for each segment

P23-9 The following excerpt is from the financial statements of H. J. Heinz Company and provides segmented geographic data:

The company is engaged principally in one line of business—processed food products—that represents more than 90% of consolidated sales. Information about the company business by geographic area is presented in the table below.

There were no material amounts of sales or transfers between geographic areas or between affiliates, and no material amounts of United States export sales.

				Foreign			
(in thousands of U.S. dollars)	Domestic	United Kingdom	Canada	Western Europe	Other	Total	Worldwide
Sales	$2,381,054	$547,527	$216,726	$383,784	$209,354	$1,357,391	$3,738,445
Operating income	246,780	61,282	34,146	29,146	25,111	149,685	396,465
Identifiable assets	1,362,152	265,218	112,620	294,732	143,971	816,541	2,178,693
Capital expenditures	72,712	12,262	13,790	8,253	4,368	38,673	111,385
Depreciation expense	42,279	8,364	3,592	6,355	3,606	21,917	64,196

Instructions

(a) Why does H. J. Heinz not prepare segment information on its products or services?

(b) Why are revenues by geographic area important to disclose?

P23-10 At December 31, 2011, Bouvier Corp. has assets of $10 million, liabilities of $6 million, common shares of $2 million (representing 2 million common shares of $1.00 par), and retained earnings of $2 million. Net sales for the year 2011 were $18 million, and net income was $800,000. As one of the auditors of this company, you are making a review of subsequent events on February 13, 2012, and you find the following.

1. On February 3, 2012, one of Bouvier's customers declared bankruptcy. At December 31, 2011, this company owed Bouvier $300,000, of which $40,000 was paid in January 2012.

2. On January 18, 2012, one of the client's three major plants burned.

3. On January 23, 2012, a strike was called at one of Bouvier's largest plants and it halted 30% of production. As of today (February 13), the strike has not been settled.

4. A major electronics enterprise has introduced a line of products that would compete directly with Bouvier's primary line, now being produced in a specially designed new plant. Because of manufacturing innovations, the competitor has been able to achieve quality similar to that of Bouvier's products, but at a price 30% lower. Bouvier officials say they will meet the lower prices, which are barely high enough to cover variable and fixed manufacturing and selling costs.

5. Merchandise traded in the open market is recorded in the company's records at $1.40 per unit on December 31, 2011. This price held for two weeks after the release of an official market report that predicted vastly excessive supplies; however, no purchases were made at $1.40. The price throughout the preceding year had been about $2.00, which was the level experienced over several years. On January 18, 2012, the price returned to $2.00 after public disclosure of an error in the official calculations of the prior December—the correction erased the expectations of excessive supplies. Inventory at December 31, 2011, was on a lower of cost or net realizable value basis.

6. On February 1, 2012, the board of directors adopted a resolution to accept the offer of an investment banker to guarantee the marketing of $1.2 million of preferred shares.

7. The company owns investments classified as trading securities accounted for using the fair value through net income model. The investments have been adjusted to fair value as of December 31, 2011. On January 21, 2012, the annual report of one of the investment companies has been issued for its year ended November 30, 2011. The investee company did not meet its earnings forecasts and the market price of the investment has dropped from $49 per share at December 31, 2011, to $27 per share on January 21, 2012.

Instructions

For each event, state how it will affect the 2011 financial statements, if at all. The company follows IFRS.

Writing Assignments

WA23-1 International Financial Reporting Standards require that publicly traded companies provide segment information based on the management approach. An operating segment must engage in activities that generate revenue and incur expenses, and discrete information is available that is regularly reviewed by the chief operating decision maker. If an operating segment meets specific criteria then it is reportable and disclosed in the notes to the financial statements.

Instructions

(a) What does financial reporting for segments of a business enterprise involve?

(b) What are the reasons for requiring financial data to be reported by segments?

(c) What are the possible disadvantages of requiring financial data to be reported by segments?

(d) What accounting difficulties are inherent in segment reporting?

WA23-2 J. J. Kersee Corporation is a publicly traded company and is currently preparing the interim financial data that it will issue to its shareholders and the Securities Commission at the end of the first quarter of its December 31, 2011 fiscal year. Kersee's financial accounting department has compiled the following summarized revenue and expense data for the first quarter of the year:

Sales	$60,000,000
Cost of goods sold	36,000,000
Variable selling expenses	2,000,000
Fixed selling expenses	1,500,000

In the first quarter, the company spent $2 million for television advertisements as a lump sum payment for the entire year. As the company believes that it will receive a benefit for the entire year for this expenditure, it has included only one quarter ($500,000) in the fixed selling expenses. Also, included in inventory is an unfavourable variance due to prices of $245,000 that has been deferred as Kersee anticipates that this will reverse before the third quarter is complete. J. J. Kersee Corporation must issue its quarterly financial statements in accordance with generally accepted accounting principles regarding interim financial reporting.

Instructions

(a) Explain whether Kersee should report its operating results for the quarter as if the quarter were an entirely separate reporting period or as if the quarter were an integral part of the annual reporting period.

(b) State how the sales, cost of goods sold, and fixed selling expenses would be reflected in Kersee Corporation's quarterly report prepared for the first quarter of the 2011 fiscal year. Briefly justify your presentation.

(c) What financial information, as a minimum, must Kersee Corporation disclose to its shareholders in its quarterly reports?

(CMA adapted)

WA23-3   The following statement is an excerpt from a document on interim financial reporting:

Interim financial information is essential to provide investors and others with timely information about the progress of the enterprise. The usefulness of such information rests on the relationship that it has to the annual results of operations. Accordingly, the Board has concluded that each interim period should be viewed primarily as an integral part of an annual period.

In general, the results for each interim period should be based on the accounting principles and practices used by an enterprise in the preparation of its latest annual financial statements unless a change in an accounting practice or policy has been adopted in the current year. The Board has concluded, however, that certain accounting principles and practices followed for annual reporting purposes may require modification at interim reporting dates so that the reported results for the interim period may better relate to the results of operations for the annual period.

Instructions

Listed below are six independent cases on how accounting facts might be reported on an individual company's interim financial reports. For each case, state whether the method that is proposed for interim reporting would be acceptable under IFRS for interim financial data. Support each answer with a brief explanation.

(a) King Limited takes a physical inventory at year end for annual financial statement purposes. Inventory and cost of sales reported in the interim quarterly statements are based on estimated gross profit rates because a physical inventory would require a stoppage of operations. The company does have reliable perpetual inventory records.

(b) Florence Limited is planning to report one fourth of its pension expense each quarter. In the current period the company had a significant settlement and has also prorated this cost over the remaining months to the end of the fiscal year.

(c) Lopez Corp. wrote inventory down to reflect lower of cost or market in the first quarter. At year end, the market exceeds the original acquisition cost of this inventory. Consequently, management plans to write the inventory back up to its original cost as a year-end adjustment.

(d) Witt Corp. realized a large gain on the sale of investments at the beginning of the second quarter. The company wants to report one third of the gain in each of the remaining quarters.

(e) Marble Limited has estimated its annual audit fee. It plans to prorate this expense equally over all four quarters.

(f) McNeil Inc. was reasonably certain that it would have an employee strike in the third quarter. As a result, it shipped heavily during the second quarter but plans to defer the recognition of the sales in excess of the normal sales volume. The deferred sales will be recognized as sales in the third quarter when the strike is in progress. McNeil management thinks this better represents normal second- and third-quarter operations.

(g) At the end of the second quarter Solace Inc. had reported an impairment loss on its goodwill related to the real estate division. At year end, this goodwill value has now increased to the amount it was prior to the writedown and the company plans to reverse this goodwill impairment loss since it is still all in the current year.

(h) Regent Corp. has a bonus plan whereby the employees will earn a bonus of 10% of the company's net income if the price of the company's share reaches a target price by the fiscal year end, which is December 31, 2011. It is now June 30, 2011, and the share price has been reached. Consequently, the company has accrued 10% of the reported net earnings for the interim period.

WA23-4   An article titled "FERF [Financial Executives Research Foundation] @65—Financial Reporting's Eternal Quest: What Do Users Want/Need?" by William Sinnett and Roland Laing, which appeared in the December 2009 issue of *Financial Executive*, discussed the decades-long debate about the constant pressure from shareholders of U.S. companies to report more and more financial information, including publishing earnings forecasts. As far back as 1972, the Securities Exchange Commission said it was reconsidering its longstanding opposition to the publication of forward-looking statements. By 2003, some 84 percent of partners in the international accounting and consulting firm Deloitte said that they had clients who published financial forecasts. In the following years, two reports co-authored by Robert J. Kueppers, a senior Deloitte executive, determined that there was no conclusion as to whether companies should release any forward-looking information. The second report, released in 2009, recommended that corporations weigh the risks and benefits of releasing specific financial forecasts. "And, as an alternative to forward-looking earnings targets, a company may favour providing robust historical information on a more real-time basis and allow investors and analysts to make their own predictions," Sinnett and Laing said of the 2009 report.

Instructions

(a) What are the risks and benefits of providing forward-looking information?

(b) What is the purpose of the safe harbour rule?

(c) Why might providing more "robust historical information on a more real-time basis" assist analysts and other users to make their own forecast?

WA23-5

Instructions

Write a brief essay highlighting the difference between IFRS and accounting standards for private enterprises noted in this chapter, discussing the conceptual justification for each.

Case

Refer to the Case Primer on the Student Website to help you answer these cases.

CA23-1   In June 2012, the board of directors for Holtzman Enterprises Inc. authorized the sale of $10 million of corporate bonds. Michelle Collins, treasurer for Holtzman Enterprises Inc., is concerned about the date when the bonds are issued. The company really needs the cash, but she is worried that if the bonds are issued before the company's year end (December 31, 2012), the additional liability will have an adverse effect on several important ratios. In July, she explains to company president Kenneth Holtzman that if they delay issuing the bonds until after December 31, the bonds will not affect the ratios until December 31, 2013. They will have to report the issuance as a subsequent event, which requires only footnote disclosure. Collins predicts that with expected improved financial performance in 2012, the ratios should be better.

Instructions

Adopt the role of Michelle Collins and discuss any issues.

Integrated Cases

IC23-1   Penron Limited (PL) is in the energy business of buying and selling gas and oil and related derivatives. It is a public company whose shares are widely held. It recently underwent a tremendous expansionary period over the past decade, and revenues quadrupled and continue to climb. Executives are remunerated using stock options, and the employee pension plan invests heavily in the company's stock. It is currently October 2011. The year end is December 31, 2011. Many of the benefit plans of the top executives vest at the end of the year (i.e., the executives will have legal entitlement to the benefits even if they leave the company). As a matter of fact, there is a concern that several of these top executives will announce that they plan to leave the company right after the year-end financial statements are released.

PL was seen as a "hot stock" by the marketplace. Numerous analysts followed the stock carefully and had been advising their clients to buy the stock as long as revenues and profits kept increasing. The third-quarter results had shown steadily increasing revenues and profits. The company had been signalling that this trend would continue through the fourth quarter.

During the fourth quarter, PL sold some of its pipelines to LPL Corporation. The pipelines had not been in use for some time and were seen as non-essential assets. Over the past two years, PL has steadily been divesting itself of non-essential assets. PL had not written the pipelines down in the financial statements since they were able to sell them and recover twice their cost. This one deal was responsible for substantially all of the fourth-quarter profits. Under the terms of the deal, the pipelines were sold for $15 million cash.

LPL Corporation was owned by the president of PL. The company had been established just before the pipeline deal was signed. Since LPL was a new company and otherwise had very few assets, it borrowed the money for the deal from the bank. The bank had requested that PL guarantee the loan, which it did.

During the year, PL issued Class A shares to certain executives of the company. The shares participate in the earnings of the entity much like the common shares of the company (i.e., dividends accrue to the shareholders out of the residual earnings after the preferred dividends have been paid). They are mandatorily redeemable if a triggering event occurs, such as the resignation or termination of the shareholder. The shares are otherwise similar to common shares in that they have no preferential rights.

During the year, the company also began the planning stages for development of a new website that will allow customers to transact with the company. A significant amount of time was spent in this planning phase to determine the feasibility and desirability of this type of customer interface. Toward the end of the year, after lengthy discussion about whether or not to go down this path, the company began to acquire software and hardware to facilitate the new website. A large amount was spent on the site's graphic design and on its content.

Instructions

Assume the role of Penron's auditors and discuss the financial reporting issues for the year ended December 31, 2011.

IC23-2 Frangipani Ltd. (FL) is a new company that has just started up in January 2011. The company is the brainchild of Frank Frangi, who is working on developing a new process for a solar-powered car. To date, most of the year has been taken up with setting up the lab and working on the problem of how to power the vehicle using solar energy. The work has been financed equally by a government-sponsored bank loan and Frank's own personal capital, which he contributed to the company in return for 100% of the common shares upon incorporation. In addition, FL sold preferred shares to family members who are anxious to see how the project (and their investment) is progressing. Frank originally thought to take a salary from the company but has not yet done so this year due to the tight cash flow situation. FL has five scientists working for it. Instead of salary, the scientists have been awarded share appreciation rights that are settleable in cash or a variable number of shares at the option of the company.

Under the terms of the government-sponsored loan, FL agreed to do the following:

- Report to the government annually on its progress, including a report on its ability to continue to operate.

- Maintain a debt-to-equity ratio of 1:1.

- The debt is forgivable if FL is successful in generating the new process within three years. The government will instead take back preferred shares.

The preferred shares have the following characteristics:

- Redeemable at the option of the company for common shares

- Redeemable at the option of the holder (in cash) if the company does not make a profit this year

During the year, FL has been selling advertising space on the company website. Frank is very interested in programming and has created a website that attracts a significant amount of traffic. The website includes several scientific and environmental blogs that many scientists and interested parties contribute to. As a matter of fact, many scientists help each other with practical and theoretical research questions. Since FL continually needs funds to further the work on the solar-powered vehicle, the advertising fees are paid upfront. FL has a clause in the advertising agreement that states the fees are non-refundable. In addition, the advertising fees are stipulated as being for one month's worth of advertising although it is commonly understood that FL displays the advertising for a year. At the end of November 2011, a significant amount of advertising dollars were received.

Frank and the scientists working on the car really feel that they have made significant breakthroughs this year and are close to reaching their goal and submitting the technology for patenting. On December 31, 2011, FL received a call from the company's patent lawyers stating that someone has already filed a patent for the technology that FL is developing. Frank was very angry to learn that it was one of the scientists who contributes to the FL blogs. Apparently someone had leaked critical information about the FL technology in an online discussion and the idea had been stolen. Frank has already contacted his friend who is a litigation lawyer and is confident he can prove the theft of the intellectual capital.

Instructions

Assume the role of the accountant for FL and discuss the financial reporting issues for the year ended December 31, 2011.

Research and Analysis

RA23-1 Thomson Reuters Corporation

In response to the investing public's demand for greater disclosure of corporate expectations for the future, safe harbour rules and legislation have been passed to encourage and protect corporations that issue financial forecasts and projections.

Access the 2009 annual report for information publisher Thomson Reuters Corporation from the company website (www.thomsonreuters.com).

Real-World Emphasis

Instructions

(a) What general expectation did the company have for the industry in 2010 for each of its divisions? How did the company plan to react to this expectation?

(b) Give examples of hard data forecasts (if any) that the company disclosed for the upcoming year (2010). What assumptions did the company use in preparing this information? What risks are involved in achieving these forecasts?

(c) What is the difference between a financial forecast and a financial projection?

RA23-2 Air Canada and British Airways plc

Access the annual report for Air Canada for the December 31, 2009 fiscal year end from the company's website (www.aircanada.com). Also, access the annual report for the year ended March 31, 2009, for British Airways plc from the company's website (www.bashares.com).

Real-World Emphasis

Instructions

(a) What specific items do the airlines discuss in their Accounting Policies notes? (Prepare a list of the headings only.)

(b) Note the similarities and differences in regard to these notes. Comment on these and relate them to the nature of the two businesses.

(c) For what lines of business or segments do the companies present segmented information? What information is provided by segment? Which note disclosure is most useful and why?

(d) Note and comment on the similarities and differences between the auditors' reports submitted by the independent auditors.

RA23-3 Thomson Reuters Corporation

Access the financial statements for the year ended December 31, 2009, for Thomson Reuters Corporation from the company's website (www.thomsonreuters.com).

Instructions

(a) What were the related-party transactions that the company had during the year?

(b) Is the disclosure adequate or is there missing information? Is this information useful?

(c) What were the subsequent events that occurred for the company? What is the cut-off date that has been used (i.e., the date of approval by the directors)?

RA23-4 Nestlé Group

Access the interim financial report for the six-month period ended June 30, 2009, for the Nestlé Group from the company's website (www.nestle.com).

Real-World Emphasis

Instructions

(a) What are the period end dates that have been reported for the statement of comprehensive income, statement of financial position, statement of changes in equity, and statement of cash flows?

(b) On what basis have these interim statements been prepared? Summarize the type of information disclosed in note 1 for accounting policies.

(c) Describe the nature of information provided in the other notes.

(d) Is this information audited?

RA23-5 SEC Conversion to IFRS

In late 2008, the Securities Exchange Commission (SEC) in the United States published its roadmap to IFRS that would look at adopting IFRS.

Read the article entitled "IFRS: Dead in the USA," by Lawrence Richter Quinn from *CA Magazine*, April 2010, which is available at www.camagazine.com.

Instructions

(a) The article suggests that the SEC has been slow in providing guidance as to whether or not IFRS will be adopted in the United States. Outlined in the article are examples of how this indecision has cost companies. Explain how these costs might be incurred and the examples provided.

(b) What are the arguments for and against the SEC requiring companies to adopt IFRS?

(c) Research what recent announcements have been made by the SEC on this topic.

Cumulative Coverage: Chapters 19 to 23

During 2011, you were hired as the Chief Financial Officer for MC Travel Inc., a fairly young travel company that is growing quickly. A key accounting staff member has prepared the financial statements, but there are a couple of transactions that have not been recorded yet because she is waiting for your guidance regarding how these transactions should be recorded. In addition, the staff member is not confident in preparing cash flow statements, so you have been asked to prepare this statement for the 2011 year. MC Travel Inc. reports under ASPE.

The transactions that have not been recorded yet are as follows.

1. On January 1, 2009, the company purchased a small hotel property in Miami for $50 million, paying $10 million in cash and issuing a 5%, $40-million bond at par to cover the balance. The bond principal is payable on January 1, 2019. When you were hired, and began to review the financial information from previous years, you quickly realized that the land portion of the total purchase price had been capitalized with the building, and depreciated. Depreciation has been incorrectly recorded on the building for 2009, 2010, and 2011, and the land is still included in the building account. The land portion of the purchase was appraised at $15 million in 2009, and the land is currently worth $17 million. The cost of the property is to be amortized over a 20-year period using the straight-line basis, and a residual value of $5 million. The company's tax rate is 30%.

2. During 2011, the president, who is also the principal shareholder in the business, transferred ownership of a vacant piece of land in the Caribbean to the company. A hotel will be constructed on this property beginning in 2012. The cost when the president purchased this property was $10 million, and the fair market value, based on a professional appraisal, at the time it was transferred to the company was $25 million. The president was issued 50,000 common shares in exchange for this land. This transaction has not yet been booked.

Additional information that you have gathered to assist in preparing the cash flow statement is as follows.

1. In 2011, equipment was purchased for $250,000. In addition, some equipment was disposed of during the year.

2. Investment income includes a dividend of $150,000 received on the temporary investment. Interest income of $106,000 was reinvested in temporary investments.

Following are the financial statements for MC Travel Inc. for the 2011 and 2010 fiscal years.

MC TRAVEL INC.
Balance Sheet—December 31

	2011	2010
ASSETS—Current assets		
Cash	$ 7,600,000	$ 5,040,000
Temporary investments	2,006,000	1,900,000
Accounts receivable	5,000,000	3,700,000
Allowance for doubtful accounts	(200,000)	(100,500)
Total current assets	14,406,000	10,539,500
Capital assets		
Land	250,000	250,000
Building and equipment	55,270,000	55,072,000
Accumulated depreciation	(7,425,000)	(4,950,000)
Total capital assets	48,095,000	50,372,000
Total assets	$62,501,000	$60,911,500
LIABILITIES AND SHAREHOLDERS' EQUITY—Current liabilities		
Accounts payable	$ 3,800,800	$ 4,100,750
Interest payable	30,000	15,000
Income taxes payable	350,000	250,000
Dividends payable	–0–	100,000
Total current liabilities	4,180,800	4,465,750
Long-term liabilities		
Long-term bank loan	1,145,000	807,000
5% bond payable—Miami property, due 2019	40,000,000	40,000,000
Future income tax liability	175,000	150,000
Total long-term liabilities	41,320,000	40,957,000
Total liabilities	45,500,800	45,422,750
Shareholders' equity		
Common shares	1,000,000	1,000,000
Retained earnings	16,000,200	14,488,750
Total shareholders' equity	17,000,200	15,488,750
Total liabilities and shareholders' equity	$62,501,000	$60,911,500

MC TRAVEL INC.
Income Statement—Year Ended December 31, 2011

Sales		$37,500,000
Expenses: Salaries and wages		5,000,000
Purchases from tour operators		22,500,000
Depreciation expense		2,500,000
Office, general, and selling expenses		3,489,800
Bad debt expenses		150,000
Interest on long-term debt		30,000
Bond interest expense		2,000,000
Total expenses		35,669,800
Income before other income and expenses		1,830,200
Investment income		256,000
Gain on sale of equipment		73,000
Income before income taxes		2,159,200
Income tax expense		647,750
Net income		$ 1,511,450

Instructions

From the information supplied, complete the necessary entries to record the two transactions that have not been recorded, and prepare a revised balance sheet and income statement for the year, keeping in mind that comparative figures will need to be restated. Once this is complete, prepare a statement of cash flows in good form using the direct method for the year ended December 31, 2011. Assume all transaction amounts have been reported in Canadian dollars.

Specimen Financial Statements

Eastern Platinum Limited

The following pages contain the financial statements, accompanying notes, and other information from the 2009 annual financial statements of Eastern Platinum Limited (Eastplats). Note 25 to the Eastplats financial statements and certain other financial information are not reproduced here but are available on WileyPLUS and the student website.

The Business

Eastplats is in the mining, exploration, and development business, with mines in South Africa. Primarily, it mines platinum and platinum group metals (referred to in the statements as "PGM").

PGM are commodities and, as such, their prices reflect supply and demand. This can be a problem for mining companies, which often have significant fixed and sunk costs (often consisting of significant exploration and development costs). Note that Eastplats has been able to decrease its cash cost per ounce from 2008.

At this point, we recommend that you take 20 to 30 minutes to scan the statements and notes to familiarize yourself with the contents and accounting elements. Throughout the following chapters, when you are asked to refer to specific parts of Eastplats' financials, do so. Then, when you have finished reading this book, we challenge you to reread Eastplats' financials to see how much greater and more sophisticated your understanding of them has become.

Deloitte.

Deloitte & Touche LLP
2800 - 1055 Dunsmuir Street
4 Bentall Centre
P.O. Box 49279
Vancouver BC V7X 1P4
Canada

Tel: 604-669-4466
Fax: 604-685-0395
www.deloitte.ca

Auditors' Report

To the Shareholders of
Eastern Platinum Limited

We have audited the consolidated statements of financial position of Eastern Platinum Limited ("the Company") as at December 31, 2009, 2008 and January 1, 2008 and the consolidated statements of income, comprehensive income (loss), changes in equity and cash flows for the years ended December 31, 2009 and 2008. These consolidated financial statements are the responsibility of the Company's management. Our responsibility is to express an opinion on these consolidated financial statements based on our audits.

We conducted our audits in accordance with Canadian generally accepted auditing standards. Those standards require that we plan and perform an audit to obtain reasonable assurance whether the financial statements are free of material misstatement. An audit includes examining, on a test basis, evidence supporting the amounts and disclosures in the financial statements. An audit also includes assessing the accounting principles used and significant estimates made by management, as well as evaluating the overall financial statement presentation.

In our opinion, these consolidated financial statements present fairly, in all material respects, the financial position of the Company as at December 31, 2009, 2008 and January 1, 2008 and the results of its operations and its cash flows for the years ended December 31, 2009 and 2008 in accordance with International Financial Reporting Standards as issued by the International Accounting Standards Board.

Deloitte & Touche LLP

Chartered Accountants
March 24, 2010

Eastern Platinum Limited

Consolidated income statements

(Expressed in thousands of U.S. dollars, except per share amounts)

	Note	Year ended December 31, 2009	Year ended December 31, 2008 (Note 25)
Revenue		$ **111,365**	$ 114,681
Cost of operations			
Production costs		**82,839**	79,961
Depletion and depreciation	8	**17,154**	14,662
		99,993	94,623
Mine operating earnings		**11,372**	20,058
Expenses			
Impairment	8	**-**	297,285
General and administrative		**10,528**	19,441
Share-based payments	17	**582**	4,625
		11,110	321,351
Operating profit (loss)		**262**	(301,293)
Other income (expense)			
Interest income		**1,786**	8,944
Finance costs	19	**(1,691)**	(3,725)
Foreign exchange loss		**(758)**	(2,155)
Loss before income taxes		**(401)**	(298,229)
Deferred income tax recovery	15	**1,623**	85,113
Net profit (loss) for the year		$ **1,222**	$ (213,116)
Attributable to			
Non-controlling interest	18	$ **(4,428)**	$ (3,735)
Equity shareholders of the Company		**5,650**	(209,381)
Net profit (loss) for the year		$ **1,222**	$ (213,116)
Earnings (loss) per share			
Basic	20	$ **0.01**	$ (0.31)
Diluted	20	$ **0.01**	$ (0.31)
Weighted average number of common shares outstanding in thousands			
Basic	20	**680,577**	677,117
Diluted	20	**687,790**	677,117

Eastern Platinum Limited
Consolidated statements of comprehensive income (loss)
(Expressed in thousands of U.S. dollars)

	December 31, 2009	December 31, 2008 (Note 25)
Net profit (loss) for the year	$ 1,222	$ (213,116)
Other comprehensive income (loss)		
Exchange differences on translating foreign operations	116,678	(169,577)
Exchange differences on translating non-controlling interest	2,467	(7,396)
Comprehensive income (loss)	$ 120,367	$ (390,089)
Attributable to		
Non-controlling interest	$ (1,961)	$ (11,131)
Equity shareholders of the Company	$ 122,328	$ (378,958)

Eastern Platinum Limited

Consolidated statements of financial position

as at December 31, 2009 and 2008, and January 1, 2008

(Expressed in thousands of U.S. dollars)

	Note	December 31, 2009	December 31, 2008 (Note 25)	January 1, 2008 (Note 25)
Assets				
Current assets				
Cash and cash equivalents		$ 7,249	$ 25,806	$ 18,818
Short-term investments		14,409	35,257	171,038
Trade and other receivables	6	29,138	9,431	32,560
Inventories	7	4,825	3,881	6,888
		55,621	74,375	229,304
Non-current assets				
Property, plant and equipment	8	634,778	505,473	815,390
Refining contract	9	14,169	12,493	18,467
Other assets	10	2,282	1,017	1,247
		$ 706,850	$ 593,358	$ 1,064,408
Liabilities				
Current liabilities				
Accounts payable and accrued liabilities	11	$ 22,919	$ 36,729	$ 22,967
Current portion of finance leases	12	926	649	748
Current loans	13	-	3,219	3,837
		23,845	40,597	27,552
Non-current liabilities				
Provision for environmental rehabilitation	14	8,152	5,598	6,224
Finance leases	12	2,850	3,014	5,057
Loans	13	-	-	3,322
Deferred tax liabilities	15	42,491	35,614	150,032
		77,338	84,823	192,187
Equity				
Issued capital	17	890,150	890,049	868,045
Equity-settled employee benefits reserve		32,336	31,827	27,428
Currency translation adjustment		(52,899)	(169,577)	-
Deficit		(250,116)	(255,766)	(46,385)
Capital and reserves attributable to equity shareholders of the Company		619,471	496,533	849,088
Non-controlling interest	18	10,041	12,002	23,133
		629,512	508,535	872,221
		$ 706,850	$ 593,358	$ 1,064,408

Approved and authorized for issue by the Board on March 24, 2010.

"David Cohen"

David Cohen, Director

"Robert Gayton"

Robert Gayton, Director

Eastern Platinum Limited

Consolidated statements of changes in equity
(Expressed in thousands of U.S. dollars, except number of shares)

	Issued capital		Equity-settled employee benefits reserve	Currency translation adjustment	Deficit	Capital and reserves attributable to equity shareholders of the parent	Non-controlling interest	Equity
	Shares	Amount						
Balance, January 1, 2008 (Note 25)	**669,031,691**	**$ 868,045**	**$ 27,428**	**$ -**	**$ (46,385)**	**$ 849,088**	**$ 23,133**	**$ 872,221**
Warrants exercised	10,824,077	21,153	-	-	-	21,153	-	21,153
Stock options exercised	670,686	851	(226)	-	-	625	-	625
Share-based payments	-	-	4,625	-	-	4,625	-	4,625
Comprehensive loss	-	-	-	(169,577)	(209,381)	(378,958)	(11,131)	(390,089)
Balance, December 31, 2008 (Note 25)	**680,526,454**	**$ 890,049**	**$ 31,827**	**$ (169,577)**	**$ (255,766)**	**$ 496,533**	**$ 12,002**	**$ 508,535**
Stock options exercised	366,871	101	(73)	-	-	28	-	28
Share-based payments	-	-	582	-	-	582	-	582
Comprehensive income	-	-	-	116,678	5,650	122,328	(1,961)	120,367
Balance, December 31, 2009	**680,893,325**	**$ 890,150**	**$ 32,336**	**$ (52,899)**	**$ (250,116)**	**$ 619,471**	**$ 10,041**	**$ 629,512**

Eastern Platinum Limited

Consolidated statements of cash flows

(Expressed in thousands of U.S. dollars)

	Note	Year ended December 31, 2009	Year ended December 31, 2008 (Note 25)
Operating activities			
Loss before income taxes		$ (401)	$ (298,229)
Adjustments to net profit for non-cash items			
Depletion and depreciation	8	17,154	14,662
Refining contract amortization	9	1,332	1,353
Impairment	8	-	297,285
Share-based payments	17	582	4,625
Interest income		(1,786)	(8,944)
Finance costs	19	1,691	3,725
Foreign exchange loss		758	2,155
Environmental expense		301	-
Net changes in non-cash working capital items			
Trade receivables		(13,169)	14,031
Inventories		22	1,391
Accounts payable and accrued liabilities		(15,135)	12,962
Cash (utilized in) generated from operations		(8,651)	45,016
Adjustments to net profit for cash items			
Realized foreign exchange gain		-	(1,157)
Interest income received		1,855	10,028
Finance costs paid		(69)	(375)
Acquisition related dividend taxes paid		(2,422)	-
Net operating cash flows		(9,287)	53,512
Investing activities			
Acquisitions, net of cash acquired	5	-	(39,589)
Maturity of short-term investments		22,647	119,360
Purchase of other assets		(929)	(42)
Property, plant and equipment expenditures		(28,955)	(143,373)
Sale of property, plant and equipment		1,552	-
Net investing cash flows		(5,685)	(63,644)
Financing activities			
Common shares issued for cash, net of share issue costs		32	22,004
Repayment of current loans		(3,065)	-
Payment of finance leases		(1,223)	(4,309)
Net financing cash flows		(4,256)	17,695
Effect of exchange rate changes on cash and cash equivalents		671	(575)
(Decrease) increase in cash and cash equivalents		(18,557)	6,988
Cash and cash equivalents, beginning of year		25,806	18,818
Cash and cash equivalents, end of year		$ 7,249	$ 25,806
Cash and cash equivalents are comprised of:			
Cash in bank		$ 7,249	$ 9,123
Short-term money market instruments		-	16,683
		$ 7,249	$ 25,806

Eastern Platinum Limited

Notes to the consolidated financial statements – years ended December 31, 2009 and 2008
(Expressed in thousands of U.S. dollars, except number of shares and per share amounts)

1. Nature of operations

Eastern Platinum Limited (the "Company") is a platinum group metal ("PGM") producer engaged in the mining, exploration and development of PGM properties located in various provinces in South Africa.

Eastern Platinum Limited is a publicly listed company incorporated in Canada with limited liability under the legislation of the Province of British Columbia. The Company's shares are listed on the Toronto Stock Exchange, Alternative Investment Market, and the Johannesburg Stock Exchange.

The head office, principal address and records office of the Company are located at 1075 West Georgia Street, Suite 250, Vancouver, British Columbia, Canada, V6E 3C9. The Company's registered address is 1055 West Georgia Street, Suite 1500, Vancouver, British Columbia, Canada, V6E 4N7.

2. Basis of preparation

In February 2009, the British Columbia and Ontario Securities Commissions granted the Company exemptive relief to adopt International Financial Reporting Standards ("IFRS") with an adoption date of January 1, 2009 and a transition date of January 1, 2008.

These consolidated financial statements, including comparatives, have been prepared using accounting policies in compliance with International Financial Reporting Standards ("IFRS") as issued by the International Accounting Standards Board ("IASB"). The disclosures concerning the transition from Canadian Generally Accepted Accounting Principles ("GAAP") to IFRS are included in Note 25.

The preparation of financial statements requires management to make judgments, estimates and assumptions that affect the application of policies and reported amounts of assets and liabilities, and revenue and expenses. The estimates and associated assumptions are based on historical experience and various other factors that are believed to be reasonable under the circumstances, the results of which form the basis of making the judgments about carrying values of assets and liabilities that are not readily apparent from other sources. Actual results may differ from these estimates.

The estimates and underlying assumptions are reviewed on an ongoing basis. Revisions to accounting estimates are recognized in the period in which the estimate is revised if the revision affects only that period or in the period of the revision and further periods if the review affects both current and future periods.

Judgments made by management in the application of IFRS that have a significant effect on the financial statements and estimates with a significant risk of material adjustment in the current and following fiscal years are discussed in Notes 3(l), 3(v), and 3(w).

3. Summary of significant accounting policies

The consolidated financial statements have been prepared under the historical cost convention, except for the revaluation of certain financial instruments. The Company's principal accounting policies are outlined below:

Eastern Platinum Limited
Notes to the consolidated financial statements – years ended December 31, 2009 and 2008
(Expressed in thousands of U.S. dollars, except number of shares and per share amounts)

3.   **Summary of significant accounting policies (continued)**

(a)   *Basis of consolidation*

These consolidated financial statements incorporate the financial statements of the Company and the entities controlled by the Company (its subsidiaries, including special purpose entities). Control exists when the Company has the power, directly or indirectly, to govern the financial and operating policies of an entity so as to obtain benefits from its activities. The financial statements of subsidiaries are included in the consolidated financial statements from the date that control commences until the date that control ceases. All significant intercompany transactions and balances have been eliminated.

Non-controlling interest in the net assets of consolidated subsidiaries are identified separately from the Company's equity. Non-controlling interest consists of the non-controlling interest at the date of the original business combination plus the non-controlling interest's share of changes in equity since the date of acquisition.

Special Purpose Entities ("SPE's") as defined in SIC 12 *Consolidation – Special Purpose Entities* are entities which are created to accomplish a narrow and well-defined objective (e.g. to act as a Black Economic Empowerment ("BEE") partner). SPE's are subject to consolidation when there is an indication that an entity controls the SPE. The Company has determined that its investment in Gubevu Consortium Investment Holdings (Pty) Ltd. ("Gubevu") is a SPE that the Company controls. The accounts of Gubevu are consolidated with those of the Company.

(b)   *Business combinations*

Business combinations that occurred prior to January 1, 2008 were not accounted for in accordance with IFRS 3 *Business Combinations* in accordance with the IFRS 1 *First-time Adoption of International Financial Reporting Standards* exemption discussed in Note 25(a).

Acquisitions of subsidiaries and businesses on, or after, January 1, 2008 are accounted for using the purchase method. The consideration for each acquisition is measured as the aggregate of the fair values (at the date of exchange) of assets given, liabilities incurred or assumed, and equity instruments issued by the Company in exchange for control of the acquiree, plus any costs directly attributable to the business combination. The acquiree's identifiable assets, liabilities and contingent liabilities that meet the conditions for recognition under IFRS 3 *Business Combinations* are recognized at their fair values at the acquisition date, except for non-current assets (or disposal groups) that are classified as held for sale in accordance with IFRS 5 *Non-current Assets Held for Sale and Discontinued Operations,* which are recognized and measured at fair value less costs to sell.

Goodwill arising on acquisition is recognized as an asset and initially measured at cost, being the excess of the cost of the acquisition over the Company's interest in the net fair value of the identifiable assets, liabilities and contingent liabilities recognized. If the Company's interest in the net fair value of the acquiree's identifiable assets, liabilities and contingent liabilities exceeds the cost of the acquisition, the excess is recognized immediately in profit or loss.

The interest of non-controlling shareholders in the acquiree is initially measured at the non-controlling shareholders' proportion of the net fair value of the assets, liabilities and contingent liabilities recognized.

Eastern Platinum Limited

Notes to the consolidated financial statements – years ended December 31, 2009 and 2008
(Expressed in thousands of U.S. dollars, except number of shares and per share amounts)

3. Summary of significant accounting policies (continued)

(c) *Presentation currency*

The Company's presentation currency is the U.S. dollar ("$"). The functional currencies of Eastern Platinum Limited and its South African subsidiaries are the Canadian Dollar and South African Rand ("ZAR"), respectively. These consolidated financial statements have been translated to the U.S. dollar in accordance with IAS 21 *The Effects of Changes in Foreign Exchange Rates.* This standard requires that assets and liabilities be translated using the exchange rate at period end, and income, expenses and cash flow items are translated using the rate that approximates the exchange rates at the dates of the transactions (i.e. the average rate for the period). Subsequent to the adoption of IFRS, all resulting translation differences are reported as a separate component of shareholders' equity titled "Cumulative Translation Adjustment".

(d) *Foreign currency translation*

In preparing the financial statements of the individual entities, transactions in currencies other than the entity's functional currency (foreign currencies) are recorded at the rates of exchange prevailing at the dates of the transactions. At each statement of financial position date, monetary assets and liabilities are translated using the period end foreign exchange rate. Non-monetary assets and liabilities are translated using the historical rate on the date of the transaction. Non-monetary assets and liabilities that are stated at fair value are translated using the historical rate on the date that the fair value was determined. All gains and losses on translation of these foreign currency transactions are included in the consolidated income statements.

(e) *Revenue recognition*

Revenue is measured at the fair value of the consideration received or receivable. The following specific criteria must be met before revenue is recognized:

(i) *Sale of goods*

Revenue from the sale of platinum group and other metals is recognized when all of the following conditions are satisfied:

- the specific risks and rewards of ownership have been transferred to the purchaser;
- the Company does not retain continuing managerial involvement to the degree usually associated with ownership or effective control over the metals sold;
- the amount of revenue can be measured reliably;
- it is probable that the economic benefits associated with the transaction will flow to the Company; and
- the costs incurred or to be incurred in respect of the sale can be measured reliably.

The sale of platinum group metals is provisionally priced such that the price is not settled until a predetermined future date based on the market price at that time. Revenue on these sales is initially recognized (when the conditions above are met) at the current market price. The difference between the present value and the future value of the current market price is recognized as interest income over the term of settlement. Subsequent to initial recognition but prior to settlement, sales are marked to market at each reporting date using the forward price for the period equivalent to that outlined in the contract. This mark to market adjustment is recorded in revenue.

Eastern Platinum Limited
Notes to the consolidated financial statements – years ended December 31, 2009 and 2008
(Expressed in thousands of U.S. dollars, except number of shares and per share amounts)

3.   **Summary of significant accounting policies (continued)**

(e)   *Revenue recognition (continued)*

(ii)   *Rental income*

Rental income from residential properties is recognized on a straight-line basis over the term of the lease.

(iii)   *Interest income*

Interest income is recognized in the income statement as it accrues, using the effective interest method.

(f)   *Share-based payments*

The Company grants stock options to buy common shares of the Company to directors, officers and employees. The board of directors grants such options for periods of up to ten years, with vesting periods determined at its sole discretion and at prices equal to or greater than the closing market price on the day preceding the date the options were granted.

The fair value of the options is measured at grant date, using the Black-Scholes option pricing model, and is recognized over the period that the employees earn the options. The fair value is recognized as an expense with a corresponding increase in equity. The amount recognized as expense is adjusted to reflect the number of share options expected to vest.

(g)   *Finance costs*

Finance costs comprise interest payable on borrowings calculated using the effective interest rate method and foreign exchange gains and losses on foreign currency borrowings.

(h)   *Income taxes*

Income tax expense consists of current and deferred tax expense. Income tax expense is recognized in the income statement.

Current tax expense is the expected tax payable on the taxable income for the year, using tax rates enacted or substantively enacted at period end, adjusted for amendments to tax payable with regards to previous years.

Deferred tax assets and liabilities are recognized for deferred tax consequences attributable to differences between the financial statement carrying amounts of existing assets and liabilities and their respective tax bases. Deferred tax assets and liabilities are measured using the enacted or substantively enacted tax rates expected to apply when the asset is realized or the liability settled.

The effect on deferred tax assets and liabilities of a change in tax rates is recognized in income in the period that substantive enactment occurs.

A deferred tax asset is recognized to the extent that it is probable that future taxable profits will be available against which the asset can be utilized. To the extent that the Company does not consider it probable that a deferred tax asset will be recovered, the deferred tax asset is reduced.

Eastern Platinum Limited
Notes to the consolidated financial statements – years ended December 31, 2009 and 2008
(Expressed in thousands of U.S. dollars, except number of shares and per share amounts)

3. **Summary of significant accounting policies (continued)**

   (h)   *Income taxes (continued)*

   The following temporary differences do not result in deferred tax assets or liabilities:
   - the initial recognition of assets or liabilities, not arising in a business combination, that does not affect accounting or taxable profit
   - goodwill
   - investments in subsidiaries, associates and jointly controlled entities where the timing of reversal of the temporary differences can be controlled and reversal in the foreseeable future is not probable.

   Deferred tax assets and liabilities are offset when there is a legally enforceable right to set off current tax assets against current tax liabilities and when they relate to income taxes levied by the same taxation authority and the Company intends to settle its current tax assets and liabilities on a net basis.

   (i)   *Earnings (loss) per share*

   Basic earnings (loss) per share is computed by dividing the net earnings (loss) available to common shareholders by the weighted average number of shares outstanding during the reporting period. Diluted earnings (loss) per share is computed similar to basic earnings (loss) per share except that the weighted average shares outstanding are increased to include additional shares for the assumed exercise of stock options and warrants, if dilutive. The number of additional shares is calculated by assuming that outstanding stock options and warrants were exercised and that the proceeds from such exercises were used to acquire common stock at the average market price during the reporting periods.

   (j)   *Comprehensive income (loss)*

   Comprehensive income (loss) is the change in the Company's net assets that results from transactions, events and circumstances from sources other than the Company's shareholders and includes items that are not included in net profit such as unrealized gains or losses on available-for-sale investments, gains or losses on certain derivative instruments and foreign currency gains or losses related to self-sustaining operations. The Company's comprehensive income (loss), components of other comprehensive income, and cumulative translation adjustments are presented in the consolidated statements of comprehensive income (loss) and the consolidated statements of changes in equity.

   (k)   *Property, plant and equipment*

   (i)   *Mining assets*

   Assets owned, mineral properties being depleted, and mineral properties not being depleted are recorded at cost less accumulated depreciation and accumulated impairment losses. All direct costs related to the acquisition, exploration and development of mineral properties are capitalized until the properties to which they relate are ready for their intended use, sold, abandoned or management has determined there to be impairment. If economically recoverable ore reserves are developed, capitalized costs of the related property are reclassified as mineral properties being depleted and amortized using the units-of-production method following commencement of production. Interest on borrowings incurred to finance mining assets is capitalized until the asset is capable of carrying out its intended use.

Eastern Platinum Limited
Notes to the consolidated financial statements – years ended December 31, 2009 and 2008
(Expressed in thousands of U.S. dollars, except number of shares and per share amounts)

3.   **Summary of significant accounting policies (continued)**

    (k)   *Property, plant and equipment (continued)*

        (i)   *Mining assets* (continued)

Mining properties and mining and process facility assets are amortized on a units-of-production basis which is measured by the portion of the mine's proven and probable ore reserves recovered during the period. Capital work-in-progress, which is included in mining assets, is not depreciated until the assets are ready for their intended use.

Although the Company has taken steps to verify title to the properties in which it has an interest, in accordance with industry standards for properties in the exploration stage, these procedures do not guarantee the Company's title. Property title may be subject to unregistered prior agreements and non-compliance with regulatory requirements.

        (ii)   *Residential properties and other property, plant and equipment*

Residential properties and other property, plant and equipment are recorded at cost less accumulated depreciation and impairment losses. These assets are depreciated using the straight-line method based on estimated useful lives, which generally range from 5 to 7 years, with the exception of residential properties and mine houses whose estimated useful lives are 50 years and office buildings whose estimated useful lives are 20 years. Land is not depreciated.

Where an item of plant and equipment comprises significant components with different useful lives, the components are accounted for as separate items of plant and equipment.

Expenditures incurred to replace a component of an item of property, plant and equipment that is accounted for separately, including major inspection and overhaul expenditures, are capitalized. Directly attributable expenses incurred for major capital projects and site preparation are capitalized until the asset is brought to a working condition for its intended use. These costs include dismantling and site restoration costs to the extent these are recognized as a provision.

The cost of self-constructed assets includes the cost of materials, direct labour and an appropriate portion of normal overheads.

The costs of day-to-day servicing are recognized in profit or loss as incurred. These costs are more commonly referred to as "maintenance and repairs."

Financing costs directly associated with the construction or acquisition of qualifying assets are capitalized at interest rates relating to loans specifically raised for that purpose, or at the weighted average borrowing rate where the general pool of group borrowings is utilized. Capitalization of borrowing costs ceases when the asset is substantially complete.

The depreciation method, useful life and residual values are assessed annually.

Eastern Platinum Limited
Notes to the consolidated financial statements – years ended December 31, 2009 and 2008
(Expressed in thousands of U.S. dollars, except number of shares and per share amounts)

3.   Summary of significant accounting policies (continued)

(k)   *Property, plant and equipment (continued)*

(iii)   *Leased assets*

Leases in which the Company assumes substantially all risks and rewards of ownership are classified as finance leases. Assets held under finance leases are recognized at the lower of the fair value and the present value of the minimum lease payments at inception of the lease, less accumulated depreciation and impairment losses. Lease payments are accounted for as discussed in Note 3(r).

(iv)   *Subsequent Costs*

The cost of replacing part of an item within property, plant and equipment is recognized when the cost is incurred if it is probable that the future economic benefits will flow to the group and the cost of the item can be measured reliably. The carrying amount of the part that has been replaced is expensed. All other costs are recognized as an expense as incurred.

(v)   *Impairment*

The Company's tangible and intangible assets are reviewed for indications of impairment at each statement of financial position date. If indication of impairment exists, the asset's recoverable amount is estimated.

An impairment loss is recognized when the carrying amount of an asset, or its cash-generating unit, exceeds its recoverable amount. A cash-generating unit is the smallest identifiable group of assets that generates cash inflows that are largely independent of the cash inflows from other assets or groups of assets. Impairment losses are recognized in profit and loss for the period. Impairment losses recognized in respect of cash-generating units are allocated first to reduce the carrying amount of any goodwill allocated to cash-generating units and then to reduce the carrying amount of the other assets in the unit on a pro-rata basis.

The recoverable amount is the greater of the asset's fair value less costs to sell and value in use. In assessing value in use, the estimated future cash flows are discounted to their present value using a pre-tax discount rate that reflects current market assessments of the time value of money and the risks specific to the asset. For an asset that does not generate largely independent cash inflows, the recoverable amount is determined for the cash-generating unit to which the asset belongs.

(vi)   *Reversal of impairment*

An impairment loss is reversed if there is an indication that there has been a change in the estimates used to determine the recoverable amount. An impairment loss is reversed only to the extent that the asset's carrying amount does not exceed the carrying amount that would have been determined, net of depreciation or amortization, if no impairment loss had been recognized. An impairment loss with respect to goodwill is never reversed.

Eastern Platinum Limited

Notes to the consolidated financial statements – years ended December 31, 2009 and 2008
(Expressed in thousands of U.S. dollars, except number of shares and per share amounts)

3.   **Summary of significant accounting policies (continued)**

(l)   *Refining contract*

The Company sells substantially all its concentrate to one customer under the terms of an off-take or refining contract. The refining contract is amortized over the original life of the contract, estimated to be fifteen years, commencing in mid 2004. An evaluation of the carrying value of the contract is undertaken whenever events or changes in circumstances indicate that the carrying amount may not be recoverable.

(m)   *Inventories*

Inventories, comprising stockpiled ore and concentrate awaiting further processing and sale, are valued at the lower of cost and net realizable value. Consumables are valued at the lower of cost and net realizable value, with replacement cost used as the best available measure of net realizable value. Cost is determined using the weighted average method and includes direct mining expenditures and an appropriate portion of normal overhead expenditure. In the case of concentrate, direct concentrate costs are also included. Net realizable value is the estimated selling price in the ordinary course of business, less the estimated costs of completion and selling expenses. Obsolete, redundant and slow moving stores are identified and written down to net realizable values.

(n)   *Short-term investments*

Short-term investments are investments which are transitional or current in nature, with an original maturity greater than three months.

(o)   *Cash and cash equivalents*

Cash and cash equivalents consist of cash on hand, deposits in banks and highly liquid investments with an original maturity of three months or less.

(p)   *Financial assets*

Financial assets are classified into one of four categories:
- fair value through profit or loss ("FVTPL");
- held-to-maturity ("HTM");
- available for sale ("AFS"); and,
- loans and receivables.

The classification is determined at initial recognition and depends on the nature and purpose of the financial asset.

(i)   *FVTPL financial assets*

Financial assets are classified as FVTPL when the financial asset is held for trading or it is designated as FVTPL.

A financial asset is classified as held for trading if:
- it has been acquired principally for the purpose of selling in the near future;
- it is a part of an identified portfolio of financial instruments that the Company manages and has an actual pattern of short-term profit-taking; or
- it is a derivative that is not designated and effective as a hedging instrument.

Eastern Platinum Limited
Notes to the consolidated financial statements – years ended December 31, 2009 and 2008
(Expressed in thousands of U.S. dollars, except number of shares and per share amounts)

3.   Summary of significant accounting policies (continued)

(p)   Financial assets (continued)

(i)   FVTPL financial assets (continued)

Financial assets classified as FVTPL are stated at fair value with any resultant gain or loss recognized in profit or loss. The net gain or loss recognized incorporates any dividend or interest earned on the financial asset. The Company does not have any assets classified as FVTPL financial assets.

(ii)   HTM investments

HTM investments are recognized on a trade-date basis and are initially measured at fair value, including transaction costs. The Company does not have any assets classified as HTM investments.

(iii)   AFS financial assets

Short-term investments and other assets held by the Company are classified as AFS and are stated at fair value. Gains and losses arising from changes in fair value are recognized directly in equity in the investments revaluation reserve. To date, these gains and losses have not been significant due to the nature of the underlying investment. As a result, the assets' carrying values approximate their fair values. Impairment losses, interest calculated using the effective interest method and foreign exchange gains and losses on monetary assets, are recognized directly in profit or loss rather than equity. When an investment is disposed of or is determined to be impaired, the cumulative gain or loss previously recognized in the investments revaluation reserve is included in profit or loss for the period.

The fair value of AFS monetary assets denominated in a foreign currency is translated at the spot rate at the statement of financial position date. The change in fair value attributable to translation differences on amortized cost of the asset is recognized in profit or loss, while other changes are recognized in equity.

(iv)   Loans and receivables

Trade receivables, loans, and other receivables that have fixed or determinable payments that are not quoted in an active market are classified as loans and receivables.

Loans and receivables are initially recognized at the transaction value and subsequently carried at amortized cost less impairment losses. The impairment loss of receivables is based on a review of all outstanding amounts at period end. Bad debts are written off during the year in which they are identified. Interest income is recognized by applying the effective interest rate, except for short-term receivables when the recognition of interest would be immaterial.

(v)   Effective interest method

The effective interest method calculates the amortized cost of a financial asset and allocates interest income over the corresponding period. The effective interest rate is the rate that discounts estimated future cash receipts over the expected life of the financial asset, or, where appropriate, a shorter period, to the net carrying amount on initial recognition.

Eastern Platinum Limited

Notes to the consolidated financial statements – years ended December 31, 2009 and 2008
(Expressed in thousands of U.S. dollars, except number of shares and per share amounts)

3.   Summary of significant accounting policies (continued)

   (p)   Financial assets (continued)

   (v)   Effective interest method (continued)

   Income is recognized on an effective interest basis for debt instruments other than those financial assets classified as FVTPL.

   (vi)   Impairment of financial assets

   Financial assets, other than those at FVTPL, are assessed for indicators of impairment at each period end. Financial assets are impaired when there is objective evidence that, as a result of one or more events that occurred after the initial recognition of the financial asset, the estimated future cash flows of the investment have been impacted.

   Objective evidence of impairment could include the following:
   - significant financial difficulty of the issuer or counterparty;
   - default or delinquency in interest or principal payments; or
   - it has become probable that the borrower will enter bankruptcy or financial reorganization.

   For financial assets carried at amortized cost, the amount of the impairment is the difference between the asset's carrying amount and the present value of the estimated future cash flows, discounted at the financial asset's original effective interest rate.

   The carrying amount of all financial assets, excluding trade receivables, is directly reduced by the impairment loss. The carrying amount of trade receivables is reduced through the use of an allowance account. When a trade receivable is considered uncollectible, it is written off against the allowance account. Subsequent recoveries of amounts previously written off are credited against the allowance account. Changes in the carrying amount of the allowance account are recognized in profit or loss.

   With the exception of AFS equity instruments, if, in a subsequent period, the amount of the impairment loss decreases and the decrease relates to an event occurring after the impairment was recognized, the previously recognized impairment loss is reversed through profit or loss. On the date of impairment reversal, the carrying amount of the financial asset cannot exceed its amortized cost had impairment not been recognized.

   (vii)   Derecognition of financial assets

   A financial asset is derecognized when:
   - the contractual right to the asset's cash flows expire; or
   - if the Company transfers the financial asset and substantially all risks and rewards of ownership to another entity.

Eastern Platinum Limited
Notes to the consolidated financial statements – years ended December 31, 2009 and 2008
(Expressed in thousands of U.S. dollars, except number of shares and per share amounts)

3. Summary of significant accounting policies (continued)

(q) *Environmental rehabilitation*

The Company recognizes liabilities for statutory, contractual, constructive or legal obligations associated with the retirement of property, plant and equipment, when those obligations result from the acquisition, construction, development or normal operation of the assets. The net present value of future rehabilitation cost estimates arising from the decommissioning of plant and other site preparation work is capitalized to mining assets along with a corresponding increase in the rehabilitation provision in the period incurred. Discount rates using a pre-tax rate that reflect the time value of money are used to calculate the net present value. The rehabilitation asset is depreciated on the same basis as mining assets.

The Company's estimates of reclamation costs could change as a result of changes in regulatory requirements, discount rates and assumptions regarding the amount and timing of the future expenditures. These changes are recorded directly to mining assets with a corresponding entry to the rehabilitation provision. The Company's estimates are reviewed annually for changes in regulatory requirements, discount rates, effects of inflation and changes in estimates.

Changes in the net present value, excluding changes in the Company's estimates of reclamation costs, are charged to profit and loss for the period.

The net present value of restoration costs arising from subsequent site damage that is incurred on an ongoing basis during production are charged to the income statement in the period incurred.

The costs of rehabilitation projects that were included in the rehabilitation provision are recorded against the provision as incurred. The cost of ongoing current programs to prevent and control pollution is charged against profit and loss as incurred.

(r) *Leases*

(i) *The Company as lessor*

Rental income from operating leases is recognized on a straight-line basis over the term of the corresponding lease. Initial direct costs incurred in negotiating and arranging an operating lease are added to the carrying amount of the leased asset and recognized on a straight-line basis over the lease term.

(ii) *The Company as lessee*

Assets held under finance leases are recognized as assets of the Company at the lower of the fair value at the inception of the lease or the present value of the minimum lease payments. The corresponding liability is recognized as a finance lease obligation. Lease payments are apportioned between finance charges and reduction of the lease obligation to achieve a constant rate of interest on the remaining liability. Finance charges are charged to profit or loss, unless they are directly attributable to qualifying assets, in which case they are capitalized.

Operating lease payments are expensed on a straight-line basis over the term of the relevant lease. Incentives received upon entry into an operating lease are recognized straight-line over the lease term.

Eastern Platinum Limited
Notes to the consolidated financial statements – years ended December 31, 2009 and 2008
(Expressed in thousands of U.S. dollars, except number of shares and per share amounts)

3. Summary of significant accounting policies (continued)

(s) Provisions

Provisions are recorded when a present legal or constructive obligation exists as a result of past events where it is probable that an outflow of resources embodying economic benefits will be required to settle the obligation, and a reliable estimate of the amount of the obligation can be made.

The amount recognized as a provision is the best estimate of the consideration required to settle the present obligation at the statement of financial position date, taking into account the risks and uncertainties surrounding the obligation. Where a provision is measured using the cash flows estimated to settle the present obligation, its carrying amount is the present value of those cash flows. When some or all of the economic benefits required to settle a provision are expected to be recovered from a third party, the receivable is recognized as an asset if it is virtually certain that reimbursement will be received and the amount receivable can be measured reliably.

(t) Employee benefits

(i) Employee post-retirement obligations – defined contribution retirement plan

The Company's South African subsidiaries operate a defined contribution retirement plan for its employees. The pension plan is funded by payments from the employees and the subsidiaries and payments are charged to profit and loss for the period as incurred. The assets of the different plans are held by independently managed trust funds. The South African Pension Fund Act of 1956 governs these funds.

(ii) Leave pay

Employee entitlements to annual leave are recognized as they are earned by the employees. A provision, stated at current cost, is made for the estimated liability at period end.

(u) Financial liabilities and equity

Debt and equity instruments are classified as either financial liabilities or as equity in accordance with the substance of the contractual arrangement.

An equity instrument is any contract that evidences a residual interest in the assets of an entity after deducting all of its liabilities. Equity instruments issued by the Company are recorded at the proceeds received, net of direct issue costs.

Financial liabilities are classified as either financial liabilities at FVTPL or other financial liabilities.

(i) Other financial liabilities

Other financial liabilities are initially measured at fair value, net of transaction costs, and are subsequently measured at amortized cost using the effective interest method, with interest expense recognized on an effective yield basis.

The effective interest method is a method of calculating the amortized cost of a financial liability and of allocating interest expenses over the corresponding period. The effective interest rate is the rate that exactly discounts estimated future cash payments over the expected life of the financial liability, or, where appropriate, a shorter period, to the net carrying amount on initial recognition.

Eastern Platinum Limited
Notes to the consolidated financial statements – years ended December 31, 2009 and 2008
(Expressed in thousands of U.S. dollars, except number of shares and per share amounts)

3.   **Summary of significant accounting policies (continued)**

(u)   *Financial liabilities and equity (continued)*

(i)   *Other financial liabilities (continued)*

The Company has classified trade and other payables, short-term financial liabilities and long-term financial liabilities as other financial liabilities.

(ii)   *Derecognition of financial liabilities*

The Company derecognizes financial liabilities when, and only when, the Company's obligations are discharged, cancelled or they expire.

(v)   *Critical accounting estimates*

Critical accounting estimates are estimates and assumptions made by management that may result in material adjustments to the carrying amount of assets and liabilities within the next financial year.

(i)   *Impairment of property, plant and equipment*

Please refer to Note 8(d).

(ii)   *Rehabilitation provision*

The future value of the provision for environmental rehabilitation was determined using an inflation rate of 7.00% (December 31, 2008 – 5.78%) and an estimated life of mine of 18 years for Zandfontein and Maroelabult (December 31, 2008 – 14 years), 1 year for Kennedy's Vale (December 31, 2008 – 1 year) and 26 years for Spitzkop. A provision for environmental rehabilitation was not recognized for Spitzkop as at December 31, 2008. The provision has been discounted to present value at a discount rate of 8.39% (December 31, 2008 – 7.09%).

(w)   *Critical accounting judgments*

Critical accounting judgements are accounting policies that have been identified as being complex or involving subjective judgments or assessments.

(i)   *Determination of functional currency*

In accordance with IAS 21 *The Effects of Changes in Foreign Exchange Rates*, management determined that the functional currencies of Eastern Platinum Limited and its South African subsidiaries are the Canadian Dollar and South African Rand ("ZAR"), respectively.

(ii)   *Useful life of assets*

The Company engaged an independent third party engineering company in South Africa to assess the life of mine ("LOM") of Barplats Mines Limited ("Barplats") in December, 2009. At December 31, 2009 the remaining LOM for Barplats was assessed at 211 months (December 31, 2008 – 171 months) based on proven and probable ore reserves. The change in remaining mine life will be evaluated each year as the reserves move to the proven and probable category.

Eastern Platinum Limited
Notes to the consolidated financial statements – years ended December 31, 2009 and 2008
(Expressed in thousands of U.S. dollars, except number of shares and per share amounts)

3.   Summary of significant accounting policies (continued)

(w)   *Critical accounting judgments (continued)*

(iii)   *Depreciation rates*

The estimated maximum useful lives of property, plant and equipment are:

Mining assets owned	
Underground and other assets	Life of mine
Mine houses	50 years
Office buildings	20 years
Plant	Life of mine
Computer equipment	3 years
Mining assets leased	5 years
Mineral properties being depleted	Life of mine
Residential properties	50 years
Properties and land	50 years

(x)   *Accounting standards issued but not yet effective*

(i)   *Effective for annual periods beginning on or after July 1, 2009*

- IFRS 2 *Share Based Payments* (revised) – revision of scope
- IFRS 3 *Business Combinations* (revised) – revision of scope and amendments to accounting for business combinations
- IAS 27 *Consolidated and Separate Financial Statements* (revised) – amendments due to IFRS 3 *Business Combinations* revisions
- IAS 38 *Intangible Assets* (revised) - amendments due to IFRS 3 *Business Combinations* revisions and measuring the fair value of an intangible asset acquired in a business combination

(ii)   *Effective for annual periods beginning on or after January 1, 2010*

- IFRS 8 *Operating Segments* (revised) – disclosure of information about segment assets

(iii)   *Effective for annual periods beginning on or after January 1, 2011*

- IAS 24 *Related Party Disclosures* (revised) – clarification of the definition of a related party

(v)   *Effective for annual periods beginning on or after January 1, 2013*

- IFRS 9 *Financial Instruments (new)* – partial replacement of IAS 39. All of IAS 39 is expected to be replaced in its entirety by the end of 2010

The Company has not early adopted these revised standards and is currently assessing the impact that these standards will have on the consolidated financial statements.

Eastern Platinum Limited

Notes to the consolidated financial statements – years ended December 31, 2009 and 2008

(Expressed in thousands of U.S. dollars, except number of shares and per share amounts)

4. Subsidiaries and associates

(a) Subsidiaries

Details of the Company's subsidiaries at December 31, 2009 are as follows:

Name of subsidiary	Principal activity	Place of incorporation and operation	Proportion of ownership interest and voting power held		
			December 31, 2009	December 31, 2008	January 1, 2008
Eastern Platinum Holdings Limited	Holding company	BVI (i)	100%	100%	100%
Eastplats Holdings Limited	Holding company	BVI (i)	100%	100%	100%
Eastplats Acquisition Co. Ltd.	Holding company	BVI (i)	100%	100%	100%
Eastplats International Incorporated	Holding company	Barbados	100%	100%	100%
Royal Anthem Investments 134 (Pty) Ltd.	Holding company	South Africa	100%	100%	100%
Spitzkop Joint Venture	Mining	South Africa	93.37%	93.37%	93.37%
Barplats Investments Limited	Mining	South Africa	87.49%	87.49%	85.02%
Spitzkop Platinum (Pty) Ltd.	Mining	South Africa	86.74%	86.74%	86.74%
Mareesburg Joint Venture	Mining	South Africa	75.5%	75.5%	75.5%
Lion's Head Platinum (Pty) Ltd.	Holding company	South Africa	51%	51%	51%
Gubevu Consortium Investment Holdings (Pty) Ltd. (ii)	Holding company	South Africa	49.99%	49.99%	42.39%

(i)   British Virgin Islands ("BVI")

(ii)   The Company has determined that its investment in Gubevu Consortium Investment Holdings (Pty) Ltd. is a Special Purpose Entity.

(b) Associates

Details of the Company's associates at December 31, 2009 are as follows:

Name of associate	Principal activity	Place of incorporation and operation	Proportion of ownership interest and voting power held		
			December 31, 2009	December 31, 2008	January 1, 2008
Afrimineral Holdings (Pty) Ltd.	Holding company	South Africa	49%	49%	49%

Eastern Platinum Limited
Notes to the consolidated financial statements – years ended December 31, 2009 and 2008
(Expressed in thousands of U.S. dollars, except number of shares and per share amounts)

5.   Acquisitions

(a)   *Acquisitions during the year ended December 31, 2008*

On December 8, 2008 the Company acquired a further 2.47% of Barplats Investments Limited ("Barplats") to increase its direct and indirect interest to 87.49%. Of the 2.47% interest, the Company acquired 0.99% directly from Barplats through the acquisition of 12,155,814 shares issued from Barplats' treasury in exchange for net cash of $6,422. This increased the Company's direct ownership in Barplats from 74% to 74.99%. The Company acquired the other 1.48% indirectly from Gubevu through the acquisition of 1,519 shares in Gubevu in exchange for net cash of $33,167. This increased the Company's direct ownership in Gubevu from 42.39% to 49.99%, and the Company's indirect ownership in Barplats from 11.02% to 12.50%.

Following these acquisitions, the Company owns directly and indirectly 87.49% of Barplats, a PGM producing company in South Africa.

Purchase price		
Acquisition of 2.47% interest in Barplats		
Cash	$	39,589
	$	39,589
Net assets acquired		
Property, plant and equipment		39,589
	$	39,589

6.   Trade and other receivables

Trade and other receivables are comprised of the following:

	December 31, 2009	December 31, 2008	January 1, 2008
Trade receivables	$ 25,839	$ 1,450	$ 27,690
Allowance for doubtful debts	(74)	(85)	(111)
	25,765	1,365	27,579
Other receivables	2,316	8,066	4,981
Current tax receivable	1,057	-	-
	$ 29,138	$ 9,431	$ 32,560

(a)   *Aging of past due, but not impaired*

The average credit period of PGM sales is 4 months. The Company has the right to request up to a 90% advance on payment, payable 1 month subsequent to sale. The Company has financial risk management policies in place to ensure that all receivables are received within the pre-agreed credit terms.

Included in trade and other receivables are receivables with a carrying value of $276 (December 31, 2008 - Nil; January 1, 2008 - $1,201) that are past due but have not been provided for. For the years ended December 31, 2009 and 2008, substantially all of the Company's PGM production was sold to one customer and there was no significant change in the credit quality of this customer over that time. The past due amounts are considered recoverable.

Eastern Platinum Limited
Notes to the consolidated financial statements – years ended December 31, 2009 and 2008
(Expressed in thousands of U.S. dollars, except number of shares and per share amounts)

6.   Trade and other receivables (continued)

(a)   Aging of past due, but not impaired (continued)

	December 31, 2009	December 31, 2008	January 1, 2008
Less than 6 months	$ 276	$ -	$ -
6 months to less than 7 months	-	-	152
7 months to less than 8 months	-	-	751
8 months and greater	-	-	298
	$ 276	$ -	$ 1,201

(b)   Movement in the allowance for doubtful debts

	December 31, 2009	December 31, 2008
Opening balance	$ 85	$ 111
Impairment losses recognized on receivables	42	10
Amounts written off during the year as uncollectible	(26)	-
Amounts recovered during the year	(43)	(7)
Foreign exchange translation gains and losses	16	(29)
Closing balance	$ 74	$ 85

(c)   Aging of impaired trade receivables

	December 31, 2009	December 31, 2008	January 1, 2008
Less than 4 months	6	1	4
Greater than 4 months	68	84	107
	$ 74	$ 85	$ 111

At December 31, 2009, receivables of $74 (December 31, 2008 - $85; January 1, 2008 - $111) were impaired and provided for. These receivables were for rental income, and impairment was determined based on payment history.

7.   Inventories

	December 31, 2009	December 31, 2008	January 1, 2008
Consumables	$ 4,549	$ 3,509	$ 5,446
Ore and concentrate	276	372	1,442
	$ 4,825	$ 3,881	$ 6,888

Production costs for the year ended December 31, 2009 was $82,839 (December 31, 2008 - $79,961). Production costs represent the cost of inventories sold during the period. This expense includes Nil (December 31, 2008 - Nil) with regards to the write-down of inventory to net realizable value, and a reduction of Nil (December 31, 2008 - Nil) with regards to the reversal of write-downs.

At December 31, 2009 and 2008, no inventories have been pledged as security for liabilities.

Eastern Platinum Limited

Notes to the consolidated financial statements – years ended December 31, 2009 and 2008
(Expressed in thousands of U.S. dollars, except number of shares and per share amounts)

8. Property, plant and equipment

	Plant and equipment owned	Plant and equipment leased	Mineral properties being depleted	Mineral properties not being depleted	Residential properties	Properties and land	TOTAL
Cost							
Balance as at January 1, 2008	$ 267,210	$ 6,603	$ 136,818	$ 535,883	$ 8,903	$ 3,897	$ 959,314
Additions							
Assets acquired	133,650	-	-	4,985	1,543	2,742	142,920
Assets acquired through step acquisition	-	-	7,236	32,353	-	-	39,589
Foreign exchange movement	(85,313)	(1,711)	(35,374)	(129,106)	(2,492)	(1,340)	(255,336)
Balance as at December 31, 2008	$ 315,547	$ 4,892	$ 108,680	$ 444,115	$ 7,954	$ 5,299	$ 886,487
Assets acquired	27,593	-	(186)	921	88	331	28,747
Disposals	(1,510)	-	-	-	-	-	(1,510)
Foreign exchange movement	84,593	1,240	27,606	101,086	2,029	1,348	217,902
Balance as at December 31, 2009	$ 426,223	$ 6,132	$ 136,100	$ 546,122	$ 10,071	$ 6,978	$ 1,131,626
Accumulated depreciation and impairment losses							
Balance as at January 1, 2008	$ 114,993	$ 1,333	$ 8,840	$ 15,666	$ 2,198	$ 894	$ 143,924
Depreciation for the year	6,791	1,112	6,648	-	111	-	14,662
Impairment loss	-	-	-	297,285	-	-	297,285
Foreign exchange movement	(30,605)	(479)	(3,091)	(39,867)	(583)	(232)	(74,857)
Balance as at December 31, 2008	$ 91,179	$ 1,966	$ 12,397	$ 273,084	$ 1,726	$ 662	$ 381,014
Depreciation for the year	11,298	1,092	4,646	-	118	-	17,154
Foreign exchange movement	24,467	633	3,722	69,238	452	168	98,680
Balance as at December 31, 2009	$ 126,944	$ 3,691	$ 20,765	$ 342,322	$ 2,296	$ 830	$ 496,848
Carrying amounts							
At January 1, 2008	$ 152,217	$ 5,270	$ 127,978	$ 520,217	$ 6,705	$ 3,003	$ 815,390
At December 31, 2008	$ 224,368	$ 2,926	$ 96,283	$ 171,031	$ 6,228	$ 4,637	$ 505,473
At December 31, 2009	$ 299,279	$ 2,441	$ 115,335	$ 203,800	$ 7,775	$ 6,148	$ 634,778

Eastern Platinum Limited

Notes to the consolidated financial statements
(Expressed in thousands of U.S. dollars, except number of shares and per share amounts)

8. Property, plant and equipment

	Crocodile River Mine (a)	Kennedy's Vale Project (b)	Spitzkop PGM Project (c)	Mareesburg Project (c)	Other property plant and equipment	TOTAL
Cost						
Balance as at January 1, 2008	$ 423,315	$ 386,352	$ 121,443	$ 28,088	$ 116	$ 959,314
Additions						
Assets acquired	137,917	257	4,728	-	18	142,920
Assets acquired through step acquisition	7,236	32,353	-	-	-	39,589
Foreign exchange movement	(126,206)	(99,853)	(24,459)	(4,794)	(24)	(255,336)
Balance as at December 31, 2008	$ 442,262	$ 319,109	$ 101,712	$ 23,294	$ 110	$ 886,487
Additions						
Assets acquired	27,826	-	826	95	-	28,747
Disposals	(1,510)	-	-	-	-	(1,510)
Foreign exchange movement	116,798	80,908	16,456	3,722	18	217,902
Balance as at December 31, 2009	$ 585,376	$ 400,017	$ 118,994	$ 27,111	$ 128	$ 1,131,626
Accumulated depreciation and impairment losses						
Balance as at January 1, 2008	$ 128,223	$ 15,666	$ -	$ -	$ 35	$ 143,924
Depreciation for the period	14,609	-	-	-	53	14,662
Impairment loss	-	297,285	-	-	-	297,285
Foreign exchange movement	(34,977)	(39,867)	-	-	(13)	(74,857)
Balance as at December 31, 2008	$ 107,855	$ 273,084	$ -	$ -	$ 75	$ 381,014
Depreciation for the period	17,130	-	-	-	24	17,154
Foreign exchange movement	29,432	69,238	-	-	10	98,680
Balance as at December 31, 2009	$ 154,417	$ 342,322	$ -	$ -	$ 109	$ 496,848
Carrying amounts						
At January 1, 2008	$ 295,092	$ 370,686	$ 121,443	$ 28,088	$ 81	$ 815,390
At December 31, 2008	$ 334,407	$ 46,025	$ 101,712	$ 23,294	$ 35	$ 505,473
At December 31, 2009	$ 430,959	$ 57,695	$ 118,994	$ 27,111	$ 19	$ 634,778

Eastern Platinum Limited

Notes to the consolidated financial statements – years ended December 31, 2009 and 2008
(Expressed in thousands of U.S. dollars, except number of shares and per share amounts)

8.   Property, plant and equipment (continued)

(a)   Crocodile River Mine ("CRM")

The Company holds directly and indirectly 87.5% of CRM, which is located on the eastern portion of the western limb of the Bushveld Complex. The Maroelabult and Zandfontein sections are currently in production. Development of the Crocette section was on hold as at December 31, 2009.

(b)   Kennedy's Vale Project ("KV")

The Company holds directly and indirectly 87.5% of KV, which is located on the eastern limb of the Bushveld Complex, near Steelpoort in the Province of Mpumalanga. It comprises PGM mineral rights on five farms in the Steelpoort Valley.

(c)   Spitzkop PGM Project and Mareesburg Project

The Company holds directly and indirectly a 93.4% interest in the Spitzkop PGM Project and a 75.5% interest in the Mareesburg Project. The Company currently acts as the operator of both the Mareesburg Platinum Project and Spitzkop PGM Project, both located on the eastern limb of the Bushveld Complex. The development of these projects was on hold as at December 31, 2009.

(d)   Impairment of property, plant and equipment

During the year ended December 31, 2008, the significant decline in platinum group metal prices triggered an impairment assessment which resulted in an impairment of $297 million on Kennedy's Vale. Future cash flows were discounted to present value at the weighted average cost of capital of 9%.

The foreign exchange rate utilized in the model is ZAR9.51 = US$1.00.

The average forecast prices utilized in the impairment model were:

		2009	2010	2011	2012	2013 +
Platinum	US$/oz	950	1,020	1,055	1,155	1,180
Palladium	US$/oz	210	225	305	385	380
Rhodium	US$/oz	1,000	980	2,785	2,895	2,830
Gold	US$/oz	870	815	650	695	680
Iridium	US$/oz	270	295	345	350	340
Ruthenium	US$/oz	190	215	240	250	245
Nickel	US$/tonne	13,850	15,875	16,210	16,285	15,915
Copper	US$/tonne	5,180	5,550	5,505	4,265	4,170
Chrome	US$/tonne	380	382	400	400	400

9.   Refining Contract

During the year ended June 30, 2006, the Company acquired a 69% interest in Barplats and assigned a portion of the purchase price to the off-take contract governing the sales of Barplats' PGM concentrate production. The initial value of the contract was $17,939. During the year ended June 30, 2007, the Company acquired an additional 5% interest in Barplats resulting in an additional allocation to the contract of $4,802 for a total aggregate value of $22,741. During the year ended December 31, 2008, the Company acquired an additional 2.47% interest in Barplats. The acquisition did not affect the aggregate value of the contract. The value of the contract is amortized over the remaining term of the contract which is 9.5 years as at December 31, 2009.

Eastern Platinum Limited
Notes to the consolidated financial statements
(Expressed in thousands of U.S. dollars, except number of shares and per share amounts)

9. Refining Contract (continued)

Cost

Balance as at January 1, 2008	$ 22,741
Foreign exchange movement	(5,891)
Balance as at December 31, 2008	$ 16,850
Foreign exchange movement	4,272
Balance as at December 31, 2009	**$ 21,122**

Accumulated amortization

Balance as at January 1, 2008	$ 4,274
Amortization for the period	1,353
Foreign exchange movement	(1,270)
Balance as at December 31, 2008	$ 4,357
Amortization for the period	1,332
Foreign exchange movement	1,264
Balance as at December 31, 2009	**$ 6,953**

Carrying amounts

At January 1, 2008	$ 18,467
At December 31, 2008	$ 12,493
At December 31, 2009	**$ 14,169**

10. Other assets

Other assets consists of a money market fund investment that is classified as available-for-sale and serves as security for a guarantee issued to the Department of Minerals and Energy of South Africa in respect of the environmental rehabilitation liability (Note 14). Changes to other assets for the year ended December 31, 2009 are as follows:

Balance, January 1, 2008	$ 1,247
Service fees	(16)
Interest income	122
Foreign exchange movement	(336)
Balance, December 31, 2008	$ 1,017
Additional investment	811
Service fees	(6)
Interest income	123
Foreign exchange movement	337
Balance, December 31, 2009	**$ 2,282**

11. Accounts payable and accrued liabilities

	December 31, 2009	December 31, 2008	January 1, 2008
Trade payables	$ **9,932**	$ 9,976	$ 6,467
Accrued liabilities	**6,849**	16,767	14,544
Taxes payable	**-**	2,388	732
Other	**6,138**	7,598	1,224
	$ **22,919**	$ 36,729	$ 22,967

The average credit period of purchases is 1 month. The Company has financial risk management policies in place to ensure that all payables are paid within the pre-agreed credit terms.

Eastern Platinum Limited
Notes to the consolidated financial statements
(Expressed in thousands of U.S. dollars, except number of shares and per share amounts)

12.   Finance leases

Finance leases relate to mining vehicles with lease terms of 5 years payable half yearly in advance. The Company has the option to purchase the vehicles for a nominal amount at the conclusion of the lease agreements. The Company's obligations under finance leases are secured by the lessor's title to the leased assets. Interest is calculated at the South African prime rate plus 1%. At December 31, 2009, the finance leases are repayable in 3 semiannual installments (December 31, 2008 – 5) of $611 (December 31, 2008 - $544) and a top-up payment of $2,450 in December 2011. The fair value of the finance lease liabilities approximated carrying value.

(a)   Minimum lease payments

	December 31, 2009	December 31, 2008	January 1, 2008
No later than 1 year	$ **1,221**	$ 1,102	$ 1,565
Later than 1 year, but no later than 5 years	**3,061**	3,644	5,599
	4,282	4,746	7,164
Less: future finance charges	**(506)**	(1,083)	(1,359)
Present value of minimum lease payments	$ **3,776**	$ 3,663	$ 5,805

(b)   Present value of minimum lease payments

	December 31, 2009	December 31, 2008	January 1, 2008
No later than 1 year	$ **926**	$ 649	$ 748
Later than 1 year, but no later than 5 years	**2,850**	3,014	5,057
	$ **3,776**	$ 3,663	$ 5,805

13.   Loans

	Note	December 31, 2009	December 31, 2008	January 1, 2008
Short-term portion	(i)	$ -	$ 3,219	$ 3,837
Long-term portion	(i)	-	-	3,322
		$ -	$ 3,219	$ 7,159

(i)   Pursuant to the Company's acquisition of a 42.39% interest in Gubevu Consortium Investment Holdings (Pty) Ltd. ("Gubevu") during the year ended June 30, 2007, the Company entered into an agreement to pay an unrelated third party certain amounts that existed in the underlying Gubevu agreements as an obligation of Gubevu. As at June 30, 2007, the total payable was ZAR 55.4 million of which half was paid in June, 2008, and the remaining amount was paid in June, 2009. The fair value of loans approximated carrying value.

14.   Provision for environmental rehabilitation

Although the ultimate amount of the environmental rehabilitation provision is uncertain, the fair value of these obligations is based on information currently available, including closure plans and applicable regulations. Significant closure activities include land rehabilitation, demolition of buildings and mine facilities and other costs.

Eastern Platinum Limited
Notes to the consolidated financial statements
(Expressed in thousands of U.S. dollars, except number of shares and per share amounts)

14.   Provision for environmental rehabilitation (continued)

The liability for the environmental rehabilitation provision at December 31, 2009 is approximately ZAR 60 million ($8,152). The liability was determined using an inflation rate of 7.00% (December 31, 2008 – 5.78%) and an estimated life of mine of 18 years for Zandfontein and Maroelabult (December 31, 2008 – 14 years), 1 year for Kennedy's Vale (December 31, 2008 – 1 year) and 26 years for Spitzkop. A provision for environmental rehabilitation was not recognized for Spitzkop as at December 31, 2008. A discount rate of 8.39% was used (December 31, 2008 – 7.09%). A guarantee of $2,282 (December 31, 2008 - $1,017) has been issued to the Department of Minerals and Energy (Note 10). The guarantee will be utilized to cover expenses incurred to rehabilitate the mining area upon closure of the mine. The undiscounted value of this liability is approximately ZAR236.3 million ($31,885).

Changes to the environmental rehabilitation provision are as follows:

Balance, January 1, 2008	$ 6,224
Revision in estimates	554
Interest expense (Note 19)	491
Foreign exchange movement	(1,671)
Balance, December 31, 2008	$ 5,598
Revision in estimates	629
Interest expense (Note 19)	443
Foreign exchange movement	1,482
Balance, December 31, 2009	**$ 8,152**

15.   Income taxes

The income tax recognized in profit or loss comprises of:

	December 31, 2009	December 31, 2008
Deferred tax recovery relating to the origination and reversal of temporary differences	$ (1,623)	$ (79,730)
Effect of changes in tax rates	-	(5,383)
Total deferred income tax recovery	$ (1,623)	$ (85,113)

Eastern Platinum Limited
Notes to the consolidated financial statements
(Expressed in thousands of U.S. dollars, except number of shares and per share amounts)

15.   **Income taxes (continued)**

The provision for income taxes reported differs from the amounts computed by applying the cumulative Canadian federal and provincial income tax rates to the loss before tax provision due to the following:

	December 31, 2009	December 31, 2008
Statutory tax rate	**30.00%**	31.00%
Expected tax recovery on net income (loss) before income tax	$ **(120)**	$ (92,452)
Difference in tax rates between foreign jurisdictions and Canada	**(9,057)**	(15,534)
Items not deductible for income tax purposes	**1,986**	2,840
Effective change in tax rates	**-**	(5,383)
Tax losses not recognized	**5,568**	32,883
Change in tax estimates	**-**	(7,467)
Deferred income tax recovery	$ **(1,623)**	$ (85,113)

The approximate tax effect of each item that gives rise to the Company's deferred tax liabilities are as follows:

	December 31, 2009	December 31, 2008	January 1, 2008
Non-capital loss carry forwards	$ **5,175**	$ 5,160	$ 5,304
Share issue costs	**1,013**	2,119	2,919
Accumulated cost base difference on assets and other	**(36,877)**	(36,880)	(143,505)
Deferred receipts	**(5,461)**	1,213	(6,416)
Deferred tax liabilities before valuation allowance	$ **(36,150)**	$ (28,388)	$ (141,698)
Less valuation allowance	**(6,341)**	(7,226)	(8,334)
Total deferred tax liabilities	$ **(42,491)**	$ (35,614)	$ (150,032)

The movement between the opening and closing balances was recognized in profit or loss.

At December 31, 2009, the Company has non-capital losses of approximately Cdn$21,713 available to apply against future Canadian income for tax purposes. In South Africa, the Company has unredeemed capital expenditures available for utilization against future mining taxable income of approximately R3,127 million, and estimated assessable tax losses of approximately R9.3 million. The South African losses do not expire unless the Company's mining activities cease. The non-capital losses will expire as follows (in thousands of Canadian dollars):

Eastern Platinum Limited
Notes to the consolidated financial statements
(Expressed in thousands of U.S. dollars, except number of shares and per share amounts)

15. Income taxes (continued)

	2009 Cdn$ (000's)	2008 Cdn$ (000's)
2011	$ 1,115	$ 1,115
2012	272	272
2013	1,592	1,595
2014	916	916
2025	3,224	3,101
2026	6,105	6,106
2027	3,393	2,551
2028	4,217	4,614
2029	879	-
	$21,713	$20,270

The Company does not have any capital losses available to apply against future capital gains in Canada.

The Company is subject to assessments by various taxation authorities which may interpret tax legislation and tax filing positions differently from the Company. The Company provides for such differences when it is probable that a taxation authority will not sustain the Company's filing position and the amount of the tax exposure can be reasonably estimated. As at December 31, 2009, no provisions have been made in the financial statements for any estimated tax liability.

16. Commitments

The Company has committed to capital expenditures on projects of approximately ZAR37 million ($4,959) as at December 31, 2009 (December 31, 2008 – ZAR 259 million, $27,925).

17. Issued capital

(a) *Authorized*

- Unlimited number of preferred redeemable, voting, non-participating shares without nominal or par value,

- Unlimited number of common shares with no par value.

(b) *Share options*

The Company has an incentive plan (the "2008 Plan"), approved by the Company's shareholders at its annual general meeting held on June 4, 2008, under which options to purchase common shares may be granted to its directors, officers, employees and others at the discretion of the Board of Directors. Under the terms of the 2008 Plan, 75 million common shares are reserved for issuance upon the exercise of options. All outstanding options at June 4, 2008 granted under the Company's previous plan (the "2005 Plan") will continue to exist under the 2008 Plan provided that the fundamental terms governing such options will be deemed to be those under the 2005 Plan. Upon adoption of the 2008 Plan, options to purchase a total of 27,525,000 common shares were available for grant under the 2008 Plan, representing 75,000,000 less the 47,475,000 outstanding options at June 4, 2008 granted under the 2005 Plan.

Eastern Platinum Limited
Notes to the consolidated financial statements
(Expressed in thousands of U.S. dollars, except number of shares and per share amounts)

17.   Issued capital (continued)

(b)   *Share options (continued)*

Under the 2008 Plan, each option granted shall be for a term not exceeding five years from the date of being granted and the vesting period is determined based on the discretion of the Board of Directors. The option exercise price is set at the date of the grant and cannot be less than the closing market price of the Company's common shares on the Toronto Stock Exchange on the day immediately preceding the day of the grant of the option.

(i)   *Movements in share options during the year*

The changes in share options during the years ended December 31, 2009 and 2008 were as follows:

	December 31, 2009		December 31, 2008	
	Number of options	**Weighted average exercise price**	Number of options	Weighted average exercise price
		Cdn$		Cdn$
Balance outstanding, beginning of year	**64,746,000**	**1.52**	46,360,000	1.94
Options granted	**695,000**	**0.57**	19,856,000	0.55
Options exercised	**(535,999)**	**0.32**	(845,000)	1.26
Options forfeited	**(5,329,167)**	**2.00**	(625,000)	1.76
Balance outstanding, end of year	**59,575,834**	**1.48**	64,746,000	1.52

(ii)   *Fair value of share options granted in the year*

The fair value of each option granted is estimated at the time of the grant using the Black-Scholes option pricing model with weighted average assumptions for grants as follows:

	2009			
	February 11	**June 30**	**November 3**	**Weighted average**
Exercise price	**Cdn$0.32**	**Cdn$0.52**	**Cdn$0.76**	**Cdn$0.57**
Closing market price on day preceding date of grant	**Cdn$0.32**	**Cdn$0.52**	**Cdn$0.76**	**Cdn$0.57**
Grant date share price	**Cdn$0.38**	**Cdn$0.52**	**Cdn$0.81**	**Cdn$0.59**
Risk-free interest rate	1.69%	1.84%	1.86%	1.83%
Expected life	**3 years**	**3 years**	**3 years**	**3 years**
Annualized volatility	78%	79%	82%	80%
Dividend rate	0%	0%	0%	0%
Grant date fair value	**Cdn$0.21**	**Cdn$0.27**	**Cdn$0.45**	**Cdn$0.32**

Exercise price is the closing market price on the day preceding the date the options were granted, as defined by the Company's 2008 share option plan.

Grant date share price is the closing market price on the day the options were granted.

Eastern Platinum Limited
Notes to the consolidated financial statements
(Expressed in thousands of U.S. dollars, except number of shares and per share amounts)

17. Issued capital (continued)

(b) Share options (continued)

(ii) Fair value of share options granted in the year (continued)

Expected volatility is based on the historical share price volatility since Eastern Platinum Limited completed its acquisition of Barplats Investment Limited on May 2, 2006, or for 3 years prior to the date of grant, whichever is shorter.

	2008			
	February 19	March 26	December 18	Weighted average
Exercise price	Cdn$3.38	Cdn$3.38	Cdn$0.32	**Cdn$0.55**
Closing market price on day preceding date of grant	Cdn$3.38	Cdn$3.32	Cdn$0.32	**Cdn$0.55**
Grant date share price	Cdn$3.38	Cdn$3.38	Cdn$0.30	**Cdn$0.53**
Risk-free interest rate	3.24%	2.67%	1.42%	**1.54%**
Expected life	3 years	3 years	3 years	**3 years**
Annualized volatility	49%	49%	76%	**74%**
Dividend rate	0%	0%	0%	**0%**
Grant date fair value	Cdn$1.22	Cdn$1.20	Cdn$0.15	**Cdn$0.23**

(iii) Share options exercised during the year

The following table outlines share options exercised during the year:

Date of issue	Number of options exercised	Exercise date	Closing share price at exercise date
December 18, 2008	6,000	May 8, 2009	$ 0.55
December 18, 2008	15,000	May 22, 2009	0.45
December 18, 2008	33,333	June 3, 2009	0.65
December 18, 2008	10,000	September 22, 2009	0.59
December 18, 2008	15,000	November 4, 2009	0.83
December 18, 2008	44,999	November 13, 2009	0.84
December 18, 2008	20,000	November 16, 2009	0.91
December 18, 2008	266,667	November 23, 2009	1.00
December 18, 2008	10,000	November 26, 2009	0.96
December 18, 2008	115,000	December 23, 2009	0.88
	535,999		$ 0.90

Eastern Platinum Limited
Notes to the consolidated financial statements
(Expressed in thousands of U.S. dollars, except number of shares and per share amounts)

17.   Issued capital (continued)

(b)   *Share options (continued)*

(iv)   *Share options outstanding at the end of the year*

The following table summarizes information concerning outstanding and exercisable options at December 31, 2009:

Options outstanding	Options exercisable	Exercise price	Remaining Contractual Life (Years)	Expiry date
		Cdn$		
6,725,000	6,725,000	1.70	1.40	May 24, 2011
250,000	250,000	1.70	1.91	November 27, 2011
19,987,500	19,987,500	1.82	2.19	March 7, 2012
17,478,334	16,598,334	0.32	3.97	December 18, 2013
60,000	20,000	0.32	4.12	February 11, 2014
400,000	400,000	0.52	4.50	June 30, 2014
215,000	71,667	0.76	4.84	November 3, 2014
13,740,000	13,740,000	2.31	7.77	October 5, 2017
90,000	90,000	2.50	7.96	December 12, 2017
460,000	440,000	3.38	8.15	February 20, 2018
170,000	130,000	3.38	8.24	March 27, 2018
59,575,834	58,452,501	1.50	4.01	

(c)   *Share purchase warrants*

The changes in warrants during the years ended December 31, 2009 and 2008 were as follows:

	December 31, 2009		December 31, 2008	
	Number of warrants	**Weighted average exercise price**	Number of warrants	Weighted average exercise price
		Cdn$		Cdn$
Balance outstanding, beginning of year	**58,485,996**	**1.80**	71,248,050	1.83
Warrants exercised	**-**	**-**	(10,824,077)	1.97
Warrants expired	**(58,485,996)**	**1.80**	(1,937,977)	2.00
Balance outstanding, end of year	**-**	**-**	58,485,996	1.80

Eastern Platinum Limited
Notes to the consolidated financial statements
(Expressed in thousands of U.S. dollars, except number of shares and per share amounts)

18. Non-controlling interest

The non-controlling interests are comprised of the following:

Balance, January 1, 2008	$	23,133
Non-controlling interests' share of loss in Barplats		(717)
Non-controlling interests' share of interest on advances to Gubevu		(3,018)
Foreign exchange movement		(7,396)
Balance, December 31, 2008	$	12,002
Non-controlling interests' share of loss in Barplats		(1,908)
Non-controlling interests' share of interest on advances to Gubevu		(2,520)
Foreign exchange movement		2,467
Balance, December 31, 2009	**$**	**10,041**

19. Finance costs

	December 31, 2009		December 31, 2008
Interest on revenue advances	$ **482**	$	1,784
Interest on finance leases	**377**		604
Interest on provision for environmental rehabilitation	**443**		491
Interest on tax	**2**		395
Other interest	**387**		451
	$ **1,691**	$	3,725

20. Diluted earnings per share

The weighted average number of ordinary shares for the purposes of diluted earnings per share reconciles to the weighted average number of ordinary shares used in the calculation of basic earnings per share as follows:

	December 31, 2009	December 31, 2008
	(in thousands)	
Weighted average number of ordinary shares used in the calculation of basic earnings per share	**680,577**	677,117
Shares deemed to be issued for no consideration in respect of:		
Options	**7,213**	-
Weighted average number of ordinary shares used in the calculation of diluted earnings per share	**687,790**	677,117

The following potential ordinary shares, outstanding at December 31, 2009, are anti-dilutive and are therefore excluded from the weighted average number of ordinary shares for the purposes of diluted earnings per share:

	December 31, 2009	December 31, 2008
	(in thousands)	
Options	**41,434**	61,053
Warrants	**-**	58,486

Eastern Platinum Limited
Notes to the consolidated financial statements
(Expressed in thousands of U.S. dollars, except number of shares and per share amounts)

21.   Retirement benefit plans

The Barplats Provident Fund is an independent, defined contribution plan administered by Liberty Life Limited in South Africa. The costs associated with the defined contribution plan included in net profit (loss) were $2,705 (December 31, 2008 - $2,308). The total number of employees in the plan at December 31, 2009 was 1,800 (December 31, 2008 – 1,460).

22.   Related party transactions

Balances and transactions between the Company and its subsidiaries have been eliminated on consolidation and are not disclosed in this note. Details of the transactions between the Company and other related parties are disclosed below.

(a)   Trading transactions

The Company's related parties consist of companies owned by executive officers and directors as follows:

	Nature of transactions
Andrews PGM Consulting	Consulting
Buccaneer Management Inc.	Management
Jazz Financial Ltd.	Management
Maluti Services Limited	General and administrative
Xiste Consulting Ltd.	Management

The Company incurred the following fees and expenses in the normal course of operations in connection with companies owned by key management and directors. Expenses have been measured at the exchange amount which is determined on a cost recovery basis.

	Note	December 31, 2009	December 31, 2008
Consulting fees	(i)	$ 232	$ 90
General and administrative expenses		48	254
Management fees		1,429	1,205
		$ 1,709	$ 1,549

(i)   The Company paid fees to a private company controlled by a director of the Company for consulting services performed outside of his capacity as a director.

(ii)   Amounts due to related parties are unsecured, non-interest bearing and due on demand. Accounts payable at December 31, 2009 included $510 (December 31, 2008 - $35) which were due to private companies controlled by officers of the Company.

(b)   Compensation of key management personnel

The remuneration of directors and other members of key management personnel during the years ended December 31, 2009 and 2008 were as follows:

	Note	December 31, 2009	December 31, 2008
Salaries and directors' fees	(i)	$ 2,695	$ 2,133
Share-based payments	(ii)	93	2,374
		$ 2,788	$ 4,507

Eastern Platinum Limited
Notes to the consolidated financial statements
(Expressed in thousands of U.S. dollars, except number of shares and per share amounts)

22.   **Related party transactions (continued)**

    (b)   *Compensation of key management personnel (continued)*

       (i)   Salaries and directors' fees include consulting and management fees disclosed in Note 22(a).

       (ii)   Share-based payments are the fair value of options granted to key management personnel, translated at the grant date foreign exchange rate.

       (iii)   Key management personnel were not paid post-employment benefits, termination benefits, or other long-term benefits during the years ended December 31, 2009 and 2008.

23.   **Segmented information**

    (a)   Operating segment - The Company's operations are primarily directed towards the acquisition, exploration and production of platinum group metals in South Africa.

    (b)   Geographic segments - The Company's assets, revenues and expenses by geographic areas for the years ended December 31, 2009 and 2008 are as follows:

Eastern Platinum Limited

Notes to the consolidated financial statements – years ended December 31, 2009 and 2008
(Expressed in thousands of U.S. dollars, except number of shares and per share amounts)

23. Segmented Information (continued)

(b) Geographic segments (continued)

	Crocodile River Mine	Kennedy's Vale	Spitzkop	Mareesburg	Other	Total South Africa	Canada	TOTAL
				December 31, 2009				
Current assets	$ 36,749	$ 176	$ 1,509	$ 45	$ 1,003	$ 39,482	$16,139	$ 55,621
Property, plant and equipment	430,959	57,695	118,994	27,111	-	634,759	19	634,778
Refining contract	14,169	-	-	-	-	14,169	-	14,169
Other Assets	2,282	-	-	-	-	2,282	-	2,282
	$ 484,159	$ 57,871	$ 120,503	$ 27,156	$ 1,003	$ 690,692	$16,158	$706,850
Property, plant and equipment expenditures	$ 27,826	$ -	$ 826	$ 95	$ -	$ 28,747	$ -	$ 28,747
Sale of property, plant and equipment	(1,510)	-	-	-	-	(1,510)	-	(1,510)
Revenue	$ 111,365	$ -	$ -	$ -	$ -	$ 111,365	$ -	$ 111,365
Production costs	(82,839)	-	-	-	-	(82,839)	-	(82,839)
Depreciation and amortization	(17,130)	-	-	-	-	(17,130)	(24)	(17,154)
General and administrative expenses	(3,397)	(2,286)	(510)	(157)	(26)	(6,376)	(4,152)	(10,528)
Share-based payment	(489)	-	-	-	-	(489)	(93)	(582)
Interest income	1,388	-	38	-	-	1,426	360	1,786
Finance costs	(1,547)	-	-	-	-	(1,547)	(144)	(1,691)
Foreign exchange gain (loss)	28	-	-	-	-	28	(786)	(758)
Profit (loss) before income taxes	$ 7,379	$ (2,286)	$ (472)	$ (157)	$ (26)	$ 4,438	$ (4,839)	$ (401)

Eastern Platinum Limited

Notes to the consolidated financial statements
(Expressed in thousands of U.S. dollars, except number of shares and per share amounts)

23. Segmented Information (continued)

(b) Geographic segments (continued)

December 31, 2008

	Crocodile River Mine	Kennedy's Vale	Spitzkop	Mareesburg	Other	Total South Africa	Canada	TOTAL
Current assets	$ 13,636	$ 2,047	$ 1,839	$ 132	$ 1	$ 17,655	$ 56,720	$ 74,375
Property, plant and equipment	334,407	46,025	101,712	23,294	-	505,438	35	505,473
Refining contract	12,493	-	-	-	-	12,493	-	12,493
Other Assets	1,017	-	-	-	-	1,017	-	1,017
	$ 361,553	$ 48,072	$ 103,551	$ 23,426	$ 1	$ 536,603	$ 56,755	$ 593,358
Property, plant and equipment expenditures	$ 137,917	$ 257	$ 4,728	$ -	$ 18	$ 142,920	$ -	$ 142,920
Sale of property, plant and equipment	-	-	-	-	-	-	-	-
Revenue	$ 114,681	$ -	$ -	$ -	$ -	$ 114,681	$ -	$ 114,681
Production costs	(79,961)	-	-	-	-	(79,961)	-	(79,961)
Depreciation and amortization	(14,609)	-	-	-	-	(14,609)	(53)	(14,662)
Impairment	-	(297,285)	-	-	-	(297,285)	-	(297,285)
General and administrative expenses	(12,317)	(1,415)	(588)	-	(18)	(14,338)	(5,103)	(19,441)
Share-based payment	(1,979)	-	-	-	-	(1,979)	(2,646)	(4,625)
Interest income	3,770	42	7	-	-	3,819	5,125	8,944
Finance costs	(3,068)	(86)	-	-	-	(3,154)	(571)	(3,725)
Foreign exchange gain (loss)	(8)	-	343	55	2	392	(2,547)	(2,155)
Profit (loss) before income taxes	$ 6,509	$(298,744)	$ (238)	$ 55	$ (16)	$ (292,434)	$ (5,795)	$ (298,229)

For the years ended December 31, 2009 and 2008, substantially all of the Company's PGM production was sold to one customer.

Eastern Platinum Limited
Notes to the consolidated financial statements
(Expressed in thousands of U.S. dollars, except number of shares and per share amounts)

24.   Financial instruments

(a)   *Management of capital risk*

The capital structure of the Company consists of equity attributable to common shareholders, comprising issued capital, equity-settled employee benefits reserve, deficit and currency translation adjustment. The Company's objectives when managing capital are to: (i) preserve capital, (ii) obtain the best available net return, and (iii) maintain liquidity.

The Company manages the capital structure and makes adjustments to it in light of changes in economic conditions and the risk characteristics of the underlying assets. To maintain or adjust the capital structure, the Company may attempt to issue new shares.

The Company is not subject to externally imposed capital requirements.

(b)   *Categories of financial instruments*

	December 31, 2009	December 31, 2008	January 1, 2008
Financial assets			
Cash and cash equivalents	$ 7,249	$ 25,806	$ 18,818
Loans and receivables			
Trade receivables	29,138	9,431	32,560
Available for sale financial assets			
Short-term investments	14,409	35,257	171,038
Other assets	2,282	1,017	1,247
	$ 53,078	$ 71,511	$ 223,663
Financial liabilities			
Other financial liabilities			
Accounts payable and accrued liabilities	$ 22,919	$ 36,729	$ 22,967
Current portion of finance leases	926	649	748
Current loans	–	3,219	3,837
Long-term portion of finance leases	2,850	3,014	5,057
Long-term loans	–	–	3,322
	$ 26,695	$ 43,611	$ 35,931

(c)   *Fair value of financial instruments*

(i)   *Fair value estimation of financial instruments*

The fair value of financial instruments traded in active markets is based on quoted market prices at the balance sheet date.

The fair values of cash and cash equivalents, short-term investments, trade receivables and accounts payable approximate their carrying values due to the short-term to maturities of these financial instruments.

The fair value of short-term debt was determined using discounted cash flows at prevailing market rates and the fair value is considered to approximate carrying value.

Eastern Platinum Limited
Notes to the consolidated financial statements
(Expressed in thousands of U.S. dollars, except number of shares and per share amounts)

24.   Financial instruments (continued)

(c)   *Fair value of financial instruments (continued)*

(ii)   *Fair value measurements recognized in the statement of financial position*

Financial instruments that are measured subsequent to initial recognition at fair value are grouped into a hierarchy based on the degree to which the fair value is observable. Level 1 fair value measurements are derived from unadjusted, quoted prices in active markets for identical assets or liabilities. Level 2 fair value measurements are derived from inputs other than quoted prices included within Level 1 that are observable for the asset or liability directly or indirectly. Level 3 fair value measurements are derived from valuation techniques that include inputs for the asset or liability that are not based on observable market data.

The Company's short-term investments and other assets are measured subsequent to initial recognition at fair value and are Level 2 financial instruments at December 31, 2009. There were no transfers between levels during the year ended December 31, 2009.

(d)   *Reclassification of financial assets*

During the year ended December 31, 2008, a short-term investment classified as held-to-maturity was sold prior to its maturity date. This tainted the Company's held-to-maturity investments and resulted in the reclassification of the Company's held-to-maturity investments, short-term investments ($35,257) and other assets ($1,017), to available for sale financial assets. The short-term investments were re-measured at fair value with any gains or losses recorded directly to other comprehensive income. The impact of the reclassification was insignificant.

(e)   *Financial risk management*

The Company's financial instruments are exposed to certain financial risks, including currency risk, interest rate risk, price risk, credit risk and liquidity risk. The Company's exposure to these risks and its methods of managing the risks remain consistent.

(i)   *Currency risk*

The Company is exposed to the financial risk related to the fluctuation of foreign exchange rates. The Company's revenues are based on US dollar PGM prices, but the Company receives revenue in South African Rand. A significant change in the currency exchange rates between the South African Rand relative to the US dollar could have an effect on the Company's results of operations, financial position and cash flows. The Company has not entered into any derivative financial instruments to manage exposures to currency fluctuations.

The carrying amount of the Company's foreign-currency denominated monetary assets at December 31, 2009, is as follows:

	December 31, 2009		December 31, 2008	
	(000's Cdn)	(000's ZAR)	(000's Cdn$)	(000's ZAR)
Financial assets				
Loans and receivables	320	213,701	552	83,410

Eastern Platinum Limited
Notes to the consolidated financial statements
(Expressed in thousands of U.S. dollars, except number of shares and per share amounts)

24.   Financial instruments (continued)

   (e)   *Financial risk management (continued)*

      (i)   *Currency risk (continued)*

The sensitivity of the Company's net earnings and other comprehensive income due to changes in the exchange rate between the South African Rand and the United States dollar, and between the Canadian dollar and the United States dollar are summarized in the tables below. The increase (decrease) in other comprehensive income is due to the effect of the exchange rate on financial instruments.

	Year ended Dec. 31, 2009	
	10% increase in ZAR to USD FX rate	10% decrease in ZAR to USD FX rate
Increase (decrease) in other comprehensive income	(2,621)	3,204

	Year ended Dec. 31, 2009	
	10% increase in Cdn to USD FX rate	10% decrease in Cdn to USD FX rate
Increase (decrease) in other comprehensive income	(2,914)	2,914

      (ii)   *Interest rate risk*

Interest rate risk is the risk that the fair value or future cash flows of a financial instrument will fluctuate because of changes in market interest rates. The Company is exposed to interest rate risk on its short-term investments. The risk that the Company will realize a loss as a result of a decline in the fair value of short-term investments is limited because these investments, although available for sale, are generally not sold before maturity. The Company monitors its exposure to interest rates and has not entered into any derivative financial instruments to manage this risk. A sensitivity analysis has not been completed for interest rate risk as it is immaterial.

      (iii)   *Price risk*

The Company is exposed to price risk with respect to fluctuations in the prices of platinum group metals. These fluctuations directly affect revenues and trade receivables. As at December 31, 2009, the Company's financial assets subject to metal price risk consist of trade receivables of $25,765 (December 31, 2008 - $1,365). Historically, the Company has not entered into any derivative financial instruments to manage exposures to price fluctuations. No such derivative financial instruments existed at December 31, 2009 and 2008.

The Company has not included a sensitivity analysis of price risk at year-end as it does not reflect the exposure experienced during the twelve months ended December 31, 2009. Presenting such an analysis would be misleading.

Eastern Platinum Limited
Notes to the consolidated financial statements
(Expressed in thousands of U.S. dollars, except number of shares and per share amounts)

24.   Financial instruments (continued)

(e)   Financial risk management (continued)

(iv)   Credit risk

Credit risk is the risk of an unexpected loss if a customer or third party to a financial instrument fails to meet its contractual obligations, and arises principally from the Company's trade receivables. The carrying value of the financial assets represents the maximum credit exposure.

The Company currently sells substantially all of its concentrate production to one customer under an off-take contract. At December 31, 2009, the Company had receivable balances associated with this one customer of $25,765 (December 31, 2008 - $1,365). The loss of this customer or unexpected termination of the off-take contract could have a material adverse effect on the Company's results of operations, financial condition and cash flows. The Company has not experienced any bad debts with this customer.

The Company minimizes credit risk by reviewing the credit risk of the counterparty to the arrangement and has made any necessary provisions related to credit risk at December 31, 2009.

(v)   Liquidity risk

Liquidity risk is the risk that the Company will not be able to meet its financial obligations as they fall due. The Company has a planning and budgeting process in place to help determine the funds required to support the Company's normal operating requirements on an ongoing basis and its expansionary plans. The Company ensures that there are sufficient funds to meet its short-term business requirements, taking into account its anticipated cash flows from operations and its holdings of cash and cash equivalents.

The Company's policy is to invest its excess cash in highly liquid, fully guaranteed, bank-sponsored instruments. The Company staggers the maturity dates of its investments over different time periods and dates to minimize exposure to interest rate changes. This strategy remains unchanged from 2008.

In the normal course of business, the Company enters into contracts that give rise to commitments for future minimum payments. The following table summarizes the Company's significant commitments and corresponding maturities.

	December 31, 2009		
	Total	<1 year	1-3
Accounts payable	$ 22,919	$ 22,919	$ -
Finance leases	4,282	1,221	3,061
Purchase commitments	881	881	-
Capital expenditures	4,077	4,077	-
	$ 32,159	$ 29,098	$ 3,061

Eastern Platinum Limited
Notes to the consolidated financial statements
(Expressed in thousands of U.S. dollars, except number of shares and per share amounts)

24.   Financial instruments (continued)

(e)   *Financial risk management (continued)*

(v)   *Liquidity risk (continued)*

	December 31, 2008		
	Total	<1 year	1-3 years
Accounts payable	$ 36,729	$ 36,729	$ -
Finance leases	4,746	1,102	3,644
Loans	3,219	3,219	-
Purchase commitments	4,751	4,751	-
Capital expenditures	23,174	22,725	449
	$ 72,619	$ 68,526	$ 4,093

	January 1, 2008		
	Total	<1 year	1-3 years
Accounts payable	$ 22,967	$ 22,967	$ -
Finance leases	7,164	1,565	5,599
Loans	7,159	3,837	3,322
Purchase commitments	2,407	2,407	-
Capital expenditures	22,741	22,741	-
	$ 62,438	$ 53,517	$ 8,921

Eastern Platinum Limited
Notes to the consolidated financial statements
(Expressed in thousands of U.S. dollars, except number of shares and per share amounts)

26.   Events after the reporting period

From January 1, 2010 to March 24, 2010:

(a)   The Company granted 2,231,000 options with an exercise price of Cdn$1.30 per share expiring on January 18, 2015.

(b)   444,831 stock options were exercised, of which 83,333 were exercised by way of cash payment at a weighted average exercise price of Cdn$0.32 for proceeds of Cdn$27, and 361,498 were exercised by way of stock appreciation rights at a weighted average exercise price of Cdn$0.35.

Table A-1

FUTURE VALUE OF 1
(FUTURE VALUE OF A SINGLE SUM)

$$FVF_{n,\,i} = (1+i)^n$$

(n) periods	2%	2½%	3%	4%	5%	6%	8%	9%	10%	11%	12%	15%
1	1.02000	1.02500	1.03000	1.04000	1.05000	1.06000	1.08000	1.09000	1.10000	1.11000	1.12000	1.15000
2	1.04040	1.05063	1.06090	1.08160	1.10250	1.12360	1.16640	1.18810	1.21000	1.23210	1.25440	1.32250
3	1.06121	1.07689	1.09273	1.12486	1.15763	1.19102	1.25971	1.29503	1.33100	1.36763	1.40493	1.52088
4	1.08243	1.10381	1.12551	1.16986	1.21551	1.26248	1.36049	1.41158	1.46410	1.51807	1.57352	1.74901
5	1.10408	1.13141	1.15927	1.21665	1.27628	1.33823	1.46933	1.53862	1.61051	1.68506	1.76234	2.01136
6	1.12616	1.15969	1.19405	1.26532	1.34010	1.41852	1.58687	1.67710	1.77156	1.87041	1.97382	2.31306
7	1.14869	1.18869	1.22987	1.31593	1.40710	1.50363	1.71382	1.82804	1.94872	2.07616	2.21068	2.66002
8	1.17166	1.21840	1.26677	1.36857	1.47746	1.59385	1.85093	1.99256	2.14359	2.30454	2.47596	3.05902
9	1.19509	1.24886	1.30477	1.42331	1.55133	1.68948	1.99900	2.17189	2.35795	2.55803	2.77308	3.51788
10	1.21899	1.28008	1.34392	1.48024	1.62889	1.79085	2.15892	2.36736	2.59374	2.83942	3.10585	4.04556
11	1.24337	1.31209	1.38423	1.53945	1.71034	1.89830	2.33164	2.58043	2.85312	3.15176	3.47855	4.65239
12	1.26824	1.34489	1.42576	1.60103	1.79586	2.01220	2.51817	2.81267	3.13843	3.49845	3.89598	5.35025
13	1.29361	1.37851	1.46853	1.66507	1.88565	2.13293	2.71962	3.06581	3.45227	3.88328	4.36349	6.15279
14	1.31948	1.41297	1.51259	1.73168	1.97993	2.26090	2.93719	3.34173	3.79750	4.31044	4.88711	7.07571
15	1.34587	1.44830	1.55797	1.80094	2.07893	2.39656	3.17217	3.64248	4.17725	4.78459	5.47357	8.13706
16	1.37279	1.48451	1.60471	1.87298	2.18287	2.54035	3.42594	3.97031	4.59497	5.31089	6.13039	9.35762
17	1.40024	1.52162	1.65285	1.94790	2.29202	2.69277	3.70002	4.32763	5.05447	5.89509	6.86604	10.76126
18	1.42825	1.55966	1.70243	2.02582	2.40662	2.85434	3.99602	4.71712	5.55992	6.54355	7.68997	12.37545
19	1.45681	1.59865	1.75351	2.10685	2.52695	3.02560	4.31570	5.14166	6.11591	7.26334	8.61276	14.23177
20	1.48595	1.63862	1.80611	2.19112	2.65330	3.20714	4.66096	5.60441	6.72750	8.06231	9.64629	16.36654
21	1.51567	1.67958	1.86029	2.27877	2.78596	3.39956	5.03383	6.10881	7.40025	8.94917	10.80385	18.82152
22	1.54598	1.72157	1.91610	2.36992	2.92526	3.60354	5.43654	6.65860	8.14028	9.93357	12.10031	21.64475
23	1.57690	1.76461	1.97359	2.46472	3.07152	3.81975	5.87146	7.25787	8.95430	11.02627	13.55235	24.89146
24	1.60844	1.80873	2.03279	2.56330	3.22510	4.04893	6.34118	7.91108	9.84973	12.23916	15.17863	28.62518
25	1.64061	1.85394	2.09378	2.66584	3.38635	4.29187	6.84847	8.62308	10.83471	13.58546	17.00000	32.91895
26	1.67342	1.90029	2.15659	2.77247	3.55567	4.54938	7.39635	9.39916	11.91818	15.07986	19.04007	37.85680
27	1.70689	1.94780	2.22129	2.88337	3.73346	4.82235	7.98806	10.24508	13.10999	16.73865	21.32488	43.53532
28	1.74102	1.99650	2.28793	2.99870	3.92013	5.11169	8.62711	11.16714	14.42099	18.57990	23.88387	50.06561
29	1.77584	2.04641	2.35657	3.11865	4.11614	5.41839	9.31727	12.17218	15.86309	20.62369	26.74993	57.57545
30	1.81136	2.09757	2.42726	3.24340	4.32194	5.74349	10.06266	13.26768	17.44940	22.89230	29.95992	66.21177
31	1.84759	2.15001	2.50008	3.37313	4.53804	6.08810	10.86767	14.46177	19.19434	25.41045	33.55511	76.14354
32	1.88454	2.20376	2.57508	3.50806	4.76494	6.45339	11.73708	15.76333	21.11378	28.20560	37.58173	87.56507
33	1.92223	2.25885	2.65234	3.64838	5.00319	6.84059	12.67605	17.18203	23.22515	31.30821	42.09153	100.69983
34	1.96068	2.31532	2.73191	3.79432	5.25335	7.25103	13.69013	18.72841	25.54767	34.75212	47.14252	115.80480
35	1.99989	2.37321	2.81386	3.94609	5.51602	7.68609	14.78534	20.41397	28.10244	38.57485	52.79962	133.17552
36	2.03989	2.43254	2.88928	4.10393	5.79182	8.14725	15.96817	22.25123	30.91268	42.81808	59.13557	153.15185
37	2.08069	2.49335	2.98523	4.26809	6.08141	8.63609	17.24563	24.25384	34.00395	47.52807	66.23184	176.12463
38	2.12230	2.55568	3.07478	4.43881	6.38548	9.15425	18.62528	26.43668	37.40434	52.75616	74.17966	202.54332
39	2.16474	2.61957	3.16703	4.61637	6.70475	9.70351	20.11530	28.81598	41.14479	58.55934	83.08122	232.92482
40	2.20804	2.68506	3.26204	4.80102	7.03999	10.28572	21.72452	31.40942	45.25926	65.00087	93.05097	267.86355

Table A-2

PRESENT VALUE OF 1

(PRESENT VALUE OF A SINGLE SUM)

$$PVF_{n,i} = \frac{1}{(1+i)^n} = (1+i)^{-n}$$

(n) periods	2%	2½%	3%	4%	5%	6%	8%	9%	10%	11%	12%	15%
1	.98039	.97561	.97087	.96156	.95238	.94340	.92593	.91743	.90909	.90090	.89286	.86957
2	.96117	.95181	.94260	.92456	.90703	.89000	.85734	.84168	.82645	.81162	.79719	.75614
3	.94232	.92860	.91514	.88900	.86384	.83962	.79383	.77218	.75132	.73119	.71178	.65752
4	.92385	.90595	.88849	.85480	.82270	.79209	.73503	.70843	.68301	.65873	.63552	.57175
5	.90583	.88385	.86261	.82193	.78353	.74726	.68058	.64993	.62092	.59345	.56743	.49718
6	.88797	.86230	.83748	.79031	.74622	.70496	.63017	.59627	.56447	.53464	.50663	.43233
7	.87056	.84127	.81309	.75992	.71068	.66506	.58349	.54703	.51316	.48166	.45235	.37594
8	.85349	.82075	.78941	.73069	.67684	.62741	.54027	.50187	.46651	.43393	.40388	.32690
9	.83676	.80073	.76642	.70259	.64461	.59190	.50025	.46043	.42410	.39092	.36061	.28426
10	.82035	.78120	.74409	.67556	.61391	.55839	.46319	.42241	.38554	.35218	.32197	.24719
11	.80426	.76214	.72242	.64958	.58468	.52679	.42888	.38753	.35049	.31728	.28748	.21494
12	.78849	.74356	.70138	.62460	.55684	.49697	.39711	.35554	.31863	.28584	.25668	.18691
13	.77303	.72542	.68095	.60057	.53032	.46884	.36770	.32618	.28966	.25751	.22917	.16253
14	.75788	.70773	.66112	.57748	.50507	.44230	.34046	.29925	.26333	.23199	.20462	.14133
15	.74301	.69047	.64186	.55526	.48102	.41727	.31524	.27454	.23939	.20900	.18270	.12289
16	.72845	.67362	.62317	.53391	.45811	.39365	.29189	.25187	.21763	.18829	.16312	.10687
17	.71416	.65720	.60502	.51337	.43630	.37136	.27027	.23107	.19785	.16963	.14564	.09293
18	.70016	.64117	.58739	.49363	.41552	.35034	.25025	.21199	.17986	.15282	.13004	.08081
19	.68643	.62553	.57029	.47464	.39573	.33051	.23171	.19449	.16351	.13768	.11611	.07027
20	.67297	.61027	.55368	.45639	.37689	.31180	.21455	.17843	.14864	.12403	.10367	.06110
21	.65978	.59539	.53755	.43883	.35894	.29416	.19866	.16370	.13513	.11174	.09256	.05313
22	.64684	.58086	.52189	.42196	.34185	.27751	.18394	.15018	.12285	.10067	.08264	.04620
23	.63416	.56670	.50669	.40573	.32557	.26180	.17032	.13778	.11168	.09069	.07379	.04017
24	.62172	.55288	.49193	.39012	.31007	.24698	.15770	.12641	.10153	.08170	.06588	.03493
25	.60953	.53939	.47761	.37512	.29530	.23300	.14602	.11597	.09230	.07361	.05882	.03038
26	.59758	.52623	.46369	.36069	.28124	.21981	.13520	.10639	.08391	.06631	.05252	.02642
27	.58586	.51340	.45019	.34682	.26785	.20737	.12519	.09761	.07628	.05974	.04689	.02297
28	.57437	.50088	.43708	.33348	.25509	.19563	.11591	.08955	.06934	.05382	.04187	.01997
29	.56311	.48866	.42435	.32065	.24295	.18456	.10733	.08216	.06304	.04849	.03738	.01737
30	.55207	.47674	.41199	.30832	.23138	.17411	.09938	.07537	.05731	.04368	.03338	.01510
31	.54125	.46511	.39999	.29646	.22036	.16425	.09202	.06915	.05210	.03935	.02980	.01313
32	.53063	.45377	.38834	.28506	.20987	.15496	.08520	.06344	.04736	.03545	.02661	.01142
33	.52023	.44270	.37703	.27409	.19987	.14619	.07889	.05820	.04306	.03194	.02376	.00993
34	.51003	.43191	.36604	.26355	.19035	.13791	.07305	.05340	.03914	.02878	.02121	.00864
35	.50003	.42137	.35538	.25342	.18129	.13011	.06763	.04899	.03558	.02592	.01894	.00751
36	.49022	.41109	.34503	.24367	.17266	.12274	.06262	.04494	.03235	.02335	.01691	.00653
37	.48061	.40107	.33498	.23430	.16444	.11579	.05799	.04123	.02941	.02104	.01510	.00568
38	.47119	.39128	.32523	.22529	.15661	.10924	.05369	.03783	.02674	.01896	.01348	.00494
39	.46195	.38174	.31575	.21662	.14915	.10306	.04971	.03470	.02430	.01708	.01204	.00429
40	.45289	.37243	.30656	.20829	.14205	.09722	.04603	.03184	.02210	.01538	.01075	.00373

Table A-3

FUTURE VALUE OF AN ORDINARY ANNUITY OF 1

$$FVF-OA_{n,\,i} = \frac{(1+i)^n - 1}{i}$$

(n) periods	2%	2½%	3%	4%	5%	6%	8%	9%	10%	11%	12%	15%
1	1.00000	1.00000	1.00000	1.00000	1.00000	1.00000	1.00000	1.00000	1.00000	1.00000	1.00000	1.00000
2	2.02000	2.02500	2.03000	2.04000	2.05000	2.06000	2.08000	2.09000	2.10000	2.11000	2.12000	2.15000
3	3.06040	3.07563	3.09090	3.12160	3.15250	3.18360	3.24640	3.27810	3.31000	3.34210	3.37440	3.47250
4	4.12161	4.15252	4.18363	4.24646	4.31013	4.37462	4.50611	4.57313	4.64100	4.70973	4.77933	4.99338
5	5.20404	5.25633	5.30914	5.41632	5.52563	5.63709	5.86660	5.98471	6.10510	6.22780	6.35285	6.74238
6	6.30812	6.38774	6.46841	6.63298	6.80191	6.97532	7.33592	7.52334	7.71561	7.91286	8.11519	8.75374
7	7.43428	7.54743	7.66246	7.89829	8.14201	8.39384	8.92280	9.20044	9.48717	9.78327	10.08901	11.06680
8	8.58297	8.73612	8.89234	9.21423	9.54911	9.89747	10.63663	11.02847	11.43589	11.85943	12.29969	13.72682
9	9.75463	9.95452	10.15911	10.58280	11.02656	11.49132	12.48756	13.02104	13.57948	14.16397	14.77566	16.78584
10	10.94972	11.20338	11.46338	12.00611	12.57789	13.18079	14.48656	15.19293	15.93743	16.72201	17.54874	20.30372
11	12.16872	12.48347	12.80780	13.48635	14.20679	14.97164	16.64549	17.56029	18.53117	19.56143	20.65458	24.34928
12	13.41209	13.79555	14.19203	15.02581	15.91713	16.86994	18.97713	20.14072	21.38428	22.71319	24.13313	29.00167
13	14.68033	15.14044	15.61779	16.62684	17.71298	18.88214	21.49530	22.95339	24.52271	26.21164	28.02911	34.35192
14	15.97394	16.51895	17.08632	18.29191	19.59863	21.01507	24.21492	26.01919	27.97498	30.09492	32.39260	40.50471
15	17.29342	17.93193	18.59891	20.02359	21.57856	23.27597	27.15211	29.36092	31.77248	34.40536	37.27972	47.58041
16	18.63929	19.38022	20.15688	21.82453	23.65749	25.67253	30.32428	33.00340	35.94973	39.18995	42.75328	55.71747
17	20.01207	20.86473	21.76159	23.69751	25.84037	28.21288	33.75023	36.97371	40.54470	44.50084	48.88367	65.07509
18	21.41231	22.38635	23.41444	25.64541	28.13238	30.90565	37.45024	41.30134	45.59917	50.39593	55.74972	75.83636
19	22.84056	23.94601	25.11687	27.67123	30.53900	33.75999	41.44626	46.01846	51.15909	56.93949	63.43968	88.21181
20	24.29737	25.54466	26.87037	29.77808	33.06595	36.78559	45.76196	51.16012	57.27500	64.20283	72.05244	102.44358
21	25.78332	27.18327	28.67649	31.96920	35.71925	39.99273	50.42292	56.76453	64.00250	72.26514	81.69874	118.81012
22	27.29898	28.86286	30.53678	34.24797	38.50521	43.39229	55.45676	62.87334	71.40275	81.21431	92.50258	137.63164
23	28.84496	30.58443	32.45288	36.61789	41.43048	46.99583	60.89330	69.53194	79.54302	91.14788	104.60289	159.27638
24	30.42186	32.34904	34.42647	39.08260	44.50200	50.81558	66.76476	76.78981	88.49733	102.17415	118.15524	184.16784
25	32.03030	34.15776	36.45926	41.64591	47.72710	54.86451	73.10594	84.70090	98.34706	114.41331	133.33387	212.79302
26	33.67091	36.01171	38.55304	44.31174	51.11345	59.15638	79.95442	93.32398	109.18177	127.99877	150.33393	245.71197
27	35.34432	37.91200	40.70963	47.08421	54.66913	63.70577	87.35077	102.72314	121.09994	143.07864	169.37401	283.56877
28	37.05121	39.85990	42.93092	49.96758	58.40258	68.52811	95.33883	112.96822	134.20994	159.81729	190.69889	327.10408
29	38.79223	41.85630	45.21885	52.96629	62.32271	73.63980	103.96594	124.13536	148.63093	178.39719	214.58275	377.16969
30	40.56808	43.90270	47.57542	56.08494	66.43885	79.05819	113.28321	136.30754	164.49402	199.02088	241.33268	434.74515
31	42.37944	46.00027	50.00268	59.32834	70.76079	84.80168	123.34587	149.57522	181.94343	221.91317	271.29261	500.95692
32	44.22703	48.15028	52.50276	62.70147	75.29883	90.88978	134.21354	164.03699	201.13777	247.32362	304.84772	577.10046
33	46.11157	50.35403	55.07784	66.20953	80.06377	97.34316	145.95062	179.80032	222.25154	275.52922	342.42945	644.66553
34	48.03380	52.61289	57.73018	69.85791	85.06696	104.18376	158.62667	196.98234	245.47670	306.83744	384.52098	765.36535
35	49.99448	54.92821	60.46208	73.65222	90.32031	111.43478	172.31680	215.71076	271.02437	341.58955	431.66350	881.17016
36	51.99437	57.30141	63.27594	77.59831	95.83632	119.12087	187.10215	236.12472	299.12681	380.16441	484.46312	1014.34568
37	54.03425	59.73395	66.17422	81.70225	101.62814	127.26812	203.07032	258.37595	330.03949	422.98249	543.59869	1167.49753
38	56.11494	62.22730	69.15945	85.97034	107.70955	135.90421	220.31595	282.62978	364.04343	470.51056	609.83053	1343.62216
39	58.23724	64.78298	72.23423	90.40915	114.09502	145.05846	238.94122	309.06646	401.44778	523.26673	684.01020	1546.16549
40	60.40198	67.40255	75.40126	95.02552	120.79977	154.76197	259.05652	337.88245	442.59256	581.82607	767.09142	1779.09031

Table A-4

PRESENT VALUE OF AN ORDINARY ANNUITY OF 1

$$PVF-OA_{n,\,i} = \dfrac{1-\dfrac{1}{(1+i)^{n}}}{i}$$

(n) periods	2%	2½%	3%	4%	5%	6%	8%	9%	10%	11%	12%	15%
1	.98039	.97561	.97087	.96154	.95238	.94340	.92593	.91743	.90909	.90090	.89286	.86957
2	1.94156	1.92742	1.91347	1.88609	1.85941	1.83339	1.78326	1.75911	1.73554	1.71252	1.69005	1.62571
3	2.88388	2.85602	2.82861	2.77509	2.72325	2.67301	2.57710	2.53130	2.48685	2.44371	2.40183	2.28323
4	3.80773	3.76197	3.71710	3.62990	3.54595	3.46511	3.31213	3.23972	3.16986	3.10245	3.03735	2.85498
5	4.71346	4.64583	4.57971	4.45182	4.32948	4.21236	3.99271	3.88965	3.79079	3.69590	3.60478	3.35216
6	5.60143	5.50813	5.41719	5.24214	5.07569	4.91732	4.62288	4.48592	4.35526	4.23054	4.11141	3.78448
7	6.47199	6.34939	6.23028	6.00205	5.78637	5.58238	5.20637	5.03295	4.86842	4.71220	4.56376	4.16042
8	7.32548	7.17014	7.01969	6.73274	6.46321	6.20979	5.74664	5.53482	5.33493	5.14612	4.96764	4.48732
9	8.16224	7.97087	7.78611	7.43533	7.10782	6.80169	6.24689	5.99525	5.75902	5.53705	5.32825	4.77158
10	8.98259	8.75206	8.53020	8.11090	7.72173	7.36009	6.71008	6.41766	6.14457	5.88923	5.65022	5.01877
11	9.78685	9.51421	9.25262	8.76048	8.30641	7.88687	7.13896	6.80519	6.49506	6.20652	5.93770	5.23371
12	10.57534	10.25776	9.95400	9.38507	8.86325	8.38384	7.53608	7.16073	6.81369	6.49236	6.19437	5.42062
13	11.34837	10.98319	10.63496	9.98565	9.39357	8.85268	7.90378	7.48690	7.10336	6.74987	6.42355	5.58315
14	12.10625	11.69091	11.29607	10.56312	9.89864	9.29498	8.24424	7.78615	7.36669	6.98187	6.62817	5.72448
15	12.84926	12.38138	11.93794	11.11839	10.37966	9.71225	8.55948	8.06069	7.60608	7.19087	6.81086	5.84737
16	13.57771	13.05500	12.56110	11.65230	10.83777	10.10590	8.85137	8.31256	7.82371	7.37916	6.97399	5.95424
17	14.29187	13.71220	13.16612	12.16567	11.27407	10.47726	9.12164	8.54363	8.02155	7.54879	7.11963	6.04716
18	14.99203	14.35336	13.75351	12.65930	11.68959	10.82760	9.37189	8.75563	8.20141	7.70162	7.24967	6.12797
19	15.67846	14.97889	14.32380	13.13394	12.08532	11.15812	9.60360	8.95012	8.36492	7.83929	7.36578	6.19823
20	16.35143	15.58916	14.87747	13.59033	12.46221	11.46992	9.81815	9.12855	8.51356	7.96333	7.46944	6.25933
21	17.01121	16.18455	15.41502	14.02916	12.82115	11.76408	10.01680	9.29224	8.64869	8.07507	7.56200	6.31246
22	17.65805	16.76541	15.93692	14.45112	13.16800	12.04158	10.20074	9.44243	8.77154	8.17574	7.64465	6.35866
23	18.29220	17.33211	16.44361	14.85684	13.48857	12.30338	10.37106	9.58021	8.88322	8.26643	7.71843	6.39884
24	18.91393	17.88499	16.93554	15.24696	13.79864	12.55036	10.52876	9.70661	8.98474	8.34814	7.78432	6.43377
25	19.52346	18.42438	17.41315	15.62208	14.09394	12.78336	10.67478	9.82258	9.07704	8.42174	7.84314	6.46415
26	20.12104	18.95061	17.87684	15.98277	14.37519	13.00317	10.80998	9.92897	9.16095	8.48806	7.89566	6.49056
27	20.70690	19.46401	18.32703	16.32959	14.64303	13.21053	10.93516	10.02658	9.23722	8.45780	7.94255	6.51353
28	21.28127	19.96489	18.76411	16.66306	14.89813	13.40616	11.05108	10.11613	9.30657	8.60162	7.98442	6.53351
29	21.84438	20.45355	19.18845	16.98371	15.14107	13.59072	11.15841	10.19828	9.36961	8.65011	8.02181	6.55088
30	22.39646	20.93029	19.60044	17.29203	15.37245	13.76483	11.25778	10.27365	9.42691	8.69379	8.05518	6.56598
31	22.93770	21.39541	20.00043	17.58849	15.59281	13.92909	11.34980	10.34280	9.47901	8.73315	8.08499	6.57911
32	23.46833	21.84918	20.38877	17.87355	15.80268	14.08404	11.43500	10.40624	9.52638	8.76860	8.11159	6.59053
33	23.98856	22.29188	20.76579	18.14765	16.00255	14.23023	11.51389	10.46444	9.56943	8.80054	8.13535	6.60046
34	24.49859	22.72379	21.13184	18.41120	16.19290	14.36814	11.58693	10.51784	9.60858	8.82932	8.15656	6.60910
35	24.99862	23.14516	21.48722	18.66461	16.37419	14.49825	11.65457	10.56682	9.64416	8.85524	8.17550	6.61661
36	25.48884	23.55625	21.83225	18.90828	16.54685	14.62099	11.71719	10.61176	9.67651	8.87859	8.19241	6.62314
37	25.96945	23.95732	22.16724	19.14258	16.71129	14.73678	11.77518	10.65299	9.70592	8.89963	8.20751	6.62882
38	26.44064	24.34860	22.49246	19.36786	16.86789	14.84602	11.82887	10.69082	9.73265	8.91859	8.22099	6.63375
39	26.90259	24.73034	22.80822	19.58448	17.01704	14.94907	11.87858	10.72552	9.75697	8.93567	8.23303	6.63805
40	27.35548	25.10278	23.11477	19.79277	17.15909	15.04630	11.92461	10.75736	9.77905	8.95105	8.24378	6.64178

Table A-5

PRESENT VALUE OF AN ANNUITY DUE OF 1

$$PVF-AD_{n,\,i} = 1 + \frac{1 - \dfrac{1}{(1+i)^{n-1}}}{i}$$

(n) periods	2%	2½%	3%	4%	5%	6%	8%	9%	10%	11%	12%	15%
1	1.00000	1.00000	1.00000	1.00000	1.00000	1.00000	1.00000	1.00000	1.00000	1.00000	1.00000	1.00000
2	1.98039	1.97561	1.97087	1.96154	1.95238	1.94340	1.92593	1.91743	1.90909	1.90090	1.89286	1.86957
3	2.94156	2.92742	2.91347	2.88609	2.85941	2.83339	2.78326	2.75911	2.73554	2.71252	2.69005	2.62571
4	3.88388	3.85602	3.82861	3.77509	3.72325	3.67301	3.57710	3.53130	3.48685	3.44371	3.40183	3.28323
5	4.80773	4.76197	4.71710	4.62990	4.54595	4.46511	4.31213	4.23972	4.16986	4.10245	4.03735	3.85498
6	5.71346	5.64583	5.57971	5.45182	5.32948	5.21236	4.99271	4.88965	4.79079	4.69590	4.60478	4.35216
7	6.60143	6.50813	6.41719	6.24214	6.07569	5.91732	5.62288	5.48592	5.35526	5.23054	5.11141	4.78448
8	7.47199	7.34939	7.23028	7.00205	6.78637	6.58238	6.20637	6.03295	5.86842	5.71220	5.56376	5.16042
9	8.32548	8.17014	8.01969	7.73274	7.46321	7.20979	6.74664	6.53482	6.33493	6.14612	5.96764	5.48732
10	9.16224	8.97087	8.78611	8.43533	8.10782	7.80169	7.24689	6.99525	6.75902	6.53705	6.32825	5.77158
11	9.98259	9.75206	9.53020	9.11090	8.72173	8.36009	7.71008	7.41766	7.14457	6.88923	6.65022	6.01877
12	10.78685	10.51421	10.25262	9.76048	9.30641	8.88687	8.13896	7.80519	7.49506	7.20652	6.93770	6.23371
13	11.57534	11.25776	10.95400	10.38507	9.86325	9.38384	8.53608	8.16073	7.81369	7.49236	7.19437	6.42062
14	12.34837	11.98319	11.63496	10.98565	10.39357	9.85268	8.90378	8.48690	8.10336	7.74987	7.42355	6.58315
15	13.10625	12.69091	12.29607	11.56312	10.89864	10.29498	9.24424	8.78615	9.36669	7.98187	7.62817	6.72448
16	13.84926	13.38138	12.93794	12.11839	11.37966	10.71225	9.55948	9.06069	8.60608	8.19087	7.81086	6.84737
17	14.57771	14.05500	13.56110	12.65230	11.83777	11.10590	9.85137	9.31256	8.82371	8.37916	7.97399	6.95424
18	15.29187	14.71220	14.16612	13.16567	12.27407	11.47726	10.12164	9.54363	9.02155	8.54879	8.11963	7.04716
19	15.99203	15.35336	14.75351	13.65930	12.68959	11.82760	10.37189	9.75563	9.20141	8.70162	8.24967	7.12797
20	16.67846	15.97889	15.32380	14.13394	13.08532	12.15812	10.60360	9.95012	9.36492	8.83929	8.36578	7.19823
21	17.35143	16.58916	15.87747	14.59033	13.46221	12.46992	10.81815	10.12855	9.51356	8.96333	8.46944	7.25933
22	18.01121	17.18455	16.41502	15.02916	13.82115	12.76408	11.01680	10.29224	9.64869	9.07507	8.56200	7.31246
23	18.65805	17.76541	16.93692	15.45112	14.16300	13.04158	11.20074	10.44243	9.77154	9.17574	8.64465	7.35866
24	19.29220	18.33211	17.44361	15.85684	14.48857	13.30338	11.37106	10.58021	9.88322	9.26643	8.71843	7.39884
25	19.91393	18.88499	17.93554	16.24696	14.79864	13.55036	11.52876	10.70661	9.98474	9.34814	8.78432	7.43377
26	20.52346	19.42438	18.41315	16.62208	15.09394	13.78336	11.67478	10.82258	10.07704	9.42174	8.84314	7.46415
27	21.12104	19.95061	18.87684	16.98277	15.37519	14.00317	11.80998	10.92897	10.16095	9.48806	8.89566	7.49056
28	21.70690	20.46401	19.32703	17.32959	15.64303	14.21053	11.93518	11.02658	10.23722	9.54780	8.94255	7.51353
29	22.28127	20.96489	19.76411	17.66306	15.89813	14.40616	12.05108	11.11613	10.30657	9.60162	8.98442	7.53351
30	22.84438	21.45355	20.18845	17.98371	16.14107	14.59072	12.15841	11.19828	10.36961	9.65011	9.02181	7.55088
31	23.39646	21.93029	20.60044	18.29203	16.37245	14.76483	12.25778	11.27365	10.42691	9.69379	9.05518	7.56598
32	23.93770	22.39541	21.00043	18.58849	16.59281	14.92909	12.34980	11.34280	10.47901	9.73315	9.08499	7.57911
33	24.46833	22.84918	21.38877	18.87355	16.80268	15.08404	12.43500	11.40624	10.52638	9.76860	9.11159	7.59053
34	24.98856	23.29188	21.76579	19.14765	17.00255	15.23023	12.51389	11.46444	10.56943	9.80054	9.13535	7.60046
35	25.49859	23.72379	22.13184	19.41120	17.19290	15.36814	12.58693	11.51784	10.60858	9.82932	9.15656	7.60910
36	25.99862	24.14516	22.48722	19.66461	17.37419	15.49825	12.65457	11.56682	10.64416	9.85524	9.17550	7.61661
37	26.48884	24.55625	22.83225	19.90828	17.54685	15.62099	12.71719	11.61176	10.67651	9.87859	9.19241	7.62314
38	26.96945	24.95732	23.16724	20.14258	17.71129	15.73678	12.77518	11.65299	10.70592	9.89963	9.20751	7.62882
39	27.44064	25.34860	23.49246	20.36786	17.86789	15.84602	12.82887	11.69082	10.73265	9.91859	9.22099	7.63375
40	27.90259	25.73034	23.80822	20.58448	18.01704	15.94907	12.87858	11.72552	10.75697	9.93567	9.23303	7.63805

Company Index

Subject Index

Credits

References to the *CICA Handbook* are reprinted (or adapted) with permission from The Canadian Institute of Chartered Accountants, Toronto, Canada. Any changes to the original material are the sole responsibility of the author (and/or publisher) and have not been reviewed or endorsed by the CICA.

Extracts adapted from *Financial Accounting: Assets* (FA2) and *Financial Accounting: Liabilities and Equities* (FA3) published by the Certified General Accountants Association of Canada © 2001 to 2008 CGA-Canada. Reproduced with permission.

CMA Canada adapted material is adapted with the permission of The Society of Management Accountants of Canada.

The information regarding Tim Hortons set forth herein are part of and/or may include (i) excerpts from financial statements included in reports filed by Tim Hortons Inc. with the U.S. Securities and Exchange Commission (SEC) and the Canadian securities administrators that have been reproduced with permission but not endorsed or confirmed by Tim Hortons, and (ii) other data and information generated by third parties unaffiliated with Tim Hortons Inc. in connection with its financial results and/or other information. Accordingly, Tim Hortons Inc. makes no representation or warranty as to, and expressly disclaims responsibility regarding, the accuracy or completeness of any of the information related to Tim Hortons, or the inquiries, analysis or interpretation regarding any such information, that is described above and/or otherwise included herein. This information should not be relied upon for purposes of trading in the securities of Tim Hortons or otherwise. You may find current financial and other information prepared by Tim Hortons Inc. at its investor relations website at www.timhortons-invest.com, or as filed with the SEC and the Canadian securities administrators at www.sec.gov and www.sedar.com, respectively.

All images are copyright© iStockphoto unless otherwise noted. **Page 906:** The Canadian Press/Mario Beauregard. **Page 958:** The Canadian Press/John Woods. **Page 1020:** TD Securities Inc. **Page 1096:** Open Text Corp. **Page 1144:** Tim Hortons Inc. **Page 1228:** The Canadian Press/Adrian Wyld. **Page 1304:** WestJet Airlines Ltd. **Page 1468:** Clearwater Seafoods Ltd.